July 11–13, 2016
Pacific Grove, CA, USA

Association for Computing Machinery

Advancing Computing as a Science & Profession

SPAA'16

Proceedings of the 28th ACM Symposium on Parallelism in Algorithms and Architectures

Sponsored by:

ACM SIGACT & ACM SIGARCH

Supported by:

Akamai & Oracle Labs

Association for
Computing Machinery

Advancing Computing as a Science & Profession

The Association for Computing Machinery
2 Penn Plaza, Suite 701
New York, New York 10121-0701

ISBN: 978-1-4503-4210-0 (Digital)

ISBN: 978-1-4503-4609-2 (Print)

Additional copies may be ordered prepaid from:

ACM Order Department
PO Box 30777
New York, NY 10087-0777, USA

Phone: 1-800-342-6626 (USA and Canada)
+1-212-626-0500 (Global)
Fax: +1-212-944-1318
E-mail: acmhelp@acm.org
Hours of Operation: 8:30 am – 4:30 pm ET

Printed in the USA

Foreword

It is my great pleasure to welcome you to the *28th ACM Symposium on Parallelism in Algorithms and Architectures.*

The goal of SPAA is to develop a deeper understanding of parallelism in all its forms, bringing together the theory and practice of parallel computing. This year's program reflects that goal, with a diverse selection of papers at the cutting edge of parallel computing. The program includes 38 regular papers and 14 brief announcements, as well as keynote talks by Michael I. Jordan and Nir Shavit.

Traditional topics in parallelism are well represented at SPAA this year. The program includes papers on parallel algorithms for classical questions (e.g., sorting and graph problems, see Sessions 9 and 14). It includes papers on scheduling parallel computations (see Session 3) and scheduling tasks in parallel systems (see Sessions 6 and 8). The program also includes papers on concurrent data structures (see Session 11), and on parallelism in distributed systems (see Session 13). These topics all have a long history at SPAA.

Over the last several years, the study of parallelism has expanded to include new models of parallel computation (e.g., Map-Reduce, see Session 1), new architectures (e.g., GPUs, see Session 9), new techniques for managing parallelism (e.g., transactional memory, see Session 4), and new types of parallel systems (e.g., programmable matter, see Session 10). These increasingly important topics are represented at SPAA this year.

The best paper award for SPAA 2016 is awarded to a paper focusing on the limitations of certain new models of parallel computation:

> **Shuffles and Circuits (On Lower Bounds for Modern Parallel Computation)**
> **by Tim Roughgarden, Sergei Vassilvitskii and Joshua Wang.**

The authors develop lower bounds on the speed of large-scale parallel computation in a model meant to capture the capabilities of Map-Reduce and Hadoop. They discover an important connection between these computations and polynomials representing boolean functions, and use this fact to show lower bounds for a variety of natural and important problems.

We would also like to recognize (in no particular order) three finalists for the best paper award:

> **Randomized approximate nearest neighbor search with limited adaptivity**
> **by Mingmou Liu, Xiaoyin Pan and Yitong Yin.**
>
> **Robust and Probabilistic Failure-Aware Placement**
> **by Madhukar Korupolu and Rajmohan Rajaraman.**
>
> **Lock-free Transactions without Aborts for Linked Data Structures**
> **by Deli Zhang and Damian Dechev**

These papers highlight the variety of exciting work in parallelism that is represented at SPAA 2016.

On behalf of the program committee, I would like to thank the many authors who submitted their work to SPAA this year. And I would like to thank the many reviewers whose work was critical to the selection process.

Seth Gilbert
SPAA '16 Program Chair

Table of Contents

Session: Parallel Algorithms

Session: Scheduling

Session: Keynote Address

Session: Scheduling and Resource Allocation

2016 Conference Organization

General Chair: Christian Scheideler *(University of Paderborn)*

Program Chair: Seth Gilbert *(National University of Singapore)*

Local Arrangements Chair: Bradley Kuszmaul *(Massachusetts Institute of Technology)*

Secretary: Jeremy Fineman *(Georgetown University)*

Treasurer: David Bunde *(Knox College)*

Publicity Chair: Nodari Sitchinava *(University of Hawaii, Manoa)*

Steering Committee:
Guy Blelloch *(Carnegie Mellon University)*
David Culler *(University of California, Berkeley)*
Frank Dehne *(Carleton University)*
Pierre Fraigniaud *(CNRS & University Paris Diderot)*
Phil Gibbons *(Carnegie Mellon University)*
Maurice Herlihy *(Brown University)*
Tom Leighton *(Massachusetts Institute of Technology & Akamai Technologies)*
Charles Leiserson *(Massachusetts Institute of Technology)*
Fabrizio Luccio *(University of Pisa)*
Friedhelm Meyer auf der Heide *(University of Paderborn)*
Gary Miller *(Carnegie Mellon University)*
Burkhard Monien *(University of Paderborn)*
Franco Preparata *(Brown University)*
Vijaya Ramachandran *(University of Texas, Austin)*
Arnold Rosenberg *(Northeastern University)*
Paul Spirakis *(CTI &University of Liverpool)*
Uzi Vishkin *(University of Maryland)*

Program Committee: Dan Alistarh *(Microsoft Research)*
Yossi Azar *(Tel Aviv University)*
Michael Bender *(Stony Brook University)*
Costas Busch *(Louisiana State University)*
Yuval Emek *(Technion)*
Antonio Fernández Anta *(IMDEA)*
Jeremy Fineman *(Georgetown University)*
Phillip Gibbons *(Carnegie Mellon University)*
Seth Gilbert *(NUS)*
Magnús M. Halldórsson *(Reykjavík University)*
Stephan Holzer *(Massachusetts Institute of Technology)*
Fabian Kuhn *(University of Freiburg)*
Yossi Lev *(Oracle Labs)*
Ishai Menache *(Microsoft Research)*
Benjamin Moseley *(Washington University in St. Louis)*
Calvin Newport *(Georgetown University)*
Merav Parter *(Massachusetts Institute of Technology)*
Boaz Patt-Shamir *(Tel Aviv University)*
Seth Pettie *(University of Michigan)*
Cynthia Phillips *(Sandia National Laboratories)*
Kirk Pruhs *(University of Pittsburgh)*
Peter Robinson *(Royal Holloway University of London)*
Thomas Sauerwald *(University of Cambridge)*
Stefan Schmid *(Aalborg University)*
Michael Scott *(University of Rochester)*
Julian Shun *(University of California, Berkeley)*
Aravind Srinivasan *(University of Maryland)*
Maxwell Young *(Mississippi State University)*

Additional reviewers:

Umut Acar
Jordi Arjona Aroca
James Aspnes
Basem Assiri
Chen Avin
Jean Claude Bajard
Jeremy Barbay
Mor Baruch
Sayan Bhattacharya
Trevor Brown
Niv Buchbinder
Kevin Buchin
Aydin Buluc
Jérémie Chalopin
Arthur Charguéraud
Luis F. Chiroque
Rezaul Chowdhury
Shumo Chu
Wyatt Clements
Ilan Cohen
Vincent Cohen-Addad
Ágnes Cseh
James Demmel
Nikhil Devanur
Aleksandar Dragojevic
Sandhya Dwarkadas
Leah Epstein
Klaus-Tycho Förster
Paweł Garncarek
Rati Gelashvili
Chryssis Georgiou
Mohsen Ghaffari
George Giakkoupis
Michael Goodrich
David Harris
James Hegeman
Zhiyi Huang
Antti Hyvärinen
Sungjin Im
Joseph Izraelevitz
Riko Jacob
Łukasz Jeż
Guoliang Jin
Hossein Jowhari
Ralf Klasing
Kirill Kogan
Christian Konrad
Kishori Konwar
Janne H. Korhonen
Amos Korman
Sebastian Krinninger
Janardhan Kulkarni
Bradley Kuszmaul
Oğuzhan Külekci
Christoph Lenzen
Jian Li
Zvi Lotker
Victor Luchangco
Brendan Lucier
Víctor M. López Millán
José Luis López-Presa
Konstantin Makarychev
Marios Mavronicolas
Avery Miller
David Mount
Cameron Musco
Danupon Nanongkai
Emanuele Natale
Nicolas Nicolaou
Debmalya Panigrahi
Evangelos Papalexakis
Miguel Peón Quirós
Miroslav Popovic
Eric Price
Rajmohan Rajaraman
Venkatesh Raman
Alan Roytman
Vivek B. Sardeshmukh
Christian Scheideler
Kevin Schewior
Roy Schwartz
Michele Scquizzato
Ohad Shamir
Gokarna Sharma
Brendan Sheridan
Subhajit Sidhanta
Harsha Simhadri
Shikha Singh
Clifford Stein
Martin Strauss
Hsin-Hao Su
Kanat Tangwongsan
Thorsten Tarrach
Christopher Thraves Caro
Vasileios Trigonakis
Mohsen Vakilian
Rob van Stee
Adi Vardi
Shai Vardi
Sergei Vassilvitskii
Frederic Wagner
Lin Wang
Ryan Yates
Yuan Zhong

Sponsors & Supporters

SPAA 2016 is sponsored & supported in part by generous contributions from the following organizations:

Sponsors: SIGACT

SIGARCH

Supporters: Akamai

Oracle Labs

Shuffles and Circuits (On Lower Bounds for Modern Parallel Computation)

Tim Roughgarden* Sergei Vassilvitskii† Joshua R. Wang*

ABSTRACT

The goal of this paper is to identify fundamental limitations on how efficiently algorithms implemented on platforms such as MapReduce and Hadoop can compute the central problems in the motivating application domains, such as graph connectivity problems.

We introduce an abstract model of massively parallel computation, where essentially the only restrictions are that the "fan-in" of each machine is limited to s bits, where s is smaller than the input size n, and that computation proceeds in synchronized rounds, with no communication between different machines within a round. Lower bounds on the round complexity of a problem in this model apply to every computing platform that shares the most basic design principles of MapReduce-type systems.

We prove that computations in our model that use few rounds can be represented as low-degree polynomials over the reals. This connection allows us to translate a lower bound on the (approximate) polynomial degree of a Boolean function to a lower bound on the round complexity of every (randomized) massively parallel computation of that function. These lower bounds apply even in the "unbounded width" version of our model, where the number of machines can be arbitrarily large. As one example of our general results, computing any non-trivial monotone graph property — such as connectivity — requires a super-constant number of rounds when every machine can accept only a sub-polynomial (in n) number of input bits s.

Finally, we prove that, in two senses, our lower bounds are the best one could hope for. For the unbounded-width model, we prove a matching upper bound. Restricting to a polynomial number of machines, we show that asymptotically better lower bounds require proving that $P \neq NC^1$.

1. INTRODUCTION

The past decade has seen a resurgence of parallel computation, and there is now an impressive array of frameworks built for working with large datasets: MapReduce, Hadoop, Pregel, Giraph, Spark, and so on. The goal of this paper is to identify fundamental limitations on how efficiently these frameworks can compute the central problems in the motivating application domains, such as graph connectivity.

Modern architectures for massively parallel computation share a number of common attributes. First, the data, or the input to the computation, is partitioned arbitrarily across all of the nodes participating in the computation. Second, computation proceeds in synchronous rounds. In every round, each machine looks at the local data available and performs some amount of computation *without communicating with other machines*. After the computation is done, a communication round begins, where each machine can send messages to other machines. Importantly, there are no restrictions on the communicating pairs — the communication pattern can be arbitrary and input-dependent. Once the communication phase is over, a new round begins. For example, for readers familiar with the MapReduce framework, the computation corresponds to the *reduce* phase, the designation of addressees to the *map* phase, and the actual communication to the *shuffle* phase.

Most previous work has focused on designing efficient algorithms for these systems. To that end, a number of models for MapReduce and its variants have been proposed; see Section 1.2 for a complete list and a detailed comparison to the present work. Since these works aspire to realizable positive results, their models aim to be faithful to a specific system, and often involve a number of system-dependent parameters and constraints that govern the algorithmic design space.

In this work, motivated by the rapidly changing landscape of the systems deployed in practice and in search of impossibility results, we take a different approach. Instead of looking for a faithful model for the system du jour, we focus on extracting the most fundamental constraints shared by all of these models and examine the consequent restrictions on feasible computations. By focusing on a single parameter, namely the *input size* for each machine, and a single benchmark, the number of *rounds* of computation, we obtain parameterized lower bounds that apply to any computing framework (past or future) that shares the same design principles.

1.1 Summary of Contributions

Our first contribution is a general model of massively parallel computation that captures the core properties common to all modern parallel processing systems. Conceptually, computation proceeds in synchronous rounds, and in each round, each machine performs an arbitrary computation on its input, and sends arbitrary information to arbitrary machines in the next round, subject only to the constraint that each machine receives at most s bits each round. In the most powerful, unbounded-width, version of our model, where the number of machines is unlimited, the only restriction is that the "fan-in" of each machine is limited to s bits,

*Stanford University. Supported in part by NSF Grant CCF-1524062.
†Google, Inc.

SPAA '16 July 11-13, 2016, Pacific Grove, CA, USA

ACM ISBN 978-1-4503-4210-0/16/07.
DOI: http://dx.doi.org/10.1145/2935764.2935799

where s is a parameter smaller than the input size n. (Unlimited extra space can be used for computations on these inputs.)

Second, we prove that computations in our model that use few rounds can be represented as low-degree polynomials over the reals. Specifically, we prove that if a function can be computed by such a computation with space s per machine in r rounds (even with unbounded width), then the function has a polynomial representation with degree at most s^r (Theorem 3.1). In particular, computing a function with a polynomial representation of degree n requires $\lceil \log_s n \rceil$ rounds. This lower bound implies, for example, that computing such a function with space $s = n^\epsilon$ per machine requires $1/\epsilon$ rounds in our model. Similarly, if s is only polylogarithmic, then $\Omega(\log n / \log \log n)$ rounds are needed. Our lower bounds also extend, with a constant-factor degradation, to randomized computations.

An obvious question is whether or not there are super-constant lower bounds on the number of rounds required to compute natural functions when the space s is polynomial in n, such as $s = \sqrt{n}$. Our third contribution is a proof that, in two senses, our lower bounds are the best one could hope for. For the unbounded-width model, our lower bound is completely tight, as every function can be computed in at most $\lceil \log_s n \rceil$ rounds in our model. But what if only a polynomial number of machines are allowed? Here, we show that better lower bounds require proving very strong circuit lower bounds. Specifically, any lower bound asymptotically larger than $\Theta(\log_s n)$ for a function in P would separate NC^1 from P, a major open question in circuit complexity (Theorem 7.1).

Fourth, by connecting MapReduce-type computations to polynomials, we can apply the sophisticated toolbox known for polynomials to reason about these computations. As one example, known results imply that every non-trivial monotone graph property can only be represented by polynomials with degree at least roughly $n^2/3$. (Here n denotes the number of vertices, and the input is given as the characteristic vector of the graph's edge set.) We therefore obtain a lower bound of approximately $\frac{1}{2} \log_s n$ on the number of rounds required for deciding any such property (Theorem 5.3), including graph connectivity.

Finally, we develop new machinery for proving lower bounds on the polynomial degree of Boolean functions, and hence on the round complexity of massively parallel computations. While polynomial degree lower bounds are of course known for many Boolean functions, we prove new (tight) lower bounds for graph problems, including undirected ST-CONNECTIVITY (Theorem 6.4). These imply an $\Omega(\log_s n)$ lower bound on the round complexity of solving these problems via any conceivable MapReduce-type system, even when the width is unbounded.

1.2 Related Work

MapReduce was introduced as a system for large scale data processing by Dean and Ghemawat [8]. As the method gained popularity, researchers began to abstract away the core features that made MapReduce successful in practice. Feldman et al. [13] introduced the *Massive Unordered Data* (MUD) model, and were the first to identify some of the restrictions imposed by the framework.

Karloff et al. [21] introduced a slightly more general model, MRC, which identified the number of synchronous rounds as the key metric for comparing any two algorithms. Furthermore, they limited the amount of parallelism allowed in the model, insisting that it be not too small, by restricting the memory of each machine to be sublinear in the input, and also not too large, by restricting the total number of machines to be sublinear in the input as well. They showed simulation results for a subclass of EREW algorithms in MRC, but left open the question of whether all NC languages can be decided in this setting. Goodrich et al. [16] further extended the simulation results to CRCW PRAMs as well as BSP algorithms [37], and gave algorithms for sorting and searching.

The MRC model in [21] only placed upper bounds on the number of machines and the space available on each, limiting both to $N^{1-\epsilon}$ for an input of size N and some fixed $\epsilon > 0$. Goodrich et al. [16] were the first to single out the total input to each machine, the key parameter of the model of the present work. This decision was later adopted by authors in proving upper bounds on the space-round trade-offs in these computations, and this parameter been variously called memory, space, and key-complexity [2, 5, 15, 26, 32].

The adoption of these models for analysis has led to a set of algorithmic tools and techniques developed for efficient computation in this setting. These include notions of filtering [26], multi-round sampling [12, 25], and coresets [3, 28], among others. Recently Fish et al. [14] introduced a uniform version of MRC, and also proved strict hierarchy theorems with respect to the computation time per processor.

The known lower bounds for explicit functions in these models concern either communication (with a fixed number of rounds) or restricted classes of algorithms (for round lower bounds). In more detail, Pietracaprina et al. [32] prove non-trivial lower bounds for matrix multiplication in a limited setting, which requires computing all elementary products (and specifically excludes Strassen-like algorithms). Similar kinds of limitations are required by [19] and [5] to prove lower bounds for a list ranking problem and relational query processing, respectively. Finally, both Beame et al. [5] and Afrati et al. [1] study, for a fixed number of rounds (usually a single round), space-communication trade-offs.

In distributed computing, the total amount of communication is often the most relevant complexity measure. For example, Woodruff and Zhang [39] and Klauck et al. [22] identify models and problems for which there is no algorithm that beats the communication benchmark of sending the entire input to a single machine. Because massively parallel systems are designed to send a potentially large amount of data in a single round, such communication lower bounds do not generally imply lower bounds for round complexity. For example, in practice, matrix multiplication is regarded as an "easy" problem in MapReduce — indeed, MapReduce was invented for precisely such computations (see e.g. [27]) — even though its solution requires total communication proportional to the size of the matrix.

1.2.1 Relation to Other Computational Models

The model proposed in this paper is closely related to several previously studied computational models.

Congested clique. Perhaps the closest model to the present work is the "congested clique" model, the special case of the CONGEST model [31] in which each pair of machines is connected by a direct link (see [11] and the references therein). The original motivation of this model was for the design and analysis of distributed algorithms, but it is also relevant to massively parallel computation. In the most commonly studied version of the model, n machines with unlimited computational power communicate in synchronized rounds. Each machine initially holds some number m of input bits, and in each round each machine can send a (different) message of w bits to every other machine. (Typically, $w = \Theta(\log n)$.) Thus, the number nw of bits that a machine can send and receive in each round automatically scales linearly with the number of machines.

In our model, we allow the number s of bits that a machine can receive in a given round to be sublinear in the total number of machines. In this sense, our model is weaker than the congested clique model (when $s = o(n)$).[1] On the other hand, MapReduce-type systems differ from distributed settings in that there is little motivation for restricting the amount of point-to-point communication in a round. In our model, a machine can receive all s of its bits in a round from a single other machine. In this sense, our model is stronger than the congested clique model (when $s = \omega(w)$). We note that Hegeman and Pemmaraju [17] show that congested clique computations can be simulated by MapReduce computations (in the model in [21]), albeit with space-per-machine proportional to the communication-per-machine in the congested clique computation. (As already noted, the latter generally scales with the number of machines, while we are generally interested in space-per-machine smaller than this.)

Drucker et al. [11] forge an interesting connection between congested clique computations and circuits. In analogy with our "barrier" result in Section 7, they prove a simulation result implying that even slightly super-constant lower bounds on the round complexity of congested clique computations for a problem in NP would imply better circuit size-depth trade-offs for such problems than are currently known (for unbounded fan-in circuits with unweighted threshold gates or with mod-m gates, e.g. $m = 6$).[2]

Circuits with medium fan-in. Another related model is "circuits with medium fan-in" — arbitrary gates with fan-in that scales with, but is smaller than, the input size — introduced recently in [18]. Our model is stronger than the one in [18], with the most significant difference being that the communication pattern in our model can be input-dependent. Our round complexity lower bounds imply depth lower bounds for the model in [18]. The focus of [18] is on circuit size (rather than depth), so the lower bounds and barriers to lower bounds identified in [18] appear incomparable to ours.

Ideal PRAMs. The much older model of "ideal CREW PRAMs" is also highly relevant to our unbounded-width model. In this model, which was introduced in [7], there is an unbounded number of processors with unbounded computational power and a shared memory. Computation proceeds in synchronous rounds. Each round, each processor can read a single memory cell and write to a single memory cell, subject to the constraint that at each time step at most one processor can write to any given memory cell. Perhaps the most intriguing result in [7] is a parallel algorithm that computes the logical OR function (and, through reductions, many other functions) in strictly fewer than $\log_2 n$ rounds. The key idea in this result is to implicitly transmit extra information by *not* writing to a memory cell. This potential "power of staying silent" is exactly what makes our lower bounds in Section 3 interesting and non-trivial. Cook et al. [7] also prove a lower bound of $\Omega(\log n)$ on the number of rounds required to compute the OR function (and many others). This lower bound translates (via a simulation argument) to a lower bound of the form $\Omega(s^{-1} \log n)$ in our model (in [7] each processor reads only one cell in each round, while in our model each machine receives s bits per round). This implied lower bound is non-trivial only when $s = o(\log n)$, and our lower bound of $\Omega(\log_s n)$ is asymptotically superior for all super-constant s.

The work of [7] also inspired Nisan [29] to introduce the fundamental concept of the "block sensitivity" of a Boolean function (the logarithm of which characterizes the ideal PRAM round complexity, up to a constant factor), which in turn is polynomially related to the decision tree complexity, degree, and approximate degree of the function [29, 30]. Our results in Section 5 rely on this circle of ideas.

Finally, our technique of characterizing parallel computations as polynomials resembles the work of Dietzfelbinger et al. [9], who used related ideas to sharpen the lower bound in [7] by a constant factor for many Boolean functions. Using the degree of the polynomial to establish lower bounds was also used by Beals et al. [4] to establish query lower bounds for quantum networks.

2. THE s-SHUFFLE MODEL

Section 2.1 develops intuition for our computational model by presenting an example, and highlights some ways in which MapReduce-type computations differ from traditional circuit computations. Section 2.2 formally defines the model. Section 2.3 proves an upper bound on the round complexity of every Boolean function in the "unbounded-width" version of our model. Only Sections 2.2 and 2.3 are essential for understanding later sections.

2.1 A Warm-Up Example

Before formally defining our model, we study a specific example, adapted from Nisan and Szegedy [30].

Example 2.1 (Silence Is Golden) Consider the Boolean function $E_{12} : \{0,1\}^3 \to \{0,1\}$ on three inputs that evaluates to 1 if and only if exactly one or two inputs are 1. Define $E_{12}^2 : \{0,1\}^9 \to \{0,1\}$ as the Boolean function that takes nine inputs, applies E_{12} to each block of three inputs, and then applies E_{12} to the results of the three blocks. For instance:

- $E_{12}^2(0,0,1,0,1,0,1,0,0) = E_{12}(1,1,1) = 0$;
- $E_{12}^2(0,0,0,1,1,0,1,1,1) = E_{12}(0,1,0) = 1$.

We next describe a remarkably efficient strategy for computing E_{12}^2 in parallel, using only machines that operate on two (ordered) bits at a time. We first show how to compute E_{12} in two "rounds." Let (x_1, x_2, x_3) denote the input. The first machine reads the bits x_1 and x_2; the second machine x_2 and x_3; and the last machine x_3 and x_1. There is also a fourth machine which belongs to "the second round." Each machine in the first round sends a 1 to the second-round machine if its inputs are 0 and 1 (in this order); otherwise, it stays silent (i.e., sends nothing). The second-round machine receives either a 1 bit (if $E_{12}(x_1, x_2, x_3) = 1$) or no bits at all (if $E_{12}(x_1, x_2, x_3) = 0$), and in all cases can correctly determine and output the value of the function.

To compute the function E_{12}^2, we use a layered version of the same idea (see also Figure 1). We think of the nine input bits as three blocks of three bits each. There are nine machines in the first round, three for each block. There are three machines in the second round, each responsible for a pair of blocks. There is a single machine in the third round, responsible for the final output.

The three bits of a block are distributed to the corresponding three first-round machines (in ordered pairs) as in the computation of E_{12}. Second-round machines have two "ports" in that their inputs are also ordered; each has a "first input" (possibly empty) and a "second input" (again, possibly empty). If the inputs of a first-round machine are 0 and 1 (in this order), then the machine sends a 1 to the two second-round machines responsible for its block; otherwise, it sends nothing. The communication pattern between the three blocks of first-round machines and the second-round machines mirrors that of the distribution of bits to first-round machines: the first second-round machine receives bits (if any) from

[1] For a simple example, suppose the machines want to compute the logical OR of their nm input bits. In the congested clique model, this problem can be solved in 1 round. In our model, when the parameter s is less than n, more than 1 round is required.

[2] To match our barrier in Section 7 of resolving NC^1 vs. P using the techniques in [11], it seems necessary to prove logarithmic (rather than just super-constant) round lower bounds for congested clique computations.

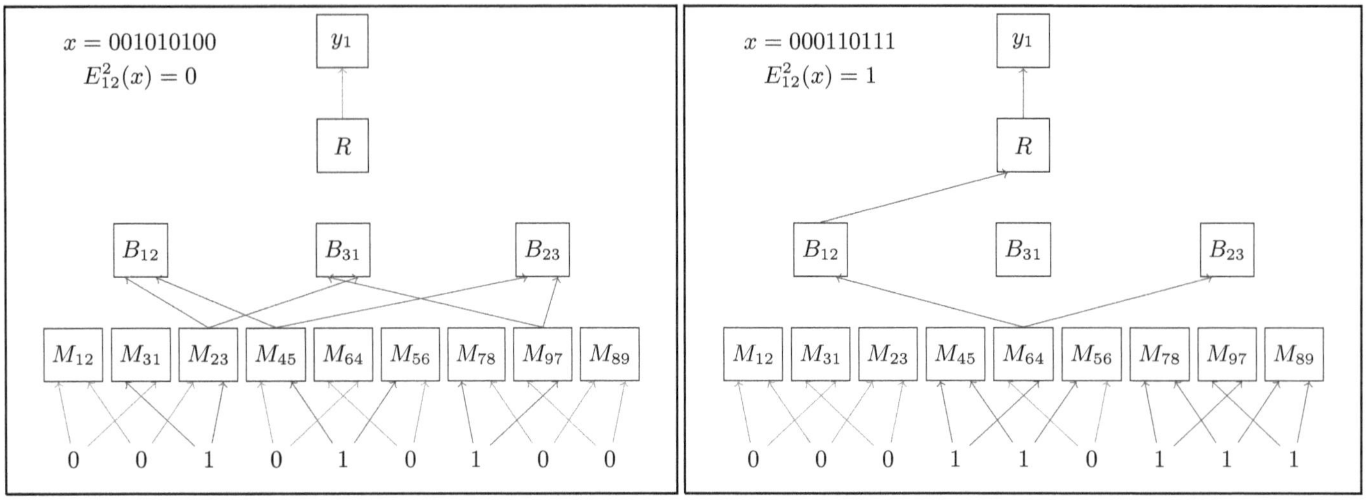

Figure 1: The parallel computation of E_{12}^2, for two different inputs. The arrows show how the machines send bits; an arrow pointing to the bottom left of a machine indicates that the bit is sent to the first port, while the bottom right indicates the second port. Notice that at most one arrow points to a given port, but the arrow that does so may change from input to input. Red arrows represent a zero bit and blue arrows represent a one bit.

the first and second blocks of first-round machines on its first and second ports, respectively; the middle second-round machine receives bits from the second and third blocks on its first and second ports, respectively; and the last second-round machine receives bits from the third and first blocks on its first and second ports, respectively. If a second-round machine receives nothing as its first input and a 1 as its second input, then it sends a 1 to the third-round machine; otherwise, it sends nothing. Finally, the third-round machine outputs 1 if it was sent a 1, and otherwise (in which case it receives nothing) it outputs 0. It is straightforward to verify that this computation correctly evaluates E_{12}^2 on all inputs. The computation uses three rounds of communication, with each machine receiving only two bits of input.

There are, unsurprisingly, many resemblances between this parallel computation and circuits — each picture in Figure 1 looks like a Boolean circuit, with machines corresponding to gates, the number of rounds corresponding to the depth, the number of machines corresponding to the size, and the number of input ports corresponding to the fan-in. We note, however, that no circuit with fan-in 2 and depth 3 (of any size) computes the function E_{12}^2, as the function depends on all nine of its inputs. This is true even for circuits with an alphabet larger than $\{0, 1\}$, such as $\{0, 1, \text{"nothing"}\}$. In general, while $\lceil \log_s n \rceil$ is an obvious lower bound on the depth of any circuit with fan-in s that computes a function that depends on all inputs, this lower bound does not necessarily hold for the number of rounds required by a MapReduce-type computation.

We emphasize that this parallel computation of E_{12}^2 can be trivially translated to a modern parallel processing infrastructure such as MapReduce (see also Appendix A). Any model that purports to capture arbitrary MapReduce-type computations, as opposed to restricted families of algorithms, should accommodate computations like the one above without significant overhead.

2.2 The Basic Model

What augmentations to standard circuit models are required to capture arbitrary MapReduce-type computations? The first two are evident from our parallel computation of E_{12}^2 in Section 2.1.

(1) The communication pattern, which plays the role of the circuit topology (i.e., which gates are connected to which), can be input-dependent. (cf., Figure 1.)

(2) Each machine has the option of staying silent and sending nothing. We refer to this as "sending a $\perp$."

At first blush, extension (2) might seem equivalent to enlarging the alphabet by one character. This is not quite correct, since $\perp$'s combine with each other and with other bits in a particular way.

Definition 2.2 ($\perp$-sum) The *$\perp$-sum* of $z_1, z_2, \ldots, z_m \in \{0, 1, \perp\}$ is:

- 1 if exactly one z_i is 1 and the rest are $\perp$;
- 0 if exactly one z_i is 0 and the rest are $\perp$;
- $\perp$ if every z_i is $\perp$;
- undefined (or invalid) otherwise.

The $\perp$-sum of m s-tuples $a_1, \ldots, a_m$ is the entry-by-entry $\perp$-sum, denoted $\odot_{i=1}^m a_i$.

Most circuit models severely restrict the computational power of each gate. This is not appropriate in the present context, where each "gate" corresponds to a general-purpose machine embedded in a MapReduce-type infrastructure. This motivates our third extension.

(3) Each machine can perform an arbitrary computation on its inputs.[3]

[3]When the goal is to prove algorithmically meaningful upper bounds, it would be sensible to restrict machines to efficient computations. Also, the total space used by a machine, both for its input and for its computations, should be small (certainly sublinear in the total input size). Given our focus on lower bounds, our allowance of arbitrary computations and unlimited scratch space on each machine only makes our results stronger.

Our formal model extends the usual notion of a circuit (with fan-in s) to accommodate (1)–(3). Our notation follows that in Vollmer [38] for circuits.

Definition 2.3 (s-SHUFFLE Computation) An *R-round s-*SHUFFLE *computation with inputs $x_1, \ldots, x_n$ and outputs $y_1, \ldots, y_k$* has the following ingredients:

1. A set V of *machines*, which includes one machine for each input bit x_i and each output bit y_i.
2. An assignment of a *round* $r(v)$ to each machine $v \in V$. Machines corresponding to input bits have round 0. Machines corresponding to output bits have round $R+1$. All other machines have a round in $\{1, 2, \ldots, R\}$.
3. For each pair (u, v) of machines with $r(u) < r(v)$, a function α_{uv} from $\{0, 1, \perp\}^s$ to $\{0, 1, \perp\}^s$.

We think of each machine as having s "ports," where each port can accept at most 1 bit. The interpretation of a function α_{uv} is: given that machine u received $\mathbf{z} = z_1, \ldots, z_s$ on its s input ports (where each $z_i \in \{0, 1, \perp\}$), it sends the message $\alpha_{uv}(\mathbf{z}) \in \{0, 1, \perp\}^s$ to the s input ports of v.[4] Thus, machine u explicitly communicates with machine v (on at least one port) if and only if at least one coordinate of $\alpha_{uv}(\mathbf{z})$ is not $\perp$. We conclude that the model supports input-dependent communication patterns, as in (1). The model also supports (2) and (3), by definition.

The output of an s-SHUFFLE computation is evaluated as one would expect, as in circuits, with the important constraint that, on every input, each input port should receive a bit (i.e., a non-$\perp$) from at most one machine.

Definition 2.4 (Result of an s-SHUFFLE Computation) The *result* of an s-SHUFFLE computation assigns a value $g(v) \in \{0, 1, \perp\}^s$ to every machine $v \in V$, and is defined inductively as follows.

1. For a round-0 machine v, corresponding to an input bit x_i, the value $g(v)$ is the s-tuple $(x_i, \perp, \perp, \ldots, \perp)$.
2. Given the value $g(u)$ assigned to every machine u with $r(u) < q$, the value assigned to a machine v with $r(v) = q$ is the $\perp$-sum, over all machines u with $r(u) < r(v)$, of the message $\alpha_{uv}(g(u))$ sent to v by u:

$$g(v) := \odot_{u\,:\,r(u)<r(v)} \alpha_{uv}(g(u)). \quad (1)$$

The result of an s-SHUFFLE computation is *valid* if every $\perp$-sum in equation (1) is well defined, and if for every machine v corresponding to an output bit y_i, the value $g(v)$ is either $(0, \perp, \perp, \ldots, \perp)$ or $(1, \perp, \perp, \ldots, \perp)$. The "0" or "1" in the first coordinate is then interpreted as the corresponding output bit y_i. Unless otherwise noted, we consider only valid s-SHUFFLE computations.

By convention, the machines corresponding to the input and output bits of the function do not contribute to the number of rounds — these are "placeholder machines" that cannot do any non-trivial computations. Translating the parallel computations in Section 2.1 of the functions E_{12} and E_{12}^2 into the formalism of Definitions 2.3 and 2.4 yields 2-round and 3-round s-SHUFFLE computations, respectively, in accordance with intuition.

The following definition is analogous to that for circuits.

[4]The model allows a machine to communicate with machines in all later rounds, not just machines in the next round. Computations of the former type can be translated to computations of the latter type by adding dummy machines, so this is not an important distinction.

Definition 2.5 (Width) The *width* of an s-SHUFFLE computation is the maximum number of machines in a round other than round 0 and the final round.

Remark 2.6 (Randomized Computations) By definition, a randomized s-SHUFFLE computation is a probability distribution over deterministic s-SHUFFLE computations.[5] We say that such a computation computes a function f if, for every input $\mathbf{x}$, the output of the computation equals $f(\mathbf{x})$ with probability at least $2/3$.

Remark 2.7 (Unordered Inputs and Larger Alphabets) Definitions 2.3 and 2.4 are easily extended to accommodate larger alphabets and unordered input ports. With these two extensions, it is straightforward to map an arbitrary r-round MapReduce computation that uses m machines with space at most s each (as formalized in [21], for example) to an $(r+1)$-round s-shuffle computation that uses $m(r+1)$ machines (not counting the machines that correspond to input and output bits). See Section 4 for formal proofs.

2.3 An Upper Bound for the Unbounded Width Model

We have argued that the s-SHUFFLE model in Definitions 2.3 and 2.4, and appropriate extensions thereof, capture arbitrary MapReduce-type computations, even those that perform exorbitant computation at each machine. What kind of lower bounds can we hope to prove for such a strong model?

To calibrate our aspirations, we next prove that, for every $s \geq 2$ and every function $f : \{0,1\}^n \to \{0,1\}^k$, f can be computed by an s-SHUFFLE computation in $\lceil \log_s n \rceil$ rounds. This upper bound requires s-SHUFFLE computations with unbounded width, and it delineates the strongest-possible lower bounds that that can be proved for the unbounded-width model. The prospects for stronger lower bounds for polynomial-width s-SHUFFLE computations are the subject of Section 7.

Proposition 2.8 For every $s \geq 2$, every function $f : \{0,1\}^n \to \{0,1\}^k$ can be computed by an s-SHUFFLE computation in $\lceil \log_s n \rceil$ rounds.

Proof (sketch): There is one machine $v_{\mathbf{x}}$ at round $\lceil \log_s n \rceil$ – the last round before the outputs – for each possible input $\mathbf{x} \in \{0,1\}^n$. Each machine $v_{\mathbf{x}}$ serves as the root of a tree of depth $\lceil \log_s n \rceil$, the machines of which are responsible for notifying $v_{\mathbf{x}}$ whether or not the input is $\mathbf{x}$. The unique machine $v_{\mathbf{x}}$ that is told that the input is indeed $\mathbf{x}$ sends the bits of the answer $f(\mathbf{x})$ to the k output machines; all other machines $v_{\mathbf{x}}$ send nothing. □

3. REPRESENTING SHUFFLES AS POLYNOMIALS

3.1 Representing the Basic Model

To prove lower bounds on the number of rounds required by an s-SHUFFLE computation, we associate each computation with a polynomial over the reals that matches (on $\{0,1\}^n$) the function it computes. We show that the number of rounds used by the computation governs the maximum degree of this polynomial, and hence

[5]This definition corresponds to "public coins," in that it allows different machines to coordinate their coin flips with no communication. One could also define a "private coins" model where each machine flips its own coins. Our lower bounds are for the stronger public-coin model, and apply to the private-coin model as a special case.

functions that correspond to polynomials of high degree cannot be computed in few rounds.

Theorem 3.1 *Suppose that an s-*SHUFFLE *computation computes the function $f : \{0,1\}^n \rightarrow \{0,1\}^k$ in r rounds. Then there are k polynomials $\{p_i(x_1,\ldots,x_n)\}_{i=1}^k$ of degree at most s^r such that $p_i(\mathbf{x}) = f(\mathbf{x})_i$ for all $i \in \{1,2,\ldots,k\}$ and $\mathbf{x} \in \{0,1\}^n$.*

PROOF. We proceed by induction on the number of rounds. We claim that for every non-output machine $v \in V$ and value $\mathbf{z} \in \{0,1,\perp\}^s$, there is a polynomial $p_{v,\mathbf{z}}(x_1,\ldots,x_n)$ that evaluates to 1 on points $\mathbf{x}$ for which the computation's assigned value $g(v)$ to v is $\mathbf{z}$ and to 0 on all other points $\mathbf{x} \in \{0,1\}^n$. Furthermore, $p_{v,\mathbf{z}}$ has degree at most $s^{r(v)}$.

The base case of the induction is for a machine v in round zero ($r(v) = 0$). Each such machine corresponds to an input bit x_i and its value $g(v)$ is $(x_i, \perp, \perp, \ldots, \perp)$. The (degree-1) polynomials for $\mathbf{z} = (0, \perp, \ldots, \perp)$ and $\mathbf{z} = (1, \perp, \ldots, \perp)$ are $p_{v,\mathbf{z}}(x_1,\ldots,x_n) = 1 - x_i$ and $p_{v,\mathbf{z}}(x_1,\ldots,x_n) = x_i$, respectively. All other values of $\mathbf{z}$ are impossible for such a machine, so they have polynomials $p_{v,\mathbf{z}}(x_1,\ldots,x_n) = 0$.

Consider a machine v that corresponds to neither an input bit nor an output bit. Fix some potential value $\mathbf{z} \in \{0,1,\perp\}^s$ of $g(v)$, and focus first on the ith coordinate of $g(v)$. When is it equal to z_i? We first consider the case where z_i is 0 or 1 (and not $\perp$). The entry $g(v)_i$ is a $\perp$-sum of the messages that machine v receives on port i from all machines in previous rounds. Hence $g(v)_i = z_i$ when a single machine in a previous round sends z_i on port i to machine v (and the rest send $\perp$'s). Consider some machine u of a previous round. It sends z_i on port i to machine v when $\alpha_{uv}(g(u))$ has an ith entry of z_i. The set of assigned values $g(u)$ to u that cause it to do this is the preimage, under α_{uv}, of the subset of $\{0,1,\perp\}^s$ containing all elements with a z_i in the ith coordinate. By our inductive hypothesis, for each value $g(u)$ in this preimage, there is a polynomial of degree at most $s^{r(v)-1}$ that indicates the inputs $\mathbf{x}$ for which u receives this value. Since u is assigned exactly one value, we can sum these polynomials together to get a polynomial (of degree at most $s^{r(v)-1}$) that indicates when u receives any value in this preimage. This polynomial indicates the inputs $\mathbf{x}$ for which u sends z_i to port i of machine v. Furthermore, since the s-SHUFFLE computation is valid, at most one machine in a previous round can send a non-$\perp$ value to v on port i. Summing over the polynomials of all machines in previous rounds yields a polynomial, still with degree at most $s^{r(v)-1}$, that indicates whether or not v received z_i on port i (from any machine).

The inputs $\mathbf{x}$ for which $g(v)_i = \perp$ are those for which no machine from a previous round sends a 0 or a 1 to v on the ith port. A polynomial for this case is just 1 minus the polynomials for the $g(v)_i = 0$ and $g(v)_i = 1$ cases. The degree of this polynomial is at most $s^{r(v)-1}$.

To obtain a polynomial that represents the inputs $\mathbf{x}$ for which $g(v) = \mathbf{z}$, we just take the product of the polynomials that represent the events $g(v)_1 = z_1, \ldots, g(v)_s = z_s$. This polynomial has degree at most $s^{r(v)}$, and this completes the inductive step.

Finally, consider a machine v that corresponds to an output bit y_i. As in the inductive step above, we can represent the first coordinate of $g(y_i)$ with a polynomial p_i of degree at most $s^{r(y_i)-1} = s^r$. Since the s-SHUFFLE computation is valid, the polynomial p_i also represents the ith output bit of the function f. □

See Section 4.1 for an extension of Theorem 3.1 to unordered inputs and larger alphabets.

The following corollary is immediate.

Corollary 3.2 *If some output bit of the function $f : \{0,1\}^n \rightarrow \{0,1\}^k$ cannot be represented by a polynomial with degree less than d, then every s-*SHUFFLE *computation that computes f uses at least $\lceil \log_s d \rceil$ rounds.*

Theorem 3.1 and Corollary 3.2 apply even to unbounded-width s-SHUFFLE computations. For functions f with $d = n$, the lower bound of $\lceil \log_s n \rceil$ in Corollary 3.2 matches the upper bound in Proposition 2.8 for arbitrary functions from $\{0,1\}^n$ to $\{0,1\}^k$.

There is a mature toolbox for bounding below the polynomial degree necessary to represent Boolean functions; we apply and contribute to this toolbox in Section 5.

3.2 Randomized Computations

We say that a polynomial $p(x_1,\ldots,x_n)$ *approximately represents* a Boolean function $f : \{0,1\}^n \rightarrow \{0,1\}$ if $|p(\mathbf{x}) - f(\mathbf{x})| \leq \frac{1}{3}$ for every $\mathbf{x} \in \{0,1\}^n$. The *approximate degree* of a Boolean function is the smallest value of d such that f can be approximately represented by a degree-d polynomial. We next give an analog of Theorem 3.1 for randomized s-SHUFFLE computations (Remark 2.6), which connects the rounds required by such computations to the approximate degree of Boolean functions.

Theorem 3.3 *Suppose that a randomized s-*SHUFFLE *computation computes the function $f : \{0,1\}^n \rightarrow \{0,1\}^k$ in r rounds. Then there are k polynomials $\{p_i(x_1,\ldots,x_n)\}_{i=1}^k$ of degree at most s^r such that $|p_i(\mathbf{x}) - f(\mathbf{x})_i| \leq \frac{1}{3}$ for all $i \in \{1,2,\ldots,k\}$ and $\mathbf{x} \in \{0,1\}^n$.*

PROOF. A randomized s-SHUFFLE computation is a distribution over deterministic computations. By Theorem 3.1, we can represent each output bit of these deterministic computations by a polynomial of degree at most s^r. The weighted averages of these polynomials, with the weights equal to the probabilities of the corresponding deterministic computations, yields polynomials $p_1,\ldots,p_k$ such that, for every i and $\mathbf{x} \in \{0,1\}^n$, $p_i(\mathbf{x})$ equals the probability that the randomized s-SHUFFLE computation outputs a 1 on the input $\mathbf{x}$. Since the randomized computation computes f in the sense of Remark 2.6, these polynomials satisfy the conclusion of the theorem. □

Corollary 3.4 *If some output bit of the function $f : \{0,1\}^n \rightarrow \{0,1\}^k$ has approximate degree at least d, then every randomized s-*SHUFFLE *computation that computes f uses at least $\lceil \log_s d \rceil$ rounds.*

Section 5 applies tools for bounding from below the approximate degree of Boolean functions to derive round lower bounds for randomized s-SHUFFLE computations.

4. LARGER ALPHABETS AND UNORDERED INPUTS

Definitions 2.3 and 2.4 are easily extended to accommodate larger alphabets and unordered input ports. With these two extensions, it is straightforward to map an arbitrary r-round MapReduce computation that uses m machines with space at most s each (as formalized in [21], for example) to an $(r+1)$-round s-shuffle computation that uses $m(r+1)$ machines (not counting the machines that correspond to input and output bits). The machines in a round of the s-shuffle computation are responsible for simulating the computation and communication that occurs in the corresponding round of the MapReduce computation. MapReduce computations operate on $\langle key; value \rangle$ pairs; the id of a machine plays the role of the key, and the alphabet in the s-shuffle computation corresponds to the set of all possible values in the MapReduce computation. See Appendix A for more details.

To formalize the extensions in more detail: with an arbitrary alphabet Σ, the input belongs to Σ^n and the output to Σ^k. Each machine u receives a value $g(u)$ and sends messages $\alpha_{uv}(g(u))$ belonging to $\{\Sigma \cup \{\perp\}\}^s$. A $\perp$-sum of m values from $\Sigma \cup \{\perp\}$ is defined in the obvious way whenever at most 1 of the values is not $\perp$ (and is undefined otherwise).

To incorporate unordered input ports, the functions α_{uv} are redefined to have domain and range equal to the multi-sets of Σ of cardinality at most s. A $\perp$-sum of such multi-sets is their union (with multiplicities adding), and is undefined if the sum of the multiplicities exceeds s.

4.1 Shuffles as Polynomials

We now outline how to modify Theorem 3.1 so that it applies to the extended model in Section 4. To represent a function $f : \Sigma^n \to \Sigma^k$, we use $k|\Sigma|$ polynomials. Every polynomial has one variable $x_{i\sigma}$ for each $i \in \{1, 2, \ldots, n\}$ and $\sigma \in \Sigma$. Inputs $\mathbf{x} \in \Sigma^n$ translate to binary $0/1$ inputs in the variable set $\{x_{i\sigma}\}$ in the obvious way. For $i \in \{1, 2, \ldots, k\}$ and $\sigma \in \Sigma$, the polynomial $p_{i\sigma}$ indicates the inputs for which the ith output bit f is σ.

In the proof of Theorem 3.1, a potential value $\mathbf{z}$ of a machine $g(v)$ is now a multi-set of Σ or size at most s, rather than an element of $\{0, 1, \perp\}^s$. We can no longer argue coordinate-by-coordinate. To extend the inductive argument in the proof, consider a machine v and suppose first that $\mathbf{z}$ is a multi-set of size exactly s. For a given partition of $\mathbf{z}$ into $\ell \le s$ non-empty sets, and a given assignment of these sets to ℓ machines in rounds before $r(v)$, the event that v receives the value $\mathbf{z}$ in precisely this way can be inductively expressed as a polynomial with degree at most $s^{r(v)}$. (Because $\mathbf{z}$ has the maximum-allowable size s and the computation is valid, the other machines must send nothing to v.) For a multi-set $\mathbf{z}$ with size less than s, the event that v receives some superset of $\mathbf{z}$ can be likewise expressed as a polynomial with degree at most s^r. Subtracting out the events corresponding to strict supersets of $\mathbf{z}$ — formally, using downward induction on the size of $\mathbf{z}$ — completes the representation of the event that $g(v) = \mathbf{z}$ as a polynomial with degree at most s^r.

Theorem 4.1 *Suppose that an s-SHUFFLE computation computes the function $f : \Sigma^n \to \Sigma^k$ in r rounds. Then for every $i \in \{1, 2, \ldots, k\}$ and $\sigma \in \Sigma$, the event that $f(\mathbf{x})_i = \sigma$ (for $\mathbf{x} \in \Sigma^n$) can be represented as a polynomial of degree at most s^r over the variable set $\{x_{i\sigma}\}_{i=1,\ldots,n,\sigma\in\Sigma}$.*

4.2 Lower Bounds

This section extends our lower bounds to non-Boolean alphabets, in two senses. The first case is when the computational problem is still boolean, but the word size allowed for intermediate computations is larger than a single bit. The second case is when the computational problem itself is encoded using a larger alphabet.

For the first case, we show that the lower bound of Corollary 3.2 applies unchanged to larger alphabets. We explore the second case in Section 6.4, where we show that for undirected ST-CONNECTIVITY the degree of the function remains large, even in the case of richer alphabets.

Corollary 4.2 *If some output bit j of the function $f : \{0,1\}^n \to \{0,1\}^k$ cannot be represented by a polynomial with degree less than d, then every s-SHUFFLE computation over the alphabet Σ that computes f uses at least $\lceil \log_s d \rceil$ rounds.*

PROOF. Suppose that some s-SHUFFLE computation over the alphabet Σ computes f in less than $\lceil \log_s d \rceil$ rounds. By Theorem 4.1, there is a polynomial p, over the variable set $\{x_{i\sigma}\}_{i\in[n],\sigma\in\Sigma}$, that represents the event when the jth output bit is 1 with degree less than d. Plugging in $(1 - x_i)$ for x_{i0}, x_i for x_{i1}, and 0 for all other variables $x_{i\sigma}$, we obtain a polynomial p' in the variables $\{x_i\}_{i\in[n]}$ with degree less than d, contradicting the assumption. We conclude that every s−SHUFFLE computation over Σ that computes f requires at least $\lceil \log_s d \rceil$ rounds. □

5. LOWER BOUNDS FOR POLYNOMIAL DEGREE

Corollary 3.2 and its extensions reduce the problem of proving lower bounds on the round complexity of s-SHUFFLE computations to proving lower bounds on the degree of a polynomial that exactly or approximately represents the function to be computed. There is a sophisticated set of tools for proving the latter type of lower bounds, which we now put to use.

5.1 Warm Up

Consider a Boolean function $f : \{0,1\}^n \to \{0,1\}$. If f can be represented by a polynomial p, meaning $f(\mathbf{x}) = p(\mathbf{x})$ for all $\mathbf{x} \in \{0,1\}^n$, then it can be represented by a multilinear polynomial (since $x_i^2 = x_i$ for $x_i \in \{0,1\}$). Recall that for every such function f, there is a unique multilinear polynomial that represents it (see e.g. [10]).[6] We call the degree of this polynomial the *degree* of the Boolean function. The maximum-possible degree is n.

For example, since the AND_n function is represented (uniquely) by the polynomial $\prod_{i=1}^n x_i$, it has the maximum-possible degree. Similarly, the OR_n function has degree n because it is represented by the polynomial $1 - \prod_{i=1}^n (1 - x_i)$. Corollary 3.2 immediately implies the following.

Corollary 5.1 *Every s-SHUFFLE computation that computes the AND_n or the OR_n function uses at least $\lceil \log_s n \rceil$ rounds.*

5.2 Monotone Graph Properties

While pinning down the precise degree of a Boolean function representing a graph problem can be a difficult task, there are powerful tools for proving loose but useful lower bounds.

The first ingredient concerns the decision tree complexity of monotone graph properties. Recall that a graph property is a property of undirected graphs that is independent of the vertex labeling. It is non-trivial if it does not assign the same value to all graphs, and monotone if adding edges cannot destroy the property. The Aanderaa-Rosenberg conjecture states that, for every non-trivial monotone graph property, the decision-tree complexity is $\Omega(n^2)$ [35]. It was first proved by Rivest and Vuillemin with a lower bound of $n^2/16$ [34], and a long line of work has yielded a lower bound of $n^2/3 - o(n^2)$ [23, 20, 24, 36].

The second ingredient is the known polynomial relationship between the decision tree complexity and the degree of a Boolean function. Specifically, Nisan and Smolensky (cited in [6]) proved that, for every Boolean function f, the decision-tree complexity of f is at most $2\deg(f)^4$, where $\deg(f)$ is the degree of f.

Combining these two ingredients with Corollary 3.2 yields the following.

[6] With a non-Boolean alphabet and the expanded variable set used in Section 4.1, there can be more than one representing polynomial. This does not affect our lower bounds; see Section 4.2.

Theorem 5.2 *For every non-trivial monotone graph property $f : \{0,1\}^{\binom{n}{2}} \to \{0,1\}$ of graphs with n vertices, every s-*SHUFFLE *computation that computes f requires at least $\frac{1}{2}\log_s n - \frac{1}{4}\log_s(6 - o(1))$ rounds.*

5.3 Approximate Degree and Randomized Computations

Recall from Corollary 3.4 that lower bounds on the approximate degree of a Boolean function translate to lower bounds on the number of rounds required by randomized s-SHUFFLE computations. It is also known that both the degree and decision tree complexity of every Boolean function are polynomially related to its approximate degree: $\deg(f) \le D(f) \le 216 \cdot \widetilde{\deg}(f)^6$, where $\widetilde{\deg}$ denotes the approximate degree [4, 30].[7] We therefore have the following analog of Theorem 5.2 for randomized computations.

Theorem 5.3 *For every non-trivial monotone graph property $f : \{0,1\}^{\binom{n}{2}} \to \{0,1\}$ of graphs with n vertices, every randomized s-*SHUFFLE *computation that computes f requires at least $\frac{1}{3}\log_s n - \frac{1}{6}\log_s(648 - o(1))$ rounds.*

In general, round lower bounds on deterministic s-SHUFFLE computations proved via Corollary 3.2 extend automatically, with a small constant-factor loss, to randomized computations.

6. LOWER BOUNDS FOR GRAPH COMPUTATIONS

The goal of this section is develop and apply a technique for showing that many problems that are important in the field of algorithms (as opposed to in Boolean function analysis) — such as graph connectivity problems — have maximum-possible degree.

Buhrman and de Wolf [6] credit Yaoyun Shi with the observation that a Boolean function has degree n if and only if the number of even solutions (i.e., assignments with an even number of 1s for which the function evaluates to 1) is not equal to the number of odd solutions. For the reader familiar with Boolean Fourier analysis, this corresponds to computing whether $\hat{f}([n])$, the function's Fourier coefficient for the set $[n]$, is nonzero. For example, the function XOR_n has no even solutions and 2^{n-1} odd solutions, so the function has degree n and hence (by Corollary 3.2) s-SHUFFLE computations require $\lceil \log_s n \rceil$ rounds to compute it.

6.1 Parity Difference Preliminaries

We first establish some notation and lemmas that simplify the proofs.

Definition 6.1 Given a set $S \subseteq \{0,1\}^n$, define the *parity difference function* as the number of even inputs in S minus the number of odd inputs in S:

$$\Phi(S) = \sum_{x \in S} \prod_i (-1)^{x_i}.$$

Define the *parity difference* of a Boolean function f on n bits by $\Phi(f) = \Phi(\{x \mid f(x) = 1\})$.

In Fourier-analytic terms, $\Phi(f)$ is exactly $2^n \hat{f}([n])$. We have the following identities.

[7] For some specific functions, better bounds are known. For example, the majority function has approximate degree $\Omega(\sqrt{n})$ [33].

Lemma 6.2 *(a) Suppose that $S \subseteq \{0,1\}^n$ and S_1, S_2 form a partition of S. Then*

$$\Phi(S) = \Phi(S_1) + \Phi(S_2).$$

(b) Suppose that $S \subseteq \{0,1\}^n$ with S the Cartesian product $S_1 \times S_2$ of sets S_1, S_2. Then

$$\Phi(S) = \Phi(S_1) \cdot \Phi(S_2).$$

PROOF. The lemma follows immediately from basic boolean Fourier analysis, if we consider the functions that represent the characteristic vectors of S, S_1, and S_2.

It is also easy to prove the lemma directly from definitions. For part (a), using the partition assumption, we have

$$\sum_{x \in S} \prod_i (-1)^{x_i} = \sum_{x \in S_1} \prod_i (-1)^{x_i} + \sum_{x \in S_2} \prod_i (-1)^{x_i}.$$

For part (b), we can split each $x \in S$ according to the product $S_1 \times S_2$ to factorize the sum:

$$\sum_{x \in S} \prod_i (-1)^{x_i} = \sum_{x^1 \in S_1} \sum_{x^2 \in S_2} \prod_i (-1)^{x_i^1} \prod_i (-1)^{x_i^2}$$
$$= \sum_{x^1 \in S_1} \prod_i (-1)^{x_i^1} \sum_{x^2 \in S_2} \prod_i (-1)^{x_i^2}.$$

□

6.2 Graph Connectivity Problems.

To apply these ideas to graph connectivity problems, we need to express graph problems as Boolean functions. One natural way is to use a $\binom{n}{2}$-variable input to represent an undirected graph on n vertices (or a $2\binom{n}{2}$-variable input for directed graphs), where each variable indicates the presence of absence of a given edge. This is effectively the adjacency matrix representation of the graph. (For lower bounds for the adjacency list representation, see Section 4.)

The CONNECTIVITY problem is: given a graph $G = (V, E)$, is there a path from every vertex to every other vertex? The related ST-CONNECTIVITY problem: given a graph $G = (V, E)$ and two vertices $s, t \in V$, is there a path from s to t? We can assume that s is the first vertex and t is the second vertex. We pinpoint the degree of both of these problems for both undirected and directed graphs. The proof strategy is similar for all four cases: we use induction on the number of vertices n, show how large problems can be decomposed into smaller problems, and use this decomposition to analyze the highest-degree Fourier coefficient.

6.3 Undirected Connectivity Functions

We begin with the undirected case (Theorems 6.3 and 6.4). Recall that to prove that a function has maximum-possible degree, it suffices to show that its parity difference is non-zero.

Theorem 6.3 *The degree of the Boolean function for undirected* CONNECTIVITY *on n vertices is $\binom{n}{2}$.*

PROOF. For a graph on n vertices, let f_n be the Boolean function for undirected CONNECTIVITY. We prove that

$$\Phi(f_n) = (-1)^{n-1}(n-1)!, \tag{2}$$

which implies the theorem.

We proceed by induction on n. The base case $n = 1$ is trivial; the graph is always connected and never has any edges, so $\Phi(f_1) = 1$.

Suppose that our inductive hypothesis is true for all smaller values of n. Consider the first vertex of our graph on n vertices. If we begin with a connected graph and remove this vertex, we obtain a partition of the remaining $n-1$ vertices into connected components. We can split the set S of all connected graphs into sets S_P which yield the same partition P of connected components when the first vertex is removed. By Lemma 6.2(a), $\Phi(S) = \sum_P \Phi(S_P)$.

Consider a particular partition P of $n-1$ vertices. Each block of the partition must be connected, and the first vertex of the graph must be connected to each partition block with at least one edge. Thus, S_P can be thought of as a cross product between the set of ways to connect the first vertex to the first block, the set of ways to connect the first block, the set of ways to connect the first vertex to the second block, the set of ways to connect the second block, and so on. By Lemma 6.2(b), it suffices to compute the parity difference of each of these sets separately, and take their product.

First, we consider the set of ways to connect the first vertex to a block with k vertices. There are k possible edges, and the only forbidden choice is the one with no edges. Hence there are 2^{k-1} odd choices but only $2^{k-1}-1$ even choices (the missing choice is even), and the parity difference of this set is -1.

By induction, the set of ways of connecting a block of size k has parity difference $(-1)^{k-1}(k-1)!$. Multiplying this with the parity difference of the set of ways that the first vertex can be connected to the block, the factor of a partition's parity difference corresponding to a block of size k is $(-1)^k(k-1)!$. The contribution of a single partition is the product of such terms, with one term per block.

Finally, we need to sum the parity differences over all partitions. Since these are all partitions of $n-1$ vertices, they all have the same sign: $(-1)^{n-1}$. We need to show that the total magnitude is $(n-1)!$ to complete the proof.

To see this, consider all $(n-1)!$ permutations of $n-1$ items. If we write them in cycle notation, we can view the cycles of a permutation as yielding a partition of $n-1$ vertices. A block of k vertices can be created by any of $(k-1)!$ possible cycles on these vertices. Multiplying over the blocks of a partition, we see that the number of permutations that map to a partition is exactly the magnitude of the parity difference of the partition. This implies that the total parity difference magnitude is the number $(n-1)1$ of permutations, which completes the inductive hypothesis and the proof. □

Theorem 6.4 *The degree of the Boolean function for undirected* ST-CONNECTIVITY *on n vertices is $\binom{n}{2}$.*

PROOF. For a graph on n vertices, et f_n be the Boolean function for undirected ST-CONNECTIVITY. We can assume that s and t are the first and second vertices. We show that $\Phi(f_n) = (-1)^{n-1}(n-2)! \neq 0$.

It is convenient to analyze $-\Phi(f_n)$ and consider all graphs in which s and t are *not* connected. Let $S_{A,B}$ be the subset of such graphs in which the connected component of s is A and the connected component of t is B. By Lemma 6.2(a), $-\Phi(f_n)$ is the sum of the $\Phi(S_{A,B})$'s for all such A, B.

Fix A and B. Both are connected, and the remainder of the vertices of the graph can have an arbitrary subset of edges within it. We can therefore think of $S_{A,B}$ as a product of the set of ways to connect A, the set of ways to connect B, and, if there are at least two vertices outside $A \cup B$, the set of ways to pick edges in the remainder of the graph. By Lemma 6.2(b), we only need to compute the parity differences of each of these sets and take their product.

First, we observe that if $V \setminus (A \cup B)$ contains more than one vertex, then the parity difference of the last set (all subsets of edges of $V \setminus (A \cup B)$) is zero. For the rest of the proof, we focus on sets A, B whose union includes all vertices, except possibly for one.

If A has a vertices and B has b vertices, then by (2) the parity difference for the set of ways to connect A is $(-1)^{a-1}(a-1)!$ and the parity difference for the set of ways to connect B is $(-1)^{b-1}(b-1)!$.

Since $V \setminus (A \cup B)$ has zero or one vertex, there are $\frac{(n-2)!}{(a-1)!(b-1)!}$ ways to choose a set A of size a and a set B of size b. (In the latter case, there are $n-2$ choices for the missing vertex, and $\binom{n-3}{a-1}$ ways of selecting the vertices that join s in A.) Thus, the total contribution to the parity difference of sets A, B with sizes a, b is $(-1)^{n-2}(n-2)!$ (if $a+b=n$) or $(-1)^{n-3}(n-2)!$ (if $a+b=n-1$). There are $n-1$ ways to choose $a \geq 1$ and $b \geq 1$ so that $a+b=n$, and $n-2$ ways to choose $a \geq 1$ and $b \geq 1$ so that $a+b=n-1$. Our final parity difference (for $-\Phi$) is

$$(n-1)(-1)^{n-2}(n-2)! + (n-2)(-1)^{n-3}(n-2)! = (-1)^{n-2}(n-2)!.$$

This completes the proof. □

6.4 Connectivity with Large Alphabets

We consider the ST-CONNECTIVITY problem, except the graph is no longer presented as an adjacency matrix as in the boolean case. Instead, we are presented with a list of m edges. We model these as m inputs from an alphabet of size $\binom{n}{2}$. We will even assume the algorithm is promised that these edges never repeat (if they could, it would be fairly easy to prove difficulty from OR). We have a bound on degree given that there are enough vertices in the graph. Note that some such condition is necessary, since too few vertices would guarantee that nodes 0 and 1 are always connected. Our vertex requirement is only a constant factor more than the minimum n to accommodate m distinct edges.

Theorem 6.5 *Let f be the function associated with the problem of undirected* ST-CONNECTIVITY *presented as an adjacency list. Any polynomial associated with this function being true has degree at least m, given $n \geq \sqrt{8m}$.*

PROOF. Again, we will show this by plugging variables into such a polynomial. Let p be a polynomial over $x_{i\sigma}$ with degree at least m which is 1 when s and t are connected and 0 otherwise.

Each edge of the input originally has $\binom{n}{2}$ possibilities, but our plan is actually to further constrain them; we promise each edge of the input will be one of two possible values. We do this in such a way that exactly one of these 2^m possibilities results in s and t being unconnected. Equivalently, we can plug in y_i, $(1-y_i)$, or 0 for every $x_{i\sigma}$ in a way such that we get the polynomial of degree at least m (we get the polynomial for OR). But the degree of p can only decrease when we perform this operation, so this contradicts our assumption about the degree of p. Hence we will have shown that no such p exists.

As usual, we assume that s and t are vertices 0 and 1. We want to choose pairs so that only one possibility does not connect 0 and 1. The first set of inputs are chosen so that this possibility connects all odd vertices and connects all even vertices. Our first input is either $(0,1)$ or $(0,2)$, our second input is either $(1,2)$ or $(1,3)$, and our third input is either $(2,3)$ or $(2,4)$. We continue in this fashion. Notice if we ever pick the first possibility, 0 and 1 must be connected. This continues so that either 0 and 1 are connected or all even vertices are connected and all odd vertices are connected. Then the remaining inputs offer an edge between vertices of opposite parity, which will connect 0 and 1, or between vertices of the same parity. Note that we never repeat an edge in this process. This yields are least $\frac{n^2}{8}$ pairs, which is more than m if $n \geq \sqrt{8m}$. □

6.5 Directed Connectivity Functions

For the more complicated case of directed graphs, we state the theorems below, but defer the proofs to the full version of the paper.

Theorem 6.6 *For a graph of n vertices, the degree of the Boolean function for directed* CONNECTIVITY *is* $2\binom{n}{2}$.

Theorem 6.7 *For a graph of n vertices, the degree of the Boolean function for directed* ST-CONNECTIVITY *n vertices is* $\binom{n}{2}$.

7. PROSPECTS FOR STRONGER LOWER BOUNDS

Our lower bounds in Section 3 and 5 apply to general unbounded-width s-SHUFFLE computations, and by Proposition 2.8 such lower bounds cannot be larger than $\lceil \log_s n \rceil$. Realizable MapReduce-type computations translate to s-SHUFFLE computations with a reasonable number of machines, so a natural question is whether or not stronger lower bounds hold for a polynomial number of machines. For example, can we prove that there is no $O(1)$-round s-SHUFFLE computation for graph connectivity problems with $s = \sqrt{n}$ and a polynomial number of machines? In this section we show that proving such stronger impossibility results requires proving circuit lower bounds.

The following result, while not difficult to prove, has significant implications for the prospects of strong lower bounds for parallel computation.

Theorem 7.1 *Consider any model of parallel computation with the following properties:*

1. *The number of machines is polynomial in the input size n.*
2. *Computation proceeds in time steps. In each time step, a machine can read $s(n) \geq 2$ bits from the input or from previous rounds of computation.*
3. *Each machine can output at least a single bit, which is a function of the $s(n)$ bits it read. The possible functions a machine can compute need only include Boolean formulas where each variable appears once.*

Suppose some problem in P cannot be solved in $O(\log_{s(n)} n)$ time steps in such a model. Then $NC^1 \subsetneq P$.

PROOF. We simply need to show that any model with these features can still simulate NC^1 circuits. Recall that NC^1 is the family of problems that can be computed by a logspace-uniform circuit family C_n of fan-in 2 with $poly(n)$ gates and $O(\log n)$ depth. Fix some such model of parallel computation. We will transform each circuit into a computation in our model which runs in $\log_{s(n)} n$ time steps. This will show that no NC^1 family computes our hypothesized problem, and hence $NC^1 \subsetneq P$, as desired.

The computation will compute the output of every circuit gate with a machine. Each time step will correspond to $\log s(n)$ layers of the circuit. For example, in the first time step, we will have a machine for every gate at depth at most $\log s(n)$. Since the circuit had fan-in 2, each gate's output can be determined from at most $s(n)$ inputs. Furthermore, the output as a function of these inputs is a Boolean formula where each of these $s(n)$ inputs appears only once. In general, in the ith time step, we have a machine for every gate at depth between $(i-1)\log s(n)$ and $i \log s(n)$. Again, these can be determined from at most $s(n)$ inputs or gates in previous time steps. We get to output gates within $O(\frac{\log n}{\log s(n)}) = O(\log_{s(n)} n)$ time steps. Each gate becomes a single machine, for $poly(n)$ machines. Figure 2 illustrates this simulation for a specific circuit of depth four. □

The barrier of $\Theta(\log_{s(n)} n)$ for lower bounds in Theorem 7.1 is the same as the lower bounds we proved, even for the unbounded-width model, in Sections 3 and 5.

Property (1) states that an arbitrarily large polynomial number of machines should be allowed. Property (2) asks for a complete communication graph and concurrent reads, and property (3) only requires fairly weak computing power per machine. s-SHUFFLE computations with a polynomial number of machines are certainly one example of a model that satisfies these assumptions. The point of Theorem 7.1 is that, more generally, the *only possible way* of proving lower bounds stronger than $\Theta(\log_s n)$ for any model of parallel computation is to either (i) prove a notoriously difficult circuit lower bound or (ii) restrict the model so much that one of the hypotheses in the theorem is not satisfied. For example, Theorem 7.1 leaves open the possibility of proving strong lower bounds for restricted classes of algorithms (this violates the third assumption); some of the previous work reviewed in Section 1.2 is of this type. Another possible approach to proving stronger lower bounds is to restrict the number of machines to be very small, for example at most constant factor larger than the minimum number n/s needed to read the input.[8]

The simulation argument in the proof of Theorem 7.1 is quite versatile. For example, it also works in the uniform setting. Since NC^1 is defined to be logspace-uniform, the lower bound barrier holds even if the model of parallel computation is restricted to logspace-uniform computations. This simulation also only blows up the width by a factor of $\log s$ from circuit to parallel computation. Hence, given a round lower bound on a width-restricted model of parallel computation, we would get a depth lower bound on a width-restricted (less so by a factor $\log s$) version of NC, which would still be an interesting result for circuit complexity. Similarly, the simulation results in the same number of machines as there were gates, so a round lower bound for a machine-restricted model of parallel computation would give a depth lower bound for a size-restricted version of NC.

8. REFERENCES

[1] Foto N. Afrati, Anish Das Sarma, Semih Salihoglu, and Jeffrey D. Ullman. Upper and lower bounds on the cost of a map-reduce computation. *PVLDB*, 6(4):277–288, 2013.

[2] Alexandr Andoni, Aleksandar Nikolov, Krzysztof Onak, and Grigory Yaroslavtsev. Parallel algorithms for geometric graph problems. In *Symposium on Theory of Computing, STOC 2014, New York, NY, USA, May 31 - June 03, 2014*, pages 574–583, 2014.

[3] MohammadHossein Bateni, Aditya Bhaskara, Silvio Lattanzi, and Vahab S. Mirrokni. Distributed balanced clustering via mapping coresets. In *Advances in Neural Information Processing Systems 27: Annual Conference on Neural Information Processing Systems 2014, December 8-13 2014, Montreal, Quebec, Canada*, pages 2591–2599, 2014.

[4] Robert Beals, Harry Buhrman, Richard Cleve, Michele Mosca, and Ronald De Wolf. Quantum lower bounds by polynomials. *Journal of the ACM (JACM)*, 48(4):778–797, 2001.

[8] Limiting the number of machines to be at most a specific function of n, rather than to an arbitrary polynomial n, has various technical drawbacks, such as losing the self-reducibility of many problems.

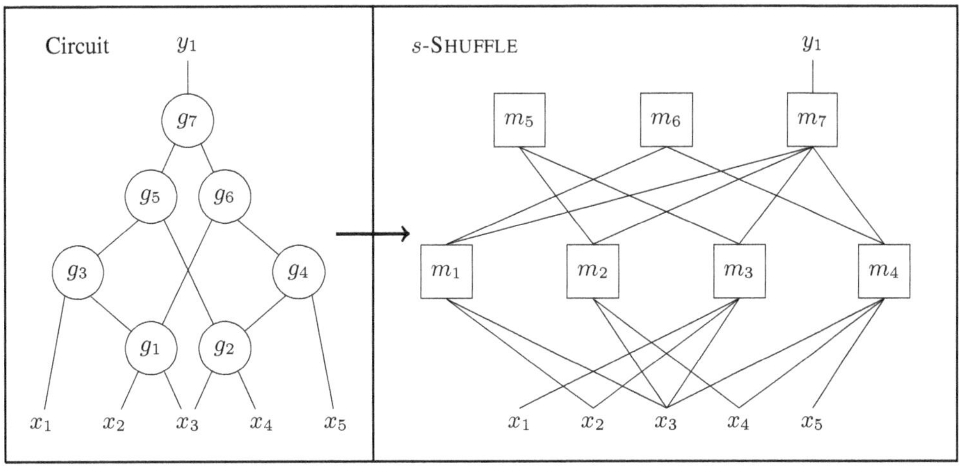

Figure 2: A depth-four circuit and its corresponding s-SHUFFLE with $s = 4$ that runs in two rounds. The number on a machine matches the number of the gate it computes.

[5] Paul Beame, Paraschos Koutris, and Dan Suciu. Communication steps for parallel query processing. In *Proceedings of the 32nd ACM SIGMOD-SIGACT-SIGART Symposium on Principles of Database Systems, PODS 2013, New York, NY, USA - June 22 - 27, 2013*, pages 273–284, 2013.

[6] Harry Buhrman and Ronald De Wolf. Complexity measures and decision tree complexity: a survey. *Theoretical Computer Science*, 288(1):21–43, 2002.

[7] Stephen Cook, Cynthia Dwork, and Rüdiger Reischuk. Upper and lower time bounds for parallel random access machines without simultaneous writes. *SIAM Journal on Computing*, 15(1):87–97, 1986.

[8] Jeffrey Dean and Sanjay Ghemawat. Mapreduce: Simplified data processing on large clusters. In *6th Symposium on Operating System Design and Implementation (OSDI 2004), San Francisco, California, USA, December 6-8, 2004*, pages 137–150, 2004.

[9] Martin Dietzfelbinger, Mirosław Kutyłowski, and Rüdiger Reischuk. Exact lower time bounds for computing boolean functions on crew prams. *Journal of Computer and System Sciences*, 48(2):231–254, 1994. Preliminary version in *SPAA '90*.

[10] R. O' Donnell. *Analysis of Boolean Functions*. Cambridge, 2014.

[11] Andrew Drucker, Fabian Kuhn, and Rotem Oshman. On the power of the congested clique model. In *Proceedings of the 2014 ACM Symposium on Principles of Distributed Computing (PODC)*, pages 367–376. ACM, 2014.

[12] Alina Ene, Sungjin Im, and Benjamin Moseley. Fast clustering using mapreduce. In *Proceedings of the 17th ACM SIGKDD International Conference on Knowledge Discovery and Data Mining, San Diego, CA, USA, August 21-24, 2011*, pages 681–689, 2011.

[13] Jon Feldman, S. Muthukrishnan, Anastasios Sidiropoulos, Clifford Stein, and Zoya Svitkina. On distributing symmetric streaming computations. In *Proceedings of the Nineteenth Annual ACM-SIAM Symposium on Discrete Algorithms, SODA 2008, San Francisco, California, USA, January 20-22, 2008*, pages 710–719, 2008.

[14] Benjamin Fish, Jeremy Kun, Ádám Dániel Lelkes, Lev Reyzin, and György Turán. On the computational complexity of mapreduce. *CoRR*, abs/1410.0245, 2014.

[15] Ashish Goel and Kamesh Munagala. Complexity measures for map-reduce, and comparison to parallel computing. *CoRR*, abs/1211.6526, 2012.

[16] Michael T. Goodrich, Nodari Sitchinava, and Qin Zhang. Sorting, searching, and simulation in the mapreduce framework. In *Algorithms and Computation - 22nd International Symposium, ISAAC 2011, Yokohama, Japan, December 5-8, 2011. Proceedings*, pages 374–383, 2011.

[17] James W. Hegeman and Sriram V. Pemmaraju. Lessons from the congested clique applied to MapReduce. *Theoretical Computer Science*, 608:268–281, 2015.

[18] Pavel Hrubes and Anup Rao. Circuits with medium fan-in. In *Proceedings of CCC*, 2015.

[19] Riko Jacob, Tobias Lieber, and Nodari Sitchinava. On the complexity of list ranking in the parallel external memory model. In *Mathematical Foundations of Computer Science 2014 - 39th International Symposium, MFCS 2014, Budapest, Hungary, August 25-29, 2014. Proceedings, Part II*, pages 384–395, 2014.

[20] Jeff Kahn, Michael Saks, and Dean Sturtevant. A topological approach to evasiveness. *Combinatorica*, 4(4):297–306, 1984.

[21] Howard J. Karloff, Siddharth Suri, and Sergei Vassilvitskii. A model of computation for MapReduce. In *Proceedings of the Twenty-First Annual ACM-SIAM Symposium on Discrete Algorithms, SODA 2010, Austin, Texas, USA, January 17-19, 2010*, pages 938–948, 2010.

[22] Hartmut Klauck, Danupon Nanongkai, Gopal Pandurangan, and Peter Robinson. Distributed computation of large-scale graph problems. In *Proceedings of the Twenty-Sixth Annual ACM-SIAM Symposium on Discrete Algorithms, SODA 2015, San Diego, CA, USA, January 4-6, 2015*, pages 391–410, 2015.

[23] Daniel J. Kleitman and D. J. Kwiatkowski. Further results on the aanderaa-rosenberg conjecture. *J. Comb. Theory, Ser. B*, 28(1):85–95, 1980.

[24] Torsten Korneffel and Eberhard Triesch. An asymptotic bound for the complexity of monotone graph properties. *Combinatorica*, 30(6):735–743, 2010.

[25] Ravi Kumar, Benjamin Moseley, Sergei Vassilvitskii, and Andrea Vattani. Fast greedy algorithms in mapreduce and streaming. In *25th ACM Symposium on Parallelism in Algorithms and Architectures, SPAA '13, Montreal, QC, Canada - July 23 - 25, 2013*, pages 1–10, 2013.

[26] Silvio Lattanzi, Benjamin Moseley, Siddharth Suri, and Sergei Vassilvitskii. Filtering: a method for solving graph problems in mapreduce. In *SPAA 2011: Proceedings of the 23rd Annual ACM Symposium on Parallelism in Algorithms and Architectures, San Jose, CA, USA, June 4-6, 2011 (Co-located with FCRC 2011)*, pages 85–94, 2011.

[27] J. Leskovec, A. Rajaraman, and J. D. Ullman. *Mining of Massive Datasets*. Cambridge, 2014. Second Edition.

[28] Vahab Mirrokni and Morteza Zadimoghaddam. Randomized composable core-sets for distributed submodular maximization. In *Symposium on Theory of Computing, STOC 2015, Portland, OR, USA*, 2015.

[29] Noam Nisan. Crew prams and decision trees. *SIAM Journal on Computing*, 20(6):999–1007, 1991.

[30] Noam Nisan and Mario Szegedy. On the degree of boolean functions as real polynomials. *Computational complexity*, 4(4):301–313, 1994.

[31] David Peleg. Distributed computing. *SIAM Monographs on discrete mathematics and applications*, 5, 2000.

[32] Andrea Pietracaprina, Geppino Pucci, Matteo Riondato, Francesco Silvestri, and Eli Upfal. Space-round tradeoffs for mapreduce computations. In *International Conference on Supercomputing, ICS'12, Venice, Italy, June 25-29, 2012*, pages 235–244, 2012.

[33] A.A. Razborov. Lower bounds on the size of bounded depth circuits over a complete basis with logical addition. *Mathematical notes of the Academy of Sciences of the USSR*, 41(4):333–338, 1987.

[34] Ronald L Rivest and Jean Vuillemin. A generalization and proof of the aanderaa-rosenberg conjecture. In *Proceedings of seventh annual ACM symposium on Theory of computing*, pages 6–11. ACM, 1975.

[35] Arnold L Rosenberg. On the time required to recognize properties of graphs: A problem. *ACM SIGACT News*, 5(4):15–16, 1973.

[36] Robert Scheidweiler and Eberhard Triesch. A lower bound for the complexity of monotone graph properties. *SIAM Journal on Discrete Mathematics*, 27(1):257–265, 2013.

[37] Leslie G. Valiant. A bridging model for parallel computation. *Commun. ACM*, 33(8):103–111, 1990.

[38] Heribert Vollmer. *Introduction to circuit complexity: a uniform approach*. Springer Science & Business Media, 1999.

[39] David P. Woodruff and Qin Zhang. When distributed computation is communication expensive. In *Distributed Computing - 27th International Symposium, DISC 2013, Jerusalem, Israel, October 14-18, 2013. Proceedings*, pages 16–30, 2013.

APPENDIX

A. SIMULATING MAPREDUCE

To illustrate the power of the s-SHUFFLE model, this appendix shows how an s-SHUFFLE computation can be used to simulate a MapReduce computation. We focus specifically on the $\mathcal{MRC}$ class defined in [21].

Recall that in the MapReduce programming paradigm, the basic unit of information is a $\langle key; value \rangle$ pair. The computation in a given round is defined by two sets of functions, mappers and reducers. A mapper, μ is a function that takes as input some number of $\langle key; value \rangle$ pairs and, independently for each such pair, produces a finite multiset of $\langle key; value \rangle$ pairs. A reducer, ρ is a function that takes as input a binary string k, representing the key, and a set of values $v_1, v_2, \ldots$, and outputs a set of $\langle key; value \rangle$ pairs, all with key k. We can think of the set of reducers as being indexed by the corresponding key k.

For the simulation below it will be useful to have an explicit bound on the size of any $\langle key; value \rangle$ pair.

Lemma A.1 *Any randomized $\mathcal{MRC}$ computation can be simulated round per round with an $\mathcal{MRC}$ computation where every $\langle key; value \rangle$ pair has at most $w = O(\log n)$ bits.*

Proof (sketch): First suppose that in a $\langle key; value \rangle$ pair, the length of the key is larger than $3 \log n$ bits. We can transform the pair into $\langle h(key); key\$value \rangle$, where h is a universal hash function onto $3 \log n$ bits. Since there are at most $n^{2-2\epsilon}$ unique keys, with high probability each long key is mapped to a unique short key, thereby keeping the logic of the computation intact.

Now consider a $\langle key; value \rangle$ pair where the value string $s = v_1 v_2 v_3 \ldots v_k$ has $k > c = w - 4 \log n$ bits. We can break the string into substrings $s_1 = v_1 v_2 \ldots v_t$, $s_2 = v_{t+1} v_{t+2} \ldots v_{2t}$, and so on. We then transform the pair $\langle key, s \rangle$ into a set of $\lceil k/c \rceil$ pairs $\langle key, u\$i\$s_i \rangle$, where u is a random $2 \log n$ bit integer, and \$ is a unique symbol. Since the length of the original string was at most $n^{1-\epsilon}$, each value now has at most w bits. Since all of these pairs have the same key they, they will be shuffled to the same reducer. Provided the integers u generated for each value string we break up are unique (a high probability event since there are at most $n^{2-\epsilon}$ pairs), the machine can use the indexes to reconstruct the original value string. □

Proposition A.2 Every r-round $\mathcal{MRC}$ computation with capacity s per mapper and reducer can be simulated by a $(r+1)$-round s-SHUFFLE computation.

Proof (sketch): We use the version of the s-SHUFFLE model with an arbitrary finite alphabet and unordered input ports (Section 4). Our alphabet Σ will be the set of all possible w-bit words. (With $w = O(\log n)$, $|\Sigma|$ is polynomial in n.)

Round $i+1$ of the s-SHUFFLE computation consists of one machine per round-i reducer of the $\mathcal{MRC}$ computation. (The space constraint of $n^{1-\epsilon}$ in the latter computation translates to a fan-in constraint of $s = n^{1-\epsilon}$ in the former computation.) Each such machine simulates the work of both the corresponding round-i reducer and the subsequent processing of the generated key-value pairs by the round-$(i+1)$ mappers. Round 1 of the s-SHUFFLE computation simulates the first mapping round of the $\mathcal{MRC}$ computation. The requisite machines corresponding to the inputs and outputs are added before the initial mappers and the final reducers. The functions α_{uv} simulate the message-passing of key-value pairs in the $\mathcal{MRC}$ computation (these are non-trivial only for pairs u, v of machines in consecutive rounds). □

Acknowledgments

We thank Noam Nisan for pointing us to several relevant references.

Parallel Algorithms for Summing Floating-Point Numbers

Michael T. Goodrich
Dept. of Computer Science
University of California, Irvine
Irvine, CA 92697 USA
goodrich@acm.org

Ahmed Eldawy
Dept. of Computer Science and Engineering
University of California, Riverside
Riverside, CA 92521 USA
eldawy@cs.ucr.edu

ABSTRACT

The problem of *exactly* summing n floating-point numbers is a fundamental problem that has many applications in large-scale simulations and computational geometry. Unfortunately, due to the round-off error in standard floating-point operations, this problem becomes very challenging. Moreover, all existing solutions rely on sequential algorithms which cannot scale to the huge datasets that need to be processed.

In this paper, we provide several efficient *parallel* algorithms for summing n floating point numbers, so as to produce a faithfully rounded floating-point representation of the sum. We present algorithms in PRAM, external-memory, and MapReduce models, and we also provide an experimental analysis of our MapReduce algorithms, due to their simplicity and practical efficiency.

1. INTRODUCTION

Floating-point numbers are a common data type for representing values that can vary widely. A (base-2) floating-point representation[1] of a number, x, is a sign bit, b, and pair of integers, (b, M, E), such that

$$x = (-1)^b \times (1 + 2^{-t}M) \times 2^{E-2^{l-1}-1},$$

where t is the number of bits allocated for M and l is the number of bits allocated for E. The value, M, is called the ***mantissa*** or ***significand*** and the value E is called the ***exponent***. For more background information on floating-point numbers, please see, e.g., the excellent survey by Goldberg [15].

In ***fixed-precision*** representations, specific values for t and l are set according to machine-architecture or established standards. For example, in the IEEE 754 standard, single-precision floating-point numbers use $t = 23$ and $l = 8$, double-precision floating-point numbers use $t = 52$ and $l = 11$, and quad-precision floating-point numbers use $t = 112$ and $l = 15$.

In ***arbitrary-precision*** representations, the number of bits, t, for the mantissa, is allowed to vary, either to be as large as a machine's memory size or to be an arbitrary value set by a user. The number, l, of bits for the exponent in such representations is typically set to be a single memory word, since a single memory word is usually sufficient to store any memory address. Examples of systems for processing arbitrary-precision floating point representations include Apfloat for Java [35], the GNU Multiple Precision (GMP) Arithmatic Library [14], the `bigfloat` type in LEDA [4], and the GNU Multiple-Precision Floating-Point (MPFR) Library [12, 19].

In either fixed-precision or arbitrary-precision representations, we do ***not*** assume in this paper that floating-point numbers are normalized so that the most significant bit of the mantissa is 1.

Given a set $X = \{x_1, x_2, \ldots, x_n\}$, of n floating-point numbers, we are interested in the design and analysis of parallel algorithms for computing a floating point number, S_n^*, that best approximates the sum

$$S_n = \sum_{i=1}^{n} x_i.$$

Moreover, we are interested in methods that are not limited to a specific fixed precision representation, such as IEEE 754 double-precision. In particular, the specific problem we are interested in is to compute the floating-point number S_n^* that is a ***faithfully rounded*** representation of S_n, where we consider the value S_n^* to be faithfully rounded as long as S_n^* is either the largest floating-point number less than or equal to S_n or the smallest floating-point number greater than or equal to S_n. For other ways of rounding floating-point numbers, please see the IEEE 754 standard.

Although the problem of accurately summing n floating-point numbers might at first seem simple, it is surprisingly challenging, due to the roundoff error inherent in floating-point arithmetic. Standard floating-point addition, which we denote as "$\oplus$," is not exact, so that for two floating-point numbers, x and y,

$$x \oplus y = (x + y)(1 + \epsilon_{x,y}); |\epsilon_{x,y}| \leq |\epsilon|,$$

where $\epsilon_{x,y}$ is a summand-specific roundoff error and ϵ is a machine-specific worst-case error term [23, 25].

[1]We take the viewpoint in this paper that floating-point numbers are a base-2 representation; nevertheless, our algorithms can easily be modified to work with other standard floating-point bases, such as 10.

SPAA'16, July 11–13, 2016, Pacific Grove, CA, USA.

ISBN 978-1-4503-4210-0/16/07...$15.00

DOI: http://dx.doi.org/10.1145/2935764.2935779

As is well-known, a standard way to sum n numbers, given the set X, is to place the numbers from X in the leaves of a binary summation tree, T, where each internal node, v, is associated with the sum of the values in v's two children, which in this case could be the $\oplus$ operation. Unfortunately, if the collection, X, of summands contains positive and negative numbers, it is NP-complete to find the summation tree, T, that utilizes only the $\oplus$ operation and minimizes the worst-case error for the sum [23]. Even for the case when all the numbers in X are positive, the optimal $\oplus$-based summation tree is a Huffman tree [23], which is not necessarily efficient to compute and evaluate in parallel. Thus, designing efficient parallel algorithms for accurately summing n floating-point numbers is a challenge.

Because of these complexity issues and the uncertainty that comes from roundoff errors, many recent floating-point summation algorithms are based on exactly computing a rounded sum of two floating point numbers, x and y, and the exact value of its error, utilizing a function,

$$\text{AddTwo}(x, y) \rightarrow (s, e_s),$$

where $s = x \oplus y$ and $x + y = s + e_s$, with s and e_s being floating point numbers in the same precision as x and y. Example implementations of the AddTwo function include algorithms by Dekker [8] and Knuth [25], both of which utilize a constant number of floating-point operations. As with these recent approaches, in this paper we take the approach of summing the numbers in X exactly and then faithfully rounding this exact sum to the an appropriate floating-point representation.

As mentioned above, because we desire precision-independent algorithms, which can work for either fixed-precision or arbitrary-precision representations, we do not take the perspective in this paper that floating-point numbers must be restricted to a specific floating-point representation, such as IEEE 754 double-precision. As is common in other precision-independent algorithms, however, we do assume that a floating-point representation is sufficiently precise so that the number, n, could itself be represented exactly as a sum of a constant number of floating-point numbers. A similar assumption is common in integer-based RAM and PRAM algorithms,[2] and poses no restriction in practice, since it amounts to saying that a memory address can be stored in $O(1)$ memory words. For example, even if all the computer storage on earth[3] were interpreted as IEEE 754 single-precision numbers and summed, we could represent the input size, n, as the (exact) sum of at most four single-precision floating-point numbers.

As a way of characterizing difficult problem instances, having the potential for significant amounts of cancellation, the ***condition number***, $C(X)$, for X, is defined as follows [34,39,40]:

$$C(X) = \frac{\sum_{i=1}^{n} |x_i|}{\left|\sum_{i=1}^{n} x_i\right|},$$

which, of course, is defined only for non-zero sums.[4] Intuitively, problem instances with large condition numbers are more difficult than problem instances with condition numbers close to 1.

Our approach for designing efficient parallel algorithms for summing n floating point numbers, even for difficult problem instances with large condition numbers, is to utilize an approach somewhat reminiscent of the classic Fast Fourier Transform (FFT) algorithm (e.g., see [3,18]). Namely, to compute the sum of n floating-point numbers, we convert the numbers to an alternative representation, compute the sum of the numbers exactly in this alternative representation, and then convert the result back to a (faithfully-rounded) floating-point number. In our case, the important feature of our alternative representation is that it allows us to compute intermediate sums without propagating carry bits, which provides for superior parallelization.

1.1 Previous Related Results

The floating-point summation problem poses interesting challenges for parallel computation, because most existing published exact-summation algorithms are inherently sequential. For instance, we are not aware of any previous parallel methods for this problem that run in worst-case polylogarithmic time.

Neal [30] describes sequential algorithms that use a number representation that he calls a ***superaccumulator*** to exactly sum n floating point numbers, which he then converts to a faithfully-rounded floating-point number. Unfortunately, while Neal's superaccumulator representation reduces carry-bit propagation, it does not eliminate it, as is needed for highly-parallel algorithms. A similar idea has been used in ExBLAS [6], an open source library for exact floating point computations. Shewchuck [33] describes an alternative representation for exactly representing intermediate results of floating-point arithmetic, but his method also does not eliminate carry-bit propagation in summations; hence, it also does not lead to efficient parallel algorithms. In addition to these methods, there are a number of inherently sequential methods for exactly summing n floating point numbers using various other data structures for representing intermediate results, including ExBLAS [6] and algorithms by Zhu and Hayes [39,40], Demmel and Hida [9,10], Rump *et al.* [34], Priest [32], and Malcolm [29]. Although the method of Demmel and Hida [10] can be carry-free for a limited number of summands, none of these sequential methods utilize a completely carry-free intermediate representation suitable for efficient parallelization. Nevertheless, Rump *et al.* [34] provide an interesting analysis that the running time of their sequential method can be estimated to depend on n and a logarithm of the condition number and other factors. Also, Demmel and Hida [10] showed that summing the numbers in a decreasing order by exponent yields a highly accurate answer, yet, the answer does not have to be faithfully-rounded.

There has also been a limited amount of previous work on parallel algorithms for summing floating-point numbers. Leuprecht and Oberaigner [28] describe parallel algorithms for summing floating-point numbers, for instance, but their methods only parallelize data pipelining, however,

[2] A PRAM is a synchronized parallel random-access machine model [21], where memory is shared between processors, so that memory accesses are exclusive-read/exclusive-write (EREW), concurrent-read/exclusive-write (CREW), or concurrent-read/concurrent-write (CRCW).

[3] As of the writing of this paper, the total computer storage on earth is estimated to be less than 8 zettabytes, that is, 8 trillion gigabytes.

[4] We could alternatively define a condition number that adds to the denominator a very small value to avoid division by zero.

and do not translate into efficient parallel methods with polylogarithmic running times or efficient algorithms in the external-memory[5] or MapReduce models.[6] Indeed, their methods can involve as many as $O(n)$ passes over the data. Kadric *et al.* [22] provide a parallel pipelined method that takes a similar approach to the algorithm of Leuprecht and Oberaigner, while improving its convergence in practice, but their method nevertheless depends on inherently sequential pipelining and iterative refinement operations. Recently, Demmel and Nguyen [11] present a parallel floating-point summation method based on using a superaccumulator, but, like the previous sequential superaccumulator methods cited above, their method does not utilize a carry-free intermediate representation; hence, it has an inherently sequential carry-propagation step as a part of its "inner loop" computation.

To our knowledge, no previous algorithm for summing floating-point numbers utilizes a carry-free intermediate representation, although such representations are known for integer arithmetic (e.g., see [31]), the most notable being the redundant binary representation (RBR), which is a positional binary representation where each position is from the set $\{-1, 0, 1\}$.

1.2 Our Results

We show in this paper that one can compute a faithfully-rounded sum, S_n^*, of n floating-point numbers with the following performance bounds.

- S_n^* can be computed in $O(\log n)$ time using n processors in the EREW PRAM model. This is the first such PRAM algorithm and, as we show, it is worst-case optimal.

- S_n^* can be computed in $O(\log^2 n \log\log\log C(X))$ time using $O(n \log C(X))$ work in the EREW PRAM model, where $C(X)$ is the condition number of X. This is the first parallel summation algorithm whose running time is condition-number sensitive.

- S_n^* can be computed in external-memory in $O(\text{sort}(n))$ I/Os, where "sort(n)" is the I/O complexity of sorting.[7]

- S_n^* can be computed in external-memory in $O(\text{scan}(n))$ I/Os, where scan(n) is the I/O complexity of scanning[8], when the size of internal memory, M, is $\Omega(\sigma(n))$, where $\sigma(n)$ is the size of our intermediate representation for the sum of n floating point numbers. This I/O performance bound is, of course, optimal for this case. Typically, $\sigma(n)$ is $O(\log n)$ in practice, due to the concentration of exponent values in real-world data (e.g., see [20, 27]) or because fixed-precision floating-point numbers have relatively small values for l, the number of bits used for exponent values, compared to n.

- S_n^* can be computed with a single-round MapReduce algorithm in $O(\sigma(n/p)p + n/p)$ time and $O(n)$ work, using p processors, with high probability, assuming p is $o(n)$.

In addition, because of the simplicity of our MapReduce algorithm, we provide an experimental analysis of several variations of this algorithm. We show that our MapReduce algorithm can achieve up-to 80X speedup over the state-of-the-art sequential algorithm. It achieves a linear scalability with both the input size and number of cores in the cluster.

2. OUR NUMBER REPRESENTATIONS

To represent the exact summation of n floating point numbers, we utilize a variety of alternative number representations. To begin, recall that a (base-2) floating-point number, x, is represented as a sign bit, b, and a pair of integers, (b, M, E), such that

$$x = (-1)^b \times (1 + 2^{-t}M) \times 2^{E-2^{l-1}-1},$$

where t is the number of bits allocated for M and l is the number of bits allocated for E. For example, for double-precision floating-point numbers in the IEEE 754 standard, $t = 52$ and $l = 11$.

Thus, for the problem of summing the n floating-point numbers in X, we could alternatively represent every floating point number, including each partial sum, as a fixed-point binary number consisting of a sign bit, $t+2^{l-1}+\lceil \log n \rceil$ bits to the left of the binary point, and $t + 2^{l-1}$ bits to the right of the binary point. Using such a representation, we would have no errors in summing the numbers in X, assuming there are no unnecessary overflows. In other words, we can consider such a fixed-point representation as a large binary integer representation, which then has its binary point shifted. Of course, such a representation would potentially waste a lot of memory, but it is nevertheless instructive to contemplate this as a possibility, as it motivates our other representations.

Although this fixed-point representation is potentially wasteful of memory, it might not actually be so bad for exactly representing partial sums of a reasonable numbers of summands of single-precision numbers. For example, in the IEEE 754 standard, single-precision 32-bit floating-point numbers can be represented as 256-bit fixed-point numbers. Thus, the memory needed for an error-free fixed-point representation of a single-precision floating-point number would occupy the same amount of space as 8 single-precision numbers. Nevertheless, an additional drawback of this representation is that, in the worst-case, there can be a lot of carry-bit propagations that occur for any addition, which negatively impacts parallel performance.

In a ***superaccumulator*** representation, as used in some previous summation approaches (e.g., see [26, 30, 32, 33, 40]), we instead represent a fixed-point (or floating-point) number as a vector, Y, of floating-point numbers, $(y_k, y_{k-1}, \ldots, y_0)$,

[5]The external-memory model [36] is a data-parallel model, where data is transferred between an internal memory of a specified size, M, and external memory in blocks of a specified size, B.

[6]A MapReduce algorithm is a coarse-grain parallel method that performs rounds that involve mapping elements to keys, assigning elements by their keys to "reducer" processors, and having those processors execute on sets of elements with the same key, possibly with a global sequential finalize phase at the end [7, 16, 24].

[7]sort$(n) = O((n/B)\log_{M/B}(n/B))$, where M is the size of internal memory and B is the block size.

[8]*scan*$(n) = O(n/B)$, where B is the block size.

such that the number, y, represented by Y is

$$y = \sum_{i=0}^{k} y_i,$$

where the numbers in Y have strictly increasing exponents, so that y_0 is the least significant number (and this summation is a true addition, with no roundoff errors).

As mentioned above, there are some interesting recent floating-point exact summation papers based on the use of superaccumulators, but these are of limited value with respect to parallel algorithms. For instance, Zhu and Hayes [40] present an inherently sequential algorithm that essentially involves adding the numbers from X one at time to an initially-zero superaccumulator and then propagating the carries to produce a faithfully-rounded sum from the most-significant entry. Neal [30] presents a similar algorithm and also discusses in passing an alternative approach based on a bottom-up parallel summation tree computation based on superaccumulators, but his parallel algorithm involves inefficiently constructing superaccumulators for every leaf, and his superaccumulators overlap by half their bits and even then are not carry-free.

In our case, we allow each y_i to be positive or negative and we add some additional conditions so that superaccumulator summations are carry-free. We do this by extending the generalized signed digit (GSD) integer representation [31] to floating-point numbers. This is a redundant representation, so that there are multiple ways of representing the same fixed-point number.

To simply our discussion, let us shift the binary point for y so that every y is an integer instead of a fixed-point number. This shift is made without loss of generality, since we can shift the binary point back to its proper place after we can computed an exact representation of the sum of numbers in X.

Next, following the GSD approach [31], we say that a superaccumulator is (α, β)***-regularized*** if

$$y_i = Y_i \times R^i,$$

for a given ***radix***, R, and each mantissa Y_i is an integer in the range $[-\alpha, \beta]$, for $\alpha, \beta \geq 2$. In particular, for our algorithms, for any fixed t, we choose R to be a power of two, $2^{t-1} > 2$, so that each y_i can be represented using a floating-point exponent storing a multiple of $t-1$ (since we assume floating-point representations are base-2 in this paper). For arbitrary-precision floating-point numbers, we likewise choose $R = 2^{t_0 - 1} > 2$, for a fixed value $t_0 \geq 2$ that is a reasonable length for the number of bits needed for a mantissa (proportional to our word size). In either case, we set

$$\alpha = \beta = R - 1.$$

This choice of the parameters, α and β, is done so that we can achieve propagation-free carrying of components of a summation, as we show next.

Our parallel algorithm for summing two superaccumulators, y and z, is as follows. First, we compute each component-wise sum of the mantissas, $P_i = Y_i + Z_i$. This sum is then reduced to an interim mantissa sum, $W_i = P_i - C_{i+1}R$, where C_{i+1} is a ***signed carry bit***, i.e., $C_{i+1} \in \{-1, 0, 1\}$, that is chosen so that W_i is guaranteed to be in the range $[-(\alpha-1), \beta-1]$. (We show below that this is always possible.) The computed mantissa sum is then performed as $S_i = W_i + C_i$, so that the resulting collection of s_i components is (α, β)-regularized and no carry-bit propagation is necessary. As the following lemma shows, taking this approach allows us to avoid propagating carries across an entire superaccumulator after each addition in a summation computation, while nevertheless representing each partial sum exactly.

LEMMA 1. *It is sufficient to choose $\alpha = \beta = R - 1$, for $R > 2$, for the resulting sum of y and z to be (α, β)-regularized, i.e., so that each S_i is in the range $[-\alpha, \beta]$.*

PROOF. Given that y and z are (α, β)-regularized, the mantissa, P_i, is in the range $[-2\alpha, 2\beta]$. We wish to show that the result, $s = y + z$, be (α, β)-regularized, that is, that each mantissa, S_i, is in the range $[-\alpha, \beta]$. Note that if $-R+1 < P_i < R-1$, then we can ensure S_i is in the range $[-\alpha, \beta]$ for any C_i in $\{-1, 0, 1\}$ by setting $C_{i+1} = 0$. So let us consider the cases when P_i is too negative or too positive.

Case 1: $P_i \geq R - 1$. Note that

$$P_i \leq 2\beta = 2R - 2.$$

Hence, we can choose $C_{i+1} = 1$, so that

$$W_i = P_i - C_{i+1}R = P_i - R \leq R - 2 = \beta - 1.$$

Moreover, $W_i \geq -1 \geq -(\alpha - 1)$, in this case, since $\alpha \geq 2$. Thus,

$$S_i = W_i + C_i \leq R - 2 + 1 \leq R - 1 = \beta,$$

and $S_i \geq -\alpha$.

Case 2: $P_i \leq -R + 1$. Note that

$$P_i \geq -2\alpha = -2R + 2.$$

Hence, we can choose $C_{i+1} = -1$, so that

$$W_i = P_i - C_{i+1}R = P_i + R \geq -R + 2.$$

Moreover, $W_i \leq 1 \leq \beta - 1$, in this case, since $\beta \geq 2$. Thus,

$$S_i = W_i + C_i \geq -R + 2 - 1 \geq -(R - 1) = -\alpha,$$

and $S_i \leq \beta$. □

This implies that, by choosing $\alpha = \beta = R - 1$, we can guarantee that the sum of two (α, β)-regularized superaccumulators can be done in parallel in constant time, with each carry going to at most an adjacent component and no further. There is a chance, of course that the sum of two superaccumulators indexed from 0 to k could result in a superaccumulator indexed from 0 to $k+1$. But this causes no problems for us, since any mantissa can hold $\Omega(\log n)$ bits; hence, one additional suparaccumulator component is sufficient for holding all the adjacent-component carries during the sum of n floating-point numbers.

An additional observation is that, since R is a power of two in our case, we can compute each W_i and C_i using simple operations involving the addition or subtraction of a power of two to a number, given P_i. Also, since we reserve an extra bit in each superaccumulator, computing P_i can be done without overflow in the standard floating-point representation of components.

Intuitively, each pair of consecutive superaccumulator components, y_i and y_{i+1}, "overlap" by one bit and each component has one additional sign bit. As an alternative to representing each y_i as a floating-point number, then, we could instead represent each number, y_i, using an integer representation, with an explicit overlap of one bit between each consecutive pair of numbers, y_i and y_{i+1}, being understood. This would allow us to save some space for what amounts to redundant exponents in the floating-point representations of the y_i's. For the sake of simplicity, however, we choose in this discussion to assume that each y_i is itself a floating-point number, with the understanding that our algorithms could be easily modified to work for the case that the numbers in Y are integers. In either case, the overlap between consecutive numbers in Y allows us to apply a lazy strategy for accumulating carry bits, without full propagation, which overcomes a shortcoming in previous representations.

One important comment is in order here. Namely, for the analysis in this paper, we are ***not*** assuming that the number, l, of bits allocated for floating-point exponents is a fixed constant; hence, our analysis does not assume that, for our floating-point numbers, the size of an equivalent fixed-point representation or superaccumulator for this number is a fixed constant.

Thus, for small numbers of arbitrary-precision floating-point numbers, it is possible that our (α, β)-regularized superaccumulators may waste space. To avoid these issues, we can represent numbers using a format we are calling a "sparse superaccumulator." Given a superaccumulator,

$$Y = (y_k, y_{k-1}, \ldots, y_0),$$

the ***sparse superaccumulator*** for Y is the vector,

$$Y' = (y_{i_j}, y_{i_{j-1}}, \ldots, y_{i_0}),$$

consisting of all the ***active*** indices in Y, for $i_0 < i_1 < \cdots < i_j$. We say that a index, i, in a superaccumulator is ***active*** if y_i is currently non-zero or has ever been non-zero in the past (when viewing a superaccumulator as an indexed data structure).

One possible parallel algorithm for summing two sparse superaccumulators, $Y' = (y_{i_{j_1}}, \ldots, y_{i_0})$ and $Z' = (z_{i_{j_2}}, \ldots, z_{i_0})$, is as follows. We first merge the active indices of Y' and Z', and we then do a summation of corresponding terms (possibly with carries into adjacent components, as needed). Note, though, that we will not propagate carries, when we use (α, β)-regularized superaccumulators. Thus, an index in the sum is active if it was active in Y' or Z' or becomes non-zero as a result of the sum. This definition is somewhat related to the adaptive floating-point representation of Shewchuk [33], which introduces sparsity and adaptivity but only for vectors of non-overlapping floating-point numbers having arbitrary exponents, rather than exponents that are powers of the radix R, as in our sparse (α, β)-regularized superaccumulator representation.

Furthermore, given a sparse superaccumulator, Y', and a parameter γ, we define the ***γ-truncated sparse superaccumulator*** for Y' to be the vector, Y'', consisting of the first (most-significant) γ entries in Y'.

3. OUR FAST PRAM ALGORITHM

The first PRAM algorithm we present is based on summing numbers represented using sparse (α, β)-regularized superaccumulators. Our method runs in $O(\log n)$ time using $O(n \log n)$ work in the EREW PRAM model, which is worst-case optimal. The details are as follows.

1. Build a binary summation tree, T, with $\lceil \log n \rceil$ depth, having each leaf i associated with a distinct floating-point number, x_i, in X. This step can be done in $O(\log n)$ time and $O(n)$ work.

2. In parallel, for each x_i, convert x_i into an equivalent (α, β)-regularized superaccumulator, x'_i. This step can be done in $O(1)$ time and $O(n)$ work, just by splitting each floating-point number into $O(1)$ numbers such that each has an exponent that is a multiple of R.

3. Perform a parallel merge-sort of the x'_i components, using their exponents as keys (not their mantissas). This creates a sorted list, $E(v)$, for each node in T, consisting of the exponents found in the subtree in T rooted at v, as well as links for each exponent, e in $E(v)$ to its predecessors in the lists for v's children and its parent. This step can be done in $O(\log n)$ time using $O(n \log n)$ work [5, 17] via the cascading divide-and-conquer technique [1], because the boundary exponents are known from the beginning.

4. Perform a parallel prefix computation to remove duplicate exponents in each $E(v)$. This step can be done in $O(\log n)$ time using $O(n \log n)$ work, since the total size of all the lists is $O(n \log n)$.

5. Using the links created in the previous step to match up corresponding components in constant-time per level, possibly adding new components that represent a carry bit moving into a component that was previously not included in the sparse representation, perform a bottom-up sparse superaccumulator summation in T. This results in a sparse superaccumulator representation of the sum being stored in the root of T. This step can be done in $O(\log n)$ time using $O(n \log n)$ work.

6. Convert the sparse (α, β)-regularized superaccumulator for the sum at the root of T into a non-overlapping superaccumulator that is $((R/2)-1, (R/2)-1)$-regularized. This amounts to a signed carry-bit propagation operation, which can be done by a parallel prefix computation (based on a simple lookup table based on whether the input carry bit is a -1, 0, or 1). We leave the details to the interested reader. This step can be done in $O(\log n)$ time using $O(n)$ work.

7. Correctly round the non-overlapping superaccumulator from the previous step into a floating-point number. This step amounts to locating the most significant non-zero component of the superaccumulator and then combining that, as needed, with its neighboring components to create a floating-point number of the appropriate size, rounding the result based on the truncated bits. This step can be done in $O(\log n)$ time using $O(n)$ work.

This gives us the following.

THEOREM 2. *Given n floating-point numbers, one can compute a faithfully-rounded representation of their sum in $O(\log n)$ time using $O(n \log n)$ work (i.e., n processors) in the EREW PRAM model. These time and processor bounds are worst-case optimal in the algebraic computation tree model.*

PROOF. We have already established the upper bounds. For the lower bounds, we show that the set equality problem can be reduced to the floating-point summation problem in $O(1)$ time using n processors. Suppose, then, that we are given two sets of n positive numbers, C and D, and wish to determine if $C = D$. Let τ be the smallest power of two greater than $\log n$. For each element c_i in C, create the floating-point number, $(-1, 1, \tau c_i)$, which represents the number, $(-1) \times 2^{\tau c_i}$. Likewise, for each element d_i in D, create the floating-point number, $(1, 1, \tau d_i)$, which represents the number, $1 \times 2^{\tau d_i}$. We claim that $C = D$ if and only if the sum of these two sets of numbers is zero. Clearly, if $C = D$, then there is a one-to-one matching between equal elements in C and D; hence, there is a matching for each floating-point number, $(-1, 1, \tau c_i)$, to a floating-point number, $(1, 1, \tau d_i)$, such that $c_i = d_i$. Therefore, the sum of all of these numbers is zero in this case. Suppose, for the "only if" case, that the sum of all these numbers is zero. Note that the exponent of any pair of floating-point numbers in our collection is either the same or differs by at least $\tau > \log n$. Thus, if two such numbers are different, they will remain different even if we multiply one of them by n. Therefore, the only way that the sum of all these numbers is zero is if each floating-point number, $(-1, 1, \tau c_i)$, in this collection, has a distinct associated floating-point number, $(1, 1, \tau d_i)$, in this collection, such that $c_i = d_i$. Therefore, if the sum of all these numbers is zero, then $C = D$. The lower-bounds follow, then, from the fact that summation is a binary operator and the set equality problem has an $\Omega(n \log n)$ lower bound in the algebraic computation tree model [2]. □

To our knowledge, this is the first PRAM method that achieves $O(\log n)$ time and an amount of work that is worst-case optimal. We note, however, that the above lower bound holds only for floating-point representations where exponents are represented with $\Omega(\log n)$ bits.

4. OUR CONDITION-NUMBER SENSITIVE PRAM ALGORITHM

In our fast PRAM algorithm, we showed that it is possible to sum two sparse superaccumulators in $O(1)$ time using n processors in the EREW PRAM model, given a sorted merge of the exponents of the components of each superaccumulator. This result also gives us the following.

LEMMA 3. *Given two truncated (α, β)-regularized sparse superaccumulators, Y_1 and Y_2, of combined size m, we can compute the sum of Y_1 and Y_2 in $O(\log m)$ time using $O(m/\log m)$ processors in the EREW PRAM model.*

PROOF. The algorithm follows from the method described above combined with an EREW PRAM method for merging two sorted lists. (E.g., see [21] for details on such computations.) □

Given this tool, we now describe our condition-number sensitive parallel algorithm for summing the floating-point numbers in X in parallel. Our method runs in polylogarithmic time using $O(n \log C(X))$ work.[9]

[9]Technically, we could have $C(X) = 1$; hence we could have $\log C(X) = 0$. As a notational convenience, therefore, we assume that the logarithms in our complexity bounds are defined to always have a minimum value of 1.

We begin with a simplified version of our algorithm from the previous section. Initialize an $O(\log n)$-depth summation tree, T, to have an element of X associated with each of its leaves. Convert each value, x_i, stored in a leaf to an equivalent sparse (α, β)-regularized superaccumulator. Perform a bottom-up parallel summation computation on T using the method of Lemma 3 to perform each pairwise summation of two sparse superaccumulators. We then complete the algorithm by a parallel prefix computation on the sparse superaccumulator for the root of T to propagate all the signed carry bits and we then convert this result to a floating-point number, as in the last two steps of our algorithm from the previous section. This simplified summation algorithm runs in $O(\log^2 n)$ time using $O(n \log n)$ work in the EREW PRAM model.

Given this template, our condition-number sensitive algorithm is as follows. Begin by setting $r = 2$. Then perform the above bottom-up parallel merge-and-sum algorithm, but do so using r-truncated sparse superaccumulators. Unlike our previous method, this one may cause lossy errors to occur, due to the restrictions to r-truncated sparse superaccumulators. So we utilize a test, which we call the "stopping condition," to determine if the result is correct and we can stop. If the stopping condition is not satisfied, however, then we set $r \leftarrow r^2$ and repeat the computation. We continue this iteration until either the stopping condition is satisfied or we have increased r so high that the final sparse superaccumulator is no longer truncated.

Before we analyze this algorithm, let us first provide the details for some sufficient stopping conditions. Let y denote the summation value computed from our method after a given iteration, where the final truncated sparse superaccumulator is

$$Y = (y_{i_1}, y_{i_2}, \ldots, y_{i_r}),$$

so that y_{i_r} is its least-significant component. Also, for the sake of simplicity, let us assume that y is positive; the method for the case when y is negative is similar. Let E_{i_r} denote the exponent for y_{i_r} and let

$$\epsilon_{\min} = \epsilon \times 2^{E_{i_r}},$$

where ϵ is the smallest mantissa that can possibly be represented in our chosen floating-point representation. Note that $\epsilon_{\min}$ is the smallest value that could be represented by y_{i_r}. A sufficient stopping condition, then, is to test whether or not

$$y = y \oplus n\epsilon_{\min} = y \oplus -n\epsilon_{\min}.$$

that is, the summation value, y, would be unchanged even after doing a floating-point addition or subtraction of n copies of a bound whose magnitude is larger than any value we truncated.

As a simplified alternative, which also works in our algorithms as a sufficient stopping condition, is to determine whether the exponent for the least significant bit in y is at least $\lceil \log n \rceil$ greater than E_{i_r}.

The reason that these tests are sufficient as stopping conditions is that when we are summing the n floating point numbers using truncated sparse superaccumulators, the largest magnitude that we can possibility truncate any summand is strictly less than $\epsilon_{\min}$. The reason for this is that, by the definition of a truncated sparse superaccumulator, if y_{i_r} is included in our final truncated sparse superaccumulator, then y_{i_r} was not truncated by any partial sum. Thus, the maximum value of the sum of all the truncated values is at most

$$n\epsilon_{\min} \leq 2^{\lceil \log n \rceil}\epsilon_{\min}.$$

Interestingly, this algorithm gives us the following condition-number sensitive result.

THEOREM 4. *Given a set, X, of n floating-point numbers, we can compute a faithfully-rounded representation of the sum of the numbers in X in time $O(\log^2 n \log\log\log C(X))$ using work that is $O(n \log C(X))$ in the EREW PRAM model, where $C(X)$ is the condition number for X.*

PROOF. The correctness for our algorithm follows immediately from the above discussion, since we terminate when we are assured of a faithfully-rounded sum for the numbers in X. We claim that the number of iterations (each of which involves squaring the truncation parameter, r) is $O(\log C(X))$. To see that this claim is true, note that

$$\log C(X) = \log\left(\sum_{i=1}^{n} |x_i|\right) - \log\left(\left|\sum_{i=1}^{n} x_i\right|\right).$$

Thus, if we represented the values, $X_1 = \sum |x_i|$ and $X_2 = |\sum x_i|$, using exact fixed-point representations, then $\log C(X)$ is proportional to the difference, δ, between the bit-position of the most significant 1-bit in the representation of X_1 and the bit-position of the most significant 1-bit in the representation of X_2. Our algorithm must therefore perform a sufficient number of iterations so that the number of bits in our truncated sparse superaccumulator for the sum is at least δ. This indeed occurs in our algorithm and, furthermore, note that our algorithm will terminate when the number of bits in our truncated sparse superaccumulator for the sum is $\Theta(\delta + \log n)$. That is, our algorithm terminates when r is $O(\log C(X))$, since we assume that floating-point numbers in our representation contain $\Omega(\log n)$ bits. Since we square r in each iteration, this implies the claimed running-time and work bounds for our parallel algorithm, since we require $O(\log\log\log C(X)))$ squarings to get r to be large enough and the total work involved is a geometric summation that adds up to $O(n \log C(X))$. □

5. EXTERNAL-MEMORY ALGORITHMS

In this section, we describe our efficient algorithms for summing n floating-point numbers in the external-memory model [36].

Suppose we are given a set X of n floating-point numbers. Our sorting-based external-memory algorithm is as follows.

1. Convert each floating-point number to an (α, β)-regularized sparse superaccumulator. This can be done with a single scan over the input, using $O(\text{scan}(n))$ I/Os.

2. Sort the components of all the sparse superaccumulators constructed in the previous step independently by their exponents. This step clearly takes $O(\text{sort}(n))$ I/Os.

3. Scan the sorted list of superaccumulator components, while maintaining a (α, β)-regularized sparse superaccumulator, S, to hold the sum. With each component, $y_{i,j}$, we add $y_{i,j}$ to S, using a localized version of the algorithm for summing two superaccumulators. Note that we do not need to store all of S in internal memory to implement this step, however, since we are processing the components in order by their exponents. Instead, we just need to keep a hot-swap buffer of S that includes the current exponent, swapping out blocks to external memory as they become full. Moreover, since summing two (α, β)-regularized superaccumulators is a carry-free operation, we don't need to worry about extra I/Os that would have otherwise been caused by carry-bit propagation. Thus, we can implement this step in $O(\text{scan}(n))$ I/Os.

4. Given the computed superaccumulator, S, which now holds the exact sum of the n floating-point numbers, perform a back-to-front scan of S to propagate signed carry bits, to convert S into a non-overlapping $((R/2)-1, (R/2)-1)$-regularized sparse superaccumulator. This step clearly requires $O(\text{scan}(n))$ I/Os.

5. Given a non-overlapping superaccumulator for the sum, we round the most significant non-zero components to produce a correctly rounded floating-point number for the sum of the n floating-point numbers in X.

This gives us the following.

THEOREM 5. *Given n floating-point numbers, we can compute a correctly-rounded floating-point representation of their sum using $O(\text{sort}(n))$ I/Os in the external-memory model, in a cache-oblivious manner.*

PROOF. We have already established the performance bounds. To establish that this algorithm can be performed in a cache-oblivious manner, we note that every step involves simple scans over lists of numbers, except for a sorting step, which itself can be done cache obliviously [13]. □

The critical step in the above external-memory algorithm, of course, is the scan to add each floating-point component to our superaccumulator. Since these components were sorted by their exponents and our superaccumulator representation is carry-free, we need only keep a "sliding window" of $O(1)$ blocks of our superaccumulator in memory as we perform this scan. Moreover, such a scan is cache-oblivious given any reasonable page eviction strategy.

If the size of our superaccumulator, $\sigma(n)$, is less than the size of internal memory, M, however, then we can utilize an even simpler algorithm. Namely, we can simply keep our entire superaccumulator stored in internal memory and process the floating-point components in any order to add each one to the superaccumulator. This observation leads to the following, then.

THEOREM 6. *Given n floating-point numbers, we can compute a correctly-rounded floating-point representation of their sum using $O(\text{scan}(n))$ I/Os in the external-memory model, in a cache-oblivious manner, if $\sigma(n) \leq M$.*

6. SIMPLE MAPREDUCE ALGORITHMS

In this section, we present a simple MapReduce [7, 16, 24] algorithm for summing n floating-point numbers. We also report on an experimental evaluation, where we assume that the input is already loaded in a Hadoop Distributed File System (HDFS) where the input is partitioned into 128 MB blocks which are stored on the local disks of cluster nodes.

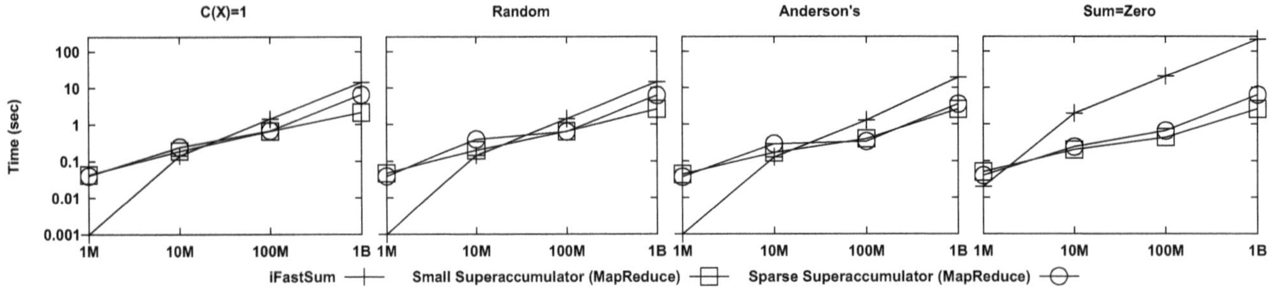

Figure 1: Total running time as the input size increases from 1 million to 1 billion numbers

Our algorithm is based on a single-round of MapReduce which takes as input a collection of floating point numbers, and produces a single floating point number that represents the correctly-rounded sum of all input numbers. In this section, we first give a high level overview of our MapReduce algorithm. Then, we describe an implementation of that algorithm using Spark [38]. Finally, we give experimental results of our implementation using large scale data.

6.1 Overview

Our MapReduce algorithm runs as a single MapReduce job as detailed below.

- Map: for each x_i, map x_i to $(r(x_i), x_i)$, where $r(x_i)$ returns an integer in the range $[1, p]$ that represents one of the available p reducers. We can simply use a random function r, which assigns each input record to a randomly chosen reducer. The function r can also be defined based on domain knowledge of X with the goal of balancing the load across the p reducers. For example, if p is $o(n)$, then this function assigns roughly $O(n/p)$ values for each reducer.
- Reduce: In the reduce phase, each reducer r_i, $i \in [1, p]$, sums up all the assigned numbers using the sequential algorithm described earlier in Section 3. The output of the reduce function is one sparse superaccumulator that represents the exact sum of the floating-point numbers assigned to r_i. After that, each reducer writes the resulting sparse superaccumulator to the output.
- Post-process: In this final step, a single machine reads back the p sparse superaccumulators produced by the p reducers and performs a final step of the sparse superaccumulator addition algorithm to add all of them into one final sparse superaccumulator. Finally, the resulting sparse superaccumulator is converted to a correctly-rounded floating point value which is written to the output as the final answer.

6.2 Implementation

We implemented the MapReduce algorithm described above using Spark [38], a modern distributed processing framework. This implementation is open source and available at https://github.com/aseldawy/sumn. We begin by loading the input from disk into the distributed memory of the cluster nodes. In this step, each machine loads the HDFS blocks that are physically stored on its local disk. Then, each machine applies a *combine* function on each block, which uses the sequential algorithm described in Section 3 to sum all numbers in each partition into one sparse superaccumulator. The goal of the combine step is to reduce the size of the data that need to be shuffled between mappers and reducers. The output of the combine function is a single key-value pair where the key is a random integer in the range $[1, p]$, and the value is the sparse superaccumulator. Then, the shuffle phase groups key-value pairs by the reducer number and assigns each group to one reducer. After that, each reducer sums up all the assigned sparse superaccumulators into one sparse superaccumulator and writes it to the intermediate output. Finally, the postprocess phase runs on the driver machine that issued the MapReduce job and it combines all sparse superaccumulators into one and writes the correctly-rounded floating point value as the final result.

6.3 Experimental Results

To test our MapReduce implementations, we carried out an experimental evaluation of the proposed MapReduce algorithm on large datasets of up to one billion numbers. The input datasets were randomly generated using four different distributions as described in [39]:

1. A set of randomly generated *positive* numbers which results in a condition number $C(X) = 1$.
2. A mix of positive and negative numbers generated uniformly at random.
3. Anderson's-ill conditioned data where a set of random numbers are generated, and then their arithmetic mean is subtracted from each number.
4. A set of numbers with real sum equal to zero.

In the four datasets, the parameter δ defines an upper bound for the range of exponents of input numbers.

We used Apache Spark 1.6.0 running on Ubuntu 14.04 and OpenJDK 1.7.0_91. For experimental repeatability, we ran all our experiments on Amazon EC2 using an instance of type 'r3.8xlarge' which has 32 cores and 244 GB of main memory running on Intel Xeon E5-2670 v2 processors [37]. We used the 32 cores to run a local cluster of 32 worker nodes inside that machine. We ran the experiments using three algorithms and measured the end-to-end running time of each one:

1. Our proposed MapReduce algorithm that uses sparse superaccumulators.

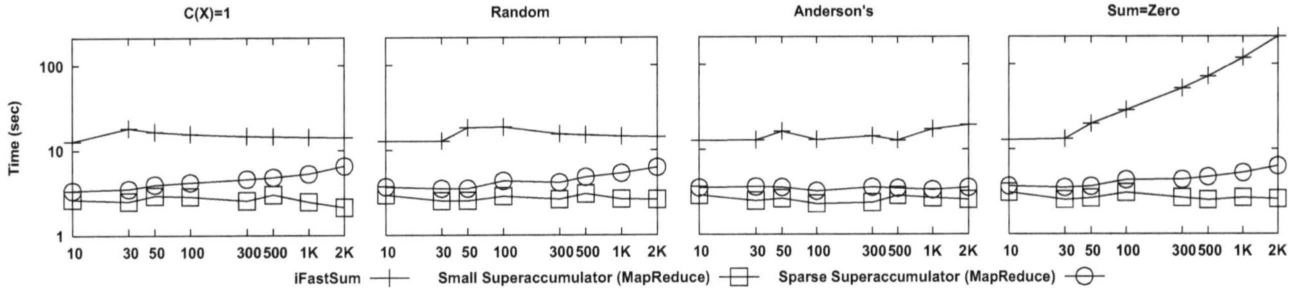

Figure 2: Total running time as the parameter δ increases from 10 to 2000

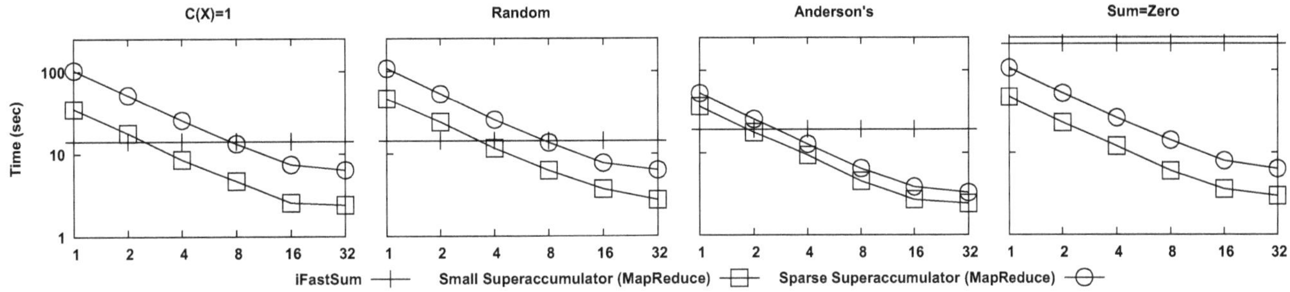

Figure 3: Total running time as the cluster size increases from 1 to 32 cores

2. A variation of our MapReduce algorithm that uses small superaccumulators [30] instead of sparse superaccumulators.
3. The state-of-the-art sequential iFastSum algorithm [40].

For the latter algorithm, we used the original C++ implementation provided by Zhu and Hayes [40], compiled using gcc 4.8.4. For all the techniques, we first generated a dataset using the random generator provided in [40] and stored it to disk. Then, we processed the same generated dataset with each algorithm one after another. We ignored the disk I/O time and focused only on the processing time. If we take the disk I/O into account, all MapReduce algorithms will be much faster due to the distributed nature of Hadoop Distributed File System (HDFS) where the machines load data in parallel from multiple disks.

Figure 1 shows the overall running time of the three algorithms as the input size increases from 1 million to 1 billion numbers, while the value of δ is fixed at 2000. In general, iFastSum is faster for processing small datasets with less than 10 million records. However, as the size of the data increases, both MapReduce implementations outperform the sequential iFastSum algorithm with up to 80x speedup. This shows a great potential for MapReduce algorithms in the problem of summing a huge array of floating point numbers. We observe that the implementation that uses small superaccumulator is slightly faster than the one that uses sparse superaccumulator. The reason for this is that each sparse superaccumulator runs on a single core, which does not allow it to realize the theoretical limit of doing $O(p)$ work in $O(1)$ time using p processors. In the future, we could investigate the use of single-instruction multiple-data (SIMD) features to achieve a higher level of parallelism. Another possibility is to use GPU processing units which can achieve massive parallelization with thousands of threads on a single chip. We believe that there is a huge potential in these two options as the design of sparse superaccumulator lends itself to these two types of parallelization where the same instruction is repeated for every index in the superaccumulator.

Figure 2 shows the running time when the parameter δ increases from 10 to 2000. Notice that the maximum possible value for δ is 2046 for double-precision floating point numbers. As the input size is 1 billion, we observe that the two MapReduce algorithms consistently outperform the sequential iFastSum algorithm. We also observe that the running time of the sparse superaccumulator algorithm slightly increases as the value of δ increases. This behavior is expected, because the increased value of δ makes the superaccumulator less sparse as the number of non-zero (active) indices increases. The only exception is with dataset No. 3, as the subtraction of the mean causes the range of exponents to decrease to about 15 even if the original δ is very large. Similar to the behavior in its original paper [39], the running time of iFastSum with dataset No. 4 increases with the value of δ. Interestingly, the small superaccumulator keeps a consistent performance regardless of the value of δ.

Figure 3 shows the end-to-end running time as the cluster size increases from 1 to 32 cores. The performance of iFastSum stays constant as it runs only on a single core. The results of this experiment shows a perfect scalability for our MapReduce algorithm, where the performance scales linearly with number of machines. The performance starts to saturate as the cluster size increases from 16 to 32 cores because the underlying processor *virtually* increases the number of running threads using the hyper-threading feature. For a small cluster with a few cores, iFastSum is faster, as it is highly tuned for sequential processing while Spark incurs extra overhead for the other algorithms. As the number of cores increases, the parallelization of MapReduce algorithms allows them to outperform iFastSum in all experimented datasets. However, the crossover point changes from one dataset to another. For example, since dataset No. 4 is the worst case for iFastSum, sparse superaccumulator proves to be faster even on a single core.

7. CONCLUSION

In this paper, we have given a number of efficient parallel algorithms for computing a faithfully rounded floating-point representation of the sum of n floating-point numbers. Our algorithms are designed for a number of parallel models, including the PRAM, external-memory, and MapReduce models. The primary design paradigm of our methods is that of converting the input values to an intermediate representation, called a sparse superaccumulator, summing the values exactly in this representation, and then converting this exact sum to a faithfully-rounded floating-point representation. Our experimental evaluation shows that our MapReduce algorithm can achieve up to 80X performance speedup as compared to the state-of-the-art sequential algorithm. The MapReduce algorithm yields lineary scalability with both the input dataset and number of cores in the cluster.

Acknowledgments

This research was supported in part by the National Science Foundation under grant 1228639, and an AWS in Education Grant. We would like to thank Wayne Hayes for several helpful discussions concerning the topics of this paper.

8. REFERENCES

[1] M. J. Atallah et al. Cascading divide-and-conquer: A technique for designing parallel algorithms. *SICOMP*, pages 499–532, 1989.

[2] M. Ben-Or. Lower bounds for algebraic computation trees. In *STOC*, pages 80–86, 1983.

[3] E. O. Brigham. *The Fast Fourier Transform and Its Applications*. Prentice-Hall, Inc., 1988.

[4] C. Burnikel et al. Exact Geometric Computation in LEDA. In *SoCG*, pages 418–419, 1995.

[5] R. Cole. Parallel merge sort. *SICOMP*, 17(4):770–785, 1988.

[6] S. Collange et al. A Reproducible Accurate Summation Algorithm for High-Performance Computing. In *Proceedings of the SIAM EX14 workshop*, 2014.

[7] J. Dean and S. Ghemawat. MapReduce: Simplified data processing on large clusters. *Commun. ACM*, 51(1):107–113, Jan. 2008.

[8] T. Dekker. A floating-point technique for extending the available precision. *Numerische Mathematik*, pages 224–242, 1971.

[9] J. Demmel and Y. Hida. Accurate and efficient floating point summation. *SIAM Journal on Scientific Computing*, 25(4):1214–1248, 2004.

[10] J. Demmel and Y. Hida. Fast and accurate floating point summation with application to computational geometry. *Numerical Algorithms*, 37(1-4):101–112, 2004.

[11] J. Demmel and H. D. Nguyen. Parallel reproducible summation. *IEEE TC*, 64(7):2060–2070, July 2015.

[12] L. Fousse et al. MPFR: A multiple-precision binary floating-point library with correct rounding. *TOMS*, June 2007.

[13] M. Frigo et al. Cache-oblivious algorithms. In *FOCS*, pages 285–297, 1999.

[14] GMPLib. GMP: the GNU multiple precision arithmetic library. https://gmplib.org/. Accessed 2015-12-16.

[15] D. Goldberg. What every computer scientist should know about floating-point arithmetic. *CSUR*, pages 5–48, Mar. 1991.

[16] M. T. Goodrich et al. Sorting, searching, and simulation in the MapReduce framework. In *Int. Symp. on Algorithms and Computation (ISAAC)*, volume 7074 of *LNCS*, pages 374–383, 2011.

[17] M. T. Goodrich and S. R. Kosaraju. Sorting on a parallel pointer machine with applications to set expression evaluation. *J. ACM*, 43(2):331–361, Mar. 1996.

[18] M. T. Goodrich and R. Tamassia. *Algorithm Design and Applications*. Wiley Publishing, 2014.

[19] G. Hanrot, V. Lefévre, P. Pélissier, P. Théveny, and P. Zimmermann. The GNU MPFR library. http://www.mpfr.org/. Accessed 2015-12-16.

[20] M. Isenburg, P. Lindstrom, and J. Snoeyink. Lossless compression of predicted floating-point geometry. *Computer-Aided Design*, pages 869–877, 2005.

[21] J. JáJá. *An Introduction to Parallel Algorithms*. Addison-Wesley, 1992.

[22] E. Kadric, P. Gurniak, and A. DeHon. Accurate parallel floating-point accumulation. In *21st IEEE Symp. on Computer Arithmetic (ARITH)*, pages 153–162, April 2013.

[23] M.-Y. Kao and J. Wang. Linear-time approximation algorithms for computing numerical summation with provably small errors. *SISC*, pages 1568–1576, 2000.

[24] H. Karloff, S. Suri, and S. Vassilvitskii. A model of computation for mapreduce. In *21st ACM-SIAM Symp. on Discrete Algorithms (SODA)*, pages 938–948, 2010.

[25] D. E. Knuth. *The Art of Computer Programming, Volume 2 (3rd Ed.): Seminumerical Algorithms*. Addison-Wesley, Boston, MA, USA, 1997.

[26] U. W. Kulisch and W. L. Miranker. The arithmetic of the digital computer: A new approach. *SIAM Review*, 28(1):1–40, 1986.

[27] A. Lacroix and F. Hartwig. Distribution densities of the mantissa and exponent of floating point numbers. In *ISCAS*, pages 1792–1795, May 1992.

[28] H. Leuprecht and W. Oberaigner. Parallel algorithms for the rounding exact summation of floating point numbers. *Computing*, 28(2):89–104, 1982.

[29] M. A. Malcolm. On accurate floating-point summation. *Commun. ACM*, 14(11):731–736, Nov. 1971.

[30] R. M. Neal. Fast exact summation using small and large superaccumulators. *arXiv ePrint*, abs/1505.05571, 2015.

[31] B. Parhami. Generalized signed-digit number systems: a unifying framework for redundant number representations. *IEEE TC*, 39(1):89–98, Jan 1990.

[32] D. Priest. Algorithms for arbitrary precision floating point arithmetic. In *10th IEEE Symp. on Computer Arithmetic (ARITH)*, pages 132–143, Jun 1991.

[33] J. Richard Shewchuk. Adaptive precision floating-point arithmetic and fast robust geometric predicates. *Discrete & Computational Geometry*, 18(3):305–363, 1997.

[34] S. M. Rump, T. Ogita, and S. Oishi. Accurate floating-point summation part i: Faithful rounding. *SIAM Journal on Scientific Computing*, 31(1):189–224, 2008.

[35] M. Tommila. Apfloat for Java. http://www.apfloat.org/apfloat_java/. Accessed 2015-12-16.

[36] J. S. Vitter. Algorithms and data structures for external memory. *TnTCS*, pages 305–474, Jan. 2008.

[37] Intel Xeon Processor E5-2670 v2. http://ark.intel.com/products/75275.

[38] M. Zaharia et al. Spark: Cluster Computing with Working Sets. In *HotCloud*, 2010.

[39] Y.-K. Zhu and W. B. Hayes. Correct rounding and a hybrid approach to exact floating-point summation. *SIAM Journal on Scientific Computing*, 31(4):2981–3001, 2009.

[40] Y.-K. Zhu and W. B. Hayes. Algorithm 908: Online Exact Summation of Floating-Point Streams. *TOMS*, pages 1–13, 2010.

Randomized Approximate Nearest Neighbor Search with Limited Adaptivity

Mingmou Liu
Nanjing University, China
MG1533028@smail.nju.edu.cn

Xiaoyin Pan
Nanjing University, China
xiaoyin.pan95@gmail.com

Yitong Yin *
Nanjing University, China
yinyt@nju.edu.cn

ABSTRACT

We study the problem of approximate nearest neighbor search in d-dimensional Hamming space $\{0,1\}^d$. We study the complexity of the problem in the famous cell-probe model, a classic model for data structures. We consider algorithms in the cell-probe model with *limited adaptivity*, where the algorithm makes k rounds of parallel accesses to the data structure for a given k. For any $k \geq 1$, we give a simple randomized algorithm solving the approximate nearest neighbor search using k rounds of parallel memory accesses, with $O(k(\log d)^{1/k})$ accesses in total. We also give a more sophisticated randomized algorithm using $O(k + (\frac{1}{k}\log d)^{O(1/k)})$ memory accesses in k rounds for large enough k. Both algorithms use data structures of size polynomial in n, the number of points in the database.

We prove an $\Omega(\frac{1}{k}(\log d)^{1/k})$ lower bound for the total number of memory accesses required by any randomized algorithm solving the approximate nearest neighbor search within $k \leq \frac{\log\log d}{2\log\log\log d}$ rounds of parallel memory accesses on any data structures of polynomial size. This lower bound shows that our first algorithm is asymptotically optimal for any constant round k. And our second algorithm approaches the asymptotically optimal tradeoff between rounds and memory accesses, in a sense that the lower bound of memory accesses for any k_1 rounds can be matched by the algorithm within $k_2 = O(k_1)$ rounds. In the extreme, for some large enough $k = \Theta\left(\frac{\log\log d}{\log\log\log d}\right)$, our second algorithm matches the $\Theta\left(\frac{\log\log d}{\log\log\log d}\right)$ tight bound for fully adaptive algorithms for approximate nearest neighbor search due to Chakrabarti and Regev [10].

Keywords

nearest neighbor search; cell-probe model; data structures; communication complexity

*State Key Laboratory for Novel Software Technology, Nanjing University, China.

SPAA '16, July 11-13, 2016, Pacific Grove, CA, USA

© 2016 ACM. ISBN 978-1-4503-4210-0/16/07...$15.00

DOI: http://dx.doi.org/10.1145/2935764.2935776

1. INTRODUCTION

Nearest neighbor search is a fundamental theoretical problem in Computer Science, with enormously many applications in diverse fields. In the nearest neighbor search problem, we are given a database B of n points from a metric space X. The goal is to preprocess them into a data structure, such that given any query point $x \in X$, an algorithm with accessing to the data structure can find a database point in B that is closest to the query point x among all database points. An extensively studied case is when the metric space is the Hamming space $X = \{0,1\}^d$.

It is conjectured that the nearest neighbor search is hard to solve by any data structures when the dimension d is high (e.g. $d \gg \log n$). This conjecture is sometimes referred as a case of the "curse of dimensionality" and is one of the central problems in the area of data structure lower bounds. It is also believed that the problem of high-dimensional nearest neighbor search remains to be intractable while either an approximation is tolerated or the algorithm is randomized, but not both at the same time [11].

The complexity of the nearest neighbor search problem, as well as many other data structure problems, is well studied in the cell-probe model [24], a classic model for the complexity of data structures. In the cell-probe model, the database is preprocessed into a data structure, stored as a table in the main memory, and upon each query, an algorithm, called the cell-probing algorithm, outputs an answer to the query after adaptively probing a number of table cells. The complexity is measured by both the size of the data structure and the number of cell-probes made by the algorithm to answer a query in the worst case. There is a substantial body of works on the cell-probe complexity of nearest neighbor search in Hamming space [6,7,13,16,19–21].

When both approximation and randomization are allowed, a seminal work of Chakrabarti and Regev [10] gives a *tight* bound for the complexity of nearest neighbor search in d-dimensional Hamming space with data structures of size polynomial in n, assuming the dimension d is high (and not too high to trivialize the problem, e.g. $(\log n)^{1.01} \leq d \leq 2^{\sqrt{\log n}}$). This fundamental result is stated informally as follows.

THEOREM 1.1 (CHAKRABARTI AND REGEV [10]). *Assume $(\log n)^{1.01} \leq d \leq 2^{\sqrt{\log n}}$. The cell-probe complexity of randomized approximate nearest neighbor search in d-dimensional Hamming space in the cell-probe model with data structure of polynomial size is $\Theta\left(\frac{\log\log d}{\log\log\log d}\right)$.*

On the other hand, when the table size becomes closer

to be linear of n, data structures such as locality-sensitive hashing (LSH) [2,12] or data-dependent LSH [3,4] achieve a cell-probe complexity of $\tilde{O}(dn^\rho)$ with data structures of size $\tilde{O}(n^{1+\rho})$ for some $0 < \rho < 1$ depending on the metric and the approximation ratio. Compared to the $\Theta\left(\frac{\log\log d}{\log\log\log d}\right)$ bound of Chakrabarti and Regev, the $\tilde{O}(dn^\rho)$ cell-probe complexity is much worse. The popularity in practice of the LSH-based data structures is due to their low space cost, and the ability to be implemented in parallel.

Take locality-sensitive hashing (LSH) as an example. The algorithm of LSH is *non-adaptive*: Each cell-probe relies only on the query but not on the information retrieved by other cell-probes. This makes all cell-probes in LSH parallelizable into one round of parallel memory accesses. And the more recent data-dependent LSH [3,4] surpasses the classic LSH in cell-probe complexity by being a little more adaptive: the algorithm retrieves a data-dependent hash function before making the second round of cell-probes, while the cell-probes in the second round are independent of each other. In contrast, the algorithm of Chakrabarti and Regev [10] is *fully* adaptive: Every cell-probe must wait for the information retrieved by the previous cell-probe to proceed.

This could give us the following intuitive image: A cell-probing algorithm is getting more clever and hence more efficient, as it is becoming more adaptive. It is then a fundamental question to study the tradeoff between the efficiency (measured by the total number of cell-probes) and adaptivity (measured by the number of rounds of parallel cell-probes) in the cell-probe model. Very little was known to this fundamental question. In [8], Brody and Larsen initiated the study of non-adaptive *dynamic* data structures, where the database receives both queries and updates. They show a foundational result that for dynamic data structures, being adaptive is critical. For static data structures, parallel cell-probes were studied in the context of low-contention data structures [5,20]. The highest cell-probe lower bound known for *non-adaptive* static data structure is the $\Omega(\log n / \log \frac{sw}{nd})$ cell-probe lower bound of Panigrahy, Talwar, and Wieder [19] for randomized approximate nearest neighbor search on a table of size s. This lower bound becomes trivial for tables of polynomial size. For cell-probe model with polynomial-sized data structures, the tradeoff between the cell-probe complexity and adaptivity is highly unknown for any static data structure problems.

Our results.

In this paper, we study the complexity of randomized approximate nearest neighbor search in the cell-probe model with limited adaptivity. We consider a natural notion of *rounds* for cell-probes, where the cell-probes in the same round are adaptive to the information retrieved in previous rounds, but non-adaptive to each other in the same round.

We give two randomized cell-probing algorithms for approximate nearest neighbor search in d-dimensional Hamming space. For both algorithms, the data structures are of polynomial size, and the cell-probes are organized into k rounds for any $k \geq 1$ (Algorithm 1) or for all sufficiently large k (Algorithm 2). The first algorithm is as follow.

THEOREM 1.2. *For any $k \geq 1$, the approximate nearest neighbor search in d-dimensional Hamming space can be solved in the cell-probe model with a data structure of polynomial size, using k rounds of parallel randomized cell-probes, with $O\left(k(\log d)^{1/k}\right)$ cell-probes in total.*

The algorithm is simple and works for all $k \geq 1$ number of rounds. Especially when $k = 1$, the algorithm is non-adaptive. Compared to the LSH which is also non-adaptive, our algorithm achieves a much better cell-probe complexity $O(\log d)$ by using a data structure of larger polynomial size.

However, when the round number k becomes large, especially at the extreme when every round has 1 cell-probe, in which case the algorithm becomes fully adaptive and has $O(\log\log d)$ total cell-probes, which is not optimal for fully adaptive algorithms by Theorem 1.1. This leads us to our second more sophisticated algorithm.

THEOREM 1.3. *For large enough k, the approximate nearest neighbor search in d-dimensional Hamming space can be solved in the cell-probe model with a data structure of polynomial size, using k rounds of parallel randomized cell-probes, with $O\left(k + \left(\frac{1}{k}\log d\right)^{O(1/k)}\right)$ cell-probes in total.*

The second algorithm is substantially more sophisticated. In the extreme, it approaches the optimal fully adaptive algorithm in Theorem 1.1 in the following sense: For some sufficiently large $k = O\left(\frac{\log\log d}{\log\log\log d}\right)$, we can implement the algorithm such that every round of the algorithm contain only 1 cell-probe.

We emphasize that these algorithms are not meant to be efficient in practice due to their expensive space costs, rather, they are parts of a theoretical endeavor to understand the complexity tradeoff between time and rounds on data structures of polynomial size. With this spirit, we prove the following lower bound for the tradeoff between cell-probe complexity and round complexity for randomized approximate nearest neighbor search.

THEOREM 1.4. *Assume $(\log n)^{1.01} \leq d \leq 2^{\sqrt{\log n}}$ and $1 \leq k \leq \frac{\log\log d}{2\log\log\log d}$. Any randomized algorithm solving the approximate nearest neighbor search in d-dimensional Hamming space in the cell-probe model with a data structure of polynomial size using k rounds of parallel randomized cell-probes must use $\Omega\left(\frac{1}{k}(\log d)^{1/k}\right)$ cell-probes in total.*

Due to this lower bound, both our algorithms achieve some optimality:

- Algorithm 1 is asymptotically optimal in cell-probe complexity for any constant number of rounds.
- Algorithm 2 approaches the asymptotically optimal tradeoff between cell-probe complexity and round complexity in the following sense: the cell-probe lower bound for any k_1-round algorithms can be approached by Algorithm 2 within $k_2 = O(k_1)$ rounds.

In addition, Algorithm 2 together with our lower bound show that the cell-probe complexity of randomized approximate nearest neighbor search undergoes a "phase transition" when the round number is within the regime $k = \Theta\left(\frac{\log\log d}{\log\log\log d}\right)$: For a small $k_1 = \Theta\left(\frac{\log\log d}{\log\log\log d}\right)$, the average number of cell-probes per each round for any k_1-round algorithm has to be a $(\log\log d)^{\Omega(1)}$, whereas for large enough $k_2 = \Theta\left(\frac{\log\log d}{\log\log\log d}\right)$, only 1 cell-probe in each round is enough for a k_2-round algorithm.

Technique.

Both our upper bounds and lower bounds rely heavily on the machineries developed in [10].

The main ideas for the upper bounds are the dimension reduction techniques developed in the pioneering works of [12, 15] and the multi-way search in [10]. Our efforts are focused on how to apply these techniques to give a *family* of algorithms approaching the smoothed tradeoff between round and cell-probe complexity. A technical innovation of [10] is to use two kinds of approximations of Hamming balls: an accurate approximation of hamming ball which is more expensive, and a coarse approximation which is cheap, to support a multi-way search with a substantial number of branchings, such that each branching is supported by one query to an accurate ball succeeded by several queries to coarse balls, which altogether consume only $O(1)$ cell-probes. Surprisingly, we discover that a simple algorithm can achieve an optimal cell-probe complexity in any constant number of rounds, using only the more expensive accurate approximation of Hamming balls. And for general round numbers, the coarse approximation of balls are employed to approach the asymptotically optimal tradeoff between rounds and cell-probes.

The lower bound is proved by the round elimination of communication protocols for the longest prefix matching problem LPM, which can be reduced to approximate nearest neighbor search. In [10], a lower bound is proved for LPM by interpreting a data structure as a communication protocol and applying round eliminations to the communication protocol, a technique that can be traced back to [1,17]. Our main observation is that k rounds of cell-probes can be represented as $2k$ rounds of communications. Although the observation is straightforward, to prove our lower bound we have to apply the techniques of [10] to adapt to non-uniform message sizes in different rounds, a setting which was rarely considered in the context of asymmetric communication complexity for data structure lower bounds. More critically, in order to get the $1/k$ exponent in our $\Omega\left(\frac{1}{k}(\log d)^{1/k}\right)$ lower bound, we are forced to exploit the round elimination of [10]. In fact, assuming $k = O\left(\frac{\log\log d}{\log\log\log d}\right)$, a lower bound with form $\Omega\left(k + \frac{1}{k^b}(\log d)^{a/k}\right)$ for any constants $a, b > 0$ is enough to imply the optimal $\Omega\left(\frac{\log\log d}{\log\log\log d}\right)$ lower bound in Theorem 1.1, whereas for our result, these constants a, b matter a lot and require much delicacy in the round elimination argument.

2. PRELIMINARIES

Approximate nearest neighbor search.

We consider the problem of *approximate nearest neighbor search* in the d-dimensional Hamming space $\mathsf{ANNS}^{\gamma}_{d,n}$. Let $\gamma > 1$ be fixed. We are given a *database* B which contains n points from the d-dimensional Hamming cube $\{0,1\}^d$. The database is preprocessed into a data structure (called the *table*). Then given any *query* point $x \in \{0,1\}^d$, the algorithm must access the data structure and output a database point $y \in B$ which is a *γ-approximate nearest neighbor* of x in B, where a point $y \in B$ is called a γ-approximate nearest neighbor of x in B if $\mathrm{dist}(x,y) \le \gamma \cdot \min_{z\in B} \mathrm{dist}(x,z)$, where $\mathrm{dist}(x,y)$ denotes the Hamming distance between x and y.

Abstractly, a *data structure problem* can be represented as a relation $\rho \subseteq \mathscr{A} \times \mathscr{B} \times \mathscr{C}$, where $\mathscr{A}, \mathscr{B}$, and $\mathscr{C}$ specify the universes for queries, databases, and answers, respectively. Given a query $x \in \mathscr{A}$ to a database $B \in \mathscr{B}$, an answer $z \in \mathscr{C}$ is correct if $(x, B, z) \in \rho$. In particular, for approximate nearest neighbor search, $\mathscr{A} = \mathscr{C} = \{0,1\}^d$, $\mathscr{B} = \binom{\{0,1\}^d}{n}$, and

$$\mathsf{ANNS}^{\gamma}_{d,n} = \big\{(x,B,z) \in \mathscr{A} \times \mathscr{B} \times \mathscr{C} \mid z \in B \wedge \forall y \in B, \mathrm{dist}(x,z) \le \gamma \cdot \mathrm{dist}(x,y)\big\}.$$

The cell-probe model.

We adopt Yao's cell-probe model [24] for static data structures. A *cell-probing scheme* $(\mathcal{A}, \mathcal{T})$ for a data structure problem $\rho \subseteq \mathscr{A} \times \mathscr{B} \times \mathscr{C}$ consists of a *cell-probing algorithm* $\mathcal{A}$ and a code (sometimes called the *table structure*) $\mathcal{T}$. Each database $B \in \mathscr{B}$ is mapped by the code $\mathcal{T} : \mathscr{B} \to \Sigma^s$ to a codeword (called a *table*) $T_B \in \Sigma^{[s]}$ of s symbols from the alphabet $\Sigma = \{0,1\}^w$. The interpretation is that each database B is preprocessed and stored as a table T_B consisting of s table *cells* (also called a *word*), with each cell storing w bits. Given an address $i \in [s]$ we use $T_B[i]$ to denote the content of the i-th cell in table T_B. Given a query $x \in \mathscr{A}$, the cell-probing algorithm $\mathcal{A}$ must output a correct answer $z \in \mathscr{C}$ such that $(x, B, z) \in \rho$, after accessing the table T_B adaptively for t times, each time reading the content of one table cell. This action of reading the content of one table cell by the cell-probing algorithm is usually called as making a *cell-probe*.

The complexity of a cell-probing scheme is captured by three parameters: namely, the *table size* s, the *word size* w, and the time cost or *cell-probe complexity* t.

Cell-probe model with limited adaptivity.

In this work, we refine the cell-probe model by considering the rounds of parallelizable cell-probes in cell-probing algorithms. Formally, a *k-round* cell-probing algorithm $\mathcal{A}$ can be described by k *lookup functions* $L_1, L_2, \ldots, L_k$ and one *truth table* A. Each lookup function L_i maps the query x and the contents of the table cells probed before round i, to a sequence of addresses indicating the set of table cells to probe in round i. In the beginning, $L_1(x) = (p^1_1, p^1_2, \ldots, p^1_{t_1}) \in [s]^{t_1}$ for some $t_1 > 0$, and for general $1 \le i \le k$:

$$L_i\left(x, \left\langle p^j_\ell, T_B[p^j_\ell]\right\rangle_{\substack{1\le j<i\\ 1\le \ell \le t_j}}\right) = (p^i_1, p^i_2, \ldots, p^i_{t_i}) \in [s]^{t_i},$$

for some $t_i > 0$, so that at round i, the algorithm makes t_i *parallel* cell-probes to the the cells p^i_ℓ, $1 \le \ell \le t_i$. And finally, the truth table A maps the contents of all the probed cells $\langle p^j_\ell, T_B[p^j_\ell]\rangle_{\substack{1\le j\le k\\ 1\le \ell\le t_j}}$, to a correct answer z satisfying that $(x, B, z) \in \rho$. The cell-probe complexity is given by $t = t_1 + t_2 + \cdots + t_k$. This formulation includes the standard definition of cell-probing scheme as a special case when $t_1 = \cdots = t_k = 1$.

Public-coin vs. private-coin cell-probing schemes.

In a (private-coin) randomized cell-probing scheme, the table is prepared by a code $\mathcal{T}$ deterministically as before, but the cell-probing algorithm $\mathcal{A}$ is a randomized algorithm. This can be considered as that the deterministic lookup functions $L_1, L_2, \ldots, L_k$ as well as the truth table A also take a sequence of random bits $r \in \{0,1\}^*$ as part of the input. We say we have a randomized cell-probing scheme $(\mathcal{A}, \mathcal{T})$ for a data structure problem $\rho \subseteq \mathscr{A} \times \mathscr{B} \times \mathscr{C}$ if for every query $x \in \mathscr{A}$ and every database $B \in \mathscr{B}$, the cell-probing algorithm outputs a correct answer $z \in \mathscr{C}$ such that $(x, B, z) \in \rho$ with probability at least 2/3. The constant 2/3 is rather arbitrary. Note that for problems such as approximate nearest neighbor search, where once the query x is known, a monotone order of the correctness between multiple answers is fixed, any positive constant success probability is enough: we can boost it to any constant accuracy $1-\epsilon$ by independent repetition of the cell-probing algorithm for constant many times *in parallel*, which will keep the asymptotic cell-probe complexity and the number of rounds of parallel cell-probes.

In this paper, all of our upper bounds will be presented first as *public-coin* randomized cell-probing schemes. For a public-coin randomized cell-probing scheme, the sequence of random bits $r \in \{0,1\}^*$ is shared between the cell-probing algorithm $\mathcal{A}$ and the table structure $\mathcal{T}$, where the table T_B^r is now determined by both the database B and the random bits r. This makes no change to the family of data structures of polynomial size: by Newman's theorem [18], a public-coin cell-probing scheme can be transformed to a standard randomized cell-probing scheme, where the randomness is private to the cell-probing algorithm.

LEMMA 2.1. *If there is a k-round public-coin randomized cell-probing scheme for a data structure problem $\rho \subseteq \mathscr{A} \times \mathscr{B} \times \mathscr{C}$ with table size s, word size w, and cell-probe complexity t, then there is a k-round randomized cell-probing scheme for ρ with table size* $(\log|\mathscr{A}|+\log|\mathscr{B}|+O(1))s$, *word size w, and cell-probe complexity t.*

PROOF. The proof is similar to the proof of Lemma 6.5 in [10], with the observation that the translation there also preserves the number of rounds. Without loss of generality, we assume that for every query to every database, the k-round public-coin randomized cell-probing scheme returns a correct answer except with an error probability at most 1/4. The k-round public-coin randomized cell-probing scheme can be seen as a k-round public coin randomized communication protocol between Alice for the cell-probing algorithm and Bob for the table, where Bob is non-adaptive thus is only response to each individual message received in the current round according to its input B in a consistent way (as a code). By Newman's theorem, the number of public random bits can be reduced to

$$\ell = \log(\log|\mathscr{A}| + \log|\mathscr{B}| + O(1))$$

while the error probability is raised to 1/3. This does not change the structure of the protocol, so it can be translated back to a k-round public-coin randomized cell-probing scheme for ρ with the same time and space complexity as before and with ℓ public random bits. We create a table T_B^r for every possible sequence of random bits $r \in \{0,1\}^\ell$ according to the public-coin cell-probing scheme. This gives us a big table of size $s \cdot 2^\ell = s(\log|\mathscr{A}| + \log|\mathscr{B}| + O(1))$, and the random bits is made private to the cell-probing algorithm. □

Notations. We use $\mathrm{dist}(\cdot,\cdot)$ to denote Hamming distance. We write log for binary logarithm and ln for natural logarithm.

3. APPROXIMATE NEAREST NEIGHBOR SEARCH IN k ROUNDS

In this section, we will give two algorithms that solve the approximate nearest neighbor search problem $\mathsf{ANNS}^{\gamma}_{d,n}$ within k rounds on a table of size $n^{O(1)}$ and word size $O(d)$:

1. a simple k-round randomized cell-probing scheme with $O(k(\log d)^{1/k})$ cell-probes;
2. a more sophisticated k-round randomized cell-probing scheme with $O(k + (\frac{1}{k}\log d)^{c/k})$ cell-probes, for any constant $c > 2$.

On the other hand, if the problem is relaxed to the approximate *near*-neighbor search problem (instead of the *nearest* neighbor search), then it was known [10] that on a table of polynomial size, the problem can be solved with 1 random cell probe, which is certainly *non-adaptive*.

Public-coin vs. private-coin in the cell-probe model.

All our three algorithms will be first presented as *public-coin* cell-probing schemes, where the random bits are shared between the cell-probing algorithm and the table, and then transformed by Lemma 2.1 to the standard randomized cell-probing schemes, where the random bits are private to the cell-probing algorithm, with the same round and cell-probe complexity and a polynomial overhead to the table size. In particular, for $\mathsf{ANNS}^{\gamma}_{d,n}$ we have the following proposition.

PROPOSITION 3.1. *If there is a k-round public-coin randomized cell-probing scheme for $\mathsf{ANNS}^{\gamma}_{d,n}$ with table size s, word size w, and cell-probe complexity t, there exists a k-round randomized cell-probing scheme for $\mathsf{ANNS}^{\gamma}_{d,n}$ with table size $O(dn \cdot s)$, word size w, and cell-probe complexity t.*

Common setup for the algorithms.

We consider only constant approximation ratio $\gamma > 1$, so without lost of generality, we can assume that $\gamma < 4$, since for larger γ our algorithms will only have better approximation. Let $\alpha \triangleq \sqrt{\gamma}$, and hence $1 < \alpha < 2$. Let $x \in \{0,1\}^d$ denote the query point and $B \subseteq \{0,1\}^d$, $|B| = n$, denote the database. We always assume that $n > d$. For $0 \le i \le \lceil \log_\alpha d \rceil\}$, let

$$B_i = \{y \in B \mid \mathrm{dist}(x,y) \le \alpha^i\}, \tag{1}$$

be the set of all database points within distance α^i of x.

DEFINITION 3.2. *Let $c_1, c_2 > 64/(1-\mathrm{e}^{(1-\alpha)/2})^2$ be constants and $1 < s < \ln\ln n$. For $0 \le i \le \lceil \log_\alpha d \rceil$, let M_i, N_i be the independent random Boolean matrices such that each entry is sampled* i.i.d. *from* Bernoulli$(\frac{1}{4\alpha^i})$, *with M_i of size $(c_1 \log n) \times d$ and N_i of size $(\frac{c_2}{s}\log n) \times d$. For $0 \le j \le i \le \lceil \log_\alpha d \rceil$, we define the sets*

$$C_i = \left\{z \in B \mid \mathrm{dist}(M_i x, M_i z) \le \delta(\alpha^i, \alpha) c_1 \log n\right\}, \tag{2}$$

$$D_{i,j} = \left\{z \in C_i \mid \mathrm{dist}(N_j x, N_j z) \le \delta(\alpha^j, \alpha)\frac{c_2}{s}\log n\right\}, \tag{3}$$

where $\delta(\beta,\alpha) = \frac{1}{2}\left(1 - \frac{1}{2\beta}\right)^\beta \left[1 - \left(1 - \frac{1}{2\beta}\right)^{(\alpha-1)\cdot\beta}\right]$.

The following lemma proved in [10] shows that C_i are approximations of the balls B_i, and D_i are also approximations in a weaker sense.

Lemma 3.3 (Chakrabarti and Regev [10]). *The following events hold simultaneously with probability at least 3/4:*

1. $B_i \subseteq C_i \subseteq B_{i+1}$ *for all* i.
2. *For all* $0 \le j \le i \le \lceil \log_\alpha d \rceil$, *at most a fraction* $n^{-1/s}$ *of* B_j *is not in* $D_{i,j}$ *and at most a fraction* $n^{-1/s}$ *of* $C_i \setminus B_{j+1}$ *is in* $D_{i,j}$.

3.1 A simple k-round protocol for ANNS

Theorem 3.4 (Theorem 1.2, restated). *Let* $\gamma > 1$ *be any constant. For* $n > d$ *and* $k \ge 1$, $\mathsf{ANNS}^{\gamma}_{d,n}$ *has a* k*-round randomized cell-probing scheme with* $O\left(k(\log d)^{1/k}\right)$ *cell-probes, table size* $n^{O(1)}$ *and word size* $O(d)$.

As mentioned earlier, the solution will be presented as a *public-coin* cell-probing scheme, which by Proposition 3.1, is then transformed to a standard randomized cell-probing scheme with the same cell-probe complexity and number of rounds on a table of polynomial size.

Without lost of generality, assume that $\gamma < 4$ and let $\alpha \triangleq \sqrt{\gamma}$. Let $x \in \{0,1\}^d$ denote the query point and $B \subseteq \{0,1\}^d$, $|B| = n$, denote the database. Recall that B_i, as defined in 1, are the sets of all database points within distance α^i of x.

There are two degenerate cases. The first case is when B_0 is not empty, which means $x \in B$. This case can be solved as a membership query of x in the set B, by the perfect hashing with 1 cell-probe to a table of size $O(n^2)$, with the random hash function as public randomness. The second degenerate case is when B_1 is not empty, which means the query point x is within distance 1 from B. This can also be solved as a membership query of x in the 1-neighborhood $N_1(B) = \{y \in \{0,1\}^d \mid \exists z \in B, \mathrm{dist}(y,z) \le 1\}$ of B, which contains at most $(d+1)n$ points, by the same method, using 1 cell-probe to a table of quadratic size with public randomness.

Note that these two instances of perfect hashing can run separately and in parallel to each other, and to the main data structure solving the non-degenerate cases, so that if a query x finds itself within B or within distance 1 from B, then the algorithm terminates and outputs the nearest neighbor. This will cost a polynomial addition to the table size and 2 more queries in the first round, but make no change to the number of rounds. For the rest, we can assume the following.

Assumption 1. $B_0 = B_1 = \emptyset$.

The goal of the main data structure is to find an i such that B_i is empty but B_{i+2} is not and output a point in B_{i+2}, assuming that $B_0 = B_1 = \emptyset$. Such a point is clearly a γ-approximate nearest neighbor of x.

For $0 \le i \le \lceil \log_\alpha d \rceil$, let M_i be the random $(c_1 \log n) \times d$ matrices sampled independently as in Definition 3.2 and $C_i \subseteq B$ the subsets of database points constructed from M_i as in Definition 3.2. The random matrices M_i are treated as the public randomness shared between the cell-probing algorithm and the table. The table who possesses the database B may construct C_i from $M_i x$ for every possible $x \in \{0,1\}^d$ (in fact, for every $M_i x \in \{0,1\}^{c_1 \log n} = [n^{c_1}]$), while the cell-probing algorithm who possesses the query point x may compute the product $M_i x$ from the actual query point x.

By Lemma 3.3, the following assumption holds with probability at least 3/4:

Assumption 2. $B_i \subseteq C_i \subseteq B_{i+1}$ *for all* i.

With this assumption, the algorithm only needs to find an i such that $C_i \ne \emptyset$ but $C_{i-1} = \emptyset$. Since $B_{i-1} \subseteq C_{i-1} = \emptyset$ and $B_{i+1} \supseteq C_i \ne \emptyset$, any point in C_i is a γ-approximation nearest neighbor of x.

Table construction.

We construct $\lceil \log_\alpha d \rceil + 1$ tables $T_0, \ldots, T_{\lceil \log_\alpha d \rceil}$. Each table T_i contains $2^{c_1 \log n} = \mathrm{poly}(n)$ many cells, where each cell corresponds to a string $j \in \{0,1\}^{c_1 \log n}$, so the total number of cells in all these tables is a polynomial of n. Here c_1 is the constant factor in the number of rows of M_i. Due to the public randomness, the table contents may depend on both the database B and the public random matrices M_i.

For every $0 \le i \le \lceil \log_\alpha d \rceil$ and every $j \in \{0,1\}^{c_1 \log n}$, the content of the j-th cell $T_i[j]$ in the i-th table T_i is given as follows:

- If there exists a datapoint $z \in B$ such that $\mathrm{dist}(j, M_i z) \le \delta(\alpha^i, \alpha) \cdot c_1 \log n$, the cell $T_i[j]$ stores an arbitrary one of such z.
- If otherwise there is no such datapoint, $T_i[j]$ stores a special symbol indicating the EMPTY.

Note that $M_i x \in \{0,1\}^{c_1 \log n}$ is a valid address for the cells in a table T_i. And for every i, the table cell $T_i[M_i x]$ stores a point from C_i if C_i is not empty, or $T_i[M_i x] = \text{EMPTY}$ if $C_i = \emptyset$.

Cell-probing algorithm.

The algorithm possesses the query point x and the public random matrices M_i. Set $\tau = c'(\log d)^{1/k}$, for a constant $c' \ge \log_\alpha 4$ so that

$$\tau \cdot \left(\frac{\tau}{2}\right)^{k-1} \ge \lceil \log_\alpha d \rceil.$$

The cell-probing algorithm consists of at most $(k-1)$ *shrinking rounds*, succeeded by one final *completion round.* And if $k = 1$, the algorithm is non-adaptive and just consists of a completion round. In every round the algorithm makes at most τ parallel cell-probes to the table. The total number of cell-probes is at most $(\tau-1)(k-1)+\tau = O(k(\log_\alpha d)^{1/k})$. The pseudocode of the cell-probing algorithm is given in Algorithm 1.

Algorithm 1 Simple k-round cell probing algorithm

```
Set τ ← (log d)^{1/k} log_α 4;
initialize l ← 0 and u ← log_α d;
while u − l ≥ τ do
    let ρ(r) ← ⌊l + (r/τ)(u − l)⌋ for 0 ≤ r ≤ τ − 1;
    retrieve T_{ρ(r)}[M_{ρ(r)}x] for 1 ≤ r ≤ τ − 1;
    if ∃ 1 ≤ r ≤ τ − 1 s.t. T_{ρ(r)}[M_{ρ(r)}x] ≠ EMPTY then
        let r* be the smallest such r;
    else
        r* ← τ;
    end if
    update l ← ρ(r* − 1) and u ← ρ(r*);
end while
retrieve T_i[M_i x] for all l + 1 ≤ i ≤ u;
i* ← min{l + 1 ≤ i ≤ u : T_i[M_i x] ≠ EMPTY};
return T_{i*}[M_{i*} x];
```

The algorithm finds a γ-approximate nearest neighbor of x by a multi-way search: it maintains two integers l and u, initially $l = 0$ and $u = \lceil \log_\alpha d \rceil$. At each round l and u are updated, satisfying the invariant that $l < u$, $C_l = \emptyset$ and $C_u \neq \emptyset$. This invariant is satisfied initially since by Assumption 1 and 2 we have $C_0 \subseteq B_1 = \emptyset$ and $C_{\lceil \log_\alpha d \rceil} \supseteq B_{\lceil \log_\alpha d \rceil} = B$. For $0 \le r \le \tau$, we denote $\rho(r) \triangleq \lfloor l + \frac{r}{\tau}(u-l) \rfloor$. The cell-probing algorithm proceeds as follows:

1. In each shrinking round: the algorithm reads the contents of $T_{\rho(r)}[M_{\rho(r)}x]$ for all $1 \le r \le \tau - 1$ in parallel, and finds those r such that $T_{\rho(r)}[M_{\rho(r)}x] \neq$ EMPTY, which means $C_{\rho(r)} \neq \emptyset$. Let r^* be the smallest such r, or let $r^* = \tau$ if no such r exists. Update l to $\rho(r^* - 1)$ and u to $\rho(r^*)$. The new gap between l and u is $\rho(r^*) - \rho(r^* - 1)$, which is at most $(u - l)/\tau + 1$.

2. Once the gap $u - l$ drops below τ, the algorithm enters the completion round: it reads the cells $T_i[M_i x]$ for all $l + 1 \le i \le u$ in parallel, finds the smallest i such that $T_i[M_i x] \neq$ EMPTY, and outputs the point stored in that cell. Such i must exist since we know $C_u \neq \emptyset$. Note that the output point is from a nonempty C_i such that $C_{i-1} = \emptyset$. With Assumption 2, it must be a γ-approximate nearest neighbor of x.

Note that in every shrinking round, l and u are updated to l' and u' respectively so that $u' - l' \le (u-l)/\tau + 1 \le 2(u-l)/\tau$ as long as $u - l \ge \tau$. And once $u - l < \tau$, the algorithm enters the completion round. Recall that $\tau \cdot (\tau/2)^{k-1} \ge \lceil \log_\alpha d \rceil$. Hence, there can be at most $(k-1)$ shrinking rounds.

3.2 A k-round protocol for ANNS for large k

THEOREM 3.5 (THEOREM 1.3, RESTATED). *Let $\gamma > 1$ and $c > 2$ be any constants. For $n > d$ and $k > 5c^2/(c-2)$, $\mathsf{ANNS}^{\gamma}_{d,n}$ has a k-round randomized cell-probing scheme with $O\left(k + \left(\frac{1}{k}\log d\right)^{c/k}\right)$ cell-probes, table size $n^{O(1)}$, and word size $O(d)$.*

As before the algorithm is also presented as a public-coin cell-probing scheme, and is transformed into a standard randomized cell-probing scheme by Proposition 3.1.

This more sophisticated algorithm reuses several components of the simple algorithm in Theorem 3.4. For $0 \le i \le \lceil \log_\alpha d \rceil$, the sets B_i and C_i, and the random matrices M_i are constructed in the same way as before. The degenerate cases when B_0 or B_1 is not empty are also handled in the same as before, so we proceed by assuming Assumption 1.

Set $s \triangleq \left(\frac{1}{4} - \frac{1}{2c}\right)k - \frac{1}{4} > 1$. We assume that $k = o(\ln \ln d)$, because for some sufficiently large $k = O(\ln \ln d / \ln \ln \ln d)$, it can be verified that our algorithm already makes $O(1)$ cell-probes per round on average, so there is no need to consider larger number of rounds after that. Hence, we have $1 < s < \ln \ln d < \ln \ln n$.

Let N_j be the random $(\frac{c_2}{s} \log n) \times d$ matrices sampled independently as in Definition 3.2 and $D_{i,j} \subseteq B$ the subsets of database points constructed from M_i and N_j as in Definition 3.2. Now the public randomness shared between the cell-probing algorithm and the table are the random matrices M_i and N_j for $0 \le j \le i \le \lceil \log_\alpha d \rceil$. We make another assumption.

ASSUMPTION 3. *For all $0 \le j \le i \le \lceil \log_\alpha d \rceil$, at most a fraction $n^{-1/s}$ of B_j is not in $D_{i,j}$ and that at most a fraction $n^{-1/s}$ of $C_i \setminus B_{j+1}$ is in $D_{i,j}$.*

By Lemma 3.3, the error probability of an algorithm that succeeds by assuming both Assumption 2 and Assumption 3 is at most 1/4.

Table construction.
We reuse the $\lceil \log_\alpha d \rceil + 1$ tables $T_0, \ldots, T_{\lceil \log_\alpha d \rceil}$ constructed in Theorem 3.4. In addition, we further construct $(\lceil \log_\alpha d \rceil + 1) \times 2^{c_1 \log n}$ *auxiliary tables* $\widetilde{T}_{i,j}$ for $0 \le i \le \lceil \log_\alpha d \rceil$ and $j \in \{0,1\}^{c_1 \log n}$. The address of each cell in an auxiliary table $\widetilde{T}_{i,j}$ corresponds to a concatenation $\overline{w} = \langle l, u, w_0, w_1, \ldots, w_s \rangle$ of:

- a pair of lower and upper thresholds $0 \le l \le u \le \lceil \log_\alpha d \rceil$;
- a special index $1 \le w_0 \le s$;
- s short strings $w_1, \ldots, w_s \in \{0,1\}^{\frac{c_2}{s} \log n}$.

Altogether these correspond to at most $(\log_\alpha d) s 2^{c_2 \log n} = \mathrm{poly}(n)$ cells in each auxiliary table. The total number of cells in all tables remains to be a polynomial of n.

For $0 \le i \le \lceil \log_\alpha d \rceil$, $j \in \{0,1\}^{c_1 \log n}$, and any address $\overline{w} = \langle l, u, w_0, w_1, \ldots, w_s \rangle$ of cells in auxiliary table $\widetilde{T}_{i,j}$, the content of the cell $\widetilde{T}_{i,j}[\overline{w}]$ is given as follows: For $1 \le r \le s$, define $\rho(r) \triangleq \lfloor l + \frac{r-1}{s-1}(u-l) \rfloor$. Let $j = M_i x$ and $w_r = N_{\rho(r)} x$ for $1 \le r \le s$. We construct the sets $C_i, D_{i,\rho(1)}, \ldots, D_{i,\rho(s)}$ since we now have complete information about the sets.

- If there exists an $1 \le r \le w_0$ such that $|D_{i,\rho(r)}| > n^{-1/s}|C_i|$, then the cell $\widetilde{T}_{i,j}[\overline{w}]$ stores the smallest such r.
- If otherwise there is no such r, the cell $\widetilde{T}_{i,j}[\overline{w}]$ stores $s + 1$.

Cell-probing algorithm.
Set $\tau = c'(\frac{1}{k}\log d)^{c/k}$ for some constant $c' \ge \log_\alpha 4$ so that

$$\left(\frac{\tau}{2}\right)^{\frac{k-1}{2} - 2s} \ge \left\lceil \frac{\log_\alpha d}{k} \right\rceil.$$

The cell-probing algorithm contains at most $(k-1)/2$ *shrinking phases*, succeeded by one final *completion round*. Each shrinking phase contains at most two rounds. In every shrinking phase the algorithm makes at most $\frac{\tau - 1}{s} + 2$ cell-probes to the table, and in the completion round it makes at most $\max\{3\tau, k\}$ parallel cell-probes. Thus the total number of cell-probes is at most

$$\begin{aligned} &\frac{k-1}{2}\left(\left\lceil \frac{\tau - 1}{s} \right\rceil + 2\right) + \max(3\tau, k) \\ =&O\left(k + \left(\frac{1}{k}\log_\alpha d\right)^{c/k}\right). \end{aligned} \quad (4)$$

The algorithm maintains two integers l and u, initially $l = 0$ and $u = \lceil \log_\alpha d \rceil$. At each shrinking phase l and u are updated, satisfying the invariant that $l < u$, $C_l = \emptyset$ and $C_u \neq \emptyset$. This invariant is satisfied initially since we have $C_0 \subseteq B_1 = \emptyset$ and $C_{\lceil \log_\alpha d \rceil} \supseteq B_{\lceil \log_\alpha d \rceil} = B$.

The aim of the algorithm is at each shrinking phase to *shrink* the gap $u-l$ by a factor of $O(\tau)$ or to *shrink* the size of C_u. When the gap $u-l$ drops below $\max\{3\tau, k\}$ the algorithm enters the completion round, where sets $C_l, \dots, C_u$ are searched simultaneously by at most $\max\{3\tau, k\}$ parallel cell-probes in one round. We claim that at each shrinking phase, the algorithm updates l and/or u in such a way that either $u'-l' \le (u-l)/\tau + 3$ or $|C_{u'}| \le n^{-1/2s}|C_u|$, where l' and u' denote the updated values of l and u, respectively.

Algorithm 2 k-round cell-probing algorithm for large k

```
Set τ ← ((1/k) log d)^{c/k} log_α 4;
initialize l ← 0 and u ← log_α d;
while u − l ≥ max{3τ, k} do
    for r ∈ [τ], let ρ(r) ← ⌊l + (r/τ)(u − l)⌋;
    for j = 1 to ⌈(τ − 1)/s⌉ do
        l_j ← ρ(1 + (j − 1)s) and u_j ← ρ(js);
        if j = ⌈(τ − 1)/s⌉ and s ∤ τ − 1 then
            w_0^j ← τ − 1 − s⌊(τ−1)/s⌋;
        else
            w_0^j ← s;
        end if
        w_q^j ← N_{ρ(1+(j−1)s+q−1)} x for 1 ≤ q ≤ w_0^j;
    end for
    retrieve T_u[M_u x];
    retrieve T̃_{u,M_u x}[w̄^j] for 1 ≤ j ≤ ⌈(τ − 1)/s⌉;
    if ∃ 1 ≤ j ≤ ⌈(τ − 1)/s⌉ s.t. T̃_{u,M_u x}[w̄^j] ≠ s+1 then
        let j* be the smallest such j;
        r* ← (j* − 1)s + T̃_{u,M_u x}[w̄^{j*}];
    else
        r* ← τ;
    end if
    if r* = 1 then
        update u ← ρ(1) + 1;
    else
        retrieve T_{ρ(r*−1)−1}[M_{ρ(r*−1)−1}]x;
        if T_{ρ(r*−1)−1}[M_{ρ(r*−1)−1}]x = EMPTY then
            update l ← ρ(r* − 1) − 1;
            if r* < τ then
                update u ← ρ(r*) + 1;
            end if
        else
            update u ← ρ(r* − 1) − 1;
        end if
    end if
end while
retrieve T_i[M_i x] for all l + 1 ≤ i ≤ u;
i* = min{l + 1 ≤ i ≤ u : T_i[M_i x] ≠ EMPTY};
return T_{i*}[M_{i*} x].
```

For $0 \le r \le \tau - 1$, we denote $\rho(r) \triangleq \lfloor l + \frac{r}{\tau}(u-l) \rfloor$. The cell-probing algorithm proceeds as follows:

1. In shrinking phase: among sets $D_{u,\rho(1)}, \dots, D_{u,\rho(\tau-1)}$, the algorithm will first find the smallest r such that $|D_{u,\rho(r)}| > n^{-1/s}|C_u|$. To find such r, the algorithm first arranges these sets into $\lceil(\tau-1)/s\rceil$ groups where each group contains up to at most s sets, with each group consumes one parallel cell-probe as follows: for every $1 \le j \le \lceil(\tau-1)/s\rceil$, let the concatenation $\overline{w}^j = \langle l_j, u_j, w_0^j, w_1^j, \dots, w_s^j \rangle$ be constructed as:
   - the lower and upper thresholds for the current group: $l_j = \rho(1+(j-1)s)$ and $u_j = \rho(js)$;
   - w_0^j gives the number of sets $D_{u,\rho(r)}$ in the current group: normally it is just s except for the last group due to the rounding, so $w_0^j = \tau - 1 - s\left\lfloor\frac{\tau-1}{s}\right\rfloor$ if $j = \lceil(\tau-1)/s\rceil$ and $s \nmid \tau - 1$, and $w_0^j = s$ if otherwise;
   - for $q = 1, 2, \dots, w_0^j$, let $w_q^j = N_{\rho(1+(j-1)s+q-1)}x$.

   The algorithm reads the contents of cells $T_u[M_u x]$ and $\widetilde{T}_{u,M_u x}[\overline{w}^j]$ for all $1 \le j \le \lceil(\tau-1)/s\rceil$ in parallel. Let j^* be the smallest j such that $\widetilde{T}_{u,M_u x}[\overline{w}^j] \ne s+1$, or $j^* = (\tau-1)/s+1$ if no such j exists. If $j^* = (\tau-1)/s+1$, let $r^* = \tau$. Otherwise let $r^* = (j^*-1)s + \widetilde{T}_{u,M_u x}[\overline{w}^{j^*}]$. Remember that $\widetilde{T}_{u,M_u x}[\overline{w}^j] = s+1$ means that all $|D_{u,l_j}|, \dots, |D_{u,\rho(1+(j-1)s+w_0-1)}| \le n^{-1/s}|C_u|$. Hence such r^* is the smallest $r \in [\tau]$ such that $|D_{u,\rho(r)}| > n^{-1/s}|C_u|$, or $r^* = \tau$ if no such r exists. There are three cases:

   (a) If $r^* = 1$ (CASE 1), the algorithm updates u to $\rho(1)+1$, leaving l unchanged, skips the second round and moves to the next phase.

   (b) Otherwise, the algorithm reads the content of cell $T_{\rho(r^*-1)-1}[M_{\rho(r^*-1)-1}x]$. If the cell is EMPTY (CASE 2), it updates l to $\rho(r^*-1)-1$ and if further $r^* < \tau$, updates u to $\rho(r^*)+1$.

   (c) If $T_{\rho(r^*-1)-1}[M_{\rho(r^*-1)-1}x] \ne$ EMPTY (CASE 3), the algorithm updates u to $\rho(r^*-1)-1$, leaving l unchanged.

2. Once the gap $u-l$ drops below $\max\{3\tau, k\}$, the algorithm enters the completion round: it reads the cells $T_i[M_i x]$ for all $l+1 \le i \le u$ in parallel, finds the smallest i such that $T_i[M_i x] \ne$ EMPTY, and outputs the point stored in that cell. Such i must exist since we know $C_u \ne \emptyset$. Note that the output point is from a nonempty C_i such that $C_{i-1} = \emptyset$. With Assumption 2, it must be a γ-approximate nearest neighbor of x.

The pseudocode of the cell-probing algorithm is given in Algorithm 2.

We now verify that at each time when the l and u are updated, the invariant that $l < u$, $C_l = \emptyset$ and $C_u \ne \emptyset$ is satisfied. First, in all three cases $l < u$ is obviously satisfied after update.

- Since in CASE 1 and CASE 3 the lower threshold l is not changed, C_l stays empty. And in CASE 2, $T_{\rho(r^*-1)-1}[M_{\rho(r^*-1)-1}x] =$ EMPTY implies that the set $C_l = C_{\rho(r^*-1)-1}$ is empty.
- In CASE 3, since $T_{\rho(r^*-1)-1}[M_{\rho(r^*-1)-1}x] \ne$ EMPTY, the set $C_u = C_{\rho(r^*-1)-1}$ is nonempty. In CASE 2 when $r^* = \tau$ the upper threshold u is not changed so that C_u stays nonempty. For the remaining cases, since $|D_{u,\rho(r^*)}| > n^{-1/s}|C_s|$, by Assumption 3, the set $D_{u,\rho(r^*)}$ must contains at least one point from $B_{\rho(r^*)+1}$. Since $B_{\rho(r^*)+1} \subseteq C_{\rho(r^*)+1}$, the set $C_u = C_{\rho(r^*)+1}$ is nonempty.

And note that in CASE 1 and CASE 2, the gap between the updated values of l and u is at most $(\lfloor l + \frac{r^*}{\tau}(l-u) \rfloor + 1) - (\lfloor l +$

$\frac{r^*-1}{\tau}(l-u)\rfloor - 1) \leq \frac{l-u}{\tau} + 3$, and in CASE 3, the size of the new C_u is $|C_{\rho_{r^*-1}-1}| \leq |B_{\rho_{r^*-1}}| \leq |D_{u,\rho_{r^*-1}}|/(1-n^{-1/s}) \leq 2|D_{u,\rho_{r^*-1}}| \leq 2n^{-1/s}|C_u|$. Therefore, in each shrinking phase, either $u' - l' \leq (u-l)/\tau + 3$ or $|C_{u'}| \leq n^{-1/2s}|C_u|$, where l' and u' denote the updated values of l and u, respectively.

Notice that as C_u stays nonempty, there are most $2s$ shrinking phases in which $|C_u|$ drops. On the other hand, as long as $u-l \geq \max(3\tau, k)$, we have $(u-l)/\tau+3 \leq 2(u-l)/\tau$. Since we choose our τ to satisfy $\frac{\log_\alpha d}{k} \leq (\tau/2)^{(k-1)/2-2s}$, there can be at most $(k-1)/2 - 2s$ shrinking phases in which $(u-l)$ shrinks by a factor of $2/\tau$. Hence, overall there can be at most $(k-1)/2$ shrinking phases. Each shrinking phase contains at most 2 rounds, where the algorithm makes $\lceil \frac{\tau-1}{s} \rceil + 1$ parallel cell-probes in the first round and one cell-probe in the second round of that phase, and at last in the completion round the algorithm makes $\max(3\tau, k)$ parallel cell-probes. The total number of cell-probes is as given by (4).

4. LOWER BOUNDS

In this section, we prove the following lower bound for k-round randomized approximate nearest neighbor search.

THEOREM 4.1 (THEOREM 1.4, RESTATED). *For any finite $c_1, c_2 > 0$, there exists a $c_3 > 0$ such that the following holds. Let $n, d \geq 1$ be sufficiently large integers such that $d \leq 2^{\sqrt{\log n}}$ and $n \leq 2^{d^{0.99}}$. Let $1 \leq k \leq \frac{\log\log d}{2\log\log\log d}$ be an integer. If $\mathsf{ANNS}^{\gamma}_{d,n}$ has a k-round randomized cell-probing scheme with table size $s \leq n^{c_1}$, word size $w \leq d^{c_2}$, such that every query is correctly answered within t total cell-probes in k rounds with probability at least 7/8, then $t > \frac{c_3}{k}(\log_\gamma d)^{1/k}$.*

The proof follows the framework given in [10]. The framework consists of three main components:

1. A reduction from $\mathsf{LPM}^{\Sigma}_{m,n}$ to $\mathsf{ANNS}^{\gamma}_{d,n}$: As observed in [10], it is impossible to prove the lower bound by considering the decision version of $\mathsf{ANNS}^{\gamma}_{d,n}$. The longest prefix match problem $\mathsf{LPM}^{\Sigma}_{m,n}$ captures the nature of $\mathsf{ANNS}^{\gamma}_{d,n}$ very well, and meanwhile, is convenient for applying the round eliminations.

2. A round elimination lemma for communication protocols for $\mathsf{LPM}^{\Sigma}_{m,n}$: Cell-probing schemes are represented as communication protocols. Eliminating a round in any communication protocol for $\mathsf{LPM}^{\Sigma}_{m,n}$ gives a weaker protocol for the same problem of a smaller scale.

3. Applying the round elimination to $\mathsf{LPM}^{\Sigma}_{m,n}$ until there is no round left yet the problem is still nontrivial.

Here a simple observation for the k-round cell-probing schemes is that k rounds of cell-probes can be simulated by $2k$ rounds of communications. Applying the above framework with this observation, for the first two component, we redo the reduction with a new choice of parameters, and reprove the round elimination lemma for general communication protocols with non-uniform message sizes in different rounds. In fact, these variations can be handled routinely by carefully going through the original proofs with new parameters and/or more generic settings. On the other hand, the most delicate part of our lower bound is our execution of the third component, which exploits the power of round eliminations. This part is in our proof of the main lower bound Theorem 4.9.

4.1 Reduction from longest prefix match

In [10], a reduction from another data structure problem, the longest prefix matching $\mathsf{LPM}^{\Sigma}_{m,n}$, to $\mathsf{ANNS}^{\gamma}_{d,n}$ is constructed.

DEFINITION 4.2 (LONGEST PREFIX MATCH). *For integers $m, n \geq 1$ and a finite alphabet Σ we define the longest prefix match problem $\mathsf{LPM}^{\Sigma}_{m,n}$ as the data structure problem that given a query $x \in \Sigma^m$ and a database $B \subseteq \Sigma^m$, $|B| = n$, an answer $z \in B$ must be returned to satisfy that z has the longest common prefix with x among all $y \in B$.*

The reduction in [10] maps instances of $\mathsf{LPM}^{\Sigma}_{m,n}$ to instances of $\mathsf{ANNS}^{\gamma}_{d,n}$ without going through the computation model, so it also applies to k-round cell-probing schemes. In order to prove our more refined lower bound, we need to guarantee the same reduction to hold for a more critical parameterization.

Fix the parameters for the problem $\mathsf{ANNS}^{\gamma}_{d,n}$. We define η and β as follows:

$$\eta \triangleq 1 - \frac{\log\log\gamma}{\log\log d} \quad \text{and} \quad \beta \triangleq 1 - \frac{c_4}{\log\log d}, \tag{5}$$

where $c_4 = 2\log 201$. Note that it holds that

$$\gamma = 2^{(\log d)^{1-\eta}}. \tag{6}$$

LEMMA 4.3 (REDUCTION FROM $\mathsf{LPM}^{\Sigma}_{m,n}$ TO $\mathsf{ANNS}^{\gamma}_{d,n}$). *Let d be a sufficiently large integer, let η and β be as defined in (5) so that γ satisfies (6), and set $m \triangleq \lfloor (\log d)^{\eta\beta} \rfloor$. Let Σ be an alphabet of size $\lceil 2^{d^{0.99}} \rceil$. If $\mathsf{ANNS}^{\gamma}_{d,n}$ has a k-round randomized cell-probing scheme with cell-probe complexity t and success probability 7/8, using table size s and word size w, then so does $\mathsf{LPM}^{\Sigma}_{m,n}$.*

Next we explain how to modify the reduction in [10] to prove this lemma.

A family of Hamming balls in $\{0,1\}^d$ is said to be γ-*separated* if the distance between any two points belonging to distinct balls in the family is more than γ times the diameter of any ball in the family. The following lemma is due to Chakrabarti *et al.* [9].

LEMMA 4.4 (REPHRASED FROM LEMMA 3.2 IN [9]). *Let $d \geq 1$ be a large enough integer, and let $\gamma > 1$. Inside a Hamming ball of radius r (where $d^{0.995} \leq r \leq d$) in $\{0,1\}^d$ there exists a γ-separated family of $\lceil 2^{d^{0.99}} \rceil$ balls, each of radius $r/(8\gamma)$.*

LEMMA 4.5 (IMPROVED FROM LEMMA 2.3 IN [10]). *Let $d \geq 1$ be a large enough integer, and let $\gamma = 2^{(\log d)^{1-\eta}} \geq 3$, as defined in (6). There exists a rooted tree $\mathcal{T}$ whose vertices are Hamming balls in $\{0,1\}^d$ and which satisfies the following properties:*

1. *If v is a child of u in $\mathcal{T}$, then as Hamming balls $v \subset u$.*

2. *Each non-leaf vertex of $\mathcal{T}$ has exactly $\lceil 2^{d^{0.99}} \rceil$ children.*

3. *Each depth-i vertex (the root being a depth-0 vertex) has radius $d/(8\gamma)^i$.*

4. *The depth-i vertices form a γ-separated family of Hamming balls, which means the distance between any two points belonging to distinct balls in the family is more than γ times the diameter of any ball in the family.*

5. *The leaves of $\mathcal{T}$ are at depth $\lfloor (\log d)^{\eta\beta} \rfloor$, where η is as defined in (5).*

PROOF. The proof is almost identical to the proof of Lemma 2.3 in [10], which follows a construction due to Chakrabarti *et al.* [9]. Note that the balls at leaves have radius of at least $d/(8\gamma)^{\lfloor (\log d)^{\eta\beta} \rfloor}$. By our choices of η and β as defined in (5), it can be verify that for large enough d,

$$\frac{d}{(8\gamma)^{\lfloor (\log d)^{\eta\beta} \rfloor}} \geq d^{0.995}.$$

Then by Lemma 4.4, we have the suitable tree $\mathcal{T}$ by a natural recursive construction. □

Given this tree $\mathcal{T}$, the reduction from $\mathsf{LPM}^{\Sigma}_{m,n}$ with the new string length $m = \lfloor (\log d)^{\beta\eta} \rfloor$ to $\mathsf{ANNS}^{\gamma}_{d,n}$ can be constructed by reusing the mapping from $\mathsf{LPM}^{\Sigma}_{m,n}$ instances to $\mathsf{ANNS}^{\gamma}_{d,n}$ instances described in the proof of Lemma 2.4 in [10] as a blackbox.

4.2 Round elimination

We now consider communication protocols between two players Alice and Bob in Yao's model of communication complexity [23]. We refer the readers to the nice textbook by Kushilevitz and Nisan [14] for formal definitions of various concepts, e.g. private-coin protocols.

We assume Alice and Bob send messages to each other alternatively. We use two vectors $\mathbf{A} = (a_1, a_2, \ldots, a_k)$ and $\mathbf{B} = (b_1, b_2, \ldots, b_k)$ to respectively denote the lengths of messages sent by Alice and Bob in each round.

DEFINITION 4.6. *Let $\mathbf{A} = (a_1, a_2, \ldots, a_k) \in \mathbb{R}^k_{\geq 0}$ and $\mathbf{B} = (b_1, b_2, \ldots, b_k) \in \mathbb{R}^k_{\geq 0}$. An $\langle \mathbf{A}, \mathbf{B}, 2k \rangle^A$-protocol is a $2k$-round communication protocol, in which Alice and Bob send messages to each other alternatively, with Alice sending the first message, with the size of Alice's i-th message being exactly $\lfloor a_i \rfloor$ bits, and the size of Bob's i-th message being exactly $\lfloor b_i \rfloor$ bits. The superscript "A" indicates that Alice sends the first message.*

For $\mathbf{A} = (a_1, \ldots, a_{k-1}) \in \mathbb{R}^{k-1}_{\geq 0}$ and $\mathbf{B} = (b_1, \ldots, b_k) \in \mathbb{R}^k_{\geq 0}$, we call such a protocol an $\langle \mathbf{A}, \mathbf{B}, 2k-1 \rangle^B$-protocol if the first message is sent by Bob.

A data structure problem $\rho \subseteq \mathscr{A} \times \mathscr{B} \times \mathscr{C}$ is naturally a communication problem: Alice is give a query $x \in \mathscr{A}$ as input, Bob is given a database $B \in \mathscr{B}$ as input, and Alice is asked to output a correct answer $z \in \mathscr{C}$ satisfying $(x, B, z) \in \rho$ after communicating with Bob. As observed in [17], any cell-probing scheme is actually a communication protocol, with Alice being the cell-probing algorithm and Bob being the table.

PROPOSITION 4.7. *If a data structure problem ρ has a randomized cell-probing scheme using table size s and word size w bits, such that every query is answered correctly within t total cell-probes in k rounds with probability $1 - \epsilon$, then ρ has a private-coin $\langle \mathbf{A}, \mathbf{B}, 2k \rangle^A$-protocol with $a_i = t_i \lceil \log s \rceil$ and $b_i = t_i w$ for every $1 \leq i \leq k$, for some $t_1, t_2, \ldots, t_k \geq 0$ that $t = \sum_{i=1}^k t_i$, such that Alice outputs a correct answer with probability at least $1 - \epsilon$.*

Here the natural interpretation is that each round of t_i many parallel cell-probes can be simulated by two rounds of communications: Alice sends the addresses of the t_i cells, each of $\lceil \log s \rceil$ bits, to Bob, and Bob responds by sending back the contents of these t_i cells, each of w bits.

Let $\mathbf{A} = (a_1, a_2, \ldots, a_k)$ and $\mathbf{B} = (b_1, b_2, \ldots, b_{k'})$ be two vectors, and $c \in \mathbb{R}$ be a number. We introduce some notations:

- let $c\mathbf{A} = (ca_1, ca_2, \ldots, ca_k)$;
- denote by $(\mathbf{A}, \mathbf{B})$, or simply $\mathbf{AB}$, the concatenation: $\mathbf{AB} = (a_1, \ldots, a_k, b_1, \ldots, b_{k'})$;
- denote by $(c, \mathbf{A})$ the concatenation of (c) and $\mathbf{A}$: $(c, \mathbf{A}) = (c, a_1, a_2, \ldots, a_k)$
- denote by $\mathbf{A}^{i-}$ the suffix of $\mathbf{A}$ starting at position i: $\mathbf{A}^{i-} = (a_i, a_{i+1}, \ldots, a_k)$.

The following is the round elimination lemma for $\mathsf{LPM}^{\Sigma}_{m,n}$ that plays a central role in proving the lower bound. The lemma is generalized from a simpler round elimination lemma in [10] to adapt to the non-uniform amount of information communicated in each round.

LEMMA 4.8 (ROUND ELIMINATION LEMMA FOR $\mathsf{LPM}^{\Sigma}_{m,n}$). *Let m, n, p, q be positive integers such that $2p \mid m$, $q \mid n$, and $n \leq |\Sigma|$. Let $0 < \epsilon, \delta < 1$ and $\mathbf{A}, \mathbf{B} \in \mathbb{R}^k_{\geq 0}$. There is a universal constant $C > 0$ such that the followings hold. Assume that $k \geq 1$ and $\frac{2a_1}{p} \geq C$. If $\mathsf{LPM}^{\Sigma}_{m,n}$ has a private-coin $\langle \mathbf{A}, \mathbf{B}, 2k \rangle^A$-protocol with error probability ϵ, then $\mathsf{LPM}^{\Sigma}_{m/2p,n/q}$ has a private-coin $\langle \mathbf{A}', \mathbf{B}', 2k-2 \rangle^A$-protocol with error probability ϵ', where*

$$\mathbf{A}' = \left(1 + \frac{2a_1}{\delta p a_2}\right) \mathbf{A}^{2-}, \quad \mathbf{B}' = \mathbf{B}^{2-},$$

$$\text{and } \epsilon' = \epsilon + 2\delta + \sqrt{b_1 2^{\frac{2a_1}{\delta p}} / q}.$$

The proof of this lemma is in the full version of the paper.

4.3 Proof of the lower bound

We now prove the communication lower bound for $\mathsf{LPM}^{\Sigma}_{m,n}$, by the round elimination tool we setup in previous sections.

THEOREM 4.9. *For any $c_1, c_2 > 0$, there exists a $c_3 > 0$ such that the followings hold. Let $n, d \geq 1$ be sufficiently large integers, and suppose that $d \leq 2^{\sqrt{\log n}}$ and $n \leq 2^{d^{0.99}}$. Let $\gamma \geq 3$ and $m = \lfloor (\log d)^{\eta\beta} \rfloor$, where η and β are as defined in (5). Let Σ be a set of cardinality $\lceil 2^{d^{0.99}} \rceil$. Let $1 \leq k \leq \frac{\log \log d}{2 \log \log \log d}$ be an integer. Let $\mathbf{A}, \mathbf{B} \in \mathbb{R}^k_{>0}$ be in the form that $a_i = c_1 t_i \log n$ and $b_i = t_i d^{c_2}$ for some $t_i > 0$ for every $1 \leq i \leq k$. If $\mathsf{LPM}^{\Sigma}_{m,n}$ has a private-coin $\langle \mathbf{A}, \mathbf{B}, 2k \rangle^A$-protocol, then $t \triangleq \sum_{i=1}^k t_i > \frac{c_3}{k} (\log_\gamma d)^{1/k}$.*

PROOF. Although $\mathbf{A} = (a_1, \ldots, a_k)$ and $\mathbf{B} = (b_1, \ldots, b_k)$, we additionally define

$$a_{k+1} \triangleq a_1, \quad b_{k+1} \triangleq b_1, \quad \text{and } t_{k+1} \triangleq t_1. \tag{7}$$

We set $\delta = \frac{1}{4k}$, $p = \frac{1}{2} m^{1/k}$, and further define

$$c_5 \triangleq \max_{1 \leq i \leq k} \frac{\log (b_i/\delta^2)}{\log n} \frac{m^{1/k}}{k t_{i+1}}.$$

By definitions of β and η in (5), we have

$$\eta\beta = 1 - \frac{c_4 + \log\log\gamma}{\log\log d} + \frac{c_4 \log\log\gamma}{(\log\log d)^2},$$

and

$$m = (\log d)^{\eta\beta} = \frac{(\log d)2^{c_4 \log\log\gamma/\log\log d}}{2^{c_4}\log\gamma} = \Theta(\log_\gamma d).$$

Therefore, assuming that $d \le 2^{\sqrt{\log n}}$ and $\gamma \ge 3$, we have

$$\begin{aligned} c_5 &= \max_{i\in[k]} O\left(\frac{(\log d)^{1/k}(\log k + \log d)}{kt_{i+1}\log n}\right) \\ &= O\left(\frac{(\log d)^2}{\log n}\right) = O(1), \end{aligned}$$

where the constant factor depends on c_2.

Furthermore, since $k \le \frac{\log\log d}{2\log\log\log d}$, it can be verified that

$$m > k^{2k}. \tag{8}$$

Now we define

$$\xi \triangleq \frac{m^{1/k}}{k} = \Theta\left(\frac{(\log_\gamma d)^{1/k}}{k}\right).$$

We start our proof by assuming $\mathsf{LPM}^{\Sigma}_{m,n}$ has a private-coin $\langle \mathbf{A}, \mathbf{B}, 2k\rangle^A$-protocol with error probability 1/8 and

$$t = c_3\xi = \xi/(c_5 + 16c_1e^{16}),$$

and derive an impossible result, which will prove that $t > c_3\xi$. For notational convenience, we ignore divisibility issues.

With the above assumption, we make the following claim.

Claim 4.10. *For any non-negative integer $i \le k$, $\mathsf{LPM}^{\Sigma}_{m_i,n_i}$ has a private-coin $\langle \mathbf{A}_i, \mathbf{B}_i, 2(k-i)\rangle^A$-protocol with error probability $\frac{1}{8} + 3i\delta$, where*

$$\begin{aligned} m_i &= \frac{ma_{i+1}}{(2p)^i a_1}, \\ n_i &= n^{1-\frac{1}{t}\sum_{j\le i} t_{j+1}}, \\ \mathbf{A}_i &= \prod_{j=1}^{i}\left(1 + \frac{2a_j}{a_{j+1}\delta p}\right)\mathbf{A}^{(i+1)-}, \\ \mathbf{B}_i &= \mathbf{B}^{(i+1)-}. \end{aligned}$$

We prove this claim by induction on i. For $i = 0$, the claim holds by our assumption. For induction hypothesis: assume the claim for an $i < k$. We then prove the claim for $i+1$.

We choose $p_{i+1} = \frac{a_{i+1}}{a_{i+2}}p$ and $q_{i+1} = n^{t_{i+2}/t}$. We claim that

$$2p_{i+1} \le m_i = \frac{ma_{i+1}}{(2p)^i a_1}. \tag{9}$$

When $i+1 = k$, this is obviously true, because $\frac{2p_k}{m_{k-1}} = \frac{2a_k p}{a_{k+1}}\frac{a_1(2p)^{k-1}}{ma_k} = 1$ since $a_{k+1} = a_1$ and $2p = m^{1/k}$, thus $2p_k = m_{k-1}$; and when $i < k-1$, we have $\frac{2p_{i+1}}{m_i} = \frac{a_1(2p)^i}{ma_{i+2}} \le \frac{a_1}{a_{i+2}m^{1/k}}$ because $2p = m^{1/k}$, and $\frac{a_1}{a_{i+2}} \le t_i \le t \le m^{1/k}$ (or otherwise $t > m^{1/k} = \Omega((\log_\gamma d)^{1/k})$ and there is nothing to prove). Therefore, $2p_{i+1} \le m_i$ holds for all i.

It is also obvious that

$$q_{i+1} \le n^{1-\frac{1}{t}\sum_{j=1}^{i} t_{j+1}} \le |\Sigma|. \tag{10}$$

On the other hand, the quantity $\frac{2a_{i,1}}{p_{i+1}}$, where $a_{i,1} = a_{i+1}\prod_{j=1}^{i}(1 + \frac{2a_j}{a_{j+1}\delta p})$ is the first entry of $\mathbf{A}_i$, is bounded as below:

$$\frac{2a_{i+1}}{p_{i+1}}\prod_{j=1}^{i}\left(1 + \frac{2a_j}{a_{j+1}\delta p}\right) \ge \frac{2a_{i+2}}{p} > \frac{2c_1\log n}{(\log d)^{1/k}},$$

which is $\omega(1)$ for $d \le 2^{\sqrt{\log n}}$. Therefore, it holds that $\frac{2a_{i,1}}{p_{i+1}} > C$ for the first entry $a_{i,1}$ of $\mathbf{A}_i$, where C is the universal constant in Lemma 4.8. Together with (9) and (10), the condition of the round elimination lemma (Lemma 4.8) is satisfied. We now apply the round elimination lemma to the protocol assumed by the induction hypothesis, to obtain a private-coin $\langle \mathbf{A}_{i+1}, \mathbf{B}_{i+1}, 2(k-i-1)\rangle^A$-protocol for $\mathsf{LPM}^{\Sigma}_{m_{i+1},n_{i+1}}$ with error probability $\frac{1}{8} + 3\delta + 2\delta + \delta'$, where

$$\delta' = \sqrt{\frac{b_{i+1}}{q_{i+1}}\exp\left(\frac{a_{i+1}\ln 2}{\delta p_{i+1}}\prod_{j=1}^{i}\left(1 + \frac{2a_j}{a_{j+1}\delta p}\right)\right)}.$$

We then show that $\delta' \le \delta$. Note that this will finish our induction and prove Claim 4.10.

By (8), we have $\delta p/2 = \frac{1}{16}m^{1/k}/k > \frac{k}{16}$, thus

$$\begin{aligned} \prod_{j=1}^{i}\left(1 + \frac{2a_j}{a_{j+1}\delta p}\right) &\le \prod_{j=1}^{k}\left(1 + \frac{2a_j}{a_{j+1}\delta p}\right) \\ &\le \left(1 + \frac{2}{\delta p}\right)^k \\ &\le \mathrm{e}^{16}. \end{aligned}$$

Where the second inequality is by the Lagrange multipliers. Therefore,

$$\delta' \le \sqrt{\frac{b_{i+1}}{q_{i+1}}2^{\frac{e^{16}a_{i+1}}{\delta p_{i+1}}}} = \sqrt{b_{i+1}}n^{8e^{16}c_1t_{i+2}k/m^{1/k} - t_{i+2}/2t}.$$

Recall that $t = c_3\xi = \xi/(c_5 + 16c_1e^{16})$ and $c_5 = \max_{1\le i\le k}\frac{\log(b_i/\delta^2)m^{1/k}}{kt_{i+1}\log n}$. We have

$$\begin{aligned} & c_5 \ge \frac{m^{1/k}\log(b_{i+1}/\delta^2)}{kt_{i+2}\log(n)} \\ \iff\ & 16c_1e^{16} - \frac{m^{1/k}\log(\delta^2/b_{i+1})}{kt_{i+2}\log(n)} \le 16c_1e^{16} + c_5 = \frac{1}{c_3} \\ \iff\ & \left(16c_1e^{16} - \frac{1}{c_3}\right)\frac{t_{i+2}k}{m^{1/k}} \le \frac{\log(\delta^2/b_{i+1})}{\log n} \\ \iff\ & \frac{16e^{16}c_1t_{i+2}k}{m^{1/k}} - \frac{t_{i+2}}{t} \le \frac{\log(\delta^2/b_{i+1})}{\log n} \\ \iff\ & \delta'^2 \le n^{16e^{16}c_1t_{i+2}k/m^{1/k} - t_{i+2}/t}b_{i+1} \le \delta^2. \end{aligned}$$

And we prove that $\delta' \le \delta$. Claim 4.10 is proved.

Now let $i = k$ in Claim 4.10. We have a private-coin protocol without message exchange between Alice and Bob but solving $\mathsf{LPM}^{\Sigma}_{1,1}$ with error probability at most $\frac{1}{8} + \frac{3}{4}$. However, this is impossible due to the following claim.

Claim 4.11. *Any private-coin protocol for $\mathsf{LPM}^{\Sigma}_{1,1}$ without message exchange can succeed with probability at most $1/|\Sigma|$ in the worst case.*

By Yao's min-max principle, it is sufficient to prove the lower bound for deterministic protocols on a uniform random inputs. Note that the only thing a deterministic Alice can do without communication is to pick a string in Σ and output it, but this can only succeed with probability at most $1/|\Sigma|$ for a random input. $\square$

Theorem 4.9 together with the translation from cell-probing scheme to communication protocol (Proposition 4.7) and the reduction from $\mathsf{LPM}^{\Sigma}_{m,n}$ to $\mathsf{ANNS}^{\gamma}_{d,n}$ (Lemma 4.3) prove the k-round cell-probe lower bound for $\mathsf{ANNS}^{\gamma}_{d,n}$ (Theorem 4.1), the main result of this section.

5. ACKNOWLEDGMENTS

This research is supported in part by NSFC grants 6127208 and 61321491. This work was done in part while YY was visiting the Simons Institute for the Theory of Computing.

6. REFERENCES

[1] M. Ajtai. A lower bound for finding predecessors in Yao's cell probe model. *Combinatorica*, 8(3):235–247, 1988.

[2] A. Andoni and P. Indyk. Near-optimal hashing algorithms for approximate nearest neighbor in high dimensions. In *Proceedings of the 47th annual IEEE Symposium on Foundations of Computer Science (FOCS)*, pages 459–468, 2006.

[3] A. Andoni, P. Indyk, H. L. Nguyen, and I. Razenshteyn. Beyond locality-sensitive hashing. In *Proceedings of the 25th annual ACM-SIAM Symposium on Discrete Algorithms (SODA)*, pages 1018–1028, 2014.

[4] A. Andoni and I. Razenshteyn. Optimal data-dependent hashing for approximate near neighbors. In *Proceedings of the 47th annual ACM on Symposium on Theory of Computing (STOC)*, pages 793–801, 2015.

[5] J. Aspnes, D. Eisenstat, and Y. Yin. Low-contention data structures. In *Proceedings of the 22nd annual ACM Symposium on Parallelism in Algorithms and Architectures (SPAA)*, pages 345–354, 2010.

[6] O. Barkol and Y. Rabani. Tighter bounds for nearest neighbor search and related problems in the cell probe model. In *Proceedings of the 32nd annual ACM Symposium on Theory of Computing (STOC)*, pages 388–396, 2000.

[7] A. Borodin, R. Ostrovsky, and Y. Rabani. Lower bounds for high dimensional nearest neighbor search and related problems. In *Proceedings of the 31st annual ACM Symposium on Theory of Computing (STOC)*, pages 312–321, 1999.

[8] J. Brody and K. G. Larsen. Adapt or die: Polynomial lower bounds for non-adaptive dynamic data structures. *Theory of Computing*, 11(19):471–489, 2015.

[9] A. Chakrabarti, B. Chazelle, B. Gum, and A. Lvov. A lower bound on the complexity of approximate nearest-neighbor searching on the hamming cube. *Discrete and Computational Geometry*, pages 313–328, 2003.

[10] A. Chakrabarti and O. Regev. An optimal randomized cell probe lower bound for approximate nearest neighbor searching. *SIAM Journal on Computing*, 39(5):1919–1940, 2010.

[11] P. Indyk. Nearest neighbors in high-dimensional spaces. 2004.

[12] P. Indyk and R. Motwani. Approximate nearest neighbors: towards removing the curse of dimensionality. In *Proceedings of the 30th annual ACM Symposium on Theory of Computing (STOC)*, pages 604–613, 1998.

[13] T. Jayram, S. Khot, R. Kumar, and Y. Rabani. Cell-probe lower bounds for the partial match problem. In *Proceedings of the 35th annual ACM Symposium on Theory of Computing (STOC)*, pages 667–672, 2003.

[14] E. Kushilevitz and N. Nisan. *Communication Complexity*. Cambridge University Press, 2006.

[15] E. Kushilevitz, R. Ostrovsky, and Y. Rabani. Efficient search for approximate nearest neighbor in high dimensional spaces. *SIAM Journal on Computing*, 30(2):457–474, 2000.

[16] D. Liu. A strong lower bound for approximate nearest neighbor searching. *Information Processing Letters*, 92(1):23–29, 2004.

[17] P. B. Miltersen, N. Nisan, S. Safra, and A. Wigderson. On data structures and asymmetric communication complexity. In *Proceedings of the 27th annual ACM Symposium on Theory of Computing (STOC)*, pages 103–111, 1995.

[18] I. Newman. Private vs. common random bits in communication complexity. *Information processing letters*, 39(2):67–71, 1991.

[19] R. Panigrahy, K. Talwar, and U. Wieder. A geometric approach to lower bounds for approximate near-neighbor search and partial match. In *Proceedings of the 49th annual IEEE Symposium on Foundations of Computer Science (FOCS)*, pages 414–423, 2008.

[20] R. Panigrahy, K. Talwar, and U. Wieder. Lower bounds on near neighbor search via metric expansion. In *Proceedings of the 51st annual IEEE Symposium on Foundations of Computer Science (FOCS)*, pages 805–814, 2010.

[21] M. Pătraşcu and M. Thorup. Higher lower bounds for near-neighbor and further rich problems. In *Proceedings of the 47th annual IEEE Symposium on Foundations of Computer Science (FOCS)*, pages 646–654, 2006.

[22] P. Sen. Lower bounds for predecessor searching in the cell probe model. In *Proceedings of the 18th IEEE annual Conference on Computational Complexity (CCC)*, pages 73–83, 2003.

[23] A. C.-C. Yao. Some complexity questions related to distributive computing. In *Proceedings of the 11th annual ACM Symposium on Theory of Computing (STOC)*, pages 209–213, 1979.

[24] A. C.-C. Yao. Should tables be sorted? *Journal of the ACM*, 28(3):615–628, 1981.

Encoding Short Ranges in TCAM Without Expansion: Efficient Algorithm and Applications*

Anat Bremler-Barr
The Interdisciplinary Center
Herzliya, Israel
bremler@idc.ac.il

Yotam Harchol
The Hebrew University
Jerusalem, Israel
yotamhc@cs.huji.ac.il

David Hay
The Hebrew University
Jerusalem, Israel
dhay@cs.huji.ac.il

Yacov Hel-Or
The Interdisciplinary Center
Herzliya, Israel
toky@idc.ac.il

ABSTRACT

We present RENÉ — a novel encoding scheme for short ranges on *Ternary content addressable memory* (TCAM), which, unlike previous solutions, does not impose *row expansion*, and uses bits proportionally to the maximal range length. We provide theoretical analysis to show that our encoding is the closest to the lower bound of number of bits used. In addition, we show several applications of our technique in the field of packet classification, and also, how the same technique could be used to efficiently solve other hard problems such as the *nearest-neighbor search* problem and its variants. We show that using TCAM, one could solve such problems in much higher rates than previously suggested solutions, and outperform known lower bounds in traditional memory models. We show by experiments that the translation process of RENÉ on switch hardware induces only a negligible 2.5% latency overhead. Our nearest neighbor implementation on a TCAM device provides search rates that are up to four orders of magnitude higher than previous best prior-art solutions.

1. INTRODUCTION

Ternary content addressable memories (TCAMs) have become highly popular in networking equipment and network processing units. TCAMs are used for high-speed IP lookup and packet classification in switches and routers [24, 45]. Software defined networking (SDN) schemes such as OpenFlow [39] rely on TCAM as the main hardware for their data path. TCAM was also suggested to be used for other computationally intensive tasks such as pattern matching [9, 19], heavy-hitters detection [35], and similarity search in databases [54].

*A preliminary version of this paper was presented in DaMoN 2015 workshop.

SPAA '16, July 11-13, 2016, Pacific Grove, CA, USA

DOI: http://dx.doi.org/10.1145/2935764.2935769

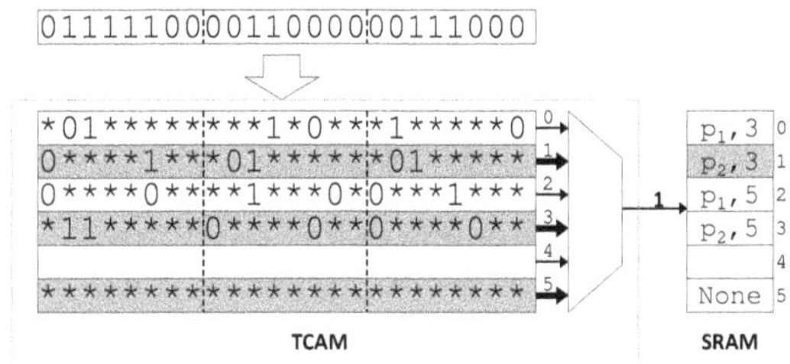

Figure 1: Diagram of the TCAM lookup process. The query is compared to all entries in parallel and the index of the first matching entry is used to find the result.

TCAM is an associative memory module. It is composed of an array of ternary words, each consisting of ternary digits, namely: 0, 1, or *. The '*' digits serve as 'wild cards' that can be matched with either '0' or '1'. Given a query word, TCAM returns the first location in the memory array that matches the query. This process is illustrated in Figure 1.

Multi-field packet classification is becoming more and more important in modern network architectures, such as SDN and *network function virtualization* (NFV) [17]. Specifically, recently suggested SDN frameworks perform more network functionalities on switches, such as load balancing [58], DDoS prevention [43], and quality of service (QoS) [53]. The initiative for NFV suggests to implement higher level tasks such as deep packet inspection and caching as virtual software services, and make traffic flow through them using smart classification rules. All such frameworks heavily rely on multi-field packet classification. Many of these fields are better expressed as ranges.

While TCAMs become more and more popular, it is still a hard problem to efficiently represent range rules on such memories. Over the last decade there has been an intense line of research on range encoding on TCAM [8, 10, 12, 13, 16, 27, 29, 31, 33, 49, 55–57]. Aside from propositions to rearchitect TCAM devices to natively support range rules [55], these solutions can roughly be classified as either *database-independent* or *database-dependent* encoding schemes. Database-independent schemes encode all possible ranges using the same technique, thus allowing fast *hot updates* [10, 27, 56]. However, these schemes use exponential TCAM row expan-

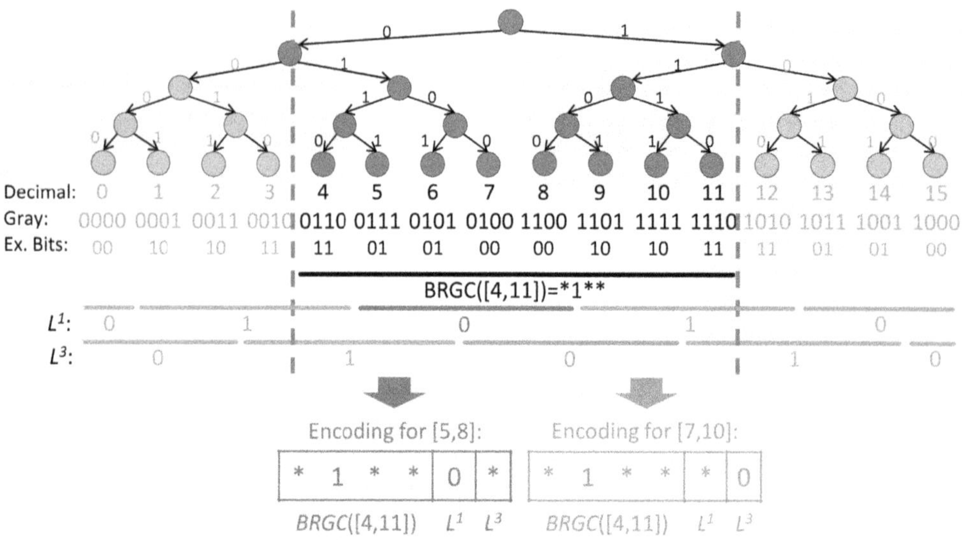

Figure 2: Toy example: A binary-reflected Gray code (BRGC) encoding tree and the encoding of ranges $[5,8]$ and $[7,10]$ using our scheme. In this example, maximal range length is 4. Ranges are divided into layers of non-overlapping ranges. Two layers contain only ranges that can be encoded using Gray code and therefore are not shown. Containing range $[4,11]$ is encoded based on the BRGC values, which forms the first left four bits. Extra bits correspond to layers: Fifth bit to layer L^1 and sixth bit to layer L^3. If a range belongs to a layer, then the value of the bit corresponding to that layer is the binary value of the range for this layer. Otherwise, that bit is set to '*'. The total number of bits is proportional to the maximal encoded length and is independent of the number of encoded ranges.

sion, where a row is expanded into several rows, exponentially to the number of range fields in it.

Database-dependent schemes trades the hot updates flexibility for more compact codes [8, 13], but usually performs well only when the number of encoded ranges is small, as the produced code is proportional to the number of ranges in database. Database-dependent schemes do not scale for large number of ranges, as we show in Section 4.1. Therefore, this paper focuses on a database-independent approach.

In this paper we present a database-independent range encoding scheme, called RENÉ - *Range Encoding with No Expansion* - that *eliminates row expansion completely* when ranges are *short enough.* The code produced by RENÉ is *proportional to the maximal range length,* not to the number of ranges, as in database-dependent schemes. In many cases, as we show in this paper, ranges are limited in length. For example, it was shown in [10] that in real-life packet classification tables more than 60% of the TCP port ranges are short. Moreover, packet classification also uses other range fields, where all ranges are short (such as IP ToS or TTL). On some fields one may apply quantization and categorization to reduce the length of ranges without hurting classification accuracy (e.g. packet length). Nonetheless, RENÉ can be combined with other approaches to represent a wider spectrum of ranges if necessary.

In addition to packet-classification, where TCAM has already been selected as de-facto industry standard, we propose in this paper using a TCAM as a co-processor to CPU in order to solve hard problems from other domains in computer science. Specifically, we show how an encoding scheme such as RENÉ, which requires no row expansion, can be used to practically and efficiently solve the *nearest neighbor search* problem and its variants, removing the infamous curse of dimensionality from them.

To our knowledge, we are the first to present a database-independent encoding scheme for short ranges on TCAM with no row expansion. In a nutshell, RENÉ divides all ranges of some length h_{max} into h_{max} layers of disjoint ranges. Using the *binary-reflected Gray code* (BRGC) [20], which was shown to be more expressive for ranges than binary representation [10], it focuses on a specific area where the encoded range is. Using additional bits, it exactly points to the encoded range inside the area in focus, where a single additional bit represents the location of the range inside the layer it belongs to. A toy example is shown in Figure 2.

Using a general conjunction operator we present next, we are able to encode all ranges with length up to h_{max}. The total length of RENÉ's code for a w-bits field, when encoding ranges of *up to* length h_{max}, is $w - \log_2(h_{max}) + h_{max} - 1$. This means that RENÉ is feasible on contemporary TCAMs for ranges up to length of 512, depending on the available space on TCAM and number of range fields. We also present a theoretical analysis and show that at least $max(h_{max} - 1, w)$ bits are required to encode short ranges of up to length h_{max} in a w-bits field. RENÉ is closer to this lower bound than any previously-suggested technique.

We show several applications for RENÉ in the area of packet classification, along with an implementation of such an application on a powerful OpenFlow switch. We also show by experiments that the penalty in latency for translating values using RENÉ is negligible.

We evaluate and experiment our nearest-neighbor algorithms on a real TCAM device and achieve search rates up to four orders of magnitude higher than previous best prior-art solutions [3,18,54].

2. BACKGROUND

2.1 Ternary Content Addressable Memory (TCAM)

Contemporary TCAM devices operate at very high rates, between hundreds of millions to more than one billion queries per second [22,46]. These devices have about 20-40 megabits of memory that can be configured to accommodate entries of up to about 640-bits wide (the wider the entry, the fewer entries can be stored on the chip).

The downsides of TCAM are that it is power hungry, tends to generate high heat (thus requiring extra cooling), and relatively expensive, compared to a standard DRAM chip. A high-density TCAM consumes 12 to $15W$ per chip when the entire memory is used [45]. However, compared to compute units and coprocessors such as CPU or GPU, TCAMs' power requirement, heating and price are actually lower, and become similar only when connecting multiple TCAMs in parallel, as usually done in high end networking equipment. For example, Intel's E7-4870 CPU consumes $130W$ [15], and Nvidia's Tesla K80 GPU consumes up to $300W$ [37]. Another downside could be that currently, a TCAM cannot be easily deployed on a standard PC, as they are manufactured for networking equipment.

However, due to their impressive adoption for networking devices, TCAMs are becoming larger, faster, less power hungry and less expensive. We speculate that this trend will continue. Inspired by the adoption of Graphics Processing Units (GPUs) for general purpose parallel computing in recent years, in Section 5 we also suggest that TCAMs may be useful for other tasks outside the networking field.

2.2 Range Encoding on TCAM

The problem of range encoding on TCAM has received considerable attention in the context of packet classification.

The traditional technique for range representation [56] is prefix expansion, where a range is represented by a set of prefixes, each of which can be stored by a single TCAM entry. The worst-case expansion ratio when using prefix expansion for a w-bit field is $2w-2$ and for an entry with d ranges it is $(2w-2)^d$. The authors of [10,27] suggest encoding schemes other than binary: In [27], the authors propose DIRPE, a hierarchical version of fence encoding. The authors of [10] propose SRGE - an encoding based on binary reflected Gray code [20]. However, these works do not reduce the range expansion to one, or, in the case of [27], it requires an infeasible exponential memory size to do that. SRGE [10] points out that more ranges can be expressed by using Gray code than when using binary representation, but it only reduces the worst case of row expansion to $2w-4$. DIRPE [27] suggests a tradeoff between row expansion and the number of bits required to code the range. For encoding without expansion, it demands the unfeasible number of 2^w-1 bits.

The database-dependent range encoding techniques design the encoding to efficiently encode the ranges that specifically appear in the database. These techniques [8,12,13,29,57] use extra bits, in addition to the w bits of the range field. The basic idea [29] is to use the extra bits as a bit map: a single extra bit is assigned to each selected range in order to avoid the need to represent it by prefix expansion. Several works [8,12,13,29,57] deal with the scalability problem of this basic technique, which requires one bit per range. However, all these solutions still require either very long rows, proportionally to the number of encoded ranges, or they trade that for row expansion. Moreover, some of these solutions demand extra logic or extra memory that makes them useless in our case, where the number of ranges is high. In [47,48] it was suggested to use negation rules on TCAM instead of row expansion, when applicable, such that rules may specify the opposite of a range and a corresponding opposite action (e.g. 'deny' instead of 'accept' in ACL). This reduces worst-case expansion factor to w but does not eliminate it, and is only applicable in certain scenarios. Other works [16,26,31–33,49] improve the overall TCAM memory requirements for classification rules, or split the rules into multiple TCAM chips [34,60]. However, these works do not focus specifically on range encoding, and can be used on top of most of the range encoding techniques including the one proposed in this paper.

Other works use TCAM for similarity search in databases. Shinde et al. [54] encode probabilistic hash functions on TCAM to implement locality-sensitive hashing [3]. Our preliminary workshop paper [7] has shown how the encoding technique presented in this paper is used to provide deterministic nearest neighbor search, as further elaborated in Section 5.

Afek et al. [1] use TCAM to implement priority queues with a constant time lookup operation and as a by-product, to provide a TCAM-based sorting algorithm with $O(n)$ time.

The limitation of all the methods has inspired a suggestion to change the TCAM hardware [55], to implement range matching directly in hardware. However this solution changes TCAM architecture dramatically, and it does not seem feasible in the near future, since TCAM is a popular memory chip that exists in tens of millions of routers and switches today. Moreover, the solution harms the flexibility of TCAM implementation, where every entry is simply encoded as a string of ternary bits, regardless of the fields type and borders.

3. ENCODING SCHEME FOR SHORT RANGES

Our goal is to encode a range up to a certain length h_{max} using a single TCAM entry of as few bits as possible. Such code will allow encoding classification rules with multiple ranges without row expansion at all.

3.1 Basic Definitions

We begin with some basic definitions that will be used throughout the rest of this section. First, we define a ternary bit-wise comparison:

DEFINITION 1. *Let $a = a_0, \ldots, a_m$ and $b = b_0, \ldots, b_m$ be two ternary words ($a_i, b_i \in \{0, 1, *\}$). a* **matches** *b, denoted $a \approx b$, if and only if for every $i \in \{0, \ldots, m\}$, either $a_i = b_i$, or a_i is $*$, or b_i is $*$.*

RENÉ encodes ranges in discrete spaces. We begin by defining an encoding function `tcode` for values and ranges. Let $\mathcal{U} = [0, 2^w) \subset \mathbb{N}_0$ be a range on the natural line. RENÉ's encoding function `tcode` encodes either a value $v \in \mathcal{U}$, or a range $R \subseteq \mathcal{U}$. It is important to note that RENÉ treats

$\mathcal{U}$ as a cyclic 'wrap-around' space and thus throughout this paper, any range $[x, y)$ refers in fact to $[x, y \bmod 2^w)$.

The result of the encoding function is either a binary word (for exact values) or a ternary word (for ranges), and we expect that a ternary match $\texttt{tcode}(v) \approx \texttt{tcode}(R)$ will imply that the value v is inside the range R. This is formally defined as follows:

DEFINITION 2. *An encoding function* tcode *is* **admissible** *if for every value $v \in \mathcal{U}$ and every range $R \subseteq \mathcal{U}$, $\texttt{tcode}(v) \approx \texttt{tcode}(R)$ if and only if $v \in R$. Furthermore, for any point $v \in \mathcal{U}$, $\texttt{tcode}(v)$ does not contain '*' symbols.*

3.2 Binary-Reflected Gray Code for TCAM

The *binary-reflected Gray code* (BRGC) [20] is a binary encoding of integers in a contiguous range such that the codes of any two consecutive numbers differ by a single bit. A b-bits BRGC is constructed recursively by reflecting a $(b-1)$-bits BRGC [1].

DEFINITION 3. *The BRGC encoding function $BRGC(v, 2^w)$ encodes a point p (where $0 \leqslant p < 2^w$) with w bits. It is defined recursively as follows:*

$$BRGC(0, 1) = \varepsilon$$

$$BRGC(p, 2^w) = \begin{cases} 0 \cdot BRGC(p, 2^{w/2}) & \text{if } p < 2^{w/2} \\ 1 \cdot BRGC(2^w - p - 1, 2^{w/2}) & \text{otherwise} \end{cases}$$

where ε is the empty word and '$\cdot$' denotes concatenation.

For example, $BRGC(4, 8) = 1 \cdot BRGC(3, 4) = 11 \cdot BRGC(0, 2) = 110 \cdot BRGC(0, 1) = 110$. An example for values in $[0, 16)$ is shown in Figure 2.

By wildcarding some of the bits of a BRGC codeword we can create a ternary range representation. For example, as can be seen in Figure 2, the ternary word `*1**` matches all values in the range $[4, 11]$. In fact, when looking at this tree representation of the BRGC encoding, we observe that all ranges that exactly contain a full sub-tree, or two adjacent full sub-trees, can be represented using a single *ternary* BRGC codeword (namely, a BRGC codeword where some of the 0-1 bits were replaced by '*' symbols).

Before formulating and proving this observation we define the following terms that will be used in the proof:

- *k-prefix* is a ternary word in which the k least significant bits are '*' and the rest are either 0 or 1.
- *k-semi-prefix* is a ternary word in which the k least significant bits are '*', one additional bit is also '*', and the rest are either 0 or 1.

We now formulate the following theorem. Due to space constraints, proofs for all theorems and lemmas in the paper appear in [6].

THEOREM 1. *If all values are BRGC-encoded, then a single ternary BRGC codeword suffices to admissibly encode a range $R = [x, y \bmod 2^w)$ if and only if there exist non-negative integers i, k, for which $x = i \cdot 2^k$ and $y = (i+2) \cdot 2^k$. Specifically, one of the following cases holds:*

1. *If i is even, the $(k+1)$ least significant bits of the codeword are *, and the rest are either 0 or 1. Thus, the ternary codeword is $(k+1)$-prefix.*
2. *If i is odd, the k least significant bits of the codeword are *, one additional bit is *, and the rest are either 0 or 1. Thus, the ternary codeword is k-semi-prefix.*

[1] The BRGC of a value x can be directly calculated using the following formula: $x \oplus (x >> 1)$, where $\oplus$ and $>>$ are the bitwise operations of XOR and Right Shift, respectively.

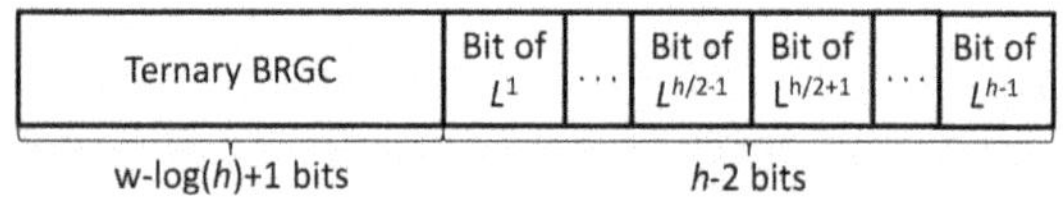

Figure 3: Encoding structure for a value or range of length h

Theorem 1 implies that when encoding ranges of length h, the $\log_2(h) - 1$ least significant bits are always '*' thus one can save TCAM space by omitting these uninformative bits.

3.3 An Encoding Function for Ranges

We call those ranges that can be encoded using a single ternary BRGC codeword *trivial ranges*, and all other ranges *nontrivial ranges*. In this section, we extend the BRGC encoding scheme so that it can encode in a single ternary word nontrivial ranges as well. We append *extra bits* to the end of BRGC codewords, as depicted in Figure 3: $w - \log_2(h) + 1$ bits are used for the binary BRGC encoding of a value $v \in \mathcal{U}$, or for the ternary BRGC encoding of some trivial range R. To encode nontrivial ranges of length $h = 2^k$ ($k \in \mathbb{N}_0$), at most $h - 2$ bits are added as extra bits.

The key idea of RENÉ is to divide all ranges of some length $h = 2^k$ ($k \in \mathbb{N}_0$) into h *layers*, such that a layer L_h^i is the set of all ranges $[x, x+h)$ for which $x \bmod h = i$. Note that two of these layers contain only trivial ranges (L_h^0 and $L_h^{2^{k-1}}$). We are left with $h - 2$ layers that contain nontrivial ranges. We assign an extra bit for each layer of nontrivial ranges. The value of this bit alternates between adjacent ranges in the same layer, such that for any pair of consecutive ranges in the same layer, the value of the bit corresponding to this layer is different. Hence, for a value $v \in \mathcal{U}$, $\texttt{tcode}(v)$ is the $1 + w - log_2(h)$ most significant bits of $BRGC(v)$, concatenated with $h-2$ extra bits. The value of the ith extra bit corresponds to layer L_h^i and is set to $\lfloor \frac{v-i}{h} \rfloor \bmod 2$.

For nontrivial ranges we define their *cover range* as follows:

DEFINITION 4. *For any nontrivial range of length $h = 2^k$ ($k \in \mathbb{N}_0$), $R = [x, x+h)$, let the* **cover range** *of R, denoted by* cover*(R), be the range $[\lfloor x/h \rfloor \cdot h, (\lfloor x/h \rfloor + 2) \cdot h)$.*

We first notice the following property of cover ranges:

LEMMA 1. *For any range $R = [x, x+h)$ of length $h = 2^k$ ($k \in \mathbb{N}_0$),* cover*(R) fully contains R.*

Note that the existence of the cover range is a unique property of the binary-reflected Gray code. The cover range $\texttt{cover}(R)$ helps us distinguish R from other ranges in the same layer. For range $R = [x, x+h) \in L_h^i$ of length $h = 2^k$ ($k \in \mathbb{N}_0$), $\texttt{tcode}(I)$ starts with the $1 + w - log_2(h)$ most

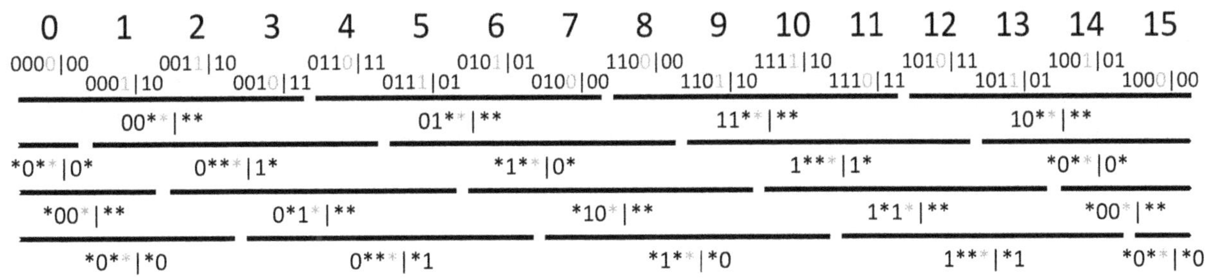

Figure 4: Encoding for all sub-ranges of length 4 and values in range $[0, 16)$. Left bits are the ternary BRGC encoding. Right bits are the extra bits for nontrivial layers. The bits in gray can be removed as explained in Section 3.2

significant bits of the ternary BRGC representation of R, if R is trivial, or of cover(R), if R is nontrivial. Then, $h-2$ extra bits are concatenated one after the other where the ith bit is either $*$ if $I \notin L_h^i$ or $\lfloor \frac{x-i}{h} \rfloor \bmod 2$ otherwise (namely, all the extra bits except one are $*$).

Our main result is that RENÉ's encoding function, `tcode` , is an *admissible encoding function* for ranges of any length $h = 2^k$ ($k \in \mathbb{N}_0$). The total length of the admissible encoding produced by `tcode` for a single value or range is hence $w - \log(h) + h - 1$.

Before proving this result (Theorem 2), we introduce the following two technical lemmas:

LEMMA 2. *If a range R is nontrivial, then no other range from the same layer is fully contained in cover(R).*

Based on this property of cover ranges, we can completely distinguish between ranges in the same layer using the extra bits we added to the ternary BRGC encoding:

LEMMA 3. *Let $R = [x, x+h)$, where $h = 2^k$, be a range in L_h^i. For every value v in cover(R), if $v \in R$, v has the same bit value as R, and if $v \notin R$, then v has the opposite bit value.*

We now turn to the main theorem.

THEOREM 2. *The function `tcode` is an admissible encoding function for ranges of length $h = 2^k$.*

Figure 4 shows the encoding of all sub-ranges of length 4 in range $[0, 16)$. Note that the first and third layers do not require extra bits, so these are both set to * in their encoding. In other layers, the corresponding extra bit alternates between ranges in the same layer. For example, the range $[1, 4]$, which cannot be encoded solely using a ternary BRGC codeword, is encoded as `0***1*`, where the fifth bit is the extra bit that corresponds to the second layer. Only points in $[1, 4]$ match this encoding.

3.4 Encoding Multiple Range Lengths

Given RENÉ's encoding function for ranges of some maximal length h_{max} we can encode, without using more bits, *all ranges whose lengths are smaller than h_{max}* as well. We define a logical conjunction operation, denoted by $\sqcap$, to encode the intersection of two ranges. The truth table of such a conjunction is given in Table 1. $\perp$ means an undefined output,

a_i	b_i	$a_i \sqcap b_i$
$*$	$*$	$*$
0	$*$	0
$*$	0	0
0	0	0
1	$*$	1

a_i	b_i	$a_i \sqcap b_i$
$*$	1	1
1	1	1
0	1	$\perp$
1	0	$\perp$

Table 1: The truth table of a ternary logical conjunction, denoted by the $\sqcap$ operator.

and we later make sure to never get such an output when using this operation. For two ternary words, $a = a_0, \ldots, a_m$ and $b = b_0, \ldots, b_m$, the conjunction $c = a \sqcap b$ is the ternary word where $c_i = a_i \sqcap b_i$. If at least one of the symbols c_i is $\perp$, then c is also marked as $\perp$ and is not defined. Note that the conjunction operation is independent of the specific encoding function.

The essence of the conjunction operation is captured in the following two lemmas:

LEMMA 4. *For any value $v \in \mathcal{U}$ and any two ranges $R_1, R_2 \subseteq \mathcal{U}$, if `tcode` is an admissible encoding function for R_1 and R_2, then `tcode`(v) $\approx$ `tcode`(R_1) $\sqcap$ `tcode`(R_2) if and only if $v \in R_1 \cap R_2$.*

LEMMA 5. *If `tcode` is an admissible encoding function for R_1 and R_2, and the result of `tcode`(R_1) $\sqcap$ `tcode`(R_2) is $\perp$ then $R_1 \cap R_2 = \emptyset$.*

Note that the other direction of Lemma 5 is not necessarily true: the conjunction of codes of two disjoint ranges may not be $\perp$.

We assume that there is a value $h_{max} = 2^{k_{max}}$, which is the maximum length we should consider. Note that any range $[x, x+h)$ of length $h < h_{max}$ (h is not necessarily a power of 2 anymore) can be written as the intersection of two ranges of length h_{max} as follows:

$$[x, x+h) = [x+h-h_{max}, x+h) \cap [x, x+h_{max}).$$

Using the conjunction operator and Lemma 4 we can construct the code for ranges of any length $h \leqslant h_{max}$, with $h_{max} - 2$ extra-bits:

$$\texttt{tcode}([x, x+h)) =$$

$$\texttt{tcode}([x+h-h_{max}, x+h)) \sqcap \texttt{tcode}([x, x+h_{max})).$$

Algorithm 1 Encoding Function for a Value v

```
function tcode (v, h_max)
                          ▷ v - value, h_max - maximal range length
    word ← BRGC(p) >> (log2(h_max) − 1)    ▷ Bitwise shift
    for i ← 0 to (h_max − 1) do
        if layer is skipped then
            continue                  ▷ Optional - encode less layers
        end if
        if layer is nontrivial (i ≠ 0 and i ≠ h_max/2) then
            b ← ⌊(v−i)/h_max⌋ mod 2
            word ← (word << 1)|b                    ▷ Bitwise OR
        end if
    end for
    return word
end function
```

We also know from Lemma 5 that $\texttt{tcode}([x, x+h))$ is not $\perp$ as the intersection is never empty.

The encoding function $\texttt{tcode}(v)$ for some value v when using any range lengths up to h_{max} is shown in Algorithm 1. When encoding a range R of length $h \leqslant h_{max}$ that is centered at some point v, Algorithm 2 is used to obtain $\texttt{tcode}(R)$.

The length of the resulting encoding of a value $v \in \mathcal{U}$ or a range $R \subseteq \mathcal{U}$ is therefore $w - \log_2(h_{max}) + h_{max} - 1$.

3.5 Running Time Analysis

Computing `tcode` for either a value or a range is simple: results only depend on the value or range themselves, and the maximal range length h_{max}. The running time of both functions, for a value and a range, is linear with h_{max}, and does not depend in the number of encoded ranges: $O(h_{max})$ when encoding a value and $O(h_{max} + h)$ when encoding a range of length $h \leqslant h_{max}$.

3.6 Lower Bound on the Number of Bits per Range

As previously recalled, Lakshminarayanan et al. [27] introduced the worst-case necessary condition of $2^w - 1$ bits to encode a w-bit range. We use this observation to introduce a lower bound for the number of bits required to encode ranges, when their lengths are limited by some upper bound h_{max}:

THEOREM 3. *In order to represent any ranges up to length h_{max} without row expansion, in a field of width w bits, at least $max(h_{max} - 1, w)$ bits are necessary.*

4. RENÉ FOR PACKET CLASSIFICATION

Range encoding on TCAM has been used for packet classification for long time. Row expansion significantly limited its usage when multiple header fields are ranges, leading vendors and administrators to avoid such situations as much as possible [41]. However, next generation SDN applications, such as load balancers, security tools, and quality of service, rely on sophisticated packet classification that is performed on the datapath itself (i.e. the switch) [5, 43, 53, 58]. Most of these solutions require range based matching on multiple header fields. We summarize several examples for such fields and metadata information that can benefit when using RENÉ:

- **TCP/UDP Port Fields:** In real-life datasets, short ranges (up to length 64) sometimes consist more than 60% of the unique ranges [10]. Thus, if a network administrator uses mainly short ranges for TCP/UDP port fields, or even for only one of these fields, RENÉ may suit their needs.

- **Network ToS (or DSCP):** In both the deprecated ToS field and the new DSCP field the precedence is set using an increasing value, and to specify one or more precedence classes, either an exact value or a short range should be used.

- **Packet Size:** Packet size (e.g. IP total length field) can be a useful piece of information for packet classification. When classifying according to this property, a categorization can be done in order to reduce range lengths. As usually one does not classify packets according to a specific length, but rather according to categories (small, medium, large, etc.), short ranges can be used to represent multiple categories. For example, a recent attack named *Tsunami SYN Flood Attack* can be identified based on the size of packets (about 1000 bytes or more) [44].

Algorithm 2 Encoding Function for a Range $[s, t]$

```
function tcode ([s, t], h_max)
                    ▷ [s, t] - range, h_max - maximal range length
    if t − s + 1 ≠ h_max then
                          ▷ Encode range as an intersection
        R1 = [s, s + h_max − 1]
        R2 = [t − h_max + 1, t]
        Γ ← {R1, R2}
    else                                 ▷ Encode range directly
        Γ ← {[s, t]}
    end if
    result ← 0
    count ← 0
    for [x, y] ∈ Γ do
        mask ← 0
        for i ← x + 1 to y do
            mask ← mask|(BRGC(i − 1) ⊕ BRGC(i))
                                     ▷ bitwise OR and XOR
        end for
        word ← BRGC(x) >> (log2(h_max) − 1)
        mask ← mask >> (log2(h_max) − 1)
        for i ← 0 to (h_max − 1) do
            if layer is skipped then
                continue          ▷ Optional - encode less layers
            end if
            if layer is nontrivial (i ≠ 0 and i ≠ h_max/2) then
                if x mod h_max ≠ i then       ▷ Irrelevant layer
                    mask ← (mask << 1)|1            ▷ Put a '*'
                    word ← word << 1
                else                     ▷ [x, y] is in this layer
                    mask ← mask << 1
                    b ← ⌊(x−i)/h_max⌋ mod 2
                    word ← (word << 1)|b
                end if
            end if
        end for
        if count > 0 then
            result ← result ⊓ (word, mask)
        else
            result ← (word, mask)
        end if
        count ← count + 1
    end for
    return result
end function
```

- **Timestamp and Counters:** Recent works suggest adding packet's metadata such as hit counters and timestamps (or time deltas) to classification data path, for example in OpenFlow switches [5]. It is likely that classification on such fields would be based on ranges and not on exact values, and thus RENÉ may be used.

- **IP Spoofing Detection:** In order to protect against IP spoofing and attacks that use this technique (e.g., DDoS), it was suggested to inspect the IP TTL value and conclude about possible spoofed packets [25, 40]. The detection is based on the fact that the TTL value does not change dramatically over short time for the same host or subnet, and these values can be found using `ping` and other tools. Thus, if a packet with IP from a known subnet comes with a TTL value that is too far from the expected value, it is classified as spoofed and dropped.

  Since the TTL value is not compared to an exact value, but rather to a short range, RENÉ can be used in order to implement IP spoofing detection on classification hardware with TCAM.

- **AS Numbering:** BGP routers and SDX [21] sometimes make classification decisions based on autonomous systems (ASes) numbers. Large ISPs and content providers usually hold multiple, consecutive AS numbers [14], which form one or more short ranges. For example, Comcast has multiple such short ranges 7015-7016, 33489-33491, 33650-33668 (in addition to five more non-consecutive AS numbers). Grouping AS numbers to ranges can reduce the total number of classification rules, as long as no row expansion is induced. RENÉ fits this goal as the ranges are short and it induces no row expansion.

4.1 Evaluation and Experiments

4.1.1 Experiment on an OpenFlow Switch

We implemented RENÉ and a sample SDN application that uses it for packet classification over the Ryu SDN controller [51]. We use a NoviFlow NoviKit 250 hardware switch that supports OpenFlow 1.3 [39] and has an internal TCAM. Our code is available at `https://github.com/yotamhc/rene`.

Classification uses OpenFlow table pipeline in the following way: First table, given a destination TCP port for a packet, writes its translation into RENÉ's encoding to the metadata field (using the OpenFlow's Write-Metadata instruction). This table is precomputed on the controller and contains up to 64K entries - an entry for each port number. Then, second table matches the packet according to the metadata only (original port information is not necessary at this stage), and forwards it accordingly.

On the same switch, when a packet is classified based on only its TCP port, without table pipeline, the total round-trip time to and from the switch, using a 1Gbps copper link, is $157\mu s$. Using our table pipeline, such round-trip takes $161\mu s$. Thus, latency increases by only 2.5%, which is a negligible factor.

4.1.2 Quantitative Evaluation

To evaluate the quality of RENÉ's encoding function `tcode` we compare it with best prior-art encoding techniques that

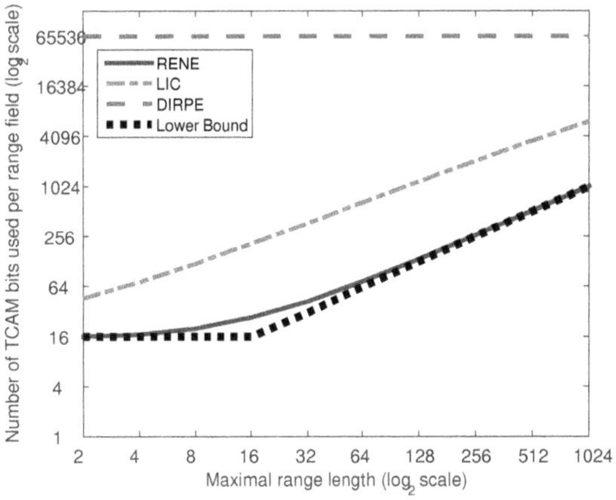

Figure 5: Analysis of the number of TCAM bits required for a 16-bits range field when representing all ranges of up to a given length.

can provide no row expansion: DIRPE [27], a database-independent encoding scheme and LIC [8], a database-dependent encoding scheme. We do not compare RENÉ to SRGE [10], for example, as it requires row expansion. We evaluate the database dependent scheme LIC both in its worst case, where all ranges are to be represented, and using a commercial classification dataset with 257 range rules. Since our goal is no expansion of TCAM entries, we compare the amount of TCAM bits required for a single range field, such that no expansion is induced whatsoever. Using the classification database, LIC performs worse than RENÉ on ranges up to length 32. When the dataset contains much higher number of ranges, LIC always performs worse than RENÉ.

Figure 5 shows the bit requirement of each encoding technique, given the maximal length of encoded ranges, assuming a 16-bits range field. In addition, it shows the lower bound of $max(h_{max}-1, w)$ bits (see Theorem 3), as a black, dotted line. Evidently, RENÉ (blue, solid line) is much closer to the lower bound than all other techniques. Moreover, the bit requirements for database-dependent techniques such as LIC [8] are higher by an order of magnitude, when *all* ranges up to a certain length should be encoded. The database-independent technique DIRPE [27] always requires $2^w - 1$ bits as it does not use the additional information on the maximal range length.

5. RENÉ FOR NEAREST NEIGHBOR SEARCH

TCAM is a powerful device with high parallelism that can also be used for tasks outside of the networking fields. Just as TCAM has broken the performance limits of packet classification and IP lookup in networking, it can also be used to break such computational limits in problems from other fields, serving as a coprocessor for the CPU, similarly to a GPU or FPGA. RENÉ can be used to implement on such TCAM applications that use the nearest-neighbor problem or its variants. We show several such variants in this section, and by experiments and simulations we show that RENÉ can improve their performance by orders of magnitudes.

Multidimensional nearest neighbor search (NN) lies at the

core of many computer science applications. In the space of integers, the problem is formally defined as follows:

DEFINITION 5. *Given a set of data points* $S = \{p_i\}_{i=1}^{n}$, $p_i \in \mathbb{Z}^d$ *and a query point* $q \in \mathbb{Z}^d$, THE NEAREST-NEIGHBOR PROBLEM *is to find the point* $s^* = \arg\min_{s \in S} D(s, q)$, *where* $D(s, q)$ *is a distance between* s *and* q.

The NN problem and its variants are utilized in a wide range of applications, such as spatial search, object recognition, image matching, image segmentation, classification and detection, to name a few [11,28,42].

When the dimensionality of the points is small, many solutions were proven to be very effective. These include mainly space partitioning techniques [52]. However, when the number of the data points is large (in the order of tens of thousands or higher) and the dimensionality is high (in the order of tens or hundreds), the exact solutions break down and produce exponential time complexity[2] [3,59]. This problem is widely known as the *curse of dimensionality*.

To overcome the curse of dimensionality, *approximated nearest neighbor* (ANN) solutions are commonly used. In particular, a c-ANN is a solution where the distance of the retrieved point from q is at most c times the true distance from the nearest point. For the ANN problem, probabilistic dimensionality reduction such as *locality sensitive hashing* (LSH) [3] was proven to be useful, with query time sublinear in n but linear in d. For very-high dimensional space this may still pose a problem [36]. Note also that the solution provided by LSH is correct only with high probability.

In this section we present super high-speed algorithms for the NN problem using TCAM as a coprocessor, and our encoding scheme RENÉ. The proposed algorithms solve the ANN problem with ℓ_∞-normed distance using *a single TCAM lookup* and linear space.

To the best of our knowledge, using TCAM for nearest neighbor search has been considered only once, by Shinde et al. [54] who proposed the TLSH scheme, where a TCAM device is utilized to implement LSH with a series of TCAM lookup cycles. Our algorithms, however, are deterministic and they provide higher throughput with less memory required on TCAM.

A simpler problem that we will use as a building block in our algorithms only searches for a neighbor close enough to the query point, or discovers that there is no such neighbor at all:

DEFINITION 6. *Given a set of points* $S = \{p_i\}_{i=1}^{n}$, $p_i \in \mathbb{Z}^d$, *and a query point* $q \in \mathbb{Z}^d$, *let* $d^* = \min_{s \in S} D(s, q)$. *The* r–NEAR-NEIGHBOR REPORT PROBLEM *is to find the point* $s' \in S$ *such that* $D(s', q) \le r$ *if* $d^* \le r$, *and to return* false *if* $d^* > r$.

Note that under ℓ_∞, a solution for the r–NEAR-NEIGHBOR REPORT PROBLEM is a data point within the d-dimensional cube of edge length $2r$ that is centered in the query point. Thus, our framework for solving c-ANN can be viewed as solving (either in parallel or sequentially) a series of r–NEAR-NEIGHBOR REPORT PROBLEM instances for increasing values of r. As pointed out in [23], this solves the c-APPROXIMATE NEAREST NEIGHBOR PROBLEM, where the approximation

[2]Exact brute-force search works in time that is linear to n and d, but is very slow for high n and d. Space partitioning techniques are exponential in d.

Algorithm 3 Encoding Function for a d-Dimensional Point

```
function TCODE(p[], d, h_max)
    word ← ε
    for i ← 1 to d do
        word ← word + tcode(p[i], h_max)
    end for
    return word
end function
```

Algorithm 4 Encoding Function for a d-Dimensional Cube

```
function TCODE(p[], d, h, h_max)
    word ← ε
    for i ← 1 to d do
        word ← word+tcode([p[i]−⌊h/2⌋ , p[i]+⌊h/2⌋], h_max)
    end for
    return word
end function
```

ratio is determined by the maximum ratio between consecutive values of r.

Using RENÉ's encoding function `tcode` , a single ternary match can determine whether a given d-dimensional point is inside a given d-dimensional cube: To encode a d-dimensional point, or a d-dimensional cube, each coordinate is encoded using the `tcode` function, and the codewords of all d coordinates are concatenated into a single ternary word. The encoding functions for a d-dimensional point and for a d-dimensional cube are shown in Algorithm 3 and in Algorithm 4, respectively.

5.1 Approximate Nearest-Neighbor Search

Our APPROXIMATE NEAREST-NEIGHBOR SEARCH algorithms solve in fact multiple instances of the r-NEAR NEIGHBOR REPORT PROBLEM for increasing values of r. In ℓ_∞, the value of r defines a cube around each data point p such that for all query points q inside that cube, p is a valid solution of the r-NEAR NEIGHBOR REPORT PROBLEM with q, and for all query points outside that cube p is not a valid solution.

Our *time-efficient method* solves the APPROXIMATE NEAREST-NEIGHBOR SEARCH in ***a single TCAM lookup***. Given a set $\mathcal{H}$ of edge lengths, let $h_{max} = \max_h \mathcal{H}$. For each point $p \in S$ and $h \in \mathcal{H}$ we store a TCAM entry representing a d-dimensional cube centered at p, with edge length h. Entries are sorted by the value of h: the smaller h is, the higher the priority of the entry.

Given a query point $q \in [0, w)^d$, we use `tcode` to build a d-dimensional point representation for maximal edge length of h_{max}, and use a *single TCAM lookup* to find the smallest cube that contains the point q. The TCAM returns the highest priority entry that matches, which is the entry of the cube that is centered at some point p, has the shortest edge length, and contains q. An example is shown in Figure 6 (left). Note that in general, p is not necessarily the exact nearest neighbor of q (as there may be more than one such cube with the same edge length h). However, the distance (under ℓ_∞) of q from its exact nearest neighbor is strictly more than $\left\lfloor \frac{1}{2} \max_{h' \in \mathcal{H}} \{h' < h\} \right\rfloor$. As we will show later, by carefully choosing the edge length set, we can obtain a $c = 1 + \varepsilon$ approximation factor, where the size of $\mathcal{H}$ is inversely proportional to ε.

In our *memory-efficient method*, the data points and query points switch roles: we store in the TCAM a single entry for each data point. The order of the entries does not matter.

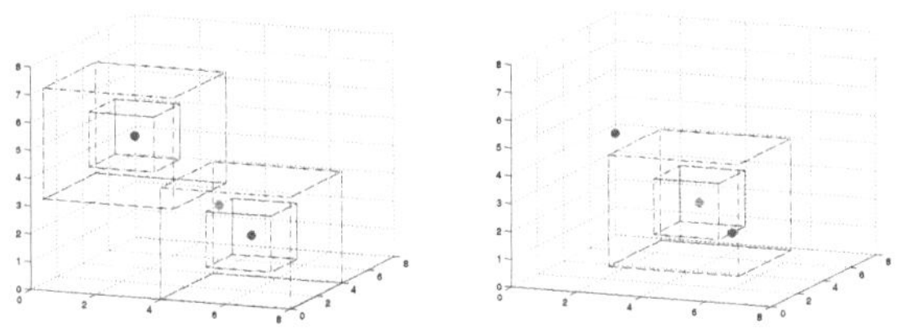

Figure 6: Illustration of the two alternative algorithms for Nearest Neighbor Search using TCAM. Left: Encoding nested cubes around each point in the database. A query is a point in this encoding, and the result is the smallest cube encompassing the query point. Right: Encoding cubes around the query points and the data is encoded as points. A query is a sequence of nested cubes in increasing edge length. The result is the first data point that matches a cube.

Upon a query q, we construct a sequence of $|\mathcal{H}|$ cubes centered in p with edge lengths in $\mathcal{H}$. Then, we perform TCAM lookups with cubes of increasing edge length values until a match is found. As in the previous method, if a point was matched with a query of edge length h, then it is a solution of the $h/2$-NEAR NEIGHBOR REPORT PROBLEM.

5.1.1 Analysis of Approximation

Let $\mathcal{H} = \{h_1, h_2, \ldots, h_{max}\}$ such that $h_i < h_j$ for each $i < j$. Matching a data point p corresponding to a cube with edge length h_i implies that $D(p,q) \leq \left\lfloor \frac{h_i}{2} \right\rfloor$ (where D is defined under ℓ_∞). Since h_i is the first edge length to be matched, $D(s^*,q) \geq \left\lfloor \frac{h_{i-1}}{2} \right\rfloor + 1$ (s^* is the exact nearest neighbor of q). This implies that under ℓ_∞, both methods solve the c-APPROXIMATE-NEAREST-NEIGHBOR PROBLEM for $c = \max_{h_i \in \mathcal{H}} \frac{\lfloor h_i/2 \rfloor}{\lfloor h_{i-1}/2 \rfloor + 1}$, where h_i is the ith smallest element in $\mathcal{H}$ and $h_1 = 1 \in \mathcal{H}$. [3]

In order to get the exact nearest neighbor in ℓ_∞, one can choose $\mathcal{H}$ to be the set of odd numbers. Reducing the size of $\mathcal{H}$ reduces the number of required entries, but decreases the quality of the results. For example, to get a c-approximate solution, $\mathcal{H}$ can consist of all even values up to $2/(c-1)$, along with the values of a geometric series starting at $2/(c-1)$, with the parameter c.

When distances are defined under ℓ_p norms, for finite values of $p \geq 1$, the approximation ratio is at most $c \cdot \sqrt[p]{d}$ in ℓ_p, where c is the approximation ratio in ℓ_∞.

5.1.2 Database Update

Our algorithms allow efficient hot updates in the lookup database (the set S). Deletion of data points is trivial (simply delete all corresponding entries from the TCAM). When using the *time-efficient method*, efficient addition of new points is possible by keeping some empty TCAM entries between entries of different edge length, by adding entries for the corresponding cubes in these empty slots. Also, one can track deletion for more empty slots. Nevertheless, this further increases space requirement.

[3] To get a bounded approximation ratio, 1 must be added to $\mathcal{H}$.

When using the *memory-efficient method*, the situation is simpler: since the order of entries is not important, point addition or deletion requires a single TCAM entry update.

5.2 Exact Nearest-Neighbor Search in ℓ_p

Our algorithms achieve $\sqrt[p]{d}$ approximate solution under ℓ_p norm. We suggest the following extension to find (exactly) the nearest neighbor under ℓ_p: For each data point $s \in S$ and for each edge length $h \in \mathcal{H}$, we *precompute* the *neighborhood set* $\mathcal{N}(s,h) = \{s' \in S \mid D_p(s,s') \leq h\sqrt[p]{d}\}$, where D_p is the distance between the two points under the p-norm. The neighborhood sets are stored in memory. Precomputing these sets is possible since datasets are relatively static and the neighborhood sets do not depend on the query points.

Since for every two points, the distance in ℓ_p is at most $\sqrt[p]{d}$ the distance in ℓ_∞, we immediately conclude that if the algorithms described in Section 5.1 return a data point s for query point q with some distance $h \in \mathcal{H}$, then the exact nearest neighbor in ℓ_p of q is in $\mathcal{N}(s,h)$.

While this method requires additional computations following the TCAM lookup, in most datasets the number of points in $\mathcal{N}(s,h)$ would be very small. In our experiments (see Section 5.5) $\mathcal{N}(s,h)$ contained only s itself for lower values of h in most cases and was small even for higher values of h. Thus, the time required to find the exact nearest neighbor is still much shorter than that required for brute-force over all points in the database.

The precomputed neighborhood sets can also be used to find k-nearest neighbors instead of only one. However, the number of neighbors in these sets might be smaller than k, so one TCAM lookup might not suffice. To find the set of k exact nearest neighbors, the lookup process should continue until k or more neighbors are found, and also until no more neighbors are found in cubes whose edge length is equal to that of previous neighbors. This process is formally described in [6, Algorithm 5], assuming a multi-match technique such as the one presented in [27] is used.

5.3 Algorithms for the Partial Match Problem

The PARTIAL MATCH PROBLEM is defined as follows:

DEFINITION 7. *Given a set of data points $S = \{p_i\}_{i=1}^n$, $p_i \in \mathbb{Z}^d$, a query point $q \in \mathbb{Z}^d$, and a subset of the dimensions $D_q \subseteq \{1,\ldots,d\}$ of size $d_q < d$,* THE PARTIAL MATCH PROBLEM *is to find the point $s^* = \arg\min_{s' \in S} D(s',q)|_{D_q}$, where $D(a,b)|_{D_q}$ is the distance between a and b under some norm in the d_q-dimensional space. Namely, for a p-norm,*

$$D(a,b)|_{D_q} = \left(\sum_{i \in D_q} |a_i - b_i|^p \right)^{1/p} .$$

This problem is useful when some features in the vector are not important for a specific query or user, and in traditional computing models it is known to be *more difficult* [4] than the nearest neighbor problem, where all relevant dimensions are given a-priori. For example, LSH (and its extension to TCAMs, TLSH [54]) cannot be used to solve this problem. However, our solution for the NN problem can be used instantly to solve the partial match problem.

Under the maximum norm ℓ_∞, a PARTIAL MATCH solution is to replace, *in the queries*, all the bits corresponding to coordinates in irrelevant dimensions with $*$ bits. We replace coordinates in queries and not for data point, as the relevant

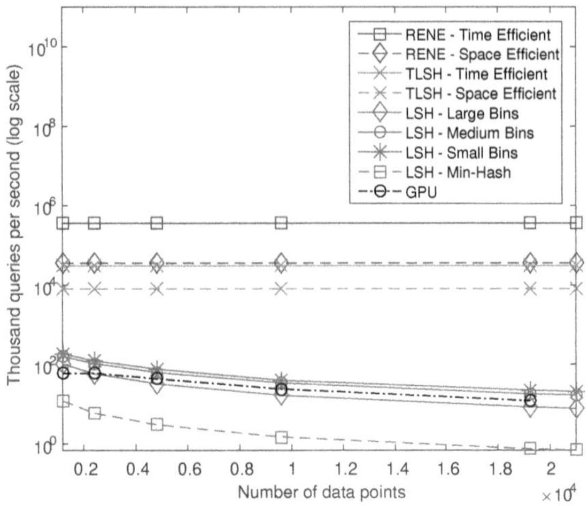

Figure 7: Throughput comparison of the various algorithms for solving the nearest neighbor problem, as a function of the size of the search database. Throughput of TCAM-based algorithms is simulated based on $360MHz$ TCAM throughput. We denote TLSH with one TCAM lookup per r-Near Neighbor Report Problem instance as *time-efficient*, and TLSH with $\log(1/\varepsilon)$ TCAM lookups per instance as *space-efficient*.

dimensions are selected per query. This technique works both for our *time-efficient* and *memory-efficient methods.*

For ℓ_p, our solution results in $\sqrt[p]{d_q}$ approximation, where d_q is the dimension of the specific query. The extensions to EXACT NEAREST NEIGHBOR SEARCH and k–NEAREST NEIGHBORS SEARCH, as described in Section 5.2, work also for this problem. The neighborhood sets are precomputed on the d-dimensional space, but queries and distance computations after queries are done on the specific d_q dimensional space. The results are still correct as distances in the d_q-dimensional space are bounded by distances in the d-dimensional space.

5.4 Geometric Clustering on TCAM

Another closely related problem that could benefit from using TCAM with RENÉ is high-dimensional geometric clustering. The k-MEANS CLUSTERING problem, for example, is usually solved as a sequence of nearest-neighbor search problems, each of these consists of a database with k d-dimensional points [30].

Algorithm [6, Algorithm 6] shows how the traditional k-MEANS CLUSTERING algorithm can be implemented on TCAM using our encoding function `tcode` , under ℓ_∞ norm. As k is usually much smaller than the number of points, this solution requires relatively low TCAM space. Still, a standard TCAM can support up to thousands of clusters using this algorithm.

5.5 Evaluation and Experimental Results

We evaluate our nearest-neighbor algorithms using an image similarity search application (using GIST [38] descriptors), on a real-life image dataset [50]. We then compare the results and performance with prior-art solutions. Our evaluation is based both on experiments with real-life TCAM devices and simulations. Each image in the dataset was encoded as a GIST vector in $\mathbb{R}^{512}$, downsampled to $\mathbb{R}^{40}$ and quantified to $\{0,\ldots,255\}^{40}$ before performing search. Images were randomly partitioned to a dataset of 21,019 images a query set of 1,000 images.

5.5.1 Experiment with a TCAM Device

Since there is no evaluation board for such devices, we used a commodity network switch (Quanta T1048-LB9) that contains a TCAM for our experiment (similarly to [54]). This switch has 48 1 Gbps ports, each handling at most $1.5M$ packets per second. TCAM is used for packet classification for OpenFlow 1.3. Using the OpenFlow interface to the switch, we mapped each entry produced by our algorithms to a set of header fields. A commercial traffic generator injected manually crafted packets that contain the queries in their headers, where each query is broken into header fields in the same way TCAM entries are stored.

We verified correctness by counting the number of matches of each TCAM entry. Using one ingress port the switch easily achieved a throughput of $1.5M$ queries per second, which is the upper bound of the link between the traffic generator and the switch (but not of the TCAM). Using 24 ingress ports we achieved throughput of $35.69M$ queries per second (almost $1.5M \times 24$). Hence, the bottleneck was not in the TCAM: If we had more ports we could have reached much higher throughput.

5.5.2 Simulation Results

We compared our results to the results of brute-force exact nearest neighbor (using MATLAB or on GPU [18]), locality sensitive hashing [3,23] (using implementation from [2]), and TLSH [54]. LSH approximated results in ℓ_2 were comparable to our approximated results in ℓ_2 only when LSH used the most complex hash functions, or when used very large bins. Both options mean longer computation time due to either more complex hash computation or much more distance computations.

Figure 7 presents a comparison of the throughput (queries per second) of CPU implementations of LSH [2], GPU implementation [18], TLSH [54] simulation, and RENÉ simulation. Each line in the figure presents the throughput of a single algorithm/implementation, as a function of the number of data points in the dataset. [4]

The required TCAM space for our *space efficient* method is $8M$ bits and for our *time efficient* method with 10 different cube sizes is $80M$ bits, with 440 bits wide entries. These requirements are available in most modern TCAM devices. TLSH requires much higher TCAM capacity and much wider TCAM entries.

6. CONCLUSIONS

While the problem of range encoding on TCAM has been deeply investigated over recent years, the proven theoretical limits on the number of bits one must use have diverted researchers to use row expansion. However, row expansion

[4]LSH implementations were ran on an Intel Core i7 2600 3.4GHz CPU. We used the same dataset and queries for our algorithms, LSH and TLSH. TCAM algorithms used 10 different cube sizes. GPU throughput is as reported in [18] for the closest lower values of n and d.

causes exponential increment in the number of TCAM entries. New applications such as SDN implementations for load balancing, security tools, and NFV frameworks use more than a few range fields. Thus, row expansion makes solutions that use it impractical.

In this paper we introduce the sub-problem of *short range encoding*, and we show that the theoretical limits on the number of required bits can be lowered in this situation. We present RENÉ: An encoding scheme for short ranges, and show that it is closer to the lower bound than any other technique. We then present multiple applications that may benefit from such short range encoding, in the area of packet classification. Furthermore, we propose to use TCAM as a co-processor for solving problems outside of the networking field, such as the nearest neighbor problem and its variants, which so far has been known to take very long time to compute. We show that using TCAM, one could solve such problems in much higher rates than previously suggested solutions, and outperform known lower bounds in traditional memory models.

Acknowledgements

This research was supported by the European Research Council under the European Union's Seventh Framework Programme (FP7/2007-2013)/ERC Grant agreement n° 259085 and the Israeli Centers of Research Excellence (I-CORE) program (Center No. 4/11).

7. REFERENCES

[1] Yehuda Afek, Anat Bremler-Barr, and Liron Schiff. Recursive design of hardware priority queues. In *SPAA*, pages 23–32, 2013.

[2] M. Aly, M. Munich, and P. Perona. Indexing in large scale image collections: Scaling properties and benchmark. In *WACV*, pages 418–425, 2011.

[3] Alexandr Andoni and Piotr Indyk. Near-optimal hashing algorithms for approximate nearest neighbor in high dimensions. *Comm. of the ACM*, 51(1):117–122, 2008.

[4] Allan Borodin, Rafail Ostrovsky, and Yuval Rabani. Lower bounds for high dimensional nearest neighbor search and related problems. In *STOC*, pages 312–321, 1999.

[5] Pat Bosshart, Dan Daly, Glen Gibb, Martin Izzard, Nick McKeown, Jennifer Rexford, Cole Schlesinger, Dan Talayco, Amin Vahdat, George Varghese, and David Walker. P4: programming protocol-independent packet processors. *CCR*, 44(3):87–95, 2014.

[6] Anat Bremler-Barr, Yotam Harchol, David Hay, and Yacov Hel-Or. Encoding short ranges in tcam without expansion: Efficient algorithm and applications. Technical report, IDC Herzliya / Hebrew University of Jerusalem, 2015. http://www.deepness-lab.org/pubs/spaa2016_tcam_techreport.pdf.

[7] Anat Bremler-Barr, Yotam Harchol, David Hay, and Yacov Hel-Or. Ultra-fast similarity search using ternary content addressable memory. In *DaMoN*, 2015.

[8] Anat Bremler-Barr, David Hay, and Danny Hendler. Layered interval codes for TCAM-based classification. *Comput. Netw.*, 56(13):3023–3039, Sep 2012.

[9] Anat Bremler-Barr, David Hay, and Yaron Koral. CompactDFA: Scalable pattern matching using longest prefix match solutions. *IEEE/ACM Trans. Netw.*, 22(2):415–428, 2014.

[10] Anat Bremler-Barr and Danny Hendler. Space-efficient TCAM-based classification using Gray coding. In *INFOCOM*, pages 1388–1396, 2007.

[11] Matthew Brown and David G Lowe. Recognising panoramas. In *ICCV*, volume 3, page 1218, 2003.

[12] Yeim-Kuan Chang and Cheng-Chien Su. Efficient TCAM encoding schemes for packet classification using gray code. In *GLOBECOM*, 2007.

[13] Hao Che, Z. Wang, Kai Zheng, and Bin Liu. DRES: Dynamic range encoding scheme for TCAM coprocessors. *Transactions on Computers*, 57(7):902–915, 2008.

[14] AS names - CIDR report. http://www.cidr-report.org/as2.0/autnums.html.

[15] Intel Corp. Intel Xeon processor E7-4870, 2011. http://ark.intel.com/products/53579/.

[16] Qunfeng Dong, Suman Banerjee, Jia Wang, Dheeraj Agrawal, and Ashutosh Shukla. Packet classifiers in ternary CAMs can be smaller. In *SIGMETRICS*, pages 311–322, 2006.

[17] ETSI. Network function virtualization, Oct 2012. http://portal.etsi.org/NFV/NFV_White_Paper.pdf.

[18] Vincent Garcia, Eric Debreuve, Frank Nielsen, and Michel Barlaud. K-nearest neighbor search: Fast GPU-based implementations and application to high-dimensional feature matching. In *ICIP*, pages 3757–3760, 2010.

[19] Ashish Goel and Pankaj Gupta. Small subset queries and bloom filters using ternary associative memories, with applications. In *SIGMETRICS*, pages 143–154, 2010.

[20] F. Gray. Pulse code communication. US Patent 2,632,058, March 17 1953 (filed November 13 1947).

[21] Arpit Gupta, Laurent Vanbever, Muhammad Shahbaz, Sean P. Donovan, Brandon Schlinker, Nick Feamster, Jennifer Rexford, Scott Shenker, Russell J. Clark, and Ethan Katz-Bassett. SDX: a software defined internet exchange. In *SIGCOMM*, pages 551–562, 2014.

[22] Cavium Inc. NEURON search processors, 2014. http://www.cavium.com/processor_NEURON-Search.html.

[23] Piotr Indyk and Rajeev Motwani. Approximate nearest neighbors: Towards removing the curse of dimensionality. In *STOC*, pages 604–613, 1998.

[24] Weirong Jiang, Qingbo Wang, and Viktor K Prasanna. Beyond TCAMs: An SRAM-based parallel multi-pipeline architecture for terabit IP lookup. In *INFOCOM*, pages 1786–1794, 2008.

[25] Cheng Jin, Haining Wang, and Kang G. Shin. Hop-count filtering: An effective defense against spoofed DDoS traffic. In *CCS*, pages 30–41, 2003.

[26] Kirill Kogan, Sergey I. Nikolenko, Ori Rottenstreich, William Culhane, and Patrick Eugster. SAX-PAC (scalable and expressive packet classification). In *SIGCOMM*, pages 15–26, 2014.

[27] Karthik Lakshminarayanan, Anand Rangarajan, and Srinivasan Venkatachary. Algorithms for advanced packet classification with ternary CAMs. In *SIGCOMM*, pages 193–204, 2005.

[28] Lin Liang, Ce Liu, Ying-Qing Xu, Baining Guo, and

Heung-Yeung Shum. Real-time texture synthesis by patch-based sampling. *ACM ToG*, 20(3):127–150, 2001.
[29] Huan Liu. Efficient mapping of range classifier into ternary-CAM. In *10th Symposium on High Performance Interconnects*, pages 95–100, 2002.
[30] Stuart P. Lloyd. Least squares quantization in PCM. pages 129–136, 1982.
[31] Chad R. Meiners, Alex X. Liu, and Eric Torng. TCAM Razor: A systematic approach towards minimizing packet classifiers in TCAMs. In *ICNP*, pages 266–275, 2007.
[32] Chad R. Meiners, Alex X. Liu, and Eric Torng. Bit Weaving: A non-prefix approach to compressing packet classifiers in TCAMs. In *ICNP*, pages 93–102, 2009.
[33] Chad R. Meiners, Alex X. Liu, and Eric Torng. Topological transformation approaches to optimizing TCAM-based packet classification systems. In *SIGMETRICS*, pages 73–84, 2009.
[34] Chad R. Meiners, Alex X. Liu, Eric Torng, and Jignesh Patel. Split: Optimizing space, power, and throughput for TCAM-based classification. In *ANCS*, pages 200–210, 2011.
[35] Masoud Moshref, Minlan Yu, Ramesh Govindan, and Amin Vahdat. DREAM: dynamic resource allocation for software-defined measurement. In *SIGCOMM*, pages 419–430, 2014.
[36] Marius Muja and David G. Lowe. Fast approximate nearest neighbors with automatic algorithm configuration. In *VISAPP*, pages 331–340, 2009.
[37] Nvidia. Tesla K80 GPU accelerator, Nov. 2014. http://international.download.nvidia.com/pdf/kepler/BD-07317-001_v04.pdf.
[38] Aude Oliva and Antonio Torralba. Modeling the shape of the scene: A holistic representation of the spatial envelope. *IJCV*, 42:145–175, 2001.
[39] Open Networking Foundation. *OpenFlow Switch Specification Version 1.3.2*, April 2013.
[40] Guy Pazi, Anat Bremler-Barr, Rami Rivlin, and Dan Touitou. Protecting against distributed denial of service attacks, 2003. US Patent App. 10/232,993.
[41] Personal communication with engineers in networking companies, 2015.
[42] James Philbin, Ondrej Chum, Michael Isard, Josef Sivic, and Andrew Zisserman. Object retrieval with large vocabularies and fast spatial matching. In *CVPR*, pages 1–8, 2007.
[43] Radware. DefenseFlow - SDN applications and DDoS attack defense, 2014. http://www.radware.com/Products/DefenseFlow/.
[44] Radware. Tsunami SYN flood attack - a new trend in DDoS attacks?, October 2014. http://blog.radware.com/security/2014/10/tsunami-syn-flood-attack/.
[45] VC Ravikumar and Rabi N Mahapatra. TCAM architecture for IP lookup using prefix properties. *Micro, IEEE*, 24(2):60–69, 2004.
[46] Renesas Electronics America Inc. 20Mbit QUAD-search content addressable memory. http://www.renesas.com/products/memory/TCAM/index.jsp.
[47] Ori Rottenstreich and Isaac Keslassy. On the code length of TCAM coding schemes. In *ISIT*, pages 1908–1912, 2010.
[48] Ori Rottenstreich and Isaac Keslassy. Worst-case TCAM rule expansion. In *INFOCOM*, 2010.
[49] Ori Rottenstreich, Issac Keslassy, Avinatan Hassidim, Haim Kaplan, and Ely Porat. On finding an optimal TCAM encoding scheme for packet classification. In *INFOCOM*, 2013.
[50] Bryan C. Russell, Antonio Torralba, Kevin P. Murphy, and William T. Freeman. Labelme: A database and web-based tool for image annotation. *Intl. Journal of Computer Vision*, 77(1-3):157–173, 2008.
[51] Ryu SDN controller, 2014. http://osrg.github.io/ryu/.
[52] Hanan Samet. *Foundations of multidimensional and metric data structures.* Morgan Kaufmann, 2006.
[53] M. Said Seddiki, Muhammad Shahbaz, Sean Donovan, Sarthak Grover, Miseon Park, Nick Feamster, and Ye-Qiong Song. FlowQoS: QoS for the rest of us. In *HotSDN*, pages 207–208, 2014.
[54] Rajendra Shinde, Ashish Goel, Pankaj Gupta, and Debojyoti Dutta. Similarity search and locality sensitive hashing using ternary content addressable memories. In *SIGMOD*, pages 375–386, 2010.
[55] E. Spitznagel, D. Taylor, and J. Turner. Packet classification using extended TCAMs. In *ICNP*, 2003.
[56] V. Srinivasan, G. Varghese, S. Suri, and M. Waldvogel. Fast and scalable layer four switching. In *SIGCOMM*, pages 191–202, 1998.
[57] J. Van Lunteren and T. Engbersen. Fast and scalable packet classification. *IEEE JSAC*, 21(4):560–571, 2003.
[58] Richard Wang, Dana Butnariu, and Jennifer Rexford. Openflow-based server load balancing gone wild. In *Hot-ICE*, 2011.
[59] Roger Weber, Hans-Jörg Schek, and Stephen Blott. A quantitative analysis and performance study for similarity-search methods in high-dimensional spaces. In *VLDB*, pages 194–205, 1998.
[60] Kai Zheng, Hao Che, Zhijun Wang, Bin Liu, and Xin Zhang. DPPC-RE: TCAM-based distributed parallel packet classification with range encoding. *IEEE Trans. Computers*, 55(8):947–961, 2006.

Invited Talk: On Computational Thinking, Inferential Thinking and Data Science

Michael I. Jordan
University of California, Berkeley
jordan@cs.berkeley.edu

ABSTRACT

The rapid growth in the size and scope of datasets in science and technology has created a need for novel foundational perspectives on data analysis that blend the inferential and computational sciences. That classical perspectives from these fields are not adequate to address emerging problems in \Big Data" is apparent from their sharply divergent nature at an elementary level|in computer science, the growth of the number of data points is a source of \complexity" that must be tamed via algorithms or hardware, whereas in statistics, the growth of the number of data points is a source of \simplicity" in that inferences are generally stronger and asymptotic results can be invoked. On a formal level, the gap is made evident by the lack of a role for computational concepts such as \runtime" in core statistical theory and the lack of a role for statistical concepts such as \risk" in core computational theory. I present several research vignettes aimed at bridging computation and statistics, including the problem of inference under privacy and communication constraints, and ways to exploit parallelism so as to trade of the speed and accuracy of inference.

SPAA '16 July 11-13, 2016, Pacific Grove, CA, USA
ACM 978-1-4503-4210-0/16/07.
http://dx.doi.org/10.1145/2935764. 2935826

Bio

Michael I. Jordan is the Pehong Chen Distinguished Professor in the Department of Electrical Engineering and Computer Science and the Department of Statistics at the University of California, Berkeley. He received his Masters in Mathematics from Arizona State University, and earned his PhD in Cognitive Science in 1985 from the University of California, San Diego. He was a professor at MIT from 1988 to 1998. His research interests bridge the computational, statistical, cognitive and biological sciences, and have focused in recent years on Bayesian nonparametric analysis, probabilistic graphical models, spectral methods, kernel machines and applications to problems in distributed computing systems, natural language processing, signal processing and statistical genetics. Prof. Jordan is a member of the National Academy of Sciences, a member of the National Academy of Engineering and a member of the American Academy of Arts and Sciences. He is a Fellow of the American Association for the Advancement of Science. He has been named a Neyman Lecturer and a Medallion Lecturer by the Institute of Mathematical Statistics. He received the IJCAI Research Excellence Award in 2016, the David E. Rumelhart Prize in 2015 and the ACM/AAAI Allen Newell Award in 2009. He is a Fellow of the AAAI, ACM, ASA, CSS, IEEE, IMS, ISBA and SIAM.

Extending the Nested Parallel Model to the Nested Dataflow Model with Provably Efficient Schedulers

David Dinh
Computer Science Division
Univ. of California, Berkeley,
Berkeley, CA 94720, USA
dinh@cs.berkeley.edu

Harsha Vardhan Simhadri
Computer Science Dept.,
Lawrence Berkeley National Lab.,
Berkeley, CA 94720, USA
harshas@lbl.gov

Yuan Tang *
School of Software, Fudan Univ.,
Shanghai Key Lab. of Intelligent
Information Processing,
Shanghai 200433, P. R. China
yuantang@fudan.edu.cn

ABSTRACT

The nested parallel (a.k.a. fork-join) model is widely used for writing parallel programs. However, the two composition constructs, i.e. "$\|$" (parallel) and ";" (serial), that comprise the nested-parallel model are insufficient in expressing "partial dependencies" in a program. We propose a new dataflow composition construct "$\rightsquigarrow$" to express partial dependencies in algorithms in a processor- and cache-oblivious way, thus extending the Nested Parallel (NP) model to the *Nested Dataflow* (ND) model. We redesign several divide-and-conquer algorithms ranging from dense linear algebra to dynamic-programming in the ND model and prove that they all have optimal span while retaining optimal cache complexity. We propose the design of runtime schedulers that map ND programs to multicore processors with multiple levels of possibly shared caches (i.e, Parallel Memory Hierarchies) and prove guarantees on their ability to balance nodes across processors and preserve locality. For this, we adapt space-bounded (SB) schedulers for the ND model. We show that our algorithms have increased "parallelizability" in the ND model, and that SB schedulers can use the extra parallelizability to achieve asymptotically optimal bounds on cache misses and running time on a greater number of processors than in the NP model. The running time for the algorithms in this paper is $O\left(\frac{\sum_{i=0}^{h-1} Q^*(\mathsf{t};\sigma\cdot M_i)\cdot C_i}{p}\right)$ on a p-processor machine, where Q^* is the parallel cache complexity of task t, C_i is the cost of cache miss at level-i cache which is of size M_i, and $\sigma \in (0,1)$ is a constant.

CCS Concepts

•**Software and its engineering** $\rightarrow$ **Parallel programming languages;** •**Theory of computation** $\rightarrow$ *Shared memory algorithms; Control primitives;*

Keywords

Parallel Programming Models, Fork-Join, Data-Flow, Nested Parallelism, Space-Bounded Scheduler, Cache-Oblivious Algorithms, Cache-Oblivious Wavefront, Numerical Algorithms, Dynamic Programming, Shared-memory multicore processors.

*All the coauthors contributed equally to this paper. Yuan Tang is the corresponding author. Part of the work was done when the author was a visiting scientist at MIT CSAIL.

SPAA '16, July 11 - 13, 2016, Pacific Grove, CA, USA

ACM ISBN 978-1-4503-4210-0/16/07...$15.00

DOI: http://dx.doi.org/10.1145/2935764.2935797

1. INTRODUCTION

A parallel algorithm can be represented by a directed acyclic graph (DAG) that contains only ***data dependencies***, without reference to the control dependencies induced by any particular programming model. We call this the ***algorithm DAG***. In an algorithm DAG, each vertex represents a piece of computation without any parallel constructs and each directed edge represents a data dependency from its source to the sink vertex. For example, Figure 1a is the algorithm DAG of the dynamic programming algorithm for the Longest Common Subsequence (LCS) problem. This DAG is a 2D array of vertices labeled $X(i,j)$, where the values with coordinates $i=0$ or $j=0$ are given. For all $i,j>0$, vertex $X(i,j)$ depends on vertices $X(i-1,j-1)$, $X(i,j-1)$ and $X(i-1,j)$. In an algorithm DAG, there are two possible relations between any pair of vertices x and y. If there is a path from x to y or from y to x, one of them must be executed before the other, i.e. they have to be serialized; otherwise, the two vertices can run concurrently.

It is often tedious to specify the algorithm DAG by listing individual vertices and edges, and in many cases the DAG is not fully known until the computation has finished. Therefore, higher level programming models are used to provide a description of a possibly dynamic DAG. One such model is the ***nested parallel programming model*** (a.k.a. the fork-join model), in which DAGs can be described via ***spawn trees***: recursive compositions based on two constructs, "$\|$" ("parallel") and ";" ("serial"). The internal nodes of the spawn tree are serial and parallel composition constructs while the leaves are strands — segments of serial code that contain no function calls, returns, or *spawn* operations. The notation a ; b is infix shorthand for a subtree of the spawn tree rooted at a node with a ";" construct with left child a and right child b; this indicates that b has a dependence on a and cannot start until a finishes. Likewise, $a \parallel b$ is an analogous construct that indicates that a and b can run concurrently. Expressing algorithms recursively in the NP model exposes their locality at various scales, enabling good schedulers to reduce the communication costs of their execution on a variety of machine configurations [1, 12, 11].

For instance, one might express the LCS algorithm in the NP model by decomposing the 2D array of vertices in the algorithm DAG into four smaller blocks, recursively solving the smaller instances of the LCS algorithms on these blocks, and composing them by specifying the dependencies between them using ; or $\|$ constructs. Figure 1 illustrates the resulting spawn tree up to two levels of recursion. For correctness, the NP model demands a serial composition between two subtrees of the spawn tree even if there is a ***partial dependency*** (or equivalently, ***partial parallelism***) between them: that is, a subset of vertices in the DAG corresponding to one of the subtrees depends on a subset of vertices corresponding to the

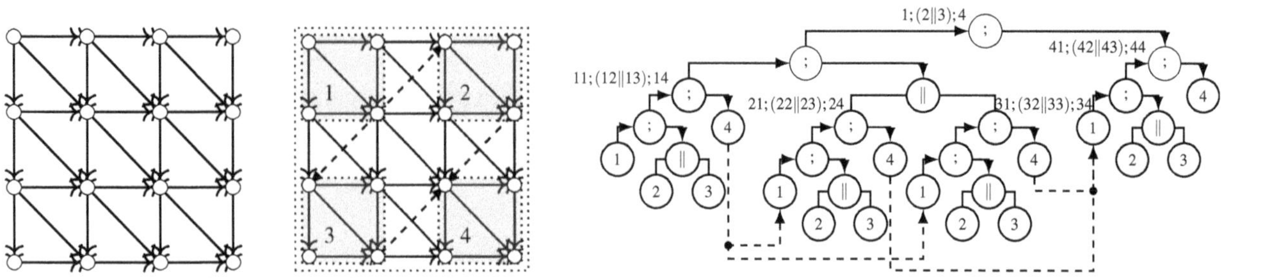

(a) Algorithm DAG (b) Divide-and-Conquer. (c) Spawn tree in the NP model

Figure 1: Algorithm DAG and the spawn tree of the LCS algorithm in the NP model. The labels 1, 2, 3, 4 correspond to the four quadrants in the recursive decomposition of the dynamic programming table. The leaves of the spawn tree are smaller LCS tasks while the internal nodes are composition constructs. Solid arrows in the algorithms DAG represents data dependencies in the algorithm DAG and control dependencies implied by the NP model in the spawn tree. The dashed arrows represent artificial dependencies induced by the NP model.

other. As a result, while the spawn tree in the NP programming model can accurately retain the data dependencies of the algorithm DAG, it also introduces many ***artificial dependencies*** that are not necessary to maintain algorithm correctness. Artificial dependencies induced by the NP programming model between subtrees of the spawn tree in Figure 1 are shown overlaid by dashed arrows onto the algorithm DAG in Figure 1b. Many parallel algorithms, including dynamic programming and direct numerical algorithms, incur an asymptotic increase in span due to the artificial dependencies introduced by the NP programming model. For example, the algorithm DAG for the LCS problem has $O(n)$ span. When expressed as a spawn tree in the NP model, its span follows the recurrence $T_\infty(n) = 3T_\infty(n/2)$, i.e., $T_\infty(n) = O(n^{1.5})$, which indicates a significant reduction in parallelism. *The insufficiency of the NP programming model in expressing partial dependencies in a spawn tree* is the fundamental reason that causes artificial dependencies between subtrees of the spawn tree. This deficiency not only limits the parallelism of such algorithms exposed to schedulers, but also makes it difficult to simultaneously optimize for multiple program complexity measures such as span and cache complexity [45]. In practice, while schedulers can take advantage of the NP model's ability to expose locality, they are unable to load balance many classes of algorithms due to reduced parallelism [43].

Our Contributions:

- **Nested Dataflow model.** We introduce a new ***fire*** construct, denoted "$\rightsquigarrow$" (pronounced "fire"), to compose subtrees in a spawn tree. This construct, in addition to the || and ; constructs, forms the ***nested dataflow (ND)*** model, an extension of the nested parallel programming model. The "$\rightsquigarrow$" construct allows us to precisely specify the partial dependence patterns in many algorithms that || and ; constructs cannot. One of the design goals of the ND programming model is to allow runtime schedulers to execute inter-processor work like a dataflow model, while retaining the locality advantages of the nested parallel model by following the depth-first order of spawn tree for intra-processor execution.
- **DAG Rewriting System (DRS).** We provide a *DAG Rewriting System* that defines the semantics of the "$\rightsquigarrow$" construct by specifying the algorithm DAG that is equivalent to a dynamic spawn tree in the ND model (see Section 2).
- **Re-designed divide-and-conquer algorithms.** We re-design several typical divide-and-conquer algorithms in the ND model eliminating artificial dependencies, thus minimizing span. The set of algorithms include dense linear algebra and dynamic programming. Section 3 presents algorithm for solving triangular systems and the LCS problem; the associated technical report [25] presents more such examples. Our critical insight is that the data dependencies in all these algorithm DAGs can be precisely described with a small set of recursive partial dependency patterns (which we formalize as *sets of fire rules*) that allows us to specify them compactly without losing any locality or parallelism. Other algorithms such as stencils and fast matrix multiplication can also be effectively described in this model.

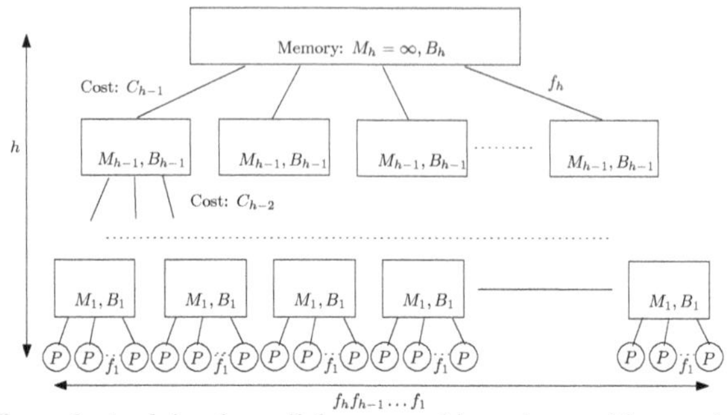

Figure 2: An h-level parallel memory hierarchy machine model.

- **Provably Efficient Runtime Schedulers.** The NP model has robust schedulers that map programs to shared-memory multicore systems, including those with hierarchical caches [17, 22, 11]. These schedulers have strong performance bounds for many programs based on complexity measures such as *work, span*, and *cache complexity* [16, 5, 10, 38, 1, 12, 11, 42]. In Section 4, we propose an extension of one such class of schedulers called the space-bounded (SB) schedulers for the ND model and provide provable performance guarantees on its performance on the Parallel Memory Hierarchy machine model (see Figure 2) — a symmetric "trees of caches" that models the multiple levels of possibly shared caches in shared memory multicore processors. We show that the algorithms in Section 3 have greater "parallelizability" in the ND model than in the NP model, and that space-bounded schedulers can use the extra parallelizability to achieve asymptotically optimal bounds on total running time on a greater number of processors than in the NP model for "reasonably regular" algorithms. Qunatitatively, suppose that the tree of caches, rooted at the DRAM, has h levels and any cache at level i has size M_i. If the input (which initially resides in DRAM) has size $N > M_{h-1}$, the SB scheduler for the ND model can efficiently use all the processors attached to up to a maximum of N^{1-c}/M_{h-1} level-$(h-1)$ caches for all the algorithms in this paper, where c is an arbitrarily small constant. When each level-i cache has at most $(M_i/M_{i-1})^{1-c}$ level-$(i-1)$ caches attached to it (and level-1 cache at most M_1^{1-c} processors), the running time is asymptotically optimal: $O\left(\left(\sum_{i=0}^{h-1} Q^*(\text{t};\sigma \cdot M_i) \cdot C_i\right)/p\right)$, where Q^* is the *parallel cache complexity* of the algorithm t, C_i is the cost of a cache miss at level-i cache, $\sigma \in (0,1)$ is a constant, and p is the number of processors. This compares favorably with the SB scheduler for the NP model [11] which, for the algorithms in the paper, requires a large input size of at least M_{h-1}^2 before it can asymptotically match the efficiency of the ND version.

2. NESTED DATAFLOW MODEL

The nested dataflow model extends the NP model by introducing an additional composition construct, "$\rightsquigarrow$", which generalizes the existing "$\|$" and "$;$" constructs. Programs in both the NP and ND models are expressed as spawn trees, where the internal nodes are the composition constructs and the leaf nodes are strands. We refer to subtrees of the spawn tree as ***tasks*** or ***function calls***. We refer to the subtree rooted at the i-th child of an internal node as its i-th ***subtask***. In both the models, larger tasks can be defined by composing smaller tasks with the "$;$" and "$\|$" constructs. The ND model allows tasks to be defined as a composition using the additional **binary** construct, "$\rightsquigarrow$", which enables the specification of "partial dependencies" between subtasks. This represents an arbitrary middle-point between the "$;$" construct (full dependency) and the "$\|$" construct (zero dependency).

For example, consider the program in Figure 3 represented by the spawn tree in Figure 4. The entire program, MAIN, is comprised of two tasks F and G. Task F is the serial composition of tasks A and C. Similarly, task G is the serial composition of B and D. Task C depends on A, which creates a partial dependency from F to G. Instead of using a "$;$" construct, which would block D until the completion of F (including both A and B), we denote the partial dependency with the "$\rightsquigarrow$" construct in Figure 4.

```
MAIN(){             F(){          G(){          ⊕ FG⇝ ⊖ = {
  F() FG⇝ G()         A() ; B()     C() ; D()     ⊕① ; ⊖①
}                   }             }             }
```

Figure 3: Code for MAIN, F, G, and a fire rule.

The partial dependency from F to G is specified with the rule $\overset{FG}{\rightsquigarrow}$. To specify that the only dependence is from A, the first subtask of F, to C, the first subtask of G, we write $⊕ \overset{FG}{\rightsquigarrow} ⊖ = \{⊕① \; ; \; ⊖①\}$. The circled values denote ***relative pedigree***, or ***pedigree*** in short, which represents the position of a nested function call in a spawn tree with respect to its ancestor [36]. We use wildcards ⊕ and ⊖ to represent the ***source*** and ***sink*** of the partial dependency. We then specify ***a set of fire rules*** to describe the partial dependence pattern of the "$\rightsquigarrow$" construct between the source and the sink nodes. In the above case, we used ⊕① to denote the first subtask of the source, ⊕; similarly, ⊖① denotes the first subtask of the sink. The semicolon indicates a full dependency between them. In the context of MAIN in Figure 3, ⊕ is bound to F and ⊖ to G, implying that there is a full dependency from Ⓕ①, which refers to A, to Ⓖ①, which refers to C. In the general case, we allow multiple rewriting rules in the definition of a fire construct, and "multilevel" pedigrees (e.g. ⊕②① denotes the first subtask of the second subtask of the source) in each rule.

In the previous example, the dependency from A to C is a full dependency; that is, the entirety of A must be completed before C can start. However, this dependency itself may be artificial. Therefore, we allow the "$\rightsquigarrow$" construct to be recursively defined using fire rules that themselves represent partial dependencies.

Consider the following divide-and-conquer algorithm for computing the matrix product $C += A \times B$, which we denote $\mathrm{MM}(A,B,C)$. Let C_{00}, C_{01}, C_{10} and C_{11} denote the top left, bottom left, top right, and the bottom right quadrants of C respectively. In the ND model, we can define $\mathrm{MM}(A,B,C)$ to be

$$
\begin{array}{ll}
((\mathrm{MM}(A_{00},B_{00},C_{00}) \,\|\, \mathrm{MM}(A_{00},B_{01},C_{01})) & //①①①\|①①② \\
\;\|\; (\mathrm{MM}(A_{10},B_{00},C_{10}) \,\|\, \mathrm{MM}(A_{10},B_{01},C_{11}))) & //①②①\|①②② \\
\overset{MM}{\rightsquigarrow} ((\mathrm{MM}(A_{01},B_{10},C_{00}) \,\|\, \mathrm{MM}(A_{01},B_{11},C_{01})) & //②①①\|②①② \\
\;\|\; (\mathrm{MM}(A_{11},B_{10},C_{10}) \,\|\, \mathrm{MM}(A_{11},B_{11},C_{11}))). & //②②①\|②②②
\end{array}
$$

Each quadrant of C is written to by two of the eight subtasks; each

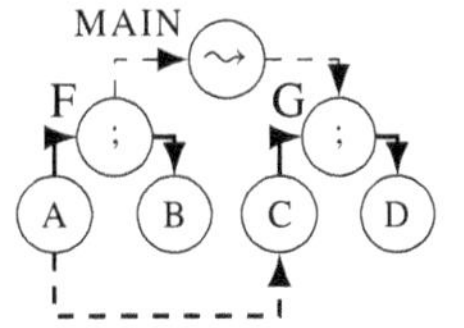

Figure 4: Spawn tree corresponding to the code in Figure 3.

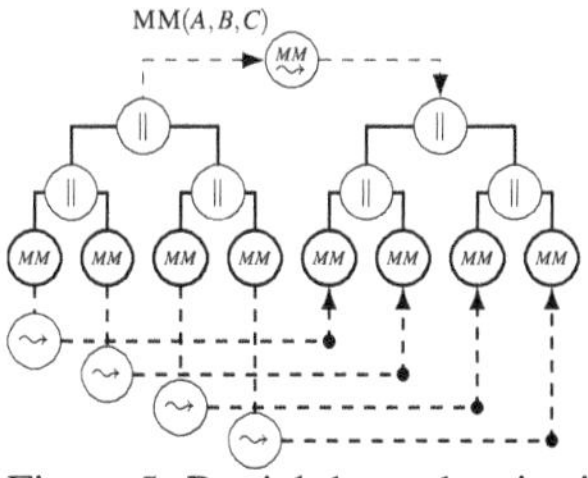

Figure 5: Partial dependencies in the recursive matrix multiply algorithm.

such pair of subtasks must be serialized to avoid a data race. For this, we might naively define the fire construct "$\overset{MM}{\rightsquigarrow}$" between the immediate subtasks of $\mathrm{MM}(A,B,C)$ with a pair of fire rules:

$$⊕ \overset{MM}{\rightsquigarrow} ⊖ \quad \{⊕① \; ; \; ⊖①, \quad ⊕② \; ; \; ⊖②\}$$

However, notice that the dependency between first subtasks (as well as second subtasks), which is expressed with "$;$" in the code above, is in reality a partial dependency. Furthermore, each of these partial dependencies has the same pattern as "$\overset{MM}{\rightsquigarrow}$". Since this pattern repeats recursively down an arbitrary number of levels, the "$\overset{MM}{\rightsquigarrow}$" construct should have been described by the fire rules:

$$⊕ \overset{MM}{\rightsquigarrow} ⊖ \quad \{⊕① \overset{MM}{\rightsquigarrow} ⊖①, \quad ⊕② \overset{MM}{\rightsquigarrow} ⊖②\}, \tag{1}$$

wherein "$;$" is replaced by "$\overset{MM}{\rightsquigarrow}$".

If the recursion terminates at the level indicated in Figure 5, the four instances of "$\overset{MM}{\rightsquigarrow}$" between leaves of the spawn tree will be interpreted as four full dependencies between the corresponding strands. If the recursion continues, the fire rules are used to further refine the dependencies. Whereas this algorithm has only one set of dependence patterns (fire rules), we will see algorithms with multiple types of fire rules in the next section.

DAG Rewriting System (DRS). We formalize the semantics of the "$\rightsquigarrow$" construct with a DRS that defines the algorithm DAG corresponding to the spawn tree given at runtime. The spawn tree can unfold dynamically at runtime by incrementally ***spawning*** new tasks – a spawn operation rewrites a leaf of the spawn tree into an internal node by adding two new leaves below. The composition construct in the internal nodes of the spawn tree imply dependencies between its subtrees. We represent these dependencies as directed ***dataflow arrows*** in the spawn tree. The equivalent algorithm DAG implied by the spawn tree is the DAG with the leaves of the spawn tree as vertices, and edges representing dataflow edges implied by both the serial and fire constructs that are incident to the leaves of the spawn tree. The DAG also grows with the spawn tree; new vertices are added to the DAG whenever new tasks are spawned, and the construct used in the spawn operation defines the edges between these new vertices in the algorithm DAG. Note that maintaining a full algorithm DAG at runtime is not necessary. To save space, one can carefully design the order of the execution of the spawn tree, and recycle the memory used to represent parts of the spawn tree that have finished executing as in [17, 34]. We will leave this for future work. Instead, we focus here on the algorithm DAG to clarify the semantics of the fire construct.

The DRS iteratively constructs the dataflow edges, and equivalently the algorithm DAG, by starting with a single vertex representing the root of the spawn tree and successively applying ***DAG rewriting rules***. Given a DAG G, a rewriting rule replaces a subgraph that is isomorphic to L with a copy of sub-graph $R = \langle V, E \rangle$, resulting in a new DAG G'. There are two rewriting rules:

1. ***Spawn Rule***: A spawn rule corresponds to a spawn operation. Any current leaf of the spawn tree corresponds to a single-vertex no-edge subgraph $L = \langle \{\mathrm{A}\}, \emptyset \rangle$ of the DAG. If it spawns, we

rewrite the leaf as a (sub)tree rooted by either a ";", "$\|$" or "$\rightsquigarrow$" in the spawn tree.[1] The root of the newly spawned (sub)tree inherits all incoming and outgoing dataflow arrows of the old leaf. For instance, if task A spawns B and C in serial, we rewrite the single-vertex, no-edge DAG L to $R = \langle\{B, \text{";"}, C\}, \overrightarrow{BC}\rangle$, where $\overrightarrow{BC}$ is a ***solid dataflow arrow*** (directed edge) from B to C ($\overrightarrow{BC}$ is actually a shorthand for all-to-all dataflow arrows from all possible descendants of B to those of C, i.e. $B \times C$). If task A calls B and C in parallel, we rewrite it as $R = \langle\{B, \text{"}\|\text{"}, C\}, \emptyset\rangle$. While the parallel construct introduces no dataflow arrows between B and C, a rewriting rule from its closest ancestor that is a "$\rightsquigarrow$" construct can introduce dataflow arrows to these two nodes according to the *fire rule*. Similar semantics apply for non-binary serial and parallel constructs. rewrite to $R = \langle\{B, \text{"}\rightsquigarrow\text{"}, C\}, E' \subseteq B \times C\rangle$, where E' is a ***dashed dataflow arrow*** and is a subset of all possible arrows from descendants of B to descendants of C to be defined by the fire rule as follows.

2. ***Fire Rule***: Given a dashed dataflow arrow between arbitrary source and sink nodes, including those from the left child of a fire construct to its right child, we (recursively) rewrite the arrow using the set of fire rules associated with it. These rules specify how the "$\rightsquigarrow$" construct is rewritten to a set of dataflow arrows between the descendants of the source and the sink nodes. There are two possible cases for rewriting:
   - If both operands A and B are strands, the dataflow arrow between them is rewritten as either "A ; B" or, if the fire construct has no rewriting rules, "A $\|$ B".
   - If the source task A of a "$\rightsquigarrow$" construct is rewritten by a spawn rule into a tree containing k subtasks, we add dataflow arrows $E' \subseteq \{A_1, \ldots A_k\} \times B$ to the resulting DAG, i.e. $R = \langle V, E \cup E'\rangle$, where the arrows in E' and their labels are determined based on the set of fire rules as follows: for a fire rule of the form $\oplus \textcircled{i} p \overset{T}{\rightsquigarrow} \ominus q$ (where p and q are some pedigrees) from A to B, we add a dataflow arrow $\oplus p \overset{T}{\rightsquigarrow} \ominus q$ from A_i to B. An analogous rule applies when the sink spawns.

From the DRS, it is evident that the binary ";" and "$\|$" constructs are special cases of the "$\rightsquigarrow$" construct. Four fire rules that recursively refine between both pairs of subtasks of $\oplus$ and $\ominus$ define the ; construct, and an empty set of rules defines "$\|$". Higher-degree ";" and "$\|$" constructs are also easily replaced by "$\rightsquigarrow$".

Work-Span Analysis. *Work-Span analysis* is commonly used to analyze the complexity of an algorithm DAG. We use T_1 to denote a task's ***work***, that is, the total number of instructions it contains. We use T_∞ to denote its ***span***, that is, the length of the critical path of its DAG. The composition rule to calculate work T_1 for all three constructs of the ND model is always a simple summation. In principle, the composition to calculate the span T_∞ for all three constructs is the maximum length of all possible paths from source to sink, i.e. the critical path. Since ";" and "$\|$" primitives have fixed semantics in all contexts, the span of tasks constructed with them can be simplified as follows: for $c = a \; ; \; b$, $T_{\infty,c} = T_{\infty,a} + T_{\infty,b}$; for $c = a \parallel b$, $T_{\infty,c} = \max\{T_{\infty,a}, T_{\infty,b}\}$. On the other hand, since the semantics of a "$\rightsquigarrow$" construct are parameterized by its set of fire rules, we have to calculate the depth of the task constructed with it on a case-by-case basis. For instance, for the code in Figure 3, we have $T_{\infty,\text{MAIN}} = T_{\infty,F \overset{FG}{\rightsquigarrow} G} = \max\{T_{\infty,A} + T_{\infty,B}, T_{\infty,A;C} + T_{\infty,D}\}$, where $T_{\infty,A;C}$ is $T_{\infty,A} + T_{\infty,C}$. If the rule "$\overset{FG}{\rightsquigarrow}$" were to place a partial dependence "$\overset{AC}{\rightsquigarrow}$" from A to C, calculating span would require further recursive analysis.

[1] A leaf with a non-constant degree parallel construct such as a parallel for loop must be rewritten as an binary tree in our model.

3. ALGORITHMS IN THE ND MODEL

We now demonstrate the advantages of the ND model by expressing typical 2-way divide-and-conquer classical linear algebra and dynamic programming algorithms in it, and deriving the necessary fire rules. We present algorithms for solving triangular systems and the LCS problem. The associated technical report [25] also presents algorithms for Cholesky factorization, LU factorization with partial pivoting and Floyd-Warshall algorithm for All-Pairs-Shortest-Paths. We demonstrate that these algorithms have improved parallelism in the ND model by proving that their span in the ND model is smaller than in the NP model and in fact matches the span of their algorithm DAG. Furthermore, the arrangement of tasks in the spawn tree for these algorithms does not change between the NP and the ND model, so that the cache complexity of the depth-first traversal is the same in both ND and NP models. In Section 4, we present more sophisticated metrics to quantify parallelism in the presence of caches; the algorithms presented here have improved parallelism according to those metrics as well.

Triangular System Solver. A Triangular System Solver $\text{TRS}(T, B)$ takes as input a lower triangular $n \times n$ matrix T and a square matrix B and outputs a square matrix X such that $TX = B$. A triangular system can be recursively decomposed as follows:

$$\begin{bmatrix} B_{00} & B_{01} \\ B_{10} & B_{11} \end{bmatrix} = \begin{bmatrix} T_{00} & 0 \\ T_{10} & T_{11} \end{bmatrix} \begin{bmatrix} X_{00} & X_{01} \\ X_{10} & X_{11} \end{bmatrix}$$
$$= \begin{bmatrix} T_{00}X_{00} & T_{00}X_{01} \\ T_{10}X_{00} + T_{11}X_{10} & T_{10}X_{01} + T_{11}X_{11} \end{bmatrix} \quad (2)$$

Equation (2) recursively solves TRS on four equally sized sub-quadrants X_{00}, X_{01}, X_{10}, and X_{11}, as graphically depicted in Figure 7. It can be expressed in the NP model as shown in Equation (3), where $\text{MMS}(A, B, C)$ represents a cache-oblivious matrix multiplication and subtraction (identical to the one presented in Section 2, except instead of computing $C += AB$ it computes $C -= AB$) with span $O(n)$ and using $O(n^2)$ space.[2]

$$\begin{aligned} X \leftarrow \text{TRS}(T, B) = &((X_{00} \leftarrow \text{TRS}(T_{00}, B_{00}) \; ; \; \text{MMS}(T_{10}, X_{00}, B_{10})) \\ &\parallel (X_{01} \leftarrow \text{TRS}(T_{00}, B_{01}) \; ; \; \text{MMS}(T_{10}, X_{01}, B_{11}))) \\ &; (X_{10} \leftarrow \text{TRS}(T_{11}, B_{10}) \parallel X_{11} \leftarrow \text{TRS}(T_{11}, B_{11})) \end{aligned} \quad (3)$$

The span of the TRS algorithm, expressed in the NP model is given by the recurrence $T_{\infty,\text{TRS}}(n) = 2T_{\infty,\text{TRS}}(n/2) + T_{\infty,\text{MMS}}(n/2)$, which evaluates to $O(n \log n)$. This is not optimal; a straightforward right-looking algorithm has a span of $O(n)$.

In Equation (4), we replace the ";" constructs from the original spawn tree with "$\rightsquigarrow$" constructs, in order to remove artificial dependencies. Because the two "$\rightsquigarrow$" constructs join different types of tasks, they have distinct types, which we denote "$\overset{TM}{\rightsquigarrow}$" and "$\overset{2TM2T}{\rightsquigarrow}$". Note that there are algorithms, e.g. Cholesky factorization, where two types of subtasks, say, TRS and MMS, have more than one kind of partial dependency pattern between them based on where they occur. Each type of fire construct has a different set of fire rules; in order to determine what these rules are, we expand an additional level of recursion to examine finer-grained data dependencies.

$$\begin{aligned} &X \leftarrow \text{TRS}(T, B) = \\ &((X_{00} \leftarrow \text{TRS}(T_{00}, B_{00}) \overset{TM}{\rightsquigarrow} \text{MMS}(T_{10}, X_{00}, B_{10})) \\ &\parallel (X_{01} \leftarrow \text{TRS}(T_{00}, B_{01}) \overset{TM}{\rightsquigarrow} \text{MMS}(T_{10}, X_{01}, B_{11}))) \\ &\overset{2TM2T}{\rightsquigarrow} (X_{10} \leftarrow \text{TRS}(T_{11}, B_{10}) \parallel X_{11} \leftarrow \text{TRS}(T_{11}, B_{11})) \end{aligned} \quad (4)$$

[2] There is also an 8-way divide-and-conquer cache-oblivious parallel algorithm of MMS that has an optimal span of $O(\log^2 n)$ but uses $O(n^3)$ space which can be used to trade off span for space complexity.

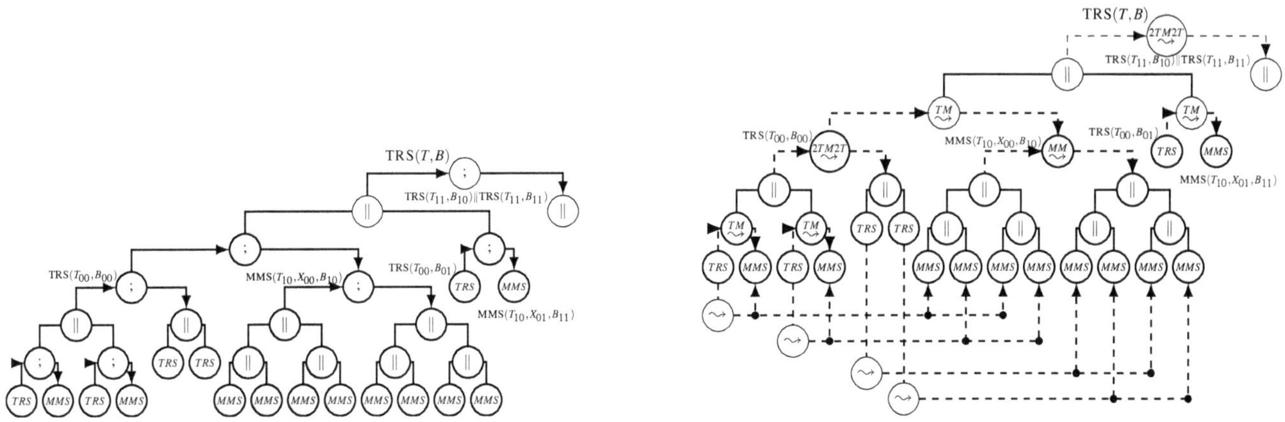

(a) Spawn tree of TRS with only "$\|$" and ";" constructs in NP model

(b) Spawn Tree of TRS with "$\rightsquigarrow$", "$\|$", and ";" constructs in ND model

Figure 6: Spawn trees of TRS in the NP and ND models. The shape of the tree and the leaves are the same between the two models, except that some of the ; constructs in NP model are relaxed with $\rightsquigarrow$ constructs and their dataflow arrows in the ND model. Dashed arrows corresponding to "$\rightsquigarrow$" constructs are recursively rewritten until both source and sink subtrees are leaves, where they are treated as solid arrows. For simplicity, the figure illustrates only dataflow arrows of type TM between the leaves, and omits dataflow arrows of other types.

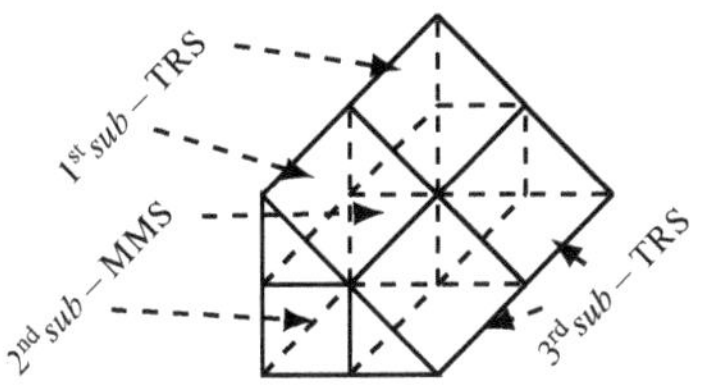

Figure 7: Geometric picture of a 2-way divide-and-conquer TRS algorithm.

Figure 8: Cross-section of the TRS algorithm DAG.

Notice that the source task of $\overset{2TM2T}{\rightsquigarrow}$ is $((X_{00} \leftarrow \mathrm{TRS}(T_{00}, B_{00}) \overset{TM}{\rightsquigarrow} \mathrm{MMS}(T_{10}, X_{00}, B_{10})) \parallel (X_{01} \leftarrow \mathrm{TRS}(T_{00}, B_{01}) \overset{TM}{\rightsquigarrow} \mathrm{MMS}(T_{10}, X_{01}, B_{11})))$, and the its sink is $(X_{10} \leftarrow \mathrm{TRS}(T_{11}, B_{10}) \parallel X_{11} \leftarrow \mathrm{TRS}(T_{11}, B_{11}))$. Since the left (analogously, right) subtask of the sink can start as soon as the matrix multiply updating B_{10} (B_{11}), which is the right subtask of the left (right) subtask of the source, is completed:

$$\oplus \overset{2TM2T}{\rightsquigarrow} \ominus = \{\oplus\textcircled{1}\textcircled{2} \overset{MT}{\rightsquigarrow} \ominus\textcircled{1}, \oplus\textcircled{2}\textcircled{2} \overset{MT}{\rightsquigarrow} \ominus\textcircled{2}\}. \quad (5)$$

Both fire constructs in the fire rules are of type "$\overset{MT}{\rightsquigarrow}$" since the dependency structure is identical: the matrix updated in the source MMS task is used as the second argument of the TRS task.

In order to determine the set of fire rules for "$\overset{MT}{\rightsquigarrow}$", we expand a pair of subtasks connected by the "$\overset{MT}{\rightsquigarrow}$" construct to an additional level of recursion. For instance, we will expand the task $\mathrm{MMS}(T_{10}, X_{00}, B_{10})$ in equation Equation (6), which (as the source) binds to $\oplus$ in $\overset{TM}{\rightsquigarrow}$, and $X_{00} \leftarrow \mathrm{TRS}(T_{11}, B_{10})$ in Equation (7), which binds to $\ominus$. In the following program, we use $A_{00,11}$ to denote the bottom right quadrant of the top left quadrant of A.

$$\begin{aligned}
&\mathrm{MMS}(T_{10}, X_{00}, B_{10}) = \qquad //\oplus \\
&((\mathrm{MMS}(T_{10,00}, X_{00,00}, B_{10,00}) \parallel \mathrm{MMS}(T_{10,00}, X_{00,01}, B_{10,01})) \\
&\quad \parallel (\mathrm{MMS}(T_{10,10}, X_{00,00}, B_{10,10}) \parallel \mathrm{MMS}(T_{10,10}, X_{00,01}, B_{10,11}))) \\
&\overset{MM}{\rightsquigarrow} ((\mathrm{MMS}(T_{10,01}, X_{00,10}, B_{10,00}) \parallel \mathrm{MMS}(T_{10,01}, X_{00,11}, B_{10,01})) \\
&\quad \parallel (\mathrm{MMS}(T_{10,11}, X_{00,10}, B_{10,10}) \parallel \mathrm{MMS}(T_{10,11}, X_{00,11}, B_{10,11}))). \quad (6)
\end{aligned}$$

$$\begin{aligned}
&X_{10} \leftarrow \mathrm{TRS}(T_{11}, B_{10}) = \qquad //\ominus \\
&((X_{00,00} \leftarrow \mathrm{TRS}(T_{11,00}, B_{10,00}) \overset{TM}{\rightsquigarrow} \mathrm{MMS}(T_{11,10}, X_{00,00}, B_{10,10})) \\
&\quad \parallel (X_{00,01} \leftarrow \mathrm{TRS}(T_{11,00}, B_{10,01}) \overset{TM}{\rightsquigarrow} \mathrm{MMS}(T_{11,10}, X_{00,01}, B_{10,11}))) \\
&\overset{2TM2T}{\rightsquigarrow} (X_{00,10} \leftarrow \mathrm{TRS}(T_{11,11}, B_{10,10}) \parallel X_{00,11} \leftarrow \mathrm{TRS}(T_{11,11}, B_{10,11})) \\
&\qquad (7)
\end{aligned}$$

The dependence of the sink task, $\ominus$, on the source task, $\oplus$, in "$\overset{MT}{\rightsquigarrow}$" is a result of requiring the value of matrix B_{10} to be updated by $\oplus$ before $\ominus$ can use it in a computation. At a more fine-grained level, we can examine which quadrant of B_{10} each subtask of $\ominus$ requires (and which subtask of $\oplus$ computes that quadrant) in order to calculate the fine-grained dependencies. For instance, consider the subtask $X_{00,00} \leftarrow \mathrm{TRS}(T_{11,00}, B_{10,00})$, whose pedigree is $\ominus\textcircled{1}\textcircled{1}\textcircled{1}$, which requires $B_{10,00}$. This quadrant of B_{10} is updated in $\mathrm{MMS}(T_{10,01}, X_{00,10}, B_{10,00})$ of the source, whose pedigree is $\oplus\textcircled{2}\textcircled{1}\textcircled{1}$. Furthermore, notice that the dependency from $\oplus\textcircled{2}\textcircled{1}\textcircled{1}$ to $\ominus\textcircled{1}\textcircled{1}\textcircled{1}$ takes the same form as the dependency from $\oplus$ to $\ominus$ itself: the matrix updated by the source is the second argument in the sink. Therefore, the fire rule for this particular dependency is $\oplus\textcircled{2}\textcircled{1}\textcircled{1} \overset{TM}{\rightsquigarrow} \ominus\textcircled{1}\textcircled{1}\textcircled{1}$. Similar reasoning gives the remaining fire rules:

$$\begin{aligned}
\oplus \overset{TM}{\rightsquigarrow} \ominus = \{&\oplus\textcircled{1}\textcircled{1}\textcircled{1} \overset{TM}{\rightsquigarrow} \ominus\textcircled{1}\textcircled{1}\textcircled{1}, \oplus\textcircled{1}\textcircled{1}\textcircled{1} \overset{TM}{\rightsquigarrow} \ominus\textcircled{1}\textcircled{2}\textcircled{1}, \\
&\oplus\textcircled{1}\textcircled{2}\textcircled{1} \overset{TM}{\rightsquigarrow} \ominus\textcircled{1}\textcircled{1}\textcircled{2}, \oplus\textcircled{1}\textcircled{2}\textcircled{1} \overset{TM}{\rightsquigarrow} \ominus\textcircled{1}\textcircled{2}\textcircled{2}, \\
&\oplus\textcircled{2}\textcircled{1} \overset{TM}{\rightsquigarrow} \ominus\textcircled{2}\textcircled{1}\textcircled{1}, \oplus\textcircled{2}\textcircled{1} \overset{TM}{\rightsquigarrow} \ominus\textcircled{2}\textcircled{2}\textcircled{1}, \\
&\oplus\textcircled{2}\textcircled{2} \overset{TM}{\rightsquigarrow} \ominus\textcircled{2}\textcircled{1}\textcircled{2}, \oplus\textcircled{2}\textcircled{2} \overset{TM}{\rightsquigarrow} \ominus\textcircled{2}\textcircled{2}\textcircled{2}\} \qquad (8) \\
\oplus \overset{2TM2T}{\rightsquigarrow} \ominus = \{&\oplus\textcircled{1}\textcircled{2} \overset{MT}{\rightsquigarrow} \ominus\textcircled{1}, \oplus\textcircled{2}\textcircled{2} \overset{MT}{\rightsquigarrow} \ominus\textcircled{2}\} \\
\oplus \overset{MT}{\rightsquigarrow} \ominus = \{&\oplus\textcircled{2}\textcircled{1}\textcircled{1} \overset{MM}{\rightsquigarrow} \ominus\textcircled{1}\textcircled{1}\textcircled{2}, \oplus\textcircled{2}\textcircled{1}\textcircled{2} \overset{MM}{\rightsquigarrow} \ominus\textcircled{1}\textcircled{2}\textcircled{2}, \\
&\oplus\textcircled{2}\textcircled{2}\textcircled{1} \overset{MT}{\rightsquigarrow} \ominus\textcircled{1}\textcircled{1}\textcircled{1}, \oplus\textcircled{2}\textcircled{2}\textcircled{2} \overset{MT}{\rightsquigarrow} \ominus\textcircled{1}\textcircled{2}\textcircled{1}\}
\end{aligned}$$

We now argue that the span of TRS in the ND model is $O(n)$, which is the span of the algorithm itself and therefore optimal. The span of an algorithm is the length of the longest path in its DAG. The algorithm DAG defined by TRS expressed in the ND model forms a periodic structure, a cross section of which can be seen in Figure 8, where squares represent matrix multiplications and triangles represent smaller TRS tasks (there are no edges between separate cross sections). The length of the longest path in the DAG, shown in blue, is $O(n)$.

We now formally prove that the algorithm we constructed in the ND model achieves this span. Let $T_{\infty,\mathrm{TRS}}(n)$ denote the span of TRS on a matrix with input size $n \times n$, and let $T_{\infty,\mathrm{TRS}\ p}(n)$ denote the span of the subtask with pedigree p descended from TRS with input size $n \times n$. Furthermore, let $T_{\infty,\overset{TM}{\rightsquigarrow}}(n)$ denote the critical path length of a TRS composed with a MMS by a "$\overset{TM}{\rightsquigarrow}$" construct, where both tasks are directly descended from a TRS of size $n \times n$. Note that it involves a TRS and a MMS, of size $n/2 \times n/2$ each.

Since replacing a fire construct with a serial construct can only increase the span, it suffices to show that a version of the problem with some fire constructs replaced with serial constructs has optimal span (this replacement can also simplify the algorithm description by allowing us to remove fire rules without making the span asymptotically worse). Replacing the "$\overset{2TM2T}{\rightsquigarrow}$" construct with ";" gives the following upper bound on the span of TRS in the ND model:

$$T_{\infty,\text{TRS}}(n) \leq T_{\infty,\text{TRS}\textcircled{1}}(n) + T_{\infty,\text{TRS}\textcircled{2}}(n). \quad (9)$$

Since the right subtask of TRS is merely the parallel composition of two TRS operations, each on a matrix of size $n/2 \times n/2$, the second term on the right reduces to the max of their (identical) spans, which is $T_{\infty,\text{TRS}\textcircled{2}}(n) = T_{\infty,\text{TRS}}(n/2)$.

The left subtask consists of two pairs (connected by a parallel composition), each consisting of a TRS task and a MMS task, connected by "$\overset{TM}{\rightsquigarrow}$" construct and done in parallel, and their spans are identical. Therefore, the first term on the right hand side of inequality 9 reduces to

$$T_{\infty,\text{TRS}\textcircled{1}}(n) = T_{\infty,\text{TRS}\textcircled{1}\textcircled{1}\textcircled{1}\overset{TM}{\rightsquigarrow}\text{TRS}\textcircled{1}\textcircled{1}\textcircled{2}}(n) = T_{\infty,\overset{TM}{\rightsquigarrow}}(n).$$

The term on the right is the maximum length among all possible paths rewritten from $\textcircled{1}\textcircled{1}\textcircled{1} \overset{\text{TM}}{\rightsquigarrow} \textcircled{1}\textcircled{1}\textcircled{2}$. There are two types of paths that could potentially be the longest. An instance of the first type is the "$\overset{TM}{\rightsquigarrow}$" composition of tasks TRS$\textcircled{1}\textcircled{1}\textcircled{1}\textcircled{1}\textcircled{1}$ $\textcircled{1}$, a TRS of size $n/4$, with TRS$\textcircled{1}\textcircled{1}\textcircled{2}\textcircled{1}\textcircled{1}$ $\textcircled{1}$, a MMS of size $n/4$, followed by a MMS of size $n/4$. This gives the first expression in the max term in the equation below. An instance of the second type is the $\overset{TM}{\rightsquigarrow}$ composition of the task TRS$\textcircled{1}\textcircled{1}\textcircled{1}\textcircled{1}\textcircled{1}$ $\textcircled{1}$, a TRS of size $n/4$, with TRS$\textcircled{1}\textcircled{1}\textcircled{1}\textcircled{1}\textcircled{1}$ $\textcircled{2}$, a MMS of size $n/4$, followed by the "$\overset{TM}{\rightsquigarrow}$" composition of TRS$\textcircled{1}\textcircled{1}\textcircled{1}\textcircled{2}\textcircled{1}$, a TRS of size $n/4$, with TRS$\textcircled{1}\textcircled{1}\textcircled{2}\textcircled{2}\textcircled{1}$ $\textcircled{1}$, a MMS of size $n/4$. This results in the second expression in the max term below.

$$T_{\infty,\overset{\text{TM}}{\rightsquigarrow}}(n) \leq \max\{T_{\infty,\overset{\text{TM}}{\rightsquigarrow}}(n/2) + T_{\infty,\text{MMS}}(n/4),\ 2T_{\infty,\overset{\text{TM}}{\rightsquigarrow}}(n/2)\}$$

For the base case of the recurrence, we simply run TRS and MM sequentially at the base case size. Therefore, we have

$$T_{\infty,\overset{\text{TM}}{\rightsquigarrow}}(1) = T_{\infty,\text{TRS}}(1) + T_{\infty,\text{MMS}}(1) = O(1).$$

Noting that $T_{\infty,\text{MMS}}(n) = O(n)$, the recurrences can be solved to show that $T_{\infty,\text{TRS}}(n) = O(n)$, which is asymptotically optimal.

One can similarly derive fire rules for composing divide-and-conquer algorithms for Cholesky factorization and LU factorization with partial pivoting in the ND model (see associated technical report [25]). Their depth is the optimal $O(n)$ for matrices of size $n \times n$. These algorithms are also cache-oblivious and have asymptotically optimal cache complexity.

LCS (Longest Common Subsequence). We now consider a divide-and-conquer algorithm for the LCS problem. Given two sequences $S = \langle s_1, s_2, \ldots, s_m \rangle$ and $T = \langle t_1, t_2, \ldots, t_n \rangle$, the goal is to find the length of longest common subsequence of S and T. LCS can be computed using the recursion in Equation (10) when $m = n$ [24] (a similar recursion can be written for the general case, $m \neq n$).[3]

$$X(i,j) = \begin{cases} 0 & \text{if } i = 0 \vee j = 0 \\ X(i-1, j-1) + 1 & \text{if } i,j > 0 \wedge s_i = t_j \\ \max\{X(i,j-1), X(i-1,j)\} & \text{if } i,j > 0 \wedge s_i \neq t_j \end{cases} \quad (10)$$

In the ND model, we express this recursion as follows (Figure 9c illustrates the spawn tree this describes):

$$\begin{aligned} X \leftarrow \text{LCS}(X) = &((X_{00} \leftarrow \text{LCS}(X_{00})) \overset{\text{HV}}{\rightsquigarrow} \\ &(X_{01} \leftarrow \text{LCS}(X_{01}) \parallel X_{10} \leftarrow \text{LCS}(X_{10}))) \\ &\overset{\text{VH}}{\rightsquigarrow} (X_{11} \leftarrow \text{LCS}(X_{11})) \end{aligned} \quad (11)$$

The partial dependencies are given by the following fire rules which are illustrated in Figures 9a and 9b:

$$\oplus \overset{\text{HV}}{\rightsquigarrow} \ominus = \{\oplus \overset{\text{H}}{\rightsquigarrow} \ominus\textcircled{1}, \oplus \overset{\text{V}}{\rightsquigarrow} \ominus\textcircled{2}\} \quad (12)$$

[3]A similar recursion applies to the pairwise sequence alignment with affine gap cost [28].

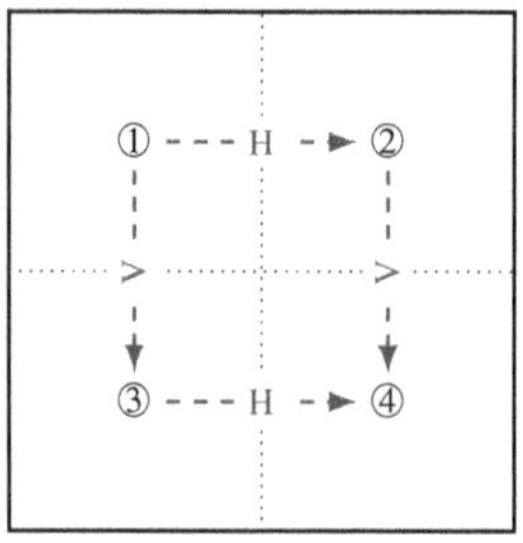

(a) Dashed arrows are defined by the algorithm in Equation (11) and fire rules in Equations (12) and (13).

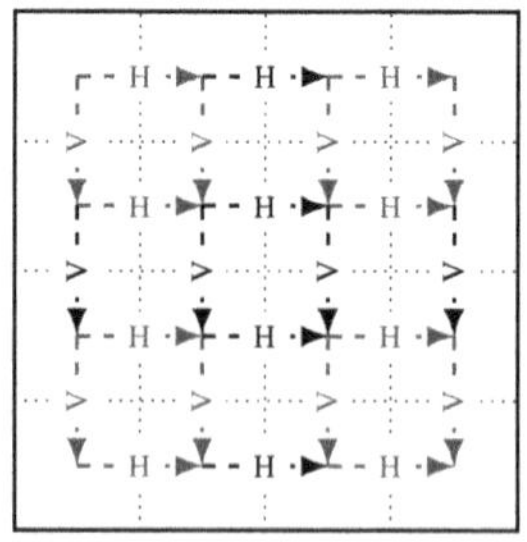

(b) Dashed arrows are rewritten by fire rules in Equations (14) and (15).

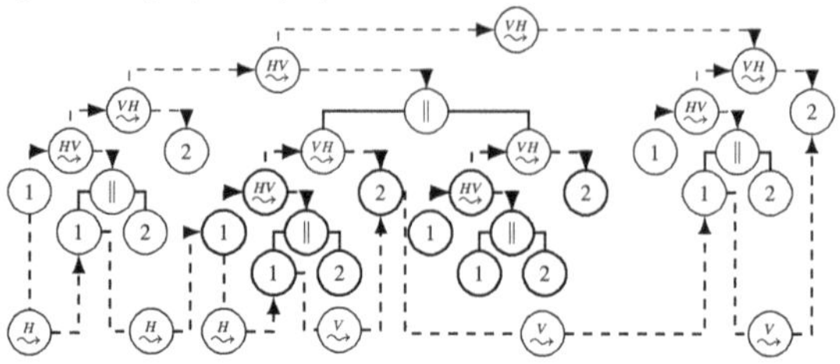

(c) Spawn tree of LCS in ND model. We only draw one "$\rightsquigarrow$" path in Figure 9b from top-left to bottom-right cell

Figure 9: DAG Rewriting and spawn tree of LCS in ND model.

$$\oplus \overset{\text{VH}}{\rightsquigarrow} \ominus = \{\oplus\textcircled{1} \overset{\text{V}}{\rightsquigarrow} \ominus, \oplus\textcircled{2} \overset{\text{H}}{\rightsquigarrow} \ominus\} \quad (13)$$

$$\oplus \overset{\text{H}}{\rightsquigarrow} \ominus = \{\oplus\textcircled{1}\textcircled{2}\textcircled{1} \overset{\text{H}}{\rightsquigarrow} \ominus\textcircled{1}\textcircled{1}, \oplus\textcircled{2} \overset{\text{H}}{\rightsquigarrow} \ominus\textcircled{1}\textcircled{2}\textcircled{2}\} \quad (14)$$

$$\oplus \overset{\text{V}}{\rightsquigarrow} \ominus = \{\oplus\textcircled{1}\textcircled{2}\textcircled{2} \overset{\text{V}}{\rightsquigarrow} \ominus\textcircled{1}\textcircled{1}, \oplus\textcircled{2} \overset{\text{V}}{\rightsquigarrow} \ominus\textcircled{1}\textcircled{2}\textcircled{1}\} \quad (15)$$

To compute the span of LCS, consider the dynamic programming table. The span is defined by the length of longest path in the DAG which runs from the top left entry to the bottom right entry. We will separately compute the length of the longest horizontal path, $T_h(n)$, and the length of the longest vertical path, $T_v(n)$. Notice that the span, $T_{\infty,LCS}(n)$, is bounded above by $T_h(n) + T_v(n)$.

Since we split an LCS problem whose dynamic programming table is of size $n \times n$ into four LCS problems of size $n/2 \times n/2$ of which the longest horizontal path covers two, we have $T_h(n) = 2T_h(n/2)$. The base case (a 1×1 matrix) only depends on three inputs, so that $T_h(1) = O(1)$. Therefore, $T_h(n) = O(n)$. Similar reasoning shows that $T_v(n) = O(n)$. As a result, $T_{\infty,LCS}(n)$ is bounded above by $O(n)$, which is optimal.

4. SPACE-BOUNDED SCHEDULERS FOR THE ND MODEL

We show that *reasonably regular* programs in the ND model, including the algorithms in Section 3 and [25], can be effectively mapped to Parallel Memory Hierarchies by adapting the space-bounded (SB) schedulers for NP programs. Regularity is a quantifiable property of the algorithm (or spawn tree) that measures how difficult it is to schedule; we will define this for programs in the ND model and show that the algorithm in Section 3 are highly regular. Space-bounded schedulers for programs in the NP model were first proposed for completely regular programs [22], improved upon and rigorously analyzed in [11], and empirically demonstrated to outperform work-stealing based schedulers for many algorithms in [43], but not for TRSM and Cholesky algorithms due to their limited parallelism in the NP model [43]. The key idea in SB schedulers is to map tasks to processors and caches in the hierarchy based on annotations regarding their memory footprint. The main result of this section is Theorem 3, which shows that the SB scheduler is able to exploit the extra parallelism exposed in the ND model.

Machine Model: Parallel Memory Hierarchy. SB schedulers are well suited for the Parallel Memory Hierarchy (PMH) machine model [4] (see Figure 2), which models the multi-level cache hierarchies and cache sharing common in shared memory multi-core architectures. The PMH is represented by a symmetric tree rooted at a main memory of infinite size. The internal nodes are caches and the leaves are processors. We refer to subtrees rooted at some cache as ***subclusters***. Each cache at level i is of the same size M_i, and has the same the number of level-$(i-1)$ caches attached to it. We call this the ***fan-out*** of level-i and denote it by the constant f_i, so that the number of processors in a h-level tree is $p_h = \prod_{i=1}^{h} f_i$. We let the constant M_0 denote the number of registers on a processor. We let C_{i-1} denote the cost parameter representing the cost of servicing a cache miss at level $(i-1)$ from level i. A cache miss that must be serviced from level j requires $C'_j = C_0 + C_1 + \cdots + C_{j-1}$ time steps. For simplicity, we let the cache block be one word long. This limitation can be relaxed and analyzed as in [11].

Terminology. A task is ***done*** when all the leaf nodes (strands) associated with its subtree have been executed. A dataflow arrow originating at a leaf node in the spawn tree is ***satisfied*** when its source node is done. A dataflow arrow originating at an internal node of the spawn tree is ***satisfied*** when all its descendants (rewritings) according to the fire rules have been satisfied. A task is ***fully ready*** or just ***ready*** when all the incoming dependencies (dataflow arrows) originating outside the subtree are satisfied. The ***size***, $s(\cdot)$, of a task or a strand is the number of distinct memory locations accessed by it. We assume that programs are statically allocated, i.e., all necessary heap space is allocated up front and freed at program termination, so that the size function is well defined. The size annotation can be supplied by the programmer or can be obtained from a profiling tool. We call a task ***M-maximal*** if its size is at most M, but its parent in the spawn tree has size $> M$. A task is level-i maximal in a PMH if it is M_i-maximal, M_i being the size of a level-i cache. Note that even though an M_i-maximal task is not ready, a M_j-maximal subtask inside it (where $j < i$) can be ready.

SB Schedulers. We define a space-bounded scheduler to be any scheduler that has the anchoring and boundedness properties [43]:

- **Anchor:** As the spawn tree unfolds dynamically, we assign and ***anchor*** ready tasks to caches in the hierarchy with respect to which they are maximal. Tasks are *allocated* a part of the subcluster rooted at the assigned cache. The anchoring property requires that all the leaves of the spawn tree of a task be executed by processors in the part of the subcluster allocated.
- **Boundedness:** Tasks anchored to a cache of size M have a total size $\le \sigma M$, where $\sigma \in (0,1)$ is a scheduler chosen constant called ***dilation parameter***.

There are several ways to maintain these properties and operate within its constraints. The approach taken in [11] is to have a task queue with each anchored task that contains its subtasks than can be potentially unrolled and anchored to the caches below it. We adopt the same approach here (outlined below for convenience) for the ND model with the **difference** being that we only anchor and run ready subtasks. In the course of execution, ready tasks are anchored to a suitable cache level (provided there is sufficient space left), and each anchored task is ***allocated*** subclusters beneath the cache, based on the size of the task. Just as in [11], a task of size S anchored at level-i cache is allocated

$$g_i(S) = \min\{f_i, \max\{1, \lfloor f_i(3S/M_i)^{\alpha'} \rfloor\}\}, \text{where } \alpha' = \min\{\alpha_{max}, 1\}$$

level-$(i-1)$ subclusters[4] where α_{max} is the parallelizability of the task, a term we will define shortly. All processors in the subclusters are required to work exclusively on this task. Initially, the root node of the spawn tree is anchored to the root of the PMH.

[4]The factor 3 in the allocation function helps in proving Thm. 3.

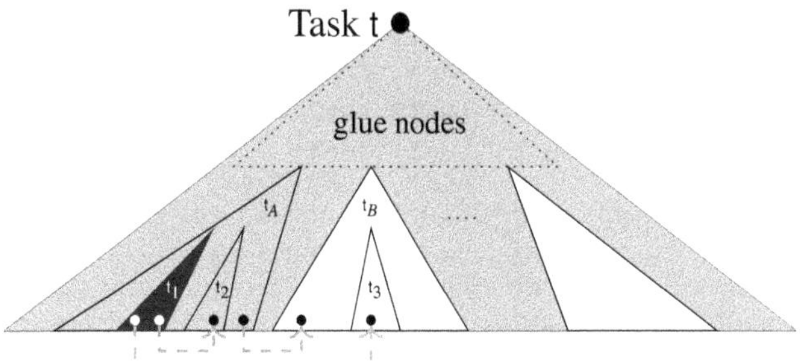

Figure 10: Use of partial parallelism in the SB scheduler. White represents tasks that are yet to start, gray represents running tasks, and black represents complete tasks. Green arrows represent dataflow arrows that may be used to start new tasks by the SB scheduler while orange dataflow arrows are not immediately used. Task t is level-i maximal; tasks t_A and t_B are level-$(i-1)$ maximal; tasks t_1, t_2, and t_3 are level-$(i-2)$ maximal. Although subtask t_1 has completed and has two outgoing dataflow edges, only t_2, which is in the same level-$(i-1)$ maximal subtask (t_A) can be started; t_3 can not immediately started until subtask t_A completes.

To find work, a processor traverses the path from the leaf it represents in the tree towards the root of the PMH until it reaches the lowest anchor it is part of. Here it checks for ready tasks in the queue associated with this anchor, and if empty, re-attempts to find work after a short wait. Otherwise, it pulls out a task from the queue. If the task is from an anchor at the cache immediately above the processor, i.e. **at an L_1 cache**, it executes the subtask by traversing the corresponding spawn tree in depth-first order. If the processor pulled this task out of an allocation at a **cache at level** $i > 1$, it does not try to execute its strands (leaves) immediately. Instead, it unrolls the spawn tree corresponding to the task using the DRS and enqueues those subtasks that are either of size $> M_{i-1}$, or not ready, in the queue corresponding to the anchor. Those subtasks that cannot be immediately worked on due to lack of space in the caches are also enqueued. However, if the processor encounters a ready task that has size less than that of a level-j cache ($j < i$), and is able to find sufficient space for it in the subcluster allocated to the anchor, the task is anchored at the level-j cache, and allocated a suitable number of subclusters below the level-j cache. The processor starts unraveling the spawn tree and finding work repeatedly. When an anchored task is done, the anchor, allocation and the associated resources are released for future tasks. We also borrow other details in the design of the space-bounded schedulers (e.g. how many subclusters are provisioned for making progress on "worst case allocations"? what fraction of cache is reserved for tasks that "skip cache levels"?) from prior work [11].

Roughly speaking, this scheduler uses the partial parallelism between level-$(i-1)$ maximal subtasks within a level-i maximal task. However, it does not use all the partial parallelism across level-$(i-2)$ subtasks, especially those dataflow arrows between level-$(i-2)$ subtasks in different level-$(i-1)$ subtasks (see Figure 10).

Metrics. We now analyze the runtime of the SB scheduler, accounting for the cost of executing the work and load imbalance, but not the overhead of the data structures needed to keep track of anchors, allocations, and the readiness of subtasks; optimizing the overhead is left for a future empirical study. The anchoring and boundedness properties help to preserve locality while trading off some parallelism. Inspired by [11, 42], we develop an analysis for the ND model to argue that the impact of the loss of parallelism due to the anchoring property on load balance is not significant.

A critical consequence of the anchoring property of the SB scheduler is that once a task is anchored to a cache, all the memory locations needed for the task are loaded only once and are not forced to be evicted until the completion of the task. This motivates the following quantification of locality. Given a task t, decompose the spawn tree into M-maximal subtasks, and "glue nodes" that hold these trees together (this decomposition is unique). Define the ***parallel cache complexity (PCC)***, $Q^*(\mathsf{t};M)$, of task t to be the sum of sizes of the maximal subtrees, plus a constant overhead from each glue node. This is motivated by the expectation that a good scheduler (such as SB) should be able to preserve locality within M-sized tasks given an cache of appropriate size, while it might be too cumbersome to preserve locality across maximal subtasks. [5] The PCC metric differs from the another common metric for locality of NP programs: the cache complexity Q_1 of the depth-first traversal in the ideal cache model [1]. Unlike Q_1, Q^* does not depend on the order of traversal, but does not capture data reuse across M-maximal subtasks, which is a smaller order term in our algorithms.

Note that M is a free parameter in this analysis. When the context is clear, we often replace the task t in the Q^* expression with a size parameter corresponding to the task, so that cache complexity is denoted $Q^*(N;M)$. With this notation we have the following bound on the cache complexity of the algorithms in Section 3.

CLAIM 1. *For dense matrices of size $N = n \times n$, the divide and conquer classical matrix multiplication and Triangular System Solve in Section 3, as well as the Cholesky and LU factorizations and the 2D analog of the Floyd-Warshall algorithm in [25] have parallel cache complexity $Q^*(N;M) = O(N^{1.5}/M^{0.5})$, when $N > M$, with the glue nodes contributing an asymptotically smaller term. The LCS algorithm has $Q^*(n;M) = O(n^2/M)$ for input of size $n > \sqrt{M}$. This is true even if the algorithms are expressed in the NP model by replacing fire constructs with the ";" construct.*

As a direct consequence of the anchoring and boundedness properties, which conservatively provision cache space, the following restatement of [11, Theorem 3] applies to the ND model.

THEOREM 1. *Suppose* t *is a task in ND program that is anchored at a level-i cache of a PMH by a SB scheduler with dilation parameter $0 < \sigma < 1$ (i.e., a SB scheduler that anchors tasks of size at most σM_j at level j). Then for all cache levels $j \leq i$, the sum of cache misses incurred by all caches at level j is at most $Q^*(\mathsf{t};\sigma \cdot M_j)$.*

In conjunction with Claim 1, this gives a bound on the communication cost of the schedulers for ND algorithms. One can verify from results on lower bounds on communication complexity [7] that these bounds are asymptotically optimal. If the scheduler is able to perfectly load balance a program at every cache level on an h level PMH with p processors, we would expect a task t to take

$$\frac{\sum_{i=0}^{h-1} Q^*(\mathsf{t};\sigma \cdot M_i) \cdot C_i}{p} \tag{16}$$

time steps to complete, where $0 < \sigma < 1$ is the dilation parameter.

However, if the algorithm does not have sufficient parallelism for the PMH or is too irregular to load balance, we would expect it take longer. Furthermore, since the number of processors assigned to a task by a SB scheduler depends on its size, unlike in the case of work-stealing scheduler, a work-span analysis of programs may not be an accurate indicator of their running time. A more sophisticated cost model that takes account of locality, parallelism-space imbalances, and lack of parallelism at different levels of recursion is necessary. In the NP model [11, Defn. 3], this was quantified

[5] This definition is a generalization of [11, Defn.2] for the ND model. The full metric measures cache complexity in terms of cache lines to model latency and is also parameterized by a second parameter B: size of a cache line. We set $B = 1$ here for simplicity. This simplification can be reversed.

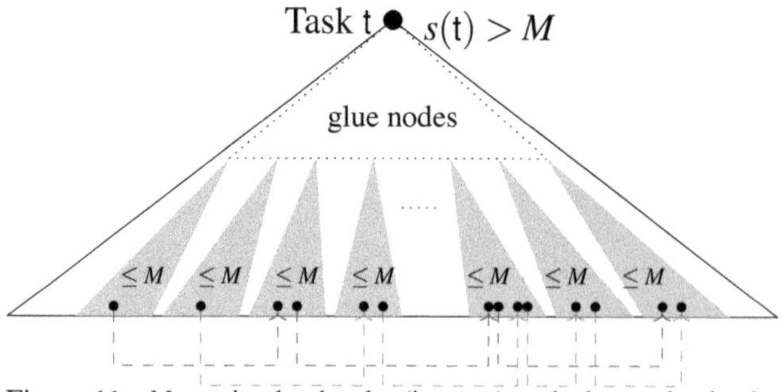

Figure 11: M-maximal subtasks (in gray) and glue nodes in the spawn tree of a task t. The PCC, $Q^*(\mathsf{t};M)$, is the sum of sizes of M-maximal subtasks plus one miss for each glue node. The red and blue sets of arrows represent two chains of dependencies in t. The ECC, $\widehat{Q}_\alpha(\mathsf{t};M)$, is determined by the maximum, among all such chains, of the sum of effective depth of M-maximal subtasks in the chain, and the ratio $Q^*(\mathsf{t};M)/s(\mathsf{t})^\alpha$ for a parameter $\alpha > 0$.

by the **effective cache complexity metric (ECC, $\widehat{Q}_\alpha$)**. We provide a new definition of this metric for the ND model. ECC attempts to capture the cost of load balancing the program on hypothetical machine with ***machine with parallelism at most*** α — a PMH which has at most $f_i \leq (M_i/M_{i-1})^\alpha$ level-$(i-1)$ caches beneath each level-i cache for all $1 \leq i \leq h$.

The metric assigns to each subtree of a spawn tree an estimate of its complexity, measured in cache miss cost equivalents, when mapped to a PMH by a SB scheduler. The estimate is based on its position in the spawn tree and its cache complexity in the PCC metric. The metric has two free parameters: α which represents the parallelism available of a hypothetical machine, and M which represents the size of one of the caches in the hierarchy with respect to which the spawn tree is being analyzed.

DEFINITION 2 (EFFECTIVE CACHE COMPLEXITY (ECC)). *Let* t *be a task in the ND model. Unroll the spawn tree of* t*, applying the DAG rewriting rules until all the leaves of the tree are M-maximal. Regard all dataflow arrows (solid or dashed) between the leaves to be dependencies (see Figure 11).*
The ECC of a M-maximal task t′*s is* $\widehat{Q}_\alpha(\mathsf{t}';M) = Q^*(\mathsf{t}';M)$.

The ECC of t *is* $\widehat{Q}_\alpha(\mathsf{t};M)$, *where* $\left\lceil \frac{\widehat{Q}_\alpha(\mathsf{t};M)}{s(\mathsf{t})^\alpha} \right\rceil =$

$$\max \begin{cases} \max_{\chi \in chains(\mathsf{t},M)} \left\{ \sum_{\mathsf{t}_i \in \chi} \left\lceil \frac{\widehat{Q}_\alpha(\mathsf{t}_i;M;\kappa)}{s(\mathsf{t}_i)^\alpha} \right\rceil \right\} & \textit{(depth dominated)} \\ \left\lceil \frac{\sum_{\mathsf{t}_i \in maximal(\mathsf{t},M)} \widehat{Q}_\alpha(\mathsf{t}_i;M)}{s(\mathsf{t})^\alpha} \right\rceil & \textit{(work dominated)} \end{cases}$$

where chains(t,M) *represents the set of chains of dependence edges between M-maximal tasks, maximal*(t,M)*, in the spawn tree of* t.

The work dominated term has the same denominator as the left hand side and thus captures the total amount of cache complexity in the spawn tree (summation over leaves). The depth dominated term captures the critical path for the SB scheduler. The term $\lceil \widehat{Q}_\alpha(\mathsf{t};M)/s(\mathsf{t})^\alpha \rceil$ is the proxy for span in our analysis and we call it the ***effective depth*** of the task t. The depth dominated ensures that the effective depth defined by ECC for a task is at least the sum of the effective depths of all M-maximal tasks along any chain between M-maximal tasks induced by DAG rewriting with respect to the fire rules. The definition of ECC is such that:

1. In the range $\alpha \in [0, \alpha_{max})$, for some algorithm-specific constant α_{max}, $\widehat{Q}_\alpha(\mathsf{t};M) \leq c_U Q^*(\mathsf{t};M)$ for all $M > M_U$, for some positive universal constants c_U, M_U.

2. On a machine with parallelism $\beta \leq \alpha_{max} - \varepsilon$ for some arbitrarily small positive constant ε, the running time of the SB scheduler is within a constant factor of the perfectly load balanced scenario in equation 16 (see Theorem 3).
3. For NP programs, it coincides with the definition in [11].

Parallelizability of an Algorithm. For the above reasons, we refer to the α_{max} of an algorithm as its ***parallelizability*** just as in [42]. The greater the parallelizability of the algorithm, the more efficient it is to schedule on larger machines. When the parallelizability of the algorithm asymptotically approaches the difference between the work and the span exponents of the algorithm, we call it ***reasonably regular***. For an input of size $N = n \times n$, TRS, Cholesky and 2D Floyd-Warshall have work exponent 1.5 and span exponent 0.5, and the difference between them is 1. In many divide-and-conquer algorithms, such as in [14], where the NP model does not induce too many artificial dependencies, the parallelizability exceeds that of largest shared memory machines available today. In such algorithms SB schedulers have been empirically shown to be effective at managing locality without compromising load balance, and as a consequence, capable of outperforming work-stealing schedulers [43]. However, this is not the case for algorithms in Section 3, which lose some parallelism when expressed in the NP model.

For example, in the NP model, the parallelizability (w.r.t. cache size M) of the cache-oblivious matrix multiplication is $\alpha_{max,MM} = 1 - \log_M(1 + c_{MM})$ for some small constant c_{MM} (see Claim 2 in Appendix of [25]), which is as high as it can be. We expect the parallelizability of nested parallel TRS algorithm to be less than $\alpha_{max,MM}$. In fact, for an $n \times n$ upper triangular T and a right hand side B of size $N = n \times n$, the parallelizability of the nested parallel TRS algorithm in Equation (3) is $1 - \log_{\min\{N/M,M\}}(1 + c_{TRS})$ (see Claim 3 in Appendix of [25]). This is smaller than the parallelizability of matrix multiplication when $N/M < M$. Since L3 caches are of the order of 10MB, the reduced parallelism adversely affects load balance even in large instances that are of the order of gigabytes (also empirically observed in [43]). When expressed in the ND model, the parallelizability of TRS improves. This can be seen in Figure 8, where the depth dominated term corresponding to the longest chain has effective depth $c(N^{0.5}/M^{0.5})M^{1-\alpha} + c'$, which is less than the work dominated term when $\alpha < 1 - \log_M(1 + c_{TRS})$. This is the parallelizability of TRS in the ND model. This is also the case for other linear algebra algorithms, including Cholesky and LU factorizations. We can similarly show that the parallelizability of LCS in the ND model is 1.

Running time analysis. The main result of this section is Theorem 3 which shows that SB schedulers can make use of the extra parallelizability of programs expressed in the ND model.

THEOREM 3. *Consider an h-level PMH with p_h processors where a level-i cache has size M_i, fanout f_i and cache miss cost C_i. Let* t *be a task such that $S(\mathrm{t};B) > f_h M_{h-1}/3$ (the scheduler allocates the entire hierarchy to such a task) with parallelizability α_{max} in the ND model. Suppose that α_{max} exceeds the parallelism of the machine by a constant. The running time of* t *is no more than:*

$$\frac{\sum_{j=0}^{h-1} \widehat{Q}_\alpha(\mathrm{t}; M_j/3) \cdot C_j}{p_h} \cdot v_h, \text{ where overhead } v_h \text{ is}$$

$$v_h = 2 \prod_{j=1}^{h-1} \left(\frac{1}{k} + \frac{f_j}{(1-k)(M_j/M_{j-1})^{\alpha'}} \right),$$

for some constant $0 < k < 1$, where $\alpha' = \min\{\alpha_{max}, 1\}$.

When the machine parallelism is no greater than the parallelizability of the algorithm in the ND model, $\widehat{Q}_\alpha(t;M) \leq c_U Q^*(M)$. Therefore, the theorem says that the algorithm runs within a constant factor (v_h) of the perfectly load balanced scenario in Equation (16). Relating this theorem to the definition of machine parallelism, we infer that for highly regular algorithms considered in this paper, the SB scheduler can effectively use up to $O(N^{1-c'}/M_{h-1})$ level-$(h-1)$ subclusters for some arbitrarily small constant $c' < 0$.

We prove this theorem using the notion of effective work, the separation lemma (lemma 5) and a work-span argument based on effective depth as in [11]. The ***latency added effective work*** is similar to the effective cache complexity, but instead of counting just cache misses at one cache level, we add the cost of cache misses at each instruction. The cost $\rho(x)$ of an instruction x accessing location m is $\rho(x) = W(x) + C'_i$, where $W(x)$ is the work, and $C'_i = C_0 + C_1 + \cdots + C_{i-1}$ is the cost of a cache miss if the scheduler causes the instruction x to fetch m from a level-i cache in the PMH. The instruction would need to incur a cache miss at level-i if it is the first instruction within the unique maximal level-i task that accesses a particular memory location. Using this per-instruction cost, we define effective work $\widehat{W}^*_\alpha(.)$ of a task using structural induction in a manner that is deliberately similar to that of $\widehat{Q}_\alpha(.)$.

DEFINITION 4 (LATENCY ADDED COST). *With cost ρ assigned to instructions, the* ***latency added effective work*** *of a task* t*, or a strand* s *nested inside a task* t *(from which it inherits space declaration) is:* strand:

$$\widehat{W}^*_\alpha(\mathrm{s}) = s(\mathrm{t})^\alpha \sum_{x \in \mathrm{s}} \rho(x).$$

task: *For task* t *of size between M_i and M_{i+1}, the l.a.e.w. is $\widehat{W}^*_\alpha(\mathrm{t})$, where* $\left\lceil \frac{\widehat{W}^*_\alpha(\mathrm{t})}{s(\mathrm{t})^\alpha} \right\rceil =$

$$\max \begin{cases} \max_{\chi \in chains(\mathrm{t},M)} \left\{ \sum_{\mathrm{t}_i \in \chi} \left\lceil \frac{\widehat{W}^*_\alpha(\mathrm{t}_i)}{s(\mathrm{t}_i)^\alpha} \right\rceil \right\} & \textit{(depth dominated)} \\ \left\lceil \frac{\sum_{\mathrm{t}_i \in maximal(\mathrm{t},M)} \widehat{W}^*_\alpha(\mathrm{t}_i)}{s(\mathrm{t})^\alpha} \right\rceil & \textit{(work dominated)} \end{cases}$$

where chains(t*, M) represents the set of chains of dependence edges between M-maximal tasks, maximal*(t*, M), in the spawn tree of* t*.*

Because of the large number of machine parameters involved ($\{M_i, C_i\}$, $i = 1 \ldots h$ etc.), it is undesirable to compute the latency added work directly for an algorithm. Instead, using induction of the structure of the task in terms of decomposition into strands and maximal tasks, one can show that the latency added effective work can be upper bounded by a sum of per (cache) level machine costs $\widehat{W}^{(i)}_\alpha(\cdot)$ that can, in turn be bounded by machine parameters and ECC of the algorithm. For $i \in [h-1]$, $\widehat{W}^{(i)}_\alpha(\mathrm{t})$ of a task t is computed exactly like $\widehat{W}^*_\alpha(\mathrm{c})$ using a different base case: for each instruction x in c, if the memory access at x costs at least C'_i, assign a cost of $\rho_i(x) = C_i$ to that node. Else, assign a cost of $\rho_i(x) = 0$. Further, we set $\rho_0(x) = W(x)$, and define $\widehat{W}^{(0)}_\alpha(\mathrm{c})$ in terms of $\rho_o(\cdot)$. It also follows from these definitions that $\rho(x) = \sum_{i=0}^{h-1} \rho_i(x)$ for all instructions x. With this notation, we have (see [25] for proof):

LEMMA 5. ***Separation Lemma****: On an h-level PMH, and for a parameter $\alpha > 0$, for a task* t *with size at least M_{h-1}, we have:*

$$\left\lceil \frac{\widehat{W}^*_\alpha(\mathrm{b})}{s(\mathrm{t})^\alpha} \right\rceil \leq \left\lceil \frac{\sum_{i=0}^{h-1} \widehat{W}^{(i)}_\alpha(\mathrm{t}).}{s(\mathrm{t})^\alpha} \right\rceil$$

With the separation lemma for the ND model, the proof of Theorem 3 follows from the two lemmas which we adapt from [11]. The first is a bound on the per level latency added effective work term in terms of the effective cache complexity. The second is a bound on the runtime in terms of the latency added effective work using a modified work span analysis akin to Brent's theorem. The proofs of these two lemmas follow the same arguments as in [11] with minor, but straightforward, modifications that account for the new definition of the ECC in the ND model.

LEMMA 6. *Consider an h-level PMH and a task (or a strand) t. If t is scheduled on this PMH using a space-bounded scheduler with dilation $\sigma = 1/3$, then $\widehat{W}^*_\alpha(t) \leq \sum_{i=0}^{h-1} \widehat{Q}_\alpha(t; M_i/3, B) \cdot C_i$.*

LEMMA 7. *Consider an h-level PMH and a task with parallelizability with α_{max} that exceeds the parallelism of the PMH by a small constant. Let $\alpha' = \min\{\alpha_{max}, 1\}$. Let N_i be a task or strand which has been assigned a set $\mathcal{U}_t$ of $q \leq g_i(S(N_i))$ level-$(i-1)$ subclusters by the scheduler. Letting $\sum_{V \in \mathcal{U}_t}(1-\mu(V)) = r$ (by definition, $r \leq |\mathcal{U}_t| = q$), the running time of N_i is at most:*

$$\frac{\widehat{W}^*_\alpha(N_i)}{rp_{i-1}} \cdot v_i, \text{where overhead } v_i = 2\prod_{j=1}^{i-1}\left(\frac{1}{k} + \frac{f_i}{(1-k)(M_i/M_{i-1})^{\alpha'}}\right),$$

for some constant $0 < k < 1$.

5. RELATED WORK AND COMPARISON

Nested Parallelism, Complexity and Schedulers. A major advantage of writing algorithms in the NP and ND models is that it exposes its locality (quantified by cache complexity) and parallelism (quantified by work and span) at different scales. This makes it possible to design schedulers that can exploit parallelism and locality in algorithms at different levels of the cache hierarchy. Initial analyses of schedulers for the NP model, such as the randomized work-stealing scheduler [17], were based only on work and span. While such analyses serve as a good indicator of their scalability and load-balancing abilities, better analyses and newer schedulers that minimize both communication costs and load balance in terms of time and cache complexities on various parallel cache configurations have been studied [1, 10, 12, 22, 11]. Many divide-and-conquer parallel cache-oblivious algorithms that can can achieve theoretically optimal bounds on cache complexity, work and span exist [14, 23]. For these NP algorithms, schedulers can achieve optimal bounds on time and communication costs.

Another advantage of the NP (and ND) algorithms is that despite being processor- and cache-oblivious, schedulers execute these algorithms well with minimal tuning; the bounds are fairly robust across cache sizes and processor counts. Tuning of algorithms for time and/or cache complexity has several disadvantages: first, the code structure becomes more complicated; second, the parameter space to explore is usually of exponential size; third, the tuned code is non-portable, i.e., separate tuning is required for different hardware systems; fourth, the tuned code may not be robust to variations and noise in the running environment. Recent work by Bender et al. [8] showed that loop based codes are not cache-adaptive, i.e., when the amount of cache available to an algorithm can fluctuate, which is usually the case in a real-world environment, the performance of tuned loop tiling based can suffer significantly. However, many runtimes and systems (e.g. Halide [41]) that map algorithms such as dense numerical algebra, stencils and memoization algorithms to parallel machines rely heavily on tuning to extract performance.

Futures, Pipelines and other Synchronization Constructs. The limitations of the NP model in expressing parallelism is known in the parallel programming community. Several approaches, such as futures [6, 26] and synchronization variables [13], were proposed to express more general classes of parallel programs.

Conceptually, the *future* construct lets a piece of computation run in parallel with the context containing it. The pointer to future can then be passed to other threads and synchronize at a later point. Several papers have studied the complexity of executing programs with futures. Greiner and Blelloch [29] discuss semantics, cost models and effective evaluations strategies with bounds on the time complexity. Spoonhower et al. [44] calculate tight bounds on the locality of work-stealing in programs with futures. The bounds show that moving from a strict NP model to programs with futures can make WS schedulers pay significant price in terms of locality. To alleviate this problem, Herlihy and Liu [31] suggest that the cache locality of future-parallel programs with work-stealing can be improved by restricting the programs to using "well-structured futures": each future is touched only once, either by the thread that created it, or by a later descendant of the thread that created it. However, it is difficult to express the algorithms in our paper as well-structured futures without losing parallelism or locality. One of the main reasons for this is that the algorithm DAGs we consider have nodes with multiple, even $O(n)$, outgoing dataflow arrows which cannot be easily translated into "touch-once" futures. Even if we were to express such DAGs with touch-once futures, the resultant DAG might be unnecessarily serialized. We seek to eliminate such artificial loss of parallelism with the ND model. Further, the analysis of schedulers for programs with futures is limited to work-stealing, which is a less than ideal candidate for multi-level cache hierarchies. To the best of our knowledge, no provably good hierarchy-aware schedulers for future-parallel programs exist.

Synchronization variables are a more general form of synchronization among threads in "computation DAG" and can be used to implement futures. Blelloch et al. [13] present the *write-once synchronization variable*, which is a variable (memory location) that can be written by one thread and read by any number of other threads. The paper also discusses an online scheduling algorithm for a program with "write-once synchronization variables" with efficient space and time bounds on the CRCW PRAM model with the fetch-and-add primitive.

Though futures or synchronization variables provide a more relaxed form of synchronization among threads in a computation DAG, thus exposing more parallelism, there are some key technical differences between these approaches and the ND model. First, the future construct fails to address the concept of "partial dependencies". A thread computing a future is "parallel", not "partially parallel", to the thread touching the future. The runtime always eagerly creates both threads before the future is computed, thus possibly wasting asymptotically more space and incurring asymptotically more cache misses. In contrast, the "$\rightsquigarrow$" construct allows the runtime the flexibility of creating "sink" tasks as required when partial dependencies are met. Second, there is no existing work on linguistic and runtime support for the recursive construction and refinement of futures over spawn trees. While many dataflow programming models have been studied and deployed in production over the last four decades [33], the automatic recursive construction of dataflow arrows over the spawn tree, which is crucial in achieving locality in a cache- and processor-oblivious fashion, is a new and unique feature of our model. Third, there are algorithms whose maximal parallelism can be easily realized using the "$\rightsquigarrow$" construct but not with futures. In the ND model, it is easy to describe algorithms in which a source can fire multiple sink nodes, and a sink node can depend on multiple sources. Such algorithms with nodes that involve multiple incoming and outgoing dataflow arrows pose problems in future-parallelism models. For instance, programming the LCS algorithm using futures without introducing artificial dependencies is very cumbersome. To eliminate artificial dependencies, this class of problems requires futures to be touched by descendants of the siblings of the node whose descendant created the future; that is, the touching thread may be created before the corresponding future thread is created. To the best of our knowledge, there is no easy scheme to pass the pointer to a future up and down the spawn tree.

Another closely related extension of the nested parallel model is "pipeline parallelism". Pipeline parallelism can be constructed by either futures (as in [15], where it was used to shorten span) or synchronization variables, or by some elegantly defined linguistic constructs [35]. The key idea in pipeline parallelism is to organize a parallel program as a linear sequence of stages. Each stage processes elements of a data stream, passing each processed data element to the next stage, and then taking on a new element before the subsequent stages have necessarily completed their processing. Pipeline parallelism cannot express all the partial dependence patterns described in this paper. To allow the expression of arbitrary DAGs, interfaces for "parallel task graphs" and schedulers for them have been studied [32, 2]. While in principle they can be used to construct computation DAGs that contain arbitrary parallelism, the work flow is more or less similar to dataflow computation without much emphasis on recursion, locality or cache-obliviousness. The same limitation is true of pipeline parallelism as well.

Other algorithms, systems and schedulers. Parallel and cache-efficient algorithms for dynamic programming have been extensively studied (e.g. [22, 27, 37, 45]). These algorithms illustrate algorithms in which it is necessary to have programming constructs that can express multiple (even $O(n)$) dataflows at each node without serialization [27]. The necessity of wavefront scheduling and designs for it have been studied in [37, 45].

Dynamic scheduling in dense numerical linear algebra on shared and distributed memories, as well as GPUs, has been studied in the MAGMA and PLASMA [3], DPLASMA [18], and PaRSEC [19] systems. The programming interface used for these systems is DaGUE [20], which is supported by hierarchical schedulers in runtimes. The DaGUE interface is a slight relaxation of the NP model that allows recursive composition of task DAGs representing dataflow within individual kernels. However, the interface does not capture the notion of partial dependencies. When DAGs of smaller kernels are composed to define larger algorithms, the dependencies are either total or null. The ability to compose kernels with partial dependency patterns is key to the ND model.

The FLAME project [30], and subsequently the Elemental project [40], provides a systematic way of deriving recursions and data dependencies in dense linear algebra from high-level expressions [9], and using them to generate data flow DAG scheduling [21]. The method proposed in these works can be adapted to find the partial dependence patterns derived by hand in this paper.

The Galois system developed at UT Austin [39] proposes a data-centric formulation of algorithms called "operator formulation". This formulation was initiated for handling irregular parallel computation in which data dependencies can change at runtime, and for irregular data structures such as graphs, trees and sets. In contrast, our approach was motivated by more regular parallel computations such as divide-and-conquer algorithms.

Acknowledgements

We thank Prof. James Demmel, Dr. Shachar Itzhaky, Prof. Charles Leiserson, Prof. Armando Solar-Lezama and Prof. Katherine Yelick for valuable discussions and their support in conducting this research. Yuan Tang thanks Prof. Xiaoyang Wang, the dean of Software School and School of Computer Science at Fudan University for general help on research environment. Yuan Tang also thanks Prof. Haibin Kan for generous financial support from grant KRH2301058. We thank the U.S. Department of Energy, Office of Science, Office of Advanced Scientific Computing Research (DoE ASCR), Applied Mathematics and Computer Science Program, grants DE-SC0010200, DE-SC-0008700, and AC02-05CH11231, for financial support, along with DARPA grant HR0011-12-2-0016, ASPIRE Lab industrial sponsors and affiliates Intel, Google, Huawei, LG, NVIDIA, Oracle, Samsung, and MathWorks.

6. REFERENCES

[1] U. A. Acar, G. E. Blelloch, and R. D. Blumofe. The data locality of work stealing. In *Proc. of the 12th ACM Annual Symp. on Parallel Algorithms and Architectures (SPAA 2000)*, pages 1–12, 2000.

[2] K. Agrawal, C. E. Leiserson, and J. Sukha. Executing task graphs using work stealing. In *IPDPS*, pages 1–12. IEEE, April 2010.

[3] E. Agullo, J. Demmel, J. Dongarra, B. Hadri, J. Kurzak, J. Langou, H. Ltaief, P. Luszczek, and S. Tomov. Numerical linear algebra on emerging architectures: The plasma and magma projects. *Journal of Physics: Conference Series*, 180(1):012037, 2009.

[4] B. Alpern, L. Carter, and J. Ferrante. Modeling parallel computers as memory hierarchies. In *Proc. Programming Models for Massively Parallel Computers*, pages 116–123. IEEE Computer Society Press, 1993.

[5] N. S. Arora, R. D. Blumofe, and C. G. Plaxton. Thread scheduling for multiprogrammed multiprocessors. In *SPAA '98*, pages 119–129, June 1998.

[6] H. C. Baker, Jr. and C. Hewitt. The incremental garbage collection of processes. In *Proceedings of the 1977 Symposium on Artificial Intelligence and Programming Languages*, pages 55–59, New York, NY, USA, 1977. ACM.

[7] G. Ballard, J. Demmel, O. Holtz, and O. Schwartz. Minimizing communication in numerical linear algebra. *SIAM J. Matrix Analysis Applications*, 32(3):866–901, 2011.

[8] M. A. Bender, R. Ebrahimi, J. T. Fineman, G. Ghasemiesfeh, R. Johnson, and S. McCauley. Cache-adaptive algorithms. In *Proceedings of the Twenty-Fifth Annual ACM-SIAM Symposium on Discrete Algorithms, SODA 2014, Portland, Oregon, USA, January 5-7, 2014*, pages 958–971, 2014.

[9] P. Bientinesi, J. A. Gunnels, M. E. Myers, E. S. Quintana-Ortí, and R. A. v. d. Geijn. The science of deriving dense linear algebra algorithms. *ACM Trans. Math. Softw.*, 31(1):1–26, Mar. 2005.

[10] G. Blelloch, P. Gibbons, and Y. Matias. Provably efficient scheduling for languages with fine-grained parallelism. *Journal of the ACM*, 46(2):281–321, 1999.

[11] G. E. Blelloch, J. T. Fineman, P. B. Gibbons, and H. V. Simhadri. Scheduling irregular parallel computations on hierarchical caches. In *Proceedings of the Twenty-third Annual ACM Symposium on Parallelism in Algorithms and Architectures*, SPAA '11, pages 355–366. ACM, 2011.

[12] G. E. Blelloch and P. B. Gibbons. Effectively sharing a cache among threads. In *Proceedings of the Sixteenth Annual ACM Symposium on Parallelism in Algorithms and Architectures*, pages 235–244. ACM, 2004.

[13] G. E. Blelloch, P. B. Gibbons, Y. Matias, and G. J. Narlikar. Space-efficient scheduling of parallelism with synchronization variables. In *Proceedings of the 9th Annual ACM Symposium on Parallel Algorithms and Architectures (SPAA)*, pages 12–23, Newport, Rhode Island, June 1997.

[14] G. E. Blelloch, P. B. Gibbons, and H. V. Simhadri. Low depth cache-oblivious algorithms. In *Proceedings of the Twenty-second Annual ACM Symposium on Parallelism in Algorithms and Architectures*, SPAA '10, pages 189–199, New York, NY, USA, 2010. ACM.

[15] G. E. Blelloch and M. Reid-Miller. Pipelining with futures. In *Proceedings of the Ninth Annual ACM Symposium on Parallel Algorithms and Architectures*, SPAA '97, pages 249–259, New York, NY, USA, 1997. ACM.

[16] R. D. Blumofe and C. E. Leiserson. Space-efficient scheduling of multithreaded computations. In *Proceedings of the Twenty Fifth Annual ACM Symposium on Theory of Computing*, pages 362–371, San Diego, California, 1993.

[17] R. D. Blumofe and C. E. Leiserson. Scheduling multithreaded computations by work stealing. *JACM*, 46(5):720–748, Sept. 1999.

[18] G. Bosilca, A. Bouteiller, A. Danalis, M. Faverge, A. Haidar, T. Herault, J. Kurzak, J. Langou, P. Lemarinier, H. Ltaief, P. Luszczek, A. Yarkhan, and J. Dongarra. Distributed dense numerical linear algebra algorithms on massively parallel architectures: Dplasma. Technical Report UT-CS-10-660, University of Tennessee Computer Science, September 2013.

[19] G. Bosilca, A. Bouteiller, A. Danalis, M. Faverge, T. Herault, and J. J. Dongarra. Parsec: Exploiting heterogeneity to enhance scalability. *Computing in Science & Engineering*, 15(6):36–45, 2013.

[20] G. Bosilca, A. Bouteiller, A. Danalis, T. Herault, P. Lemarinier, and J. Dongarra. Dague: A generic distributed {DAG} engine for high performance computing. *Parallel Computing*, 38(1-2):37 – 51, 2012. Extensions for Next-Generation Parallel Programming Models.

[21] E. Chan and F. D. Igual. Runtime data flow graph scheduling of matrix computations with multiple hardware accelerators, FLAME Working Note #50, October 2010.

[22] R. Chowdhury, F. Silvestri, B. Blakeley, and V. Ramachandran. Oblivious algorithms for multicores and network of processors. *Journal of Parallel and Distributed Computing (Special issue on best papers from IPDPS 2010, 2011 and 2012)*, 73(7):911–925, 2013. A preliminary version appeared in IPDPS '10.

[23] R. Cole and V. Ramachandran. Efficient resource oblivious algorithms for multicores. *CoRR*, abs/1103.4071, 2011.

[24] T. H. Cormen, C. E. Leiserson, R. L. Rivest, and C. Stein. *Introduction to Algorithms*. MIT Press, 3rd edition, 2009.

[25] D. Dinh, H. V. Simhadri, and Y. Tang. Extending the nested parallel model to the nested dataflow model with provably efficient schedulers. *CoRR*, abs/1602.04552, 2016.

[26] D. Friedman and D. Wise. Aspects of applicative programming for parallel processing. *Computers, IEEE Transactions on*, C-27(4):289–296, April 1978.

[27] Z. Galil and K. Park. Parallel algorithms for dynamic programming recurrences with more than $O(1)$ dependency. *Journal of Parallel and Distributed Computing*, 21:213–222, 1994.

[28] O. Gotoh. An improved algorithm for matching biological sequences. *Journal of Molecular Biology*, 162:705–708, 1982.

[29] J. Greiner and G. E. Blelloch. A provably time-efficient parallel implementation of full speculation. *ACM Trans. Program. Lang. Syst.*, 21(2):240–285, Mar. 1999.

[30] J. A. Gunnels, F. G. Gustavson, G. M. Henry, and R. A. van de Geijn. FLAME: Formal Linear Algebra Methods Environment. *ACM Transactions on Mathematical Software*, 27(4):422–455, Dec. 2001.

[31] M. Herlihy and Z. Liu. Well-structured futures and cache locality. In *Proceedings of the 19th ACM SIGPLAN Symposium on Principles and Practice of Parallel Programming*, PPoPP '14, pages 155–166. ACM, 2014.

[32] T. Johnson, T. A. Davis, and S. M. Hadfield. A concurrent dynamic task graph. *Parallel Comput.*, 22(2):327–333, 1996.

[33] W. M. Johnston, J. R. P. Hanna, and R. J. Millar. Advances in dataflow programming languages. *ACM Comput. Surv.*, 36(1):1–34, Mar. 2004.

[34] I.-T. A. Lee, S. Boyd-Wickizer, Z. Huang, and C. E. Leiserson. Using memory mapping to support cactus stacks in work-stealing runtime systems. In *Proceedings of the 19th International Conference on Parallel Architectures and Compilation Techniques*, PACT '10, pages 411–420, New York, NY, USA, 2010. ACM.

[35] I.-T. A. Lee, C. E. Leiserson, T. B. Schardl, J. Sukha, and Z. Zhang. On-the-fly pipeline parallelism. In *Proceedings of the Twenty-fifth Annual ACM Symposium on Parallelism in Algorithms and Architectures*, SPAA '13, pages 140–151, New York, NY, USA, 2013. ACM.

[36] C. E. Leiserson, T. B. Schardl, and J. Sukha. Deterministic parallel random-number generation for dynamic-multithreading platforms. In *Proceedings of the 17th ACM SIGPLAN Symposium on Principles and Practice of Parallel Programming*, PPoPP '12, pages 193–204, New York, NY, USA, 2012. ACM.

[37] S. Maleki, M. Musuvathi, and T. Mytkowicz. Parallelizing dynamic programming through rank convergence. In *Proceedings of the 19th ACM SIGPLAN Symposium on Principles and Practice of Parallel Programming*, PPoPP'14, pages 219–232, New York, NY, USA, 2014. ACM.

[38] G. Narlikar. *Space-Efficient Scheduling for Parallel, Multithreaded Computations*. PhD thesis, Carnegie Mellon University, Pittsburgh, PA, May 1999.

[39] K. Pingali, D. Nguyen, M. Kulkarni, M. Burtscher, M. A. Hassaan, R. Kaleem, T.-H. Lee, A. Lenharth, R. Manevich, M. Méndez-Lojo, D. Prountzos, and X. Sui. The tao of parallelism in algorithms. In *Proceedings of the 32Nd ACM SIGPLAN Conference on Programming Language Design and Implementation*, PLDI '11, pages 12–25. ACM, 2011.

[40] J. Poulson, B. Marker, R. A. van de Geijn, J. R. Hammond, and N. A. Romero. Elemental: A new framework for distributed memory dense matrix computations. *ACM Trans. Math. Softw.*, 39(2):13:1–13:24, Feb. 2013.

[41] J. Ragan-Kelley, C. Barnes, A. Adams, S. Paris, F. Durand, and S. Amarasinghe. Halide: A language and compiler for optimizing parallelism, locality, and recomputation in image processing pipelines. In *Proceedings of the 34th ACM SIGPLAN Conference on Programming Language Design and Implementation*, PLDI '13, pages 519–530. ACM, 2013.

[42] H. V. Simhadri. *Program-Centric Cost Models for Locality and Parallelism*. PhD thesis, CMU, 2013.

[43] H. V. Simhadri, G. E. Blelloch, J. T. Fineman, P. B. Gibbons, and A. Kyrola. Experimental analysis of space-bounded schedulers. *Transactions on Parallel Computing*, 3(1), 2016. A preliminary version appeared in SPAA '14.

[44] D. Spoonhower, G. E. Blelloch, P. B. Gibbons, and R. Harper. Beyond nested parallelism: Tight bounds on work-stealing overheads for parallel futures. In *Proceedings of the Twenty-first Annual Symposium on Parallelism in Algorithms and Architectures*, SPAA '09, pages 91–100, New York, NY, USA, 2009. ACM.

[45] Y. Tang, R. You, H. Kan, J. J. Tithi, P. Ganapathi, and R. A. Chowdhury. Cache-oblivious wavefront: Improving parallelism of recursive dynamic programming algorithms without losing cache-efficiency. In *PPoPP'15*, San Francisco, CA, USA, Feb.7 – 11 2015.

A Practical Solution to the Cactus Stack Problem

Chaoran Yang
Department of Computer Science
Rice University
chaoran@rice.edu

John Mellor-Crummey
Department of Computer Science
Rice University
johnmc@rice.edu

ABSTRACT

Work-stealing is a popular method for load-balancing dynamic multithreaded computations on shared-memory systems. In theory, a randomized work-stealing scheduler can achieve near linear speedup when the computation has sufficient parallelism and requires stack space that is linear in the number of processors. In practice, however, work-stealing runtimes sacrifice interoperability with serial code to achieve these bounds. For example, both Cilk and Cilk++ prohibit a C function from calling a Cilk function. Other work-stealing runtime systems that do not have this restriction either lack a strong time bound, which might cause them to deliver little or no speedup in the worst case, or lack a strong space bound, which might lead to an excessive memory footprint. This problem was previously described as the *cactus stack problem*.

In this paper, we present *Fibril*, a new multithreading library that supports a fork-join programming model using work-stealing. Fibril solves the cactus stack problem by (1) implementing on a cactus stack that conforms to the calling conventions of serial code and (2) returning unused memory pages of suspended stacks to the operating system to bound consumption of physical memory. Theoretically, Fibril achieves strong bounds on both time and memory usage without sacrificing interoperability with serial code. Empirically, Fibril achieves up to 3× the performance of Intel Cilk Plus and up to 8× the performance of Intel Threading Building Blocks for the 12 benchmarks we evaluated.

Keywords

Work-stealing; cactus stack; interoperability.

1. INTRODUCTION

Work-stealing is a standard technique for load balancing parallel tasks in multicore systems. Many parallel programming models employ work-stealing to support dynamic task parallelism, including Cilk [8], OpenMP 3.0 [3], Threading Building Blocks (TBB) [15], Java Fork/Join Framework [9], Task Parallel Library [11], and X10 [5]. Work-stealing enables an efficient implementation that guarantees bounds on both time and stack space. For a class of computations, Blumofe and Leiserson [4] prove strong time and space bounds when stealing is unrestricted. Let T_1 be the running time of a deterministic parallel computation on one processor, i.e., its *work*, and let T_∞ be its ideal running time on an infinite number of processors, i.e., its *span*. Then a randomized work-stealing scheduler can perform the computation on P processors in expected time

$$T_p \leq T_1/P + c_\infty T_\infty, \tag{1}$$

where c_∞ is a constant value called *span overhead*. This bound guarantees *linear speedup* when $P \ll T_1/T_\infty$, that is, the number of processors P is much less than the computation's average parallelism T_1/T_∞. Moreover, if S_1 is the stack space of a serial execution, a randomized work-stealing scheduler can execute the computation on P processors using stack space

$$S_p \leq PS_1. \tag{2}$$

This bound guarantees that the stack space usage in a parallel execution is at worst *linear* in the number of processors.

For a program written in an Algol-like programming language, such as C, its execution can be thought of as a depth-first traversal of its *invocation tree*. If a function instance A calls a function instance B,[1] A is the parent of B in the invocation tree. When a processor executes a function, it allocates an *activation frame* that stores local data, including arguments and local variables for that function. A processor frees an activation frame when it returns from that function. For a serial execution of a program, activation frames can be allocated using a simple *linear stack*. In a linear stack, a function call advances the stack pointer to allocate a new frame on the top of the stack; when the function returns, it restores the stack pointer to its value for the parent frame, freeing the child frame.

When a program executes in parallel, however, a linear stack is insufficient. In a parallel execution, multiple children of a function may exist simultaneously; their activation frames form a tree of stacks, namely a *cactus stack*. A cactus stack is essentially an N-ary tree in which each node has a pointer to its parent node. Each node in a cactus stack is a linear stack that allocates and frees activation frames by manipulating a stack pointer. If a frame creates a new child while another child still exists, it allocates a new stack to

[1]In the rest of the paper, we use the term *function* instead of *function instance* where there is no room for ambiguity.

SPAA'16, July 11–13, 2016, Pacific Grove, California, USA.

ISBN 978-1-4503-4210-0/16/07...$15.00
DOI: http://dx.doi.org/10.1145/2935764.2935787

store the new child's activation frame with a parent pointer that points to itself.

Cactus stacks are a key building block in parallel runtime systems. Ideally, a cactus stack implementation should:

- support full interoperability with serial binaries compiled to use a linear stack,
- enable a scheduler to achieve nearly perfect linear speedup on computations with ample parallelism, and
- consume a bounded amount of stack space that is practical for general-purpose systems.

It is difficult for work-stealing runtimes to achieve all three criteria at the same time. For example, Cilk [8] guarantees the time bound and space bound, however it forbids a C function from calling Cilk functions. Interoperability with serial code, aka *serial-parallel reciprocity*, is important for building reusable software. Common design patterns, such as *visitor* and *observer* patterns, use callback functions to communicate between objects. One cannot use these patterns if the visitor or observer's callback invokes a Cilk function. TBB [15] is interoprable with serial code. However, to avoid consuming potentially unbounded stack space, TBB restricts a worker to steal only frames that are deeper on the stack than its own suspended frame; this may lead to sub-linear speedup for some computations. Lee et al. [10] refer to the problem of achieving the three aforementioned criteria simultaneously as the *cactus stack problem*. They presented a solution that leverages a *thread-local memory mapping* (TLMM) mechanism. TLMM enables threads in a process to map different physical memory pages for the same region of the process's virtual address space. Sadly, no existing operating systems supports TLMM, which makes Lee et al.'s approach impractical on systems running conventional kernels.

This paper presents a practical solution to the cactus stack problem. We designed a library-based work-stealing system, *Fibril*, that supports a fork-join programming model. Fibril uses a cactus stack that is fully interoperable with serial code that uses a linear stack. Fibril achieves a strong time bound $T_p \leq T_1/P + c_\infty T_\infty$, where $c_\infty = O(S_1 + D)$, and a strong space bound $S_p \leq P(S_1 + D)$. In both bounds, D is the *Fibril depth* (defined in Section 4.4) of a Fibril program.

The contribution of Fibril is two-fold. First, we present a cactus stack implementation that is more efficient than existing work-stealing systems. Second, we present a stack management technique that maintains a strong space bound without sacrificing a strong time bound. Fibril's cactus stack may use up to DPS_1 pages of virtual address space, which is practical for systems that use a 64-bit address space.

Section 2 explains the cactus stack problem in work-stealing runtime systems. Section 3 describes existing approaches for managing cactus stacks in work-stealing systems. Section 4 describes the implementation of Fibril in detail. Section 5 presents an evaluation of Fibril. Section 6 presents our conclusions.

2. BACKGROUND

We investigate the cactus stack problem in the context of a fork-join programming model. In this model, a programmer expresses logical parallelism using a `fork` construct. When a function A initiates a `fork` to perform an asynchronous call to a function B, A may continue to execute without waiting for B to complete. We refer to the callee B at a `fork` as a child *task* and the caller A as its *parent*. A `join` construct synchronizes between a parent and its child tasks, suspending execution of the parent until all of its children complete.

We consider the cactus stack problem in the context of a work-stealing scheduler, which executes a computation expressed in a fork-join programming model on a finite set of hardware threads, called *workers*. In particular, we consider the randomized work-stealing scheduler proposed by Blumofe and Leiserson [4]. Cilk and its descendants, Cilk++ and Intel Cilk Plus, use such a scheduler in their runtime system to support their fork-join programming models.

In Cilk's work-stealing scheduler, each worker maintains a double-ended queue, known as a *deque*. A worker pushes the parent frame onto its deque at a `fork` (`cilk_spawn`) and pops it when the task completes.[2] When a worker runs out of work, it becomes a *thief* and steals from the top of a randomly selected worker's deque. We refer to the worker that has its parent frame stolen as a *victim*. When a worker steals a frame, it executes the frame until it encounters a `join` (`cilk_sync`). At a `join`, the current frame is *suspended* if any of its child tasks have not yet completed; otherwise, the worker continues with the frame. If a thief steals a frame, the victim will fail when attempting to pop the frame from its deque. Then the victim will attempt to *resume* the stolen frame, expecting that the thief has completed the frame. If the resumption succeeds, the victim executes the stolen frame starting at the `join`; otherwise, it becomes a thief and performs randomized stealing.

Blumofe and Leiserson [4] have shown that Cilk's work-stealing scheduler can execute a computation on P workers in expected time $T_p \leq T_1/P + c_\infty T_\infty$. Their proof of the time bound indicates that, to achieve near-linear speedup, each worker needs to be either working and making progress on the T_1/P term, or randomly stealing and making progress on the T_∞ term with high probability. If any worker were to wait, or candidate frames for stealing are restricted, the time bound would cease to hold, resulting in sublinear speedup on a program with sufficient parallelism.

Cilk's work-stealing scheduler maintains the so-called *busy-leaves* property [4], which states that during the execution of the computation, every extant leaf of the invocation tree has a worker executing it. The busy-leaves property leads to the space bound of PS_1, since any path from a leaf to the root of the invocation tree corresponds to a path in the cactus stack, no path can require more than S_1 space, and there can be at most P leaves active at a time.

We analyze the cactus stack problem under the assumption that a work-stealing scheduler cannot move a frame to a different address in memory once it is allocated as moving a frame will invalidate all pointers to variables in the frame.[3] Under this restriction, if a worker fails to pop from its deque and finds the frame on top of its stack suspended, it cannot move the frame out of its stack. The worker also cannot

[2] Some work-stealing schedulers push a child frame created by a `fork` onto a worker's local deque and continue executing the parent frame after the `fork`. We do not consider such schedulers in this paper because they may require an unbounded amount of space for bookkeeping.

[3] Some work-stealing programming models forbid users from creating a pointer to a local variable and hence do not have this restriction. Other work-stealing systems leverage the help of a managed environment that can update pointers when frames are moved. However we assume a native runtime environment in this paper.

use its stack space to execute a stolen task because the suspended frame may be resumed, allocating more frames on the stack before the stolen task completes. A naive approach to construct a cactus stack would be to allocate a new stack to execute the stolen task; however, this approach may lead to an impractically large number of stacks since each stack may contain as little as a single frame in the worst case. Cilk and Cilk++ allocate frames of Cilk functions in heap to avoid having a suspended frame tie up a stack. However, this requires Cilk functions to use a custom calling convention that is not compatible with the standard calling conventions. Therefore a Cilk program is not fully interoperable with serial code.

3. RELATED WORK

In this section, we describe various approaches to the cactus stack problem used by existing work-stealing runtimes. To summarize, these work-stealing runtimes address the cactus stack problem by either sacrificing one of the three criteria of a cactus stack or relying on custom operating system extensions. Therefore, we do not consider them as practical solutions to the cactus stack problem.

Cilk [8] and Cilk++ [12] use heap-allocated activation frames for Cilk functions. For normal C functions, Cilk stack allocates their activation frames. Cilk forbids a C function from calling a Cilk function to prevent stack frames from being suspended. This restriction helps Cilk to maintain a strong space bound, however sacrifices serial-parallel reciprocity.

Intel Cilk Plus [16] does not forbid a C function from calling a Cilk function. In Cilk Plus, a worker executes stolen frames on empty stacks acquired from a pool of stacks. The stack pool contains a bounded number of stacks. When the stack pool is empty, a thief has to refrain from stealing until some worker returns a stack to the pool. This implementation choice sacrifices the theoretical time bound of randomized work stealing to provide a tight space bound. Lee et al. [10] state that the theoretical space bound of using a new stack for each stolen frame is DPS_1, where D is the depth of a Cilk application. Therefore, to avoid staling due to a shortage of stacks, executing an application in Cilk Plus on a large number of workers may require an impractically large number of stacks.

A different approach is to allocate activation frames, both called or forked, on a linear stack. In particular, if a worker has a suspended frame on top of its stack, it steals a frame and executes it using its remaining stack space. In this case, the scheduler cannot resume the suspended frame until the stolen frame completes since the suspended frame may allocate new frames on the stack when resumed. This restriction violates the busy-leaves property because a suspended frame that is ready to resume is an extant leaf of the invocation tree and no worker is working on it. Violating the busy-leaves property can cause each worker's stack to grow impractically large. To prevent a worker's stack from growing beyond S_1, one can restrict a worker to only steal frames with a depth greater than the depth of the current suspended frame in the invocation tree. This form of stealing, called *depth-restricted stealing*, sacrifices the time bound. Sukha [17] has shown that there exist computations for which a depth-restricted stealing scheduler cannot execute faster than a sequential execution. TBB [15] uses a strategy that is similar to depth-restricted stealing.

A technique called *leapfrogging* can be applied to conserve stack space when implementing a cactus stack. Wagner and Calder proposed the leapfrogging technique to implement *futures* [18]. The logic behind leapfrogging is that if a worker has a suspended frame on its stack, it can steal a frame that is a descendant of the suspended frame and execute it using its remaining stack space. It is safe to reuse the stack in this way because the suspended frame will not resume until all its descendants complete, including the stolen frame. Because leapfrogging restricts a thief to steal only descendant tasks of the suspended frames on its stack, it is more restrictive than depth-restricted stealing. Therefore, Sukha's lower bound [17] applies to leapfrogging as well. Agrawal et al. [1] endorsed this idea for Cilk, but they did not show an empirical evaluation of the approach.

Lee et al. [10] addressed the cactus stack problem by modifying the operating system kernel to provide support for thread-local memory mapping (TLMM). TTLM designates a region of a process's virtual address space as "local" to each thread, i.e. each worker may map different memory pages to the TLMM region. Lee et al. created a work-stealing runtime system, Cilk-M, by using TLMM to implement the cactus stack in Cilk's runtime system. In Cilk-M, each worker executes on a stack that resides in the TLMM region. Whenever a thief steals a frame, it moves the memory pages that contain the stolen frame and the ancestor frames — the stack prefix — to its stack. Because stacks reside in the TLMM region, a thief can place the stolen stack prefix at the same virtual address as it was allocated. Therefore, pointers to local variables in the stack prefix are still valid. There are two major drawbacks of the TLMM approach. First, TLMM is currently not supported by any existing operating system. Second, since a worker's stack resides in the TLMM region, variables allocated on a worker's stack are not addressable by other workers. This restriction means shared data structures that allocate storage on the stack, such as MCS locks [14], do not work in Cilk-M.

4. FIBRIL

We present *Fibril*, a lightweight multithreading library to support a fork-join programming model. The design of Fibril closely follows that of Cilk. Fibril's randomized work-stealing scheduler behaves similarly to Cilk's scheduler as described in Section 2. Nevertheless, there are two major differences between Cilk and Fibril. First, Fibril is a pure C library that does not require a custom compiler front-end. Instead, Fibril exposes its interface as C macros, leveraging the C preprocessor to generate parallel code for a Fibril program. Second, unlike Cilk, which forbids a C function from calling a Cilk function, Fibril functions are fully interoperable with C functions. Fibril realizes our solution to the cactus stack problem by maintaining a strong time bound, a strong space bound, and serial-parallel reciprocity.

Section 4.1 introduces Fibril's API. Section 4.2 describes how Fibril exploits the standard x86-64 calling conventions to construct a cactus stack for parallel execution. Section 4.3 presents the implementation of Fibril's work-stealing scheduler. Section 4.4 analyzes the theoretical time and space bounds of Fibril's scheduler.

4.1 Fibril's API

We use an example to show how to use Fibril to parallelize a serial program using a fork-join programming model.

```
1  int fib(int n) {
2    if (n < 2) return n;

3    int x, y;
4    x = fib(n - 1);
5    y = fib(n - 2);

6    return x + y;
7  }

8  fibril int parfib(int n) {
9    if (n < 2) return n;

10   fibril_t fr;
11   fibril_init(&fr);

12   int x, y;
13   fibril_fork(&fr, x, parfib, (n - 1));
14   y = parfib(n - 2);

15   fibril_join(&fr);
16   return x + y;
17 }
```

Listing 1: A function `fib` and its parallel version `parfib` implemented in Fibril. Fibril macros are shown in *italic* font.

Listing 1 shows a serial function, `fib`, which computes a Fibonacci number recursively, and a Fibril function, `parfib`, which is a parallel implementation of `fib` using Fibril.

Fibril requires that one label a *Fibril function* — a functions that forks or joins tasks — with the `fibril` keyword (line 8). The `fibril` keyword instructs compilers to generate code for the function that conforms to a calling convention that permits parallel execution (described in Section 4.2). Unlike Cilk, which restricts that a Cilk function can only be spawned, one can either fork a Fibril function (line 13) or call the function directly (line 14).

Before forking or joining a Fibril function, one should declare (line 10) and initialize (line 11) a variable of type `fibril_t`, namely a *Fibril frame*. A Fibril frame synchronizes child tasks and stores the execution state of their parent task. To fork a function, one invokes the `fibril_fork` macro with (1) an initialized Fibril frame, (2) a variable to receive the return value, unless the function returns `void`, (3) the name of the function to fork, and (4) the arguments to the function wrapped within parenthesis (line 13). Logically, `fibril_fork` creates a child task that executes in parallel with its parent. One can use the same Fibril frame to fork multiple functions. To join the forked functions on a Fibril frame, one invokes the `fibril_join` macro with the Fibril frame as an argument (line 15). Logically, `fibril_join` blocks the execution of its caller until all functions forked with the Fibril frame as their parent complete.

Like Cilk, the design of Fibril's API follows the *C elision* rule proposed by Frigo et al. [8]. If we expand `fibril_init` and `fibril_join` to empty statements, and `fibril_fork` to a function call, we will have a syntactically and semantically correct serial program.

Unlike other library based multithreading systems, such as Posix threads, Fibril's API does not require Fibril functions to use a uniform function signature. Using a uniform function signature forces the parent function to pass arguments to a forked function via memory, which is more costly than passing arguments via registers. Therefore, Fibril's API is not only flexible to use, but also permits a low overhead implementation of `fibril_fork`, which can be used to create fine-grained parallelism.

Position	Contents	Frame
`8n+16(%rbp)`	B's memory argument b_n	linkage region
	...	
`16(%rbp)`	B's memory argument b_0	
`8(%rbp)`	B's return address	B's frame
`0(%rbp)`	A's `%rbp` value	
`-8(%rbp)`	B's local variables	
	...	
`0(%rsp)`	(unspecified variable size)	
`-8(%rsp)`	C's memory argument c_n	linkage region
	...	
`-8n-8(%rsp)`	C's memory argument c_0	

Figure 1: Stack organization on x86-64 systems. `%rbp`: frame pointer register; `%rsp`: stack pointer register. High address is at top of the figure.

4.2 Fibril's calling conventions

A calling convention defines how a function receives arguments from its caller, how it returns a result, and how a function's state is preserved across function calls. Different compilation units are interoperable only when they conform to the same calling convention. An architecture's Application Binary Interface (ABI) defines the calling conventions that a binary compiled for the architecture should use. We designed Fibril to work on the x86-64, aka AMD64, architecture. In this section, we describe x86-64 architecture's calling conventions [13]. We then explain the implementation of Fibril's cactus stack, which supports x86-64 calling conventions to enable parallel execution of a Fibril function. In the end, we describe Fibril's context switch scheme which leverages x86-64 calling conventions to reduce overhead. Fibril can be ported to non x86-64 systems with minor changes.

4.2.1 x86-64's linear stack and Fibril's cactus stack

Figure 1 shows a snapshot of the stack organization on x86-64 systems. The snapshot is taken when a thread is executing function B. B was called by function A, and is calling function C. A thread's run-time stack contains the stack frames of live function instances. A function's stack frame contains its return address, the value of its parent's frame pointer, and storage for its local variables. Typically, when a function makes a function call, it passes the callee's arguments in registers. For arguments that cannot be passed in a register, it allocates a *linkage region* between the caller and the callee to pass these arguments. When a thread executes a function, it accesses its stack using two registers: `%rbp` and `%rsp`. In Figure 1, the thread uses `%rbp`, aka the frame pointer, with positive offsets to access memory arguments and the stack frame of the current function B. When B calls C, the thread decrements `%rsp`, aka the stack pointer, pushing memory arguments to be passed to its callee C onto the stack, then decrements `%rsp` again to allocate C's stack frame.

Using both a frame pointer and a stack pointer allows a stack frame to be of an unspecified variable size. Using two pointers to manipulate the stack frames enables us to use this calling convention to construct a cactus stack. In Fib-

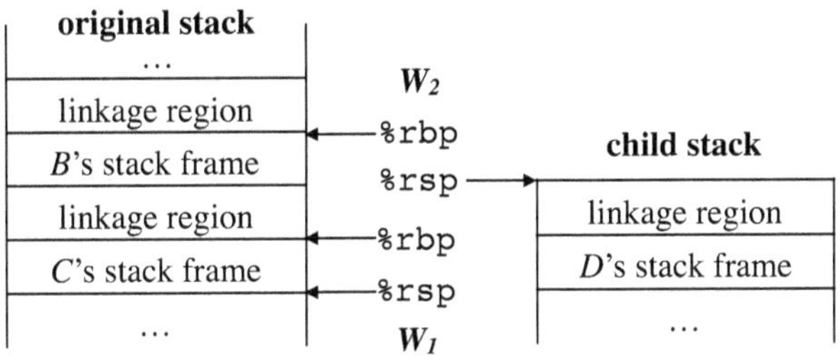

Figure 2: Fibril's cactus stack organization.

ril, when a thread W_1 forks a function C and a thief W_2 steals C's parent B, W_2 resumes execution of B on B's original stack using a new stack pointer (`%rsp`) that points to the top of a new stack. Figure 2 illustrates this situation. In this case, W_2 can access B's stack frame and memory arguments via using its frame pointer (`%rbp`). When W_2 calls or forks another child function C, C's memory arguments and stack frame will be allocated on the new stack, avoiding a collision with C's frame on the original stack. In this way, we construct a cactus stack that allows multiple children of a function to exist simultaneously. When W_2 returns from B, we restore its stack pointer to its original value pointing to the original stack.

When the size of a function's frame is known at compile time, the x86-64 ABI allows the function to avoid using `%rbp` as a frame pointer for the fixed-size frame. This optimization saves the instructions to push and pop `%rbp` in a function's prologue and epilogue; it also allows `%rbp` to be used as a general-purpose register. Nevertheless, omitting a function's frame pointer disallows it to be executed on a non-linear stack. Therefore, Fibril assumes a Fibril function always retains a frame pointer. Some compilers, such as GCC, provide a function attribute that instructs the compiler to use a frame pointer when generating code for a function. Fibril expands the `fibril` macro into such an attribute. For compilers that do not provide this feature, one can define a dummy variable that is a variable-length array in the Fibril function to achieve the same effect.

4.2.2 Enabling context switch in Fibril

The x86-64 ABI classifies all registers in an x86-64 system into two categories: a *caller-saved* register, whose value must be preserved by the caller, and a *callee-saved* register, whose value must be preserved by the callee. When a function uses a callee saved register, it must save the register's value in its stack frame in its prologue and restore the value in its epilogue. There are six callee-saved registers on x86-64: `%rbp`, `%rbx`, and `%r12` through `%r15`; all other registers are caller-saved registers.

Fibril exploits these rules to implement a low-overhead context switch scheme to save and resume a Fibril frame's execution state. Listing 2 shows the code for the `parfib` function in Listing 1 with Fibril's macros expanded. In Fibril, a context switch may only happen at a `fibril_fork` or a `fibril_join`. Specifically, if a worker W_1 forks B and W_2 steals the parent A, it resumes A's execution starting from the instruction immediately after the `fibril_fork`; if a worker resumes A after A's children complete, it executes A starting from the instruction immediately after the `fibril_join` that corresponds to the fork.

```
18 typedef struct {
19   int lock;
20   int count;
21   struct { void * rbp, rsp, rip; } state;
22   void * stack;
23 } fibril_t;

24 int parfib(int n) {
25   if (n < 2) return n;

26   fibril_t fr;
27   { // fibril_init(&fr);
28     fr.lock = 0;
29     fr.count = 0;
30   }

31   int x, y;
32   { // fibril_fork(&fr, x, fib, (n - 1));
33     fr.state.rbp = get_frame_pointer();
34     fr.state.rsp = get_stack_pointer();
35     void fork_parfib(int a1, int * ret, fibril_t * f) {
36       f->state.rip = get_return_address();
37       _fibril_push(f);
38       *ret = parfib(a1);
39       if (!_fibril_pop()) _fibril_resume(f);
40     }
41     fork_parfib(n - 1, &x, &fr); clobber_regs();
42   }
43   y = fib(n - 2);

44   if (fr.count > 0) { // fibril_join(&fr);
45     fr.state.rbp = get_frame_pointer();
46     fr.state.rsp = get_stack_pointer();
47     _fibril_join(&fr); clobber_regs();
48   }
49   return x + y;
50 }

51 void _fibril_join(fibril_t * f) {
52   f->state.rip = get_return_address();
53   _fibril_resume(f);
54 }
```

Listing 2: `parfib` with Fibril macros expanded. Names with `_fibril_` prefix are Fibril's runtime routines. Functions shown in *italic* font are implemented using compiler extensions.

To preserve a frame's execution context at a fork or a join, we need to save the values of all registers. For caller-saved registers, since the calling convention requires the compiler to save them before a function call, we rely on the compiler to save them by implementing both `fibril_fork` and `fibril_join` as function calls. In particular, Fibril expands `fibril_fork` into a call to a task-specific nested function (line 41) and expands a `fibril_join` into a call to a Fibril runtime routine `_fibril_join` inside an `if`-block (line 47). GCC implements nested functions using several strategies: (1) when a nested function can be inlined, GCC inlines the function; (2) if the nested function cannot be inlined and it references a variable of its enclosing function, GCC generates a trampoline for the nested function and the nested function uses a general purpose register to reference its enclosing function's variables; (3) if the nested function cannot be inlined and does not reference variables in its enclosing function, GCC treats the nested function as a normal function. Fibril uses a `noinline` attribute to mark the nested function to prevent the compiler from inlining it, therefore GCC will generate code that follows the standard calling conventions for our task-specific nested function, which saves the caller-saved registers before a fork.

For callee-saved registers, we add a special instruction `clobber_regs` to accompany the calls to `fibril_fork` and `fibril_join`. `clobber_regs` is an inline assembly instruction that tells the compiler that the prior call may modify callee-saved registers, causing the compiler to generate code that saves these registers before the call.

Fibril only explicitly saves a frame's frame pointer, `%rbp`, its stack pointer, `%rsp`, and its return address, `%rip`. These values are accessed using GNU builtin functions. Since Fibril does not use a custom compiler frontend, it requires these compiler extensions to generate nested functions, clobber registers, and read the value of the frame pointer, stack pointer, and return address of a frame. However, these extensions are fairly standard; both the GNU C Compiler and the Intel C Compiler support these features.

4.3 Fibril's work-stealing scheduler

We divide the address space of a Fibril program into two spaces: the *application space* and the *scheduler space*. A Fibril program executes its *application code* — user-defined functions and code generated by Fibril's macros — in the application space. For routines of Fibril's work-stealing scheduler, shown in Listing 3, Fibril executes them in the scheduler space. In particular, each worker uses an alternative stack to execute the work-stealing scheduler to avoid collision with threads executing the application code. The `_fibril_resume` function, called when a `pop` fails (line 39) or at a `_fibril_join` (line 47), is the entry point to the scheduler space; it switches a worker's context to the scheduler space and invokes `schedule`. We omit the code for `_fibril_resume` from this paper.

In Fibril, each worker is uniquely identified using a thread-local variable `_wid`. Fibril represents a worker's state using a pair (`stack`, `deque`). A worker's `stack` is a pointer to the stack the worker should use to execute application code. A worker uses its `deque` to `push` and `pop` tasks. We omit the implementation of Fibril's deque, including `push`, `pop`, and `steal`, since it is the same as Cilk's deque [8], which employs Dijkstra's protocol for mutual exclusion [7].

A Fibril frame (defined in line 18) contains a `count` that records the number of pending child tasks of the frame. A frame's `count` is zero initially. When a frame is stolen for the first time, the thief increments the frame's count twice (line 88 and 89) to account for both the parent frame and the child task that was forked earlier.

When a worker completes a child task and attempts to resume its parent by calling `_fibril_resume`, it enters the scheduler space and calls `schedule`. `schedule` first locks the frame the worker is attempting to resume, then decrements the frame's `count`.

If the frame still has pending children, i.e., `count` is larger than zero, the scheduler has to perform randomized stealing to find a task for the worker to execute. Before the worker starts stealing, however, it should check whether the suspended frame resides on top of its current stack (line 62). If the frame is on top of the worker's stack, the worker `unmap`s the unused portion of its current stack and clears the stack from its worker state (line 64). The unused space starts at the stack's address and ends at the page boundary that is just above the top of the stack. It is safe to unmap unused memory pages of the stack because no worker will access the unused space until one resumes the suspended frame. When a worker steals a frame, it will take a stack from a stack pool to execute the stolen frame (line 93).

```
55 typedef struct { deque_t * deque; void * stack; } worker_t;
56 __thread int _wid;
57 worker_t * _workers;

58 void schedule(fibril_t * f) {
59   worker_t * w = _workers[_wid];
60   lock(f);
61   if (--f->count > 0) {
62     if (f->stack == w->stack) {
63       unmap(f->stack, PAGE_ALIGN(f->state.rsp));
64       w->stack = NULL;
65     }
66     unlock(f);
67     random_steal(w);
68   } else {
69     unlock(f);
70     if (f->stack != w->stack) {
71       put_stack_into_pool(w, w->stack);
72       remap(f->stack, PAGE_ALIGN(f->state.rsp));
73       w->stack = f->stack;
74     }
75     execute(f, f->state.rsp);
76   }
77 }

78 void random_steal(worker_t * w) {
79   worker_t * victim; fibril_t * f;
80   while (1) {
81     victim = _workers[rand() % NPROCS];
82     lock(v->deque);
83     f = steal(victim->deque);
84     if (f == NULL) unlock(victim->deque);
85     else break;
86   }
87   lock(f); unlock(victim->deque);
88   if (f->count++ == 0) {
89     f->count += 1;
90     f->stack = victim->stack;
91   }
92   unlock(f);
93   if (!w->stack) w->stack = take_stack_from_pool(w);
94   execute(f, w->stack + STACK_SIZE);
95 }

96 void execute(fibril_t * f, void * rsp) {
97   set_stack_pointer(rsp);
98   set_frame_pointer(f->state.rbp);
99   set_return_address(f->state.rip);
100 }
```

Listing 3: The implementation of Fibril's scheduler.

If all children of the frame that the scheduler is trying to resume have completed, i.e., `count` becomes zero, the worker can resume the frame. If the stack the frame resides on is not the stack the worker is using (line 70), the worker puts its current stack into the stack pool and *remap*s the memory pages of the suspended stack. Then it uses the frame's stack to execute the frame.

Eventually, the scheduler will call `execute` on a frame to transfer the control back to the application space and execute the frame. Note that if the frame is a stolen frame, the worker will execute the frame using a stack pointer that points to the top of a new stack (line 94).

Implementation of unmap/remap.

There are two ways to implement the `unmap`/`remap` routine in Listing 3. Many operating systems provides an interface to change the memory mapping of a virtual address range. For example, Linux provides an `mmap` system call that changes the memory mapping of a virtual address range. To unmap, one can call mmap to change the mappings of the unused address space to an empty dummy file. Since the dummy file will not be accessed, these mappings will not consuem physical memory or incur I/O activity. Note that we cannot implement unmap by calling munmap to free the unused memory pages because the operating system (OS) may give the unused virtual address space back to the memory allocator. Changing the mappings of the unused stack space to a dummy file preserves the address space but frees the physical memory pages. In remap, we can call mmap again to obtain anonymous pages from the OS for the unused portion of the stack.

This approach assumes that a multithreaded process's underlying virtual memory subsystem allows operations that change non-overlapping memory regions of a shared address space to execute concurrently. Unfortunately, most operating systems today serialize these operations. Specifically, widely used OS kernels, such as Linux and FreeBSD, use a single lock per shared address space. System calls that change the shared address space, such as mmap, need to acquire the lock before applying changes.[4] Therefore, mmap will become a bottleneck for Fibril, since multiple workers may call unmap/remap at the same time on different stacks.

On Unix-like systems, one can implement unmap using the madvise system call with the MADV_DONTNEED flag. madvise(..., MADV_DONTNEED) tells the OS that the memory pages of a specified address range are no longer needed and the OS may choose to free the pages. This approach gives the OS the flexibility to free the memory pages lazily, which may yield better performance if the OS has memory to spare and does not need to reclaim the memory pages.[5] More importantly, calling madvise with MADV_DONTNEED does not acquire the address space lock to free the memory pages, which permits concurrent unmap calls. When unmap is implemented using madvise, remap becomes an no-op. Accessing the unmapped address range will trigger a page fault then the OS will allocate a memory page for the accessed address.

4.4 Theoretical bounds

Because Fibril changes the memory mapping to conserve memory footprint, there is a gap between a Fibril program's physical memory and virtual address usage. We analyze bounds on the physical and virtual space separately. We measure space in memory pages, the size of which we leave unspecified. We define the **stack depth** of a Fibril program to be the number of memory pages on the stack in a serial execution of the program. We define the **Fibril depth** of a Fibril program to be the maximum number of Fibril frames on any path from the root to a leaf of the program's invocation tree. We show the following theorems regarding the space and time requirements of a Fibril program.

THEOREM 4.1. *For a Fibril program with stack depth S_1 and Fibril depth D, the Fibril scheduler can execute the program on P processors using DPS_1 pages of virtual address space.*

PROOF. Fibril maintains the busy-leaves property. This implies that, at any given time, the number of leaves in the invocation tree is bounded by P. The stack frames along a path from the root of the invocation tree to a leaf may reside on different stacks. Since a path changes to a different stack only when resuming a stolen Fibril frame, each path may span at most D stacks. Moreover, because each of these stacks may grow to be as large as S_1, each path may use DS_1 virtual address space. Therefore, the bound on the virtual address space is DPS_1. □

Although the bound on virtual address space can be very large for an execution with a deep Fibril depth, it is practical on 64-bit systems because the virtual address space is significantly larger than any realistic value of DPS_1.

THEOREM 4.2. *For a Fibril program with stack depth S_1 and Fibril depth D, the Fibril scheduler can execute the program on P processors using $P(S_1 + D)$ pages of physical memory.*

PROOF. Because the Fibril scheduler maintains the busy-leaves property, the number of leaves in the program's invocation tree is bounded by P. For a path from the root of the invocation tree to a leaf, the stack frames on the path may span multiple stacks. Since a path can only change to a different stack at a Fibril frame, each path may span at most D stacks. Because Fibril unmaps the unused pages of a stack, each dormant stack only contains memory pages that hold stack frames. Because stack frames may not align with page boundaries, there may be a partially unused page at the top of each stack. Since there are at most D stacks, there can be at most D such partially unused pages on a path. Since the stack frames on each path may consume up to S_1 pages, the total number of pages a path may use is $S_1 + D$. Therefore, the program uses at most $P(S_1 + D)$ memory pages. □

Fibril's physical memory bound is a strong bound. Comparing with Blumofe and Leiserson's space bound, it only adds a constant overhead D per processor, staying well below the border of practicality. Fibril's physical memory bound is also a loose bound since it counts every non-leaf frame in the invocation tree more than once. Moreover, we should not expect that every Fibril frame will be stolen. For a program with sufficient parallelism, the number of steals is usually much less than the number of forks.

THEOREM 4.3. *For a Fibril program with work T_1 and span T_∞, the Fibril scheduler can execute the program on P processors in expected time $T_p \le T_1/P + c_\infty T_\infty$, where $c_\infty = O(S_1 + D)$.*

The proof of Fibril's time bound needs complex theoretical analysis that is beyond the scope of this paper. Fibril's time bound trades the constant span overhead c_∞ on the span term of Cilk's time bound for an overhead that is linear in the program's depth $S_1 + D$. This increased overhead reflects the cost of unmapping and remapping a stack's unused memory pages. We consider the cost of changing the mappings of an address space to be linear in the number of mappings it changes. In the worse case, every steal might

[4] In principle, if two mmaps operate on non-overlapping memory regions, these operations should be perfectly parallelizable. Clements et al. applied this principle in the design of a scalable address space for multithreaded applications, called *RadixVM* [6].

[5] Currently, the Linux implementation of madvise(..., MADV_DONTNEED) always frees the memory pages. But this may change in the future.

Table 1: The description of the 12 benchmarks.

Benchmark	Input	Description
cholesky	4000/40000*	Cholesky decomposition
fft	2^{26}	Fast Fourier transformation
fib	42	Recursive Fibonacci
heat	2048×500	Jacobi heat diffusion
integrate	$10^4 (\epsilon = 10^{-9})$	Quadrature adaptive integration
knapsack	32	Recursive knapsack
lu	4096	LU decomposition
matmul	2048	Matrix multiply
nqueens	14	Count ways to place N queens
quicksort	10^8	Parallel quicksort
rectmul	4096	Rectangular matrix multiply
strassen	4096	Strassen matrix multiply

*: 40000 is the number of non-zero values in the matrix.

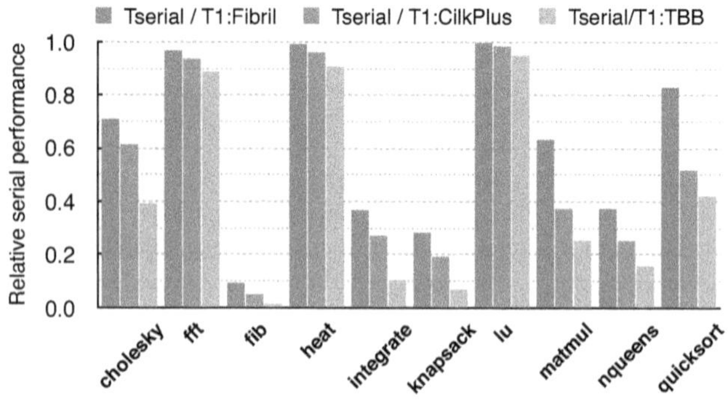

Figure 3: The relative performance on one thread.

cause the scheduler to change the mappings of a worst-case stack of depth S_1+D. One may prove Fibril's time bound by applying the proof techniques of Blumofe and Leiserson [4] or those of Arora et al. [2].

Like the space bound, Fibril's time bound is also a loose bound because not every steal will cause an `unmap` action. Fibril does not unmap a stack if the worker that executes on the stack completes later than the thief who steals the frame on top of the stack. The bound is also a strong bound; it guarantees that a program with sufficient parallelism achieves near-perfect linear speedup. We consider a program has sufficient parallelism if $T_1/T_\infty \gg O(S_1+D)P$.

5. EVALUATION

To evaluate Fibril's performance, we implemented Fibril on an x86-64 architecture. There are three concerns that we investigate in our empirical study:

1. how Fibril's performance compares with other work-stealing runtime systems,
2. whether Fibril's `unmap/remap` routine incurs significant overhead, and
3. how effective is Fibril's `unmap/remap` in reducing the memory footprint of a parallel program.

To address these concerns, we compare Fibril with Intel Cilk Plus [16] and Thread Building Blocks (TBB) [15]. Because Cilk Plus's work-stealing scheduler is similar to that of Fibril, it serves as a fair point of comparison. Intel TBB is similar to Fibril because it is also a library-based implementation of a work-stealing scheduler. We evaluate Fibril using 12 benchmarks. Table 1 briefly describes each benchmark and lists the input size we used for each of them in our experiments. These benchmarks are a representative subset of the benchmarks used in previous studies of work-stealing. We evaluate two variants of Fibril: **Fibril** and **Fibril (w/o unmap)**, where Fibril implements `unmap` using `madvise(..., MADV_DONTNEED)` and Fibril (w/o unmap)'s `unmap` is an no-op. In both versions, `remap` is an no-op.

General Setup.

We ran all experiments on an Intel Haswell system with two 18-core 2.3 GHz CPUs with 2-way simultaneous multi-threading on each core, with a total of 72 hardware threads. The total memory available on the system is 128 GBytes. The operating system ran on the machine is Red Hat Enterprise Linux Server 7.0 (Maipo) with kernel version 3.16.7. All code, both Fibril and the benchmarks, are compiled with GCC 5.2.0. Since GCC 5.2.0 comes with native support for Cilk Plus, we also used it to compile the Cilk Plus versions of the benchmarks. We used Intel TBB 4.4 Update 4 in our experiments. We compiled all code with `-O2` optimization. We performed all experiments ten times and recorded the mean execution time and the maximum stack usage of all ten runs. The standard deviation of our results is negligible. All experiments use 4KB memory pages and 1M stacks. Cilk Plus by default limits the maximum number of stacks its workers can use to 2400. We do not pin threads to physical cores to allow the OS to migrate workers among cores when it sees an oppertunity.

Serial Performance.

Figure 3 shows the relative performance of Fibril, Cilk Plus, and TBB versions of the benchmark on a single thread. We normalize each performance number ($1/T_1$:Fibril, $1/T_1$:CilkPlus, and $1/T_1$:TBB) with the performance of the serial version of the benchmark ($1/T_{serial}$). A number below one indicates that the benchmark's parallel version is slower than its serial version. For instance, the performance of `matmul` using Fibril on one thread is approximately 40% slower than the performance of the serial `matmul`. For all benchmarks we tested, Fibril outperforms both Intel Cilk Plus and TBB. In particular, The Fibril versions of `fib`, `integrate`, `knapsack`, `matmul`, `nqueens`, and `quicksort` outperform those of Cilk Plus by **1.9**×, **1.3**×, **1.5**×, **1.7**×, **1.4**×, and **1.6**×, respectively, and those of TBB by **6.0**×, **3.6**×, **4.2**×, **2.5**×, **2.3**×, and **2.0**×, respectively. These results indicate that Fibril's calling conventions have lower overhead than those of Cilk Plus. Since `fft`, `heat`, `lu`, `rectmul`, and `strassen` perform a large amount of floating point computation within each task, the serial overhead of fork and join operations becomes insignificant. Therefore, the performance of different versions of these benchmarks is almost the same.

Parallel Performance.

Figure 4 shows the performance of the benchmarks on 1–72 threads. We assume the ideal speedup a benchmark achieves is $P\times$ on P threads. Fibril greatly outperforms both Cilk Plus and TBB for most of the benchmarks. In particular, the Fibril versions of `choleskey`, `fib`, `integrate`, `knapsack`, `matmul`, and `nqueens` outperform those of Cilk Plus by **1.4**×, **2.8**×, **1.8**×, **2.2**×, **2.3**×, and **2.1**×, respectively, and those of TBB by **3.0**×, **7.9**×, **4.5**×, **4.8**×, **4.3**×, and **2.8**×, respectively. For other

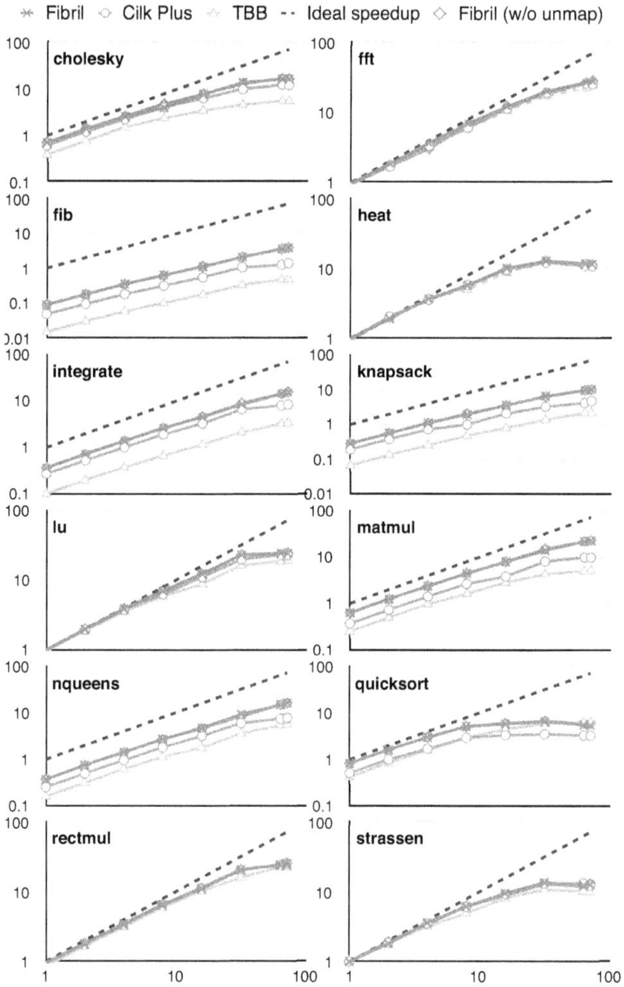

Figure 4: The speedup on 1–72 threads. The X axis are the number of threads, and Y axis values are T_{serial}/T_P, where T_P is the execution time on P threads.

benchmarks, their Fibril versions perform better or similar to their Cilk Plus and TBB versions. Since Cilk Plus's limitation on the total number of stacks a program can use is never reached in our experiments, Fibril's speedup over Cilk Plus is a result of Fibril's better serial performance. Figure 4 also shows that the performance difference between Fibril and Fibril (w/o unmap) is negligible. This indicates that our approach to bound the memory usage is of minimal overhead.

Table 2 lists the average number of key actions performed on 72 threads. Table 2 shows that not every successful steal in Fibril will cause an `unmap` operation. The percentage of steals that cause an `unmap` in Fibril varies from 33% to 92% among the 12 benchmarks. Table 2 also shows that Fibril's `unmap` results in an increase in the number of page faults. This is because a page that is returned to the OS may be accessed again when the suspended frame on the stack is resumed. However, the increase in the number of page faults does not incur significant overhead because the Fibril (w/o unmap) version performs the same as Fibril as shown in Figure 4.

Table 2: Profile of key operations on 72 threads.

	steals	unmaps	page faults		
	Fibril	Fibril	Fibril	Cilk Plus	TBB
cholesky	6568K	2795K	89K	31K	193K
fft	81K	63K	2392K	1475K	346K
fib	20K	12K	6K	3K	9K
heat	579K	452K	10K	10K	9K
integrate	22K	19K	5K	3K	5K
knapsack	13K	12K	1K	2K	1K
lu	2440K	1384K	41K	2K	5K
matmul	92K	62K	13K	10K	69K
nqueens	37K	12K	19K	3K	4K
quicksort	7263K	4005K	1299K	693K	66K
rectmul	43K	33K	3012K	2712K	6472K
strassen	25K	9K	9336K	9494K	23926K

Table 3: Stack space usage in Fibril.

Application	D	S_1	$S_1 + D$	$S_{72}/72$
cholesky	10	2	12	4.82
fft	19	5	24	13.90
fib	41	3	44	8.46
heat	12	1	13	4.49
integrate	32	3	35	8.76
knapsack	32	3	35	5.71
lu	8	2	10	4.92
matmul	10	2	12	4.90
nqueens	14	3	17	6.19
quicksort	69	4	73	9.89
rectmul	24	3	27	9.31
strassen	6	2	8	4.79

Stack Space Utilization.

Table 3 shows the stack footprint of the benchmarks using Fibril on 72 threads. For comparison, we also list the theoretical space bound per thread ($S_1 + D$) in the table. Overall, Fibril's actual stack usage is well below its theoretical bound. Specifically, all of the benchmarks use less than 60% of the stack space of their theoretical bound. This confirms that the space bound in Theorem 4.2 is loose.

Table 4 shows the resident set size (RSS) and stack usage of the benchmarks on 72 threads. The RSSes of Fibril benchmarks are similar to those of Cilk Plus. This may be because Fibril uses more stacks than Cilk Plus to execute these computations. Comparing with TBB, Fibril uses much less memory to execute the same computations.

6. CONCLUSIONS

It is very important for a work-stealing framework to implement a cactus stack that provides interoperability and strong bounds in both time and space. Sacrificing any one of the three criteria can compromise a work-stealing framework's usability or performance. The TLMM approach by Lee et al. [10] is not a viable solution for today's commodity operating systems because it requires custom OS support that is unavailable. Our cactus stack implementation is the first solution to the cactus stack problem that is practical and efficient for use in common systems. We have demonstrated its practicability and efficiency both theoretically and empirically in this paper. Our theoretical bounds ensure a Fibril program's memory usage stays within the range of practicability and guarantee near-linear speedup given sufficient parallelism. Our empirical evaluation shows that Fib-

Table 4: **The RSS and stack usage on 72 threads.**

	ΔRSS / Max RSS			# of stacks	
	Fibril	C.P.	TBB	Fibril	C.P.
cholesky	84/95	81/91	173/184	346	333
fft	1540/2055	1546/2060	1639/2154	334	321
fib	3/6	3/5	108/111	315	297
heat	36/65	31/31	139/175	323	314
integrate	3/6	3/5	97/100	326	310
knapsack	3/6	3/5	106/109	316	326
lu	3/134	3/133	92/224	356	348
matmul	11/54	14/57	123/167	356	348
nqueens	5/5	3/3	113/116	352	314
quicksort	385/769	391/775	883/883	340	323
rectmul	513/772	680/938	1026/1285	335	333
strassen	2434/2694	2762/3020	2603/2862	343	329

C.P.=Cilk Plus. The RSS are reported in MBs. Δ RSS=the incremental RSS during the computation; this excludes the physical memory used for input data and libraries.

ril's approach to bound memory usage is of minimal overhead and Fibril outperforms the-state-of-art work-stealing frameworks on most benchmarks.

7. ACKNOWLEDGMENTS

This work was supported in part by the DOE Office of Science's Advanced Scientific Computing Research Program through Cooperative Agreement number DE-SC0008883. Experiments were performed on a dual-socket Intel Haswell system on loan from Intel.

8. REFERENCES

[1] K. Agrawal, I.-T. A. Lee, and J. Sukha. Brief announcement: Serial-parallel reciprocity in dynamic multithreaded languages. In *Proceedings of the Twenty-second Annual ACM Symposium on Parallelism in Algorithms and Architectures*, SPAA '10, pages 186–188, New York, NY, USA, 2010. ACM.

[2] N. S. Arora, R. D. Blumofe, and C. G. Plaxton. Thread scheduling for multiprogrammed multiprocessors. In *Proceedings of the Tenth Annual ACM Symposium on Parallel Algorithms and Architectures*, SPAA '98, pages 119–129, New York, NY, USA, 1998. ACM.

[3] E. Ayguade, N. Copty, A. Duran, J. Hoeflinger, Y. Lin, F. Massaioli, X. Teruel, P. Unnikrishnan, and G. Zhang. The design of OpenMP tasks. *Parallel and Distributed Systems, IEEE Transactions on*, 20(3):404–418, March 2009.

[4] R. D. Blumofe and C. E. Leiserson. Scheduling multithreaded computations by work stealing. *J. ACM*, 46(5):720–748, Sept. 1999.

[5] P. Charles, C. Grothoff, V. Saraswat, C. Donawa, A. Kielstra, K. Ebcioglu, C. von Praun, and V. Sarkar. X10: An object-oriented approach to non-uniform cluster computing. In *Proceedings of the 20th Annual ACM SIGPLAN Conference on Object-oriented Programming, Systems, Languages, and Applications*, OOPSLA '05, pages 519–538, New York, NY, USA, 2005. ACM.

[6] A. T. Clements, M. F. Kaashoek, and N. Zeldovich. RadixVM: Scalable address spaces for multithreaded applications. In *Proceedings of the 8th ACM European Conference on Computer Systems*, EuroSys '13, pages 211–224, New York, NY, USA, 2013. ACM.

[7] E. W. Dijkstra. Solution of a problem in concurrent programming control. *Commun. ACM*, 8(9):569–, Sept. 1965.

[8] M. Frigo, C. E. Leiserson, and K. H. Randall. The implementation of the Cilk-5 multithreaded language. In *Proceedings of the ACM SIGPLAN 1998 Conference on Programming Language Design and Implementation*, PLDI '98, pages 212–223, New York, NY, USA, 1998. ACM.

[9] D. Lea. A Java fork/join framework. In *Proceedings of the ACM 2000 Conference on Java Grande*, JAVA '00, pages 36–43, New York, NY, USA, 2000. ACM.

[10] I.-T. A. Lee, S. Boyd-Wickizer, Z. Huang, and C. E. Leiserson. Using memory mapping to support cactus stacks in work-stealing runtime systems. In *Proceedings of the 19th International Conference on Parallel Architectures and Compilation Techniques*, PACT '10, pages 411–420, New York, NY, USA, 2010. ACM.

[11] D. Leijen, W. Schulte, and S. Burckhardt. The design of a task parallel library. In *Proceedings of the 24th ACM SIGPLAN Conference on Object Oriented Programming Systems Languages and Applications*, OOPSLA '09, pages 227–242, New York, NY, USA, 2009. ACM.

[12] C. E. Leiserson. The Cilk++ concurrency platform. In *Proceedings of the 46th Annual Design Automation Conference*, DAC '09, pages 522–527, New York, NY, USA, 2009. ACM.

[13] M. Matz, J. Hubicka, A. Jaeger, and M. Mitchell. System V application binary interface AMD64 architecture processor supplement. http://www.x86-64.org/documentation/abi.pdf, October 2013.

[14] J. M. Mellor-Crummey and M. L. Scott. Algorithms for scalable synchronization on shared-memory multiprocessors. *ACM Trans. Comput. Syst.*, 9(1):21–65, Feb. 1991.

[15] J. Reinders. *Intel Threading Building Blocks: Outfitting C++ for Multi-core Processor Parallelism.* O'Reilly Media, Inc., 2007.

[16] A. D. Robison. Composable parallel patterns with Intel Cilk Plus. *Computing in Science and Engg.*, 15(2):66–71, Mar. 2013.

[17] J. Sukha. Brief announcement: A lower bound for depth-restricted work stealing. In *Proceedings of the Twenty-first Annual Symposium on Parallelism in Algorithms and Architectures*, SPAA '09, pages 124–126, New York, NY, USA, 2009. ACM.

[18] D. B. Wagner and B. G. Calder. Leapfrogging: A portable technique for implementing efficient futures. In *Proceedings of the Fourth ACM SIGPLAN Symposium on Principles and Practice of Parallel Programming*, PPOPP '93, pages 208–217, New York, NY, USA, 1993. ACM.

Latency-Hiding Work Stealing

Scheduling Interacting Parallel Computations with Work Stealing

Stefan K. Muller
Carnegie Mellon University
Pittsburgh, PA, USA
smuller@cs.cmu.edu

Umut A. Acar
Carnegie Mellon University
Pittsburgh, PA, USA
umut@cs.cmu.edu

ABSTRACT

With the rise of multicore computers, parallel applications no longer consist solely of computational, batch workloads, but also include applications that may, for example, take input from a user, access secondary storage or the network, or perform remote procedure calls. Such operations can incur substantial latency, requiring the program to wait for a response. In the current state of the art, the theoretical models of parallelism and parallel scheduling algorithms do not account for latency.

In this work, we extend the dag (Directed Acyclic Graph) model for parallelism to account for latency and present a work-stealing algorithm that hides latency to improve performance. This algorithm allows user-level threads to suspend without blocking the underlying worker, usually a system thread. When a user-level thread suspends, the algorithm switches to another thread. Using extensions of existing techniques as well as new technical devices, we bound the running time of our scheduler on a parallel computation. We also briefly present a prototype implementation of the algorithm and some preliminary empirical findings.

1. INTRODUCTION

Recent hardware advances have brought shared-memory parallelism to the mainstream. These advances have motivated significant research and development in programming languages and language extensions for parallelism, including OpenMP, Cilk [15], Fork/Join Java [22], Habanero Java [19], TPL [23], TBB [20], X10 [10], parallel ML [14], and parallel Haskell [21], many of which have had significant impact. In these systems, the programmer expresses parallelism at an abstract level without directly specifying how to create threads and map them onto processors.

In such parallel languages, the runtime system creates the user-level threads, which we simply refer to as threads (they are also known as tasks, strands, sparks, etc.), and relies on a *scheduler* to map the threads onto the processors. The scheduler does not require *a priori* knowledge of the thread structure—it works online as part of the runtime system. The efficiency and performance of a parallel language crucially depends on the scheduler. Many theoretical results have been shown for parallel scheduling, including bounds on runtime and space use [7, 16, 26] as well as locality [1, 6]. Furthermore, the schedulers have been shown to be very effective in practice [15, 2, 30].

The focus of both the theory and experimental analysis of parallel scheduling has been on scheduling computations where threads, once started, are not expected to perform latency-incurring operations, such as waiting for a request from a client or waiting for a response from a remote machine. Popular parallel scheduling algorithms such as work stealing are therefore non-preemptive: they run a thread to completion, never changing to another thread without completing one. This is generally adequate in the traditional applications of parallelism, such as in high-performance computing, where workloads are heavily computational. In such workloads, operations rarely incur latency and thus techniques such as busy-waiting or blocking can be used without significantly harming performance.

Modern workloads of multicore and parallel hardware, however, are not solely computational but also include applications that communicate with external agents such as the user, the file system, a remote client or server, etc. For example, a parallel server may communicate with clients to obtain requests and fulfill them. Since the client may not respond to a request immediately, threads in such an application can incur latency. In such applications, allowing the scheduler to preempt the latency-bound thread and run another thread that can perform useful work could greatly improve performance by *hiding* the latency.

Latency hiding is a classic technique performed by operating system (OS) schedulers. Silbershatz and Galvin's book presents a comprehensive review of these techniques [27]. These techniques, however, are unlikely to carry over to parallel scheduling of user-level threads for several reasons. First, a typical parallel scheduler must carefully control the order in which threads are executed, since it is likely scheduling interdependent threads, while a typical OS scheduler schedules independent jobs which are less sensitive to such ordering. Second, OS schedulers manage a relatively small number of jobs (in the hundreds or perhaps thousands), whereas a typical parallel scheduler will have to manage many more (millions or more) threads. Third, operating system schedulers can use a relatively large scheduling quantum (granularity), whereas parallel schedulers usually schedule fine-grained threads that can perform tiny amounts of work.

SPAA '16, July 11-13, 2016, Pacific Grove, CA, USA

DOI: http://dx.doi.org/10.1145/2935764.2935793

In this paper, we propose a model that represents mathematically the behavior of parallel computations that can incur latency and develop a *latency-hiding* scheduling algorithm for such computations. With our scheduling algorithm, a user-level thread that incurs latency can *suspend*, allowing another thread to run in its place.

Our model (Section 2) extends a standard model of parallel computations as Directed Acyclic Graphs, or dags, by allowing edges of the dag to include non-unit weights that represent the *latency* incurred by an instruction. Computational instructions (e.g., integer or floating point arithmetic) incur no latency. This is represented with unit-weight or *light* edges. Operations that communicate, such as I/O operations, remote procedure calls, or messaging primitives can incur latency, which is represented with non-unit weight *(heavy)* edges. We define the *span* or the *depth* of such a weighted computation dag to include the latency, by calculating the longest weighted path in the dag. As in the traditional model, we use the term *work* to refer to the total computational work of the dag, excluding edge weights.

Our scheduling algorithm (Section 3), like traditional work-stealing algorithms, uses deques (double-ended queues) to store the ready threads to be executed. Instead of one deque per worker, however, our algorithm can use many deques per worker to keep track of suspended threads which were switched out in favor of other work. Our algorithm is online and does not require knowledge of the dag or the edge weights (latencies) but requires knowing which edges are heavy and which edges are light.

To analyze the efficiency of the algorithm, in addition to the traditional notions of work and span, we rely on a notion of *suspension width*, which measures the number of heavy edges that cross a source-sink partition of the computation dag. Suspension width is related to the notion of *s-t* cuts in flow algorithms.

For a dag with W work, S span and $U \geq 1$ suspension width, we prove that the latency-hiding work-stealing algorithm yields a P-processor runtime bound of

$$O\left(\frac{W}{P} + SU(1 + \lg U)\right),$$

amortized and in expectation (Section 3). When $U = 0$, all edges are light (with weight 1). In this case, our algorithm behaves identically to standard work stealing, achieving the bound $O\left(\frac{W}{P} + S\right)$. We note that, in our bounds, work W does not include latency, indicating that our scheduler is able to avoid incurring any latency that does not fall on the critical path (S) of the computation.

We have completed a prototype implementation of the algorithm and obtained some preliminary empirical results (Section 6). These results show that, for computations with significant latency, latency-hiding work stealing can improve speedups compared to the standard work-stealing algorithm, which does not hide latency. Our evaluation also suggests that the factors involving U in the runtime bound might not hinder practical speedups and that our algorithm can handle computations with large numbers of suspended threads.

2. WEIGHTED DAG MODEL

We extend the traditional Directed Acyclic Graph (dag) model of parallel computations to account for computations that may suspend. Throughout the paper, we mostly follow the terminology of Arora, Blumofe, and Plaxton [5].

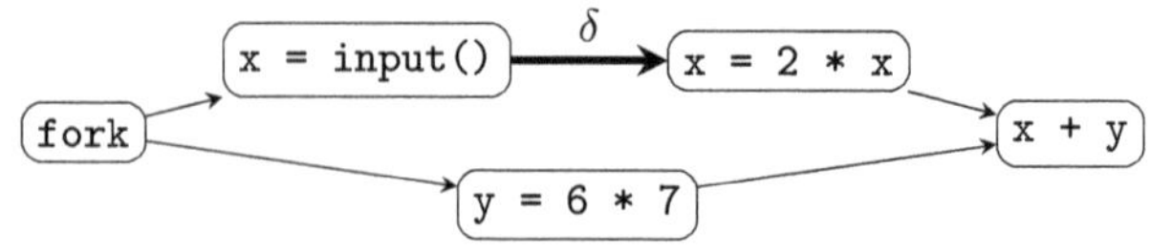

Figure 1: An example weighted dag

We represent a multithreaded/parallel computation with a weighted dag. Vertices of the dag represent single instructions of a thread, each of which is assumed to perform one *step* of work. Operations that require more than one step of work can be represented by a chain of instructions. An edge from u to v indicates a dependence between instructions u and v, requiring u to be executed before v. In a multithreaded or parallel program, an edge from u to v can originate from three conditions: (1) u comes before v within a single program thread; (2) u spawns a new thread whose first instruction is v, (3) the threads containing u and v synchronize, e.g., via a join, requiring u to execute before v. We order the edges in the dag such that when a vertex u spawns a new thread whose first instruction is v, v is the *right child* and the other child, which is the continuation of u in the same thread, is the *left child.*

We label each edge with its latency, a positive integer weight, and write (u, v, δ) for an edge from u to v with weight δ. If $\delta = 1$, then we refer to the edge as a *light* edge. In this case, there is no latency between u and v, and thus v may be scheduled and use the results of u immediately after u executes. If $\delta > 1$, then we refer to the edge as a *heavy* edge. In this case, there is a δ-step latency between u and v, and v may use the results of u only after δ steps. Thus v cannot be scheduled to execute for at least δ steps.

As an example, consider a toy parallel program that creates two threads. The first thread multiplies 6×7 and returns the result. The second thread requests an integer x from the user, doubles x, and returns it. The program then waits for both threads to complete and adds the returned values. Since the user may not respond immediately, the reading of the variable x incurs a latency. Figure 1 shows the dag for an execution of this program where reading the input x takes δ steps. Throughout the paper, the weight of 1 is omitted from light edges, and these are drawn as thin lines while heavy edges are drawn as thick lines. This example demonstrates a common use case of the model in which instructions, like `input()` of the example, perform a unit of work and start an operation (a console input, file read, network operation, etc.) that takes $\delta - 1$ time steps to complete. Such an operation is easily modeled, as in the figure, by a vertex whose outgoing edge(s) has/have weight δ. In the rest of this paper, our examples will be drawn from this simple form of latency-incurring operation, though the model might allow for more general forms of latency.

We make several assumptions regarding dags:

- A dag has exactly one *root*, which has in-degree zero, and exactly one *final vertex*, which has out-degree zero.
- The out-degree (number of outgoing edges) of a vertex is at most two, i.e., an instruction may spawn or synchronize with at most one other thread.
- If vertex v has a heavy incoming edge, i.e., there exists an edge (u, v, δ) with $\delta > 1$, then v has in-degree 1.
- The dag is deterministic, that is, its structure is in-

dependent of the decisions made by the scheduler. In the case of weighted dags, this assumption requires that the latency of an instruction does not depend on when the instruction is executed.

The first two assumptions are common in the literature. The third assumption seems to cause no loss of generality, because a vertex with multiple heavy in-edges can be replaced with multiple vertices, with edges distributed to meet this restriction. The final assumption could be relaxed by considering the set of possible dags and stating time bounds and other properties in terms of the worst case over all possible dags, but we do not consider this here.

We say that a vertex is *enabled* when all of its parents have executed and it is *ready* when it is enabled and all latency requirements expire. Consider a vertex v and let u be the last parent of v to execute. If the edge (u, v, δ) is light, then v is enabled and ready immediately after u is executed. If the edge (u, v, δ) is heavy, then v is enabled immediately after u is executed, but ready only δ steps after u is executed. (Note that by the third assumption above, v has only one heavy in-edge.)

We define the *span* of a weighted dag to be the longest *weighted* path in the dag. If a dag has no heavy edges, then this reduces to the traditional, unweighted notion of span (which simply counts the edges along a path). We define the *work* of a weighted dag as the total number of vertices in the dag. The definition of the work is unchanged from the traditional model—weights do not count toward the work.

To analyze our scheduling algorithm on weighted dags, we introduce a new measure, U, the *suspension width*, of a dag.

DEFINITION 1 (SUSPENSION WIDTH). *Consider a parallel computation represented by a dag $G = (V, E)$ with vertices V and edges $E \subset V \times V \times \mathbb{N}$. Let s be the root vertex and t be the final vertex of G. Let $\mathcal{P}$ be the set of all partitions (S, T) of G (where $S \uplus T = V$ and S and T each induce a connected subdag of G) such that $s \in S$ and $t \in T$. We define the suspension width of G as the maximum number, over all partitions, of heavy edges that cross the partition. More precisely,*

$$U = \max_{(S,T)\in\mathcal{P}} |\{(u, v, \delta) : u \in S, v \in T, (u, v, \delta) \in E \mid \delta > 1\}| .$$

The suspension width of a dag is the maximum number of heavy edges that cross a source-sink partition. This notion is similar to an *s-t cut* in flow networks, which inspires our notation. The main differences are that s-t cuts generally do not require that the cut induce connected components and they include all source-to-sink edges, rather than certain (heavy) edges as we do here.

The suspension width is relevant to scheduling of weighted dags because it is the maximum number of vertices that can be suspended at any point during the run of the computation. To see this, at the end of step i of the execution, let S_i consist of the instructions that have been executed and T_i consist of the instructions that have not been executed. By construction, $S_i \uplus T_i = V$ and S_i contains the root vertex and T_i contains the final vertex. The suspended vertices at the end of step i are exactly those in the set

$$\{v \mid (u, v, \delta) \in E, u \in S_i, v \in T_i, \delta > 1\}$$

Since each suspended vertex has exactly one in-edge, the number of suspended vertices is equal to the number of heavy edges crossing the partition (S_i, T_i) which, by definition is no greater than U.

Offline scheduling problem. Given a dag and a number P of processors (workers), a *schedule* is an assignment of vertices of the dag to worker-step pairs (p, i), such that each worker executes at most one vertex per step and each vertex is ready when it is executed.

The *offline scheduling problem* requires finding a short schedule for a computation represented by a given weighted or unweighted dag on P workers. For unweighted dags, finding an optimal solution is NP-hard [31], but Brent [8] showed that a "level-by-level" schedule on P workers has length within a factor of two of optimal. Future work [12] proved a similar bound for *greedy schedules*, which are defined by keeping all workers busy on steps when there are at least P ready vertices.

We now generalize these results to show that a greedy schedule gives us a similar bound for weighted dags.

THEOREM 1. *Consider a parallel computation with work W and span S. Any greedy schedule of this computation for P workers has length at most $\frac{W}{P} + S$.*

Our proof, which appears in the companion technical report [25], uses much the same technique as the ABP proof for unweighted dags [5]. The intuition is that, if all workers are busy at a step, then they are "making progress" on the work of the computation, but if any workers are idle on a step, then they are "making progress" on the span by executing all vertices at a level in the dag and/or "counting down" the latencies of heavy edges. Our bound is slightly different from that of ABP, $\frac{W}{P} + S\frac{P-1}{P}$, since in weighted dags, at any step, it is possible for all workers to be idle and waiting for suspended vertices, whereas with unweighted dags, at least one worker must be busy at each step.

Online scheduling problem. The *online scheduling problem* for unweighted or weighted dags requires scheduling a dag as its structure is revealed during the execution. In particular, a scheduler operates in *rounds*. On each round, a scheduler may execute an instruction v and learn what new vertices become enabled and possibly ready as a result. Executing v may enable the children of v but not all children of v become ready immediately because they may suspend due to a heavy incoming edge. Furthermore, in the case of weighted dags, the scheduler does not know the edge weights of heavy edges and thus does not know how long it will be before suspended vertices become ready, though it does know whether outgoing edges are heavy or light.

In the rest of the paper, we present an algorithm that solves the online parallel scheduling problem for weighted dags, and an analysis of this algorithm. Our analysis uses the completed dag, including edge weights, in an *a posteriori* fashion, but the scheduler does not use this information since, in general, such information is usually not available in a realistic computation.

3. ALGORITHM

Our algorithm is a variant of work stealing and, as such, uses deques to store the ready vertices to be executed. Instead of one deque per worker (thread), however, our algorithm can use many deques per worker, only one of which is *active* at a time. To obtain work, the worker pops a vertex from the bottom of its active deque. If the worker successfully removes a vertex from the bottom of its deque, it executes that vertex in one step. The execution of the vertex may enable zero, one or two new vertices. If a newly enabled vertex is ready, then it is executed or pushed onto the bottom of the deque in the usual way. If however, the vertex suspends (corresponding to a heavy edge in the dag), the algorithm pairs the suspended vertex with the active deque—the suspended vertex *belongs* to the active deque—and goes back to its active deque to obtain work. If a worker finds its deque to be empty, it first checks if it owns another deque that can become active. If so, it switches to that deque. Otherwise, it becomes a *thief.* To obtain work, a thief randomly chooses any deque and attempts to remove, or *steal*, the vertex at the top of the chosen deque, the *victim.* When a thief successfully steals a vertex, it starts a new deque and makes the new deque its active deque.

The algorithm outlined above is almost complete, except for one crucial point: it does not deal with suspended vertices that resume (become ready). In every round, our scheduler checks for suspended vertices that have resumed since the last round. Since there can be arbitrarily many resumed vertices at a check point, a worker cannot handle them by itself without harming performance. To solve this problem, new work is injected into the computation that will execute the resumed vertices in parallel. More specifically, the scheduler partitions the resumed vertices according to the deques to which they belong and, for each deque, spawns a function that will, in a parallel `for` loop, execute the resumed vertices belonging to that deque.

Figure 3 shows the pseudocode for the algorithm, which we now describe in more detail.

Deques and Sets. Each worker *owns* a collection of deques. Each deque is either *ready*, if it has work, or *suspended* if it is empty and there is a suspended vertex which will eventually be returned to it. At any point, one of the deques of each worker is designated as the *active deque.* The worker also has a set `readyDeques` of its (non-active) ready deques, and a set `resumedDeques` of deques for which a suspended vertex has resumed since the last round. A summary of state changes of deques is shown in Figure 2. Table 1 lists the operations and fields we require for operating on deques, sets of deques, and sets of vertices. We assume that all listed operations take (possibly amortized) constant time. In addition, we assume iteration (using `for` loops) over sets is possible and, in particular, that *parallel* operations over vertex sets are possible (using `pfor` loops) in linear work and logarithmic span in the size of the set.

Several implementations of work-stealing deques exist (e.g. [5, 11, 2]) which provide the required guarantees. Our setting satisfies the requirements of these implementations since each deque is always owned by the same single worker. At the end of this section, we describe an implementation of the other required data structures.

Suspended Vertices. When a vertex v suspends and the active deque is q, a callback `callback(v, q)` is installed to be run when v resumes [1]. The callback adds v to the set `q.resumedVertices`, which tracks the (newly) resumed vertices belonging to q, decrements `q.suspendCtr` to indicate that q has one fewer suspended vertex and, if this has not already been done, adds q to the set of resumed deques.

[1]In practice, this may be implemented by, e.g. signal handlers or polling in a separate (system) thread.

Member	Description
	Deques q
`q.popTop()`	Pop the top vertex of deque `q`
`q.popBottom()`	Pop the bottom vertex of `q`
`q.pushBottom(v)`	Push `v` to the bottom of `q`
`q.free()`	Free the deque `q`
`q.suspendCtr`	A counter of q's suspended vertices
`q.resumedVertices`	A set of q's resumed vertices
`newDeque()`	Create a new, empty deque
`randomDeque()`	Return *any* allocated deque
	Deque sets `qs`
`qs.add(q)`	Add `q` to set `qs`
`qs.removeAny()`	Remove any deque from `qs`
`qs.remove(q)`	Remove `q` from `qs`
	Vertex sets `vs`
`vs.add(v)`	Add `v` to set `vs`
`vs.clear()`	Clear the set `vs`
`vs.size`	The size of set `vs`

Table 1: Deque and set interfaces

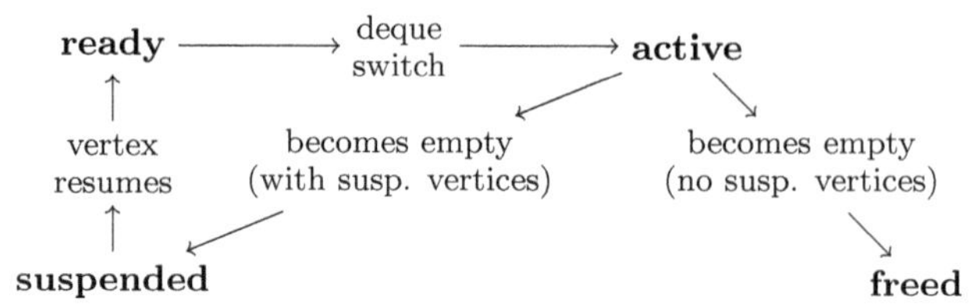

Figure 2: Transitions of deque states

The function `addResumedVertices()` iterates over the set of resumed deques. For each such deque q, a closure is allocated which executes all of the resumed vertices for q in a parallel `for` loop. This closure is encapsulated in a new vertex, which is pushed onto the bottom of q. Finally, q is added to the set of ready deques for this worker.

Scheduling loop. Execution starts by setting one worker's `assignedVertex` to the root of the computation and setting the `activeDeque` of every worker to an empty deque (Line 25 in Figure 3). Execution then jumps to execute the main scheduler loop, shown between lines 31 and 56 of Figure 3. We refer to one iteration of the loop as a *round* of the scheduler. If a worker has an assigned vertex on a round, it takes the following actions:

1. Execute the vertex to get zero, one or two (possibly suspended) children.
2. Handle the right child (if present). If it is suspended, the function `handleChild` increments the suspension counter of the active deque and installs the callback. Otherwise, the child is pushed onto the bottom of the active deque.
3. Call `addResumedVertices()`.
4. Handle the left child (if present) as described above.

Actions 2, 3 and 4 are done in this order so that the left child will have higher priority than the right child and the pfor tree. This ensures that our scheduler is not preemptive: the current task continues running until it finishes.

```
function callback(v, q)
  q.resumedVertices.add(v)
  q.suspendCtr = q.suspendCtr - 1
  if (q.resumedVertices.size == 1)
    resumedDeques.add(q)

function addResumedVertices()
  for (q in resumedDeques)
    v = vertex({ pfor (u in q.resumedVertices)
                   u.execute() })
    q.pushBottom(v)
    readyDeques.add(q)
    resumedDeques.remove(q)
    q.resumedVertices.clear()

function handleChild(v)
  q = activeDeque
  if (v.isSuspended)
    v.installCallback(callback(v, q))
    q.suspendCtr = q.suspendCtr + 1
  else
    q.pushBottom(v)

// Assign root to worker zero.
assignedVertex = NULL
activeDeque = newDeque()  // Initial deque
if (self == WorkerZero)
  assignedVertex = rootVertex

// Run scheduling loop.
while (!computationDone)
  // Execute assigned vertex.
  if (assignedVertex <> NULL)
    (left, right) = assignedVertex.execute()
    if (right <> NULL)
      handleChild(right)
    addResumedVertices()
    if (left <> NULL)
      handleChild(left)
    assignedVertex = activeDeque.popBottom()
  else
    if (activeDeque.suspendCtr = 0)
      activeDeque.free()
      activeDeque = NULL
    // First, try to resume a ready deque.
    new = readyDeques.removeAny()
    if (new <> NULL)
      activeDeque = new
    else  // Make steal attempt.
      victim = randomDeque()
      assignedVertex = victim.popTop()
      if (assignedVertex <> NULL)
        activeDeque = newDeque()
    addReadyVertices()
    if (assignedVertex == NULL)
      assignedVertex = activeDeque.popBottom()
```

Figure 3: Pseudocode for the scheduling algorithm

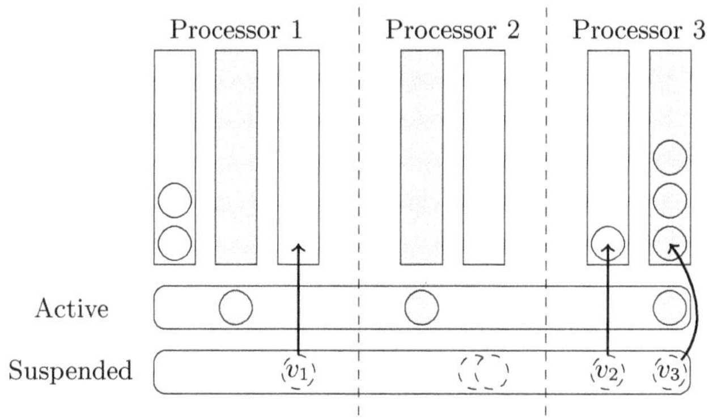

Figure 4: Illustration of work stealing

If a worker doesn't have an assigned vertex, it attempts to switch its active deque to another ready deque. If successful, the new deque becomes the active deque and its bottom vertex becomes the assigned vertex. If all deques are suspended, the worker becomes a thief and steals the top vertex from a randomly chosen deque (note that, unlike in most conventional work stealing schedulers, a steal targets deques and not workers; the victim deque is chosen uniformly at random from all deques). If the steal is successful, `newDeque()` is called to generate a new active deque; the children (if any) of the stolen vertex will be pushed to this new deque. Finally, whether a deque switch or steal attempt occurred, `addResumedVertices()` is called.

Figure 4 illustrates an example state of the scheduler. Active deques and vertices are shown with gray backgrounds. Suspended vertices are shown as dashed circles below the deque with which they are associated. Suppose that, in the next round, suspended vertices v_1, v_2 and v_3 will resume and be returned to their respective deques. Assuming none of the active vertices enable new work, the active deques of processors 1 and 2 will become empty. Processor 1 will switch its active deque. Processor 2 will steal work from one of the other processors and create a new deque. Processor 3 will continue working from its active deque.

Deque and Set implementation. To implement the operations of Table 1 efficiently, the algorithm maintains a global (across all workers) array of deques, called `gDeques`. This may be a growable array (resizes will require a full synchronization and should be rare, in order to amortize the cost of the synchronization and the copy) or, if acceptable for the application, a fixed-size array. There is also a global counter, `gTotalDeques`, which indicates the array index of the next deque to be allocated.

Each worker p maintains a set `emptyDeques` of indices of deques previously owned by p which have been freed by `free()`. Whenever possible, `newDeque()` will reuse a deque from `emptyDeques` rather than allocating a new one. If no empty deques are available, it increments `gTotalDeques` using an atomic fetch-and-add (or other synchronization primitives). The next deque in the array is allocated and becomes the active deque. This implementation of `newDeque()` is shown in Figure 5. The implementation of `free()` does not actually deallocate the deque, but simply adds it to the `emptyDeques` set. The array implementation makes the implementation of `randomDeque()` quite straightforward: it simply chooses a random index between 0 (inclusive) and

```
function newDeque()
  dequeToReturn = emptyDeques.removeAny()
  if (dequeToReturn == NULL)
    i = fetch_and_add(gTotalDeques, 1)
    gDeques[i] = new Deque
    dequeToReturn = gDeques[i]
  return dequeToReturn
```

Figure 5: The newDeque function

`gTotalDeques` (exclusive). The chosen deque may have been "freed", in which case the steal will fail. Since our worst-case asymptotic analysis assumes that the maximum number of deques are allocated, the (somewhat loose) upper bound we prove is not impacted by stealing from freed deques. Our implementation (Section 6) uses a more optimized policy.

A set of deques may be implemented as a doubly-linked list, allowing for constant-time removal. Since removal is not necessary for sets of vertices, but parallel operations (for which lists are unsuitable) are, vertex sets may be implemented as growable arrays, with amortized constant-time addition. In a language with garbage collection, `clear` can be implemented in constant time by simply destroying the pointer to the array. Without garbage collection, the cost of freeing each element can be charged to the corresponding calls to `add`, and so the amortized cost of the three operations will still be constant.

4. ANALYSIS

To bound the running time of the latency-hiding work-stealing scheduler, we first bound the number of rounds in terms of the work of the computation and the number of steal attempts. Based on this result, in Sections 4.1 and 4.2, we establish an upper bound of $O(\frac{W}{P} + SU(1 + \lg U))$ on the expected number of rounds by bounding the number of steal attempts. Our analysis is based on an analysis of work stealing for dedicated environments [3], which simplifies the analysis of Arora et al. [5] for multiprogrammed environments. Finally, in Section 4.3, we use an amortization argument to show that, on average, each round takes constant time. This gives the desired bound on the running time.

We first establish an upper bound on the number of rounds in an execution in terms of the work of the computation and the number of steal attempts (Lemma 1). Our proof accounts for deque switches performed during execution and the additional work injected into the computation to process the resumed vertices. Such additional work comes in the form of the parallel `for` (`pfor`) loops that execute resumed vertices. For n resumed vertices, such a `pfor` loop unfolds into a tree, which we call a *pfor tree* (its vertices are *pfor vertices*) with $\lg n$ span and n leaves, each of which executes one of the resumed vertices (which itself expands into a dag).

LEMMA 1. *Consider a parallel computation with work W and span S executed on P workers by our algorithm. The number of rounds taken to complete the computation is at most $4\frac{W}{P} + \frac{R}{P}$, where R is the number of steal attempts.*

PROOF. At each round, each worker places a token into one of three buckets: the *work bucket* if it executes an instruction (including a pfor vertex), the *switch bucket* if it switches deques or the *steal bucket* if it attempts to steal. At the end of the computation, the number of tokens in the work bucket is equal to $W + W_{pfor}$, where W_{pfor} is the number of pfor vertices. Since a (binary) tree has at most as many internal vertices as leaves and the leaves of a pfor tree are included in W, we have $W + W_{pfor} \leq 2W$. At a round i, if worker p places a token in the switch bucket, it now has an active deque which is ready, and an assigned vertex. It will therefore place a token in the work bucket on round $i + 1$, so at the end of the computation, there are at most as many tokens in the switch bucket as there are in the work bucket, and the number of tokens in these two buckets together is at most $4W$. By definition, the number of tokens in the steal bucket is exactly R. Since P tokens are placed per round, the number of rounds is as desired. □

Given this result, to bound the number of rounds, it suffices to bound the number of steal attempts by $O(PSU(1+\lg U))$.

4.1 Enabling trees and the potential function

An *enabling tree* is a tree derived from a computation dag, which represents the relationship between vertices in a particular execution. As opposed to the computation dag, an enabling tree is a purely runtime notion and there can be many possible enabling trees for a given dag. Enabling trees are not constructed by the algorithm; we simply use them as technical devices for the analysis. In the unweighted case (e.g. [5]), an edge (u, v) of the dag is an *enabling edge* and is included in the enabling tree if executing u enables v. In this way, tracing up from the leaves of the enabling tree gives a record of when vertices were added to deques.

We extend the concept of an enabling tree to account for heavy edges in a way that will be made precise later in this section. In keeping with the intuitive notion of an enabling tree described above, suspended vertices should be added to the enabling tree at the point at which they become ready. This means that heavy edges will not appear in the enabling tree. Consider the computation dag shown in Figure 6(a). When heavy edges and non-enabling light edges are removed from the dag, the suspended vertices that are the targets of these edges (vertices 4 and 9) will have no parent in the dag. This induces a spanning tree consisting of the components of the dag that are connected with only light edges, shown in Figure 6(b). Suppose that, after vertex 3 executes, vertex 4 resumes. We then consider vertex 3 to have enabled vertices 4, 5 and 6 and place vertex 4 in the enabling tree accordingly[2]. If after vertex 5 executes, vertex 9 becomes ready, this relationship is represented in the enabling tree as well. The final enabling tree is shown in Figure 6(c).

The above discussion glosses over two points. First, the construction violates our assumption that vertices have at most two outgoing edges. This is easily solved by adding an additional vertex and distributing the outgoing edges accordingly, a process sometimes called "ternarization". The

[2]The term "enabling tree", which comes from prior work, unfortunately clashes with our terminology, in which vertex 4 was already enabled and is now ready. One way to make sense of this is to think of the enabling tree as building up an unweighted program which is consistent with the execution of the weighted program. For example, the behavior of our scheduler on the example dag "looks like" the behavior of standard work stealing on a dag where vertex 3 is a 3-way fork enabling vertices 4, 5 and 6 (where the out-degree restriction is temporarily relaxed to allow this).

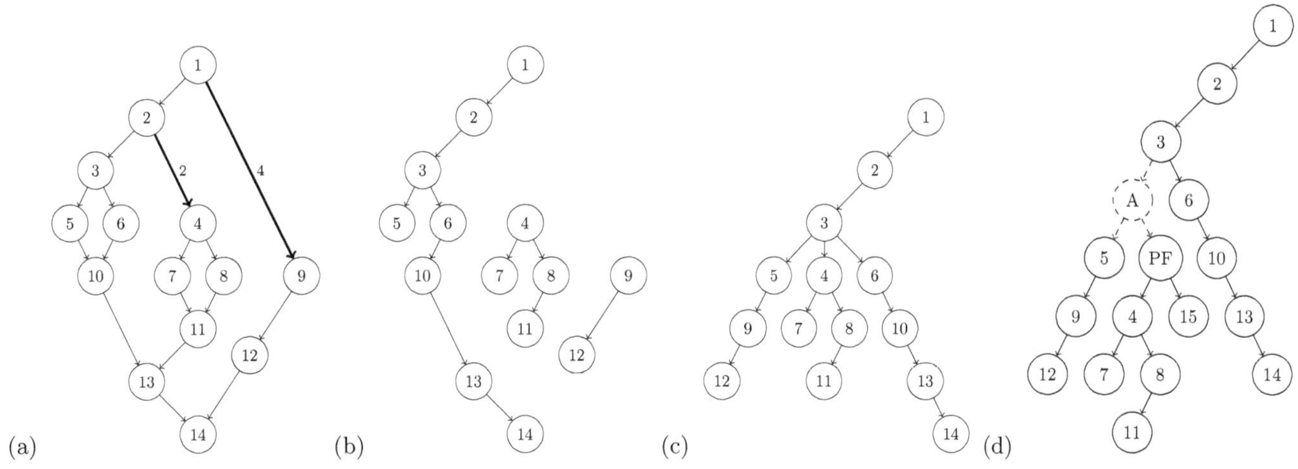

Figure 6: Construction of a possible enabling tree: (a) the input dag (b) spanning forest of the light-edge components (c) the enabling tree (d) the enabling tree with restricted out-degree and pfor trees (assuming a new vertex 15, which resumes at the same time as vertex 4)

exact construction will be detailed below. Second, if multiple suspended vertices resume at the same time, they are not added to the enabling tree directly. Rather, the root of the pfor tree is added at the correct location and it will, in turn, spawn all of the suspended vertices (and their dags). In the context of the example, suppose that there is another vertex, 15, which resumes in the same round as vertex 4. Figure 6(d) shows an enabling tree including an auxiliary vertex A to reduce the out-degree of vertex 3 and a pfor vertex PF, which spawns vertices 4 and 15.

At a more precise level, construction of the enabling tree proceeds as follows. All vertices and all enabling edges (which are all light) are included in the enabling tree. To determine where to add pfor trees in the enabling tree, we proceed by cases on whether the pfor is added to the active deque or a non-active deque. If a pfor vertex v' is added to the active deque, then the scheduler just executed a vertex u from the active deque. Proceed by cases on what kinds of children, if any, u enables. If u enables no children, we simply add an *auxiliary edge* $(u, v', 1)$ to join the pfor tree to u. If u had a left child v, we add an *auxiliary vertex* u' and *auxiliary edges* $(u, u', 1)$, $(u', v', 1)$ and $(u', v, 1)$, where v is considered the left child of u'. If u had a right child r, the edge $(u, r, 1)$ is unchanged. In Figure 6(d), vertex 3 is u, vertex 5 is v, PF is v' and vertex 6 is r.

In the second case, suppose a pfor tree rooted at v' is added to a non-active deque q, and let i be the round in which it is added. If q is non-empty, let u be the bottom vertex in q and j be the round in which it was added to the deque. If q is empty, let u be the last instruction to execute from q and j be the round in which it executed. To maintain the intuitive property that the enabling tree can be used as a record of additions to the deques, we wish to add v' as a descendant of u in the enabling tree. However, it is also important for the analysis to make sure that v' is at a depth in the enabling tree corresponding to when it is added to the deque. To account for the time between when u was executed or added to the deque and when v' is added, we add a chain of $i - j - 1$ auxiliary vertices $u_1, \ldots, u_{i-j-1}$ and auxiliary edges

$$(u, u_1, 1), (u_1, u_2, 1), \ldots (u_{i-j-1}, v, 1)$$

The *depth* $d(v)$ of v in the enabling tree is the length of the path from the root to v in the enabling tree. The depth $d_G(v)$ of v in the original dag G is the length of the longest weighted path from the root to v in G. Let S^* (the "enabling span") be the longest path in the enabling tree at the end of the computation. Observe that, by the time a suspended vertex whose incoming edge has weight δ becomes ready, the worker will not have proceeded deeper than δ levels in the dag (it may even have proceeded fewer, if it backtracked), and so the pfor tree for a suspended vertex v will be reinserted into the enabling tree at a depth no more than a factor of $\lg U$ greater than $d_G(v)$, even considering auxiliary and and pfor vertices. Thus, the enabling span is $O(S(1 + \lg U))$. This key fact will be a direct result of Lemma 2, which shows a number of invariants about the enabling tree and the execution of the scheduler.

LEMMA 2. *Consider an execution of a multithreaded computation represented by a dag G, which results in an enabling tree with enabling span S^*. At the end of a round i, the following conditions hold:*

1. *For all vertices $u \in G$ already executed or currently ready, $d(u) \leq (2 + \lg U)d_G(u)$.*
2. *For all ready or executed pfor vertices u which have depth d in a pfor tree, $d(u) \leq (2 + \lg U)d_G(v) - \lg U + d$ for all v in the pfor tree of u.*
3. *Let u be a suspended vertex whose parent u' came from deque q, with the in-edge (u', u, δ) for some δ, and which was enabled in round $i - k$, for $k \geq 0$. If v was the last instruction executed from deque q and was executed in round $i - j$, for $j \geq 0$, then $d(v) \leq (2 + \lg U)d_G(u') + 2k - j$.*
4. *Let u be a suspended vertex whose parent u' came from deque q, with the in-edge (u', u, δ) for some δ, and which was enabled in round $i - k$, for $k \geq 0$. If v is the assigned vertex of p, then $d(v) \leq (2 + \lg U)d_G(u') + 2(k + 1)$.*
5. *Let $v_1, \ldots, v_k$ be the vertices in any deque, from bottom to top and v_0 be the assigned vertex if this deque is the active deque of a worker. Let $u_0, \ldots, u_k$ be their*

parents in the enabling tree. For all $1 \leq i \leq k$, vertex u_i is an ancestor of u_{i-1} in the enabling tree, and this ancestor relationship is proper for $i > 1$.

The proof appears in the companion technical report [25]. It is now straightforward to show that the enabling tree is no more than a factor of $\lg U$ deeper than the original dag.

COROLLARY 1. *Consider a computation represented by a dag G with span S. When run to completion using the scheduler, if the enabling tree has enabling span S^*, then $S^* \in O(S(1 + \lg U))$.*

PROOF. Let v be the deepest vertex in the enabling tree (that is, $d(v) \geq d(u)$ for all u in the enabling tree). By definition, $S^* = d(v)$. The deepest vertex in the enabling tree will be in G (it will not be a auxiliary vertex or a pfor vertex, since these always have descendants which are in G). By condition 1 of Lemma 2, we have

$$S^* = d(v) \leq (2 + \lg U) d_G(v) \leq (2 + \lg U)S \leq 2S(1 + \lg U)$$

□

We now define the potential function which we will use to show the bound on the number of steal attempts. Let $w(v) = S^* - d(v)$ be the *weight* of a vertex v and define the potential of v at round i as follows:

$$\phi_i(v) = \begin{cases} 3^{2w(v)-1} & v \text{ is assigned at the start of round } i \\ 3^{2w(v)} & \text{otherwise} \end{cases}$$

Each non-active deque with suspended vertices has an extra potential

$$\phi_i^E(q) = \begin{cases} 2 \cdot 3^{2w(v)-2j} & q \text{ is empty} \\ & \text{and last executed } v \text{ in round } i-j \\ 2 \cdot 3^{2w(v)-2j} & v \text{ is the bottom vertex of } q \\ & \text{and was added in round } i-j \\ 0 & q \text{ is the active deque} \end{cases}$$

The extra potential decreases over time, simulating the execution of the chains of auxiliary vertices added to the enabling tree when suspended deques resume. The total potential of a deque q with vertices $v_1, \ldots, v_k$ is:

$$\Phi_i(q) = \phi_i^E(q) + \Sigma_{j=1}^k \phi_i(v_j)$$

4.2 Bounding steal attempts

At the beginning of a round i, let

- A_i be the set of assigned vertices.
- D_i be the set of ready deques.
- S_i be the set of suspended deques.
- $\Phi_i(A_i) = \Sigma_{v \in A_i} \phi_i(v)$
- $\Phi_i(D_i) = \Sigma_{q \in D_i} \Phi_i(q)$
- $\Phi_i(S_i) = \Sigma_{q \in S_i} \Phi_i(q)$
- $\Phi_i = \Phi_i(A_i) + \Phi_i(D_i) + \Phi_i(S_i)$

We note that Φ_i is the total potential for the computation at the start of round i. At the start of the computation, the computation consists only of the root, which has weight S^*, so the potential is 3^{2S^*-1}. At the end of the computation, no vertices are remaining, so the final potential is 0.

The next two lemmas show important properties of the potential function: first, that a constant fraction of the total potential of a deque sits at the top of the deque, accessible to a steal. Next, that executing a vertex decreases the total potential by a constant fraction of that vertex's potential.

LEMMA 3 (TOP-HEAVY DEQUES). *Consider any round i and any deque $q \in D_i$. The topmost vertex in q's deque contributes at least 2/3 of the total potential of q.*

PROOF. It can be shown from Condition 5 of Lemma 2 that if $v_1, \ldots, v_k$ are the vertices of q, then $w(u_1) < \cdots < w(u_k)$. The lemma follows from this fact and the definition of the potential function. □

LEMMA 4. *Consider any round i and let $v \in A_i$.*

$$\Phi_i - \Phi_{i+1} \geq \frac{5}{9}\phi_i(v)$$

PROOF. By cases on what scheduler actions follow the execution of v. □

Furthermore, potential does not increase during computation. The proof of this lemma appears in the companion technical report [25].

LEMMA 5. *For any round i, $\Phi_{i+1} \leq \Phi_i$.*

Lemma 6 is used to show how steal attempts decrease the potential. See [5] for the proof.

LEMMA 6 (BALLS AND WEIGHTED BINS). *Suppose that P balls are thrown independently and uniformly at random into P bins, where for $i = 1, \ldots, P$, bin i has a weight W_i. The total weight is $W = \Sigma_{i=1}^P W_i$. For each bin i, define the random variable X_i as*

$$X_i = \begin{cases} W_i & \textit{if some ball lands in bin } i \\ 0 & \textit{otherwise} \end{cases}$$

If $X = \Sigma_{i=1}^P X_i$, then for any β in the range $0 < \beta < 1$, we have $Pr[X \geq \beta W] > 1 - \frac{1}{(1-\beta)e}$.

To show the bound on steal attempts, we divide the computation into *phases*, with at least $P(U + 1)$ steal attempts in each phase. We will then bound the number of phases. The reason U is relevant in this bound is that, at any time, each worker may have up to $U+1$ deques, each of which may be targeted by a steal. In the parlance of the Balls and Bins Lemma, there are thus $O(PU)$ bins (deques) into which we throw balls (steal attempts). We first show this bound on the number of deques. In the proof, we consider the implementation of `newDeque()` given at the end of Section 3, in which deques are never deallocated but are recycled.

LEMMA 7. *At all times during execution of the scheduler, no worker owns more than $U + 1$ allocated deques.*

PROOF. By induction on the sequence of actions taken by the scheduler. The only action that adds a deque is a call to `newDeque()`, which only occurs on a steal. A steal only occurs if there are no ready deques, and `newDeque()` only allocates a new deque if there are no empty deques (including the active deque, which will have just been added to the list if it is not suspended). Therefore, if a new deque is allocated, all deques owned by the worker must be suspended. There can be at most U such deques. □

We now show that any phase, with constant probability, decreases the total potential by a constant fraction of the potential in the deques.

Lemma 8. *Consider any round i and any later round j such that at least $P(U+1)$ steal attempts occur from rounds i (inclusive) to j (exclusive). Then*

$$Pr[\Phi_i - \Phi_j \geq \frac{2}{9}\Phi_i(D_i)] > \frac{1}{4}$$

Proof. Suppose a steal in round $k > i$ targets a non-empty deque $q \in D_i$, of which v is the top vertex. After round k, vertex v will be assigned (by the thief or by the victim or another thief if there is contention). By Lemma 3, v contributes at least $\frac{2}{3}$ of the potential of q, and assigning it decreases its potential, so

$$\Phi_i(q) - \Phi_{i+1}(q) \geq \frac{2}{3}\phi_i(v) \geq \frac{2}{3}\frac{2}{3}\Phi_i(q) = \frac{4}{9}\Phi_i(q)$$

Next, we use the Balls and Bins Lemma to establish the total decrease in potential. In the setting of the lemma, let $W_q = \frac{4}{9}\Phi_i(q)$ if $q \in D_i$ and $W_q = 0$ otherwise. Therefore, in the setting of the lemma, X is the total decrease in potential after $P(U+1)$ steal attempts and $W = \frac{4}{9}\Phi_i(D_i)$. By the lemma, using $\beta = \frac{1}{2}$, we have

$$Pr[\Phi_j - \Phi_i \geq \frac{2}{9}\Phi_i(D_i)] > 1 - \frac{1}{(1-\frac{1}{2})e} > \frac{1}{4}$$

□

Putting the above results together shows the desired bound on the number of steal attempts.

Theorem 2. *Consider a computation with work W, span S and suspension width $U > 1$. The number of rounds taken by the latency-hiding work-stealing scheduler on P workers is $O(\frac{W}{P} + SU(1+\lg U))$ in expectation.*

Proof. Consider a phase which consists of the rounds $[i, j)$. Let $u \in A_i$. After u is executed on round i, the potential drops by at least $\frac{5}{9}\phi_i(u)$ (by Lemma 4), so we have $\Phi_i - \Phi_j \geq \frac{5}{9}\Phi_i(A_i)$.

Let $q \in S_i$. By the definition of the potential, for some k,

$$\begin{aligned} \Phi_i(q) - \Phi_j(q) &\geq 2 \cdot 3^{2w(v)-2(i-k)} - 2 \cdot 3^{2w(v)-2(j-k)} \\ &= (1 - 3^{2(j-i)})\Phi_i(q) \\ &> \tfrac{8}{9}\Phi_i(q) \end{aligned}$$

Summing over all deques in S_i, $\Phi_i - \Phi_j \geq \frac{8}{9}\Phi_i(S_i)$.

From Lemma 8, we know that $Pr[\Phi_i - \Phi_j \geq \frac{2}{9}\Phi_i(D_i)] > \frac{1}{4}$, so since $\Phi_i = \Phi_i(D_i) + \Phi_i(A_i) + \Phi_i(S_i)$, with probability at least $\frac{1}{4}$, the potential decreases by a factor of at least $\frac{2}{9}$.

Define a *successful* phase to be a phase in which the total potential decreases by a factor of at least $\frac{2}{9}$. Since the starting potential is 3^{2S^*-1} and the final potential is 0 and potential is always an integer, we require at most

$$(2S^* - 1)\log_{9/7} 3 < 10S^* - 5 \in O(S^*) \in O(S(1 + \lg U))$$

successful phases. Since each phase has $\Theta(PU)$ steal attempts, there are $O(PSU(1+\lg U))$ steal attempts in expectation. The desired bound on the number of rounds follows from Lemma 1. □

For the case $U = 1$, no pfor trees will be added and each worker will maintain exactly one deque because when a worker's deque becomes empty, it will always be freed and subsequently reused for the stolen work. A bound of $O(\frac{W}{P} + S)$ rounds for this case can be shown using the same techniques as for the unweighted case [3, 5]

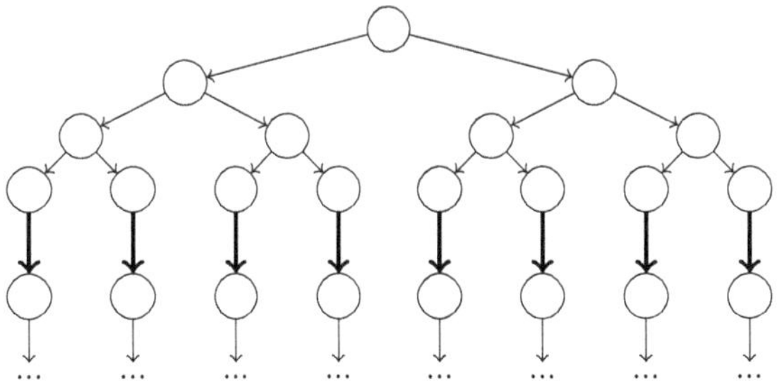

Figure 7: Partial dag for map and reduce

```
function distMapReduce(f, g, id, lo, hi)
  n = hi - lo
  if n = 0 then return id
  else if n = 1 then
    x = getValue(lo) // May suspend
    return f(x)
  else
    piv = (lo + hi) / 2
    (res1, res2) =
      fork2(distMapReduce(f, g, id, lo, piv),
            distMapReduce(f, g, id, piv, hi))
    return g(res1, res2)
```

Figure 8: Example: distributed map and reduce.

4.3 Running time

Each round of the scheduler takes (amortized) time $O(1)$.

Theorem 3. *If I_p is the number of instructions executed by worker p, then $I_p \in O(\frac{W}{P} + SU(1 + \lg U))$.*

Proof. All operations outside of calls to `addResumedVertices()` and callbacks are constant-time. We amortize the non-constant work done by a worker over the rest of the work done by the worker. In particular, we "charge" the work done for a suspended vertex v to v's parent (which was executed by the same worker and spawns at most two children). See the companion technical report for a more detailed version of the proof. □

5. EXAMPLES

The two examples in this section illustrate an application of our techniques and also show how to achieve extremal values of U, which is relevant because the time bound of our scheduler depends on U.

Distributed map and reduce. Consider a computation in which we wish to map a function $f(x)$ over each of a large set of n values x, and then combine the resulting values with an associative binary operation $g(x, y)$ with identity *id*. To introduce latency, suppose that each value is stored on a different remote server (or must be obtained from a remote user). Pseudocode for this example is shown in Figure 8. In this computation, it is possible for each of the n calls to `getValue()` to be suspended at once, and so $U = n$. The top of the dag for this example is shown in Figure 7.

Server. For an example that minimizes U, consider a program similar to the map and reduce example, but which takes its inputs one-by-one from a user. This code appears

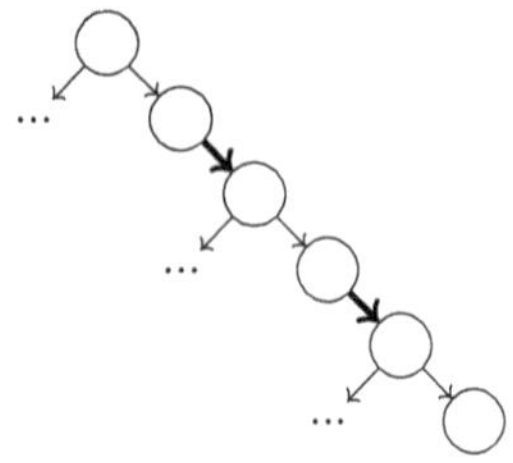

Figure 9: Partial dag for the "server"

```
function server(f, g)
  input = getInput() // May suspend
  if input = "Done" then return 0
  else
    (res1, res2) = fork2(f(input), server(f, g))
    return g(res1, res2)
```

Figure 10: Example: the "server"

in Figure 10. The code gets input from the user. If the user enters "Done", the identity value is returned up the tree. If the user enters a number x, the computation forks; in parallel, $f(x)$ is computed, and a recursive instance of the server is run. In the end, all of the branches join and the values are reduced with g. In this computation, getting user input may incur a substantial amount of latency. However, `server()` is not called recursively until after `getInput()` returns, and so only one operation may be suspended at a time and $U = 1$. Part of this dag is shown in Figure 9, with ... indicating branches that lead to $f(x)$ computations.

6. IMPLEMENTATION

We have developed a proof-of-concept implementation of our scheduling algorithm by extending a more traditional work-stealing algorithm developed by Spoonhower et al. [29, 28] for a parallel implementation of Standard ML. The language has support for fork-join parallelism and futures. Their scheduler and our extension are written entirely in Standard ML. Our implementation largely follows the description in Section 3 with a few exceptions.

- As usual, our scheduler operates at the granularity of threads rather than instructions and is only invoked when the current thread ends, requires synchronization (with another thread) or suspends.
- Suspended threads are placed in a list, tagged with the event on which they are waiting. Each event is polled when the scheduler is invoked. The overhead of this operation is acceptable for reasonable suspension widths and task granularities.
- We sometimes use theoretically less efficient data structures or policies, favoring simplicity and practicality.
- Rather than targeting a random deque, steals target a worker and then choose randomly from that worker's *ready deques*. This requires synchronization between the two workers but decreases the number of failed steals because steals won't target empty deques.

6.1 Preliminary experiments

We implemented a variant of the map and reduce example of Section 5 and performed a preliminary experimental evaluation. In our implementation of this benchmark, we calculate the Fibonacci number of each input using the naive recursive parallel Fibonacci algorithm and sum the results modulo a large constant. In order to control the latency associated with taking each input, the benchmark simulates a latency of δ milliseconds by sleeping for δ milliseconds and then immediately returning 30. Thus each Fibonacci calculation computes the 30th Fibonacci number. We have run this benchmark using both our latency-hiding scheduler and Spoonhower's traditional work-stealing scheduler.

Figure 11 shows the self-speedup curves for our scheduler, labeled LHWS, and the standard work-stealing scheduler, labeled WS. For all curves, the speedup shown is relative to the one-processor run of WS. In all of these experiments, the number of elements (remote server connections)is 5,000. Note that, in this example, this is equal to the suspension width. The first (leftmost) plot shows the case when the latency δ is 500ms (a very high latency, which might represent waiting for user input or for data which requires some computation on a remote server). This plot shows that latency-hiding work stealing delivers superlinear speedups, as much as 3 times larger speedup than standard work stealing. The superlinear speedups are expected with latency hiding because the standard work stealer does not hide latency. In the second plot, δ is 50ms. Latency-hiding still provides substantial speedup benefit. The third plot shows that, when δ is smaller (1ms), there is less benefit to hiding latency. In the limit, if latency is expected to be small, programmers might wish to wait for operations to complete.

7. RELATED WORK

We know of relatively little other work that has considered the problem of scheduling user-level parallel computations which involve operations that may incur a latency.

In terms of the models and analysis presented, perhaps the most closely related work to ours is BATCHER [4], which uses work stealing to schedule threads that perform accesses on a concurrent data structure. In order to avoid synchronizing concurrent accesses, accesses are batched and performed all at once. As a result, an operation on the data structure will block, incurring a latency, until the next batch of operations is executed. A major difference with our work is that, in BATCHER, the scheduler decides when to execute a batch and thus has some control over latency, whereas our scheduler has no control over the latency of an operation. Another difference is that their scheduling algorithm employs two deques per worker, whereas in our algorithm the number of deques can grow dynamically based on the suspension width of the dag and the scheduling decisions.

Many other variants of work stealing have been considered in the literature (e.g., [9, 17, 15, 7, 2]). Mattheis, et al. [24] investigate modifications to work stealing in order to make it suitable for real-time applications, in particular stream processing. They focus on minimizing the completion time (response time) of particular threads; the latency incurred by threads themselves is not considered. Spoonhower [28] presents a comprehensive treatment of work stealing and considers variants with multiple deques per worker. The goal of these variations is to minimize the number of *deviations* from a single-processor depth-first order. In one variation, when a thread waits for another thread or future, the entire deque is suspended and a new one is created. In another,

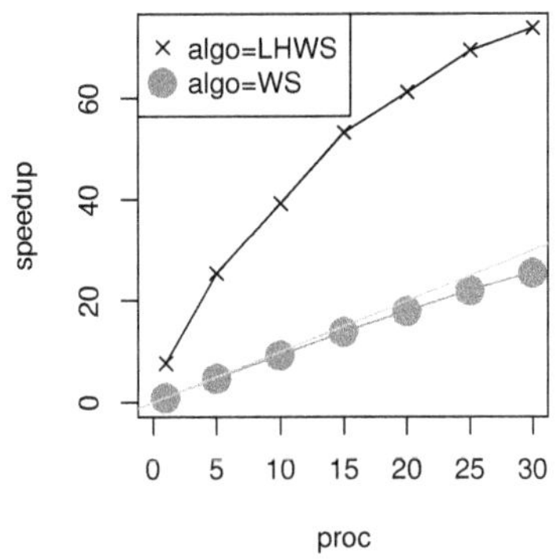

$\delta = 500\text{ms}$

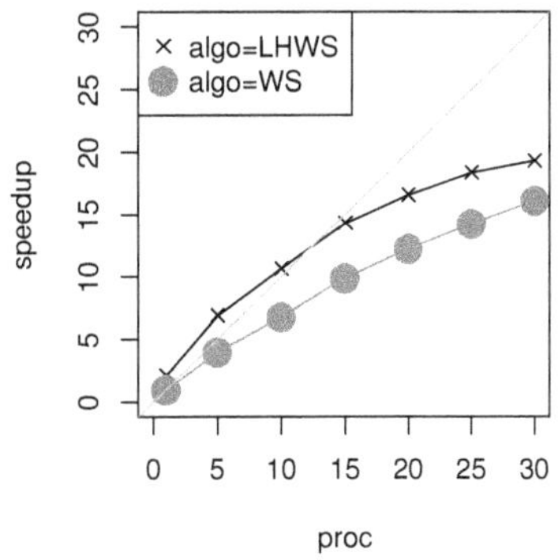

$\delta = 50\text{ms}$

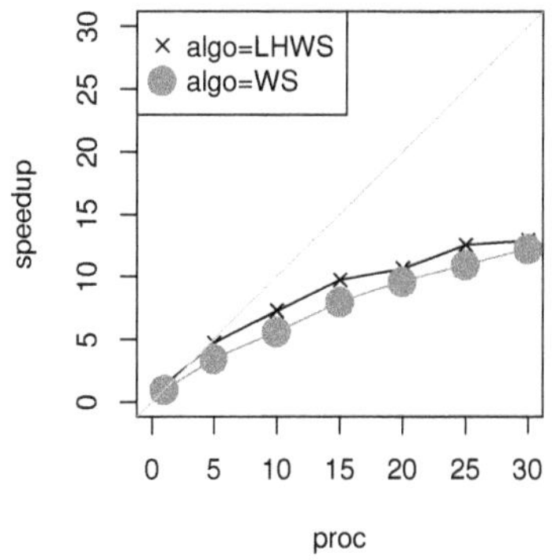

$\delta = 1\text{ms}$

Figure 11: Experimental results of prototype implementation

when a suspended thread resumes, a new deque is created to execute it. Neither of these exactly corresponds to our approach, where a delay does not suspend an entire deque, and new deques are created on steals, not resumes.

In more remotely related work, scheduling for reduced latency has been an important consideration in queuing-theoretic scheduling. For an excellent review of this vast literature, we refer the interested reader to Harchol-Balter's book [18]. The focus of the research in this area is minimizing the latency of a job, i.e., the response time, rather than scheduling a single parallel job that includes operations that can incur latency, which is our focus. Most of the work on queuing-theoretic scheduling considers sequential jobs. One exception is the work on gang scheduling in the context of supercomputing. Feitelson, Rudolph and Schwiegelshohn have a nice survey on this topic [13]. Gang scheduling focuses primarily on the problem of scheduling parallel jobs on a number of processors, rather than scheduling a single parallel job for fast completion.

Many systems use lightweight threads, which allow latency hiding but have higher overhead than fine-grained tasks. As an intermediate approach, Concurrent Cilk [32] schedules tasks using work stealing, but lazily promotes tasks to lightweight threads when they perform blocking operations. Since this is essentially accomplished by blocking the deque of the suspended task and spawning a new lightweight worker thread to start on a new deque, the approach is similar to our algorithm, but Concurrent Cilk spawns new worker threads more eagerly than our algorithm creates new deques. Our approach, which continues to schedule suspended tasks as fine-grained tasks, also avoids the additional state and thread-scheduling overhead associated with (even lightweight) threads.

8. CONCLUSION

In this work, we have extended the traditional dag model of parallel computation to model computations with latency-incurring operations such as I/O, secondary storage access and communication with remote machines. We have also developed a *latency-hiding work-stealing* scheduler, which can efficiently schedule latency-incurring computations without stalling workers when one thread incurs latency and suspends. Our algorithm generalizes standard work-stealing schedulers to use multiple deques per worker, and reduces to the standard algorithm on computations in which no threads suspend. Our theoretical analysis shows that the scheduler is able to hide latency from the typically dominant "work" component but can incur an overhead for latency that falls on the critical path. Finally, our prototype implementation and initial evaluation give evidence that this approach can be practical and has the potential to significantly improve the performance of computations that perform latency-incurring operations without penalizing the computations that don't incur such latency.

Acknowledgments

This research is partially supported by the National Science Foundation under grant numbers CCF-1320563 and CCF-1408940 and by Microsoft Research.

We would also like to thank Guilherme Rito for his contributions to early versions of this work, as well as Guy Blelloch, Robert Harper, Angelina Lee and the anonymous reviewers for their helpful feedback.

References

[1] U. A. Acar, G. E. Blelloch, and R. D. Blumofe. The data locality of work stealing. *Theory of Computing Systems (TOCS)*, 35(3):321–347, 2002.

[2] U. A. Acar, A. Charguéraud, and M. Rainey. Scheduling parallel programs by work stealing with private deques. In *ACM SIGPLAN Symposium on Principles and Practice of Parallel Programming (PPOPP)*, 2013.

[3] U. A. Acar and S. K. Muller. A proof of work stealing for dedicated multiprocessors. Technical Report CMU-CS-16-114, Carnegie Mellon University School of Computer Science, Dec. 2016.

[4] K. Agrawal, J. T. Fineman, K. Lu, B. Sheridan, J. Sukha, and R. Utterback. Provably good scheduling for parallel programs that use data structures through

implicit batching. In *Proceedings of the 26th ACM Symposium on Parallelism in Algorithms and Architectures*, SPAA '14, pages 84–95, 2014.

[5] N. S. Arora, R. D. Blumofe, and C. G. Plaxton. Thread scheduling for multiprogrammed multiprocessors. *Theory Comput. Syst.*, 34(2):115–144, 2001.

[6] G. E. Blelloch, J. T. Fineman, P. B. Gibbons, and H. V. Simhadri. Scheduling irregular parallel computations on hierarchical caches. In *Proceedings of the 23rd ACM Symposium on Parallelism in Algorithms and Architectures*, SPAA '11, pages 355–366, 2011.

[7] R. D. Blumofe and C. E. Leiserson. Scheduling multithreaded computations by work stealing. *J. ACM*, 46:720–748, Sept. 1999.

[8] R. P. Brent. The parallel evaluation of general arithmetic expressions. *J. ACM*, 21(2):201–206, 1974.

[9] F. W. Burton and M. R. Sleep. Executing functional programs on a virtual tree of processors. In *Functional Programming Languages and Computer Architecture (FPCA '81)*, pages 187–194. ACM Press, Oct. 1981.

[10] P. Charles, C. Grothoff, V. Saraswat, C. Donawa, A. Kielstra, K. Ebcioglu, C. von Praun, and V. Sarkar. X10: an object-oriented approach to non-uniform cluster computing. In *Proceedings of the 20th annual ACM SIGPLAN conference on Object-oriented programming, systems, languages, and applications*, OOPSLA '05, pages 519–538. ACM, 2005.

[11] D. Chase and Y. Lev. Dynamic circular work-stealing deque. In *ACM Symposium on Parallelism in Algorithms and Architectures*, SPAA '05, pages 21–28, 2005.

[12] D. L. Eager, J. Zahorjan, and E. D. Lazowska. Speedup versus efficiency in parallel systems. *IEEE Transactions on Computing*, 38(3):408–423, 1989.

[13] D. G. Feitelson, L. Rudolph, and U. Schwiegelshohn. Parallel job scheduling - A status report. In *Job Scheduling Strategies for Parallel Processing (JSSPP), 10th International Workshop*, pages 1–16, 2004.

[14] M. Fluet, M. Rainey, J. Reppy, and A. Shaw. Implicitly threaded parallelism in Manticore. *Journal of Functional Programming*, 20(5-6):1–40, 2011.

[15] M. Frigo, C. E. Leiserson, and K. H. Randall. The implementation of the Cilk-5 multithreaded language. PLDI '98, pages 212–223, 1998.

[16] J. Greiner and G. E. Blelloch. A provably time-efficient parallel implementation of full speculation. *ACM Trans. Program. Lang. Syst.*, 21(2):240–285, Mar. 1999.

[17] R. H. Halstead, Jr. Implementation of MultiLisp: Lisp on a multiprocessor. In *Proceedings of the 1984 ACM Symposium on LISP and functional programming*, LFP '84, pages 9–17. ACM, 1984.

[18] M. Harchol-Balter. *Performance Modeling and Design of Computer Systems: Queueing Theory in Action.* Cambridge University Press, 2013.

[19] S. M. Imam and V. Sarkar. Habanero-Java library: a Java 8 framework for multicore programming. In *2014 International Conference on Principles and Practices of Programming on the Java Platform Virtual Machines, Languages and Tools, PPPJ '14, Cracow, Poland, September 23-26, 2014*, pages 75–86, 2014.

[20] Intel. Intel threading building blocks. 2011.

[21] G. Keller, M. M. Chakravarty, R. Leshchinskiy, S. Peyton Jones, and B. Lippmeier. Regular, shape-polymorphic, parallel arrays in Haskell. In *Proceedings of the 15th ACM SIGPLAN international conference on Functional programming*, ICFP '10, pages 261–272, 2010.

[22] D. Lea. A Java fork/join framework. In *Proceedings of the ACM 2000 conference on Java Grande*, JAVA '00, pages 36–43, 2000.

[23] D. Leijen, W. Schulte, and S. Burckhardt. The design of a task parallel library. In *Proceedings of the 24th ACM SIGPLAN conference on Object Oriented Programming Systems Languages and Applications*, OOPSLA '09, pages 227–242, 2009.

[24] S. Mattheis, T. Schuele, A. Raabe, T. Henties, and U. Gleim. Work stealing strategies for parallel stream processing in soft real-time systems. In *Proceedings of the 25th International Conference on Architecture of Computing Systems*, ARCS'12, pages 172–183, Berlin, Heidelberg, 2012. Springer-Verlag.

[25] S. K. Muller and U. A. Acar. Latency-hiding work stealing. Technical Report CMU-CS-16-112, Carnegie Mellon University School of Computer Science, May 2015.

[26] G. J. Narlikar and G. E. Blelloch. Space-efficient scheduling of nested parallelism. *ACM Transactions on Programming Languages and Systems*, 21, 1999.

[27] A. Silberschatz, P. B. Galvin, and G. Gagne. *Operating system concepts (7. ed.).* Wiley, 2005.

[28] D. Spoonhower. *Scheduling Deterministic Parallel Programs.* PhD thesis, Carnegie Mellon University, Pittsburgh, PA, USA, 2009.

[29] D. Spoonhower, G. E. Blelloch, R. Harper, and P. B. Gibbons. Space profiling for parallel functional programs. In *International Conference on Functional Programming*, 2008.

[30] O. Tardieu, B. Herta, D. Cunningham, D. Grove, P. Kambadur, V. Saraswat, A. Shinnar, M. Takeuchi, and M. Vaziri. X10 and APGAS at petascale. In *Proceedings of the ACM SIGPLAN Symposium on Principles and Practice of Parallel Programming*, PPoPP '14, pages 53–66, 2014.

[31] J. Ullman. NP-complete scheduling problems. *Journal of Computer and System Sciences*, 10(3):384 – 393, 1975.

[32] C. Zakian, T. A. K. Zakian, A. Kulkarni, B. Chamith, and R. R. Newton. Concurrent Cilk: Lazy promotion from tasks to threads in C/C++. In *The 28th International Workshop on Languages and Compilers for Parallel Computing (LCPC 2015)*, 09/2015 2015.

Provably Good and Practically Efficient Parallel Race Detection for Fork-Join Programs

Robert Utterback* Kunal Agrawal* Jeremy T. Fineman† I-Ting Angelina Lee*

*Washington University in St. Louis
*{robert.utterback, kunal, angelee}@wustl.edu

†Georgetown University
†jfineman@cs.georgetown.edu

ABSTRACT

If a parallel program has ***determinacy race(s)***, different schedules can result in memory accesses that observe different values — various race-detection tools have been designed to find such bugs. A key component of race detectors is an algorithm for ***series-parallel (SP) maintenance***, which identifies whether two accesses are logically parallel.

This paper describes an asymptotically optimal algorithm, called ***WSP-Order***, for performing SP maintenance in programs with fork-join (or nested) parallelism. Given a fork-join program with T_1 work and T_∞ span, WSP-Order executes it while also maintaining SP relationships in $O(T_1/P + T_\infty)$ time on P processors, which is asymptotically optimal. At the heart of WSP-Order is a work-stealing scheduler designed specifically for SP maintenance.

We also implemented C-RACER, a race-detector based on WSP-Order within the Cilk Plus runtime system, and evaluated its performance on five benchmarks. Empirical results demonstrate that when run sequentially, it performs almost as well as previous best sequential race detectors. More importantly, when run in parallel, it achieves almost as much speedup as the original program without race-detection.

Categories and Subject Descriptors

F.2.2 [**Analysis of Algorithms and Problem Complexity**]: Nonnumerical Algorithms and Problems—*Sequencing and scheduling*; D.1.3 [**Programming Techniques**]: Concurrent Programming—*Parallel programming*; D.2.5 [**Software Engineering**]: Testing and Debugging—*Testing tools*; E.1 [**Data Structures**]: *Distributed data structures*

Keywords

series-parallel maintenance, determinacy race, race detection, work stealing, order-maintenance data structures

1. INTRODUCTION

A ***determinacy race*** [14] (or a ***general race*** [29]), occurs when two or more logically parallel instructions access the same memory location, and at least one of the accesses is a write. Determinacy races can lead to nondeterministic program behaviors, and as such they are often bugs.[1]

Over the years, researchers have proposed several algorithms [26, 14, 31, 32, 5] for performing race detection "on the fly" as the program executes. These race detectors provide a fairly strong correctness guarantee — for a given input, they report a race if and only if the program contains a race on that input. In general, on-the-fly race detectors include two important components: (1) an ***SP-maintenance data structure*** for maintaining and querying series-parallel relationships between strands of a parallel program online; and (2) a ***memory access history*** that keeps track of (one or two) previous readers and writers for each memory location. On each memory access, the race detector checks whether the current access is logically parallel with these previous accesses to determine whether a race exists.

Since Mellor-Crummey's seminal work [26], most on-the-fly race detectors have adopted similar schemes for maintaining the access history. Where they differ significantly is in how they perform SP maintenance. Not only can SP maintenance significantly impact the overall running time of race detection, but it may dictate that the program (with race detection) must run sequentially. All prior SP-maintenance algorithms have performance drawbacks — either they must execute the program serially [14, 31], they limit the parallelism of the execution [5], or they have high worst-case overhead [26, 32] on memory accesses.

This paper describes ***WSP-Order***, an asymptotically optimal SP-maintenance algorithm for fork-join programs that runs in parallel. Specifically, let T_1 be the ***work***, or sequential running time, of a deterministic computation[2], and let T_∞ be its ***span***[3], or its running time on an infinite number of processors. Then WSP-Order executes the computation while correctly maintaining SP-relationships in expected time $O\left(\frac{T_1}{P} + T_\infty\right)$ on P processors. Since running the computation without SP maintenance also takes $\Omega(\frac{T_1}{P} + T_\infty)$ time, this is the best possible bound and guarantees linear speedup when the computation's parallelism is $\Omega(P)$.

Adding the standard access-history algorithm to WSP-Order, we get a correct and efficient parallel race-detection algorithm. The access history has some inherent overheads due to concurrent updates on reads; therefore, it is diffi-

[1]In contrast, a ***data race*** occurs when the atomicity of critical sections is violated [29].

[2]Henceforth, we shall use the term ***computation*** to refer to a program given a fixed input.

[3]Span is sometimes called critical-path length or depth.

SPAA '16, July 11-13, 2016, Pacific Grove, CA, USA

© 2016 ACM. ISBN 978-1-4503-4210-0/16/07...$15.00

DOI: http://dx.doi.org/10.1145/2935764.2935801

cult to provide good guarantees for race-detection on a weak contention model. Assuming a constant-time priority-write primitive [36], a race detector with WSP-Order executes a program with full race detection (including access history) in expected $O\left(\frac{T_1}{P} + T_\infty\right)$. To our knowledge, this is the first asymptotically optimal parallel race-detection algorithm.

SP Maintenance: WSP-Order achieves its running time through a nontrivial integration of a modified work-stealing scheduler [6] and a parallel version of SP-Order, an SP-maintenance algorithm proposed by Bender et al. [5]. At a high-level, SP-Order uses a pair of order-maintenance (OM) data structures [9, 4] to perform SP maintenance. When running sequentially, SP-Order is asymptotically optimal since OM data structures support constant-time operations. However, it is not immediately clear how to produce an efficient parallel version of SP-Order due to its reliance on the shared OM data structures. To compensate, Bender et al. [5] propose a significantly more complicated algorithm allowing parallel execution, but it has non-constant overhead.

WSP-Order achieves optimal performance without modifying the SP-order algorithm itself. Instead, we modify the scheduler and the OM data structures. A key insight is that SP-Order uses OM data structures in a well structured way — concurrent accesses to the data structures do not logically conflict; therefore, in principle, concurrent updates to the data structure can generally proceed without concurrency control. Occasionally, however, the OM data structures undergo ***relabel operations***, wherein a large portion of the data structure is modified. These relabels, which are necessary to achieve the optimal performance bounds, do conflict with concurrent operations. Coping with relabels in the OM data structure is the main challenge in parallelizing SP-order and achieving asymptotically optimal performance.

The high-level ideas behind WSP-Order are to (1) forbid concurrent accesses during relabels, but otherwise allow all concurrent OM operations to proceed without any significant concurrency control; (2) use parallelism within relabel operations to ensure that they can finish quickly; (3) modify the scheduler to prioritize relabels; and (4) ensure that relabels do not occur "too frequently" by relabeling more eagerly. As we shall see in later sections, these four modifications are sufficient to achieve provably good performance.

Race Detector: Based on WSP-Order, we implemented a race detector, ***C-RACER***, in Cilk Plus [20], a multi-threaded language that supports fork-join parallelism. Empirical results on five benchmarks indicate that C-RACER outperforms an existing state-of-the-art race detector for Cilk Plus [21]. They bear out the claim that WSP-Order is asymptotically optimal — when executing on 16-cores, C-RACER achieves speedups similar to the computation without C-RACER. A breakdown of overheads shows that, the C-RACER's overheads are mostly incurred in access-history management, and the WSP-Order indeed incurs minimal overhead, less than 2× the baseline across benchmarks.

Outline: Section 2 provides background about work stealing, race detection, and OM data structures. Sections 3 and 4 describes the design and theoretical analysis of WSP-Order. Section 5 shows empirical results for C-RACER. Sections 6 and 7 provide related work and conclusions.

2. BACKGROUND

In this section, we start by describing the parallel control constructs for generating fork-join parallelism and the work-stealing scheduler. Next, we describe the abstract data type for the order-maintenance (OM) data structure and how SP-Order uses the it to perform SP-maintenance. We then review how a parallel race detector maintains an access history and detects races. Finally, we describe the order-maintenance data structures and their complexity.

Fork-Join Programs: We will use Cilk Plus keywords to explain the fork-join model; other languages have similar constructs. Parallelism is created using `cilk_spawn`. When a function instance F ***spawns*** another function instance G by preceding the invocation with `cilk_spawn`, the ***continuation*** of F — the statements after the spawning of G — may execute in parallel with G without waiting for G to return. Instruction `cilk_sync` acts as a local barrier; the control flow cannot move past a `cilk_sync` in function F until functions previously spawned by F have returned.

A parallel computation can be represented as a directed acyclic graph (dag). Each node in the dag is a ***strand*** — a sequence of instructions that contain no parallel primitives and therefore must execute sequentially. Nodes become ***ready*** to execute when all their predecessors have executed.

For fork-join computations, the dag is ***series parallel*** [14], meaning that it can be generated by repeated series and parallel composition. A race detector must maintain series-parallel relationships between strands. Formally, a strand x is ***logically precedes*** strand y if and only if there is a directed path from x to y in the computation dag. If there is no directed path in either direction, the two strands are ***logically parallel***.

Work-Stealing Scheduler: During execution, a ***work-stealing*** scheduler [6, 17] dynamically load balances a parallel computation across available ***worker*** threads. Each worker maintains a ***deque***, double-ended queue; when a worker creates new strands, they are placed on this worker's deque. When it completes its current strand, it takes work from the bottom of the deque. If its deque becomes empty, the worker becomes a ***thief*** and randomly chooses a ***victim*** worker to ***steal*** from. Given a computation with work T_1 and span T_∞, a work-stealing scheduler executes it in expected time $\frac{T_1}{P} + O(T_\infty)$ on P processors [6].

Order Maintenance Abstract Data Type: An ***order-maintenance (OM)*** data structure maintains a total order of elements subject to the following operations.

- PRECEDES(x,y): Given pointers to x and y, return *true* if x precedes y in the total order and *false* otherwise.
- INSERT(x,y_1,y_2): given a pointer to existing element x, splice-in new elements y_1 and y_2, in that order, *immediately* after x in the total order. Thus, x and all its predecessors of x precede y_1 and y_2, while all successors of x succeed y_1 and y_2.

It is possible to solve order maintenance in $O(1)$ time per operation[9, 4]. The amortized solutions are simpler (and sufficient for our purposes), but it is possible to achieve the same bounds in the worst case [9, 4].

The SP-Order Algorithm: SP-Order [5] uses two order-maintenance data structures to maintain two different total orderings — called ***English*** and ***Hebrew*** — of all strands in the computation. Figure 1 shows pseudocode for SP-Order.[4]

[4]The original description of SP-Order is with respect to a series-parallel parse tree; we adopt an operational description here.

In the frame of each function F, SP-Order has pointers to elements in English and Hebrew structures representing its currently executing strand. On spawns, it creates nodes for three new strands: the newly spawned function, the continuation strand, and the strand immediately after the corresponding `cilk_sync` (this last one need only be created for the first spawn of the sync block). These three new elements are inserted after the current strand in both orderings. In the English ordering their order is spawn then continuation then sync. In the Hebrew ordering, their order is continuation then spawn then sync. These orderings are sufficient to determine SP relationships; a strand x logically precedes strand y if and only if x precedes y in both orderings.

```
On F spawning G :
if first-spawn = true
  first-spawn = false
  create OM-ELEMENT for F.sync.e and F.sync.h
  OM-INSERT(Eng, F.curr.e, F.sync.e)
  OM-INSERT(Heb, F.curr.h, F.sync.h)
create OM-ELEMENT for G.curr.e, G.curr.h,
F.cont.e, and F.cont.h
OM-INSERT(Eng, F.curr.e, G.curr.e, F.cont.e)
OM-INSERT(Heb, F.curr.h, F.cont.h, G.curr.h)
F.curr.e = F.cont.e;
F.curr.h = F.cont.h

On F passing cilk_sync :
first-spawn = true
F.curr.e = F.sync.e
F.curr.h = F.sync.h

On F calling child H :
H.curr.e = F.curr.e
H.curr.h = F.curr.h

On a called child H returning to F :
F.curr.e = H.curr.e
F.curr.h = H.curr.h
```

Figure 1: The SP-Order algorithm. SP-Order maintains two OM data structures, *Eng* and *Heb*. For a function F, elements representing the currently executing strand are in $F.curr.e$ and $F.curr.h$. $F.cont.e$ and $F.cont.h$ represent F's continuation strand after the spawning of G. $F.sync.e$ and $F.sync.h$ represent the strand after the corresponding `cilk_sync` in F.

We use the SP-Order's SP-maintenance algorithm without modification; therefore, the correctness guarantee follows from correctness of SP-Order (presented in [5]) In addition, while SP-Order was described as sequential algorithm, it works in parallel out of the box if we can insert and query into the English and Hebrew structures concurrently. (The question is performance.)

Detecting Races Using SP-Order: The second main component of a race detector is the access history. WSP-Order maintains an access history, briefly overviewed here, similar to that used by Mellor-Crummey's [26] race detector. For a parallel race detector, it is sufficient for the access history to record the last writer w and two readers — the "left-most" reader lr and the "right-most" reader. When a strand s writes to ℓ, the race detector now performs three queries in the SP-maintenance structure, reporting a race if any s is logically parallel with any of lr, rr, or w. If not, s becomes the last writer. If s reads ℓ, s is only compared against w to find a race as before. However, additional queries are necessary to see if s is the new leftmost reader lr or rightmost reader rr. Since multiple reads can occur in parallel even in a race-free program, more than one reader could try to update these locations concurrently. Therefore, the parallel race detector needs to protect these objects using locks or atomic primitives like compare-and-swap or priority writes.

Overview of Order-Maintenance Implementations: Efficient implementations of order maintenance can provide $O(1)$ time per operation [9, 4] for both inserts and queries using two main insights. First, these use a ***two-level data structure***. Each element is stored in a ***bottom level structure*** which contains a ***group*** of consecutive elements. The groups (i.e., pointers to bottom-level structures) are organized into a single ***top-level structure***. Second, each element and each group has an integer label L_B and L_T, respectively; group labels are unique and element labels within a group are unique. The OM data structure maintains the invariant that element x precedes element y in the total order if and only if (1) $L_T(group(x)) < L_T(group(y))$, or (2) $group(x) = group(y)$ and $L_B(x) < L_B(y)$. Therefore, the PRECEDES query only requires two label comparisons.

An INSERT(x,y) is implemented by trying to inserting y immediately after x in x's bottom-level structure and assigning y a unique label between x and x's successor in the group. If y can be assigned a label, then the insert completes in $O(1)$ time. If y cannot be assigned a label e.g., x's successor has label $L_B(x) + 1$, then the group is ***full***, triggering a ***relabel operation***. A relabel operation consists of two steps: (1) The full group is ***split*** into potentially many groups, the elements therein are assigned new labels that are "spaced apart" allowing for fast future inserts. (2) The (pointers to) the newly created groups are inserted into the top-level structure. During this step, the top level structure is potentially ***rebalanced*** and the group labels may be changed to accommodate these new groups. There are a few details and many different labeling schemes exist, but the important features are (1) the amortized cost of a split is $O(1)$ per insert, and (2) each group contains $\Omega(\lg n)$ elements, so the total number of splits and top-level insertions is $O(n/\lg n)$. The cost of inserting new groups into top-level structure is $O(\lg n)$ on average; combining these features, the amortized cost per insert is $O(1)$.

3. EFFICIENT PARALLEL SP-ORDER

This section discusses how to get an efficient, parallel implementation of SP-order by modifying both the work-stealing runtime system and the OM data structures. Here we present the theoretically optimal design; in our implementation (see Section 5), we slightly modified both the runtime system and the OM data structure for both ease of programming and practical performance.

3.1 Overview

Multiple challenges are involved in obtaining a theoretically efficient parallel SP-Order. First, SP-maintenance may perform *a lot* of OM operations since every spawn or sync translates into OM inserts and each memory access translates to multiple OM queries (see Section 2). In the worst case, the number of inserts and the number of queries can both be $\Theta(T_1)$, where T_1 is the work of the computation. Since all P processors can be continually pounding on the

```
INSERT(x,y) // executed by worker w
1  y_inserted = false
2  repeat
3    g = GROUP(x)
4    if IS_FULL(g)
5      if TRY_ACQUIRE(global_lock)
6        // push RELABEL onto DS deque and
7        START_RELABEL() // switch to DS deque
8      else
9        JOIN_RELABEL() // switch to DS deque
10   elseif TRY_ACQUIRE(w.local_lock)
11     INSERT_INTO_GROUP(g,x,y)
12     y_inserted = true
13     if IS_HEAVY(g)
14       ADD_TO_HEAVY_GROUPS(g)
15     RELEASE_LOCK(w.local_lock)
16   else // local lock not acquired, relabel in progress
17     JOIN_RELABEL() // switch to DS deque
18 until y_inserted = true

RELABEL() // invariant: global lock is held
1  parallel for each worker w
2    ACQUIRE(w.local_lock) // spin until successful
3  Build array H of all heavy groups
4  parallel for each index i of H
5    PARALLEL_SPLIT(H[i])
6  PARALLEL_REBALANCE_TOPLEVEL()
7  parallel for each worker w
8    RELEASE(w.local_lock)
9  RELEASE_LOCK(global_lock)
```

Figure 2: Pseudocode for the insert and the relabel procedures of the OM data structure.

data structures, it is natural to expect an overhead of at least $\Omega(\lg P)$ to coordinate the accesses. Indeed, most concurrent data structures have such overheads (or worse). Nevertheless, our approach avoids this overhead.

A key idea of our approach is to bypass the expensive coordination for most OM operations (inserts and queries). Doing so seems impossible for a general concurrent data structure — after all, some coordination is required to guarantee correctness — but extra structural properties of both SP-Order and the order-maintenance data structures help us. Three key observations that lead to our good design:

1. In SP-Order, all OM insertions are with respect to the strand currently being executed by that worker. Thus, there are no logical conflicts between any concurrent insertions.
2. Barring splits due to relabels, inserting into a bottom-level structure requires only local changes. Consequently, as long as no splits are in progress, concurrent inserts may safely operate on disjoint locations in bottom-level structures.
3. Queries are just comparing labels and groups. As long as no labels or groups are changing, queries and inserts can occur concurrently.

Given these insights, the main idea is simple: resort to a slow concurrency-control mechanisms only during a relabeling.

Even with the reduced concurrency control, a second challenge remains: relabels can be large operations and potentially block inserts and queries. Executing all relabel operations sequentially would make it impossible to provide good speedup. Therefore, (1) we design an OM data structure that implements parallel relabels; and (2) we modify a work-stealing scheduler to prioritize relabels and properly move processors between working on the computation and the ongoing relabel operation as needed. The combination of the two strategies helps speed-up the relabel process.

Finally, the last challenge is that, with a traditional OM data structure, there may be as many as $\Theta(n/\lg n)$ relabel events over the lifetime of an n-element order-maintenance structure. Since a parallel relabel operation incurs $\Theta(\lg n)$ span and each relabel occurs one after another, all relabels together would incur $O(n)$ span, which can be as bad as $O(T_1)$. To allay this problem, we must somehow reduce the number and frequency of distinct relabel events. Recall that, during a relabel, a full group (as implemented by a bottom-level structure) is split into multiple groups. Our solution is to introduce a more aggressive process — once a relabel is triggered, instead of just splitting the full group, we also split all groups that are "heavy," or full enough. This aggressive splitting also introduces more parallelism into the relabel process, since multiple groups can be split in parallel.

In summary, the four main components of our solution are (1) reducing concurrency control except on relabels, (2) parallelizing the relabels, (3) modifying the work-stealing scheduler to prioritize relabels, and (4) reducing the frequency of distinct relabel operations by splitting more aggressively.

The remainder of this section explains each of these in detail. We first explain the mechanism for reducing concurrency control and the scheduler modifications. Then we describe the implementation of the OM data structure used by WSP-Order. Finally, we present how to perform fewer relabels and how to do relabels in parallel.

3.2 Reducing Concurrency Control

To reduce concurrency control, WSP-Order uses a two-level locking scheme. Each processor/worker has a ***local lock*** that it must acquire before performing any data-structure operation (insert or query). There is also a single ***global lock*** to protect relabel. When a relabel is in progress, the relabel process acquires the global lock as well as all the local locks. Therefore, a relabel cannot be concurrent with any insert or query; however, inserts and queries from different workers can proceed concurrently with each other.

Figure 2 shows the pseudocode for the underlying INSERT operation used by OM-INSERT. When a worker w is trying to insert element y after element x, it first checks to see if the group that x belongs to is already full (line 4). If so, w either triggers a relabel process (line 7) if one is not in progress (the global lock is free), or it joins the ongoing one (line 9). If the group is not full, w proceeds to acquire its local lock (line 10) and perform the insert (line 11). If the local lock is not free, a relabel is in progress, and w joins the relabel (line 17). If the local lock is free, the insert always succeeds since the group was not full before the insert. The insert may cause the group to become heavy or full, however, in which case the group is marked as heavy (line 14) and will be split in the next relabel. (We will describe the condition a group being heavy and the relabel process in later subsections.)

There are a few subtleties in the code shown. First, checking if the group is full must be in the loop, since even though w may join an ongoing relabel process, that relabel process may not include g (for instance, the relabel process started before g became heavy). In this case, g remains full after this particular relabel operation finishes, and w will need to recheck g for fullness and possibly start the another relabel operation. Second, the local-lock acquire must also be in the loop, since w may fail to acquire the lock, join the relabel, and must retry the insert again when the relabel ends. Finally, since RELABEL is a parallel operation, the worker who initiated RELABEL's may not be the one who executes its final instruction. Therefore, it is important to release the global lock at the end of RELABEL (as opposed to in INSERT after START_RELABEL returns).[5]

3.3 Scheduler Support to Prioritize Relabels

Since an ongoing relabel prevents other concurrent OM operations, we want an ongoing relabel to finish quickly; moreover, workers blocked on an insert or query should help with the relabel instead of being idle. To prioritize relabels, we modify the work-stealing scheduler as follows. Each worker has two deques, a ***core deque*** and a ***DS deque***. The DS deque is only used to hold work associated with the parallel relabel, and the core deque holds all other work of the program. When workers steal work from some other worker's core deque, they place it on their own core deque, and when they steal work from some worker's DS deque, they place it on their own DS deque. Initially all workers perform work stealing on core deques as usual, switching to the DS deque when starting a parallel relabel operation.

In general, workers prioritize the DS deque, enabling relabels to finishes quickly. In particular, when a worker w starts a relabel (START_RELABEL in line 7), w suspends the current strand, switches to the DS deque to work on relabel, and does not return until discovering that the relabel has finished. Likewise, when a worker w fails to acquire a global or local lock (i.e., a relabel is in progress), w invokes JOIN_RELABEL (in lines 9 and 17), which suspends the current strand, switches to work-steal on the DS deque until the relabel finishes. Finally, when the current deque is empty, w checks the global lock before performing a steal attempt. If the global lock is held, it starts work stealing on the DS deques. If the global lock is free, it operates on the core deque, resuming any suspended strand. If the core deque is empty, it starts work stealing from core deque.

3.4 The OM Data Structure Implementation

Before we describe the parallel relabel and how we reduce its frequency, we must first describe in more detail the implementation of the OM data structure used in WSP-Order.

Bottom-level structure: In sequential versions of OM data structure, the bottom-level structures are typically implemented as linked lists. WSP-Order, however, must iterate over all elements in parallel during relabels. Therefore, in WSP-Order, these are implemented as unbalanced binary tree where each internal node has exactly two children. All the OM elements are stored in the leaves. Each element has an integer label corresponding to its root-to-leaf path (as in a trie), i.e., 0 for left child and 1 for right child, with the root starting from the high-order bit of a b-bit machine word. Any unused trailing bits are implicitly 0s. Each element also stores its depth in the tree (i.e., the logical label length) and its group identifier.

To insert a new element y after an existing element x, first assign y the same group as x. Next, create a new internal node with x and y as the left and right children, respectively, and splice that node in place of x in the tree. Next, assign y the label induced by its root-to-leaf path by appending a 1 to x's label, i.e., $L_B(y) = L_B(x) + 2^{b-depth(x)}$. Finally, record y's depth and implicitly refine the precision of x's label by incrementing x's depth. It is not hard to see that y's label correctly matches the root-to-leaf path to y and that these updates can be performed in constant time. Note that the label induced by x's path does not change since 0s are appended regardless, so concurrent queries on x are not affected by the update.

The structure is considered ***full*** when the depth of any node reaches b — in this case, we no longer have space to insert another node immediately after the currently inserted node while keeping the number of bits in the label at most b. At this point, a relabel is triggered. During a relabel, all the full bottom level structures are ***split*** — that is, all the elements from a full bottom-level structure are partitioned between multiple structures of smaller depth. This leads to a change in labels of all these elements.

Top-level structure: WSP-Order needs to operate on the top-level structure in parallel, so a structure like Dietz's original tree-based version [10] is most appropriate. Here, we describe the basic sequential structure for concreteness, and while some of the details differ slightly from previously published structures, we are not claiming any new ideas here.

The top-level structure is a balanced binary tree where each internal node has exactly two children. Like the bottom-level structures, all elements are stored in the leaves, and each element is explicitly labeled according to its root-to-leaf path. The elements (leaves) of the top-level structure are (pointers to) the bottom-level groups. Since the top-level structure can be much larger than bottom-level structures, we must maintain a balanced tree to ensure that labels fit in a machine word. Therefore, the easy insertion algorithm described earlier is not sufficient. On the other hand, all inserts into the top-level structure occur inside relabel operations, so they are protected by the global lock.

Since the labels of elements change whenever its root-to-leaf path changes, rotation-based balancing schemes do not readily apply. Instead, most implementations of the top-level structure use some form of weight balance. For each node, WSP-Order maintains a ***size*** corresponding to the number of leaves in the node's subtree, and a ***depth*** corresponding to the distance from the root to the node. We say that a node r is ***out of balance*** if some specific conditions on $size(r)$ are not met. When a node becomes out of balance, the entire subtree rooted at r must be rebuilt. It is not important to understand the specific condition used — there are many balance conditions that would work, e.g., scapegoat trees [3, 18]. Rebuilding the appropriate subtree can be easily implemented as parallel tree walks, with $O(size(r))$ work, which is sufficient to achieve $O(\log n)$ work per top-level insert [3, 18].

3.5 Reducing Relabel Frequency

WSP-Order reduces the frequency of relabels by proactively splitting any bottom-level structures that are "not full, but close enough" whenever a relabel occurs. In particular, we say that a bottom-level structure is ***heavy*** when its depth reaches $b/2$, where b is the number of bits in a word. This small change adds much-needed parallelism to relabels by allowing multiple splits to occur during a single relabel.

We make two changes to keep track of heavy lists. First, each bottom-level structure has a bit flag to indicate whether

[5]Our locking implementation allows a lock to be acquired and released by different workers.

the structure is heavy. Second, each worker has a local array that stores a list of heavy groups to be read when performing a relabel. When a worker w performs an insertion that results in a $\geq b/2$-bit label, w performs a test-and-test-and-set on the heavy bit. If w manages to set the bit, then a pointer to this group is added to w's local array of heavy groups; otherwise, w does not retry. This procedure ensures that a heavy group is stored on only one worker's local array and trivially takes $O(1)$ time.

3.6 Parallel Relabels

We now describe how to parallelize the relabel operation. Recall that a relabel operation splits each the heavy groups (bottom-level structures) into potentially many groups and inserts elements representing newly creating groups into the top-level structure, also rebalancing the top-level structure.

Figure 2 also shows the high-level control flow for the RELABEL procedure. It first acquires all local locks in parallel. These lock acquisitions are blocking, retrying until successful. Second, all heavy lists from P workers' local arrays are concatenated in parallel using prefix sums (line 3). Next, in parallel, we split all heavy groups. Since groups may be large, each split is further parallelized using two parallel, recursive tree walks. The first walk calculates the size of the subtree of each internal node. (These calculations are performed in postorder, i.e., when returning from recursive tree walks.) Given a size-m bottom-level tree, the second walk splits the tree into $\Theta(m/b)$ shallow, fully balanced bottom-level trees of size $\Theta(b)$ and depth $\Theta(\lg b)$. One method is to write all elements into an array in order (in parallel) using size information at internal nodes to determine array offsets, split the array into subarrays of $\Theta(b)$ elements, and then recursively build shallow balanced trees of these segments. Pointers to these new groups are stored in an array attached to the original group's node, for easy parallel access.

Rebalancing the top-level tree in parallel is more complicated. Since we split the heavy groups into multiple groups, some leaves in the top level tree (corresponding to groups that were just split) now represent multiple groups and the ancestors of these nodes have a different size now. We must be careful when updating sizes to avoid race conditions on the internal nodes. The process is as follows:

1. For each split group in parallel (i.e., a parallel loop over the list of heavy groups), follow the leaf-to-root path up the tree, marking all ancestor nodes via test-and-set (no locks needed because the races are benign).
2. Recursively walk down the tree in parallel, only along the marked paths, updating the sizes of internal nodes in postorder as before. For the base case, the size of each modified leaf is the number of new bottom-level structures into which that group was split.
3. Recursively walk down the tree again in parallel, stopping the recursion at each branch that finds an out-of-balance node. Note that there may be many out of balance nodes, but starting from the root finds all the highest ones.
4. Rebuild all out-of-balance subtrees in parallel. Similar to bottom-level tree splits, we can first recursively build an array of leaves, and then use this array to construct a new balanced subtree.

Finally, all marked nodes are unmarked in parallel, all heavy arrays emptied in parallel, and then all local locks released in parallel before releasing the global lock.

4. PERFORMANCE ANALYSIS

This section analyzes the running time of a program augmented with WSP-Order to perform SP-maintenance. Our analysis divides the execution into phases. A ***core phase*** is a period during which only core work (the original computation) and inserts and queries to OM data structures occur, but no relabels. A core phase ends when a relabel operation begins, at which point a ***relabel phase*** begins; it ends when the relabel finishes and the next core phase begins.

As long as inserts and queries (apart from relabel) take $O(1)$ time, it is not hard to see that the total time spent in core phases is $T_P = O(T_1/P + T_\infty)$ in expectation for a program with T_1 work and T_∞ span on P processors, following from a standard work stealing analysis [6]. The challenge is stitching together the core phases and the relabel phases. The crux of the argument is to leverage the fact that relabels are provably infrequent, and hence the number of relabel phases is $O(T_P/\log n)$. We then apply a work-stealing analysis to each relabel phase to conclude that they also take $O(T_1/P + T_\infty)$ time overall.

4.1 Performance Model

For our theoretical analysis, we make the following modeling assumptions. These assumptions are common in the related literature but not always called out explicitly.

First, our base model is a transdichotomous RAM [16], meaning that (1) b-bit machine words support standard arithmetic and bit operations in constant time, and (2) all pointers fit in a single word. Therefore $b > \lg n$, and all top-level labels fit in a constant number of machine words. Similarly, $b > \lg P$. Second, we assume that all processors operate at the same speed, e.g., that workers are not swapped out to run an operating-system task. Third, for SP maintenance and work stealing, the basic atomic primitive is a compare-and-swap (CAS). We assume that each CAS completes (possibly failing) in constant time regardless of contention. Finally, we assume that lock (which can be implemented using CAS9) are somewhat fair. That is, if worker w_1 is spinning on a lock, and worker w_2 releases the lock, then we assume that w_1 acquires the lock before w_2 can reacquire it. In WSP-Order, there is never more than one worker spinning on a lock, so this assumption is reasonable. All these assumptions are for performance only, not correctness.

4.2 Core Phases

We argue that OM operations during core phases are fast and bound the total time in core phases.

LEMMA 4.1. *Each data-structure operation performed during a core phase completes in $O(1)$ time and does not conflict with any other operations.*

PROOF. By definition, during the core phase the global lock is not held, and no relabels occur. Thus, an insert operation consists of 1) acquiring the processor's local lock, 2) performing an insert into a bottom-level structure, 3) potentially performing a test-and-set on a group and adding a heavy group to the processor local array of heavy groups, and 4) releasing the local lock. Since there is no competition on local locks when the global lock is not held and test-and-sets are constant-time, each step takes $O(1)$ time. All inserts add new elements after the element representing currently executing strand in the OM structures. Since each strand is executed by a different processor, concurrent inserts operate with respect to different insertion points and there are no conflicts during inserts. Queries are similar, modulo the details of the query itself which also takes $O(1)$ time. To see that inserts do not conflict with queries, it is enough to observe that 1) all queries by SP-order query elements that have already been inserted into the OM structures, and 2) in the absence of relabels, inserts do not change labels of any existing elements. □

LEMMA 4.2. *Consider a P-processor execution of a series-parallel computation augmented to perform SP-maintenance. Let T_1 and T_∞, respectively, denote the work and span of the underlying* a posteriori *computation DAG not counting the SP-maintenance operations. Then the total time spent in core phases, including SP-maintenance operations, is $T_P = O(T_1/P + T_\infty)$ in expectation.*[6]

PROOF. First, create a ***augmented core DAG*** by augmenting every node in the computation DAG by $O(1)$ to reflect the worst-case time of any OM operation apart from relabels (with constant chosen according to Lemma 4.1).

Observe that, using standard work-stealing [6], the augmented core DAG executes in $O(T_1/P+T_\infty)$ expected time on P processors. It remains only to confirm that the execution of core phases is no worse than executing the augmented core DAG. In particular, consider the execution with all relabel phases elided. By Lemma 4.1, all data-structure operations during this subexecution take $O(1)$ time. Moreover, when a processor starts working on its DS deque (only during a relabel phase), it simply suspends works on its core deque and resumes where it left off at the start of the next core phase. The execution thus corresponds to a work-stealing execution of the augmented core DAG, except that some nodes (finished during relabel phases) may be removed for free; specifically some processors (those neither stealing nor performing data-structure operations) may continue to make progress on their core deques during relabel phases, which only improves the time bound of core phases. □

4.3 Relabel Phases

We next analyze the work and span of relabel phases, which we can use to get total time spent in relabel phases by applying a work-stealing analysis. We will subdivide the phases further to consider the running time.

LEMMA 4.3. *The amortized work complexity of each order-maintenance insert is $O(1)$.*

PROOF. This analysis is very similar to the standard order-maintenance analyses, e.g., [9]. The only difference is in our parallel implementations of the structures.

Consider any bottom-level tree that is split, i.e., that is heavy at the start of the relabel phase, and m be the number of elements (leaves) in the tree. The split is implemented as several (parallel) tree walks, so the work is asymptotically the number of nodes in the tree. Since each internal node has 2 children, the number of internal nodes is less than m. The total work is thus $O(m)$.

To get $O(1)$ work per element, we need to charge this $O(m)$ work against $\Omega(m)$ new insertions. Again consider the bottom-level tree. When this tree was created (the result of a previous split), it had $m' = \Theta(b)$ elements, and it was as balanced as possible, i.e., having depth $\lg b + O(1)$. Since it is now heavy, its depth has grown to $b/2$, meaning that it has experienced at least $\Omega(b)$ inserts. We charge the cost of the split against these insertions. That is, we divide the $O(m)$ cost by the $m - m'$ new insertions. Since $m' = O(b)$ and $m - m' = \Omega(b)$, we conclude that $m - m' = \Omega(m)$. The work per insertion is thus $O(m/(m - m')) = O(1)$.

The analysis of rebalancing the top-level structure is similar to that of scapegoat trees [18], where the amortized work of an insert is $O(\lg n)$ as long as the cost of rebuilding a subtree is linear in its size. In WSP-Order, the parallel rebalance process has two components 1) following leaf-to-root paths for each top-level insert, giving a worst-case cost of $O(\lg n)$ per top-level insert, and 2) tree walks, giving cost linear in size of the subtrees walked, which yields $O(\lg n)$ amortized work per the standard analysis. Adding these gives $O(\lg n)$ amortized work per top-level insert. Since each bottom-level structure contains $\Omega(b)$ elements, the number of top-level inserts is $O(n/b)$ and giving the cost per insertion of $O((1/b)\lg n) = O((1/\lg n)\lg n) = O(1)$. □

LEMMA 4.4. *The span of each relabel is $O(b)$, where b is the number of bits in a machine word.*

PROOF. The algorithm first acquires all P local locks. Since local locks are fair, it never has to wait for more than 1 operation to finish before it gets a lock and all non-relabel operations finish in $O(1)$ time. Therefore, it can acquire all local locks in parallel with $O(\lg P)$ span. Concatenating each worker's local list of heavy nodes and then splitting these list in parallel can be done with span $O(\lg P + \lg n)$. Next, bottom-level splits take $O(b)$ to perform divide and conquer on the trees. Finally, the top-level rebuilding has $O(\lg n)$ span to walk up the tree and $O(\lg n)$ span to perform the rebuilding tree walks. Adding these up gives $O(\lg P + \lg n + b) = O(b)$ by the transdichotomous assumption. □

To bound the time in relabel phases, we subdivide the phases further. A ***busy subphase*** occurs while at least $P/2$ processors are still working on the core deques, i.e., since the beginning of this relabel phase, they have neither stolen nor tried to acquire a the local lock to perform data-structure operations. The remainder of the relabeling phase is the ***stealing subphase***, i.e., when most processors are either working off or trying to steal from DS deques. Note that each relabel phase has at most one busy subphase and one stealing subphase the busy subphase starts at the beginning of the relabel phase, and the stealing subphase persists to the end. But it is possible for a relabel phase to be entirely a busy subphase or entirely a stealing subphase.

LEMMA 4.5. *Consider a relabel phase consisting of a w-work relabel. The expected time spent in the stealing subphase is $O(w/P+b)$, where b is the size of a machine word.*

PROOF. By definition of a stealing phase, at least $P/2$ processors are performing work stealing on the DS deque. We can thus apply the work-stealing theorems to a dag with $w+P$ work and b span (Lemma 4.4), where the P work comes from the work of acquiring/releasing all P local locks. This gives expected time $O((w + P)/P + b) = O(w/P + b)$. □

[6]In fact, this bound can be extended to a high probability bound as in [6]. Specifically, with probability at least $1 - \epsilon$, the time is $O(T_1/P + T_\infty + \lg P + \lg(1/\epsilon))$.

4.4 Total Time across Relabel Phases

Consider the time bound in Lemma 4.5. The work term, $O(w/P)$, is good — the work is low (according to Lemma 4.3) and the term implies linear speedup. The problem is the span term of $O(b)$. Specifically, if there are too many relabel phases, e.g., n/b of them, then all we have concluded is that the total time spent in relabel phases is $O(n)$, and we would be better off just running sequentially.

To get a good bound on runtime, we argue next there are not too many relabel phases. We do so by arguing that core phases have to be long.

LEMMA 4.6. *Let T_P be the total time spent in core phases. Then there are at most $O(T_P/b)$ relabel phases.*

PROOF. In 1 timestep of a core phase, each worker can perform at most one insert into the bottom-level structures. Since each insert is to a different node in the tree, the depth of a bottom-level tree increases by at most 1 per timestep.

In addition, at the start of a core phase, all bottom-level trees have depth at most $b/2$. In particular, any trees deeper than $b/2$ are marked as heavy and split during a relabel phase. When split, any new bottom-level trees are built with a height of $\lg b + O(1) < b/2$ for sufficiently large b. Since, by definition, a core phase ends when some bottom-level tree reaches depth b, each core phase requires at least $b/2$ time. It follows that the number of core phases (and hence the number of relabel phases) is at most $O(T_P/b)$ □

We are now ready to sum the time across all relabel phases. We consider the busy and stealing subphases separately.

LEMMA 4.7. *The total time in busy subphases is $O(T_1/P + T_P/b)$, where T_1 is the work of the computation DAG not counting data-structure operations, P is the number of processors, and T_P is the total time of the core phases.*

PROOF. By definition, a busy phase is the time during which at least $P/2$ processors are working on the main computation. Ignoring failed lock acquisitions, each step makes $\Omega(P)$ progress towards the work of the augmented core DAG. Unfortunately, some steps may be unproductive, namely when the local lock acquisition fails. But this can only happen once per processor per relabel phase, after which point the worker shifts to the DS deque. Moreover, all attempts to acquire the lock take $O(1)$ time. The total work, including failed lock acquisitions, is $O(T_1 + PT_P/b)$, where the T_P/b is the number of phases from Lemma 4.6. Dividing by the $P/2$ yields the claim. □

LEMMA 4.8. *The total expected time in stealing subphases is $O(n/P + T_P)$, where n is the number of strands in the computation DAG, P is the number of processors, and T_P is the total time of the core phases.*

PROOF. Applying Lemma 4.5 across relabel phases, the total time across all k stealing phases is $O\left(\sum_{i=1}^{k}(w_i/P + b)\right)$, where w_i is the work of the ith stealing phase. By Lemma 4.3, $\sum_i w_i = O(n)$. By Lemma 4.6, the number of phases is $k = O(T_P/b)$. We're thus left with $O\left(\sum_{i=1}^{k}(w_i/P) + \sum_{i=1}^{k} b\right) = O(n/P + (T_P/b)b)$, which proves the claim. □

4.5 Total Time

Finally, we get the overall running time by adding the time for core phases and relabel phases together.

THEOREM 4.9. *Consider P-processor execution of a series-parallel computation augmented with WSP-Order. Let T_1 and T_∞, respectively, denote the work and span of the underlying* a posteriori *computation DAG, not counting the SP-maintenance operations. The completion time, including SP-maintenance operations, is $O\left(\frac{T_1}{P} + T_\infty\right)$ in expectation.*

PROOF. From Lemma 4.2, the total time in core phases is $T_P = O(T_1/P + T_\infty)$ in expectation. Adding the time in busy and relabel subphases as given in Lemmas 4.7 and 4.8, we get a total time of $O(T_P + (T_1/P + T_p/b) + (n/P + T_P)) = O(T_1/P + T_\infty)$ since $n = O(T_1)$. □

Since executing the computation without maintaining series-parallel relationships also takes $\Omega(\frac{T_1}{P} + T_\infty)$ time, this bound is asymptotically optimal, in expectation.

4.6 Performance of Race Detection

As described in Section 2, in addition to SP-maintenance, a parallel race detector must also maintain an access history which stores one writer w and two readers, lr and rr for each memory location ℓ. When a strand s reads (or writes to) ℓ, it uses the OM data structure to check if s is in parallel with w (or lr or rr) and reports a race if it is. Since each query in SP-Order takes $O(1)$ time, this race-detection operation takes $O(1)$ time per memory access.

There is, however, one subtlety. Strands also update the access history if certain conditions are met, recording their identities. Since concurrent writers only occur in the presence of a race, contention on the last writer is not a performance problem. The readers, however, are another story. Multiple strands reading ℓ simultaneously may be "left of" ℓ's current leftmost reader lr. This means that we need some concurrency control on the access history to avoid losing important updates. Note that this is an issue in all race detectors that run in parallel.

Fortunately, the "left of" (and "right of") relations induce total orders, and only the "leftmost" ("rightmost") reader's update need be performed. One can implement these relations using a priority-write primitive [36]. If priority updates complete in $O(1)$ time, which seems to match performance when the number of locations being updated is large [36], access history updates only adds $O(1)$ work per read. Under that assumption, our race detection algorithm, including the access history, runs in $O(T_1/P + T_\infty)$ expected time.

5. EMPIRICAL EVALUATION

This section evaluates the practical performance of a parallel race detector, C-RACER, that employs WSP-Order for SP-maintenance. We briefly overview the implementation of C-RACER and present experimental results that evaluate C-RACER's overhead and scalability. The results show that a program augmented with WSP-Order (but not access history) generally runs less than 2× slower compared with the baseline running without race detection. Full C-RACER also scales well, tracking the speedups obtained by the baseline and outperforming ***Cilkscreen*** [21], a well-engineered, state-of-the-art serial race detector from Intel when running on two or more cores. Finally, we also measured the frequency of relabel operations, and the results indicate that relabels occur infrequently and the eager splitting of heavy groups can indeed help.

Overview of Implementation: Our parallel race detector, C-RACER, contains multiple components: (1) WSP-

Order including a modified work-stealing runtime system as described in Section 3.3 as well as an implementation of the OM data structure that does parallel relabels and eagerly splits heavy groups; (2) compiler instrumentation for Cilk Plus's parallel constructs and memory accesses; and (3) an implementation of the access history. WSP-Order is based on an implementation of BATCHER [1], which was originally developed by modifying MIT Cilk [17], and we have ported it to Cilk Plus by modifying the Cilk Plus runtime. The instrumentation resembles previous work on tool annotations for Cilk Plus [38]; we have used the instrumentation developed for Cilkprof [34], which is implemented in a branch of LLVM/Clang compiler that contains Cilk Plus language extensions [19]. This branch of LLVM/Clang also implements ThreadSanitizer [35], which provides instrumentation for memory accesses. C-RACER'S access history is maintained with a word (four-byte) granularity.

The actual implementation of C-RACER differs from the theoretical algorithm presented in Section 3 in a few ways. First, in the theoretical algorithm, if the global lock is held, workers always join a relabel operation when they steal. In our implementation, a stealing worker joins a relabel in progress with 50% probability. This scheduling strategy provides the same theoretical guarantees, but the full proof requires an analysis similar to BATCHER [1]. Second, we have implemented the bottom-level groups in the OM data structure as linked lists rather than trees, and the way we assign labels and marking lists heavy treats the lists as flattened trees. Thus the splits of the bottom-level groups are sequential. Third, instead of performing several traversals of the upper-level tree to determine size information, we walk up the tree only once, using atomic fetch-and-add instructions to increment the size of each node. Fourth, as mentioned in Section 2, parallel readers may update the access history for a given location concurrently, and the theoretical algorithm assumes the use of priority write [36]. In practice, we simply acquire a lock whenever we need to update the location of in the access history, with separate locks for the last writer, left-most reader, and right-most reader per memory location. The last three modifications potentially reduce the theoretical parallelism of the computation. However, they improve the overall performance due to lower overheads.

Experimental Setup: We used five benchmarks from the Cilk-5 distribution [17] to evaluate C-RACER. `matmul` performs divide-and-conquer matrix multiplication, `cilksort` runs a parallel mergesort, `fft` calculates a fast-fourier transform, `heat` performs heat diffusion, and `cholesky` calculates the Cholesky decomposition of a matrix.

We ran our experiments on an Intel Xeon E5-2665 with 16 2.40-GHz cores on two sockets; 64 GB of DRAM; two 20 MB L3 caches, each shared among 8 cores; and private L2- and L1-caches of sizes 2 MB and 512 KB, respectively. Running time are in seconds as a mean of five runs. The standard deviation was within 2% of the mean for most configurations, with a maximum of 8% for `cholesky`.

5.1 Overhead and Scalability

To evaluate the overhead of C-RACER, we compare the following configurations:

- **baseline:** execution without race detection;
- **WSP-Order:** execution augmented with WSP-Order but not the access history management.
- **full:** execution running C-RACER with full race detection (i.e., including both WSP-Order and the access history).

We obtain the WSP-Order configuration of C-RACER by turning on only the instrumentation for Cilk Plus's parallel control constructs but not memory accesses, allowing us to measure the overhead of only SP-maintenance (including relabel operations), but not include overheads due to access history management.

We also compare with the execution times of these benchmarks running with ***Cilksan***, a serial race detector that implements the SP-bags algorithm [14] for SP-maintenance, and with ***Cilkscreen*** [21], a well-engineered, state-of-the-art serial race detector from Intel that implements the SP-bags algorithm but instrumented using PIN [25], a binary instrumentation framework from Intel, instead of compiler instrumentation. We have implemented Cilksan for fair comparison, since unlike Cilkscreen, Cilksan uses the same compiler instrumentation and access history management as C-RACER; the only difference between Cilksan and C-RACER is the SP-maintenance algorithm used.

Table 1 presents running times of the different configurations. First, note that the overheads due to WSP-Order (SP-maintenance only) shows minimal overhead compared with the baseline. The benchmark with the highest overhead is `fft`, with 1.78 times overhead. This indicates that WSP-Order can be implemented efficiently. Most of the C-RACER overhead actually comes from the management of access history — full C-RACER incurs another 30–132× overhead, with `heat` being the worst case. This is expected because the WSP-Order performs additional work only at parallel control constructs and function boundaries, whereas the access history management incurs additional overhead on every memory access, and for most applications, the number of memory accesses far exceeds the number of `cilk_spawn`, `cilk_sync`, and function boundaries. The overhead for `heat` is particularly bad, for C-RACER as well as Cilksan and Cilkscreen, since compute-to-memory-access ratio is low.

Across all benchmarks, Cilksan outperforms Cilkscreen, so we compare to Cilksan. The ratio of C-RACER execution time to Cilksan's is generally less than 1.5. As column `full(16)` shows, however, C-RACER utilizes parallelism to significantly outperform Cilksan when running on 16 cores. In fact, as long as the application has some parallelism, C-RACER outperforms Cilksan on 2 or more cores.

To evaluate how well WSP-Order and C-RACER scale, Table 2 shows the speedup for each benchmark as we vary the number of cores used. For most benchmarks, our implementation of WSP-Order scales with the baseline, verifying the theory presented in sections 3 and 4. The exception is `cholesky`, which executes many spawns but only a small amount of work in each strand. In addition, the C-RACER also scales as the number of processors increases, generally at the same rate as the baseline program.

5.2 Detailed Breakdown of Overhead

Figure 3 shows a breakdown of the overheads due to various components of C-RACER for the `fft` benchmark. Due to lack of space, we present this breakdown only for `fft`. We chose `fft` due to the relatively high number of inserts and relabels required, which allows us to show meaningful results here. The x-axis shows the number of cores used, and the y-axis shows the aggregate processing time (i.e., number of cores used × wall-clock time) in seconds. As

	base	WSP-Order	full(1)	full(16)	Cilksan	Cilkscreen
matmul	15.69	16.22 (1.03×)	499.61 (31.84×)	31.79 (2.03×)	408.49 (26.04×)	922.23 (58.78×)
cilksort	3.20	3.38 (1.06×)	113.29 (35.40×)	10.81 (3.38×)	73.71 (23.03×)	99.82 (31.19×)
fft	18.34	32.73 (1.78×)	878.17 (47.88×)	81.34 (4.44×)	523.94 (28.57×)	991.29 (54.05×)
heat	7.33	7.73 (1.05×)	1026.70 (140.07×)	79.55 (10.85×)	726.89 (99.17×)	1202.29 (164.02×)
cholesky	5.96	7.44 (1.25×)	687.88 (115.42×)	45.45 (7.63×)	666.66 (111.86×)	962.34 (161.47×)

Table 1: Execution times for five benchmarks, in seconds. The `full(16)` column shows the execution time of the full configuration of C-RACER running on 16 cores. All other columns show the execution time on a single core. The numbers in parenthesis indicates the overhead comparing with the baseline running serially.

		P				
		2	4	8	12	16
matmul	base	2.00	3.99	7.97	11.88	15.64
	WSP-Order	1.98	3.95	7.87	11.68	15.56
	full	2.00	3.98	7.95	11.82	15.71
cilksort	base	1.99	3.98	7.81	11.17	13.37
	WSP-Order	1.98	3.94	7.71	10.82	13.31
	full	1.92	3.51	6.25	8.19	10.48
fft	base	1.77	3.43	6.12	8.16	9.60
	WSP-Order	1.80	3.31	6.06	8.20	10.00
	full	1.71	3.27	6.43	8.81	10.80
heat	base	1.99	3.63	5.22	7.09	6.71
	WSP-Order	1.98	3.56	5.44	6.62	7.33
	full	2.06	3.86	7.43	10.71	12.91
cholesky	base	1.99	3.96	7.83	11.31	14.69
	WSP-Order	1.86	3.54	6.65	8.73	10.28
	full	1.98	3.87	7.64	11.44	15.13

Table 2: Speedup over the sequential version when running with different configurations. For each configuration, the speedup is computed with respect to the running time of the same configuration running on one core.

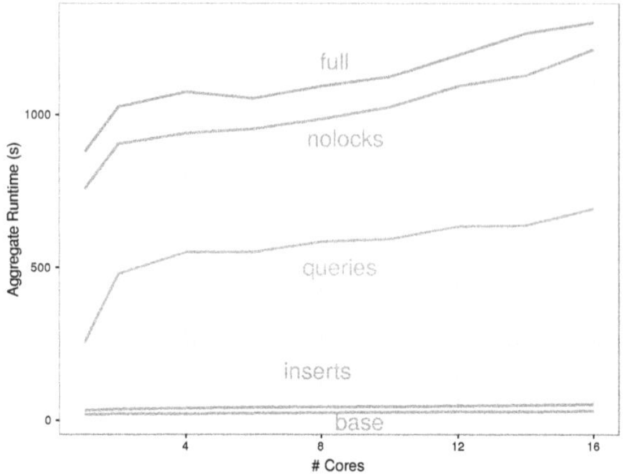

Figure 3: Detailed breakdown of C-RACER overheads for fft, in seconds. The lines `base` and `inserts` show the overall processing time when running the baseline and inserts configuration described earlier. The line `queries` shows the processing time after including the overhead for queries on top of the inserts configuration. The line `nolocks` shows the processing time of C-RACER running in full configuration but does not acquire locks when updating the shadow memory. The line `full` shows the overall processing time of C-RACER running in the full configuration.

the WSP-Order line shows, access history contributes the bulk of the overhead. The other three lines break down the overheads of various components of maintaining the access history. As explained in Section 2, the access history records three strands per memory location and on every access, the race detector queries both OM data structures with the current strands and all three strands, updating the access history as necessary. As shown in breakdown, half of the overhead of access history management is due to the 6 queries and the other half is due to checking and updating the access history. Moreover, whenever a strand s tries to update the shadow memory, it must acquire a lock. This locking overhead (the gap between lines `nolocks` and `full`) appears to be relatively small.

5.3 Effect of Eagerly Splitting Heavy Groups

We now analyze the effect of our modification to OM data structure where instead of only splitting full bottom-level groups, we eagerly split heavy groups. Recall that a tree is full when its depth reaches b and we set the heavy threshold as 50%; that is, a tree is considered heavy when it has depth $b/2$. In practice, we have implemented the bottom-level groups using lists, which means that we mark a list heavy when we discover a label with $b/2$ bits used before trailing 0s. We ask a few different questions here: (1) Does the eager splitting reduce the total number of relabels? (2) How many more splits do we get due to eagerly splitting trees? (3) What effect does the heavy threshold have on the number of relabels and the number of splits?

Table 3 shows the stats of relabel operations for three benchmarks running with C-RACER on 16 cores. These numbers are from a single run; general trends are similar across runs. We varied the heavy threshold (described here as the percentage of the total bits in a label — 64 in our case). For the most part, relabels occur infrequently; in fact, we omit the results for `matmul` and `cilksort` because their executions contain no relabels even for very large input sizes. For `heat` and `cholesky`, some relabels occur but not many. We see that the total number of heavy groups decreases as we increase the heavy threshold, but the number of relabels does not change. This makes sense, since with a lower threshold, more groups get marked as heavy early, but no relabel is triggered until some group becomes full.

The interesting one is `fft`, which triggers the most relabels among all our benchmarks. When the heavy threshold is 1 (last row) — that is, we only split full nodes — as expected, most relabels split only a single heavy group; very occasionally, a couple of heavy groups may become full concurrently and causes a relabel to split more than one group. Even by just decreasing the threshold to be .875, we already see that the median of the number of heavy groups increase to 5.7 and the number of relabels reduces dramatically. This trend continues as we decrease the heavy threshold. This result demonstrates that when many groups can become full dur-

	fft				heat				cholesky			
threshold	relabels	median	max	total	relabels	median	max	total	relabels	median	max	total
0.25	1567	18	40	32207	24	3	4	54	22	4	5	66
0.375	1576	15	27	21905	24	1	1	24	22	2	4	56
0.5	1614	19	22	20270	24	1	1	24	22	1	2	31
0.625	1642	12	22	18959	24	1	1	24	22	1	2	31
0.75	1725	7	17	17345	24	1	1	24	22	1	2	24
0.875	2838	4	11	11285	24	1	1	24	22	1	1	22
1	7985	1	3	8090	24	1	1	24	22	1	1	22

Table 3: The effects of varying the heavy threshold when running C-RACER 16 cores. The first column for a given benchmark shows the number of relabels. The other columns provide information about the number of heavy groups — the median and maximum for individual relabels, and the total number of heavy groups split across all relabels.

ing the execution, eager splitting indeed helps in decreasing the number of relabels.

6. RELATED WORK

Netzer [29] formalized definitions for determinacy and data races. Static checking for races has been studied in [12, 27, 13], while [8, 28, 2] investigate post-mortem analysis. Research on race detectors for general parallel computations include [15, 33, 30, 11]. In addition to English-Hebrew labeling and SP-Order (and the related SP-hybrid), many algorithms have been proposed for on-the-fly race detection for series-parallel programs. Offset-span labels[26] are shorter than English-Hebrew labels, but still not bounded by a constant. The Nondeterminator race detector [14] runs serially and uses Tarjan's nearly linear-time least-common-ancestor algorithm [37] to simulate the SP-parse tree of a computation. Raman et al. [31] develop a race detection algorithm for async-finish parallelism and implement it in Habanero Java [7]. Raman et al. [32] developed an simple parallel algorithm that maintains the entire computations tree; while it provides good empirical results, it provides no theoretical guarantees. That implementation takes advantage of compiler optimizations to avoid instrumenting all memory access; we have not yet applied such optimizations. Lastly, in contrast to existing race detectors for fork-join computations, TARDIS [22, 24] does not explicitly keep track of the series-parallel relationships among strands. Instead, it employees a log-based access set and detects races by intersecting the access sets of logically parallel subcomputations at the join point. Moreover, it does not provide provably good time bounds as intersecting the access sets can lead to an asymptotic increase in the span of the computation.

Our runtime modification — the idea of switching between two deques — also exists in the BATCHER runtime [1]. BATCHER is a runtime scheduler augmented specifically for programs that use shared data structures. In particular, BATCHER allows the programmer to replace concurrent data structures by certain (non-concurrent) batched data structures.[7] The runtime automatically batches operations and allows workers that are blocked on a batch to help it complete. One possible way to parallelize SP-Order would apply BATCHER directly with a batched OM data structure. Unfortunately, roughly speaking, BATCHER itself adds $\Omega(\lg P)$ work/time to each data-structure access — therefore, even with an efficient OM data structure, it seems impossible to achieve an optimal SP-maintenance algorithm using BATCHER directly.

[7]A batched data structure supports, e.g., inserting a set of elements instead instead of inserting elements one by one.

7. CONCLUDING REMARKS

WSP-Order maintains series-parallel relationships in parallel and without any asymptotic slowdown for fork-join programs. In addition, our implementation of C-RACER provides good speedup in practice. One aspect we have not discussed is deletion from the order-maintenance data structures. In WSP-Order and in C-RACER, once a strand is inserted it will never be removed, even though it may never be used again. Performing some kind of garbage collection on such nodes may improve memory usage. In addition, WSP-Order is designed for series-parallel programs; it would be interesting to consider race detection for broader classes of parallelism, such as pipeline parallelism [23].

Acknowledgments

This research was supported in part by National Science Foundation grants CCF-1527692, CCF-1218017, CCF-1150036, CCF-1218188, and CCF-1314633. We thank the referees for their excellent comments.

8. REFERENCES

[1] Kunal Agrawal, Jeremy T. Fineman, Kefu Lu, Brendan Sheridan, Jim Sukha, and Robert Utterback. Provably good scheduling for parallel programs that use data structures through implicit batching. SPAA '14, pages 84–95, New York, NY, USA, 2014. ACM.

[2] Todd R. Allen and David A. Padua. Debugging fortran on a shared memory machine. ICPP '87, pages 721–727, aug 1987.

[3] Arne Andersson. Improving partial rebuilding by using simple balance criteria. WADS '89, pages 393–402, London, UK, UK, 1989. Springer-Verlag.

[4] Michael A. Bender, Richard Cole, Erik D. Demaine, Martin Farach-Colton, and Jack Zito. Two simplified algorithms for maintaining order in a list. ESA '02, pages 152–164, London, UK, UK, 2002. Springer-Verlag.

[5] Michael A. Bender, Jeremy T. Fineman, Seth Gilbert, and Charles E. Leiserson. On-the-fly maintenance of series-parallel relationships in fork-join multithreaded programs. SPAA '04, pages 133–144, New York, NY, USA, 2004. ACM.

[6] Robert D. Blumofe and Charles E. Leiserson. Scheduling multithreaded computations by work stealing. *Journal of the ACM*, 46, 1999.
[7] Vincent Cavé, Jisheng Zhao, Jun Shirako, and Vivek Sarkar. Habanero-java: The new adventures of old x10. PPPJ '11, pages 51–61, New York, NY, USA, 2011. ACM.
[8] Jong-Deok Choi, Barton P. Miller, and Robert H. B. Netzer. Techniques for debugging parallel programs with flowback analysis. *ACM Trans. Program. Lang. Syst.*, 13(4):491–530, October 1991.
[9] P. Dietz and D. Sleator. Two algorithms for maintaining order in a list. STOC '87, pages 365–372, New York, NY, USA, 1987. ACM.
[10] Paul F. Dietz. Maintaining order in a linked list. STOC '82, pages 122–127, New York, NY, USA, 1982. ACM.
[11] Tayfun Elmas, Shaz Qadeer, and Serdar Tasiran. Goldilocks: A race and transaction-aware java runtime. PLDI '07, pages 245–255, New York, NY, USA, 2007. ACM.
[12] Perry A. Emrath and David A. Padua. Automatic detection of nondeterminacy in parallel programs. PADD '88, pages 89–99, New York, NY, USA, 1988. ACM.
[13] Dawson Engler and Ken Ashcraft. Racerx: Effective, static detection of race conditions and deadlocks. SOSP '03, pages 237–252, New York, NY, USA, 2003. ACM.
[14] Mingdong Feng and Charles E. Leiserson. Efficient detection of determinacy races in cilk programs. SPAA '97, pages 1–11, New York, NY, USA, 1997. ACM.
[15] Cormac Flanagan and Stephen N. Freund. Fasttrack: Efficient and precise dynamic race detection. PLDI '09, pages 121–133, New York, NY, USA, 2009. ACM.
[16] Michael L. Fredman and Dan E. Willard. Surpassing the information theoretic bound with fusion trees. *J. Comput. Syst. Sci.*, 47(3):424–436, December 1993.
[17] Matteo Frigo, Charles E. Leiserson, and Keith H. Randall. The implementation of the cilk-5 multithreaded language. PLDI '98, pages 212–223, New York, NY, USA, 1998. ACM.
[18] Igal Galperin and Ronald L. Rivest. Scapegoat trees. SODA '93, pages 165–174, Philadelphia, PA, USA, 1993. Society for Industrial and Applied Mathematics.
[19] Intel Corporation. CilkPlus/LLVM. http://cilkplus.github.io/, 2013.
[20] Intel Corporation. Intel® Cilk™ Plus Language Extension Specification, Version 1.2, September 2013. Document 324396-003US.
[21] Intel Corporation. An introduction to the cilk screen race detector., November 2013.
[22] Weixing Ji, Li Lu, and Michael L. Scott. Tardis: Task-level access race detection by intersecting sets. WoDet '13, Houston, TX, USA, 2013.
[23] I-Ting Angelina Lee, Charles E. Leiserson, Tao B. Schardl, Jim Sukha, and Zhunping Zhang. On-the-fly pipeline parallelism. SPAA '13, pages 140–151, New York, NY, USA, 2013. ACM.
[24] Li Lu, Weixing Ji, and Michael L. Scott. Dynamic enforcement of determinism in a parallel scripting language. PLDI '14, pages 519–529, Edinburgh, United Kingdom, 2014. ACM.
[25] Chi-Keung Luk, Robert Cohn, Robert Muth, Harish Patil, Artur Klauser, Geoff Lowney, Steven Wallace, Vijay Janapa Reddi, and Kim Hazelwood. Pin: Building customized program analysis tools with dynamic instrumentation. PLDI '05, pages 190–200, New York, NY, USA, 2005. ACM.
[26] John Mellor-Crummey. On-the-fly detection of data races for programs with nested fork-join parallelism. Supercomputing '91, pages 24–33, New York, NY, USA, 1991. ACM.
[27] John Mellor-Crummey. Compile-time support for efficient data race detection in shared-memory parallel programs. PADD '93, pages 129–139, New York, NY, USA, 1993. ACM.
[28] Robert Netzer and Barton P. Miller. Detecting data races in parallel program executions. In *In Advances in Languages and Compilers for Parallel Computing, 1990 Workshop*, pages 109–129. MIT Press, 1989.
[29] Robert H. B. Netzer and Barton P. Miller. What are race conditions?: Some issues and formalizations. *ACM Lett. Program. Lang. Syst.*, 1(1):74–88, March 1992.
[30] Eli Pozniansky and Assaf Schuster. Multirace: Efficient on-the-fly data race detection in multithreaded c++ programs: Research articles. *Concurr. Comput. : Pract. Exper.*, 19(3):327–340, March 2007.
[31] Raghavan Raman, Jisheng Zhao, Vivek Sarkar, Martin Vechev, and Eran Yahav. Efficient data race detection for async-finish parallelism. RV'10, pages 368–383, Berlin, Heidelberg, 2010. Springer-Verlag.
[32] Raghavan Raman, Jisheng Zhao, Vivek Sarkar, Martin Vechev, and Eran Yahav. Scalable and precise dynamic datarace detection for structured parallelism. PLDI '12, pages 531–542, New York, NY, USA, 2012. ACM.
[33] Stefan Savage, Michael Burrows, Greg Nelson, Patrick Sobalvarro, and Thomas Anderson. Eraser: A dynamic data race detector for multi-threaded programs. SOSP '97, pages 27–37, New York, NY, USA, 1997. ACM.
[34] Tao B. Schardl, Bradley C. Kuszmaul, I-Ting Angelina Lee, William M. Leiserson, and Charles E. Leiserson. The cilkprof scalability profiler. SPAA '15, pages 89–100, Portland, Oregon, USA, June 2015. ACM.
[35] Konstantin Serebryany and Timur Iskhodzhanov. Threadsanitizer: Data race detection in practice. WBIA '09, pages 62–71, New York, NY, USA, 2009. ACM.
[36] Julian Shun, Guy E. Blelloch, Jeremy T. Fineman, and Phillip B. Gibbons. Reducing contention through priority updates. PPoPP '13, pages 299–300, New York, NY, USA, 2013. ACM.
[37] Robert Endre Tarjan. Applications of path compression on balanced trees. *Journal of the ACM*, 26(4):690–715, October 1979.
[38] Intel Cilk Plus Development Team. Intrinsics for Low Overhead Tool Annotations. Technical report, November 2011.

Brief Announcement: Dynamic Determinacy Race Detection for Task Parallelism with Futures

Rishi Surendran
Rice University
rishi@rice.edu

Vivek Sarkar
Rice University
vsarkar@rice.edu

ABSTRACT

Existing dynamic determinacy race detectors for task-parallel programs are limited to programs with strict computation graphs, where a task can only wait for its descendant tasks to complete. In this paper, we present the first known determinacy race detector for non-strict computation graphs with futures. The space and time complexity of our algorithm are similar to those of the classical SP-bags algorithm, when using only structured parallel constructs such as spawn-sync and async-finish. In the presence of point-to-point synchronization using futures, the complexity of the algorithm increases by a factor determined by the number of future operations, which includes future task creation and future get operations. The experimental results show that the slowdown factor observed for our algorithm relative to the sequential version is in the range of 1.00× – 9.92×, which is very much in line with slowdowns experienced for fully strict computation graphs.

1. INTRODUCTION

Current dynamic race detection algorithms for task parallelism are limited to parallel constructs in which a task may synchronize with the parent task [5] or an ancestor task [8, 9]. However, current parallel programming models include parallel constructs that support more general synchronization patterns. For example, the OpenMP depends clause allows tasks to wait on previously spawned sibling tasks and the future construct in X10, HJ, C# and C++11 enables a task to wait on any previously created task to which the waiter task has a reference. Algorithms based on vector clocks [1] are impractical for these constructs because either the vector clocks have to be allocated with a size proportional to the maximum number of simultaneously live tasks (which can be unboundedly large) or precision has to be sacrificed by assigning one clock per processor or worker thread, thereby missing potential data races when two tasks execute on the same worker. In this paper, we present the first known sound and precise dynamic determinacy race detector for non-strict computation graphs with futures.

Our work addresses parallel programming models that can support combinations of functional-style futures and imperative-style tasks. Specifically, our race detection algorithm supports async-finish constructs for imperative-style parallelism and future construct for functional-style parallelism. The statement "`async { S }`" causes the parent task to create a new child task to execute `S` asynchronously with the remainder of the parent task. The statement "`finish { S }`" causes the parent task to execute `S` and then wait for the completion of all asynchronous tasks created within `S`. Each dynamic instance T_A of an async task has a unique *Immediately Enclosing Finish (IEF)* instance F of a finish statement during program execution, where F is the innermost finish containing T_A. A future [6] refers to an object that acts as a proxy for a result that may initially be unknown because the computation of its value may still be in progress as a parallel task. The statement, "`future<T> f = async<T> Expr;`" creates a new child task to evaluate `Expr` asynchronously, where `T` is the type of the expression `Expr`. In this case, `f` contains a handle to the return value (future object) for the newly created task and the operation `f.get()` can be performed to obtain the result of the future task. If the future task has not completed as yet, the task performing the `f.get()` operation blocks until the result of `Expr` becomes available.

The remainder of this brief announcement is organized as follows. Section 2 defines a determinacy race for our programming model. Section 3 presents our approach for determinacy race detection for parallel programs with futures, and Section 4 discusses the experimental results for our race detection algorithm.

2. DATA RACES AND DETERMINISM

We define a data race for programs containing async, finish, and future constructs in terms of the ***computation graph*** [2], and as a preamble to defining determinacy races. A computation graph models the execution of a parallel program as a graph, where each node in a computation graph corresponds to a step, where a step is defined as follows:

Definition 1. *A step is a maximal sequence of statement instances such that no statement instance in the sequence includes the start or end of an async, finish or a get operation.*

The edges in computation graph represent parallel control dependences. There are three different types of edges in a

SPAA '16, July 11-13, 2016, Pacific Grove, CA, USA

ACM ISBN 978-1-4503-4210-0/16/07.
DOI: http://dx.doi.org/10.1145/2935764.2935815

computation graph (akin to those in a fully strict computation graph):

1. **Continue Edges** capture the sequencing of steps within a task. All steps in a task are connected by continue edges.
2. **Spawn Edges** represent the parent-child relationship among tasks. When task A creates task B, a spawn edge is inserted from the step that ends with the async in task A to the step that starts task B.
3. **Join Edges** represent the synchronization among tasks. When task A performs a get on future B, a join edge is inserted from the last step of B to the step in task A that immediately follows the `get()` operation. Join edges are also inserted from the last step of every task to the step in the ancestor task immediately following the Immediately Enclosing Finish (IEF). A join edge from task B to task A is referred to as ***tree join*** if A is an ancestor of B; otherwise, it is referred to as a ***non-tree join***.

Definition 2. *A step u is said to precede step v, denoted as* $u \prec v$, *if there exists a path from u to v in the computation graph.*

We use the notation $u \nprec v$ to denote that there is no path from step u to step v in the computation graph.

Definition 3. *A data race may occur between steps u and v, iff both u and v access a common memory location, at least one of which is a write and* $u \nprec v$ *and* $v \nprec u$.

We say that a parallel program is *functionally deterministic* if it always computes the same answer when given the same inputs. By default, any sequential computation is expected to be deterministic with respect to its inputs; if the computation interacts with the environment (e.g., a GUI event such as a mouse click, or a system call like System.nanoTime()) then the values returned by the environment are also considered to be inputs to the computation. Further, we refer to a program as *structurally deterministic* if it always computes the same computation graph, when given the same inputs. Finally, following past work [7]we say that a program is *determinate* if it is both functionally and structurally deterministic. If a parallel program is written using only async, finish, and future constructs, *and is guaranteed to never exhibit a data race*, then it must be determinate, i.e., both functionally and structurally deterministic. Note that all data-race-free programs written using async, finish and future constructs are guaranteed to be determinate, but it does not imply that all racy programs are non-determinate.

3. RACE DETECTION APPROACH

Our race detection algorithm detects races on-the-fly during a depth-first serial execution of the input program. A dynamic race detector needs to provide mechanisms that answers two questions: for any pair of memory accesses, at least one of which is a write 1) can the two accesses logically execute in parallel? 2) do they access the same memory location? To answer the first question, we introduce a program representation referred to as *dynamic task reachability graph* which is presented in Section 3.1. Similar to most race detectors, we use a shadow memory mechanism to answer the second question which is presented in Section 3.2. Section 3.3 presents a high-level view of our algorithm.

3.1 Dynamic Task Reachability Graph

The dynamic task reachability graph represents the reachability information at task-level instead of step-level. It uses the following three ideas for encoding reachability information between steps in the computation graph of the input program:

- *Disjoint set representation of tree joins:* The reachability information between tasks which are connected by tree join edges is captured using a disjoint set data structure. Two tasks A and B are in the same set if and only if B is a descendant of A and there is a path in the computation graph from B to A which includes only tree-join edges and continue edges. Any m operations on n sets take a total of $O(m\ \alpha(m, n))$ time where α is the inverse Ackermann's function.
- *Interval encoding of spawn tree:* To efficiently store and query reachability information from a task to its descendants, we use a labeling scheme [4], where each task is assigned a label according to the preorder and postorder numbering scheme. The values are assigned according to the order in which the tasks are visited during a depth-first-traversal of the *spawn tree*, where the nodes in the spawn tree correspond to each of the tasks and edges represent the parent-child spawn relationship. Ancestor-descendant relationship queries between task pairs can be answered by checking if the interval of one task subsumes the interval of the other task.
- *Immediate predecessors+significant ancestor representation of non-tree joins:* The non-tree joins in the computation graph are represented in the dynamic task reachability graph as follows:
  - *immediate predecessors*: For each non-tree join from task A to task B, B stores A in the set of predecessors.
  - *lowest significant ancestor*: We define the *significant ancestors* of task A as the set of ancestors of A which has performed at least one non-tree join operation. For each task, we store only the lowest significant ancestor.

3.2 Shadow Memory

Our algorithm maintains a shadow memory M_s for every shared memory location M. M_s contains the following fields

- *writer*, a reference to a task that wrote to M. M_s.*writer* is initialized to *null* and is updated at every write to M. It refers to the task that last wrote to M.
- *readers*, a set of references to tasks that read M. M_s.*readers* is initialized to $\emptyset$ and is updated at reads of M. It contains references to all future tasks that read M in parallel since the last write to M. It also contains a reference to one non-future (async) task which read M since the last write to M.

3.3 Algorithm

As the input program executes in serial, depth-first order the race detection algorithm performs additional operations whenever one of the following actions occurs: task creation, task return, `get()` operation, shared memory read and shared memory write. Determinacy races are detected when a read or write to a shared memory location occurs. When a write to a memory location M is performed by step

Benchmark	Description	Input Size	Seq (millisecs)	Racedet (millisecs)	Slowdown
Series-af	Fourier coefficient analysis using async-finish	Size C	483,224	484,746	1.00
Series-future	Fourier coefficient analysis using futures	Size C	487,134	487,985	1.00
Crypt-af	IDEA encryption algorithm using async-finish	Size C	15,375	119,504	7.77
Crypt-future	IDEA encryption algorithm using futures	Size C	15,517	128,234	8.26
Jacobi	2 dimensional 5-point stencil using futures	2048 x 2048	3,402	27,388	8.05
Smith-Waterman	Sequence alignment using futures	10000	3,488	34,558	9.92
Strassen	Strassen's algorithm using futures	1024 x 1024	30,811	33,618	5.35

Table 1: Runtime overhead for determinacy race detection. **Seq** is the sequential execution time in milliseconds and **Racedet** is the execution time with race detection enabled in milliseconds. **Slowdown** is the slowdown due to race detection (**Racedet/Seq**).

u, the algorithm checks if the previous *writer* or the previous *readers* in the shadow memory space may execute in parallel with the currently executing step and reports a race. It updates the *writer* shadow space of M with the current task and removes any task S if $S \prec u$. When a read to a memory location M is performed by step u, the algorithm checks if the previous *writer* in the shadow memory space may execute in parallel with the currently executing step and reports a race. It adds the current task to the set of readers of M and removes any task S if $S \prec u$. Given tasks A and B, our algorithm determines if they can execute in parallel by inspecting the dynamic task reachability graph. The algorithm does this by traversing only the non-tree edges and using the disjoint set and interval labels to answer reachability queries along paths with spawn and tree join edges.

Our race detection algorithm can be implemented to check a program that executes in time T on one processor for determinacy races in $O(T\ (f+1)\ (n+1)\ \alpha(T, a+f))$ time using $O(a+f+n+v\ (f+1))$ space, where a is the number of async tasks and f is the number of future tasks created by the program, n is the number of non-tree joins performed by the program and v is the number of shared memory locations referenced by the program.

4. EXPERIMENTAL RESULTS

The race detector was implemented as a new Java library for detecting determinacy races in HJ [3] programs containing async, finish, and future constructs. The benchmarks written in HJ were instrumented for race detection during a bytecode-level transformation pass implemented on HJ's Parallel Intermediate Representation (PIR). The instrumentation pass adds the necessary calls to our race detection library at async, finish, and future boundaries, future get operations, and also on reads and writes to shared memory locations.

Our experiments were conducted on a 16-core Intel Ivybridge 2.6 GHz system with 48 GB memory, running Red Hat Enterprise Linux Server release 7.1, and Sun Hotspot JDK 1.7. To reduce the impact of JIT compilation, garbage collection, and other JVM services, we report the mean execution time of 10 runs repeated in the same JVM instance for each data point.

The results of our evaluation are given in Table 1. The first column lists the benchmark name. The fourth column (Seq) reports the average execution time of the sequential (serial elision) version of the benchmark, and the following column (Racedet) reports the average execution time of a 1-processor execution of the parallel benchmark using the determinacy race detection algorithm introduced in this paper. Finally, the Slowdown column reports the ratio of the Racedet and Seq values. The slowdowns for Series-af and Crypt-af are comparable to the slowdowns reported for the ESP-Bags algorithm that only supported async and finish, thereby showing that our determinacy race detector does not incur additional overhead for async/finish constructs relative to state-of-the-art implementations. The slowdown for Crypt-future is higher than that of Crypt-af because of two reasons: 1) the additional number of memory accesses due to the future references and 2) the average number of readers stored in the shadow memory is higher, because of the presence of future tasks. The slowdowns for Jacobi, Smith-Waterman, and Strassen (8.05×, 9.92×, and 5.35×) are positively correlated with the number of shared memory accesses, the average number of readers stored in the shadow memory, and 1/Seq.

5. REFERENCES

[1] Utpal Banerjee, Brian Bliss, Zhiqiang Ma, and Paul Petersen. A theory of data race detection. In *PADTAD '06*, pages 69–78, New York, NY, USA, 2006. ACM.

[2] Robert D. Blumofe and Charles E. Leiserson. Scheduling multithreaded computations by work stealing. *J. ACM*, 46(5):720–748, September 1999.

[3] Vincent Cavé, Jisheng Zhao, Jun Shirako, and Vivek Sarkar. Habanero-java: the new adventures of old x10. In *PPPJ '11*, pages 51–61, New York, NY, USA, 2011. ACM.

[4] P. Dietz and D. Sleator. Two algorithms for maintaining order in a list. In *STOC '87*, pages 365–372, New York, NY, USA, 1987. ACM.

[5] Mingdong Feng and Charles E. Leiserson. Efficient detection of determinacy races in Cilk programs. In *SPAA '97*, pages 1–11, New York, NY, USA, 1997. ACM.

[6] Robert H. Halstead, Jr. Multilisp: A language for concurrent symbolic computation. *ACM Trans. Program. Lang. Syst.*, 7(4):501–538, 1985.

[7] Richard M. Karp and Raymond E. Miller. Parallel program schemata. *J. Comput. Syst. Sci.*, 3(2):147–195, May 1969.

[8] Raghavan Raman, Jisheng Zhao, Vivek Sarkar, Martin Vechev, and Eran Yahav. Efficient data race detection for async-finish parallelism. *Formal Methods in System Design*, 41(3):321–347, December 2012.

[9] Raghavan Raman, Jisheng Zhao, Vivek Sarkar, Martin Vechev, and Eran Yahav. Scalable and precise dynamic datarace detection for structured parallelism. In *PLDI '12*, pages 531–542, New York, NY, USA, 2012. ACM.

RUBIC: Online Parallelism Tuning for Co-located Transactional Memory Applications

Amin Mohtasham
amohtasham@gsd.inesc-id.pt

João Barreto
joao.barreto@tecnico.ulisboa.pt

INESC-ID Lisboa/ Instituto Superior Técnico, Universidade de Lisboa, Portugal

ABSTRACT

With the advent of Chip-Multiprocessors, Transactional Memory (TM) emerged as a powerful paradigm to simplify parallel programming. Unfortunately, as more cores become available in commodity systems, the scalability limits of a wide class of TM applications become more evident.

Hence, online parallelism tuning techniques were proposed to adapt the optimal number of threads of TM applications. However, state-of-the-art solutions are exclusively tailored to single-process systems with relatively static workloads, exhibiting pathological behaviors in scenarios where multiple multi-threaded TM processes contend for the shared hardware resources.

This paper proposes RUBIC, a novel parallelism tuning method for TM applications in both single and multi-process scenarios that overcomes the shortcomings of the preciously proposed solutions. RUBIC helps the co-running processes adapt their parallelism level so that they can efficiently space-share the hardware.

When compared to previous online parallelism tuning solutions, RUBIC achieves unprecedented system-wide fairness and efficiency, both in single- and multi-process scenarios. Our evaluation with different workloads and scenarios shows that, on average, RUBIC enhances the overall performance by 26% with respect to the best-performing state-of-the-art online parallelism tuning techniques in multi-process scenarios, while incurring negligible overhead in single-process cases. RUBIC also exhibits unique features in converging to a fair and efficient state.

Categories and Subject Descriptors

D.1.3 [**Software**]: Programming Techniques *Concurrent Programming*

Keywords

concurrency control; feedback-driven systems; resource allocation; software transactional memory

SPAA '16, July 11-13, 2016, Pacific Grove, CA, USA

© 2016 ACM. ISBN 978-1-4503-4210-0/16/07... $15.00

DOI: http://dx.doi.org/10.1145/2935764.2935770

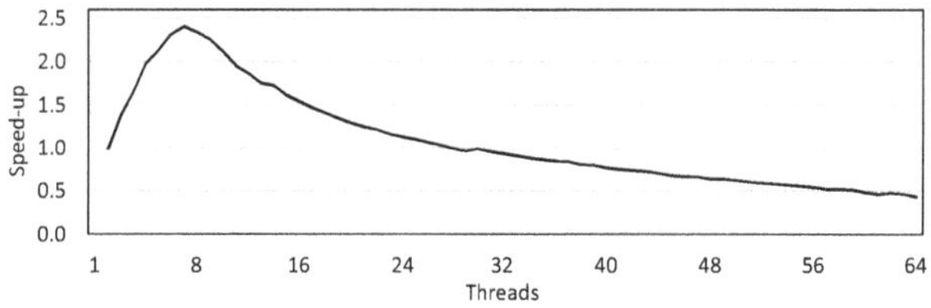

Figure 1: Intruder's throughput deteriorates after 7 parallel threads.

1. INTRODUCTION

Transactional Memory (TM) has emerged as a powerful paradigm to simplify parallel programming. Building on the abstraction of atomic transactions, and freeing the programmer from the complexity of conventional synchronization schemes, TM has proven capable of simplifying the development and verification of concurrent programs by avoiding the pitfalls of manual, lock-based synchronization, enhancing code reliability and boosting productivity. After intense research during the last decade, TM has reached the maturity required for mainstream adoption. Notable evidences of this trend include the software implementations in the gcc compiler [1], the upcoming version of the C++ standard [2], and best-effort hardware TM support in mainstream and high-end processors from major chip manufacturers.

Unfortunately, as more and more cores become available in commodity systems, the scalability limits of a wide class of TM applications become more evident. Taking STAMP [3] as a well-known benchmark suite, most applications reach a performance peak after a certain number of threads; to make things worse, many such applications even observe performance drops after such a peak [4]. For example, Figure 1 shows Intruder achieves the highest speed-up with only 7 parallel threads on a 4-socket 64-core machine, without using any explicit thread placement policy, and on average of 50 runs. As the number of threads goes beyond the peak point, the performance deteriorates such that, at 64 threads, the throughput becomes less than half of the sequential execution's throughput.

The limited scalability of the parallel workloads on modern multi/many-core processors implies 3 important observations: (i) running a parallel workload with as many threads as the number of hardware (h/w) contexts can lead to a significant waste of the hardware resources; (ii) there must be a mechanism that finds the optimal number of threads for a given workload and maximizes the speed-up;

(iii) to fully utilize the hardware, co-locating multiple TM parallel applications will become increasingly common [5, 6].

Recently, a number of works have proposed online techniques that aim at finding optimal parallelism level in *malleable* TM applications [7, 8, 4, 9]. Malleable applications are flexible applications and can set their parallelism level prior to or during their execution [10]. These constitute the vast majority of the applications that are found in the reference TM benchmarks [3, 11]. Online solutions usually employ online feedback-driven techniques together with hill-climbing techniques to learn about the workload and find its optimal parallelism level. In contrast to offline approaches, online solutions are particularly appealing because they are well-suited for workloads that are not known a priori or dynamic execution environments.

Nevertheless, the current state-of-the-art in online parallelism tuning techniques is designed for and evaluated in single-process scenarios. Although such techniques are implicitly *assumed* to also work well in multiple-process situations, our experimental results (presented in Section 4) show that they actually exhibit alarmingly poor performance when multiple TM processes run concurrently in the same machine. This pathological behavior is explained by some fundamental issues that arise when one considers a system of multiple parallel processes instead of a single one, as follows.

Oversubscription: a system becomes oversubscribed when its total number of computationally-intensive software (s/w) threads exceeds the number of h/w contexts. In an oversubscribed system, the overall performance degrades, mainly due to frequent context switches and increased cache trashing. Apart from this, a TM-application, specially, suffers from oversubscription due to prolonged transaction execution time and increased conflict likelihood, hence losing throughput[12]. In a single-process scenario, a parallelism tuning technique can easily avoid oversubscription by putting a hard limit on the number of s/w threads. However, in a multi-process environment, things are not that straightforward, as all the co-running processes need to somehow coordinate to keep the total number of s/w threads below the oversubscription point.

System-wide optimization: for a single process, the obvious goal is to simply maximize some performance metric (e.g., throughput, speed-up, etc.). However, in a multi-process system, the main goal is to optimize the whole system's performance. With such a system, the overall performance is usually defined as an aggregate function of each process' performance. Considering the limited hardware resources (i.e. h/w contexts), to maximize a given overall performance function, some processes may be required to give up some of their resources to the other processes (e.g. to those that achieve higher speed-up). *Sacrificing* a single for the sake of a whole is not aligned with the goals of the current parallelism tuning methods, where each process greedily tries to maximize its performance, regardless of the system's overall performance (Section 2 elaborates on this behavior).

Fairness: when it comes to resource allocation, establishing fairness immediately becomes a major issue. While, intuitively, in a fair system, all processes must receive *enough* resources to make some progress, defining and quantifying fairness is far from trivial. There exist several definitions for fairness and choosing each one affects the system's performance differently. For instance, one can define fairness as *equality*, while another actually finds equality unfair and allocates more resources to processes that contribute more to the system's overall performance (a.k.a. proportional fairness). In the context of resource allocation, for a given definition of fairness, the system's performance function is defined in such a way that it reflects the fairness requirements of that system as well [13, 14]. Nonetheless, as the state-of-the-art parallelism tuning methods do not consider maximizing any system-wide performance function, the fairness characteristics of such methods, when applied in multi-process environments, is totally unknown.

This paper proposes RUBIC, a highly adaptive online parallelism tuning method for malleable TM applications that overcomes all of the aforementioned shortcomings of the current tuning techniques in single and multi-process environments. We believe this is a key breakthrough, as it enables elastic systems composed of multiple TM-based applications that adaptively space-share h/w contexts amongst themselves, efficiently and fairly, at no extra cost with regard to the state-of-the-art techniques.

Inspired by the well-studied problem of flow/congestion control in data networks, RUBIC employs a sophisticated online feedback loop control within each running process that makes unilateral decisions only based on that process' local observations. That is to say that our solution does not rely on a central entity, nor does it require any sort of communication between running processes.

Our experimental results show that RUBIC can substantially boost the system's overall performance when compared to solutions previously proposed to single-process settings. At the same time, RUBIC is highly responsive to changes in the system and its convergence to an efficient and fair allocation is impressively fast, unlike the state-of-the-art methods.

Although this paper focuses on TM workloads, our solution is not limited to TM applications. In fact, any malleable parallel application can benefit from RUBIC.

The rest of this paper is structured as follows. Section 2 elaborates on the shortcomings of the state-of-the-art methods and illustrates the rationale behind RUBIC. Section 3 describes RUBIC in detail. Section 4 shows how our proposed method acts in practice and how it outperforms the state-of-the-art. Finally, Section 5 surveys related work and Section 6 concludes.

2. THE NEED FOR SPEED AND FAIRNESS

In this section, we explain why the existing solutions, originally designed for single-process environments, are not suitable for multi-process systems. Then, we describe the rationale behind RUBIC to understand what makes RUBIC an adequate solution for parallelism tuning in multi-process environments.

Online parallelism tuning techniques usually employ a feedback loop to control the parallelism. A controller loop constantly monitors a performance metric (e.g. throughput) and makes the appropriate decision regarding the new parallelism level (i.e. number of s/w threads), based on the received feedback from the last decision. A decision can be either increasing or decreasing the parallelism level. Depending on the decision, the new level L_N is obtained through the functions f_{INC} and f_{DEC}, which are used for increasing and decreasing the parallelism level, respectively. Both functions accept the current level, L_C, as the input parameter.

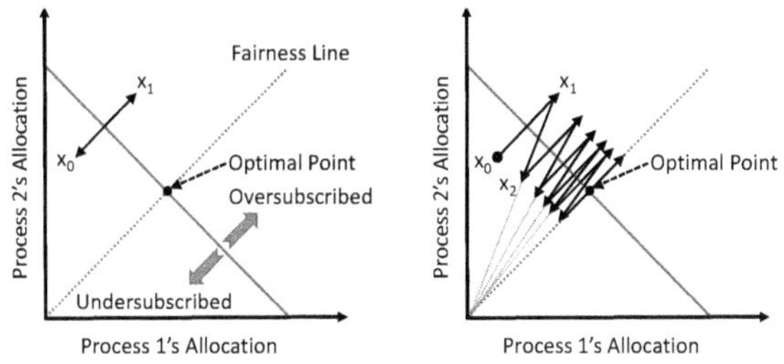

(a) AIAD (b) AIMD

Figure 2: The convergence behavior of a system with two malleable processes, using different tuning schemes. AIMD converges to the optimal point.

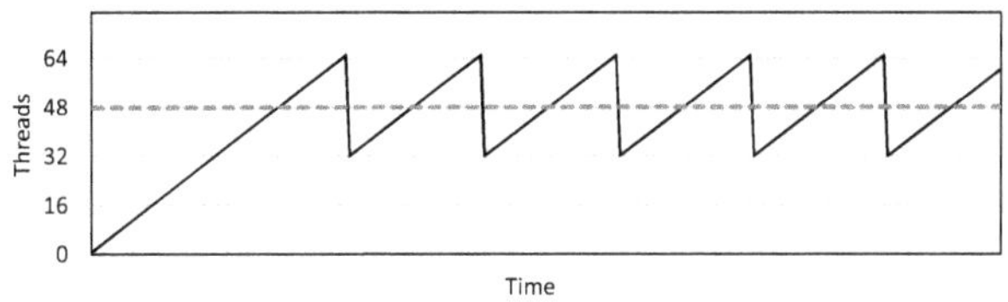

Figure 3: The expected behavior of an AIMD-based model ($\alpha = 0.5$) on a 64-core machine (the dashed line represents the average thread count).

The choice of functions f_{INC} and f_{DEC} defines the behavior of a parallelism tuning technique.

Existing solutions rely on simple linear functions for both increasing and decreasing purposes [4, 7]. At each step, the parallelism level is *additively* increased or decreased by a constant value Δl, which is usually set to 1. Therefore, we refer to this model as *AIAD* (additive-increase/additive-decrease).

AIAD gives the controller excellent capabilities to gradually explore the solution space and to find the optimal parallelism level in a single-process environment. However, in the following, we question the capabilities of AIAD-based schemes in multi-process environments, and show why such models do not converge to a system-wide fair and efficient state.

2.1 Additive vs. Multiplicative Decrease

Figure 2a shows the behavior of AIAD in a two-process system. Starting from an arbitrary point X_0, which is in the undersubscribed region, both processes additively increase their parallelism level. Therefore, the system's state moves along, at an angle of 45°, to point X_1, which is above the oversubscription line, and the system becomes oversubscribed. As a result, both processes shall notice some performance loss and additively reduce their parallelism level. Consequently, the system's state moves back, along at an angle of 45°, to the starting point, X_0, and the same additive increase phase happens. Therefore, the system's state oscillates between points X_0 and X_1 and never converges to the optimal point, at which the resources would be fairly allocated to both processes.

Inspired by congestion control techniques in data networks [15], we can solve the convergence issue by replacing the additive decrease phase with a *multiplicative decrease* (MD) one. In other words, instead of decreasing the

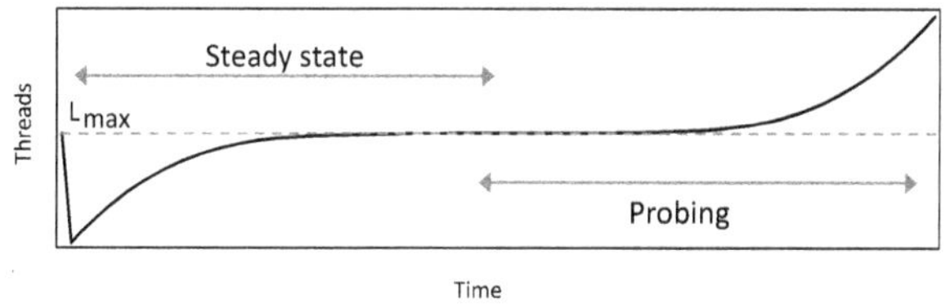

Figure 4: A cubic growth function includes a steady state phase (below L_{max}) and a probing phase (above L_{max}).

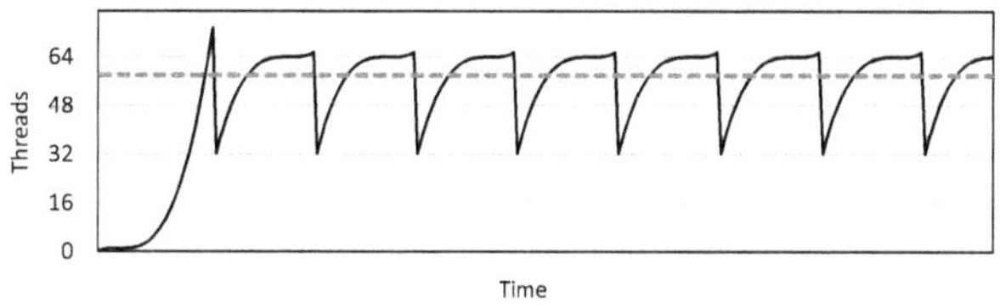

Figure 5: The expected behavior of a CIMD-based model ($\alpha = 0.5, \beta = 0.1$) on a 64-core machine. CIMD has a fast convergence due to its initial probing phase and achieves higher average utilization than AIMD (the dashed line represents the average thread count).

parallelism level by one, the new level is obtained by multiplying the current level by a positive constant factor, α, where $0 < \alpha < 1$. We refer to this model as *AIMD*.

Figure 2b shows how switching from AIAD to AIMD affects the convergence behavior of the system. Starting from the same point, X_0, similarly to AIAD, the system's state moves to point X_1. However, as the system becomes oversubscribed, both processes multiplicatively reduce their parallelism level and the system's state moves toward the line joining X_1 and the origin to point X_2, which is below the oversubscription line. This cycle repeats and, eventually, the system's state oscillates around the optimal point, which is the goal.

Therefore, in order to have multiple processes converge to a fair and efficient state, the linear decrease function that is used by the state-of-the-art solutions should be replaced by a multiplicative decrease one.

2.2 Additive vs. Cubic Increase

Multiplicative decrease in parallelism level solves the convergence issue. Nevertheless, it introduces a new problem to the system: the oscillations around the optimal point are expensive and cause overall undersubscription.

Figure 3 shows the behavior of a single highly-scalable process, using an AIMD controller ($\alpha = 0.5$), running on a 64-core machine. Each time the parallelism level exceeds 64, the controller detects some performance drop and multiplicatively decreases the parallelism level. Therefore, the new parallelism level is set to 32 (or close to it). At this point, the system is half-loaded and the controller, again, incrementally increases the parallelism level until it goes beyond 64 and the system oscillates around the optimal point (i.e. 64).

In this example, the average parallelism level is 48, depicted by the dashed-line in Figure 3, which means 25% of the h/w cores (16 out of 64) are left unused. In other words, the system is undersubscribed rather than operating at full capacity, due to using a multiplicative decrease function.

To enhance the system utilization, we can resort to a new growth function: a cubic function that was initially used in the context of congestion/flow control techniques in data networks [16]. More specifically, the growth function is obtained by the following equation:

$$L_{cubic} = L_{max} + \beta\big(\Delta t_{max} - \sqrt[3]{L_{max} \times \alpha/\beta}\big)^3 \quad (1)$$

where L_{max} depicts the last parallelism level at which a performance loss was observed and Δt_{max} denotes the time since that performance loss; α is a constant multiplication factor that reduces the parallelism level to αL_{max} (as in AIMD); and, finally β is a constant scaling factor that controls the growth rate of the parallelism level.

Figure 4 shows the growth behavior of a cubic function after an MD phase at L_{max}, based on Equation (1). The parallelism level increases very fast upon an MD phase. Then, its growth slows down as it gets closer to L_{max}; becoming almost zero when the parallelism level reaches L_{max}. This phase is the *steady state* phase. During this phase, the controller tries to stabilize the parallelism level and to keep it close to L_{max} (i.e. near the oversubscription point).

As the time passes and the parallelism level exceeds L_{max}, the controller increases the growth rate and starts the *probing* phase. The probing phase indicates the possibility of free resources in the system. During this phase, the controller looks for a new oversubscription point, by taking longer and longer steps.

Figure 5 shows the expected behavior of a single and highly-scalable process, using a controller with *cubic-increase-/multiplicative-decrease* (CIMD) functions, on a 64-core machine. At the beginning, L_{max} is set to 1. As the parallelism level gets away from 1, the probing phase starts until the first performance loss, due to oversubscription, is observed around 64 threads. At this point, L_{max} is set to the observed oversubscription level, an MD phase occurs, and the steady state phase keeps the parallelism level close to L_{max} (e.g., 64). In this example, the average parallelism level is close to 60, which implies the system utilization is enhanced from 75% with AIMD to 94% with cubic growth.

Based on what we discussed in this section, we claim that to enable the fair and efficient parallelism tuning in both single- and multi-process environments, the growth and reduction functions used in the state-of-the-art solutions must be revised. More specifically, we propose to replace the AIAD scheme used in the current solutions with a CIMD scheme.

3. PARALLELISM TUNING WITH RUBIC

In this section, we present RUBIC: the first parallelism tuning solution that is tailored for both single- and multi-process environments.

We assume each process includes a pool of s/w worker threads and runs a malleable parallel workload. The process' parallelism level can be tuned by activating or blocking the threads inside the thread-pool. As soon as a s/w thread completes its current task, it picks a new task from a task queue, until all tasks have been completed. The worker thread can then terminate, or block until there are new tasks available. In order to access shared data, tasks use transactions that ensure safe synchronization of concurrent accesses to the data.

3.1 The RUBIC Algorithm

Each process runs a monitoring thread that is responsible for running the RUBIC controller. This thread is created with a higher priority than other threads inside the thread-pool. This ensures that the monitoring thread gets to perform its duty even when the system is oversubscribed.

The controller periodically measures the process' throughput (e.g., commit-rate) and updates the T_c variable, in a loop. At the end of each iteration, the value of T_c is stored in T_p, to be used in the next round (i.e., iteration).

We assume the time between two measurements is long enough so an active worker thread can finish at least one task within that time. To measure the throughput, each worker thread maintains a local counter. Upon finishing a task, a worker thread increases its counter by one. At each round, the monitoring thread reads all the thread-local counters from the thread-pool and calculates T_c. This determines the process throughput in the period that is just completing.

It is worth noting that, for each thread-local counter variable, only that thread can update such counter; the monitoring thread only reads from those counters. Therefore, maintaining the thread-specific throughput counters is very lightweight; no atomic instructions are necessary.

After each measurement, the controller compares T_c with T_p. Should T_c be greater than or equal to T_p, the controller increases the parallelism level according to the cubic growth function in Equation 1. Conversely, in the case of a performance loss, a multiplicative reduction function calculates the new level.

Algorithms 1 and 2 show how the monitoring thread and the other threads inside the thread-pool co-operate in order to change the parallelism level.

To change a process' parallelism level, we augment each worker thread's metadata with a semaphore and a unique integer identifier $tid \in [0..S-1]$, where S is the size of that process' thread-pool. The number of active threads is maintained in a process-wide global variable, named L_{RUBIC}. The monitoring thread adjusts the parallelism level by changing the value of L_{RUBIC}.

At the application initialization, the parallelism level is set to minimum (1 thread). This means that only the first worker thread (i.e., $tid = 0$) is allowed to run tasks at the beginning and the rest must be blocked. Also, all thread semaphores are initialized to 0 (lines 2-5 in Algorithm 1).

Before acquiring a task from the task queue, each thread compares its *tid* with the global variable L_{RUBIC}. If *tid* is greater than L_{RUBIC}, it means the thread must be blocked. Hence, the thread waits on its semaphore, which was initialized to 0, and blocks (lines 8-10 in Algorithm 1). Otherwise, the thread acquires a task, if any, and executes.

It is noteworthy that the normal task acquisition flow does not include any system calls and the $Wait$ call only happens when a thread must block.

3.2 The Increase Function

The lines 6-15 in Algorithm 2 show how RUBIC increases the parallelism level, based on Equation 1 in Section 2.2.

In the round immediately after a cubic growth, the controller runs an additive increase phase and increments the parallelism level just by one. This enables the controller to compare two adjacent levels and to make more accurate decisions. The variable *growth* is used to interleave cubic and linear growth phases, in Algorithm 2.

Algorithm 1 Applied changes to the legacy instrumentation

```
procedure INITIALIZATION
    L_RUBIC = 1
    for each thread do
        thread.semaphore = 0
    end for
end procedure

procedure ACQUIRETASK(thread)
    if (thread.tid ≥ L_RUBIC) then
        Wait(thread.semaphore)
    end if
    //The rest remains unchanged...
end procedure
```

Finally, the controller signals the blocked worker threads that must be awakened in this round. It also stores the value of T_c in T_p to be used in the next round (lines 20-23 in Algorithm 2).

3.3 The Reduction Function

Should the throughput drop, RUBIC decreases the parallelism level (lines 25-35 in Algorithm 2).

The reduction function also interleaves two phases: a multiplicative phase and a linear one. This hybrid technique is used to avoid unnecessary multiplicative phases as much as possible. The main rationale behind this is as follows. A performance drop can be due to: (i) passing the workload's optimal parallelism level in the growth phase; or (ii) dynamic changes in the running workload or available hardware resources. This happens when, for example, a new process joins the system.

Whenever there is a performance drop, RUBIC first assumes the slowdown is caused by passing the workload's optimal parallelism level. Therefore, it linearly decreases the parallelism (lines 31-32), instead of a multiplicative decrease.

If a linear decrease does not produce the desired outcome, and the performance loss still persists in the next round, a multiplicative decrease happens (lines 26 to 29).

The variable *reduction* enables the interleaving between the two phases above.

4. EVALUATION

In this section we evaluate RUBIC. The purpose of this evaluation is to thoroughly analyze the behavior of our technique in static/dynamic and single-/multi-process environments. The main examined features are: performance, efficiency, fairness and adaptability. Throughout our experiments, we show how RUBIC outperforms the existing solutions in all the above features.

4.1 The System's Performance Function

As stated earlier in Section 1, in a multi-process environment, one must consider two main factors for optimal resource allocation: (i) the system's overall performance, rather than each process' performance alone; and (ii) fairness to ensure all processes get some fair share of the system and no process starves.

Therefore, we must define the system's overall performance function so that it reflects both aforementioned features. To do so, we resort to Nash's solution for the bargaining problem (NSBP) [13].

Algorithm 2 Adaptive parallelism algorithm in the monitoring thread

```
1: growth ← CUBIC, reduction ← LINEAR, T_p ← 0
2: while running do
3:     Sleep(TIME_PERIOD)
4:     T_c ← CalculateCurrentThroughput()
5:     if (T_c ≥ T_p) then
6:         L_p ← L_RUBIC
7:         if (growth = CUBIC) then
8:             Δt_max ← Δt_max + 1
9:             L_cubic ←
10:                L_max + β(Δt_max − ∛(L_max × α/β))^3
11:            L_RUBIC ← max(L_cubic, L_RUBIC + 1)
12:            growth ← LINEAR
13:        else
14:            L_RUBIC ← L_RUBIC + 1
15:            growth ← CUBIC
16:        end if
17:        if (T_p ≠ 0) then
18:            reduction ← LINEAR
19:        end if
20:        for each thread where L_p ≤ tid < L_RUBIC do
21:            Signal(thread.semaphore)
22:        end for
23:        T_p ← T_c
24:    else
25:        Δt_max ← 0
26:        if (reduction = MULTIPLICATIVE) then
27:            L_max ← L_RUBIC
28:            L_RUBIC ← αL_RUBIC
29:            reduction ← LINEAR
30:        else
31:            L_RUBIC ← L_RUBIC − 2
32:            reduction ← MULTIPLICATIVE
33:        end if
34:        growth ← LINEAR
35:        T_p ← 0
36:    end if
37: end while
```

For a process ρ, running a parallel workload ω, we define the speed-up function of the process ρ ($S_\rho(\omega)$) as the ratio between the process's obtained throughput ($T_\rho(\omega)$), and the measured throughput of a sequential execution of the workload ω, in a single process configuration ($T_{seq}(\omega)$). In other words, $S_\rho(\omega) = \frac{T_\rho(\omega)}{T_{seq}(\omega)}$.

Based on NSBP, in a system with N running processes, where each one is running workload ω_ρ, the system's overall performance is defined as the product of all process' speed-up (i.e. $\prod_{\rho=1}^{N} S_\rho(\omega_\rho)$).

For example, it can be easily shown that in a contended system running identical processes, equally sharing the hardware between the processes maximizes the system's overall performance.

4.2 The Efficiency Function

We also define a process's efficiency (E) as the ratio between its achieved speed-up (S) and its parallelism level (L) (i.e. the number of active threads)[17]. Thus, for a process ρ, running a workload ω: $E_\rho(\omega) = \frac{S_\rho(\omega)}{L_\rho(\omega)}$.

Similarly to the system's performance function, we define the systems's total efficiency as the product of all running process, which is expressed as: $\prod_{\rho=1}^{N} E_\rho(\omega_\rho)$

4.3 Allocation Policies

We compare our results to those gathered by different policies referred as *Greedy*, *EqualShare*, *F2C2* [4], and *EBS* [7]. EBS and F2C2 are almost identical and they both implement an AIAD-based controller. The only difference is that,

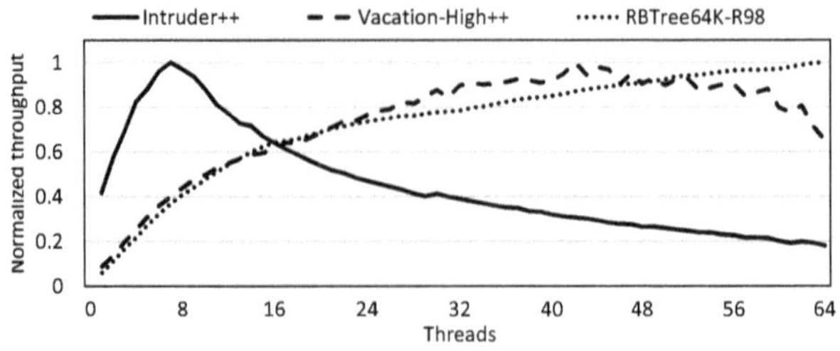

Figure 6: The scalability graph of the evaluated workloads.

F2C2 benefits from an initial exponential growth phase for faster convergence to the optimal level. By this mechanism, the controller initially doubles the parallelism level instead of increasing it by 1. After the first performance loss, F2C2 halves the parallelism level and switches to pure AIAD until the end, as in EBS.

With Greedy, each process tries to take over all the hardware by spawning as many parallel threads as the h/w contexts.

In EqualShare, each process takes an equal share of the h/w context, regardless of its workload. This policy relies on a central entity to decide upon the number of threads in each process. It is the simplest heuristic we could use to avoid oversubscription. Nevertheless, EqualShare is naïve, since it ignores the running workloads and provides each process with the same amount of h/w contexts, even if some processes actually do not require those many contexts.

Finally, in our implementation of RUBIC, the α and β constants, in Equation (1) from Section 2, are set to 0.8 and 0.1, respectively, to obtain the best results.

4.4 Methodology and Workloads

We evaluated the policies in a 4-socket machine consisting of AMD Opteron 6272 CPUs, each with 16 cores, where each core runs one thread, resulting in 64 h/w contexts and total memory of 32GB, running Linux kernel 3.2.0-58.

The monitoring thread measures the commit-rate every 10 milliseconds.

We have implemented all the policies and incorporated them into the RSTM transactional framework [18], using SwissTM [19] as the underlying TM runtime. We consider three different benchmarks: Vacation and Intruder from the STAMP benchmark suite [3] and the Red-Black-Tree micro benchmark (with 64K elements and 98% look-up operations). These well-known benchmarks are chosen to represent applications from a wide scalability spectrum, ranging from poorly to highly scalable workloads.

Furthermore, for the sake of simplicity, the thread placement is left to the OS's default policy.

Figure 6 shows the scalability graph of each benchmark. In this graph, we measure the throughput in terms of transaction commit-rate as the number of parallel threads grows from 1 to 64. To make the results from each benchmark comparable, the values are normalized relatively to the peak throughput that was measured in each workload.

It should be noted that the choice of the host machine, underlying parallelism runtime and the benchmark does not affect the conclusions we draw next. This observation stems from the fact that our techniques only depend on the scalability curve defined by each running process. The only requirement is that the scalability graph of the workloads must monotonically increase until its peak point.

The metric we use to calculate throughput is commit-rate, measured by the number of commits per second for each process. We use the throughput values to calculate the performance and the efficiency metrics that are previously defined in sections 4.1 and 4.2.

Each experiment lasts for 10 seconds and performance results are the average of 50 repeated experiments to minimize the evaluation noise.

We run the experiments in both pairwise and single-process settings. In the pairwise execution, two co-running processes run distinct workloads, with the same starting time. This results into three pairs of workloads. In a single process setting, a single process runs either of the workloads.

4.5 Performance Results

We now present the obtained performance results of all allocation policies.

4.5.1 Pairwise Execution

Figure 7 depicts the system's overall metrics for the pairwise execution of the workloads.

Figure 7a shows the system's total speed-up with each workload pair and the geometric average of all three pairwise experiments. It is evident that for all workload pairs and also on average, RUBIC achieves the best results, while Greedy proves to be the worst policy. The poor performance of Greedy is due to ignoring the running workloads and oversubscribing the system, as expected.

EqualShare performs poorly too, as it also neglects the running workloads. This is especially evident in the workload pairs that include *Intruder*, where the 32 h/w contexts allocated to this workload cause severe performance loss for the running process and the system's overall performance, consequently. EqualShare performs better with the *Vac/RBT* pair. This is because both running workloads scale up to 32 threads. Hence, no workload suffers from performance loss, due to over-allocation. Nonetheless, even with this workload pair, EqualShare is not the best policy, as it still suffers from ignoring the running workloads and improper resource allocation.

Surprisingly, unlike what we initially expected, EBS and F2C2 perform very differently. With all workload pairs, EBS outperforms F2C2. Furthermore, with the *Int/Vac* pair, EBS's performance is comparable to RUBIC's. This is because, with this pair, running both workloads at their peak parallelism level does not oversubscribe the system. Therefore, the greedy characteristic of EBS neither oversubscribes the system nor leads to unfair resource allocation. However, this situation is not the case for the other pairs, where RUBIC outperforms EBS because of EBS's unfair allocation and oversubscription.

On average over all pairwise experiments, RUBIC enhances the system's overall performance by 26% and 500% with regard to the second-best policy (EBS) and the worst policy (Greedy), respectively.

The total numbers of running s/w threads in the system are depicted in Figure 7b. We expected all adaptive policies to keep the total number of threads below the oversubscription line (the dashed line). Perhaps surprisingly, only RUBIC meets our expectation. In fact, except for the *Int/Vac* pair, where EBS maintains the total number of threads be-

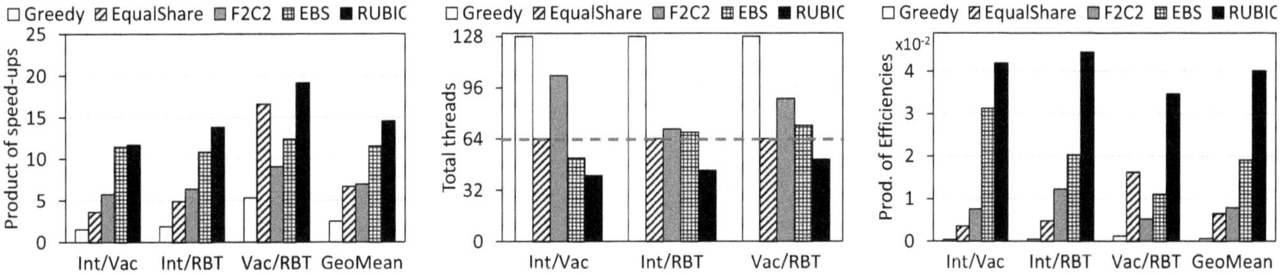

(a) Total performance (b) Total number of threads (c) Total efficiency

Figure 7: The system's overall metrics in pairwise execution of the workloads.

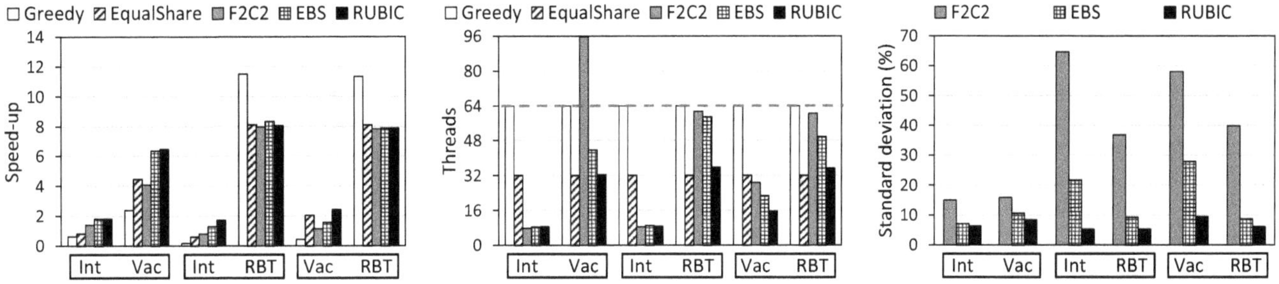

(a) Per-process speed-ups (b) Per-process threads (c) Per-process threads std. deviation

Figure 8: The system's per-process metrics in pairwise execution of the workloads (in graph (c) lower is better).

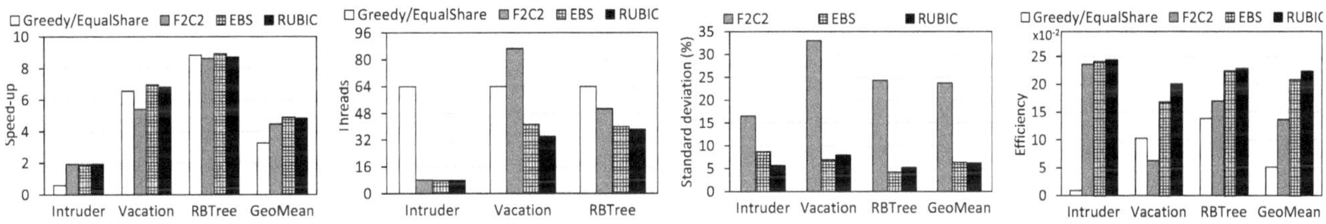

(a) Speed-up (b) No. of threads (c) Threads std. deviation (d) Process efficiency

Figure 9: Process-specific metrics for single-process execution of the workloads (in graph (c) lower is better).

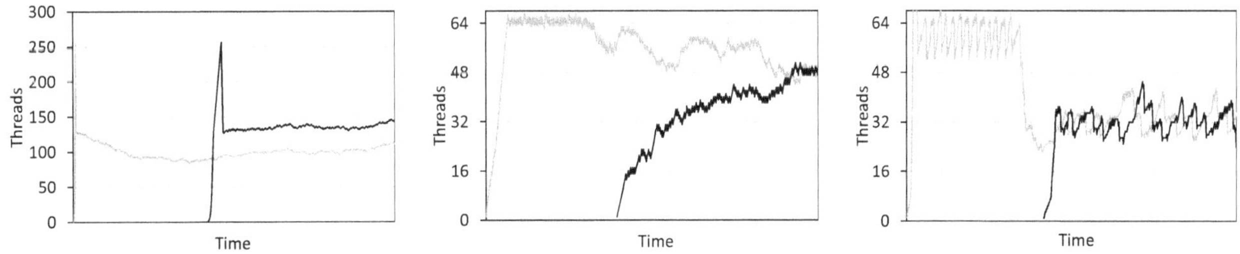

(a) F2C2 (b) EBS (c) RUBIC

Figure 10: Number of active threads over time, in 2 homogeneous processes with different arrival time. With F2C2 and EBS techniques, the processes are greedy and oversubscribe the system to get more computational power. But, with RUBIC, the processes reach a fair equilibrium without oversubscribing the hardware.

low 64, EBS and F2C2 cannot keep the system's overall state below the oversubscription line. This is caused by the greedy nature of these policies, where co-running processes with scalable workloads get involved in a race over resources and oversubscribe the system.

Due to higher performance and lower resource consumption, RUBIC is theoretically expected to be the most efficient policy as well. The total efficiency results in Figure 7c confirm that expectation. As in the performance results, EBS comes after RUBIC as the second-most efficient policy, while Greedy is the least efficient one.

On average over all pairwise experiments, RUBIC proves to be 2 and 66 times more efficient than the second-most efficient policy (EBS) and the least efficient policy (Greedy), respectively.

Figure 8 demonstrates the per-process statistics of the pairwise execution of the workloads. This information helps us better understand the superior overall performance of RUBIC. In the graphs, each workload pair is specified by a rectangle and each 2-bar group represents a whole pairwise experiment.

Interestingly, in Figure 8a (and unlike Figure 7a), Greedy does not always lead to the worst speed-up. In fact, the *RBT* workload always achieves the highest speed-up with Greedy, when compared to other policies. However, taking a look at *RBT*'s counterparts in the pairwise execution, Greedy achieves very low speed-up for both *Intruder* and *Vacation* workloads. This justifies Greedy's very low overall performance.

Comparing RUBIC's per-process speed-up statistics, in Figure 8a, to EBS's, they both have comparable speed-up gains running the *Int/Vac* pair. Nevertheless, *RBT*'s counterparts always gain higher speed-up with RUBIC. This is due to the fairness characteristic of RUBIC. In other words, RUBIC slightly sacrifices a very scalable process' performance to achieve a much higher speed-up gain on a less scalable process (e.g., 1% of *RBT*'s speed-up in exchange for 10% improvement in *Intruder*). Figure 8c shows how RUBIC allocates less threads to *RBT* to reduce the pressure on its *Intruder* and *Vacation* counterparts. Consequently, both *Intruder* and *Vacation* experience a performance boost, which highly affects the system's overall performance.

This interesting feature of RUBIC is also known as *proportional fairness*, which is a well-studied topic in the context of resource allocation in distributed systems [14].

Furthermore, Figure 8b proves RUBIC to be the most stable adaptive policy. In this figure, the lowest standard deviation in resource allocation, across all 50 repetitions of each experiment, belongs to RUBIC. On the contrary, F2C2 is the most unstable adaptive solution.

It is worth nothing that the unexpected poor performance and low stability of F2C2 stem from the initial exponential growth phase. By this initial phase, a process can fall onto a performance plateau, where the AIAD-based technique cannot exit from, preventing the controller from ever converging. This is visible, for example, when running the workload pair *Int/Vac*, since *Vacation*'s parallelism level goes beyond the number of h/w contexts and never falls back (Figure 8c).

4.5.2 Single-process Execution

Although RUBIC originally targets multi-process environments, it is also relevant to evaluate it in single-process scenarios.

It should be noted that in single-process scenarios, EqualShare and Greedy become identical, as they both give all the hardware to a single running process.

Figure 9a depicts the achieved speed-up of all the policies, running either of the workloads. For all the workloads and also on average, RUBIC's speed-up is always comparable with the best performing policy.

Figure 9b shows that RUBIC achieves the aforementioned speed-up by allocating slightly less threads to the running process. However, RUBIC's thread allocation is always the closest one to the best performing policy (i.e. EBS).

Furthermore, on average, RUBIC is the most stable policy, by having the lowest standard deviation in its allocation results throughout the repeated experiments, depicted in Figure 9c. Nevertheless, the same figure suggests that EBS's stability is very comparable to RUBIC.

4.6 Convergence

This section analyzes the convergence behavior of RUBIC and the other parallelism tuning solutions.

To do so, we conduct the following experiment: two processes, P1 and P2, run an identical workload. However, these process have different arrival times. P2 arrives 5 seconds after P1 starts running and the whole experiment lasts for 10 seconds.

We record each process' parallelism level during the experiment. Then we see how P1 behaves before P2's arrival and how both processes behave as P2 joins the system.

To make the running processes actually fight over resources, we chose to use a conflict-free red-back-tree workload (i.e. 100% read-only transactions). This workload is highly scalable and scales up to the number of h/w contexts, in a single-process scenario. However, with 2 running processes a fair and efficient allocation state is when the processes equally share the hardware and each uses 32 s/w threads.

Figure 10 shows the behavior of different online policies in the aforementioned experiment. We see that each policy behaves very differently from the others.

In Figure 10a, F2C2 exhibits a pathological behavior: neither before, nor after P2's arrival, the system converges to an efficient state. The initial growth phase exponentially increases the parallelism level to beyond the number of h/w contexts. Then, the F2C2 controller gets stuck on a performance plateau, and very slowly decreases the parallelism level, but never converges to 64 threads. As P2 arrives, P2 falls into the same plateau. Interestingly, upon P2's arrival, P1 changes its behavior and starts slowly increasing its parallelism level, as well as P2. In fact, after P2's arrival, both processes fall into a race and greedily increase their resource usage.

In Figure 10b, EBS performs the best before P2's arrival (unlike F2C2). P1's parallelism level gradually converges to 64 threads and remains steady at that level. But, as P2 joins the system, both processes behave rather randomly and they do not converge to the optimal allocation, which is 32 threads per process.

Figure 10c depicts RUBIC's impressive convergence behavior. In the beginning, P1 runs the initial probing phase and quickly converges to 64 threads. From this point on, P2 oscillates around the optimal level (e.g., 64) until P2 joins the system. P2's cubic probing phase coincides with several multiplicative decreases from P1's side. Therefore, both processes, almost immediately, get close to 32 threads and both start oscillating around the optimal allocation line (i.e. 32 threads), until the end of the experiment, unlike the other tuning policies.

5. RELATED WORK

While not a new topic, the problem of adaptive parallelism tuning has received stronger attention in recent years due to the emergence of multi/many-core architectures.

Didona *et. al.* [7] propose an exploration-based scaling (EBS) method to dynamically find the best parallelism level for TM applications. They use transaction commit-rate as the performance measure and try to maximize the throughput by dynamically changing the number of active threads, taking a hill-climbing approach. Recently, Ravichandran *et. al.* [4] introduced F2C2-STM, another adaptive parallelism method. F2C2-STM is similar to Didona's work, except for an initial exponential-growth phase that allows a faster convergence. We compared our results of RUBIC to those of EBS and F2C2-STM in Section 4.

Heiss *et. al.* [20] also take a similar hill-climbing approach to find the optimal parallelism level in transactional database systems.

Ansari *et. al.* [8] and Chan *et. al.* [9] suggest techniques to increase the efficiency of TM applications by limiting the wasted computational power caused by aborted transactions. These methods try to keep the ratio of committed transactions above a predefined threshold by dynamically changing the number of active threads. However, such techniques are not targeted at maximizing the system throughput neither in single-process nor in multi-process environments, as they only limit the amount of wasted work.

Mohtasham *et. al.* [21] propose an online parallelism tuning technique that is based on additive increase and multiplicative decrease phases. However, as discussed in Section 2, this method is unstable and underutilizes the system.

Pusukuri *et. al.* [22] introduce a kernel-level solution to find the near-optimal number of threads for a single parallel application. This method is based on profiling the application offline to find its best parallelism point. However, as it is offline, it is not able to cope with dynamic changes in workload or available hardware resources.

Also, there exists a body of research trying to improve the performance of TM by introducing contention management or transactional scheduling elements to a transactional runtime [23, 24, 25]. Although these approaches may share the concept of scheduling with our work in a broad sense, they focus on rescheduling transactions (threads) inside a single process, while we focus on the interferences between multiple processes. In fact such research works are orthogonal and complementary to ours.

Mohtasham *et. al.* [26] formalize and solve the resource allocation problem for co-existing transactional memory applications, by introducing FRAME. FRAME is a centralized and offline method; hence to obtain the optimal allocation, it requires thorough knowledge of the co-running workloads, which is far from trivial. Similarly, Creech *et. al.* [17] solves the resource allocation problem for co-running OpenMP processes with SCAF.

Rughetti *et. al.* [27, 28] use machine learning techniques to predict the best parallelism level in software and hardware transaction memory. These techniques need a learning phase and are not completely online. Also, due to their dependence on the learning phase, such techniques may only perform well in single-process scenarios.

There is significant work on adaptive parallelism tuning for data-parallel languages, which shares some goals with our proposal [29]. However, there are crucial differences between such context and the one that this paper considers. Most importantly, contention across tasks within a job in data-parallel programs is rare or inexistent; whereas TM applications inherently share data, thus their threads are highly prone to interferences such as data conflicts. Moreover, where TM applications typically run a pool of active threads that is mostly stable, data-parallel programs dynamically unfold a directed acyclic graph of tasks, hence can quickly oscillate between different parallelism levels. Therefore, the assumptions underlying adaptive scheduling techniques for data-parallel languages are not directly applicable to the TM programs.

Furthermore, in the context of task scheduling and aside from the classic schedulers [30], there exists a plethora of contention-aware scheduling techniques [31, 32, 5]. Such methods try to come up with an efficient solution to map software threads to hardware cores and minimize the cross-thread interferences. These methods are orthogonal to the parallelism tuning problem. That is to say, contention-aware schedulers do not change the number of threads in the parallel processes and, given a fixed set of active threads, these methods merely aim at finding the best thread-to-core mapping. Therefore, our solution can complement such schedulers with the ability to limit the total number of active software threads in the system.

6. CONCLUSION AND FUTURE WORK

Transactional memory has proved itself as an elegant and easy-to-use alternative to traditional lock-based methods. Although TM solutions are known to be scalable on multicore processors, due to the inherent workload contention, many TM applications cannot scale up to the ever-increasing parallelism available on commodity many-core machines. In fact, most TM workloads not only stop scaling after peaking at a certain parallelism level, but also start losing performance after that peak.

Hence, it becomes increasingly important to devise effective approaches to dynamically tune each process' parallelism in order to reach the maximum throughput.

This problem has received recent attention. However, the state-of-the-art solutions are tailored to and evaluated considering single-process scenarios, thus neglecting the dynamics of the system, the running workload and fairness in multiprocess environments.

This paper proposes RUBIC: a decentralized method for adaptive parallelism tuning for co-located transactional multithreaded processes. Our evaluation with different workloads and scenarios shows that RUBIC enhances the system's performance compared to the state-of-the-art parallelism tuning solutions in multi-process environments, while exhibiting considerably faster convergence and higher fairness.

Although this paper focuses on the specific case of programs based on the transactional memory paradigm, RUBIC is extensible to any type of malleable application. The key insight is that, as long as there are meaningful and precise ways of measuring the throughput of each process, it can serve as the input to RUBIC. In future work, we plan to extend RUBIC to support a wider range of the target applications, including non-transactional and non-malleable parallel applications.

7. ACKNOWLEDGMENTS

This work has been partially supported by Fundação para a Ciência e Tecnologia (FCT) through the project with the reference UID/CEC/50021/2013.

8. REFERENCES

[1] W. Ruan, T. Vyas, Y. Liu, and M. Spear, "Transactionalizing legacy code: An experience report using GCC and memcached," *ACM SIGARCH Computer Architecture News*, 2014.

[2] V. Luchangco, M. Wong, H. Boehm, *et al.*, "Transactional memory support for C++," 2014.

[3] C. C. Minh, J. Chung, C. Kozyrakis, and K. Olukotun, "STAMP: Stanford transactional applications for multi-processing," IISWC'08, 2008.

[4] K. Ravichandran and S. Pande, "F2C2-STM: Flux-based feedback-driven concurrency control for STMs," IPDPS'14, IEEE, 2014.

[5] T. Harris, M. Maas, and V. J. Marathe, "Callisto: co-scheduling parallel runtime systems," EuroSys'14, ACM, 2014.

[6] S. Peter, A. Schüpbach, P. Barham, *et al.*, "Design principles for end-to-end multicore schedulers," HotPar'10, USENIX Association, 2010.

[7] D. Didona, P. Felber, D. Harmanci, P. Romano, and J. Schenker, "Identifying the optimal level of parallelism in transactional memory applications," in *Networked Systems*, Springer Berlin Heidelberg, 2013.

[8] M. Ansari, M. Luján, C. Kotselidis, *et al.*, "Robust adaptation to available parallelism in transactional memory applications," in *Transactions on High-Performance Embedded Architectures and Compilers III*, Springer, 2011.

[9] K. Chan, K. T. Lam, and C.-L. Wang, "Adaptive thread scheduling techniques for improving scalability of software transactional memory," PDCN'11, ACTA Press., 2011.

[10] D. Feitelson and L. Rudolph, "Toward convergence in job schedulers for parallel supercomputers," in *Job Scheduling Strategies for Parallel Processing*, Springer Berlin Heidelberg, 1996.

[11] R. Guerraoui, M. Kapalka, and J. Vitek, "STMBench7: A benchmark for software transactional memory," EuroSys'07, ACM, 2007.

[12] W. Maldonado, P. Marlier, P. Felber, *et al.*, "Scheduling support for transactional memory contention management," in *ACM Sigplan Notices*, ACM, 2010.

[13] J. F. Nash Jr, "The bargaining problem," *Econometrica: Journal of the Econometric Society*, 1950.

[14] F. P. Kelly, A. K. Maulloo, and D. K. Tan, "Rate control for communication networks: shadow prices, proportional fairness and stability," *Journal of the Operational Research society*, 1998.

[15] D. M. Chiu and R. Jain, "Analysis of the increase and decrease algorithms for congestion avoidance in computer networks," *Computer Networks and ISDN systems*, 1989.

[16] S. Ha, I. Rhee, and L. Xu, "CUBIC: a new TCP-friendly high-speed TCP variant," *ACM SIGOPS Operating Systems Review*, 2008.

[17] T. Creech, A. Kotha, and R. Barua, "Efficient multiprogramming for multicores with SCAF," MICRO-46, ACM, 2013.

[18] V. J. Marathe, M. F. Spear, C. Heriot, A. Acharya, D. Eisenstat, W. N. Scherer III, and M. L. Scott, "Lowering the overhead of nonblocking software transactional memory," TRANSACT'06, 2006.

[19] A. Dragojević, R. Guerraoui, and M. Kapalka, "Stretching transactional memory," PLDI'09, ACM, 2009.

[20] H. Heiss and R. Wagner, "Adaptive load control in transaction processing systems," VLDB'91, Morgan Kaufmann Publishers Inc., 1991.

[21] A. Mohtasham and J. Barreto, "Brief announcement: Fair adaptive parallelism for concurrent transactional memory applications," SPAA'15, ACM, 2015.

[22] K. Pusukuri, R. Gupta, and L. Bhuyan, "Thread reinforcer: Dynamically determining number of threads via OS level monitoring," IISWC'11, 2011.

[23] R. Guerraoui, M. Herlihy, and B. Pochon, "Toward a theory of transactional contention managers," PODC'05, ACM, 2005.

[24] W. N. Scherer, III and M. L. Scott, "Advanced contention management for dynamic software transactional memory," PODC'05, ACM, 2005.

[25] R. M. Yoo and H.-H. S. Lee, "Adaptive transaction scheduling for transactional memory systems," SPAA'08, ACM, 2008.

[26] A. Mohtasham, R. Filipe, and J. Barreto, "FRAME: Fair resource allocation in multi-process environments," ICPADS'15, IEEE, 2015.

[27] D. Rughetti, P. Di Sanzo, A. Pellegrini, B. Ciciani, and F. Quaglia, "Tuning the level of concurrency in software transactional memory: An overview of recent analytical, machine learning and mixed approaches," in *Transactional Memory. Foundations, Algorithms, Tools, and Applications*, Springer, 2015.

[28] D. Rughetti, P. Romano, F. Quaglia, and B. Ciciani, "Automatic tuning of the parallelism degree in hardware transactional memory," EuroPar'14, Springer, 2014.

[29] K. Agrawal, Y. He, W. J. Hsu, and C. E. Leiserson, "Adaptive scheduling with parallelism feedback," PPoPP'06, ACM, 2006.

[30] A. S. Tanenbaum and H. Bos, *Modern operating systems*. Prentice Hall Press, 2014.

[31] S. Zhuravlev, J. C. Saez, S. Blagodurov, A. Fedorova, and M. Prieto, "Survey of scheduling techniques for addressing shared resources in multicore processors," *ACM Computing Surveys (CSUR)*, 2012.

[32] A. Merkel, J. Stoess, and F. Bellosa, "Resource-conscious scheduling for energy efficiency on multicore processors," in *EuroSys'10*, ACM, 2010.

Extending TM Primitives using Low Level Semantics

Mohamed M. Saad
Virginia Tech
msaad@vt.edu

Roberto Palmieri
Virginia Tech
robertop@vt.edu

Ahmed Hassan
Virginia Tech
hassan84@vt.edu

Binoy Ravindran
Virginia Tech
binoy@vt.edu

ABSTRACT

Transactional Memory (TM) has recently emerged as an optimistic concurrency control technique that isolates concurrent executions at the level of memory reads and writes, therefore providing an easy programming interface. However, such transparency could be overly conservative from an application-level perspective. In this work, we propose an extension to the classical TM primitives (read and write) to capture program code semantics (e.g., conditional expressions) while maintaining the same level of programming abstraction. We deployed this extension on two state-of-the-art STM algorithms and integrated it into the GCC compiler and the RSTM software framework. Results showed speedups of up to 4× (average 1.6×) on different applications including micro benchmarks and STAMP.

Keywords

Transactional Memory, Semantics, GCC

1. INTRODUCTION

Transactional Memory (TM) is a programming abstraction for accessing shared memory data without exposing any lock interfaces to the application so that difficulties and drawbacks such as deadlock, livelock, and priority inversion are prevented. With TM, programmers organize blocks of code that access shared memory addresses as atomic sections (or *transactions*) in which reads and writes appear to take effect instantaneously. As a common pattern, each transaction maintains its own read-set and write-set to detect conflicts with other concurrent transactions. When a conflict happens, a contention manager [22] resolves it by aborting one transaction and allowing the other to proceed to commit, yielding (the illusion of) atomicity. TM was originally proposed in hardware (HTM) [21] and later in software (STM) [35].

In order for a TM implementation to be generic, conflicts are usually detected at the level of memory addresses. For this reason, the TM abstraction can be expressed using four instructions: `TM_BEGIN`, `TM_END`, `TM_READ`, and `TM_WRITE`. The first two identify the transaction boundaries while the last two define the barriers for every memory read and write that occurs within those boundaries. TM algorithms differ in the way those instructions are implemented. Although frameworks may add other features, such as allowing external aborts, non-transactional reads/writes, or irrevocable operations, the above four instructions are used to form the body of most TM solutions.

Despite TM's high programmability and generality, its performance is still not yet as good as (or better than) optimized manual implementations of synchronization. To overcome that, researchers have investigated various approaches with different design choices. Regarding STM, they mostly varied the internal granularity of locking and/or validation of accessed memory addresses. Examples of those solutions include coarse-grained mutual exclusion of commit phases, as used in NOrec [11]; compact bloom filters [6] to track memory accesses, as used in RingSTM [36]; and fine-grained ownership records, as used in TL2 [12]. On the other hand, current HTM processors [30, 7] have a "best effort" nature because transactions are not guaranteed to progress in HTM (even if they are executed alone without any actual concurrency). That is why an efficient software "fallback" path is needed (i.e., hybrid TM) when hardware transactions repeatedly fail [13]. Recent literature proposes many compelling solutions that make the fallback path fast under different conditions [10, 31, 8, 13, 25, 4].

The key commonality of all the aforementioned approaches is that they do not challenge the main objective of TM itself, which is providing generality at the application level. This is also the reason why those smart and advanced solutions still retain some of the fundamental inefficiency of TM. On the other hand, providing high performance in multi-threaded applications before the advent of TM, when thread synchronization was manually done using fine-grained locks and/or lock-free designs, depended upon the specific application semantics. For example, identifying the critical sections and the best number of locks to use are design choices that can be made only after deeply knowing the semantics of the application itself (i.e., what the application does).

A related question that arises in this regard is: *Is there some room for including semantics in TM frameworks without sacrificing their generality?* If the answer is "yes", which is what we claim and assess in this paper, then we will finally be able to overcome one of the main obstacles that has existed alongside TM since its early stages, and boost its performance accordingly. Recent literature provides a few

SPAA '16, July 11-13, 2016, Pacific Grove, CA, USA

DOI: http://dx.doi.org/10.1145/2935764.2935794

semantic-based concurrency controls, which will be detailed in Section 2. However, they either solve specific application patterns [33], break the high abstraction of TM [20, 15], or are orthogonal to TM [19, 18].

Motivated by the above question, this paper provides three major contributions. First, we identify a set of semantics that can be included in TM frameworks without impacting the generality of the TM abstraction (we call them *TM-friendly* semantics), and we extend the existing TM API to include such semantics. Second, we show how to modify STM algorithms to exploit such semantic-based APIs. Finally, we illustrate how we embedded those extensions in compiler passes (using GCC) so that the application developing experience will not be altered.

Regarding the first point, with TM-friendly semantics we mean those optimizations that can be decoupled from the application layer. In particular, this paper focuses on optimizing conditional statements (e.g., `if x > 0`) and increments/decrements (e.g., x++), which are commonly used in legacy applications. More details about those semantics are presented in Section 3.

The second contribution involves deploying those TM-friendly semantics with existing state-of-the-art STM algorithms. Roughly, STM algorithms can be classified into two groups according to the technique used for validating transactions. The first group uses *version-based* validation, where each memory location keeps a version number that is used to identify memory changes. The second group uses *value-based* validation, where the content of each location itself is leveraged to detect memory modifications. For value-based algorithms, we propose *semantic validation* as a generalization of value-based validation, allowing TM frameworks to define a specific validator for the semantic-based instructions. For version-based approaches, we propose a methodology for adapting them to allow a hybrid (i.e., version/semantic) validation mechanism. In Section 4, we show how to modify NOrec [11] (a value-based algorithm) and TL2 [12] (a version-based algorithm) to include semantics. Then, in Section 5, we discuss the correctness of those new algorithms.

Our last contribution is to integrate semantic APIs and their corresponding STM algorithms into current TM frameworks. We propose two approaches to achieve that:

- The first approach is to implement semantic extensions entirely as a *compiler pass*, thus not exposing any API additions to the programmer. This approach has the advantages of being entirely transparent and retaining backward compatibility with existing applications that leverage GCC's transactional API.
- The second approach involves exposing the new semantic APIs as TM interfaces. These new APIs give conscious programmers an opportunity to better exploit semantics while developing concurrent applications. Clearly, this approach increases the chance of achieving higher performance, with the cost of reducing, although marginally, the programmability level.

Since each of those two solutions fits specific interests, we assess both of them in this paper. We assess the latter solution (which is easier to implement) by enriching the API of the RSTM [24] framework with our semantics. Regarding the former, we show in Section 6 how we modified the compilation passes of GCC to provide full compilation support with limited overhead in terms of both compilation process and execution time. In Section 7, we evaluated our semantic-based TM (using both RSTM and GCC) with the following applications: Bank, a benchmark that simulates a multithreading application where threads mostly perform money transfers; LRU-Cache, a benchmark that simulates a software cache with the least-recently-used replacement policy; a hash-table benchmark; and the STAMP benchmark suite [28]. The results show that enabling semantics boosts performance consistently, yielding a peak of 4× improvement when semantics is highly exploited. Also, contrasting the performance trend of GCC experiments with that of RSTM experiments allows understanding the consequences of moving the whole TM framework, including our semantic extensions, into the compiler level.

All the implementations used in this paper, including the new version of GCC and RSTM, are available as open-source projects at http://www.hyflow.org.

2. RELATED WORK

Not surprisingly, the trials to include semantics in TM started in the literature as early as TM itself. In fact, the potential objective of the first TM proposal, as can be easily inferred from the title of the first TM paper [21], was providing architectural support for lock-free data structures. However, the approach proposed in that paper, as well as subsequent approaches, was fairly general because its main objective was improving programmability. As a result, the performance of TM could not compete with handcrafted (i.e., very optimized) fine-grained and lock-free designs.

In the last decade, involving semantics to improve TM performance has been an important topic, addressed by approaches such as open nested transactions [29], elastic transactions [15], specialized STM [14], and early release [20]. The main downside of all those attempts is that they move the entire burden of providing optimizations to the programmer, and propose a modified framework to accept those programmer modifications. Since TM has been mainly proposed to make concurrency control as transparent as possible from the programmer's standpoint, the practical adoption of the above approaches remained limited. The innovations presented in this paper overcome those issues by providing solutions that preserve the generality of TM, do not give up optimizations and semantics, and cope with the current state-of-the-art TM implementations.

Another research direction focused on developing collections of transactional blocks (essentially data structure operations) that perform better than the corresponding "naive" TM-based counterparts (i.e., when the sequential specification of a data structure is made concurrent using TM). Methodologies like transactional boosting [19, 18], consistency oblivious programming [3, 5], semantic locking [16], and partitioned transactions [38] are examples of that direction. Despite the promising results, those approaches remain isolated from TM as synchronization abstractions and appear as standalone components designed mainly for data structures.

Involving compilers in TM's concurrency control is currently becoming mandatory given the enhanced GCC release [37], which includes TM support. However, to the best of our knowledge, very few works addressed the issue of detecting TM-friendly semantics at compilation time similar to what we propose in this paper. Among them, one recent approach proposes a new *read-modify-write* instruction to handle some programming patterns in TM [33]. However, that approach still addresses specific execution patterns and does not generalize the problem like our attempt in this paper, which rather pushes more in the direction of abstracting the problem and providing a comprehensive solution to inject semantics into existing TM frameworks.

3. TM-FRIENDLY API

In this section we show the proposed semantics that can be injected into TM frameworks without hampering the generality of TM itself. As mentioned before, TM defines two language/library constructs for reading (`TM_READ`) and writing (`TM_WRITE`) memory addresses. In most cases, these constructs enforce a "conservative" conflict resolution policy; two concurrent transactions are said to be conflicting if they access the same address and at least one access is a write. Algorithm 1 gives an example that shows why such a policy may be too conservative due to lack of semantics.

Algorithm 1 Two transactions conflicting at the memory level but not at the semantic level.

```
                    Initially x = y = 5
TM_BEGIN(T1)
if x > 0 || y > 0 then
   // Do reads/writes ...
                              TM_BEGIN(T2)
                              x++
                              y--
                              TM_END
TM_END
```

In this example, when T_1 executes its first line, existing TM algorithms save x and y in the read-set. Starting from this point, in order to preserve consistency, most TM implementations force T_1 to abort as soon as any concurrent change in x or y occurs. This abort can be triggered during the validation of T_1's next read (e.g., in NOrec), when T_1 tries to commit (e.g., in TL2), or immediately (e.g., in Intel HTM processors). In that specific example, since T_2 writes to x and y and commits before T_1 reaches its commit phase, most TM implementations force T_1 to abort. However, T_1 has no real issue at the semantic level and can safely commit since the boolean result of the conditional expression still holds, which means that the conflict triggered by the TM framework is a "false conflict" at the semantic level.

`TM_GT(address, value|address)`	greater than
`TM_GTE(address, value|address)`	greater or equals
`TM_LT(address, value|address)`	less than
`TM_LTE(address, value|address)`	less or equals
`TM_EQ(address, value|address)`	equals
`TM_NEQ(address, value|address)`	not equals
`TM_INC(address, value)`	increment
`TM_DEC(address, value)`	decrement

Table 1: Extended TM Constructs.

Examples like the above motivated us to design extensions to the traditional transactional constructs that enrich the TM programming model. Those constructs are classified according to their semantics into two categories (summarized in Table 1). The first category includes *conditional operators*, which take two operands and return a boolean state of the conditional expression. The operands in this category can be two addresses or an address and a value. At the memory level, a traditional execution of those constructs inside a transaction implies one or two calls to `TM_READ` (depending upon the type of operands). Using our constructs, we consider the whole expression as one semantic operation, and the safety of the enclosing transaction is preserved by validating that the return value of the condition remains the same until the transaction commits. The second category includes increment/decrement operations, which take an address and an offset as arguments. Unlike the first category, the traditional way of handling transactional increment/decrement involves both `TM_READ` and `TM_WRITE`. In our solution, leveraging semantics means invoking one semantic operation that performs the actual read only at commit time, which allows for more concurrency.

Including those semantic operations in TM frameworks is appealing for two reasons. First, they are commonly used in applications, as we show later with some examples. Second, the integration can be entirely done at compilation time, where the compiler can detect semantic operators and translate them.

An interesting feature of the semantic operations listed in Table 1 is that they can compose by having more than one operator and/or more than one variable in the conditional expression. For example, the scenario shown in Algorithm 1 can be further enhanced if the whole conditional expression (i.e., `TM_READ(x) > 0 || TM_READ(y) > 0`) is considered as one semantic read operation. In this example, if the condition was initially `true` and then a concurrent transaction modifies only one variable, either x or y, to be negative, considering the clause as a whole avoids aborting T_1 given the `OR` operator. A similar enhancement consists of allowing complex expressions in conditional statements (e.g., `x + y > 0`), where modifications on multiple variables may compensate each other so that the return value of the overall expression remains unchanged. Although supporting such complex expressions is appealing because it may save additional aborts, integrating them into algorithm designs and GCC may add overheads in terms of compilation process and execution time. For that reason, we currently do not support those complex expressions, and we plan for further investigation on them. A more detailed discussion about those operations is in the technical report [34].

3.1 TM-friendly semantics in action

To further support the need of injecting semantics into the classical TM abstraction, we now show examples from real benchmarks and applications whose performance can be enhanced by our semantic TM extensions. These examples are clearly not exhaustive, but they are representative of programming patterns used in concurrent programming.

Hashtable with open addressing. Operations in such a hash table usually start by probing the table in order to find a matching index for a given hash value. This function can be enhanced by our approach because it consists of a chain of conditional expressions that check specific semantics and do not impose certain values of `state` or `set` (e.g., it may only require the checked cells to be not free and either flagged as removed or having a different value from the hashed one). On the other hand, when using the classical read/write TM constructs, concurrent changes to the accessed cells will abort the probing transaction. Considering semantics through our proposed extensions avoid such aborts. Algorithm 2 depicts pseudocode of the probing method and its transformed semantic version.

Algorithm 2 Using our semantic constructs to enhance hash table probing.

```
TM_BEGIN
  ▷ Using our constructs: while (TM_NEQ(states[index], FREE) && (TM_EQ(states[index], REMOVED) || TM_NEQ(set[index], value))
while TM_READ(states[index]) != FREE && (TM_READ(states[index]) == REMOVED || TM_READ(set[index]) != value) do
  index = (index + probe)
return TM_READ(states[index]) == FREE ? -1 : index;
TM_END
```

Algorithm 3 Using our semantic constructs to enhance dequeue operation.

```
TM_BEGIN
                 ▷ Using our constructs: If (TM_EQ(head, tail))
if TM_READ(head) != TM_READ(tail) then
  return false;
item = array[TM_READ(head) % array_size];
                 ▷ Using our constructs: TM_INC(head, 1);
TM_WRITE(head, TM_READ(head) + 1)
return true;
TM_END
```

Queues. Any efficient concurrent queue implementation should let an `enqueue` operation execute concurrently with a `dequeue` operation if the queue is not empty. However, this case is not allowed using traditional TM constructs because the `dequeue` operation compares the head with the tail in order to detect the special case of an empty queue. Algorithm 3 shows how we re-enable this level of concurrency in an array-based queue using our constructs.

Algorithm 4 Using our semantic constructs to enhance reservations in the Vacation benchmark.

```
TM_BEGIN
for n = 0; n < ids.length; n++ do
  res = tablePtr.find(ids[n]);
                 ▷ Using our constructs: TM_GT(res.numFree, 0)
  if TM_READ(res.numFree) > 0 then
                 ▷ Using our constructs: TM_GT(res.price, max_price)
    if TM_READ(res.price) > max_price then
      max_price = TM_READ(res.price);
      max_id = id;
reservation = tablePtr.find(max_id);
                 ▷ Using our constructs: TM_INC(res.numFree, -1)
TM_WRITE(res.numFree, TM_READ(res.numFree) - 1));
TM_END
```

Vacation. This application is included in the STAMP suite [28] and simulates a travel reservation system. The workload consists of clients' reservations; each client uses a coarse-grained transaction to execute its session. Vacation has two main operation profiles: making a reservation and updating offers (e.g., price changes). Although the reservation profile checks the common attributes of the offer (e.g., the number of free slots and the range of price), most of those checks are semantic and do not seek specific values. Using the classical (more conservative) TM model, any update on offers will conflict with all concurrent reservations because of those conditional statements. Using our semantic extensions, as depicted in Algorithm 4, the reservation will not abort as long as the outcomes of the comparison conditions hold (e.g., `number of free slots > 0` and `price > max_price`). The key idea, which also explains well the intuition behind our proposal, is that a reservation does not use the exact value of price or the amount of available resources, it just checks if the price is in the right range and resources are still available.

Kmeans. Kmeans is another STAMP application, which

Algorithm 5 Using our semantic constructs to enhance the Kmeans benchmark.

```
TM_BEGIN
  ▷ Using our constructs: TM_INC(*new_centers_len[index], 1);
TM_WRITE(*new_centers_len[index],
TM_READ(*new_centers_len[index]) + 1);
for j = 0; j < nfeatures; j++ do
        ▷ Using our constructs: TM_INC(new_centers[index][j],
feature[i][j]));
   TM_WRITE(new_centers[index][j],
TM_READ(new_centers[index][j]) + feature[i][j]));
TM_END
```

implements a clustering algorithm that iterates over a set of points and groups them into clusters. The main transactional overhead is in updating the cluster centers, which can be enhanced using our *TM_INC* operation, as shown in Algorithm 5.

4. SEMANTIC-BASED TM ALGORITHMS

The first step towards injecting semantics into STM algorithms is to find an abstract way to define them. The semantic operations listed in Table 1 can be seen as the implementation of two abstract methods:

```
bool cmp(operator, address, val)
void inc(address, delta)
```

where `cmp` and `inc` represent the semantic actions that replace the normal TM behavior (`delta` can be positive or negative to support increment and decrement). In this abstraction, we restrict `cmp` operations in Table 1 to those that have an address and a value as arguments. However, as we show in Section 6, our compilation pass also detects the address-address case and translates it to a specific API call. Extending the STM algorithms presented in this section to cover the address-address case is straightforward, thus we do not include it to simplify the presentation.

In this section, we show how we integrate the above two abstract methods into two state-of-the-art STM algorithms: NOrec [11] and TL2 [12].

4.1 S-NOrec

NOrec is an STM algorithm that exploits value-based validation to eliminate the need for fine-grained locks. A transaction stores the values it reads as metadata in a local read-set and validates this read-set before every read, as well as at the commit phase of writing transactions. The commit phase is protected by a single global timestamped lock. The validation procedure succeeds if all accessed addresses have the same values as what is saved in the read-set.

We extend NOrec to support our constructs as shown in Algorithm 6 (we call the new algorithm S-NOrec), mainly by executing `cmp` and `inc` using additional procedures. The main difference between `read` and `cmp` is that `read` appends the normal address/value pair to the read-set (line 41) while

Algorithm 6 S-NOrec

```
1: procedure Validate(Transaction tx)
2:     time = global_lock
3:     if (time & 1) != 0 then go to 2 end if
4:     for each (addr, operation, val ) in reads do
5:         if ! (addr OP val) then                      ▷ Semantic validation
6:             Abort()
7:     if time != global lock then go to 2 end if
8:     return time
9: end procedure
10: procedure ReadValid(Address addr, Transaction tx)
11:     val = *addr
12:     while snapshot != global lock do
13:         snapshot = Validate(tx)
14:         val = *addr
15:     return val
16: end procedure
17: procedure RAW(Address addr, Transaction tx)
18:     if writes[addr].type = INCREMENT then
19:         val = ReadValid(addr, tx)                    ▷ Promote increment
20:         reads.append(address, val, EQUALS)
21:         writes[addr] = ( entry.value + val, WRITE )
22:     return writes[addr].value
23: end procedure
24: procedure Start(Transaction tx)
25:     do
26:         snapshot = global_lock
27:     while (snapshot & 1) ≠ 0
28: end procedure
29: procedure Compare(Address addr, Operation op, Value operand, Transaction tx)
30:     if writes[addr] ≠ ϕ then
31:         return RAW(addr, tx) OP operand
32:     val = ReadValid(addr, tx)
33:     result = (val OP operand)
34:     reads.append(addr, operand, result ? OP : Inverse(OP))
35:     return result
36: end procedure
37: procedure Read(Address addr, Transaction tx)
38:     if writes[addr] ≠ ϕ then
39:         return RAW(addr, tx)
40:     val = ReadValid(addr, tx)
41:     reads.append(addr, val, EQUALS)
42:     return val
43: end procedure
44: procedure Increment(Address addr, Value delta, Transaction tx)
45:     if writes[addr] ≠ ϕ then
46:         writes[addr] = ( entry.value + delta, entry.type )
47:     else
48:         writes[addr] = ( delta, INCREMENT )
49: end procedure
50: procedure Write(Address addr, Value value, Transaction tx)
51:     writes[addr] = ( value, WRITE )
52: end procedure
```

`cmp` saves the conditional expression (or its inverse if the condition is `false`) in the read-set (line 34). To simplify the `validate` procedure, we consider `read` as a semantic `TX_EQ` operation. Consequently, the `validate` procedure (lines 1-9) becomes a generalization of the original NOrec that uses a semantic validation instead of the original value-based one.

Both `read` and `cmp` read the address using a special procedure, called `readValid` (lines 10-16), that performs a read-set validation (if the global timestamp changed) to ensure the consistency of the current state of the read-set.

Supporting `inc` operations requires storing the delta (i.e., incremented or decremented value) in the write-set, and applying it at commit time. In practice, we support `inc` by overloading NOrec's write-set. In particular, a flag is added to each write-set entry to indicate whether it stores a standard write or an increment.

The cases where a variable is read/written (either semantically or non-semantically) by two different operations in the same transaction are handled by S-NOrec as follows:

- *write after write:* If an `inc` is preceded by a `write` or an `inc`, the new delta is accumulated over the entry's value without changing the entry's flag (line 46). If a `write` is preceded by a `write` or an `inc`, it just overwrites the value and changes the flag to indicate a `write` operation (line 51).
- *read after write:* Both `compare` and `read` check the write-set first for read-after-write conflicts (lines 31 and 39). If the write-set entry is an increment, the `inc` is promoted to traditional `read` and `write` operations (see lines 19-21). The read part of the promotion is also done using the `readValid` procedure (line 19).
- *write after read:* This case is inherently covered because the value of the address will be validated anyway at commit time (because of the read) before the write takes place. It does not matter if the read/write operations are semantic or non-semantic.
- *read after read:* We add two different entries in the read-set for each read. Although this approach looks redundant and may nullify the gain of adopting a semantic validation if one read is semantic and the other is non-semantic, the overhead of discovering duplicates may not be negligible in the normal cases.

S-NOrec is the first STM algorithm, to the best of our knowledge, that supports `cmp` operations. For `inc` operations, a recent approach discusses supporting a pattern similar to our proposal [33]. Interestingly, in contrast with [33], S-NOrec maintains the same privatization and publication properties [26] of the original NOrec algorithm, since it still uses the global timestamp at commit time. In fact, there is no considerable overhead of S-NOrec over NOrec with respect to both processing time and memory occupied, as it only adds the read-set operation type and the write-set flag to the algorithm's metadata.

4.2 S-TL2

TL2 is an STM algorithm that maps shared memory locations to a table of ownership records (`orecs`). Writing transactions lock the `orecs` of their write-set entries at commit instead of acquiring a global lock as in NOrec. Because of that, writing transactions can commit concurrently as long as they access different `orecs`, and hence TL2 is known to scale better than NOrec. To validate reads, TL2 leverages: *i)* a global timestamp, which is atomically incremented by each writing transaction at commit; *ii)* a *start_version* for each transaction, which is set at the beginning of the transaction by snapshotting the global timestamp; and *iii)* an *orec_version* for each `orec`, which is modified by the writing transaction at commit time. This way, validation is done simply by ensuring that the *orec_version* of a newly read address is less than the *start_version* of the transaction, and revalidating the *orec_versions* of the whole read-set at commit time (only if the transaction is a writing transactions).

Algorithm 7 depicts our extended version of TL2 (called S-TL2). The write-set handlers (`inc`, `write` and `raw`) are similar to Algorithm 6, so we did not show them in Algorithm 7. On the other hand, supporting the `cmp` operation in

Algorithm 7 S-TL2

```
1: procedure Start(Transaction tx)
2:     tx.start_version = global_timestamp
3: end procedure
4: procedure Compare( Address addr, Operation op,
5:             Value operand, Transaction tx)
6:     if writes[addr] ≠ φ then
7:         return RAW(addr, tx)
8:     orec = getOrec(addr)
9:     L1 = orec.version
10:    if tx.reads.isEmpty() then            ▷ Phase 1: No reads yet
11:        if orec.lock ∉ {tx, φ} then
12:            go to 8                       ▷ Wait until unlocked
13:        val = *addr
14:        L2 = orec.version
15:        if L1 ≠ L2 then
16:            go to 8                       ▷ Retry read
17:        result = (val OP operand)         ▷ Add to compare-set
18:        compares.append(addr, operand, result ? OP : Inv(OP))
19:        if L1 > start_version then
20:            time = global_timestamp
21:            ValidateCompareSet()
22:            if time != global_timestamp then
23:                go to 20                  ▷ Retry validation
24:            else
25:                start_version = time      ▷ Extend start_version
26:    else                ▷ Phase 2: At least one pervious read occur
27:        if orec.lock ∉ {tx, φ} then
28:            Abort()
29:        val = *addr
30:        L2 = orec.version
31:        if L1 > start_version ∨ L1 != L2 then
32:            Abort()
33:        result = (val OP operand)         ▷ Add to compare-set
34:        compares.append(addr, operand, result ? OP : Inv(OP))
35:    return result
36: end procedure
37: procedure Read(Address addr, Transaction tx)
38:    if writes[addr] ≠ φ then
39:        return RAW(addr, tx)
40:    orec = getOrec(addr)
41:    L1 = orec.version
42:    if orec.lock ∉ {tx, φ} then
43:        Abort()
44:    val = *addr
45:    L2 = orec.version
46:    if L1 > start_version ∨ L1 != L2 then
47:        Abort()
48:    reads.append(orec)                    ▷ Add to read-set
49:    return val
50: end procedure
51: procedure ValidateReadSet(Transaction tx)
52:    for each (orec) in tx.reads do
53:        if orec.lock ∉ {tx,φ} ∨ orec.version > start_version then
54:            Abort()
55: end procedure
56: procedure ValidateCompareSet(Transaction tx)
57:    for each (addr, operation, val ) in tx.compares do
58:        current = *addr
59:        orec = getOrec(addr)
60:        if orec.version > start_version then
61:            if orec.lock ∉ {tx,φ} then
62:                repeat until orec.lock = φ    ▷ Wait until unlocked
63:            if !(current OP val) then         ▷ Semantic validation
64:                Abort()
65: end procedure
66: procedure Commit(Transaction tx)
67:    AcquireWriteSetLocks(tx)
68:    time = global_timestamp
69:    if start_version ≠ time then
70:        ValidateCompareSet(tx)
71:    if !CAS(global_timestamp, time, time+1) then
72:        go to 68                  ▷ Retry compare-set validation
73:    if start_version + 1 ≠ time then
74:        ValidateReadSet(tx)
75:    WriteBack(tx, time + 1)
76:    ReleaseWriteSetLocks(tx)
77: end procedure
```

S-TL2 is more complex than S-NOrec. The first issue is that the actual addresses and their values are not saved in the read-set; only the corresponding `orecs` are saved. To solve this problem, we first define a separate *compare-set* for saving `cmp` operations whose structure is similar to S-NOrec's read-set. In particular, a `read` operation saves the `orec` of the address in the read-set (line 48), and a `cmp` operation saves the actual address along with the information about the compare operation in the compare-set (lines 18 and 34).

The second problem is that we now have two ways of validating reads: the first relies on value-based validation (for `cmp` operations), while the second relies on the relation between the *read_version* of an `orec` and the *start_version* of the enclosing transaction (for `read` operations). To address this issue in an efficient way, we split the execution into three phases. The first phase starts from the transaction begin until the first `read` operation. The second one starts from the first `read` until right before commit. The last phase is the commit phase.

In the first phase, before the first `read` operation, `cmp` operations can be optimized similar to S-NOrec (lines 10-25): the transaction's *start_version* is not used, and rather the compare-set is validated after each `cmp` operation (line 21). If this validation succeeds, the transaction's *start_version* is extended (line 25). This way, we allow semantic validations as long as no `read` operation is executed yet. Another optimization, although less important, is when the address's `orec` is observed to be locked by a concurrent transaction. In this case, the `cmp` operation waits until the `orec` is unlocked instead of aborting the transaction (line 62). In those cases, we employ a timeout mechanism (not shown in the algorithm) to avoid starvation. This optimization makes sense only for `cmp` operations. This is because for `read` operations, observing a locked `orec` means that its *orec_version* will likely be updated before it is unlocked, which also means that the read will be invalidated and the transaction will be aborted anyway. The same optimization is made when a concurrent transaction changes the *orec_version* while reading the variable (line 16), and also when the global-timestamp is changed during the compare-set validation (line 23).

In the second phase, after the first `read` operation, `cmp` operations have to preserve consistency with previous reads, and therefore the transaction's *start_version* cannot be extended anymore. That is why, in this phase, both `read` (lines 37-50) and `cmp` (lines 26-34) validate that the newly read address (even if inside a `cmp` operation) is consistent with the previous reads, by comparing the *orec_version* with the transaction's *start_time* as the original TL2 does.

The commit phase is depicted in lines 66-77. In TL2, the commit phase starts by locking the writes' `orecs` and atomically incrementing the global timestamp. Then the reads are re-validated. If validation succeeds, writes are published and then locks are released. The commit phase of S-TL2 differs from that of TL2 in two points: *i)* the way reads are validated; *ii)* the way the global timestamp is incremented.

Regarding the first point, the read-set and the compare-set are validated differently using `ValidateReadSet` (lines 51-

55) for the former and ValidateCompareSet (lines 56-65) for the latter. Specifically, when the *read_version* of an orec is greater than the *start_version* of the transaction, which means that the value of the address may have been changed, ValidateReadSet aborts the transaction (line 54), while ValidateCompareSet re-computes the expression and aborts only if the return value changes (line 64).

Second, if a concurrent transaction starts its commit phase during ValidateCompareSet, the compare-set has to be re-validated. This is important because the return value of one cmp operation may be affected by this new commit, and thus ValidateCompareSet procedure may return an incorrect result. Lines 68-72 depict how we achieve that (the order of lines is important here): the global timestamp is snapshotted, ValidateCompareSet is called, and then the global timestamp is incremented using CAS instead of using AtomicFetchAndAdd. If the CAS fails, validation is retried. It is worth to note that this mechanism is not needed for ValidateReadSet because it conservatively aborts the transaction if any orec in the read-set has changed.

S-TL2 requires adding a compare-set as well as a flag in the write-set in addition to the original metadata of TL2. An additional source of overhead is that cmp operations may involve calling ValidateCompareSet, whose execution time is linear with respect the size of the compare-set itself. However, as we show in the evaluation, those overheads are mostly dominated by the performance gain due to avoiding unnecessary aborts.

5. CORRECTNESS

The correctness of a TM algorithm is usually inferred by proving that all histories it generates are *opaque* [17]. We infer the correctness of S-NOrec and S-TL2 in the same way.

We start by roughly recalling some definitions related to opacity, borrowed from [17], to make the presented intuitions self-contained. A history $\mathcal{H}$ is a sequence of operations issued by transactions on a set of shared objects. Intuitively, we say that a history $\mathcal{H}$ is *sequential* if no two transactions are concurrent. A sequential specification of a shared object *ob*, called *Seq(ob)*, is the set of all sequences of operations on *ob* that are considered correct when executed sequentially. A sequential history is *legal* if, for every shared object *ob*, the subsequence of operations on *ob* in $\mathcal{H}$ is in *Seq(ob)*. Two histories are *equivalent* if they contain the same transactions with the same operations and the same return values. Given a history $\mathcal{H}$, $Complete(\mathcal{H})$ indicates the set of histories obtained by committing or aborting every commit-pending transaction in $\mathcal{H}$, and aborting every other live transaction in $\mathcal{H}$. A history $\mathcal{H}$ is *opaque* if any history in $Complete(\mathcal{H})$ is equivalent to a legal sequential history $\mathcal{S}$ that preserves the *real-time order* of $\mathcal{H}$.

The definition of opacity is general enough to be applied on shared objects with generic APIs, as long as every shared object has a well-defined *sequential specification* based on those APIs. However, as we mentioned before, most TMs consider the *read-write register* abstraction with two APIs: a read operation, which takes no argument and returns the current state of the register, and a *write* operation, which takes a value v as argument and always returns *ok*. This simple scheme implies a trivial sequential specification for each register x, as defined in [17]: *the set of all sequences of read and write operations on x such that every read operation returns the value given as an argument to the latest preceding write operation (the initial value is the default).*

Although this simple scheme best fits shared memory models, it does not match the API of our *semantic-based* TM because it does not distinguish between reads/writes that are made within a comparison/increment expression and all other reads/writes. That is why the first step towards proving the correctness of our algorithms is to define the new abstraction for our TM. Our TM algorithms (S-Norec and S-TL2) implement a TM whose shared *registers* export four operations: **read**, which takes no argument and returns the current state of the register; **write**, which takes a value v as an argument and returns always *ok*; **inc**, which takes a value d as an argument and returns always *ok*; and **cmp**, which takes a value *v_cmp* and an operator type *Op* whose value is given from the enum {==, !=, >, >=, <, <=} as arguments and returns *true* or *false*.

The sequential specification of a register x in our TM, $Seq(x)$, is defined as follows: the set of all sequences of **read**, **write**, **cmp**, and **inc** operations on x, such that:

- every **read** operation returns $v + \sum d$, where v is the value given as an argument to the latest preceding **write** operation, w, and $\sum d$ is the sum of the values given as arguments to every **inc** between the **read** operation and w;
- every **cmp** operation returns the boolean value of the expression (v *Op v_cmp*), where v is the return value of the corresponding **read** operation.

Algorithm 8 A history that is opaque with our API.

```
                    Initial values are 0
TM_BEGIN(T1)
if x >= 0 then
                                  TM_BEGIN(T2)
                                  x = 1
                                  y = 1
                                  TM_END
   z = y;
TM_END
```

Algorithm 8 gives an example that clarifies the importance of defining a new abstraction for our TM. Using the original *read-write register* abstraction, the corresponding history has two possible equivalent sequential histories ($T_1 \rightarrow T_2$ and $T_2 \rightarrow T_1$), and both of them are not legal because T_1 returns an illegal value for y in the former and an illegal value for x in the latter. However, using our (correct) abstraction, $T_2 \rightarrow T_1$ is an equivalent legal sequential history because x is read using cmp and the return value of this cmp is legal, which means that the history is opaque.

Another interesting example to assess the correctness of S-NOrec and S-TL2 is shown in Algorithm 9. The history of this example is not opaque even with the new API because the value of x at the moment of executing the cmp operation was different from its value when the transaction read y.

Based on the two cases in Algorithms 8 and 9, it is easy to understand the idea behind proving opacity of histories containing cmp operations, which is proving that: *i)* the address read inside each cmp is consistent with all the previous reads at the moment of computing the return value of the conditional expression, and *ii)* this return value does not change until the transaction commits (even if the value of the address becomes inconsistent).

Proving that a history containing inc operations is opaque is easier to infer. This is because the read part of inc can be

Algorithm 9 A history that is not opaque with our API.

Initial values are 0

```
TM_BEGIN(T1)
z = y
                              TM_BEGIN(T2)
                              x = 1
                              y = 1
                              TM_END
if x >= 1 then
    z = 1
TM_END
```

deferred to the commit phase where the address is locked, and thus the whole `inc` operation is considered as a `write` operation during the transaction execution. The only exception for that is when the address accessed by an `inc` operation is also accessed by another operation in the same transaction. In the following two sections, we show how those cases are covered by S-NOrec and S-TL2.

5.1 Correctness of S-NOrec

Based on the opacity definition, the correctness of S-NOrec can be inferred if we identify the *legal* sequential history $\mathcal{S}$ that is equivalent to a generic history $\mathcal{H}$ generated at any point of its execution (after completing $\mathcal{H}$). Roughly, $\mathcal{H}$ may contain committed transactions (either read-only or writing) and live transactions (considering aborted transaction as live right before they trigger the abort call). $\mathcal{S}$ is identified, similar to NOrec, as follows: committed writing transactions are serialized when they CAS the global timestamp at commit; and both read-only and live transactions are serialized when the validation of their last finished `read`/`cmp` succeeds (i.e., after the committed writing transaction that sets the global timestamp with the value returned at line 8).

The history $\mathcal{S}$ remains legal with the existence of `cmp` operations because of the following reasons: *i)* every address is initially read consistently using `readValid` procedure in all `read`, `cmp`, and `RAW` calls; and *ii)* the semantic validation made after each read and during commit guarantees that the return values of each `cmp` remain the same.

The existence of `inc` operations also does not affect the legality of $\mathcal{S}$ because: *i)* at commit time, `inc` is handled exactly like `write`, which is safe because the transaction has an exclusive access to the address (in fact commit phases in NOrec are executed serially); and *ii)* live transactions that execute `inc` along with other operations on the same address are always consistent because the read operations (`read` and `cmp`) check the write-set first and promote the `inc` operation if needed, and the write operations (`write` and `inc`) properly override the write-set entry.

5.2 Correctness of S-TL2

The legal equivalent serialization of a history generated by S-TL2 is slightly different from TL2. In fact, handling `inc` operations does not affect the serialization because of the same reasons mentioned for S-NOrec. However, we identify two differences that arise due to `cmp` operation.

First, committed writing transactions are serialized in TL2 when they atomically increment the timestamp. In S-TL2, this atomic increment is replaced with a `CAS` operation which forms the new serialization point (line 71). Using `CAS` instead of `AtomicFetchAndAdd` is needed because it is not legal for a transaction to observe the writes of any transaction that increments the global timestamp after it. Note that it is guaranteed that the transaction observes the writes of all transactions that increment the timestamp before it, because the `orecs` of the write-set entries are locked before incrementing the timestamp (line 67) and the transaction waits until those `orecs` are unlocked.

Second, the serialization of read-only and live transactions depends on the phase they are executing. If the transaction is in the first phase, before any `read` operation, the serialization point is, similar to S-NOrec, when the validation during the last `cmp` operation succeeds (more specifically, when *start_version* is advanced at line 25). That is because all the committed writing transactions so far did not change the return value of all `cmp` operations. On the other hand, if the transaction is in the second phase, after the first `read` operation, it is serialized similar to TL2, namely before all writing transactions that commit with a timestamp greater than its *start_version*. That is legal because: *i)* all `cmp` operations in the first phase are consistent up to the current value of *start_version*; and *ii)* all `read` and `cmp` operations in the second phase use this *start_version* in validation.

6. INTEGRATION WITH GCC

GCC has supported STM since version 4.7 and HTM since version 4.9. The integration of TM into GCC resulted in adding `_transaction_atomic` to the constructs of C/C++ [2, 23]. Statements within a `_transaction_atomic` block are translated by GCC to the appropriate TM calls that follow an Application Binary Interface (ABI) similar to the TM ABI proposed by Intel [1]. Those calls are handled according to the TM algorithm chosen by the programmer. The implementation of those TM algorithms is encapsulated in the *libitm* library[1].

The first, straightforward, step we made towards embedding our semantic interfaces is adding three semantic operations to *libitm*'s ABI (see Table 2). The first two operations, `_ITM_S2R` and `_ITM_S1R`, handle `cmp` operation with address-address and address-value modes, while `_ITM_SW` handles `inc` operation. Then, we deployed our S-NOrec algorithm as an additional TM algorithm in the *libitm* library, and implemented the new ABI operations as described in Section 4.1. Due to lack of a TL2 implementation that matches the baseline we used to construct our S-TL2, we plan the integration of S-TL2 as a future work. Besides, in the TM algorithms currently existing in *libitm* library, those new operations are implemented by delegating their execution to the classical read and write handlers.

`_ITM_S2R`*type*	address-address semantic read operation
`_ITM_S1R`*type*	address-value semantic read operation
`_ITM_SW`*type*	semantic write operation

Table 2: Extended GCC ABI.

The next, more complicated, step is to detect the code patterns of our semantic operations (`cmp` and `inc`) during compilation. We do that after GCC generates the GIMPLE [27] representation of the program. GIMPLE is a language independent, tree-based representation that uses 3-operands expressions (except for function calls) in Static Single Assignment (SSA) [9] form. We chose GIMPLE to deploy our

[1]We use GCC 5.3 and *libitm* libraries from https://github.com/mfs409/transmem, which include NOrec.

optimization passes for two reasons. First, GIMPLE is both architecture and language independent, thus optimizing it is considered a transparent *middle-end* optimization. Second, GIMPLE uses temporary variables to put its expressions in 3-operand form, where every variable is assigned only once. This form simplifies dependency analysis.

The `tm_mark` pass is one of the optimization passes on the GIMPLE representation where statements that perform transactional memory operations are replaced with the appropriate TM built-ins. We extended this pass to detect the code patterns of `cmp` and `inc` operations as follows.

- *cmp:* For any conditional expression we track the origins of its two operands along the GIMPLE tree. If one origin refers to a direct transactional memory access and the other refers to either a literal value or a local variable, then we replace the condition with a call to the `_ITM_S1R` built-in. If the two origins refer to direct transactional memory accesses, we use `_ITM_S2R`.
- *inc:* For any transactional write, we track the origin of its right hand side, and if it is calculated using a mathematical "+" or "-" equation, we track both its operands. If the origin of one of them is a transactional read to the same written address and the origin of the second operand is either a literal value or a local variable, we call the `_ITM_SW` built-in instead of generating the transactional write. At this stage, the original transactional read of the `inc` still exists and has to be removed. We did so by developing another optimization pass, named `tm_optimize`, that removes TM read calls for *never-live variables*, since the read part of every `inc` becomes one of those *never-live variables* reads after replacing the write part with our call. This pass is made in a conservative way; it does not remove a read if there is no guarantee that it is *never-live*.

A side optimization that our `tm_optimize` pass performs is removing any TM read that is part of a never-live assignment, even if it is not originally part of an `inc` operation. The current GCC version does not perform any *liveness optimization* or *dead assignment identification* on the transactional code, therefore it does not remove such reads.

Another important note is that cases where a shared variable is involved in both semantic (i.e., `cmp` and `inc`) and non-semantic (i.e., `read` and `write`) operations of the same transaction are handled by the TM algorithm as mentioned in Section 4 (see lines 31 & 46 of Algorithm 6, and line 7 of Algorithm 7), therefore it is not needed to detect those cases in the compiler passes.

One of the advantages of our optimizations is that they reduce the number of TM calls from two to one when using `_ITM_S2R` or `_ITM_SW`. Such reduction has a visible impact on application performance; in fact, TM calls are costly because GCC performs three indirect calls per TM call. Also, our pass does not require complex alias analysis for tracking the operands origin because we look for simple expression patterns that usually reside in the same basic block.

7. EVALUATION

We tested our extended semantic-based TM on a set of micro-benchmarks, as well as applications of the STAMP suite [28]. We conducted our experiments on an AMD machine equipped with 2 Opteron 6168 CPUs, each with 12 cores running at 1.9 GHz. The total memory available is 12 GB. We reported the throughput for the micro-benchmarks, and the application execution time for STAMP, by varying the number of threads executing concurrently. We reported the results for both RSTM and GCC implementations.

Table 3 shows the average number of invocations per operation type in the used benchmarks. They are measured at runtime using RSTM because it provides more flexibility to extract statistics than GCC. In this table, semantic and non-semantic algorithms are contrasted to give an intuition about the number of read and write operations saved by applying our semantic constructs. Reduction is substantial, which enables performance improvement as showed later.

7.1 RSTM-based implementations

In the following experiments, depicted in Figure 1, throughput/time and abort rate were computed for NOrec and TL2 in both their semantic and original (i.e., non-semantic) versions.

Micro benchmarks. In our first set of experiments we considered three micro benchmarks: Hashtable with Open Addressing, Bank, and Least Recently Used (LRU) Cache.

Hashtable with Open Addressing. The workload in this experiment was a collection of *set* and *get* operations, where each transaction performed 10 set/get operations. Both S-NOrec and S-TL2 exploited our semantic extensions in the probing procedure, as depicted in Algorithm 2. As a result, and as shown in Table 3, all `read` operations were transformed into semantic `cmp` operations. This reduced the number of aborts significantly (Figure 1b), which directly raised the throughput (up to 4× speedup) in both algorithms (Figure 1a).

Bank. Each transaction performs multiple transfers (at most 10) between accounts with an overdraft check (i.e., skip the transfer if account balance is insufficient). In the semantic version of the benchmark, the reads/writes were transformed into `cmp` and `inc` operations. As shown in Figure 1c, exploiting semantics helps S-NOrec to outperform NOrec at low-contention (1-8 threads). However, when contention increases, both NOrec and S-NOrec degrade and perform similarly. This is mainly because the probability of having true conflicts increases, and transactions start to abort even if they are semantically validated. Moreover, due to the overhead of semantic validation, S-NOrec performs slightly worse in some cases. In TL2, concurrent commits are allowed, thus it scales better than NOrec. Similarly, S-TL2 benefits from the underlying semantics and performs 20% better than TL2, and incurs 25% fewer aborts.

LRU Cache. This benchmark simulates an $m \times n$ cache with least-frequently-used replacement policy. The cache uses m cache lines, and each line contains n buckets. Each bucket stores both the data and the hit frequency. Each transaction either sets or looks up multiple entries in the cache. Table 3 shows that 93% of the `read` operations were transformed into `cmp` operations. Accordingly, as shown in Figures 1e and 1f, S-NOrec reduced the aborts dramatically and achieved up to 2× speedup. S-TL2 was not improved much (only 25% speedup). The reason is that the non-transformed reads in S-TL2 prevented it from advancing its snapshot (i.e., it makes the first phase described in Section 4.2 shorter); thus, any compare operations had to preserve the snapshot identified by the *start_version* and the overall behavior becomes similar to TL2.

STAMP. STAMP is a suite of applications designed for evaluating in-memory concurrency controls. We did not show the results of three applications (`Genome`, `Intruder`,

	Hashtable		Bank		LRU		Vacation		Kmeans		Labyrinth		Yada		SSCA2		Genome		Intruder	
	base	*semantic*	*base*	*semantic*	*base*	*semantic*	*base*	*semantic*	*base*	*semantic*	*base*	*semantic*	*base*	*semantic*	*base*	*semantic*	*base*	*semantic*	*base*	*semantic*
Read	3440	0	22.5	0.05	173	12	14704	13714	25	0	176	4	142	135	2	1	84	84	28.5	28.5
Write	6.2	6.2	12.7	0	19.7	19.7	28.5	12	25	0	173	173	21.4	21.4	2	1	3	3	2.6	2.6
Compare	-	3440	-	10	-	161	-	989.5	-	0	-	172	-	7	-	0	-	0.06	-	0
Increment	-	0	-	12.7	-	0.03	-	16.7	-	25	-	0	-	0	-	1	-	0.01	-	0
Promote	-	0	-	0.05	-	0.01	-	15.7	-	0	-	0	-	0	-	0	-	0	-	0

Table 3: Average Number of Operations per Transaction.

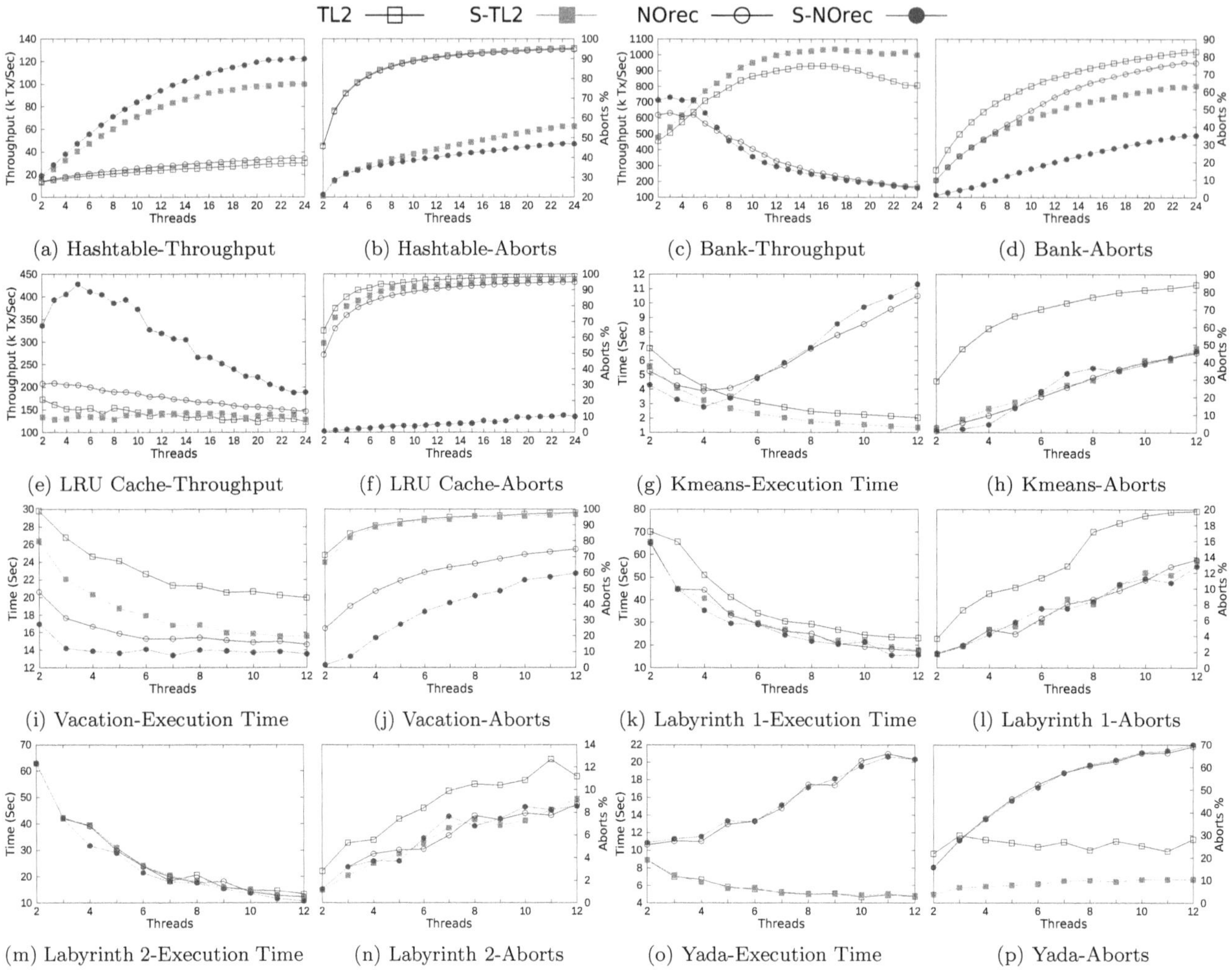

Figure 1: Micro Benchmarks and STAMP Applications using RSTM.

and **SSCA2**) because we found that the semantic operations per transaction were very limited (see Table 3). Hence, there was no difference in both abort rate and throughput in those three applications, which is expected since both the overhead and the potential gain depend on having semantic operations. We also excluded **Bayes** because of its nondeterministic behavior. Since the performance saturated at a high number of threads in all tested applications, we show the results only up to 12 threads.

Kmeans is a clustering algorithm that iterates over a set of points and associate them to clusters. The main computation is in finding the nearest point, while shared data updates occur at the end of each iteration. As illustrated in Algorithm 5, updating the centroid is changed by transforming all **writes** into **increments**. S-NOrec and S-TL2 achieve 25%-40% speedup (Figure 1g). However, at a high number of threads, both NOrec and S-NOrec saturate and start to degrade in performance, which indicates a high contention workload due to the coarse-grained locking. Consequently, starting from 8 threads, S-NOrec performs slightly worse than NOrec (see Figure 1g) because it adds an overhead that is not exploited to reduce the abort rate (see Figure 1h).

Vacation is a travel reservation system using an in-memory database. The workload consists of client reservations. This application emulated an OLTP workload. The reservation procedure was optimized as in Algorithm 4; however, only 7% of the reads were transformed into compares. This is because most of the **read** operations are part of the internal

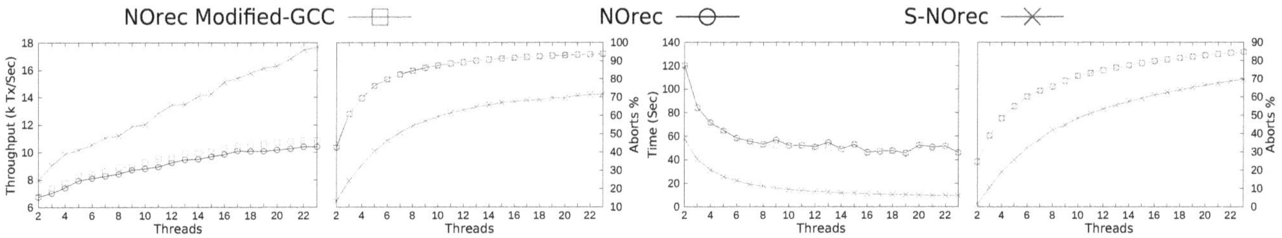

(a) Hashtable-Throughput (b) Hashtable-Aborts (c) Vacation-Execution Time (d) Vacation-Aborts

Figure 2: Hashtable and STAMP Vacation using GCC.

red-black tree operations. Additionally, almost all the `inc` operations were promoted to `read` and `write` operations because of an additional sanity check performed by the transaction. Although these two factors limited the gain of using the benchmark semantics, both S-NOrec and S-TL2 consistently outperformed the original algorithms.

Labyrinth is a multi-path maze solver. The maze is represented as a three-dimensional uniform grid, and each thread tries to connect input pairs by a path of adjacent maze points. Upon finding a path, it is highlighted in a shared output grid. Different checks along the routing path (e.g., *isEmpty*, *isGarbage*) were transformed into semantic `cmp` operations, which allowed S-TL2 to outperform TL2 by 20%-50% speedup and to save half of the aborts (see Figures 1k & 1l). Both S-NOrect and NOrec perform similarly, which indicates that transactions that fail in NORec's value-based validation also fail in S-NOrec's semantic validation. In [32], an optimized version of Labyrinth was proposed, where some non-transactional operations (memory copy) are moved outside the transaction, which in effect reduces the transaction size. Figures 1m & 1n show the performance in this new version. Although S-TL2 still has lower abort rate, the returned gain in performance became insignificant because most of the work was moved outside transactions.

Yada is a mesh triangulation benchmark implementing Ruppert's algorithm. Threads iterate over the mesh and try to produce a smoother one by identifying triangles whose minimum angle is below some threshold. NOrec's behavior is similar to `Labyrinth`. Interestingly, although S-TL2 reduced the number of aborts, throughput was not affected (Figures 1o & 1p). Our measurements revealed that the reason for this behavior is in the aborted transactions. Although resolving the semantic conflicts of transactions in S-TL2 allowed them to proceed with execution, true conflicts caused most of them to abort later. Therefore, the length of the aborted transactions in S-TL2 became longer than TL2 without real benefit (since transactions eventually aborted). This is similar to what happened in Bank.

7.2 GCC-based implementations

Now we discuss the results of the above experiments using our modified GCC instead of RSTM. As mentioned in Section 6, in these experiments we focus on NOrec and S-NOrec. We also added one more version of NOrec that uses our modified GCC API but does not handle them semantically. The only difference between this version and NOrec is that, in the former, the applications calls our semantic API and internally delegates them to the normal reads/writes of NOrec, while the latter calls NOrec's API directly.

The results in Figure 2 follow the same trends described above with RSTM (due to space limitations, we move some results to the technical report [34]). As before, our semantic extensions help improve performance in all benchmarks. Compared to RSTM, the actual throughput values decreased. This is mainly because GCC speculates every read and write within the `_transaction_atomic` blocks, while RSTM speculates only addresses accessed using its transactional `TM_READ` and `TM_WRITE` APIs. However, GCC algorithms scale better than RSTM algorithms, mainly because of the internal optimizations in GCC, such as using more efficient structures to store and handle metadata. Interestingly, using our modified GCC, even without exploiting semantics ("NOrec Modified-GCC"), we observe some performance improvement due to decreasing the overall number of TM calls.

8. CONCLUSIONS

In this paper, we show that generality of TM does not always contradict application semantics. We did so by identifying *TM-friendly* semantics and proposing an approach to inject them in current TM algorithms and frameworks. We also integrated our work in GCC and provide full compiler support for them. Our experimental results depicted a promising improvement over the base algorithms. We plan to extend this line of research by investigating more on including HTM algorithms and supporting more complex semantic patterns.

9. ACKNOWLEDGMENTS

Authors would like to thank Marina Sadini and Yuzhong Wen for their support in integrating our extensions into GCC. We also thank our anonymous reviewers for their valuable comments. This work is partially supported by Air Force Office of Scientific Research (AFOSR) under grant FA9550-14-1-0187.

10. REFERENCES

[1] Intel transactional memory compiler and runtime application binary interface. https://software.intel.com/sites/default/files/m/5/a/2/a/f/8097-Intel_TM_ABI_1_0_1.pdf, 2008.

[2] A.-R. Adl-Tabatabai, T. Shpeisman, and J. Gottschlich. Draft specification of transactional language constructs for c++, 2009.

[3] Y. Afek, H. Avni, and N. Shavit. Towards consistency oblivious programming. In *OPODIS*, pages 65–79, 2011.

[4] Y. Afek, A. Matveev, O. R. Moll, and N. Shavit. Amalgamated lock-elision. In *DISC*, pages 309–324, 2015.

[5] H. Avni and B. C. Kuszmaul. Improving HTM scaling with consistency-oblivious programming. In *TRANSACT*, 2014.

[6] B. H. Bloom. Space/time trade-offs in hash coding with allowable errors. *Commun. ACM*, 13(7):422–426, July 1970.

[7] H. W. Cain, M. M. Michael, B. Frey, C. May, D. Williams, and H. Le. Robust architectural support for transactional memory in the power architecture. In *ISCA*, pages 225–236, 2013.

[8] I. Calciu, T. Shpeisman, G. Pokam, and M. Herlihy. Improved single global lock fallback for best-effort hardware transactional memory. In *TRANSACT*, 2014.

[9] R. Cytron, J. Ferrante, B. K. Rosen, M. N. Wegman, and F. K. Zadeck. An efficient method of computing static single assignment form. In *POPL*, pages 25–35, 1989.

[10] L. Dalessandro, F. Carouge, S. White, Y. Lev, M. Moir, M. L. Scott, and M. F. Spear. Hybrid NOrec: A case study in the effectiveness of best effort hardware transactional memory. In *ASPLOS*, pages 39–52, 2011.

[11] L. Dalessandro, M. F. Spear, and M. L. Scott. NOrec: Streamlining STM by abolishing ownership records. In *PPoPP*, pages 67–78, 2010.

[12] D. Dice, O. Shalev, and N. Shavit. Transactional locking II. In *DISC*, pages 194–208, 2006.

[13] N. Diegues and P. Romano. Self-tuning Intel transactional synchronization extensions. In *ICAC*, pages 209–219, 2014.

[14] A. Dragojevic and T. Harris. STM in the small: trading generality for performance in software transactional memory. In *EuroSys*, pages 1–14, 2012.

[15] P. Felber, V. Gramoli, and R. Guerraoui. Elastic transactions. In *DISC*, pages 93–107, 2009.

[16] G. Golan-Gueta, G. Ramalingam, M. Sagiv, and E. Yahav. Automatic scalable atomicity via semantic locking. In *PPoPP*, pages 31–41, 2015.

[17] R. Guerraoui and M. Kapalka. On the correctness of transactional memory. In *PPoPP*, pages 175–184, 2008.

[18] A. Hassan, R. Palmieri, and B. Ravindran. Optimistic transactional boosting. In *PPoPP*, pages 387–388, 2014.

[19] M. Herlihy and E. Koskinen. Transactional boosting: A methodology for highly-concurrent transactional objects. In *PPoPP*, pages 207–216, 2008.

[20] M. Herlihy, V. Luchangco, M. Moir, and W. N. Scherer III. Software transactional memory for dynamic-sized data structures. In *PODC*, pages 92–101, 2003.

[21] M. Herlihy and J. E. B. Moss. Transactional memory: Architectural support for lock-free data structures. In *ISCA*, pages 289–300, 1993.

[22] W. N. S. III and M. L. Scott. Advanced contention management for dynamic software transactional memory. In *PODC*, pages 240–248, 2005.

[23] V. Luchangco, M. Wong, H. Boehm, J. Gottschlich, J. Maurer, P. McKenney, M. Michael, M. Moir, T. Riegel, M. Scott, et al. Transactional memory support for c++. 2014.

[24] V. Marathe, M. Spear, C. Heriot, A. Acharya, D. Eisenstat, W. Scherer III, and M. Scott. Lowering the overhead of nonblocking software transactional memory. In *TRANSACT*, 2006.

[25] A. Matveev and N. Shavit. Reduced hardware norec: A safe and scalable hybrid transactional memory. In *ASPLOS*, pages 59–71, 2015.

[26] V. Menon, S. Balensiefer, T. Shpeisman, A. Adl-Tabatabai, R. L. Hudson, B. Saha, and A. Welc. Practical weak-atomicity semantics for java stm. In *SPAA*, pages 314–325, 2008.

[27] J. Merrill. Generic and gimple: A new tree representation for entire functions. In *Proceedings of the 2003 GCC DevelopersâĂŹ Summit*, pages 171–179, 2003.

[28] C. C. Minh, J. Chung, C. Kozyrakis, and K. Olukotun. STAMP: Stanford transactional applications for multi-processing. In *IISWC*, pages 35–46, 2008.

[29] Y. Ni, V. Menon, A. Adl-Tabatabai, A. L. Hosking, R. L. Hudson, J. E. B. Moss, B. Saha, and T. Shpeisman. Open nesting in software transactional memory. In *PPoPP*, pages 68–78, 2007.

[30] J. Reinders. Transactional synchronization in Haswell. http://software.intel.com/en-us/blogs/2012/02/07/transactional-synchronization-in-haswell/, 2013.

[31] T. Riegel, P. Marlier, M. Nowack, P. Felber, and C. Fetzer. Optimizing hybrid transactional memory: The importance of nonspeculative operations. In *SPAA*, pages 53–64, 2011.

[32] W. Ruan, Y. Liu, and M. Spear. Stamp need not be considered harmful. In *TRANSACT*, 2014.

[33] W. Ruan, Y. Liu, and M. F. Spear. Transactional read-modify-write without aborts. *TACO*, 11(4):63:1–63:24, 2014.

[34] M. M. Saad, R. Palmieri, A. Hassan, and B. Ravindran. Extending TM primitives using low level semantics. Technical report, ECE Dept., Virginia Tech, May 2016. www.hyflow.org/pubs/spaa16-saad-TR.pdf.

[35] N. Shavit and D. Touitou. Software transactional memory. In *PODC*, pages 204–213, 1995.

[36] M. F. Spear, M. M. Michael, and C. von Praun. RingSTM: scalable transactions with a single atomic instruction. In *SPAA*, pages 275–284, 2008.

[37] Transactional Memory Specification Drafting Group. Draft specification of transactional language constructs for C++, version 1.1, February 2012. Available http://www.open-std.org/jtc1/sc22/wg21/docs/papers/2013/n3725.pdf.

[38] L. Xiang and M. L. Scott. Software partitioning of hardware transactions. In *PPoPP*, pages 76–86, 2015.

Investigating the Performance of Hardware Transactions on a Multi-Socket Machine

Trevor Brown*
University of Toronto
tabrown@cs.toronto.edu

Alex Kogan
Oracle Labs
alex.kogan@oracle.com

Yossi Lev
Oracle Labs
yossi.lev@oracle.com

Victor Luchangco
Oracle Labs
victor.luchangco@oracle.com

ABSTRACT

The introduction of hardware transactional memory (HTM) into commercial processors opens a door for designing and implementing scalable synchronization mechanisms. One example for such a mechanism is transactional lock elision (TLE), where lock-based critical sections are executed concurrently using hardware transactions. So far, the effectiveness of TLE and other HTM-based mechanisms has been assessed mostly on small, single-socket machines.

This paper investigates the behavior of hardware transactions on a large two-socket machine. Using TLE as an example, we show that a system can scale as long as all threads run on the same socket, but a single thread running on a different socket can wreck performance. We identify the reason for this phenomenon, and present a simple adaptive technique that overcomes this problem by throttling threads as necessary to optimize system performance. Using extensive evaluation of multiple microbenchmarks and real applications, we demonstrate that our technique achieves the full performance of the system for workloads that scale across sockets, and avoids the performance degradation that cripples TLE for workloads that do not.

Keywords

hardware transactional memory, nonuniform memory access, lock elision, concurrent data structures, locks

1. INTRODUCTION

To perform well on modern multiprocessor systems, applications must exploit the increasing core count on these systems by executing operations concurrently on different cores without introducing too much overhead in synchronizing these operations. Recent systems have introduced *hardware transactional memory* (HTM) [20] to support efficient synchronization, and previous work has shown that it can be used effectively [2, 12, 16–18, 26, 34]. However, until recently, HTM has been available only on relatively small single-socket systems. For this paper, we investigated the behavior of HTM on a large multi-socket machine and observed that its behavior differs from that of smaller systems in ways that present challenges for scaling the performance on the larger machine.

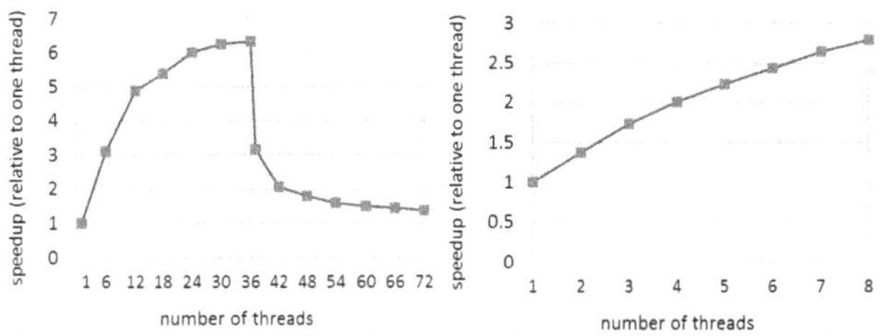

Figure 1: AVL tree microbenchmark on a large HTM system (left), and a small HTM system (right). The workload is 100% updates with key range [0, 2048).

For example, consider the graph on the left in Figure 1, which shows the speedup over single-thread execution of a microbenchmark in which we repeatedly insert and delete nodes in an AVL tree [1]. Operations on the tree are protected by a single lock, to which we apply *transactional lock elision* (TLE) [13], a popular technique for exploiting HTM in which lock-based critical sections are executed concurrently using hardware transactions, implemented on top of the Intel Haswell TSX/RTM interface. The machine has two sockets, each with 18 hyperthreaded cores, for a total of 72 threads. We bind threads so that the first 36 all run on one socket, and the last 36 threads run on the other socket. (This microbenchmark is described in more detail in Section 3.) As we can see, performance improves until we reach 36 threads, though the scaling is more moderate after 12 threads. However, as soon as any thread executes on the second socket, the performance drops dramatically. Performance continues to decline until the machine is saturated, at which point its performance is barely better than with a single thread. These results are in stark contrast to those shown on the right, from a similar experiment on a smaller single-socket machine (4 hyperthreaded cores), whose performance continues to improve until the machine is saturated.

Not all benchmarks exhibit this pathology: with only lookup operations (i.e., a read-only workload), for example,

*This work was done while Trevor Brown was an intern at Oracle Labs.

SPAA '16, July 11-13, 2016, Pacific Grove, CA, USA
© 2016 ACM. ISBN 978-1-4503-4210-0/16/07...$15.00
DOI: http://dx.doi.org/10.1145/2935764.2935796

performance scales all the way to 72 threads (i.e., the full capacity of the machine). We experimented with a variety of microbenchmarks to identify the causes of this performance pathology, as well as other differences between the behaviors of HTM on the large and small machines. In this paper we describe several of these experiments and their results, and the conclusions we draw from them.

Informed by these results, we explored several ways, described in the latter half of this paper, to use HTM effectively on the multi-socket machine. The technique we found most effective is to adaptively throttle the number of threads to optimize performance. At a high level, the idea is to profile TLE performance and decide, separately for each lock, whether critical sections protected by that lock should be executed by threads on multiple sockets, or only on a single socket. We implemented this idea entirely in a library providing a lock API, thus requiring no changes to the code that uses traditional lock-based synchronization. Using multiple microbenchmarks and a number of real applications, including STAMP [27], ccTSA [4] and paraheap-k [21], we show that this simple approach avoids sharp performance degradation for workloads that do not scale beyond one socket while exploiting additional sockets for workloads that do scale. We describe this technique in detail and present experimental results that demonstrate its effectiveness.

2. BACKGROUND

The machine we are studying is an Oracle Server X5-2, a two-socket system with two Intel Xeon E5-2699 v3 processors. Each processor has 18 cores, each with 2 hardware threads (i.e., 72 threads in all), running Ubuntu 15.04 at 2.30GHz. Because of its two-socket design, this machine has *non-uniform memory access* (NUMA): Cores on the same processor share an L3 cache, so communication between threads running on the same processor is much faster than inter-socket communication. For comparison, the other (smaller) machine we used in Figure 1 is a single-socket 4-core hyperthreaded Haswell Core i7-4770 (also with 2 threads per core, so 8 threads in all) running Oracle Linux 7 at 3.40GHz.

Both systems provide "best effort" hardware transactional memory (HTM): transactions are not guaranteed to *commit*, but any transaction that commits appears to other threads to have been executed atomically. A transaction that does not commit is *aborted*: its writes to memory are discarded and are never made visible to other threads. A transaction that aborts sets a condition code indicating the cause, and then jumps to a fallback code path specified at the beginning of the transaction. This condition code allows us to distinguish, for instance, between transactions that abort because some internal buffer overflowed and those that abort due to conflict with another thread. It also includes a hint bit that indicates whether, according to the hardware, the transaction is likely to succeed if retried.

We use transactional lock elision (TLE) [13] implemented on top of the Intel Haswell TSX/RTM interface as a vehicle to study the behavior of HTM. TLE is a practical synchronization technique for exploiting HTM that can be applied without requiring changes to code that uses traditional lock-based synchronization: it co-opts the *LockAcquire* and *LockRelease* operations that bracket a critical section, attempting to elide the lock acquisition (and subsequent release) by executing within a transaction. If the transaction commits, it ensures that the critical section executes without interference from other threads. If the transaction aborts, the critical section may be retried in another transaction or it may be executed in the traditional fashion by acquiring the lock. (To avoid executing concurrently with a critical section executed under lock, a transaction executing a critical section must check that the associated lock is free and abort otherwise.) If the transaction aborts and the hint bit is not set (typically, if the abort is due to overflow), it is common to not retry at all [3,16].

Numerous studies have observed that TLE provides nearly ideal speedups when applied to workloads in which threads have few data conflicts and transactions do not overflow [12, 18, 26, 28, 34]. However, when these conditions do not hold, the performance of TLE deteriorates quickly. Several recent papers have suggested ways to improve the performance of TLE in these scenarios, employing various approaches such as adaptively tuning retry policies [12, 16] and introducing auxiliary locks [2, 17]. All these papers, however, evaluated TLE and suggested improvements using relatively small, single-socket machines.

Most of our experiments use TLE applied to an AVL tree implementation that uses a single global lock to synchronize access to the tree. An AVL tree [1] is a balanced binary search tree that ensures that the heights of the left and right subtrees of any node differ by at most 1. Whenever an operation disrupts this balance (by adding or deleting a node), it "rotates" the node and/or its ancestors to restore the balance. Most insert and delete operations do not conflict with other operations because they update only a few nodes at the bottom of the tree, but a few operations may rebalance even the root node, conflicting with every other operation.

The effects of NUMA on the performance of multithreaded systems has been an area of active research in the past few decades [6–8, 22, 23, 32, 33]. This research is motivated by the observation that remote memory accesses and remote cache misses (i.e., cache misses served from another cache located on a different socket) are expensive, and therefore should be reduced. Dice et al. [15], for instance, achieve this goal through the design of a series of NUMA-aware *cohort locks*, which allow threads running on the same socket to pass the lock among themselves (and thus exploit cache locality within the socket) before releasing the lock so that it can be acquired by a thread on a different socket. Other researchers attempt to colocate threads and the data they access through thread migration [6, 24] or data migration and replication [33].

Prior work in various contexts has considered restricting concurrency to improve system performance. Multiple papers, for instance, observe that using fewer threads than the available cores can lead to better performance [9,29,30], and suggest ways to tune the number of running threads to achieve that. In the context of software transactional memory, several papers consider contention management mechanisms that throttle some of the conflicting software transactions to increase the chance that remaining transactions succeed [5,35]. In the context of TLE, Diegues et al. [17] suggest using *core locks*, which synchronize between hardware transactions running on the same core when those transactions abort due to overflow. In the same context, Afek et al. [2] consider adding an auxiliary lock to TLE, which is acquired by conflicting transactions. The above-mentioned cohort locks [15] are perhaps most relevant to the concurrency restriction ideas that we consider in this paper. They throttle threads running on sockets other than the one holding the lock, thus sacrificing short-term fairness for higher throughput.

Delegation is another approach aimed at reducing remote cache misses. The idea of delegation is to mediate access to a data structure or critical section by one or more server threads, which execute requests from client threads. Client and server threads communicate via message passing implemented on top of shared memory. As an example, Lozi et al. [25] propose structuring a client-server system in which server threads running on dedicated cores execute critical sections on behalf of client threads. Calciu et al. [8] investigate different approaches for implementing message passing and show that while delegation can be effective, the communication overhead of message passing often outweighs its benefits. In the context of software transactional memory, Hassan et al. [19] investigate the idea of dedicating a number of server threads to perform commit phase of software transactions executed by client threads.

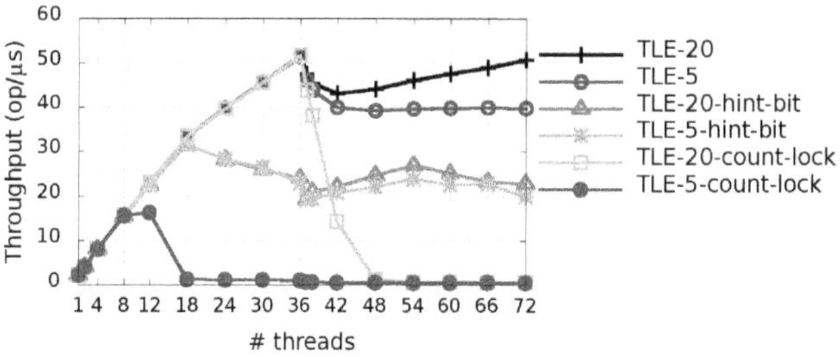

(a) TLE using different retry policies

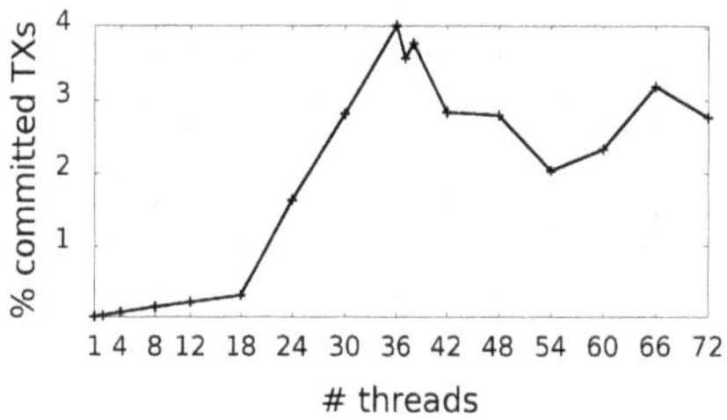

(b) Percent of transactions in *TLE-20* that commit after at least one failure with hint bit not set

Figure 2: An AVL tree on a large HTM system. The workload is 100% updates with key range $[0, 131072)$.

3. HTM ON A LARGE MACHINE

In this section, we present and analyze the results of several experiments we ran to better understand the behavior of HTM on the large (72-thread) NUMA system. In Section 3.1, we make observations that are not due to NUMA effects, but rather to the larger number of cores in our system. Section 3.2 details findings that are more NUMA-specific.

In most of these experiments, threads repeatedly invoke insert, delete and lookup operations on implementations of an abstract set (e.g., an AVL tree) using a key selected uniformly at random from a specified key range. The set is prefilled with approximately half the keys. We specify the percentage of lookup operations, with the remaining operations being evenly split between insert and delete operations (collectively update operations) to keep the set approximately half filled. Unless otherwise specified, we pin the threads to cores so that the first 18 threads are executed by different cores on the first socket, and the next 18 are executed with hyperthreading on the same cores. (Thus, all threads execute on a single socket when there are 36 or fewer threads.) The next 36 threads are pinned similarly to cores on the second socket. (We discuss alternative pinning policies in Section 5.)

3.1 Going beyond 8–12 cores

We tested whether the conventional wisdom about retry polices in TLE on small systems is appropriate for the large system. Figure 2(a) shows the results of a microbenchmark on the large HTM system wherein threads perform insertions and deletions (i.e., no lookup operations) in an AVL tree with key range $[0, 131072)$ (i.e., containing approximately 65536 keys) using different retry policies. (This tree fits in the L3 cache but is large enough that concurrent operations are unlikely to conflict.) *TLE-5-hint-bit* implements a policy commonly used in small HTM systems: we attempt to execute a critical section using a transaction up to 5 times before falling back to the lock. We do not count attempts that fail because the lock is held by another thread (in which case the transaction is not retried until the lock is released in order to avoid the *lemming effect* [14]). However, if a transaction aborts and the hint bit is not set by hardware, we fall back to the lock immediately (recall that this bit is set if, according to the hardware, the transaction is likely to succeed if retried). *TLE-20-hint-bit* implements the same policy except that 20 attempts are allowed before falling back to the lock. *TLE-5* and *TLE-20* are similar except that they ignore the hint bit (i.e., they do not fall back to the lock immediately when a transaction aborts and the hint bit is not set). Finally, *TLE-5-count-lock* and *TLE-20-count-lock* also ignore the hint bit, but they do count attempts that fail because the lock is held by another thread.

Perhaps surprisingly, contrary to the common belief that a transaction that fails with the hint bit not set (which in most cases happens due to overflow) will continue to fail if it is retried, we observed that subsequent attempts may succeed. Thus, falling back immediately when a transaction aborts with the hint bit not set caused threads to fall back to the lock unnecessarily. Eliminating this "optimization" significantly improves performance. (Compare, for example, the curves for *TLE-20* and *TLE-20-hint-bit*.) This improvement shows up after 18 threads, suggesting that hyperthreading may cause transient overflow failures. Indeed, the percentage of transactions that commit after a previous attempt failed with the hint bit not set, shown in Figure 2(b), rises sharply when there are more than 18 threads. (The graph for transactions committing after a previous attempt failed due to overflow is similar.) Although this percentage never exceeds 4%, this result emphasizes the greater cost of falling back to the lock on a system running more than a dozen threads: Because a thread that takes the lock blocks every other thread, in a large system, it pays to tolerate more failed transactions to avoid taking the lock.

Allowing 20 transactional attempts rather than only 5 (compare the curves for *TLE-20* and *TLE-5*) also improves performance, though to a lesser extent. To determine whether raising the limit on transactional attempts beyond 20 might improve performance even more, we experimented with vary-

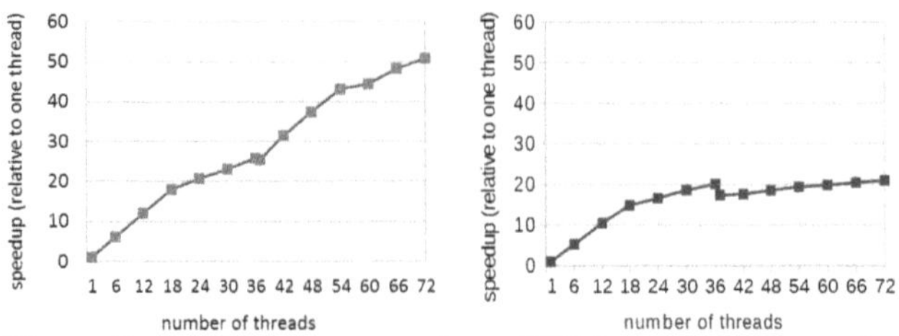

Figure 3: An AVL tree on a large HTM system. The workload is 100% lookup on the left, and 2% updates (i.e., 98% lookups) on the right, with key range [0, 2048).

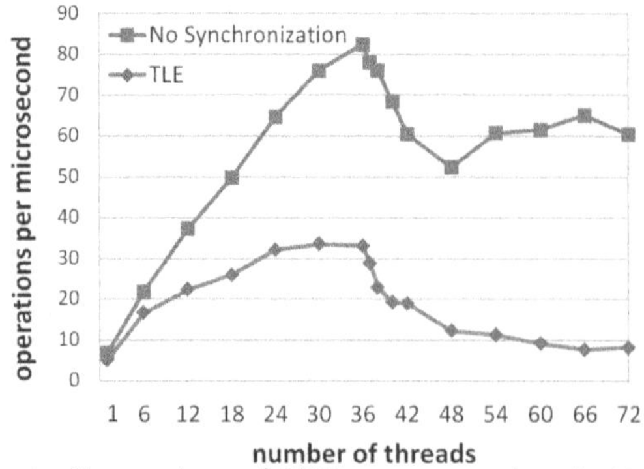

Figure 4: Comparison of TLE vs. no synchronization in a workload doing search-and-replace operations on an AVL tree with key range [0, 4096).

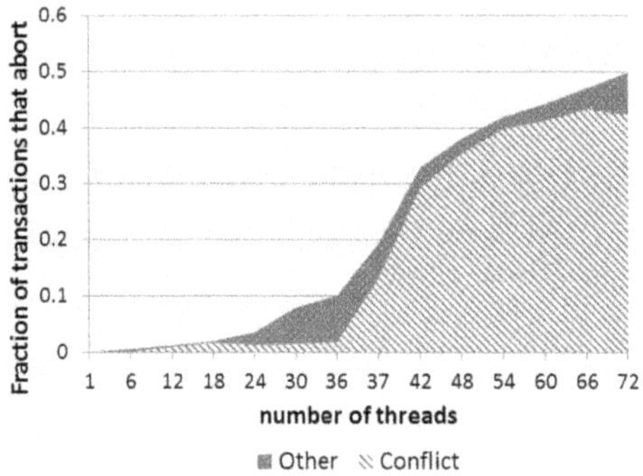

Figure 5: Abort rate for the TLE curve in Figure 4. (Note: the x-axis is not to scale near x=37).

ing the limit over a wide range, up to hundreds of millions of retries, and we were not able to consistently improve performance beyond that achieved with 20 attempts. In the rest of this paper, unless otherwise specified, we report on results for *TLE-20*.

The curves for *TLE-5-count-lock* and *TLE-20-count-lock* show the importance of the anti-lemming-effect optimization. *TLE-5-count-lock* scales well up to 8 threads, the typical capacity of small systems, but collapses after just 12 threads. Allowing more retries in *TLE-20-count-lock* delays this collapse, but nonetheless, more data conflicts arise as the number of threads grows, leading more threads to acquire the lock. This in turn causes the lemming effect, which hurts performance.

3.2 How NUMA affects HTM

For the workload depicted in Figure 2, performance does not significantly decrease when threads run on two sockets. This is because operations on a large AVL tree are lightly contended, and most of them succeed in HTM on the first attempt. In a smaller tree, however, concurrent operations are more likely to conflict, and thus the performance suffers greatly once threads execute on the second socket. We already saw this in Figure 1, which depicted *TLE-20* in an AVL tree with key range [0, 2048): Adding a single thread on the second socket cut performance in half, and performance at 72 threads was reduced almost to that of a single thread. This drop in performance is caused by NUMA effects (i.e., the increased latency of inter-socket communication).

It is possible to scale to the full capacity of the large HTM system. As an example, in a read-only workload, TLE scales all the way to 72 threads. However, performing just 2% updates flattens the curve after 36 threads, completely negating the benefit of the second socket (see Figure 3).

Although NUMA effects are well known to negatively impact performance, this impact is amplified by the use of HTM. Figure 4 shows the results of a simple experiment in which threads repeatedly search for a randomly chosen key and then write the key found in the last node visited by this search into the key field of that node. (This might not be the key chosen because that key may not be in the set). This *search-and-replace* operation can be implemented without any synchronization because it does not actually change the key (i.e., it writes the same value that is already in the field). As we can see from this figure, NUMA effects impact TLE much more than the algorithm with no synchronization. With 36 threads, the algorithm with no synchronization is 12.1x faster than with a single thread, but only 8.9x faster with 72 threads, a 26% decrease in performance. However, the TLE algorithm experiences a much larger (75%) drop in performance when going from 36 to 72 threads (6.4x faster than a single thread with 36 threads vs. 1.6x faster with 72 threads).

To understand why TLE suffers so greatly from NUMA effects, consider Figure 5, which shows how many transaction attempts aborted, and the reasons (i.e., the condition code) they did so. The fraction of transactions that abort dramatically increases as threads are added on the second socket, from 10% at 36 threads to 33% at only 42 threads. Beyond 36 threads, the vast majority of these aborts are reported by hardware as data conflicts.

We hypothesize that these aborts occur because cross-socket cache invalidations lengthen the time needed to complete a transaction, which, in turn, lengthens the "window of contention" during which it may conflict with other transactions, increasing the likelihood of such conflicts. In contrast, when a cacheline is invalidated by a thread on the same socket, it can be restored much more quickly because the threads share an L3 cache.

Our hypothesis explains why performance is poor with even a single thread on the second socket (operations performed on the second socket cause expensive cache misses on the first socket), why read-only workloads scale on both sockets (threads do not cause cross-socket cache invalidations), and why the impact of NUMA effects on *TLE-20* is more severe in Figure 1 than in Figure 2 (in the small tree, there is a higher chance of conflicts, and operations complete more frequently, so more cache invalidations occur).

To check our hypothesis, we ran a 36-thread *single-socket* experiment that added some artificial delay (spinning) just

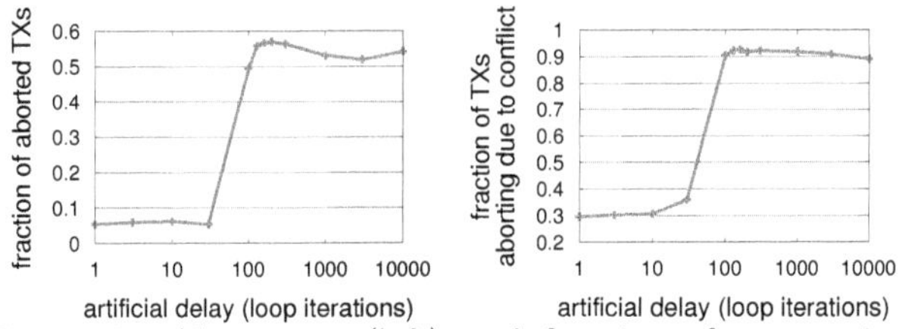

Figure 6: Abort rate (left) and fraction of transactions aborting due to conflict (right) for a 36-thread single-socket experiment in which delay is inserted before committing each transaction. The workload is 100% updates in an AVL tree with key range [0, 131072).

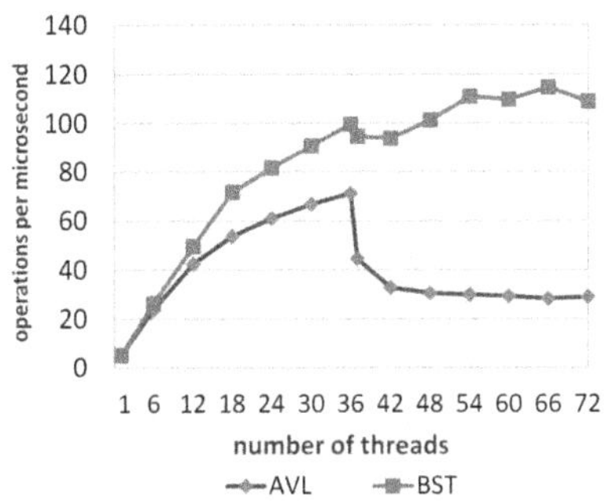

Figure 7: Comparison between an AVL tree and a leaf-oriented BST, with 20% updates and key range [0, 2048).

before committing each transaction.[1] The results in Figure 6 show that, with a certain amount of delay, the abort rate jumps significantly, mimicking the results on two sockets, and that once the abort rate increases, most transactions that abort do so because of conflicts, mimicking the phenomenon in Figure 5. These results provide strong evidence for our hypothesis.

Our hypothesis predicts that NUMA effects will be less significant for unbalanced leaf-oriented trees, where each update modifies a leaf, or the parent of a leaf. In such a tree, threads can only cause cross-socket cache invalidations near leaves, so the top of the tree is likely to remain cached. We tested this prediction by comparing the AVL tree to an unbalanced leaf-oriented binary search tree. As we can see in Figure 7, which shows the result of a workload with 20% updates and a key range of [0, 2048), the leaf-oriented BST scales much better than the AVL tree.

An alternative explanation for this behavior is that a transaction may abort whenever it experiences a last-level cache (LLC) miss (as it does, for example, whenever it experiences a page fault). To rule out this possibility, we designed a simple experiment in which a single thread allocates a one gigabyte array of bytes, and then iterates over the cells of this array, starting a transaction, reading a word, and committing. Because this array is too large to fit in cache, many of the thread's reads cause LLC misses. There is one complication: Whenever a thread reads a location in memory, modern Intel processors fetch the entire cache line containing the memory location, and also prefetch the next cache line. To avoid prefetching effects, the thread skips two cache lines (128 bytes) in between each pair of reads. In this experiment, almost all the $\frac{2^{30}}{128} = 2^{23}$ reads should incur a LLC miss, and we confirmed (using the Linux tool **perf**) that the number of LLC misses was approximately 2^{23}. However, there were fewer than 100 transactional aborts, which proves that LLC misses do not necessarily cause transactions to abort. We did a similar experiment to rule out the possibility that *cross-socket* LLC misses cause transactions to abort.

[1]The delay was implemented by varying a number of loop iterations, each consisting of a small, constant number of instructions. The average length of successful transactions increased from about 61ns (without the delay) to about 43μs (with the maximal delay of 10K iterations). Even with the maximal delay, transactions are short enough so that the chance for aborts imposed by context switch interrupts is negligible.

4. DEALING WITH NUMA

4.1 Considered approaches

In this section, we briefly describe a few unsuccessful approaches we tried to deal with NUMA effects, and then concentrate on one simple technique that did work.

One approach to deal with NUMA effects is to delegate each operation to the socket on which it should ideally execute (i.e., the socket on which most of its accesses would be local). If a thread gets an operation that should be executed on a different socket, it packages it up and sends it to the other socket. We implemented a number of delegation algorithms, in which we manually decided which socket to send each AVL tree operation to by checking whether its key fell into the lower or upper half of the key range. The results showed that while delegation doubled performance *per unit of time spent executing delegated operations*, the overhead of coordination between threads was too high. This experience echoes the results of previous work, which has shown that the benefit of delegation is often outweighed by the overhead of implementing it [8]. We were able to extract some benefit from delegation by packing multiple operations into a single critical section (reducing the relative overhead due to the increased size of each critical section). In future work, we plan to explore better delegation techniques and ways to apply them generically and with reduced overheads.

Another approach to deal with NUMA effects is to restrict the concurrency of threads executing on different sockets. For instance, one might allow only a few threads to run on the second socket. However, as Figure 1 shows, even a single thread running on the second socket can cripple performance. Alternatively, one might force threads on the second socket to backoff before retrying an aborted transaction. We tried this approach early in our exploration, and we found that performance improved only when the backoff was so long that the second socket was almost completely starved. Although starving the second socket avoids performance degradation beyond 36 threads, it yields poor performance for workloads that scale on two sockets.

The most effective solution we found builds on the observation that, for many workloads, the best performance is achieved either when only threads on one socket are allowed to execute (i.e., starving threads on the other socket) or when all threads regardless of socket are allowed to execute. We exploit this observation by periodically profiling TLE performance to determine, for each lock L, whether it is better to allow any thread to execute critical sections protected by L or to restrict concurrency to threads on one socket at a time. The results of this profiling is used to guide when a thread is allowed to execute critical sections outside

```
type Lock {
  lock_t lockData; // original lock metadata

  long acquisitions[][];
    // acquisitions[i][m] = #lock acquisitions
    //    for thread i and mode m
  int fastestMode;
  int alternateMode;
  long fastestModeSlice;
    // time slice out of each quantum for which
    // the lock mode should be fastestMode
  long  lastProfStart = 0;
    // when this lock was profiled for the last time
}
```

Figure 8: *Lock* data structure.

of the profiling phase. In particular, if we determine that it is better to restrict concurrency, then after profiling, we cycle through the sockets, allowing only threads from one socket at a time to execute critical sections protected by L, with the amount of time allocated to each socket determined by their relative performance as measured during the profiling. Critically, throttling decisions are made on a per-lock basis, and as we demonstrate in Section 5, our solution may choose to use all available sockets for some locks, and alternate between sockets for others. In the remainder of this section, we provide a high-level description of our implementation, which we call NATLE (for NUMA-aware TLE).

4.2 NATLE implementation

For simplicity, we assume a two-socket system, but it is straightforward to extend this implementation to systems with more sockets. NATLE allows performance tuning through a number of configurable parameters (such as the number of TLE attempts, the length and the frequency of the profiling period, etc.), which we currently set to fixed values that work reasonably well for our benchmarks. Of course, some applications may benefit by using different settings. Dynamically adapting these settings is left for future work.

For the NATLE implementation, we augment each lock with a *mode* that specifies which threads may execute critical sections protected by that lock. In our two-socket system, there are three possible modes: In mode 0 or mode 1, only threads on socket 0 or 1, respectively, may execute the critical section (threads on the other socket are delayed until the mode changes); in mode 2, threads on either socket may do so. In general, the number of modes is equal to the number of sockets plus one.

The running time is conceptually divided into cycles; each cycle is composed of a profiling phase and a post-profiling phase. The profiling phase is equally divided between different modes. The post-profiling phase is equally divided into quanta, and each quantum is split (based on relative performance during profiling) between two modes corresponding to two sockets (or treated as one unit if the favorable mode of operation found during profiling is using both sockets). In our implementation, the length of the profiling time in each cycle was 30ms; thus, each mode was profiled for 10ms. The length of each quantum was set to the length of the profiling time (30ms), and we used 9 quanta per cycle. Thus, the length of each cycle was 300ms, with 10% of this time allocated to profiling.

Figure 8 provides details on the *Lock* data structure maintained by NATLE. The *Lock* data structure contains the metadata of the original (pthread) lock implementation (*lockData*), the start time of the last profiling phase (*lastProfStart*), the fastest mode (i.e., the mode in which the most critical sections were executed) as determined by the most recent profiling session (*fastestMode*), the relative length of the quantum allocated to the fastest mode (*fastestModeSlice*) and an *acquisitions* collection, which is used for profiling. The last two bits in the *lastProfStart* field identify the stage of the profiling phase: 0 indicates that profiling is on but the profiling data (stored in *acquisitions*) has not yet been initialized; 1 indicates that profiling is on and the data has been initialized; 2 indicates that profiling is done but the profiling data has not yet been aggregated; 3 is when the profiling done and the profiling data has been aggregated. In the pseudocode, `S(x)` denotes the last two bits of `x`, and the tuple `<x,y>` denotes the value obtained by setting the last two bits of `x` to `y`.

```
int LockAcquire(Lock *lock) {
  int repetitions=0;
  while (repetitions++ < REPETITIONS_THRESHOLD) {
    // check if we are allowed to acquire the lock
    int mode = getMode(lock);
    if (mode == NUM_MODES-1 || mode == getSocket()) {
      ++lock->acquisitions[getTid()][mode];
      // call the underlying TLE implementation
      return LockAcquireTLE(lock);
    }
    wait for a while
  }
  // call the underlying TLE implementation
  return LockAcquireTLE(lock);
}

int LockRelease(Lock *lock) {
  // just call the underlying TLE implementation
  return LockReleaseTLE(lock);
}
```

Figure 9: LockAcquire and LockRelease.

The *acquisitions* collection stores, for each thread and mode, the number of times the critical section was executed by that thread in that mode since the last profiling phase began. In each cycle, when the profiling phase is finished, the data in this collection is aggregated and used to decide which mode is fastest and for how long it should be used, for each lock. For simplicity, we assume that an upper bound is known on the number of threads, and we implement *acquisitions* using an array with one slot for each thread and mode. One could eliminate this assumption by using, e.g., a linked list in which each thread maintains its statistics in a separate node.

As usual with TLE, we co-opt the *LockAcquire* and *LockRelease* operations that bracket the critical section to attempt to elide the lock acquisition and release using transactions. The details of these operations as implemented in NATLE are given in Figure 9. While the *LockRelease* operation in NATLE is simply a wrapper for the underlying TLE implementation, a thread executing *LockAcquire* must now first check the mode of the lock to determine whether it is allowed to execute the critical section. This is done by calling the auxiliary *getMode* function (see Figure 10).

To determine the mode of the lock, the thread in *getMode* reads the current system time[2] and determines at what part of the current cycle it is. If it is in the profiling phase, it ensures that profiling data has been initialized by calling *start-*

[2]To reduce overhead, the system time may be cached in a thread-local variable and read less frequently.

```
int getMode(Lock *l) {
  long start = startTime; // shared variable, set
      once when it is read for the first time
  long now = getCurrentTime();
  long timeIntoCycle = (now - start) % CYCLE_LEN;
  if (timeIntoCycle < PROFILING_LEN) {
    startProfiling(l, now - timeIntoCycle);
    return timeIntoCycle / (PROFILING_LEN/NUM_MODES);
  } else {            // profiling is finished
    finalizeProfiling(l);

    if (l->fastestModeSlice == 1 ||
      ((timeIntoCycle - PROFILING_LEN) % QUANTUM_LEN
          < l->fastestModeSlice * QUANTUM_LEN))
      return l->fastestMode;

    return l->alternateMode;
  }
}

void startProfiling(Lock *l, long profStart) {
  long t = l->lastProfStart;
  while (t < <profStart,1>) {
    if (t < <profStart,0> &&
        CAS(&l->lastProfStart, t, <profStart,0>)) {
      // reset learning counters
      set all entries of l->acquisitions to 0
      // signal that profiling data is initialized
      CAS(&l->lastProfStart, <profStart,0>,
          <profStart,1>);
      return;
    }
    t = l->lastProfStart;
  }
}
```

Figure 10: Auxiliary functions for getting the current mode and starting a new profiling phase.

Profiling and returns the mode corresponding to the current time. If it is in the post-profiling phase, it ensures that the profiling data has been finalized by calling *finalizeProfiling*.

The profiling functions are shown in Figures 10 and 11. In *startProfiling*, the thread compares the current time with the value of *lastProfStart* stored in the lock. If the initialization is required, it atomically sets (using CAS) the *lastProfStart* to the current time and resets the entries of the *acquisitions* collection to 0. In *finalizeProfiling*, if the data has not been finalized (determined by checking the last two bits of the *lastProfStart* field stored in the lock), the thread toggles these bits (using CAS), signaling other threads that it is in the process of summarizing profiling data, which it does by calling *computeBestLockModes*. There, if it finds out that most acquisitions took place in the mode allowing both sockets to run, it sets *fastestMode* to 2 and *fastestModeSlice* to 1; otherwise, it sets *fastestMode* to the mode with the most acquisitions and sets *fastestModeSlice* to the ratio of the number of acquisition in the *fastestMode* to the total number of acquisition in that mode and in the mode $1 - fastestMode$ (i.e., the mode corresponding to the other socket).

To avoid cases where insufficient profiling data (e.g., during warmup time) may lead to a suboptimal decision of using only one of the sockets, we use a threshold (set to 256); if the total number of lock acquisitions in all modes falls below that threshold, *fastestMode* is set to 2 (and *fastestModeSlice* is set to 1). (For simplicity, this optimization is omitted from the pseudo-code.)

After calling *finalizeProfiling*, the thread decides (in *getMode*) based on the current time and the values of *fastestMode* and *fastestModeSlice* on the current mode for the lock.

```
void finalizeProfiling(Lock *l) {
  long t = l->lastProfStart;
  // check if the profiling data has been finalized
      already
  if (S(t) == 3) return;

  if (S(t) == 1 &&
      CAS(&l->lastProfStart, <t,1>, <t,2>)) {
    computeBestLockModes(l);
    CAS(&l->lastProfStart, <t,2>, <t,3>;
  } else
    while (S(t) == 2 &&
      <t,0> == <l->lastProfStart,0>) {
      t = l->lastProfStart;
    }
}

void computeBestLockModes(Lock *l) {
  // compute fastest mode for the given lock
  long acqs[];
  for (int m = 0; m < NUM_MODES; m++) {
    // sum acquisitions in mode m for all threads
    acqs[m] = 0;
    for (int j = 0; j < NUM_THREADS; j++) {
      acqs[m] += l->acquisitions[j][m];
    }
  }
  l->fastestMode = index of largest element of acqs
  l->alternateMode = index of second largest
                      element of acqs

  if (l->fastestMode == NUM_MODES-1) {
    // both sockets run in fastest mode, so no need
        to alternate modes
    l->fastestModeSlice = 1;
  } else {
  // Only one socket runs in fastest mode. Divide
      quantum between fastest and alternate modes.
  l->fastestModeSlice = acqs[l->fastestMode] /
    (acqs[l->fastestMode] +
      acqs[1 - l->fastestMode]);
  }
}
```

Figure 11: Auxiliary functions for finalizing a profiling phase and computing modes for a post-profiling phase.

If the mode returned by *getMode* is the one corresponding to the socket on which this thread is running (which can be found through a library call and is stored in a thread-local variable) or corresponding to the mode that allows both sockets to run, the thread proceeds with the underlying TLE operation. Otherwise, if the current mode corresponds to the socket different from the one on which the thread is running, the thread spins for a while (or yields) and then repeats from the beginning of the *LockAcquire* function. To avoid pathological cases (e.g., when a thread continuously misses the times when the corresponding lock is in the mode that would allow it to run), the number of repetitions is limited by a large constant. To accommodate possible thread migrations, each thread infrequently (e.g., every 1K attempts to execute *LockAcquire*) rechecks the socket on which it is running. Critically, even if the thread decides to run in the "wrong" mode, correctness is preserved, and only performance may be affected (for limited time, until the thread finds out the real mode it should run with). Also, note that NATLE does not assume any specific underlying TLE implementation. While in our evaluation in Section 5 we use a common TLE implementation (denoted as *TLE-20* in Section 3.1), other variants are possible, e.g., a TLE implementation that performs contention management using an auxiliary lock [2].

5. EXPERIMENTAL RESULTS

5.1 Data structure microbenchmarks

In this section, we present a selection of results from a large suite of microbenchmarks. We implemented the set data type (i.e., supporting insert, delete, and search operations) in three different ways, as an AVL tree, as an unbalanced binary search tree (BST), and as a skip-list. Each implementation has a single lock that protects every operation, and we used two variants of TLE to implement this lock. The first variant (which we simply call TLE) is the common implementation described in Section 3.1, in which a thread makes 20 attempts using HTM before falling back to a (test-and-test-and-set) lock. The second variant is the NATLE algorithm described in Section 4 implemented on top of this common TLE implementation.

Each data point in our graphs is an average of five timed trials, each lasting approximately 10 seconds. In each trial, a fixed number of threads repeatedly invoke operations with keys drawn uniformly at random from a fixed key range with a specified proportion of update vs. search operations. Before a trial begins, the data structure is prefilled so that it contains half of its key range, and among the update operations, inserts and deletes are equally likely, so the data structure remains approximately half full. As mentioned in Section 3, we pin the first 36 threads to one socket and the next 36 to the other socket. In all experiments, we use an HTM-friendly memory allocator [10]. To reduce noise from the power management system, the machine was set up in performance mode (i.e., the power governor was disabled, while all cores were brought to the highest frequency) with turbo mode disabled.

Figure 12 shows the results of several experiments on AVL trees. First consider the graphs on the left, in which threads do not do any "external work" between operations. For the read-only workload (top left graph), both TLE variants scale (the reductions in slope from 18 to 36 threads and from 54 to 72 threads occur because of hyperthreading). However, NATLE achieves about 27% less throughput than TLE due to periodic profiling overhead and time sampling, which are redundant in this case because the best performance is achieved by simply using both sockets. Tuning the frequency and the length of profiling, as well as the frequency of time sampling is possible, but is left for future work.

In more realistic settings, threads typically perform some work between consecutive operations on a shared data structure. We emulate this external work by having each thread call a short function a random number of times; this random number is chosen from some preset range (e.g., $[0, 256)$). The graphs on the right side of Figure 12 show the results of experiments with such external work on the AVL tree. In the read-only workload and a single-thread experiment, the external work reduces the throughput of TLE (and NATLE) by about 2/3. At the same time, the gap between NATLE and TLE in this workload shrinks to less than 13%.

When we introduce update operations, both TLE and NATLE do not scale as well, and this worsens as the proportion of updates increases. However, once threads start to execute on the second socket (i.e., when there are more than 36 threads), TLE's throughput drops dramatically, whereas NATLE manages to stay closer to the peak throughput achieved at 36 threads. This is true with or without external work. In summary, NATLE can exploit both sockets for workloads

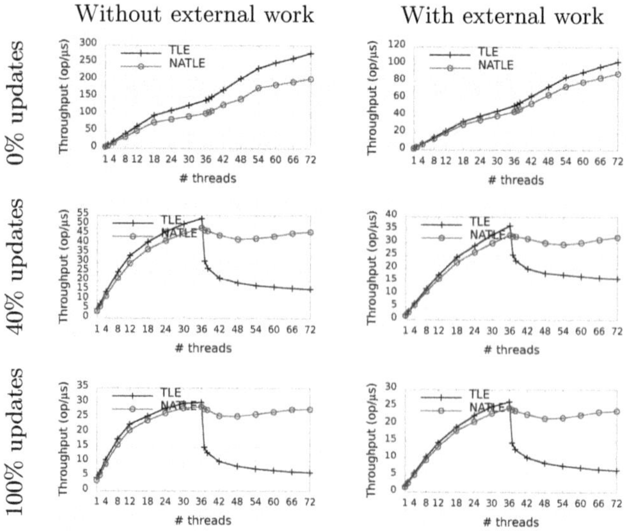

Figure 12: Experimental results for AVL trees. The key range is $[0, 2048)$.

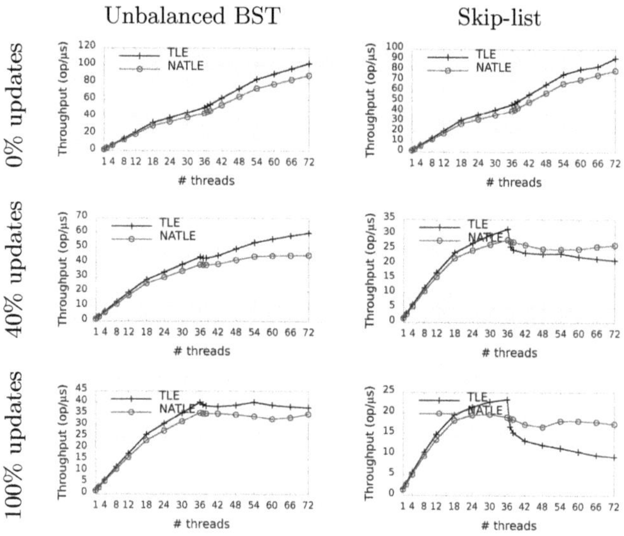

Figure 13: Experimental results for unbalanced BSTs (left) and skip-lists (right). The key range is $[0, 2048)$.

that scale on both sockets with TLE (e.g., the read-only workload), but unlike TLE, it exhibits little or no performance degradation when using cores on both sockets for workloads that do not scale.

The results for experiments with unbalanced BSTs and skip lists are provided in Figure 13. There, threads perform the same amount of external work as in the right part of Figure 12. Interestingly, TLE performance in unbalanced BSTs is not prone to the NUMA effects as operations do not rotate the tree and thus always modify only nodes at or near tree leaves. Indeed, the NATLE profiling statistics show that the number of critical section executions is slightly larger when both sockets are used, and thus it chooses to use both sockets. However, as Figure 14 demonstrates, reducing the key range increases the chance for a data conflict between tree operations, which in turn makes TLE susceptible to the NUMA effect. In this case, NATLE is able to avoid the performance degradation. Its profiling statistics show

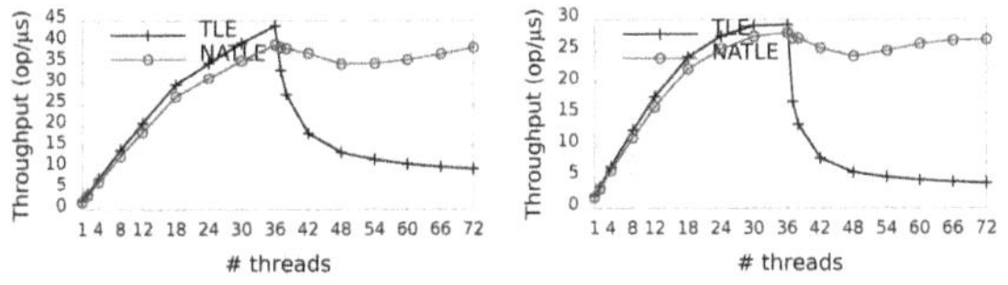

(a) 40% updates (b) 100% updates

Figure 14: Experimental results for unbalanced BSTs with key range [0, 128).

Pin to alternating sockets No pinning

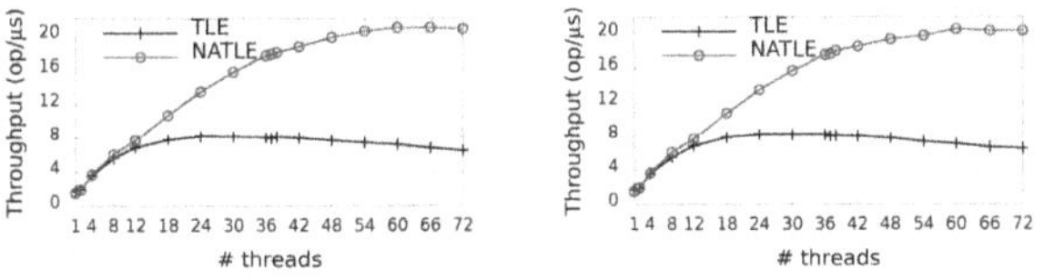

Figure 15: Experimental results for AVL trees with different thread pinning policies. The workload is 100% updates with key range [0, 2048).

that using one socket at a time is by far more efficient that using both sockets. Along with that, the performance of skip lists (cf. Figure 13) is more like AVL trees, although the performance degradation of TLE is slightly less dramatic.

We also experimented with several different policies for pinning threads. In Figure 15, we show graphs using two alternative pinning policies for workloads with 100% updates, key range [0, 2048), and the same amount of external work as in right part of Figure 12. For the graph on the left, threads are pinned to alternating sockets (i.e., even-numbered threads are pinned to cores on socket 0 and odd-numbered threads are pinned to cores on socket 1). For the graph on the right, threads are not pinned; rather, the operating system decides placement. The similarity between these two graphs suggests that the Linux scheduler attempts to evenly distribute the load across sockets. Since the workload does not scale on two sockets, the benefit of NATLE is more significant, and is evident earlier (starting at eight threads).

Although the benchmarks we have considered thus far use only one lock, NATLE can profile and throttle threads for applications that use multiple locks, and it does so independently for each lock. That is, the mode(s) selected for each lock is determined separately for each lock based on the statistics gathered for that lock during the profiling phase. For example, in Figure 16, we show the results of an experiment in which there are two AVL trees, both with key range [0, 2048). Half of the threads invoke only update operations on one tree; the other half invoke only search operations on the other tree. (We only run this experiment with even numbers of threads.) As before, threads are pinned to spread across the cores of a single socket as much as possible (i.e., until there are more than 18 threads), and then use hyperthreading before spilling over onto the other socket. When there are more than 36 threads, we ensure that there are equal numbers of threads accessing each tree. In other words, the first 36 threads (divided equally between two groups) run on the first socket, and the remaining threads (again, divided equally between two groups) run on the second socket.

Note that these two groups of threads are accessing different trees, so threads in one group never conflict with threads in the other group. To simplify the evaluation, we want both groups of threads to have approximately the same throughput (when running without contention). Since search operations are generally much faster than update operations, we achieve this by adding external work between invocations of the search operations.

We know from Figure 12 that the workload with 100% updates does not scale on two sockets, whereas the workload with 0% updates does. Thus, the threads doing update operations should be throttled so that at any time, only threads from one socket are accessing the update-only tree. In contrast, the threads doing search operations should not be throttled: threads executing on different sockets can, and should, access the read-only tree concurrently.

The graphs in Figure 16 show the combined throughput of both groups of threads, and also the contribution of each group to that combined throughput. NATLE significantly outperforms TLE when there are more than 36 threads because it throttles the update-only threads but not the search-only threads. The graphs that break out performance by data structure (two rightmost charts in Figure 16) show that the drop at 38 threads for TLE occurs mostly because of a drop in the performance of the tree with updates operations. At the same time, NATLE keeps scaling by avoiding this drop.

5.2 STAMP

In this section, we present results with STAMP [27], a common benchmarking suite for transactional memory programs. We evaluate the version of the suite provided by Ruan et al. [31], which includes a number of code modifications that allow adaptation to the standard transactional memory interface. Note that NATLE does not require the latter, however, it can be used with transactional programs as long as the transactional runtime configured to simply use a pthread lock for each transaction. This is exactly what we have done by overwriting the transactional runtime implementation library (libitm) provided with GCC.

The results for various STAMP benchmarks and standard workloads are shown in Figure 17. (We omit the results for the bayes benchmark since it highly depends on the order of various parallel computations and thus exhibits high variance; this fact was noted in [34].) These benchmarks report the total runtime, hence the lower result is better.

STAMP benchmarks appear to be very sensitive to cross-socket contention: In 7 out of 9 charts the runtime of TLE skyrockets when the number of threads exceeds the capacity of one socket. In all these cases, however, NATLE is able to maintain roughly the same performance across all thread counts beyond 36.

5.3 ccTSA

The ccTSA software is an open source implementation of a de novo gene sequence assembler [4]. It gets an input file with DNA segments and tries to assemble the whole genome by looking for overlap between the segments. It uses a lock-protected hash-map to store subsequences of DNA segments during their processing. ccTSA achieves good scalability on real genome data by splitting the main hash-map data structure into thousands of smaller hash-maps, each protected by its own lock. For our evaluation, however, we are using the

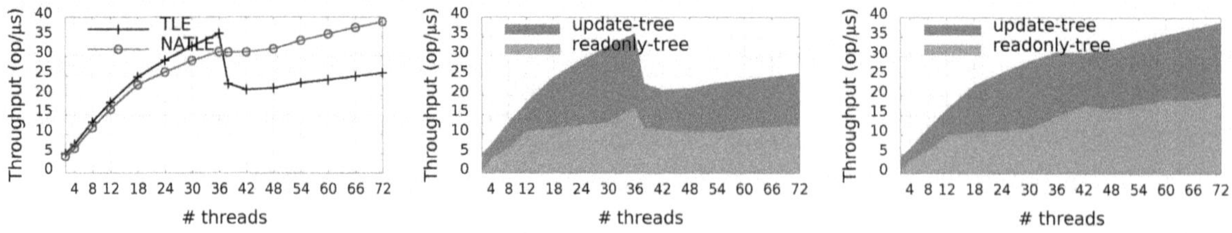

(a) Total throughput (b) Break-down for TLE (c) Break-down for NATLE

Figure 16: Experimental results for a workload involving two AVL trees. The left graph compares the performance of the TLE algorithms. The other two area graphs each show a single algorithm, and break out the performance of *each data structure*. The area graphs are *stacked*, meaning that the top of the upper area represents the aggregate performance for both trees.

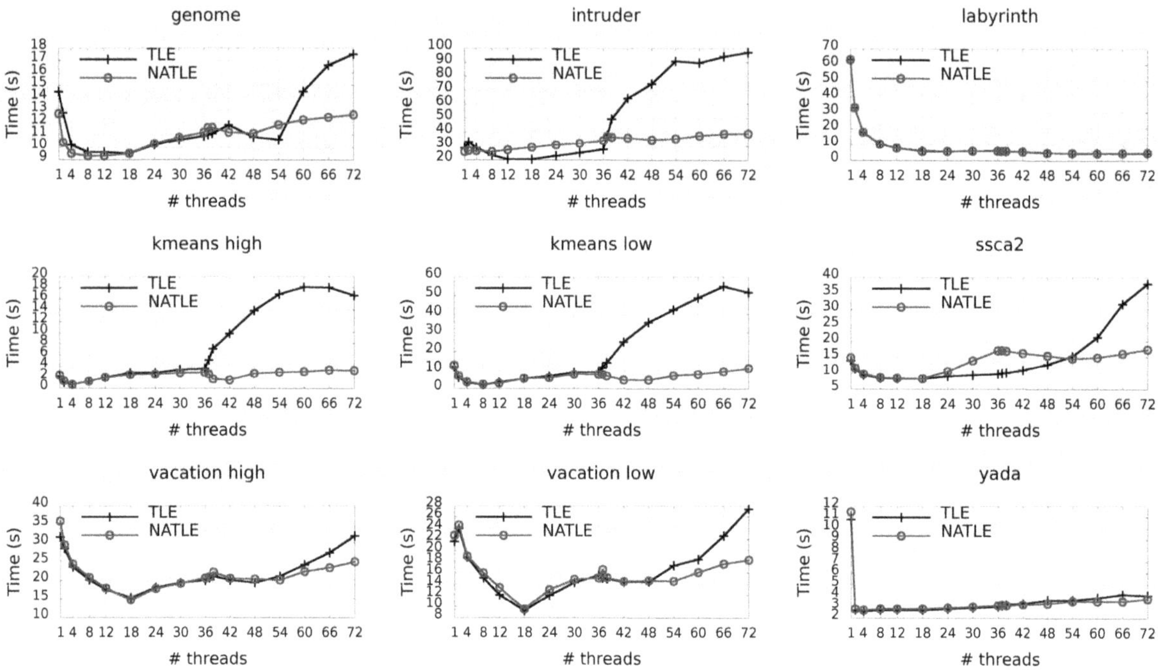

Figure 17: Experimental results with STAMP.

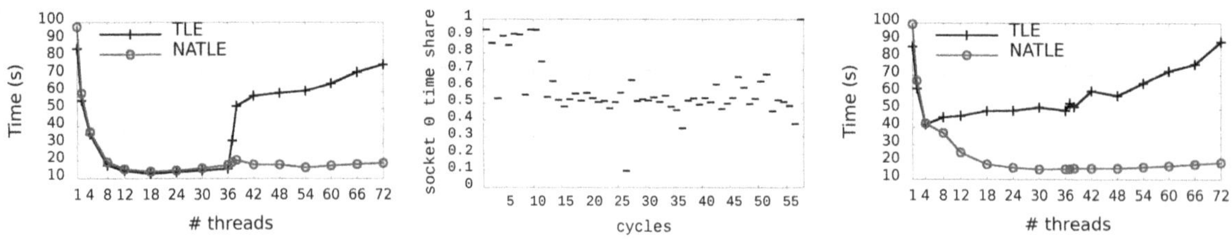

(a) Total runtime (with pinning) (b) Time allocation for socket 0 when running with 72 threads (with pinning) (c) Total runtime (without pinning)

Figure 18: Experimental results with ccTSA.

transactified version of ccTSA [11], which simplifies the design of the original implementation and uses a single (lock-protected) hash-map. Comparing to the original lock-based implementation, this version achieves better single-thread performance when used with locks, and performs more than twice better at any thread count when the lock is elided using TLELib (see [11] for details).

For our evaluation we use DNA segments from the E.coli organism that were provided with the original software, and configure ccTSA (e.g., the size of subsequences) with the same configuration as reported in [11]. Figure 18(a) compares the performance of ccTSA with TLE and NATLE using our usual pinning policy. Both variants scale well up to 18 threads and then keep stable performance up to 36 threads. When the number of threads exceeds the capacity of one socket, however, the runtime of TLE jumps, almost reaching the level of the single thread. In contrast, NATLE decides to throttle periodically one of the sockets, maintaining the same level of performance up to 72 threads.

Data shown in Figure 18(b) sheds some light on the decisions taken by NATLE in a run with 72 threads. The x-axis corresponds to runtime cycles (as a reminder, NATLE divides the running time into cycles and profiles performance at the beginning of each cycle), while the y-axis corresponds to the ratio of running time allocated in each quantum of the corresponding cycle for socket 0. Based on these results, one can see that for the majority of cycles, NATLE decides to allocate roughly half of the quantum time to each of the two sockets. The decision is taken based on the profiling, which shows that for these cycles, socket throttling is more effective than using both sockets at the same time.

We also show the results of running this benchmark without pinning threads (see Figure 18(c)). In this case, the benefit of using NATLE becomes evident much earlier because the cctsa benchmark does not scale across sockets.

5.4 paraheap-k

paraheap-k is a small (less than 1000 lines of code) parallel heap-based application for calculating k-means clusters [21]. It has been developed in the context of studying astronomical data to process efficiently galactic spectral data with the task of finding galactic components. paraheap-k gets as in input a file with galactic coordinates and uses a configurable number of threads to calculate iteratively k centroids. The calculation process stops once the ratio of data points that maintains an association with the same centroid across subsequent iterations goes above a configurable threshold (99.9%, by default). At the end, the position of calculated centroids as well as the data point association is written to output files.

Overall, the paraheap-k application has 7 critical sections, 6 of which are very short (just update a shared counter) and another one inserts a data point into the heap. Furthermore, the application uses multiple locks, making it an interesting use case for the evaluation of NATLE. The results of this evaluation with the usual pinning policy are shown in Figure 19(a). We measured the time of the actual data processing, i.e., we did not include the time to read the provided input file and output the results.

Despite the fact that NATLE statistics show that for most parts of executions with more than 36 threads, using one socket at a time yielded substantially higher throughput then when using both sockets, the benefit of NATLE over

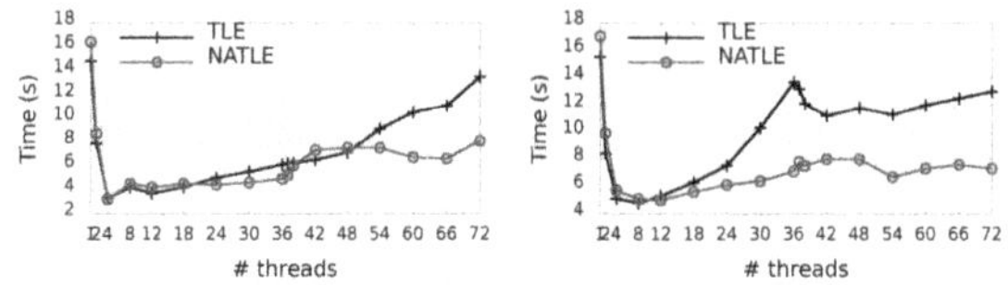

(a) With pinning (b) Without pinning

Figure 19: Experimental results with paraheap-k.

TLE is relatively moderate. We believe this is a result of the way this benchmark creates and uses multiple worker threads. Specifically, while all other benchmarks considered so far create their working threads once and at the beginning of their runs, paraheap-k does so in every processing iteration (there are more than a dozen iterations per run), and in fact, does so twice per iteration (to associate data points with centroids, and then to recalculate the position of those centroids once the data association phase is done). Each time a new thread is created, it is pinned according to the pinning policy, and the overhead of this pinning becomes substantial when it is done frequently, eliminating most of the benefits achieved by NATLE in reducing conflicts between threads running on different sockets. The results of the evaluation without pinning confirm this hypothesis (see Figure 19(b)). There, the benefit of NATLE is much more substantial, and it becomes evident at 18 threads.

6. CONCLUSION

In this paper, we have presented results of experiments we have done in an investigation into the behavior of HTM on a large 72-thread dual-socket machine. We have shown that some recommendations and common usage patterns for HTM on smaller single-socket machines do not carry over to larger machines. In particular, the NUMA characteristics of the multi-socket machine can have dramatic effects on the performance of applications that use HTM: for some applications, using all 72 threads on the machine yields behavior that is only marginally better than that of single-threaded execution. On the other hand, other applications may scale to the full capacity of the machine.

Based on these observations, we proposed a technique for more effective use of HTM on large NUMA machines by adaptively throttling threads as necessary to optimize performance based on profiling information collected during execution. Our experiments show that our technique achieves the full performance of both sockets for workloads that scale, and avoids the performance degradation that cripples TLE for workloads that do not.

7. REFERENCES

[1] G. Adelson-Velsky and E. Landis. An algorithm for the organization of information. *Soviet Mathematics Doklady*, 3:1259–1263, 1962.

[2] Y. Afek, A. Levy, and A. Morrison. Software-improved hardware lock elision. In *Proc. ACM PODC*, pages 212–221, 2014.

[3] Y. Afek, A. Matveev, O. R. Moll, and N. Shavit. Amalgamated lock-elision. In *Proc. DISC*, pages 309–324, 2015.

[4] J. H. Ahn. ccTSA: A Coverage-Centric Threaded Sequence Assembler. *PLoS ONE*, 7(6), June 2012.

[5] E. Atoofian. Improving performance of software transactional memory through contention locality. *J. Supercomput.*, 64(2):527–547, 2013.
[6] S. Blagodurov, S. Zhuravlev, M. Dashti, and A. Fedorova. A case for NUMA-aware contention management on multicore systems. In *Proc. USENIX ATC*, 2011.
[7] W. Bolosky, R. Fitzgerald, and M. Scott. Simple but effective techniques for NUMA memory management. *SIGOPS Oper. Syst. Rev.*, 23(5):19–31, Nov. 1989.
[8] I. Calciu, D. Dice, T. Harris, M. Herlihy, A. Kogan, V. J. Marathe, and M. Moir. Message passing or shared memory: Evaluating the delegation abstraction for multicores. In *Proceedings of the International Conference on Principles of Distributed Systems OPODIS*, pages 83–97, 2013.
[9] G. Chadha, S. Mahlke, and S. Narayanasamy. When less is more (LIMO): Controlled parallelism for improved efficiency. In *Proc. International Conference on Compilers, Architectures and Synthesis for Embedded Systems (CASES)*, pages 141–150, 2012.
[10] D. Dice, T. Harris, A. Kogan, and Y. Lev. The influence of malloc placement on TSX hardware transactional memory. *CoRR*, 2015.
[11] D. Dice, A. Kogan, and Y. Lev. Refined transactional lock elision. In *Proc. ACM PPoPP*, pages 19:1–12, 2016.
[12] D. Dice, A. Kogan, Y. Lev, T. Merrifield, and M. Moir. Adaptive integration of hardware and software lock elision techniques. In *Proc. ACM SPAA*, pages 188–197, 2014.
[13] D. Dice, Y. Lev, M. Moir, and D. Nussbaum. Early experience with a commercial hardware transactional memory implementation. In *Proc. ACM ASPLOS*, pages 157–168, 2009.
[14] D. Dice, Y. Lev, M. Moir, D. Nussbaum, and M. Olszewski. Early experience with a commercial hardware transactional memory implementation. Technical report, Sun Labs, 2009.
[15] D. Dice, V. J. Marathe, and N. Shavit. Lock cohorting: A general technique for designing NUMA locks. *TOPC*, 1(2):13, 2015.
[16] N. Diegues and P. Romano. Self-tuning Intel transactional synchronization extensions. In *Proceedings of the International Conference on Autonomic Computing (ICAC)*, pages 209–219, 2014.
[17] N. Diegues, P. Romano, and S. Garbatov. Seer: Probabilistic scheduling for hardware transactional memory. In *Proc. ACM SPAA*, pages 224–233, 2015.
[18] N. Diegues, P. Romano, and L. Rodrigues. Virtues and limitations of commodity hardware transactional memory. In *Proceedings of the 23rd International Conference on Parallel Architectures and Compilation (PACT)*, pages 3–14, 2014.
[19] A. Hassan, R. Palmieri, and B. Ravindran. Remote transaction commit: Centralizing software transactional memory commits. *IEEE Transactions on Computers*, pages 26–33, 2015.
[20] M. Herlihy and E. Moss. Architectural support for lock-free data structures. In *Proc. International Symposium on Computer Architecture (ISCA)*, pages 289–300, 1993.
[21] M. Jenne, O. Boberg, H. Kurban, and M. Dalkilic. Studying the milky way galaxy using paraheap-k. *Computer*, 47(9):26–33, 2014.
[22] R. P. LaRowe, Jr., C. S. Ellis, and M. A. Holliday. Evaluation of NUMA memory management through modeling and measurements. *IEEE Transactions on Parallel and Distributed Systems*, 3:686–701, 1991.
[23] B. Lepers, V. Quema, and A. Fedorova. Thread and memory placement on NUMA systems: Asymmetry matters. In *Proc. USENIX ATC*, 2015.
[24] T. Li, D. Baumberger, D. A. Koufaty, and S. Hahn. Efficient operating system scheduling for performance-asymmetric multi-core architectures. In *Proc. ACM/IEEE Supercomputing*, pages 1–11, 2007.
[25] J.-P. Lozi, F. David, G. Thomas, J. Lawall, and G. Muller. Remote core locking: Migrating critical-section execution to improve the performance of multithreaded applications. In *Proc. USENIX ATC*, 2012.
[26] A. Matveev and N. Shavit. Reduced hardware lock elision. In *Proceedings of 6th Workshop on the Theory of Transactional Memory (WTTM)*, 2014.
[27] C. C. Minh, J. Chung, C. Kozyrakis, and K. Olukotun. STAMP: stanford transactional applications for multi-processing. In *Proceedings of the International Symposium on Workload Characterization (IISWC)*, pages 35–46, 2008.
[28] T. Nakaike, R. Odaira, M. Gaudet, M. Michael, and H. Tomari. Quantitative Comparison of Hardware Transactional Memory for Blue Gene/Q, zEnterprise EC12, Intel Core, and POWER8. In *Proc. ACM/IEEE ISCA*, 2015.
[29] K. K. Pusukuri, R. Gupta, and L. N. Bhuyan. Thread reinforcer: Dynamically determining number of threads via os level monitoring. In *Proc. IEEE International Symposium on Workload Characterization (IISWC)*, pages 116–125, 2011.
[30] A. Raman, H. Kim, T. Oh, J. W. Lee, and D. I. August. Parallelism orchestration using dope: The degree of parallelism executive. In *Proc. ACM PLDI*, pages 26–37, 2011.
[31] W. Ruan, Y. Liu, and M. Spear. STAMP need not be considered harmful. In *Proceedings of ACM SIGPLAN Workshop on Transactional Computing (TRANSACT)*, 2014.
[32] L. Tang, J. Mars, X. Zhang, R. Hagmann, R. Hundt, and E. Tune. Optimizing Google's warehouse scale computers: The NUMA experience. In *Proc. IEEE HPCA*, pages 188–197, 2013.
[33] B. Verghese, S. Devine, A. Gupta, and M. Rosenblum. Operating system support for improving data locality on CC-NUMA compute servers. *SIGOPS Oper. Syst. Rev.*, 30(5):279–289, 1996.
[34] R. M. Yoo, C. J. Hughes, K. Lai, and R. Rajwar. Performance evaluation of Intel® transactional synchronization extensions for high-performance computing. In *International Conference for High Performance Computing, Networking, Storage and Analysis (SC)*, 2013.
[35] R. M. Yoo and H.-H. S. Lee. Adaptive transaction scheduling for transactional memory systems. In *Proc. ACM SPAA*, pages 169–178, 2008.

Brief Announcement: Transactional Data Structure Libraries*

Alexander Spiegelman
Technion, Israel
sashas@tx.technion.ac.il

Guy Golan-Gueta
Yahoo Research, Israel
ggolan@yahoo-inc.com

Idit Keidar
Technion and Yahoo Research, Israel
idish@ee.technion.ac.il

ABSTRACT

We introduce *transactions* into libraries of concurrent data structures; such transactions can be used to ensure atomicity of sequences of data structure operations. By restricting transactional access to a well-defined set of data structure operations, we strike a balance between the ease-of-programming of transactions and the efficiency of custom-tailored data structures. We exemplify this concept by designing and implementing a library supporting transactions on any number of maps, sets (implemented as skiplists), and queues. Our library offers efficient and scalable transactions, which are an order of magnitude faster than state-of-the-art transactional memory toolkits. Moreover, our approach treats stand-alone data structure operations (like *put* and *enqueue*) as first class citizens, and allows them to execute with virtually no overhead, at the speed of the original data structure library.

Motivation

Data structures are the bricks and mortar of computer programs. They are generally provided via highly optimized libraries. Since the advent of the multi-core revolution, many efforts have been dedicated to building *concurrent data structure libraries (CDSLs)* [2], which are so-called "thread-safe". Thread-safety is usually interpreted to mean that each individual data structure operation (e.g., *insert, contains, push, pop*, and so on) executes atomically, in isolation from other operations on the same data structure.

Unfortunately, simply using atomic operations is not always "safe". Many concurrent programs require a number of data structure operations to jointly execute atomically. As an example, consider a server that processes requests to transfer money to bank accounts managed in a CDSL. If several threads process requests in parallel, then clearly, atomicity of individual CDSL operations does not suffice for safety: two concurrent threads processing transfers to the same account may read the same balance at the start of their respective operations, causing one of the transfers to be lost.

This predicament has motivated the concept of memory *transactions*, which appear to execute atomically (all-or-nothing) and in isolation (so no partial effects of on-going transactions are observed). A transaction can either *commit*, in which case all of its updates are reflected to the rest of the system, or *abort*, whereby none of its updates take effect. Transactions have been used in DBMSs for decades, and are broadly considered to be a programmer-friendly paradigm for writing concurrent code. Numerous academic works have developed *software transactional memory (STM)* toolkits. Moreover, some (limited) hardware support for transactions is already available.

Nevertheless, as of today, general-purpose transactions are not practical. STM incurs too high a overhead and hardware transactions are only "best effort". And in both cases, abort rates can be an issue. Thus, with the exception of eliding locks in short critical sections, transactions are hardly used in industry today. CDSLs, despite their more limited semantics, are far more popular. Efficient CDSL implementations are available for many programming languages and are widely adopted.

Contributions

Our goal in this paper is to provide transaction semantics for CDSLs without sacrificing performance. We introduce the concept of a *transactional CDSL (TDSL)*, which supports bundling sequences of data structure operations into atomic transactions. Individual operations are seen as *singleton transactions* (*singletons* for short). TDSLs provide *composability*; for example, a transaction may invoke operations on two different maps and a queue. But unlike STM approaches, atomicity only encompasses the TDSL's operations, whereas other memory accesses are not protected.

Restricting the transactional alphabet to a well-defined set of operations (e.g., *enqueue, dequeue, insert, remove*, and *contains*) is the key to avoiding the notorious overhead associated with STM. We show that we can benefit from this restriction in three ways:

1. First, while a TDSL implementation *may* use standard STM techniques, it can also apply CDSL-like custom-tailored optimizations that rely on the specific data structure's semantics and organization in order to improve efficiency and reduce the abort rate. For example, it can employ STM-like read-set tracking and validation, but reduce the read-set size to include only memory locations that induce real semantic conflicts.

*The full paper has been accepted to PLDI 2016 [3].

SPAA '16 July 11-13, 2016, Pacific Grove, CA, USA

ACM ISBN 978-1-4503-4210-0/16/07.
DOI: http://dx.doi.org/10.1145/2935764.2935805

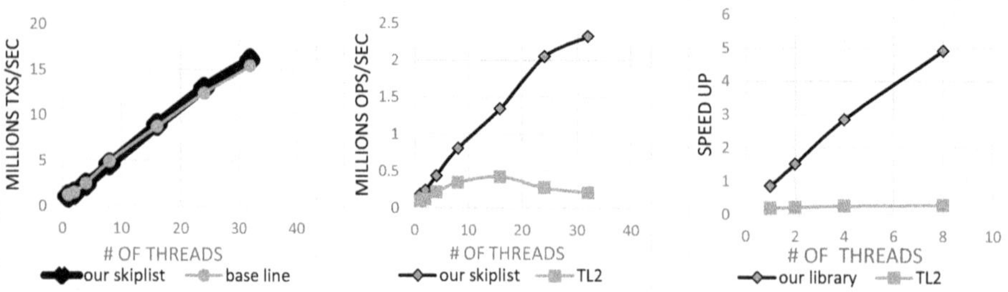

Singletons, micro-benchmark. Update-only workload. Transactions, mico-benchmark. Update-only workload. Intruder. Speedup over sequential execution.

Figure 1: Representative results of our TDSL evaluation.

Another example is to use transactional access to a core data structure that ensures correctness but does not support fast lookup, and complement it with a non-transactional index for fast lookup.

2. Second, a TDSL can employ different STM strategies for managing different data structures within the same library. For example, transactional access to maps is amenable to optimistic concurrency control, since operations in concurrent transactions are unlikely to conflict. But when queues are used inside transactions, contention is frequent, and so a pessimistic solution is often more efficient.

3. Third, a TDSL can treat singletons as first class citizens – it can spare them the transaction management overhead altogether, and save programmers the need to deal with their aborts.

In our full paper [3] we exemplify these three ideas by presenting example TDSL algorithms for popular data structures – maps, sets (implemented as skiplists), and queues – as well as compositions thereof. In addition, we generalize this concept, and discuss a generic approach for composing TDSLs with each other as well as with STM toolkits such as TL2 [1]. Such a composition can provide, on the one hand, high performance transactions comprised of data structure operations, and on the other hand, fully general transactions, including ones that access scalars.

API and semantics

A TDSL is simply a CDSL with added support for transactions. Its API provides, in addition to CDSL operations (like *insert* and *enqueue*), *TX-begin* and *TX-commit* operations. The added operations are delineations – library operations invoked between a *TX-begin* and the ensuing *TX-commit* pertain to the same transaction[1]. However, other memory accesses made in this span to locations outside the library do not constitute part of the transaction. We assume that the shared data structure's state is only manipulated via the TDSL's API.

The library may *abort* a transaction during any of the operations, resulting in an exception. In case of abort, none of the transaction's operations is reflected in the data structure. Applications using the library need to catch abort exceptions, at which point they typically restart the aborted transaction.

We consider transactions that further provide, meaning that even transactions that are deemed to abort are not allowed to see inconsistent states of the data structure partially reflecting concurrent transactions' updates.

It is important to note that a TDSL is, in particular, a CDSL, and legacy code may continue to use its operations outside of transactions. Library operations invoked outside transactions are treated as singletons. Singletons cannot abort, and so legacy code can continue to use the original thread-safe library operations. The semantics of singletons relative to other transactions is preserved. In other words, each run has a *linearization* encompassing all of its transactions and singletons.

Evaluation

We compare the singletons of our transactional skiplist to custom-tailored concurrent skiplist CDSL operations, and evaluate transactions of skiplist operations using our TDSL relative to a state-of-the-art STM. In addition, we evaluate our library with Intruder, a transactional benchmark that performs signature-based network intrusion detection.

In Figure 1(a), we compare our singletons to the baseline in order to assess the overhead inflicted on stand-alone operations by our transaction support; comparison with additional CDSLs is given in the full paper [3]. In Figure 1 (b), we compare our transactions to the TL2 implementation provided with Synchrobench and in Figure 1 (c) we compare an Intruder implementation using our library to the STAMP Intruder.

Our evaluation shows that we can get ten-fold faster transactions than STMs in update-dominated workloads accessing sets, and at the same time cater stand-alone operations, (i.e., singletons), in par with state-of-the-art CDSLs. In addition, it shows that Intruder runs up to 17x faster than using a state-of-the-art STM.

References

[1] Dave Dice, Ori Shalev, and Nir Shavit. Transactional locking ii. In *Distributed Computing*. Springer, 2006.

[2] Maurice Herlihy and Nir Shavit. *The art of multiprocessor programming*. Morgan Kaufmann, 2008.

[3] Alexander Spiegelman, Guy Golan-Gueta, and Idit Keidar. Transactional data structure libraries. To

[1]In principle, a transaction may end in a programmer-initiated abort, but we omit this option for simplicity of the exposition.

Cache-Adaptive Analysis

Michael A. Bender [†] Erik D. Demaine[‡] Roozbeh Ebrahimi[§] Jeremy T. Fineman[¶]
Rob Johnson[†] Andrea Lincoln[‖] Jayson Lynch[‡] Samuel McCauley[†]

ABSTRACT

Memory efficiency and locality have substantial impact on the performance of programs, particularly when operating on large data sets. Thus, memory- or I/O-efficient algorithms have received significant attention both in theory and practice. The widespread deployment of multicore machines, however, brings new challenges. Specifically, since the memory (RAM) is shared across multiple processes, the effective memory-size allocated to each process fluctuates over time.

This paper presents techniques for designing and analyzing algorithms in a cache-adaptive setting, where the RAM available to the algorithm changes over time. These techniques make analyzing algorithms in the cache-adaptive model almost as easy as in the external memory, or DAM model. Our techniques enable us to analyze a wide variety of algorithms — Master-Method-style algorithms, Akra-Bazzi-style algorithms, collections of mutually recursive algorithms, and algorithms, such as FFT, that break problems of size N into subproblems of size $\Theta(N^c)$.

We demonstrate the effectiveness of these techniques by deriving several results:

- We give a simple recipe for determining whether common divide-and-conquer cache-oblivious algorithms are optimally cache adaptive.
- We show how to bound an algorithm's non-optimality. We give a tight analysis showing that a class of cache-oblivious algorithms is a logarithmic factor worse than optimal.
- We show the generality of our techniques by analyzing the cache-oblivious FFT algorithm, which is not covered by the above theorems. Nonetheless, the same general techniques can show that it is at most $O(\log\log N)$ away from optimal in the cache adaptive setting, and that this bound is tight.

These general theorems give concrete results about several algorithms that could not be analyzed using earlier techniques. For example, our results apply to Fast Fourier Transform, matrix multiplication, Jacobi Multipass Filter, and cache-oblivious dynamic-programming algorithms, such as Longest Common Subsequence and Edit Distance.

Our results also give algorithm designers clear guidelines for creating optimally cache-adaptive algorithms.

This research was supported in part by NSF grants CCF 1114809, CCF 1217708, CCF 1218188, CCF 1314633, IIS 1247726, IIS 1251137, CNS 1408695, and CCF 1439084; MADALGO - Center for Massive Data Algorithmics, a Center of the Danish National Research Foundation; and a Stanford Graduate Fellowship.

[†]Department of Computer Science, Stony Brook University, Stony Brook, NY 11794-4400, USA. Email: {bender, rob, smccauley}@cs.stonybrook.edu.

[‡]MIT Computer Science and Artificial Intelligence Laboratory, 32 Vassar Street, Cambridge, MA 02139, USA. Email: {edemaine,jaysonl}@mit.edu.

[§]Google Inc., 1600 Amphitheatre Parkway, Mountain View, CA 94043 USA. Email: rebrahimi@google.com.

[¶]Department of Computer Science, Georgetown University, 37th and O Streets, N.W., Washington D.C. 20057, USA. Email: jfineman@cs.georgetown.edu.

[‖]Department of Computer Science, Stanford University, Palo Alto, CA 94305 USA. Email: andreali@cs.stanford.edu.

SPAA '16, July 11 - 13, 2016, Pacific Grove, CA, USA

ISBN 978-1-4503-4210-0/16/07...$15.00

DOI: http://dx.doi.org/10.1145/2935764.2935798

1. INTRODUCTION

Memory fluctuations are the norm on most computer systems. Each process's share of memory changes dynamically as other processes start, stop, or change their own demands for memory. This phenomenon is particularly prevalent on multi-core computers.

External-memory computations especially suffer from these fluctuations. Examples include:

- joins and sorts in a database management system (DBMS),
- irregular, I/O-bound, shared-memory parallel programs,
- cloud computing services running on shared hardware,

and essentially any external-memory computation running on a time-sharing system.

Database and scientific computing researchers and practitioners have recognized this problem for over two decades [9, 18, 19], and have developed many sorting and join algorithms [15, 20, 21, 25–27] that offer good empirical performance when memory changes size dynamically. However, most of these algorithms are designed to perform well in the common case, but perform poorly in the worst case [3, 4].

In contrast to this reality, most of today's performance models for external-memory computation assume a *fixed internal memory size* M (see, e.g., [24]) and hence algorithms designed in these models cannot cope when M changes. This means that most external-memory algorithms cannot take advantage of memory freed by other processes, and can begin thrashing if the system takes back too much memory.

Thus, there is a gap between the state of the world, where memory fluctuations are the rule, and today's tools for designing and analyzing external-memory algorithms, which assume fixed internal-memory sizes.

Barve and Vitter [3, 4] took the first major step towards closing this gap by showing that worst-case, external-memory bounds are possible in an environment where the cache[1] changes size. Barve and Vitter generalized the DAM (disk-access machine) model [1] to allow the memory size M to change periodically. They give optimal algorithms for sorting, FFT, matrix multiplication, LU decomposition, permutation, and buffer trees. Their work shows that it is possible to specially design intricate algorithms to handle adaptivity, but stops short of giving a general framework.

Bender et al. [7] took the next major step towards closing this gap between theoretical performance models and real systems. They formally define the cache-adaptive model,[2] and prove that some—but not all—optimal cache-oblivious[3] algorithms [13, 14, 22] remain optimal when the cache changes size dynamically. Specifically, if a recursive cache-oblivious algorithm performs $O(1)$ block transfers in addition to its recursive calls, then it is optimally cache adaptive. So is lazy funnel sort [8], despite not fitting this recursive pattern. Bender et al.'s results are encouraging. Because cache-oblivious algorithms are well understood, frequently easy to design, and widely deployed, there is hope that provably good cache-adaptive algorithms can also be deployed in the field.

On the other hand, open questions remain. In particular, the primary contribution of Bender et al. [7] was proposing a computational model rather than an analysis technique. Is there an algorithmic toolkit for cache-adaptive analysis so that future engineers could write their own cache-oblivious algorithms and then quantify their adaptivity? How can we analyze more general forms of recursive algorithms, e.g., in the common case where the additive term is $\omega(1)$? (Examples include cache-oblivious FFT, some versions of cache-oblivious matrix multiply and mutually recursive cache-oblivious dynamic programming algorithms such as LCS [10], Edit Distance [10], and Jacobi Multipass Filter [22].) How can we prove that a recursive algorithm is *not* optimally cache adaptive? For such algorithms, how far are they from optimality? The point of the present paper is to help answer these and other questions.

[1]We use "cache" to refer to the smaller level in any two-level hierarchy. Because this paper emphasizes RAM and disk, we use the terms "internal memory," "RAM," and "cache" interchangeably.

[2]The cache-adaptive model allows memory to change size more rapidly and unpredictably than the model of [3, 4], meaning that cache-adaptive results are more likely to hold up in the real world.

[3]***Cache-oblivious*** algorithms are not parameterized by the memory hierarchy, yet they often achieve provably optimal performance for any *static* hierarchy; see Section 2.

Results

The contribution of this paper is a set of tools that make analyzing the performance of recursive algorithms in the cache-adaptive setting almost as easy as analyzing their performance in the DAM [1] or cache-oblivious/ideal-cache models [13, 14, 22]. Analyzing the performance of many algorithms in the cache-adaptive model boils down to mechanically transforming the recurrence relation for the algorithm's I/O complexity, solving this new recurrence, and comparing the result to a problem-specific lower bound: if these bounds are asymptotically equal, then the algorithm is optimal; if they are not, then their ratio bounds how far the algorithm is from optimal.

Our techniques are general. They can analyze a wide variety of algorithms: Master-method-style algorithms [11], Akra-Bazzi-style algorithms [2], algorithms made of several mutually recursive functions, and algorithms, such as cache-oblivious FFT, that break a problem of size N into subproblems of size $\Theta(N^c)$.

Our results provide easy guidelines for cache-adaptive-algorithm designers. For example, in the case of linear-space-complexity Master-method-style algorithms, our results give an easy rule: if you want your algorithm to be optimal in the cache-adaptive model, then it can perform linear scans of size up to $O(N^c)$, where $c < 1$, in addition to its recursive calls. See Theorem 7.3 for the detailed criteria.

Our results suggest that the problem of designing and analyzing algorithms that adapt to memory fluctuations is tractable. The cache-adaptive model places almost no restrictions on how much and when memory can change size, so results in the model can carry over to most real-world systems. Despite this generality, our method enables algorithm designers to easily evaluate performance in this model.

We demonstrate our techniques by deriving several concrete results. (Below N refers to the input size.)

- We establish that cache-obliviousness does not always lead to cache-adaptivity using a variation of the cache-oblivious naïve matrix multiplication algorithm of Frigo et al. [13]. While this variation is optimal in the DAM model, it is a $\Theta(\log N)$ factor away from optimal in the cache-adaptive model. This result serves as a concrete example of our more general techniques.
- We completely characterize when a Master-method-style linear-space-complexity algorithm is optimal in the cache-adaptive model; see Theorem 7.3. We show that when such an algorithm is DAM-optimal, it is at most an $O(\log N)$-factor slower than optimal in the cache-adaptive model.
- More generally, we completely characterize when a set of mutually recursive linear-space-complexity Akra-Bazzi-style algorithms are optimal in the cache-adaptive model (Theorem 6.10 and Theorem 6.11).

  We apply these theorems to show the cache-adaptive optimality of mutually recursive algorithms such as the cache-oblivious dynamic programming algorithms of Chowdhury and Ramachandran [10] for Longest Common Subsequence and Edit Distance, and Prokop's cache-oblivious Jacobi Multipass Filter Algorithm [22].
- We show that the same techniques can be used to analyze non-Akra-Bazzi-style algorithms. As an example, we show that the cache-oblivious FFT algorithm [13] is $O(\log \log N)$ away from optimal.

Paper overview. The rest of the paper is organized as follows. Section 2 reviews the cache-adaptive model. Section 3 axiomatizes the notion of a progress bound, which are used in many DAM optimality proofs.

Section 4 works through the analysis of a version of the cache-oblivious matrix multiply algorithm of Frigo et al. [13]. This example shows how our results apply to a classic cache-oblivious algorithm, and demonstrates the key ideas behind our techniques. Section 5 generalizes these ideas to an easy-to-use recipe for performing cache-adaptive analysis.

Section 6 gives a high-level overview of the core technical idea of the paper. We show how to bound the progress an algorithm can make on any memory profile. Section 7 describes our main cache-adaptive optimality characterization theorems. We give an optimal cache-adaptivity characterization theorem for collections of mutually recursive Akra-Bazzi-style algorithms. The proofs for the theorems given in Section 7 appear in the full version of this paper.

The paper ends with a summary of concrete results about specific algorithms that can be obtained using our methods.

2. CACHE-ADAPTIVE MODEL, DEFINITIONS, AND ANALYTICAL TOOLS

The ***cache-adaptive*** model [7] is the same as the DAM model [1] except that memory may change size after each I/O (i.e., after each cache miss).[4] Thus, the size of memory is not a constant, but rather a function $m(t)$ giving the size of memory (in blocks) after the tth I/O. We also use $M(t) = B \cdot m(t)$ to represent the size, in words, of memory at time t. We call $m(t)$ and $M(t)$ ***memory profiles*** in blocks and words, respectively.

Optimality in the cache-adaptive model mirrors optimality in the DAM model. On every memory profile, an optimal algorithm has worst-case I/O complexity within a constant factor of any other algorithm's worst-case I/O complexity.

However, in the cache-adaptive model it does not make sense to compare two algorithms' running times directly. That is, given a profile $m(t)$ and two algorithms A and B, we cannot compare A and B's performance by simply running them on $m(t)$ and comparing their running times. To see why, suppose B performs one dummy I/O and then runs A. By any reasonable definition, B's running time should be asymptotically no worse than A's. But consider an input I and profile $m(t)$ that drops to very little memory as soon as $A(I)$ finishes. Now B may finish arbitrarily later than A.

Thus, we formalize optimality by comparing algorithms using ***speed augmentation***. Rather than granting an algorithm extra time, we allow it to perform multiple I/Os per time step in our analysis. Speed augmentation is a theoretical tool to ensure that algorithms are compared on profiles that provide the same overall resources up to a constant factor. Thus, rather than saying one algorithm is (say) twice the speed of another, we say that it performs equally well on hardware with half the latency. This gives the same intuition as classic asymptotic analysis while being meaningful in the cache-adaptive model.

Definition 2.1. *Giving an algorithm A,* ***c-speed augmentation*** *means that A may perform c I/Os in each step of the memory profile.*

In order to make the definition of optimality in the CA model as strong as possible, we allow algorithms to query $m(t)$, even into the future. Thus, an optimal algorithm in the CA model is asymptotically as fast as any other algorithm, even one that can see the future size of memory and plan accordingly.[5]

However, allowing algorithms to query the memory profile creates a problem: a P/poly algorithm may be able to use the memory profile as a "reference string" to speed up its computations on some memory profiles. We rule out this behavior by only permitting ***memory-monotone*** algorithms:

Definition 2.2. *A* ***memory monotone*** *algorithm runs at most a constant factor slower when given more memory.*

Memory monotonicity is a weak restriction: all cache-oblivious algorithms are memory monotone, as are LRU, the optimal offline paging algorithm, and many other paging algorithms. Memory monotone also includes almost all "reasonable" DAM-model algorithms. One notable exception is FIFO paging [6], which was recently shown not to be memory monotone [12].

Definition 2.3. *An algorithm A that solves problem P is* ***optimal*** *in the cache-adaptive model if there exists a constant c such that on all memory profiles and all sufficiently large input sizes N, the worst-case running time of a c-speed-augmented A is no worse than the worst-case running time of any other (non-augmented) memory-monotone algorithm.*

As in the DAM model, memory augmentation is needed to show that LRU is constant competitive. We also use memory augmentation to simplify our analyses.

Definition 2.4. *For any memory profile m, we define a* ***c-memory augmented*** *version of m as the profile $m'(t) = cm(t)$. Running an algorithm A with* ***c-memory augmentation*** *on the profile m means running A on the c-memory augmented profile of m.*

If an algorithm is not parameterized by M or B, then we say it is ***cache-oblivious***. These algorithms are designed to perform well without knowing the size of memory.

When analyzing cache-oblivious algorithms in the CA model, we assume that the system performs automatic page replacement. Belady's algorithm [5] turns out to be an optimal offline paging algorithm in the CA model and the least-recently-used (LRU) policy is $O(1)$-competitive with resource augmentation [7].

The performance bounds for cache-oblivious algorithms commonly rely on a so-called ***tall-cache*** assumption, which means that there is a value $H(B)$, polynomial in B, such that $M \geq H(B)$. For example, for cache-oblivious sorting or matrix transpose, $H(B) = \Theta(B^2)$ [13]. We support these kinds of analyses in the CA model as follows.

Definition 2.5. *In the CA model, we say that a memory profile M is* ***H-tall*** *if for all $t \geq 0$, $M(t) \geq H(B)$.*

Definition 2.6. *Algorithm A has* ***space complexity*** *$f(N)$ if for all problems of size N, the number of distinct memory locations accessed by A while processing I is $\Theta(f(N))$.*

Space complexity is often defined as the maximum memory location indexed. This definition is slightly more general.

[4]We use I/Os as a proxy for time because we are studying I/O-bound algorithms—the algorithm spends most of its time performing these I/Os (see [7]).

[5]Note that while our model allows the algorithms to see the future memory, the cache-oblivious algorithms presented here do not take advantage of this—in fact, they are not even aware of the present size of memory.

3. PROGRESS BOUNDS: HOW MUCH AN ALGORITHM CAN DO ON A PROFILE

This section axiomatizes the notion of ***progress bounds***, which are used in many lower-bound proofs in the DAM model, and develops tools to easily port progress bounds from the DAM model to the CA model.

In the DAM model, a ***progress bound*** $\rho(M,T)$ for a problem P gives an upper bound on the amount of progress that any algorithm can make towards solving an instance of P given M words of memory and T I/Os. A ***progress requirement function*** $R(N)$ gives a lower bound on the amount of progress any algorithm must make in order to solve all problem instances of size N. In the DAM model, the I/O complexity of any algorithm must be at least $\Omega(T \cdot R(N)/\rho(M,T))$.

Example 3.1. *The DAM sorting lower bound [1] says that, after sorting each block, a comparison-based sorting algorithm learns at most $O(B\log(M/B))$ bits of information per I/O, given M memory, and must learn $\Omega(N\log N)$ bits to sort. Thus, $R(N) = \Omega(N\log N)$ and $\rho(M,T) = O(TB\log(M/B))$. Hence sorting in the DAM model takes at least $R(N)/\rho(M,1) = \Omega(\frac{N}{B}\log_{M/B} N)$ I/Os.*

Example 3.2. *The DAM matrix multiplication lower bound [16, 17, 23] states that, given M memory and M/B I/Os, no naive matrix multiplication algorithm can perform more than $O(M^{3/2})$ elementary multiplications, and multiplying two $\sqrt{N}\times\sqrt{N}$ matrices requires performing $\Theta(N^{3/2})$ elementary multiplications. Thus $\rho(M,M/B) = M^{3/2}$ and $R(N) = \Theta(N^{3/2})$. Consequently, multiplying two $\sqrt{N}\times\sqrt{N}$ matrices requires $\frac{M}{B}R(N)/\rho(M,\frac{M}{B}) = \Omega(MN^{3/2}/(BM^{3/2})) = \Omega(\frac{N^{3/2}}{B\sqrt{M}})$ I/Os.*

We first generalize the notion of progress bounds to arbitrary profiles. Given an arbitrary memory profile $M(t)$, we write $\rho(M)$ as the upper bound on progress that any algorithm can make on an instance of problem P when given memory profile $M(t)$.

Most[6] progress bounds developed in the DAM model also apply to the CA model because they are "memory-less", i.e., the bound $\rho(M,t)$ applies no matter what the size or content of memory was before the t I/Os in question. In fact, in the full version of this paper, we give a general method for deriving progress bounds from DAM lower bounds based on the red pebble game [23].

The only challenge to using DAM progress bounds on arbitrary memory profiles in the CA model is that some bounds apply only to time-spans during which memory does not change size. For example, the matrix multiply progress bound is defined only for M/B I/Os during which memory is always of size M.

We solve this problem using ***square profiles***. A profile $m(t)$ is square if time can be decomposed into a sequence of regions $t_0 < t_1 < \dots$ such that $m(t) = t_{i+1} - t_i$ for all $t \in [t_i, t_{i+1})$. Square profiles are useful because we can apply progress bounds, like the matrix multiply progress bound, to each square independently and sum to get a bound on the progress that any algorithm can make on the entire profile. We use the notation $\square_M$ to denote a square of size M words by M/B I/Os, and we denote a square profile with squares of size $M_1,\dots,M_k$ as $\square_{M_1} \| \cdots \| \square_{M_k}$. We generalize ρ from the DAM model to squares as $\rho(\square_M) = \rho(M, M/B)$.

[6]In fact, all that we have found.

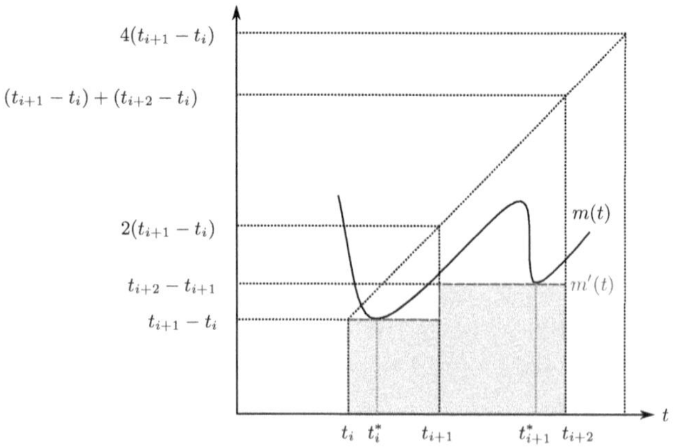

Figure 1: The inner square profile of memory profile $m(t)$.

We can then generalize these bounds to arbitrary profiles by using ***inner square profiles*** [7]. The inner square profile of a profile M is constructed by greedily packing the largest-possible squares under M from left to right, as shown in Figure 1. Square profiles enable us to compute bounds on the amount of progress that any algorithm can make on an arbitrary memory profile.

Definition 3.3. *For a memory profile m, the **inner square boundaries** $t_0 < t_1 < t_2 < \dots$ of m are defined as follows: Let $t_0 = 0$. Recursively define t_{i+1} as the largest integer such that $t_{i+1} - t_i \le m(t)$ for all $t \in [t_i, t_{i+1})$. The **inner square profile** of m is the profile m' defined by $m'(t) = t_{i+1} - t_i$ for all $t \in [t_i, t_{i+1})$ (see Figure 1).*

Bender et al. [7] proved the following useful lemma about inner square profiles.

Lemma 3.4. *Let m be a memory profile where $m(t+1) \le m(t)+1$ for all t. Let $t_0 < t_1 < \dots$ be the inner square boundaries of m, and m' be the inner square profile of m.*

1. *For all t, $m'(t) \le m(t)$.*
2. *For all i, $t_{i+2} - t_{i+1} \le 2(t_{i+1} - t_i)$.*
3. *For all i and $t \in [t_{i+1}, t_{i+2})$, $m(t) \le 4(t_{i+1} - t_i)$.*

The following definitions axiomatize two technical but obvious properties of progress functions: (1) that profiles with more time and memory can support more progress, and (2) that the progress possible on a square profile is just the sum of the progress possible on each of its squares.

Intuitively, we say that one profile is ***smaller*** than another, i.e., offers less memory and/or time, if it can be cut into pieces, each of which fits underneath a corresponding piece of the other.

Definition 3.5. *Let M and U be any two profiles of finite duration. We say that **M is smaller than U, $M \prec U$,** if there exist profiles $L_1, L_2 \dots L_k$ and $U_0, U_1, U_2 \dots U_k$, such that $M = L_1 \| L_2 \dots \| L_k$ and $U = U_0 \| U_1 \| U_2 \dots \| U_k$, and for each $1 \le i \le k$,*
(i) *if d_i is the duration of L_i, U_i has duration $\ge d_i$, and*
(ii) *as standalone profiles, L_i is always below U_i.*

Definition 3.6. *A function $\rho : \mathbb{N}^* \to \mathbb{N}$ is **monotonically increasing** if for any profiles M and U, $M \prec U$ implies $\rho(M) \le \rho(U)$.*

Second, we assume that the progress on a square profile should be, essentially, the sum of the progress possible on each square.

Definition 3.7. *Let $M_1 \| M_2$ indicate concatenation of profiles M_1 and M_2. A monotonically increasing function $\rho : \mathbb{N}^* \rightarrow \mathbb{N}$ is* ***square-additive*** *if (i) $\rho(\square_M)$ is bounded by a polynomial in M, and (ii) $\rho(\square_{M_1} \| \cdots \| \square_{M_k}) = \Theta(\sum_{i=1}^{k} \rho(\square_{M_i}))$.*

With these requirements in mind, we can axiomatize the notion of progress bound.

Definition 3.8. *A problem has a* ***progress bound*** *if there exists a monotonically increasing polynomial-bounded* ***progress-requirement function $R : \mathbb{N} \rightarrow \mathbb{N}$*** *and a square-additive* ***progress limit function $\rho : \mathbb{N}^* \rightarrow \mathbb{N}$*** *such that: For any profile M, if $\rho(M) < R(N)$, then no memory-monotone algorithm running under profile M can solve all problem instances of size N.*

We also refer to the progress limit function ρ as the ***progress function*** or ***progress bound***.

3.1 Optimally-Progressing Algorithms

In this paper, we prove that algorithms are optimal (or non-optimal) by analyzing whether they always make within a constant factor of the maximum possible progress on a profile. An algorithm is ***optimally progressing*** if, for every usable profile m that is just long enough for the algorithm to solve all problems of size N, $\rho(m) = O(R(N))$. We first define what it means for a profile to be "usable" and "just long enough" and then define optimally progressing formally.

The CA model allows memory to increase or decrease arbitrarily from one time step to the next. However, since an algorithm can only load one block into memory per time step, its memory usage can only increase by one block per time step.

Definition 3.9. *An h-tall memory profile m is* ***usable*** *if $m(0) = h(B)$ and if m increases by at most 1 block per time step, i.e. $m(t+1) \leq m(t) + 1$ for all t.*

Definition 3.10. *For an algorithm A and problem instance I we say a profile M of length ℓ is* ***I-fitting*** *if A requires exactly ℓ time steps to process input I on profile M. A profile M is* ***N-feasible for A*** *if A, given profile M, can complete its execution on all instances of size N. We further say that M is* ***N-fitting for A*** *if it is N-feasible and there exists at least one instance I of size N for which M is I fitting. (When A is understood, we will simply say that M is N-feasible, N-fitting, etc.)*

Definition 3.11. *For an algorithm A, integer N, and N-feasible profile $M(t)$, let $M_N(t)$ denote the N-fitting prefix of M. We say that algorithm A with tall-cache requirement H is* ***optimally progressing with respect to a progress bound ρ*** *(or simply optimally progressing if ρ is understood) if, for every integer N and N-feasible H-tall usable profile M, $\rho(M_N) = O(R(N))$.*

The following two lemmas show that usable profiles and square profiles support essentially the same amount of progress. This implies that, if a memory-monotone algorithm is optimally progressing on all usable profiles, then it is optimally progressing on all square profiles, and vice versa. This enables us to focus exclusively on square profiles, which are easier to analyze, when proving algorithms optimal (or non-optimal) in the CA model.

Lemma 3.12. *If ρ is square additive and M is a usable profile with inner square profile M', then $\rho(M) = \Theta(\rho(M'))$.*

Proof. Since ρ is monotonic and $M'(t) \leq M(t)$ for all t, $\rho(M') \leq \rho(M)$. Let $M'_{4,4}$ be the 4-speed and 4-memory augmented version of M'. Since ρ is square-additive and since $\rho(\square_N)$ is bounded by a polynomial in N, $\rho(M'_{4,4}) = O(\rho(M'))$.

We prove that $M \prec M'_{4,4}$. Thus, by monotonicity of ρ,

$$\rho(M') \leq \rho(M) \leq \rho(M'_{4,4}) = O(\rho(M')),$$

which means that $\rho(M) = \Theta(\rho(M'))$.

Let $M[S_i]$ denote the profile M restricted to the interval S_i. Let $k+1$ be the number of inner squares in M'. Define $L_1 = M[S_1 \cup S_2], L_2 = M[S_3], \ldots, L_k = M[S_{k+1}]$, and note that $M = L_1 \| L_2 \| \ldots \| L_k$. Also, define U_i to be a 4-speed 4-memory augmented version of square S_i and allow $U'_k = U_k \| U_{k+1}$. Notice that $M'_{4,4} = U_1 \| U_2 \| \ldots U_{k-1} \| U'_k$.

In order to prove that $M \prec M'_{4,4}$, we show that each U_i, $1 \leq i \leq k-1$ satisfies the three conditions of Definition 3.5, and U'_k satisfies the first two conditions of Definition 3.5.

We start by considering U_1 and L_1. If M is $H(B)$-tall, by Definition 3.9 we have that $M(0) = H(B)$. By Definition 3.3, we have that $t_1 = H(B)$ and since $m(t+1) \leq m(t) + 1$, we have that for all $t \in [0, t_1)$, $M(t) \leq 2t_1$. Moreover, by Lemma 3.4, we know that S_2 is at most twice as long as S_1 and for all $t \in [t_1, t_2)$, $M(t) \leq 4(t_1 - t_0) = 4|S_1|$. Hence, $t_2 \leq 3t_1$, and for all $t \in [0, t_2)$, $M(t) \leq 4|S_1|$. Because U_1 is a 4-speed 4-memory augmented version of S_1, we have that (i) U_1 has a longer duration than $L_1 = M[S_1 \cup M_2]$, and that (ii) L_1 is below U_1.

Similarly, for each U_i, $2 \leq i \leq k$, by Lemma 3.4, we know that S_{i+1} is at most twice as long as S_i and for all $t \in [t_{i+1}, t_{i+2})$, $M(t) \leq 4(t_{i+1} - t_i) = 4|S_i|$. Because U_i is a 4-speed 4-memory augmented version of S_i, we have that (i) U_i has a longer duration than $L_i = M[S_{i+1}]$, and that (ii) L_i is below U_i.

By repeating the above argument for U_k, we see that (i) U_k has a longer duration than $L_k = M[S_{k+1}]$, and that (ii) L_k is below U_k. This means that $U'_k = U_k \| U_{k+1}$ also satisfies both of the above conditions. Therefore, we have shown that $M \prec M'_{4,4}$ and the lemma is complete. □

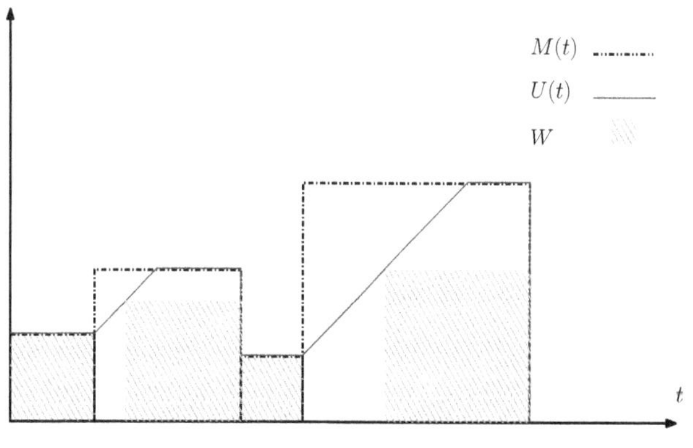

Figure 2: The usable profile beneath each square profile.

Lemma 3.13. *Let ρ be square additive. For every H-tall square memory profile M, there exists a* usable *memory profile U below M such that $\rho(U) = \Theta(\rho(M))$.*

Proof. Let $M = \square_{M_1} \| \square_{M_2} \| \ldots \square_{M_k}$ be any square profile. We construct a usable profile U as follows. We set $U(x) = H(B) + x$ for $x \in [0, \leq M_1 - H(B)]$ and $U(x) = M_1$ for $x \in (M_1 - H(B), M_1)$. For $i \geq 2$, U does the following on the interval $[t_i, t_i + M_i)$ covered by the ith square of M,

(i) If $M_i \leq M_{i-1}$, we let $U(x) = M_i$ for $x \in [t_i, t_i + M_i)$.

(ii) If $M_i > M_{i-1}$, let $U(x) = M_{i-1}+x$ for $x \in [t_i, t_i+M_i - M_{i-1}]$ and $U(x) = M_i$ for $x \in (t_i+M_i-M_{i-1}, t_i+M_i)$.

See Figure 2 for an illustration. Clearly we have $U \prec M$, so by monotonocity of ρ, we have that $\rho(U) \leq \rho(M)$.

We now argue that $\rho(U) = \Omega(\rho(M))$. To exhibit this, we show that there exist mutually disjoint squares $\square_{W_i}$, that all fit below U and for each i, $\square_{W_i}$ is at most 2 times shorter than $\square_{M_i}$. Since each $\square_{W_i}$ fits below U, we have that $W \prec U$ where $W = \square_{W_1} \| \square_{W_2} \| \ldots \square_{W_k}$. On the other hand, since ρ is square-additive, ρ is bounded by a polynomial and thus $\rho(\square_{W_i}) = \Theta(\rho(\square_{M_i}))$. Square-additivity of ρ also means that $\rho(W) = \Theta(\rho(M))$. Since $\rho(W) \leq \rho(U)$ the statement follows.

It remains to show that such $\square_{W_i}$ exist for each i. For each i, if $\square_{U_i} = \square_{M_i}$ (as in case (i) above), we allow $\square_{W_i} = \square_{M_i}$. Otherwise (as in case (ii) above), we let $\square_{W_i}$ be a square that is grown from the rightmost point of $\square_{M_i}$ diagonally to left until it touches U, see Figure 2. Note that because U increases linearly at the beginning of $\square_{M_i}$ until it reaches M_i, the point of $\square_{W_i}$ intersecting U is always on or above the diagonal of $\square_{M_i}$. Therefore, the height of W_i is at least 1/2 the height of M_i. □

Thus, between Lemma 3.12 and Lemma 3.13 we are able to use square profiles for both upper and lower bounds without loss of generality.

Finally, our proofs focus on showing that an algorithm is optimally progressing. This lemma justifies this focus—showing that an algorithm is optimally progressing is sufficient to show that it is cache-adaptive.

Lemma 3.14. *If an algorithm A is optimally progressing, then it is optimally cache adaptive.*

While optimally progressing is sufficient for adaptivity, we do not know if it is necessary—it remains an open question if there are algorithms that are optimally cache-adaptive but not optimally progressing. On the other hand, *progress optimality* and *competitive optimality* are equivalent in the DAM model. (See the full version for the proof.)

4. MATRIX MULTIPLY: A TALE OF TWO ALGORITHMS

This section provides a concrete example of our approach by working through the analysis of two cache-oblivious matrix multiplication algorithms.

We analyze two variants of the cache-oblivious matrix multiplication algorithm of Frigo et al. [13], which we call MM-INPLACE and MM-SCAN. Both algorithms divide each input matrix into four submatrices and perform eight recursive calls to compute submatrix products. Both run in $O(N^{3/2}/\sqrt{M}B)$ I/Os in the DAM model, which is optimal [16,17].

Remarkably, only MM-INPLACE is optimally cache adaptive; MM-SCAN is a $\Theta(\log(N/B^2))$ factor away from being optimal in the cache-adaptive model. This shows that cache-oblivious algorithms are not always cache adaptive.

The two algorithms differ in how they combine the eight matrix sub-products. MM-SCAN adds the eight matrix sub-products in one final linear scan, yielding a recurrence of $T(N) = 8T(N/4) + \Theta(1 + N/B)$ in DAM. MM-INPLACE computes the eight matrix sub-products "in place," adding the results of elementary multiplications into the output matrix as soon as it computes them, and yielding a recurrence of $T(N) = 8T(N/4) + O(1)$ in the DAM model. Both algorithms require a tall cache of $\Theta(B^2)$ and both recurrences have the same solution in the DAM model.

However, the linear scans of MM-SCAN are wasteful if they execute when memory is plentiful. For each input size N, we can construct a profile W_N^* that causes MM-SCAN to run inefficiently by giving the algorithm lots of memory during its scans, when it can't use it, and very little memory at other times. As a result, the profile W_N^* will have a recursive structure that mimics that of MM-SCAN: where MM-Scan performs a linear scan of size $\Theta(N)$, W_N^* will contain a square of size $\Theta(N)$. When MM-SCAN performs a recursive call on a problem of size $N/4$, W_N^* will have a copy of $W_{N/4}^*$. Hence $\rho(W_N^*)$, the progress possible on W_N^*, will satisfy a recurrence relation very similar to the recurrence relation for MM-SCAN. Where MM-SCAN's recurrence relation has a term of the form $\Theta(N/B)$, corresponding to a linear scan of size N, $\rho(W_N^*)$'s recurrence will have a term of the form $\rho(\square_N)$. This will enable us to solve explicitly for $\rho(W_N^*)$, yielding a concrete counter-example to the optimality of MM-SCAN.

Theorem 4.1. *The cache-oblivious matrix multiplication algorithm* MM-SCAN *is a $\Omega(\log(N/B^2))$ factor away from being optimal when solving problem instances of size N.*

Sketch. We show in Theorem 7.3 that MM-INPLACE is optimally progressing; intuitively, this is because nearly all of its computation time is spent in recursive calls.

The construction of W_N^* works as follows. Let $\lambda = \Theta(B^2)$ be the tall cache requirment for MM-SCAN. Memory starts out at size λ. Whenever MM-SCAN starts a linear scan of size $L \geq 2\lambda$ with λ memory, it will necessarily incur $\Theta((L-\lambda)/B) = \Theta(L/B)$ page faults, no matter how memory changes size during the scan. Thus we can increase memory to size $\Theta(L)$ for the next $\Theta(L/B)$ time steps. At the last time step of the linear scan, we drop memory back to λ.

We now compute $\rho(W_N^*)$. From Example 3.2, no naive matrix multiply algorithm can do more than $O(M^{3/2})$ elementary multiplications given M words of memory and M/B I/Os [23]. Thus $\rho(\square_M) = \Theta(M^{3/2})$. Since the top-level recursion performs a linear scan of size $\Theta(N)$, W_N^* contains a square of size $\Theta(N)$, which contributes $\Theta(\rho(\square_N))$ to $\rho(W_N^*)$. Further, W_N^* contains eight copies of $W_{N/4}^*$—one for each recursive call made by MM-SCAN. Thus $\rho(W_N^*)$ satisfies the recurrence

$$\rho(W_N^*) = 8\rho(W_{N/4}^*) + \Theta(\rho(\square_N)) = 8\rho(W_{N/4}^*) + \Theta(N^{3/2})$$

with base case $\rho(W_N^*) = \Theta(B^{3/2})$ when $N = O(B^2)$. Thus $\rho(W_N^*) = \Theta(N^{3/2}\log(N/B^2))$. Since MM-SCAN finishes at the last time step of W_N, W_N is N-fitting for MM-SCAN.

A problem of size N requires $R(N) = \Theta(N^{3/2})$ total multiplications. Since MM-SCAN only makes $O(N^{3/2})$ progress on W_N^* but W_N^* supports $\Theta(N^{3/2}\log(N/B^2))$ progress, MM-SCAN is $\Omega(\log(N/B^2))$ less than optimally progressing. □

5. A GENERAL RECIPE FOR ANALYZING ALGORITHMS IN THE CA MODEL

We now explain how to generalize the construction from Section 4 to obtain a simple recipe for testing whether a recursive linear-space cache-oblivious algorithm is optimally progressing.

The method from Section 4 can be used to construct a profile W_N^* for any cache-oblivious algorithm. Whenever $\rho(W_N^*) = \omega(R(N))$, the algorithm is not optimal.

The main technical challenge of this paper is to show that W_N^* is, for many algorithms, the worst possible profile, up to constant factors. Thus, an algorithm is optimally progressing if and only if $\rho(W_N^*) = O(R(N))$.

Since $\rho(W_N^*)$ satisfies, by construction, a recurrence that we can easily derive from the program's structure, this gives us an easy way to analyze Master-method-style cache-oblivious algorithms in the CA model.

1. Write down the recurrence for $T(N)$, the algorithm's I/O complexity in the DAM model:
$$T(N) = aT(N/b) + \Theta(N^c/B).$$
2. Derive the recurrence for $\rho(W_N)$ by replacing terms of the form $T(X)$ with $\rho(W_X)$ and terms corresponding to linear scans of size X with $\rho(\square_X)$:
$$T(N) = aT(N/b) + \Theta(N^c/B)$$
$$\Downarrow$$
$$\rho(W_N) = a\rho(W_{N/b}) + \Theta(\rho(\square_{N^c})).$$
3. Solve the recurrence for $\rho(W_N)$.
4. Compare the solution to $R(N)$. If $\rho(W_N) = O(R(N))$, then the algorithm is optimal. Otherwise, their ratio bounds how far the algorithm is from optimal.

In fact, we can explicitly solve the recurrence to obtain a simple theorem characterizing when linear-space complexity cache-oblivious Master-method-style algorithms are optimally progressing in the CA model (see Theorem 7.2).

The same basic technique works for Akra-Bazzi-style algorithms and even for collections of mutually-recursive Akra-Bazzi-style algorithms (see Theorem 6.10). Although Theorem 6.10 looks complex, the basic idea is the same.

1. Write down the recurrence relation for the I/O complexity of the algorithm.
2. Derive three new recurrences by performing the transformations specified in Theorem 6.10.
3. Solve these recurrences and compare to $R(N)$.

We explore these generalizations in Sections 6 and 7.

6. BOUNDING THE WORST-CASE PROFILE

This section formalizes the recipe described in Section 5. We first define the structure of algorithms covered by our theorems and then prove bounds on the progress possible on their worst-case profiles.

We first need to formalize the notion of a ***linear scan***. When a cache-efficient recursive algorithm is not making recursive calls, the work it does must be I/O efficient. We refer to this work as a ***linear scan***. Note that under our definition, a linear scan need not access a sequence of consecutive elements, as in a classical linear scan. However, it must be efficient—accessing $\Omega(B)$ useful locations on average, plus $O(1)$ additional I/Os.

Definition 6.1. *We say that algorithm L is a* ***linear scan of size ℓ*** *if it accesses ℓ distinct locations, it performs $\Theta(\ell)$ memory references, and its I/O complexity is $\Theta(1+\ell/B)$.*

This definition captures a wide variety of efficient cache-oblivious behaviors. Note that, in the definition, a linear scan might not access every element of its input (e.g., a search for a specific item in an array), it might not access the pages in sequential order (e.g., cache-oblivious matrix transpose [13]), and the order of accesses can be data-dependent (e.g., the merge operation from merge-sort).

Note that some linear scans and algorithms are I/O efficient only under a tall-cache assumption. For example, for cache-oblivious sorting or matrix transpose, $H(B) = \Theta(B^2)$ [13]. Thus the definition of a scan depends implicitly on the memory profile.

A particular type of linear scans only access a small number of locations. This may occur when, for example, an algorithm does $O(1)$ work at the beginning of a recursive call to set up the computation, or when recursive calls decrease the size of the linear scan below the block size.

Definition 6.2. *When the size of a linear scan in an invocation of an algorithm is $\leq B$, we refer to it as an* ***overhead*** *reference. An overhead reference costs $\Theta(1)$ I/Os.*

We can now define the class of algorithms covered by our theorems. Briefly, these algorithms are collections of mutually recursive Akra-Bazzi-style algorithms, i.e. they make a constant number of recursive calls on sub-problems a constant factor smaller than their input, and perform linear scans. This class covers everything from simple algorithms, such as the matrix multiplication algorithms described earlier, to advanced cache-oblivious algorithms, such as the cache-oblivious longest-common-subsequence (LCS) and Edit Distance algorithms of Chowdhury and Ramachandran [10], and the cache-oblivious Jacobi Multipass Filter algorithm of Prokop [22].

Definition 6.3. *Let $0 \leq c_j \leq 1$ and $f_j \geq 1$ be constants for $j = 1,\ldots,e$. Also let $a_{ji} > 0$, and $0 < b_{ji} < 1$ be constants for $j = 1,\ldots,e$, and $i = 1,\ldots,f_j$. Algorithms $A_1,\ldots,A_e$ are* ***generalized compositional regular (GCR) algorithms*** *if, for all i, A_j on an input of size N*

(i) *makes $\boldsymbol{a_{ji}}$ calls to algorithm $\boldsymbol{A_{ji}}$ on subproblems of size $\boldsymbol{b_{ji}N}$. Algorithm A_{ji} is one of $A_1,\ldots,A_e$.*

(ii) *performs $\Theta(1)$ linear scans before, between, or after its calls, where the size of the biggest linear scan is $\Theta(N^{c_j})$.*

Algorithms $A_1,\ldots,A_e$ are ***perfect*** *generalized compositional regular (PGCR) algorithms, if for every j the size of all of A_j's linear scans is $\Theta(N^{c_j})$.*

We can now define the worst-case profile for an algorithm.

Definition 6.4. *Algorithm* ***A's worst-case profile for inputs of size N*** *among all profiles that are λ-tall is*

$$W_{A,N,\lambda} = \text{argmax}\{\rho(M) \mid M \text{ is } N\text{-fitting, } \lambda\text{-tall, usable}\}.$$

When λ is omitted, we assume that λ equals the tall-cache requirement for A, $H(B)$,

$$W_{A,N} = W_{A,N,H} = \text{argmax}\{\rho(M) \mid M \textit{ is } N\textit{-fitting, } H\textit{-tall, usable}\}. \quad (1)$$

The following lemma, which follows directly from the definitions, enables us to analyze algorithms by looking at only their worst-case profiles.

Lemma 6.5. *If $\rho(W_{A,N,\lambda}) = O(R(N))$, then A is optimally progressing on all λ-tall profiles.*

When combined with Lemma 3.12, the above lemma means we can analyze algorithms by looking at only their worst-case square profiles.

The worst-case profile, or its inner square profile, does not have to respect the recursive structure of A. For example, squares can cross recursive boundaries, cover multiple recursive invocations, span multiple linear scans, etc. Any analysis based solely on the recursive structure of the algorithm must handle the fact that the profile may not nicely line up with the algorithm.

To solve this problem, we first establish a mapping from squares of any N-fitting square profile to recursive calls and linear scans performed by A.

The following definition defines three conditions under which the progress from a square can be charged to a linear scan, recursive call, or overhead reference.

Definition 6.6. *When A executes on a square profile $M(t)$, we say a square S of M* ***overlaps*** *a linear scan L if at least one memory reference of L is served during S. Similarly, we say S* ***encompasses*** *A's execution on a subproblem if every memory reference A makes while solving the subproblem is served during S. Finally, we say S* ***contains*** *an overhead reference R if at least half of the references of R are served during S.*

We now define when we can charge every square of a profile to a linear scan, recursive call, or overhead reference.

Definition 6.7. *Let $A_1, \ldots, A_e$ be generalized compositional regular (GCR) algorithms all with linear space complexity. We say that a square profile M of length ℓ is* ***N-chargeable with respect to A_j***, *if every square S of M satisfies at least one of the following three properties when M is considered with respect to A_j's execution on any problem instance of size N that takes exactly ℓ steps to process.*

(i) S encompasses *an execution of any of $A_1, \ldots, A_e$ on a subproblem of size $\Theta(|S|)$.*

(ii) S overlaps *a linear scan of size $\Omega(|S|)$.*

(iii) S contains $\Theta(|S|/B)$ *overhead references.*

Finally, we prove that, for GCR algorithms with linear space complexity, every profile is N-chargeable.

Lemma 6.8. *Let e be a constant and let $A_1, \ldots, A_e$ be* perfect generalized compositional regular (PCGR) algorithms, *all with linear space complexity. Then every N-fitting square profile for A_j is N-chargeable with respect to A_j.*

To see why, consider a square of size S that does not overlap a linear scan of size $\Omega(S)$. Such a square must contain entire executions that access $\Theta(S)$ distinct locations. And since all the algorithms have linear space complexity, any execution that touches $\Theta(S)$ distinct locations must be on a subproblem of size $\Theta(S)$. (See the full version for the complete proof.)

Finally, we bound the size of boxes that contain mostly overhead references, which means that they can be ignored when analyzing many algorithms.

Lemma 6.9. *Let $A_1, \ldots, A_e$ be a set of generalized compositional regular algorithms all with linear space complexity and let $q = \max\{b_{ji}\}$. Let M be an N-chargeable profile with respect to A_j. Each square of M that does not satisfy property (i) nor property (ii) in Definition 6.7 has size $O\left(B \log_{1/q} X(S)\right)$.*

These two lemmas give us the "recurrence-rewriting" rule outlined in Section 5. The progress on each square of a profile can be charged to either (1) a linear scan of size at least as large as the square, (2) a subproblem of size proportional to the square, or (3) overhead references, although in the last case the square cannot be very large. Theorem 6.10 (at the top of the next page) summarizes this result.

The following theorem, proven in the full version, gives a corresponding lower bound on the progress of the worst-case profile. While Theorem 6.10 can show that an algorithm is optimally progressing, Theorem 6.11 gives a recipe to prove that an algorithm is not optimally progressing.

Theorem 6.11. *Suppose $A_1, \ldots, A_e$ are generalized compositional regular algorithms with linear space complexity, tall-cache requirement $H(B)$, and progress bound ρ. Let $\lambda = \max\{H(B), (B \log_{1/b} B)^{1+\varepsilon}\}$, where ε is any constant larger than 0. When all $c_j = 1$, the bound in Theorem 6.10 is tight, meaning that $\rho(W_{A_j,N,\lambda})$, is $\Theta(\mathcal{T}_j(N) + \mathcal{U}_j(N) + \mathcal{V}_j(N))$.*

7. OPTIMALITY CRITERIA FOR MANY MASTER-METHOD-STYLE ALGORITHMS

Theorem 6.10, Theorem 6.11, and Lemma 6.5 provide an easy way to test whether a linear-space GCR algorithm is optimally progressing: derive the recurrences on $\mathcal{T}_i$, $\mathcal{U}_i$, and $\mathcal{V}_i$ from the structure of the algorithm, solve the recurrences, and check whether $\mathcal{T}_i(N) + \mathcal{U}_i(N) + \mathcal{V}_i(N) = O(R(N))$.

Although we can't give a general solution for all possible $\mathcal{T}_i$, $\mathcal{U}_i$, and $\mathcal{V}_i$, we can use this method to derive a simple test for Master-method-style algorithms.

We first define the class of Master-theorem-style algorithms covered by our optimality criterion. Note that this class is more general than the constant-overhead recursive (COR) form algorithms covered by previous work [7]. Note also that $c \leq 1$ is implied by the linear space restriction.

Definition 7.1. *Let $a \geq 1/b$, $0 < b < 1$, and $0 \leq c \leq 1$ be constants. A linear-space algorithm is* ***(a, b, c)-regular*** *if, for inputs of sufficiently large size N, it makes*

(i) *exactly* ***a*** *recursive calls on subproblems of size* ***bN***, *and*

(ii) $\Theta(1)$ *linear scans before, between, or after recursive calls, where the size of the biggest scan is $\Theta(N^c)$.*

We will prove that a DAM-optimal linear-space-complexity (a, b, c)-regular algorithm is optimal in the CA model if and only if $c < 1$. We first solve the recurrence from Theorem 6.10 for the special case of (a,b,c)-regular algorithms to get a simple bound on $\rho(W_N)$.

Theorem 6.10. *Let $0 \leq c_j \leq 1$ and $f_j \geq 1$ be constants for $j = 1, \ldots, e$. Also let $a_{ji} > 0$, and $0 < b_{ji} < 1$ be constants for $j = 1, \ldots, e$, and $i = 1, \ldots, f_j$. Suppose $A_1, \ldots, A_e$ are generalized compositional regular algorithms all with linear space complexity, tall-cache requirement $H(B)$, and progress bound ρ.*
Let $b = \max\{b_{ji}\}$ and $\lambda \geq H(B)$ be constants. Then there exist functions $\mathcal{T}_1, \ldots, \mathcal{T}_e$; $\mathcal{U}_1, \ldots, \mathcal{U}_e$; $\mathcal{V}_1, \ldots, \mathcal{V}_e$ such that the progress of the worst-case λ-tall profile for A_j, $\rho(W_{A_j,N,\lambda})$, is $O(\mathcal{T}_j(N) + \mathcal{U}_j(N) + \mathcal{V}_j(N))$ and the $\mathcal{T}_j$, $\mathcal{U}_j$ and $\mathcal{V}_j$ satisfy the recurrences

$$\mathcal{T}_j(N) = \begin{cases} \max\left\{\rho(\square_N), \sum_{i=1}^{f_j} a_{ji}\mathcal{T}_{ji}(b_{ji}N)\right\} & \text{if } \lambda < N \\ \Theta(\rho(\square_\lambda)) & \text{if } N \leq \lambda; \end{cases}$$

$$\mathcal{U}_j(N) = \begin{cases} \Theta\left(\rho(\square_{N^{c_j}})\right) + \sum_{i=1}^{f_j} a_{ji}\mathcal{U}_{ji}(b_{ji}N) & \text{if } N = \Omega(\lambda) \text{ and } N^{c_j} = \Omega(\lambda) \\ \sum_{i=1}^{f_j} a_{ji}\mathcal{U}_{ji}(b_{ji}N) & \text{if } N = \Omega(\lambda) \text{ and } N^{c_j} \neq \Omega(\lambda) \\ 0 & \text{if } N \neq \Omega(\lambda); \end{cases}$$

$$\mathcal{V}_j(N) = \begin{cases} \sum_{i=1}^{f_j} a_{ji}\mathcal{V}_{ji}(b_{ji}N) & \text{if } B\log_{1/b} N = \Omega(\lambda) \text{ and } N^{c_j} > B \\ \Theta(\rho(\square_{B\log_{1/b} N})) + \sum_{i=1}^{f_j} a_{ji}\mathcal{V}_{ji}(b_{ji}N) & \text{if } B\log_{1/b} N = \Omega(\lambda) \text{ and } N^{c_j} \leq B \\ 0 & \text{if } B\log_{1/b} N \neq \Omega(\lambda). \end{cases}$$

where $\mathcal{T}_{ji}$, $\mathcal{U}_{ji}$ and $\mathcal{V}_{ji}$ are one of $\mathcal{T}_1, \ldots, \mathcal{T}_e$; $\mathcal{U}_1, \ldots, \mathcal{U}_e$; $\mathcal{V}_1, \ldots, \mathcal{V}_e$ depending on the structure of A_j.

Theorem 7.2. *Let A be an (a, b, c)-regular algorithm with linear space complexity and tall-cache requirement $H(B)$. Suppose that A is optimal in the DAM model for a problem with progress bound $\rho(\square_X) = \Theta(X^p)$, where p is a constant. Assume that $B \geq 4$. Pick an $\varepsilon > 0$, and let $d = 3(1+\varepsilon)$ and $\lambda = \max\{H(B), (dB\log_{1/b} B)^{1+\varepsilon}\}$.*
Then, $\rho(W_{A,N,\lambda})$ is bounded by $O(\mathcal{X}(N))$, where

$$\mathcal{X}(N) = \begin{cases} \Theta\left(N^{\log_{1/b} a}\log_{1/b}\frac{N}{\lambda}\right) & \text{if } c = 1 \\ \Theta\left(N^{\log_{1/b} a}\right) & \text{otherwise.} \end{cases}$$

The following rule for optimality of (a, b, c)-regular algorithms can be derived by comparing $\mathcal{X}(N)$ with $R(N)$.

Theorem 7.3. *Suppose A is an (a, b, c)-regular algorithm with tall-cache requirement $H(B)$ and linear space complexity. Suppose also that, in the DAM model, A is optimally progressing for a problem with progress bound $\rho(\square_N) = \Theta(N^p)$, for constant p. Assume $B \geq 4$. Let $\lambda = \max\{H(B), ((1+\varepsilon)B\log_{1/b} B)^{1+\varepsilon})\}$, where $\varepsilon > 0$.*

1. *If $c < 1$, then A is optimally progressing and optimally cache-adaptive among all λ-tall profiles.*
2. *If $c = 1$, then A is $\Theta\left(\log_{1/b}\frac{N}{\lambda}\right)$ away from being optimally progressing and $O\left(\log_{1/b}\frac{N}{\lambda}\right)$ away from being optimally cache-adaptive.*

8. APPLYING OUR TECHNIQUES

The techniques presented in this paper provide cookbook methods for designing and analyzing a wide variety of cache-adaptive algorithms. Figure 3 summarizes the result of analyzing several algorithms using this method. In addition to analyzing algorithms that did not fit the requirements of previous analysis techniques, our approach enables us improve on previous results by reducing the tall-cache requirements for some algorithms.

The analysis of FFT is similar to the technique described above, but requires a separate proof because FFT breaks problems of size N into subproblems of size $\sqrt{N}$. The proof uses the same idea: we determine the worst-case profile using a charging argument, and use it to analyze the algorithm's performance. This shows that the technique is useful even when Theorem 6.10 does not apply. See the full version for complete proofs of all these results.

Algorithm	Tall Cache	Ratio to Optimal
RECURSIVE-LCS	$O((B\log_2 B)^{1+\varepsilon})$	$\Theta(1)$
EDIT-DISTANCE	$O((B\log_2 B)^{1+\varepsilon})$	$\Theta(1)$
JACOBI	$O((B\log_2 B)^{1+\varepsilon})$	$\Theta(1)$
MM-INPLACE	$O(B^2)$	$\Theta(1)$
FW-APSP	$O(B^2)$	$\Theta(1)$
M-TRANSPOSE	$O(B^2)$	$\Theta(1)$
FFT	$O(B^2)$	$\Theta(\log\log(N/B^2))$

Figure 3: Adaptivity of several cache-oblivious algorithms. All but FFT can be analyzed using the technique described above. The analysis of FFT is similar, but requires a separate analysis because FFT breaks problems of size N into subproblems of size $\sqrt{N}$.

9. CONCLUSION

This paper revisits one of the most important, but also most difficult, problems in the design, analysis, and deployment of external-memory algorithms. We show that designing and analyzing cache-adaptive algorithms is tractable.

But our results have broader implications for the cache adaptive model itself.

In order for a computational model to be truly useful, (1) it needs to capture an important phenomenon that people care about, (2) its predictions have to be true-to-life, and (3) it has to be simple enough to work with. There are dozens of theoretical models capturing different aspects of memory-hierarchy performance. The DAM [1] and cache-oblivious [13, 14, 22] models have been so successful because they satisfy these criteria so effectively.

The cache-adaptive model is already known to satisfy two of these criteria. It captures the important phenomenon of changes in cache size, which can strongly affect the performance of algorithms on concurrent systems. It is true to life because it imposes no unrealistic restrictions on changes in the size of memory.

We believe that, by making it easy to analyze many algorithms in the cache-adaptive model, the tools developed in this paper provide the final piece necessary for the cache-adaptive model to join the ranks of truly useful models, such as the DAM and cache-oblivious models.

10. REFERENCES

[1] A. Aggarwal and S. Vitter, Jeffrey. The input/output complexity of sorting and related problems. *Communications of the ACM*, 31(9):1116–1127, Sept. 1988.

[2] M. Akra and L. Bazzi. On the solution of linear recurrence equations. *Computational Optimization and Applications*, 10(2):195–210, 1998.

[3] R. Barve and J. S. Vitter. External memory algorithms with dynamically changing memory allocations. Technical report, Duke University, 1998.

[4] R. D. Barve and J. S. Vitter. A theoretical framework for memory-adaptive algorithms. In *Proc. 40th Annual Symposium on the Foundations of Computer Science (FOCS)*, pages 273–284, 1999.

[5] L. A. Belady. A study of replacement algorithms for a virtual-storage computer. *IBM Journal of Research and Development*, 5(2):78–101, June 1966.

[6] L. A. Belady, R. A. Nelson, and G. S. Shedler. An anomaly in space-time characteristics of certain programs running in a paging machine. *Communications of the ACM*, 12(6):349–353, 1969.

[7] M. A. Bender, R. Ebrahimi, J. T. Fineman, G. Ghasemiesfeh, R. Johnson, and S. McCauley. Cache-adaptive algorithms. In *Proc. 25th Annual ACM-SIAM Symposium on Discrete Algorithms (SODA)*, pages 958–971, 2014.

[8] G. S. Brodal and R. Fagerberg. Cache oblivious distribution sweeping. In *Proc. 29th International Colloquium on Automata, Languages and Programming (ICALP)*, pages 426–438. Springer-Verlag, 2002.

[9] K. P. Brown, M. J. Carey, and M. Livny. Managing memory to meet multiclass workload response time goals. In *Proc. 19th International Conference on Very Large Data Bases (VLDB)*, pages 328–328. Institute of Electrical & Electronics Engineers (IEEE), 1993.

[10] R. A. Chowdhury and V. Ramachandran. Cache-oblivious dynamic programming. In *Proc. 17th annual ACM-SIAM Symposium on Discrete Algorithms (SODA)*, pages 591–600. ACM, 2006.

[11] T. Cormen, C. Leiserson, R. Rivest, and C. Stein. *Introduction To Algorithms*. MIT Press, 2001.

[12] P. Fornai and A. Iványi. FIFO anomaly is unbounded. *CoRR*, abs/1003.1336, 2010.

[13] M. Frigo, C. E. Leiserson, H. Prokop, and S. Ramachandran. Cache-oblivious algorithms. In *Proc. 40th Annual Symposium on the Foundations of Computer Science (FOCS)*, pages 285–298, 1999.

[14] M. Frigo, C. E. Leiserson, H. Prokop, and S. Ramachandran. Cache-oblivious algorithms. *ACM Transactions on Algorithms*, 8(1):4, 2012.

[15] G. Graefe. A new memory-adaptive external merge sort. Private communication, July 2013.

[16] J.-W. Hong and H. T. Kung. I/O complexity: The red-blue pebble game. In *Proc. 13th Annual ACM Symposium on the Theory of Computation (STOC)*, pages 326–333, 1981.

[17] D. Irony, S. Toledo, and A. Tiskin. Communication lower bounds for distributed-memory matrix multiplication. *Journal of Parallel and Distributed Computing*, 64(9):1017–1026, 2004.

[18] R. T. Mills. *Dynamic adaptation to CPU and memory load in scientific applications*. PhD thesis, The College of William and Mary, 2004.

[19] R. T. Mills, A. Stathopoulos, and D. S. Nikolopoulos. Adapting to memory pressure from within scientific applications on multiprogrammed cows. In *Proc. 8th International Parallel and Distributed Processing Symposium (IPDPS)*, page 71, 2004.

[20] H. Pang, M. J. Carey, and M. Livny. Memory-adaptive external sorting. In *Proc. 19th International Conference on Very Large Data Bases (VLDB)*, pages 618–629. Morgan Kaufmann, 1993.

[21] H. Pang, M. J. Carey, and M. Livny. Partially preemptible hash joins. In *Proc. 5th ACM SIGMOD International Conference on Management of Data (COMAD)*, page 59, 1993.

[22] H. Prokop. Cache oblivious algorithms. Master's thesis, Department of Electrical Engineering and Computer Science, Massachusetts Institute of Technology, June 1999.

[23] J. E. Savage. *Models of Computation: Exploring the Power of Computing*. Addison-Wesley Longman Publishing Co., Inc., 1st edition, 1997.

[24] J. S. Vitter. Algorithms and data structures for external memory. *Foundations and Trends in Theoretical Computer Science*, 2(4):305–474, 2006.

[25] H. Zeller and J. Gray. An adaptive hash join algorithm for multiuser environments. In *Proc. 16th International Conference on Very Large Data Bases (VLDB)*, pages 186–197, 1990.

[26] W. Zhang and P.-A. Larson. A memory-adaptive sort (MASORT) for database systems. In *Proc. 6th International Conference of the Centre for Advanced Studies on Collaborative research (CASCON)*, pages 41–. IBM Press, 1996.

[27] W. Zhang and P.-A. Larson. Dynamic memory adjustment for external mergesort. In *Proc. 23rd International Conference on Very Large Data Bases (VLDB)*, pages 376–385. Morgan Kaufmann Publishers Inc., 1997.

Parallel Algorithms for Asymmetric Read-Write Costs

Naama Ben-David[†] Guy E. Blelloch[†] Jeremy T. Fineman[‡] Phillip B. Gibbons[†]
Yan Gu[†] Charles McGuffey[†] Julian Shun[*]

[†]Carnegie Mellon University [‡]Georgetown University [*]UC Berkeley

{nbendavi,guyb,gibbons,yan.gu,cmcguffe}@cs.cmu.edu
jfineman@cs.georgetown.edu jshun@eecs.berkeley.edu

ABSTRACT

Motivated by the significantly higher cost of writing than reading in emerging memory technologies, we consider parallel algorithm design under such asymmetric read-write costs, with the goal of reducing the number of writes while preserving work-efficiency and low span. We present a nested-parallel model of computation that combines (i) small per-task stack-allocated memories with symmetric read-write costs and (ii) an unbounded heap-allocated shared memory with asymmetric read-write costs, and show how the costs in the model map efficiently onto a more concrete machine model under a work-stealing scheduler. We use the new model to design reduced-write, work-efficient, low-span parallel algorithms for a number of fundamental problems such as reduce, list contraction, tree contraction, breadth-first search, ordered filter, and planar convex hull. For the latter two problems, our algorithms are output-sensitive in that the work and number of writes decrease with the output size. We also present a reduced-write, low-span minimum spanning tree algorithm that is nearly work-efficient (off by the inverse Ackermann function). Our algorithms reveal several interesting techniques for significantly reducing shared memory writes in parallel algorithms without asymptotically increasing the number of shared memory reads.

1. INTRODUCTION

We are on the cusp of the emergence of a new wave of nonvolatile memory technologies that are projected to become the dominant type of main memory in the near future [1, 2, 40, 54]. A key property of these new memory technologies (e.g., phase-change memory, spin-torque transfer magnetic RAM, and memristor-based resistive RAM) is their asymmetric read-write costs: Writes can be an order of magnitude or more higher energy, higher latency, and lower (per-module) bandwidth than reads [3, 8, 11, 12, 15, 22, 23, 32, 33, 36, 46, 52]. This high cost for writes motivates the design of models that reflect this asymmetry and "write-efficient" algorithms that perform well under such models by reducing their number of writes.

Prior work has studied read-write asymmetries in several contexts. Work targetting NAND Flash memory [9, 24, 25, 44, 45, 51] has focused on the fact that on NAND Flash chips (i) bits can only be cleared by incurring the overhead of erasing a large block of memory and/or (ii) individual cells can quickly wear out due to too many writes to the cell. Emerging memories, in contrast, can write arbitrary bytes in-place and system software can use the virtual-to-physical mapping to balance application writes across individual physical cells. Other prior work has targeted database query processing [18, 50, 51] or systems considerations [19, 32, 39, 53, 55, 56]. Our recent paper [12] defined an Asymmetric PRAM model that differs from the classic PRAM in charging $\omega > 1$ for writes (reads are unit cost), as well as a variety of external-memory-style models that transfer data in blocks. Write-efficient algorithms were presented for sorting, FFT and matrix multiplication. Our follow-on paper [11] presented write-efficient *sequential* algorithms for a number of fundamental problems, and defined the sequential (M, ω)-Asymmetric RAM model that combines a small symmetric-cost memory of size M with a large asymmetric-cost memory. Finally, Carson et al. [15] recently presented a number of interesting results for models with asymmetric read-write costs. Specifically, they considered (i) sequential algorithms on a model with a small symmetric memory and a large asymmetric memory, both cache-oblivious and not, and (ii) parallel algorithms on a distributed memory model where the last level of the memory hierachy on each node has asymmetric read-write costs. On the latter model, they presented upper and lower bounds for various linear algebra problems and direct N-body methods, restricted to the class of "communication-avoiding" algorithms, i.e., parallel algorithms that minimize the (unweighted) sum of reads and writes.

In this paper, we focus on parallel algorithm design under asymmetric read-write costs, extending prior work in two important ways. First, we define the Asymmetric Nested-Parallel model, which combines features of the sequential (M, ω)-Asymmetric RAM model and the popular nested-parallel model but with a distinctive memory allocation scheme. Specifically, it is comprised of small stack-allocated memories with symmetric read-write costs and an unbounded heap-allocated shared memory with asymmetric read-write costs. Stack-allocated memory is allocated by a task, available to the task and any children it forks, but is invalid when the task finishes. We show that the model, with its costs analyzed based on the computation DAG (with no notions of processors or scheduling) maps efficently onto a more concrete machine model, when using a work-stealing scheduler. In particular, the model's careful accounting for task memory usage yields good bounds on the number of writes incurred during a steal, because it can accurately capture the true working set sizes that need to be transferred. Note that our use of small amounts of symmetric memory along with the large asymmetric memory matches the expected reality of real machines.

Second, we use the new model to design the first reduced-write, work-efficient, low-span (a.k.a., low-depth) parallel algorithms for

SPAA '16, July 11-13, 2016, Pacific Grove, CA, USA

 ISBN 978-1-4503-4210-0/16/07. . . $15.00

DOI: http://dx.doi.org/10.1145/2935764.2935767

Table 1: Results for the Asymmetric Nested-Parallel Model

problem	work	span
reduce	$\Theta(n + \omega)$	$\Theta(\log n + \omega)$
ordered filter	$\Theta(n + \omega k)\dagger$	$O(\omega \log n)\dagger$
list contraction	$\Theta(n)$	$O(\omega \log n)\dagger$
tree contraction	$\Theta(n)$	$O(\omega \log n)\dagger$
minimum spanning tree	$O(\alpha(n)m + \omega n \log(\min(\frac{m}{n}, \omega)))\dagger$	$O(\omega \operatorname{polylog}(m))\dagger$
2D convex hull	$O(n(\log k + \omega \log\log k))\ddagger$	$O((\omega + \log k) \cdot \log^2 n \log\log h)\dagger$
BFS tree	$\Theta(m + \omega n)\ddagger$	$O(\omega \mathcal{D} \log n)\dagger$

ω=write cost; k=output size; †=with high probability; α=inverse Ackerman; m=number of edges; ‡=expected; $\mathcal{D}$=graph diameter

reduce, list contraction, tree contraction, breadth-first search (BFS), ordered filter, and planar convex hull. For the latter two problems, our algorithms are output-sensitive in that the work and number of writes decrease with the output size. We also present a reduced-write, low-span minimum spanning tree (MST) algorithm that is nearly work-efficient (off by the inverse Ackermann function). See Table 1 for a summary of our results. All of these algorithms significantly reduce the number of writes over the best prior algorithms, e.g., by a factor of ω for list/tree contraction. While some of these results are relatively straightforward, our algorithms for tree contraction, MST, and convex hull are more novel. Our algorithms reveal several interesting techniques for significantly reducing shared memory writes in parallel algorithms without asymptotically increasing the number of shared memory reads, such as the random exponential growing-with-filtering technique used in MST and BFS, the balanced tree partitioning technique used in tree contraction, and the pre-bucketed divide-and-conquer technique used in convex hull.

2. ASYMMETRIC NESTED-PARALLEL

In this paper we use a parallel variant of the (M, ω)-Asymmetric RAM (ARAM) model [11] to analyze algorithms. The (M, ω)-ARAM is a sequential RAM with two memories: a small symmetric memory of size M for which both reads and writes take unit time, and a large asymmetric memory of unbounded size for which reads take unit time but writes take time $\omega > 1$. We extend the model to allow for multiple parallel tasks. Our goal is to allow for dynamic parallelism and to analyze algorithms using work and span (also called depth or critical path length). We therefore use the nested-parallel model [10] extended with asymmetric memory, which we refer to as the *Asymmetric Nested-Parallel* (NP) model. We include some detail on the model because there are some subtleties on how the small symmetric memory is defined in a dynamically parallel model, and some care was given to the particular formulation we give here. We also describe a more concrete machine model and map costs from the Asymmetric NP model to it.

2.1 Asymmetric NP model

In the nested-parallel model a computation starts and ends with a single ***root*** task. Each task has a constant number of registers, and runs a standard instruction set from a random access machine (RAM), except it has one additional instruction called FORK. The FORK instruction takes an integer n and creates n ***child*** tasks, which can run in parallel. Child tasks get a copy of the parent's register values, with one special register getting an integer from 1 to n indicating which child it is. The parent task suspends until all its children finish[1] at which point it continues with the registers in the same state as when it suspended, except the program counter advanced by one. We say that a computation has ***binary branching*** if $n = 2$. In the model a computation can be viewed as a (series-parallel) DAG in the standard way. We assume every instruction has a weight (cost). The ***work*** (W) is the sum of the weights of the instructions, and the ***span*** (D) is the weight of the heaviest path. The ***nesting depth*** (δ) is the maximum depth of forked tasks during the computation.

In the ***Asymmetric Nested-Parallel*** (NP) model we assume a stack allocated symmetric small memory, and a heap allocated asymmetric large memory. ***Stack allocated*** memory is memory allocated by a task, available to the task and its children, but invalid when the task finishes. It is under this model, for example, that the memory bounds for work stealing are shown [13]. ***Heap allocated*** memory is allocated by a task and can be accessed by any other task, including ancestor tasks (it is completely shared memory). Each instruction has weight one, except writes to the heap memory, which have weight $\omega \geq 1$ (in practice, $\omega \gg 1$).[2] When doing analysis of an algorithm, the term "writes" will be used to refer to the number of writes to heap allocated memory. In this paper we assume the amount of stack memory allocated by all but the leaf tasks (tasks with no forks) is constant. The amount of symmetric stack memory a leaf task can allocate is bounded by a parameter M_l. This separation into stack and heap allocated memory, and the distinction between leaf and non-leaf tasks for stack memory size, is made both because it is a convenient model for using the different memories, and also because it enables an efficient mapping onto a fixed number of processors, as justified below.

Note that the Asymmetric NP is an algorithmic cost model, as opposed to a machine model, enabling reasoning about nested-parallel computations without worrying about mapping the computation to machines. We address this scheduling issue next.

2.2 Scheduling Asymmetric NP Computations

This section shows that the algorithmic cost metrics of Asymmetric NP are sufficiently descriptive to capture the performance of Asymmetric NP computations when using good schedulers.

The Asymmetric NP model has been designed in a manner that yields an efficient mapping to an (M, ω)-***Asymmetric PRAM*** [12] machine model. In this model, there are P processors, each running its own instructions using a small symmetric ***local*** memory of size M. The processors share an unbounded asymmetric ***global*** memory, to which concurrent reads and writes are allowed. We also allow any processor to read the local memory of another processor (concurrently), but not to write to it. A request to read the local memory of another processor is viewed as requiring a write out to the global memory in order to enable the read, and hence is charged ω. On each processor any write to the global memory also takes ω time. All other instructions take unit time. For synchronizing we assume an atomic fetch-and-add to the global memory that can be performed in constant span and work linear in the number of processors.

The challenge with Asymmetric NP computations is that stack variables must be written out to global memory before tasks can be migrated to a different processor from the one that forked it.

[1] We assume, as in the RAM, there is a FINISH instruction.

[2] We treat the write cost, ω, as a parameter in our model in order to highlight its impact on algorithm design and analysis. To further highlight, we also state bounds on the number of writes in each of our algorithms. Because of our interest in practical algorithms, we seek algorithms where the constant factors hidden by the Big-O notation are small, so that the gains from using fewer writes matter.

The naïve approach would forego the stack and instead write all $O(1)$ stack variables for non-leaf tasks directly to global memory, making each FORK cost $\Theta(\omega)$. For fine-grained parallelism especially, where the number of FORKs for an algorithm with work W is $\Omega(W)$, this approach would yield running time no better than $\Omega(\omega W/P)$. In other words, one may as well consider every instruction a write if adopting the naïve scheduler.

Here we show that a variant of a work-stealing scheduler [13] achieves $O(W/P+\omega D)$ expected time when limited to binary forking. In standard (symmetric-memory) work stealing, each worker (or processor) maintains a double-ended queue called a deque of tasks that are ready to execute. Whenever a worker executes a (binary) FORK instruction, the processor continues working on the "left" child task and places the "right" child on the bottom of its deque. When a worker completes a task by executing its FINISH instruction, there are two options. If that task enabled another one, i.e., the completed task was the last outstanding child of its parent, then the worker continues working on the now-enabled parent. Otherwise, the worker removes the bottom task from its deque and executes it. If the deque is empty, the worker instead ***steals***, meaning that it chooses a random victim processor and takes the task from the top of that processor's deque if the deque is non-empty. In the event that the steal is unsuccessful, the worker will continue to attempt to steal until it successfully steals a task or the computation is finished.

In the Asymmetric NP model, working locally on a deque is cheap, and in general stack frames need not be written out. For example, if the entire computation runs sequentially on one processor, then no stack-related writes occur (assuming that the local memory is large enough to hold the stack depth).

There are still some challenges, however, most notably on steals. Because a task has access to any stack variables of its ancestor tasks, any unwritten stacks of ancestor tasks must be written out to global memory when a steal occurs. This situation is particularly challenging to analyze as it may cause steals to take time proportional to ω times the nesting depth. To cope with this challenge, Lemma 2.1 shows that a simple modification to work stealing results in at most a constant number of frames needing to be written. We assume that a steal request somehow interrupts its target task (e.g., all tasks can regularly poll to check if there are any outstanding steal requests), and if work is available, the registers for the stolen task and relevant ancestors are written to the asymmetric global memory. There is a similar potential issue when a task completes: its return value must be written to its parent task, which may no longer be local, and hence a write to global memory could be required.

LEMMA 2.1. *There exists a variant of work stealing such that on each steal (or steal attempt), only $O(1)$ stack frames are written to global memory.*

PROOF. The lemma can be achieved either by modifying work stealing or by an equivalent program transformation. The program transformation is as follows. Transform every FORK into two FORKs as follows. First FORK two tasks: the left child performs the intended FORK, which we call a forking task, and the right child is a dummy task that does nothing. The dummy task is inserted onto the deque, whereas the worker continues on to execute the forking task. (In Cilk-like work-stealing, e.g., [13], expressing the FORK as two "spawns" followed by a "sync" would automatically create a similar dummy task as a continuation from the second spawn.)

We claim that for the topmost task on the deque (i.e., the one that can be stolen), at most its parent and grandparent have not already been written out to global memory. In order for a task to be on the deque and hence stealable, it must be the right child of its parent. A simple induction shows that for any task on a deque, all right children of ancestors have either been stolen already or are on the same deque. (A similar claim is proven as Lemma 3 in [7].) Thus, a steal need only write-out the frames corresponding to the longest right-only path in the computation graph. The longest is three nodes, which we can show by cases. A forking task is always the left child and hence not stealable. A real task (i.e., one existing before the transformation) is always the child of a forking task, so it can have at most one unwritten ancestor frame: the parent forking task. A dummy task is always the right child of a real task, so stealing a dummy task could entail writing out three frames. □

THEOREM 2.2. *Consider a computation in the Asymmetric NP model with binary branching factor, W work, D span, δ nesting depth, and M_l leaf stack memory. There exists a work-stealing scheduler that executes the computation in $O(W/P+\omega D)$ expected time on a P-processor $(O(\delta)+M_l,\omega)$-Asymmetric PRAM.*

PROOF. We adopt the potential-based analysis from [7]. But we need to modify the argument to cope with the fact that (1) steals involve writing out to global memory, and (2) finishing tasks may also entail writing out to global memory, i.e., if the parent frame is in global memory.

The main idea of the original potential-based analysis [7] is as follows. On each timestep, each processor places a token in either a work bucket, if it is making progress on a task, or a steal bucket, if it is attempting to steal. Since at most W units of progress can be made on tasks, there are at most W work tokens. Moreover, every processor places a token on each timestep, so the parallel running time is the total number of tokens divided by P. It follows that if S steal attempts occur during the course of the execution, then the running time is $O(W/P + S/P)$. One can bound $S = O(PD)$ in expectation through a clever potential analysis [7]. The details are not important here, but the main idea is that each $\Theta(P)$ steal attempts are "likely" to steal the shallowest ready tasks, and hence progress is made on the span of the computation. Thus, the expected running time is $O(W/P + D)$ in the symmetric memory setting where writes are constant time.

In our case, a steal attempt does not correspond to a constant-time event. Instead, we may need to write out several stack frames. By Lemma 2.1, a steal occupies two processors for at most $O(\omega)$ timesteps. Thus, the cost of a steal token is increased by this much. We must also account for the fact that work in the computation may increase elsewhere if writes to global memory occur. In particular, assuming local memory is large enough to hold the entire stack (i.e., $O(\delta) + M_l$)), the only additional writes that occur are when a child returns to a parent task that resides in global memory, i.e., it has been stolen. This event corresponds to a more expensive write token, but the number of these heavy write tokens is bounded by the number of steals. We thus have a total running time that is $O(W/P + \omega S/P)$, where S is the number of steal attempts. The potential analysis on the number of steal attempts [7] can be applied to the augmented computation as usual, and we are left with an expected running time of $O(W/P + \omega D')$, where $D' \leq 2D$ is the span of the augmented computation created using the process described in Lemma 2.1. □

The above theorem provides justification for charging only unit cost for FORK, and for example, means that the standard reduce via a binary tree incurs only $\Theta(n + \omega)$ work instead of $\Theta(\omega n)$ work on the Asymmetric NP, as discussed in Section 3. Note also that our separate accounting for leaf stack memory in the Asymmetric NP model, and the observation that the non-leaf tasks of all the algorithms in this paper each allocate only $O(1)$ stack memory, means that the bound in the lemma is only a constant number of writes per steal, whereas without the separate accounting, it would be $O(M_l)$ writes per steal.

Bulk-Synchronous Computations. Many of the algorithms in this paper are ***bulk-synchronous*** algorithms for which there is only one level of nesting ($\delta = 1$). The root task proceeds in a sequence of R rounds. In each round i it forks n_i child tasks (each a leaf) and waits for them to finish. The root task can run arbitrary computation between such rounds. We define the iteration count I as $\sum_{i=1}^{R} n_i$. The following lemma for scheduling bulk-synchronous algorithms provides additional support for the model.

LEMMA 2.3. *A bulk-synchronous computation with arbitrary branching on the Asymmetric NP model with W work, D span, R rounds, I iteration count, and M_l leaf stack memory, can be simulated on an $(O(M_l), \omega)$-Asymmetric PRAM with P processors in $O((W + \omega I)/P + D + \omega R)$ time.*

PROOF. The idea is that the root task runs on some processor and when it gets to a fork, it sets up the registers for the children and sets a count to n. The processors then grab tasks by decrementing this count (using the fetch-and-add). When the count reaches zero idle processors quit for that round and wait for a later round when it is again set to some non-zero number. A separate counter can be used to detect when all processors are done, and the processor that detects termination can continue with the root task. The additional work done for accessing the counter is $O(\omega I)$ and the charge to the span is $O(\omega R)$ so using Brent's scheduling principle [14], ($T \leq W/P + D$), we have the given time bounds.

Each child task takes $O(M_l)$ local memory. Since the nesting depth is one, the total memory needed by a child task is $O(M_l + 1)$. This gives the memory bound. □

3. BASIC PARALLEL PRIMITIVES

In this section we consider two basic parallel primitives. We note that some primitives inherently require as many writes as reads. For example, all prefix sums needs to write out all the sums. However, when they are used as a step for some other purpose, then the final generation of the values can be folded into whatever needs the values. This idea is used in the output sensitive filter described below.

3.1 Reduce

Summing a sequence of values with respect to an associative function $f(x, y)$ is surely the most common parallel function. Of course it only requires a single result so it should be possible to make it write efficient. In the Asymmetric NP there are two methods to do this. The first is simply to use a divide-and-conquer algorithm that recurses on the two halves in parallel, and when they return add the two results. The base case can either be a single element or $O(\log n)$ elements, and then sum those elements sequentially. A fork can be used to generate two child tasks for the calls. The interesting feature of our model is that this will only require a single write, which is to write the final answer. All other computation can be done in the constant space per task stack space. This may seem impossible since the processors need to communicate. Recall, however, that when we simulate the Asymmetric NP (with binary branching) on a machine, we account for the steals in the cost. These steals are communicating the values among processors. The divide-and-conquer algorithm leads to the following result.

LEMMA 3.1. *The reduction of n elements can be done in $\Theta(n + \omega)$ work and $\Theta(\log n + \omega)$ span using $\Theta(1)$ writes on the Asymmetric NP model.*

A second way to do a reduce is with bulk-synchronous steps. The first step forks n/ω tasks, each of which sums ω values and writes its sum to large memory. This can be repeated $\log_\omega n$ times to get the sum. The resulting algorithm does $\Theta(n + \omega)$ work and has $\Theta(\omega \log_\omega n)$ span.

3.2 Output-Sensitive Ordered Filter

Given an array A of size n and a predicate ρ on the elements of A, we want to filter out the entries $x \in A$ for which $\rho(x) = 0$, and get a new array A' of size $k \leq n$, where k is the number of elements $x \in A$ for which $\rho(x) = 1$ and A' preserves the relative order of the elements in A. In the classic nested-parallel model, this is easily done in linear work and logarithmic span by first creating a new array that holds the result of applying ρ to each element, computing a prefix sum on that array to determine the position in A' of each element to be moved, and then moving those elements. However, this requires $\Theta(n)$ writes. In the Asymmetric NP model, this number of writes can be problematic; there exist algorithms where the number of writes depends on k rather than n except for the filtering step.

Our goal is an (output-sensitive) ordered filter algorithm whose writes are proportional to the output size rather than the input size, thereby matching the lower bound on writes. We show the following result:

LEMMA 3.2. *Ordered filter on an array of size n such that k elements satisfy the given predicate can be done in $\Theta(n+\omega k)$ work and $O(\omega \log n)$ span using $\Theta(k)$ writes w.h.p. on the Asymmetric NP model.*

Our algorithm proceeds as follows: we first apply a REDUCE operation with ρ to find k, and allocate an array B of size $O(k)$. Recall that in our model, a reduce operation takes only $O(1)$ writes.

If $k \leq \frac{n}{\log n}$, then we hash the k entries, along with their indices in A into B. This takes only $O(k)$ writes and can be done efficiently in parallel, since we expect few collisions. We then sort the array by the original indices to get an array A' of size k that preserves the elements' relative order in the input array. Because there are less than $\frac{n}{\log n}$ entries, we can sort them in $O(n + \omega k)$ work and $O(\omega \log n)$ span w.h.p., using a write-efficient parallel sorting algorithm [12].

If $k > \frac{n}{\log n}$, we divide the array into k equal parts, and then in parallel process each part sequentially. This sequential filtering need only write each non-filtered element once, and it takes $O(\log n + \omega)$ span since each part is small. Finally, we concatenate the results to get our output array. This concatenation can be done in $O(\omega \log n)$ span by counting the elements in each part and using a prefix sum to find starting indices for each part's output in the final array. Since the prefix sum is only applied to the set of k parts, it uses only $O(k)$ writes.

4. LIST AND TREE CONTRACTION

In this section we introduce efficient parallel algorithms for list and tree contraction that reduce the number of writes without increasing the reads. In both problems, our goal is to divide up the problem into sub-problems that can be processed in parallel. We say that an ***equal partition*** of a structure of size n is a partition into $O(s)$ contiguous parts, each of which is of size $O(n/s)$ for some $s \leq n$. For example, the partition based on m-critical nodes in [26] is an equal partition.

The list contraction algorithm we present is relatively simple, and uses a common approach to partition the problem size using random samples. Tree contraction however, becomes more challenging when we limit the writes to main memory. We are not aware of any existing tree contraction algorithms (even sequential ones) that solve the problem using bounded local memory. Furthermore, designing a parallel version is hard because we cannot explicitly

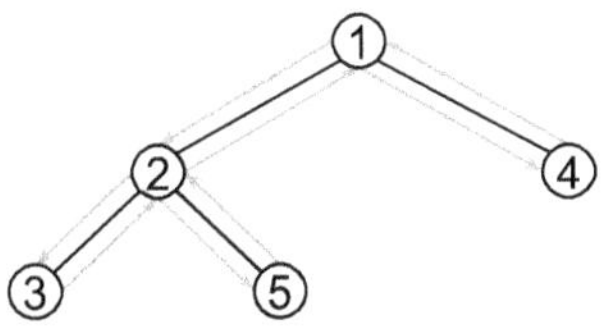

Figure 1: The Euler tour of this rooted binary tree is $(1, 2, 3, 2, 5, 2, 1, 4, 1)$, obtained by following the arrows on the edges starting at the root node 1.

record information on the tree nodes (this would require too many writes).

Previous parallel tree contraction algorithms use either a top-down approach [34, 42, 43, 48] or a bottom-up approach [26]. All of them require a linear number of writes, and we are unaware of any non-trivial modifications to these algorithms that can reduce the number of writes to $o(n)$. To solve this problem, our algorithm a uses a bottom-up approach. It is based on a new tree-partition algorithm that, instead of partitioning the tree based on sub-tree sizes as done in [26], uses the Euler tour as a tool to refine our partition after randomly selecting sample nodes. Then we prove that the partition we get is an equal partition using a surprisingly simple argument. With this partitioning of the tree, we can combine a sequential space-bounded tree contraction algorithm that we describe with any of the existing tree contraction algorithms to obtain a write-efficient parallel tree contraction algorithm in the Asymmetric NP model.

4.1 List Contraction

A linked list is a list of nodes in which each node has a pointer to the next node in the list. A segment on the linked list is defined as the elements between two given nodes. The list contraction problem is to contract a linked list of length n into a single node (possibly combining values). It has many applications, including list ranking and Euler tours [34]. Sequentially, we can just loop over all nodes by following the pointers which takes a linear number of reads and work, and a constant number of writes to main memory. In the symmetric setting ($\omega = 1$), the standard parallel approach using random mate [5] requires $O(\log n)$ span and linear reads and writes.

Our algorithm partitions the list in two steps. In the first step, each element in the list is randomly marked with probability s/n for some parameter s. Then in the second step, we start with each marked node, and in parallel, follow the list with the pointers and mark every $\lfloor n/s \rfloor$'th element. The longest chain we have to follow here has length $O((n \log n)/s)$ w.h.p., which can be shown using a Chernoff bound. Now clearly all segments between two consecutively marked nodes have size no more than $\lfloor n/s \rfloor$. With the marked nodes, we contract all segments in parallel, with each one done sequentially (terminating when the next marked node is encountered). After that, a standard symmetric version of parallel list contraction is applied on the marked nodes. Each step of the algorithm performs $O(s)$ writes.

The new list contraction algorithm takes linear work, $O(\omega + (n \log n)/s)$ span, and $O(s)$ writes in the Asymmetric NP model. This algorithm is efficient when running on a share-memory machine with $p = O(n/(\omega \log n))$ cores. In this case we can just plug in $s = n/\omega$ and get the bounds shown in Table 1. The list partition routine described above is used as a subroutine in our tree contraction algorithm described next.

4.2 Tree Contraction

The tree contraction problem is to contract a tree with n nodes into a single node (possibly combining node values), and has many applications in parallel computing [34, 42, 43]. We assume that

Algorithm 1 A parallel tree partitioning algorithm.

Input: A rooted binary tree T.
Output: $O(s)$ partition nodes.

1: Apply the parallel list partitioning algorithm on the Euler tour of tree T and mark no more than $O(s)$ tree nodes such that each sublist has length less than n/s
2: **for each** marked node v **do**
3: Traverse the Euler tour from the position of v's last appearance to the next marked node v'
4: Mark the highest node in this range
5: **return** all marked nodes

the input is a rooted binary tree and each tree node has pointers to its parent, left child, and right child (if they exist). When the tree is viewed as a directed graph that contains two directed edges for each edge in the tree, the Euler tour [49] of the tree is an Eulerian circuit of the directed graph (see Figure 1 for an example). It can be constructed implicitly: given the current node and the previous edge, we can check whether the previous edge is from the parent or child of the current node, and according to this information, decide which edge to take next. We define a ***component*** of a tree to be a set of tree nodes that are connected. A subtree is a component, but not vice versa.

In the symmetric setting ($\omega = 1$) doing tree contraction sequentially in linear work is trivial, and classic parallel tree contraction algorithms [34, 42, 43, 26] take $O(\log n)$ span and $O(n)$ writes. However, many applications, such as arithmetic expression evaluation and subtree size queries on a set of tree nodes, have a sublinear output size. Thus, a natural question to ask is whether we can design a parallel tree contraction algorithm with a sublinear number of writes. We describe such an algorithm in this section.

4.2.1 A new tree partitioning algorithm

The goal of this algorithm is to find $O(s)$ partition nodes such that each tree component has size at most n/s. The high-level idea of the algorithm is to compute an equal partition of the Euler tour and mark the lowest common ancestor of each component as a partition node. The pseudocode is provided in Algorithm 1, and we explain the details below.

Since we cannot afford to store information per node, our solution is to run the parallel list partitioning algorithm described in Section 4.1 on the Euler tour of the tree. However, generating the Euler tour is too expensive, as it would require a linear number of writes. Thus, we need to simulate the parallel list partitioning algorithm. We do so as follows. First, we randomly sample $O(s)$ nodes on the tree. Then, from each sampled tree node, we follow the Euler tour in every direction in parallel. In each direction, we mark every $\lfloor n/(3s) \rfloor$'th element along the path, until we reach the next sampled node on the Euler tour. This step is similar in the list partitioning algorithm, but each node may correspond to multiple (up to three) different locations in the Euler tour, so we traverse the list from all different locations. In expectation, the distance between two samples will be at most $O((n/s) \log n)$ w.h.p. We will mark another $O(s)$ nodes during the second step. This process corresponds to Line 1 of the pseudocode.

With the $O(s)$ marked nodes, the algorithm now finds and marks $O(s)$ ***partition nodes***, which corresponds to Lines 2–4 of Algorithm 1. A partition node is the highest node (closest to the root) in a tree component consisting of tree nodes in a segment of the Euler tour. For every segment that starts with the first or second appearance of a marked interior node v, the partition node is just the first node in the segment, because the segment cannot go beyond the subtree of v and it terminates no later than the next appearance of v in the Euler

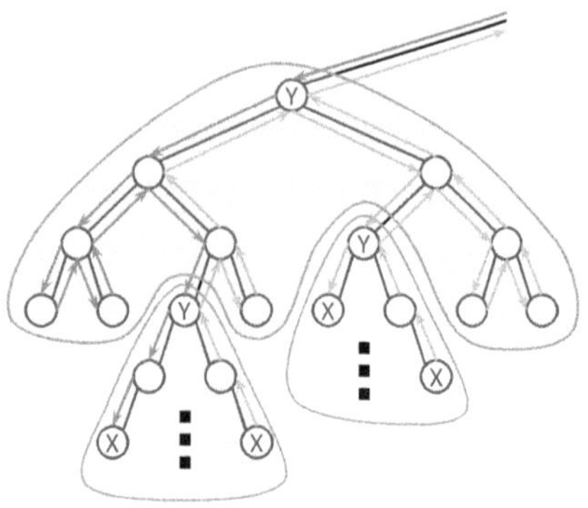

Figure 2: An example of how the tree is partitioned into components. A component consists of tree nodes from at most three segments of the Euler tour.

tour. Hence, we need to do nothing for these segments since the partition nodes are already marked. We only consider the segments that start with the last appearances of marked nodes. The partition node of each such segment can be computed with constant space by traversing through the segment: we always maintain a pointer p to the highest node so far in the traversal. We start by pointing at the first node in the segment, and whenever we go from our current top node to its parent in the traversal, we update p to point to its parent as well. When the traversal finishes, the node pointed by p is marked. It is easy to see that this marked node is the highest node in the segment.

The partition nodes provide a partitioned tree with $O(s)$ components if we form the tree components by ignoring edges from all partition nodes to their parents. We now show that this partition is an equal partition.

LEMMA 4.1. *The marked nodes generated in Algorithm 1 partition the tree such that each tree component contains at most n/s tree nodes.*

PROOF. We prove this by showing that each component consists of tree nodes from at most three segments of the Euler tour, which is shown in Figure 2. Recall that in the algorithm, we marked every $\lfloor n/3s \rfloor$'th element in the Euler tour, so showing this suffices to prove our claim.

In Figure 2, nodes marked by the list partitioning algorithm are shown with the letter "X", and the newly-added partition nodes corresponding to the highest nodes in each segment are marked with "Y". Both types of nodes are considered *marked nodes*. We claim that for each tree component rooted by either an X node or a Y node (e.g., the blue region in Figure 2), there exist at most two subtrees (e.g., the two yellow regions in Figure 2) that contain marked nodes and are rooted at nodes that are direct children of this component. More specifically, there will be at most one such subtree in each of the left and right subtrees of the root node (we will refer to these two subtrees as *left-side and right-side marked subtrees*). The segment from the last X node in the left subtree (if it exists) on the Euler tour to the first X node in the right subtree (if it exists) marks the root of this component. To see that there is at most one subtree on each side, assume for the sake of contradiction that there are two marked nodes on the same side of the root but not in the same marked subtree (yellow region). Then the lowest common ancestor of these two nodes will be marked as a Y node. This node is assumed to be in this component (the blue region) but actually it will be marked and removed from this component, which leads to a contradiction.

Hence, each component only consists of nodes from at most three segments from the Euler tour. The first segment is the one that enters this component in the Euler tour, and ends at the first X node (based on the Euler tour) in the left-side marked subtree, which is shown as the red arrows in Figure 2. The second segment is illustrated as the orange arrows, starting from the last X node in the left-side marked subtree and ending in the first X node in the right-side marked subtree. The last segment, shown as the green arrows, is symmetric to the first segment and leaves this part from the last X node. If there are no marked node in the left side, then the first and second segments are merged into one, and similarly on the right side. Thus each component consists of vertices from at most three segments of the Euler tour.

Since we can guarantee that each segment has size no more than $n/3s$, each tree component contains no more than n/s nodes. □

The overall cost is the sum of the cost of partitioning the Euler tour and the cost of traversing a subset of the segments (starting for the up-edge of each X node). This takes linear work, $O(s)$ writes and $O((n/s)\log n)$ span w.h.p.

Remark: Notice that our tree partition is done by removing (actually ignoring) edges but not vertices (as done in [26]) since this is more efficient on both work and writes in practice. This algorithm also works on all constant-degree trees. However, for an arbitrary tree our algorithm would not work. In fact, if the given tree is a star, then there does not exist any equal partition of non-constant ($\omega(1)$) size, which means that no top-down approaches by tree partitioning will give a write-efficient solution in this case. Therefore, a preprocessing step that converts the input to a binary tree with linear writes is required before running our algorithm, but if the tree contraction is run multiple times on a given tree, there is still an advantage in using this algorithm.

4.2.2 A sequential algorithm

We now discuss a sequential and space-bounded tree contraction algorithm that will be used as a subroutine in our parallel algorithm. Previous tree contraction algorithms [42, 43, 48, 26] take either linear space or linear writes to the main memory, which is too costly in the asymmetric setting. Instead we would like to design an algorithm that uses a small amount of local (small) memory and performs no writes to main memory. The tool we use is the tree partitioning algorithm discussed in the previous section, which can be used to partition a tree into components of size no more than n/s using $O(s)$ writes. Our algorithm then contracts each tree component down to a single node, and after that we apply a standard tree contraction algorithm on the marked nodes. To restrict the number of components as well as the size of the components so that all intermediate results fit into a small memory and require no writes, the we recursively apply the tree partitioning algorithm until each component fits in small memory. Suppose that the cutoff size for the base case of the recursion is c. Then the required small memory size is $O(s\log_s(n/c)+c)$, and the work and number of reads is $O(n\log_s(n/c))$. By setting s to either $O(\epsilon n^\epsilon)$ or some constant greater than 1, we obtain the following lemma.

LEMMA 4.2. *The sequential algorithm presented above contracts a tree of size n requiring $O(1)$ writes, and using a small memory of size $O(n^\epsilon)$ and linear work, where $0<\epsilon<1$, or a small memory of size $O(\log n)$ and $O(n\log n)$ work and reads.*

4.2.3 A parallel algorithm

We now describe a parallel tree-contraction algorithm that uses the tree partitioning algorithm and sequential tree contraction algorithm as subroutines.

The high-level idea for the parallel algorithm is to first partition the tree into small, almost equal-sized components using the tree partitioning algorithm, and then contract each component independently in parallel using the sequential contraction algorithm. Finally, we use a standard parallel tree contraction algorithm to contract the remaining nodes. This step requires a number of writes proportional to the number of remaining nodes, which is much smaller than the original tree size. The algorithm takes s as a parameter and consists of three steps as described below.

Step 1: Tree Partitioning. The first part of the algorithm computes a tree partition such that each component has size $O(n/s)$, where s is a parameter of the algorithm. This step requires $O(n)$ work, $O(\omega + (n \log n)/s)$ span w.h.p. and $O(s)$ writes, if implemented by Algorithm 1.

Step 2: Tree Contraction on Components. With the partition nodes computed in Step 1, we now have a set of components each with size at most $O(n/s)$. Since the tree components are themselves trees, we can apply our sequential tree contraction algorithm on each of them. The contraction is restricted to be inside each component by not contracting any partition node. Also, we leave the root node of each component uncontracted. After contraction, each component's root has at most one left and one right child, which is either the marked child (the Y nodes in the yellow regions in Figure 2) or the a descendant of the root that is in the component (if no marked child on the side). Hence, if the local memory has size $O((n/s)^\epsilon)$, this step takes linear time and $O(n/s)$ span, and yields an intermediate contracted tree with no more than $O(s)$ nodes.

Step 3: Contraction of Remaining Nodes. In the last step, we apply any existing parallel tree contraction algorithm with linear work and logarithmic span to contract the tree generated from the last step to a single node. This step costs $O(s)$ reads, writes and work, and $O(\omega \log n)$ span.

To reduce the number of writes without increasing the asymptotic work complexity, we choose $s = n/\omega$. Hence, the size of the components is at most ω. The following theorem gives the cost of our parallel tree contraction algorithm.

THEOREM 4.3. *Algorithm 1 can be used to contract a tree with size n using $O(n)$ work, $O(\omega \log n)$ span and $O(n/\omega)$ writes with $O(\omega^\epsilon)$ local memory in the Asymmetric NP model.*

5. MINIMUM SPANNING TREES

This section extends Karger, Klein and Tarjan's (KKT) [35] sequential linear-work randomized algorithm for minimum spanning tree/forest. At a high level, their algorithm proceeds as follows: Randomly sample half of the edges, and calculate a minimum spanning forest on these sampled edges. Use the sampled forest to filter out edges that cannot be part of the overall minimum spanning forest. Specifically, identify all edges $e = (x, y)$ of the graph such that e is the heaviest edge on the cycle it closes in the sampled forest. These edges are discarded. Next, recurse on the remaining graph and perform a constant number "Borůvka steps" to reduce the number of nodes in the graph. The proof that this algorithm runs in linear work hinges on two main facts: first, that the filtering can be done in linear work, and second, that the number of edges filtered out is large in expectation. We will use the following definitions in this section.

DEFINITION 1. *For a given tree T in the graph, and two vertices $x, y \in V$, the path connecting x and y in T (if such a path exists) is denoted by $\tau(x, y)$.*

DEFINITION 2. *An edge $e = (x, y)$ is said to be* ***heavy*** *with respect to a tree T on the graph if e closes a cycle in T and it is the heaviest edge in that cycle. That is, $w(e) \geq \max(w(e') \mid e' \in \tau(x, y))$. Any edge that is not heavy with respect to T is said to be* ***light*** *with respect to T.*

Recall the well-known *cycle property* of MSTs: a tree T is an MST in a graph G if and only if every non-tree edge closes a cycle in T and is the maximum weight edge on that cycle. Therefore, if all edges of a graph not in T are heavy, then T is an MST of that graph.

The filtering-out of heavy edges is achieved via minimum spanning tree verification algorithms. These algorithms take a tree and a graph as input and determine whether the tree is an MST in the graph. They operate by labeling each edge as light or heavy with respect to the tree. There is extensive work on the verification of minimum spanning trees, and several algorithms are known to operate in linear work [21, 37, 31]. The KKT algorithm then throws out any edges labelled heavy by the verification algorithm, and recurses on the remainder of the graph.

To be efficient, the KKT algorithm requires that when a minimum spanning forest is built on a random subset of the graph, a large fraction of edges in the remaining graph can be filtered out. They show that this holds using the following lemma:[3]

LEMMA 5.1 (SAMPLING LEMMA). *For a random subset $R \subseteq E$ of size r, and a random subset $S \subseteq E$ of size s, the expected number of edges in S that are light with respect to the MST of R is less than sn/r.*

Using this lemma, Karger et al. prove that their algorithm requires $O(m)$ work with high probability.

5.1 Write-efficient MST

Our goal is to find an MST algorithm that minimizes the number of writes performed without significantly increasing the number of reads. A slight modification of Borůvka's algorithm yields an algorithm which executes in $O(m \log n + \omega n)$ work in the (M, ω)-ARAM model [11]. That is, we can achieve the optimal number of writes ($O(n)$) using $O(m \log n)$ reads. However, we want to find an algorithm that more closely matches the optimal work of the algorithm of Karger et al. [35].

We present an MST algorithm that uses the KKT algorithm as a subroutine, and requires $O(\alpha(n)m)$ reads (where $\alpha(\cdot)$ is the inverse Ackermann function) and $O(n \log(\min(m/n, \omega)))$ writes, resulting in $O(\alpha(n)m + \omega n \log(min(m/n, \omega)))$ work.

The algorithm is iterative, and proceeds as follows. It begins by taking an $O(n)$ sized random sample of the edges and running KKT on them to find a minimum spanning forest of the sampled graph. Then, in each round, it takes a random sample that is twice as large as the previous one, filters out the edges in the sample that are heavy with respect to the most recently calculated spanning forest, and then runs KKT again on the remaining part of the sample. In each such round, with high probability, we will only be left with $O(n)$ edges from the sample that pass the filtering, and so each round will need $O(n)$ writes. The algorithm proceeds in this way until the final sample includes all edges in the graph. The pseudocode for this algorithm is presented in Algorithm 2.

5.2 Analysis

We start with a sample set S of edges with size $\max(2n, m/\omega)$, and run the KKT algorithm on this sample to calculate a minimum spanning forest on it. We then double the size of the sample set in

[3]The statement of this lemma is a slight variation of the version given in [17] and is different from the original paper [35].

Algorithm 2 Write efficient MST algorithm

Input: A graph $G = (V, E)$.
Output: An MST with a set T of edges.

```
sampleSize ← max(2n, m/ω)
Edge set T ← {}
while sampleSize < m do
    The set of light edges S_L ← {}
    for s ← 1 to sampleSize do
        Randomly pick an edge e ∈ E
        if e cannot be filtered with respect to T then
            S_L ← S_L + {e}
    T ← KKT(S_L ∪ T)
    sampleSize ← 2 · sampleSize
S_L ← {}
for all e ∈ E do                     ▷ Take all edges in final round
    if e cannot be filtered with respect to T then
        S_L ← S_L + {e}
T ← KKT(S_L ∪ T)
return T
```

each round and recalculate, until all edges are processed. However, to save writes, instead of storing all the samples, we use an online filtering algorithm to throw out the edges that are heavy, and only keep the light sample edges. We sample slightly (a constant factor) more than our desired sample size to account for collisions. Note that once the sample size is linear in m, we can sample by flipping a coin with appropriate probabilities for each edge, without increasing the algorithm's total work. We define the edge set S_L to be the subset of S that contains light edges (with respect to the current spanning forest in this round), and the edge set S_H to be the subset consisting of heavy edges. Clearly, $S = S_H \cup S_L$.

LEMMA 5.2. *At the end of round i of the algorithm, we have a minimum spanning forest on $\Theta(2^{i-1}\max(n, m/\omega))$ edges of the graph in expectation.*

PROOF. In round i, we have at least $\Theta(2^{i-1}\max(2n, m/\omega))$ sample edges in expectation, but only build a minimum spanning forest using the edges in S_L, along with the tree we already have. Let T be the set of edges in the current forest, as shown in the pseudocode. Note that by the definition of heavy edges, T is a minimum spanning forest in the graph whose edge set is $S_H \cup T$. Therefore, the MST of $T \cup S_L$ is also a minimum spanning forest on $T \cup S_L \cup S_H$. □

Therefore, at the end of round $\lceil \log_2(\min(m/n, \omega)) \rceil$, we have an MST on the entire graph, and we are done. Note that in the last round, we simply consider all of the edges (without sampling) to ensure that we've seen every edge.

LEMMA 5.3. *In every round, the expected size of S_L, the number of edges that pass the filtering, is $\Theta(n)$.*

PROOF. By Lemma 5.2, the MST used to filter edges in round i is a minimum spanning forest on at least $c_1 2^{i-1} n$ edges in expectation for some constant c_1. The sample size in round i is $c_2 2^i n$ in expectation for some constant c_2. By the Sampling Lemma, the expected size of S_L in round i is less than $\frac{sn}{r} = \frac{c_2(2^i n)n}{c_1 2^{i-1} n} = \Theta(n)$. □

By Lemmas 5.2 and 5.3, it is easy to see that, excluding any work needed for the filtering, the total number of writes required for this algorithm is $O(n\log(\min(m/n, \omega)))$, and the number of reads is $\sum_{i=1}^{\lceil \log_2(\min(m/n,\omega)) \rceil} \Theta(2^i n) = O(m)$.

Ideally, we would like the filtering step to take no more than $O(n)$ writes per round, and a constant number of reads per edge. There are several MST verification algorithms that take work linear in the number of edges [21, 37, 31]. However, all of these algorithms also take $O(m)$ writes, and are therefore not suitable for us. Alon and Schieber [4] present an online algorithm for minimum spanning tree verification that operates in $O(n)$ preprocessing work, and then $\alpha(n)$ work per queried edge. The queries are done through a look-up in the data structure built in the preprocessing stage, and require no writes. Using their algorithm allows us to execute the entire write-efficient MST algorithm in $O(n\log(\min(m/n, \omega)))$ writes and $O(\alpha(n)m)$ reads.

Alon and Schieber also prove a matching lower bound for the problem of answering online tree product queries, which is a generalization of the MST verification problem. However, they show this lower bound looking at the worst case query. It may be possible to improve upon this result by considering the query time amortized over all of the edges.

5.3 Parallel Analysis

We can parallelize each of the steps of the algorithm. Clearly, the sampling of edges can be done in parallel in constant span. We then use a parallel version of Alon and Schieber's algorithm [4] to filter out heavy edges. This takes polylogarithmic span. Cole et al. [20] presented a parallel version of the KKT algorithm that takes linear work and polylogarithmic span, which we can use instead of the sequential version whenever we call KKT. So simply by using the parallel versions of these algorithms, we achieve a work-efficient polylogarithmic span algorithm (we only sample $O(\log(\min(m/n, \omega)))$ times, and the span is only increased by a factor of $O(\log(\min(m/n, \omega)))$).

However, we need to be precise with the number of writes required in the parallel version. After using Alon and Schieber's algorithm to check whether each sampled edge can be filtered out, we need to pack out the edges that passed the filtering to use them in the next round of the algorithm. A standard packing algorithm would execute a number of writes proportional to the total size of the sample, which is too many writes for us. For this, we use the output sensitive filter algorithm presented in Section 3.2.

We thus obtain the following theorem:

THEOREM 5.4. *Given a graph G with m edges and n vertices, an MST of G can be found in $O(\alpha(n)m + \omega n\log(\min(m/n, \omega)))$ work, $O(\omega\ \mathrm{polylog}(n))$ span and $O(n\log(\min(m/n, \omega)))$ writes w.h.p. in the Asymmetric NP model, where $\alpha(\cdot)$ is the inverse Ackerman function.*

6. OUTPUT-SENSITIVE CONVEX HULL

The ***planar convex hull*** problem takes as input a set of points in 2D and generates the smallest polygon (represented as a list of segments) that contains all of the points. The fastest algorithms for computing a convex hull either require $O(n\log n)$ work if the algorithm is insensitive to the output size, or $O(n\log h)$ work, where h is the number of points on the hull. Naive implementations of these algorithms would require $O(n\log n)$ or $O(n\log h)$ reads/writes, respectively, while the minimum number of writes required is much lower since only the h points and segments on the hull need to be written. Our goal in this section is to develop work-efficient parallel algorithms where the number writes is asymptotically lower than the number of reads.

Several algorithms first sort the points by increasing x-coordinate, and then apply a $O(n)$ work step on the sorted points to compute the hull (see, e.g., [30, 6]). We note that we can trivially obtain an

Algorithm 3 OUTPUT-SENSITIVE (UPPER) CONVEX HULL

Input: A set of n two-dimensional points in general position.

1: Place the points into h buckets each of size $O(n/h)$, where the x-coordinates of all points in bucket $i \in [0, \min(h-1)]$ are less than the x-coordinates of all points in buckets $j > i$.
   (a) Pick $\Theta(h \log n)$ random samples, sort them, and use every $(\log n)$'th sample as a splitter.
   (b) Have the remaining points each do a binary search on the splitters to determine which bucket they belong to.
   (c) Use prefix sums to determine and appropriate offsets into buckets for each point.
   (d) Have all points write to the appropriate offset into their bucket.

2: If there is only one bucket B, search up the tree of bridges and perform one of the following:
   (a) If all points in the buckets are on or below a bridge, then do nothing.
   (b) If there are points in B not covered by a bridge, then apply a standard output-sensitive convex hull algorithm on an input containing points in the bucket and the points forming the bridges $Br_{B,L}$ and $Br_{B,R}$.

3: Split points into two sets, L and R, where L contains points in the first $\lceil h/2 \rceil$ buckets, and R contains the remaining points.

4: Find the bridge between L and R.

5: Recursively apply Steps 2–5 on each of L and R, storing the bridge computed in each sub-problem as the left and right child, respectively, of the bridge in Step 4.

6: Obtain final solution by traversing down the tree of bridges.

algorithm with $O(n \log n)$ reads and $O(n)$ writes, by first using a write-efficient sort [12], followed by the same post-processing step that takes $O(n)$ reads/writes. The sort can be done in $O(\omega \log n)$ span w.h.p. [12], and the post-processing step can be done in parallel in $O(n)$ work and $O(\omega \log n)$ span [29].

6.1 An output-sensitive algorithm

Obtaining a write-efficient output-sensitive convex hull algorithm with $O(n \log h)$ work requires more effort because we can no longer directly apply a comparison sort. We now describe how to obtain an algorithm with $O(n \log h)$ reads and $O(n \log \log h)$ writes.

Our algorithm uses divide-and-conquer and borrows ideas from [38, 16]. We first assume that we know the value of h and that $h = O(n/\log n)$ (to make oversampling work); we will remove these assumptions later. We also assume without loss of generality that no points have the same x-coordinate. We describe how to compute the upper hull (the hull above the line from the leftmost point to the rightmost point) and the lower hull can be computed analogously. The main steps of the algorithm are shown in Algorithm 3.

The algorithm is a divide-and-conquer algorithm but to avoid data movement we approximately pre-sort the points. In particular, we split the points into h buckets each of size $O(n/h)$, where the x-coordinates of all points in bucket $i \in [0, h-1]$ are less than the x-coordinates of all points in buckets $j > i$. By picking $\Theta(h \log n)$ samples, sorting them, and using every $(\log n)$'th element as a splitter, the buckets can be shown to have size $O(n/h)$ w.h.p. using Chernoff bounds. This step is described as Step 1 of Algorithm 3.

If the input contains a single bucket, then we have reached the base case (Step 2), which we will describe how to handle shortly. Otherwise, the algorithm splits the points into approximately two halves, L and R (Step 3). This step requires no data movement, since the points have already been placed into their respective buckets.

We then find the ***bridge*** of the upper hull between L and R, which is a line passing through a point in each set such that all points lie below the line (Step 4). The bridge can be found by solving the following two-dimensional linear program, where the bridge is the line $y = \alpha x + \beta$ and x_{mid} is the x-coordinate of a vertical line between L and R (which can be computed as a value arbitrarily close to the x-coordinate of the splitter element [41]):

$$\begin{aligned} \text{minimize} \quad & \alpha x_{mid} + \beta \\ \text{subject to:} \quad & \alpha x_{p_i} + \beta \geq y_{p_i} \quad \forall i \in L \cup R \end{aligned}$$

We describe how to solve 2D linear programs write-efficiently in Section 6.3.

The bridge found in Step 4 is stored as the root of a tree of bridges, and we recursively compute the tree of bridges on each of L and R in Step 5.

We now describe the base case, when there is only a single bucket B. The bucket searches up the tree of bridges, and considers any bridge whose x-range intersects with the bucket's x-range. A bridge can either lie on or above all points in B, have only a left endpoint in B, or have only a right endpoint in B. If we find any bridge that covers all of B, then no new convex hull edges will be generated from B and we are done. Otherwise, we find the one or two bridges that cover the most points in the bucket, and solve a subproblem with points in B and the up-to-two bridges using a standard $O(n \log h)$-work output-sensitive convex hull algorithm.

Call the set of the bridges with a left endpoint in the bucket $Br_{B,L}$, and the set of bridges with a right endpoint in the bucket $Br_{B,R}$. We wish to include the bridge in each set that covers the most points in the bucket. For a bridge $b \in Br_{B,L}$, let p_b be the endpoint of b in bucket B. The bridge in $Br_{B,L}$ that satisfies this criteria is a bridge b with the minimum value of x_{p_b}, since all points in B are below the bridge, and bridges $b \in Br_{B,L}$ cover all points in B with x-coordinate greater than x_{p_b}. If there are ties, then any bridge with x_{p_b} equal to the minimum value suffices. Similarly, the bridge in $Br_{B,R}$ that satisfies this criteria is a bridge b with the maximum value of x_{p_b}. Both of these bridges can be found during the search up the tree of bridges.

To obtain the final solution (Step 6), we start at the root of the tree of bridges, include the bridge in the solution, and recursively include into the solution the bridges in the descendants of the root that have not been already covered by a previously included bridge. To determine whether to include a bridge, we can search up the tree to see whether it has been covered. If the base case is reached, then all bridges formed from the set of points in the bucket are included.

Cost analysis.

We now analyze the cost of Algorithm 3. Step 1a can be done using write-efficient sorting [12] in $O(\omega \log n)$ span w.h.p. using $O(n \log h)$ reads and $O(n)$ writes. Step 1b takes $O(n \log h)$ reads, $O(n)$ writes, and $O(\omega + \log h)$ span. Steps 1c takes $O(n)$ reads and writes, and $O(\omega \log n)$ span. Finally, Step 1d, takes $O(n)$ reads and writes, and $O(1)$ span. So the cost for this pre-processing is $O(n \log h)$ reads, $O(n)$ writes and $O(\omega \log n)$ span w.h.p.

The number of levels of recursion of Steps 2–5 is $O(\log h)$ w.h.p. since there are h buckets at the beginning and each sub-problem contains half as many buckets.

Step 2 takes $O(\log h)$ reads, $O(1)$ writes, and $O(\omega + \log h)$ span to find $Br_{B,L}$ and $Br_{B,R}$ per bucket. Summed over all buckets, this takes $O(h \log h)$ reads, $O(h)$ writes and $O(\omega + \log h)$ span. Each sub-problem solved using a standard output-sensitive algorithm contains $O(n/h)$ points, and only generates segments on the upper convex hull of the original point set, since we included the bridges coming in from both sides of the bucket. The total number of operations is $\sum_{i=1}^{h} O((n/h)\log(1+h_i))$, where h_i is the number of points on the hull in bucket i and $h = \sum_{i=1}^{h} h_i$. The sum is maximized when all h_i's are equal, giving a total of $O(n)$ reads and writes. The algorithm of Kirkpatrick and Seidel [38] can be parallelized to take $O(n \log h)$ work and $O(\omega \log^2 n)$ span [27]. Note that the algorithm that we apply on the buckets on must take $O(n \log h)$ work overall for the value of h that we guessed, not the number of points on the actual convex hull. Once the amount of work done on the buckets exceeds cn for some constant c, we can assume that our guess of h is wrong, and terminate. To keep track of the work, we can modify the Kirkpatrick and Seidel algorithm that we use on the buckets to increment a shared counter in global memory whenever an operation is performed, and also check the counter before performing an operation and if it is above cn then terminate. The total number of reads/writes for maintaining the counter is cn, which is within our bounds.

Step 3 requires constant work/span since the points are pre-sorted, and Step 4 requires $O(n)$ reads, $O(\log n)$ writes, and $O((\omega + \log n)\log n)$ span w.h.p. as shown in Section 6.3. There are $O(\log h)$ levels of recursion so the overall number of reads in this step is $O(n \log h)$ in expectation. The number of writes from this step satisfies the recurrence $W(n) = 2W(n/2) + O(\log n)$ which solves to $O(n)$. The total span is $O((\omega + \log n)\log n \log h)$ as each of the two recursive calls in Step 5 can be executed in parallel.

In Step 6, the searches up the tree take $O(\log h)$ reads and $O(1)$ writes for a total of $O(h \log h)$ reads and $O(h)$ writes. The span is $O((\omega + \log h)\log h)$.

Overall, the algorithm requires $O(n \log h)$ reads, $O(n)$ writes, and $O((\omega + \log h)\log^2 n)$ span w.h.p.

As done in [16], to remove the assumption that we know h, we will repeatedly guess h and apply the above algorithm until our guess is above the true value of h. On the i'th application of the algorithm, our guess will be $h^* = 3^{2^i}$, so in total we require $O(\log \log h)$ iterations until $h^* \geq h$. The number of reads per iteration is $\sum_{i=0}^{O(\log\log h)} O(n \log 3^{2^i}) = O(n \log h)$. The number of writes is $O(n)$ per iteration, for a total of $O(n \log \log h)$. Finally, the span is $O((\omega + \log h)\log^2 n \log\log h)$ w.h.p. To remove the assumption that $h = O(n/\log n)$, once our guess of h exceeds $cn/\log n$ for some constant c we call the output-insensitive algorithm described earlier, which takes $O(n \log n) = O(n \log h)$ reads, $O(n)$ writes, and $O(\omega \log n)$ span w.h.p. We obtain the following theorem.

THEOREM 6.1. *A planar convex hull can be computed with $O(n(\log h+\omega \log\log h))$ expected work, $O((\omega+\log h)\log^2 n \log\log h)$ span w.h.p., and $O(n \log\log h)$ writes w.h.p. under the Asymmetric NP model.*

6.2 Another output-sensitive algorithm

Here we describe an algorithm with $O(nh)$ reads, $O(n)$ writes, and $O((\omega + \log n)\log n)$ span w.h.p., obtained by modifying the algorithm of Kirkpatrick and Seidel [38]. Their original algorithm finds a bridge on the two halves of the points, uses the bridge to filter out a constant fraction of the points, and recursively finds the hull of the remaining points on each half. The number of levels of recursion is $O(\log h)$ and the number of sub-problems solved is h. Their algorithm as described takes $O(n \log h)$ reads and writes, and $O(\log n \log h)$ span.

Our goal is to reduce the number of writes. Instead of moving the points such that points for a sub-problem are contiguous, we just inspect all of the points each time we need to find a bridge in a subproblem. Furthermore, we do not filter out any points. Therefore, each time we need to find the bridge, we use the 2D linear programming algorithm in Section 6.3, taking $O(n)$ reads and $O(\log n)$ writes. The number of times we solve the 2D linear program is h, giving a total of $O(nh)$ reads and $O(h \log n)$ writes. We can find the splitters that divide the points approximately evenly, which is needed for the linear program, by taking a random sample of $\min(n, h \log n)$ elements at the beginning, sorting them, and using every $(\log n)$'th element as a splitter, as done in our first algorithm. This takes $O(n \log h)$ reads, $O(n)$ writes, and $O(\omega \log n)$ span w.h.p. in total. Since the 2D linear programming algorithm requires a randomized order, we generate a random permutation of the constraints at the beginning, and use it throughout the algorithm, taking $O(n)$ reads and writes and $O(\omega \log n)$ span. The two recursive calls can happen in parallel, so the span is $O((\omega + \log n)\log n \log h)$ w.h.p. To reduce the overall number of writes to $O(n)$, if the algorithm has not terminated after $O(\log\log n)$ levels of recursion (after $O(n \log n)$ reads and $O(\log^2 n)$ writes have been done in solving the LPs), we can switch to the output-insensitive algorithm that takes $O(n \log n)$ reads and $O(n)$ writes. This gives the following theorem.

THEOREM 6.2. *A planar convex hull can be computed with $O(n(\min(h, \log n)+\omega))$ expected work, $O((\omega+\log n)\log n \log h)$ span w.h.p., and $O(n)$ writes under the Asymmetric NP model.*

6.3 2D linear programming for convex hull

We use Seidel's randomized incremental algorithm [47] for 2D linear programming, which we first review. We assume there are bounding planes such that the solution is not unbounded. The algorithm inserts the constraints incrementally, in a random order, maintaining the optimum point so far. For each added constraint it checks if it makes the current optimum infeasible; if so, it finds the best feasible solution satisfying all constraints added so far, and otherwise the old optimum point is kept. The new optimum must lie on the halfplane defining the newly added constraint, and can be found by finding the best point among all intersections between previous constraints and the newly added constraint (a one-dimensional linear program). If the points are given in random order, then the probability that the i'th constraint makes the optimum point infeasible is at most $2/i$. Checking against all previous constraints to find a new optimum takes $O(i)$ work, so the overall work is $\sum_{i=1}^{n} O(i)\cdot(2/i) = O(n)$ in expectation.

We assume that the constraints are given in a random order. For our algorithms, this requirement can be satisfied by generating a random permutation of the points at the beginning in $O(\omega \log n)$ span w.h.p. and $O(n)$ reads and writes [42], and using it to order the constraints throughout the algorithm.

The only time writing is required is when a new optimum needs to be found. In expectation, this will happen at most $\sum_{i=1}^{n} 2/i = O(\log n)$ times. A high probability bound can be obtained using Chernoff bounds. The 1D linear program, which involves maximum/minimum operations, can be solved using the reduce primitive from Section 3 using $O(1)$ writes, so the number of writes is $O(\log n)$ overall. To parallelize this, we add the constraints in rounds, where the k'th round processes the next 2^k unprocessed constraints. Processing a set of constraints in a round involves repeatedly finding the lowest-indexed constraint that makes the current optimum infeasible (a tight constraint), finding a new optimum by adding the tight constraint, and removing it and all lower-indexed constraints from the set. Finding the lowest-indexed constraint can be done with a reduce, and as discussed before finding the new optimum can also be done with a reduce, taking $O(2^k)$ reads and $O(1)$ writes. The expected number of times this process is repeated is equal to the number of constraints in the set that cause a new optimum to be computed, which on round k is at most

$\sum_{j=2^k}^{2^{k+1}-1}(2/j) \le 2^k \cdot (2/2^k) = O(1)$, so each round takes $O(2^k)$ reads and $O(1)$ writes. The span per round is $O(\omega + \log n)$ for reduce. There are a total of $O(\log n)$ rounds until all constraints are processed. This gives a parallel algorithm for solving 2D linear programming, given constraints in a randomized order, that requires $O(n)$ reads in expectation, $O(\log n)$ writes w.h.p., and $O((\omega + \log n)\log n)$ span w.h.p. Note that for convex hull, we are reusing the permutation throughout the algorithm, so the probabilities are not independent among sub-problems. However, the span and number of writes are w.h.p., so we can take a union bound on the failure probability over the h sub-problems and still get a high probability bound. The number of reads is an expectation and so is unaffected. This gives the following lemma.

LEMMA 6.3. *When constraints are given in a random order, 2D linear programming can be done with $O(n + \omega \log n)$ expected work, $O((\omega + \log n)\log n)$ span w.h.p., and $O(\log n)$ writes w.h.p. under the Asymmetric NP model.*

7. BREADTH-FIRST SEARCH

The *breadth-first search* (BFS) problem takes as input an unweighted graph $G = (V, E)$ and a source vertex r, and returns breadth-first search tree rooted at r containing all vertices reachable from r. This section describes a parallel write-efficient BFS algorithm. We will use the notation $n = |V|$ and $m = |E|$. The standard sequential BFS algorithm is write-efficient, but not parallel. It requires $O(m + \omega n)$ work, including $O(n)$ writes (the minimum number of writes required for BFS). On the other hand, the standard parallel level-synchronous BFS algorithm of [10] is not write-efficient, requiring $O(m)$ writes. The algorithm explores the graph in parallel, where round i visits all vertices at a distance i away from r (we call the vertices newly explored in round $i-1$ the *frontier* for round i). Each frontier vertex visits and writes to all of its unexplored neighbors in parallel, which causes additional writes when multiple frontier vertices attempt to visit the same vertex simultaneously. This algorithm uses $O(\omega(m + n))$ work, $O(\omega\mathcal{D}\log^* n)$ span w.h.p. (using approximate compaction [28]), and $O(m + n)$ writes, where $\mathcal{D}$ is the diameter of the input graph.

We now present an algorithm for BFS that runs in $O(m + \omega n)$ work and $O(\omega\mathcal{D}\log n)$ span using only $O(n)$ writes in expectation. The algorithm works like level-synchronous BFS, but makes use of exponential delaying algorithm when visiting the vertices in a round to reduce collisions (and writes) on a shared neighbor. In exponential delaying exploration takes place in iterations, where on each iteration we process a fraction of the vertices on the frontier. We first randomize the order of the frontier vertices, and then on the first iteration we process the first vertex and on iteration $i > 1$, we process the next 2^{i-2} vertices on the frontier. During the exploration process, a vertex checks to see if its neighbor has been visited and only updates that neighbor if it was not visited in a prior round or a prior iteration in the same round.

We now show that the number of writes for this algorithm is $O(n)$ in expectation. Consider a vertex v that is adjacent to the current frontier and has not yet been visited. Let F be the number of vertices on the frontier (without loss of generality, assume it is a power of 2), let $N_F(v)$ be the number of in-neighbors v has on the frontier. We will use $\alpha = 1 - (N_F(v)/F)$ for notational convenience. The probability that v is first visited in iteration 1 is α and in iteration $i > 1$ is:

$$(1-\alpha^{2^{i-2}})\alpha\prod_{j=2}^{i-1}\alpha^{2^{j-2}} = (1-\alpha^{2^{i-2}})\alpha^{2^{i-2}}$$

The expected number of vertices that attempt to visit v in iteration 1 is $N_F(v)/F = 1 - \alpha$ and in iteration $i > 1$ is $2^{i-2}(1-\alpha)$. Summing the expectations over all iterations gives:

$$(1-\alpha)\alpha + \sum_{i=2}^{\log F} 2^{i-2}(1-\alpha)(1-\alpha^{2^{i-2}})\alpha^{2^{i-2}}$$
$$< O(1) + \sum_{i=2}^{\log F} 2^{i-2}\alpha^{2^{i-2}} = O(1)$$

where we use $\sum_{x=1}^{\infty} xa^x = O(1)$ for $0 \le a < 1$. This shows that the expected number of writes to a vertex is $O(1)$, and the expected number of writes overall is $O(n)$.

Randomly permuting the vertices sums to linear work overall and $O(\omega \log n)$ span w.h.p. per round [42]. The $\log n$ iterations used in the exponential delaying also contributes $O(\omega\mathcal{D}\log n)$ to the span per round. Thus the overall span is $O(\omega\mathcal{D}\log n)$. The number of reads remains $O(m + n)$, which gives the following theorem.

THEOREM 7.1. *For a graph with n vertices, m edges, and diameter $\mathcal{D}$, our write-efficient breadth-first search algorithm requires $O(m + \omega n)$ work in expectation, $O(\omega\mathcal{D}\log n)$ span w.h.p., and $O(n)$ writes in expectation on the Asymmetric NP model.*

8. CONCLUSION

In this paper we have studied parallel algorithms that are efficient in terms of how many writes they do to main memory. The research is motivated in large part by new memory technologies in which writing is more expensive than reading. We believe, however, that reducing writes is of interest even without this motivation, both out of theoretical interest, and because there are other practical reasons to reduce writes (e.g., reducing cache-coherence traffic). We defined the Asymmetric Nested-Parallel model that enables algorithm analysis in the popular work-span framework while accounting for the extra cost of writes. Our bounds for a slight variant of work stealing schedulers showed that the Asymmetric NP bounds map directly and efficiently to the (M, ω)-Asymmetric PRAM machine model.

Our paper presented several novel techniques for designing write-efficient parallel algorithms. One is to process a geometrically increasing number of elements in a sequence of rounds with the property that each round enables filtering of writes from future rounds (as was done for MST and BFS). Another is to pre-bucket elements for divide-and-conquer (as was done for convex hull). A third is a technique for partitioning a tree into balanced connected components (as was done for tree contraction). The advantage of these approaches is that they are work-efficient, low-span, and significantly reduce writes. We expect that the techniques will be useful in designing other write-efficient parallel algorithms.

Acknowledgments

This research was supported in part by NSF grants CCF-1314590, CCF-1314633 and CCF-1533858, the Intel Science and Technology Center for Cloud Computing, and the Miller Institute for Basic Research in Science at UC Berkeley.

9. REFERENCES

[1] HP, SanDisk partner on memristor, ReRAM technology. http://www.bit-tech.net/news/hardware/2015/10/09/hp-sandisk-reram-memristor, Oct. 2015.

[2] Intel and Micron produce breakthrough memory technology. http://newsroom.intel.com/community/intel_newsroom/blog/2015/07/28/intel-and-micron-produce-breakthrough-memory-technology, July 2015.

[3] A. Akel, A. M. Caulfield, T. I. Mollov, R. K. Gupta, and S. Swanson. Onyx: A prototype phase change memory storage array. In *HotStorage*, 2011.

[4] N. Alon and B. Schieber. Optimal preprocessing for answering on-line product queries. *Technical Report, Tel Aviv University*, 1987.

[5] R. J. Anderson and G. L. Miller. A simple randomized parallel algorithm for list-ranking. *Inf. Proc. Letters*, 1990.

[6] A. M. Andrew. Another efficient algorithm for convex hulls in two dimensions. *Inf. Proc. Letters*, 1979.

[7] N. S. Arora, R. D. Blumofe, and C. G. Plaxton. Thread scheduling for multiprogrammed multiprocessors. In *SPAA*, 1998.

[8] M. Athanassoulis, B. Bhattacharjee, M. Canim, and K. A. Ross. Path processing using solid state storage. In *ADMS*, 2012.

[9] A. Ben-Aroya and S. Toledo. Competitive analysis of flash-memory algorithms. In *ESA*, 2006.

[10] G. E. Blelloch. Programming parallel algorithms. *Commun. ACM*, 39, 1996.

[11] G. E. Blelloch, J. T. Fineman, P. B. Gibbons, Y. Gu, and J. Shun. Efficient algorithms under asymmetric read and write costs. *arXiv preprint arXiv:1511.01038*, 2015.

[12] G. E. Blelloch, J. T. Fineman, P. B. Gibbons, Y. Gu, and J. Shun. Sorting with asymmetric read and write costs. In *SPAA*, 2015.

[13] R. D. Blumofe and C. E. Leiserson. Scheduling multithreaded computations by work stealing. *JACM*, 46(5), 1999.

[14] R. P. Brent. The parallel evaluation of general arithmetic expressions. *JACM*, 21(2), 1974.

[15] E. Carson, J. Demmel, L. Grigori, N. Knight, P. Koanantakool, O. Schwartz, and H. V. Simahdri. Write-avoiding algorithms. In *IPDPS*, 2016.

[16] T. M. Chan. Optimal output-sensitive convex hull algorithms in two and three dimensions. *Discrete & Computational Geometry*, 16(4), 1996.

[17] T. M. Chan. Backwards analysis of the Karger-Klein-Tarjan algorithm for minimum spanning trees. *Inf. Proc. Letters*, 67(6), 1998.

[18] S. Chen, P. B. Gibbons, and S. Nath. Rethinking database algorithms for phase change memory. In *CIDR*, 2011.

[19] S. Cho and H. Lee. Flip-N-Write: A simple deterministic technique to improve PRAM write performance, energy and endurance. In *MICRO*, 2009.

[20] R. Cole, P. N. Klein, and R. E. Tarjan. Finding minimum spanning forests in logarithmic time and linear work using random sampling. In *SPAA*, 1996.

[21] B. Dixon, M. Rauch, and R. E. Tarjan. Verification and sensitivity analysis of minimum spanning trees in linear time. *SIAM J. on Computing*, 21(6), 1992.

[22] X. Dong, N. P. Jouupi, and Y. Xie. PCRAMsim: System-level performance, energy, and area modeling for phase-change RAM. In *ICCAD*, 2009.

[23] X. Dong, X. Wu, G. Sun, Y. Xie, H. Li, and Y. Chen. Circuit and microarchitecture evaluation of 3D stacking magnetic RAM (MRAM) as a universal memory replacement. In *DAC*, 2008.

[24] D. Eppstein, M. T. Goodrich, M. Mitzenmacher, and P. Pszona. Wear minimization for cuckoo hashing: How not to throw a lot of eggs into one basket. In *SEA*, 2014.

[25] E. Gal and S. Toledo. Algorithms and data structures for flash memories. *ACM Computing Surveys*, 37(2), 2005.

[26] H. Gazit, G. L. Miller, and S.-H. Teng. *Optimal tree contraction in the EREW model*. Springer, 1988.

[27] M. R. Ghouse and M. T. Goodrich. Fast randomized parallel methods for planar convex hull construction. *Computational Geometry*, 7(4), 1997.

[28] J. Gil, Y. Matias, and U. Vishkin. Towards a theory of nearly constant time parallel algorithms. In *FOCS*, 1991.

[29] M. T. Goodrich. Finding the convex hull of a sorted point set in parallel. *Inf. Proc. Letters*, 26(4), 1987.

[30] R. L. Graham. An efficient algorithm for determining the convex hull of a finite planar set. *Inf. Proc. Letters*, 1972.

[31] T. Hagerup. An even simpler linear-time algorithm for verifying minimum spanning trees. In *Graph-Theoretic Concepts in Computer Science*. Springer, 2010.

[32] J. Hu, Q. Zhuge, C. J. Xue, W.-C. Tseng, S. Gu, and E. Sha. Scheduling to optimize cache utilization for non-volatile main memories. *IEEE Transactions on Computers*, 63(8), 2014.

[33] www.slideshare.net/IBMZRL/theseus-pss-nvmw2014, 2014.

[34] J. Jaja. *Introduction to Parallel Algorithms*. Addison-Wesley Professional, 1992.

[35] D. R. Karger, P. N. Klein, and R. E. Tarjan. A randomized linear-time algorithm to find minimum spanning trees. *JACM*, 42(2), 1995.

[36] H. Kim, S. Seshadri, C. L. Dickey, and L. Chu. Evaluating phase change memory for enterprise storage systems: A study of caching and tiering approaches. In *FAST*, 2014.

[37] V. King. A simpler minimum spanning tree verification algorithm. *Algorithmica*, 18(2), 1997.

[38] D. G. Kirkpatrick and R. Seidel. The ultimate planar convex hull algorithm? *SIAM J. on Computing*, 15(1), 1986.

[39] B. C. Lee, E. Ipek, O. Mutlu, and D. Burger. Architecting phase change memory as a scalable DRAM alternative. In *ISCA*, 2009.

[40] J. S. Meena, S. M. Sze, U. Chand, and T.-Y. Tseng. Overview of emerging nonvolatile memory technologies. *Nanoscale Research Letters*, 2014.

[41] N. Megiddo. Linear programming in linear time when the dimension is fixed. *JACM*, 31(1), 1984.

[42] G. Miller and J. Reif. Parallel tree contraction and its application. In *FOCS*, 1985.

[43] G. Miller and J. Reif. Parallel tree contraction part 2: Further applications. *SIAM J. on Computing*, 20(6), 1991.

[44] S. Nath and P. B. Gibbons. Online maintenance of very large random samples on flash storage. *VLDB J.*, 19(1), 2010.

[45] H. Park and K. Shim. FAST: flash-aware external sorting for mobile database systems. *J. of Systems and Software*, 82(8), 2009.

[46] M. K. Qureshi, S. Gurumurthi, and B. Rajendran. *Phase Change Memory: From Devices to Systems*. Morgan & Claypool, 2012.

[47] R. Seidel. Small-dimensional linear programming and convex hulls made easy. *Discrete & Computational Geometry*, 6(3), 1991.

[48] J. Shun, Y. Gu, G. E. Blelloch, J. T. Fineman, and P. B. Gibbons. Sequential random permutation, list contraction and tree contraction are highly parallel. In *SODA*, 2015.

[49] R. E. Tarjan and U. Vishkin. Finding biconnected componemts and computing tree functions in logarithmic parallel time. In *FOCS*, 1984.

[50] S. D. Viglas. Adapting the B^+-tree for asymmetric I/O. In *ADBIS*, 2012.

[51] S. D. Viglas. Write-limited sorts and joins for persistent memory. *Proc. VLDB Endowment*, 7(5), 2014.

[52] C. Xu, X. Dong, N. P. Jouppi, and Y. Xie. Design implications of memristor-based RRAM cross-point structures. In *DATE*, 2011.

[53] B.-D. Yang, J.-E. Lee, J.-S. Kim, J. Cho, S.-Y. Lee, and B.-G. Yu. A low power phase-change random access memory using a data-comparison write scheme. In *ISCAS*, 2007.

[54] Yole Developpement. Emerging non-volatile memory technologies, 2013.

[55] P. Zhou, B. Zhao, J. Yang, and Y. Zhang. A durable and energy efficient main memory using phase change memory technology. In *ISCA*, 2009.

[56] O. Zilberberg, S. Weiss, and S. Toledo. Phase-change memory: An architectural perspective. *ACM Computing Surveys*, 45(3), 2013.

Brief Announcement: Preserving Happens-before in Persistent Memory *

Joseph Izraelevitz Hammurabi Mendes Michael L. Scott
University of Rochester, Rochester, NY, USA
{jhi1,hmendes,scott}@cs.rochester.edu

ABSTRACT

Nonvolatile, byte-addressable memory (NVM) will soon be commercially available, but registers and caches are expected to remain transient on most machines. Without careful management, the data preserved in the wake of a crash are likely to be inconsistent and thus unusable.

Previous work has explored the semantics of instructions used to push the contents of cache to NVM. These semantics comprise a "memory persistency model," analogous to a traditional "memory consistency model." In this brief announcement we introduce *explicit epoch persistency*, a memory persistency model that captures the current and expected semantics of Intel x86 and ARM v8 persistent memory instructions. We also present a construction that augments any data-race-free program (for release consistency or any stronger memory model) in such a way that preserved data are guaranteed to represent a consistent cut in the happens-before graph of the program's execution.

1. INTRODUCTION

Nonvolatile, byte-addressable memory (NVM) is expected to be common in coming years. Caches and registers, however, are likely to remain in SRAM for some time to come. While NVM offers the opportunity to keep persistent data in main memory (not just in the file system), the fact that recent updates to registers and cache may be lost during a power failure means that the data in main memory, if not carefully managed, may not be consistent at recovery time.

Maintaining a consistent state in NVM requires special care to order main memory updates. Several libraries have been designed to support transactional updates of persistent state [3,7,12]. Similarly, some high performance data structures [11,13] carefully control concurrent updates to ensure that the persistent portion of a data structure remains consistent.

*This work was supported in part by NSF grants CNS-1319417, CCF-1337224, and CCF-1422649, and by support from the IBM Canada Centres for Advanced Study.

SPAA'16, July 11–13, 2016, Pacific Grove, CA, USA.

ACM ISBN 978-1-4503-4210-0/16/07.
DOI: http://dx.doi.org/10.1145/2935764.2935810

Concurrent and crash-resilient programs are closely connected: both must ensure that state can safely be read concurrently—either by a "real" thread during normal execution or by a conceptual "recovery thread" [10] that sees the post-crash state. By leveraging this connection, we can ensure that the happens-before ordering of the concurrent program is seen by the recovery thread.

Specifically, we present a construction that augments any properly synchronized concurrent program in a way that forces stores to be written back to NVM in an order consistent with happens-before. Our construction assumes that the input program is data-race free under release consistency or some stronger memory model. It further assumes that the hardware supports what we call *explicit epoch persistency*, a relaxed memory persistency model [10] that captures current and forthcoming processors in the Intel x86 and ARM v8 product lines. As output, our construction produces a program that guarantees that the contents of NVM in the wake of a crash will always represent a state that might have been seen by some concurrent reader thread during pre-crash execution. For nonblocking linearizable concurrent objects, this state will be one from which execution could reasonably continue. For programs using locks or other blocking mechanisms, additional machinery (e.g., redo or undo logs) will be required.

1.1 Consistency

On a machine with *relaxed consistency*, writes to a single location are totally ordered across threads, and each thread sees its own writes (to all locations) in program order [5]. Absent explicit synchronization, however, threads may see each others' writes in arbitrary order. In this work we consider a *release consistent* model with str (*store*), ld (*load*), str_rel (*store release*), ld_acq (*load acquire*), and CAS (*compare-and-swap*) instructions. The last three of these are synchronization instructions. They appear, across all threads and locations, to execute in some total order such that, transitively, (1) each ld_acq or CAS appears to other threads to occur before any subsequent instructions in its own thread; (2) each str_rel or CAS appears to other threads to occur after any previous instructions in its own thread; and (3) each str_rel or CAS appears, to all threads, to occur before the next ld_acq or CAS in synchronization order that touches the same location.

This model corresponds closely to that of the ARM v8 instruction set. For purposes of our construction, it can also be considered to subsume the model of Intel's x86 instruction set, where str_rel is emulated by an ordinary str, and where ld_acq is emulated with ⟨mfence; ld⟩ to force ordering with respect to any previous strs that serve as str_rel. Absent a cross-thread str_rel/CAS–to–ld_acq/CAS dependence, we make no assumptions about when (or even if) the stores of one thread will become visible to the loads of another.

1.2 Persistency

Given transient registers and caches but persistent main memory, an instruction set must give the programmer control over the order and timing by which information becomes persistent. The instructions used to control this ordering and timing embody a memory *persistency model* [10]. Persistency may be independent of consistency, and controlled by different instructions. In particular, acquires and releases on current and forthcoming machines are expected to have no bearing on the order in which data are persisted; they may, however, interact with the persistency instructions.

We introduce an *explicit epoch persistency* model. Unlike previous, *implicit* versions of epoch persistency, which assume that the hardware will force dirty data back when necessary to preserve ordering [4,8,10], our model captures the behavior of both ARM and x86, and requires that programs employ explicit writes-back when ordering is required. As noted above, we also consider a release-consistent model of transient memory, rather the more restrictive TSO [4,8] or sequential consistency [10] of prior work.

Under explicit epoch persistency, threads control the ordering and timing of persistency using three special instructions. A *persist write-back* (pwb) initiates write-back of a specified location to persistent memory, but does not block. A subsequent *persist fence* (pfence) enforces an ordering between previous and subsequent writes-back in the current thread. Finally, a *persist sync* (psync) blocks until all preceding pfences in the current thread have become persistent.

In the absence of fences, pwb instructions are allowed to reorder with respect to both ordinary and synchronization instructions. At the same time,

- each pwb is ordered with respect to (i) each preceding or subsequent pfence in its thread;
- for any given thread and location, each pwb is ordered with respect to (ii) each preceding str/str_rel, (iii) each preceding ld/ld_acq, and (iv) each preceding pwb of the same location in the same thread; and
- for any given thread, each pfence is ordered with respect to (v) each preceding ld_acq and (vi) each subsequent str_rel in that thread.

We also assume three other properties: First, writes-back persist atomically at some specified granularity [4]: their values cannot be torn across a fixed size. For generality, we assume here that a full-word write-back appears in its entirety or not at all in the wake of a crash. On real machines, atomicity is likely to be guaranteed at larger granularity—e.g., the width of a cache line. Second, persists to a given location respect coherence: the programmer need never worry that a newly persisted value will subsequently be overwritten by the write-back of some earlier value. Third, stored locations can "leak" back to persistence at any point after a store; in effect, extraneous pwbs can be inserted at will by the hardware or runtime system. Like explicit pwbs, these extraneous pwbs respect coherence and ordering.

Table 1 summarizes the mapping of our persistence instructions to the x86 and ARM ISAs. Neither instruction set currently distinguishes between pfence and psync, though both may do so at some point in the future. For now, ordering requires that the current thread wait for values to reach persistence.

Explicit Epoch Persistency	*Intel x86 [6]*	*ARM v8 [1]*
pwb *addr*	CLWB *addr*	DC CVAC *addr*
pfence	SFENCE PCOMMIT* SFENCE*	DSB†
psync	‘ ’	‘ ’

Table 1: Equivalent instruction sequences for explicit epoch persistency.

*Required if memory controller buffer is transient.

†Requires persistent memory controller buffer; transient memory buffers are unsupported on ARM v8 at this time.

2. TRANSFORMATION

Our transformation takes a transient concurrent program annotated for release consistency and turns it into an equivalent program for explicit epoch persistency. This transformation preserves the happens-before ordering of the original concurrent program—that is, in the event of a crash, the values present in persistent memory are guaranteed to represent a consistent cut in the happens-before partial order of the original program.

Our transformation is as follows:

1. Immediately after every str, write back the written value by issuing a pwb.
2. Immediately before a str_rel, issue a pfence; immediately after a str_rel, write back the written value by issuing a pwb.
3. Immediately after an ld_acq, write back the loaded value by issuing a pwb, then issue a pfence.
4. Handle acquire–release CAS instructions as both str_rel and ld_acq: immediately before the CAS, issue a pfence; after the CAS, write back the loaded value by issuing a pwb, then issue another pfence.
5. Take no persistence action on lds.
6. Before taking any I/O action, issue a psync to ensure all changes have reached persistent storage.

2.1 Argument for Correctness

Let $O = x.ins_t(params)$ denote an instruction ins that is performed by thread t on memory location x, with parameters $params$. Let $\mathcal{M}$ be the set of *memory instructions* {ld, str, ld_acq, str_rel, CAS}, and $\mathcal{P}$ the set of *persistence instructions* {pwb, pfence, psync}. For any $O = x.ins_t(params)$, with $ins \in \mathcal{M}$, let $P = x.px_t^O$ denote the persistence operation with $px \in \mathcal{P}$ associated with the transformation of operation O. Note that $x.px_t^O$ is well-defined and unique, given our transformation. We treat $x.\mathsf{CAS}_t(a,b)$ as an atomic $\langle O1; O2\rangle = \langle x.\mathsf{str\_rel}_t(b);\ x.\mathsf{ld\_acq}_t(a)\rangle$ pair), transformed to $\mathsf{pfence}_t^{O1}; \langle O1;\ O2\rangle;\ x.\mathsf{pwb}_t^{O1,O2}; \mathsf{pfence}_t^{O2}$.

For every memory location x, we have a total order of values written to x, as memory is coherent. Without loss of generality, assume that the i-th value written to x is i, and its initial value is 0. Operations in our execution history are partially ordered by the *happens-before* relation, denoted $\prec$, respecting the constraints of the memory and persistence models. We wish to show that, in the wake of a crash, the contents of persistent memory will always respect the happens-before order of str and str_rel instructions in the pre-crash execution.

Assume the contrary: $\exists A = x.\mathit{st1}_t(a)$, $B = y.\mathit{st2}_u(b)$, with $\mathit{st1}, \mathit{st2} \in \{\mathsf{str}, \mathsf{str\_rel}\}$, such that $A \prec B$, but in the wake of a crash, B is seen to have persisted while A has not. Without loss of generality, we may assume that A and B are *consecutive* operations—that is, $\nexists C : A \prec C \prec B$ (otherwise, if C has persisted, proceed with C in place of B or, if C has not persisted, with C in place of A).

Let $W_B = y.\mathsf{pwb}_u(b)$ be the write-back that persisted B. Our starting assumption implies that $\nexists W_A = x.\mathsf{pwb}_v(a') \prec W_B$, with $a' \geq a$. Note the arbitrary issuing thread in W_A.

In the discussion below, we write $\prec^{(i,\ldots,vi)}$ to justify a happens-before statement based on ordering properties (i) through (vi), enumerated in Section 1.2. The following cases are exhaustive:

1. If $t = u$ and $\mathit{st2} = \mathsf{str}$, then $y = x$ (otherwise $A \not\prec B$, since A and B are consecutive). In this case, we have $y.\mathsf{pwb}^A_t(a) \prec^{(iv)} y.\mathsf{pwb}^B_t(b)$.
2. If $t = u$ and $\mathit{st2} = \mathsf{str\_rel}$, either $y = x$ or $y \neq x$. In either case, we have $x.\mathsf{pwb}^A_t(a) \prec^{(i)} \mathsf{pfence}^B_t \prec^{(vi)} B \prec^{(ii)} y.\mathsf{pwb}^B_t(b)$.
3. If $t \neq u$, then $\mathit{st1} = \mathsf{str\_rel}$, or we contradict the fact that A and B are consecutive. Hence, $[A = x.\mathsf{str\_rel}_t(a)] \prec [L = x.\mathsf{ld\_acq}_u(a)] \prec [B = y.s2_u(b)]$. However,
   (a) $A \prec L$, so $A \prec L \prec^{(iii)} x.\mathsf{pwb}^L_u(a') \prec^{(i)} \mathsf{pfence}^L_u$, with $a' \geq a$ since writes-back are coherent; and
   (b) $L \prec B$, so $\mathsf{pfence}^L_u \prec^{(i)} y.\mathsf{pwb}_u(b)$.

   Therefore, $x.\mathsf{pwb}^L_u(a') \prec \mathsf{pfence}^L_u \prec y.\mathsf{pwb}^B_u(b)$.

In all three cases, we have contradicted the starting assumption that $\nexists W_A \prec W_B$. That is, for any consecutively ordered stores A and B, if $W_B = y.\mathsf{pwb}_u(b)$ persists into memory, some $W_A = x.\mathsf{pwb}_v(a')$ also persists into memory, and becomes visible before W_B does. Between any consecutive stores, we have a pwb and a pfence (cases 2 and 3), or their persistence respects coherence (case 1).

3. CONCLUSIONS AND FUTURE WORK

Explicit epoch persistency, we believe, accurately captures the semantics that can be expected of forthcoming NVM systems. Our construction demonstrates that simple, mechanical transformations can preserve the happens-before order of properly synchronized programs, leading to meaningful post-crash memory contents. More specifically, in the wake of a crash, the contents of memory will reflect some consistent cut of the happens-before graph of pre-crash execution. For nonblocking concurrent objects, this cut represents a valid static state of the object, which can be trivially recovered [9]. For blocking objects, if the cut interrupts a failure-atomic or critical section, additional recovery mechanisms may be needed to roll the cut forward or backward [3, 7, 12] to reach a consistent state [2].

In ongoing work, we are continuing to investigate the notion of correctness for persistent programs and to develop programming methodologies to (1) reduce the cost of persistence for nonblocking concurrent objects, (2) preserve the consistency of blocking objects, and (3) support the composition of atomic operations into larger ACID transactions—atomic, consistency-preserving, isolated, and persistent (durable).

4. REFERENCES

[1] ARM Limited. ARM Cortex-A series programmer's guide for ARMv8-A. Technical Report DEN0024A:ID050815, ARM Limited, Mar. 2015.

[2] H.-J. Boehm and D. Chakrabarti. Persistence programming models for non-volatile memory. Technical Report HP-2015-59, HP Labs, Aug. 2015.

[3] D. R. Chakrabarti, H.-J. Boehm, and K. Bhandari. Atlas: Leveraging locks for non-volatile memory consistency. In *Proc. of the 2014 ACM Intl. Conf. on Object Oriented Programming Systems Languages and Applications*, Portland, OR, USA, 2014.

[4] J. Condit, E. B. Nightingale, C. Frost, E. Ipek, B. Lee, D. Burger, and D. Coetzee. Better I/O through byte-addressable, persistent memory. In *Proc. of the ACM 22nd Symp. on Operating Systems Principles*, Big Sky, MT, USA, 2009.

[5] K. Gharachorloo, D. Lenoski, J. Laudon, P. Gibbons, A. Gupta, and J. Hennessy. Memory consistency and event ordering in scalable shared-memory multiprocessors. In *Proc. of the 17th Intl. Symp. on Computer Architecture*, Seattle, WA, USA, 1990.

[6] Intel Corporation. Intel architecture instruction set extensions programming reference. Technical Report 319433-022, Intel Corporation, Oct. 2014.

[7] J. Izraelevitz, T. Kelly, and A. Kolli. Failure-atomic persistent memory updates via JUSTDO logging. In *Proc. of the 21st Intl. Conf. on Architectural Support for Programming Languages and Operating Systems*, Atlanta, GA, USA, 2016.

[8] A. Joshi, V. Nagarajan, M. Cintra, and S. Viglas. Efficient persist barriers for multicores. In *Proc. of the 48th Intl. Symp. on Microarchitecture*, 2015.

[9] F. Nawab, D. R. Chakrabarti, T. Kelly, and C. B. Morrey III. Procrastination beats prevention: Timely sufficient persistence for efficient crash resilience. In *Proc. of the 18th Intl. Conf. on Extending Database Technology*, Brussels, Belgium, Mar. 2015.

[10] S. Pelley, P. M. Chen, and T. F. Wenisch. Memory persistency. In *Proc. of the 41st Intl. Symposium on Computer Architecture*, Piscataway, NJ, USA, 2014.

[11] S. Venkataraman, N. Tolia, P. Ranganathan, and R. H. Campbell. Consistent and durable data structures for non-volatile byte-addressable memory. In *Proc. of the 9th USENIX Conf. on File and Storage Technologies*, Berkeley, CA, USA, 2011.

[12] H. Volos, A. J. Tack, and M. M. Swift. Mnemosyne: Lightweight persistent memory. In *Proc. of the 16th Intl. Conf. on Architectural Support for Programming Languages and Operating Systems*, Newport Beach, CA, USA, 2011.

[13] J. Yang, Q. Wei, C. Chen, C. Wang, K. L. Yong, and B. He. NV-Tree: Reducing consistency cost for NVM-based single level systems. In *Proc. of the 13th USENIX Conf. on File and Storage Technologies*, Santa Clara, CA, USA, Feb. 2015.

Brief Announcement: Approximating the I/O Complexity of One-Shot Red-Blue Pebbling

Timothy Carpenter*
Dept. of Computer Science and Engineering
The Ohio State University
Columbus, OH USA
carpenter.454@osu.edu

Fabrice Rastello
Inria
Univ. Grenoble Alpes, LIG, F-38000 Grenoble, France
CNRS, LIG, F-38000 Grenoble, France
Fabrice.Rastello@inria.fr

P. Sadayappan†
Dept. of Computer Science and Engineering
The Ohio State University
Columbus, OH USA
saday@cse.ohio-state.edu

Anastasios Sidiropoulos*
Dept. of Computer Science and Engineering
Dept. of Mathematics
The Ohio State University
Columbus, OH USA
sidiropoulos.1@osu.edu

ABSTRACT

Red-blue pebbling is a model of computation that captures the complexity of I/O operations in systems with external memory access. We focus on one-shot pebbling strategies, that is without re-computation. Prior work on this model has focused on finding upper and lower bounds on the I/O complexity of certain families of graphs. We give a polynomial-time bi-criteria approximation algorithm for this problem for graphs with bounded out-degree. More precisely, given a n-vertex DAG that admits a pebbling strategy with R red pebbles and I/O complexity opt, our algorithm outputs a strategy using $O(R \cdot \log^{3/2} n)$ red pebbles, and I/O complexity $O(\mathsf{opt} \cdot \log^{3/2} n)$. We further extend our result to the generalization of red-blue pebble games that correspond to multi-level memory hierarchies. Finally, we complement our theoretical analysis with an experimental evaluation of our algorithm for red-blue pebbling.

Keywords

red-blue pebble game; I/O complexity; memory hierarchy; approximation algorithms

1. INTRODUCTION

Pebbling games are a powerful abstraction for analyzing the complexity of computations [13, 12]. We focus on the *red-blue* pebble game, as introduced in [7], which is used to capture the I/O complexity of computations in the presence of external memory. We are interested in *one-shot* pebbling, that is without re-computation.

The rules of the red-blue pebble game are as follows: The input consists of a DAG G. Initially, all input vertices (i.e. with in-degree zero) have a blue pebble. (R1) A red pebble can be placed in any vertex that contains a blue pebble. (R2) A blue pebble can be placed in any vertex that has a red pebble. (R3) A red pebble can be placed in any vertex whose all immediate predecessors have red pebbles. (R4) A pebble can be removed form any vertex. A terminal configuration is one where all output vertices (i.e. of out-degree zero) have blue pebbles. Intuitively, red pebbles correspond to (limited) internal memory, while blue pebbles correspond to (unlimited) external storage. The *I/O complexity* of a pebbling is the number of times that transitions according to rules (R1) and (R2) are performed. One-shot pebbling means that rule (R3) can be performed at most once for each vertex. We remark that this is also known as *red-blue-white* pebbling (see [5] for details).

Most prior work on red-blue pebble games is focused on obtaining upper and lower bounds on the I/O complexity of specific families of graphs, such as pyramids [14], diamonds, butterflies, matrix multiplication graphs, and so on [5].

Recent results in pebbling study the approximability of the minimum number of pebbles required for a given input DAG, for various pebble games [2, 12]. We obtain a bi-criteria approximation algorithm for the I/O complexity of red-blue pebble games with a given number of red pebbles. More precisely, let $\mathsf{opt}_R(G)$ be the minimum I/O complexity for red-blue pebblings of G with R red pebbles. We give a polynomial-time algorithm which given a DAG G of bounded out-degree and some $R > 0$, outputs a pebbling strategy for G using $O(R \cdot \log^{3/2} n)$ red pebbles, with I/O complexity $O(\mathsf{opt}_R(G) \cdot \log^{3/2} n)$.

We further extend our algorithm to the generalization

*Supported by NSF under award CAREER-1453472 and grant CCF-1423230.
†Supported in part by DOE award DE-SC0012489

SPAA '16 July 11-13, 2016, Pacific Grove, CA, USA

ACM ISBN 978-1-4503-4210-0/16/07.
DOI: http://dx.doi.org/10.1145/2935764.2935807

of red-blue pebble games for multi-level memory hierarchy given in [15].

Finally, we evaluate our algorithm experimentally. In some cases we obtain pebbling strategies that outperform the best-known theoretical upper bounds.

2. PRELIMINARIES

A *directed vertex separator* of a directed graph $G = (V, E)$ is a partition (A, B, S) of V such that there are no edges between A and B, and all edges between S and B are directed from S to B. We define the *size* of the separator to be $|S|$. We say that (A, B, S) is α*-balanced*, for some $0 < \alpha < 1$ if $\max\{|A|, |B|\} \leq \alpha|V|$.

It can be shown that such separators exist in any DAG G by splitting some topological ordering into sets A, B around any point in the ordering, and moving any vertex of A with a child in B to the separator S. Using an approximation algorithm for directed sparsest-cut and the reduction described in [10], it is possible to find a directed balanced separator (A, B, S) of G which approximately minimizes the ratio $|S|/\min\{|S \cup A|, |S \cup B|\}$.

A bi-criteria ρ-approximation for minimum directed balanced vertex separator is an algorithm that outputs a directed α-balanced separator, of size at most $\rho \cdot b$, where b is the size of a minimum 1/2-balanced directed vertex separator, for some universal constant $\alpha > 0$. For the remained of this paper, let $\alpha = 1/4$, and let $\rho^* > 0$ be such that there exists a polynomial time bi-criteria ρ^*-approximation algorithm for minimum directed balanced vertex separator. The actual value of ρ^* will depend on the class of graphs under consideration. For some $X \subseteq V$ we denote by $G[X]$ the vertex-induced subgraph of G on X.

3. THE APPROXIMATION ALGORITHM

The following is a modified version of the algorithm in [10] for approximating the minimum black pebbling cost.

Algorithm 1 Ordering algorithm

Input: DAG G.
Output: Ordering of V.

If $|V| \leq 1$ then output the unique ordering of V.

Otherwise, compute a bi-criteria ρ-approximate directed 1/4-balanced vertex separator (A, B, S) of G. Recursively order $G[A \cup S]$ and $G[B]$, and output the ordering of G as the ordering of $G[A \cup S]$ followed by $G[B]$.

We now describe our algorithm for one-shot red-blue pebbling: We first use Algorithm 1 to find an ordering π of V. The order in which vertices are first pebbled red is determined by π. If at some step of the pebbling there are no unused red pebbles when one is needed, then from the set of vertices with red pebbles, we find the vertex v with the longest span before the next child will be pebbled (ties broken arbitrarily), and we pebble v blue. For all $v, v' \in V$ such that $\pi(v') = \pi(v) + 1$, after pebbling v and before pebbling v', pebble red any parents of v' that are pebbled blue. When all the children of a vertex v have been pebbled, the red pebble is removed from v. This completed the description of the red-blue pebbling algorithm.

THEOREM 1. *Let $G = (V, E)$ be a n-vertex DAG with maximum out-degree d. Then the red-blue pebbling algorithm on G outputs a pebbling strategy using $O(R \cdot \rho^* \cdot \log n)$ red pebbles with I/O complexity $O(d \cdot \rho^* \cdot \mathsf{opt}_R(G) \cdot \log n)$.*

From [1] we have $\rho^* = O(\sqrt{\log n})$. Thus we obtain the following.

COROLLARY 1. *Let G be a n-vertex directed acyclic graph with maximum out-degree d. There exists a polynomial-time algorithm that for any $R > 0$, computes a red-blue pebbling strategy for G using $O(R \cdot \log^{3/2} n)$ red pebbles with I/O complexity $O(\mathsf{opt}_R(G) \cdot d \cdot \log^{3/2} n)$.*

4. EXTENSION TO MULTI-LEVEL MEMORY HIERARCHIES

The memory hierarchy model extends red-blue pebbling by adding several types of pebbles, organized into levels $1, \ldots, k$. Let $P_1, \ldots, P_k$ be the number of pebbles at each level, and $P_k = \infty$. Each level $i > 1$ has an I/O cost c_i associated with using a pebble. The following rules govern the placement and removal of pebbles from vertices: (M1) A pebble on level $1 < i < k$ can only be placed on a vertex to replace a pebble of level $i - 1$ or $i + 1$. A level-1 pebble can only be placed (M2) on a source vertex, (M3) a vertex with a level-2 pebble, or (M4) a vertex whose parents all hold a level-1 pebble. (M5) A level-k pebble may only be placed on a vertex holding a level-$(k - 1)$ pebble. Pebbles of any level may be removed at any time. The pebbling is completed only when all vertices have been pebbled. Notice that when $k = 2$, the memory hierarchy model coincides with red-blue pebbling. The one-shot version of this model is obtained by allowing rule (M4) to be performed at most once per vertex.

We now describe our algorithm for finding a hierarchical pebbling strategy. Let $G = (V, E)$ be the input DAG. We first use Algorithm 1 to find a topological ordering π of G. The ordering π determines the order in which each vertex is pebbled. If v is the next vertex to be pebbled, we ensure that all parents of v hold a level-1 pebble. If there is only one level-1 pebble available when one is needed, we free up an addition pebble as follows: From the set of vertices holding a level-1 pebble, identify a vertex u with the longest span in π before the next child of u is pebbled, and transition u to level 2. When any $u \in V$ is being transitioned to a level-i pebble, we consider the following cases:

(1) There are at least two level-i pebbles available. In this case, give u a level-i pebble.

(2) There is only one level-i pebble available.

(2.1) There is a vertex r with a level-i pebble, and r has a longer span than u. Transition r to a level-$(i + 1)$ pebble, and give u a level-i pebble.

(2.2) There is no vertex r with a level-i pebble and longer span than u. Pebble u using the last level-i pebble, and transition u to a level-$(i + 1)$ pebble.

For all $v \in V$, once the last child of v has been pebbled, release the pebble v holds. This completes the description of the algorithm.

Let $\mathsf{opt}(G)$ be the minimum total I/O complexity of any pebbling strategy for G with $P_1, \ldots, P_{k-1}$ pebbles at level $1, \ldots, k - 1$. The following Theorem summarizes our result on the performance of the above algorithm.

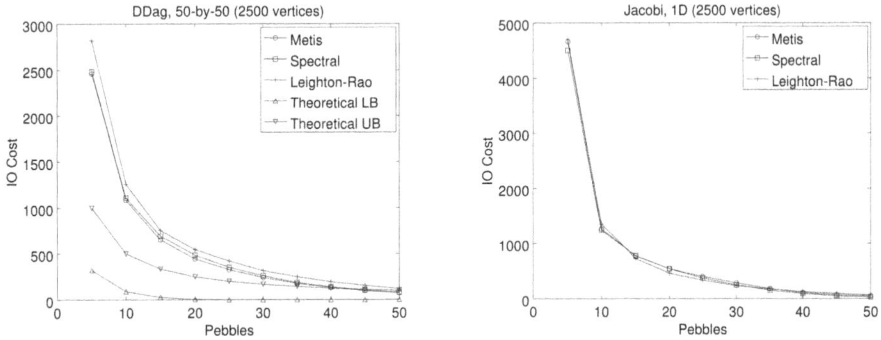

Figure 1: Performance of Algorithm 1 on the diamond graph of size 50×50 (left) and the 1-dimensional Jacobi graph on 2500 vertices (right).

THEOREM 2. *Let G be a n-vertex DAG with maximum out-degree d. The hierarchical pebbling algorithm for G outputs a pebbling strategy using $O(P_i \cdot \rho^* \cdot \log n)$ level-i pebbles for each $i < k$ and has I/O complexity $O(d \cdot \rho^* \cdot \mathsf{opt}(G) \cdot \log n)$.*

5. EXPERIMENTAL EVALUATION

We have experimentally evaluated our algorithm on various DAGs. The most computationally intensive step is finding balanced directed vertex separators. Unfortunately, most widely available graph partitioning software works only on undirected graphs[1]. We have implemented three algorithms for this step: The first one is the directed version of the approximation algorithm due to [11], using the faster combinatorial algorithm for maximum concurrent flow from [16]. The second one is a heuristic based on the METIS graph partitioning library for undirected graphs [8]. The third implementation is a heuristic based on spectral partitioning of undirected graphs.

Figure 1 depicts the results on the 50×50 diamond graph (i.e. the DAG obtained from the grid by orienting all edges from left to right and from top to bottom) and the 1-D Jacobi graph. We observe that, in either case, the choice of graph partitioning algorithm does not significantly affect the I/O complexity. Figure 1 also includes the best previously known theoretical upper and lower bounds (see [5]) for the diamond graph. Interestingly, our implementations using METIS and spectral partitioning outperform the theoretical upper bound when the number of red pebbles is at least 45.

6. REFERENCES

[1] A. Agarwal, M. Charikar, K. Makarychev, and Y. Makarychev. $O(\sqrt{\log n})$ approximation algorithms for min uncut, min 2cnf deletion, and directed cut problems. In *Proc. of the 37th Annual ACM Symposium on Theory of Computing*, STOC '05, 2005.

[2] P. Austrin, T. Pitassi, and Y. Wu. Inapproximability of treewidth, one-shot pebbling, and related layout problems. In *Approximation, Randomization, and Combinatorial Optimization. Algorithms and Techniques*, pages 13–24. Springer, 2012.

[3] D. A. Bader, H. Meyerhenke, P. Sanders, and D. Wagner. Graph partitioning and graph clustering - 10th DIMACS implementation challenge workshop.

[1]This is one of the main open problems emphasized in the 10th DIMACS Implementation Challenge [3].

[4] S. M. Chan, M. Lauria, J. Nordstrom, and M. Vinyals. Hardness of approximation in PSPACE and separation results for pebble games. In *Proc. of IEEE 56th Ann. Symp. on Found. of Comp. Science*, 2015.

[5] V. Elango, F. Rastello, L.-N. Pouchet, J. Ramanujam, and P. Sadayappan. Data access complexity: The red/blue pebble game revisited. Technical report, OSU-CISRC-7/13-TR16, Ohio State University, 2013.

[6] U. Feige, M. Hajiaghayi, and J. R. Lee. Improved approximation algorithms for minimum-weight vertex separators. In *Proc. of the 37th Annual ACM Symp. on Theory of Comp.*, STOC '05, 2005.

[7] J.-W. Hong and H. T. Kung. I/O complexity: The red-blue pebble game. In *Proc. of the 13th Annual ACM Symposium on Theory of Computing*, 1981.

[8] G. Karypis and V. Kumar. Metis–unstructured graph partitioning and sparse matrix ordering system, version 2.0. 1995.

[9] G. Karypis and V. Kumar. A fast and high quality multilevel scheme for partitioning irregular graphs. *SIAM J. Sci. Comput.*, 20(1):359–392, December 1998.

[10] P. Klein, A. Agrawal, R. Ravi, and S. Rao. Approximation through multicommodity flow. In *Proc. of the 30th Ann. Symp. on Found. of Comp. Science*, 1989.

[11] T. Leighton and S. Rao. Multicommodity max-flow min-cut theorems and their use in designing approximation algorithms. *J. ACM*, 46(6):787–832, 1999.

[12] J. Nordstrom. New wine into old wineskins: A survey of some pebbling classics with supplemental results. *Foundations and Trends in Theoretical Computer Science. http://people.csail.mit.edu/jakobn*, 2010.

[13] N. Pippenger. *Advances in pebbling*. Springer, 1982.

[14] D. Ranjan, J. Savage, and M. Zubair. Upper and lower I/O bounds for pebbling r-pyramids. *Journal of Discrete Algorithms*, 14:2–12, 2012.

[15] J. E. Savage. Extending the hong-kung model to memory hierarchies. In *Computing and Combinatorics*, pages 270–281. Springer, 1995.

[16] F. Shahrokhi and D. W. Matula. The maximum concurrent flow problem. *Journal of the ACM (JACM)*, 37(2):318–334, 1990.

General Profit Scheduling and the Power of Migration on Heterogeneous Machines

Sungjin Im
University of California - Merced
Merced, CA 95343
sim3@ucmerced.edu

Benjamin Moseley
Washington University in St. Louis.
St. Louis, MO 63130
bmoseley@wustl.edu

ABSTRACT

In this paper we consider the power of migration in heterogeneous machines settings and general profit scheduling. We begin by showing that on related machines or on related machines with restricted assignment that any migratory algorithm can be simulated by a non-migratory algorithm given $1+\epsilon$ speed augmentation and $O(\frac{1}{\epsilon})$ and $O(\frac{1}{\epsilon^2})$ machine augmentation, respectively, for any $0 < \epsilon \leq 1$. Similar results were only known in the case of identical machines and our results effectively show that migration does not give too much additional power to an algorithm, even in heterogeneous environments. Our results are constructive and can be computed efficiently in the offline setting. We complement our result by showing that there exists migratory schedules on related machines which require $\Omega(\frac{1}{\epsilon})$ machine augmentation with $(1+\epsilon)$-speed to be simulated by any non-migratory scheduler for any $0 < \epsilon \leq 1/2$, showing that machine augmentation without speed augmentation is insufficient for a non-migratory scheduler to simulate a migratory scheduler.

We then use these results to study general profit scheduling where a set of n jobs arrive over time online and every job i has a function $g_i(t)$ specifying the profit of completing job i at time t. The goal of the schedule is to maximize the total profit obtained. We give a $(1+\epsilon)$-speed $O(\frac{1}{\epsilon^2})$-competitive algorithm in the *unrelated* machines setting for any $\epsilon > 0$ when compared against a non-migratory adversary. Previous results were only known in the identical machines setting. As an example of the usefulness of the previous results on migration, they with the results on genral profit scheduling give a $(1+\epsilon)$-speed $O(\frac{1}{\epsilon^4})$-competitive algorithm for general profit scheduling when comparing against a migratory algorithm on related machines with restricted assignment for any $\epsilon > 0$.

SPAA '16, July 11-13, 2016, Pacific Grove, CA, USA

DOI: http://dx.doi.org/10.1145/2935764.2935771

1. INTRODUCTION

In online scheduling theory a fundamental area of research focuses on designing algorithms for completing a set of jobs to maximize the amount of profit obtained. In one of the most basic formulations of this problem, there are n jobs that arrive over time and each job i arrives at some time r_i. Each of these jobs i is associated with a profit w_i and a deadline d_i. If the job i is completed by its deadline then a profit of w_i is obtained and no profit is obtained for the job otherwise. This problem is known as maximizing throughput (or throughput maximization).

Throughput maximization has been extensively studied in the case where the jobs are to be scheduled on a single machine and preemption is allowed. In this case, every job has some processing time p_i. This line of work has resolved the complexity of the problem and it is known that the optimal deterministic competitive ratio is $\Theta(\delta)$ where δ is ratio of the maximum to minimum density of a job [3, 4, 11, 13]. The density of a job is $\frac{w_i}{p_i}$, which intuitively is the profit obtained for each unit of the job processed. The optimal randomized competitive ratio is $\Theta(\min\{\log \delta, \log \Delta\})$ where Δ is the ratio of the maximum to minimum job size [6, 10].

Unfortunately, these results can be viewed as unsatisfying since they depend on δ and Δ, which could be super polynomial in the size of the problem instance. In this face of these strong lower bound, previous work has resorted to a resource augmentation analysis where the algorithm is given extra speed over the adversary [7]. An algorithm is said to be s-speed c-competitive if it can process jobs an s factor faster than the adversary and achieves a profit within $1/c$ factor of the optimal solution. Using resource augmentation, a $(1+\epsilon)$-speed $O(f(\epsilon))$-competitive algorithm is known for any fixed $\epsilon > 0$ where f is a function of only ϵ [7].

Work has also considered this problem in more general machine environments [10, 6, 12, 8]. One such environment is the *identical* machines setting. In this case, the jobs can be scheduled on a set of m machines and every job has the same processing time no matter which machine the job is processed on. In this setting, a $(1+\epsilon)$-speed $O(1)$ competitive algorithms are known for any fixed constant $\epsilon > 0$ [12, 8]. Interestingly, as far as the authors are aware, competitive online algorithms have not been discovered in more general environments, such as related machine, restricted assignment or unrelated machines. In the related machines setting each machine i runs at a speed s_i and the processing time of a job on a machine is $\frac{p_i}{s_i}$. In restricted assignment setting, a job i can only be processed on some subset of the machines and has processing time p_i on each machine it can be processed on. Finally, the unrelated machines setting is the most general model where the processing time of job i on machine j is $p_{i,j}$ and the processing times of jobs on machines are arbitrary.

Relatively recently, the throughput problem was generalized to the following problem, which we refer to as *general profit scheduling*. In this problem, instead of each job i having a weight, it is associated with its own *individual* function $g_i(t)$. The value $g_i(t)$ specifies the profit of completing job i at time t and the goal is to maximize $\sum_{i \in [n]} g_i(C_i)$ where C_i is the completion time of job i under some schedule. In past work, the *only assumption* made of the functions $g_i(t)$ is that they are non-increasing or, in other words, there should be no incentive to complete a job later. For this very general problem, $(1+\epsilon)$-speed $O(\frac{1}{\epsilon})$-competitive algorithm is known on a single machine [2] as well as on identical machines [12].

A question that is intimately tied with the problems of maximizing throughput, general profit scheduling, and many other problems is what power does an algorithm gain by using *migration*? That is, when scheduling on more than one machine, a preemptive algorithm could be allowed to migrate a job between the machines. The question is can an algorithm leverage this power to obtain significantly better schedules than an algorithm which must process each job on exactly one machine?

In general, a migratory algorithm can feasibly complete more jobs than a non-migratory scheduler in the throughput setting. Interestingly, it has been shown that this power is fairly limited. In particular, an algorithm was shown in [8] which can convert any feasible migratory schedule on m identical machines to a a scheduler that is non-migratory using $6m$ machines. The schedule ensures that every job is completed only earlier than in the migratory schedule. This immediately implies that there exists a non-migratory scheduler that can achieve profit within $1/6$ of any non-migratory scheduler for throughput and general profit scheduling without any additional machine or speed augmentation. To see this, consider doing the conversion and then only choosing to schedule jobs on the m machine that achieve the largest profit. In general this fundamental result shows that for effectively any reasonable objective, one can convert a migratory scheduler to a non-migratory scheduler with a small amount of machine augmentation. Other results that study the power of migration can be found in [5, 9].

This line of work on profit scheduling problems and on the power of migration has left open many intriguing questions. Do there exist competitive algorithms for throughput maximization in heterogeneous machine settings such as related machine, restricted assignment or unrelated machines? Could these be extended to find algorithms for general profit scheduling in these settings? Finally, what is the power of migration on heterogeneous machines? In this paper, we work towards answering these questions.

Results: Our work begins by addressing the question of converting migratory schedules to non-migratory schedules on heterogeneous machines. We say that a non-migratory schedule *simulates* a migratory schedule if the following three properties hold (1) every job is processed only after its arrival; (2) every job is completed only possibly earlier in the non-migratory schedule; and (3) each job is processed on at most one machine. Our main result for the conversion is for the related machines with restricted assignment setting where machines have different speeds and each job can only be processed on some subset of the machines.

THEOREM 1.1. *For any migratory schedule on m related machines with restricted assignment there exists a non-migratory schedule that simulates this schedule when every machine i is given a $(1+\epsilon)$ factor additional speed and there are $O(\frac{1}{\epsilon^2})$ copies of each machine for any $0 < \epsilon \leq 1$.*

While a similar result for the related machines setting (with no restricted assignment) (see Theorem 2.4) easily follows with a small observation from the previous work [1] on minimizing maximum weighted flowtime on related machines, we use different techniques to obtain a more general result. Succinctly, the result in [1] can be viewed as a clever generalization of the 'slow-fit' algorithm on minimizing makespan on related machines where each job is scheduled on the slowest machine it can be – to handle jobs arriving over time, a laminar family of intervals is defined, and a careful volume argument is performed. On the other hand, we cannot use a greedy rule to assign jobs to machines since jobs can be placed on different subsets of machines. Due to this, we create a network flow for jobs of similar sizes, and obtain an integral flow which readily translates into an actual assignment. Here we carefully use the constraints imposed on intervals that form a laminar family, and show no machines get too large volume on any interval in the laminar family. The main challenge is to ensure the volume does not accrue too much over multiple assignments coming from different network flows. The conversion is constructive and offline.

To complement our positive results, we further show that machine augmentation is insufficient without speed augmentation on related machines (even without restricted assignment) unlike the identical machine result of [8]. This shows that our conversion results are essentially tight for any fixed ϵ.

THEOREM 1.2. *There exists a migratory schedule on related machines such that any non-migratory schedule with $(1+\epsilon)$-speed requires $\Omega(\frac{1}{\epsilon})$-machine augmentation for any $0 \leq \epsilon \leq 1/2$.*

We leave the case for unrelated machines as an interesting open question, but note that it appears to require new techniques beyond those used in our work.

With these results in place, we work towards discovering competitive non-migratory schedulers for throughput and general profit scheduling on heterogeneous machines. We show that the novel results of [2] on a single machine, can be generalized to the full extent of unrelated machines.

THEOREM 1.3. *There exists a non-migratory schedule on unrelated machines with $(1+\epsilon)$-speed that achieves a $O(\frac{1}{\epsilon^2})$-competitive for general profit scheduling when compared against a non-migratory adversary.*

With these results, we can compare against a non-migratory adversary on related machines with restricted assignment using only $(1+\epsilon)$ speed augmentation and no machine augmentation. Indeed, for any migratory optimal solution one can use Theorem 1.2 to convert it to a migratory schedule with $(1+\epsilon)$ speed augmentation and $O(\frac{1}{\epsilon^2})$ machine augmentation. Then, for each machine of the original schedule, choose the copy which achieves the highest profit in the non-migratory schedule to get a $(1+\epsilon)$-speed $O(\frac{1}{\epsilon^2})$-competitive non-migratory scheduler. One can then compare against migratory schedule to derive the following corollary.

COROLLARY 1.4. *There exists a non-migratory schedule on related machines with restricted assignment with $(1+\epsilon)$-speed that achieves a $O(\frac{1}{\epsilon^4})$-competitive for general profit scheduling when compared against a migratory adversary.*

Organization: We begin by studying how to covert migratory schedules to non-migratory schedules in Section 2 and in Section 2.2 we show a lower bound on the machine augmentation needed for converting a migratory schedule to a non-migratory schedule in the related machines setting. In Section 3 we study the general profit scheduling problem on unrelated machines when comparing against a non-migratory adversary.

2. RELATIONSHIP BETWEEN MIGRATORY AND NON-MIGRATORY SCHEDULES

In this section we begin by showing how to covert a migratory schedule to a non-migratory schedule in the related machines setting. Later in the section, we will discuss the related machines with restricted assignment setting. Throughout this section, we assume that we are given a migratory schedule on either related machines or related machines with restricted assignment. Given this migratory we define d_i to be the time the schedule completes job i. We will refer to this as job i's deadline and the time interval $[r_i, d_i]$ as job i's window. The window for a job, is the feasible times our scheduler can execute the job. Note that this time is completely dependent on the given migratory schedule. Our goal is to show a scheduler which completes all jobs by their deadlines, while ensuring every job is executed on only one machine.

We begin by defining formally the definition of the type of speed and machine augmentation we will use in the conversion.

DEFINITION 2.1. *We say that a schedule is feasible with s-speed μ-machine augmentation if all jobs are completed during their respective windows (and at any point in time no job is scheduled on more than one machine) when each machines has μ identical copies and all machines run s times faster than their original speed.*

In the following lemma, we consider the following situation. Say one has a schedule which ensures that all jobs are scheduled without using migration. The schedule can be infeasible by allowing a job to be executed before its arrival and after its deadline, but the interval the job is executed during can be bounded by $(d_i - r_i)$. Then we can use such a schedule to construct a feasible non-migratory schedule.

LEMMA 2.2. *For any constant $\delta < 1$, consider a schedule on a single machine with speed s where each job j is scheduled during time the interval $[r_j - \frac{1}{\delta}(d_j - r_j), d_j+\frac{1}{\delta}(d_j-r_j)]$, which we call j's $(1/\delta)$-extended window. Further, assume that in this schedule $d_j - r_j \geq cp_j$ for all jobs j for some constant $c > 0$. Then, for any $\gamma > \frac{1}{c} - 1$, there exists a non-migratory schedule on $\lfloor (2/\delta+3)s/(1+\gamma-\frac{1}{c})+1 \rfloor = O(\frac{s}{(1+\gamma-\frac{1}{c})\delta})$ identical parallel machines running with speed $1+\gamma$ where each job is scheduled on a single machine (i.e., in a non-migratory way) during the time interval $[r_j, d_j]$. Further, such a schedule can be found in polynomial time.*

PROOF. For notational simplicity, let $\ell_j := d_j - r_j$ and $m := \lfloor (2/\delta+3)s/(1+\gamma-\frac{1}{c}) \rfloor +1$. We construct a desired non-migratory schedule as follows. Consider jobs in increasing order of their window sizes, and schedule each job j on an arbitrary machine that has enough idle times to preemptively process the job before its deadline and after its arrival. Observe that job j can not be assigned to machine i only if the machine processes at least $(1+\gamma-\frac{1}{c})\ell_j$ volume of work for jobs of smaller windows during $[r_j, d_j]$ since machines run with speed $(1+\gamma)$ and $d_j - r_j \leq cp_j$. We show that we can always find a machine to process each job j.

For the sake of contradiction, say j is the first job we couldn't schedule. Then, every machine must process at least $(1+\gamma-\frac{1}{c})\ell_j$ volume of work during $[r_j, d_j]$ for jobs of smaller window than job j. Such jobs arrive no earlier than $r_j - \ell_j$ and no later than d_j, meaning that they must be completed by time $d_j + \ell_j(1+1/\delta)$ under the given schedule on a single machine. Hence we found a set of jobs of total volume at least $(1+\gamma-\frac{1}{c})\ell_j m$ that must be completed during $[r_j - (1+1/\delta)\ell_j, d_j + \ell_j(1+1/\delta)]$ on a *single* machine of speed s. Since the given schedule can process at most $(2/\delta+3)s\ell_j$ volume of work during the interval, we obtain $m \leq (2/\delta+3)s/(1+\gamma-\frac{1}{c})$, which is a contradiction. □

We note that the relationship between migratory and non-migratory schedules on related machines easily follows from the following theorem from [1] and Lemma 2.2.

THEOREM 2.3. *[1] There is a $O(1/\epsilon^4)$-competitive non-migratory algorithm to minimize maximum weighted flow time on related machines with $1+\epsilon$ speed* *augmentation for any $0 < \epsilon \le 1$. The competitive ratio holds even against a migratory optimal schedule. Furthermore, every job i is scheduled on a machine j such that $\frac{p_i}{s_j} \le \frac{1}{w_i}$, where w_i is the weight of job i and assuming that the optimal solution objective is at most 1.*

THEOREM 2.4. *For any migratory schedule on m related machines there exists a non-migratory schedule that simulates this schedule when every machine i is given $O(1+\epsilon)$ factor additional speed and there are $O(\frac{1}{\epsilon})$ copies of each machine for any $0 < \epsilon \le 1$.*

PROOF. For each job j, define its weight w_j to be $1/(d_j - r_j)$. Note that the given migratory schedule has the maximum weighted flow time of $(d_j - r_i)w_j = 1$. Theorem 2.3 implies the existence of a non-migratory schedule with 2-speed that has the maximum weighted flow time of at most $O(1)$. Note that in this non-migratory schedule each job must complete by time $r_j + O(1)/w_j = r_j + O(1) \cdot (d_j - r_j)$. Applying Lemma 2.2 with $\delta = O(1)$, $c = 1$ and $s = 2$ on each machine together with jobs on it, we can find a non-migratory schedule with $1+\gamma$ speed and $O(1/\gamma)$-machine augmentation. □

2.1 Related Machines with Restricted Assignment

We now consider the more challenging case where machines have different speeds and each job only can be assigned to a subset of machines. We call this setting as related machines setting with restricted assignment. The remainder of this section is devoted to proving Theorem 1.1. As before, we consider an arbitrary migratory schedule and set d_i to be the time job i is completed in the migratory schedule. Our goal will be to construct a non-migratory schedule that completes each job i during $[r_i, d_i]$.

For simplicity, we will use slowness factor instead of speeds – a machine with slowness factor s requires sp time steps to complete a job of size p. To begin with, we change the original migratory schedule in the following manner. Let $0 \le \epsilon < 1$ be some constant. We want to convert the schedule to another schedule that ensures a job i is only scheduled on machines j where $d_i - r_i \ge \frac{s_j p_i}{1+\epsilon}$. This is so that later we can apply Lemma 2.2. Note that $s_j p_i$ is the processing time of job i on machine j. To do this, notice that the total aggregate amount any job i can be processed on all machines j where $d_i - r_i < \frac{s_j p_i}{1+\epsilon}$ is $\frac{1}{1+\epsilon} p_i$ because a job can only be processed on one machine at any point in time and the job is completed during $[r_i, d_i]$. Using this, we can remove any portion of a job that is processed on any machine where $d_i - r_i < \frac{s_j p_i}{1+\epsilon}$. Then we use $\frac{1+\epsilon}{\epsilon}$ speed augmentation on each machine to ensure every job i is fully processed on machines j where $d_i - r_i \ge \frac{s_j p_i}{1+\epsilon}$. Then the total amount a job is processed on these faster machines is at least $p_i(1 - \frac{1}{1+\epsilon})\frac{1+\epsilon}{\epsilon} = p_i$.

To clarify notation for remainder of the proof, we scale the slowness of machines such that machine j has slowness $s'_j := s_j \cdot \frac{\epsilon}{1+\epsilon}$ and work with these new speeds. Note that now $d_i - r_i \ge \frac{s'_j p_i}{\epsilon}$ for any machine j job i is processed on. Now, we assume that each job i is further restricted so that it cannot be processed on a machine j where $d_i - r_i < \frac{s'_j p_i}{\epsilon}$. We will work with the modified instance. To show our main theorem, we will later reduce this $O(\frac{1}{\epsilon})$ speed augmentation by using additional machine augmentation.

Consider any machine j. For each machine j we create a laminar family of intervals: Intervals of length 1, $(0,1), (1,2), (2,3), \ldots$ are at the lowest level, and those of length 2^h, $(0, 2^h)$, $(1 \cdot 2^h, 2 \cdot 2^h)$, $(2 \cdot 2^h, 3 \cdot 2^h), \ldots$ are at the hth lowest level – the top level interval should be long enough to cover the whole schedule. The created intervals for machine j are denoted as $\mathcal{I}_j$. We let $I(j, k', l)$ denote the interval $[(l-1) \cdot 2^{k'}, l \cdot 2^{k'}]$ in $\mathcal{I}_i$.

We create a single-source-single-sink network flow graph G_k for *all* jobs with size in $[2^{k-1}, 2^k)$ as follows. The source and sink nodes are denoted as $q_{k,s}$ and $q_{k,t}$, respectively. There is a unique node for each job i where $p_i \in [2^{k-1}, 2^k)$; for notational simplicity, we also refer to the node as job node i. The source node $q_{k,s}$ is connected to each job node j with capacity 1. For each machine j we create a node for each interval in $\mathcal{I}_j$. Again, we abuse the notation $I(j, k', l)$ to denote the node created for the interval $I(j, k', l) \in \mathcal{I}_j$. Each job node i is connected to the interval node $I(j, k', l)$ if the following conditions hold: (1) The interval $I(j, k', l)$ intersects $[r_i, d_i]$; (2) job i is allowed to be scheduled on machine j (this is, j is not a restricted machine for job i); and $s'_j 2^k \in [2^{k'-1}, 2^{k'})$. The capacity of these edges are 1. We note that the set of interval nodes a job is connected to corresponds to the machines and time intervals where the job can be feasibly processed in the modified migratory schedule and the length of these intervals are within a factor 4 of the processing time of i on j.

Before we move to explaining how interval nodes are connected, we define $\tilde{x}_{kjI}$ to be the total fractional number of jobs of size in $[2^{k-1}, 2^k)$ processed on machine j during time interval I. In other words, $\tilde{x}_{kjI} = \sum_{i \,:\, p_i \in [2^{k-1}, 2^k)} \frac{p'_{i,j}}{p_i}$ where $p'_{i,j}$ is the amount job i is processed on machine j in the migratory schedule. Each interval node $I(i, k', l)$ is connected to its unique parent interval node $I(j, k'+1, \lceil l/2 \rceil)$ with capacity $\lceil \tilde{x}_{kjI} \rceil$ where $I = I(j, k', l)$. The top level interval node I' for machine j is connected to the sink node $q_{k,t}$ with capacity equal to $\lceil \tilde{x}_{kjI'} \rceil$. This completes the description of G_k.

We now explain how to find a non-migratory schedule using the network flow graphs we constructed above. We observe that there is a fractional flow respecting the capacity constraints for each graph G_k such that one unit of flow is pushed through each job node. Such a flow is achieved by a natural flow where an edge from each job node i with size in $[2^{k-1}, 2^k)$ sends flow directly to an interval node $I = I(j, k', l)$, for machine j, equal to the fractional amount job i processed during $I(j, k', l)$ on machine j. A total of unit flow is pushed from each job node i. The flow on other edges are defined following flow conservation. The total flow passing through an interval node I will be exactly $\tilde{x}_{kjI}$. For each G_k we find an integral max flow respecting the capacities. This integral flow can be interpreted as an assignment $\mathcal{A}$ of jobs i with size in $[2^{k-1}, 2^k)$ to intervals $I(j,k',l)$ where $s'_j 2^k \in [2^{k'-1}, 2^{k'})$. That is, a job i is matched to an interval I such that node i is directly connected to the interval node I. We say job i is matched to interval I if the node for I is directly connected to the node for j and a unit of flow passes from node i to node I. Our goal is to use this assignment to construct a feasible non-migratory schedule.

We observe that the discovered assignment $\mathcal{A}$ has the following properties. Recall that $\tilde{x}_{kjI}$ is the fractional number of jobs of size 2^k assigned to interval I on machine j.

CLAIM 2.5. *Let $\bar{x}_{kjI}$ denote the integer number of jobs of size in $[2^{k-1}, 2^k)$ assigned to an interval I on machine j under the assignment $\mathcal{A}$. Then, $\mathcal{A}$ has the following properties.*

1. $\bar{x}_{kjI} - \tilde{x}_{kjI} \leq 1$.
2. *$\mathcal{A}$ assigns each job i with size $p_i \in [2^{k-1}, 2^k)$ to a unique machine j and interval $I(j,k',l)$ whose length $2^{k'}$ is such that $s'_j 2^k \in [2^{k'-1}, 2^{k'})$. Further j is a feasible machine for i.*
3. *If $\mathcal{A}$ assigns job i to I, then the interval I is completely contained in $[r_j - 4(d_j - r_j), d_j + 4(d_j - r_j)]$.*

PROOF. The first property is immediate from the fact that $\mathcal{A}$ is derived from a flow respecting the capacity constraints. The second property follows from the fact that job node i is only directly connected to intervals nodes corresponding to machines that i can be feasibly scheduled on and have the desired length. To see why the third property holds, recall that in the modified migratory schedule job i can only be processed on machines j where $d_i - r_i \geq \frac{s'_j p_i}{\epsilon}$. Thus if job i is matched to an interval $I(j,k',l)$ on machine j then the length of $I(j,k',l)$, $2^{k'}$, must be less than $2s'_j 2^k \leq 4s'_j p_i \leq 4\epsilon(d_i - r_i) \leq 4(d_i - r_i)$. By definition of the flow networks, a job node i is only connected to interval nodes where $I(j,k',l)$ intersects $[r_j, d_j]$. Therefore, i's 4-extended window must include I. □

We now show that any interval $I(j,k',l)$ does not get assigned a lot more volume of jobs than it can handle over the assignment generated by combining the matchings from each graph G_k.

LEMMA 2.6. *Fix any machine j and consider an interval $I(j,k',l)$. Let $J(j,k',l)$ be the set of all jobs matched to an interval $I(j,k,l) \subseteq I(j,k',l)$, including $I(j,k',l)$ itself over all matchings found. The total processing time of the jobs in $J(j,k',l)$ on machine j, $s'_j \sum_{i \in J(j,k',l)} p_i$, is less than $4s'_j 2^{k'}$.*

PROOF. Fix any machine j and an interval $I(j,k',l)$. Consider a flow graph G_k and let k'' be such that $s'_j 2^k \in [2^{k''-1}, 2^{k''})$ and $k'' \leq k'$. Let $I = I(j,k',l)$. Notice that the total number of jobs with $p_i \in [2^{k-1}, 2^k)$ matched in G_k to an interval $I(j,k'',l) \subseteq I(j,k',l)$ is at most $\lceil \tilde{x}_{kjI} \rceil$. This is because node $I = I(j,k',l)$ in G_k has one outgoing edge of capacity $\lceil \tilde{x}_{kjI} \rceil$ and all flow through nodes $I(j,k'',l)$ where $I(j,k'',l) \subseteq I(j,k',l)$ must pass through node $I(j,k',l)$. We see that, $s'_j \sum_{i \in J(j,k',l), p_i \in [2^{k-1}, 2^k)} p_i \leq 2^{k''} \lceil \tilde{x}_{kjI} \rceil \leq 2^{k''}(\tilde{x}_{kjI} + 1)$.

Now our goal is to aggregate the processing time of all jobs over all matchings found to bound the processing time of jobs in $J(j,k',l)$. We see that,

$$\begin{aligned} & s'_j \sum_{i \in J(j,k',l)} p_i \\ \leq & \sum_{k \,:\, s'_j 2^k \in [2^{k''-1}, 2^{k''}), k'' \leq k'} 2^{k''}(\tilde{x}_{kjI} + 1) \\ \leq & \; 2^{k'+1} + \sum_{k \,:\, s'_j 2^k \in [2^{k''-1}, 2^{k''}), k'' \leq k'} 2^{k''} \tilde{x}_{kjI} \\ \leq & \; 2^{k'+1} + 2^{k'+1} \end{aligned}$$

The last inequality follows from the fact that the migratory schedule was able to processed a $\tilde{x}_{kjI}$ fraction of jobs of size in $[2^{k''-1}, 2^{k''})$ during $I(j,k',l)$ where $s'_j 2^k \in [2^{k''-1}, 2^{k''})$. □

We now apply Lemma 2.2 for each machine j. Recall that we scaled each machine's slowness to be $s'_j = s_j \frac{\epsilon}{1+\epsilon}$ at the beginning of the proof. We now want to convert back to the original problem instance while ensuring we have a feasible schedule. Notice that if each machine j runs with slowness $s'_j/4$ it can complete all jobs i such that i is only processed during $[r_j - 4(d_j - r_j), d_j + 4(d_j - r_j)]$ by the previous lemma. Further, we know by definition of the problem instance $d_i - r_i \geq \frac{s'_j p_i}{\epsilon} = \frac{s_j p_i}{1+\epsilon}$. We can then applying Lemma 2.2 for each machine j by assuming job i has processing time $s_j p_i$ on machine j, and setting $\delta = \frac{1}{4}$, $s = \frac{4(1+\epsilon)}{\epsilon}$, $c = \frac{1}{1+\epsilon}$ and $\gamma = 1 + 2\epsilon$. This give a desired non-migratory schedule where each machine j has speed-$(1+2\epsilon)s_j$ and there are $O(1/\epsilon^2)$ copies of machine j, which completes the proof of Theorem 1.1.

2.2 Lower Bound on Machine Augmentation

In this section, our goal is to show Theorem 1.2, showing that at least $\Omega(\frac{1}{\epsilon})$ machine augmentation is needed to covert a migratory schedule to a non-migratory schedule in the related machines setting.

Proof of [Theorem 1.2] Fix any constant $0 < \epsilon \leq 1/2$ and consider the following problem instance. There are n jobs of size 1 that are all released at time 0. There is a set M_1 of n speed-1 machines and a set M_2 of ϵn speed-5 machines. This completes the description of the instance.

First we show that there exists a migratory schedule that completes all of the jobs by time $1 - 2\epsilon$. Partition the jobs into groups $G_1, G_2, \ldots G_{\epsilon n}$ such that each group contains at most $\frac{1}{\epsilon}$ jobs. In the schedule, the jobs in group G_i is associated with a unique machine in M_2. Additionally, every job is associated with a unique machine in M_1. Each job in G_i is processed on the associated machine in M_2 for $\frac{\epsilon}{2}$ time steps during $[0, \frac{1}{2}]$. This can be done by say round robining the jobs in G_i on the machine. Every time step where a job is not being processed on a machine in M_2 the job is processed on its unique machine in M_1. Now we show that the jobs are competed by time $1 - 2\epsilon$. Indeed, each job receives $\frac{\epsilon}{2} \cdot 5$ amount of processing by a machine in M_2 and in the remaining $1 - \frac{\epsilon}{2} - 2\epsilon$ time steps during $[0, 1 - 2\epsilon]$ the jobs are processed on a machine in M_1 of speed 1. Thus, the amount of processing completed on a job is $\frac{\epsilon}{2}5 + 1 - \frac{\epsilon}{2} - 2\epsilon = 1$.

Now consider any non-migratory schedule with speed augmentation $1+\epsilon$ and at most $\frac{1}{10\epsilon}$ machine augmentation. Let M_1' denote all of machines of speed $1+\epsilon$ in this schedule and M_2' denote the machines of speed $5(1+\epsilon)$. We will show that this schedule will not be able to complete all of the jobs by time $1 - 2\epsilon$. First notice that no job can be scheduled on a machine in M_1' because then the job will not complete until time $\frac{1}{1+\epsilon} > 1 - 2\epsilon$ for $0 < \epsilon \leq 1$. Thus, all of the jobs are scheduled on machines in M_2'. There are $\frac{1}{10\epsilon} \cdot \epsilon n = \frac{n}{10}$ such machines. Thus there must be some machine that is assigned 10 jobs. However, these jobs then do not finish until time $10/(5(1+\epsilon)) > 1 - 2\epsilon$. □

We note that in the proof that one machines with two different speeds are needed and the speeds are bounded by a constant factor of each other. Notice that this theorem implies the following corollary.

COROLLARY 2.7. *Machine augmentation (and no speed augmentation) is insufficient to convert a migratory schedule to a non-migratory schedule.*

3. PROFIT SCHEDULING ON UNRELATED MACHINES

In this section, we consider the following general profit scheduling problem in the online setting. There is a set of m unrelated machines. There are n jobs which arrive over time where job i has release time is r_i and each job i is associated with a function $g_i(t)$. The function $g_i(t)$ specifies the profit of completing job i at time t and the only assumption made on g_i is that it is non-increasing. That is, there should be no additional profit for making a job wait longer to be completed. Notice the each job has its own *individual* profit function. Each job i has a processing time $p_{i,j}$ on machine j. The goal of scheduler, which completes each job i at a time C_i, is to maximize $\sum_{i\in[n]} g_i(C_i)$.

We now define our algorithm which is inspired by [2, 12]. We assume the algorithm is given $1+\epsilon$ speed augmentation for some $\epsilon > 0$ and we compare against a non-migratory adversary. The algorithm is non-migratory and when a job arrives it commits to the machine that will schedule the job. However, since we are in the profit setting, the scheduler may later decide not to schedule the job at all since there maybe higher profit jobs to schedule. When a job arrives the scheduler will associate it with a set of intervals I_i, which is intuitively are the times the scheduler is allowed to schedule the job. These intervals will be fixed the moment a job arrives as well as the machine the job is to be scheduled on. Let $A_j(t)$ be the set of all jobs which have been assigned to machine j by the algorithm by time t and let m_i denote the machine job i is assigned to. Note that the processing time of job i in the algorithm's schedule is then p_{i,m_i}. The total aggregate length of the intervals in I_i will be exactly $\frac{1+\epsilon/2}{1+\epsilon}p_{i,m_i}$. Implicit in the intervals I_i will be a time t_i where the algorithm hopes to complete job i by. We call this the *tentative* completion time. Given the tentative completion time of job i, let $w_i = g_i(t_i)$ be the potential profit of job i if we complete it before this completion time. Note that since g_i is non-decreasing, if we complete i before t_i the algorithm obtains at least w_i profit for job i. Finally, we define the *density* of job i to be $\frac{w_i}{p_{i,m_i}}$, the potential profit of the job in the algorithm's schedule divided by the processing time.

Now consider when job i arrives at time r_i. The algorithm considers each machine j and time t. When considering i and t, the algorithm tests if on machine j the time t is a good candidate tentative completion time. Let $w_i = g_i(t)$ be the potential profit of completing job i at time t. For a fixed constant α, to be set later, let $S(\frac{w_i}{\alpha})$ be the set of jobs assigned to machine j with density at least $\frac{w_i}{\alpha}$. Let I be the set of maximal time intervals during $[r_j, t]$ that do not overlap with any interval in $I_{i'}$ for a job $i' \in S(\frac{w_i}{\alpha})$. The time t is feasible if the total length of intervals in I is at least $\frac{1+\epsilon/2}{1+\epsilon}p_{i,j}$. After testing this for all machines and times, the algorithm assigns job i to the machine j with the *earliest* feasible tentative completion time and sets I_i to be the set of associated intervals for the machine and time. Note that there is always such a feasible time by allowing t to be sufficiently large.

So far, we have specified how to assign jobs to machine. As for which job to execute on each machine, at time t on machine j the algorithm schedules the job i which has the highest density *and* t is contained in some interval in I_i.

3.1 Analysis

We begin by making a few observations about the algorithm, similar to what was shown in [2].

CLAIM 3.1. *Consider any job i and machine j (which i may or may not have been assigned to). Let t be any time where $t \geq r_i + p_{i,j}$ and the algorithm sets the tentative completion time of i to be strictly later than t. Let L be the amount of time during $[r_i, t]$ which is contained in time intervals in any $I_{i'}$ associated with a job i' assigned to machine j which has density at least $\frac{g_i(t)}{\alpha p_{i,j}}$. It must be the case that $L \geq \frac{\epsilon/2}{1+\epsilon}(t - r_i)$.*

PROOF. If L is less than $\frac{\epsilon/2}{1+\epsilon}(t - r_i)$ than t is a feasible time for job i. Since t is earlier than the tentative completion time job i, this contradicts the definition of the algorithm. □

CLAIM 3.2. *For any two jobs i and i' assigned to the same machine j where I_i and $I_{i'}$ contain intervals that overlap then $u_i > \alpha\frac{w_{i'}}{p_{i',j}}$ or $u_{i'} > \alpha\frac{w_i}{p_{i,j}}$.*

PROOF. The proof of the previous claim follows by definition of I_i and $I_{i'}$. □

Let C be the set of jobs completed by the algorithm. We begin by showing that the profit of the job's completed by the algorithm is close to the profit that algorithm would have obtained if it completed all jobs by their tentative completion times.

LEMMA 3.3. *The total profit obtained for jobs in C is at least as much as $(1 - \frac{2+\epsilon}{4\epsilon(\alpha-1)}) \sum_{i\in[n]} w_i$, which is $(1 - \frac{2+\epsilon}{4\epsilon(\alpha-1)})$ multiplied by the total profit the algorithm would have obtained if it completed all jobs by the tentative completion time.*

PROOF. We will utilize a charging scheme separately for each machine j. For each job i in C we allocated w_i units of profit. This profit will be transferred to other jobs ensuring that every job i' receives $(1 - \frac{2+\epsilon}{4\epsilon(\alpha-1)})w_{i'}$ units of profit, proving the lemma. For any time t, let $X_{t,j}$ be the set of jobs i assigned to machine j that has an interval in I_i which contains t. The job i with the highest density in $X_{t,j}$ transfers profit to the other jobs in $X_{t,j}$ an amount of $(\frac{1+\epsilon}{2\epsilon})\frac{w_i}{p_{i,j}}$ for t.

The proof will follow by showing that each job must have w_i units of profit assigned to it and by showing that not too much profit is transferred out of the job. For each job in C, it is assigned w_i units of profit. For any job i assigned to machine j which is not completed, it must be the case that the algorithm was executing a more dense job for $\frac{\epsilon}{2(1+\epsilon)}p_{i,j}$ units of time contained in I_i by definition of the algorithm. Knowing that any job i' is only executed at a time during an interval $I_{i'}$, the total credit transferred to i is at least $\frac{1+\epsilon}{2\epsilon}p_{i,j}(\frac{1+\epsilon}{2\epsilon})\frac{w_i}{p_{i,j}} = w_i$. Thus, every job is assigned w_i profit.

Now, we show that no job i has $\frac{2+\epsilon}{4\epsilon(\alpha-1)}w_i$ profit transferred to other jobs. Consider any time t and machine j. By Claim 3.2 it is the case that the jobs i' in $X_{t,j}$ have geometrically decreasing densities on machine j. Let i be the job in $X_{t,j}$ with the highest density. The total profit transferred from job i at time t is $(\frac{1+\epsilon}{2\epsilon})\frac{w_i}{p_{i,j}}\sum_{k=1}^{\infty}\frac{1}{\alpha^k} \leq (\frac{1+\epsilon}{2\epsilon(\alpha-1)})\frac{w_i}{p_{i,j}}$. Knowing that the total amount of time in I_i is $\frac{1+\epsilon/2}{1+\epsilon}p_{i,j}$ the total amount transferred out of job i is $\frac{1+\epsilon/2}{1+\epsilon}p_{i,j}(\frac{1+\epsilon}{2\epsilon(\alpha-1)})\frac{w_i}{p_{i,j}} = \frac{2+\epsilon}{4\epsilon(\alpha-1)}w_i$. Thus, every job i is finally assigned $(1 - \frac{2+\epsilon}{4\epsilon(\alpha-1)})w_i$ profit. □

We have now shown that the total profit the algorithm obtains is close to the total profit the algorithm would have received if it completed jobs by their tentative completion times. Our final goal is to bound the total profit the algorithm would have obtained if it completed jobs by their tentative completion time by the profit the adversary obtains, which will complete the analysis. Let $P^*(X)$ be the profit he adversary obtains for a set of jobs X and $P(X)$ be the profit the algorithm obtains for a set of jobs in X if it completed the jobs in X by their tentative completion times. Let A_1 be the set of jobs i where the algorithm sets the tentative completion time i to earlier than when the adversary completes i. Let A_2 be the remaining jobs. Clearly $P(A_1) \geq P^*(A_1)$ since the jobs' profit functions are non-increasing. Thus, our goal is to bound $P^*(A_2)$ by the profit the algorithm obtains.

Consider some machine j. Let $A^*_{2,j}$ (resp. $A_{2,j}$) be the set of jobs the adversary (resp. algorithm) processes on machine j that are contained in A_2 and similarly let $A^*_{1,j}$ (resp. $A_{1,j}$) be the jobs the adversary (resp. algorithm) processes on machine j that are contained in A_1. Our goal will be to bound the profit the adversary receives for these jobs by the total profit the algorithm would have received if it completed all jobs assigned to machine j by their tentative deadline. Let C^*_i be the completion time of job i in the adversary's schedule and let $w^*_i = g_i(C^*)$ be the profit the adversary obtains for job i. Let $L^*_j(u)$ denote the total length of time where the adversary is scheduling a job on machine j whose density in the adversary schedule is at least u. That is, $\frac{w^*_i}{p_{i,j}} \geq u$ for a job i assigned to machine j in the adversary's schedule. Let $L_j(\frac{u}{\alpha})$ be the total length of times t such that there is at least one job i in the algorithm's schedule assigned to j where t is contained in an interval in I_i and $\frac{w_i}{p_{i,j}} \geq \frac{u}{\alpha}$.

LEMMA 3.4. *For all machines j and all $u > 0$, $L^*_j(u) \leq \frac{4(1+\epsilon)}{\epsilon}L(\frac{u}{\alpha})$*

PROOF. Fix a machine j. We define $[r_i, C^*_i]$ to be the window of job i in the adversary's schedule. Let W^*_j be the set of windows for jobs in $A^*_{2,j}$ whose density $\frac{w^*_j}{p_{i,j}}$ is at least u in the adversary's schedule. Let M be a minimum subset of jobs in $A^*_{2,j}$ where $\frac{w^*_j}{p_{i,j}} \geq u$ whose windows span every time contained in a window in W^*_j. By minimality, it is the case that no three job in M contain the same time in their window. Thus, we can partition M into two sets M_1 and M_2 such that no two jobs in M_1 (respectively M_2) have overlapping windows. Without loss of generality, assume that the total length of the windows for jobs in M_1 is longer. Note that the length of the windows in M_1 is at least half of the total amount of time contained in the union of the windows in W^*_j.

Now consider any job i in M_1. We know that the adversary scheduled job i on machine j during $[r_i, C^*_i]$ and therefore $C^*_i - r_i \geq p_{i,j}$. Further, we know that since $i \in A^*_{2,j}$ the algorithm's tentative completion time of i is later than C^*_i. Thus, by Claim 3.1 it must be the case that the amount of time during $[r_i, C^*_i]$ which is contained in some interval in $I_{i'}$ for a job i' assigned to machine j by the algorithm whose density is at least $\frac{w^*_i}{\alpha p_{i,j}}$, is at least $\frac{\epsilon/2}{1+\epsilon}(C^*_i - r_i)$. Knowing that this holds for all jobs in M_1 and M_1 is at least half of the total amount of time content in the union of jobs in W^*_j, we have the lemma. □

Now we are ready to bound $P^*(A^*_{2,j})$, the total profit the adversary obtains for jobs in A_2 processed on machine j by $P(A_{1,j} \cup A_{2,j})$ the profit the algorithm would obtain if it completed all jobs by their tentative completion time which were assigned to machine j.

LEMMA 3.5. $P^*(A^*_{2,j}) \leq \frac{\alpha 4(1+\epsilon)}{\epsilon}P(A_{1,j} \cup A_{2,j})$

PROOF. Consider the set of jobs in $A^*_{2,j}$. Let $k = |A^*_{2,j}|$ and consider sorting the jobs in $A^*_{2,j}$ from

$1, 2, \ldots k$ by their densities in the adversary's schedule $\frac{w_i^*}{p_{i,j}}$ in decreasing order. For ease of notation let there be a job $k+1$ where $\frac{w_{k+1}^*}{p_{k+1,j}} = 0$. By Lemma 3.4 we know that for every u, $L_j^*(u) \leq \frac{4(1+\epsilon)}{\epsilon} L(\frac{u}{\alpha})$. In particular, for $u = \frac{w_i^*}{p_{i,j}}$ for a job $i \in A_{2,j}^*$, it is the case that

$$\sum_{i' \in A_{2,j}^*, i' \leq i} p_{i',j} = L_j^*(\frac{w_i^*}{p_{i,j}}) \leq \frac{4(1+\epsilon)}{\epsilon} L(\frac{\frac{w_i^*}{p_{i,j}}}{\alpha}) \quad (1)$$

$$= \frac{4(1+\epsilon)}{\epsilon} \sum_{i' \in A_{1,j} \cup A_{2,j}, \frac{w_i^*}{p_{i,j}\alpha} \leq \frac{w_{i'}}{p_{i',j}}} p_{i',j}. \quad (2)$$

Using this, we have the following,

$$\begin{aligned}
P^*(A_{2,j}^*) &= \sum_{i \in A_{2,j}^*} w_i^* \\
&= \sum_{i \in A_{2,j}^*} p_{i,j} \sum_{i' \in A_{2,j}^*, i' \geq i} (\frac{w_{i'}^*}{p_{i',j}} - \frac{w_{i'+1}^*}{p_{i'+1,j}}) \\
&\qquad [\text{Telescoping summation and } \tfrac{w_{k+1}^*}{p_{k+1,j}} = 0] \\
&= \sum_{i \in A_{2,j}^*} (\frac{w_i^*}{p_{i,j}} - \frac{w_{i+1}^*}{p_{i+1,j}}) \sum_{i' \in A_{2,j}^*, i' \leq i} p_{i',j} \\
&\leq \frac{4(1+\epsilon)}{\epsilon} \sum_{i \in A_{2,j}^*} (\frac{w_i^*}{p_{i,j}} - \frac{w_{i+1}^*}{p_{i+1,j}}) \\
&\qquad \cdot \sum_{i' \in A_{1,j} \cup A_{2,j}, \frac{w_i^*}{p_{i,j}\alpha} \leq \frac{w_{i'}}{p_{i',j}}} p_{i',j} \quad [\text{Equation (2)}] \\
&= \frac{4(1+\epsilon)}{\epsilon} \sum_{i \in A_{1,j} \cup A_{2,j}} p_{i,j} \\
&\qquad \cdot \sum_{i' \in A_{2,j}^*, \frac{w_{i'}^*}{\alpha p_{i',j}} \leq \frac{w_i}{p_{i,j}}} (\frac{w_{i'}^*}{p_{i,j}} - \frac{w_{i'+1}^*}{p_{i'+1,j}}) \\
&\leq \frac{4(1+\epsilon)}{\epsilon} \sum_{i \in A_{1,j} \cup A_{2,j}} p_{i,j} \alpha \frac{w_i}{p_{i,j}} \\
&\leq \frac{\alpha 4(1+\epsilon)}{\epsilon} \sum_{i \in A_{1,j} \cup A_{2,j}} w_i \\
&= \frac{\alpha 4(1+\epsilon)}{\epsilon} P(A_{1,j} \cup A_{2,j})
\end{aligned}$$

□

THEOREM 3.6. *There is a $(1+\epsilon)$-speed $O(\frac{1}{\epsilon^2})$-competitive algorithm for any $0 < \epsilon \leq 1$ on related machine.*

PROOF. The total profit obtained by the adversary is $\sum_{j=1}^m P^*(A_1^*) + P^*(A_2^*)$. By definition, we know that $\sum_{j=1}^m P^*(A_1^*)$ is a most the profit the algorithm obtains for jobs in A_1, $\sum_{j=1}^m P(A_{1,j})$. By Lemma 3.5 we know that $P^*(A_{2,j}^*) \leq \frac{\alpha 4(1+\epsilon)}{\epsilon} P(A_{1,j} \cup A_{2,j})$. Thus, $\sum_{j=1}^m P^*(A_1^*) + P^*(A_2^*) \leq (1 + \frac{\alpha 4(1+\epsilon)}{\epsilon}) \sum_{j=1}^m P(A_{1,j} \cup A_{2,j})$.

Now recall that $P(A_{1,j} \cup A_{2,j})$ is the total profit the algorithm would obtain for all jobs assigned to machine j if they were completed by their tentative completion time and C is the set of jobs completed by the algortihm. By Lemma 3.3 we know that $\sum_{j=1}^m P(A_{1,j} \cup A_{2,j}) \leq (\frac{4\epsilon(\alpha-1)-(2+\epsilon)}{4\epsilon(\alpha-1)}) \sum_{i \in C} w_i$. Thus, we have that $\sum_{j=1}^m P^*(A_1^*) + P^*(A_2^*) \leq (1 + \frac{\alpha 4(1+\epsilon)}{\epsilon})(\frac{4\epsilon(\alpha-1)-(2+\epsilon)}{4\epsilon(\alpha-1)}) \sum_{i \in C} w_i$. Setting $\alpha = 1 + \frac{1}{\epsilon}$ completes the proof. □

Acknowledgements

S. Im was supported in part by NSF grant CCF-1409130. B. Moseley was supported in part by a Google Research Award and a Yahoo Research Award.

4. REFERENCES

[1] S. Anand, Karl Bringmann, Tobias Friedrich, Naveen Garg, and Amit Kumar. Minimizing maximum (weighted) flow-time on related and unrelated machines. In *Automata, Languages, and Programming - 40th International Colloquium, ICALP 2013*, pages 13–24, 2013.

[2] Nikhil Bansal, Ho-Leung Chan, and Kirk Pruhs. Competitive algorithms for due date scheduling. *Algorithmica*, 59(4):569–582, 2011.

[3] Sanjoy K. Baruah, Gilad Koren, Decao Mao, Bhubaneswar Mishra, Arvind Raghunathan, Louis E. Rosier, Dennis Shasha, and Fuxing Wang. On the competitiveness of on-line real-time task scheduling. *Real-Time Systems*, 4(2):125–144, 1992.

[4] Sanjoy K. Baruah, Gilad Koren, Bhubaneswar Mishra, Arvind Raghunathan, Louis E. Rosier, and Dennis Shasha. On-line scheduling in the presence of overload. In *Symposium on Foundations of Computer Science*, pages 100–110, 1991.

[5] Ho-Leung Chan, Tak Wah Lam, and Kar-Keung To. Non-migratory online deadline scheduling on multiprocessors. In *Proceedings of the Fifteenth Annual ACM-SIAM Symposium on Discrete Algorithms, SODA 2004, New Orleans, Louisiana, USA, January 11-14, 2004*, pages 970–979, 2004.

[6] Bala Kalyanasundaram and Kirk Pruhs. Fault-tolerant real-time scheduling. *Algorithmica*, 28(1):125–144, 2000.

[7] Bala Kalyanasundaram and Kirk Pruhs. Speed is as powerful as clairvoyance. *J. ACM*, 47(4):617–643, 2000.

[8] Bala Kalyanasundaram and Kirk Pruhs. Eliminating migration in multi-processor scheduling. *J. Algorithms*, 38(1):2–24, 2001.

[9] Chiu-Yuen Koo, Tak Wah Lam, Tsuen-Wan Ngan, and Kar-Keung To. Extra processors versus future information in optimal deadline scheduling. *Theory Comput. Syst.*, 37(3):323–341, 2004.

[10] Gilad Koren and Dennis Shasha. MOCA: A multiprocessor on-line competitive algorithm for real-time system scheduling. *Theor. Comput. Sci.*, 128(1&2):75–97, 1994.

[11] Gilad Koren and Dennis Shasha. Dover: An optimal on-line scheduling algorithm for overloaded uniprocessor real-time systems. *SIAM J. Comput.*, 24(2):318–339, 1995.

[12] Kirk Pruhs and Clifford Stein. How to schedule when you have to buy your energy. In *Approximation, Randomization, and Combinatorial Optimization. Algorithms and Techniques, 13th International Workshop, APPROX 2010, and 14th International Workshop, RANDOM 2010, Barcelona, Spain, September 1-3, 2010. Proceedings*, pages 352–365, 2010.

[13] Gerhard J. Woeginger. On-line scheduling of jobs with fixed start and end times. *Theor. Comput. Sci.*, 130(1):5–16, 1994.

The Power of Migration in Online Machine Minimization*

Lin Chen
Magyar Tudományos Akadémia (MTA SZTAKI)
Budapest, Hungary
chenlin198662@gmail.com

Nicole Megow
Technische Universität München
Zentrum Mathematik
Garching, Germany
nmegow@ma.tum.de

Kevin Schewior
Technische Universität München
Zentrum Mathematik
Garching, Germany
schewior@ma.tum.de

ABSTRACT

In this paper we investigate the power of migration in online scheduling on multiple parallel machines. The problem is to schedule preemptable jobs with release dates and deadlines on a minimum number of machines. We show that migration, that is, allowing that a preempted job is continued on a different machine, has a huge impact on the performance of a schedule. More precisely, let m be the number of machines required by a migratory solution; then the increase in the number of machines when disallowing migration is unbounded in m. This complements and strongly contrasts previous results on variants of this problem. In both the offline variant and a model allowing extra speed, the power of migration is limited as the increase of number of machines and speed, respectively, can be bounded by a small constant.

In this paper, we also derive the first non-trivial bounds on the competitive ratio for non-migratory online scheduling to minimize the number of machines without extra speed. We show that in general no online algorithm can achieve a competitive ratio of $f(m)$, for any function f, and give a lower bound of $\Omega(\log n)$. For agreeable instances and instances with "loose" jobs, we give $\mathcal{O}(1)$-competitive algorithms and, for laminar instances, we derive an $\mathcal{O}(\log m)$-competitive algorithm.

1. INTRODUCTION

It is a central problem in operating real-time systems to schedule preemptable jobs that arrive online over time with hard deadlines on multiple identical processors. When a job is preempted, it can resume processing at any time later. A schedule is *migratory* if a preempted job may continue processing on a different machine, whereas in a *non-migratory* schedule each job is processed by exactly one machine. In practice, non-migratory schedules are highly favored because migration may cause a significant overhead in communication and synchronization and it increases the risk of cache-failures. On the other hand, migratory schedules may be easier to design and have a better performance.

In this paper we investigate the power of migration in online scheduling with the objective of minimizing the number of machines. We show that migration has a huge impact on the performance of a schedule. More precisely, we construct instances with n jobs which can be processed by a migratory offline schedule on m machines, while any online non-migratory schedule requires at least $\max\{\Omega(\log n), f(m)\}$ machines for any function f. Informally speaking, preempting jobs is not worth it if we do not allow migration. Indeed, if migration is allowed then there is an online algorithm that finds a schedule on $\mathcal{O}(m \log m)$ machines [4], while otherwise not even an exponential number of machines (in m) is sufficient.

Our result complements and strongly contrasts previous results on the offline variant of our problem and on online scheduling with extra speed. Indeed, for those problems it has been shown that migration is actually of limited power [3, 7]; more details are given below. Our result also settles an open question raised in [3].

Leveraging the result on the offline variant of our problem [7], our lower-bound construction can be used to show the same bounds also on the *competitive ratio* of online non-migratory scheduling, that is, comparing an online non-migratory schedule to the optimal *non-migratory* schedule. In fact, these bounds are the first non-trivial bounds on the competitive ratio for online non-migratory scheduling to minimize the number of machines.

For relevant special cases of the problem, we show that the power of migration is much weaker. We derive an $\mathcal{O}(\log m)$-competitive non-migratory algorithm for instances with laminar time windows and even $\mathcal{O}(1)$-competitive algorithms for instances with agreeable time windows or "loose" jobs with a processing time being at most a constant fraction of the time window.

Further related results.

The online machine minimization problem under free migration has been investigated extensively by Phillips et al. [10]. For a natural greedy algorithm called *Least Laxity First* (LLF), they show a competitive ratio of $\mathcal{O}(\log \Delta)$ whereas the even simpler and classic *Earliest Deadline First* (EDF) algorithm, has a lower bound of $\Omega(\Delta)$. Both algorithms may preempt and migrate jobs many times. Only recently, a more sophisticated algorithm with competitive

*This research was supported by the German Science Foundation (DFG) under contract ME 3825/1. The third author was supported by the DFG within the research training group 'Methods for Discrete Structures' (GRK 1408).

SPAA '16, July 11-13, 2016, Pacific Grove, CA, USA
© 2016 ACM. ISBN 978-1-4503-4210-0/16/07...$15.00
DOI: http://dx.doi.org/10.1145/2935764.2935786

ratio $\mathcal{O}(\log m)$ has been derived [4]. Despite this improvement, there remains a huge gap to the best known lower bound on the competitive ratio of 5/4 [10].

The non-preemptive (and thus non-migratory) variant of the problem is hopeless in terms of competitiveness. Saha [11] ruled out the existence of an algorithm with competitive ratio $f(m)$, for any computable function f. She gave a lower bound of $\Omega(\log \Delta)$ or n on the competitive ratio, complemented by an $\mathcal{O}(\log \Delta)$-competitive algorithm. (An upper bound of n is obvious.) However, in the special case of unit processing times, which was also studied implicitly in the context of energy minimization [1], the optimal online algorithm has the exact competitive ratio of $e \approx 2.72$ [1,5].

In the related speed-augmentation problem, an online algorithm has access to higher-speed machines instead of a larger number of machines than the offline adversary. This problem under free migration is quite well understood in the sense that online algorithms with a speed requirement of roughly 2 are known [9,10]. Also trade-offs between speed and machine augmentation were considered for this setting in [9].

For non-migratory online scheduling, there only exist results involving speed augmentation. Chan, Lam, and To [3] gave an algorithm with speed requirement 5.828 in the pure speed-augmentation model, that is, using the same number of machines as the offline migratory optimum. Concerning trade-offs, they also give an algorithm that requires $\lceil(1+1/\varepsilon)^2\rceil \cdot m$ speed-$(1+\varepsilon)^2$ machines for any $\varepsilon > 0$. They state as an open question if there exists a non-migratory online algorithm using only $f(m)$ speed-1 machines, where f is a function on m, on instances for which there is a migratory optimum solution on m machines [3].

The power of migration for machine minimization has been investigated also in the offline setting, in which all jobs are known in advance [7,8]. In particular, Kalyanasundaram and Pruhs [7] have shown that any migratory solution on m machines can be transformed into a non-migratory solution on $6m - 5$ machines.

It is noteworthy that the preemptive migratory offline problem can be solved in polynomial time by modeling it as a linear program or maximum flow problem [6].

Our contribution.

Our main result is to rule out the existence of non-migratory online algorithms that can guarantee to find a schedule using a number of machines, that is independent of the number of jobs n or their processing times. More precisely, any non-migratory online algorithm may require $\Omega(\log n)$ many machines, whereas a migratory schedule on $m \geq 3$ machines exists. Note that when allowing migration, then it is possible to construct a feasible online schedule on $\mathcal{O}(m \log m)$ machines [4].

To the best of our knowledge, our lower bound is the first non-trivial result on the non-migratory scheduling problem without speed augmentation, and it answers an open question raised in [3]. We derive the lower bound by a recursive construction in which any *non-migratory* online algorithm spreads jobs over machines in such a way that releasing another job forces it to open a new machine. This is inherently different from previous lower-bound constructions [9,10] (for *migratory* algorithms), in which any algorithm (using too little resources) is forced to open a new machine because it has delayed the wrong jobs and needs to finish too much aggregate volume by a certain deadline.

Our lower-bound result does not only complement previous results on the power of migration, it also strongly contrasts them. Firstly, in the offline setting of our problem, every migratory schedule can be transformed into a non-migratory one by increasing the number of machines only by a small constant factor [7]. Secondly, a small (factor 5.83) increase in the speed is sufficient for an online algorithm to find a non-migratory schedule on the same number of machine, m, as the optimal migratory schedule [3]. Thus, migration has a rather negligible power in offline scheduling or when having extra speed, but it has a huge impact—even unbounded in m—for our online problem.

Competitive analysis is the major concept for evaluating the performance of online algorithms. Instead of comparing the performance of an online non-migratory algorithm with an optimal *migratory* schedule, one compares here with an optimal *non-migratory* schedule. A close connection between both ratios is not too difficult to see, and we describe our further results using the notion of competitive ratios. Indeed, we give the first competitiveness results for our non-migratory scheduling complementing earlier results that required speed-augmentation [3].

- Our strong lower bound above, implies a general lower bound of $\Omega(\log n)$ on the competitive ratio for non-migratory scheduling.

However, we identify a number of special cases which admit $\mathcal{O}(\log m)$- or even $\mathcal{O}(1)$-competitive algorithms.

The first special case occurs if all jobs have a processing time that is at most a constant fraction, say $\alpha \in (0,1)$, of the respective job time interval. We call these jobs α-loose.

- For instances consisting only of α-loose jobs we give an $\mathcal{O}(1)$-competitive algorithm. The high-level idea is very simple. We use a known algorithm with a performance guarantee based on speed-augmentation from [3] as a black box. To do so, we increase the processing times of our jobs by a certain factor (guided by the guaranteed speed-factor) and apply the black-box algorithm. Then we transform back the resulting schedule into a feasible schedule on unit-speed machines for the original instance. The tricky part is to relate the minimum number of machines required by the original instance to the number needed by the modified instance. Our key result is an upper bound on this increase, which might be of independent interest.

Other special cases are agreeable and laminar instances which are widely believed to be the most important complementary special cases for scheduling jobs with time intervals. Instances are *agreeable*, if no intersecting time windows are fully contained in one another. For *laminar* instances it holds that whenever the time windows of two jobs intersect then they are fully contained in each other.

- We provide an $\mathcal{O}(\log m)$-competitive algorithm for laminar instances. With the above result for α-loose jobs, we only need to consider the remaining jobs. For those we design an algorithm which is inspired by an $\mathcal{O}(\log m)$-competitive algorithm for the general preemptive problem [4] and from which we carefully eliminate migration.

- For agreeable instances, we achieve a competitive ratio of $\mathcal{O}(1)$. Our algorithm is very simple and constructs even a non-preemptive solution. One may wonder, if agreeable instances are even trivial to solve. We answer this negatively by giving the first non-trivial lower bound, $6 - 2\sqrt{6} \approx 1.10$, on the competitive ratio for agreeable instances, even for the migratory problem.

Note that these positive results for special cases also justify the complexity of our lower-bound construction; a construction as simple as the one in Saha's lower bound for the non-preemptive problem [11], in which all jobs are α-loose and form a laminar instance, is not possible in our case.

Outline.

In Section 2, we formally define the problem and give some structural results. We construct the strong lower bound in Section 3. In Section 4, we give an $\mathcal{O}(1)$-competitive algorithm for instances consisting of α-loose jobs. We derive $\mathcal{O}(\log m)$- and $\mathcal{O}(1)$-competitive algorithms for laminar and agreeable instances in Sections 5 and 6, respectively.

2. PRELIMINARIES

Problem definition.

We are given a set of n jobs where each job $j \in \{1, 2, \dots, n\}$ has a processing time $p_j \in \mathbb{Q}$, a release date $r_j \in \mathbb{Q}$ which is the earliest possible time at which the job can be processed, and a deadline $d_j \in \mathbb{Q}$ by which it must be completed. The task is to determine a feasible preemptive schedule on a minimum number of identical parallel machines. In a feasible schedule each job j is scheduled for p_j units of time within the time window $[r_j, d_j)$. Each machine can process at most one job at the time, and no job is running on multiple machines at the same time. We allow job preemption, i.e., a job can be preempted at any moment in time and may resume processing later. We distinguish migratory and non-migratory preemptive schedules. In a migratory schedule, a preempted job may resume processing on an arbitrary machine, whereas in the non-migratory setting, each job is processed on exactly one machine.

In this paper we focus our investigations on the performance of non-migratory online algorithms compared to a migratory offline optimum. However, we note a direct connection to *competitive analysis*, the standard method to evaluate the performance of online algorithms; see, e.g., [2]. The difference is that in competitive analysis we compare the performance of an online algorithm with an optimal offline solution within the *same* problem setting with respect to migration (and or preemption). In this paper, we give first non-trivial bounds on the competitive ratio of non-migrative online algorithms. In general, we call an online algorithm *ρ-competitive* if m' machines with $m' \leq \rho \cdot \mathsf{OPT}$ suffice to guarantee a feasible solution for any instance that admits a feasible schedule on OPT machines.

Throughout this paper we assume that the optimum number of machines is known to the online algorithm. It has been shown in [4] that we can do so at the loss of a small constant factor in the competitive ratio.

Notation.

We denote the *(processing) interval* of job j by $I(j) = [r_j, d_j)$, and we say j *covers* each time point $t \in I(j)$. For a set of jobs S, we define $I(S) = \cup_{j \in S} I(j)$. For $I = \cup_{i=1}^{k} [a_i, b_i)$ where $[a_1, b_1), \dots, [a_k, b_k)$ are pairwise disjoint, we define the *length* of I to be $|I| = \sum_{i=1}^{k} (b_i - a_i)$.

We distinguish jobs by the relation between processing volume of a job and the length of its interval. We call a job *α-loose*, for some $\alpha < 1$, if $p_j \leq \alpha(d_j - r_j)$ and *α-tight* otherwise.

The *laxity* of a job j is defined as $\ell_j = d_j - r_j - p_j$. The remaining processing time of j at time t is denoted by $p_j(t)$.

Characterization of the optimum.

The optimal number of machines can be characterized based on the work load of jobs to be processed in certain time intervals [4]. Interestingly, in [4] only the lower bound on m was used. Now, in this new work we crucially employ the exact characterization, that is, lower and upper bound.

Given a finite union of intervals $I \subset \mathbb{R}$, let the *contribution* of a job j to I be $C(j, I) := \max\{0, |I \cap I(j)| - \ell_j\}$, i.e., the least amount of processing that j receives during I in any feasible schedule. Let the contribution of a job set S to I, denoted by $C(S, I)$, be the sum of the individual contributions of jobs in S.

THEOREM 1 ([4]). *Let m be the minimum number of machines needed to schedule a given job set S feasibly. There exists a finite union of intervals I with $\lceil C(S, I)/|I| \rceil = m$ but none with $\lceil C(S, I)/|I| \rceil > m$.*

Power of migration and competitive ratio.

The performance of non-migratory online scheduling compared to migratory offline scheduling is closely related to the competitive ratio for non-migrative scheduling. In fact, we observe that they are equal up to a constant factor.

LEMMA 1. *Let f and g be functions in m, the optimal number of machines in a migratory schedule. The following two statements are equivalent for some $g \in \Theta(f)$.*

(a) There is an online algorithm that computes a non-migratory schedule on $f(m) \cdot m$ machines for any instance, for which there is a migratory schedule on m machines.

(b) There is a $g(m)$-competitive online algorithm for non-migratory scheduling.

To see that, the following result by Kalyanasundaram and Pruhs [7] will become handy.

THEOREM 2 ([7]). *Any feasible migratory schedule on m machines can be turned (offline) into a feasible non-migratory schedule on $6m - 5$ machines.*

PROOF OF LEMMA 1. For a given instance, let m be the number of machines used in an optimal migratory schedule and let OPT be the number of machines in an optimal non-migratory solution. Clearly, $m \leq \mathsf{OPT}$. Furthermore, Theorem 2 implies $\mathsf{OPT} \leq 6m - 5$.

Suppose there is an online algorithm that computes a non-migratory schedule on $k \leq f(m) \cdot m \leq f(m) \cdot \mathsf{OPT}$ and, thus, the algorithm is $f(m)$-competitive for non-migratory scheduling. We conclude that (a) implies (b).

To see the reverse direction, assume that there is a $g(m)$-competitive algorithm for non-migratory scheduling. This algorithm finds a non-migratory schedule using at most $g(m) \cdot \mathsf{OPT} < g(m) \cdot 6m$ many machines, which is $f(m) \cdot m$ for some $g \in \Theta(f)$. Thus, (b) implies (a). $\square$

3. A STRONG LOWER BOUND

We prove the following theorem.

THEOREM 3. *Let $m \geq 3$. For every (deterministic) non-migratory online algorithm, there is an instance on n jobs such that the algorithm requires $\Omega(\log n)$ machines.*

We inductively define an adversarial strategy that forces any non-migratory online algorithm to use an unbounded number of machines while (offline) the resulting instance has a migratory schedule on three machines which even has some idle intervals. This is made formal in the following key lemma which directly implies the theorem.

LEMMA 2. *For every non-migratory online algorithm A and $k \in \mathbb{N}$, there is an instance I_k with $\mathcal{O}(2^k)$ jobs and a critical time t_0 such that:*

(i) In the schedule computed by A, there are at time t_0 unfinished critical jobs $j_1, \ldots, j_k \in I_k$ assigned to k different machines.

(ii) There is a feasible schedule of I_k on three machines with the following properties. Two machines are idle within $[t_0, t_0 + \varepsilon)$ for some $\varepsilon > 0$. The other one is continuously idle from t_0 on.

The base of our inductive proof is easy to see. The intuition for the induction step is the following. Given I_k as above, we obtain I_{k+1} by first releasing I_k, forcing the online algorithm to open k different machines. We then release I'_k, a scaled-down copy of I_k which can be handled during the idle intervals of the offline schedule, and we distinguish two cases. Firstly, if the online algorithm uses $k + 1$ machines to schedule both I_k and I'_k, we will be able to select a suitable subset of the critical jobs of I_k and I'_k to obtain the critical jobs of I_{k+1}. Secondly, if the online algorithm uses the same k machines to schedule both I_k and I'_k, we release a new job. This job will be designed to be in conflict with each of the critical jobs of I'_k and will thus require the online algorithm to open a new machine for the new job. The new job and the critical jobs of I_k will then be the critical jobs of I_{k+1}.

Before we give the formal proof of the lemma, we introduce some notation: The latest time when a job j has to be assigned to a machine and the earliest time when it can be finished are denoted by $a_j = r_j + \ell_j$ and $f_j = d_j - \ell_j$, respectively.

PROOF OF LEMMA 2.. We define the instances I_k depending on constants $\alpha \in (1/2, 1)$ and $\beta \in (0, 1/2)$, which will later be chosen appropriately. For the sake of intuition, α and β can be thought of constants very close to 1 and 0, respectively.

Clearly, I_1 exists. We define I_2: At time 0, we release job j_1 with $p_{j_1} = \alpha$ and $d_{j_1} = 1$. From a_{j_1} on, we start additionally releasing *short* jobs: For the i-th short job j, we set $r_j = a_{j_1} + (i-1) \cdot \beta$, $p_j = \alpha\beta$, and $d_j = a_{j_1} + i\beta$. We ensure that our choice of α and β fulfills

$$\left\lfloor \frac{f_{j_1} - a_{j_1}}{\beta} \right\rfloor \cdot \alpha\beta > \ell_{j_1}, \tag{1}$$

implying that the total processing time of short jobs that have to be scheduled within $[a_j, f_j) \subsetneq I(j_1)$ will eventually add up to more than the laxity of of j_1. This ensures that A has to schedule some short job on a different machine than j_1. We define j_2 to be the first such job, let $t_0 := a_{j_2}$, and stop releasing jobs then.

Given Equation (1), we check (i) and (ii) for critical jobs j_1, j_2 and critical time t_0: By definition of j_1 and j_2, they are assigned to different machines by A. Using $t_0 = a_{j_2} < f_{j_1}$ (implied by Equation (1)) and $t_0 = a_{j_2} < f_{j_2}$ (implied by $\alpha > 1/2$), both jobs are not finished at time t_0, that is, we get (i). On the other hand, an offline schedule could simply run job j_1 on one machine and all short jobs on another machine. Since for all jobs j holds $p_j < d_j - r_j$, they can be preempted within some interval $[t_0, t_0 + \varepsilon)$. This shows (ii).

We check that Equation (1) can indeed be made true: Using the definition of a_j, f_j, and ℓ_j, we obtain that Equation (1) is equivalent to

$$\left\lfloor \frac{2\alpha - 1}{\beta} \right\rfloor \cdot \alpha\beta > 1 - \alpha,$$

which, for instance, is true for $\alpha = 3/4$ and $\beta = 1/4$.

For $k > 2$, we define I_k inductively. Suppose the lemma is true for $k - 1$. We start by applying the lemma once, creating $k - 1$ critical jobs $j_1, \ldots, j_{k-1}$ that are not finished by A and assigned to $k - 1$ different machines at the critical time t_0. Also, there is a feasible schedule of I_k on three machines such that machine 1 and 2 are idle within some $[t_0, t_0 + \varepsilon)$ with $\varepsilon > 0$ while machine 3 is continuously idle from t_0 on. Recall that $p_j(t)$ is defined to be the remaining processing time of a job j at time t. We define

$$\varepsilon' := \min \left\{ \varepsilon, p_{j_1}(t_0), \ldots, p_{j_{k-1}}(t_0) \right\} > 0 \tag{2}$$

to be the largest ε' such that within $[t_0, t_0 + \varepsilon')$ no job j_i for $i \in \{1, \ldots, k-1\}$ can get finished by A and machine 1 and 2 can still be idle in a feasible schedule. We apply the lemma with $k - 1$ another time in a scaled-down way such that the latest deadline (i.e., that of the job released first) occurring in this sub-instance I'_k is $t_0 + \varepsilon'/2$. We call the corresponding critical jobs and time $j'_1, \ldots, j'_{k-1}$ and t'_0, respectively, and distinguish two cases:

Case 1: The jobs $j_1, \ldots, j_{k-1}$ and $j'_1, \ldots, j'_{k-1}$ are scheduled by A on different sets of machines. By using the induction hypothesis, there is a job j'_i such that $j_1, \ldots, j_{k-1}, j'_i$ are scheduled on k different machines. By our choice of ε' and the induction hypothesis for I'_k, these jobs are not finished by the critical time t'_0, implying (i). We also show (ii): Again by our choice of ε', only I'_k has to be scheduled within $[t_0, t_0 + \varepsilon'/2)$. By the induction hypothesis regarding I'_k, there is a schedule of this sub-instance with the following property: Two machines are idle within $[t'_0, t'_0 + \varepsilon'')$ for some $\varepsilon'' > 0$ and the other machine is continuously idle from t'_0 on. Since we can again choose to leave machine 3 continuously idle from t'_0 on, we get (ii).

Case 2: The jobs $j_1, \ldots, j_{k-1}$ and $j'_1, \ldots, j'_{k-1}$ are scheduled by A on the same set of machines. Then we additionally release exactly one job $j^\star$ at time t'_0 with deadline $t_0 + \varepsilon'$. We choose

$$p_{j^\star} \in \Big(t_0 + \varepsilon' - t'_0 - \min_{i=1,\ldots,k-1} p_{j'_i}(t'_0), \\ t_0 + \varepsilon' - t'_0 \Big),$$

ensuring that $j^\star$ cannot be scheduled on the same machine as any j'_i for $i \in \{1, \dots, k-1\}$ (lower bound on $p_{j^\star}$) and that it has strictly positive initial laxity (upper bound on $p_{j^\star}$). We further make sure that

$$p_{j^\star} > t_0 + \frac{\varepsilon'}{2} - t'_0,$$

meaning that $j^\star$ cannot be finished at time $t_0 + \varepsilon'/2$ (note that $p_{j^\star}$ still exists since $t_0 + \varepsilon'/2 - t'_0 < t_0 + \varepsilon' - t'_0$). We release no further jobs and claim that (i) and (ii) hold with critical jobs $j_1, \dots, j_{k-1}, j^\star$ and critical time $t''_0 := t_0 + \varepsilon'/2$.

We first show (i): Consider the schedule computed by A. By the induction hypotheses for I_{k-1} and our choice of ε', at time t''_0 the jobs $j_1, \dots, j_{k-1}$ are not finished and scheduled on $k-1$ different machines. Using the assumption that $j'_1, \dots, j'_{k-1}$ are scheduled on exactly the same set of machines as $j_1, \dots, j_{k-1}$ and the fact that $j^\star$ cannot be scheduled on the same machine as any j'_i for $i \in \{1, \dots, k-1\}$, the jobs $j_1, \dots, j_{k-1}, j^\star$ are scheduled on k different machines. By construction of $j^\star$, it is not finished by time t''_0 either.

To create a schedule obeying the condition in (ii), we schedule the whole instance except for $j^\star$ according to Part (ii) of the induction hypothesis (for both I_{k-1} and I'_{k-1}). Using that the latest deadline in I'_{k-1} is $t_0 + \varepsilon'/2$, in this schedule, machine 3 is continuously idle from t'_0 on and machine 1 (and 2) within $[t_0 + \varepsilon'/2, t_0 + \varepsilon')$. We schedule $j^\star$ within $[t'_0, t_0 + \varepsilon'/2)$ on machine 3 and afterwards on machine 1, starting it on machine 1 as late as possible. Since $j^\star$ has positive initial laxity, this again leaves an idle period $[t''_0, t''_0 + \varepsilon'')$ for $\varepsilon'' > 0$ on machines 1 and 2. Also, machine 3 is continuously idle from time t''_0 on, meeting the requirements of (ii). We illustrate this schedule in Figure 1.

We finally note that we have indeed $\mathcal{O}(2^k)$ jobs in the resulting instance: I_2 has a constant number of jobs, and for I_k we release I_{k-1} twice plus at most one additional job, showing that I_k has $\mathcal{O}(2^k)$ jobs. $\square$

Using Lemma 1, we obtain a similar theorem concerning competitive ratio. We get the following more explicit statement by directly applying Theorem 2.

THEOREM 4. *Consider instances with n jobs that have a feasible non-migratory offline schedule on* OPT *machines, where* OPT ≥ 13 *is fixed. Every (deterministic) non-migratory online algorithm requires $\Omega(\log n)$ machines.*

PROOF. Suppose there is a non-migratory online algorithm A on $o(\log n)$ machines. Using Lemma 2, we obtain instances with n jobs on which A uses more than $\Omega(\log n)$ machines and which have feasible (migratory) schedules on 3 machines. Using Theorem 2, we can turn these schedules into a feasible non-migratory schedules on $6 \cdot 3 - 5 = 13$ machines. We obtain a contradiction to the assumption that A only requires $o(\log n)$ machines. $\square$

4. A CONSTANT-COMPETITIVE ALGORITHM FOR LOOSE JOBS

In this section, we consider instances consisting of loose jobs, i.e., jobs j with $p_j \leq \alpha \cdot (d_j - r_j)$ for arbitrary constant $\alpha \in (0,1)$. The main theorem of this section is the following.

THEOREM 5. *For any fixed $\alpha \in (0,1)$, there is a non-migratory online algorithm on $\mathcal{O}(m)$ machines for instances consisting only of α-loose jobs.*

The key to proving the result is a reduction to a speed-augmentation problem on m machines.

THEOREM 6. *Suppose there is a non-migratory online algorithm* A *on $f(m)$ speed-s machines for general instances. Then, for every fixed $\alpha \in (0, 1/s)$, there is a non-migratory online algorithm on $f(\mathcal{O}(m))$ (unit-speed) machines for instances consisting only of α-loose jobs.*

The proof idea is as follows. To schedule α-loose jobs (for $\alpha < 1/s$) without additional speed, we increase the processing time of each job from the input instance by a factor of s. We denote the set of jobs with modified processing times by J^s. Note that the resulting instance is feasible in the sense that $p_j \leq d_j - r_j$ for all jobs j. We apply the speed-s algorithm to this instance. Whenever a job is scheduled in the resulting schedule, our algorithm schedules the corresponding job from the original instance on the respective machine.

To analyze our algorithm, we have to relate the minimum numbers of machines needed for scheduling the original instance J and for scheduling the instance with increased processing times J^s, respectively. To do so, we introduce two auxiliary job types. For some $\gamma \in (0,1)$ and every job j, we define two jobs $j_\gamma^{\lhd}, j_\gamma^{\rhd}$ with

$$I(j_\gamma^{\lhd}) := [r_j, d_j - \gamma\ell_j),\ p_{j_\gamma^{\lhd}} := p_j$$
$$\text{and } I(j_\gamma^{\rhd}) := [r_j + \gamma\ell_j, d_j),\ p_{j_\gamma^{\rhd}} := p_j,$$

that is, we remove a γ-fraction of the laxity from either side of j's feasible time window. We further define $J_\gamma^{\lhd} := \{j_\gamma^{\lhd} \mid j \in J\}$ and $J_\gamma^{\rhd} := \{j_\gamma^{\rhd} \mid j \in J\}$. The following lemma relates the number of machines needed for scheduling J to that needed for scheduling $J_\gamma^{\lhd}$ and $J_\gamma^{\rhd}$, and it may be of independent interest. Here we denote by $m(S)$ the minimum number of machines needed to schedule an instance S.

LEMMA 3. *For every instance J and $\gamma \in (0,1)$, we have*

$$m(J_\gamma^{\lhd}) \leq \frac{1}{1-\gamma} \cdot m(J) + 1$$
$$\text{and } m(J_\gamma^{\rhd}) \leq \frac{1}{1-\gamma} \cdot m(J) + 1. \tag{3}$$

PROOF. We show the statement for $J_\gamma^{\rhd}$, and the proof for $J_\gamma^{\lhd}$ is symmetric. According to Theorem 1, there exists a finite union of intervals I such that $m(J_\gamma^{\rhd}) = \lceil C(J_\gamma^{\rhd}, I)/|I| \rceil$. Without loss of generality, we can assume $I = [g_1, h_1) \cup \dots \cup [g_k, h_k)$ with $h_i < g_{i+1}$ for all $i = 1, \dots, k-1$. To derive the relationship between $m(J_\gamma^{\rhd})$ and $m(J)$, we expand I to a superset (and also finite union of intervals) $\mathrm{ex}(I)$ such that $|\mathrm{ex}(I)| = |I|/(1-\gamma)$. We will show for each job $j \in J$ with $C(j_\gamma^{\rhd}, I) > 0$ that $C(j, \mathrm{ex}(I)) \geq C(j_\gamma^{\rhd}, I)$. This will imply

$$\begin{aligned} m(J_\gamma^{\rhd}) - 1 &\leq \frac{C(J_\gamma^{\rhd}, I)}{|I|} = \frac{\sum_{j\in J} C(j_\gamma^{\rhd}, I)}{|I|} \\ &\leq \frac{\sum_{j\in J} C(j, \mathrm{ex}(I))}{(1-\gamma)\cdot|\mathrm{ex}(I)|} = \frac{1}{1-\gamma} \cdot \frac{C(J, \mathrm{ex}(I))}{|\mathrm{ex}(I)|} \\ &\leq \frac{1}{1-\gamma} \cdot m(J), \end{aligned}$$

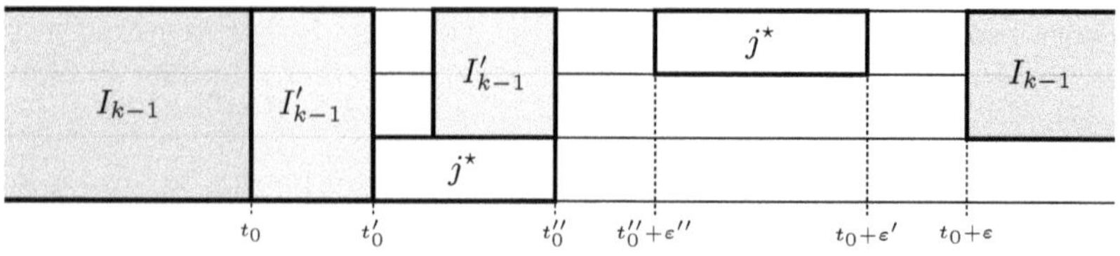

Figure 1: The optimal schedule constructed in Case 2 of the proof of Lemma 2. Recall $t''_0 = t_0 + \varepsilon'/2$.

where we use the other direction of Theorem 1 in the last step. Hence, Inequality (3) will follow.

The expanding works as follows. Given I as above, we expand each of the intervals $[g_i, h_i)$ to $[g'_i, h_i)$ with $g'_i \leq g_i$ and obtain $\text{ex}(I) := [g'_1, h_1) \cup \cdots \cup [g'_k, h_k)$. We start at the rightmost interval $[g'_k, h_k)$ and try to set $g'_k := h_k - (h_k - g_k)/(1-\gamma)$. If this would, however, produce an overlap between $[g'_k, h_k)$ and $[g_{k-1}, h_{k-1})$, we set $g'_k := h_{k-1}$ as well as $\delta_k := h_{k-1} - (h_k - (h_k - g_k)/(1-\gamma))$ and try to additionally expand $[g_{k-1}, h_{k-1})$ by δ_k instead. After that, we continue this procedure until $i = 1$. More formally, we let $h_0 = -\infty$ as well as $\delta_{k+1} = 0$, and for all $i = k, \ldots, 1$ we set

$$g'_i := \max\left\{h_{i-1}, h_i - \left(\frac{h_i - g_i}{1-\gamma} + \delta_{i-1}\right)\right\}$$

$$\text{and } \delta_i := \max\left\{0, h_{i-1} - \left(h_i - \left(\frac{h_i - g_i}{1-\gamma} + \delta_{i-1}\right)\right)\right\}.$$

Obviously, indeed $|\text{ex}(I)| = |I|/(1-\gamma)$.

We show $C(j, \text{ex}(I)) \geq C(j^{\triangleright}_{\gamma}, I)$ for all $j \in J$ with $C(j^{\triangleright}_{\gamma}, I) > 0$. By the definition of contribution, we have

$$\begin{aligned} C(j, \text{ex}(I)) &= \max\{0, |\text{ex}(I) \cap I(j)| - \ell_j\} \\ \text{and} \quad C(j^{\triangleright}_{\gamma}, I) &= \max\{0, |I \cap I(j^{\triangleright}_{\gamma})| - \ell_{j^{\triangleright}_{\gamma}}\} \\ &= \max\{0, |I \cap I(j^{\triangleright}_{\gamma})| - (1-\gamma) \cdot \ell_j\}, \end{aligned}$$

that is, we can restrict to showing $|\text{ex}(I) \cap I(j)| \geq |I \cap I(j^{\triangleright}_{\gamma})| + \gamma \ell_j$. Next, we define $I' := I \cap I(j^{\triangleright}_{\gamma})$. Using the fact that $I' \subseteq I$ implies $\text{ex}(I') \subseteq \text{ex}(I)$, it even suffices to show

$$|\text{ex}(I') \cap I(j)| \geq |I'| + \gamma \ell_j. \tag{4}$$

To see this, we distinguish two cases:

Case 1: The leftmost point of $\text{ex}(I')$ is left of r_j. Since the leftmost point of I' was not left of $r_j + \gamma \ell_j$, $[r_j, r_j + \gamma \ell_j)$ is a subset of $\text{ex}(I')$. Consequently, we have $|\text{ex}(I') \cap I(j)| - |I' \cap I(j)| \geq \gamma \ell_j$. Using $|I' \cap I(j)| = |I'|$, the claim follows.

Case 2: The leftmost point of $\text{ex}(I')$ is not left of r_j. By the way our expanding works, we have that $\text{ex}(I')$ takes up a length of $|I' \cap I(j)|/(1-\gamma)$ within $I(j)$. Plugging $|I'| > \ell_{j^{\triangleright}_{\gamma}} = (1-\gamma) \cdot \ell_j$, which follows since $C(j^{\triangleright}_{\gamma}, I) > 0$, into that, we also obtain $|\text{ex}(I') \cap I(j)| - |I' \cap I(j)| \geq \gamma \ell_j$. Again using $|I' \cap I(j)| = |I'|$, the claim follows.

This completes the proof. □

We apply this lemma to get a similar statement about jobs with an in increased processing time, J^s, which might be of independent interest. Formally, for $j \in J$, let j^s denote a copy of job j with a processing time increased by a factor s, and $J^s := \{j^s \mid j \in J\}$.

LEMMA 4. *Let $s \geq 1$. For every instance J consisting only of α-loose jobs for some fixed $\alpha \in (0, 1/s)$, we have $m(J^s) = \mathcal{O}(m(J))$.*

PROOF. We investigate the number of machines required to schedule J^s: To do so, we define

$$\delta := \frac{1 - \alpha s}{\lceil s \rceil} \cdot (d_j - r_j).$$

Note that $\ell_{j^s} \geq (1 - \alpha s) \cdot (d_j - r_j) > 0$ and thus

$$0 < \delta \leq \frac{\ell_{j^s}}{\lceil s \rceil}. \tag{5}$$

Further, for every job $j \in J$, we define $\lceil s \rceil$ different jobs $j_1, \ldots, j_{\lceil s \rceil}$ with

$$\begin{aligned} I(j_i) &:= [r_j + (i-1) \cdot (p_j + \delta), r_j + i \cdot (p_j + \delta)), \\ p_{j_i} &:= p_j \\ &\quad \text{for all } i < \lceil s \rceil \\ \text{and } I(j_{\lceil s \rceil}) &:= [r_j + (\lceil s \rceil - 1) \cdot (p_j + \delta), r_j + s \cdot p_j + \lceil s \rceil \delta)), \\ p_{j_{\lceil s \rceil}} &:= (s - \lceil s \rceil + 1) \cdot p_j. \end{aligned}$$

Furthermore let $J_i := \{j_i \mid j \in J\}$ for all i. Now note that, for showing $m(J^s) = \mathcal{O}(m(J))$, it suffices to show that $m(J_i) = \mathcal{O}(m(J))$ for all i. This is because we have $I(j_i) \subseteq I(j^s)$ for all i, $I(j_i) \cap I(j_{i'}) \neq \emptyset$ for all i, i', and $\sum_i p_{j_i} = p_{j^s}$, which can be easily checked. Thus any feasible schedule of $J_1, \ldots, J_{\lceil s \rceil}$ on $\mathcal{O}(m(J))$ machines each can be transformed into a feasible schedule of J^s on $\lceil s \rceil \cdot \mathcal{O}(m(J)) = \mathcal{O}(m(J))$ by scheduling each j^s whenever any j_i is scheduled in the respective schedule.

We show that indeed $m(J_i) = \mathcal{O}(m(J))$ for all i. We first show this for $i < \lceil s \rceil$: Note that, using Inequality 5, we have $\ell_{j_i} = \delta = \beta \ell_j > 0$ for all $j \in J$ and constant $\beta > 0$. Thus, by applying Lemma 3 up to two times to shorten the time window from both sides, $m(J_i) = \mathcal{O}(m(J))$. For $i = \lceil s \rceil$, first note that the above reasoning also works for $J'_{\lceil s \rceil} := \{j'_{\lceil s \rceil} \mid j \in J\}$ with

$$\begin{aligned} I(j'_{\lceil s \rceil}) &:= [r_j + (s-1) \cdot p_j + (\lceil s \rceil - 1) \cdot \delta, \\ &\qquad r_j + s \cdot p_j + \lceil s \rceil \delta)), \\ p_{j'_{\lceil s \rceil}} &:= p_j, \end{aligned}$$

that is, $m(J'_{\lceil s \rceil}) = \mathcal{O}(m(J))$. Now clearly any feasible schedule of $J'_{\lceil s \rceil}$ can be transformed into one of $J_{\lceil s \rceil}$ without increasing the number of machines by scheduling each $j_{\lceil s \rceil}$ whenever $j'_{\lceil s \rceil}$ is scheduled unless $j_{\lceil s \rceil}$ is finished, implying $m(J_{\lceil s \rceil}) \leq m(J'_{\lceil s \rceil}) = \mathcal{O}(m(J))$. □

We now apply the preceding lemma in the proof of Theorem 6.

PROOF OF THEOREM 6. To schedule J only having α-loose jobs with constant $\alpha < 1/s$, we first transform J into J^s. Using Lemma 4, by applying A to J^s, we obtain a non-migratory schedule of J^s on $f(m(J^s)) = f(\mathcal{O}(m(J)))$ speed-s processors. We transform this schedule into a non-migratory schedule of J on $f(\mathcal{O}(m(J)))$ speed-1 machines by replacing each j^s by j for all j, which does not violate feasibility by the definition of j^s. □

We are now ready to utilize an algorithm due to Chan, Lam, and To [3] for which they prove an upper bound on the required number of machines that scales with the given speed—even for speeds arbitrarily close to 1.

THEOREM 7 (CHAN, LAM, AND TO [3]). *For every $\varepsilon > 0$, there is a non-migratory online algorithm on $\lceil(1 + 1/\varepsilon)^2\rceil$ speed-$(1 + \varepsilon)^2$ machines.*

Indeed, it suffices to plug Theorem 7 as a black box into Theorem 6 to obtain Theorem 5. By applying Lemma 1, we also get the following result for the competitive ratio.

THEOREM 8. *For any fixed $\alpha \in (0, 1)$, there there is an $\mathcal{O}(1)$-competitive non-migratory online algorithm for instances consisting only of α-loose jobs.*

5. AN O(log m)-COMPETITIVE ALGORITHM FOR LAMINAR INSTANCES

In this section, we consider *laminar* instances in which for any two jobs j, j' with $I(j) \cap I(j') \neq \emptyset$, it holds that $I(j) \subseteq I(j')$ or $I(j') \supseteq I(j)$. We prove the following result.

THEOREM 9. *There exists an online algorithm that produces a non-migratory solution on $\mathcal{O}(m \log m)$ machines for laminar instances.*

For ease of presentation, we assume throughout this section that jobs are indexed from 1 to n in accordance with their release dates: We assume $j < j'$ implies $r_j \leq r_{j'}$. If $r_j = r_{j'}$, we assume that $j < j'$ implies $d_j \geq d_{j'}$. We say that j *dominates* j' (denoted as $j \succ j'$) if $j < j'$ and $I(j) \supseteq I(j')$. We also say j' *is dominated* by j and denote this as $j' \prec j$.

5.1 Description of the Algorithm

It suffices to consider α-tight jobs for some fixed $\alpha \in (0, 1)$. The remaining α-loose jobs are scheduled on a separate set of $\mathcal{O}(m)$ machines as described in the previous section (cf. Theorem 5).

Job Assignment.

We open m' machines and will later see that we can choose $m' = \mathcal{O}(m \log m)$. At every release date, the arriving jobs are immediately assigned to their machines in order of job indices. Each job is assigned to exactly one machine, that is, we obtain a non-migratory schedule. Consider some job j. If there is a machine that has no job j' with $I(j) \cap I(j') \neq \emptyset$ assigned to it, we assign j to any such machine. Otherwise we execute the following procedure.

Consider any machine and the jobs j' assigned to it with $I(j) \cap I(j') \neq \emptyset$. Based on the laminarity of the instance and the order in which we assign jobs, all these j' dominate j and are ordered linearly by $\prec$. Consequently, there exists a unique $\prec$-minimal job among them, which is said to be currently *responsible* on the considered machine. Consider the set of currently responsible jobs of *all* machines. Again, by laminarity of the instance, these jobs form a chain $c_1(j) \prec \cdots \prec c_{m'}(j)$. We call $c_i(j)$ the i-th *candidate* of j.

We now want to select a candidate $c_i(j)$ and assign j to the same machine as $c_i(j)$. Consider the laxity of a candidate, which can be viewed as a *budget* for delaying the jobs. Since $I(j) \subseteq I(c_i(j))$, it is a necessary criterion that the budget of $c_i(j)$ suffices to schedule both j and the jobs j' with $I(j') \subseteq I(c_i(j))$ that have been assigned to the same machine earlier. Intuitively, we would also like to minimize the candidate that we pick w.r.t. $\prec$ so as to save the budget of jobs with larger time windows. However, it fails to greedily assign jobs to the machine of their $\prec$-minimal candidate that fulfills the above necessary criterion. This can be shown using a well-known class of difficult (laminar) instances [10, Theorem 2.13].

Instead we use a more sophisticated balancing scheme similar to that in [4]: We partition the budget of each candidate into m' equally-sized (sub-)budgets. For every i, we only consider the i-th budget of $c_i(j)$ when assigning j. When picking $c_i(j)$ and assigning j to the same machine, we charge not just p_j but $|I(j)| \geq p_j$ to the i-th budget of $c_i(j)$. This policy ensures that, as long as no budget becomes negative, there is a feasible schedule under the current assignment (cf. Lemma 5).

We make this more formal: We call a job j' that has been assigned to the machine of its h-th candidate $c_h(j')$ the h-th *user* of $c_h(j')$. We denote the set of all h-th users of a (candidate) job j' by $U_h(j')$, for all h. Note that at any time the h-th budget of j' has been charged exactly $|I(j'')|$ for all its users j''. To assign j, we select the smallest i such that the i-th budget of $c_i(j)$ can still pay for $|I(j)|$, that is,

$$\frac{\ell_{c_i(j)}}{m'} - \sum_{j' \in U_i(c_i(j))} |I(j')| \geq |I(j)|. \tag{6}$$

If we find such an i, we assign j to $c_i(j)$ (and thereby add j to $U_i(c_i(j))$ and charge $|I(j)|$ to the i-th budget of $c_i(j)$). If we do not find such an i, the assignment of j *fails*. In the analysis, we will show that the latter case will never happen if m' is chosen large enough.

Scheduling.

At any time and on each machine, we process an arbitrary unfinished job assigned to it with minimum deadline. It will later turn out (cf. Lemma 5) that there is always a *unique* such job.

5.2 Analysis of the Algorithm

We first show that our algorithm obtains a feasible schedule if no job assignment has failed. Then we give a proof of the fact that the job assignment never fails on instances that admit a feasible schedule. As a byproduct, we get a simplification of our scheduling rule.

LEMMA 5. *Suppose the job assignment does not fail for any job. We have the following two properties.*

(i) Our algorithm produces a feasible schedule.

(ii) At any time and on each machine, there are no two unfinished jobs with the same deadline.

PROOF. Consider some machine. We first show (ii) by induction on the jobs assigned to this machine in order of their indices. The induction base is clear. So assume the statement holds until some job j gets assigned to the considered machine.

The statement is obviously fulfilled if no other unfinished job on the considered machine has deadline d_j. So suppose $j^\star$ with $d_{j^\star} = d_j$ exists. We note that then the candidate j' of j must (also) have deadline d_j: Otherwise, using the laminarity of the instance, we have $d_{j^\star} < d_{j'}$ and thus $j' \succ j^\star$ and j' cannot be the $\prec$-minimal job whose interval contains r_j. Since j is assigned to the machine of its candidate j', one sub-budget and thus the total budget of j' must be at least $|I(j)|$ right before j is assigned. Consider the state of j' and its users at this time. Using Part (ii) of the induction hypothesis, j' was so far only preempted at some time t when there was a user j'' of it with $t \in I(j'')$. Thus, it was processed for at least

$$\begin{aligned}&\Big(|I(j')| - (d_{j'} - r_j)\Big) - \sum_{i=1}^{m'} |I(U_i(j'))|\\ \geq &\Big(|I(j')| - (d_{j'} - r_j)\Big) - \big(\ell_{j'} - |I(j)|\big)\\ = &|I(j')| - \ell_{j'} = p_{j'},\end{aligned}$$

using $d_j = d_{j'}$ in the second step. Hence j' is finished at time r_j, a contradiction.

To see (i), consider some job j and note that, by applying (ii), whenever it is preempted at some time t, there must be a user j' of j with $t \in I(j')$. According to Inequality (6), j is thus preempted for no longer than

$$\sum_{i=1}^{m'} |I(U_i(j))| \leq \sum_{i=1}^{m'} \sum_{j' \in U_i(j)} |I(j')| \leq m' \cdot \frac{\ell_j}{m'} = \ell_j.$$

Therefore, j can be processed for p_j time units. □

It remains to show that the job assignment never fails for some $m' = \mathcal{O}(m \log m)$. The proof idea is as follows: We assume the algorithm fails to assign a job $j^\star$. Then we select a critical job set and, by a load argument on this set, derive a contradiction to the existence of a feasible (migratory) schedule on m machines. Intuitively, this set is a minimal subset of the instance that still causes the failure. Note that this construction resembles the one from [4]. Indeed, the careful choice of our set allows us to use a lower bound introduced in [4] which is based on such a critical set.

We initialize $G_{m'} := \{j^\star\}$. Given G_i, we construct F_i and G_{i-1} in the following way. First, F_i is defined to be the set of all $\prec$-maximal i-th candidates of jobs in G_i. Subsequently, G_{i-1} is constructed by adding all the i-th users of jobs in F_i to G_i. Formally,

$$F_i := M_\prec\big(\{c_i(j) \mid j \in G_i\}\big)$$
$$\text{and } G_{i-1} := G_i \cup \bigcup_{j \in F_i} U_i(j),$$

where $M_\prec$ is the operator that picks out the $\prec$-maximal elements from a set of jobs: $M_\prec(S) := \{j \in S \mid \nexists j' : j \prec j'\}$. After m' many such iterations, that is, when $G_0, F_1, \ldots, F_{m'}$ have been computed, we set $F_0 := M_\prec(G_0)$.

We define

$$F := F_0 \cup F_1 \cup \cdots \cup F_{m'} \text{ and } T := \bigcup_{j \in F_0} I(j),$$

where we call (F, T) a *witness set*. The idea is to show that (F, T) obeys the following definition for suitably chosen parameters. This is the basis for applying a lower bound from [4] which we state below.

DEFINITION 1 ([4]). *Let F' be a set of α-tight jobs and let T' be a non-empty finite union of disjoint intervals. For some $\mu \in \mathbb{N}$ and $\beta \in (0,1)$, a pair (F', T') is called (μ, β)-critical if*

(i) each $t \in T'$ is covered by at least μ distinct jobs in F',
(ii) and $|T' \cap I(j)| \geq \beta \ell_j$ for any $j \in F'$.

This will allows us to use the following result as a lower bound on the optimum number of machines m.

THEOREM 10 ([4]). *If there exists a (μ, β)-critical pair, then $m = \Omega\left(\frac{\mu}{\log 1/\beta}\right)$.*

To do so, we first show some structural properties of (F, T) that will be useful later. Towards this, we define the following notation. For two job sets S_1 and S_2, we write $S_1 \prec S_2$ if, for each $j_1 \in S_1$, there is a $j_2 \in S_2$ with $j_1 \prec j_2$.

LEMMA 6. *For any witness set (F, T), we have the following structural properties:*

(i) We have $F_0 \prec \cdots \prec F_{m'}$.
(ii) The sets $F_0, \ldots, F_{m'}$ are pairwise disjoint.

PROOF. To see (i), we define $C_i := \{c_i(j) \mid j \in G_i\}$, for every $1 \leq i \leq m'$, and $C_0 := G_0$. We first show $C_{i-1} \prec C_i$ for every $1 \leq i \leq m'$. For $i = 1$, this directly follows from the construction. Consider $2 \leq i \leq m'$. Let j be an arbitrary job in C_{i-1}, which is then an $(i-1)$-th candidate of some job in G_{i-1}, say, job j'. According to the construction, we have $j' \in G_i$, or j' is the i-th user of some job in $F_i \subseteq C_i$. In both cases, C_i contains the i-th candidate of job j', which dominates job j. Hence, $C_{i-1} \prec C_i$. Since F_{i-1} and F_i are obtained from C_{i-1} and C_i only by deleting dominated jobs, $F_{i-1} \prec F_i$ follows.

Consider property (ii) and suppose there is some $j \in F_i \cap F_{i'}$ for some $i < i'$. Then, by (i), there is also a job $j' \in F_{i'}$ with $j \prec j'$, contradicting the fact that $F_{i'}$ only contains $\prec$-maximal elements. □

We are ready to show that (F, T) is indeed a critical pair.

LEMMA 7. *The witness set (F, T) is a (μ, β)-critical pair for $\mu = m'$, $\beta = 1/m'$.*

PROOF OF LEMMA 7. We first consider Property (1) of a (μ, β)-critical pair. Given Lemma 6, it is obvious that every $t \in I(j)$ for $j \in F_0$ is covered by at least m' distinct jobs.

Concerning Property 1 of a (μ, β)-critical pair, we have

$$T = \bigcup_{j \in F_0} I(j) = \bigcup_{j \in M_\prec(G_0)} I(j) = \bigcup_{j \in G_0} I(j)$$

according to the definition of T. Furthermore, G_0 contains all the the i-th users of jobs in F_i, hence $|T \cap I(j)| \geq \ell_j / m'$ for any $j \in F_i$. □

We now use Lemma 7 and Theorem 10 to get a lower bound on m and thereby an upper bound on m'.

PROOF OF THEOREM 9. We show that, for a sufficiently large constant c and $m' = cm \log m$, our algorithm always produces feasible schedules. According to Lemma 5, it suffices to show that the job assignment procedure never fails. Suppose it does fail. Then we derive the witness set (F, T), which is a $(m', 1/m')$-critical pair (G, T) by Lemma 7. Using Theorem 10, we get $m = \Omega(\mu/\log 1/\beta) = \Omega(m'/\log m')$, which is a contradiction if $m' = cm \log m$ for sufficiently large c, that is, for some $m' = \mathcal{O}(m \log m)$ the algorithm never fails and thus always produces feasible schedules. □

Lemma 1 implies the following result for the competitive ratio.

THEOREM 11. *There is an $\mathcal{O}(\log m)$-competitive non-migratory online algorithm for laminar instances.*

6. AGREEABLE INSTANCES

Consider an instance J in which any two jobs $j, j' \in J$ are *agreeable*, that is, $r_j < r_{j'}$ implies $d_j \leq d_{j'}$. We also call J agreeable.

6.1 A constant-competitive non-preemptive algorithm

For agreeable instances, we derive an online algorithm that only uses $\mathcal{O}(m)$ machines. In fact, we show an even a stronger result in the context of non-*preemptive* scheduling.

THEOREM 12. *There exists an online algorithm that produces a non-preemptive solution on $32.70 \cdot m$ machines for agreeable instances.*

The idea is to again treat α-loose and -tight jobs separately for fixed $\alpha \in (0, 1)$. To obtain a non-migratory (but not necessarily non-preemptive) algorithm for α-loose jobs, note that we could simply use Theorem 6. To derive a non-preemptive algorithm, we will utilize the following theorem that has been shown for arbitrary (not necessarily agreeable) instances in the context of migratory scheduling. Given m' machines, the algorithm EDF schedules at any time m' unfinished jobs with the smallest deadlines.

THEOREM 13 ([4]). *Let $\alpha \in (0, 1)$. EDF is an online algorithm that produces a feasible (possibly migratory) solution on $m/(1-\alpha)^2$ machines for any instance that consists only of α-loose jobs.*

Now notice that EDF on agreeable instances never preempts jobs that have already started because the jobs released later have a larger deadline. This directly implies the following corollary.

COROLLARY 1. *Let $\alpha \in (0, 1)$. EDF is an online algorithm that produces a non-preemptive schedule on $m/(1-\alpha)^2$ machines for any agreeable instance that consists only of α-loose jobs.*

Consider α-tight jobs. We use the following simple algorithm MediumFit: Any job j runs exactly in the interval $[r_j + \ell_j/2, d_j - \ell_j/2)$, independently of all other jobs. Note that this algorithm is meaningful in the sense that running j in $[r_j + \ell_j, d_j)$ or $[r_j, d_j - \ell_j)$ does *not* yield a schedule on $\mathcal{O}(m)$ machines.

The analysis MediumFit works via a load argument.

LEMMA 8. *Let $\alpha \in (0, 1)$. MediumFit is an online algorithm that produces a non-preemptive solution on $16m/\alpha$ machines for any agreeable instance that consists only of α-tight jobs.*

PROOF. Consider an arbitrary time t and all jobs j' that are run by MediumFit at this time, among which we let j be a job with minimum laxity. We estimate their contributions to the interval(s)

$$I = [r_j - 2\ell_j, r_j + 2\ell_j) \cup [d_j - 2\ell_j, d_j + 2\ell_j),$$

which has a total length of at most $8\ell_j$. Distinguish two cases for each j' that is run at t.

Case 1: We have $|I(j')| \geq 2\ell_j$. As $I(j')$ contains r_j or d_j, we have $|I \cap I(j')| \geq 2\ell_j$. Given that $\ell_{j'} \leq \ell_j$, j' contributes at least $2\ell_j - \ell_{j'} \geq \ell_j$ to I.

Case 2: We have $|I(j')| < 2\ell_j$. As a consequence $I(j') \subseteq I$. Observe that $|I(j')| \geq \ell_j/2$ holds because both j and j' are run at time t by MediumFit. As j' is α-tight, its contribution to I is at least $\alpha\ell_j/2$.

Let n_1 and n_2 be the number of jobs corresponding to the above two cases, respectively. Then the contribution of the $n_1 + n_2$ jobs to I is at least

$$(n_1 + \alpha n_2/2) \cdot \ell_j \geq (n_1 + n_2) \cdot \alpha\ell_j/2.$$

Using Theorem 1, the total contribution is upper bounded by $m|I| \leq 8m\ell_j$, implying $n_1 + n_2 \leq 16m/\alpha$. □

Corollary 1 and Lemma 8 imply a non-preemptive solution on $m/(1-\alpha)^2 + 16m/\alpha$ machines, which attains its minimum at approximately $32.70 \cdot m$ for $\alpha \approx 0.63$. Theorem 12 follows. For the competitive ratio, we get the following result by Lemma 1.

THEOREM 14. *There is an $\mathcal{O}(1)$-competitive non-migratory online algorithm for agreeable instances.*

6.2 A non-trivial lower bound

We complement the upper-bound result with the first non-trivial lower bound for agreeable instances. We can even restrict to instances where all jobs have the same processing time.

THEOREM 15. *For any $\varepsilon > 0$, there is no online algorithm that produces a migratory solution on $(6 - 2\sqrt{6} - \varepsilon) \cdot m \approx 1.10 \cdot m$ machines for agreeable instances where all jobs have identical processing times.*

The lower-bound instances have a structure similar to existing ones for general instances [9, 10]. We say that an algorithm is *behind* by $w \geq 0$ at some time t if the following three properties hold:

(i) An optimal schedule could have finished all jobs released so far at time t.
(ii) The work unfinished by the algorithm is at least w.
(iii) We have $d_j \leq t + 1$ for all jobs released so far.

To prove the theorem, we will iteratively apply the following lemma.

LEMMA 9. *Consider an online algorithm* A *that uses* $(6 - 2\sqrt{6} - \varepsilon)m$ *machines for some* $\varepsilon > 0$. *There is a* $\delta > 0$ *with the following property.*

Let t *be a time at which* A *is behind by* w. *Then jobs can be released (in an agreeable way) such that there is a time* $t' > t$ *at which* A *is behind by* $w + \delta$.

PROOF. Define $\beta := (6 - 2\sqrt{6} - \varepsilon) - 1$. We choose some $\alpha \in [0, 1] \cap \mathbb{Q}$ that is yet to be optimized, and we assume that $\alpha m \in \mathbb{N}$. At time t, we release m jobs j with $p_j = 1$ and $d_j = t + 1 + \alpha$ (type-1 jobs) and αm jobs j with $p_j = 1$ and $d_j = t + 2$ (type-2 jobs). We will now show that there is a $\delta > 0$ such that A is behind by $w + \delta$ at time $t' = t + 1 + \alpha$. Observe that it suffices to give a lower bound of $w + \delta$ on the work that is left of type-1 jobs at time $t + 1 + \alpha$.

First note that $(1 - \alpha)m$ jobs j with $p_j = 1$ and $d_j = t + 2$ could be released at time $t + 1$ without violating feasibility of the instance. This leaves at most $(\alpha + \beta)m$ machines for processing the type-1 jobs within $[t + 1, t + 1 + \alpha)$, i.e., a total capacity of $(\alpha^2 + \alpha\beta)m$. Thus, the type-2 jobs can receive $(\alpha^2 + \alpha\beta)m + \beta m - w$ of processing within $[t, t + 1)$, amounting to $(\alpha^2 + \alpha\beta)m + \beta m - w + \alpha^2 m$ within $[t, t + 1 + \alpha)$. Consequently, at time $t' = t + 1 + \alpha$, the work left of type-1 jobs is at least

$$\alpha m - ((\alpha^2 + \alpha\beta)m + \beta m - w + \alpha^2 m) = w + \delta.$$

First note that δ is independent of w. Now the requirement $\delta > 0$ is equivalent to

$$\beta < \frac{\alpha - 2\alpha^2}{1 + \alpha}.$$

Maximizing the right-hand side of this inequality over the real numbers yields a maximum of $5 - 2\sqrt{6}$ for $\alpha = (\sqrt{6} - 2)/2 \approx 0.25$. By continuity of the right-hand side and definition of β, we can choose a rational α that makes the inequality true. This proves the lemma. □

We are ready to prove the theorem.

PROOF OF THEOREM 15. Suppose there exists some online algorithm A that uses $(6 - 2\sqrt{6} - \varepsilon)m$ machines. Clearly, for the empty instance and at time 0, A is behind by 0. Now applying Lemma 9 sufficiently often forces A to be behind by w at some time t where w exceeds the available capacity of $6 - 2\sqrt{6} - \varepsilon$ in $[t, t + 1)$. □

7. CONCLUSION

We have investigated the power of migration in online machine minimization. Surprisingly, it has turned out that, without allowing migration, the online machine requirement is unbounded in m even when $m = 3$ whereas with migration $\mathcal{O}(m \log m)$ machines suffice for any m [4]. A tight upper bound remains open. The currently best upper bound we are aware of, is $\mathcal{O}(\log \Delta)$, with Δ being the largest ratio of processing times, and it is obtained by a non-preemptive algorithm [11].

We remark that our lower bound leaves open if for $m = 2$ there is an online non-migratory algorithm using $\mathcal{O}(1)$ machines. Note that such an algorithm exists if we allow migration [4], but it is ruled out if we do not allow to preempt [11].

We also presented online algorithms for restricted instances, namely loose, agreeable, and laminar instances, that that construct non-migratory schedules using only $\mathcal{O}(m \log m)$ (or even $\mathcal{O}(m)$) machines. It remains an open question whether $o(m \log m)$ machines suffice for laminar instances when migration is not allowed.

8. REFERENCES

[1] N. Bansal, T. Kimbrel, and K. Pruhs. Speed scaling to manage energy and temperature. *J. ACM*, 54(1), 2007.

[2] A. Borodin and R. El-Yaniv. *Online Computation and Competitive Analysis*. Cambridge University Press, 1998.

[3] H. Chan, T. W. Lam, and K. To. Nonmigratory online deadline scheduling on multiprocessors. *SIAM J. Comput.*, 34(3):669–682, 2005.

[4] L. Chen, N. Megow, and K. Schewior. An $\mathcal{O}(\log m)$-competitive algorithm for online machine minimization. In *ACM-SIAM Symposium on Discrete Algorithms (SODA)*, pages 155–163, 2016.

[5] N. R. Devanur, K. Makarychev, D. Panigrahi, and G. Yaroslavtsev. Online algorithms for machine minimization. *CoRR*, abs/1403.0486, 2014.

[6] W. A. Horn. Some simple scheduling algorithms. *Naval Research Logistics Quarterly*, 21(1):177–185, 1974.

[7] B. Kalyanasundaram and K. Pruhs. Eliminating migration in multi-processor scheduling. *J. Algorithms*, 38(1):2–24, 2001.

[8] G. Koren, E. Dar, and A. Amir. The power of migration in multiprocessor scheduling of real-time systems. *SIAM Journal on Computing*, 30(2):511–527, 2000.

[9] T. W. Lam and K.-K. To. Trade-offs between speed and processor in hard-deadline scheduling. In *ACM-SIAM Symposium on Discrete Algorithms (SODA)*, pages 623–632, 1999.

[10] C. A. Phillips, C. Stein, E. Torng, and J. Wein. Optimal time-critical scheduling via resource augmentation. *Algorithmica*, 32(2):163–200, 2002.

[11] B. Saha. Renting a cloud. In *IARCS Conference on Foundations of Software Technology and Theoretical Computer Science (FSTTCS)*, pages 437–448, 2013.

Fair Online Scheduling for Selfish Jobs on Heterogeneous Machines

Sungjin Im
University of California, Merced
Merced, CA 95343
sim3@ucmerced.edu

Janardhan Kulkarni
Microsoft Research
Redmond, WA 98052
jakul@microsoft.com

ABSTRACT

Scheduling jobs on multiple machines has numerous applications and has been a central topic of research in the scheduling literature. Recently, much progress has been made particularly in online scheduling with the development of powerful analysis tools. In this line of wok a centralized scheduler typically dispatches jobs to machines to exploit the given resources the best to achieve the best system performance which is measured by a certain global scheduling objective. While this approach has been very successful in attacking scheduling problems of growing complexity, the underlying assumption that jobs follow a centralized scheduler may not be realistic in certain scheduling settings.

In this paper we initiate the study of online scheduling for selfish jobs in the presence of multiple machines. Selfish behavior of jobs is a common aspect observed in the absence of a centralized scheduler. We explore this question in the unrelated machines setting, arguably one of the most general multiple machine models. In this model each job can have a completely different processing time on each machine. Motivated by several practical scenarios, we assume that when a job arrives it *chooses the machine that completes the job the earliest* i.e. minimizes the flow time of the job. The goal is to design a local scheduling algorithm on each machine with the goal of minimizing the total (weighted) flow time. We show that the algorithm Smoothed Latest Arrival Processor Sharing, which was introduced in a recent work by Im et al. [27, 28], yields an $O(1/\epsilon^2)$-competitive schedule when given $(1+\epsilon)$ speed. We also extend our result to minimize total flow-time plus energy consumed. To show this result we establish several interesting properties of the algorithm which could be of potential use for other scheduling problems.

1. INTRODUCTION

Processing jobs using multiple resources is a fundamental scheduling problem that arises in various forms in many disciplines. Such settings are prevalent and found in server farms and data centers which consist of a large number of machines. At a smaller scale, chips are equipped with multiple heterogeneous cores, and the number of cores per chip is expected to grow exponentially to deliver high throughput with less energy consumption. Routers and middleboxes are common computing resources to process packets in network. When resources are viewed as abstract machines, numerous applications can be captured by this setting.

SPAA '16, July 11-13, 2016, Pacific Grove, CA, USA

DOI: http://dx.doi.org/10.1145/2935764.2935773

Not surprisingly, multiple machines scheduling has been a central topic of research in the theoretical scheduling community. One of the most general multiple machines settings is the unrelated machine model. In this model, there are m machines and n jobs, and each job j arrives at time r_j. Each job j may have an arbitrary processing requirement (size) of p_{ij} on each machine i and is associated with weight w_j which stands for its importance. The unrelated machines setting captures and generalizes identical machines and related machines where machines run in different speeds. When multiple jobs compete to be processed earlier, one needs to prioritize between jobs according to a global scheduling objective. Perhaps the most popular objective in online setting is to minimize the average (or equivalently total) weighted flow time of jobs, where the flow time of a job j is defined as the length of time a job waits before it is completed since its arrival, multiplied by its weight w_j.

The problem of minimizing the average weighted flow time of jobs on unrelated machines has been extensively studied both in online and offline settings; we give an extensive survey of known results in Section 1.4. Much of the approximation and online algorithms literature on the problem, however, has taken a system-centric and centralized view of the problem. In this view, the jobs arriving into the system are assumed to be altruistic, and are at the discretion of a centralized scheduler that attempts to achieve high overall system performance. Although this model is a fair abstraction of scheduling jobs within an operating system or across different cores of a single machine, it does not capture scheduling constraints arising in data centers or other cloud services [34]. In many applications, implementing centralized and monolithic scheduling algorithms is not always possible. Furthermore, in many scenarios jobs behave selfishly by choosing machines that give them the earliest completion time. The selfish behavior of jobs may arise because the jobs are submitted by self-interested clients or simply as a consequence of a dispatch rule which is decentralized and greedy. The examples for latter case include, webpage requests are usually dispatched to server farms that are least loaded[12], and DNS query requests are routed to DNS servers with the least service time. Selfish behavior may impact the performance of the system and has to be taken into consideration when designing scheduling policies.

Much of the work on selfish scheduling of jobs has been considered mainly in the setting of coordination games, first introduced in a seminal paper [16]. In this setting, each machine declares a strongly local scheduling policy. The strategy of each job consists of choosing the machine which minimizes its own completion time. Each job knows the processing lengths of other jobs and hence this induces a game amongst the jobs. The objective in the coordination mechanisms is to design scheduling policies which have small Price of Anarchy (PoA) [33]. PoA measures the degradation in the social cost (objective function) at an equilibrium (typically Nash Equilibrium or Correlated Equilibrium) compared to the offline optimum which can assign each job to any machine. Coordination mechanisms have been extensively studied in the context of scheduling for the makespan objectives [4, 11, 10, 31]. Recently, Cole et al. [17] studied the coordination mechanisms for minimizing the weighted completion objective, and showed that many scheduling policies such as Shortest Job First, Round Robin and their weighted extensions to lead to games with constant PoA when all release dates are same (In this case, a job's completion time is equal to its flow time).

While coordination games provide valuable insight on the effect of selfish jobs, the assumption that jobs reach a NE is not very realistic in many settings, especially for scheduling jobs that arrive online. In these applications, it is unlikely that an arriving job will have the complete knowledge of other jobs that will arrive in future, hence studying the cost at a Nash Equilibrium may not be the right solution concept. Also in many cases, jobs make one-time decision on which machine they are assigned to (as in the DNS example), and are not reassigned.

Unfortunately, there has been very little work on designing efficient scheduling algorithms for greedy jobs in online setting. Now that resources are growing both in complexity and quantity, we believe that developing scheduling algorithms for greedy jobs for various objectives is of increasing importance. In this paper we take the initiative in this direction. Following our discussion, we assume that upon the arrival each job *selfishly and irrevocably selects a machine which minimizes its own flow time looking at only the sets of jobs assigned to each machine*. We also require that each machine can run only a *strongly local* scheduling policy that makes its scheduling decisions based only on the set of jobs assigned to it (independent of the processing lengths of jobs on other machines). Local scheduling policies are more desirable since they can save communication cost between machines and are easier to implement. We will consider unrelated machines, and will refer to this setting as scheduling of greedy jobs on unrelated machines. In this paper we would like to explore the following concrete questions:

Are there strongly local online scheduling policies for the unrelated machine setting that are constant competitive for total weighted flow objective? Can we design scheduling algorithms that align the best moves for the overall system with that of individual jobs?

1.1 Our Results and Contributions

Our main result is that Smoothed Latest Arrival Processor Sharing (SLAPS), and its weighted version, recently introduced by Im et al [27, 28], answers the above questions in the affirmative in the resource augmentation model. In resource augmentation model, the online algorithm is allowed to run each machine $(1+\epsilon)$ times faster and is compared to an optimal offline scheduler that runs at a unit speed [32]. Without resource augmentation, the competitive ratio of any online algorithm can be unbounded [23]. An online algorithm is said to be *scalable* if it is $O(poly(1/\epsilon))$-competitive for all $\epsilon > 0$, and finding a scalable algorithm is in general considered to be the ultimate goal when there is a strong lower bound on competitive ratio without speed augmentation.

Our main result is the following.

- For the problem of minimizing the weighted flow time of greedy jobs on unrelated machines, we show that Weighted SLAPS is $(1+\epsilon)$-speed $O(1/\epsilon^2)$-competitive for any $0 < \epsilon \leq 1$ (Theorem 3.1).

We prove several crucial properties of SLAPS that leads to the desired result. We believe that these properties may be of independent interest in analyzing SLAPS for other scheduling problems.

Recently, another important research direction in scheduling theory has been designing energy efficient algorithms. Dynamic speed scaling is a widely studied setting where machines can be run faster by consuming more energy. In this setting, one of the most widely studied models is where a machine consumes energy s^α when run at a speed of s. The goal of an energy efficient scheduler is to minimize total weighted flow time plus total energy consumed.

Our next result is an energy efficient algorithm in our setting.

- For the problem of minimizing the weighted flow time plus energy of greedy jobs on unrelated machines, we give a strongly local scheduling policy that is $O(\alpha^2)$-competitive (Theorem 4.1).

To the best of our knowledge, these are the first positive results for scheduling greedy jobs online in the multiple machines setting (even in the simplest identical machines case) for any scheduling objectives except minimizing the maximum flow time when all jobs arrive at time 0 (makespan). We note that when the scheduler can assign each job to any machine, the best known results for each of the above problems are a $(1+\epsilon)$-speed $O(1/\epsilon)$-competitive algorithm and a $O(\alpha/\log\alpha)$-competitive algorithm, respectively [2, 35, 19]. Perhaps, it is surprising that one can obtain results that nearly match the best known results even when jobs behave selfishly.

1.2 Limitations of Previous Approaches

The first scalable algorithm for minimizing weighted flow time on unrelated machine was given by Chadha et al. in a breakthrough result [13]. The algorithm in [13] had two properties which are highly desirable in multiple machines scheduling – *immediate dispatch* and *non-migration*. That is, the scheduler immediately dispatches an incoming job to a machine, and the job never migrates to other machines. Furthermore, their algorithm consisted of two surprisingly simple components: each machine runs the Highest Density First (the density of a job is defined as the ratio of its weight to size), and the dispatch rule is to assign each incoming job to the machine that increases the objective the least. Later, Anand et al. [2] improved this result via a novel dual fitting argument to obtain a slightly better competitive ratio, and extended their result to dynamic speed scaling setting.

The scheduling algorithms Highest Density First (HDF) or Highest Residual Density First (HRDF) that were used to get a (centralized) scalable algorithm by [13, 2], however, result in a competitive ratio as high as $\Omega(n)$ even when given any constant speed augmentation in our setting (We defer the proof to the full version.) The main reason for this catastrophic degradation in the performance is because the best move for individual jobs can be very different from the best move for the overall system. In particular, the greedy dispatch rule – assign incoming job to the machine that increase the objective by the least– is very crucial and a common ingredient in the works of [13, 26, 2]. Hence, it would be natural to ask the question: Is the greedy dispatch rule robust? How critical is it to minimize the increase in the objective when assigning jobs to machines?

Indeed, one can show that if the dispatch rule repeatedly makes a non-optimal decision in dispatching jobs, even if it is a constant factor off from the optimal decision, the resulting schedule could be far from the optimum without substantial speed augmentation. This is the case no matter what algorithm each machines uses. Thus, it is imperative that any algorithm in our setting has to unify the best moves for the overall system and for individual jobs.

Then probably the first algorithm one would try will be Round Robin (RR) – for a while let us assume that jobs are unweighted to simplify our discussion. Intuitively, RR processes all jobs at the same rate, so the overall system performance will be less susceptible to jobs selfish behavior. This intuition turns out to be true, and one can show that RR achieves a constant competitive ratio for average flow time when given $(2+\epsilon)$-speed. However, RR is known to be not scalable [32]. Similarly, it is easy to show a lower bound of $\Omega(n)$ on Shortest Elapsed Time First (SETF) even with constant speed augmentation. The next natural candidate algorithm will be then Latest Arrival Processor Sharing (LAPS) which was first introduced by Edmonds and Pruhs in a beautiful result and was shown to be scalable for the average flow time objective in a fairly general scheduling setting [21]. The algorithm LAPS generalizes RR, and round-robins among a fraction of the most recently arriving jobs; the fraction is given as a parameter. Although LAPS was developed for scheduling for jobs of different parallelizability [21], it has been proven to be very useful in other scheduling contexts, in particular broadcast scheduling [7, 20]. However, when it comes to multiple (heterogeneous) machines scheduling, LAPS has a serious weakness that the increase of the objective due to a new job's arrival cannot be easily bounded. In a nutshell, it is because LAPS processes only jobs within a 'boundary' and this makes it very hard to measure the increase. Perhaps this is the reason why there is no work that used LAPS in non-identical machines settings [1].

SLAPS **and its properties.** We use SLAPS (and its weighted version), recently introduced by Im et al [27, 28], to overcome this issue. What SLAPS distinguishes itself from LAPS the most is its *proportional invariance*. The proportional invariance property states that the relative speed of two jobs does not change upon the arrival of new jobs into the machine. This simple property turns out to be very important in the analysis of SLAPS. In particular, using the proportional invariance property we establish that the flow time of a newly arriving job *closely* approximates the increase in the objective. We call this crucial property of SLAPS as *bounded externality*. Hence, when machines run SLAPS, individual job's greedy behavior leads to (approximately) globally good behavior. This is our key idea in obtaining scalable algorithm when jobs are greedy. This also answers the question (iii).

SLAPS seems to inherit many important properties of LAPS which has been very useful for various scheduling problems, for example see [7, 20, 14, 22]. One of those properties is that the scheduling decision is made only based on the *ordering of the arrival time* of currently existing jobs. This is a very unique property that LAPS has (and its special case, RR). In some cases, this counter intuitive scheduling decision makes the analysis a lot easier compared to other algorithms that use time-varying feature such as remaining processing times. SLAPS also makes its scheduling decisions only using the relative arrival ordering of jobs, and it seems that it can be used in all the places where LAPS was used to obtain the same results.

Finally, in terms of the service provided to individual jobs, we think SLAPS is more closer to Round Robin, which can be thought as a fair scheduling algorithm, than any other scheduling algorithm. One intuitive way of defining fairness is to let a job wait for at most a period of time in proportion to its size. The idea is to distinguish between jobs asking for different amount of resources, and this was the key intuition behind the total stretch objective which is the sum of each job's flow time divided by its size [9, 6]. In SLAPS, when a new job arrives, each existing job gets delayed by an amount up to a constant times the job's size, unlike LAPS (See Section 2). For these reasons, we believe that SLAPS is perhaps a more useful generalization of RR compared to LAPS.

[1]The only exception is [25] that used LAPS to show a scalable algorithm for average flow time on related machines. But the algorithm in [25] is migratory, which is very different from our setting.

1.3 Our technical contributions

Our analysis uses the elegant dual fitting framework introduced recently by Anand et al. [2]. So far our discussion was mainly on the difficulty arising due to the gap between the best moves for individual jobs and for entire system performance. Another challenge in obtaining a scalable algorithm in our setting is that we have to *directly argue with integral flow time* of jobs. Fractional flow time is a very useful relaxation of flow time and simplifies the analysis substantially, especially when potential functions are used [13, 30]. Another view of flow time of a job is to pay a unit cost/penalty for each unit of time for which the job waits. In fractional flow time, the penalty is only for the remaining portion of the job size (fractional weighted of a job is the remaining portion multiplied the job's weight). Roughly speaking, fractional flow time allows us to view each job as consisting of infinitesimal sized pieces, and hence any work on the job completes some pieces of the job. In general, fractional flow time is easier to handle. Hence it is now a standard approach to obtain a scheduling algorithm first for fractional flow time and convert it to integral flow using additional round of speed augmentation, for example [13, 30].

One crucial property needed in the analysis in [2] for minimizing the weighted flow time + energy was the monotonicity property of the underlying algorithm we discussed. Since HRDF (weighted version of Shortest Remaining Processing Time First) is not monotone, for the analysis of the total weighted flow time plus energy objective, [2] used Highest Density First (HDF) in place of HRDF. Unfortunately, HDF is the algorithm inspired by the fractional flow time view, and hence the analysis was done first on fractional flow time. This type of analysis cannot be used for our problem since the quantity each individual job seeks to minimize is its integral flow, not fractional flow. Hence throughout the analysis we need to argue only with the integral flow time. A consequence of this restriction is that, we can not use multiple rounds of speed augmentation typically seen in the analysis of many scheduling algorithms for flow time.

1.4 Other Related Work

Minimizing the average weighted flow time of jobs on unrelated machines has been extensively studied in the offline setting as well. The problem is known to be NP-hard to approximate within a factor of $\Omega(\log P)$ even when all machines are identical, i.e. p_{ij} is the same for all i [24]. Here P is the ratio of the maximum to the minimum job size. The current best result is by Bansal and Kulkarni [8] that achieves an approximation factor of $O(\log n \log P)$.

In the online setting, Avrahami and Azar [3] were first to consider immediate-dispatch non-migratory schedules for minimizing the flow time in the identical machine environment. Chekuri et al. [15] gave the first scalable algorithm for this setting. [15, 13] show that one can obtain a scalable algorithm by assigning jobs to identical machines at random. For the unrelated machine setting, the first scalable algorithm for minimizing weighted flow time on unrelated machine was given by Chadha et al. in a breakthrough result [13]. Extensions to the l_k-norms of the flow time on unrelated machines were considered in [29, 2]. Later, Anand et al. [2] improved these results via a novel dual fitting argument to obtain a slightly better competitive ratio.

Unfortunately, non-migratory algorithms do not lead any bounded competitive ratio for the objective of minimizing flow-time on unrelated machines in the non-clairvoyant setting [25]. On the other hand, if an algorithm is allowed to change the assignment of jobs over time, then scalable algorithms were obtained by Im et al in [27, 28]. In the setting we consider, however, migrating jobs over time is not allowed.

The flow-time objectives have also been considered when machines can change their speed by consuming more energy. The most common objective studied in this line of work is to minimize total weighted flow time plus total energy consumed. This objective offers a natural trade-off between weighted flow time and energy consumed [1]. Namely, one can improve the overall system performance by consuming more energy, and vice versa. For this objective, in the unrelated machines setting, Anand et al. [2] gave an $O(\alpha^2)$-competitive algorithm when each machine consumes energy s^α when it runs in speed s. Here the speed of the machine is set to the total (fractional) [2] weight of the jobs remaining at that time following the single machine scheduling result by Bansal et al. [5]. Intuitively, this is a natural way to balance two competing objectives, weighted flow time and energy since at each time the remaining jobs incur a total cost equal to their weight.

Much of the work on selfish scheduling of jobs has been considered in the setting of coordination games first introduced in a seminal paper [16]. In this setting, each machine declares a strongly local scheduling policy. The strategy of each job consists of choosing the machine which minimizes its own completion time. Each job knows the processing lengths of other jobs and hence this induces a game amongst the jobs. The objective in the coordination mechanisms is to design scheduling policies which have small Price of Anarchy (PoA) [33]. PoA measures the degradation in the social cost(objective function) at an equilibrium (typically Nash Equilibrium or Correlated Equilibrium) compared to the offline optimum which can assign each job to any machine. Coordination mechanisms have been extensively studied in the context of scheduling for the makespan objectives [4, 11, 10, 31]. Recently, Cole et al. [17] studied the coordination mechanisms for minimizing the weighted completion objective and showed that many scheduling policies such as Shortest Job First, Round Robin and their weighted extensions to lead to games with constant PoA when all release dates are same (In this case, a job's completion time is equal to its flow time).

However, our proposed model differs from the coordination mechanism model in many significant ways. In the coordination mechanisms, each job has the complete information of the system and knows the size and release dates of other jobs. Furthermore, it is a simultaneous move game. That is, jobs move around until they reach an equilibrium (which may take exponential steps and but is assumed to happen instantaneously). On the other hand, in our model jobs arrive online and each arriving job only knows about the set of jobs already present in the system. The jobs choose a machine looking at only the current state of the system. Hence the resulting configuration of jobs on machines need not be a Nash Equilibrium. We believe that our setting is a more realistic model of real world applications.

[2]The difference between fractional and integral weights will be discussed at the end of Section 1.1.

2. ALGORITHM SMOOTH LATEST ARRIVAL PROCESSOR SHARING (SLAPS) AND ITS PROPERTIES

To make our presentation more readable, we first describe the unweighted version of the algorithm (SLAPS) and discuss how it can be extended to weighted jobs in Section 2.2. See [27, 28] for more details. For the total flow time objective, the algorithm SLAPS is exactly the algorithm that will run on all machines. Also for the objective of total flow time plus energy, this algorithm will be used with appropriate dynamic speed scaling. The algorithm SLAPS is non-clairvoyant and local in the sense that if it is run on a machine, its scheduling decision relies only on the jobs assigned to the machine. Hence we will not need to refer to a specific machine to describe SLAPS. Our algorithm SLAPS is parameterized by a non-negative integer k, and we may use SLAPS_k to highlight the parameter it uses. Let $A(t)$ denote the set of alive jobs at time t. Order the jobs in $A(t)$ in increasing order of their arrival time. Let $\pi_{j,t}$ denote job j's rank at time t in this order. Here the earliest arriving job in $A(t)$ has rank 1 and the latest arriving job in $A(t)$ has rank $|A(t)|$. We assume without loss of generality that all jobs have distinct arrival times by breaking ties arbitrarily but consistently. Let $s \geq 1$ denote the speed that the algorithm is given. We distribute the total processing power available among the jobs in $A(t)$ by giving each job j the following speed:

$$h_j(t) := s \cdot \frac{\pi_{j,t}^k}{1^k + 2^k + ... + (|A(t)|)^k}, \tag{1}$$

We will refer $h_j(t)$ as j's share or speed at time t. Observe that the total share of all jobs in $A(t)$ is exactly s (when $A(t) \neq \emptyset$). This completes the description of the algorithm that each machine runs.

It is worth noting that SLAPS_0 is exactly ROUND ROBIN (RR).

2.1 Properties of SLAPS

We discuss several interesting properties of the algorithm SLAPS which will be useful throughout the analysis. We first summarize these useful properties in words. The formal description can be found below and in Lemma 3.2.

- Proportional Invariance: The *relative* speed that each job gets does not change when more jobs arrive.
- Bounded Externality: The total delay seen by all the jobs already present in the system (increase in the total flow time) upon arrival of a new job is bounded by the flow time of the newly arriving job, assuming it is the last job arriving into the system. See Lemma 3.2.
- Monotonicity: Consider two schedules σ and σ' where the set of jobs in σ is a subset of jobs in σ'. Then, at any point in time, if a job j is alive in both schedules, j is processed only slower in σ'. Further, at any time, σ' has no less alive jobs than σ.

In order to formally describe the above properties, we need to define some notation. Consider a set of jobs S say at time t. Now consider another set S' of alive jobs which arrive later than all jobs in S. Jobs in $S \cup S'$ are possibly partially processed. Let $h_j^S(t)$ denote job j's share of speed when the algorithm has only the jobs in S in its current queue $A(t)$. Similarly, define $h_j^{S \cup S'}(t')$ for the case where the algorithm has only the jobs in $S \cup S'$ in its current queue $A(t')$ at some time t'. Here we are implicitly assuming that the algorithm's instantaneous scheduling decision is oblivious to the remaining job sizes.

Proportional Invariance. For any two jobs $j, j' \in S$ and any time instants t and t' it is the case that $h_j^S(t)/h_{j'}^S(t) = h_j^{S \cup S'}(t')/h_{j'}^{S \cup S'}(t')$.

The property follows from the definition of SLAPS since each newly arriving job slows down the jobs in the set S by exactly the same factor. An interesting consequence of this property is that there exists an one-to-one mapping of time instants between two schedules such that remaining sizes of jobs in the set S are exactly the same.

Now fix time any time t, and consider two sets S and S' defined as above. Let σ denote the schedule induced when the algorithm works on jobs in S from time t. Likewise, σ' denote the schedule induced when the algorithm works on jobs in S from time t and jobs in S' arrive later than t. Let $h_j^{(\cdot)}$ denote the job j's share of speed in the schedule specified in the superscript. Let $n_j^{(\cdot)}$ denote the number (total weight) of alive jobs in the schedule specified in the superscript. Note that we added σ to $A(\tau)$ as superscript to emphasize that $A^\sigma(\tau)$ denotes the set of alive jobs at time τ in schedule σ.

Monotonicity. For any time $\tau \geq t$, $n_\tau^\sigma \leq n_\tau^{\sigma'}$. Also for any job $j \in A^\sigma(\tau)$, $h_j^\sigma(\tau) \geq h_j^{\sigma'}(\tau)$.

The monotonicity property follows from the definition of SLAPS since the rank of existing jobs does not change due to new jobs arrival but some portion of the processing power is given to new jobs. We stated these properties formally since there is a similar property that does not hold: when some jobs are completed, every job's speed can only increase. Although this seemingly-true property holds when $k = 0$ (RR), it is not the case for general k. We prove the bounded externality property in Lemma 3.2.

2.2 Weighted Version of SLAPS

In this section we extend the algorithm SLAPS to work for weighted jobs. The main intuition is to think of a job j of weight w_j as w_j copies of unweighted job with the same arrival time. Then the share of job j is defined as the total share of job j's copies; we assume wlog that w_j is an integer. More formally, define $\bar{w}_j := \sum_{j' \in A(t): r_{j'} \leq r_j} w_{j'}$, and $f(x) := 1^k + 2^k + \ldots + x^k$. Let j' be the job that arrives the latest before job j. Then job j's share is defined as $h_j(t) := s \cdot \frac{f(\bar{w}_j) - f(\bar{w}_{j'})}{f(\bar{w}_j)}$. Note that when jobs have unit weights, this definition is exactly the same as the one given for unweighted jobs.

We state a useful inequality that is used frequently in the analysis.

Proposition 2.1 *Consider any integer $k \geq 0$, and $n \geq 1$. Then it follows*

$$\frac{k+1}{n+k+1} \leq \frac{n^k}{1^k + 2^k + \ldots + n^k} \leq \frac{k+1}{n}$$

PROOF. To show the first inequality we use $1^k + 2^k + \ldots + (n-1)^k \leq \int_{x=0}^{n} x^k dx = n^{k+1}/(k+1)$. For the second, use $1^k + 2^k + \ldots + n^k \geq \int_{x=0}^{n} x^k dx$. □

3. TOTAL (AVERAGE) FLOW TIME

In this section we show that SLAPS induces a scalable algorithm (schedule) when each job chooses to go to the machine that minimizes its flow time. In order to present our analysis more transparently, we proceed our analysis assuming all jobs are unweighted, i.e. $w_j = 1$, and the analysis for weighted jobs is presented is similar and we omit the proof in this version. We remind the reader that each job's decision is also myopic in the sense that its decision is made solely based on the current status of machines without considering future jobs. As mentioned before, our model is immediate-dispatch and non-migratory: every job chooses the machines immediately upon its arrival, and no job migrates to other machines once assigned to a machine. We prove the following theorem. For simplicity, $1/\epsilon$ is assumed to be an integer.

Theorem 3.1 *Suppose that the online algorithm is given $1 + 3\epsilon$ speed for any $0 < \epsilon \leq 1$. If all machines run* SLAPS$_k$ *where $k = 1/\epsilon$, the resulting schedule is $O(1/\epsilon^2)$-competitive for the objective of average flow time of all jobs.*

We begin our analysis by proving the bounded externality property of SLAPS. We will show that the increase in total flow time due to job j's arrival and the flow time of job j (assuming no more jobs arrive) are comparable. Let $F_{ij}(r_j)$ denote the flow time of job j when it chooses machine i at time r_j assuming that no more jobs arrive. Let Δ_{ij} denote the increase in the total flow time. More precisely, Δ_{ij} is the increase of flow time of all jobs that are in the queue of machine i upon the arrival of job j plus job j's flow time $F_{ij}(r_j)$. We remark once more that Δ_{ij} and $F_{ij}(r_j)$ are defined assuming that j is the last job on machine i.

Lemma 3.2 $\Delta_{ij} \leq (k+2) F_{ij}(r_j)$.

PROOF. For notational simplicity, consider any fixed machine i, and re-index jobs so that every job j' in $A_i(t)$ has rank j'. Let $1, 2, \ldots, n$ be the jobs in $A_i(t)$. Throughout the proof we drop the machine i from the notation if there is no confusion from the context. Let $n+1$ be the newly arriving job. The proportional invariance property of SLAPS states that all jobs are slowed down by exactly the same factor upon the arrival of a new job. This allows us to define a mapping between the schedules before and after the new job $n+1$ arrives.

Let σ denote the schedule of jobs $1, 2, \ldots, n$ on machine i defined from time r_{n+1} assuming that no more jobs arrive, and σ' the schedule of jobs $1, 2, \ldots, n, n+1$. The schedule σ' is also defined from time r_{n+1} assuming that no more jobs arrive. Let C' denote the completion time of job $n+1$ in σ'. We can define a one-to-one map between the time steps in two schedules σ and σ' with the same remaining processing times of jobs $1, 2, \ldots, n$. Formally, let $(q_1^\sigma(t), q_2^\sigma(t), \ldots q_n^\sigma(t))$, denote the vector of remaining processing times of jobs in the schedule σ and similarly define $(q_1^{\sigma'}(t), q_2^{\sigma'}(t), \ldots q_n^{\sigma'}(t))$. For every time instant t in the schedule σ, we find the corresponding time instant t' in σ' such that, vector of remaining processing times of jobs are equal. Note that, this mapping is only possible due to proportional invariance property of SLAPS. Define the unique function $g(t) : [r_{n+1}, C] \rightarrow [r_{n+1}, C']$ that maps time steps in σ to σ'. Here C denotes the time step in σ corresponding to the time C' in σ'. It is easy to see that $C' \geq C$ due to the monotonicity property of SLAPS. Let $g^{-1}(t)$ denote the time step in σ corresponding to t in σ'.

Consider any infinitesimal time interval $[t, t + \mathrm{d}t)$ in $[r_{n+1}, C']$ where no job is completed. Obviously, flow time of job $n+1$ is $F_{n+1}(r_{n+1}) := C' - r_{n+1}$. Now we look at how much the schedule σ slows down during $[t, t+\mathrm{d}t)$ compared to σ'. That is, we will compare the length of two intervals, $[t, t+\mathrm{d}t)$ and $[g^{-1}(t), g^{-1}(t+\mathrm{d}t))$. The new job $n+1$ slows down other jobs processing, and each alive job in $1, 2, \ldots, n$ experiences a delay of $\mathrm{d}t - (g^{-1}(t+\mathrm{d}t) - g^{-1}(t))$. Let n_t be the number of alive jobs amongst $1, 2, \ldots, n$ in σ during $[t, t+\mathrm{d}t)$. From the definition (1) we know that each job (except $n+1$) is processed in σ' at a slower rate as it is in σ, and the exact slow down factor is

$\frac{1^k+2^k+...+n_t^k}{1^k+2^k+...+n_t^k+(n_t+1)^k}$. Hence the total increase of flow time during $[t, t+\mathrm{dt})$ in σ' from σ is at most,

$$\begin{aligned}
& \frac{(n_t+1)^k}{1^k+2^k+...+(n_t+1)^k} \cdot n_t \cdot \mathrm{dt} + \mathrm{dt} \qquad (2) \\
\leq \quad & (k+1) \cdot \frac{n_t}{n_t+1} \cdot \mathrm{dt} + \mathrm{dt} \leq (k+2)\mathrm{dt}
\end{aligned}$$

The quantity consists of two parts: the first part is due to the increase of flow of "old" jobs and the second (dt) is part of the flow time of job $n+1$. The first inequality is due to Proposition 2.1. We charge the first part to the second, which completes the proof. □

3.1 Dual Fitting

To prove Theorem 3.1, we use the dual fitting framework in [2]. We first write a linear programming relaxation of the problem $\mathsf{LP}_{\mathsf{primal}}$ described below which was first given by [2]. It has a variable x_{ijt} for each machine $i \in [m]$, each job $j \in [n]$ and each unift time slot $t \geq r_j$. If the machine i processes the job j during the whole time slot t, then this variable is set to 1. The first constraint says that every job has to be completely processed. The second constraint says that a machine cannot process more than one unit of jobs during any time slot. Note that the LP allows a job to be processed simultaneously across different machines.

$$\text{Min} \sum_j \sum_i \sum_{t \geq r_j} w_j \cdot \left(\frac{t-r_j}{p_{ij}} + \frac{1}{2}\right) \cdot x_{ijt} \qquad (\mathsf{LP}_{\mathsf{primal}})$$

$$\begin{aligned}
\sum_i \sum_{t \geq r_j} \frac{x_{ijt}}{p_{ij}} &\geq 1 && \forall j \\
\sum_{j : t \geq r_j} x_{ijt} &\leq 1 && \forall i, t \\
x_{ijt} &\geq 0 && \forall i, j, t : t \geq r_j
\end{aligned}$$

We briefly discuss how the objective function lower bounds the total weighted flow time of a feasible integral schedule where each job is processed on a single machine. For more details see [2]. Say job j is assigned to machine i. In the objective function, one can easily see the term $\sum_{t \geq r_j} w_j \cdot (\frac{t-r_j}{p_{ij}}) \cdot x_{ijt}$ is at most job j's weighted flow time due to the first constraint. In fact, the quantity is the fractional weighted flow time of the job j, which is well known to be at most its integral weighted flow time, minus $w_j p_{ij}/2$. The remaining term $\sum_{t \geq r_j} w_j \cdot (1/2) \cdot x_{ijt}$ equals $w_j p_{ij}/2$. Hence, $\mathsf{LP}_{\mathsf{primal}}$ is a valid relaxation. We note that the '1/2' in the objective is crucial since otherwise the LP can cheat by processing a job simultaneously on a lot of machines, thereby paying very little for the job.

Now we write the dual of the above linear program.

$$\text{Max} \sum_j y_j - \sum_i \sum_t z_{it} \qquad (\mathsf{LP}_{\mathsf{dual}})$$

$$\begin{aligned}
\frac{y_j}{p_{ij}} - z_{it} &\leq w_j\left(\frac{t-r_j}{p_{ij}} + \frac{1}{2}\right) && \forall i, j, t : t \geq r_{ij} \\
y_j &\geq 0 && \forall j \\
z_{it} &\geq 0 && \forall i, t
\end{aligned}$$

Setting dual variables: We proceed our analysis by defining the dual variables as follows. As mentioned before, we will assume that all jobs have weight 1, and extend to arbitrary weights later. Say job j chose to go to machine i. We set y_j to be $1/8$ times the flow time of job j at the time of its arrival assuming that no more jobs arrive, i.e. $y_j = F_{ij}(r_j)/8$. We set z_{it} to be $1/8(k+3)$ times the total number of alive jobs at the time t on machine i, i.e. $z_{it} = \frac{n_{it}}{8(k+3)}$ where n_{it} denotes the total number of jobs that are alive at time t on machine i.

Bounding the dual objective: By Lemma 3.2 we know that $\sum_j y_j$ is $1/8(k+2)$ times the total flow time. Also due to the well known fact that the sum of number of alive jobs over all times equals the total flow time, we conclude that $\sum_i \sum_t z_{it} = F^A/8(k+3)$, where F^A is the total flow time of all jobs in our algorithm. Therefore, the dual objective is $\Omega(1/k^2) = O(\epsilon^2)$ times the total flow time, which establishes the competitive ratio claimed in Theorem 3.1, if the dual variables satisfy all the constraints.

It now remains to show that this definition of dual variables satisfies the dual constraints. Note that we need to satisfy the dual constraint for any pair of job j and machine i. We consider two cases.

Case 1: Job j chooses machine i. We first show the constraint is satisfied assuming that job j is the job arriving the last, then later will lift this assumption using the monotonicity property of SLAPS.

For any time $t \in [r_j, r_j + F_{ij}(r_j)]$, $F_{ij}(r_j) - (t - r_j)$ is the remaining flow time of job j. We observe that the speed with which the job j is processed can only increase as time passes. This follows from the proposition stated below and noting that j is the highest ranked job.

Proposition 3.3 *$n^k/(1^k + 2^k + ... + n^k)$ is decreasing in n.*

PROOF. We view $n^k/(1^k + 2^k + ... + n^k)$ as $\frac{\sum_{l \in [n]} l^k - (l-1)^k}{\sum_{l \in [n]} l^k}$. We use the following: given positive a_i, b_i such that $\frac{a_1}{b_1} \geq \frac{a_2}{b_2} \geq ... \geq \frac{a_l}{b_l}$, it follows that $\frac{\sum_{l' \in [l-1]} a_i}{\sum_{l' \in [l-1]} b_i} \geq \frac{\sum_{l' \in [l]} a_i}{\sum_{l' \in [l]} b_i}$. Hence it suffices to show $\frac{l^k - (l-1)^k}{l^k} = 1 - (1 - 1/l)^k$ is decreasing in l, which is indeed the case. □

Hence we deduce that $F_{ij}(r_j) - (t - r_j) \leq p_{ij}/h_{ij}(t)$ where $h_{ij}(t)$ is the speed job j gets at time t. Also we know by Proposition 2.1 that for all $t \geq r_j$, $h_{ij}(t) \geq s \cdot \frac{n_{it}^k}{\sum_{l=1}^{n_{it}} l^k} \geq s \cdot \frac{k+1}{n_{it}+k+1}$.
Hence we get,

$$\begin{aligned}
\frac{8y_j - (t-r_j)}{p_{ij}} &= \frac{F_{ij}(r_j) - (t-r_j)}{p_{ij}} \\
\leq \quad & \frac{1}{h_{ij}(t)} \leq \frac{1}{s} \cdot (1 + \frac{n_{it}}{k+1}) \\
= \quad & \frac{1}{s}(1 + \frac{k+3}{k+1} \cdot 8z_{it}) \leq 1 + 8z_{it}
\end{aligned}$$

Note that we used the facts that $s = 1 + 3\epsilon$ and $k = 1/\epsilon$. Arranging terms shows the dual constraints are satisfied.

We now explain why the assumption that no more jobs arrive after j is w.l.o.g. Note that y_j relies only on the jobs arriving no later than job j, hence has no dependency on jobs arriving after job j. Finally, the monotonicity property of SLAPS states that for any *fixed* time $t \geq r_j$, when more jobs arrive into machine i, the number of alive jobs at time t on machine i, n_{it} can only increase. Hence, if more jobs arrive, it only gives more slack to the dual constraint.

Case 2: Job j chooses a machine other than i. Say that job j chose to go to machine $i' \neq i$. As in the previous case, we can without loss of generality assume that no more jobs arrive. Throughout the analysis we will be concerned with two schedules σ and σ'. The first schedule σ is the real schedule which describes how jobs are processed on machine i since time r_j. The second schedule is a fictitious schedule on machine i obtained if job j were assigned to machine i, rather i'. The proof from the case one implies that dual constraints are satisfied if we were to consider the schedule σ'. However, we need to work with schedule σ. One cause of concern is that the number of alive jobs in σ may be much less than the number of alive jobs in σ'. However, by carefully mapping the two schedules we show that this is not the case.

As we did in the proof of Lemma 3.2 we can define one-to-one mapping between σ and σ' so that the two schedules have exactly the same remaining processing time for all jobs except j which are assigned to machine i. We will use $g(t)$ to denote the unique time step in σ' corresponding to t in σ. We let C' denote job j's completion time in σ'. Let $C = g^{-1}(C')$. Consider any time $t \in [r_j, C]$. Consider an infinitesimal time interval $[t, t + \mathrm{d}t)$ in $[r_j, C]$. We note that the length of the interval in σ' corresponding to $[t, t + \mathrm{d}t)$ in σ is at most

$$\mathrm{d}t + \frac{(n_{it}+1)^k}{1^k + 2^k + ... + n_{it}^k}\mathrm{d}t \leq \mathrm{d}t + \frac{k+1}{n_t}(1 + \frac{1}{n_{it}})^k \mathrm{d}t \quad (3)$$

where n_{it} is the number of alive jobs at time t on machine i in schedule σ. This is because every alive job in σ is processed slower than in σ' by a factor of $(\sum_{l=1}^{n_{it}} l^k)/(\sum_{l=1}^{n_{it}+1} l^k)$. The inequality is due to Proposition 2.1.

Note that job j is alive at time $g(t)$ in schedule σ', and that is the only difference from the schedule σ at time t. We now consider two cases. If $n_t \geq k + 1$, (3) is at most 4dt. Now suppose that $n_{it} < k+1$. Since job j has the highest rank, the fraction the job j gets from the total speed s in σ' is at least $(n_{it} + 1)^k/(1^k + 2^k + ... + (n_{it} + 1)^k) \geq \frac{k+1}{k+1+n_{it}+1} \geq 1/2$ by Proposition 2.1. Hence the total length of such time steps is at most $2p_{ij}$. Hence we have shown that for any $t \in [r_j, C)$,

$$g(t) - t \leq 4(t - r_j) + 2p_{ij} \quad (4)$$

We are now ready to complete our analysis.

$$\begin{aligned}
\frac{8y_j - (t - r_j)}{p_{ij}} &= \frac{F_{i'j}(r_j) - (t - r_j)}{p_{ij}} \\
&\leq \frac{F_{ij}(r_j) - (t - r_j)}{p_{ij}} \quad \text{[Since job } j \text{ chose } i' \text{ over } i] \\
&= \frac{F_{ij}(r_j) - (g(t) \quad r_j) + (g(t) - t)}{p_{ij}} \\
&\leq \frac{1}{s}(1 + \frac{n_{it}+1}{k+1}) + \frac{(g(t) - t)}{p_{ij}} \quad (5) \\
&\leq 2 + 8z_{it} + \frac{4(t - r_j)}{p_{ij}} + 2 \quad (6)
\end{aligned}$$

The inequality in (5) follows from the same argument in the previous case since σ' is constructed by assigning job j to i. Here note that the '1' is added to n_{it} to count job j. The inequality (6) follows from (4). By rearranging terms, we complete the analysis.

4. EXTENSION TO TOTAL FLOW + ENERGY

In this section we extend the online greedy scheduling problem to the speed scaling setting. In this setting, each machine's speed can be adjusted dynamically, and consumes power s^α when it runs with speed s where $\alpha > 1$ is a constant which is uniform to all machines. The goal is to design local scheduling policy and a dynamic speed scaling algorithm to minimize the total flow time plus energy consumption. We aim to prove the following theorem.

Theorem 4.1 *There exists an online algorithm such that when each machine runs the algorithm, and each job goes to the machine that minimizes its flow time without considering future jobs, the resulting schedule is $O(\alpha^2)$-competitive for the problem of minimizing the total flow time plus energy in the unrelated machines setting.*

4.1 Algorithm

As before, each machine will run SLAPS$_k$ with $k = \lceil \alpha \rceil$. In the analysis, for simplicity, we will assume that α is an integer greater than 1; this assumption can be easily removed, and the same analysis goes through. The speed of machine i at time t is set to $n_{it}^{1/\alpha}$. Here n_{it} denotes the total number of alive jobs at time t that are assigned to machine i. For the sake of analysis, we will assume that each machine gets more speed by factor $s = \max(\frac{k+3}{k}, \frac{(k+1)(k+2)}{k+3})$ if $\alpha < 4$ and $s = \frac{k+3}{k}$ otherwise, than it should get for consuming n_{it}. That is, each machine i consumes power equal to n_{it} and gets speed $s \cdot n_{it}^{1/\alpha}$. Note that the total power is equal to s^α times the total flow time. However, this is only $O(1)$ times the cost of flow time. Hence we will focus on bounding the total flow time, and factor in the energy cost at the end of analysis. Our algorithm for setting the speed at each time instant is same as the one used in [5, 23].

4.2 Analysis of Total Flow + Energy

In this section we give the proof of theorem 4.1. Taking similar steps as in the analysis of the average flow time objective, we will show that the increase in total flow time due to job j's arrival and the flow time of job j at the time of arrival are comparable. We use the same notation $F_{ij}(r_j)$ and Δ_{ij}. We prove a similar bound as one in the Lemma 4.2 taking into consideration the effect of dynamic speed scaling.

Lemma 4.2 $\Delta_{ij} \leq (k + 2)F_{ij}(r_j)$.

PROOF. The proof is similar to that of Lemma 4.2, hence we will omit few details and highlight the differences. Recall that, σ denotes the schedule of jobs $1, 2, ..., n$ on machine i defined from time r_{n+1} assuming that no more jobs arrive, and σ' the schedule of jobs $1, 2, ..., n, n+1$. Note that, jobs are renamed to match their rank and $n + 1$ is the latest arriving job. Let $g(t) : [r_{n+1}, C] \to [r_{n+1}, C']$ be the function which maps time steps in σ to σ' where remaining processing lengths of jobs are same. Unlike in the case of proof of Lemma 4.2, here two schedules run at different speeds. However, proportional invariance property still holds and it is easy to see that every job is slowed by exactly the same amount. Hence, $g(t)$ is well defined.

Consider any infinitesimal time interval $[t, t + \mathrm{d}t)$ in $[r_{n+1}, C']$ where no job is completed. Clearly, flowtime of job $n + 1$ is $F_{n+1}(r_{n+1}) := C - r_{n+1}$. Now we look at how much the schedule σ' slows down during $[t, t + \mathrm{d}t)$ compared to σ during $[g^{-1}(t), g^{-1}(t + \mathrm{d}t))$. The new job $n + 1$ slows down other jobs, and recall that delay seen by each job is $dt-(g^{-1}(t+\mathrm{d}t)-g^{-1}(t))$. Here we also need to consider the fact that machine i runs at speed $n_{it}^{1/\alpha}$ in σ and $(n_{it} + 1)^{1/\alpha}$ in σ'. It is easy to see that the slow down factor is

$$\frac{1^k + 2^k + ... + n_{it}^k}{1^k + 2^k + ... + n_{it}^k + (n_{it} + 1)^k} \cdot \frac{(n_{it} + 1)^{1/\alpha}}{n_{it}^{1/\alpha}}$$

Here the second term $\frac{(n_{it}+1)^{1/\alpha}}{n_{it}^{1/\alpha}}$ is greater than 1, hence we can ignore it in lower bounding the slow down factor. Therefore, rest of the analysis remains exactly the same as in the proof of Lemma 4.2. This completes the proof.

□

4.3 Dual Fitting Analysis for Total Flow + Energy

We write a convex programming relaxation for the average flow plus energy objective. At a high level, this formulation is essentially the same as the one presented in [2] but is easier to work with and interpret. Due to this, we modestly simplify the analysis and make it exactly similar to analysis of the flow time objective. As noted earlier, since each job chooses the machine which minimizes its flow time upon its arrival, we no longer can afford to work with the fractional flow time of jobs unlike the previous works.

Consider the convex program $\mathsf{CP}_{\mathsf{primal}}$ described below. It has a variable x_{ijt} for each machine $i \in M$, each job $j \in J$ and each unit time-slot $t \geq r_j$. If the machine i processes the job j during the whole time slot t, then this variable is set to 1. It has a variable s_{it} for each machine i and each time slot t. The variable s_{it} indicates the speed used by machine i at time t.

$$\text{Min} \sum_j \sum_i \sum_{t \geq r_j} w_j \cdot x_{ijt} \cdot \left(\frac{t - r_j}{p_{ij}} + \frac{1}{2} \right) + \sum_i \sum_t s_{it}^{\alpha} \qquad (\mathsf{CP}_{\mathsf{primal}})$$

$$\begin{aligned} \sum_i \sum_{t \geq r_j} \frac{x_{ijt}}{p_{ij}} &\geq 1 && \forall j \\ \sum_{j : t \geq r_j} x_{ijt} &\leq s_{it} && \forall i, t \\ x_{ijt} &\geq 0 && \forall i, j, t : t \geq r_j \end{aligned}$$

The first constraint says that every job has to be completely processed. The second constraint says that a machine cannot process more than s_{it} units of the jobs during any time slot. Note that the convex program allows a job to be processed simultaneously across different machines. The first term in the objective is a lower bound on the *total cost* of any feasible schedule was shown in [2]. We would like to point out that the first term in the objective does not lower bound the total flow time of jobs. The second term is obviously the total power consumed. Hence this convex program is at most $O(1)$ times the cost of optimal solution.

We derive the dual of the above convex program by following the template outlined in [18]. In the dual objective, the second part is the conjugate function of $\sum_i \sum_t s_{it}^{\alpha}$.

$$\text{Max} \sum_j y_j - (1 - \frac{1}{\alpha}) \cdot \alpha^{\frac{1}{1-\alpha}} \sum_i \sum_t u_{it}^{\frac{\alpha}{\alpha-1}} \qquad (\mathsf{CP}_{\mathsf{dual}})$$

$$\begin{aligned} \frac{y_j}{p_{ij}} - z_{it} &\leq w_j\left(\frac{t - r_j}{p_{ij}} + \frac{1}{2}\right) && \forall i, j, t : t \geq r_j \\ z_{it} &\leq u_{it} \\ y_j &\geq 0 && \forall j \\ z_{it} &\geq 0 && \forall i, t \end{aligned}$$

Setting the dual variables: Our analysis will be based on dual fitting. Again, we first study unweighted jobs and extend it to weighted jobs. Say job j chose to go to machine i. We set y_j to be $1/8$ times the flow time of job j at the time of its arrival assuming that no more jobs arrive, i.e. $y_j = F_{ij}(r_j)/40$. We set z_{it} and u_{it} to be $1/8(k+3)$ fraction of the number of jobs alive at the time t on machine i, i.e. $z_{it} = u_{it} = \frac{n_{it}^{(\alpha-1)/\alpha}}{8(k+3)}$ where n_{it} denotes the total number of jobs that are alive at time t on machine i.

Bounding the dual objective: We first show that from our definition of dual variables the dual objective is $\Omega(1/\alpha^2)$ times the total flow time of our algorithm, denoted by F^A.

$$\begin{aligned} &\text{OPT} \\ \geq\ & \sum_j y_j - (1 - \frac{1}{\alpha}) \cdot \alpha^{\frac{1}{1-\alpha}} \cdot \sum_i \sum_t u_{it}^{\frac{\alpha}{\alpha-1}} \\ \geq\ & \sum_j \frac{1}{8} F_{ij}(r_j) - (1 - \frac{1}{\alpha}) \cdot \alpha^{\frac{1}{1-\alpha}} \cdot \frac{1}{8(k+3)^{\alpha/(\alpha-1)}} \sum_i \sum_t n_{it} \\ \geq\ & \frac{1}{8(k+2)} F^A - \frac{1}{8(k+3)} F^A \quad \text{[By Lemma 4.2]} && (7) \\ =\ & \Omega(1/k^2) F^A = \Omega(1/\alpha^2) F^A && (8) \end{aligned}$$

This establishes that the dual objective is at least $\Omega(1/\alpha^2)$ times the total flow time. Moreover, the energy cost of our schedule is at most s^{α} times the total flow time, which we noted is at most $O(1)$ times the cost of flow time. Therefore, if we prove that dual constraints are satisfied, it follows from the weak duality theorem for convex programs and $\epsilon = 1/\lceil \alpha \rceil$ that the competitive ratio of our algorithm is at most $O(\alpha^2)$.

It now remains to show that this definition of dual variables satisfies the dual constraints. Note that we need to satisfy the dual constraints for any pair of job j and machine i. We consider two cases.

Case 1: *Job j chooses machine i.* We first observe that given the following lemma, it suffices to show that the constraint is satisfied assuming that job j is the last arriving job. This is because, our definition of y_j does not change upon arrival of new jobs and as a consequence of the following lemma, for any *fixed* time, z_{it} can only increase when more jobs arrive.

Lemma 4.3 *Consider two schedules σ and σ' such that:*

- *In both schedules, the same set of jobs arrive before the job j arrives.*
- *In σ, the job j is the last arriving job while in σ' some jobs arrive after job j arrives.*

Then at all times $t \geq r_j$, every job with arrival time at most r_j has been processed more in σ than in σ'.

PROOF. By the proportional invariance property, we observe that all jobs arriving before r_j are processed at the same relative rate in both schedules. Reindex the jobs such that any job l has the rank l. Let total number of alive jobs be n. If a new job is added, the speed of job l will change from, $l^k \cdot n^{1/\alpha}/(1^k + 2^k + ... + n^k)$ to $l^k \cdot (n+1)^{1/\alpha}/(1^k + 2^k + ... + (n+1)^k)$.

We will show that,

$$\frac{n^{1/\alpha}}{1^k + 2^k + ... + n^k} \geq \frac{(n+1)^{1/\alpha}}{1^k + 2^k + ... + (n+1)^k}$$

This will prove that any 'old' job's (jobs with release time at most r_j) speed can only decrease when new jobs arrive. Hence the lemma will follows. Toward this end, we use the following: given positive a_i, b_i such that $\frac{a_1}{b_1} \geq \frac{a_2}{b_2} \geq ... \geq \frac{a_l}{b_l}$, it follows that

$\frac{\sum_{l' \in [l-1]} a_i}{\sum_{l' \in [l-1]} b_i} \geq \frac{\sum_{l' \in [l]} a_i}{\sum_{l' \in [l]} b_i}$, and observe that it suffices to show that

$$\frac{(n+1)^{1/\alpha} - n^{1/\alpha}}{(n+1)^k}$$

is decreasing. This can be easily verified by differentiating the function. □

Hence we focus on the case when j is the last arriving job and show that all the dual constraints are satisfied.

Proposition 4.4 *The function $n^{1/\alpha} \cdot \frac{k+1}{n+k+1}$ is non-decreasing in the interval $[1, k + 1/\alpha - 1)$ and it is non-increasing everywhere else for all positive n.*

PROOF. We omit the details as this can be easily verified by looking at the derivate of the function. □

Consider the speed at which job j is processed at time t. Using Prooposition 2.1 we have,

$$h_{ij}(t) \geq s \cdot \frac{n_{it}^k}{\sum_{l=1}^{n_{it}} l^k} \cdot n_{it}^{1/\alpha} \geq s \cdot \frac{k+1}{n_{it}+k+1} \cdot n_{it}^{1/\alpha}$$

Let $h = s \cdot \min(\frac{k+1}{n_{it}+k+1} \cdot n_{it}^{1/\alpha}, \frac{k+1}{k+2})$. From Proposition 4.4 we conclude that, $h \leq h_{ij}(t)$ for all times $t \geq r_j$. For any time $t \in [r_j, r_j + F_{ij}(r_j)]$, $F_{ij}(r_j) - (t - r_j)$ measures the remaining flow time of job j. We observe that,

$$F_{ij}(r_j) - (t - r_j) \leq \frac{p_{ij}(t)}{h}$$

This follows from a) The right hand side of the inequality measures the projected flow time of the job $j$if it continues to get the speed h. b) However, the speed job j gets is lower bounded by h by Proposition 4.4. Now we consider two cases to show that dual constraints are satisfied.

Case a): $\alpha > 4$. In this case, note that we can assume without loss of generality that $h = s \cdot \frac{k+1}{n_{it}+k+1} \cdot n_{it}^{1/\alpha}$. This is because due to Proposition 4.4, the function increases in only the range $[1, 2)$ and then starts decreasing. However, if there is only one job it gets the entire speed, it is easy to see that dual constraints are trivially satisfied. Consider,

$$\frac{8y_j - (t - r_j)}{p_{ij}} = \frac{F_{ij}(r_j) - (t - r_j)}{p_{ij}} \leq \frac{1}{h_{ij}(t)} \leq \frac{1}{h}$$
$$\leq \frac{1}{s} \cdot (1 + \frac{n_{it}}{k+1}) \cdot n_{it}^{-1/\alpha} = \frac{1}{s}(1 + \frac{k+3}{k+1} \cdot 8z_{it}) \leq 1 + 8z_{it}$$

Note that we used the fact that $s \geq \frac{k+3}{k}$. Arranging terms shows the dual constraint is satisfied.
Case b): $\alpha \leq 4$. Suppose $h = s \cdot \frac{k+1}{k+2}$ since we already showed the other case. Then we have,

$$\frac{8y_j - (t - r_j)}{p_{ij}} = \frac{F_{ij}(r_j) - (t - r_j)}{p_{ij}} \leq \frac{1}{h_{ij}(t)} \leq \frac{1}{h}$$
$$\leq \frac{1}{s} \cdot \frac{k+2}{k+1} \cdot n^{1-1/\alpha} \leq \frac{1}{s} \cdot \frac{k+2}{k+1} \cdot 8(k+3) \cdot z_{it} \leq 1 + 8z_{it}$$

Again we used the fact that, $s \geq \frac{(k+3)(k+2)}{k+1}$ and $k = \alpha \leq 4$. This concludes the first case (1).

Case 2: *Job j chooses a machine other than i.* Say that job j chose to go to machine $i' \neq i$. As in the previous case, we can without loss of generality assume that no more jobs arrive. Throughout the analysis we will be concerned with two schedules σ and σ'.The first schedule σ is the real schedule which describes how jobs are processed on machine i since time r_j. The second schedule is a fictitious schedule on machine i obtained if job j were assigned to machine i, rather i'.

We define an one-to-one mapping from time steps in σ to time steps σ' so that in both schedules all jobs except j have exactly the same remaining processing times at two corresponding times. We will use $g(t)$ to denote the unique time step in σ corresponding to t in σ'. We can obtain the same relation as we did in the second case in showing dual constraints are satisfied in Section 3. The only difference is to take into account dynamic speed scaling, but it turns out that the quantity $g(t) - t$ measuring the delay due to job j can only decrease with dynamic speed scaling. Intuitively, in σ' the machine will run faster in the dynamic speed scaling setting compared to the static speed scaling setting.

$$g(t) - t \leq (t - r_j) + 2p_{ij} \tag{9}$$

We are now ready to complete our analysis.

$$\begin{aligned}
&\frac{8y_j - (t - r_j)}{p_{ij}} \\
=\ &\frac{F_{i'j}(r_j) - (t - r_j)}{p_{ij}} \\
\leq\ &\frac{F_{ij}(r_j) - (t - r_j)}{p_{ij}} \quad \text{[Since job } j \text{ chose } i' \text{ over } i\text{]} \\
=\ &\frac{F_{ij}(r_j) - (g(t) - r_j) + (g(t) - t)}{p_{ij}} \\
\leq\ &1 + 8z_{it} + 1 + \frac{(g(t) - t)}{p_{ij}} &(10) \\
\leq\ &8z_{it} + \frac{t - r_j}{p_{ij}} + 4 &(11)
\end{aligned}$$

The inequality (10) follows from the same argument in the previous case since σ' is constructed by assigning job j to i. Here note that the '1' is added to n_{it} to count job j. The inequality (11) follows from (9). By rearranging terms, we complete the analysis.

Acknowledgements

Part of this works was done while the authors were at Duke, where S. Im was supported in part by NSF grant CCF-1008065, and J. Kulkarni by NSF grants CCF-1408784, IIS- 1447554, and CCF-1348696. Later, S. Im continued this work at UC Merced supported in part by NSF grant CCF-1409130.

5. REFERENCES

[1] Susanne Albers and Hiroshi Fujiwara. Energy-efficient algorithms for flow time minimization. *ACM Transactions on Algorithms*, 3(4), 2007.

[2] S. Anand, Naveen Garg, and Amit Kumar. Resource augmentation for weighted flow-time explained by dual fitting. In *SODA*, pages 1228–1241, 2012.

[3] Nir Avrahami and Yossi Azar. Minimizing total flow time and total completion time with immediate dispatching. In *SPAA '03: Proceedings of the fifteenth annual ACM symposium on Parallel algorithms and architectures*, pages 11–18, 2003.

[4] Yossi Azar, Kamal Jain, and Vahab Mirrokni. (almost) optimal coordination mechanisms for unrelated machine scheduling. In *Proceedings of the nineteenth annual*

ACM-SIAM symposium on Discrete algorithms, SODA '08, pages 323–332, Philadelphia, PA, USA, 2008. Society for Industrial and Applied Mathematics.

[5] Nikhil Bansal, Ho-Leung Chan, and Kirk Pruhs. Speed scaling with an arbitrary power function. In *Proceedings of the twentieth Annual ACM-SIAM Symposium on Discrete Algorithms*, SODA '09, pages 693–701, Philadelphia, PA, USA, 2009. Society for Industrial and Applied Mathematics.

[6] Nikhil Bansal and Mor Harchol-Balter. Analysis of srpt scheduling: investigating unfairness. In *SIGMETRICS/Performance*, pages 279–290, 2001.

[7] Nikhil Bansal, Ravishankar Krishnaswamy, and Viswanath Nagarajan. Better scalable algorithms for broadcast scheduling. In *ICALP (1)*, pages 324–335, 2010.

[8] Nikhil Bansal and Janardhan Kulkarni. Minimizing flow-time on unrelated machines. In *Proceedings of the Forty-Seventh Annual ACM on Symposium on Theory of Computing, STOC 2015, Portland, OR, USA, June 14-17, 2015*, pages 851–860, 2015.

[9] Michael A. Bender, Soumen Chakrabarti, and S. Muthukrishnan. Flow and stretch metrics for scheduling continuous job streams. In *SODA*, pages 270–279, 1998.

[10] Ioannis Caragiannis. Better bounds for online load balancing on unrelated machines. In *SODA*, pages 972–981, 2008.

[11] Ioannis Caragiannis. Efficient coordination mechanisms for unrelated machine scheduling. In *SODA*, pages 815–824, 2009.

[12] Valeria Cardellini, Michele Colajanni, and Philip S. Yu. Request redirection algorithms for distributed web systems. *IEEE Trans. Parallel Distrib. Syst.*, 14(4):355–368, April 2003.

[13] Jivitej S. Chadha, Naveen Garg, Amit Kumar, and V. N. Muralidhara. A competitive algorithm for minimizing weighted flow time on unrelatedmachines with speed augmentation. In *Symposium on Theory of Computing*, pages 679–684, 2009.

[14] Ho-Leung Chan, Jeff Edmonds, and Kirk Pruhs. Speed scaling of processes with arbitrary speedup curves on a multiprocessor. *Theory Comput. Syst.*, 49(4):817–833, 2011.

[15] Chandra Chekuri, Ashish Goel, Sanjeev Khanna, and Amit Kumar. Multi-processor scheduling to minimize flow time with epsilon resource augmentation. In *STOC*, pages 363–372, 2004.

[16] G. Christodoulou, E. Koutsoupias, and A. Nanavati. Coordination mechanisms. *Theor. Comput. Sci.*, 410(36):3327–3336, August 2009.

[17] Richard Cole, José R. Correa, Vasilis Gkatzelis, Vahab Mirrokni, and Neil Olver. Inner product spaces for minsum coordination mechanisms. In *Proceedings of the 43rd annual ACM symposium on Theory of computing*, STOC '11, pages 539–548, New York, NY, USA, 2011. ACM.

[18] Nikhil R. Devanur. Fisher markets and convex programs.

[19] Nikhil R. Devanur and Zhiyi Huang. Primal dual gives almost optimal energy efficient online algorithms. In *Proceedings of the Twenty-Fifth Annual ACM-SIAM Symposium on Discrete Algorithms, SODA 2014, Portland, Oregon, USA, January 5-7, 2014*, pages 1123–1140, 2014.

[20] Jeff Edmonds, Sungjin Im, and Benjamin Moseley. Online scalable scheduling for the ℓ_k-norms of flow time without conservation of work. In *ACM-SIAM Symposium on Discrete Algorithms*, 2011.

[21] Jeff Edmonds and Kirk Pruhs. Scalably scheduling processes with arbitrary speedup curves. In *ACM-SIAM Symposium on Discrete Algorithms*, pages 685–692, 2009.

[22] Kyle Fox, Sungjin Im, and Benjamin Moseley. Energy efficient scheduling of parallelizable jobs. In *SODA*, pages 948–957, 2013.

[23] N. Garg and A. Kumar. Better algorithms for minimizing average flow-time on related machines. In *ICALP (1)*, 2006.

[24] Naveen Garg and Amit Kumar. Minimizing average flow-time : Upper and lower bounds. In *FOCS*, pages 603–613, 2007.

[25] Anupam Gupta, Sungjin Im, Ravishankar Krishnaswamy, Benjamin Moseley, and Kirk Pruhs. Scheduling heterogeneous processors isn't as easy as you think. In *Proceedings of the Twenty-Third Annual ACM-SIAM Symposium on Discrete Algorithms*, SODA '12, pages 1242–1253. SIAM, 2012.

[26] Anupam Gupta, Ravishankar Krishnaswamy, and Kirk Pruhs. Scalably scheduling power-heterogeneous processors. In *ICALP (1)*, pages 312–323, 2010.

[27] Sungjin Im, Janardhan Kulkarni, and Kamesh Munagala. Competitive algorithms from competitive equilibria: non-clairvoyant scheduling under polyhedral constraints. In *Symposium on Theory of Computing, STOC 2014, New York, NY, USA, May 31 - June 03, 2014*, pages 313–322, 2014.

[28] Sungjin Im, Janardhan Kulkarni, Kamesh Munagala, and Kirk Pruhs. Selfishmigrate: A scalable algorithm for non-clairvoyantly scheduling heterogeneous processors. In *55th IEEE Annual Symposium on Foundations of Computer Science, FOCS 2014, Philadelphia, PA, USA, October 18-21, 2014*, pages 531–540, 2014.

[29] Sungjin Im and Benjamin Moseley. An online scalable algorithm for minimizing ℓ_k-norms of weighted flow time on unrelated machines. In *ACM-SIAM Symposium on Discrete Algorithms*, 2011.

[30] Sungjin Im, Benjamin Moseley, and Kirk Pruhs. A tutorial on amortized local competitiveness in online scheduling. *SIGACT News*, 42(2):83–97, 2011.

[31] Nicole Immorlica, Li (Erran) Li, Vahab S. Mirrokni, and Andreas S. Schulz. Coordination mechanisms for selfish scheduling. *Theor. Comput. Sci.*, 410(17):1589–1598, April 2009.

[32] Bala Kalyanasundaram and Kirk Pruhs. Speed is as powerful as clairvoyance. *Journal of the ACM*, 47(4):617–643, 2000.

[33] Elias Koutsoupias and Christos H. Papadimitriou. Worst-case equilibria. In *STACS*, pages 404–413, 1999.

[34] Malte Schwarzkopf, Andy Konwinski, Michael Abd-El-Malek, and John Wilkes. Omega: flexible, scalable schedulers for large compute clusters. In *SIGOPS European Conference on Computer Systems (EuroSys)*, pages 351–364, Prague, Czech Republic, 2013.

[35] Nguyen Kim Thang. Lagrangian duality in online scheduling with resource augmentation and speed scaling. In *Algorithms - ESA 2013 - 21st Annual European Symposium, Sophia Antipolis, France, September 2-4, 2013. Proceedings*, pages 755–766, 2013.

Scheduling Parallelizable Jobs Online to Minimize the Maximum Flow Time

Kunal Agrawal Jing Li Kefu Lu Benjamin Moseley
Washington University in St. Louis.
{kunal, li.jing, kefulu, bmoseley}@wustl.edu

ABSTRACT

In this paper we study the problem of scheduling a set of dynamic multithreaded jobs with the objective of minimizing the maximum latency experienced by any job. We assume that jobs arrive online and the scheduler has no information about the arrival rate, arrival time or work distribution of the jobs. The scheduling goal is to minimize the maximum amount of time between the arrival of a job and its completion — this goal is referred to in scheduling literature as *maximum flow time*. While theoretical online scheduling of parallel jobs has been studied extensively, most prior work has focussed on a highly stylized model of parallel jobs called the "speedup curves model." We model parallel jobs as *directed acyclic graphs*, which is a more realistic way to model dynamic multithreaded jobs.

In this context, we prove that a simple First-In-First-Out scheduler is $(1+\epsilon)$-speed $O(\frac{1}{\epsilon})$-competitive for any $\epsilon > 0$. We then develop a more practical work-stealing scheduler and show that it has a maximum flow time of $O(\frac{1}{\epsilon^2}\max\{\mathrm{OPT}, \ln(n)\})$ for n jobs, with $(1+\epsilon)$-speed. This result is essentially tight as we also provide a lower bound of $\Omega(\log(n))$ for work stealing. In addition, for the case where jobs have weights (typically representing priorities) and the objective is minimizing the maximum weighted flow time, we show a non-clairvoyant algorithm is $(1+\epsilon)$-speed $O(\frac{1}{\epsilon^2})$-competitive for any $\epsilon > 0$, which is essentially the best positive result that can be shown in the online setting for the weighted case due to strong lower bounds without resource augmentation.

After establishing theoretical results, we perform an empirical study of work-stealing. Our results indicate that, on both real world and synthetic workloads, work-stealing performs almost as well as an optimal scheduler.

1. INTRODUCTION

In today's systems, response time, or latency, is often a very important measure of performance. For interactive services on clouds and servers, the platform scheduler is often interested in minimizing the maximum latency experienced by a job once it has been submitted to be processed. In addition, these services often run on large parallel machines with many processors and it is important to utilize these parallel machines efficiently to process these requests. In this paper, we consider the problem of minimizing the maximum latency or ***maximum flow time***. Formally, given n parallel jobs and a parallel machine with m processors, the scheduling goal is to minimize the amount of time between a job's arrival and its completion, over all jobs. We consider the online version of this problem, where jobs arrive dynamically. The objective of maximum flow time is the natural generalization of the makespan[1] objective to the case where jobs arrive over time. We also assume that the scheduler has no knowledge of the job arrival times or work distribution.

This paper focuses on parallel programs expressed through *dynamic multithreading*[2] (see [9, Ch. 27]), which is common in many parallel languages and libraries, such as Cilk dialects [14, 19], Intel TBB [25], Microsoft Parallel Programming Library [7] and OpenMP [23]. In these parallel languages, programmers express algorithmic parallelism, through linguistic constructs such as "spawn" and "sync," "fork" and "join," or parallel for loops. On the other hand, programmers do not need to provide any mapping from subcomputations to processors — it is the job of the scheduler to execute the work of each job onto processors efficiently.

Scheduling a single dynamic multithreaded program has been studied extensively in the parallel computing literature. Parallel runtime systems generally use work-stealing as a scheduler since it is known to be an efficient scheduler for such programs both theoretically and in practice [14, 5]. A single parallel program having W *work* — the running time on 1 processor, and P *critical-path length* — the length of the critical path (the longest path in the program), can be executed in $O(W/m + P)$ (expected) time on m processors (or workers) using a work-stealing scheduler. This running time is asymptotically optimal and guarantees linear speedup for programs with sufficient parallelism.

However, the problem of how to schedule these parallel programs in multiprogrammed environments where a quality of service guarantee must be provided is not well studied. There has been some prior work on how to allocate processors to programs in a fair and efficient manner [1] and some further work on using it to provide mean completion time

SPAA '16, July 11-13, 2016, Pacific Grove, CA, USA

DOI: http://dx.doi.org/10.1145/2935764.2935782

[1]The makespan of a schedule is the time that last job completes and this objective is popular when all jobs arrive at the same time.

[2]Dynamic multithreading is also called fork-join parallelism.

guarantees [16] and average flow time guarantees [2], but none of the work considers maximum flow time.

On the other hand, the multiprogrammed scheduling problem is well-studied for the case where each job is sequential, i.e. can only use one processor at a time. In particular, it is known that the algorithm First-In-First-Out (FIFO) is $(3/2 - \frac{1}{m})$-competitive [3, 4]. A related problem that has been considered for sequential jobs is when jobs have weights where weight represents some sort of priority of the job (not necessarily correlated with the job's work). In this case, the scheduler is interested in minimizing the maximum weighted flow time. For this setting, it is known that any algorithm is $\Omega(W^{.4})$-competitive where W is the ratio of the maximum weight to minimum weight. This is true even when jobs are sequential and unit sized [8].

Due to this strong lower bound, previous work has considered a *resource augmentation* analysis [20] where the algorithm is given extra speed over the adversary. An ***s-speed c-competitive*** algorithm achieves a competitive ratio of c when given processors s times the speed of the optimal schedule. An ideal algorithm is $(1+\epsilon)$-speed $O(f(\epsilon))$-competitive for any $\epsilon > 0$ where $f(\epsilon)$ is some function that only depends on ϵ. That is, an algorithm which achieves constant competitiveness with the minimum possible resource augmentation. Such an algorithm is referred to as *scalable*. Finding a scalable algorithm is the best positive result one can hope for when strong lower bounds exists without resource augmentation. For jobs with weights, a scalable algorithm is known when jobs are sequential [8].

In this paper, we present several theoretical results for minimizing maximum flow time for dynamic multithreaded jobs. These are the first known non-trivial results for maximum flow time in the DAG model. We refer the reader to Section 8 for work in related parallel models. All of the algorithms considered in this paper are *non-clairvoyant*, meaning that they have no prior knowledge of the size or structure of the jobs or when they arrive. In particular, our contributions are as follows:

1. We start with an idealized FIFO scheduler — at each time step, FIFO looks at jobs in the order of arrival and allocates each job as many processors it can use until it runs out of jobs or processors. We prove that FIFO is $(1+\epsilon)$-speed $O(\frac{1}{\epsilon})$-competitive (Section 3).
2. We then generalize the result to work stealing (Section 4). Work stealing is a practical and efficient scheduler that is used in many parallel languages and libraries. In comparison, an implementation of the ideal FIFO scheduler is likely to have high overhead since it is centralized and potentially preempts jobs and re-allocates processors at every time step. For work stealing, we prove that a version of it, called *admit-first*, is scalable for "reasonable jobs". In particular, we show that admit-first with $(1+\epsilon)$-speed has maximum flow time $O(\frac{1}{\epsilon^2}\max\{\text{OPT}, \ln(n)\})$ over n jobs for any fixed $\epsilon > 0$ with high probability. Note that if any job has span $\Omega(\lg n)$ or work $\Omega(m \lg n)$, then $\text{OPT} \geq \ln n$ and admit-first is scalable with $(1+\epsilon)$-speed $O(\frac{1}{\epsilon^2})$-competitive with high probability.
3. We introduce a generalization of admit-first scheduler, called steal-k-first. Our goal in this generalization is to design a work-stealing scheduler that is closest to FIFO since intuitively FIFO is the 'right' scheduling policy for maximum flow time, but is inefficient in implementation. Steal-k-first is parameterized by k. Intuitively as k becomes larger, this algorithm becomes closer to the FIFO scheduler. Theoretically, this scheduler is $(k+1+\epsilon)$)-speed $O(\frac{1}{\epsilon^2}\max\{\text{OPT}, \ln(n)\})$-competitive for any $\epsilon > 0$ and $k \geq 0$. It reduces to admit-first when $k = 0$.
4. We also provide a lower bound showing that the competitive ratio of work-stealing is $\Omega(\lg n)$ — that is, if all jobs are tiny with work $o(\lg n)$, then work stealing cannot be scalable due to the randomization involved (Section 5). This shows that our upper bound is close to being tight.
5. We implemented admit-first and steal-k-first in Thread Building Block (TBB) and compare their performance with a simulated optimal scheduler on realistic and synthetic workloads. Evaluation results shows that a work stealing scheduler (especially steal-k-first) have comparable performance to the optimal scheduler (Section 6).
6. Finally, we consider the case where jobs have weights and show a non-clairvoyant algorithm Biggest-Weight-First (BWF) is $(1+\epsilon)$-speed $O(\frac{1}{\epsilon^2})$-competitive for any $\epsilon > 0$, which is the best positive result that can be shown in the online setting for the weighted case (Section 7).

2. PRELIMINARIES

In the online scheduling problem of multiple jobs, n jobs arrive over time and are scheduled on m identical processors. Each job J_i has an arrival (release) time r_i, which is the first time an online scheduler is aware of the job. Each job could have a weight w_i — this weight is known to the scheduler when the job arrives and may not be correlated to the work of the job. For the unweighted setting, $w_i = 1$ for all jobs.

When analyzing the performance of a scheduling algorithm, we denote c_i as the completion time of job J_i in the algorithm's schedule. We denote $F_i = c_i - r_i$ as the flow time of job J_i in the algorithm's schedule. The goal of the scheduler is to minimize $\max_{i \in [n]} w_i F_i$.

A dynamic multithreaded job J_i can be represented as a ***Directed-Acyclic-Graph (DAG)*** G_i. Each node (task) v in G_i has an associated processing time p_v and the node must be processed sequentially on a processor for p_v time to be completed. A node in G_i cannot be executed until all of its predecessors in G_i have been executed. We say that a node is *ready* if all of its predecessors have been processed. Multiple ready nodes for the same job can be scheduled simultaneously. A job is completed only once all of the nodes in its DAG have been completely processed. Note that we do not assume that the scheduler knows the DAG in advance; in fact, the DAG unfolds dynamically as the job executes.

Symbol	Definition
c_i	completion time of job J_i in schedule
r_i	arrival time of job J_i
F_i	flowtime of job J_i
P_i	the critical path length of J_i
m	the number of processors
w_i	the weight of job J_i
OPT	optimal schedule and also optimal objective

Table 1: Symbols and Definitions

Dynamic multithreaded jobs can be characterized by two important parameters. The ***critical-path length*** P_i of job J_i is defined to be the execution time of J_i if it were scheduled continuously on an infinite number of processors. Alternatively, it is defined to be the length of the longest path in G_i, where each node v in the longest path contributes p_v to the length of the path. Note that P_i is a lower bound on the execution time of J_i for any scheduler. The ***Work*** W_i of job J_i is the execution time on 1 processor; or alternatively, the sum of the processing times of all the nodes in the DAG. We summarize some of the notations in Table 1.

The following proposition is well-known and has been shown in several works, for example [22]. The proposition states that any time a scheduler is working on all the ready nodes for some job J_j, then the scheduler must be decreasing the remaining critical path of J_j.

PROPOSITION 2.1. *If during each time step during a time interval $[t', t]$, a scheduler of speed s is always scheduling all available nodes for a job J_j, then the scheduler reduces the critical path length of J_i by $s(t - t')$.*

Difficulties of Analyzing Algorithms in the DAG Model. For scheduling sequential jobs, previous analyses for maximum flow time follows by showing that the algorithm A under consideration cannot fall behind for more than mp_{max} where p_{max} is the maximum processing time of a job. The is because either the algorithm A has less than m jobs and so there can be at most mp_{max} total work for unsatisfied jobs in its queue; or it has more than m jobs, but then the algorithm A cannot fall behind much since it will always be using all m processors.

Unfortunately, this argument is no longer straightforward for DAGs. To see this, consider unweighted flow time and let OPT denote the objective of the optimal solution. Note that in the sequential setting, $\text{OPT} \geq p_{max}$. In contrast, in the DAG model, some jobs could have work $\Theta(m\text{OPT})$. Now, even if the algorithm A under consideration has fewer than m unsatisfied jobs, it can have a total work of $\Theta(m^2\text{OPT})$ in its queue — allowing it to fall very far behind OPT. Thus, it is difficult to directly bound the amount of work an algorithm falls behind the OPT just as a function of the number of jobs in the algorithm's schedule. To prove that the algorithm does not fall far behind the optimal solution, a necessary condition for an algorithm to be competitive for maximum flow time, we instead identify times where the algorithm must not be too far behind the optimal solution and then show that the algorithm must not fall behind much further following those times.

On an additional note, most previous work on scheduling parallel jobs is in the arbitrary speedup curves model (see Section 8) for some details) and uses a potential function argument (see [17] for a tutorial). Unfortunately, there are currently no known potential function proofs for maximum flow time unlike for other objectives.

3. UNWEIGHTED MAXIMUM FLOW TIME USING FIFO

In this section our goal is to prove the following theorem stating that the algorithm First-In-First-Out (FIFO) is $(1+\epsilon)$-speed $O(\frac{1}{\epsilon})$-competitive for minimizing the maximum unweighted flow time for any $0 < \epsilon < 1$.

THEOREM 3.1. *First-in-First-Out (FIFO) is $(1+\epsilon)$ speed $O(\frac{1}{\epsilon})$ competitive for minimizing the maximum unweighted flow time for any $\epsilon > 0$.*

FIFO is defined as follows. At any time t, FIFO orders the jobs in increasing order by their arrival time, breaking ties arbitrarily. The algorithm then assigns all of the ready nodes for the first job to unique processors, then recursively does the same for the next job in the list. This continues until all processors have been assigned some node or there are no more ready nodes available. The algorithm may have a choice on which ready nodes of a job to schedule if the job has more ready nodes than the number of processors that have not been assigned to a node when the job is considered. In this case, we assume the scheduler chooses an arbitrary set of ready nodes from the job.

The rest of this section is devoted to proving Theorem 3.1. We assume for the remaining of this section that FIFO is given $(1 + \epsilon)$-speed for some constant $0 < \epsilon < 1$ and we will show that FIFO is $\frac{3}{\epsilon}$ competitive. To show this, assume for the sake of contradiction that FIFO is more than $\frac{3}{\epsilon}$-competitive and we consider the instance for which FIFO does not achieve a competitive ratio of $\frac{3}{\epsilon}$. Let J_i be the job with the maximum flow F_i at this instance, so $\text{OPT} < \frac{\epsilon}{3}F_i$ by assumption. Since no jobs that arrive later than J_i has any effect on how or when J_i is scheduled due to FIFO's scheduling policy, in our instance J_i is the last job to arrive.

We begin by showing that during the time interval job J_i is alive in FIFO's schedule, the processors must be busy for most of the interval. We define one ***time step*** as the time period for a s-speed processor to execute one unit of work. In other words, in one time step m processors with speed s can finish m work of jobs. Note that on processors with different speeds, the length of a time step will be different. Hence, the number of time steps on a s-speed processor in T time is sT, while it is T on unit speed processor.

LEMMA 3.2. *During the interval $[r_i, c_i]$ in FIFO's schedule, there can be no more than $\frac{\epsilon}{3}F_i$ time steps where not all m processors are busy working on jobs.*

PROOF. For the sake of contradiction, suppose there is at least $\frac{\epsilon}{3}F_i$ time steps during $[r_i, c_i]$ where not all processors are busy. Consider FIFO's scheduling policy. Anytime during $[r_i, c_i]$ where FIFO is not processing nodes on every processor, FIFO must be scheduling all of the ready nodes of J_i. Due to this, at these times FIFO is working on the critical path length of J_i by Proposition 2.1. Let this path length be P_i, then we have $P_i \geq \frac{\epsilon}{3}F_i$.

Also note that OPT cannot finish a job in less time than its critical-path length, this leads to $\text{OPT} \geq P_i \geq \frac{\epsilon}{3}F_i$, so the competitive ratio is $\frac{F_i}{\text{OPT}} \leq \frac{3}{\epsilon}$, a contradiction. □

The previous lemma shows that for most of the time steps in $[r_i, c_i]$ FIFO has m processors busy working. In the next lemma, we show that the work done by FIFO during $[r_i, c_i]$ is concentrated on jobs which did not arrive before $r_i - F_i$. We define ***processor idling steps*** to be the aggregate number of time steps per processor where the processor is not working on any job. Hence, during one time step that not all m processors are busy working, there can be at most m processor idling steps in total.

LEMMA 3.3. *During $[r_i, c_i]$, FIFO does more than $m(1 + \frac{\epsilon}{3})F_i$ work on jobs which arrived after $r_i - F_i$.*

PROOF. Since J_i is the job with the maximum flow time F_i, all previous jobs must have had less flow time than F_i. Therefore, all jobs which received any processing during $[r_i, c_i]$ must have arrived at earliest $r_i - F_i$.

Now to complete the lemma we calculate the total work done during $[r_i, c_i]$. From Lemma 3.2 the number of processor idling steps is at most $m\frac{\epsilon}{3}F_i$ during $[r_i, c_i]$. Since the processors have speed $1+\epsilon$, the total work that is done during $[r_i, c_i]$ is at least

$$m(1+\epsilon)F_i - m\frac{\epsilon}{3}F_i > m(1+\frac{\epsilon}{3})F_i$$

which completes the lemma. □

Using the previous lemmas we can complete the proof.

Proof of Theorem 3.1 We consider the work of the optimal schedule. OPT achieves a flow time of $\text{OPT} < \frac{\epsilon F_i}{3}$ from the assumption that FIFO does not achieve a competitive ratio of $\frac{3}{\epsilon}$.

Consider all the jobs which arrived during $[r_i - F_i, r_i]$, OPT must finish every such job before $r_i + \frac{\epsilon}{3}F_i$. During the interval $[r_i - F_i, r_i + \frac{\epsilon}{3}F_i]$ the optimal schedule can do at most $m(1+\frac{\epsilon}{3})F_i$ work with 1 speed.

However from Lemma 3.3 the jobs which arrive after $r_i - F_i$ have more than $m(1+\frac{\epsilon}{3})F_i$ work. Hence the optimal schedule cannot possibly finish all jobs by time $r_i + \frac{\epsilon}{3}F_i$, a contradiction. □

4. UNWEIGHTED MAXIMUM FLOW TIME USING WORK STEALING

In this section, we consider a variation of work stealing, called steal-k-first work stealing scheduler, the formal definition of which will be discussed later. Our goal is to show the following theorem.

THEOREM 4.1. *The maximum unweighted flow time of the steal-k-first work stealing scheduler with $(k+1+(k+2)\epsilon)$ speed is $O(\frac{1}{\epsilon^2}\max\{\text{OPT}, \ln n\})$ for any $k \geq 0$ and any $0 < \epsilon < \frac{1}{k+2}$ with high probability.*

By scaling the constant ϵ using the constant k in Theorem 4.1, we can trivially get the Corollary below.

COROLLARY 4.2. *The maximum unweighted flow time of the steal-k-first work stealing scheduler with $(k+1+\epsilon)$ speed is $O(\frac{1}{\epsilon^2}\max\{\text{OPT}, \ln n\})$ for any $k \geq 0$ and any $0 < \epsilon < 1$ with high probability.*

For a version of steal-k-first, namely admit-first, where the constant $k = 0$, we have the following result.

COROLLARY 4.3. *The maximum unweighted flow time of the admit-first work stealing scheduler with $(1+\epsilon)$ speed is $O(\frac{1}{\epsilon^2}\max\{\text{OPT}, \ln n\})$ for any $0 < \epsilon < 1$ with high probability. In particular, if $\text{OPT} \geq \ln n$, then the scheduler is $(1+\epsilon)$-speed $O(\frac{1}{\epsilon^2})$-competitive with high probability.*

Work Stealing for a Single Job. The work stealing scheduler [5] is a distributed scheduler for scheduling a single parallel program. It dispatches work dynamically, rather than statically. Scheduling is done in a distributed manner, which results in scalability and lower overhead. Specifically, the runtime system creates a worker thread for every available core. Each worker maintains a local double-ended queue, called *deque*. When a worker generates new work (enables a ready node from the job's DAG), it pushes the work onto the bottom of its deque. When a worker finishes its current node, it pops a ready node from the bottom of its deque. If the local deque is empty, the worker becomes a *thief* and randomly picks a *victim* worker and tries to steal work from the top of the victim's deque. We assume that it takes a unit time step to steal work between workers.

Note that most of the time, workers work off their own queues and don't need to communicate with each other. Hence, this randomized work-stealing strategy is very effective in practice and the amount of scheduling and synchronization overhead is small. Therefore, work stealing is the default strategy used for executing parallel DAGs in many parallel runtime systems such as Cilk Plus, TBB, X10, and PPL [5, 19, 25, 28, 7].

Theoretically, however, because of this randomized and distributed characteristic, work stealing is not a strictly greedy strategy. However, work stealing provides strong probabilistic guarantees of linear speedup for a single job. Researchers have shown that work-stealing is provably efficient with high-probability when scheduling a single job [5].

Work Stealing for Multiple Jobs. Though work stealing scheduler is designed for scheduling a single job, we can extend it to scheduling multiple jobs in a straightforward way. In addition to the deque of each worker, a global FIFO queue is dedicated for the arrival and admission of new jobs. When a new job is released, it is inserted into the tail of the global queue. A worker will *admit* a job by popping if from the head of the global queue in a FIFO order.

Under different admission strategies, workers could choose to steal work or admit a job in different manners. In this paper, we consider a strategy, namely ***steal-k-first work stealing***, in which each worker always tries to randomly steal first and only tries to admit a new job if there are k consecutive unsuccessful steal attempts for some constant $k \geq 0$. Now we analyze the theoretical performance of steal-k-first and we present its empirical performance in Section 6.

Intuitions for Proving Theorem 4.1. As discussed in Section 2, to prove steal-k-first is competitive for maximum flow time, we need to show that it does not fall far behind the optimal schedule. We assume for the sake of contradiction that it does at some time t. Then we go back in time to a point t' where the algorithm was not far behind the optimal solution. This time is carefully defined by recursively going back in time ensuring (1) that the algorithm is always doing a significant amount of work during $[t', t]$ and (2) that we can actually find t' while ensuring (1) is true. After finding such a time t', we are able to show that while the algorithm may fall far behind the optimal schedule during $[t', t]$ due to not taking advantage of the parallelizability of jobs, it eventually is able to do a large amount of work. With faster speed, it catches up and this allows us to bound its performance. Before formally proving the theorem, we first show that steal-k-first does not idle much when there are jobs to execute.

Idling Steps in Steal-k-First. We define ***processor idling steps*** to be the aggregate number of time steps per processor where the processor is not working on a job (and is stealing instead). WLOG, we assume that each steal attempt takes 1 time step. To bound the idling time in steal-k-first's schedule, we first state a theorem from [5], which provides the bound on the time that a work stealing scheduler spends on stealing during the execution of a *single* job.

LEMMA 4.4. *During the time interval $[e_i, c_i]$ where e_i and c_i are the execution start time and completion time of a job J_i respectively, the expected number of steal attempts is bounded by $32mP_i$ where P_i is the critical-path length and m is the number of processors. Moreover, for any $\delta > 0$, the number of steal attempts is bounded by $64mP_i + 16\ln(1/\delta)$ with probability at least $1 - \delta$.*

Although the Lemma above only applies to the case of a single job, by extending it we can obtain a useful lemma for the case with n jobs. In the following lemma, let e_i denote the time that job J_i is admitted from the global queue by a processor. This is the first time the job is started.

LEMMA 4.5. *For a time interval that lies between the start time e_i and completion time c_i of a job J_i, with probability at least $1 - \frac{1}{n}$, the number of processor idling steps is bounded by $64mP_i + 32\ln(n) \leq 64m\text{OPT} + 32\ln(n)$.*

PROOF. Consider Lemma 4.4 and choose $\delta = \frac{1}{n^2}$. The probability of any job J_i exceeding the idling time bound $64mP_i + 16\ln(n^2) = 64mP_i + 32\ln(n)$ during $[e_i, c_i]$ is $\frac{1}{n^2}$. This idling time bound holds for any time interval that is between $[e_i, c_i]$. Union bounding over all n jobs and subtracting from 1 yields the probability in the lemma. □

W will use the following lemma to later bound the idling time due to steal attempts between the arrival time r_i and the start time e_i of a job J_i.

LEMMA 4.6. *Under steal-k-first with a speed of $s = k+1+(k+2)\epsilon$, the number of idling steps during a time interval $[t', t]$ that is contained in $[r_i, e_i]$, the time between when a job arrives and is removed from the global queue, is at most $\frac{k}{k+1}(k+1+(k+2)\epsilon)m(t-t') + km$.*

PROOF. Every time a processor has more than k steal attempts, the processor will do one unit of work. Thus for any time interval of length $(t - t')$ there can be at most a $s\frac{k}{k+1}(t-t') + k$ steal attempts per processor. The lemma follows by aggregating over all processors. □

Now we can bound the amount of work steal-k-first does. We say that a job J_i ***spans*** a time interval $[t_a, t_{a-1}]$, if its release time $r_i \leq t_a$ and its completion time $c_i \geq t_{a-1}$.

LEMMA 4.7. *If a job spans a time interval $[t_a, t_{a-1}]$, then steal-k-first work stealing with speed $k+1+(k+2)\epsilon$ does at least $\frac{k+1+(k+2)\epsilon}{k+1}m(t_b - t_a) - (km + 64m\text{OPT} + 32\ln(n))$ work with probability at least $1 - \frac{1}{n}$.*

PROOF. By definition, $[t_a, t_{a-1}]$ lies between $[r_i, c_i]$. From Lemma 4.6, the number of idling steps during $[t_a, e_i]$ is at most $\frac{k}{k+1}(k+1+(k+2)\epsilon)m(e_i - t_a) + km \leq \frac{k}{k+1}(k+1+(k+2)\epsilon)m(t_{a-1} - t_a) + km$. From Lemma 4.5, the number of idling steps during $[e_i, t_b]$ is at most $64m\text{OPT} + 32\ln(n)$ with probability at least $1 - \frac{1}{n}$.

Thus, during $[t_a, t_{a-1}]$ the amount that work steal-k-first with speed $k+1+(k+2)\epsilon$ does is at least

$$(k+1+(k+2)\epsilon)\, m(t_{a-1} - t_a) - (64m\text{OPT} + 32\ln(n))$$
$$- \left(\frac{k}{k+1}(k+1+(k+2)\epsilon)\, m(t_{a-1} - t_a) + km\right)$$
$$= \frac{k+1+(k+2)\epsilon}{k+1} m(t_b - t_a) - (km + 64m\text{OPT} + 32\ln(n))$$

with probability at least $1 - \frac{1}{n}$. □

Time Intervals in Steal-k-First. The main challenge in analyzing steal-k-first is that it is difficult to show that the remaining processing time of jobs in its queue is comparable to that of OPT's queue. Rather than directly bounding the differences between the two queues as done in previous section, we will construct a set of time intervals where steal-k-first must be busy most of the time. Using the assumption that steal-k-first has resource augmentation, we will draw a contradiction by showing that steal-k-first has completed a large amount of work which is even more than the total amount of work available during a time interval.

From here on, our goal is to show that the steal-k-first with $(k+1+(k+2)\epsilon)$-speed achieves a maximum flow time of $O(\frac{1}{\epsilon^2}\max\{\text{OPT}, \ln(n)\})$ with high probability. To simplify the proof, we rewrite the objective to eliminate the max and show instead that steal-k-first achieves a maximum flow of $\frac{65}{\epsilon^2}(\text{OPT} + \ln(n) + k)$, $k \geq 0$ is a constant and $0 < \epsilon < \frac{1}{k+2}$.

Let J_i be the job in steal-k-first's schedule with the maximum flow time F_i. Recall that r_i and c_i are the arrival and completion time of J_i, respectively. To show contradiction, we assume that $F_i \geq \frac{65}{\epsilon^2}(\text{OPT} + \ln(n) + k)$.

We will recursively define a set of time intervals

$$T = \{[t', t_\beta], [t_\beta, t_{\beta-1}], [t_{\beta-1}, t_{\beta-2}] \ldots [t_1, t_0], [t_0, r_i], [r_i, c_i]\}$$

where $t' \leq t_\beta \leq t_{\beta-1} \leq \ldots \leq t_1 \leq t_0 \leq r_i \leq c_i$. To illustrate the time intervals, Figure 1 shows an example execution trace of steal-k-first.

Let t_0 be the arrival time of the earliest arriving job among the jobs that are not finished by steal-k-first right before time r_i. For instance, in Figure 1 there are two jobs (job J_0 and job J_q) that are active right before r_i. Among then, job J_0 has the earliest arrival time, so t_0 is defined using it. If there are no jobs right before r_i, let $t_0 = r_i$. Now we define further intervals recursively. Given the time t_{a-1}, we want to define t_a. If $t_{a-1} - t_a \leq \epsilon F_i$, then we are done defining intervals; otherwise, we define t_a as the arrival time of the earliest arriving job among those that are not finished by steal-k-first right before time t_{a-1}. We say that a certain job J_a ***defines*** an interval $[t_a, t_{a-1}]$, if it is the earliest arriving job unsatisfied by steal-k-first right before t_{a-1} and t_a is its arrival time.

Note that this process of defining intervals will always terminate. The procedure terminates when $t_{a-1} - t_a \leq \epsilon F_i$, which must happen if one goes back to the first time a job arrives. We let β denote the maximum value that a takes during this inductive definition. Hence, $[t_\beta, t_{\beta-1}]$ is the earliest time interval defined in this scheme. Moreover, the arrival time t' of the earliest arriving job among those that are unfinished right before time t_β satisfies $t' - t_\beta \leq \epsilon F_i$. As in Figure 1, interval $[t', t_\beta]$ is the first such interval that has length less than ϵF_i.

Work Done by Steal-k-First. We intend to show that steal-k-first does a lot of work during the interval $[t_\beta, c_i]$. In fact, we will show that if the assumption of $F_i \geq \frac{65}{\epsilon^2}(\text{OPT} + \ln(n) + k)$ is true, then steal-k-first would have done more work than the total work of all jobs that are active during $[t_\beta, c_i]$, which is not possible and leads to a contradiction.

To do so, we partition $[t_\beta, c_i]$ into two sets of time intervals, specifically $S_1 = \{[t_a, t_{a-1}], \forall\, 0 < a \leq \beta\} \cup \{[t_0, r_i]\}$ during $[t_\beta, r_i]$, and $S_2 = \{[r_i, c_i]\}$. We first show that for intervals in S_1, steal-k-first does more work than OPT.

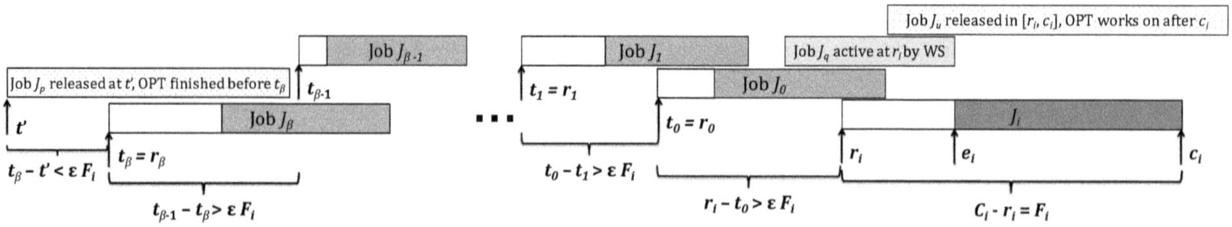

Figure 1: An example execution trace of work-stealing identifying jobs' release and completion times.

LEMMA 4.8. *For any time interval $[t_a, t_{a-1}] \in S_1$ during $[t_\beta, r_i]$, with probability at least $1 - \frac{1}{n}$ the work that steal-k-first does is more than $m(t_{a-1} - t_a)$, which is as much as OPT does.*

PROOF. By definition, there is a job J_a which defines this time interval. Specifically, this job spans the time interval. According to Lemma 4.7, we know that with probability $1 - \frac{1}{n}$ the amount of work steal-k-first does is at least $\frac{k+1+(k+2)\epsilon}{k+1} m(t_{a-1} - t_a) - (km + 64m\text{OPT} + 32\ln(n))$.

Recall that by assumption that $F_i > \frac{65}{\epsilon^2}(\text{OPT} + \ln(n) + k)$ and by definition that $(t_{a-1} - t_a) > \epsilon F_i$, we have

$$\begin{aligned}(t_{a-1} - t_a) > \epsilon F_i > &\frac{65}{\epsilon}(\text{OPT} + \ln(n) + k)\\ =&\frac{1}{\epsilon}\frac{1}{m}(65km + 65m\text{OPT} + 65m\ln(n))\\ >&\frac{1}{\epsilon}\frac{1}{m}(km + 64m\text{OPT} + 32\ln(n))\end{aligned}$$

Hence, $(km + 64m\text{OPT} + 32\ln(n)) < \epsilon m(t_{a-1} - t_a)$

Thus during any time interval $[t_a, t_{a-1}]$ in S_1, the work done by steal-k-first (with speed $k + 1 + (k+2)\epsilon$) on jobs is at least:

$$\begin{aligned}&\frac{k+1+(k+2)\epsilon}{k+1} m(t_{a-1} - t_a) - (km + 64m\text{OPT} + 32\ln(n))\\ &> m(t_{a-1} - t_a) + \frac{(k+2)\epsilon}{k+1} m(t_{a-1} - t_a) - \epsilon m(t_{a-1} - t_a)\\ &= m(t_{a-1} - t_a) + \frac{\epsilon}{k+1} m(t_{a-1} - t_a)\end{aligned}$$

Clearly OPT with only 1 speed can only do at most $m(t_{a-1} - t_a)$ work during this time interval. □

We now show that for S_2, steal-k-first does a lot of work too.

LEMMA 4.9. *During $[r_i, c_i] \in S_2$, the amount of work that steal-k-first does on jobs is more than $mF_i + \epsilon mF_i + m\text{OPT}$ with probability $1 - \frac{1}{n}$.*

PROOF. Consider the work that steal-k-first does during $[r_i, c_i]$. By definition this interval has a length of F_i and we know that J_i spans this interval. Directly applying Lemma 4.7, we derive that with probability $1 - \frac{1}{n}$ the amount of work done by steal-k-first during $[r_i, c_i]$ is at least

$$\begin{aligned}&\frac{k+1+(k+2)\epsilon}{k+1} mF_i - (km + 64m\text{OPT} + 32\ln(n))\\ =&mF_i + \epsilon mF_i + \frac{\epsilon}{k+1} mF_i - (km + 64m\text{OPT} + 32\ln(n))\end{aligned}$$

By definition, $0 < \epsilon < \frac{1}{k+2}$, so $\frac{1}{k+1}\frac{1}{\epsilon} > 1$. Also recall that by assumption that $F_i > \frac{65}{\epsilon^2}(\text{OPT} + \ln(n) + k)$, we have

$$\begin{aligned}\frac{\epsilon}{k+1} mF_i >&\frac{m}{k+1}\frac{65}{\epsilon}(\text{OPT} + \ln(n) + k)\\ >&65m(\text{OPT} + \ln(n) + k)\\ >&(km + 64m\text{OPT} + 32\ln(n)) + m\text{OPT}\end{aligned}$$

Hence, $\frac{\epsilon}{k+1} mF_i - (km + 64m\text{OPT} + 32\ln(n)) > m\text{OPT}$. Therefore, the amount of work done by steal-k-first during $[r_i, c_i]$ is more than $mF_i + \epsilon mF_i + m\text{OPT}$ with probability $1 - \frac{1}{n}$. □

We need one more critical argument to complete the analysis. The reason we defined these time intervals inductively is to identify the jobs that are active under steal-k-first during $[t_\beta, c_i]$. The total volume of these jobs is bounded by the work that OPT can finish. However, just showing that steal-k-first does more work than OPT during $[t_\beta, c_i]$ will not suffice, as OPT could have done part of this work either before t_β or after c_i. As shown in Figure 1, the two jobs (job J_p and job J_u) in dotted shade are executed by steal-k-first during $[t_\beta, c_i]$, while OPT finished job J_p before t_β and started working on job J_u after c_i. The next lemma bounds the maximum amount of work that are available for steal-k-first to work on during $[t_\beta, c_i]$.

LEMMA 4.10. *For jobs that are active under steal-k-first during $[t_\beta, c_i]$, their total amount of work is at most $m(r_i - t_\beta) + m(\epsilon F_i + \text{OPT} + F_i)$.*

PROOF. By definition, $[t_\beta, c_i]$ consists of time intervals of S_1 during $[t_\beta, r_i]$ and time interval of $S_2 = \{[r_i, c_i]\}$. Also recall that the length of interval $[r_i, c_i]$ is F_i. Hence, the total length of $[t_\beta, c_i]$ is $(r_i - t_\beta) + F_i$.

Moreover, by definition of t_β, the earliest arriving job that is unsatisfied by steal-k-first just before time t_β must have arrived no earlier than time $t_\beta - \epsilon F_i$. Thus, the jobs that are active under steal-k-first during $[t_\beta, c_i]$ all arrived during $[t_\beta - \epsilon F_i, c_i]$.

Further, all these jobs have an optimal maximum flow time no more than OPT under the optimal scheduler. Therefore, OPT must be able to complete all of them by time $c_i + \text{OPT}$. Knowing that OPT can only work on these jobs during $[t_\beta - \epsilon F_i, c_i + \text{OPT}]$, the total amount of work of those jobs can have volume at most $m(r_i - t_\beta) + m(\epsilon F_i + \text{OPT} + F_i)$. □

Finally, we are ready to complete the proof.

Proof of Theorem 4.1 To prove the theorem, we consider the jobs that are active under steal-k-first during $[t_\beta, c_i]$. By Lemma 4.10, we know that the total amount of work of these jobs, denoted as X, is bounded: $X \leq m(r_i - t_\beta) + m(\epsilon F_i + \text{OPT} + F_i)$. Note that these jobs are the only ones available for steal-k-first to work on during $[t_\beta, c_i]$. Therefore, during

$[t_\beta, c_i]$ steal-k-first cannot do more than X work even with speedup.

On the other hand, consider the minimum amount of work that steal-k-first must have done during $[t_\beta, c_i]$, denoted as Y, assuming that $F_i > \frac{65}{\epsilon^2}(\text{OPT} + \ln(n) + k)$ is true. We will see that $Y > X$, which leads to a contradiction.

From Lemma 4.8, we know that during $[t_\beta, r_i]$ the amount of work steal-k-first does is more than

$$m\left(\sum_{0<a\leq\beta}(t_{a-1} - t_a) + (r_i - t_0)\right) = m(r_i - t_\beta)$$

From Lemma 4.9, we know that during $[r_i, c_i]$, steal-k-first does more than $mF_i + \epsilon mF_i + m\text{OPT}$ work. Thus, for interval $[t_\beta, c_i]$, we get $Y > m(r_i - t_\beta) + mF_i + \epsilon mF_i + m\text{OPT}$.

Now we compare X and Y:

$$\begin{aligned} Y - X >& m(r_i - t_\beta) + mF_i + \epsilon mF_i + m\text{OPT} \\ &- m(r_i - t_\beta) - m(\epsilon F_i + \text{OPT} + F_i) > 0 \end{aligned}$$

Hence, $Y > X$. In other words, if the assumption of F_i is true, during $[r_i, c_i]$ steal-k-first must have done more work than the total available work, which gives a contradiction.

Thus, we obtain the theorem. □

Discussion about Steal-k-First. Note that for steal-k-first work stealing with $k = 0$, instead of steal first, this scheduler will in fact admit all jobs from the global queue first. We denote this special case as ***admit-first***. From Theorem 4.1, we know that the theoretical performance of steal-k-first is better with smaller constant k. Hence, admit-first has the best theoretical performance and is $O(\frac{1}{\epsilon^2})$-competitive with high probability with $1 + \epsilon$ speed, as it guarantees that a job's execution is not delayed by unnecessary random stealing.

However, as shown in Section 6 steal-k-first for a relatively large k performs better than admit-first empirically. Intuitively, if there is any job available for stealing, then in expectation m consecutive random steal attempts would be able to find the stealable work. Thus, for $k \geq m$, steal-k-first better approximates FIFO, which we know works well.

In contrast, in admit-first jobs could run sequentially when there are more than m unfinished jobs. During these times, jobs at the end of the global queue take long time to be admitted and they further take longer time to finish sequential execution in the worst case. Hence, this could increase the maximum flow time of the system.

Moreover, steal-k-first requires a speed of more than $(k + 1)$ theoretically to be competitive, mainly due to the worst case scenario where each job has a unit time of work but takes k stealing steps to admit. However, in practice, jobs have much larger work and the constant k steal attempts for admitting a job is negligible in practice.

5. WORK STEALING LOWER BOUND

In this section we give a lower bound for the work stealing algorithm. We show that in the online setting, the scheduler when given any constant speed is $\Omega(\log n)$ competitive. This shows that our upper bound analysis of the algorithm is effectively tight.

LEMMA 5.1. *Work stealing is $\Omega(\log n)$-competitive for maximum flow time in the online setting when given any constant resource augmentation.*

PROOF. Let n be an input parameter and let the number of machines be $m = \log n$. Let s be a constant specifying the resource augmentation given to work stealing. The schedule consists of n jobs, which are identical. A job consists of one task which is the predecessor of $m/10$ independent tasks. Note that the total work of the job is $m/10 + 1$ and can be competed by a 1 speed scheduler scheduler in 2 time steps. A single job is released at multiples of $2m$ starting at time 0. Note that even if a job is executed sequentially, it will complete in only $m/10 + 1$ time steps. Thus, these jobs do not have overlapping times where multiple jobs are alive in any non-idling schedule.

Now fix any job and consider the probability that the job executes completely sequentially by a work stealing scheduler. This occurs if every steal attempt fails to find the processor holding the tasks for the job. In a single time step, the probability that $m - 1$ processors do not successfully steal is $(1 - \frac{1}{m-1})^{m-1} \geq \frac{1}{2e}$ for sufficiently large m. The probability that all processors fail to steal for $m/10$ time steps is greater than $(\frac{1}{2e})^{m/10}$.

Now consider the expected number of jobs which execute sequentially by work stealing. There are $n = 2^m$ jobs released. The expected number of jobs to execute sequentially is $2^m(\frac{1}{2e})^{m/10} \geq 1$. Thus, the expected maximum flow time of work stealing with s speed is $\frac{m/10+1}{s} = \frac{\log n}{s}$. Knowing that the optimal solution has maximum flow time 2 and $s = O(1)$, the lemma follows. □

6. EXPERIMENTAL RESULTS FOR UNWEIGHTED MAXIMUM FLOW TIME

In this section we present the experimental results using realistic and synthetic workloads to compare the performance of OPT and two work stealing strategies: (1) *Admit-first* where workers preferentially admit jobs from the global queue and only steal if the queue is empty, and (2) *Steal-k-first* where workers preferentially steal and only admit a new job if k steal attempts fail (we use $k = 16$). Our experiments indicate that steal-k-first performs better and is almost comparable to an optimal scheduler.

Setup: We conduct experiments on a server with dual eight-core Intel Xeon 2.4Ghz processors with 64GB main memory. The server runs Linux version 3.13.0, with processor throttling, sleeping, and hyper-threading disabled. The work-stealing algorithms are implemented in Intel Thread Building Block (TBB) [25] version 4.3, a well-engineered popular work stealing runtime library. We extended TBB to schedule multiple jobs arriving online by adding a global FIFO queue for admitting jobs and we implement both admit-first and steal-k-first.

Since we do not know the optimal scheduler, we must approximate it using a simulated scheduler by reducing a parallel scheduling problem to a sequential scheduling problem on a single processor. In particular, for this lower bound, we assume that there is no preemption overhead and that each job can get linear speedup (fully parallelizable). Therefore, we can execute each job one at a time assuming it is a sequential job with execution time equal to its W/m where W is its total work. We then run all jobs using FIFO which is optimal in this setting. When jobs are fully parallelizable, this reduces the problem to the case where there is only one machine. In this setting, it is well known that FIFO is opti-

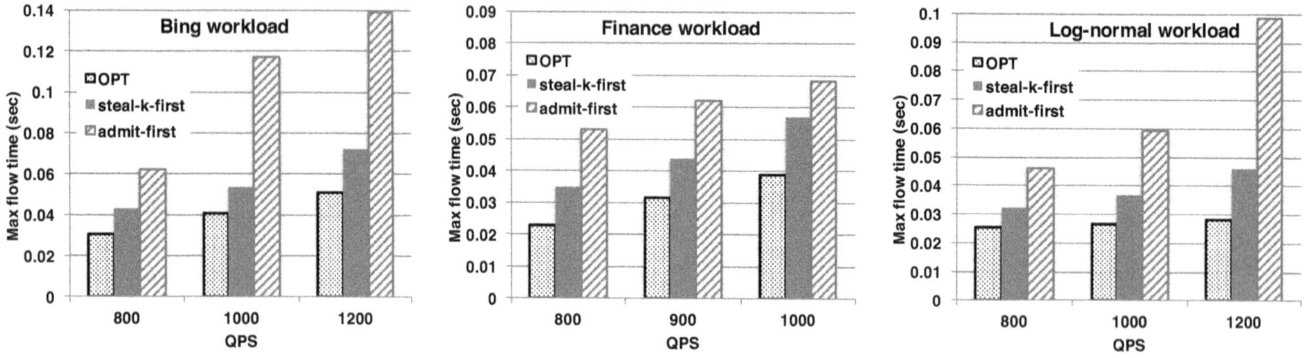

(a) Bing workload (b) Finance workload (c) Log-normal workload

Figure 2: Experimental results comparing the maximum flow time running on three work distributions with three different load settings and scheduled using simulated OPT, steal-k-first, and admit-first (from left to right). Note that the scale of the y-axis for the figures differ. From all different settings, OPT has the smallest max flow time, while admit-first has the largest max flow time.

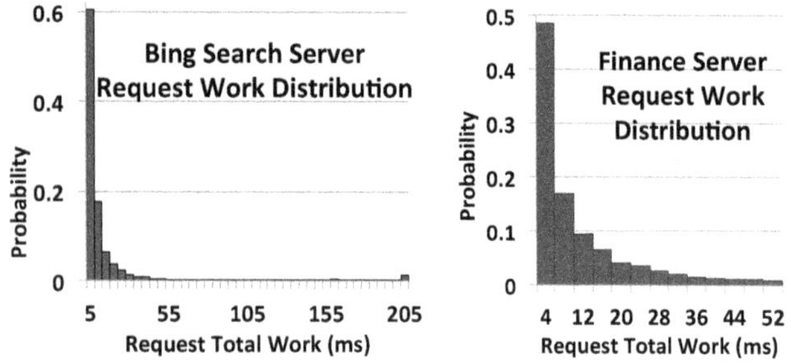

(a) Bing search (b) Finance server

Figure 3: Work distribution of two workload: Bing web search [21] and an option pricing finance server [26].

mal for maximum flow time [8]. Thus, this scheduler has the performance for maximum flow time that is at least as good as any feasible scheduler, including the optimal schedule.

Workloads: We evaluate different strategies on work distributions from two real-world applications shown in Figure 3 and additional synthetic workloads with log-normal distribution. Henceforth we shall refer to workload generated from the three distributions as the *Bing workload*, the *finance workload* and the *log-normal workload*, respectively. For each distribution, we select a set of queries-per-second, QPS, to generate workloads with low ($\sim 50\%$), medium ($\sim 60\%$), and high ($\sim 70\%$) machine utilization respectively, and the inter-arrival time between jobs is generated by a Poisson process with a mean equal to $1/QPS$. Each job contains CPU-intensive computation and is parallelized using parallel for loops. $100,000$ jobs are used to obtain a single point in the experiments.

Figure 2 shows the experimental results comparing simulated OPT, steal-k-first and admit-first under three different work distributions and three different load settings (i.e., query-per-second). The experiments indicate that, even though our results on OPT are lower bounds on maximum flow time, steal-k-first performs comparably to OPT — matching our intuition that it is a closer approximation for maximum flow time, as discussed at the end of Section 4.

Recall that steal-k-first has worse theoretical performance than admit-first. However, in practice, admit-first generally performs worse in terms of maximum flow time and the performance difference increases as load increases (for instance, for Bing and log-normal workloads with high utilization, admit first has twice the maximum flow). This matches our intuition — at higher loads, admit-first executes jobs more or less sequentially, while steal-first provides parallelism to already admitted jobs before admitting new jobs. Therefore steal-first is closer to FIFO in that it tries to execute jobs that arrived earlier with more parallelism. Therefore, in practice, steal-first is likely to be a good implementation for schedulers that want to minimize maximum flow time without incurring the large overheads of FIFO.

7. MAXIMUM WEIGHTED FLOW TIME

In this section our goal is to prove that the algorithm Biggest-Weight-First (BWF) is a scalable algorithm for minimizing the maximum weighted flow time.

THEOREM 7.1. *Biggest-Weight-First (BWF) is $(1+\epsilon)$ speed $O(\frac{1}{\epsilon^2})$ competitive for minimizing the maximum weighted flow for any $\epsilon > 0$.*

BWF is defined as follows, which is similar to FIFO except that priority is given to the jobs with the biggest weight. At any time t, BWF orders the jobs in decreasing order by their weight, breaking ties arbitrarily. The algorithm then assigns all of the ready nodes for the first job to some processor, then recursively does the same for the next job in the list. This continues until all processors have been assigned some node or there are no more ready nodes available. Like FIFO, BWF may have a choice on which ready nodes of a job to schedule if the job has more ready nodes than the number of processors which have not been assigned to a node when the job is considered. In this case, we assume the scheduler chooses an arbitrary set of ready nodes.

The reminder of this section is devoted to proving Theorem 7.1. For the rest of this section, we assume that BWF is given $(1+3\epsilon)$-speed for some constant $0 < \epsilon < \frac{1}{3}$ and we will show that BWF is $\frac{3}{\epsilon^2}$ competitive. Fix any sequence of jobs and let OPT denote the optimal schedule on this instance as well as the optimal maximum weighted flow time. Let F_a^* be the flow time of a job J_a in OPT.

Let J_i be the job in BWF's schedule with the maximum weighted flow time w_iF_i. For the sake of contradiction, we assume that $w_iF_i > \frac{3}{\epsilon^2}\text{OPT}$. Since $\text{OPT} = w_iF_i^*$, $F_i > \frac{3}{\epsilon^2}F_i^*$, where F_i^* is the flow time of J_i in OPT. By comparing the weight w_i of job J_i, any jobs with weight at least w_i are referred as ***heavy*** jobs, and any jobs with less weight than w_i are referred as ***light*** jobs.

Time Intervals in BWF. Similar to the time intervals specified in Section 4, we will inductively define a set of time intervals

$$T = \{[t', t_\beta], [t_\beta, t_{\beta-1}], [t_{\beta-1}, t_{\beta-2}] \dots [t_1, t_0], [t_0, r_i], [r_i, c_i]\}$$

where $t' \leq t_\beta \leq t_{\beta-1} \leq \dots \leq t_1 \leq t_0 \leq r_i \leq c_i$.

Recall that r_i and c_i are the arrival and completion time of J_i, respectively. Consider the *heavy* jobs that BWF is scheduling right before r_i. Let t_0 be the arrival time of the *earliest* arriving one of those jobs. If there are no heavy jobs right before r_i, let $t_0 = r_i$. Now we define further intervals recursively. Given the times t_{a-1}, we want to define t_a. If $t_{a-1} - t_a \leq \epsilon F_i$, then we are done defining time intervals; otherwise, we define t_a to be the arrival time of the earliest arriving heavy job J_a that are unsatisfied under BWF right before time t_{a-1}. Again if there are no heavy jobs unsatisfied by BWF just before time t_{a-1} then let $t_a = t_{a-1}$. We let β denote the maximum value that a takes during this inductive definition. Hence, $[t_\beta, t_{\beta-1}]$ is the earliest time interval defined in this scheme.

Note that this process of defining intervals is almost the same as in Section 4. The only difference is that the job J_a, which defines the interval $[t_a, t_{a-1}]$, is the earliest unfinished *heavy* job under *BWF*. We only consider heavy jobs, because under BWF only heavy jobs can preempt job J_i and other heavy jobs and any light jobs can only execute when all the available nodes of all the active heavy jobs are already executing by some processors. Thus, when analyzing the flow time of J_i and other heavy jobs, we can ignore the remaining light jobs, since light jobs cannot in interfere the execution of heavy ones. Hence, the processor idling steps in the remaining of this section is refering to the time steps where a processor is not working on nodes corresponding to heavy jobs.

We begin the proof by showing that during all time intervals between $[t_\beta, r_i]$, BWF is using most time steps to process nodes for heavy jobs.

LEMMA 7.2. *During any interval $[t_a, t_{a-1}]$ where $a \leq k$, the number of processor idling steps (where a processor is not working on nodes corresponding to heavy jobs) is at most $m\frac{\epsilon^2}{3}F_i$.*

PROOF. For the sake of contradiction, assume that this is not true. Then consider the job that defines $[t_a, t_{a-1}]$ and let this job be J_a. By definition this heavy job arrived at t_a and is still being processed at time t_{a-1}. From BWF's scheduling policy, every time step during $[t_a, t_{a-1}]$, where some processors find no nodes from heavy jobs to work on, all ready nodes of J_a are being scheduled. Hence the processors are decreasing the remaining critical path of J_a at these times by Proposition 2.1. Since the job is not finished until at t_{a-1}, this job must have a critical-path length P_a longer than $P_a > t_{a-1} - t_a > \frac{\epsilon^2}{3}F_i$. Also since J_a is a heavy job and $w_a \geq w_i$ and by assumption $w_iF_i > \frac{3}{\epsilon^2}\text{OPT}$, its weighted flow time is at least

$$w_a(t_{a-1} - t_a) > w_a\frac{\epsilon^2}{3}F_i \geq w_i\frac{\epsilon^2}{3}F_i > \frac{\epsilon^2}{3}\frac{3}{\epsilon^2}\text{OPT} \geq \text{OPT}$$

However, OPT cannot complete a job faster than its critical-path length, so $F_a^* \geq P_a$. Further, J_a's weighted flow time under OPTis at most the maximum weighted flow time OPT. We have

$$\text{OPT} \geq w_aF_a^* \geq w_aP_a > w_a(t_{a-1} - t_a) > \text{OPT}$$

This gives a contradiction. □

Using the previous lemma, we bound the aggregate amount of work done by BWF on heavy jobs during $[t_\beta, r_i]$.

LEMMA 7.3. *During $[t_\beta, r_i]$, the amount of work that BWF does on heavy jobs is more than $m(1 + 2\epsilon)(r_i - t_\beta)$.*

PROOF. From Lemma 7.2, we know that there are only $m\frac{\epsilon^2}{3}F_i$ processor idling steps where a processor is not working on nodes corresponding to heavy jobs during any time interval $[t_a, t_{a-1}]$. In addition, we know $t_{a-1} - t_a > \epsilon F_i$, since $a \leq \beta$. Hence, the work done by BWF (with $1 + 3\epsilon$ speed) on heavy jobs during $[t_a, t_{a-1}]$ is at least:

$$\begin{aligned}
&m(1 + 3\epsilon)(t_{a-1} - t_a) - m\frac{\epsilon^2}{3}F_i \\
>&m(1 + 3\epsilon)(t_{a-1} - t_a) - m\frac{\epsilon}{3}(t_{a-1} - t_a) \\
>&m(1 + 2\epsilon)(t_{a-1} - t_a)
\end{aligned}$$

Summing over all the intervals yields the lemma. □

Similarly, we can bound the amount of work done by BWF on heavy jobs during $[r_i, c_i]$.

LEMMA 7.4. *During $[r_i, c_i]$, the amount of work that BWF does on heavy jobs is more than $m(1 + 2\epsilon)F_i$.*

PROOF. By assumption, $F^* < \frac{\epsilon^2}{3}F_i$. Since OPT cannot finish a job in less time than its critical-path length, job J_i has $P_i \leq F_i^* < \frac{\epsilon^2}{3}F_i$. From Proposition 2.1, we can derive that the number of processor idling steps where a processor is not working on heavy jobs is at most mP_i. Hence, the amount of work done by BWF during $[r_i, c_i]$ is at least $m(1 + 3\epsilon)F_i - mP_i > m(1 + 3\epsilon)F_i - m\frac{\epsilon^2}{3}F_i > m(1 + 2\epsilon)F_i$, since $\epsilon < \frac{1}{3}$. □

Now we bounds the maximum amount of work that are available for BWF to work on during $[t_\beta, c_i]$.

LEMMA 7.5. *For jobs that are active under BWF during $[t_\beta, c_i]$, their total amount of work is at most $m(r_i - t_\beta) + m(1 + \epsilon + \frac{\epsilon^2}{3})F_i$.*

PROOF. By definition, the total length of $[t_\beta, c_i]$ is $(r_i - t_\beta) + F_i$. Moreover, by definition of t_β, the earliest arriving heavy job that is unsatisfied BWF just before time t_β must have arrived no earlier than time $t_\beta - \epsilon F_i$. Thus, the heavy jobs that are active under BWF during $[t_\beta, c_i]$ all arrived during $[t_\beta - \epsilon F_i, c_i]$.

Furthermore, all these heavy jobs have an optimal maximum weighted flow time no more than OPT under the optimal scheduler, i.e., $\text{OPT} \geq F_a^*w_a$. By definition of a heavy job $w_a \geq w_i$ and by assumption $w_iF_i > \frac{3}{\epsilon^2}\text{OPT}$, we have $w_aF_i \geq w_iF_i > \frac{3}{\epsilon^2}\text{OPT} > \frac{3}{\epsilon^2}F_a^*w_a$. Thus, the flow time F_a^* of these heavy jobs under the optimal schedule is $F_a^* < \frac{\epsilon^2}{3}F_i$.

Therefore, OPT must be able to complete all of them by time $c_i + \frac{\epsilon^2}{3}F_i$. Knowing that OPT can only work on these jobs during $[t_\beta - \epsilon F_i, c_i + \frac{\epsilon^2}{3} F_i]$, the total amount of work of those jobs can have volume at most $m(r_i - t_\beta + F_i) + m(\epsilon F_i + \frac{\epsilon^2}{3} F_i) = m(r_i - t_\beta) + m(1 + \epsilon + \frac{\epsilon^2}{3}) F_i$. □

Finally, we are ready to complete the proof.

Proof of Theorem 7.1 To prove the theorem, we consider the heavy jobs that are active under BWF during $[t_\beta, c_i]$. By Lemma 7.5, we know that the total amount of work of these jobs, denoted as X, is bounded: $X \leq m(r_i - t_\beta) + m(1 + \epsilon + \frac{\epsilon^2}{3}) F_i$. Note that these jobs are the only ones available for BWF to work on, so during $[t_\beta, c_i]$ BWF cannot do more than X work even with speedup.

On the other hand, consider the minimum amount of work that BWF must have done during $[t_\beta, c_i]$, denoted as Y, assuming that $w_i F_i > \frac{3}{\epsilon^2}\mathrm{OPT}$ is true. We will see that $Y > X$, which leads to a contradiction.

From Lemma 7.3, we know that during $[t_\beta, r_i]$ the amount of work BWF does is more than $m(1 + 2\epsilon)(r_i - t_\beta)$ From Lemma 7.4, we know that during $[r_i, c_i]$, BWF does more than $m(1 + 2\epsilon) F_i$ work. Thus, for interval $[t_\beta, c_i]$, we get $Y > m(r_i - t_\beta) + m(1 + 2\epsilon) F_i$.

Now we compare X and Y and note that $\epsilon < \frac{1}{3}$:

$$\begin{aligned} Y - X > & m(r_i - t_\beta) + m(1 + 2\epsilon) F_i \\ & - m(r_i - t_\beta) - m(1 + \epsilon + \frac{\epsilon^2}{3}) F_i > 0 \end{aligned}$$

Hence, if the assumption of $w_i F_i$ is true, then during $[r_i, c_i]$ BWF must have done more work than the total available work, which gives a contradiction. By scaling ϵ, we obtain the theorem. □

Remarks. The result of weighted flow time can be applied to maximum stretch. In the sequential setting, weighted flow time captures maximum stretch by setting the weight to be the inverse of the processing time. In other words, the flow of a job is scaled by the inverse of its processing time in the stretch objective for sequential jobs. However, stretch is not well-defined for DAG jobs. In particular, should the flow time be scaled by the inverse of the total work or the critical path length? Although there are two natural interpretations of the stretch in the DAG setting, both of them can be still captured by weighted flow time. Since BWF is $(1 + \epsilon)$-speed $O(\frac{1}{\epsilon^2})$-competitive for maximum weighted flow time and there are strong lower bounds without speed augmentation, so this result can be viewed as essentially the best positive theoretical result for maximum stretch.

8. RELATED WORK

In scheduling theory, two dominant models have emerged for modeling the parallelizability of jobs. One model is the Directed-Acyclic-Graph (DAG) model, which was considered in this paper. This model is a good model for representing parallel programs written using programming languages and libraries designed for this purpose, and, due to this the model is well connected to practice [5, 14, 13, 12, 6].

The other model considered is known as the arbitrary speed-up curves setting when online and sometimes referred to as the malleable task setting when offline. In the arbitrary speed-up curves setting, each job J_j consists of μ_j phases and the ith phase is associated with a tuple $(p_{i,j}, \Gamma_{i,j}(m'))$. The value of $p_{i,j}$ is the work of the ith phase for job j and $\Gamma_{i,j}(m')$ is a speed-up function that specifies the rate $p_{i,j}$ is processed at when job J_j is given m' processors when in the ith phase. The phases of the job must be processed sequentially and $\Gamma_{i,j}$ specifies the parallelizability of J_i during phase i. It is generally assumed that $\Gamma_{i,j}$ is a non-decreasing sublinear function.

Both models have been widely considered both online and offline. However, it is important to note that the models are fundamentally different and there does not appear to be a straightforward way of translating results from one model to the other. In particular, in the DAG setting, the realized parallelizability of a job, at any point in time, depends on the nodes of the job that are free to execute. That is, the nodes whose predecessors have been previously processed. The realized parallelizability, or number of ready nodes, depends not only on how much work on the job has been complete in the past, but also *which* nodes were processed. Due to this, one cannot map an arbitrary DAG to a set of speed-up curves since the parallelizability of a job in the speed-up curves model only depends on the amount of work previously processed. Alternatively, in the speed-up curves model, it could be the case that a job has a speed up function of $\Gamma(m') = \sqrt{m'}$. In this case, a job is processed at a rate of $\sqrt{m'}$ when given m' processors for any $1 \leq m' \leq m$. In the DAG setting, one cannot simulate this speed-up curves since the parallelizability of a job is essentially linear up to the number of nodes ready to be scheduled.

The results mentioned in Section 1 on minimizing the maximum (weighted) flow time were all for the case where jobs are sequential. When jobs are parallelizable, few online algorithmic techniques are known to have strong performance guarantees for maximum flow time, unlike for other objectives such as average flow time [11]. The only positive result on maximum flow time is for the arbitrary speed-up curves setting, where a $(1 + \epsilon)$-speed $O(\log n)$-competitive algorithm for unweighted flow time was shown [24]. This result is complemented by a lower bound showing that no algorithm can be s-speed $o(\log n)$-competitive for any constant resource augmentation $s > 0$. The lower bound is somewhat surprising because average flow time, typically thought of as a harder objective than maximum flow time, admits an $O(1)$-competitive algorithm with constant resource augmentation [11]. Thus, this result on maximum flow time seems to close the problem and rules out hope for a $O(1)$-competitive algorithm even with resource augmentation. Our result, which provides $O(1)$-competitive algorithm with $1+\epsilon$ speed augmentation is the first to cleanly separate the DAG model from the arbitrary speed-up curves model for any objective.

Work on the speed-up curves setting has also considered other objectives. A $(1+\epsilon)$ speed $O(\frac{1}{\epsilon})$-competitive algorithm for any $\epsilon > 0$ is known for average flow time [11]. Without resource augmentation, an $O(\log P)$-competitive algorithm is known assuming polynomial speed-up functions under some assumptions of the jobs parallelizability [18]. For the ℓ_k-norms of flow time, a $(1 + \epsilon)$ speed $O(\frac{k}{\epsilon^{2k+1}})$ for any $\epsilon > 0$ is known [10, 15]. Notice that maximum flow time is captured by the ℓ_k-norms for sufficiently large k, but here the competitive ratio grows with k. For maximum flow time a $(1+\epsilon)$-speed $O(\log n)$-competitive is known with a matching lower bound on any algorithm given $O(1)$ speed augmentation [24].

For the DAG scheduling setting, little is known online. Recently some works have considered algorithms in the real time scheduling setting [27, 22].

9. CONCLUSION

The DAG model has been influential in design of theoretically good and practically efficient schedulers for executing single parallel program. In this paper, we give the first results in this model for maximum flow time, an important scheduling metric, for multiprogrammed environment where jobs arrive online. This work opens up many interesting further questions. For instance, is resource augmentation absolutely necessary for DAG jobs? Also, are there online algorithms with strong performance guarantees for other objectives such as the ℓ_k-norms of flow time? Our results also show that the online scheduling of parallel programs in the DAG model differs from the arbitrary speed-up curves setting. It would be of interest to further explore connections and differences between these two models.

Acknowledgment

This research was supported in part by a Google Research Award, a Yahoo Research Award, NSF awards CCF-1337218, CCF-1218017, and CCF-1150036.

10. REFERENCES

[1] Kunal Agrawal, Charles E Leiserson, Yuxiong He, and Wen Jing Hsu. Adaptive work-stealing with parallelism feedback. *ACM Trans. Computer Syst.*, 26(3):7, 2008.

[2] Kunal Agrawal, Jing Li, Kefu Lu, and Benjamin Moseley. Scheduling parallel DAG jobs online to minimize average flow time. In *SODA '16*, pages 176–189, 2016.

[3] Christoph Ambühl and Monaldo Mastrolilli. On-line scheduling to minimize max flow time: an optimal preemptive algorithm. *Oper. Res. Lett.*, 33(6):597–602, 2005.

[4] Michael A. Bender, Soumen Chakrabarti, and S. Muthukrishnan. Flow and stretch metrics for scheduling continuous job streams. In *SODA '98*, pages 270–279, 1998.

[5] Robert D. Blumofe and Charles E. Leiserson. Scheduling multithreaded computations by work stealing. *JACM*, 46(5):720–748, 1999.

[6] F. Warren Burton and M. Ronan Sleep. Executing functional programs on a virtual tree of processors. In *FPCA*, pages 187–194. ACM, 1981.

[7] Colin Campbell and Ade Miller. *A Parallel Programming with Microsoft Visual C++: Design Patterns for Decomposition and Coordination on Multicore Architectures.* Microsoft Press, 2011.

[8] Chandra Chekuri, Sungjin Im, and Benjamin Moseley. Online scheduling to minimize maximum response time and maximum delay factor. *Theory of Computing*, 8(1):165–195, 2012.

[9] Thomas H Cormen, Charles E Leiserson, and Ronald L Rivest. *Introduction to algorithms.* MIT press, 2009.

[10] Jeff Edmonds, Sungjin Im, and Benjamin Moseley. Online scalable scheduling for the ℓ_k-norms of flow time without conservation of work. In *SODA '11*, pages 109–119, 2011.

[11] Jeff Edmonds and Kirk Pruhs. Scalably scheduling processes with arbitrary speedup curves. *ACM Trans. Algo.*, 8(3):28, 2012.

[12] Rainer Feldmann, Peter Mysliwietz, and Burkhard Monien. Studying overheads in massively parallel min/max-tree evaluation. In *SPAA '94*, pages 94–103, 1994.

[13] Vincent W. Freeh, David K. Lowenthal, and Gregory R. Andrews. Distributed Filaments: Efficient fine-grain parallelism on a cluster of workstations. In *OSDI '94*, pages 201–213. USENIX, 1994.

[14] Matteo Frigo, Charles E. Leiserson, and Keith H. Randall. The implementation of the Cilk-5 multithreaded language. In *PLDI*, pages 212–223, 1998.

[15] Anupam Gupta, Sungjin Im, Ravishankar Krishnaswamy, Benjamin Moseley, and Kirk Pruhs. Scheduling jobs with varying parallelizability to reduce variance. In *SPAA '10*, pages 11–20, 2010.

[16] Yuxiong He, Wen-Jing Hsu, and Charles E Leiserson. Provably efficient online nonclairvoyant adaptive scheduling. *IEEE Trans. Parallel Distrib. Syst.*, 19(9):1263–1279, 2008.

[17] Sungjin Im, Benjamin Moseley, and Kirk Pruhs. A tutorial on amortized local competitiveness in online scheduling. *SIGACT News*, 42(2):83–97, 2011.

[18] Sungjin Im, Benjamin Moseley, Kirk Pruhs, and Eric Torng. Competitively scheduling tasks with intermediate parallelizability. In *SPAA '14*, pages 22–29, 2014.

[19] Intel. Intel CilkPlus, Sep 2013. https://www.cilkplus.org/.

[20] Bala Kalyanasundaram and Kirk Pruhs. Speed is as powerful as clairvoyance. *J. ACM*, 47(4):617–643, 2000.

[21] Saehoon Kim, Yuxiong He, Seung-won Hwang, Sameh Elnikety, and Seungjin Choi. Delayed-dynamic-selective (DDS) prediction for reducing extreme tail latency in web search. In *WSDM '15*, pages 7–16, 2015.

[22] Jing Li, Jian-Jia Chen, Kunal Agrawal, Chenyang Lu, Christopher D. Gill, and Abusayeed Saifullah. Analysis of federated and global scheduling for parallel real-time tasks. In *ECRTS '14*, pages 85–96, 2014.

[23] OpenMP. OpenMP Application Program Interface v4.0, July 2013. http://http://www.openmp.org/mp-documents/OpenMP4.0.0.pdf.

[24] Kirk Pruhs, Julien Robert, and Nicolas Schabanel. Minimizing maximum flowtime of jobs with arbitrary parallelizability. In *WAOA '10*, pages 237–248, 2010.

[25] James Reinders. *Intel threading building blocks: outfitting C++ for multi-core processor parallelism.* O'Reilly Media, 2010.

[26] Shaolei Ren, Yuxiong He, Sameh Elnikety, and Kathryn S McKinley. Exploiting processor heterogeneity in interactive services. In *ICAC '13*, pages 45–58, 2013.

[27] Abusayeed Saifullah, David Ferry, Jing Li, Kunal Agrawal, Chenyang Lu, and Christopher D. Gill. Parallel real-time scheduling of dags. *IEEE Trans. Parallel Distrib. Syst.*, 25(12):3242–3252, 2014.

[28] Olivier Tardieu, Haichuan Wang, and Haibo Lin. A work-stealing scheduler for x10's task parallelism with suspension. In *PPoPP '12*, 2012.

Brief Announcement: A QPTAS for Non-preemptive Speed-scaling

Sungjin Im
EECS, University of California, Merced
Merced, CA
sim3@ucmerced.edu

Maryam Shadloo
EECS, University of California, Merced
Merced, CA
mshadloo@ucmerced.edu

ABSTRACT

Modern processors typically allow dynamic speed-scaling offering an effective trade-off between high throughput and energy efficiency. In a classical model, a processor/machine runs at speed s when consuming power s^α where $\alpha > 1$ is a constant. Yao et al. [FOCS 1995] studied the problem of completing all jobs before their deadlines on a single machine with the minimum energy in their seminal work and gave a nice polynomial time algorithm. The influential work has been extended to various settings. In particular, the problem has been extensively studied in the presence of multiple machines as multi-core processors have become dominant computing units.

However, when jobs must be scheduled *non-preemptively*, our understanding of the problem remains fairly unsatisfactory. Often, preempting a job is prohibited since it could be very costly. Previously, a $O((w_{\max}/w_{\min})^\alpha)$-approximation was known for the non-preemptive setting where $w_{\max}$ and $w_{\min}$ denote the maximum and minimum job sizes, respectively. Even when there is only one machine, the best known approximation factor had a dependency on α. In this paper, for any fixed $\alpha > 1$ and $\epsilon > 0$, we give the *first* $(1+\epsilon)$-approximation for this problem on multiple machines which runs in $n^{O(\text{polylog}(n))}$ time where n is the number of jobs to be scheduled.

1. INTRODUCTION

Energy efficiency is considered a primary goal in modern scheduling at various scales [1]. Energy dissipation is a main concern in mobile devices. Cumulative energy cost over a long time period can easily exceed the hardware procurement cost. At a larger scale, for example, in data centers, the importance of energy conservation is well illustrated by the following quote:

> What matters most to the computer designers at Google is not speed, but power, low power, because data centers can consume as much electricity as a city.
>
> - Dr. Eric Schmidt, CEO of Google [21].

SPAA '16 July 11-13, 2016, Pacific Grove, CA, USA

ACM ISBN 978-1-4503-4210-0/16/07.
DOI: http://dx.doi.org/10.1145/2935764.2935824

Various methods have been developed to save energy while meeting/optimizing certain qualities of services [18, 1]. One of the most widely used technologies is dynamic speed-scaling where each individual machine can run in different speeds depending on the energy it consumes. A machine can run slowly when processing small workload, and run faster to process high volume of incoming jobs by consuming more power.

Yao et al. studied a fundamental scheduling problem on a single machine with dynamic speed-scaling capabilities in their seminal work [22]. In the problem, which we call THE ENERGY-EFFICIENT DEADLINE SCHEDULING PROBLEM (EDS), there are n jobs. Each job j has a release time r_j, deadline d_j, and work volume w_j that must be completed during its lifespan (r_j, d_j) on the given single machine. When the machine runs in speed s at time instant t, the machine consumes power $P(s) = s^\alpha$, where $\alpha > 1$ is a constant. A job j completes when it gets processed by w_j units. The goal is to complete all jobs during their respective lifespans while minimizing the total energy consumption. For EDS, Yao et al. gave an elegant polynomial time algorithm. The influential work has been extended to multiple machines [11, 2, 4, 7, 6].

However, all the aforementioned works assume that preemption is allowed for free, meaning that a job being processed can be interrupted to process other jobs and can be resumed later. While preemption is very useful for optimizing certain objectives, it is prohibited in some applications – preempting and resuming a job can be very costly, or may not be allowed due to the way the system works. Unfortunately, non-preemptive scheduling is fundamentally different from preemptive scheduling and gives a lot of algorithmic challenges. For example, adding a job j of small lifespan may change the schedule drastically by forcing other jobs to either complete before j starts or to start after j completes.

Indeed, the EDS problem becomes strongly NP-hard without preemption [5] – we will call the EDS problem with no preemption EDS-N. The best approximation known for EDS-N is $(1+\epsilon)\tilde{B}_\alpha$ due to [8]. Here $\tilde{B}_\alpha := \sum_{k=0}^{\infty} \frac{k^\alpha/e}{k!}$ is the generalized Bell number which grows exponentially in α. A key idea of the $(1+\epsilon)\tilde{B}_\alpha$-approximation was to forbid certain 'enclosing' using a clever configuration LP and rounding scheme. That is, each job j is allowed to start at time a_j and end at time b_j only when the interval (a_j, b_j) includes no other jobs lifespans. However, this constraint is no longer valid when there are multiple machines, rendering the configuration LP inapplicable. Prior to our work the best approximation factor of any polynomial or quasi-polynomial time algorithms known for EDS-N in the multiple machines setting was $\Omega((w_{\max}/w_{\min})^{\alpha})$ [15, 8], where $w_{\max}$ and $w_{\min}$ denote the maximum and minimum job sizes, respectively. The dependency on $w_{\max}/w_{\min}$ was unavoidable in the previous work since machines had to run at a rate of $\Theta(w_{\max}/w_{\min})$ to treat jobs as if they were of an equal size.

1.1 Our result

Our main result is the following.

THEOREM 1. *For the problem* ENERGY-EFFICIENT DEADLINE SCHEDULING WITH NO PREEMPTION *(EDS-N), for any $\epsilon > 0$, there exists a $(1+\epsilon)$-approximation algorithm which runs in $n^{O\left(\frac{4^{\alpha}\log^3 n}{\epsilon^2}\right)}$ time. Further, this result holds even when there are an arbitrary number of identical machines.*

As mentioned before, the best known approximation factor prior to our work had an exponential dependency on α. Further, no constant approximations were known even for a fixed α when there are more than one machine. Although we only present our result for identical machines, we note that our result can be easily extended to a constant number of heterogeneous machines.

Hence a natural looming question was if one could obtain an approximation arbitrarily close to the optimum. We answer this question positively by giving the first $(1+\epsilon)$-approximation, albeit with a quasi-polynomial running time. This is the first $(1+\epsilon)$-approximation for the general case. Previously, polynomial time algorithms were known for instances where all jobs are unit sized [3, 16] or jobs have agreeable deadlines [22]. [1] Quasi-polynomial-time approximation schemes (QPTAS) were known only for restricted instances where jobs lifespans form a laminar structure [5, 16]. That is, for any two distinct jobs, one job's lifespan is completely included in the other's, or the two have disjoint lifespans. The dynamic programming used in [5, 16] strongly relies on the fact that laminar instances have a tree representation. In contrast, our work makes no assumptions on instances, and our approach is very different. Our result implies that EDS-N might admit a PTAS.

1.2 Overview of our algorithm and analysis

Our algorithm is inspired by the dynamic programming framework in [17], which addressed various scheduling objectives, particularly completing as many jobs as possible before their deadlines. A simple yet useful observation made in [17] was that if we know that the scheduling intervals $\mathcal{T}$ where jobs $\mathcal{J}$ are scheduled (but neither the actual assignment of jobs to the intervals, nor the assignment of intervals to machines), then we can find a feasible schedule by finding a matching between $\mathcal{J}$ and $\mathcal{T}$ and greedily packing the intervals $\mathcal{T}$ into machines. This observation allowed [17] to focus on finding a 'good' set $\mathcal{T}$ of intervals that admits a matching between $\mathcal{J}$ and $\mathcal{T}$. Hence [17] used dynamic programming to find such a set. However, to make the dynamic programming efficient, [17] made use of a novel sketching scheme, and was able to find a set $\mathcal{T}$ of intervals that admits a 'fractional' matching between $\mathcal{J}$ and $\mathcal{T}$ where every job is matched by one unit, while every interval in $\mathcal{T}$ is matched by at most $1+\epsilon$ units; here a mild speed augmentation was used and such a fractional matching was said to have congestion $1+\epsilon$. Then, using the integrality of matching, [17] was able to find an intermediate schedule where each interval in $\mathcal{T}$ schedules at most two jobs, which was turned into a feasible schedule by either doubling the speed or the number of machines.

We obtain our QPTAS by carefully adapting this idea for EDS-N. First, observe that it is not enough to find a set $\mathcal{T}$ of scheduling intervals that admits a fractional matching with congestion $1+\epsilon$: Since our objective is minimizing total energy consumption, we will try to find a minimum cost integral matching where the edge between a job of size w and an interval of size p has cost $p(w/p)^{\alpha}$, which is exactly the energy needed to schedule the job on the interval. As in [17], in the integral matching, two jobs may have to be scheduled on the same interval. If we double the speed to convert it into a feasible schedule, we may have to use 2^{α} factor more energy in the worst scenario. Hence, for each pair of w and p, we will keep track of which intervals $\mathcal{T}'$ of length p are used to accommodate (matched with) jobs $\mathcal{J}'$ of size w. The matching between $\mathcal{J}'$ and $\mathcal{T}'$ we find has an additional nice property that only a few scheduling intervals in $\mathcal{T}'$ schedule more than one job from $\mathcal{J}'$. Then, the energy overhead for doubling the machines speed on such intervals can be charged to energy used on other intervals. The actual algorithm is slightly more complicated, but this is a high-level idea.

To discuss other difficulties and how our work is different from [17], we illustrate our dynamic programming at a high level. Suppose the time horizon is $(0, N)$, i.e. all jobs release times and deadlines are between 0 and N. For simplicity, assume that there is only one machine. We first guess the job j_m that is processed at the middle time $N/2$ (if such a job exists). Then, we need to decide which jobs should be scheduled before j_m and after. But such decisions can be exponentially many. This is where [17] uses sketches. The sketching scheme in [17] shows that jobs can be grouped if they have 'similar' release times, deadlines, and sizes. More precisely, it was shown that (1) if there is a feasible schedule for the original instance, then there is a feasible schedule for the instance simplified via the sketch, and (2) if a set of scheduling intervals admits a fractional matching with a congestion 1 for the simplified instance, then it admits a fractional matching with a congestion $(1+\delta)^h$ for the original instance where h is the depth of divide-and-conquer tree in the dynamic programming. Hence, if the dynamic programming has $O(\text{polylog}(n))$ levels and by setting $\delta = O(1/\text{polylog}(n))$ we can find good execution intervals with a small congestion.

However, we need to carefully adapt this dynamic programming to the speed scaling setting since each job can be processed for a very long or short period of time compared to its size. For example, we need to guess how long the middle job is processed in each iteration of the dynamic programming. Further, when some quantities such as job sizes are not polynomially bounded, the number of levels can be super-polylogarithmic. [17] handles this issue by showing that inflexible jobs, whose sizes are not so small compared to their lifespans, are the main concern, and flexible jobs of specific size w are involved in sketching at most $O(\log n)$ levels. Intuitively, flexible jobs are easy to schedule

[1] The instance is said to be agreeable if for any two jobs j and j', $r_j \le r_{j'}$, then $d_j \le d_{j'}$.

since they only need to use machines for short during their lifespans. In our setting, we have to adapt the notion of flexible/inflexible jobs in connection to energy consumption since how long jobs are processed can be very different from their sizes. Additionally, there are many details that should be carefully handled.

1.3 Other related work

We first discuss previous work on the preemptive case. As mentioned earlier, [22] gave a polynomial time algorithm for EDS when there is a single machine. The algorithm was refined in [19, 20]. When there are multiple machines, one can think of two cases, migratory and non-migratory, depending on whether a job can be scheduled on more than one machine or not. Migratory schedule was studied and polynomial-time algorithms were given in [11, 2, 4]. The algorithm in [11] was based on mathematical programing and the others were combinatorial. [6] studied the case when machines are heterogeneous in both migratory and non-migratory settings. In particular, [6] gave a $(1+\epsilon)\tilde{B}_\alpha$-approximation for heterogeneous machines when the schedule is migratory and preemptive.

We now shift our discussion to non-preemptive scheduling. Constant approximations depending on α are known for the single machine case [5, 6, 15]. The current best approximation ratio $(1+\epsilon)\tilde{B}_\alpha$ is due to [8]. [15] gives a $(w_{\max}/w_{\min})^{O(\alpha)}$ approximation when there are multiple machines, and their work can handle heterogeneous machines.

Finally, we briefly discuss other work on non-preemptive scheduling when machines have fixed speeds. Several $O(1)$-approximations [10, 14, 17] are known for the throughput objective where each job has some profit, and the goal is to maximize the total profit of the jobs completed by their deadlines. The problem of scheduling all jobs with the minimum number of machines was studied in [12, 13, 17]. Flow time objectives were studied in [9, 17].

Acknowledgements

This work was supported in part by NSF grant CCF-1409130.

2. REFERENCES

[1] S. Albers. Energy-efficient algorithms. *Commun. ACM*, 53(5):86–96, 2010.

[2] S. Albers, A. Antoniadis, and G. Greiner. On multi-processor speed scaling with migration. In *SPAA*, pages 279–288. ACM, 2011.

[3] E. Angel, E. Bampis, and V. Chau. Throughput maximization in the speed-scaling setting. *arXiv preprint arXiv:1309.1732*, 2013.

[4] E. Angel, E. Bampis, F. Kacem, and D. Letsios. Speed scaling on parallel processors with migration. In *Euro-Par 2012 Parallel Processing*, pages 128–140. Springer, 2012.

[5] A. Antoniadis and C.-C. Huang. Non-preemptive speed scaling. *J. of Scheduling*, 16(4):385–394, Aug. 2013.

[6] E. Bampis, A. Kononov, D. Letsios, G. Lucarelli, and M. Sviridenko. Energy efficient scheduling and routing via randomized rounding. In *FSTTCS*, pages 449–460, 2013.

[7] E. Bampis, D. Letsios, and G. Lucarelli. Green scheduling, flows and matchings. In *Algorithms and Computation*, pages 106–115. Springer, 2012.

[8] E. Bampis, D. Letsios, and G. Lucarelli. Speed-scaling with no preemptions. In *Algorithms and Computation*, pages 259–269. Springer, 2014.

[9] N. Bansal, H.-L. Chan, R. Khandekar, K. Pruhs, B. Schieber, and C. Stein. Non-preemptive min-sum scheduling with resource augmentation. In *FOCS*, pages 614–624, 2007.

[10] A. Bar-Noy, S. Guha, J. Naor, and B. Schieber. Approximating the throughput of multiple machines in real-time scheduling. *SIAM J. Comput.*, 31(2):331–352, 2001.

[11] B. D. Bingham and M. R. Greenstreet. Energy optimal scheduling on multiprocessors with migration. In *ISPA*, pages 153–161. IEEE, 2008.

[12] J. Chuzhoy, S. Guha, S. Khanna, and J. S. Naor. Machine minimization for scheduling jobs with interval constraints. In *FOCS*, pages 81–90, 2004.

[13] J. Chuzhoy and J. Naor. New hardness results for congestion minimization and machine scheduling. *J. ACM*, 53(5):707–721, 2006.

[14] J. Chuzhoy, R. Ostrovsky, and Y. Rabani. Approximation algorithms for the job interval selection problem and related scheduling problems. *Math. Oper. Res.*, 31(4):730–738, 2006.

[15] V. Cohen-Addad, Z. Li, C. Mathieu, and I. Milis. Energy-efficient algorithms for non-preemptive speed-scaling. In *Approximation and Online Algorithms*, pages 107–118. Springer, 2014.

[16] C.-C. Huang and S. Ott. New results for non-preemptive speed scaling. In *Mathematical Foundations of Computer Science 2014*, pages 360–371. Springer, 2014.

[17] S. Im, S. Li, B. Moseley, and E. Torng. A dynamic programming framework for non-preemptive scheduling problems on multiple machines [extended abstract]. In *SODA*, pages 1070–1086, 2015.

[18] S. Irani and K. Pruhs. Algorithmic problems in power management. *SIGACT News*, 36(2):63–76, 2005.

[19] M. Li, B. J. Liu, and F. F. Yao. Min-energy voltage allocation for tree-structured tasks. *Journal of Combinatorial Optimization*, 11(3):305–319, 2006.

[20] M. Li, A. C. Yao, and F. F. Yao. Discrete and continuous min-energy schedules for variable voltage processors. *PNAS*, 103(11):3983–3987, 2006.

[21] J. Markoff and S. Lohr. Intel's huge bet turns iffy, new york times, september 29, 2002.

[22] F. Yao, A. Demers, and S. Shenker. A scheduling model for reduced cpu energy. In *FOCS*, pages 374–382. IEEE, 1995.

Invited Talk: A Multicore Path to Connectomics-on-Demand

Nir Shavit
Massachusetts Institute of Technology
and Tel-Aviv University
shanir@csail.mit.edu

ABSTRACT

Connectomics is an emerging field of neurobiology that uses cutting edge machine learning and image processing to extract brain connectivity graphs from electron microscopy images. It has long been assumed that the processing of connectomics data will require mass storage and farms of CPUs and GPUs and will take months if not years. This talk shows the feasibility of designing a high-throughput connectomics-on-demand system that runs on a multicore machine with less than 100 cores and extracts connectomes at the terabyte per hour pace of modern electron microscopes. Building this system required solving algorithmic and performance engineering issues related to scaling machine learning on multicore architectures, and may have important lessons for other problem spaces in the natural sciences, where until now large distributed server or GPU farms seemed to be the only way to go.

Bio

Nir Shavit received B.Sc. and M.Sc. degrees in Computer Science from the Technion|Israel Institute of Technology in 1984 and 1986, and a Ph.D. in Computer Science from the Hebrew University of Jerusalem in 1990. Shavit is a coauthor of the book The Art of Multiprocessor Programming, is a winner of the 2004 Gödel Prize in theoretical computer science for his work on applying tools from algebraic topology to model shared memory computability, and a winner of the 2012 Dijkstra Prize for the introduction and first implementation of software transactional memory. He is a past program chair of the ACM Symposium on Principles of Distributed Computing (PODC) and the ACM Symposium on Parallelism in Algorithms and Architectures (SPAA). He has recently become interested in computational neurobiology, and in particular is involved in developing new ways of using high performance computing to analyze data in order to uncover the microscopic structure and function of neural tissue.

SPAA '16 July 11-13, 2016, Pacific Grove, CA, USA
ACM 978-1-4503-4210-0/16/07.
http://dx.doi.org/10.1145/2935764.2935825

Robust and Probabilistic Failure-Aware Placement

Madhukar Korupolu
Google Research
mkar@google.com

Rajmohan Rajaraman*
Northeastern University
rraj@ccs.neu.edu

ABSTRACT

Motivated by the growing complexity and heterogeneity of modern data centers, and the prevalence of commodity component failures, this paper studies the *failure-aware placement problem* of placing tasks of a parallel job on machines in the data center with the goal of increasing availability. We consider two models of failures: adversarial and probabilistic. In the adversarial model, each node has a weight (higher weight implying higher reliability) and the adversary can remove any subset of nodes of total weight at most a given bound W and our goal is to find a placement that incurs the least disruption against such an adversary. In the probabilistic model, each node has a probability of failure and we need to find a placement that maximizes the probability that at least K out of N tasks survive at any time.

For adversarial failures, we first show that (i) the problems are in Σ_2, the second level of the polynomial hierarchy, (ii) a basic variant, that we call RobustFAP, is co-NP-hard, and (iii) an all-or-nothing version of RobustFAP is Σ_2-complete. We then give a PTAS for RobustFAP, a key ingredient of which is a solution that we design for a fractional version of RobustFAP. We then study fractional RobustFAP over hierarchies, denoted HierRobustFAP, and introduce a notion of *hierarchical max-min fairness* and a novel *Generalized Spreading* algorithm which is simultaneously optimal for all W. These generalize the classical notion of *max-min fairness* to work with nodes of differing capacities, differing reliability weights and hierarchical structures. Using randomized rounding, we extend this to give an algorithm for integral HierRobustFAP.

For the probabilistic version, we first give an algorithm that achieves an additive ε approximation in the failure probability for the single level version, called ProbFAP, while giving up a $(1+\varepsilon)$ multiplicative factor in the number of failures. We then extend the result to the hierarchical version, HierProbFAP, achieving an ε additive approximation in failure probability while giving up an $(L+\varepsilon)$ multiplicative factor in the number of failures, where L is the number of levels in the hierarchy.

*Supported in part by NSF grants CNS-1217981, CCF-1422715, and CCF-1535929, and a Google Research Award.

SPAA '16, July 11 - 13, 2016, Pacific Grove, CA, USA

ISBN 978-1-4503-4210-0/16/07...$15.00
DOI: http://dx.doi.org/10.1145/2935764.2935802

1. Introduction

Modern datacenters are becoming increasingly complex and heterogeneous [3, 6, 11, 36]. Machines, racks, network switches, storage drives and other hardware equipment of different generations and capabilities often co-exist in the data center – leading to heterogeneity both in capacities as well as failure characteristics. The use of commodity hardware and the large scale of these data centers makes failures a common occurence and software systems need to plan and design for them [3, 38, 41].

In fact, the book on warehouse scale computing [3] devotes a whole chapter to failure and fault tolerance. Machines in the data center are often arranged in hierarchies [2, 6, 39] – with racks and top-of-rack (ToR) switches which are then inter-connected via network and power hierarchies. The components of these hierarchies are also prone to failure – due to hardware defects, planned and unplanned outages.

Several recent systems papers address the question of failures and the need to improve reliability in the presence of failures. [16, 34, 37] analyze failures in large disk drive and distributed installations. [17, 38, 42, 44] analyze failures of machines and network elements in large data centers, including Microsoft data centers over the course of a year. [6, 39, 40] study correlated failures in data centers due to failure of common nodes such as network and power domains. Decreased availability due to failures causes service downtimes and also hurts reputation for cloud service providers.

In recent work, [6, 39] addressed the problem of placing tasks of a parallel job (such as MapReduce [10], Spark [45]) among machines in a hierarchical data center so as to increase availability. However the treatment is informal and the proposed heuristics are evaluated experimentally without theoretical analysis.

Given this increasingly important context, in this paper, we initiate the formal definition of *failure-aware placement problem* and study its theoretical complexity and approximation algorithms. This models the common scenario in modern data centers where a job (such as MapReduce [10], Spark [45]) arrives with multiple identical tasks that need to be placed on machines in the data center. These can be either *batch jobs* that perform computations over large data sets and terminate when finished or *service jobs* that run indefinitely serving user requests [8, 36, 41]. The tasks of the job can be executed in parallel among machines in the data center. Both the machines and the hardware domains that connect them (racks, switches, busducts, power nodes) are prone to failure. Jobs have availability requirements – such as a minimum number of tasks that need to be up and running at any time – to make quick progress and also to meet service level agreements. When a job arrives, the goal of the *failure aware placement system* is to allocate its tasks among machines so as to improve availability.

While we present our results in the context of tasks and machines, the concepts are general and apply to storage and other contexts as well. From a storage point of view, failure rates and disk drive characteristics have been studied in [34, 16, 37]. Error correcting codes are often used to store data among nodes in such a way that as long as k of n chunks are available, the original data can be reconstructed [18, 25, 35]. However, the related problem of how to place the n chunks among the available nodes so as to maximize the probability of k chunks surviving has received little attention [27]. A good failure-aware placement algorithm can increase data availability and thereby reduce the amount of redundant storage required.

1.1 Problem Setup

We formulate two classes of problems for failure-aware placement: *robust (adversarial)* and *probabilistic*. The first class of problems focuses on *robustness* by associating each domain with a weight representing its reliability (higher weight implies higher reliability), and allowing an adversary to remove (i.e., cause failures in) a subset of domains with total weight bounded by a given failure budget W. The goal is to determine a placement of N tasks among machines such that the maximum number of tasks that fail, taken over all adversary's choices of failing domains, is minimized. The second class of failure-aware problems considers probabilistic failures by associating a failure probability with each domain. The goal here is to determine a placement of N tasks among machines such that the probability that more than a given number F of tasks fail is minimized.

We study several variants of failure-aware placement under the above two classes. In addition to differences in the nature of failures (adversarial or probabilistic), these variants differ in the organization of the failure domains (single-level or hierarchical), the kind of adversary (fractional or integral), and the kind of placement (fractional or integral). In all of these variants, we focus on the case where all the tasks have the same size. Many of the modern data parallel batch processing systems (such as MapReduce [10], Spark [45]) have jobs with multiple (tens to thousands of) tasks of the same size running on different machines [36, 41]. They are launched using a config file which specifies the resource requirements for each task and the number of tasks (e.g., see [41], Section 2.3). User-facing jobs also often have multiple instances of the same size running on different machines, and they use a load balancer in front to distribute load evenly among them.

1.2 Overview of results and techniques

We now formally define the specific problems we study, and summarize our results and techniques. In each formulation, we have a set $\mathcal{F}$ of failure domains which includes machines and internal nodes in case of a hierarchy, and a job with N identical tasks that just arrived and needs to be placed. We have a capacity C_i for each domain, representing the number of tasks of the job that can be placed in the domain. We define a placement as a map $P : \mathcal{F} \to \mathbb{N}$ with $0 \le P(i) \le C_i$ for each domain i, $0 \le i \le |\mathcal{F}|$. For a subset D of disjoint domains, we define $P(D) = \sum_{i \in D} P(i)$.

Adversarial failures. We first consider the robust variants with adversarial failures.

Definition 1. (Placement against adversarial failures) *Given a nonnegative integer W, and for each i in $\mathcal{F}$ an integer weight w_i, the goal of* RobustFAP *is to place N tasks subject to capacity constraints so as to minimize the maximum number of tasks placed on any subset of domains with total weight at most W.*

For a given set S of domains, let $w(S)$ denote the sum of the weights of the domains in S. Formally, the goal of RobustFAP is to find a placement P that optimizes $\min_P \max_{S:w(S)\le W} \sum_{i\in S} P(i)$.

Hardness of RobustFAP and related problems. As formulated, it is unclear whether RobustFAP is in NP because the inner maximization is an NP-complete integer knapsack problem. Since the decision version of RobustFAP is of the form $\exists P \forall S$, where P refers to a placement, and S to the choice of an adversary, the problem is in Σ_2, the second level of the polynomial hierarchy [32, Chapter 17].

Theorem 1. *The decision version of* RobustFAP *is co-NP-hard. (Section 2)*

To better understand the complexity of RobustFAP, we consider a variant which we call AllOrNoneRobustFAP, which is identical to RobustFAP, except that we require that the placement P be *whole*: for any domain i, $P(i) = 0$ or $P(i) = C_i$; i.e., we either use the entire capacity of a domain or do not use it at all. AllOrNoneRobustFAP belongs to the class of bilevel knapsack problems, which have gathered interest in recent work [7, 14, 15].

Theorem 2. AllOrNoneRobustFAP *is Σ_2-complete, and NP-hard if input weights are unary. (Section 2)*

Algorithms for RobustFAP and related variants. As a step toward an approximation algorithm for RobustFAP, we first consider a fractional variant.

Definition 2 (Fractional RobustFAP). *The problem* FracRobustFAP *is identical to* RobustFAP, *except that the actions of both the placement algorithm and the adversary can be fractional. Formally, we seek a fractional placement $P : \mathcal{F} \to \mathbb{R}$ optimizing* $\min_{P:P(\mathcal{F})\ge N} \max_{x\in[0,1]^n : x\cdot w \le W} x \cdot P$.

Note that the notion of robustness is different in the RobustFAP and FracRobustFAP problems. In RobustFAP, an adversary can take down any subset of domains with total weight bounded by W. In FracRobustFAP, an adversary can take down any fraction (say $x(i)$) of any domain i, as a result of which the number of failed tasks in the domain is $x(i)$ times the number of tasks allocated to i; the sole constraint is that the total fractional weight of the failed domains, $\sum_i x(i)w_i$, is bounded by W. We show that the classic notion of weighted max-min fair allocation [19, 28, 33] is simultaneously optimal for all weights W for FracRobustFAP.

THEOREM 3. *The weighted max-min fair allocation is simultaneously optimal for all W for* FRACROBUSTFAP. *(Section 3)*

Our main result here is a PTAS for ROBUSTFAP that combines the algorithm for FRACROBUSTFAP with a careful enumeration of placements according to how allocations are made to domains. We also present a PTAS for ALLORNONEROBUSTFAP, which places it alongside the bilevel knapsack problem DNEG [7] in the class of Σ_2-complete problems that surprisingly admit polynomial-time approximation schemes.

THEOREM 4. *There exist PTASes for* ROBUSTFAP *and* ALLORNONEROBUSTFAP. *(Section 3)*

Failure domain hierarchies. Thus far, we have assumed a flat organization of the failure domains. We next generalize the problem to failure domain hierarchies, in which we have a failure domain tree $\mathcal{T}$, with machines at the leaves and internal nodes of the tree representing failure domains. Each node v has a weight w_v representing its reliability, and a capacity C_v representing the maximum number of tasks that can placed in the subtree rooted at that node. Failure of an internal node v causes the whole subtree rooted at v and the tasks placed in that subtree to be unavailable.

DEFINITION 3. (FRACTIONAL PLACEMENT AGAINST ADVERSARIAL FAILURES IN HIERARCHIES) *The goal of* HIERFRACROBUSTFAP *is to compute a fractional placement of N tasks among machines in a hierarchy such that the capacity constraints are satisfied and the maximum number of tasks that can fail due to a fractional adversary with weight bound W is minimized.*

Our second main result is a new placement algorithm for HIERFRACROBUSTFAP, which computes a placement that is *simultaneously optimal* for all weight budget bounds W. Our algorithm, which we call *Generalized Spreading*, introduces the concept of *hierarchical max-min fairness* that applies to nodes of different capacities, different reliability weights and a hierarchical structure, and could be useful in other domains.

THEOREM 5. *The Generalized Spreading algorithm is optimal for all W for* HIERFRACROBUSTFAP. *(Section 4)*

We then consider the integral problem HIERROBUSTFAP, and show in Section 4, that a randomized rounding of the Generalized Spreading algorithm solution yields a solution for HIERROBUSTFAP with performance guarantees against oblivious adversaries.

Probabilistic failures in domain hierarchies. The next class of failure-aware placement problems we study is with probabilistic failures: where we model failures by having, for each domain, a probability of failure for that domain.

DEFINITION 4. (PLACEMENT UNDER PROBABILISTIC FAILURES) *In* PROBFAP, *we are given a set of N tasks, and a set of domains $\mathcal{F}$, and for each domain i, a probability p_i of the domain failing. The goal is to find a placement of tasks to machines subject to capacity constraints so as to minimize the probability that the number of tasks that fail exceeds a given failure bound of F.*

The probability that the number of tasks failing in a given placement exceeds F is given by

$$Pr_P(F) = \sum_{D \subseteq \mathcal{F}: P(D) \geq F} \prod_{i \in D} p_i \prod_{i \in \mathcal{F} - D} (1 - p_i).$$

where D is the set of domains that fail and the summation is over all possible subsets D of $\mathcal{F}$. The goal of PROBFAP then is to find a placement P that minimizes $Pr_P(F)$.

We then extend the problem formulation to hierarchies of domains. In HIERPROBFAP, we have a failure domain tree $\mathcal{T}$, each node v of which has a probability p_v of failing, and a capacity C_v representing the maximum number of tasks that can placed in the subtree rooted at that node. If a domain v fails, then the entire subtree under it is unavailable, implying that all the tasks placed in the domain fail. Given a bound F on the number of failed tasks, the goal of HIERPROBFAP is to allocate N tasks to the machines in the hierarchy subject to capacity constraints so as to minimize the probability that the number of failed tasks exceeds F.

Our main result here is a bicriteria approximation algorithm for PROBFAP and HIERPROBFAP. Our solution approach builds on the stochastic knapsack framework of Li and Yuan [24] to handle dependencies among knapsack items and hierarchical constraints on the allocations.

THEOREM 6. *There exists a polynomial-time algorithm for* HIERPROBFAP, *which computes, for any given constant $\varepsilon > 0$, a placement of N tasks such that the probability that the number of failed tasks is at most $(L+\varepsilon)F$ is at least $OPT - \varepsilon$ where OPT is the maximum achievable probability for the given failure bound F, and L is the number of levels in the hierarchy. (Section 5)*

The remainder of the paper is organized as follows. Section 1.3 reviews related work. Section 2 contains hardness results. Section 3 presents PTASes for ROBUSTFAP and ALLORNONEROBUSTFAP. Section 4 presents results for HIERFRACROBUSTFAP and HIERROBUSTFAP. Section 5 presents results for PROBFAP and HIERPROBFAP. Section 6 closes with open problems stemming from our work. Due to space constraints, we have omitted many of the proofs in this paper. We refer the reader to the full paper for missing proofs and details [21].

1.3 Related work

To the best of our knowledge, our specific formulations for failure-aware placement are new. We now review related results in the theory, operations research, and systems communities, and highlight the differences between our work and past work.

Max-min fairness. The notion of max-min fairness and its generalizations, including weighted max-min fairness and generalized processor sharing, have been used in networking [19, 28, 33]. The basic idea is to allocate resources among multiple players such that any attempt to further increase the allocation of one player necessarily results in the decrease in allocation of some other player with an equal or smaller allocation. Max-min fairness and its variants are used in process and network schedulers to allow multiple packet flows to share bandwidth fairly [12]. We show in Section 3.1 that the optimal placement for FRACROBUSTFAP is a weighted max-min fair one. For hierarchies the problem is more involved due to the corelations among the different levels of the hierarchy. To address this, we introduce the concept of hierarhical max-min fairness in the *Generalized Spreading* algorithm of Section 4.

Bilevel knapsack. The ALLORNONEROBUSTFAP problem has similarities to the bilevel knapsack problems which model decision makers at multiple levels [13, 43]. A bilevel knapsack problem has two players: a leader and a follower.

First, a leader fixes the values of their variables with the aim of optimizing their objective. Next, the follower reacts by setting their variables with the aim of optimizing their objective, under the constraints imposed by the leader. The variants studied earlier differ in the objective functions and variables under control of the leader and follower [14, 15, 26]. Dempe and Richter [14] study a variant in which the leader controls the capacity of the knapsack while the follower decides which items are packed in the knapsack. In the variant labeled DNeg [15], both players have a knapsack of their own, and the follower can only choose from items that the leader did not pick. Our ALLORNONEROBUSTFAP problem has similarity to DNeg [15], however the particular combination of constraints and objective functions are different and as a result the complexity results for one do not directly translate to the other. Our Σ_2-completeness and PTAS for ALLORNONEROBUSTFAP build on ideas from [7]. The ROBUSTFAP problem has a different structure and uses additional ideas.

Stochastic knapsack and chance-constrained optimization. The placement problem under probabilistic failures resembles the category of chance-constrained optimization [29, 30], which involves constraints and objectives determined by probability of certain events. One consequence of having such chance constraints is that they define a non-convex set, making it difficult to apply general optimization techniques [29]. This challenge applies to PROBFAP and HIERPROBFAP as well. A number of algorithms have been developed for chance-constrained optimization [1, 4, 20, 30, 31], however, these do not yield any provable approximations for our problems of interest. Our solution approach for PROBFAP and HIERPROBFAP builds on the stochastic optimization framework of Li and Yuan [24] which uses a Poisson approximation technique [22]. Other recent work on stochastic knapsack and related problems includes [5, 23].

Finally, the recent work of [9] studies a distributed storage problem, which is a stochastic knapsack problem in which the unknown variables that are being determined are real-valued. Using structural results from the study of linear threshold functions, they give a unicriterion additive PTAS for their storage problem. In contrast, we focus on the discrete version of the related placement problem, and obtain a bicriteria additive PTAS for constant-depth network hierarchies with probabilistic failures.

2. Hardness of placement under adversarial failures

In this section, we establish the hardness of ROBUSTFAP and ALLORNONEROBUSTFAP: Theorems 1 and 2.

2.1 Hardness of ROBUSTFAP

Recall that, in the decision version of ROBUSTFAP, our goal is to decide if there exists a placement such that for any subset S of domains with weight at most W, the total number of tasks allocated to the domains in S is at most F.

Proof of Theorem 1: Our co-NP-hardness proof is by a reduction from the NP-hard partition problem. Let I be an instance of the partition problem consisting of a set S of n integers $\{a_i : 1 \leq i \leq n\}$ such that $\sum_i a_i$ equals an even number $2W$. The goal of the partition problem is to determine if there exists a subset T of S such that the sum of the elements in T equals W.

Given I, we construct the following instance I' of ROBUSTFAP. We have one domain for each element of S, with the capacity C_i and the reliability weight $w(i)$ of the ith domain both equal to a_i, for $1 \leq i \leq n$. We set (i) N, number of tasks we need to place, to $2W$, (ii) the adversary's weight budget to W, and (ii) F, the maximum number of allowed failures, to $W - 1$.

We now show that I' has a placement with maximum failures $W - 1$ if and only if I cannot be partitioned into two sets of equal size. First note that there is exactly one feasible placement of N tasks: place a_i tasks in domain i. Also for each subset X of domains, the number of tasks allocated as well as the weight are both equal to $\sum_{i\in X} a_i$. Therefore, a placement with maximum failures $W-1$ exists if and only if I cannot be partitioned into two sets of equal size thus establishing the co-NP-hardness.

2.2 Hardness of ALLORNONEROBUSTFAP

We now establish Theorem 2, the hardness of ALLORNONEROBUSTFAP. Clearly, ALLORNONEROBUSTFAP is in Σ_2. We show that it is Σ_2-hard via a reduction from the Σ_2-complete problem SUBSETSUMINTERVAL. Our proof is similar to the proof given in [7], that establishes this result for DNEG, a different variant of bilevel knapsack which is incomparable to ALLORNONEROBUSTFAP. We refer the reader to [21] for the proof.

3. Polynomial-time approximation schemes for ROBUSTFAP and ALLORNONEROBUSTFAP

We first consider the fractional variant FRACROBUSTFAP and show in Section 3.1 that it can be solved optimally using weighted max-min fair allocations. We then present PTASes for ROBUSTFAP and ALLORNONEROBUSTFAP, using the solution to FRACROBUSTFAP for the former.

3.1 FRACROBUSTFAP: Weighted max-min fair allocations

We begin with FRACROBUSTFAP, as defined in Definition 2. Consider the *weighted max-min fair allocation*, a fractional placement that satisfies the following *fairness property*: if a domain i gets less than its "fair share" compared to another domain j, it is only because i is full. More formally, for any i and j, if $P(i)/w_i < P(j)/w_j$, then $P(i) = C_i$. Such a placement can be computed by the following algorithm.

1. Set $N' = N$, and for each domain i, $C'_i = C_i$.
2. Repeat the following until $N' = 0$:
    1. Let $D = \{i : C'_i > 0\}$ and $w(D) = \sum_{i\in D} w_i$
    2. For each domain i in D: place $a_i = \min\{C'_i, N'w_i/w(D)\}$ tasks on i and set $C'_i = C'_i - a_i$
    3. Set $N' = N' - \sum_i a_i$

Note that the above allocation is a fractional placement. We show that the weighted max-min fair allocation is in fact simultaneously optimal for all weight bounds W. This result is somewhat implicit in previous fair allocation works [28, 33]. In the full paper [21], we include detailed proofs for the sake of completeness, and to place the results in our failure-aware placement context.

LEMMA 1. *For any* FRACROBUSTFAP *instance with weight bound* W*, there exists an optimal allocation that satisfies max-min fairness.*

PROOF. For any placement P not satisfying the fairness property, we define the *low-ratio* as the $\min_i k_i/w_i$ over all i such that $k_i < C_i$, yet there exists a j for which $k_j/w_j > k_i/w_i$. Suppose, for the sake of contradiction, that there does not exist any optimal allocation satisfying the fairness property. Let P be an optimal allocation for the weight bound W, with the highest low-ratio.

Let i denote the arg-min for the low-ratio minimization, and let j be such that $k_i/w_i < k_j/w_j$ and yet $k_i < C_i$. Consider an alternative placement P' that is identical to P except that $P'(i) = P(i) + \varepsilon$ and $P'(j) = P(j) - \varepsilon$, for a sufficiently small $\varepsilon > 0$ satisfying $(P(i) + \varepsilon)/w_i < (P(j) - \varepsilon)/w_j$. Let s' be any knapsack of weight W and value v' built from P'. Consider the knapsack s that is identical to s' except that $s_i = s'_i - \varepsilon$ and $s_j = s'_j + \delta w_i(P(j) - \varepsilon)/(w_j(P(i)+\varepsilon))$, where $\delta = \min(s'_i, w_j(P(i)+\varepsilon)/(w_i(P(j)-\varepsilon))$. By construction, s has the same weight as s'. By our assumption on ε, $w_i(P(j)-\varepsilon)/(w_j(P(i)+\varepsilon))$ is at least δ, so the value of s is at least that of s'. Finally, either $\delta = s'_i$ or $\delta \geq \varepsilon$, and $\delta w_i(P(j)-\varepsilon)/(w_j(P(i)+\varepsilon)) \leq \varepsilon$, which together imply that s is a knapsack that can be built from P. Thus, for every knapsack of weight W and value v in P', we have a knapsack of weight W and value at least v in P, implying that P' is a placement that is also optimal and has a higher low-ratio than P. This contradicts our assumption that P had the higher low-ratio, completing the proof. □

LEMMA 2. *For any* FRACROBUSTFAP *instance, there is a unique weighted max-min fair allocation.*

Lemmas 1 and 2 establish the following Theorem.

THEOREM 7. *For a single level of failure domains with weight vector* $(w_1, \ldots, w_m)$ *and capacity vector* $(C_1, \ldots, C_m)$*, the weighted max-min fair allocation is simultaneously optimal for all weight bounds* W *for* FRACROBUSTFAP. □

3.2 ROBUSTFAP and ALLORNONEROBUSTFAP

For ROBUSTFAP one can easily construct instances to show that no (integral) placement can be simultaneously optimal for all weight bounds [21]. Given the "universal" optimality of the weighted max-min fair allocation for FRACROBUSTFAP, it is natural to explore its integer variants for ROBUSTFAP. One integer variant of ROBUSTFAP that we consider is the *rounded fair* placement: (i) compute the weighted max-min fair allocation P_f; (ii) let D be the set of domains that have a non-integer assignment, and $k < |D|$ equal to the integer $\sum_{i \in D}(P_f(i) - \lfloor P_f(i) \rfloor)$; (iii) set new placement P'_f as follows: $P'_f(i) = \lceil P_f(i) \rceil$ for i belonging to an arbitrary k-size subset of D, and $P'_f(i) = \lfloor P_f(i) \rfloor$ for all other i. We immediately observe that $P'_f(i) < P_f(i) + 1$ for all i. Though the rounded fair placement does not directly yield a PTAS, it plays a central role in our PTAS construction below.

We now describe our PTAS for ROBUSTFAP. Recall that the goal of ROBUSTFAP is to determine a placement P that minimizes the maximum of $P(T)$, over all subsets T of $\mathcal{F}$ with total weight at most W, such that (i) $P(\mathcal{F}) = N$, and (ii) for each $i \in \mathcal{F}$, $P(i) \leq C_i$. Consider the decision version of ROBUSTFAP: does there exist a placement such that for any subset T of domains whose weight is at most W, the sum of tasks assigned to domains in T is at most F? We give a poly-time algorithm that either determines that there does not exist any such placement, or returns a placement such that for any subset T of $\mathcal{F}$ whose weight is at most W, the sum of tasks placed in T is at most $(1+\varepsilon)F$. We then obtain a PTAS for ROBUSTFAP via a binary search over F, invoking the above decision algorithm at each step.

Grouping of capacities and allocations. We constrain the placements to only allocate for each domain i a number of tasks that is either at most $\lceil 1/\varepsilon \rceil$, or the floor of an integer power of $(1+\varepsilon)$, or C_i. We say that an allocation to a particular domain is *small* if it is at most $\lceil 1/\varepsilon \rceil$, *large* if it is not small and at least εF, and *medium* otherwise. We say that a placement P is monotonic if for any two domains i and j, if $w_i < w_j$ and $P(j) < C_j$, then $P(i) \leq P(j)$.

LEMMA 3. *There exists a monotonic placement, optimal for* ROBUSTFAP.

PROOF. For any placement P, we define the number of *inversions* of P as the number of pairs (i, j) such that $w_i < w_j$, $P(j) < C_j$, and $P(i) > P(j)$. The number of inversions lies between 0 and $n(n-1)/2$, where n is the number of domains. A monotonic placement has no inversions. Let P be an optimal placement that has the least number of inversions. If this number is 0, we are done. Otherwise, we will derive a new optimal placement that has fewer inversions, thus contradicting the assumption and establishing the lemma.

Let (i, j) be any inversion in P. We define a new placement P' which is identical to P except that $P'(j)$ equals $\min\{C_j, P(i)\}$, and $P'(i) = P(i) - (P'(j) - P(j))$. By construction, all capacity constraints are maintained. It is not hard to see, that the number of inversions of P' is less than that of P. We now show that P' is also optimal. Let T' denote the set of domains selected by the adversary against P'. Clearly, $w_{T'} \leq W$. If either T' has both i and j or has neither i nor j, then the adversary can select exactly the same set T' against P and achieve the same value. If T' has i but not j, then the adversary can select exactly the same set T' against P and achieve a value of $F' - P'(i) + P(i) > F'$. Finally, if T' has j but not i, then the adversary can select the set $T' - \{j\} \cup \{i\}$, with weight at most $W + w_i - w_j \leq W$, against P and achieve a value of $F' - P'(j) + P(i) \geq F'$. Thus, the value achieved by the adversary against P is at least that against P', thus completing the proof. □

Controlling large allocations. Since a large allocation is at least εF and at most F, it follows from our grouping of allocations that there are at most $g(\varepsilon) = \log_{1+\varepsilon}(1/\varepsilon) = O(\ln(1/\varepsilon)/\varepsilon)$ values to choose from for a large allocation. Since we are restricting to monotonic placements, there are at most $n^{g(\varepsilon)}$ different ways in which large allocations can be assigned to the domains, where n is the number of domains. Each way yields a partial placement: it specifies the exact allocation for all domains that have large allocations, while the small and medium allocations are undetermined. Given one such partial monotonic solution J, the adversary selects a subset of at most $\lceil 1/\varepsilon \rceil$ domains with large allocations, subject to the weight constraint. Thus, for a given J, the set $K(J)$ of choices for the adversary has size at most $n^{1/\varepsilon+1}$.

Enumerating small allocations. Restricting to monotonic placements allows us to bound the number of ways in which we can make small allocations. Suppose we sort the domains in nondecreasing order of weights: i.e., $w_1 \leq \ldots \leq w_n$. Then, the small allocations are completely characterized by $t = \lceil 1/\varepsilon \rceil + 1$ indices $0 = i_0 \leq i_1 \leq \ldots \leq i_{t-1} \leq n$ such that every domain in the interval (i_{j-1}, i_j) has exactly $\min\{C_i, j\}$ tasks. Clearly, the number of ways we can determine these small allocations is $n^{O(1/\varepsilon)}$. In the remainder, we fix one choice S of the small allocations.

Determining medium allocations. Thus far, we have fixed a partial placement that assigns large allocations to some domains, and small allocations to others, and the adversary has selected a subset of the domains with large allocations. It remains to assign medium allocations. Let N' denote the number of tasks that remains to be assigned, and let $\mathcal{F}'$ denote the set of domains for which an allocation has not been determined. Note that the weight of each domain in $\mathcal{F}'$ is at most that of each domain that has already been assigned a large allocation. We need to consider the value achieved by an adversary that selects domains with medium and small allocations. Since all these domains have at most εF tasks, an adversary can achieve a value within an εF additive amount of the optimal by ordering the domains in increasing order of their density, and selecting a prefix of this sequence until no more domains can be added. We refer to this adversary as the *prefix adversary.*

Since we are restricting to medium allocations, we first place $\lceil 1/\varepsilon \rceil$ tasks in each domain in $\mathcal{F}'$, and set the capacity of each domain i in $\mathcal{F}'$ to be $\min\{\varepsilon F, C_i\}$. If the number of tasks already placed exceeds N', then the current partial assignment is not part of an $(1 + \varepsilon)$-optimal solution. Otherwise, we assign the remaining tasks using the rounded fair placement, which assigns to each domain in $\mathcal{F}'$ at most one more task than the weighted max-min fair allocation. Since the number of tasks in any medium allocation is at least $\lceil 1/\varepsilon \rceil$, this additional task per domain with a medium allocation can cause only an extra ε fraction task failures, as compared with the weighted max-min fair allocation, which is optimal against all fractional adversaries. As we argued above, the prefix adversary is within an additive εF of an optimal fractional adversary. Consequently, for medium allocations, the value achieved by the rounded fair placement is within an additive εF of optimal against any adversary.

Putting it together. We enumerate over partial monotonic placements J in which the large allocations are fixed, an adversarial choice from the set $K(J)$ that determines which domains with large allocations to fail, a small allocation S, and run the rounded fair placement procedure for medium allocations. For each of these choices, we calculate the number of tasks failed by a weight W-bounded adversary, and determine if there exists a solution with at most $(1 + \varepsilon)F$ failures. Given the polynomial size of J, $K(J)$, and the number of small allocations, we obtain a PTAS for ROBUSTFAP.

PTAS for ALLORNONEROBUSTFAP. Recall that in ALLORNONEROBUSTFAP we have a set $\mathcal{F}$ of failure domains, a weight w_i and capacity C_i for each domain i, and an integer N. The goal of ALLORNONEROBUSTFAP is to determine a subset S of domains whose capacity is at least N such that the maximum, over any subset T of S whose weight is at most W, of the sum of capacities of domains in T is minimized. As in Section 3.2, we give a polynomial-time approximate algorithm for the decision problem and then give a PTAS for the optimization problem by doing a binary search. Due to space constraints, we defer the algorithm description and proofs to the full paper [21].

4. Hierarchical ROBUSTFAP

We now present the *Generalized Spreading* algorithm for HIERFRACROBUSTFAP in Sections 4.1 and 4.2. We then use the Generalized Spreading algorithm to develop a randomized algorithm for HIERROBUSTFAP in Section 4.3.

4.1 HIERFRACROBUSTFAP: Hierarchical max-min fairness

Recall that in HIERFRACROBUSTFAP we have a failure domain tree, with machines at the leaves and internal nodes representing failure domains. We now develop a hierarchical notion of max-min fairness. Given a fractional placement P and node v, let $P(v)$ denote the number of tasks placed by P in the subtree rooted at v. Given a placement P, for any leaf u, and any subtree T containing u, let $p_u(T, P)$ denote

$$\max_{\text{ancestor } v \text{ of } u \text{ in } T} P(v)/w_v.$$

We refer to $p_u(T, P)$ as the *vulnerability* of u in T. Note that this definition generalizes the analogous ratio used for defining fairness in the single-level case in Section 3.1. We say that a placement P is *hierarchical max-min fair* if for any pair of leaf nodes i and j, and any subtree T containing i and j, if $p_i(T, P) < p_j(T, P)$, then $P(i) = C_i$. By definition, any hierarchical max-min fair placement, when restricted to any subtree, is also hierarchical max-min fair.

In the following lemmas, we show that a hierarchical max-min fair optimal solution exists for every weight bound, and establish the existence of a unique hierarchical max-min fair placement for a given number of tasks; this solution is hence simultaneously optimal for all weight bounds. We defer the proofs of the lemmas to Section 4.4 after we present a polynomial-time algorithm to compute the hierarchical max-min fair placement in Section 4.2.

LEMMA 4. *For any instance of* HIERFRACROBUSTFAP *and weight bound W, there exists a hierarchical max-min fair optimal solution.*

LEMMA 5. *For any instance of* HIERFRACROBUSTFAP, *there exists a unique hierarchical max-min fair allocation.*

4.2 Generalized spreading for HIERFRACROBUSTFAP

We now present an algorithm for computing the hierarchical max-min fair allocation for HIERFRACROBUSTFAP. Our algorithm incrementally allocates tasks to the leaf nodes, while always maintaining the fairness property. *The intuition is best captured by thinking of directing fluid (tasks) into each of the leaf nodes in such way that the next infinitesimal unit goes to that node which has the least vulnerability.* Since vulnerability increases with the assignment of tasks, that node will soon have more vulnerability than some of the other nodes, in which case the next infinitesimal unit goes to another node. Repeating this process will yield the desired allocation. How do we convert the above intuition into a finite efficient procedure? The key challenge in implementing this algorithm is that the rate of increase for different leaf nodes is different, depending on their vulnerability, and not even constant for any given node.

An iteration of Generalized Spreading. Let P be a given current hierarchical max-min fair allocation, and we would like to add more tasks. We proceed in a bottom-up manner, and compute the following for each node j: (i) vector v_j giving the relative rates for the leaves in the subtree rooted at j by which we can increment their allocation (subject to capacity constraints); (ii) a scalar upper bound $u_j > 0$ indicating the (fractional) number of tasks that we can allocate using the relative rates v_j; and (iii) $maxr_j(x)$, a linear function over a scalar variable x yielding the maximum vulnerability in the subtree rooted at j. We show how to compute the above three quantities for a node j, given the same for the children of j.

Computation at the leaves. For any leaf l, we set v_l (which is simply a scalar) to be 1, u_l to be the remaining capacity of l, and $maxr_l(x)$ to be $(P(l) + x)/w_l$.

Recursive computation of v_j, u_j, and $maxr_j$. Fix an internal node j and let H_j denote the set of children of j. We first define function $r_i(x)$ to be the ratio $(P(j)+x)/w_j$. Fix a child i in H_j. If $r_j(0) > maxr_i(0)$, then this implies that the vulnerability at j exceeds that inside the subtree rooted at i. So we set $r_i^*(x) = r_j(x)$ and u_i^* to be the minimum of u_i and the smallest x_i such that $r_j(x_i) \leq maxr_i(x_i)$ (the point at which the ratios switch); otherwise, we set $r_i^*(x) = maxr_i(x)$ and u_i^* to be u_i.

Let i be an arbitrary child of j that is not full. Consider equating $r_i^*(x_i)$ with $r_l^*(x_l)$ for all non-full children l in H_j. By the fairness of the current placement and the definition of fairness from Section 4.1, if i and l are both not full, then $r_i^*(0) = r_l^*(0)$. Since these equations are linear, we can obtain a solution to the set of equations such that x_l for each l is a scalar multiple of x_i. We now set v_j to be the vector obtained by the putting together $x_l v_l$, over all children l of j, scaled so that the sum of the values equals 1. We next set u_j to be the minimum of the remaining capacity at j and the minimum, over all l, of $u_l^*/v_j(l)$, where $v_j(l)$ is the sum, over all leaf nodes m_l in the subtree rooted at l, of $(v_j)_{m_l}$. Finally, we set $maxr_j(x) = r_i^*(x)$.

Updating the placement. Using the above computation in a bottom-up manner, we compute for the root node t: v_t, u_t, and $maxr_t(x)$. We set P to be the new allocation given by the vector sum $P + v_t \min\{u_t, N - |P|\}$, where we use $|P|$ here to denote the number of tasks allocated in P.

We repeat the above process until the required number of tasks have been allocated. By design, the algorithm maintains the fairness property. In each iteration, either a node reaches capacity or a new node achieves the maximum vulnerability bound. This leads to a polynomial bound on the number of iterations. Combining this with Lemmas 5 and 4 yields the theorem.

THEOREM 8. *The generalized spreading algorithm computes in polynomial time a fractional placement that is simultaneously optimal for all W for* HIERFRACROBUSTFAP.

4.3 Randomized algorithm for HIERROBUSTFAP

Though the generalized spreading algorthm is inherently "continuous" it suggests natural algorithms for HIERROBUSTFAP. One discrete version of generalized spreading for HIERROBUSTFAP is to execute the same high-level incremental procedure, but allocating units of tasks in each iteration, as opposed to fractions. An analysis of this algorithm is an open problem. We now present a basic randomized rounding of generalized spreading that offers performance guarantees against oblivious adversaries.

Suppose P is the fractional placement returned by generalized spreading. We number the machines in the hierarchy in order (say left to right in appearance in the domain tree) so that all the machines belonging to a domain appear contiguously. With machine i, we associate the interval $I(i) = [\sum_{j=1}^{i-1} P(j), \sum_{j=1}^{i} P(j))$. We select a number ρ uniformly at random from $[0, 1]$. Consider the set $K = \{k + \rho : k \in \mathbf{Z}\}$. In our solution, the number of tasks we place in machine i equals the size of the intersection $I(i) \cap K$.

We now analyze the guarantee provided by the above randomized algorithm. For any machine i, the expected number of tasks placed on i equals the number of tasks $P(i)$ since it exactly equals the length of the interval $I(i)$. By linearity of expectation, the expected number of tasks placed on any set S of domains is $P(S)$. Therefore, for any weight bound W, if the optimal solution to HIERFRACROBUSTFAP achieves an objective of A_W^*, then for any subset S of domains of weight at most W, the expected number of tasks placed by the randomized algorithm on the domains in S is at most A_W^*. Furthermore, for any domain, the number of tasks placed on the domain is within one of that placed by the optimal fractional solution. This yields the following lemma.

LEMMA 6. *For any weight bound W, let A_W^* denote the objective value achieved by the optimal solution to* HIERFRACROBUSTFAP. *There exists a randomized algorithm for computing a placement for* HIERROBUSTFAP *such that for any W and any subset S of domains of total weight W, the expected number of tasks placed in S is at most A_W^*.*

4.4 Proofs for Lemmas 4 and 5

We start with characterizing an optimal adversary. The adversary's maximization problem for a given placement P is given in Equation 1 below, where $P(u)$ denotes the number of tasks placed by P in the subtree rooted at u.

$$A(P) = \max \sum_u x_u P(u) \tag{1}$$

$$\begin{aligned}
\sum_u x_u w_u &\leq W \\
\sum_{u \in anc(v)} x_u &\leq 1 \text{ for every machine } v \\
x_u &\leq 1 \text{ for every domain } u \\
x_u &\geq 0 \text{ for every domain } u
\end{aligned}$$

The following two lemmas provide insight into a solution to the adversary's maximization problem.

LEMMA 7. *Given any placement P, there exists an optimal solution x for the adversary in which there exists at most one node v such that x_v is not 0 and the sum of x_u, over all ancestors u of v, is in $(0, 1)$.*

PROOF. Let x be an optimal extreme point solution to the LP (an optimal vertex of the associated polytope). For any u, if x_u is 0 we remove x_u from the LP and u from the hierarchy; for any x_u that is 1, we add $P(u)$ as a constant into the LP objective and constraints, and remove the subtree rooted under u. We thus have an LP with number of variables equal to the number of nodes in the resulting forest, and the number of constraints equal to one more than twice the number of nodes. Since the number of tight constraints in an extreme point solution equals the number of variables and none of the range constraints are tight, it follows that all but at most one of the sum constraints are tight, thus completing the proof of the desired claim. □

LEMMA 8. *Given any placement P, there exists an optimal solution x for the adversary in which there exists at most one node v such that x_v is in $(0,1)$.*

PROOF. By Lemma 7, there exists an optimal solution x for the adversary in which there is at most one node v such that x_v is not 0 and the sum of x_u, over all ancestors u of v, is in $(0,1)$. We refer to such as node v, if it exists, as an *outlier*. Let S be the set of nodes such that for each s in S, $x_s \in (0,1)$. Fix an s in S. If there exists an ancestor s' of s such that $x_{s'}$ is non-zero, then s' is an outlier; otherwise, s is an outlier. Given that there is at most one outlier, if $|S| > 1$, then there exists a unique node t in S such that (a) t is an outlier and an ancestor for all nodes in S, (b) no node in $S - t$ is an ancestor of any other node in $S - t$, and (c) for every s in $S - t$, x_s equals $1 - x_t$.

We now argue that x can be transformed into another optimal solution x' for the adversary which satisfies the claim of the corollary. We consider three cases. In the first case $w_t < w(S - t)$, where $w(S - t)$ is the sum of the weights of the nodes in $S - t$. In this case, we set x'_t to be $x_t + \varepsilon$ and x'_s to be $x_s - \varepsilon'$, where $\varepsilon > \varepsilon' > 0$ is a real made sufficiently small. The weight constraint is maintained by the adversary by making ε' and ε sufficiently small, while the objective values increases, yielding a contradiction. In the second case, we have $w_t > w(S - t)$. Let $\varepsilon_t = \delta/w_t$ and $\varepsilon_s = \delta/w(S - t)$. If $P(t)/w_t \geq P(S - t)/w(S - t)$, then we set $x'_t = x_t + \varepsilon_t$ and $x'_s = x_s - \varepsilon_s$ for all $s \in S - t$. Otherwise, we set $x'_t = x_t - \varepsilon_t$ and $x'_s = x_s + \varepsilon_s$ for all $s \in S - t$. By the setting of ε_s and ε_t, the weight constraint for the adversary is satisfied. And in either of the two subcases, the objective value of the adversary improves, yielding a contradiction.

We are finally left with the case $w_t = w(S - t)$. In this case, we set $x_t = 1$ and $x_s = 0$ for all $s \in S - t$. Clearly, the weight constraint is satisfied, and the objective value of the adversary remains the same, establishing the desired claim of the corollary. □

LEMMA 9. *Given any placement P and any weight bound W, in every optimal adversarial solution x, for any two leaf nodes i and j and any subtree T containing i and j, if $p_i(T,P) > p_j(T,P)$, then $y_i(T,x) \geq y_j(T,x)$.*

PROOF. The proof is by contradiction. Let i and j be two leaves and T be a subtree containing them such that $p_i(T,P) > p_j(T,P)$ and $y_i(T,x) < y_j(T,x)$. Since $y_i(T,x) < y_j(T,x)$, there must exist an ancestor r of j in T such that $x_r > 0$. Let q denote the ancestor of i that is the argmax of $\max_{\text{ancestor } l \text{ of } i \text{ in } T} P(l)/w_l$. Then, we have $P(q)/w_q = p_i(T,P) > p_j(T,P) \geq P(r)/w_r$. We also have $x_q \leq y_i(T,x) < y_j(T,x) \leq 1$. Consider an alternative adversarial solution x' that is identical to x except that $x'_r = x_r - \varepsilon$, $x'_q = x_q + w_r/w_q$, for $\varepsilon \leq \min\{1 - x_q, x_r\}$. The difference between the total value of the knapsack x' and that of x equals $\varepsilon w_r k_q/w_q - \varepsilon k_r$, which is positive since $k_q/w_q > k_r/w_r$. This contradicts the assumption that x is optimal, thus completing the proof of the lemma. □

Proof of Lemma 4: Let P be an optimal (fractional) placement for the weight bound W. Suppose, for the sake of contradiction, that there does not exist any optimal hierarchical max-min fair allocation. We consider any linear order $<$ of all of the subtrees of the hierarchy in which $T_1 < T_2$ whenever T_1 is a subtree of T_2. For any allocation P, let muf(P) denote the minimum subtree, according to this linear order, such that P is not hierarchical max-min fair within that subtree. By our assumption, such a subtree exists. Let lvs(P) denote the number of leaves i in muf(P) such that $p_i(\text{muf}(P),P)$ equals $\max_{j \in \text{muf}(P)} p_j(\text{muf}(P),P)$.

Let P denote an optimal allocation with lexicographically minimum with respect to the triple

$$(\text{muf}(P), \max_{j \in \text{muf}(P)} p_j(\text{muf}(P),P), \text{lvs}(P)).$$

Let T equal muf(P). We thus have two leaf nodes i and j of T such that j has the maximum vulnerability in T and $p_i(T,P) < p_j(T,P)$ and yet, $P(i) < C_i$. We argue now by contradiction that i and j belong to two different proper subtrees of T. If i and j belong to the same proper subtree, say T', of T, then since P is hierarchical max-min fair within T', $p_i(T',P) \geq p_j(T',P)$, which also implies that $p_i(T,P) \geq p_j(T,P)$ leading to a contradiction.

Let i and j belong to proper subtrees rooted at say u and v, respectively; we refer to these trees as T_u and T_v, respectively. By our assumption the allocations within both T_u and T_v are hierarchical max-min fair. Consider an alternative allocation P' that is identical to k except that an $\varepsilon > 0$ amount of tasks are added to the tree rooted at u, and an amount decreased from the tree rooted at v. We do this following the algorithm defined above; this is feasible since the allocation P, restricted to u (or v), is hierarchical max-min fair and hence produced by the algorithm (following our assumption about T being muf(P)). The amount is chosen sufficiently small such that $(P(u)+\varepsilon)/w_u < (P(v)+\varepsilon)/w_v$, and $P'(l) \leq C_l$ for all l in the tree rooted at u, and $P'(l) \geq 0$ for all l in the tree rooted at v. Clearly, P' is a valid allocation. Furthermore, since j has maximum vulnerability in P, P' has either a smaller maximum vulnerability than P or P' has fewer leaf nodes with the maximum vulnerability value. In either case, P' is lexicographically smaller with respect to the metric given above. We now derive a contradiction by arguing that P' is also an optimal allocation.

Let s' be an optimal knapsack of weight W and value v' built from P'. Note that j has the largest vulnerability in the tree rooted at v and i has the largest vulnerability in the tree rooted at u. Since j has higher vulnerability than u, we obtain from Lemma 9 that s' will select at least as much fraction of j and the other leaves in T_v with the highest vulnerability than of i and the other leaves in T_u with the highest vulnerability. Since the amount of the former is less in P' than in P by ε, while that of the latter is more in P' than in P by ε, we obtain that the value of the knapsack s' against allocation P is at least that of s' against P'. Thus, for any weight W, an optimal weight-W knapsack against P has at least as much value as an optimal weight-W knapsack against P'. Hence, P' is optimal and lexicographically smaller than P, contradicting our assumption about P. This completes the proof of the lemma.

For any leaf u and subtree T containing u, and knapsack solution x to the adversarial maximization problem, let

$y_u(T,x)$ denote the sum, over all ancestors v of u in T, of x_v.

Proof of Lemma 5: The proof is by induction on the height of the hierarchy. For the induction basis (hierarchies of height 1), the claim follows from the single-level case. For the induction step, consider any hierarchy of height h. For a given number N, let, if possible, there be two distinct hierarchical max-min fair solutions P and P'. Since the claim is true for hierarchies of height smaller than h, it follows that there exist two children u and v of the root such that $P(u) > P'(u)$ while $P(v) < P'(v)$. So there must exist an incomplete leaf node, say i, under P in the tree rooted at v, and an incomplete leaf node, say j, under P' in the tree rooted at u. We thus have $p_i(v,P) \geq p_j(u,P')$ and $p_i(v,P') \leq p_j(u,P)$. But since $P(v) < P(v)$ and $P(u) > P'(u)$, and the unique hierarchical max-min fair allocations for the two hierarchies rooted at v and u, respectively, have the property that the vulnerability of an incomplete leaf node only increases with the number of tasks, we have $p_i(v,P') > p_i(v,P)$ and $p_j(u,P) > p_j(u,P')$. These inequalities together yield a contradiction, completing the induction step and the proof of the lemma.

5. Probabilistic failures: Bicriteria approximations

We now present bicriteria polynomial-time approximations for ProbFAP and HierProbFAP. In particular, our algorithm for ProbFAP achieves an ε additive approximation in the failure probability, while giving up a $(1+\varepsilon)$ multiplicative factor in the number of failures. We next extend the result to hierarchies by giving an algorithm for HierProbFAP, which achieves an ε additive approximation in failure probability, while giving up a $(L+\varepsilon)$ multiplicative factor in the number of failures, for L-level hierarchies, where L is a constant.

5.1 Single-level case: ProbFAP

Our solution approach here builds on the stochastic optimization framework of Li and Yuan [24]. For each domain i and integer b in $[0, C_i]$, we introduce an item (i,b) with associated random variable $X(i,b)$, capturing the fraction of failed tasks if domain i fails, that has the following distribution:

$$X(i,b) = \begin{cases} 0 & \text{with probability } 1-p_i \\ \frac{b}{N} & \text{with probability } p_i \end{cases}$$

Define U as the universe of all items; i.e., $U = \{(i,b) : i \in \mathcal{F}, 0 \leq b \leq C_i\}$. We define a subset S of U as feasible if (a) for each $i \in \mathcal{F}$, there is exactly one item of the form (i,b) in S; and (b) $\sum_{(i,b)\in S} b = N$.

For a feasible solution S, define $X(S) = \sum_{(i,b)\in S} X(i,b)$. ProbFAP is then exactly the *threshold probability maximization problem* where we aim to maximize $\Pr[X(S) \leq F/N]$. Li and Yuan show that a PTAS for an associated multi-dimensional exact version of the problem implies an approximation scheme for the threshold probability maximization problem. Their framework, however, assumes that the random variables $X()$ are mutually independent. This is not true for our problem since while $X(i,b)$ is independent of $X(j,b')$ for any $i \neq j$, b, b', the variables $X(i,b)$ and $X(i,b')$ are not independent of each other. Fortunately, in our problem any feasible set of items consists of at most one item of the form (i,b) for any given i; so, the random variables associated with the items in any feasible set are all mutually independent. We use this fact to extend the Li-Yuan framework for the single-level case.

We now present the mechanism of classifying items as light or heavy, discretizing the size distributions of light items, enumerating all possible heavy item sets, and signatures of light item sets.

Item classification. Call an item (i,b) *light* if $E[X(i,b)] \leq \varepsilon^{10}$, and *heavy* otherwise.

Discretization. For item (i,b), we define variable $\tilde{X}(i,b)$ that takes values in $\{s_j = j\varepsilon^5 : 0 \leq j \leq \lfloor 1/\varepsilon^5 \rfloor\}$. We map $X(i,b)$ to $\tilde{X}(i,b)$ as follows. If $X(i,b) > \varepsilon^4$, then $\tilde{X}(i,b) = \lfloor X(i,b)/\varepsilon^5 \rfloor \varepsilon^5$. For $X(i,b) \leq \varepsilon^4$, we find a d such that $\varepsilon^4 \cdot \Pr[X(i,b) \geq d | X(i,b) \leq \varepsilon^4] = E[X(i,b)|X(i,b) \leq \varepsilon^4]$, and set $\tilde{X}(i,b) = 0$ for $0 \leq X(i,b) < d$ and $\tilde{X}(i,b) = \varepsilon^4$ for $d \leq X(i,b) \leq \varepsilon^4$. It is easy to show that for any feasible set of items, the distribution of the sum of the discretized variables for the set is close to that for the original variables.

Lemma 10 ([24, Lemma 2.2]). *For any set S of items such that $E[X(S)] \leq 3/\varepsilon$, for any k, we have*

$$|\Pr[X(S) \leq k] - \Pr[\tilde{X}(S) \leq k]| = O(\varepsilon).$$

Enumeration of heavy item sets. We enumerate all possible heavy item sets H with $E[X(H)] < 3/\varepsilon$. Each heavy item set is of constant cardinality, hence the number of such sets is polynomial. In the remainder, we can assume a fixed heavy item set H.

Signatures. For an item (i,b), we define its signature to be the vector $(\pi_{i,b}(s_1), \ldots, \pi_{i,b}(s_{z-1}))$, where

$$\pi_{i,b}(s) = \frac{\varepsilon^6}{n} \left\lfloor \frac{n}{\varepsilon^6} \cdot \Pr[\tilde{X}(i,b) = s] \right\rfloor$$

for all s in $\{s_1, s_2, \ldots, s_{z-1}\}$. We define the signature of a set of items to be the coordinate-wise sum of the signatures of the individual items in the set. A key claim [24, Lemma 2.3] shows that it is sufficient to consider signatures whose components add up to at most $3/\varepsilon$, and enumerate signatures for set of light items. The proof of this lemma relies on the Poisson approximation theorem for sums of independent random variables [22]. Since we apply the Possion approximation theorem for random variables associated with the items in any feasible set, the independence of these variables continues to hold, the same lemma holds.

Lemma 11. *Let S_1 and S_2 be two sets of light items, with the same signature, and $E[\tilde{X}(S_1)] \leq 3/\varepsilon$, $E[\tilde{X}(S_2)] \leq 3/\varepsilon$. Then, the total variation distance between $X(S_1)$ and $X(S_2)$ is $O(\varepsilon)$.*

Using Lemmas 10 and 11, we then obtain the equivalent of Theorem 1.1 of [24]: If there is a pseudopolynomial algorithm for determining whether, for a given weight bound $\mathcal{W}$, there is a feasible solution of weight $\mathcal{W}$ for a given instance of ProbFAP where individual elements have weights, then there is a polynomial-time approximation algorithm for ProbFAP that finds a feasible solution S such that $\Pr[X(S) \leq (1+\varepsilon)F/N] \geq \mathrm{OPT} - \varepsilon$, where OPT is the maximum value achieveable for $\Pr[X(S) \leq F/N]$, for any feasible S.

Algorithm for an exact version of ProbFAP. In the exact version of ProbFAP, each element (i,b) of U is associated with a weight $\omega_{i,b}$, where the weight will represent the item signature we have defined above. We are given a weight constraint W and we would like to determine if there is a feasible solution S such that $\sum_{(i,b)\in S} \omega_{i,b} = \mathcal{W}$. Note that $\mathcal{W}$ represents the overall signature we desire for the set of light items. We define $\Pi(X, M, j)$ to be a predicate that is true if it is possible to assign tasks to domains 1 through j so that the total weight of the assignment is exactly X. We set up a dynamic program as follows: $\Pi(0,0,0)$ is true; $\Pi(X, M, j)$ is true if $\Pi(X - w(i,b), M - b, j-1)$ is true for any $0 \le b \le C_j$, and false otherwise. It can be seen that the above can be computed in time polynomial in the number of tasks N, the number of possible weight values, and the number of domains n. Furthermore, the algorithm extends to the scenario where the weights are constant-dimensional vectors, as is the case with the signatures; the exponent in the polynomial time grows with the dimension of the weight vectors. Finally, note that our algorithm as presented is polynomial in N, not the size of N. We apply the standard method of restricting b values in the items (i,b) to rounded powers of $(1+\varepsilon)$. This causes us another factor of $(1+\varepsilon)$ loss in the number of failed tasks, and yields the following single-level special case of Theorem 6.

THEOREM 9. *For any $\varepsilon > 0$, there exists a polynomial time algorithm that runs in time $n^{poly(1/\varepsilon)}$ and returns a feasible placement of N tasks such that*

$$\Pr[\text{number of failed tasks } \le (1+\varepsilon)F] \ge \mathrm{OPT} - \varepsilon,$$

where OPT *is the maximum probability, over any placement of N tasks, that the number of failed tasks is at most F.*

5.2 Hierarchical case: HIERPROBFAP

We next consider the hierarchical version, HIERPROBFAP. For each node i, we define an item (i,b) for each $0 \le b \le C_i$. As before, we have the associated random variable $X(i,b)$, that takes value 0 with the probability that at least one of its ancestor domains fails, and b/N otherwise. The $X(i,b)$ variables are no longer independent, even for different i. This is because nodes share ancestor domains.

One approach to this problem is to solve multiple stochastic knapsack problems, one for each of the L levels, using the single-level algorithm of Section 5.1 and then select the best of all the solutions. This approach is unlikely to yield any useful approximation guarantees, however, since the solution for any one level may perform poorly for other levels. We present an approximation algorithm that considers the multiple level problems in an integrated manner and identifies a single solution that performs close to the optimal at each level. Let $P_\ell(E)$ denote the probability of event E, over the failure events of domains at level ℓ; that is,

$$P_\ell(E) = \Pr[E| \text{ no domain at any level } i \ne \ell \text{ fails}].$$

For subproblem at level ℓ, we enumerate a polynomial number of solutions to find all feasible solutions S_ℓ such that $P_\ell(X(S_\ell) \le (1+\varepsilon/L)F/N) \le \mathrm{OPT}_\ell - \varepsilon/L$, where OPT_ℓ is the maximum probability, over any placement of N tasks, that the number of failed tasks due to failures exclusively at level ℓ is at most F. By our enumeration of the solutions, we will identify *a single solution* S such that $P_\ell(X(S) \le (1+\varepsilon)F/N) \ge \mathrm{OPT}_\ell - \varepsilon/L$ *for each* ℓ. By combining the bound over all the levels, we will establish that S satisfies

$$\Pr[X(S) \le (L+\varepsilon)F/N] \ge \mathrm{OPT} - \varepsilon.$$

For each level, as in Section 5.1, we classify items as light or heavy based on their expected size, discretize the size distributions for light items, and enumerate all possible heavy item sets and signatures for light item sets. The item classification and discretization is the same as in Section 5.1. The heavy item sets and the dynamic program we set up to process the light item sets across all levels in an integrated manner are described below.

Enumeration of heavy item sets. We enumerate all possible heavy item sets H with $E[X(H)] < 3/\varepsilon$ at each level. Each heavy item set is of constant cardinality, hence the number of distinct heavy sets at each level is polynomial. Since the number of levels is constant, there is a polynomial number of ways to select a heavy item set at each level.

Dynamic programming. Fix a heavy item set H_ℓ for each level ℓ of the hierarchy. Fix a signature σ_ℓ for each level ℓ of the hierarchy. Recall that each signature is a vector with $O(\varepsilon^{-5})$ coordinates, and the value of each coordinate is bounded by $O(n)$.

Our goal now is to determine whether there is a selection of items so that L_ℓ is the set of light items selected at level ℓ, $H_\ell \cup L_\ell$ is feasible for each ℓ, and $Sg(L_\ell) = \sigma_\ell$ for each ℓ; here, $Sg(I)$ of a set I of light items denotes the signature of the set. We set up a dynamic program that determines if there is a feasible selection of light items satisfying the preceding condition. Let $\lambda(v)$ denote the level of node v in the hierarchy. For a given node v, positive integer i at most the number of children of v, and sequence of signature vectors $\sigma_1, \sigma_2, \ldots, \sigma_{\lambda(v)}$, we define $\Phi(v, i, \sigma_1, \ldots, \sigma_{\lambda(v)})$ to be true if there exists a feasible selection of light items for the subtree consisting of v, the first i children of v, and their descendants such that the signature of the set of light items at level ℓ, $1 \le \ell \le \lambda(v)$, equals σ_ℓ. We compute $\Phi()$ using the following dynamic program. For a leaf node v we set

$$\Phi(v, 0, \sigma) = \begin{cases} \textbf{true} & \text{if } \sigma = (0,0,\ldots) \text{ or } \exists b : Sg(\{(v,b)\}) = \sigma \\ \textbf{false} & \text{otherwise.} \end{cases}$$

For an internal node v, let $d(v)$ denote the number of children of v, and let v_i denote the ith child of v, numbered in an arbitrary order. For internal node v, we compute that for $i > 0$ $\Phi(v, i, \sigma_1, \ldots, \sigma_{\lambda(v)})$ equals

$$\bigvee_{\sigma'_1,\ldots,\sigma'_{\lambda(v)-1}} (\Phi(v, i-1, \sigma_1 - \sigma'_1, \ldots, \sigma_{\lambda(v)-1} - \sigma'_{\lambda(v)-1}, \sigma_{\lambda(v)}) \\ \wedge \Phi(v_i, d(v_i), \sigma'_1, \ldots, \sigma'_{\lambda(v)-1})),$$

where we note that $\lambda(v_i) = \lambda(v) - 1$. Finally, $\Phi(v, 0, \sigma_1, \ldots, \sigma_{\lambda(v)})$ is exactly the single-level problem for node v in which we determine if there exists an selection of light items for the domains v_1 through $v_{d(v)}$ such that the heavy items selected for this subset of domains, together with the light items form a feasible solution for this set of domains, and the signature of the light item set matches $\sigma_{\lambda(v)}$.

Final output. We have written the above dynamic program as a predicate; it is straightforward to extract an actual solution that satisfies the condition desired in Φ. Thus, after solving the dynamic program, for any combination of signatures σ_i at level i, for $i \le \ell$, if there exists a solution that has the signature σ_i at level i, for $i \le \ell$, we obtain one such solution. Among these, we select one solution that has the highest product $\prod_l P_\ell(X_\ell(S) \le (1+\varepsilon)F/N)$, which we can estimate using the signatures, as in the single-level subproblem.

Analysis of the algorithm. Since the number of different signature values is polynomial ($n^{O(\varepsilon^{-5})}$) and the number of levels is a constant, the total number of different inputs for which Φ is being computed is polynomial in n. This ensures that in polynomial time, we determine a feasible solution S of items such that at each level ℓ, the signature of S matches that of a globally optimal solution, say S^*. If $X_\ell(S)$ (resp., $X_\ell(S^*)$ denotes the number of failed tasks in S (resp., S^*) due to failures in level ℓ, then Lemma 11 implies that at each level ℓ the variation distance between $\tilde{X}_\ell(S)$ and $\tilde{X}_\ell(S^*)$ is $O(\varepsilon)$. Together with Lemma 10, we get

$$P_\ell(X_\ell(S) \leq (1+\varepsilon)F/N) \geq \mathrm{OPT}_\ell - O(\varepsilon) \qquad (2)$$

where OPT_ℓ is the maximum probability, over any placement of N tasks, that the number of failed tasks due to failures exclusively at level ℓ is at most F. Since the failure events at each of the failure domains are independent of one another, $\prod_\ell \mathrm{OPT}_\ell$ is an upper bound on maximum probability OPT, over any placement of N, that the number of failed tasks due to failures at all levels is at most F. Here we have used the fact that for the total number of failures to be at most F, the number of failures at each level need to be at most F. We thus obtain

$$\begin{aligned}\Pr[X(S) \leq (L+\varepsilon)F/N] &\geq \prod_\ell P_\ell(X_\ell(S) \leq (1+\varepsilon/L)F/N) \\ &\geq \prod_\ell (\mathrm{OPT}_\ell - O(\varepsilon/L)) \\ &\geq \mathrm{OPT} - O(\varepsilon),\end{aligned}$$

where in the second step, we invoke Equation 2, with ε replaced by ε/L. This gives us Theorem 6, restated below.

THEOREM 10 (RESTATEMENT OF THEOREM 6). *For any $\varepsilon > 0$, there exists a polynomial time algorithm for* HIERPROBFAP *over an L-level hierarchy that runs in time $n^{poly(L,1/\varepsilon)}$ and returns a feasible placement such that*

$$\Pr[\textit{number of failed tasks} \leq (L+\varepsilon)F] \geq \mathrm{OPT} - O(\varepsilon),$$

where OPT *is the maximum probability, over any placement of N tasks, that the number of failed tasks is at most F.*

6. Conclusions and open problems

In this paper, we formulate and initiate the study of *failure-aware placement* for hierarchical data centers under adversarial and probabilistic failures. For both classes, we give hardness results and approximation algorithms for multiple variants: based on *generalized spreading* for HIERROBUSTFAP and Poisson approximation for HIERPROBFAP.

One natural question is to improve the approximation guarantees and design more practical implementations for some of the variants. In particular, the approximation factor in the bicriteria PTAS for HIERPROBFAP grows linearly in the number of levels. While this is reasonable for current datacenters (which typically have three to four levels of hierarchy), it would be interesting to see if the approximation factor can be made sublinear or even independent of number of levels. Similarly, our PTASes incur high running times (e.g., for ROBUSTFAP, a standard implementation would take time $O(n^{(3+ln(1/\varepsilon))/\varepsilon})$ time), and it is important to design practical implementations of PTASes that trade off approximation guarantees for simplicity.

On a related note, our study here has focused on identical tasks of the same size. It will be interesting to extend this to an on-line sequence of jobs of possibly different sizes. A further extension would be to consider dynamic task migrations to improve availability as jobs finish and leave.

Acknowledgments

We would like to thank Gerhard Woeginger for providing insights into the results of [7], and sharing a full version of their paper.

7. References

[1] S. Agrawal, Y. Ding, A. Saberi, and Y. Ye. Price of correlations in stochastic optimization. *Operations Research*, 60:243–248, February 2012.

[2] Mohammad Al-Fares, Alexander Loukissas, and Amin Vahdat. A scalable, commodity data center network architecture. In *ACM SIGCOMM Computer Communication Review*, volume 38, pages 63–74. ACM, 2008.

[3] Luiz André Barroso and Urs Hölzle. The datacenter as a computer: An introduction to the design of warehouse-scale machines. *Synthesis lectures on computer architecture*, 4:1–108, 2009.

[4] D. Bertsimas and M. Sim. The price of robustness. *Operations Research*, 52, 2004.

[5] A. Bhalgat, A. Goel, and S. Khanna. Improved approximation results for stochastic knapsack problems. In *SODA*, 2011.

[6] P. Bodik, I. Menache, M. Chowdhury, P. Mani, D. A. Maltz, and I. Stoica. Surviving failures in bandwidth-constrained datacenters. In *Proceedings of the ACM SIGCOMM 2012 conference on Applications, technologies, architectures, and protocols for computer communication*, 2012.

[7] Alberto Caprara, Margarida Carvalho, Andrea Lodi, and Gerhard J. Woeginger. A complexity and approximability study of the bilevel knapsack problem. In *Integer Programming and Combinatorial Optimization*, pages 98–109. 2013.

[8] Min Chen, Shiwen Mao, and Yunhao Liu. Big data: A survey. *Mobile Networks and Applications*, 19(2):171–209, 2014.

[9] C. Daskalakis, A. De, I. Diakonikolas, A. Moitra, and R. Servedio. A polynomial-time approximation scheme for fault-tolerant distributed storage. In *SODA*, 2014.

[10] J. Dean and S. Ghemawat. Mapreduce: Simplified data processing on large clusters. *Communications of the ACM*, 51:107–113, 2008.

[11] Christina Delimitrou and Christos Kozyrakis. QoS-Aware Scheduling in Heterogeneous Datacenters with Paragon. In *ACM Transactions on Computer Systems (TOCS)*, 2013.

[12] A. Demers, S. Keshav, and S. Shenker. Analysis and simulation of a fair queueing algorithm. *SIGCOMM Comput. Commun. Rev.*, 19(4):1–12, August 1989.

[13] S. Dempe. *Foundations of bilevel programming.* Kluwer Academic Publishers, 2002.

[14] S. Dempe and K. Richter. Bilevel programming with knapsack constraint. *Central European Journal of Operations Research*, 2000.

[15] S. DeNegre. *Interdiction and discrete bilevel linear programming.* PhD thesis, Lehigh University, 2011.

[16] D. Ford, F. Labelle, F. I. Popovici, M. Stokely, V. A. Truong, L. Barroso, C. Grimes, and S. Quinlan. Availability in globally distributed storage systems. In *Proceedings of Operating Systems Design and Implementation (OSDI)*, 2010.

[17] P. Gill, N. Jain, and N. Nagappan. Understanding network failures in data centers: measurement, analysis, and implications. In *ACM SIGCOMM Computer Communication Review*, 2011.

[18] M. Gribaudo, M. Iacono, and D. Manini. Improving reliability and performances in large scale distributed applications with erasure codes and replication. *Future Generation Computer Systems*, 2015.

[19] S. Keshav. *An Engineering Approach to Computer Networking: ATM Networks, the Internet, and the Telephone Network*. Addison-Wesley Longman Publishing Co., Inc., Boston, MA, USA, 1997.

[20] O. Klopfenstein and D. Nace. A robust approach to the chance-constrained knapsack problem. *Operations Research Letters*, 36, 2008.

[21] M. Korupolu and R. Rajaraman. Robust and probabilistic failure-aware placement, 2016.

[22] L. Le Cam. An approximation theorem for the Poisson binomial distribution. *Pacific Journal of Mathematics*, 10:1181–1197, 1960.

[23] J. Li and A. Deshpande. Maximizing expected utility for stochastic combinatorial optimization problems. In *FOCS*, 2011.

[24] J. Li and W. Yuan. Stochastic combinatorial optimization via Poisson approximation. In *STOC*, 2013.

[25] Florence Jessie MacWilliams and Neil James Alexander Sloane. *The theory of error-correcting codes*, volume 16. Elsevier, 1977.

[26] R. Mansi, C. Alves, J. de Carvalho, and S. Hanafi. An exact algorithm for bilevel 0-1 knapsack problems. *Mathematical Problems in Engineering*, 2012.

[27] K. A. Mills, R. Chandrasekaran, and N. Mittal. Algorithms for replica placement in high-availability storage. In *ArXiv preprint arXiv:1503.02654*, 2015.

[28] J. Nagle. On packet switches with infinite storage. *IEEE Transactions on Communications*, 35, 1987.

[29] A. Nemirovski and A. Shapiro. Convex approximations of chance constrained programs. *SIAM Journal of Optimization*, 17, 2006.

[30] E. Nikolova. Approximation algorithms for offline risk-averse combinatorial optimization. In *APPROX*, 2010.

[31] B. K. Pagnoncelli, S. Ahmed, and A. Shapiro. Sample average approximation method for chance-constrained programming: Theory and applications. *Journal of Optimization theory and Applications*, 142, 2009.

[32] Christos Papadimitriou. *Computational Complexity*. Addison-Wesley, 1994.

[33] A. Parekh and R. Gallager. A generalized processor sharing approach to flow control in integrated services networks: the single-node case. *IEEE/ACM Transactions on Networking*, 1, 1993.

[34] Eduardo Pinheiro, Wolf-Dietrich Weber, and Luiz André Barroso. Failure trends in a large disk drive population. In *FAST*, pages 17–23, 2007.

[35] James S Plank et al. A tutorial on reed-solomon coding for fault-tolerance in raid-like systems. *Softw., Pract. Exper.*, 27:995–1012, 1997.

[36] C. Reiss, A. Tumanov, G. Ganger, R. Katz, and M. Kozych. Heterogeneity and dynamicity at scale: Google trace analysis. In *ACM Symposium on Cloud Computing*, 2012.

[37] B. Schroeder, E. Pinheiro, and W. D. Weber. Dram errors in the wild: a large-scale field study. In *ACM SIGMETRICS Performance Evaluation Review*, volume 37, pages 193–204, 2009.

[38] Bianca Schroeder and Garth A Gibson. Understanding failures in petascale computers. In *Journal of Physics: Conference Series*, volume 78, page 012022. IOP Publishing, 2007.

[39] M. Sedaghat, E. Wadbro, J. Wilkes, S. De Luna, O. Seleznjev, and E. Elmroth. Die-hard: Reliable scheduling to survive correlated failures in cloud data centers. In *Proceedings of IEEE/ACM International Symposium on Cluster, Cloud and Grid Computing (CCGrid)*, 2016.

[40] D. Tang and R. K. Iyer. Analysis and modeling of correlated failures in multicomputer systems. In *IEEE Transactions on Computers*, volume 41, pages 567–577, 1992.

[41] A. Verma, L. Pedrosa, M. Korupolu, D. Oppenheimer, E. Tune, and J. Wilkes. Large-scale cluster management at Google with Borg. In *Proceedings of the European Conference on Computer Systems (EuroSys)*, Bordeaux, France, 2015.

[42] K. V. Vishwanath and N. Nagappan. Characterizing cloud computing hardware reliability. In *ACM Symposium on Cloud Computing, SOCC*, 2010.

[43] H. von Stackelberg. *The theory of market economy.* Oxford University Press, 1952.

[44] P. Yalagandula, S. Nath, H. Yu, P. B. Gibbons, and Seshan S. Beyond availability: Towards a deeper understanding of machine failure characteristics in large distributed systems. In *Proceedings of the Workshop on Real, Large Distributed Systems (WORLDS âĂŹ04)*, 2004.

[45] M. Zaharia, M. Chowdhury, M . J. Franklin, S. Shenker, and I. Stoica. Spark: cluster computing with working sets. In *Proceedings of the 2nd USENIX conference on Hot topics in cloud computing*, 2010.

Brief Announcement: Flexible Resource Allocation for Clouds and All-Optical Networks*

Dmitriy Katz
IBM T.J. Watson Research Center, Yorktown Heights NY 10598, USA
katzrog@us.ibm.com

Baruch Schieber
IBM T.J. Watson Research Center, Yorktown Heights NY 10598, USA
sbar@us.ibm.com

Hadas Shachnai†
Dept. of Computer Science Technion
Haifa 3200003, Israel
hadas@cs.technion.ac.il

ABSTRACT

Motivated by the cloud computing paradigm, and by key optimization problems in all-optical networks, we study two variants of the classic job interval scheduling problem, where a reusable resource is allocated to competing job intervals in a *flexible* manner. Each job, J_i, requires the use of up to $r_{max}(i)$ units of the resource, with a profit of $p_i \geq 1$ accrued for each allocated unit. The goal is to feasibly schedule a subset of the jobs so as to maximize the total profit. The resource can be allocated either in *contiguous* or *non-contiguous* blocks. These problems can be viewed as flexible variants of the well known *storage allocation* and *bandwidth allocation* problems.

We show that the contiguous version is strongly NP-hard, already for instances where all jobs have the same profit and the same maximum resource requirement. We derive the best possible positive result for such instances, namely, a *polynomial time approximation scheme (PTAS)*. We further show that the contiguous variant admits a $(\frac{5}{4} + \varepsilon)$-approximation algorithm, for any fixed $\varepsilon > 0$, on instances whose job intervals form a *proper* interval graph. At the heart of the algorithm lies a non-standard parameterization of the approximation ratio itself. For the non-contiguous case, we uncover an interesting relation to the *paging* problem that leads to a simple $O(n \log n)$ algorithm for *uniform* profit instances of n jobs.

Keywords

Flexgrid all-optical networks; cloud computing; scheduling; paging; flexible storage allocation; bandwidth allocation

1. BACKGROUND

Interval scheduling has a wide range of applications in computer science and in operations research (see, e.g., [8]). We study two variants of the problem, where a reusable resource is allocated to competing job intervals in a *flexible* manner. The input to our problems consists of a set $\mathcal{J}$ of n jobs, where each job $J_i \in \mathcal{J}$ is associated with a half open real interval $[s_i, e_i)$, along which it requires the use of a limited resource. The amount of resource allocated to J_i can take any value up to $r_{max}(i)$, and the profit accrued for each allocated unit is $p_i \geq 1$. The total amount of resource allocated at any time cannot exceed the available amount, $W > 0$.

In the *flexible bandwidth allocation problem* (FBAP), we seek a feasible allocation which maximizes the total profit. In the *flexible storage allocation problem* (FSAP), we add the requirement that the allocation to each job is a *contiguous* block of the resource.

Motivation. Scheduling problems of this ilk arise naturally in scenarios where activities require a portion of an available resource with some revenue associated with the allocated amount. In the cloud computing paradigm the resource can be servers in a large computing cluster, storage capacity, or bandwidth allocated to time-critical jobs (see, e.g. [6]).

In *flexgrid* all-optical networks, the resource is the available spectrum of light that is divided into frequency intervals of variable width (see, e.g., [5]). Several high-speed signals connecting different source-destination pairs may share a link, provided they are assigned disjoint sub-spectra (see, e.g., [10]). Given a path network and a set of connection requests, represented by intervals, each associated with a profit per allocated spectrum unit and a maximum bandwidth requirement, we need to feasibly allocate frequencies to the requests, with the goal of maximizing the total profit. In the FBAP variant the sub-spectra allocated to each request need not be contiguous, while in the FSAP variant each request requires a contiguous frequency spectrum.

Related Work. The classic interval scheduling problem, where each interval requires all of the resource for its execution, is solvable in $O(n \log n)$ time [1]. The *storage allocation problem* (SAP), which is strongly NP-hard, was first studied in [1, 9]. Bar-Noy *et al.* [1] presented an approximation algorithm that yields a ratio of 7, with subsequent improvements and results for subclasses of instances. The best known result is a $(2 + \varepsilon)$-approximation algorithm due to [11]. The *bandwidth allocation problem* (BAP) is known to be strongly NP-hard, already for uniform profits [4]. The best known result for BAP is an LP-based $(2 + \varepsilon)$-approximation algorithm due to Chekuri *et al.* [3]. Both BAP and SAP have been studied also in the *nonuniform* resource case, where the amount of available resource may change over time (see [7] and the references therein).

†This work was partly carried out during a visit to DIMACS supported by the National Science Foundation under grant number CCF-1144502.

*A detailed version of this paper can be found in [7].

SPAA '16 July 11-13, 2016, Pacific Grove, CA, USA

ACM ISBN 978-1-4503-4210-0/16/07.
DOI: http://dx.doi.org/10.1145/2935764.2935806

The *flexible* variants of SAP and BAP were introduced by Shalom *et al.* [13]. The authors study instances where each job interval J_i has a minimum and a maximum resource requirement, satisfying $0 \leq r_{min}(i) < r_{max}(i) \leq W$, for which they show that FBAP can be solved in polynomial time. The paper also presents a $\frac{4}{3}$-approximation algorithm for FSAP instances in which the input graph is proper, and $r_{min}(i) \leq \lceil \frac{r_{max}(i)}{2} \rceil$, for all i. The paper [12] shows that FSAP is NP-hard even when $r_{min}(i) = 0$ for all i, and presents a $(2 + \varepsilon)$-approximation algorithm for such instances. In the more general case, where each interval has a minimum and a maximum resource requirement, FBAP and FSAP can be approximated within factor 3 and $3 + \varepsilon$, respectively [11].

2. OUR CONTRIBUTION

For FBAP we uncover an interesting relation to the *paging* problem that leads to a simple $O(n \log n)$ algorithm for *uniform* profit instances. This improves the running time of the algorithm for FBAP due to [13], which uses flow techniques.

THEOREM 1. *Algorithm Paging_FBA runs in $O(n \log n)$ time and finds an optimal allocation for FBAP instances with arbitrary $r_{min}(i) < r_{max}(i)$, and $p_i = 1$ for all $1 \leq i \leq n$.*

For FSAP we present approximation algorithms for several subclasses, as well as an improved hardness result.

THEOREM 2. *FSAP admits a $(\frac{5}{4} + \varepsilon)$-approximation algorithm on any instance in which the job intervals form a proper interval graph.*

THEOREM 3. *FSAP is strongly NP-hard even if $r_{max}(i) = 3$ and $p_i = 1$, for all $1 \leq i \leq n$, and W is not divisible by 3.*

We derive the best possible positive result for such instances.

THEOREM 4. *FSAP admits a PTAS on instances where $r_{max}(i) = \texttt{Max}$ for some $1 \leq \texttt{Max} \leq W$, and $p_i = 1$ for all $1 \leq i \leq n$.*

3. GENERALIZED FBAP AND PAGING

Consider a generalized version of FBAP, where each job J_i has also a lower bound $r_{min}(i)$ on the amount of resource it is allocated. We show that when all jobs have the same profit per allocated resource unit, the problem can be solved by an efficient algorithm based on Belady's well known algorithm for offline paging [2]. We use *coloring* terminology when referring to the assignment of resource to the jobs, and each available resource unit is represented by a distinct color.

We view the available colors as slots in fast memory, and each job (interval) J_i as $r_{max}(i)$ pairs of requests for pages in the main memory. Each such pair of requests is associated with a distinct page: one request at s_i and one at $e_i - 1$. We now apply Belady's offline paging algorithm: if a page remains in the fast memory between the two times it was requested, then the color that corresponds to its fast memory slot is allocated to the corresponding job. To ensure feasibility, at least $r_{min}(i)$ colors are allocated to each J_i. The optimality of the paging algorithm implies the optimality of the solution for our FBA instance.

The algorithm, Paging_FBA, is implemented iteratively by scanning the endpoints of the intervals from left to right. When Paging_FBA scans s_i, it first assigns $r_{min}(i)$ colors to J_i, starting with the available colors. If less than $r_{min}(i)$ colors are available at s_i, Paging_FBA examines the intervals intersecting J_i at s_i in decreasing order of right endpoints, and feasibly decreases the number of colors assigned to the corresponding jobs and reassigns them to J_i, until J_i is allocated $r_{min}(i)$ colors. The feasibility of the instance implies that so many colors can be reassigned.

Next, Paging_FBA allocates up to $r_{max}(i) - r_{min}(i)$ additional colors to job J_i. If $r_{max}(i) - r_{min}(i)$ colors are available at s_i, then they are assigned to J_i. Otherwise, Paging_FBA follows Belady's algorithm to potentially assign additional colors to J_i. Paging_FBA examines the intervals intersecting J_i at s_i, and in case there are such intervals with right endpoint larger than e_i, it feasibly decreases the number of colors assigned to intervals with the largest right endpoints (furthest in the future), and increases the number of colors assigned to J_i, up to $r_{max}(i)$.

When Paging_FBA scans e_i, the right endpoint of an interval J_i, the colors assigned to J_i are released and become available.

Acknowledgments. We thank Magnús Halldórsson and Viswanath Nagarajan for valuable discussions.

4. REFERENCES

[1] A. Bar-Noy, R. Bar-Yehuda, A. Freund, J. Naor, and B. Schieber. A unified approach to approximating resource allocation and scheduling. *JACM*, 48(5):735–744, 2000.

[2] L. A. Belady. A study of replacement algorithms for virtual-storage computer. *IBM Systems Journal*, 5(2):78–101, 1966.

[3] C. Chekuri, M. Mydlarz, and F. B. Shepherd. Multicommodity demand flow in a tree and packing integer programs. *ACM Transactions on Algorithms*, 3(3), 2007.

[4] M. Chrobak, G. J. Woeginger, K. Makino, and H. Xu. Caching is hard - even in the fault model. *Algorithmica*, 63(4):781–794, 2012.

[5] O. Gerstel. Flexible use of spectrum and photonic grooming. In *Photonics in Switching*, 2010.

[6] N. Jain, I. Menache, J. Naor, and J. Yaniv. A truthful mechanism for value-based scheduling in cloud computing. In *SAGT*, pages 178–189, 2011.

[7] D. Katz, B. Schieber, and H. Shachnai. Flexible resource allocation for clouds and all-optical networks. http://arxiv.org/abs/1605.04982.

[8] A. W. Kolen, J. K. Lenstra, C. H. Papadimitriou, and F. C. Spieksma. Interval scheduling: A survey. *Naval Research Logistics*, 54(5):530–543, 2007.

[9] S. Leonardi, A. Marchetti-Spaccamela, and A. Vitaletti. Approximation algorithms for bandwidth and storage allocation problems under real time constraints. In *FSTTCS*, pages 409–420, 2000.

[10] R. Ramaswami, K. N. Sivarajan, and G. H. Sasaki. *Optical Networks: A Practical Perspective*. Morgan Kaufmann Publisher Inc., San Francisco, 2009.

[11] H. Shachnai, A. Voloshin, and S. Zaks. Flexible bandwidth assignment with application to optical networks. In *MFCS*, 2014.

[12] H. Shachnai, A. Voloshin, and S. Zaks. Optimizing bandwidth allocation in flex-grid optical networks with application to scheduling. In *IPDPS*, 2014.

[13] M. Shalom, P. Wong, and S. Zaks. Profit maximization in flex-grid all-optical networks. In *SIROCCO*, 2013.

Clairvoyant Dynamic Bin Packing for Job Scheduling with Minimum Server Usage Time

Runtian Ren and Xueyan Tang
School of Computer Science and Engineering
Nanyang Technological University
Singapore 639798
{RENR0002, asxytang}@ntu.edu.sg

ABSTRACT

The MinUsageTime Dynamic Bin Packing (DBP) problem targets at minimizing the accumulated usage time of all the bins in the packing process. It models the server acquisition and job scheduling issues in many cloud-based systems. Earlier work has studied MinUsageTime DBP in the non-clairvoyant setting where the departure time of each item is not known at the time of its arrival. In this paper, we investigate MinUsageTime DBP in the clairvoyant setting where the departure time of each item is known for packing purposes. We study both the offline and online versions of Clairvoyant MinUsageTime DBP. We present two approximation algorithms for the offline problem, including a 5-approximation Duration Descending First Fit algorithm and a 4-approximation Dual Coloring algorithm. For the online problem, we establish a lower bound of $\frac{1+\sqrt{5}}{2}$ on the competitive ratio of any online packing algorithm. We propose two strategies of item classification for online packing, including a classify-by-departure-time strategy and a classify-by-duration strategy. We analyze the competitiveness of these strategies when they are applied to the classical First Fit packing algorithm. It is shown that both strategies can substantially reduce the competitive ratio for Clairvoyant MinUsageTime DBP compared to the original First Fit algorithm.

Keywords

Dynamic bin packing, job scheduling

1. INTRODUCTION

Job scheduling is a fundamental issue in many cloud-based systems. In a typical scenario, each cloud server has a fixed capacity of computational resources. Each job requires a certain amount of computational resources to run on a cloud server from its arrival time to its departure time. Since the total resource demand of the jobs running on a server cannot exceed its capacity, a limited number of jobs can be processed concurrently on each cloud server. Thus, a sufficient number of cloud servers need to be acquired to handle a given set of jobs. On the other hand, the cost of renting a cloud server is normally proportional to its running hours by "pay-as-you-go" billing [1]. Therefore, it is important to acquire cloud servers and schedule jobs on the cloud servers in an effective way to minimize the total renting cost of the servers. Such a server acquisition and job scheduling problem can be modeled as the MinUsageTime Dynamic Bin Packing (DBP) problem, which was first defined by Li *et al.* [19, 17]. The MinUsageTime DBP problem aims at minimizing the total usage time of all the bins in the packing process. The jobs and cloud servers in the aforementioned job scheduling problem correspond to the items and bins respectively in MinUsageTime DBP. Li *et al.* [19, 17, 24] studied MinUsageTime DBP in the non-clairvoyant setting where the departure time of each item is not known at the time of its arrival. They analyzed the competitiveness of several classical bin packing algorithms for online Non-Clairvoyant MinUsageTime DBP, including an Any Fit family of algorithms (which open a new bin only when no current open bin can accommodate an incoming item), First Fit and Best Fit (which are two particular Any Fit algorithms).

In this paper, we study the MinUsageTime DBP problem in the clairvoyant setting where the departure time of each item is known for packing purposes. This is possible in real applications such as cloud gaming where the ending times of game sessions can be predicted with reasonable accuracy for certain games [18], and data analytics systems where jobs are mostly recurring [21, 12]. We consider both the offline and online versions of the Clairvoyant MinUsageTime DBP problem.[1] In the offline version, the information of all the items to pack (including item sizes, arrival times and departure times) is assumed known, whereas in the online version, the items must be placed into bins as they arrive without any knowledge of future item arrivals. Clairvoyant MinUsageTime DBP can also be viewed as a generalized interval scheduling problem. In the interval scheduling problem with bounded parallelism [10], a set of interval jobs are to be processed. Each job should be assigned to run on a machine from its arrival time to its departure time. Each machine can simultaneously process at most a fixed number of g jobs, where g stands for the machine capacity. A machine is considered busy when there is at least one job running on it. The interval scheduling problem aims at minimizing the total busy time of all the machines for processing the given set of interval jobs. Our Clairvoyant MinUsageTime DBP problem generalizes the above interval scheduling problem in that items are allowed to have arbitrary sizes, so the maximum number of items that can be placed in a bin is not fixed.

Previous work on MinUsageTime DBP. Li *et al.* [19, 17] analyzed the competitiveness of several classical bin packing algo-

SPAA '16, July 11-13, 2016, Pacific Grove, CA, USA
© 2016 ACM. ISBN 978-1-4503-4210-0/16/07...$15.00
DOI: http://dx.doi.org/10.1145/2935764.2935775

[1] We remark that it does not really make sense to study the offline version of the Non-Clairvoyant MinUsageTime DBP problem since by definition, item departure times are not known for packing purposes in the non-clairvoyant setting.

rithms for Non-Clairvoyant MinUsageTime DBP. It was shown that the competitive ratio of any Any Fit packing algorithm cannot be better than $\mu + 1$, where μ is the ratio of the maximum item duration to the minimum item duration. The competitive ratio of Best Fit packing is not bounded for any given μ. The competitive ratio of First Fit packing has an upper bound of $2\mu + 7$. A Hybrid First Fit algorithm that classifies and packs items based on their sizes can achieve a competitive ratio within $\frac{8}{7}\mu + \frac{55}{7}$ when μ is not known and within $\mu + 5$ when μ is known. Kamali *et al.* [13] later showed that Next Fit packing has a competitive ratio bounded above by $2\mu + 1$. Recently, Tang *et al.* [24] conducted an improved competitive analysis for First Fit packing and established a new upper bound of $\mu + 4$ on its competitive ratio. All the above results are for the MinUsageTime DBP problem in the non-clairvoyant setting. To the best of our knowledge, there has been no study on the MinUsageTime DBP problem in the clairvoyant setting.

Contributions of this paper. In this paper, we investigate the Clairvoyant MinUsageTime DBP problem. We first study approximation algorithms for the offline Clairvoyant MinUsageTime DBP problem. We show that a Duration Descending First Fit algorithm can achieve an approximation ratio within 5. We develop a Dual Coloring algorithm and show that it has an approximation ratio bounded above by 4. We then study the online Clairvoyant MinUsageTime DBP problem. We establish a lower bound of $\frac{1+\sqrt{5}}{2}$ on the competitive ratio of any online packing algorithm. We propose two strategies of item classification for online Clairvoyant MinUsageTime DBP, including a classify-by-departure-time strategy and a classify-by-duration strategy. We apply these strategies to First Fit packing (which is the best known online algorithm in the non-clairvoyant setting) and analyze their competitiveness. If the minimum and maximum item durations are not known, classify-by-departure-time First Fit can achieve a competitive ratio within $\frac{\rho}{\Delta} + \frac{\mu\Delta}{\rho} + 3$, where ρ is an algorithm parameter of classification and Δ is the minimum item duration, and classify-by-duration First Fit can achieve a competitive ratio within $\alpha + \lceil log_{\alpha}\mu \rceil + 4$, where α is the max/min item duration ratio of each item category. If the minimum and maximum item durations are known, classify-by-departure-time First Fit can achieve a competitive ratio within $2\sqrt{\mu} + 3$, and classify-by-duration First Fit can achieve a competitive ratio within $\min_{n \geq 1} \mu^{\frac{1}{n}} + n + 3$. Numerical results show that both classification strategies can substantially reduce the competitive ratio for Clairvoyant MinUsageTime DBP compared to the original First Fit packing algorithm.

2. RELATED WORK

The classical DBP problem, which was first defined by Coffman *et al.* [9], aims at minimizing the maximum number of bins concurrently used in the packing process. A large amount of research work has been carried out to analyze the competitiveness of various algorithms for classical DBP [9, 6, 7]. However, classical DBP does not consider the duration of bin usage. In contrast, the MinUsageTime DBP problem defined by Li *et al.* [19, 17] aims to minimize the accumulated bin usage time.

As mentioned, interval scheduling with bounded parallelism [10, 20, 23, 14, 8] is also related to our MinUsageTime DBP problem. Flammini *et al.* [10] presented a 4-approximation algorithm for interval scheduling with bounded parallelism. They also developed a greedy algorithm with an approximation ratio of 2 for the special case where no interval is properly contained in another. Mertzios *et al.* [20] studied two versions of interval scheduling with bounded parallelism: one scheduling minimization version for minimizing the total busy time of machines to process all jobs and one resource allocation maximization version for maximizing the number of jobs processed under a busy time budget. For the scheduling minimization problem, they proposed an improved $(2 - \frac{1}{g})$-approximation algorithm for the special case where no interval is properly contained in another. They also proposed a $\frac{g \cdot H_g}{H_g + g - 1}$-approximation algorithm (H_g is the g-th harmonic number) for the special case where any two job intervals intersect. Chang *et al.* [8] outlined two 2-approximation algorithms for the problem of interval scheduling with bounded parallelism based on the work of Alicherry *et al.* [4] and Kumar *et al.* [15]. They also proposed a GREEDYTRACKING algorithm which has an approximation ratio of 3. The aforementioned work all focused on the offline version of interval scheduling. Shalom *et al.* [23] investigated the online version of interval scheduling with bounded parallelism, in which interval jobs are scheduled to run on machines when they arrive without any knowledge of future job arrivals. They proposed a BucketFirstFit algorithm and showed that it has a competitive ratio bounded by $(2\alpha + 2) \cdot \lceil \log_{\alpha} \mu \rceil$, where μ is the max/min length ratio of job intervals and α is an algorithm parameter. All the above work on interval scheduling assumes that the jobs all have the same resource demands which are equal to $\frac{1}{g}$ of the machine capacity for a given integer g. In contrast, our MinUsageTime DBP problem considers items (jobs) with arbitrary sizes (demands). As shall be discussed later, some of our analysis implies significant improvement to the existing result of online interval scheduling. Khandekar *et al.* [14] considered scheduling flexible jobs whose intervals may not be fixed. Each job is associated with a release time, a deadline, a processing time (length), and a demand for machine capacity. A First_Fit_with_Demands algorithm was proposed to divide jobs into narrow and wide ones based on their demands and the algorithm was shown to achieve an approximation ratio of 5. Our Clairvoyant MinUsageTime DBP problem is similar to this one, but we focus on interval jobs whose starting and ending times are fixed. We propose a 5-approximation algorithm different from [14] (without dividing jobs according to their demands) and a new 4-approximation algorithm for Clairvoyant MinUsageTime DBP. Moreover, besides packing items in an offline manner, we also study online Clairvoyant MinUsageTime DBP.

3. PRELIMINARIES

3.1 Notations and Definitions

We first define some key notations for this paper. For any time interval I, we use I^- and I^+ to denote the left and right endpoints of I respectively. For technical reasons, we shall view intervals as half-open, i.e., $I = [I^-, I^+)$. Let $l(I) = I^+ - I^-$ denote the length of time interval I.

For any item r, let $I(r)$ denote the time interval from r's arrival to its departure. We say that item r is *active* during interval $I(r)$, and refer to $I(r)$ as the *active interval* of r. The length of $I(r)$ is known as the *item duration*. Let $s(r)$ denote the size of item r. The product of the size and duration of item r, i.e., $s(r) \cdot l(I(r))$ represents its *time-space demand*. For a list of items $\mathcal{R}$, we use $d(\mathcal{R})$ to denote the total time-space demand of all the items in $\mathcal{R}$, i.e., $d(\mathcal{R}) = \sum_{r \in \mathcal{R}} s(r) \cdot l(I(r))$. In addition, we refer to the time duration in which at least one item in $\mathcal{R}$ is active as the *span* of $\mathcal{R}$ and denote it by $span(\mathcal{R})$ (see Figure 1). Let $\mu = \frac{\max_{r \in \mathcal{R}} l(I(r))}{\min_{r \in \mathcal{R}} l(I(r))}$ denote the ratio of the maximum item duration to the minimum item duration among all the items in $\mathcal{R}$.

We assume that the items are not allowed to move from one bin to another during their active intervals. For example, in highly interactive applications such as cloud gaming [11, 3, 2, 16], it is not

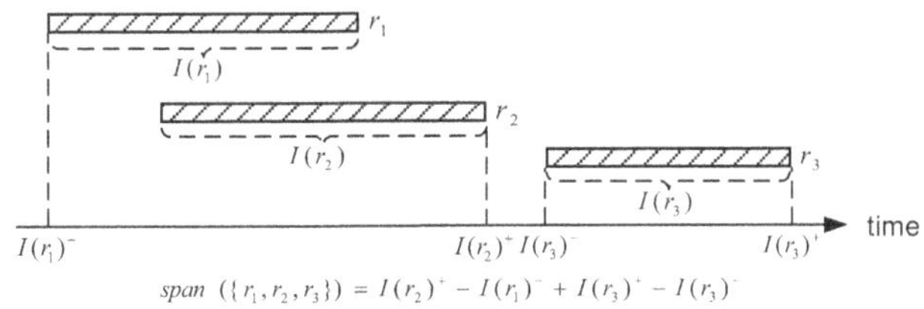

Figure 1: Span of an item list

preferable to migrate game instances from one server to another during execution as migration causes interruption to game play. At any time in the packing process, the total size of all the active items placed in a bin, known as the *bin level*, cannot exceed the bin capacity. The usage time of a bin is defined as the span of all the items placed in it. The objective of MinUsageTime DBP is to minimize the total usage time of all the bins.

3.2 Approximation and Competitive Ratios

The performance of an approximation algorithm and an online algorithm is often characterized by their *approximation ratio* and *competitive ratio* respectively, i.e., the worst-case ratio between the objective function value of a solution constructed by the algorithm and the objective function value of an optimal solution [5, 25].

We give three lower bounds on the total bin usage time of an optimal packing solution to the MinUsageTime DBP problem. These bounds shall be used in deriving the approximation ratios or competitive ratios of our algorithms. Without loss of generality, we assume that the bins all have unit capacity. Given a list of items $\mathcal{R}$, let $OPT(\mathcal{R}, t)$ denote the minimum achievable number of bins into which all the active items at time t can be repacked. Then, the total bin usage time of an optimal offline adversary that can repack everything at any time is given by

$$OPT_{total}(\mathcal{R}) = \int_{\bigcup_{r \in \mathcal{R}} I(r)} OPT(\mathcal{R}, t)\, dt,$$

where $\bigcup_{r \in \mathcal{R}} I(r)$ is the time period corresponding to the span of $\mathcal{R}$. It is easy to obtain the following lower bounds on $OPT_{total}(\mathcal{R})$:

PROPOSITION 1. $OPT_{total}(\mathcal{R}) \geq d(\mathcal{R})$.

PROPOSITION 2. $OPT_{total}(\mathcal{R}) \geq span(\mathcal{R})$.

PROPOSITION 3. $OPT_{total}(\mathcal{R}) \geq \int_{\bigcup_{r \in \mathcal{R}} I(r)} \lceil S(t) \rceil\, dt$, *where $S(t)$ is the total size of all the active items at time t.*

The first bound is derived by assuming that no capacity of any bin is wasted at any time, where $d(\mathcal{R})$ is the total time-space demand of all the items in $\mathcal{R}$. The second bound is derived from the fact that at least one bin must be used at any time when at least one item is active. The above two bounds have been given in the earlier work [19, 17]. The third bound is a new one motivated by [8]. It exploits the fact that the number of open bins must be at least $\lceil S(t) \rceil$ at any time t. Obviously, the third bound is tighter than the first two bounds.

4. APPROXIMATION ALGORITHMS FOR CLAIRVOYANT MINUSAGETIME DBP

We start by studying the offline problem of Clairvoyant MinUsageTime DBP. Note that when all the items have the same arrival times and the same departure times, Clairvoyant MinUsageTime DBP reduces to the classical bin packing problem since minimizing the total bin usage time is equivalent to minimizing the number of bins opened. Thus, it is obvious that Clairvoyant MinUsageTime DBP is NP-hard. In the following, we present and analyze two approximation algorithms for Clairvoyant MinUsageTime DBP. Without loss of generality, we shall assume that the minimum item duration is 1, and the maximum item duration is μ ($\mu \geq 1$).

4.1 Duration Descending First Fit Algorithm

Our first algorithm is called *Duration Descending First Fit* and it works as follows. First, all the items are sorted in the descending order of their durations. Then, the items are placed one at a time according to the first fit rule. That is, each item is placed in the bin of the smallest index that can accommodate the item throughout its duration, where the bins are indexed according to their opening order by the execution of the packing algorithm. If no opened bin can accommodate the item throughout its duration, a new bin is opened for it. This algorithm was also used by [10] for interval scheduling with bounded parallelism and shown to have an approximation ratio of 4 when all jobs (items) have the same resource demands (sizes). In such a special case, the maximum number of jobs that can be concurrently processed by each machine (i.e., the machine capacity) is fixed. If the machines have capacity g, each machine can essentially be viewed as a collection of g mini-machines each with capacity 1. These g mini-machines are then considered separately in the analysis of [10]. In contrast, in our MinUsageTime DBP problem, items can have arbitrary sizes so that the maximum number of items that can be placed in each bin is not predictable and it may also vary at different times. Thus, the analysis of [10] is not directly applicable to MinUsageTime DBP since it is impossible to divide each bin into mini-bins. Inspired by [10], in what follows, we present a new analysis to show that Duration Descending First Fit has an approximation ratio of 5 for MinUsageTime DBP. Our key observation is that whenever a new bin is opened to pack an item r, there must exist at least one moment in r's duration such that the level of an earlier opened bin plus the size of r is larger than the bin capacity.

Suppose that a total of m bins $b_1, b_2, \ldots, b_m$ are used by the Duration Descending First Fit algorithm to pack a list of items $\mathcal{R}$. The bins are indexed in their opening order, i.e., b_1 is the first bin opened by the Duration Descending First Fit algorithm and b_m is the last bin opened by the algorithm. For each bin b_k, let $\mathcal{R}_k$ denote the set of the items packed into b_k. Then, by definition, the usage time of b_k is $span(\mathcal{R}_k)$. Thus, the total bin usage time of Duration Descending First Fit is given by $\sum_{k=1}^{m} span(\mathcal{R}_k)$.

Consider any item set $\mathcal{R}_k$ ($k \geq 2$). We reduce $\mathcal{R}_k$ to a subset $\mathcal{R}'_k$ by removing any item whose duration is completely contained in the duration of another item. In this way, the items left in $\mathcal{R}'_k$ satisfy the following property: let n denote the number of items in $\mathcal{R}'_k$ and let $r_1, r_2, \ldots, r_n$ be the items sorted according to their arrival times, i.e., $I(r_1)^- < I(r_2)^- < \cdots < I(r_n)^-$, then it holds that $I(r_1)^+ < I(r_2)^+ < \cdots < I(r_n)^+$. Otherwise, if $I(r_x)^+ \geq I(r_y)^+$ for some $x < y$, the duration of item r_y is fully contained in the duration of item r_x, which contradicts the definition of $\mathcal{R}'_k$. It is easy to see that reducing $\mathcal{R}_k$ to $\mathcal{R}'_k$ does not shorten the usage time of bin b_k, i.e., $span(\mathcal{R}_k) = span(\mathcal{R}'_k)$.

As shown in Figure 2, we can split $\bigcup_{r \in \mathcal{R}'_k} I(r)$ into n disjoint periods at the arrival times of the items:

$$X(r_1) = [I(r_1)^-, \min\{I(r_2)^-, I(r_1)^+\}),$$
$$X(r_2) = [I(r_2)^-, \min\{I(r_3)^-, I(r_2)^+\}),$$
$$\ldots\ldots$$

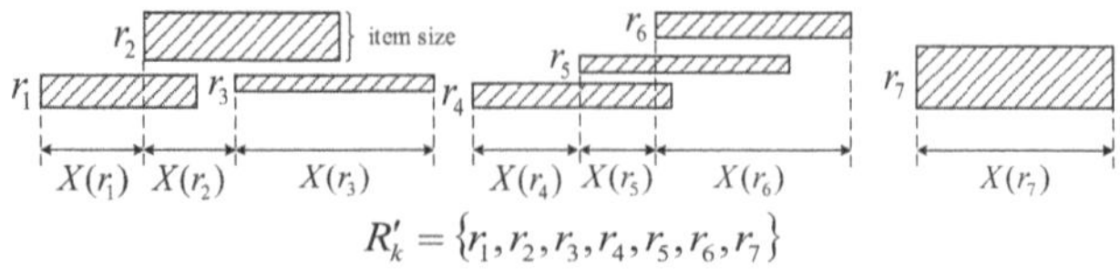

Figure 2: Splitting $\bigcup_{r\in\mathcal{R}'_k} I(r)$ for bin b_k

$$\begin{aligned} X(r_{n-1}) &= [I(r_{n-1})^-, \min\{I(r_n)^-, I(r_{n-1})^+\}), \\ X(r_n) &= [I(r_n)^-, I(r_n)^+). \end{aligned}$$

We refer to the above periods as the X-periods of items r_1, r_2, $\cdots$, r_n respectively. Obviously, the total length of the X-periods is $span(\mathcal{R}'_k)$, i.e., $\sum_{i=1}^n l(X(r_i)) = span(\mathcal{R}'_k)$. We define

$$d_k = \sum_{i=1}^n s(r_i) \cdot l(X(r_i)).$$

Apparently, d_k is a lower bound on the total time-space demand of all the items placed in bin b_k since the X-period of each item is shorter than or equal to the active interval of the item:

$$\begin{aligned} d_k &\le \sum_{i=1}^n s(r_i) \cdot l(I(r_i)) \\ &= d(\mathcal{R}'_k) \\ &\le d(\mathcal{R}_k). \end{aligned} \tag{1}$$

By the definition of Duration Descending First Fit, when each item r_i in $\mathcal{R}'_k$ ($k \ge 2$) is placed in bin b_k, there must exist at least one moment t_i, such that the level of bin b_{k-1} at time t_i plus the size of item r_i is larger than 1 (the bin capacity). Let $W(r_i)$ be the set of all the active items in bin b_{k-1} at time t_i when item r_i is placed in bin b_k by the Duration Descending First Fit algorithm. By the algorithm definition, each item in $W(r_i)$ must have a duration no shorter than that of r_i. We define

$$d_k^* = \sum_{i=1}^n \Big(\sum_{r\in W(r_i)} s(r) \cdot l(X(r_i)) \Big).$$

It then follows that

$$\begin{aligned} d_k + d_k^* &= \sum_{i=1}^n \Big(s(r_i) + \sum_{r\in W(r_i)} s(r) \Big) \cdot l(X(r_i)) \\ &> \sum_{i=1}^n 1 \cdot l(X(r_i)) \\ &= span(\mathcal{R}'_k) \\ &= span(\mathcal{R}_k). \end{aligned} \tag{2}$$

We next show that d_k^* is bounded by $3 \cdot d(\mathcal{R}_{k-1})$, where $d(\mathcal{R}_{k-1})$ is the total time-space demand of all the items placed in bin b_{k-1}.

LEMMA 1. $d_k^* \le 3 \cdot d(\mathcal{R}_{k-1})$.

Proof: Please refer to the extended version of this paper [22]. □

It follows from (1), (2) and Lemma 1 that

$$span(\mathcal{R}_k) < d(\mathcal{R}_k) + 3 \cdot d(\mathcal{R}_{k-1}).$$

Note that the above inequality holds for any item set $\mathcal{R}_k$ where $k \ge 2$. As a result, we have

$$\begin{aligned} \sum_{k=2}^m span(\mathcal{R}_k) &< \sum_{k=2}^m \big(d(\mathcal{R}_k) + 3 \cdot d(\mathcal{R}_{k-1})\big) \\ &< \sum_{k=1}^m d(\mathcal{R}_k) + 3 \cdot \sum_{k=1}^m d(\mathcal{R}_k) \\ &= d(\mathcal{R}) + 3 \cdot d(\mathcal{R}) \\ &= 4 \cdot d(\mathcal{R}), \end{aligned}$$

where $d(\mathcal{R})$ is the total time-space demand of all the items.

Therefore, the total bin usage time of Duration Descending First Fit satisfies

$$\begin{aligned} \sum_{k=1}^m span(\mathcal{R}_k) &= \Big(\sum_{k=2}^m span(\mathcal{R}_k) \Big) + span(\mathcal{R}_1) \\ &< 4 \cdot d(\mathcal{R}) + span(\mathcal{R}) \\ &\le 4 \cdot OPT_{total}(\mathcal{R}) + OPT_{total}(\mathcal{R}) \\ &= 5 \cdot OPT_{total}(\mathcal{R}), \end{aligned}$$

where the last inequality follows from the bounds given in Propositions 1 and 2. Thus, we have the following conclusion.

THEOREM 1. *The Duration Descending First Fit algorithm is a 5-approximation algorithm for Clairvoyant MinUsageTime DBP.*

4.2 Dual Coloring Algorithm

In this section, we develop a *Dual Coloring* algorithm for Clairvoyant MinUsageTime DBP and show that it has an approximation ratio of 4. Our algorithm is motivated by the Simple algorithm described in [15] for the Fiber Minimization problem which aims to construct a cost-effective optical fiber network to meet demands. A recent study [8] indicated that the Simple algorithm can also be used for interval scheduling with bounded parallelism and has an approximation ratio of 2 for it. In the context of interval scheduling, this algorithm works by considering a machine that can process g jobs concurrently as a collection of g mini-machines each with capacity 1. It allocates jobs and schedules them on one mini-machine at a time. However, this approach is not guaranteed to produce a feasible solution for our MinUsageTime DBP problem as the number of items that can be simultaneously placed in each bin is not fixed and should be dynamically determined as packing progresses. The arbitrary sizes of items make it challenging to distribute items among bins to produce a quality solution.

Our Dual Coloring algorithm divides the items in a list $\mathcal{R}$ into two groups: a small group $\mathcal{R}_S$ and a large group $\mathcal{R}_L$. $\mathcal{R}_S$ contains all the items of size no larger than $\frac{1}{2}$, and $\mathcal{R}_L$ contains all the items of size larger than $\frac{1}{2}$. These two groups of items are packed separately. The large items are packed arbitrarily and the bins used to pack large items do not further pack any small item. The small items are packed by first constructing a demand chart. As shown in Figure 3, the horizontal dimension of the demand chart represents the time, which ranges over the span of the item list. The vertical dimension of the demand chart represents the space demand. The height of the demand chart at any time t is given by the total size of all the small items that are active at time t. With the demand chart, the small items are then packed in two phases. In Phase 1, all the small items are placed in the demand chart such that no three items overlap together. In Phase 2, the small items are packed into bins according to their positions in the demand chart.

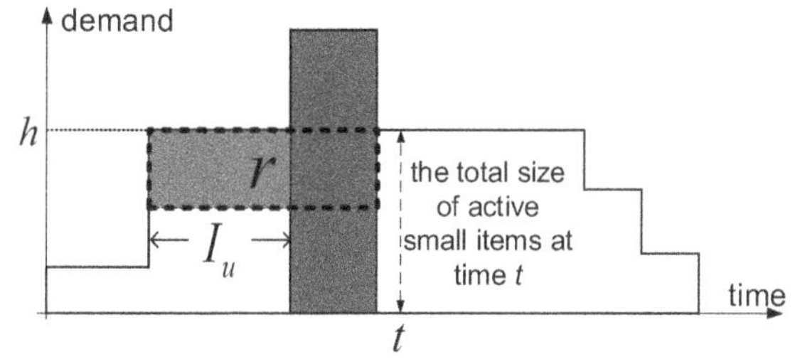

Figure 3: Item placement in demand chart

Phase 1 Item placement in demand chart

1: $M \leftarrow$ {the total size of all active small items at time $t \mid t \in \cup_{r \in \mathcal{R}_S} I(r)$} and $\mathcal{J} \leftarrow \mathcal{R}_S$
2: **while** $M \neq \emptyset$ **do**
3:    Find the maximum altitude $h \in M$ to examine
4:    Let R, B and U be the respective sets of all maximal red, blue and uncolored intervals at altitude h
5:    **while** $U \neq \emptyset$ **do**
6:       Pick an uncolored interval $I_u \in U$
7:       **if** $\exists\, r \in \mathcal{J}$ such that $I(r) \cap I_u \neq \emptyset$ and $\forall\, I \in U \cup R \backslash \{I_u\}, I(r) \cap I = \emptyset$ **then**
8:          Place r at altitude h and delete r from $\mathcal{J}$
9:          Color the rectangle $\{I(r) \cap I_u\} \times (h - s(r), h]$ red
10:          Delete I_u from U
11:          **if** $I_u^- < I(r)^-$ **then**
12:             Add $[I_u^-, I(r)^-)$ into U
13:          **if** $I_u^+ > I(r)^+$ **then**
14:             Add $[I(r)^+, I_u^+)$ into U
15:          **if** $h > s(r)$ and $(h - s(r)) \notin M$ **then**
16:             Add $(h - s(r))$ into M
17:       **else**
18:          Color the rectangle $I_u \times (0, h]$ blue
19:          Delete I_u from U
20:    Delete h from M

In Phase 1, each item r placed in the demand chart occupies a rectangle covering its active interval $I(r)$ in the time dimension and of height $s(r)$ in the demand dimension. Thus, the area occupied by each item r is equal to its time-space demand $s(r) \cdot l(I(r))$. To simplify presentation, we say that an item r is placed at altitude h in the demand chart if it occupies the range $(h - s(r), h]$ in the demand dimension. The area of the demand chart is gradually colored either red or blue as items are placed. To place items, the Dual Coloring algorithm examines a collection of altitudes from high to low in the demand chart. Let M denote the collection of altitudes to examine. Initially, M contains all possible total sizes of active small items at different times (step 1), i.e., all the ceiling altitudes in the demand chart. In each iteration, the algorithm examines the next (maximum) altitude h in M (step 3). Based on its coloring status, the horizontal line at altitude h in the demand chart is divided into three sets of intervals: red, blue and uncolored (step 4). For each uncolored interval I_u, the algorithm looks for an item r (not yet placed) whose active interval $I(r)$ intersects with I_u but does not intersect with any other uncolored interval and any red interval (step 7). If there is no such item, all the area below I_u in the demand chart is colored blue (step 18). If such an item r exists, r is placed at altitude h (step 8) (see Figure 3 for an example). The uncolored area covered by r is then colored red (step 9). For convenience of algorithm presentation, we intentionally leave r's lower boundary uncolored for identifying uncolored intervals in the subsequent examination. The altitude of r's lower boundary, i.e., $h - s(r)$, is added into M (step 16) as other items may be able to be placed immediately below r at altitude $h - s(r)$. The examination of an altitude h proceeds until there is no more uncolored interval (step 5). Phase 1 completes when all altitudes in M have been examined (step 2).

We now prove that Phase 1 runs in polynomial time. Note that the total size of active small items can change only upon item arrivals and departures. Thus, the initial set M (the set of all possible total sizes of active small items over time) contains at most $2 \cdot |\mathcal{R}_S|$ different altitudes, where $|\mathcal{R}_S|$ is the number of small items (step 1). Subsequently, the placement of each item introduces at most one additional altitude to examine (step 16). Therefore, the total number of altitudes examined in Phase 1 is bounded by $3 \cdot |\mathcal{R}_S|$. In the examination of each altitude, the total number of red, blue and uncolored intervals is bounded by $O(|\mathcal{R}_S|)$ because the endpoints of each interval must correspond to item arrivals and/or departures. There are at most $|\mathcal{R}_S|$ items to check for each uncolored interval, and checking the eligibility of each item for placement takes $O(|\mathcal{R}_S|)$ time. So, the time complexity for examining each altitude is bounded by $O(|\mathcal{R}_S|^3)$. As a result, the total time complexity of Phase 1 is bounded by $O(|\mathcal{R}_S|^4)$.

Phase 1 gives rise to the following properties of item placement in the demand chart. The complete proofs of these properties are given in the extended version of this paper [22].

LEMMA 2. *After Phase 1, the entire area of the demand chart is colored.*

Proof Sketch: This claim is proved by showing that when the examination of an altitude h completes, all the area between altitude h and the next altitude h^- to examine ($h^- < h$) is colored. □

LEMMA 3. *Whenever an item r is placed at an altitude h in Phase 1, the rectangle occupied by r is within the demand chart.*

Proof Sketch: It is obvious that r's left boundary (at time $I(r)^-$), right boundary (at time $I(r)^+$) and upper boundary (at altitude h) are within the demand chart. Thus, we only need to check r's lower boundary (at altitude $h - s(r)$). It can be shown that r's lower boundary must also be within the demand chart. □

LEMMA 4. *All the small items are placed in the demand chart after Phase 1.*

LEMMA 5. *No three items overlap together in their placement of Phase 1.*

In Phase 2, to pack items into bins, the demand chart is partitioned into stripes of height $\frac{1}{2}$ each as shown in Figure 4. Let $S_S(t)$ denote the total size of all active small items at time t. Then, the total number of stripes is given by $m = \lceil 2 \cdot \max_{t \in \cup_{r \in \mathcal{R}_S} I(r)} S_S(t) \rceil$ (step 1), where $\max_{t \in \cup_{r \in \mathcal{R}_S} I(r)} S_S(t)$ is the maximum height of the demand chart. The algorithm creates $(2m - 1)$ bins to pack items, among which m bins are used for items placed completely within individual stripes in Phase 1 and the other $(m - 1)$ bins are used for items placed across stripes. Specifically, for each stripe, since the height of the stripe is $\frac{1}{2}$ and no three items overlap together in their placement (Lemma 5), the total size of all the items placed completely within the stripe is bounded by 1 at any time. Thus, they can be accommodated by one bin (step 6). On the other hand, note that the size of each small item is bounded by $\frac{1}{2}$. This implies that an item can cross at most two stripes in the placement by Phase 1. For each pair of neighboring stripes, by Lemma 5, at

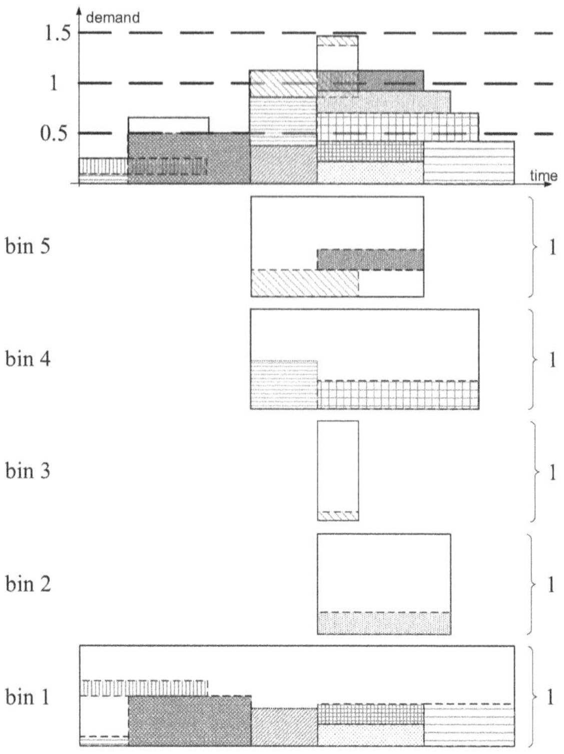

Figure 4: Item packing

Phase 2 Item packing

1: $m \leftarrow \lceil 2 \cdot \max_{t \in \cup_{r \in \mathcal{R}_S} I(r)} S_S(t) \rceil$
2: Create $2m - 1$ bins
3: **for** each item r **do**
4: Let h be the altitude where r is placed in the demand chart
5: **if** $\frac{k-1}{2} \leq h - s(r) < h \leq \frac{k}{2}$ for some k $(1 \leq k \leq m)$ **then**
6: Pack item r into the k-th bin
7: **if** $h - s(r) < \frac{k}{2} < h$ for some k $(1 \leq k < m)$ **then**
8: Pack item r into the $(m + k)$-th bin

most two items can cross them concurrently at any time, so their total size is bounded by 1. Therefore, all the items placed across a pair of neighboring stripes can be accommodated by one bin (step 8). Since there are $(m-1)$ pairs of neighboring stripes, we need at most $(m-1)$ bins to pack all the items placed across stripes. It is easy to see that the time complexity of Phase 2 is $O(|\mathcal{R}_S|)$, where $|\mathcal{R}_S|$ is the number of small items.

Now, let's compute the bin usage time of the Dual Coloring algorithm. In Phase 2 of packing small items, the number of stripes produced at each time point t is $\lceil 2S_S(t) \rceil$. Thus, the number of open bins for packing small items at time t is at most $2\lceil 2S_S(t) \rceil - 1$, among which $\lceil 2S_S(t) \rceil$ bins are used for items placed within individual stripes and $\lceil 2S_S(t) \rceil - 1$ bins are used for items placed across stripes. So, the total bin usage time for packing small items is bounded by $\int_{\cup_{r \in \mathcal{R}_S} I(r)} (2\lceil 2S_S(t) \rceil - 1)\, \mathrm{d}t$.

Recall that large items are packed arbitrarily and the size of each large item is greater than $\frac{1}{2}$. Let $S_L(t)$ denote the total size of all active large items at time t. Then, the number of active large items at time t is smaller than $2 \cdot S_L(t)$. As a result, the number of open bins for packing large items at time t is at most $\lfloor 2S_L(t) \rfloor$. So, the total bin usage time for packing large items is bounded by $\int_{\cup_{r \in \mathcal{R}_L} I(r)} \lfloor 2S_L(t) \rfloor\, \mathrm{d}t$.

Therefore, the total bin usage time of the Dual Coloring algorithm is bounded by

$$\int_{\cup_{r \in \mathcal{R}_L} I(r)} \lfloor 2S_L(t) \rfloor\, \mathrm{d}t + \int_{\cup_{r \in \mathcal{R}_S} I(r)} (2\lceil 2S_S(t) \rceil - 1)\, \mathrm{d}t.$$

THEOREM 2. *The Dual Coloring algorithm is a 4-approximation algorithm for Clairvoyant MinUsageTime DBP.*

Proof Sketch: Let $S(t)$ denote the total size of all active items at time t. Following algebra, it can be shown that at any time t, the total number of open bins is bounded by $4\lceil S(t) \rceil$. Therefore,

$$\int_{\cup_{r \in \mathcal{R}_L} I(r)} \lfloor 2S_L(t) \rfloor\, \mathrm{d}t + \int_{\cup_{r \in \mathcal{R}_S} I(r)} (2\lceil 2S_S(t) \rceil - 1)\, \mathrm{d}t$$
$$\leq \int_{\cup_{r \in \mathcal{R}} I(r)} 4\lceil S(t) \rceil\, \mathrm{d}t$$
$$\leq 4 \cdot OPT_{total}(\mathcal{R}),$$

where the last inequality follows from the bound given in Proposition 3. Please refer to the extended version of this paper [22] for the complete proof. □

5. ONLINE ALGORITHMS FOR CLAIRVOYANT MINUSAGETIME DBP

Earlier work has established a lower bound μ on the competitive ratio of any online packing algorithm for Non-Clairvoyant MinUsageTime DBP where the departure times of items are not known when they are placed in bins [13, 17]. In Clairvoyant MinUsageTime DBP, with additional information of item departure times, it is possible to design more competitive online packing algorithms. In this section, we first present a lower bound on the competitive ratio of any online packing algorithm for Clairvoyant MinUsageTime DBP. Then, we propose two strategies of item classification to improve the competitiveness of online packing for Clairvoyant MinUsageTime DBP. The first strategy is called *classify-by-departure-time* and the second strategy is called *classify-by-duration*. We apply these two strategies to First Fit packing (the best known online algorithm in the non-clairvoyant setting) and analyze their competitiveness. To facilitate presentation, we say that a bin is *opened* in an online packing process when it receives the first item. When all the items in a bin depart, the bin is *closed*.

5.1 A lower bound of online packing algorithms

THEOREM 3. *For Clairvoyant MinUsageTime DBP, no deterministic online packing algorithm can achieve a competitive ratio lower than* $\frac{1+\sqrt{5}}{2}$.

Proof: At time 0, let two items of size $\frac{1}{2} - \varepsilon$ arrive, where $0 < \varepsilon < \frac{1}{2}$ is a small value. The duration of the first item is x and the duration of the second item is 1 $(x > 1)$. We consider two cases as shown in Figure 5. In case A, the item list to pack contains the above two items only. In case B, another two items of size $\frac{1}{2} + \varepsilon$ arrive at time τ ($\tau > 0$ is a small value), where the duration of the third item is x and the duration of the fourth item is 1. Obviously, the optimal solution for case A is to place the first two items in the same bin, which gives a total bin usage time of x. The optimal solution for case B is to place the first and third items in one bin

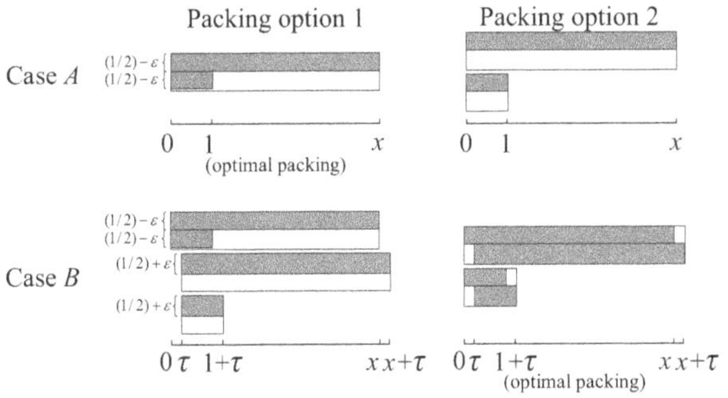

Figure 5: Two cases for online packing

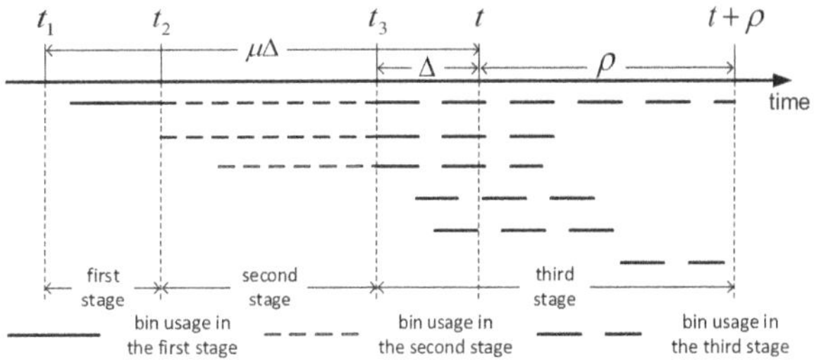

Figure 6: Time-space demands in three stages

and the second and fourth items in another bin, which gives a total bin usage time of $x + \tau + 1 + \tau = x + 1 + 2\tau$.

Note that any deterministic online packing algorithm always packs the first two items in the same way for both cases A and B, since the knowledge of the third and fourth items is not available when packing the first two items in case B. As shown in Figure 5, if an algorithm places the first two items in the same bin, this bin will not be able to accommodate any later item. Since the next two items in case B have size $\frac{1}{2} + \varepsilon$ each, two additional bins are needed to pack them separately. Thus, the total bin usage time for case B is $x + x + 1 = 2x + 1$, resulting in a ratio of $\frac{2x+1}{x+1+2\tau}$ to the optimal solution, which approaches $\frac{2x+1}{x+1}$ as τ approaches 0. On the other hand, if an algorithm places the first two items in two bins separately, then the resultant ratio to the optimal solution for case A is $\frac{x+1}{x}$. Therefore, the competitive ratio of any deterministic online packing algorithm must be at least $\min\{\frac{x+1}{x}, \frac{2x+1}{x+1}\}$. When $x = \frac{1+\sqrt{5}}{2}$, the value of $\min\{\frac{x+1}{x}, \frac{2x+1}{x+1}\}$ reaches the maximum at $\frac{x+1}{x} = \frac{2x+1}{x+1} = \frac{1+\sqrt{5}}{2}$. Hence, the theorem is proven. □

5.2 Classify-by-Departure-Time Strategy

When the departure times of the items are not known at the times of their packing, it is likely that items with very different departure times are packed into the same bin. As a result, after the items with early departure times leave, the remaining items may cause the bin to keep open at some low bin level for a long time, preventing the bin from being closed timely. This can introduce significant but unnecessary bin usage time. To reduce the bin usage time, we propose a classify-by-departure-time strategy to pack the items based on their departure times: the items with similar departure times are considered for placement in the same bin. In this way, the items in a bin would depart at around the same time, after which the bin can be closed timely. As such, the total bin usage time can be saved.

In our classify-by-departure-time strategy, the time is split into intervals of length ρ each, where $\rho > 0$ is a constant. We classify all the items into categories according to their departure times. Each category contains all the items that depart in a time interval of length ρ. Without loss of generality, in our analysis, we assume that the times when there is at least one active item constitute a continuous interval. If they form multiple disjoint intervals, then the entire item list can be broken into multiple sublists with disjoint spans and our analysis can be applied to each sublist separately.

Given an item list $\mathcal{R}$, the above classification produces $\lceil \frac{span(\mathcal{R})}{\rho} \rceil$ categories of items. Without loss of generality, suppose that the first item of $\mathcal{R}$ arrives at time 0, and the last item of $\mathcal{R}$ departs at time $span(\mathcal{R})$. Then, the first category consists of the items departing in the time interval $(0, \rho]$, the second category consists of the items departing in the time interval $(\rho, 2\rho]$, and so on. The category of each item can be determined at the time of its arrival since the departure time of the item is known. We apply the First Fit algorithm to pack the items in each category separately. In First Fit, when a new item arrives, if there are one or more open bins that can accommodate it, the new item is placed in the bin which was opened earliest among these bins. Otherwise, if no open bin can accommodate the new item, a new bin is opened to receive the item.

Next, we study the competitive ratio of the classify-by-departure-time First Fit algorithm. Let Δ denote the minimum item duration and $\mu\Delta$ ($\mu \geq 1$) denote the maximum item duration. Consider a category in which the items depart in a time interval $(t, t + \rho]$. To analyze the bin usage time of packing all the items in the category, we divide the time-space demand of the items into three parts. As shown in Figure 6, We first define t_1 as the time point that is $\mu\Delta$ time units before the beginning of the departure time interval, i.e., $t_1 = t - \mu\Delta$. Since the maximum item duration is $\mu\Delta$, all the items in the category must arrive from t_1 onwards. We then define t_3 as the time point that is Δ time units before the beginning of the departure time interval, i.e., $t_3 = t - \Delta$. We further define t_2 as the time point between t_1 and t_3 when the second bin is opened to pack the items in the category. If no second bin is opened by time t_3, i.e., there is at most one open bin up to time t_3, we define $t_2 = t_3$. The time-space demand of the items in the category is then broken into those over the following three stages: the first stage is from time t_1 to t_2; the second stage is from time t_2 to t_3; and the third stage is from time t_3 to $t + \rho$.

Now, we analyze the bin usage times and the time-space demands in these three stages separately. In the first stage, by definition, there is at most one open bin. Since the length of the first stage is $t_2 - t_1 \leq t_3 - t_1 = (t - \Delta) - (t - \mu\Delta) = (\mu - 1)\Delta$, the bin usage time in the first stage of an item category is bounded by $(\mu - 1)\Delta$. Recall that there are $\lceil \frac{span(\mathcal{R})}{\rho} \rceil$ item categories. For the first item category, i.e., the items departing in the interval $(0, \rho]$, there is no bin usage in its first stage since it is beyond the span of the item list $\mathcal{R}$. Thus, the total bin usage time in the first stages of all the item categories (denoted by $usage_A$) is bounded by

$$\begin{aligned} usage_A &\leq (\mu - 1)\Delta \cdot \left(\left\lceil \frac{span(\mathcal{R})}{\rho} \right\rceil - 1 \right) \\ &< (\mu - 1)\Delta \cdot \frac{span(\mathcal{R})}{\rho} \\ &= \frac{(\mu - 1)\Delta}{\rho} \cdot span(\mathcal{R}). \end{aligned} \quad (3)$$

In the second stage, at least two bins are opened. The following lemma establishes a lower bound on the average bin level in the second stage.

LEMMA 6. *At any moment in the second stage, the average level of all the open bins must exceed $\frac{1}{2}$.*

Proof: Please refer to the extended version of this paper [22]. $\square$

Lemma 6 implies that at any moment in the second stage, the total size of all the active items is at least half the total capacity of all open bins. Thus, the bin usage time in the second stage is bounded by twice the time-space demand of the items over the second stage. This holds for all the item categories. Let $usage_B$ denote the total bin usage time in the second stages of all the item categories, and let d_B denote the total time-space demand of the items over these stages. Then, we have

$$usage_B < 2 \cdot d_B. \tag{4}$$

Finally, we analyze the third stage. Suppose that a total of m bins $b_1, b_2, \ldots, b_m$ are used by the First Fit algorithm to pack the items of a category in the third stage. Assume that the bins are indexed in the temporal order of their openings, i.e., b_1 is the first opened bin and b_m is the last opened bin. For each bin b_i, if b_i is opened before time t_3, let I_i denote the period of b_i's usage from t_3 to its closing. If b_i is opened after time t_3, let I_i denote the entire usage period of b_i from its opening to closing. Then, the bin usage time in the third stage is given by $\sum_{i=1}^{m} l(I_i)$.

For each bin b_i, let E_i be the latest closing time of all the bins that are opened before b_i, i.e., $E_i = \max\{I_j^+ | 1 \le j < i\}$. We divide period I_i into two parts: I_i^L and I_i^R, where I_i^L is the period $[I_i^-, \min\{I_i^+, E_i\})$ (if $E_i \le I_i^-$, then $I_i^L = \emptyset$) and $I_i^R = I_i - I_i^L = [\min\{I_i^+, E_i\}, I_i^+)$ is the remaining period. For the first opened bin b_1, we define $E_1 = I_1^-$ so that $I_1^L = \emptyset$ and $I_1^R = I_1$. Apparently, we have $l(I_i) = l(I_i^L) + l(I_i^R)$ for each I_i. Therefore, the bin usage time in the third stage can be rewritten as $\sum_{i=1}^{m} l(I_i) = \sum_{i=1}^{m} l(I_i^L) + \sum_{i=1}^{m} l(I_i^R)$.

We shall refer to $\sum_{i=1}^{m} l(I_i^L)$ as the *left bin usage time* and $\sum_{i=1}^{m} l(I_i^R)$ as the *right bin usage time*. Obviously, for any two different bins b_i and b_j ($1 \le i \ne j \le m$), it holds that $I_i^R \cap I_j^R = \emptyset$. Thus, it is easy to see that the right bin usage time is bounded by the duration of the third stage, i.e., $t+\rho-t_3 = t+\rho-(t-\Delta) = \rho+\Delta$. This applies to all the item categories.

Moreover, for the first item category (i.e., the items departing in the interval $(0, \rho]$), there is no bin usage in the first Δ time units of the third stage (i.e., from time $-\Delta$ to 0) as it is beyond the span of the item list $\mathcal{R}$. So, its right bin usage time is bounded by ρ.

Similarly, for the last item category, the departure time interval is $\big((\lceil \frac{span(\mathcal{R})}{\rho} \rceil - 1) \cdot \rho, \lceil \frac{span(\mathcal{R})}{\rho} \rceil \cdot \rho\big]$, and the third stage is from time $(\lceil \frac{span(\mathcal{R})}{\rho} \rceil - 1) \cdot \rho - \Delta$ to $\lceil \frac{span(\mathcal{R})}{\rho} \rceil \cdot \rho$. There is bin usage only within the first $\Delta + span(\mathcal{R}) - (\lceil \frac{span(\mathcal{R})}{\rho} \rceil - 1) \cdot \rho$ time units of the third stage as the rest is beyond the span of the item list $\mathcal{R}$. Hence, the right bin usage time for the last item category is bounded by $\Delta + span(\mathcal{R}) - (\lceil \frac{span(\mathcal{R})}{\rho} \rceil - 1) \cdot \rho$.

Thus, the total right bin usage time in the third stages of all the item categories is bounded by

$$\begin{aligned}
&\rho + \Big(\Big\lceil \frac{span(\mathcal{R})}{\rho} \Big\rceil - 2\Big) \cdot (\rho + \Delta) \\
&\quad + \Big(\Delta + span(\mathcal{R}) - \Big(\Big\lceil \frac{span(\mathcal{R})}{\rho} \Big\rceil - 1\Big) \cdot \rho\Big) \\
&= span(\mathcal{R}) + \Big(\Big\lceil \frac{span(\mathcal{R})}{\rho} \Big\rceil - 1\Big) \cdot \Delta \\
&< span(\mathcal{R}) + \frac{span(\mathcal{R})}{\rho} \cdot \Delta \\
&= \frac{\rho + \Delta}{\rho} \cdot span(\mathcal{R}).
\end{aligned}$$

Next, we examine the left bin usage time in the third stage. We shall derive a lower bound on the time-space demand over the third stage as a function of the left bin usage time in order to bound the competitiveness of the latter. This derivation is an extension of our recent analysis of the original First Fit algorithm [24].

For each open bin b_i where $I_i^L \ne \emptyset$, we find the first item r_i with size less than $\frac{\Delta}{\rho+2\Delta}$ (if any) among all the items placed in bin b_i by the end of I_i^L and let a_i denote the arrival time of item r_i. We consider the following three subperiods $I_i^{L_1}$, $I_i^{L_2}$ and $I_i^{L_3}$, whose union covers the whole I_i^L, i.e., $I_i^L \subseteq I_i^{L_1} \cup I_i^{L_2} \cup I_i^{L_3}$. $I_i^{L_1}$ denotes the period from the beginning of I_i to r_i's arrival, $I_i^{L_2}$ denotes a period of length Δ immediately after r_i's arrival (such a period must exist since item r_i stays in bin b_i for at least Δ time units) and $I_i^{L_3}$ denotes the remaining period in I_i^L if any. Note that r_i may arrive before the third stage starts (i.e., before time t_3) or during the third stage (i.e., after time t_3). If r_i arrives before time t_3, then $I_i^{L_1} = \emptyset$, $I_i^{L_2} = [t_3, t)$ and $I_i^{L_3} = [t, I_i^{L+})$ (for example, bin b_2 in Figure 7). If r_i arrives after time t_3, then $I_i^{L_1} = [I_i^-, a_i)$, $I_i^{L_2} = [a_i, a_i + \Delta)$ and $I_i^{L_3} = [a_i + \Delta, \max\{a_i + \Delta, I_i^{L+}\})$ (for example, bins b_3 and b_5 in Figure 7). Obviously, before the arrival of r_i, the level of bin b_i must be at least $\frac{\Delta}{\rho+2\Delta}$ high if it is open. Thus, b_i's bin level is at least $\frac{\Delta}{\rho+2\Delta}$ high in $I_i^{L_1}$. If no item with size less than $\frac{\Delta}{\rho+2\Delta}$ is placed in bin b_i by the end of I_i^L, we define $I_i^{L_1} = I_i^L$, $I_i^{L_2} = \emptyset$ and $I_i^{L_3} = \emptyset$ (for example, bin b_4 in Figure 7). In this case, again, b_i's bin level is at least $\frac{\Delta}{\rho+2\Delta}$ high in $I_i^{L_1}$. For notational convenience, if $I_i^L = \emptyset$, we also define $I_i^{L_1} = I_i^L = \emptyset$, $I_i^{L_2} = \emptyset$ and $I_i^{L_3} = \emptyset$. Based on the above definitions, we have the following properties:

PROPOSITION 4. *For each bin b_i, if $I_i^{L_1} \ne \emptyset$, b_i's bin level is at least $\frac{\Delta}{\rho+2\Delta}$ high in $I_i^{L_1}$.*

PROPOSITION 5. *For each bin b_i, if $I_i^L \ne \emptyset$ and an item of size less than $\frac{\Delta}{\rho+2\Delta}$ is placed in b_i by the end of I_i^L, then $I_i^{L_2} \ne \emptyset$. Otherwise, $I_i^{L_2} = \emptyset$ and $I_i^{L_3} = \emptyset$.*

To bound the time-space demand, we define the concepts of *supplier bin* and *supplier period*. For each bin b_i where $I_i^L \ne \emptyset$ and an item of size less than $\frac{\Delta}{\rho+2\Delta}$ is placed in b_i by the end of I_i^L, there must exist at least one bin b_h opened before b_i and closed after time a_i, i.e., the arrival time of item r_i. Otherwise, by definition, we have $E_i = \max\{I_j^+ \mid 1 \le j < i\} \le a_i$ and hence a_i should belong to I_i^R rather than I_i^L. Among all such bins opened before bin b_i and closed after time a_i, we define the last opened bin (the bin with the highest index) as the supplier bin of b_i. Consider the following three cases of r_i's arrival time.

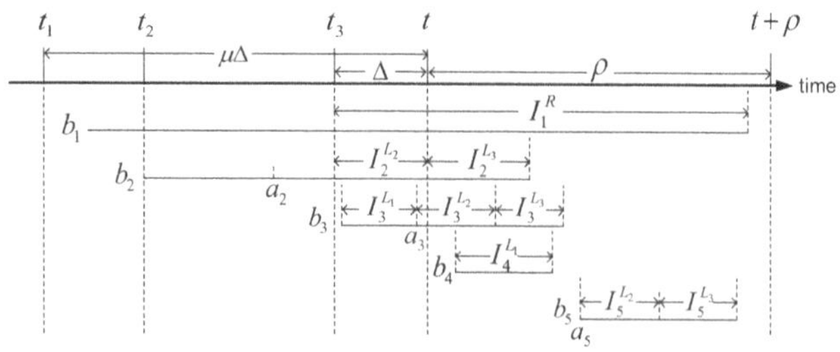

Figure 7: Definitions of $I_i^{L_1}$, $I_i^{L_2}$ and $I_i^{L_3}$

Case 1: Item r_i arrives on or before time t_3, i.e., $a_i \leq t_3$. In this case, b_i's supplier bin must be b_{i-1} since the open bins of the item category can only be closed in the interval $(t, t+\rho]$ in which the items depart. For example, in Figure 7, b_2's supplier bin is b_1. According to the First Fit packing algorithm, at the moment of a_i, the sum of the levels of b_{i-1} and b_i is higher than 1 (the bin capacity). This implies b_{i-1}'s level at time a_i is higher than $1 - s(r_i)$. We define the time interval $[t_3, t)$ associated with bin b_{i-1} as the supplier period of bin b_i and denote it by P_i. Note that the level of b_{i-1} never decreases before t. Also note that the length of period I_i^{L2} is Δ, and item r_i stays in bin b_i throughout I_i^{L2}. Let $d(P_i)$ denote the total time-space demand of the items in b_i's supplier bin over the supplier period P_i, and let $d(I_i^{L2})$ denote the total time-space demand of the items in bin b_i over the period I_i^{L2}. It follows that

$$\begin{aligned} d(P_i) + d(I_i^{L2}) &> \big(1 - s(r_i)\big) \cdot l(P_i) + s(r_i) \cdot l(I_i^{L2}) \\ &= \big(1 - s(r_i)\big) \cdot \Delta + s(r_i) \cdot \Delta \\ &= \Delta. \end{aligned}$$

Case 2: Item r_i arrives between time t_3 and t, i.e., $t_3 < a_i < t$. In this case, b_i's supplier bin must also be b_{i-1} since no open bin is closed before time t. For example, in Figure 7, b_3's supplier bin is b_2. We define the time interval $[t_3, a_i + \Delta)$ associated with bin b_{i-1} as the supplier period of bin b_i and denote it by P_i. Following similar arguments to Case 1, at the moment of a_i, the level of b_{i-1} is higher than $1 - s(r_i)$. All the items in b_{i-1} at that time remain in b_{i-1} till at least time t. Recall that each item resides in the system for at least Δ time units. Thus, each item in b_{i-1} at time a_i must stay for a duration at least Δ time units long in the time interval $[a_i - (\Delta - (t - a_i)), t + (\Delta - (t - a_i))) = [t_3, a_i + \Delta)$. Also note that item r_i stays in bin b_i throughout I_i^{L2}. Therefore,

$$d(P_i) + d(I_i^{L2}) > \big(1 - s(r_i)\big) \cdot \Delta + s(r_i) \cdot \Delta = \Delta.$$

Case 3: Item r_i arrives on or after time t, i.e., $a_i \geq t$. For example, $a_5 \geq t$ in Figure 7 and b_5's supplier bin is b_1. Again, the supplier bin of b_i must have a level higher than $1 - s(r_i)$ at time a_i. We define the time interval $[a_i - \Delta, a_i + \Delta)$ associated with the supplier bin as the supplier period of bin b_i and denote it by P_i. Since each item stays in the system for at least a duration of Δ time units, we have $d(P_i) > \big(1 - s(r_i)\big) \cdot \Delta$ and $d(I_i^{L2}) \geq s(r_i) \cdot \Delta$. Thus,

$$d(P_i) + d(I_i^{L2}) > \big(1 - s(r_i)\big) \cdot \Delta + s(r_i) \cdot \Delta = \Delta.$$

So far, we have created a supplier period P_i for each bin b_i where $I_i^L \neq \emptyset$ and an item with size less than $\frac{\Delta}{\rho+2\Delta}$ is placed in b_i by the end of I_i^L. The total time-space demand over periods P_i and I_i^{L2} is at least Δ, i.e.,

$$d(P_i) + d(I_i^{L2}) \geq d(P_i) + s(r_i) \cdot l(I_i^{L2}) > \Delta. \tag{5}$$

If multiple bins share the same supplier bin, their supplier periods may overlap. We group the bins $b_2, b_3, \ldots, b_m$ according to their supplier bins. Let $\mathcal{G}$ be the set of all the bin groups. Consider a bin group $H \in \mathcal{G}$. Suppose there are s bins $b_{j_1}, b_{j_2}, \ldots, b_{j_s}$ in H that share the same supplier bin. Without loss of generality, suppose that $j_1 < j_2 < \cdots < j_s$. We first analyze the total length of the periods $I_{j_1}^{L2} \cup I_{j_1}^{L3}, I_{j_2}^{L2} \cup I_{j_2}^{L3}, \ldots, I_{j_s}^{L2} \cup I_{j_s}^{L3}$ together with the supplier period P_{j_1} of the first bin b_{j_1} in the group.

LEMMA 7. *The total length of the supplier period P_{j_1} together with periods $I_{j_1}^{L2} \cup I_{j_1}^{L3}, I_{j_2}^{L2} \cup I_{j_2}^{L3}, \ldots, I_{j_s}^{L2} \cup I_{j_s}^{L3}$ is bounded by $\rho + 2\Delta$.*

Proof: Please refer to the extended version of this paper [22]. □

In what follows, we shall refer to the lowest-indexed bin in each group $H \in \mathcal{G}$ as its *flag bin* and denote its index by $f(H)$ (i.e., $f(H) = j_1$ in the above discussion).

Lemma 7 together with (5) imply that for each bin group $H \in \mathcal{G}$, we have

$$\begin{aligned} &\frac{\Delta}{\rho + 2\Delta} \cdot \Big(l(P_{f(H)}) + \sum_{b_j \in H} l(I_j^{L2} \cup I_j^{L3})\Big) \\ &\leq \frac{\Delta}{\rho + 2\Delta} \cdot (\rho + 2\Delta) \\ &< d(P_{f(H)}) + s(r_{f(H)}) \cdot l(I_{f(H)}^{L2}) \\ &\leq d(P_{f(H)}) + d(I_{f(H)}^{L2}). \end{aligned} \tag{6}$$

To compute the aggregate time-space demand of the periods $P_{f(H)}$ and $I_{f(H)}^{L2}$ for all the bin groups, we need to study the possible overlaps between the periods of different bin groups. Note that the time-space demands repeatedly counted in the overlapping parts are all due to items $r_{f(H)}$'s that have sizes less than $\frac{\Delta}{\rho+2\Delta}$. Also note that the bin levels are at least $\frac{\Delta}{\rho+2\Delta}$ high in the L_1-periods (Proposition 4). It can finally be shown that (see the extended version of this paper [22] for the complete derivation)

$$\frac{\Delta}{\rho + 2\Delta} \cdot \sum_{i=1}^{m} l(I_i^L) \leq \sum_{i=1}^{m} d(I_i). \tag{7}$$

Since the above inequality holds for all the item categories, the total left bin usage time over the third stages of all the item categories is bounded by $(\frac{\rho}{\Delta} + 2) \cdot d_C$, where d_C denotes the total time-space demand of the items over these periods. Putting together the left and right bin usage times, the total bin usage time in the third stages of all the item categories (denoted by $usage_C$) is bounded by

$$usage_C \leq \Big(\frac{\rho}{\Delta} + 2\Big) \cdot d_C + \frac{\rho + \Delta}{\rho} \cdot span(\mathcal{R}). \tag{8}$$

By definition, $d_B + d_C$ is capped by the total time-space demand $d(\mathcal{R})$ of the entire item list $\mathcal{R}$. Therefore, adding up the bin usage times in the three stages of all the item categories (i.e., (3), (4) and (8)) and according to Propositions 1 and 2, the total bin usage time of the classify-by-departure-time First Fit algorithm satisfies

$$\begin{aligned} &usage_A + usage_B + usage_C \\ &< 2 \cdot d_B + \Big(\frac{\rho}{\Delta} + 2\Big) \cdot d_C + \frac{\mu\Delta + \rho}{\rho} \cdot span(\mathcal{R}) \\ &\leq \Big(\frac{\rho}{\Delta} + 2\Big) \cdot (d_B + d_C) + \frac{\mu\Delta + \rho}{\rho} \cdot span(\mathcal{R}) \\ &\leq \Big(\frac{\rho}{\Delta} + 2\Big) \cdot d(\mathcal{R}) + \frac{\mu\Delta + \rho}{\rho} \cdot span(\mathcal{R}) \\ &\leq \Big(\frac{\rho}{\Delta} + 2\Big) \cdot OPT_{total}(\mathcal{R}) + \frac{\mu\Delta + \rho}{\rho} \cdot OPT_{total}(\mathcal{R}) \\ &= \Big(\frac{\rho}{\Delta} + \frac{\mu\Delta}{\rho} + 3\Big) \cdot OPT_{total}(\mathcal{R}). \end{aligned} \tag{9}$$

There exists an optimal value of the algorithm parameter ρ that minimizes the factor $\frac{\rho}{\Delta} + \frac{\mu\Delta}{\rho} + 3$. If the minimum and maximum item durations are known prior to packing, ρ can be set to $\sqrt{\mu}\Delta$ so that $\frac{\rho}{\Delta} + \frac{\mu\Delta}{\rho} + 3$ reaches the minimum value of $2\sqrt{\mu} + 3$. Therefore, we have the following conclusion.

THEOREM 4. *For Clairvoyant MinUsageTime DBP, if the minimum and maximum item durations are not known, the classify-*

by-departure-time First Fit algorithm has a competitive ratio of $\frac{\rho}{\Delta} + \frac{\mu\Delta}{\rho} + 3$, where ρ is the length of the departure time interval for each item category and Δ is the minimum item duration. If the minimum and maximum item durations are known, the classify-by-departure-time First Fit algorithm can achieve a competitive ratio of $2\sqrt{\mu} + 3$.

5.3 Classify-by-Duration Strategy

In our recent work, we have established an upper bound of $\mu + 4$ on the competitive ratio of First Fit packing for Non-Clairvoyant MinUsageTime DBP [24]. Observing that the competitive ratio of First Fit packing is a linear function of the max/min item duration ratio μ, we propose another classify-by-duration strategy to make the packing algorithm more competitive by reducing the max/min ratio of item durations. Specifically, we classify the items into categories such that the max/min item duration ratio for each category is a given constant α. Given a base item duration b, each category includes all the items with durations between $b \cdot \alpha^{i-1}$ and $b \cdot \alpha^i$ for an integer i. Suppose that the max/min item duration for the entire item list $\mathcal{R}$ is μ. Then, there can be up to $\lceil log_\alpha \mu \rceil + 1$ non-empty item categories produced by the classification.[2] Let $\mathcal{R}_1$, $\mathcal{R}_2, \mathcal{R}_3, \ldots, \mathcal{R}_{\lceil log_\alpha \mu \rceil + 1}$ denote these item categories. Since the departure time (and thus the duration) of each item is known at the time of its arrival, the category of the item can be determined at the time of its assignment. We use First Fit packing to pack the items in each category $\mathcal{R}_i$ separately.

In our proof that First Fit packing is $(\mu+4)$-competitive for Non-Clairvoyant MinUsageTime DBP [24], we have established that the total bin usage time of First Fit packing is bounded by

$$(\mu + 3) \cdot d(\mathcal{R}) + span(\mathcal{R}),$$

where $\mathcal{R}$ is the item list packed by First Fit, and $d(\mathcal{R})$ and $span(\mathcal{R})$ are the total time-space demand and the span of $\mathcal{R}$ respectively.

Thus, by applying the classify-by-duration First Fit algorithm, the bin usage time of packing all the items in each category $\mathcal{R}_i$ $(i = 1, 2, 3, \ldots, \lceil log_\alpha \mu \rceil + 1)$ is bounded by

$$(\alpha + 3) \cdot d(\mathcal{R}_i) + span(\mathcal{R}_i).$$

Therefore, the total bin usage time of classify-by-duration First Fit packing for the entire item list $\mathcal{R}$ is bounded by

$$(\alpha + 3) \cdot \sum_{i=1}^{\lceil log_\alpha \mu \rceil + 1} d(\mathcal{R}_i) + \sum_{i=1}^{\lceil log_\alpha \mu \rceil + 1} span(\mathcal{R}_i). \quad (10)$$

Note that $d(\mathcal{R}) = \sum_{i=1}^{\lceil log_\alpha \mu \rceil + 1} d(\mathcal{R}_i)$ and for any $1 \leq i \leq \lceil log_\alpha \mu \rceil + 1$, by definition, $span(\mathcal{R}_i) \leq span(\mathcal{R})$. As a result, the total bin usage time is bounded by

$$(\alpha + 3) \cdot d(\mathcal{R}) + (\lceil log_\alpha \mu \rceil + 1) \cdot span(\mathcal{R}).$$

By Propositions 1 and 2, it follows that the total bin usage time of classify-by-duration First Fit packing is bounded by

$$(\alpha + \lceil log_\alpha \mu \rceil + 4) \cdot OPT_{total}(\mathcal{R}).$$

If the minimum and maximum item durations are known prior to packing, the base item duration b can be set to match the minimum item duration and the ratio α can be set to $\mu^{\frac{1}{n}}$ such that there are exactly n item categories produced by the classification. In this case, the total bin usage time of classify-by-duration First Fit packing is bounded by $(\mu^{\frac{1}{n}} + n + 3) \cdot OPT_{total}(\mathcal{R})$. Given a value of μ, there exists an optimal number of item categories that minimizes the factor $\mu^{\frac{1}{n}} + n + 3$, which can be found numerically. Therefore, we have the following result.

THEOREM 5. *For Clairvoyant MinUsageTime DBP, if the minimum and maximum item durations are not known, the classify-by-duration First Fit algorithm has a competitive ratio of $\alpha + \lceil log_\alpha \mu \rceil + 4$, where α is the max/min item duration ratio for each item category. If the minimum and maximum item durations are known, the classify-by-duration First Fit algorithm can achieve a competitive ratio of $\min_{n \geq 1} \mu^{\frac{1}{n}} + n + 3$.*

We remark that our result significantly improves the existing one of online interval scheduling with bounded parallelism. Shalom *et al.* [23] proposed a BucketFirstFit algorithm that classifies interval jobs according to their lengths and applies First Fit to each category of jobs. They showed that BucketFirstFit has a competitive ratio of $(2\alpha + 2) \cdot \lceil log_\alpha \mu \rceil$, where μ is the max/min length ratio of all job intervals and α is the max/min length ratio of job intervals in each category. Our result implies that BucketFirstFit can achieve a competitive ratio of $\alpha + \lceil log_\alpha \mu \rceil + 4$ which is asymptotically lower than $(2\alpha + 2) \cdot \lceil log_\alpha \mu \rceil$. Our result is also much more general in that we allow items to have arbitrary sizes while the analysis of [23] is restricted to jobs with the same resource demands.

5.4 Numerical results

In this section, we compare the competitive ratios of the classify-by-duration and classify-by-departure-time strategies based on the results of Theorems 4 and 5. Suppose that the minimum and maximum item durations are known prior to packing. Figure 8 shows the best achievable competitive ratios of the classify-by-departure-time and classify-by-duration First Fit algorithms at their respective optimal parameter settings of ρ and n for different max/min item duration ratios μ. For comparison purposes, we also include in Figure 8 the competitive ratio of the original First Fit packing algorithm in the non-clairvoyant setting which is given by $\mu + 4$.

It can be seen that the First Fit algorithms with item classification can achieve asymptotically much lower competitive ratios compared to the original First Fit algorithm. When $\mu < 4$, the classify-by-departure-time strategy has a lower competitive ratio than the classify-by-duration strategy. When $\mu > 4$, the classify-by-duration strategy has a lower competitive ratio than the classify-by-departure-time strategy. This implies that it may be possible to design an even more competitive packing algorithm by combining these two strategies of item classification. Items can first be classified by their durations to reduce the max/min ratio of item durations

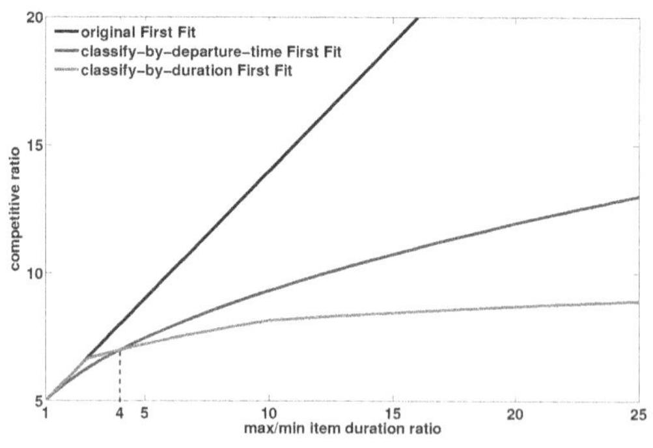

Figure 8: Comparison between classify-by-departure-time and classify-by-duration First Fit

[2]For example, if $\alpha = 2$ and the minimum and maximum item durations are 1.5 and 4.5 respectively, there are $\lceil log_2 3 \rceil + 1 = 3$ non-empty item categories: $[1, 2)$, $[2, 4)$ and $[4, 8)$.

and then be further classified by their departure times for packing. We leave the design of such an algorithm as our future work.

6. CONCLUDING REMARKS

In this paper, we have studied both the offline and online versions of the Clairvoyant MinUsageTime DBP problem. One direction for future work is to design a more competitive online packing algorithm by combining the two proposed item classification strategies for Clairvoyant MinUsageTime DBP. We shall also analyze how inaccurate estimates of item durations would impact the competitiveness. Another direction is to extend the Clairvoyant MinUsageTime DBP problem to model flexible jobs that have release times and deadlines and do not have to be processed immediately upon arrival. Finally, we are also interested in extending MinUsageTime DBP to multiple resource dimensions.

7. ACKNOWLEDGMENTS

This work is supported by Singapore Ministry of Education Academic Research Fund Tier 2 under Grant MOE2013-T2-2-067, and Academic Research Fund Tier 1 under Grant 2013-T1-002-123.

8. REFERENCES

[1] Amazon EC2 pricing. http://aws.amazon.com/ec2/pricing/.

[2] Gaikai. http://www.gaikai.com/.

[3] Onlive. http://www.onlive.com/.

[4] M. Alicherry and R. Bhatia. Line system design and a generalized coloring problem. In *ESA 2003: European Symposium on Algorithms*, pages 19–30. Springer, 2003.

[5] A. Borodin and R. El-Yaniv. *Online computation and competitive analysis*, volume 53. Cambridge University Press Cambridge, 1998.

[6] J. W.-T. Chan, T.-W. Lam, and P. W. Wong. Dynamic bin packing of unit fractions items. *Theoretical Computer Science*, 409(3):521–529, 2008.

[7] J. W.-T. Chan, P. W. Wong, and F. C. Yung. On dynamic bin packing: An improved lower bound and resource augmentation analysis. *Computing and Combinatorics*, pages 309–319, 2006.

[8] J. Chang, S. Khuller, and K. Mukherjee. LP rounding and combinatorial algorithms for minimizing active and busy time. In *Proceedings of the 26th ACM Symposium on Parallelism in Algorithms and Architectures (SPAA)*, pages 118–127, 2014.

[9] E. G. Coffman, Jr, M. R. Garey, and D. S. Johnson. Dynamic bin packing. *SIAM Journal on Computing*, 12(2):227–258, 1983.

[10] M. Flammini, G. Monaco, L. Moscardelli, H. Shachnai, M. Shalom, T. Tamir, and S. Zaks. Minimizing total busy time in parallel scheduling with application to optical networks. In *Proceedings of the 23rd IEEE International Parallel and Distributed Processing Symposium (IPDPS)*, pages 1–12, 2009.

[11] C.-Y. Huang, K.-T. Chen, D.-Y. Chen, H.-J. Hsu, and C.-H. Hsu. GamingAnywhere: the first open source cloud gaming system. *ACM Transactions on Multimedia Computing, Communications, and Applications*, 10(1):10, 2014.

[12] V. Jalaparti, P. Bodik, I. Menache, S. Rao, K. Makarychev, and M. Caesar. Network-aware scheduling for data-parallel jobs: Plan when you can. In *Proceedings of the 2015 ACM Conference on Special Interest Group on Data Communication (SIGCOMM)*, pages 407–420, 2015.

[13] S. Kamali and A. López-Ortiz. Efficient online strategies for renting servers in the cloud. In *SOFSEM 2015: Theory and Practice of Computer Science*, pages 277–288. Springer, 2015.

[14] R. Khandekar, B. Schieber, H. Shachnai, and T. Tamir. Minimizing busy time in multiple machine real-time scheduling. In *FSTTCS 2010: Foundations of Software Technology and Theoretical Computer Science*, pages 169–180. Springer, 2010.

[15] V. Kumar and A. Rudra. Approximation algorithms for wavelength assignment. In *FSTTCS 2005: Foundations of Software Technology and Theoretical Computer Science*, pages 152–163. Springer, 2005.

[16] Y. Li, Y. Deng, R. Seet, X. Tang, and W. Cai. MASTER: Multi-platform application streaming toolkits for elastic resources. In *Proceedings of the 23rd ACM International Conference on Multimedia (MM)*, pages 805–806, 2015.

[17] Y. Li, X. Tang, and W. Cai. On dynamic bin packing for resource allocation in the cloud. In *Proceedings of the 26th ACM Symposium on Parallelism in Algorithms and Architectures (SPAA)*, pages 2–11, 2014.

[18] Y. Li, X. Tang, and W. Cai. Play request dispatching for efficient virtual machine usage in cloud gaming. *IEEE Transactions on Circuits and Systems for Video Technology*, 25(12):2052–2063, 2015.

[19] Y. Li, X. Tang, and W. Cai. Dynamic bin packing for on-demand cloud resource allocation. *IEEE Transactions on Parallel and Distributed Systems*, 27(1):157–170, 2016.

[20] G. B. Mertzios, M. Shalom, A. Voloshin, P. W. Wong, and S. Zaks. Optimizing busy time on parallel machines. In *Proceedings of the 26th IEEE International Parallel and Distributed Processing Symposium (IPDPS)*, pages 238–248, 2012.

[21] Q. Pu, G. Ananthanarayanan, P. Bodik, S. Kandula, A. Akella, P. Bahl, and I. Stoica. Low latency geo-distributed data analytics. In *Proceedings of the 2015 ACM Conference on Special Interest Group on Data Communication (SIGCOMM)*, pages 421–434, 2015.

[22] R. Ren and X. Tang. Clairvoyant dynamic bin packing for job scheduling with minimum server usage time (extended version).
Available at http://www.ntu.edu.sg/home/asxytang/.

[23] M. Shalom, A. Voloshin, P. W. Wong, F. C. Yung, and S. Zaks. Online optimization of busy time on parallel machines. *Theoretical Computer Science*, 560:190–206, 2014.

[24] X. Tang, Y. Li, R. Ren, and W. Cai. On first fit bin packing for online cloud server allocation. In *In Proceedings of the 30th IEEE International Parallel and Distributed Processing Symposium (IPDPS)*, 2016.

[25] V. V. Vazirani. *Approximation algorithms*. Springer Science & Business Media, 2013.

Brief Announcement: Improved Approximation Algorithms for Scheduling Co-Flows*

Samir Khuller
Computer Science Department
University of Maryland, College Park
samir@cs.umd.edu

Manish Purohit
Computer Science Department
University of Maryland, College Park
manishp@cs.umd.edu

ABSTRACT

Co-flow scheduling is a recent networking abstraction introduced to capture application-level communication patterns in datacenters. In this paper, we consider the offline co-flow scheduling problem with release times to minimize the total weighted completion time. Recently, Qiu, Stein and Zhong [8] obtained the first constant approximation algorithms for this problem with a deterministic $\frac{67}{3}$-approximation and a randomized $(9 + \frac{16\sqrt{2}}{3}) \approx 16.54$-approximation. In this paper, we improve upon their algorithm to yield a deterministic 12-approximation algorithm. For the special case when all release times are zero, we obtain a deterministic 8-approximation and a randomized $(3 + 2\sqrt{2}) \approx 5.83$-approximation.

1. INTRODUCTION

Applications designed for data-parallel computation frameworks such as MapReduce, Hadoop, and Spark usually alternate between computation and communication stages. Typically, intermediate data generated by a computation stage needs to be transferred across machines during a communication stage (called "shuffle" in MapReduce) for further processing. Chowdhury and Stoica [2] introduce *co-flows* as a networking abstraction to represent the collective communication requirements of a job. Every job j is associated with a set of flow demands (called as a co-flow) and the job j is said to be satisfied once *all* of its demands are met.

Due to significant potential gains in datacenter throughput, co-flow scheduling has been a topic of active research [3, 4, 8, 10] since its introduction. Although the heuristics developed by Chowdhury et al [4, 3] perform very well in practice, they do not admit provable worst-case guarantees. Even in the offline setting, when all jobs are known in advance, no $O(1)$ approximation algorithm was known until recently. Qiu, Stein and Zhong [8] obtain a deterministic $\frac{67}{3}$ approximation and a randomized $(9 + \frac{16\sqrt{2}}{3})$ approximation for the problem of minimizing the weighted completion time.

*This work is supported by NSF grant CCF 1217890.

SPAA '16 July 11-13, 2016, Pacific Grove, CA, USA

ACM ISBN 978-1-4503-4210-0/16/07.
DOI: http://dx.doi.org/10.1145/2935764.2935809

For the special case when all release times are zero, Qiu et al. [8] demonstrate improved bounds of $\frac{64}{3}$ (deterministic) and $(8 + \frac{16\sqrt{2}}{3})$ (randomized).

1.1 Problem Setting

A datacenter is modeled as a single $m \times m$ *non-blocking* switch, i.e., it is comprised of m *input ports* and m *output ports*. For simplicity, we assume that all ports have unit capacity - i.e., at most one unit of data can be transferred through any port at a time.

A co-flow is defined as a collection of parallel flow demands that share a performance goal. Each co-flow j has weight w_j, release time r_j, and is represented as a $m \times m$ integer matrix $D^j = [d^j_{io}]$ where the entry d^j_{io} represents the number of data units that must be transferred from input port i to output port o for co-flow j.

A co-flow j is available to be scheduled at its release time r_j and is said to be completed when all the flows in the matrix D^j have been scheduled. We assume that time is slotted and data transfer within the switch is instantaneous. Since each input port i can transmit at most one unit of data and each output port o can receive at most one unit of data in each time slot, a feasible schedule for a single time slot is described by a matching. Our goal is to find a feasible, integral schedule that minimizes the total, weighted completion time of the co-flows, i.e. minimize $\sum_j w_j C_j$.

1.2 Connection to Concurrent Open Shop

The co-flow scheduling problem as described above generalizes the well-studied concurrent open shop problem [7, 1, 5, 6, 9]. In the concurrent open shop problem, we have a set of m machines and each job j with weight w_j is composed of m tasks $\{t^j_i\}^m_{i=1}$, one on each machine. Let p^j_i denote the processing requirement of task t^j_i. A job j is said to be completed once all its tasks have completed. Any machine can perform at most one unit of processing at a time. The objective is to find a feasible schedule that minimizes the total weighted completion time of jobs. An LP-relaxation using completion time variables yields a 2-approximation algorithm for concurrent open shop scheduling when all release times are zero [1, 5, 6] and a 3-approximation algorithm for arbitrary release times [5, 6]. It can be seen that the concurrent open shop problem is a special case of co-flow scheduling when the demand matrices D^j for all co-flows j are diagonal [4, 8].

1.3 Our Contribution

The main algorithmic contribution of this paper is the

following improved approximation guarantee for the offline co-flow scheduling problem.

THEOREM 1. *There exists a deterministic 12-approximation algorithm for co-flow scheduling with release times and a deterministic 8-approximation algorithm for co-flow scheduling without release times.*

THEOREM 2. *There exists a randomized* $(3+2\sqrt{2}) \approx 5.83$-*approximation algorithm for co-flow scheduling without release times.*

2. APPROXIMATION ALGORITHMS

For every co-flow j and input port i, we define the load $L_i^j = \sum_{o=1}^{m} d_{io}^j$ to be the total amount of data that co-flow j needs to transmit through port i. Similarly, we define $L_o^j = \sum_{i=1}^{m} d_{io}^j$ for every co-flow j and output port o. Our algorithm consists of the following two stages.

2.1 Reduction to Concurrent Open Shop:

Let $\mathcal{I}$ denote an instance of the co-flow scheduling problem. We now construct an instance $\mathcal{I}'$ of the concurrent open shop scheduling problem on $2m$ machines (one for each port) and n jobs (one for each co-flow). For a job j, set $p_s^j = L_s^j$, i.e., the processing requirement of job j on a machine s is set to be the load of the co-flow j on the corresponding port. Let $OPT(\mathcal{I})$ denote the cost of an optimal co-flow schedule and $OPT(\mathcal{I}')$ denote the cost of an optimal, preemptive concurrent open shop schedule for the instance $\mathcal{I}'$.

LEMMA 1. $OPT(\mathcal{I}') \leq OPT(\mathcal{I})$

PROOF. Let S^* denote an optimal co-flow schedule for instance $\mathcal{I}$. For a co-flow j and port s, let T_s^j denote the set of time slots when data corresponding to co-flow j is being processed (either input or output) at port s as per schedule S^*. Now processing one unit of the corresponding job j on machine s in the concurrent open shop instance $\mathcal{I}'$ at all times in T_s^j leads to a feasible schedule. □

Let $\bar{C}_j$ denote the completion time of job j in an approximate schedule for the concurrent open shop instance $\mathcal{I}'$. Further, let us assume without loss of generality that the co-flows are ordered so that the following holds.

$$\bar{C}_1 \leq \bar{C}_2 \leq \ldots \leq \bar{C}_n \tag{1}$$

The following statements now hold from the feasibility of the schedule and Equation (1).

$$\bar{C}_k \geq r_k + \max_s p_s^k, \qquad 1 \leq k \leq n \tag{2}$$

$$\bar{C}_k \geq \max_s \sum_{j \leq k} p_s^j, \qquad 1 \leq k \leq n \tag{3}$$

COROLLARY 1. $\sum_j w_j \bar{C}_j \leq 3 \times OPT(\mathcal{I})$. *Further if all release times are zero, then* $\sum_j w_j \bar{C}_j \leq 2 \times OPT(\mathcal{I})$

PROOF. The concurrent open shop scheduling problem with release times has well-known 3-approximation algorithms [6, 5] that also yield a 2-approximation when all release times are zero. We remark that these approximation algorithms also yield guarantees with respect to the optimal *preemptive* schedule. Combining any of these algorithms with Lemma 1 yields the corollary. □

2. Scheduling Co-flows:

The following two lemmas by Qiu et al. [8] show that grouping co-flows in geometrically increasing groups based on the approximate completion times ($\bar{C}_j$) and then scheduling the consolidated co-flows sequentially yields a provably good co-flow schedule.

LEMMA 2 ([8]). *Given a permutation of co-flows that satisfies conditions* (2) *and* (3), *there exists a deterministic algorithm that yields a feasible co-flow schedule such that for every co-flow* k, $C_k(alg) \leq 4\bar{C}_k$ *where* $C_k(alg)$ *is the completion time of co-flow* k *in the co-flow schedule.*

LEMMA 3 ([8]). *Given a permutation of co-flows that satisfies condition* (3) *and* $r_k = 0$ *for all co-flows* k, *there exists a randomized algorithm that yields a feasible co-flow schedule such that for every co-flow* k, $C_k(alg) \leq (\frac{3}{2} + \sqrt{2})\bar{C}_k$.

Theorems 1 and 2 now follow from Corollary 1 and Lemmas 2 and 3 respectively.

3. REFERENCES

[1] Z.-L. Chen and N. G. Hall. Supply chain scheduling: Conflict and cooperation in assembly systems. *Operations Research*, 55(6):1072–1089, 2007.

[2] M. Chowdhury and I. Stoica. Coflow: A networking abstraction for cluster applications. In *Proceedings of the 11th ACM Workshop on Hot Topics in Networks*, pages 31–36. ACM, 2012.

[3] M. Chowdhury and I. Stoica. Efficient coflow scheduling without prior knowledge. In *Proceedings of the 2015 ACM Conference on Special Interest Group on Data Communication*, pages 393–406. ACM, 2015.

[4] M. Chowdhury, Y. Zhong, and I. Stoica. Efficient coflow scheduling with varys. In *Proceedings of the 2014 ACM Conference on SIGCOMM*, SIGCOMM '14, pages 443–454, New York, NY, USA, 2014. ACM.

[5] N. Garg, A. Kumar, and V. Pandit. Order scheduling models: Hardness and algorithms. In *FSTTCS 2007: Foundations of Software Technology and Theoretical Computer Science*, pages 96–107. Springer, 2007.

[6] J. Y.-T. Leung, H. Li, and M. Pinedo. Scheduling orders for multiple product types to minimize total weighted completion time. *Discrete Applied Mathematics*, 155(8):945–970, 2007.

[7] M. Mastrolilli, M. Queyranne, A. S. Schulz, O. Svensson, and N. A. Uhan. Minimizing the sum of weighted completion times in a concurrent open shop. *Operations Research Letters*, 38(5):390–395, 2010.

[8] Z. Qiu, C. Stein, and Y. Zhong. Minimizing the total weighted completion time of coflows in datacenter networks. In *Proceedings of the 27th ACM Symposium on Parallelism in Algorithms and Architectures*, SPAA '15, pages 294–303, New York, NY, USA, 2015. ACM.

[9] G. Wang and T. E. Cheng. Customer order scheduling to minimize total weighted completion time. *Omega*, 35(5):623–626, 2007.

[10] Y. Zhao, K. Chen, W. Bai, M. Yu, C. Tian, Y. Geng, Y. Zhang, D. Li, and S. Wang. Rapier: Integrating routing and scheduling for coflow-aware data center networks. In *Computer Communications (INFOCOM), 2015 IEEE Conference on*, pages 424–432. IEEE, 2015.

Online Packet Scheduling for CIOQ and Buffered Crossbar Switches*

Kamal Al-Bawani
Department of Computer Science
RWTH Aachen University
Germany
kbawani@cs.rwth-aachen.de

Matthias Englert
DIMAP and Department of Computer Science
University of Warwick
UK
englert@dcs.warwick.ac.uk

Matthias Westermann
Department of Computer Science
TU Dortmund
Germany
matthias.westermann@cs.tu-dortmund.de

ABSTRACT

We consider the problem of online packet scheduling in Combined Input and Output Queued (CIOQ) and buffered crossbar switches. In the widely used CIOQ switches, packet buffers (queues) are placed at both input and output ports. An $N \times N$ CIOQ switch has N input ports and N output ports, where each input port is equipped with N queues, each of which corresponds to an output port, and each output port is equipped with only one queue. In each time step, arbitrarily many packets may arrive at each input port, and only one packet can be transmitted from each output port. Packets are transferred from the queues of input ports to the queues of output ports through the internal fabric. Buffered crossbar switches follow a similar design, but are equipped with additional buffers in their internal fabric. In either model, our goal is to maximize the number or, in case the packets have weights, the total weight of transmitted packets.

Our main objective is to devise online algorithms that are both competitive and efficient. We improve the previously known results for both switch models, both for unweighted and weighted packets.

For unweighted packets, Kesselman and Rosén (J. Algorithms '06) give an online algorithm that is 3-competitive for CIOQ switches. We give a faster, more practical algorithm achieving the same competitive ratio. In the buffered crossbar model we also show 3-competitiveness, improving the previously known ratio of 4.

For weighted packets, we give 5.83- and 14.83-competitive algorithms with an elegant analysis for CIOQ and buffered crossbar switches, respectively. This improves upon the previously known ratios of 6 and 16.24.

*The second and third author's work was supported by ERC Grant Agreement No. 307696.

SPAA '16, July 11 - 13, 2016, Pacific Grove, CA, USA

ISBN 978-1-4503-4210-0/16/07...$15.00

DOI: http://dx.doi.org/10.1145/2935764.2935792

Keywords

Online algorithms; competitive analysis; scheduling; buffer management; CIOQ switches; buffered crossbar switches

1. INTRODUCTION

In the widely used *Combined Input and Output Queued (CIOQ) switches*, packet buffers (queues) are placed at both input and output ports. An $N \times N$ CIOQ switch has N input ports and N output ports. Each input port is equipped with N queues, each of which corresponds to an output port, and each output port is equipped with only one queue. The switching fabric of the switch connects the input ports with the output ports and are used to transfer packets from the queues of input ports to the queues of output ports. Figure 1 depicts an example of a CIOQ switch.

When a packet arrives at a CIOQ switch, it is first tagged with the following information: the value that represents its class of service, i.e., its priority, the input port through which it enters the switch, and the output port through which it has to leave the switch. Packets proceed inside the switch in the following way. They are first stored in the queues of the input ports, such that each packet is stored in the queue that corresponds to its output port. After that, they are transferred from input to output ports through the switching fabric, and reside in the queues of the output ports until they are eventually sent out of the switch. However, queues inside the switch are of limited capacities and there may be bursts of packets arriving which exceed the capacities. Thus, queues may overflow. Typically, packets are transferred through the switching fabric with a rate that is S times the rate of transmission, i.e., they are transferred through the switching fabric over S cycles of speed in each time step. We call S the speedup of the switch. It is worth noting here that we consider non-FIFO queues, i.e., packets can be stored in and released from queues in any arbitrary order.

Closely related to CIOQ switches, another type of switch architecture, the so-called *buffered crossbar switches*, is obtained by adding further queues at the crosspoints of the switching fabric. More specifically, for every queue at the input ports, an additional queue is placed at the switching fabric and dedicated to accommodate packets that are transferred from the input queue before they later on are transferred further to the corresponding output port. The number of those crossbar queues is proportional to the number of crosspoints, i.e., N^2, but it has been shown that the adoption of crossbar queues significantly decreases the

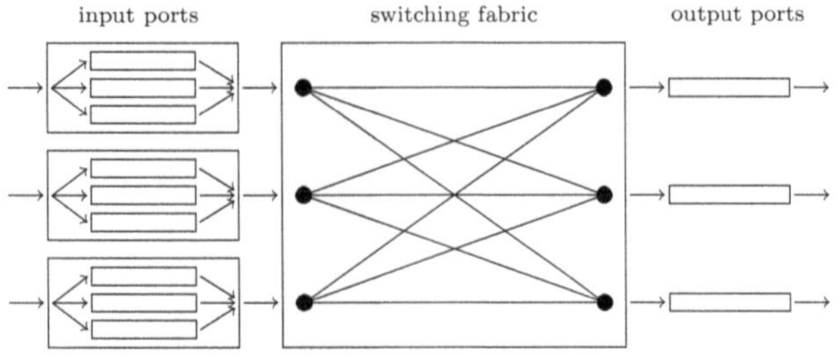

Figure 1: CIOQ switch — An example with $N = 3$

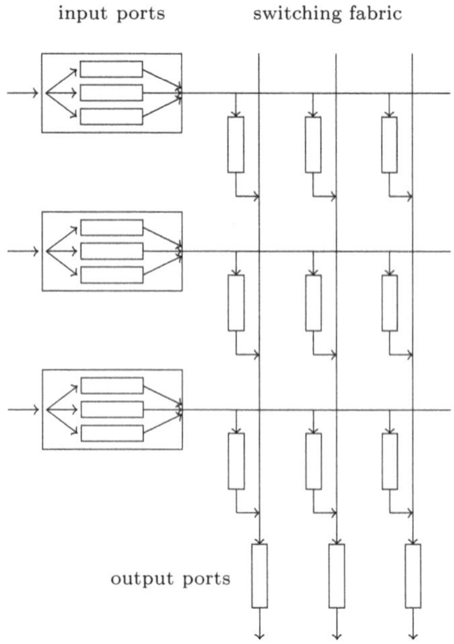

Figure 2: Buffered crossbar switch — An example with $N = 3$

scheduling overhead of CIOQ switches. Figure 2 depicts an example of a buffered crossbar switch.

Packet scheduling in both CIOQ and buffered crossbar switches has been extensively studied in the networking literature (see, e.g., [9, 10]). The design and analysis of scheduling algorithms in that line of research is mostly based on prior assumptions about the traffic distribution, e.g., Poisson-like distributions. However, it has been shown that Internet traffics do not necessarily adhere to such particular distributions (see, e.g., [26, 28]). We do not make any prior assumptions about the arrival behavior of packets, and instead resort to the framework of competitive analysis [27], which is the typical worst-case analysis used to assess the performance of *online* algorithms, i.e., algorithms whose input is revealed piece by piece over time, and the decision they make in each time step is irrevocable.

In competitive analysis, the benefit, in our case the switch's throughput, of an online algorithm is compared to the benefit of an optimal algorithm OPT which is assumed to know the entire input sequence in advance. An online algorithm ONL is called *c-competitive* if, for each input sequence σ, the benefit of OPT over σ is at most c times the benefit of ONL over σ. The value c is also called the *competitive ratio* of ONL.

1.1 Our Contribution

Our objective in the CIOQ model is twofold: to devise online algorithms that are both competitive and efficient. All online algorithms known for this problem are based on computing a maximum matching in each scheduling cycle, and thus are far from being efficient for real-world switches. We present new algorithms that are significantly more efficient and yet achieve the best competitive ratios known for this problem.

In each scheduling cycle, a bipartite graph is induced from the current configuration of the input and output queues, where the vertices of the left-hand side correspond to the input ports, and the vertices of the right-hand side correspond to the output ports. An edge (i, j) indicates that a packet can be transferred from the i-th input port to the j-th output port. Clearly, a matching in this graph corresponds to an admissible schedule for the current scheduling cycle.

We present two online algorithms in this model: Greedy Matching (GM) for the unit-value case, i.e., where all packets have the same value, and Preemptive Greedy (PG) for the general-value case. Both algorithms are based on greedy maximal matching computations, i.e., we construct a matching incrementally by adding edges, one by one, until no more edges can be added. This is much more efficient than computing the maximum matchings that have been used in previous works. Moreover, computing maximal matchings complies more with the current practice in distributed systems where packet scheduling has to perform in real time.

With respect to competitiveness, we show in Section 2.1 that GM is 3-competitive for any speedup, and thus it achieves the best competitive ratio known for this problem [22]. In Section 2.2, we show that PG has a competitive ratio of $3 + 2\sqrt{2} \approx 5.828$ for any speedup, which improves upon the previously known competitive ratio of 6 [23].

To obtain these results in an elegant way, we manipulate the queues of an optimal offline algorithm such that certain invariants in relation to our online algorithms are maintained. The techniques we use in the analysis of GM and PG also allow us to achieve improved upper bounds in the related model of buffered crossbar switches. For the unit-value case of this model, Kesselman et al. [20] present a greedy algorithm, which we call Crossbar Greedy Unit (CGU), with a competitive ratio of 4 for any speedup. We improve on this result and show that CGU is indeed 3-competitive. For the general-value case, they give an algorithm that is 16.24-competitive for any speedup. We present a slightly different algorithm, Crossbar Preemptive Greedy (CPG), and show that it achieves a competitive ratio of $12 + 2\sqrt{2} \approx 14.828$ for any speedup.

A similar analysis technique has been successfully used by Jeż et al. [18] for other packet scheduling related problems. However, in that work the buffer is manipulated in such a way that the optimal algorithm and the online algorithm always have an identical buffer content. In our proofs, we maintain different invariants.

1.2 Related Work

For the general-value case of CIOQ switches with FIFO queues, i.e., packets are stored and released in order of their arrival, Kesselman and Rosén [22] give two algorithms with competitive ratios of $4 \cdot S$ and $8 \cdot \min\{k, 2 \log \alpha\}$, where k is the number of distinct packet values and α is the ratio between the largest and the smallest packet value. The latter result was improved by Azar and Richter [7] where they give an algorithm with a competitive ratio of 8 for any speedup. Kesselman et al. [21] show that this algorithm is 7.47-competitive. For the buffered crossbar model with FIFO queues, Kesselman et al. [19] give a 19.95-competitive algorithm for any speedup.

The model of input queued switches (IQ) consists of m queues of the same capacity B and one output port. It is worth noticing that CIOQ switches generalize this model since if the speedup is 1 and only one input port is in use, CIOQ and IQ switches become equivalent. In the unit-value case of the IQ model, Azar and Richter [6] provide a lower bound of $2-1/m$ on the competitive ratio of any deterministic algorithm. Clearly, this lower bound carries over to the CIOQ model. Further results on the IQ model can be found in [3, 4, 5, 8, 17].

The problem of packet scheduling (also known as buffer management) has also been studied under several other models. For example, the multi-queue model with shared memory [1, 14, 15], the multi-queue model with class segregation [2], the single-queue (FIFO) model [12], and the bounded delay model, where packets have deadlines besides their values [11, 24]. Comprehensive and up-to-date surveys on this problem and its variants can be found in [13, 16, 25].

1.3 Models and Notations

We consider a CIOQ switch with N input ports and N output ports. Each input port has N queues and each output port has one queue. We call the queues at the input ports the *input queues* and those at the output ports the *output queues*. An input queue that is placed at input port i ($i = 1, \dots, N$) and corresponds to output port j ($j = 1, \dots, N$) is denoted by Q_{ij}. An output queue that is placed at output port j ($j = 1, \dots, N$) is denoted by Q_j. For any input or output queue Q, the capacity of Q is denoted by $B(Q)$, and $Q(t)$ denotes the set of packets that reside in Q at time t. All queues in the switch are non-FIFO, i.e., packets may be stored in and released from queues in any arbitrary order.

An input instance of this problem is a sequence of packets arriving at the switch in an online manner, i.e., packets that arrive at time t are not known before t. All packets have the same size. For each packet p in the input sequence, $v(p)$, $\text{arr}(p)$, $\text{in}(p)$, and $\text{out}(p)$ denote p's value, arrival time, input port, and output port, respectively, where $\text{in}(p)$ and $\text{out}(p)$ take on values between 1 and N.

Time is discretized into steps of unit length, and each of these time steps is divided into three phases; namely, arrival, scheduling and transmission phases. In the *arrival phase*, arbitrarily many packets may arrive at the switch. An arriving packet p is either *accepted* and thus inserted in queue Q_{ij}, where $i = \text{in}(p)$ and $j = \text{out}(p)$, or it is *rejected*, i.e., discarded.

In the *scheduling phase*, a set of packets that are stored in input queues are transferred to their corresponding output queues through the switching fabric of the switch. These transfers take place in internal time cycles which we call the *scheduling cycles*. We say that a switch has a speedup S when it is capable of performing S scheduling cycles within a single time step. we denote the s-th cycle of time step t by $t[s]$, for $s = 1, \dots, S$. In any scheduling cycle, a matching between input and output ports is computed, such that at most one packet is released from each input port and at most one packet is admitted to each output port. More specifically, when a packet p is transferred from queue Q_{ij} in scheduling cycle $t[s]$, it is forwarded through the switching fabric to queue Q_j, and no packet except p is released from input port i or forwarded to output port j in $t[s]$.

Finally, in the *transmission phase*, at most one packet is sent out from each output queue, i.e., transmitted to its next destination on the network.

Preemption is allowed, i.e., a packet that was previously inserted into a queue can be *preempted*, i.e., discarded, before it is sent. Therefore, a packet may be lost in one of two occasions: rejection upon its arrival, or preemption after getting stored in a queue.

The benefit made by an online algorithm ONL on an input sequence σ is denoted by $\text{ONL}(\sigma)$, and is defined as the total value of packets that ONL sends from the output queues. We aim at maximizing this benefit. An algorithm that knows the entire input beforehand and makes the maximum benefit on any sequence is denoted as OPT. An online algorithm ONL is *c-competitive* if $\text{OPT}(\sigma) \leq c \cdot \text{ONL}(\sigma)$ for any input sequence σ.

Finally, the time that precedes the first arrival of the sequence is denoted as time 0. We assume that the queues of any algorithm are all empty at time 0.

Buffered crossbar switches are obtained by adding further queues at the crosspoints of the switching fabric. A crossbar queue that is placed at the crosspoint of input port i ($i = 1, \dots, N$) and output port j ($j = 1, \dots, N$) is denoted by C_{ij}. Again, all queues in the switch are non-FIFO, i.e., packets may be stored in and released from queues in any arbitrary order.

All other notations and conventions of the CIOQ model hold also for the buffered crossbar model. However, each cycle of the scheduling phase in the buffered crossbar model is divided into two subphases: the *input subphase* and the *output subphase*. In the input subphase, packets can be transferred from any input queue Q_{ij} to its corresponding crossbar queue C_{ij}, such that at most one packet is transferred from each input port i. In the output subphase, packets can be transferred from any crossbar queue C_{ij} to its corresponding output queue Q_j, such that at most one packet is transferred to each output port j.

2. CIOQ SWITCHES

2.1 Unit-Value Case

In this case, all packets have the same value 1. Thus, our goal is to maximize the number of transmitted packets. In the following, we present the Greedy Matching algorithm (GM).

> **Arrival phase:** For every arriving packet p with $\text{in}(p) = i$ and $\text{out}(p) = j$, accept p if Q_{ij} is not full; otherwise, reject p.
>
> **Scheduling phase:** In every scheduling cycle $t[s]$, a bipartite graph $G_{t[s]} = (U, V, E)$ is induced from the current configuration of the switch, where $U = \{u_1, \dots, u_N\}$, $V = \{v_1, \dots, v_N\}$ and an edge $(u_i, v_j) \in E$ if and only if the input queue Q_{ij} is not empty and the output queue Q_j is not full at $t[s]$.
>
> A greedy matching $M_{t[s]}$ is then computed on $G_{t[s]}$ in the following way: Start with an empty

matching and iterate over all edges of E. Add an edge e to the current matching if e does not violate the matching property.

After $M_{t[s]}$ is computed, for each edge $(u_i, v_j) \in M_{t[s]}$, the head packet of Q_{ij} is transferred to Q_j.

Transmission phase: For every non-empty output queue Q_j, send the packet at the head of Q_j.

The next theorem shows that GM is 3-competitive for any speedup.

THEOREM 1. *The competitive ratio of* GM *is at most 3 for any speedup.*

From now on, we fix an input sequence σ, and, for any input or output queue Q, we reserve the notation Q for the online algorithm and use Q^* to denote the corresponding queue of the offline algorithm OPT.

First, without loss of generality, we assume that OPT is greedy in transmission events, i.e, it sends a packet from an output queue as long as its queue is not empty. Obviously, as OPT knows in advance which packets it is going to send, holding packets back in output queues, rather than sending them as early as possible, cannot improve its benefit.

Now, we modify OPT in a way that does not decrease its benefit of σ. Specifically, at the end of each scheduling cycle $t[s]$, i.e., immediately after OPT performs its scheduling policy, we apply the following two modifications on the configuration of OPT in the given order:

MODIFICATION 2.1.1. *Suppose that* GM *transfers a packet from Q_{ij} and* OPT *does not transfer any packet from Q^*_{ij} in $t[s]$. If Q^*_{ij} is not empty in $t[s]$, we release a packet p from Q^*_{ij} and send it directly out of the switch, i.e., through an imaginary channel. In this case, p is called a* privileged packet of Type 1 *and it contributes to the benefit of the optimal algorithm.*

MODIFICATION 2.1.2. *Suppose that* OPT *transfers a packet p to Q^*_j and* GM *does not transfer any packet to Q_j in $t[s]$. If Q_j is not full in $t[s]$, we send p directly out of the switch. In this case, we call p a* privileged packet of Type 2 *and it contributes to the benefit of the optimal algorithm.*

Clearly, these modifications do not decrease the benefit of the optimal algorithm. They can only make it stronger by allowing it to send packets directly from input ports to outside the switch without being enqueued in output ports. The input and output queues will respectively become shorter in this case and thus the optimal algorithm may accept more new packets.

Before we continue, we introduce further notations. We call packets that OPT schedules through the normal channels, i.e., they are not privileged, *normal* packets. We use S^* and P^* to denote the sets of OPT's normal and privileged packets, respectively. Clearly, the benefit of OPT is given by $|P^*| + |S^*|$. We also use S to denote the set of packets sent by GM. Thus, we want to show that $|P^*| + |S^*| \leq 3|S|$.

We now show how to derive the competitive ratio of 3. First, we show in Lemma 1 how Modifications 2.1.1 and 2.1.2 are used to preserve the following invariant: At any time, each queue in GM is no shorter than its counterpart in OPT. Therefore, for any time step t and output port j, if OPT sends a packet from j in t, GM must also send a packet from j in t. Hence, $|S^*| \leq |S|$. After that, we show by Lemma 3 that $|P^*| \leq 2|S|$. Thus, the proof of Theorem 1 follows directly from these two lemmas.

LEMMA 1. *For any $i, j \in \{1, \ldots, N\}$ and any time t, the following inequalities hold:*

I1. $|Q^*_{ij}(t)| \leq |Q_{ij}(t)|$

I2. $|Q^*_j(t)| \leq |Q_j(t)|$

PROOF. Inequalities I1 and I2 can be shown by a simple induction over time. Let the induction base be at time 0, i.e., before the sequence starts. All queues are empty at this time and thus I1 and I2 hold. Assume now that they hold for any time up to time $t-1$. We next show that they hold for t as well.

Clearly, queues change in arrival, scheduling and transmission events only. So, we assume that t is the time immediately after an event τ that is either an arrival, scheduling or transmission event.

Assume τ is an arrival event. Clearly, output queues do not change in arrival events and thus I2 holds for this case. For I1, the only critical case is when the arriving packet is rejected by GM and accepted by OPT. However, the input queue of GM must be full in this case and thus I1 still holds.

Now, let τ be a scheduling event. Here, the only critical case for I1 is when GM transfers a packet from Q_{ij} while OPT does not transfer anything from Q^*_{ij}. However, either Q^*_{ij} is empty in this case or it cannot happen due to Modification 2.1.1. For I2, the only critical case is when OPT inserts a packet into Q^*_j while GM does not insert anything into Q_j. However, either Q_j is full in this case or it cannot happen due to Modification 2.1.2.

Finally, assume τ is a transmission event. Clearly, the input queues do not change in transmission events and thus I1 holds for this case. For I2, the only critical case is when GM sends a packet from Q_j while OPT does not send anything from Q^*_j. However, since we assume that OPT is greedy at sending, its output queue must be empty in this case and thus I2 still holds. □

The following lemma shows that if Modification 2.1.2 takes place, GM must transfer a packet from the same input port.

LEMMA 2. *Suppose that, in $t[s]$,* OPT *transfers a packet p from Q^*_{ij} to Q^*_j and* GM *does not transfer any packet to Q_j. If Q_j is not full in $t[s]$, then* GM *transfers a packet p' from $Q_{ij'}$ in $t[s]$, where $j' \neq j$.*

PROOF. Recall the bipartite graph $G_{t[s]}$ and the corresponding matching $M_{t[s]}$ which are induced from the configuration of GM right before performing the scheduling cycle $t[s]$.

Assume that Q_j is not full in $t[s]$. By Inequality I1 of Lemma 1, since OPT transfers p from Q^*_{ij} in $t[s]$, GM must have at least one packet in Q_{ij}. Therefore, an edge (u_i, v_j) must be in E. Nevertheless, since GM does not transfer any packet to Q_j, (u_i, v_j) is not in $M_{t[s]}$. Since $M_{t[s]}$ is a maximal matching, there must exist an edge $(u_i, v_{j'})$, for $j' \neq j$, such that $(u_i, v_{j'}) \in M_{t[s]}$. Hence, a packet p' is transferred from $Q_{ij'}$ in $t[s]$. □

LEMMA 3. *The following inequality holds:*

$$|P^*| \leq 2\,|S| \ .$$

PROOF. We carry out the following mapping scheme from P^* to S in each scheduling cycle $t[s]$.

1. Let p be a privileged packet of Type 1 that is sent by OPT from Q^*_{ij} in $t[s]$. By Modification 2.1.1, GM transfers a packet p' from Q_{ij} in $t[s]$. Map p to p'.

2. Let p be a privileged packet of Type 2 that is sent by OPT from Q^*_{ij}. By Lemma 2, GM transfers a packet p' from $Q_{ij'}$ in $t[s]$, where $j' \neq j$. Map p to p'.

Clearly, this mapping scheme is feasible, i.e., each packet $p \in P^*$ is mapped to a packet $q \in S$. Furthermore, at most two privileged packets can be mapped to each packet $q \in S$. To see that, let q be a packet transferred by GM from Q_{ij} in a scheduling cycle $t[s]$. Clearly, q can get mapped only in $t[s]$, provided that OPT sends privileged packets in this time. By Modifications 2.1.1 and 2.1.2, OPT can send at most 2 privileged packets from input port i in $t[s]$: one of Type 1 if OPT's queue of Q^*_{ij} is not empty, and one of Type 2 if it transfers a packet from another queue $Q^*_{ij'}$. Thus, these two privileged packets are mapped to q. □

2.2 General-Value Case

For the case of arbitrary packet values, we present the Preemptive Greedy algorithm (PG) that is a variant of a 6-competitive algorithm given by Kesselman and Rosén [23]. We show next that PG has a competitive ratio of $3 + 2\sqrt{2} \approx 5.828$ for any speedup.

Before we describe PG formally, we introduce further notations. Let $g_{ij}(t)$ denote the packet with the greatest value in Q_{ij} at time t, and $l_{ij}(t)$ (resp. $l_j(t)$) denote the packet with the least value in Q_{ij} (resp. Q_j) at time t. Additionally, let $\beta \geq 1$ be a parameter of the algorithm that will be determined later.

Arrival phase: If a packet p arrives at time t with $\text{in}(p) = i$ and $\text{out}(p) = j$, accept p if

$$|Q_{ij}(t)| < B(Q_{ij}) \bigvee v(l_{ij}(t)) < v(p) \ ;$$

otherwise, reject p. If p is accepted while $|Q_{ij}(t)| = B(Q_{ij})$, then $l_{ij}(t)$ is preempted.

Scheduling phase: In every scheduling cycle $t[s]$, a weighted bipartite graph $G_{t[s]} = (U, V, E, w)$ is induced from the current configuration of the switch, where $U = \{u_1, \ldots, u_N\}$, $V = \{v_1, \ldots, v_N\}$, an edge $(u_i, v_j) \in E$ if and only if

$$|Q_{ij}(t[s])| > 0 \bigwedge \Big(|Q_j(t[s])| < B(Q_j) \bigvee v(g_{ij}(t[s])) > \beta\, v(l_j(t[s])) \Big) \ ,$$

and the weight of (u_i, v_j) is given by $w(u_i, v_j) = v(g_{ij}(t[s]))$.

A greedy matching $M_{t[s]}$ is then computed on $G_{t[s]}$ in the following way: Start with an empty matching and iterate over all edges of E in a descending order of their weights. Add an edge e to the current matching if e does not violate the matching property.

After $M_{t[s]}$ is computed, for each edge $(u_i, v_j) \in M_{t[s]}$, the packet $g_{ij}(t[s])$ is transferred to Q_j. If $g_{ij}(t[s])$ is transferred while $|Q_j(t[s])| = B(Q_j)$, then $l_j(t[s])$ is preempted.

Transmission phase: For every non-empty output queue Q_j, send the packet with the greatest value in Q_j.

As described above, unlike the algorithm given in [23], PG computes a maximal weighted matching in each scheduling cycle rather than a maximum weighted matching.

THEOREM 2. *For $\beta = \sqrt{2}+1$, the competitive ratio of* PG *is at most $3 + 2\sqrt{2} \approx 5.828$ for any speedup.*

First, we fix an input sequence σ. Without loss of generality, we make the following assumptions about OPT:

A1. OPT is greedy in scheduling and transmission events, i.e, when it transfers or sends a packet p from an input or output queue, it chooses p as the one with the greatest value in the queue.

A2. OPT is work-conserving at output ports, i.e., it sends a packet from every non-empty output queue in each transmission event.

Obviously, as OPT knows in advance which packets it is going to send, it does not matter for OPT in which order these packets are released from queues or when they are transmitted from output queues. Now, based on the greediness of both PG and OPT, we make another harmless assumption:

A3. In all input and output queues, PG and OPT store packets in the order of their values, where the packet with the greatest value is at the queue's head and the one with the least value is at the queue's tail.

Similarly to the unit-value case, we modify OPT without decreasing its benefit. Specifically, at the end of each scheduling cycle $t[s]$, i.e., immediately after OPT performs its scheduling policy, we apply the following modifications on the configurations of OPT:

MODIFICATION 2.2.1. *Suppose that* PG *transfers a packet from Q_{ij} and* OPT *does not transfer any packet from Q^*_{ij} in $t[s]$. If Q^*_{ij} is not empty in $t[s]$, we release the head packet p of Q^*_{ij}, i.e., the packet with the greatest value in Q^*_{ij}, and send it directly out of the switch. In this case, we call p* a privileged packet of Type 1 *and it contributes to the benefit of the optimal algorithm.*

MODIFICATION 2.2.2. *If* OPT *transfers a packet p to Q^*_j and* PG *transfers a packet q to Q_j in $t[s]$ with $v(q) < v(p)$, we send p directly out of the switch. In this case, we call p* a privileged packet of Type 2 *and it contributes to the benefit of the optimal algorithm.*

MODIFICATION 2.2.3. *Suppose that* OPT *transfers a packet p to Q^*_j and* PG *does not transfer any packet to Q_j in $t[s]$. If Q_j is not full in $t[s]$ or $v(p) > \beta\, v(l_j(t[s]))$, we send p directly out of the switch. In this case, we call p* a privileged packet of Type 3 *and it contributes to the benefit of the optimal algorithm.*

Note that Modifications 2.2.2 and 2.2.3 are closely related and dealing with them separately is only for ease of exposition.

Let $\delta_{ij}(k,t)$ (resp. $\delta_j(k,t)$) denote the packet at position k in Q_{ij} (resp. Q_j) at time t, where position 1 corresponds to the head of the queue. Let $\delta^*_{ij}(k,t)$ and $\delta^*_j(k,t)$ be the corresponding notations for OPT. The following lemma shows that each packet in an OPT's input queue is aligned to a packet of the same or greater value in the corresponding input queue of PG, and each packet p in an OPT's output queue is aligned to a packet q in the corresponding output queue of PG, where $v(p) \leq \beta v(q)$.

LEMMA 4. *For any $i, j \in \{1, \ldots, N\}$ and any time t, the following inequalities hold:*

I1. $v(\delta^*_{ij}(k,t)) \leq v(\delta_{ij}(k,t))$, *for* $k = 1, \ldots, |Q^*_{ij}(t)|$

I2. $v(\delta^*_j(k,t)) \leq \beta\, v(\delta_j(k,t))$, *for* $k = 1, \ldots, |Q^*_j(t)|$

PROOF. Inequalities I1 and I2 can be shown by a simple induction over time. Let the induction base be at time 0, i.e., before the sequence starts. All queues are empty at this time and thus I1 and I2 hold. Assume now that they hold for any time up to time $t-1$. We next show that they hold for time t as well.

Clearly, input queues change only in arrival, scheduling or transmission events. So, we assume that t is the time immediately after an event τ which is either an arrival, scheduling or transmission event. In the following, we will argue only for *I*2. The argument for *I*1 is analogous, and we will put the main differences between [ ] at the respective positions.

Before we start, we say that a packet $p \in Q^*_j(t)$ is in a legal alignment, if p is aligned in time t to a packet $q \in Q_j(t)$ with $v(p) \leq \beta v(q)$. Clearly, it suffices to show that any packet $p \in Q^*_j(t)$ is in a legal alignment. We distinguish between two cases:

Case I2.1 $p \in Q^*_j(t-1)$. Thus, by induction, p is aligned in $t-1$ to a packet $q \in Q_j(t-1)$ with $v(p) \leq \beta v(q)$ [resp. $v(p) \leq v(q)$]. We need to show in this case that p either remains in the same alignment in t or it changes to another legal alignment. Assumption A3 implies that any packet p from $t-1$ either remains in its position in time t, moves one step ahead (if a packet, that is in front of p, is sent from the queue) or moves one step back (if a new packet is inserted in front of p).

Assume now that p remains in its position in t but q moves. Note that neither q nor any packet in front of it can be released from the queue in time t; otherwise, by Assumption A2 [resp. Modification 2.2.1], some packet would be also released from Q^*_j, which makes p move one step ahead. Thus, q can only move back in t. In this case, however, the packet q' that is directly in front of q is aligned with p. Since $v(q) \leq v(q')$, p is again in a legal alignment.

Next, assume that p moves one step ahead in t. In this case, p either remains in a legal alignment with q (in case q moves ahead as well) or it aligns with a packet that is in front of q in $t-1$ and thus makes again a legal alignment.

Finally, assume that p moves one step back in t. Thus, a packet p' must be inserted in front of p, implying that $v(p) \leq v(p')$. Note that the insertion of p' happens only in one of two cases: (i) if a packet r with $v(r) \geq v(p')$ is inserted into Q_j (by Modifications 2.2.2), or (ii) if Q_j is full in t and $v(p') \leq \beta v(l_j(t))$ (by Modifications 2.2.3). Let k denote the position of the alignment (p,q) in time $t-1$. In case (i), either (1) r is inserted in a position $k' \leq k$, and thus p will be aligned again with q in t, or (2) r is inserted in a position $k' > k$, and thus p will be aligned with some packet q' in t. Clearly, the second case implies that $v(r) \leq v(q')$. Since $v(p) \leq v(p') \leq v(r)$, then $v(p) \leq v(q')$. Hence, p is in a legal alignment in either case.

In case (ii), since Q_j is full in t, p must be aligned with some packet q' in t. Clearly, $v(l_j(t)) \leq v(q')$. Moreover, since $v(p') \leq \beta v(l_j(t))$, $v(p) \leq v(p') \leq \beta v(q')$. Thus, p makes a legal alignment with q'. [The respective cases for I1 are: case (i) p' is also inserted into Q_{ij}, thus $r = p'$ in the above argument, and case (ii) Q_{ij} is full in t and $v(l_j(t)) \geq v(p')$.]

Case I2.2 $p \notin Q^*_j(t-1)$. Thus, p is a new packet that is inserted in the queue in time t. Again, note that the insertion of p into Q^*_j happens only in one of two cases: (i) if a packet r with $v(r) \geq v(p)$ is inserted into Q_j (by Modification 2.2.2), or (ii) if Q_j is full in t and $v(p) \leq \beta v(l_j(t))$ (by Modifications 2.2.3). In case (ii), since Q_j is full in t, p must be aligned with a packet q in t. Since $v(p) \leq \beta v(l_j(t))$, $v(p) \leq \beta v(q)$. Thus, p makes a legal alignment with q.

Now, consider case (i). Let k denote the position at which p is inserted. If $k = 1$, p is aligned with the most valuable packet in Q_j in t. Since r is in Q_j in time t, p must be aligned with a packet of value at least $v(r) \geq v(p)$. Now suppose $k > 1$. Let p' be the packet that is directly in front of p in t. Clearly, $p' \in Q^*_j(t-1)$ and $v(p) \leq v(p')$. Furthermore, let q' be the packet aligned with p' in time $t-1$. Thus, $v(p) \leq v(p') \leq \beta v(q')$. Additionally, let q be the packet at position k in Q_j in time $t-1$ (assume $q = \emptyset$, if this is an empty position in Q_j).

Note that (1) r is inserted in position k, and thus p will be aligned with r in t, (2) r is inserted in a position $k' < k$, and thus p will be aligned with q' in t, or (3) r is inserted in a position $k' > k$, and thus p will be aligned with q in t. Clearly, the last case implies that $q \neq \emptyset$ and that $v(q) \geq v(r) \geq v(p)$. Therefore, we have $v(p) \leq v(r)$ in the first case, $v(p) \leq \beta v(q')$ in the second, and $v(p) \leq v(q)$ in the third. Hence, p is in a legal alignment in any case.

[The respective cases for I1 are: case (i) p is also inserted into Q_{ij}, thus $r = p$ in the above argument, and case (ii) Q_{ij} is full in t and $v(l_j(t)) \geq v(p)$.] □

Similarly to the analysis of the unit-value case, granting OPT with privileged packets must be done carefully, so that the total value of privileged packets remains within a certain factor of the total value of packets that PG sends. Obviously, each privileged packet of Type 1 can be paired with a packet that PG transfers from the same input queue. In the following two lemmas, we show that such a pairing is feasible for privileged packets of Type 2 and 3 as well. Of course, as packets of PG may be preempted after being transferred to output queues, some pairs can be destructed. However, we will show in Lemma 7 how to fix this problem.

LEMMA 5. *If* OPT *transfers a packet p from Q^*_{ij} to Q^*_j and* PG *transfers a packet q to Q_j in $t[s]$ with $v(q) < v(p)$, then* PG *transfers a packet p' from $Q_{ij'}$ in $t[s]$ with $j' \neq j$ and $v(p') \geq v(p)$.*

PROOF. Recall the bipartite graph $G_{t[s]}$ and the corresponding matching $M_{t[s]}$ which are induced from the configuration of PG right before performing the scheduling cycle $t[s]$.

By Inequality I1 of Lemma 4, since OPT transfers p from Q^*_{ij} in $t[s]$, PG must have at the head of Q_{ij} a packet r with $v(r) \geq v(p)$. Obviously, $v(r) > v(q)$ and thus $q \neq r$. As a result, q must be transferred from an input queue $Q_{i'j}$ with $i' \neq i$. Moreover, since q is inserted in Q_j, the edge $(u_{i'}, v_j) \in E$, and either $|Q_j(t[s])| < B(Q_j)$ or $v(q) > \beta v(l_j(t[s]))$. Thus, it holds also for r that either $|Q_j(t[s])| < B(Q_j)$ or $v(r) > \beta v(l_j(t[s]))$. Hence, the edge $(u_i, v_j) \in E$ as well, and clearly $w(u_i, v_j) \geq w(u_{i'}, v_j)$. This implies that (u_i, v_j) is considered before $(u_{i'}, v_j)$ during the computation of $M_{t[s]}$. However, since (u_i, v_j) is not in the matching, the node u_i must have been matched before considering (u_i, v_j), and thus there exists an edge $(u_i, v_{j'})$, for $j' \neq j$, that is inserted in the matching before considering (u_i, v_j). As a result, a packet p' is transferred from $Q_{ij'}$, and it must hold that $w(u_i, v_{j'}) \geq w(u_i, v_j)$. Hence, $v(p') \geq v(r) \geq v(p)$. □

The proof of the following lemma is analogous to that of Lemma 5.

LEMMA 6. *Suppose that, in $t[s]$, OPT transfers a packet p from Q^*_{ij} to Q^*_j and PG does not transfer any packet to Q_j. If Q_j is not full in $t[s]$ or $v(p) > \beta v(l_j(t[s]))$, then PG transfers a packet p' from $Q_{ij'}$ in $t[s]$ with $j' \neq j$ and $v(p') \geq v(p)$.*

Now, recall Inequality I2 of Lemma 4. It implies that if OPT sends a packet of value v from some output queue at some time, PG must send a packet of at least v/β from the same output queue at the same time. Let S (resp. S^*) denote the set of all packets that PG (resp. OPT) sends from output queues. Thus,

$$\sum_{p \in S^*} v(p) \leq \beta \sum_{p \in S} v(p) \ .$$

Moreover, let P^* denote the set of all privileged packets, of all types, that OPT sends directly out of the switch. The next lemma shows that

$$\sum_{p \in P^*} v(p) \leq \frac{2\beta}{\beta - 1} \sum_{p \in S} v(p) \ .$$

Thus, we can conclude the competitive ratio of PG as follows

$$\begin{aligned} \text{OPT}(\sigma) &= \sum_{p \in S^*} v(p) + \sum_{p \in P^*} v(p) \\ &< \beta \sum_{p \in S} v(p) + \frac{2\beta}{\beta - 1} \sum_{p \in S} v(p) \\ &= \left(\beta + \frac{2\beta}{\beta - 1}\right) \text{PG}(\sigma) \ . \end{aligned}$$

Finally, it is easy to verify that the optimal value for β is $\sqrt{2} + 1$, resulting in a competitive ratio of $3 + 2\sqrt{2} \approx 5.828$.

LEMMA 7. *The following inequality holds:*

$$\sum_{p \in P^*} v(p) \leq \frac{2\beta}{\beta - 1} \sum_{p \in S} v(p) \ .$$

PROOF. We consider the following mapping scheme:

1. Let p be a privileged packet of Type 1 that is sent by OPT from Q^*_{ij} in scheduling cycle $t[s]$. By Modification 2.2.1, PG transfers a packet p' from Q_{ij} in $t[s]$, and by Inequality I1 of Lemma 4, $v(p) \leq v(p')$. Map p to p'.
2. Let p be a privileged packet of Type 2 that is sent by OPT from Q^*_{ij} in scheduling cycle $t[s]$. By Lemma 5, PG transfers a packet p' from $Q^*_{ij'}$ in $t[s]$ with $j' \neq j$ and $v(p) \leq v(p')$. Map p to p'.
3. Let p be a privileged packet of Type 3 that is sent by OPT from Q^*_{ij} in scheduling cycle $t[s]$. By Lemma 6, PG transfers a packet p' from $Q^*_{ij'}$ in $t[s]$ with $j' \neq j$ and $v(p) \leq v(p')$. Map p to p'.
4. Let q be a packet that is preempted from an output queue Q_j by another packet p'. For each privileged packet p that is mapped to q, re-map p to p'.

As shown above, this mapping scheme is feasible, i.e., each packet $p \in P^*$ is mapped to a packet $p' \in S$. Now, it remains to show that the total value of privileged packets that are mapped to each packet $p' \in S$ is at most $\frac{2\beta}{\beta-1} v(p')$.

For any packet $p' \in S$, p' can get mapped in two events: when it is scheduled and when it preempts a packet from an output queue.

Assume that p' is scheduled from $Q_{ij'}$ to $Q_{j'}$ during scheduling cycle $t[s]$. Now, assume that OPT transfers a packet from Q^*_{ij} to Q^*_j during $t[s]$. Clearly, we can only send one privileged packet p_1 of Type 1 from $Q^*_{ij'}$ in $t[s]$ (in case $j \neq j'$). Furthermore, we can only send from Q^*_{ij} either a privileged packet p_2 of Type 2 (in case PG transfers a packet q to Q_j with $v(q) < v(p_2)$), or a privileged packet p_3 of Type 3 (in case PG does not transfer any packet to Q_j). Hence, at most two privileged packets may be sent during $t[s]$ from each input port i. Since privileged packets are mapped only to packets that are transferred by PG from the same input port during the same scheduling cycle, at most two packets from $\{p_1, p_2, p_3\}$ can be mapped to p'. Furthermore, as shown in the mapping scheme above, the value of any of these privileged packets is at most the value of p'. Thus, the total value of privileged packets that are mapped to p' when it is scheduled is at most $2\,v(p')$.

Assume now that p' is the m-th packet in a chain of packets $q_0, \ldots, q_m$ in which packet q_n preempts packet q_{n-1}, for $1 \leq n \leq m$. Let $x(q_n)$ denote the total value of privileged packets that are mapped to a packet q_n after it preempts q_{n-1}. Thus, the total value of privileged packets that are mapped to p' is given by $x(q_m)$. Note that q_0 does not preempt any packet and thus the total value of privileged packets that are mapped to q_0 is at most $2\,v(q_0)$. Thus, $x(q_m)$ can be given by the following recursion:

$$\begin{aligned} &x(q_0) \leq 2\,v(q_0) \ \text{and} \\ &x(q_n) \leq 2\,v(q_n) + x(q_{n-1}) \ , \ \text{for } 0 < n \leq m \ . \end{aligned}$$

Solving this recursion, we obtain that

$$x(q_m) \leq 2 \sum_{n=0}^{m} v(q_n) \ .$$

Note also that $v(q_{n-1}) \leq v(q_n)/\beta$, for $1 \leq n \leq m$. Hence, we can rewrite $x(q_m)$ as follows:

$$\begin{aligned} x(q_m) &\leq 2v(q_m) \sum_{n=0}^{m} (1/\beta)^n \\ &\leq \frac{2\beta}{\beta - 1} v(q_m) \ . \end{aligned}$$

□

3. BUFFERED CROSSBAR SWITCHES

3.1 Unit-Value Case

For the case where all packets have value 1, Kesselman et al. [20] considered the following algorithm, which we call Crossbar Greedy Unit (CGU). The arrival and transmission phases of CGU are the same as those of GM (Section 2.1). In the scheduling phase, CGU works as follows.

> **Scheduling phase:** We divide every scheduling cycle $t[s]$ into two subphases:
>
> - **Input subphase**: For each input port i, choose an arbitrary input queue Q_{ij} which satisfies
>
> $$|Q_{ij}(t[s])| > 0 \bigwedge |C_{ij}(t[s])| < B(C_{ij}) ,$$
>
> and transfer its head packet.
>
> - **Output subphase**: For each output queue Q_j, choose an arbitrary crossbar queue C_{ij} which satisfies
>
> $$|Q_j(t[s])| < B(Q_j) \bigwedge |C_{ij}(t[s])| > 0 ,$$
>
> and transfer its head packet.

The next theorem shows that CGU is 3-competitive for any speedup.

THEOREM 3. *The competitive ratio of* CGU *is at most 3 for any speedup.*

First, we fix an input sequence σ. Again, we modify OPT in a way that does not decrease its benefit over σ. Specifically, at the end of each scheduling cycle $t[s]$, i.e., immediately after OPT performs its scheduling policy, we apply the following modifications on the configuration of OPT in the given order:

> MODIFICATION 3.1.1. *Suppose that* CGU *transfers a packet from Q_{ij} and* OPT *does not transfer any packet from $Q^*_{ij} \neq \emptyset$ in $t[s]$. We transfer a packet p from Q^*_{ij} in $t[s]$. If C^*_{ij} is not full in $t[s]$, p is transferred to C^*_{ij}. Otherwise, p is sent directly out of the switch. In either case, p is called a* privileged packet *and it contributes to the benefit of the optimal algorithm.*

> MODIFICATION 3.1.2. *Suppose that* CGU *transfers a packet to C_{ij} and* OPT *does not transfer any packet to C^*_{ij} in $t[s]$. If C^*_{ij} is not full in $t[s]$ and no privileged packet is transferred to C^*_{ij} by Modification 3.1.1 in $t[s]$ (possibly because* CGU *transfers from Q_{ij} while Q^*_{ij} is empty), we generate a new packet and insert it into C^*_{ij}. Such a new packet is called an* extra packet *of Type 1 and it contributes to the benefit of the optimal algorithm.*

> MODIFICATION 3.1.3. *Suppose that* OPT *transfers a packet from C^*_{ij} and* CGU *does not transfer any packet from C_{ij} in $t[s]$. If C_{ij} is not empty in $t[s]$, we generate a new packet and insert it into C^*_{ij}. Such a new packet is called an* extra packet *of Type 2 and it contributes to the benefit of the optimal algorithm.*

Note that extra packets are not used in the analysis of the algorithms presented in Section 2 for the CIOQ model. Next, we show how the above modifications are used to show a set of invariants that is different from the invariants shown in Section 2.1.

LEMMA 8. *For any time t and any $i, j \in \{1, \ldots, N\}$, the following inequalities hold:*

I1. $|Q_{ij}(t)| \geq |Q^*_{ij}(t)|$

I2. $|C^*_{ij}(t)| \geq |C_{ij}(t)|$

PROOF. We show Inequalities I1 and I2 by a simple induction over time. Let the induction base be at time 0, i.e., before the sequence starts. All queues are empty at this time and all inequalities hold. Assume now that they hold for any time up to time $t-1$. We next show that they hold for t as well.

Clearly, input and crossbar queues change only in arrival and scheduling events. So, we assume that t is the time immediately after an event τ which is either an arrival or a scheduling event.

Assume τ is an arrival event. Clearly, crossbar queues do not change in arrival events and thus I2 holds for this case. For I1, the only critical case is when the arriving packet is rejected by CGU and accepted by OPT. However, the input queue of CGU must be full in this case and thus I1 still holds.

Now, let τ be a scheduling event. Here, the only critical case for I1 is when CGU transfers a packet from Q_{ij} while OPT does not transfer any packet from Q^*_{ij}. However, either Q^*_{ij} is empty in this case or it cannot happen due to Modification 3.1.1. For I2, the first critical case is when CGU inserts a packet into C_{ij} while OPT does not insert any packet into C^*_{ij}. However, either C^*_{ij} is full in this case or it cannot happen due to Modification 3.1.2. The second critical case for I2 is when OPT transfers a packet from C^*_{ij} while CGU does not transfer any packet from C_{ij}. However, either C_{ij} is empty in this case or the size of C^*_{ij} does not decrease due to Modification 3.1.3. □

In the following, we use $S^*_{t[s]}$ to denote the set of OPT's *normal* packets in the input subphase of $t[s]$. These are packets that OPT schedules through the normal channels, i.e., they are not privileged, and are part of the original input sequence, i.e., they are not extra. On the other hand, we use $S_{t[s]}$ to denote the set of packets that CGU schedules in the input subphase of cycle $t[s]$, i.e., from input queues to crossbar queues.

LEMMA 9. *For any scheduling cycle $t[s]$, $|S^*_{t[s]}| \leq |S_{t[s]}|$.*

PROOF. We want to show that in the input subphase of any scheduling cycle $t[s]$, if OPT transfers a normal packet from an input port i, CGU also transfers a packet from i.

Assume that OPT transfers a normal packet p from Q^*_{ij} (to C^*_{ij}) in $t[s]$. Thus, by I1 and I2 of Lemma 8, Q_{ij} is not empty and C_{ij} is not full in $t[s]$ (Note that OPT would not schedule a packet to a full crossbar queue, as all packets are of the same value). Hence, CGU transfers a packet from either Q_{ij} or another $Q_{ij'}$ in $t[s]$. □

Let $P^*_{t[s]}$ denote the set of OPT's privileged and extra packets (of either type) that occur in scheduling cycle $t[s]$.

We consider the following mapping scheme from $P^*_{t[s]}$ to $S_{t[s]}$. For packets that are inserted in CGU's output queues, we use the notion of a *marked* packet. Initially, all packets are unmarked.

1. Let p be a privileged packet that is transferred by OPT from Q^*_{ij} in scheduling cycle $t[s]$. By Modification 3.1.1, CGU transfers a packet q from Q_{ij} in $t[s]$. Map p to q.

2. Let p be an extra packet of Type 1 that is inserted into C^*_{ij} in the input subphase of scheduling cycle $t[s]$. By Modification 3.1.2, CGU transfers a packet q into C_{ij} in $t[s]$. Map p to q.

3. Let p be an extra packet of Type 2 that is inserted into C^*_{ij} in the output subphase of scheduling cycle $t[s]$. By Modification 3.1.3, C_{ij} is not empty in $t[s]$, and OPT transfers a packet p' to Q^*_j. Thus, Q^*_j is not full right before $t[s]$. Now, let q be the first unmarked packet in Q_j, i.e., the nearest to the queue's head. Map p to q and then mark q. Note that q can be the packet that CGU may insert into Q_j in $t[s]$.

Next, we show that the mapping scheme is feasible, i.e., each packet $p \in P^*_{t[s]}$ is mapped to a packet $q \in S_{t[s]}$. Clearly, Steps 1 and 2 are feasible. We show now that Step 3 is feasible as well. Let $M_j(t)$ denote the set of marked packets in Q_j at time t, for any $1 \leq j \leq N$. We first show the following lemma.

LEMMA 10. *At any time t, $|M_j(t)| \leq |Q^*_j(t)|$.*

PROOF. We show the claim by induction over the scheduling and transmission events. Clearly, $M_j(t)$ and $Q^*_j(t)$ change only in these events.

Assume first that t is a transmission event. The only critical scenario in this event is that OPT sends a packet from Q^*_j while CGU does not send a marked packet. If that happens, then either CGU sends an unmarked packet or it does not send any packet at all. The first case cannot happen while $|M_j(t)| > 0$ since marked packets are always at the front of the queue. The second case is safe because it implies that Q_j is empty and thus $|M_j(t)| = 0$.

Now, assume that t is a scheduling event. The only critical scenario in this event is that a packet q is marked in Q_j while OPT does not insert any packet into Q^*_j. However, according to Step 3 of the mapping scheme, marking q implies that OPT transfers a packet p' from C^*_{ij} to Q^*_j. Thus, this scenario cannot happen in scheduling events. □

Now, to show that Step 3 of the mapping scheme is feasible, we need to show that at least one packet is unmarked in Q_j in the scheduling cycle $t[s]$. For the sake of contradiction, assume that all packets in Q_j are marked or Q_j is empty in $t[s]$. The first thing that follows from this assumption is that CGU does not insert any packet into Q_j in $t[s]$ (because otherwise the inserted packet would be initially unmarked).

Recall from Step 3 that C_{ij} is not empty in $t[s]$. Thus, since no packet is inserted into Q_j, Q_j must be full in $t[s]$. Hence, since all packets are marked by assumption, $|M_j(t)| = B(Q_j)$, where t is the time right before $t[s]$. Thus, by Lemma 10, $|Q^*_j(t)| = B(Q^*_j)$ as well. However, this contradicts with the fact that OPT inserts p' into Q^*_j in $t[s]$. Hence, at least one packet is unmarked in Q_j in the scheduling cycle $t[s]$, and thus Step 3 is feasible.

LEMMA 11. *For any scheduling cycle $t[s]$, $|P^*_{t[s]}| \leq 2\,|S_{t[s]}|$.*

PROOF. As shown above, the mapping scheme is feasible for each scheduling cycle $t[s]$. So, it remains to show that at most two packets from $P^*_{t[s]}$ are mapped to any packet $q \in S_{t[s]}$.

Consider a packet $q \in S_{t[s]}$. Let Q_{ij} be the input queue from which q is transferred in the scheduling cycle $t[s]$. Obviously, q may get mapped by: (i) a privileged packet p that is transferred from Q^*_{ij} in $t[s]$, (ii) an extra packet p' of Type 1 that is inserted into C^*_{ij} in the input subphase of $t[s]$, and (iii) an extra packet p'' of Type 2 that is inserted into $C^*_{i'j}$ in the output subphase of $t[s]$, with $i \neq i'$. Therefore, at most three packets can be mapped to q during its entire lifespan.

Assume now, for the sake of contradiction, that both p and p' are mapped to q. According to Modification 3.1.2, since an extra packet p' is inserted into C^*_{ij}, C^*_{ij} cannot be full in $t[s]$. However, by Modification 3.1.1, p must be transferred to C^*_{ij} in this case and not directly to outside the switch. Hence, by Modification 3.1.2, no extra packet is generated in $t[s]$ in this case and thus p' does not exist, leading to a contradiction. □

Now, as CGU does not preempt packets, each packet which CGU schedules in an input subphase must be eventually sent, and thus it contributes to the benefit of CGU. Hence, $\text{CGU}(\sigma) = \sum_{t[s]} |S_{t[s]}|$. Furthermore, note that $\text{OPT}(\sigma) = \sum_{t[s]} |S^*_{t[s]}| + |P^*_{t[s]}|$. Therefore, the proof of Theorem 3 follows immediately from Lemma 9 and 11.

3.2 General-Value Case

For the case of arbitrary packet values, we present the Crossbar Preemptive Greedy algorithm (CPG) that is a variant of a 16.24-competitive algorithm given by Kesselman et al. [20].

Recall the notations $g_{ij}(t)$, $l_{ij}(t)$, and $l_j(t)$ that we used with algorithm PG (Section 2.2). Let $gc_{ij}(t)$ and $lc_{ij}(t)$ be the corresponding notations for crossbar queue C_{ij}, i.e., the packet with the greatest value and the packet with the least value, respectively, in C_{ij} at time t. Additionally, let $\beta \geq 1$ and $\alpha \geq 1$ be two parameters of the algorithm that will be determined later. If $\beta = \alpha$, our algorithm will be the same as the algorithm given in [20]. However, we show that to minimize the competitive ratio for this algorithm, these two parameters must take on different values.

The arrival and transmission phases of CPG are the same as those of PG. In the scheduling phase, CPG works as follows.

Scheduling phase: We divide every scheduling cycle $t[s]$ into two subphases:

- **Input subphase**: For each input port i, let J be defined as follows:

$$J = \Big\{ j : |Q_{ij}(t[s])| > 0 \bigwedge \Big(|C_{ij}(t[s])| < B(C_{ij}) \bigvee v(g_{ij}(t[s])) > \beta\, v(lc_{ij}(t[s])) \Big) \Big\} \ .$$

  If $J \neq \emptyset$, choose Q_{ij} such that for all $j' \in J$,

$$j \in J \bigwedge v(g_{ij}(t[s])) \geq v(g_{ij'}(t[s])) \ .$$

  Transfer $g_{ij}(t[s])$ to C_{ij}. If $|C_{ij}(t[s])| = B(C_{ij})$, preempt $lc_{ij}(t[s])$ first.

- **Output subphase**: For each output queue Q_j, choose a crossbar queue C_{ij} such that for all $i' \neq i$,

$$|C_{ij}(t[s])| > 0 \bigwedge v(gc_{ij}(t[s])) \geq v(gc_{i'j}(t[s])) \ .$$

If the following condition is satisfied

$$|Q_j(t[s])| < B(Q_j) \bigvee v(gc_{ij}(t[s])) > \alpha\, v(l_j(t[s])),$$

transfer $gc_{ij}(t[s])$ to Q_j. If $|Q_j(t[s])| = B(Q_j)$, preempt $l_j(t[s])$ first.

Note that all ties in CPG are broken arbitrarily.

THEOREM 4. *For $\beta = 2\sqrt{2} - 1$ and $\alpha = 2\sqrt{2}$, the competitive ratio of* CPG *is at most $12 + 2\sqrt{2} \approx 14.828$ for any speedup.*

The proof of Theorem 4 is omitted due to space limitations.

4. REFERENCES

[1] W. Aiello, A. Kesselman, and Y. Mansour. Competitive buffer management for shared-memory switches. *ACM Transactions on Algorithms*, 5(1):Article 3, 2008.

[2] K. Al-Bawani and A. Souza. Buffer overflow management with class segregation. *Information Processing Letters*, 113(4):145–150, 2013.

[3] S. Albers and M. Schmidt. On the performance of greedy algorithms in packet buffering. *SIAM Journal on Computing*, 35(2):278–304, 2006.

[4] Y. Azar and A. Litichevskey. Maximizing throughput in multi-queue switches. *Algorithmica*, 45(1):69–90, 2006.

[5] Y. Azar and Y. Richter. The zero-one principle for switching networks. In *Proc. of the 36th ACM Symp. on Theory of Computing (STOC)*, pages 64–71, 2004.

[6] Y. Azar and Y. Richter. Management of multi-queue switches in QoS networks. *Algorithmica*, 43:81–96, 2005.

[7] Y. Azar and Y. Richter. An improved algorithm for CIOQ switches. *ACM Transactions on Algorithms*, 2(2):282–295, 2006.

[8] M. Bienkowski and A. Madry. Geometric aspects of online packet buffering: An optimal randomized algorithm for two buffers. In *Proc. of the 8th Latin American Symp. on Theoretical Informatics (LATIN)*, pages 252–263, 2008.

[9] S.-T. Chuang, A. Goel, N. McKeown, and B. Prabhakar. Matching output queueing with a combined input output queued switch. *IEEE Journal on Selected Areas in Communications*, 17:1030–1039, 1999.

[10] S.-T. Chuang, S. Iyer, and N. McKeown. Practical algorithms for performance guarantees in buffered crossbars. In *Proc. of the 24th IEEE Conf. on Computer Communications (INFOCOM)*, pages 981–991, 2005.

[11] M. Englert and M. Westermann. Considering suppressed packets improves buffer management in QoS switches. In *Proc. of the 18th Annual ACM-SIAM Symp. on Discrete Algorithms (SODA)*, pages 209–218, 2007.

[12] M. Englert and M. Westermann. Lower and upper bounds on FIFO buffer management in QoS switches. *Algorithmica*, 53(4):523–548, 2009.

[13] L. Epstein and R. van Stee. Buffer management problems. *SIGACT News*, 35(3):58–66, 2004.

[14] P. T. Eugster, A. Kesselman, K. Kogan, S. I. Nikolenko, and A. Sirotkin. Essential traffic parameters for shared memory switch performance. In *Proc. of the 22nd International Colloquium on Structural Information and Communication Complexity (SIROCCO)*, pages 61–75, 2015.

[15] P. T. Eugster, K. Kogan, S. I. Nikolenko, and A. Sirotkin. Shared memory buffer management for heterogeneous packet processing. In *Proc. of the 34th IEEE International Conference on Distributed Computing Systems (ICDCS)*, pages 471–480, 2014.

[16] M. H. Goldwasser. A survey of buffer management policies for packet switches. *SIGACT News*, 41:100–128, 2010.

[17] T. Itoh and N. Takahashi. Competitive analysis of multi-queue preemptive QoS algorithms for general priorities. *IEICE Transactions on Fundamentals of Electronics, Communications and Computer Sciences*, E89-A(5):1186–1197, 2006.

[18] Ł. Jeż, F. Li, J. Sethuraman, and C. Stein. Online scheduling of packets with agreeable deadlines. *ACM Transactions on Algorithms*, 9(1):Article 5, 2012.

[19] A. Kesselman, K. Kogan, and M. Segal. Packet mode and QoS algorithms for buffered crossbar switches with FIFO queuing. *Distributed Computing*, 23(3):163–175, 2010.

[20] A. Kesselman, K. Kogan, and M. Segal. Best effort and priority queuing policies for buffered crossbar switches. *Chicago Journal of Theoretical Computer Science*, 2012(5):1–14, 2012.

[21] A. Kesselman, K. Kogan, and M. Segal. Improved competitive performance bounds for CIOQ switches. *Algorithmica*, 63(1–2):411–424, 2012.

[22] A. Kesselman and A. Rosén. Scheduling policies for CIOQ switches. *Journal of Algorithms*, 60(1):60–83, 2006.

[23] A. Kesselman and A. Rosén. Controlling CIOQ switches with priority queuing and in multistage interconnection networks. *Journal of Interconnection Networks*, 9(1–2):53–72, 2008.

[24] F. Li, J. Sethuraman, and C. Stein. Better online buffer management. In *Proc. of the 18th Annual ACM-SIAM Symp. on Discrete Algorithms (SODA)*, pages 199–208, 2007.

[25] S. I. Nikolenko and K. Kogan. Single and multiple buffer processing. *Encyclopedia of Algorithms*, pages 1–9, 2014.

[26] V. Paxson and S. Floyd. Wide-area traffic: the failure of Poisson modeling. *IEEE/ACM Transactions on Networking*, 3(3):226–244, 1995.

[27] D. Sleator and R. Tarjan. Amortized efficiency of list update and paging rules. *Communications of the ACM*, 28(2):202–208, 1985.

[28] A. Veres and M. Boda. The chaotic nature of TCP congestion control. In *Proc. of the 19th IEEE Conf. on Computer Communications (INFOCOM)*, pages 1715–1723, 2000.

Brief Announcement: Energy Optimization of Memory Intensive Parallel Workloads

Chhaya Trehan
chhaya.dhingra@gmail.com
Queen's University, Belfast

Hans Vandierendonck
h.vandierendonck@qub.ac.uk
Queen's University, Belfast

Georgios Karakonstantis
g.karakonstantis@qub.ac.uk
Queen's University, Belfast

Dimitrios S. Nikolopoulos
d.nikolopoulos@qub.ac.uk
Queen's University, Belfast

ABSTRACT

Energy consumption is an important concern in modern multicore processors. The energy consumed during the execution of an application can be minimized by tuning the hardware state utilizing knobs such as frequency, voltage etc. The existing theoretical work on energy minimization using Global DVFS (Dynamic Voltage and Frequency Scaling), despite being thorough, ignores the energy consumed by the CPU on memory accesses and the dynamic energy consumed by the idle cores. This article presents an analytical energy-performance model for parallel workloads that accounts for the energy consumed by the CPU chip on memory accesses in addition to the energy consumed on CPU instructions. In addition, the model we present also accounts for the dynamic energy consumed by the idle cores. We present an analytical framework around our energy-performance model to predict the operating frequencies for global DVFS that minimize the overall CPU energy consumption. We show how the optimal frequencies in our model differ from the optimal frequencies in a model that does not account for memory accesses. We further show how the memory intensity of an application affects the optimal frequencies.

Keywords

Energy Optimization; Global DVFS; Memory Intensive

1. INTRODUCTION

Energy consumption and performance turn out to be the two most important and contradicting design criteria for modern multicore processors. The power consumption of a CMP(Chip Multi Processor) is an increasing function of the operating frequency of the chip and thus can be reduced by reducing the frequency. Dynamic Voltage and Frequency Scaling (DVFS) is a popular energy minimization technique. Most of the theoretical work on the energy-delay trade off deals with the *local* DVFS [3], where frequency can be set separately for each core. We study the problem of energy minimization under a performance constraint using global DVFS where all the cores on the chip are set to run on the same frequency. While local DVFS has more freedom in choosing clock frequencies and can therefore save more energy, it is not easy to implement. Often when we think of parallelism, we think of performance gains and we tend to ignore its ramifications on energy consumption. The fact that we can gain performance by increasing parallelism allows us to save energy by reducing the frequency without violating a performance constraint. The relationship of parallelism with energy and performance was first studied by Sangyeun and Melhem in [2]. Gerards et al further formalized the problem for task graphs [3]. They showed that using a single clock frequency during the execution of an application does not lead to optimal energy consumption. They presented an approach for varying the frequency according to the variations in the amount of parallelism where a separate frequency is assigned to each number of active cores. The analytical model of [3], however, completely ignores the energy consumed by the CPU while it waits for data accesses to the main memory. Since it does not account for the time overhead of the access latency of memory, it can lead to an imprecise estimate of the slack between the time to completion and the given performance budget. The CPU energy optimization techniques that save energy by decreasing the operating frequencies of the cores at the cost of an increased delay need to be tuned to account for the memory access latencies. Another assumption in [3] is that the frequency of the idle cores can be brought down to zero. This is not always possible in reality, the idle cores can't be completely shut down and do consume some dynamic energy. In this article, we present a new model for the energy and performance of multicore systems that accounts for the energy consumed by the CMP while waiting for memory accesses in addition to the energy consumed on CPU instructions without ignoring the dynamic energy consumed by the idle cores.

Application Model: We consider a parallel application consisting of a set of N tasks. The application can be depicted as a DAG (Directed Acyclic Graph) where the nodes represent the tasks and the (Directed) edges represent the precedence constraints. A task is characterized by its compute workload and the data workload. The compute work load of a task is the number of clock cycles required to perform its computations and its data workload is the number of memory accesses it has to make. We assume an applica-

SPAA '16 July 11-13, 2016, Pacific Grove, CA, USA

ACM ISBN 978-1-4503-4210-0/16/07.
DOI: http://dx.doi.org/10.1145/2935764.2935811

tion wide parameter called data to CPU quotient d which is the ratio of data to compute workloads of the application.

Power Model: We consider two components of power, the *dynamic power* and the *static power*. Assuming f is the frequency of the CMP at some time t, the dynamic power of an active core at time t can be expressed as $p_{DynamicActive}(f) = c1f^{\alpha}$. The constant $c1 > 0$ is a characteristic of the computing platform and $2 \leq \alpha \leq 3$. At any given point in time, an inactive core consumes relatively less dynamic power owing to its reduced activity factor. We model this difference in dynamic power of active and inactive cores by assuming that the constant $c1$ for inactive cores is less than the $c1$ for active cores. Assuming $c1'$ to be the constant for inactive cores such that the ratio $K = \frac{c1'}{c1} < 1$, the dynamic power of an inactive core can be expressed as $p_{DynamicInactive}(f) = c1'f\alpha$. The static power can be expressed as $p_{Static}(f) = c2f + c3$. The equation for the total power at a given point in time, with m active cores at frequency f is:

$$p_m(f) = [m + k(M-m)]c1f^{\alpha} + c2f + c3 \quad (1)$$

From this point on, we will denote $[m + k(M-m)]$ as m'. Dividing equation 1 on both sides by f gives energy per CPU cycle which we denote as $\bar{p}_m$, where

$$\bar{p}_m(f) = m'c1f^{\alpha-1} + c2 + \frac{c3}{f} \quad (2)$$

The overall energy consumption of an application can be expressed in terms of its amount of parallelism. We refer the reader to go through [3] to fully appreciate the concept of power modeling in terms of parallelism. For an application with N tasks running on a CMP with M cores, its amount of parallelism for a given schedule can be defined formally as a vector $[w_1, w_2, ...w_m...w_M]$, where w_m is the total number of CPU cycles for which exactly m cores are active. Using the idea that a constant frequency for a fixed number of active cores leads to an optimal energy consumption, the task of energy optimization is reduced to finding a vector $f = [f_1, f_2, ...f_m...f_M]$, where f_m is the optimal frequency for m active cores . For a given amount of parallelism w_m, $(w_m d)t_a$ is the duration for which the CPU waits for memory accesses, where t_a is the memory access latency. The additional cycles expended per core on memory accesses for w_m is thus $w_m dt_a f_m$. The total energy consumed by the CPU in terms of parallelism and the corresponding frequencies can be expressed as $E_{total} = \sum_{m=1}^{M}[\bar{p}_m(f_m)(w_m + w_m dt_a f_m)]$. The time to completion can be expressed as $t_{completion} = \sum_{m=1}^{M} \frac{w_m}{f_m} + \sum_{m=1}^{M} w_m dt_a$.

2. MAIN RESULTS

We investigate how do the optimal frequencies relate to the memory intensity of an application and whether and how the relationship between optimal frequencies and the number of active cores changes in the presence of memory accesses. We present our main results in the form of three lemmas.

LEMMA 1. *It holds for every pair $n, m \in \{1, 2, ...M\}$ such that $m \geq n$ and $w_m, w_n > 0$: for an optimal solution $f = [f1, f2, ...f_M]$ to the constrained energy optimization problem, $\frac{f_m}{f_n}$ lies in the interval $[\sqrt[\alpha]{\frac{n'}{m'}}, 1]$.*

Ignoring the static energy, $\frac{f_m}{f_n}$ lies in the interval $[\sqrt[\alpha]{\frac{n'}{m'}}, \sqrt[\alpha+1]{\frac{n'}{m'}}]$.

LEMMA 2. *for an optimal solution $f = [f1, f2, ...f_M]$ to the constrained energy optimization problem without the static energy, the following holds for every pair $n, m \in \{1, 2, ...M\}$ with $w_m, w_n > 0$:*

$$\sqrt[\alpha]{m'[\alpha - 1 + \alpha dt_a f_m]}f_m = \sqrt[\alpha]{n'[\alpha - 1 + \alpha dt_a f_n]}f_n$$

Lemma 2 shows the relationship between the frequencies for two different parallel regions. This is in contrast to the corresponding relationship in [3], which is, $\sqrt[\alpha]{n}f_n = \sqrt[\alpha]{m}f_m$. Including d and k, makes the relation more precise.

The next step is to analytically relate an optimal frequency for any parallel region to the optimal frequency of the serial region. Lemma 3 gives such a relation for $\alpha = 2$.

LEMMA 3. *For $\alpha = 2$, the ratio $x_m = \frac{f_m}{f_1}$, of the optimal frequency f_m for a parallel region of the schedule with m active cores and the optimal frequency f_1 for the serial region is a solution to the following cubic equation:*

$$\frac{m'}{1'}2dt_a f1x_m^3 + \frac{m'}{1'}x_m^2 - (2dt_a f1 + 1) = 0 \quad (3)$$

where $1'$ is a constant equal to $KM + (1 - K)$

Note that it is possible for a schedule to have no serial region at all. The purpose of expressing x_m in terms of f_1 is to help understand by how much does the frequency for a given parallelizm differ from f_1. One can think of f_1 as a *reference* frequency for a given hardware and application combination. For the sake of analysis, we call the term $2dt_a f_1$, the *memory overload factor*. A careful analysis of equation 3 in relation to the memory overload factor reveals that, as memory overhead increases, the optimal frequency for m active cores tends to be inversely proportional to $\sqrt[3]{m}$. Without accounting for the memory accesses, the optimal frequency for m active cores is inversely proportional to $\sqrt[2]{m}$. Thus, accounting for memory accesses does not allow as much reduction in frequencies for parallel regions as predicted in [3]. This confirms that the energy savings predicted by [3] are over optimistic especially in the case of memory intensive applications running on a slow hardware on a tight performance budget. In general, from theorem 1 and generalizing the above exposition, it can be established that the optimal frequency for m active cores for a memory intensive application (with $\alpha dT_a f_1$ sufficiently large) is inversely proportional to $\sqrt[\alpha+1]{m}$.

3. REFERENCES

[1] A. Benoit, P. Renaud-Goud, and Y. Robert. Models and complexity results for performance and energy optimization of concurrent streaming applications. *International Journal of High Performance Computing Applications*, 25(3):261–273, 2011.

[2] S. Cho and R. Melhem. On the interplay of parallelization, program performance, and energy consumption. *Parallel and Distributed Systems, IEEE Transactions on*, 21(3):342–353, March 2010.

[3] J. L. H. Marco E.T. Gerards and J. Kuper. On the interplay between global dvfs and scheduling tasks with precedence constraints. *IEEE TRANSACTIONS ON COMPUTERS*, 64(06), 2015.

Just Join for Parallel Ordered Sets

Guy E. Blelloch
Carnegie Mellon University
guyb@cs.cmu.edu

Daniel Ferizovic
Karlsruhe Institute of Technology
dani93.f@gmail.com

Yihan Sun
Carnegie Mellon University
yihans@cs.cmu.edu

ABSTRACT

Ordered sets (and maps when data is associated with each key) are one of the most important and useful data types. The set-set functions union, intersection and difference are particularly useful in certain applications. Brown and Tarjan first described an algorithm for these functions, based on 2-3 trees, that meet the optimal $\Theta\left(m \log\left(\frac{n}{m}+1\right)\right)$ time bounds in the comparison model (n and $m \leq n$ are the input sizes). Later Adams showed very elegant algorithms for the functions, and others, based on weight-balanced trees. They only require a single function that is specific to the balancing scheme—a function that joins two balanced trees—and hence can be applied to other balancing schemes. Furthermore the algorithms are naturally parallel. However, in the twenty-four years since, no one has shown that the algorithms, sequential or parallel are asymptotically work optimal.

In this paper we show that Adams' algorithms are both work efficient and highly parallel (polylog span) across four different balancing schemes—AVL trees, red-black trees, weight balanced trees and treaps. To do this we use careful, but simple, algorithms for JOIN that maintain certain invariants, and our proof is (mostly) generic across the schemes.

To understand how the algorithms perform in practice we have also implemented them (all code except JOIN is generic across the balancing schemes). Interestingly the implementations on all four balancing schemes and three set functions perform similarly in time and speedup (more than 45x on 64 cores). We also compare the performance of our implementation to other existing libraries and algorithms.

1. INTRODUCTION

Ordered sets and ordered maps (sets with data associated with each key) are two of the most important data types used in modern programming. Most programming languages either have them built in as basic types (e.g. python) or supply them as standard libraries (C++, C# Java, Scala, Haskell, ML). These implementations are based on some form of balanced tree (or tree-like) data structure and, at minimum, support lookup, insertion, and deletion in logarithmic time. Most also support set-set functions such as union, intersection, and difference. These functions are particularly useful when using parallel machines since they can support parallel bulk updates. In this paper we are interested in simple and efficient parallel algorithms for such set-set functions.

The lower bound for comparison-based algorithms for union, intersection and difference for inputs of size n and $m \leq n$, and returning an ordered structure[1], is $\log_2 \binom{m+n}{n} = \Theta\left(m \log\left(\frac{n}{m}+1\right)\right)$. Brown and Tarjan first matched these bounds, asymptotically, using a sequential algorithm based on red-black trees [12]. Although designed for merging, the algorithm can be adapted for union, intersection and difference with the same bounds. However, the Brown and Tarjan algorithm is complicated, and completely sequential.

Adams later described very elegant algorithms for union, intersection, and difference, as well as other functions based on a single function, JOIN [1, 2] (see Figure 1). JOIN(L, k, R) takes a key k and two ordered sets L and R such that $L < k < R$ and returns the union of the keys [30, 28]. It can be used to implement JOIN2(L, R), which does not take the key in the middle, and SPLIT(T, k), which splits a tree at a key k returning the two pieces and a flag indicating if k is in T (See Section 4). With these three functions, union, intersection, and difference (as well as insertion, deletion and other functions) are almost trivial. Because of this, at least three libraries use Adams' algorithms for their implementation of ordered sets and tables (Haskell [21] and MIT/GNU Scheme, and SML).

Adam's original algorithms implemented JOIN using weight-balanced trees[2]. JOIN can also be implemented using other balance criteria. Sleator and Tarjan describe an algorithm for JOIN based on splay trees which runs in amortized logarithmic time [28]. Tarjan describes a version for red-black tree that runs in worst case logarithmic time [30].

Surprisingly, however, there have been almost no results on bounding the work (time) of Adams' algorithms, in general nor on specific tree types. Adams informally argues that his algorithms take $O(n+m)$ work for weight-balanced tree, but that is a very loose bound. Blelloch and Reid-Miller later show that similar algorithms for treaps [7], are optimal for work (i.e. $\Theta\left(m \log\left(\frac{n}{m}+1\right)\right)$), and are also parallel. Their algorithms, however, are specific for treaps. The problem with bounding the work of Adams' algorithms, is that just bounding the time of SPLIT, JOIN and JOIN2 with logarithmic costs is not sufficient.[3] One needs additional properties of the trees.

SPAA '16, July 11-13, 2016, Pacific Grove, CA, USA

DOI: http://dx.doi.org/10.1145/2935764.2935768

[1] By "ordered structure" we mean any data structure that can output elements in sorted order without any further comparisons—e.g., a sorted array, or a binary search tree.

[2] Adams' version had some bugs in maintaining the balance, but these were later fixed [16, 29].

[3] Bounding the cost of JOIN, SPLIT, and JOIN2 by the logarithm of the *smaller tree* is probably sufficient, but implementing a data structure with such bounds is very much more complicated.

```
split(T, k) =
  if T = Leaf then (Leaf, false, Leaf)
  else (L, m, R) = expose(T);
    if k = m then (L, true, R)
    else if k < m then
      (L_L, b, L_R) = split(L, k);
      (L_L, b, join(L_R, m, R))
    else (R_L, b, R_R) = split(R, k);
      (join(L, m, R_L), b, R_R)

splitLast(T) =
  (L, k, R) = expose(T);
  if R = Leaf then (L, k)
  else (T', k') = splitLast(R);
    (join(L, k, T'), k')

join2(T_L, T_R) =
  if T_L = Leaf then T_R
  else (T'_L, k) = splitLast(T_L);
    join(T'_L, k, T_R)

insert(T, k) =
  (T_L, m, T_R) = split(T, k);
  join(T_L, k, T_R)

delete(T, k) =
  (T_L, m, T_R) = split(T, k);
  join2(T_L, T_R)

union(T1, T2) =
  if T1 = Leaf then T2
  else if T2 = Leaf then T1
  else (L2, k2, R2) = expose(T2);
    (L1, b, R1) = split(T1, k2);
    T_L = union(L1, L2) || T_R = union(R1, R2);
    join(T_L, k2, T_R)

intersect(T1, T2) =
  if T1 = Leaf then Leaf
  else if T2 = Leaf then Leaf
  else (L2, k2, R2) = expose(T2);
    (L1, b, R1) = split(T1, k2);
    T_L = intersect(L1, L2) || T_R = intersect(R1, R2);
    if b = true then join(T_L, k2, T_R)
    else join2(T_L, T_R)

difference(T1, T2) =
  if T1 = Leaf then Leaf
  else if T2 = Leaf then T1
  else (L2, k2, R2) = expose(T2);
    (L1, b, R1) = split(T1, k2);
    T_L = difference(L1, L2) || T_R = difference(R1, R2);
    join2(T_L, T_R)
```

Figure 1: Implementing UNION, INTERSECT, DIFFERENCE, INSERT, DELETE, SPLIT, **and** JOIN2 **with just** JOIN. EXPOSE **returns the left tree, key, and right tree of a node. The || notation indicates the recursive calls can run in parallel. These are slight variants of the algorithms described by Adams [1], although he did not consider parallelism.**

The contribution of this paper is to give the first work-optimal bounds for Adams' algorithms. We do this not only for the weight-balanced trees, but for three other balancing schemes: AVL trees, red-black trees and treaps. We analyze exactly the algorithms in Figure 1. We show that with appropriate (and simple) implementations of JOIN for each balancing scheme, we achieve asymptotically optimal bounds on work. These bounds hold when either input tree is larger (this was surprising to us). Furthermore the algorithms have $O(\log n \log m)$ span (parallel time), and hence are highly parallel. To prove the bounds on work we show that our implementations of JOIN satisfy certain conditions based on a rank we define for each tree type. In particular the cost of JOIN must be proportional to the difference in ranks of two trees, and the rank of the result of a join must be at most one more than the maximum rank of the two arguments.

In addition to the theoretical analysis of the algorithms, we implemented parallel versions of all of the algorithms on all four tree types and describe experiments. Our implementation is generic in the sense that we use common code for the algorithms in Figure 1, and only wrote specialized code for each tree type for the JOIN function. Our implementations of JOIN are as described in this paper. We compare performance across a variety of parameters. We compare across the tree types, and interestingly all four balance criteria have very similar performance. We measure the speedup on up to 64 cores and achieve close to a 46-fold speedup. We compare to other implementations, including the set implementation in the C++ Standard Template library (STL) for sequential performance, parallel weight-balanced B-trees (WBB-trees) [14] and the multi-core standard template library (MCSTL) [15] for parallel performance, and to previously reported results on concurrent balanced trees [11]. The conclusion from the experiments is that although not always as fast as (WBB-trees) [14] on uniform distributions, the generic code is quite competitive, and on keys with a skewed overlap (two Gaussians with different means), our implementation is much better than all the other baselines. Our times are very much faster than the concurrent balanced trees, but this is perhaps not fair since concurrent trees are not asymptotically efficient requiring at least $\Omega(m \log n)$ work instead of $\Theta\left(m \log\left(\frac{n}{m}+1\right)\right)$.

Related Work.

Parallel set operations on two ordered sets have been well-studied. Paul, Vishkin, and Wagener studied bulk insertion and deletion on 2-3 trees in the PRAM model [26]. Park and Park showed similar results for red-black trees [25]. These algorithms are not based on JOIN and are not work efficient, requiring $O(m \log n)$ work. Katajainen [18] claimed an algorithm with $O\left(m \log\left(\frac{n}{m}+1\right)\right)$ work and $O(\log n)$ span using 2-3 trees, but it appears to contain some bugs in the analysis [7]. Blelloch and Reid-Miller described a similar algorithm as Adams' (as well as ours) on treaps with optimal work (in expectation) and $O(\log n)$ span (with high probability) on a EREW PRAM with scan operations. This implies $O(\log n \log m)$ span on a plain EREW PRAM, and $O(\log n \log^* m)$ span on a plain CRCW PRAM. The pipelining that is used is quite complicated. Akhremtsev and Sanders [4] recently describe an algorithm for array-tree UNION based on (a, b)-trees with optimal work and $O(\log n)$ span on a CRCW PRAM. Our focus in this paper is in showing that very simple algorithms are work efficient and have polylogarithmic span, and less with optimizing the span.

Many researchers have considered concurrent implementations of balanced search trees (e.g., [19, 20, 11, 23]). None of these are work efficient for UNION since it is necessary to insert one tree into the other requiring at least $\Omega(m \log n)$ work.

2. PRELIMINARIES

A *binary tree* is either a `Leaf`, or a node consisting of a *left* binary tree T_L, a value (or key) v, and a *right* binary tree T_R, and denoted $\texttt{Node}(T_L, v, T_R)$. The *size* of a binary tree, or $|T|$, is 0 for a `Leaf` and $|T_L| + |T_R| + 1$ for a $\texttt{Node}(T_L, v, T_R)$. The *weight* of a binary tree, or $w(T)$, is one more than its size (i.e., the number of leaves in the tree). The *height* of a binary tree, or $h(T)$, is 0 for a `Leaf`, and $\max(h(T_L), h(T_R)) + 1$ for a $\texttt{Node}(T_L, v, T_R)$. *Parent, child, ancestor* and *descendant* are defined as usual (ancestor and descendant are inclusive of the node itself). The *left spine* of a binary tree is the path of nodes from the root to a leaf always following the left tree, and the *right spine* the path to a leaf following the right tree. The *in-order values* of a binary tree is the sequence of values returned by an in-order traversal of the tree.

A *balancing scheme* for binary trees is an invariant (or set of invariants) that is true for every node of a tree, and is for the purpose of keeping the tree nearly balanced. In this paper we consider four balancing schemes that ensure the height of every tree of size n is bounded by $O(\log n)$. For each balancing scheme we define the *rank* of a tree, or $r(T)$.

AVL trees [3] have the invariant that for every $\texttt{Node}(T_L, v, T_R)$, the height of T_L and T_R differ by at most one. This property implies that any AVL tree of size n has height at most $\log_\phi(n+1)$, where $\phi = \frac{1+\sqrt{5}}{2}$ is the golden ratio. For AVL trees $r(T) = h(T) - 1$.

Red-black (RB) trees [5] associate a color with every node and maintain two invariants: (the red rule) no red node has a red child, and (the black rule) the number of black nodes on every path from the root down to a leaf is equal. Unlike some other presentations, we do not require that the root of a tree is black. Our proof of the work bounds requires allowing a red root. We define the *black height* of a node T, denoted $\hat{h}(T)$ to be the number of black nodes on a downward path from the node to a leaf (inclusive of the node). Any RB tree of size n has height at most $2\log_2(n+1)$. In RB trees $r(T) = 2(\hat{h}(T) - 1)$ if T is black and $r(T) = 2\hat{h}(T) - 1$ if T is red.

Weight-balanced (WB) trees with parameter α (also called BB[α] trees) [24] maintain for every $T = \texttt{Node}(T_L, v, T_R)$ the invariant $\alpha \le \frac{w(T_L)}{w(T)} \le 1 - \alpha$. We say two weight-balanced trees T_1 and T_2 have *like* weights if $\texttt{Node}(T_1, v, T_2)$ is weight balanced. Any α weight-balanced tree of size n has height at most $\log_{\frac{1}{1-\alpha}} n$. For $\frac{2}{11} < \alpha \le 1 - \frac{1}{\sqrt{2}}$ insertion and deletion can be implemented on weight balanced trees using just single and double rotations [24, 8]. We require the same condition for our implementation of JOIN, and in particular use $\alpha = 0.29$ in experiments. For WB trees $r(T) = \lceil \log_2(w(T)) \rceil - 1$.

Treaps [27] associate a uniformly random priority with every node and maintain the invariant that the priority at each node is no greater than the priority of its two children. Any treap of size n has height $O(\log n)$ with high probability (w.h.p)[4]. For treaps $r(T) = \lceil \log_2(w(T)) \rceil - 1$.

For all the four balancing schemes $r(T) = \Theta(\log(|T|+1))$. The notation we use for binary trees is summarized in Table 1.

A *Binary Search Tree* (BST) is a binary tree in which each value is a key taken from a total order, and for which the in-order values are sorted. A *balanced BST* is a BST maintained with a balancing scheme, and is an efficient way to represent ordered sets.

[4]Here w.h.p. means that height $O(c \log n)$ with probability at least $1 - 1/n^c$ (c is a constant).

Notation	Description
$\lvert T\rvert$	The size of tree T
$h(T)$	The height of tree T
$\hat{h}(T)$	The black height of an RB tree T
$r(T)$	The rank of tree T
$w(T)$	The weight of tree T (i.e, $\lvert T\rvert + 1$)
$p(T)$	The parent of node T
$k(T)$	The value (or key) of node T
$L(T)$	The left child of node T
$R(T)$	The right child of node T
$\texttt{expose}(T)$	$(L(T), k(T), R(T))$

Table 1: Summary of notation.

Our algorithms are based on nested parallelism with nested fork-join constructs and no other synchronization or communication among parallel tasks.[5] All algorithms are deterministic. We use work W and span (or depth) S to analyze asymptotic costs, where the work is the total number of operations and span is the critical path. We use the simple composition rules $W(e_1 \,||\, e_2) = W(e_1) + W(e_2) + 1$ and $S(e_1 \,||\, e_2) = \max(S(e_1), S(e_2)) + 1$. For sequential computation both work and span compose with addition. Any computation with W work and S span will run in time $T < \frac{W}{P} + S$ assuming a PRAM (random access shared memory) with P processors and a greedy scheduler [10, 9].

3. THE JOIN FUNCTION

Here we describe algorithms for JOIN for the four balancing schemes we defined in Section 2. The function $\text{JOIN}(T_L, k, T_R)$ takes two binary trees T_L and T_R, and a value k, and returns a new binary tree for which the in-order values are a concatenation of the in-order values of T_L, then k, and then the in-order values of T_R.

As mentioned in the introduction and shown in Section 4, JOIN fully captures what is required to rebalance a tree and can be used as the only function that knows about and maintains the balance invariants. For AVL, RB and WB trees we show that JOIN takes work that is proportional to the difference in rank of the two trees. For treaps the work depends on the priority of k. All versions of JOIN are sequential so the span is equal to the work. Due to space limitations, we describe the algorithms, state the theorems for all balancing schemes, but only show a proof outline for AVL trees.

```
joinRight(T_L, k, T_R) =
  (l, k', c) = expose(T_L);
  if h(c) ≤ h(T_R) + 1 then
    T' = Node(c, k, T_R);
    if h(T') ≤ h(l) + 1 then Node(l, k', T')
    else rotateLeft(Node(l, k', rotateRight(T')))
  else
    T' = joinRight(c, k, T_R);
    T'' = Node(l, k', T');
    if h(T') ≤ h(l) + 1 then T''
    else rotateLeft(T'')

join(T_L, k, T_R) =
  if h(T_L) > h(T_R) + 1 then joinRight(T_L, k, T_R)
  else if h(T_R) > h(T_L) + 1 then joinLeft(T_L, k, T_R)
  else Node(T_L, k, T_R)
```

Figure 2: AVL JOIN algorithm.

[5]This does not preclude using our algorithms in a concurrent setting.

```
joinRightRB(T_L, k, T_R) =
  if (r(T_L) = ⌊r(T_R)/2⌋ × 2) then
    Node(T_L, ⟨k, red⟩, T_R);
  else
    (L', ⟨k', c'⟩, R')=expose(T_L);
    T' = Node(L', ⟨k', c'⟩, joinRightRB(R', k, T_R));
    if (c'=black) and (c(R(T')) = c(R(R(T')))=red) then
      c(R(R(T')))=black;
      T''=rotateLeft(T')
    else T''

joinRB(T_L, k, T_R) =
  if ⌊r(T_L)/2⌋ > ⌊r(T_R)/2⌋ then
    T' =joinRightRB(T_L, k, T_R);
    if (c(T')=red) and (c(R(T'))=red) then
      Node(L(T'), ⟨k(T'), black⟩, R(T'))
    else T'
  else if ⌊r(T_R)/2⌋ > ⌊r(T_L)/2⌋ then
    T' =joinLeftRB(T_L, k, T_R);
    if (c(T')=red) and (c(L(T'))=red) then
      Node(L(T'), ⟨k(T'), black⟩, R(T'))
    else T'
  else if (c(T_L)=black) and (c(T_R)=black) then
    Node(T_L, ⟨k, red⟩, T_R)
  else Node(T_L, ⟨k, black⟩, T_R)
```

Figure 3: RB JOIN algorithm.

```
joinRightWB(T_L, k, T_R) =
  (l, k', c)=expose(T_L);
  if (balance(|T_L|, |T_R|) then Node(T_L, k, T_R));
  else
    T' = joinRightWB(c, k, T_R);
    (l_1, k_1, r_1) = expose(T');
    if like(|l|, |T'|) then Node(l, k', T')
    else if (like(|l|, |l_1|)) and (like(|l| + |l_1|, r_1)) then
      rotateLeft(Node(l, k', T'))
    else rotateLeft(Node(l, k', rotateRight(T')))

joinWB(T_L, k, T_R) =
  if heavy(T_L, T_R) then joinRightWB(T_L, k, T_R)
  else if heavy(T_R, T_L) then joinLeftWB(T_L, k, T_R)
  else Node(T_L, k, T_R)
```

Figure 4: WB JOIN algorithm.

```
joinTreap(T_L, k, T_R) =
  if prior(k, k_1) and prior(k, k_2) then Node(T_L, k, T_R)
  else (l_1, k_1, r_1)=expose(T_L);
    (l_2, k_2, r_2)=expose(T_R);
    if prior(k_1, k_2) then
      Node(l_1, k_1, joinTreap(r_1, k, T_R))
    else Node(joinTreap(T_L, k, l_2), k_2, r_2)
```

Figure 5: Treap JOIN algorithm.

AVL trees. Pseudocode for AVL JOIN is given in Figure 2 and illustrated in Figure 6. Every node stores its own height so that $h(\cdot)$ takes constant time. If the two trees T_L and T_R differ by height at most one, JOIN can simply create a new $\texttt{Node}(T_L, k, T_R)$. However if they differ by more than one then rebalancing is required. Suppose that $h(T_L) > h(T_R)+1$ (the other case is symmetric). The idea is to follow the right spine of T_L until a node c for which $h(c) \leq h(T_R) + 1$ is found (line 3). At this point a new $\texttt{Node}(c, k, T_R)$ is created to replace c (line 4). Since either $h(c) = h(T_R)$ or $h(c) = h(T_R) + 1$, the new node satisfies the AVL invariant, and its height is one greater than c. The increase in height can increase the height of its ancestors, possibly invalidating the AVL invariant of those nodes. This can be fixed either with a double rotation if invalid at the parent (line 6) or a single left rotation if invalid higher in the tree (line 11), in both cases restoring the height for any further ancestor nodes. The algorithm will therefore require at most two rotations.

LEMMA 1. *For two AVL trees T_L and T_R, the AVL* JOIN *algorithm works correctly, runs with $O(|h(T_L) - h(T_R)|)$ work, and returns a tree satisfying the AVL invariant with height at most $1 + \max(h(T_L), h(T_R))$.*

Proof outline. Since the algorithm only visits nodes on the path from the root to c, and only requires at most two rotations, it does work proportional to the path length. The path length is no more than the difference in height of the two trees since the height of each consecutive node along the right spine of T_L differs by at least one. Along with the case when $h(T_R) > h(T_L) + 1$, which is symmetric, this gives the stated work bounds. The resulting tree satisfies the AVL invariants since rotations are used to restore the invariant (details left out). The height of any node can increase by at most one, so the height of the whole tree can increase by at most one. □

Red-black Trees. Tarjan describes how to implement the JOIN function for red-black trees [30]. Here we describe a variant that does not assume the roots are black (this is to bound the increase in rank by UNION). The pseudocode is given in Figure 3. We store at every node its black height $\hat{h}(\cdot)$. The first case is when $\hat{h}(T_R) = \hat{h}(T_L)$. Then if both $k(T_R)$ and $k(T_L)$ are black, we create red $\texttt{Node}(T_L, k, T_R)$, otherwise we create black $\texttt{Node}(T_L, k, T_R)$. The second case is when $\hat{h}(T_R) < \hat{h}(T_L) = \hat{h}$ (the third case is symmetric). Similarly to AVL trees, JOIN follows the right spine of T_L until it finds a black node c for which $\hat{h}(c) = \hat{h}(T_R)$. It then creates a new red $\texttt{Node}(c, k, T_R)$ to replace c. Since both c and T_R have the same height, the only invariant that can be violated is the red rule on the root of T_R, the new node, and its parent, which can all be red. In the worst case we may have three red nodes in a row. This is fixed by a single left rotation: if a black node v has $R(v)$ and $R(R(v))$ both red, we turn $R(R(v))$ black and perform a single left rotation on v. The update is illustrated in Figure 7. The rotation, however can again violate the red rule between the root of the rotated tree and its parent, requiring another rotation. The double-red issue might proceed up to the root of T_L. If the original root of T_L is red, the algorithm may end up with a red root with a red child, in which case the root will be turned black, turning T_L rank from $2\hat{h} - 1$ to $2\hat{h}$. If the original root of T_L is black, the algorithm may end up with a red root with two black children, turning the rank of T_L from $2\hat{h} - 2$ to $2\hat{h} - 1$. In both cases the rank of the result tree is at most $1 + r(T_L)$.

LEMMA 2. *For two RB trees T_L and T_R, the RB* JOIN *algorithm works correctly, runs with $O(|r(T_L) - r(T_R)|)$ work, and returns a tree satisfying the red-black invariants and with rank at most $1 + \max(r(T_L), r(T_R))$.*

The proof is similar as Lemma 1.

Weight Balanced Trees. We store the weight of each subtree at every node. The algorithm for joining two weight-balanced trees is similar to that of AVL trees and RB trees. The pseudocode is shown in Figure 4. The `like` function in the code returns true if

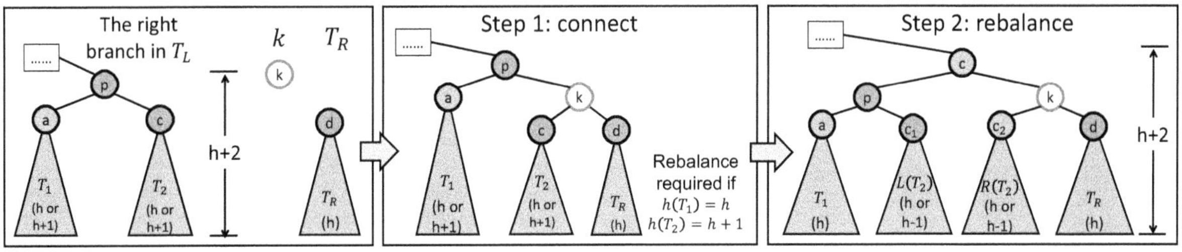

Figure 6: An example for JOIN on AVL trees ($h(T_L) > h(T_R) + 1$). We first follow the right spine of T_L until a subtree of height at most $h(T_r) + 1$ is found (i.e., T_2 rooted at c). Then a new $\texttt{Node}(c, k, T_R)$ is created, replacing c (Step 1). If $h(T_1) = h$ and $h(T_2) = h + 1$, the node p will no longer satisfy the AVL invariant. A double rotation (Step 2) restores both balance and its original height.

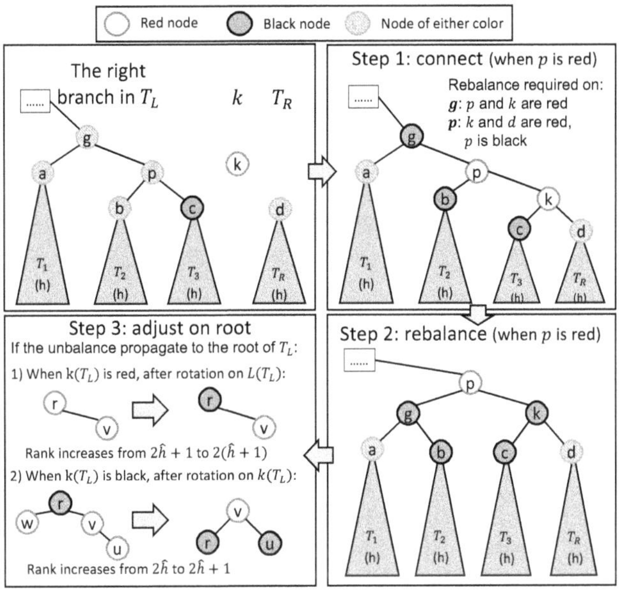

Figure 7: An example of JOIN on red-black trees ($\hat{h} = \hat{h}(T_L) > \hat{h}(T_R)$). We follow the right spine of T_L until we find a black node with the same black height as T_R (i.e., c). Then a new red $\texttt{Node}(c, k, T_R)$ is created, replacing c (Step 1). The only invariant that can be violated is when either c's previous parent p or T_R's root d is red. If so, a left rotation is performed at some black node. Step 2 shows the rebalance when p is red. The black height of the rotated subtree (now rooted at p) is the same as before ($h + 1$), but the parent of p might be red, requiring another rotation. If the red-rule violation propagates to the root, the root is either colored red, or rotated left (Step 3).

the two input tree sizes are balanced, and false otherwise. If T_L and T_R have like weights the algorithm returns a new $\texttt{Node}(T_L, k, T_R)$. Suppose $|T_R| \leq |T_L|$, the algorithm follows the right branch of T_L until it reaches a node c with like weight to T_R. It then creates a new $\texttt{Node}(c, k, T_R)$ replacing c. The new node will have weight greater than c and therefore could imbalance the weight of c's ancestors. This can be fixed with a single or double rotation (as shown in Figure 8) at each node assuming α is within the bounds given in Section 2.

LEMMA 3. *For two α weight-balanced trees T_L and T_R and $\alpha \leq 1 - \frac{1}{\sqrt{2}} \approx 0.29$, the weight-balanced* JOIN *algorithm works correctly, runs with $O(|\log(w(T_L)/w(T_R))|)$ work, and returns a*

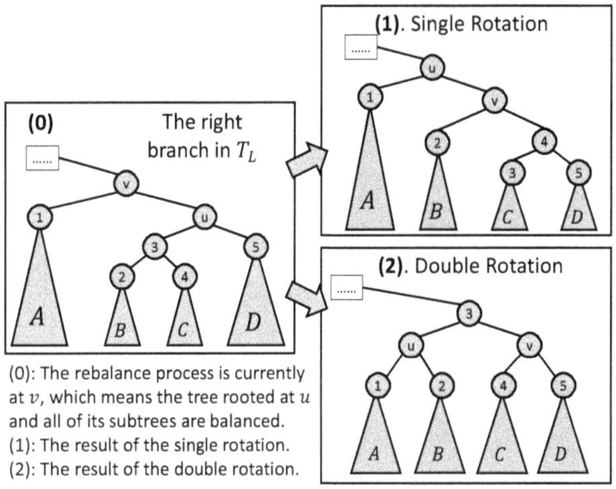

Figure 8: An illustration of single and double rotations possibly needed to rebalance weight-balanced trees. In the figure the subtree rooted at u has become heavier due to joining in T_L and its parent v now violates the balance invariant.

tree satisfying the α weight-balance invariant and with rank at most $1 + \max(r(T_L), r(T_R))$.

The proof is shown in the full version of our paper (on arXiV) [6].

Treaps. The treap JOIN algorithm (as in Figure 5) first picks the key with the highest priority among k, $k(T_L)$ and $k(T_R)$ as the root. If k is the root then the we can return $\texttt{Node}(T_L, k, T_R)$. Otherwise, WLOG, assume $k(T_L)$ has a higher priority. In this case $k(T_L)$ will be the root of the result, $L(T_L)$ will be the left tree, and $R(T_L)$, k and T_R will form the right tree. Thus JOIN recursively calls itself on $R(T_L)$, k and T_R and uses result as $k(T_L)$'s right child. When $k(T_R)$ has a higher priority the case is symmetric. The cost of JOIN is therefore the depth of the key k in the resulting tree (each recursive call pushes it down one level). In treaps the shape of the result tree, and hence the depth of k, depend only on the keys and priorities and not the history. Specifically, if a key has the tth highest priority among the keys, then its expected depth in a treap is $O(\log t)$ (also w.h.p.). If it is the highest priority, for example, then it remains at the root.

LEMMA 4. *For two treaps T_L and T_R, if the priority of k is the t-th highest among all keys in $T_L \cup \{k\} \cup T_R$, the treap* JOIN *algorithm works correctly, runs with $O(\log t + 1)$ work in expectation and w.h.p., and returns a tree satisfying the treap invariant with rank at most $1 + \max(r(T_L), r(T_R))$.*

From the above lemmas we can get the following fact for JOIN.

THEOREM 1. *For AVL, RB and WB trees* JOIN(T_L, k, T_R) *does* $O(|r(T_L) - r(T_R)|)$ *work. For treaps* JOIN *does* $O(\log t)$ *work in expectation if k has the t-th highest priority among all keys. For AVL, RB, WB trees and treaps,* JOIN *returns a tree T for which the rank satisfies* $\max(r(T_L), r(T_R)) \leq r(T) \leq 1 + \max(r(T_L), r(T_R))$.

4. OTHER FUNCTIONS USING JOIN

In this section, we describe algorithms for various functions that use just JOIN. The algorithms are generic across balancing schemes. The pseudocodes for the algorithms in this section is shown in Figure 1.

Split. For a BST T and key k, SPLIT(T, k) returns a triple (T_L, b, T_R), where T_L (T_R) is a tree containing all keys in T that are less (larger) than k, and b is a flag indicating whether $k \in T$. The algorithm first searches for k in T, splitting the tree along the path into three parts: keys to the left of the path, k itself (if it exists), and keys to the right. Then by applying JOIN, the algorithm merges all the subtrees on the left side (using keys on the path as intermediate nodes) from bottom to top to form T_L, and merges the right parts to form T_R. Figure 9 gives an example.

THEOREM 2. *The work of* SPLIT(T, k) *is* $O(\log |T|)$ *for all balancing schemes described in Section 3 (w.h.p. for treaps). The two resulting trees* T_L *and* T_R *will have rank at most* $r(T)$.

PROOF. We only consider the work of joining all subtrees on the left side. The other side is symmetric. Suppose we have l subtrees on the left side, denoted from bottom to top as $T_1, T_2, \ldots T_l$. We have that $r(T_1) \leq r(T_2) \leq \cdots \leq r(T_l)$. As stated above, we consecutively join T_1 and T_2 returning T_2', then join T_2' with T_3 returning T_3' and so forth, until all trees are merged. The overall work of SPLIT is the sum of the cost of $l-1$ JOIN functions.

For AVL trees, red-black trees and weight-balanced trees, recall Theorem 1 that we have $r(T_i') \leq r(T_i) + 1$, so $r(T_i') \leq r(T_i) + 1 \leq r(T_{i+1}) + 1$. According to Theorem 1, the work of a single operation is $O(|r(T_{i+1}) - r(T_i')|)$. The overall complexity is $\sum_{i=1}^{l} |r(T_{i+1}) - r(T_i')| \leq \sum_{i=1}^{l} r(T_{i+1}) - r(T_i') + 2 = O(r(T)) = O(\log |T|)$.

For treaps, each JOIN uses the key with the highest priority since the key is always on a upper level. Hence by Lemma 4, the complexity of each JOIN is $O(1)$ and the work of split is at most $O(\log |T|)$ w.h.p.

Also notice that when getting the final result T_L and T_R, the last step is a JOIN on two trees, the larger one of which is a subtree of the original T. Thus the rank of the two trees to be joined is of rank at most $r(T) - 1$, according to Theorem 1 we have $r(T_L)$ and $r(T_R)$ at most $r(T)$. □

Join2. JOIN2(T_L, T_R) returns a binary tree for which the in-order values is the concatenation of the in-order values of the binary trees T_L and T_R (the same as JOIN but without the middle key). For BSTs, all keys in T_L have to be less than keys in T_R. JOIN2 first finds the last element k (by following the right spine) in T_L and on the way back to root, joins the subtrees along the path, which is similar to SPLIT T_L by k. We denote the result of dropping k in T_L as T_L'. Then JOIN(T_L', k, T_R) is the result of JOIN2. Unlike JOIN, the work of JOIN2 is proportional to the rank of both trees since both SPLIT and JOIN take at most logarithmic work.

THEOREM 3. *The work of* JOIN2(T_L, T_R) *is* $O(r(T_L)+r(T_R))$ *for all balancing schemes described in Section 3 (bounds are w.h.p for treaps).*

Union, Intersect and Difference. UNION(T_1, T_2) takes two BSTs and returns a BST that contains the union of all keys. The algorithm uses a classic divide-and-conquer strategy, which is parallel. At each level of recursion, T_1 is split by $k(T_2)$, breaking T_1 into three parts: one with all keys smaller than $k(T_2)$ (denoted as L_1), one in the middle either of only one key equal to $k(T_2)$ (when $k(T_2) \in T_1$) or empty (when $k(T_2) \notin T_1$), the third one with all keys larger than $k(T_2)$ (denoted as R_1). Then two recursive calls to UNION are made in parallel. One unions $L(T_2)$ with L_1, returning T_L, and the other one unions $R(T_2)$ with R_1, returning T_R. Finally the algorithm returns JOIN$(T_L, k(T_2), T_R)$, which is valid since $k(T_2)$ is greater than all keys in T_L are less than all keys in T_R.

The functions INTERSECT(T_1, T_2) and DIFFERENCE(T_1, T_2) take the intersection and difference of the keys in their sets, respectively. The algorithms are similar to UNION in that they use one tree to split the other. However, the method for joining is different. For INTERSECT, JOIN2 is used instead of JOIN if the root of the first *is not* found in the second. For DIFFERENCE, JOIN2 is used anyway because $k(T_2)$ should be excluded in the result tree. The base cases are also different in the obvious way.

THEOREM 4 (MAIN THEOREM). *For all four balance schemes mentioned in Section 3, the work and span of the algorithm (as shown in Figure 1) of* UNION, INTERSECT *or* DIFFERENCE *on two balanced BSTs of sizes m and n* ($n \geq m$) *is* $O\left(m \log\left(\frac{n}{m} + 1\right)\right)$ *and* $O(\log n \log m)$ *respectively (the bound is in expectation for treaps).*

A generic proof of Theorem 4 working for all the four balancing schemes will be shown in the next section.

The work bound for these algorithms is optimal in the comparison-based model. In particular considering all possible interleavings, the minimum number of comparisons required to distinguish them is $\log \binom{m+n}{n} = \Theta\left(m \log\left(\frac{n}{m} + 1\right)\right)$ [17].

Other Functions. Many other functions can be implemented with JOIN. Pseudocode for INSERT and DELETE was given in Figure 1. For a tree of size n they both take $O(\log n)$ work.

5. THE PROOF OF THE MAIN THEOREM

In this section we prove Theorem 4, for all the four balance schemes (AVL trees, RB trees, WB trees and treaps) and all three set algorithms (UNION, INTERSECT, DIFFERENCE) from Figure 1. For this purpose we make two observations. The first is that all the work for the algorithms can be accounted for within a constant factor by considering just the work done by the SPLITs and the JOINs (or JOIN2s), which we refer to as *split work* and *join work*, respectively. This is because the work done between each split and join is constant. The second observation is that the split work is identical among the three set algorithms. This is because the control flow of the three algorithms is the same on the way down the recursion when doing SPLITs—the algorithms only differ in what they do at the base case and on the way up the recursion when they join.

Given these two observations, we prove the bounds on work by first showing that the join work is asymptotically at most as large as the split work (by showing that this is true at every node of the recursion for all three algorithms), and then showing that the split work for UNION (and hence the others) satisfies our claimed bounds.

We start with some notation, which is summarized in Table 2. In the three algorithms the first tree (T_1) is split by the keys in the second tree (T_2). We therefore call the first tree the *decomposed*

[6]The nodes in $T_d(v)$ form a subset of T_d, but not necessarily a subtree. See details later.

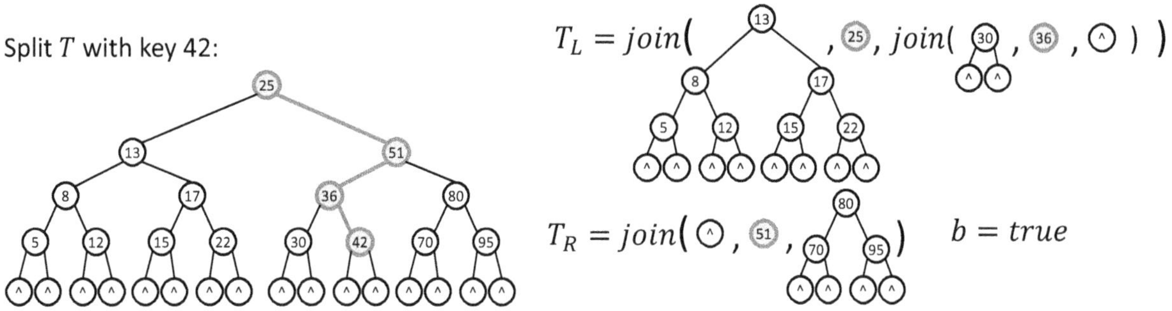

Figure 9: An example of SPLIT in a BST with key 42. We first search for 42 in the tree and split the tree by the searching path, then use JOIN to combine trees on the left and on the right respectively, bottom-top.

Notation	Description
T_p	The pivot tree
T_d	The decomposed tree
n	$\max(\|T_p\|, \|T_d\|)$
m	$\min(\|T_p\|, \|T_d\|)$
$T_p(v), v \in T_p$	The subtree rooted at v in T_p
$T_d(v), v \in T_p$	The tree from T_d that v splits[6]
s_i	The number of nodes in layer i
v_{kj}	The j-th node on layer k in T_p
$d(v)$	The number of nodes attached to a layer root v in a treap

Table 2: Descriptions of notations used in the proof.

tree and the second the *pivot tree*, denoted as T_d and T_p respectively. The tree that is returned is denoted as T_r. Since our proof works for either tree being larger, we use $m = \min(|T_p|, |T_d|)$ and $n = \max(|T_p|, |T_d|)$. We denote the subtree rooted at $v \in T_p$ as $T_p(v)$, and the tree of keys from T_d that v splits as $T_d(v)$ (i.e., $\text{SPLIT}(v, T_d(v))$ is called at some point in the algorithm). For $v \in T_p$, we refer to $|T_d(v)|$ as its *splitting size*.

Figure 10 (a) illustrates the pivot tree with the splitting size annotated on each node. Since SPLIT has logarithmic work, we have,

$$\text{split work} = O\left(\sum_{v \in T_p} (\log |T_d(v)| + 1)\right),$$

which we analyze in Theorem 6. We first, however, show that the join work is bounded by the split work. We use the following Lemma, which is proven in the appendix.

LEMMA 5. *For T_r =UNION(T_p, T_d) on AVL, RB or WB trees, if $r(T_p) > r(T_d)$ then $r(T_r) \leq r(T_p) + r(T_d)$.*

THEOREM 5. *For each function call to* UNION, INTERSECT *or* DIFFERENCE *on trees $T_p(v)$ and $T_d(v)$, the work to do the* JOIN *(or* JOIN2*) is asymptotically no more than the work to do the* SPLIT.

PROOF. For INTERSECT or DIFFERENCE, the cost of JOIN (or JOIN2) is $O(\log(|T_r| + 1))$. Notice that DIFFERENCE returns the keys in $T_d \backslash T_p$. Thus for both INTERSECT and DIFFERENCE we have $T_r \subseteq T_d$. The join work is $O(\log(|T_r| + 1))$, which is no more than $O(\log(|T_d| + 1))$ (the split work).

For UNION, if $r(T_p) \leq r(T_d)$, the JOIN will cost $O(r(T_d))$, which is no more than the split work.

Consider $r(T_p) > r(T_d)$ for AVL, RB or WB trees. The rank of $L(T_p)$ and $R(T_p)$, which are used in the recursive calls, are at least $r(T_p) - 1$. Using Lemma 5, the rank of the two trees returned by the two recursive calls will be at least $(r(T_p) - 1)$ and at most $(r(T_p) + r(T_d))$, and differ by at most $O(r(T_d)) = O(\log |T_d| + 1)$. Thus the join cost is $O(\log |T_d| + 1)$, which is no more than the split work.

Consider $r(T_p) > r(T_d)$ for treaps. If $r(T_p) > r(T_d)$, then $|T_p| \geq |T_d|$. The root of T_p has the highest priority among all $|T_p|$ keys, so on expectation it takes at most the $\frac{|T_p|+|T_d|}{|T_p|} \leq 2$-th place among all the $|T_d| + |T_p|$ keys. From Lemma 4 we know that the cost on expectation is $\mathbb{E}[\log t] + 1 \leq \log \mathbb{E}[t] + 1 \leq \log 2 + 1$, which is a constant. □

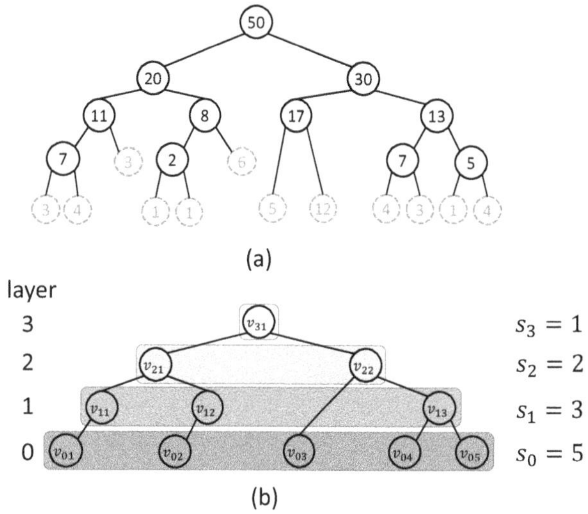

Figure 10: An illustration of splitting tree and layers. The tree in (a) is T_p, the dashed circle are the exterior nodes. The numbers on the nodes are the sizes of the tree from T_d to be split by this node, i.e., the "splitting size" $|T_d(v)|$. In (b) is an illustration of layers on an AVL tree.

This implies the total join work is asymptotically bounded by the split work.

We now analyze the split work. We do this by layering the pivot tree starting at the leaves and going to the root and such that nodes in a layer are not ancestors of each other. We define layers based on the ranks and denote the size of layer i as s_i. We show that s_i shrinks geometrically, which helps us prove our bound on the split work. For AVL and RB trees, we group the nodes with rank i in layer i. For WB trees and treaps, we put a node v in layer i iff v has rank i and v's parent has rank strictly greater than i. Figure 10 (b) shows an example of the layers of an AVL tree.

DEFINITION 1. *In a BST, a set of nodes V is called a* disjoint set *if and only if for any two nodes v_1, v_2 in V, v_1 is not the ancestor of v_2.*

LEMMA 6. *For any disjoint set $V \subseteq T_p$, $\sum_{v\in V} |T_d(v)| \le |T_d|$.*

The proof of this Lemma is straightforward.

LEMMA 7. *For an AVL, RB, WB tree or a treap of size N, each layer is a disjoint set, and $s_i \le \frac{N}{c^{\lfloor i/2 \rfloor}}$ holds for some constant $c > 1$.*

PROOF. For AVL, RB, WB trees and treaps, a layer is obviously a disjoint set: a node and its ancestor cannot lie in the same layer.

For AVL trees, consider a node in layer 2, it must have at least two descendants in layer 0. Thus $s_0 \ge 2s_2$. Since an AVL tree with its leaves removed is still an AVL tree, we have $s_i \ge 2s_{i+2}$. Since s_0 and s_1 are no more than N, we can get that $s_i < \frac{N}{2^{\lfloor i/2 \rfloor}}$.

For RB trees, the number of black nodes in layer $2i$ is more than twice as many as in layer $2(i+1)$ and less than four times as many as in layer $2(i+1)$, i.e., $s_{2i} \ge 2s_{2i+2}$. Also, the number of red nodes in layer $2i+1$ is no more than the black nodes in layer $2i$. Since s_0 and s_1 are no more than N, $s_i < \frac{N}{2^{\lfloor i/2 \rfloor}}$.

For WB trees and treaps, the rank is defined as $\lceil \log_2(w(T)) \rceil - 1$, which means that a node in layer i has weight at least $2^i + 1$. Thus $s_i \le (N+1)/(2^i+1) \le N/2^i$. □

Not all nodes in a WB tree or a treap are assigned to a layer. We call a node a *layer root* if it is in a layer. We attach each node u in the tree to the layer root that is u's ancestor and has the same rank as u. We denote $d(v)$ as the number of descendants attached to a layer root v.

LEMMA 8. *For WB trees and treaps, if v is a layer root, $d(v)$ is less than a constant (in expectation for treaps). Furthermore, the random variables $d(v)$ for all layer roots in a treap are i.i.d. (See the proof in the Appendix.)*

By applying Lemma 7 and 8 we prove the split work. In the following proof, we denote v_{kj} as the j-th node in layer k.

THEOREM 6. *The split work in* UNION, INTERSECT *and* DIFFERENCE *on two trees of size m and n is $O\left(m\log\left(\frac{n}{m}+1\right)\right)$.*

PROOF. The total work of SPLIT is the sum of the log of all the splitting sizes on the pivot tree $O\left(\sum_{v\in T_p} \log(|T_d(v)|+1)\right)$. Denote l as the number of layers in the tree. Also, notice that in the pivot tree, in each layer there are at most $|T_d|$ nodes with $|T_d(v_{kj})| > 0$. Since those nodes with splitting sizes of 0 will not cost any work, we can assume $s_i \le |T_d|$. We calculate the dominant term $\sum_{v\in T_p} \log(|T_d(v)|+1)$ in the complexity by summing the work across layers:

$$\sum_{k=0}^{l}\sum_{j=1}^{s_k} \log(|T_d(v_{kj})|+1) \le \sum_{k=0}^{l} s_k \log\left(\frac{\sum_j |T_d(v_{kj})|+1}{s_k}\right) = \sum_{k=0}^{l} s_k \log\left(\frac{|T_d|}{s_k}+1\right)$$

We split it into two cases. If $|T_d| \ge |T_p|$, $\frac{|T_d|}{s_k}$ always dominates 1. we have:

$$\begin{aligned}
\sum_{k=0}^{l} s_k \log\left(\frac{|T_d|}{s_k}+1\right) &= \sum_{k=0}^{l} s_k \log\left(\frac{n}{s_k}+1\right) && (1)\\
&\le \sum_{k=0}^{l} \frac{m}{c^{\lfloor k/2 \rfloor}} \log\left(\frac{n}{m/c^{\lfloor k/2 \rfloor}}+1\right) && (2)\\
&\le 2\sum_{k=0}^{l/2} \frac{m}{c^k} \log\frac{n}{m/c^k}\\
&\le 2\sum_{k=0}^{l/2} \frac{m}{c^k} \log\frac{n}{m} + 2\sum_{k=0}^{l/2} k\frac{m}{c^k}\\
&= O\left(m\log\frac{n}{m}\right) + O(m)\\
&= O\left(m\log\left(\frac{n}{m}+1\right)\right) && (3)
\end{aligned}$$

If $|T_d| < |T_p|$, $\frac{|T_d|}{s_k}$ can be less than 1 when k is smaller, thus the sum should be divided into two parts. Also note that we only sum over the nodes with splitting size larger than 0. Even though there could be more than $|T_d|$ nodes in one layer in T_p, only $|T_d|$ of them should count. Thus we assume $s_k \le |T_d|$, and we have:

$$\begin{aligned}
\sum_{k=0}^{l} s_k \log\left(\frac{|T_d|}{s_k}+1\right) &= \sum_{k=0}^{l} s_k \log\left(\frac{m}{s_k}+1\right) && (4)\\
&\le \sum_{k=0}^{2\log_c \frac{n}{m}} |T_d| \log(1+1)\\
&\quad + \sum_{k=2\log_c \frac{n}{m}}^{l} \frac{n}{c^{\lfloor k/2 \rfloor}} \log\left(\frac{m}{n/c^{\lfloor k/2 \rfloor}}+1\right) && (5)\\
&\le O\left(m\log\frac{n}{m}\right) + 2\sum_{k'=0}^{\frac{l}{2}-\log_c \frac{m}{n}} \frac{m}{c^{k'}} \log c^{k'}\\
&= O\left(m\log\frac{n}{m}\right) + O(m)\\
&= O\left(m\log\left(\frac{n}{m}+1\right)\right) && (6)
\end{aligned}$$

From (1) to (2) and (4) to (5) we apply Lemma 7 and the fact that $f(x) = x\log(\frac{n}{x}+1)$ is monotonically increasing when $x \le n$.

For WB trees and treaps, the calculation above only includes the log of splitting size on layer roots. We need to further prove the total sum of the log of all splitting size is still $O\left(m\log\left(\frac{n}{m}+1\right)\right)$. Applying Lemma 8, the expectation is less than:

$$\begin{aligned}
&\mathbb{E}\left[2\sum_{k=0}^{l}\sum_{j=1}^{x_k} d(v_{kj}) \log((T_d(v_{kj})+1)\right]\\
&= \mathbb{E}[d(v_{kj})] \times 2\sum_{k=0}^{l}\sum_{j=1}^{x_k} \log((T_d(v_{kj})+1)\\
&= O\left(m\log\left(\frac{n}{m}+1\right)\right)
\end{aligned}$$

For WB trees $d(v_{kj})$ is no more than a constant, so we can also come to the same bound.

To conclude, the split work on all four balancing schemes of all three functions is $O\left(m\log\left(\frac{n}{m}+1\right)\right)$. □

THEOREM 7. *The total work of* UNION, INTERSECT *or* DIFFERENCE *of all four balancing schemes on two trees of size* m *and* n $(m \geq n)$ *is* $O\left(m \log\left(\frac{n}{m}+1\right)\right)$.

This directly follows Theorem 5 and 6.

THEOREM 8. *The span of* UNION *and* INTERSECT *or* DIFFERENCE *on all four balancing schemes is* $O(\log n \log m)$. *Here* n *and* m *are the sizes of the two tree.*

PROOF. For the span of these algorithms, we denote $D(h_1, h_2)$ as the span on UNION, INTERSECT or DIFFERENCE on two trees of height h_1 and h_2. According to Theorem 5, the work (span) of SPLIT and JOIN are both $O(\log |T_d|) = O(h(T_d))$. We have:

$$D(h(T_p), h(T_d)) \leq D(h(T_p) - 1, h(T_d)) + 2h(T_d)$$

Thus $D(h(T_p), h(T_d)) \leq 2h(T_p)h(T_d) = O(\log n \log m)$. □

Combine Theorem 7 and 8 we come to Theorem 4.

6. EXPERIMENTS

To evaluate the performance of our algorithms we performed several experiments across the four balancing schemes using different set functions, while varying the core count and tree sizes. We also compare the performance of our implementation to other existing libraries and algorithms.

Experiment setups and baseline algorithms.

For the experiments we use a 64-core machine with 4 x AMD Opteron(tm) Processor 6278 (16 cores, 2.4GHz, 1600MHz bus and 16MB L3 cache). Our code was compiled using the `g++` 4.8 compiler with the Cilk Plus extensions for nested parallelism. The only compilation flag we used was the `-O2` optimization flag. In all our experiments we use keys of the double data type. The size of each node is about 40 bytes, including the two child pointers, the key, the balance information, the size of the subtree, and a reference count. We generate multiple sets varying in size from 10^4 to 10^8. Depending on the experiment the keys are drawn either from an uniform or a Gaussian distribution. We use μ and σ to denote the mean and the standard deviation in Gaussian distribution. Throughout this section n and m represent the two input sizes for functions with two input sets $(n \geq m)$.

We test our algorithm by comparing it to other available implementations. This includes the sequential version of the set functions defined in the C++ Standard Template Library (STL) [22] and STL's `std::set` (implemented by RB tree). To see how well our algorithm performs in a parallel setting, we compare it to parallel WBB-trees [14] and the MCSTL library [15], both supporting array-tree UNION.

Comparing the balancing schemes and functions.

To compare the four balancing schemes we choose UNION as the representative operation. Other operations give similar results. We compare the schemes across varying thread counts and sizes.

Figure 11 (a) shows the runtime of UNION for varying tree sizes and all four balancing schemes on 64 cores. The times are very similar across the balancing schemes, differing by no more than 10%.

Figure 11 (b) shows the speedup curves for UNION on a varying number of cores with both inputs of size 10^8. All balancing schemes achieve a speedup of about 45 on 64 cores, and about 30 on 32 cores. The less-than-linear speedup beyond 32 cores is not due to lack of parallelism, since when we ran the same experiments on significantly smaller input (and hence less parallelism) we get very similar curves (not shown). Instead it seems to be due to saturation of the memory bandwidth.

We use the AVL tree as the representative tree to compare different functions. Figure 11 (c) compares time for the UNION, INTERSECT and DIFFERENCE functions. The size of the larger tree is fixed (10^8), while the size of the smaller tree varies from 10^4 to 10^8. As the plot indicates, the three functions have very similar performance.

The experiments are a good indication of the performance of different balancing schemes and different functions, while controlling other factors. The conclusion is that all schemes perform almost equally on all the set functions. It is perhaps not surprising that all balancing schemes achieve similar performance because the dominant cost is in cache misses along the paths in the tree, and all schemes keep the trees reasonably balanced. The AVL tree is always slightly faster than the other trees and this is likely due to the fact that they maintain a slightly stricter balance than the other trees, and hence the paths that need to be traversed are slightly shorter. For different set functions the similar performance is also as expected given the similarity of the code.

Comparing to sequential implementations.

The STL supports `set_union`, `set_intersection`, and `set_difference` on any container class, including sets based on red-black trees, and sorted vectors (arrays). Since the STL does not offer any parallel version of these functions we could only use it for sequential experiments. For two inputs of size n and m, $m \leq n$, it takes $O(m+n)$ time on `std::vectors` by moving from left to right on the two inputs, comparing the current values, and writing the lesser to the end of the output, and $O((n+m)\log(n+m))$ time on `std::set` by inserting the elements in one set into the other. In the case of `std::set` we can do better by inserting elements from the smaller set into the larger, leading a time of $O(m \log(n+m))$. This is also what we do in our experiments. For vectors we stick with the available `set_union` implementation.

Figure 11 (d) gives a comparison of times for UNION. For equal lengths our implementation is about a factor of 3 faster than the set variant (red-black trees), and about 8 times slower than the vector variant. This is not surprising since we are asymptotically faster than their red-black tree implementation, and their array-based implementation just reads and writes the values, one by one, from flat arrays, and therefore has much less overhead and much fewer cache misses. For taking the union of smaller and larger inputs, our UNION is orders of magnitude faster than either STL version. This is because their theoretical work bound ($O(m+n)$ and $O(m \log(m+n))$ is worse than our $O(m \log(n/m+1))$, which is optimal in the comparison model.

Comparing to parallel implementations..

To see how well our algorithm performs in a parallel setting, we compare it to parallel WBB-trees [14] and the MCSTL library [15]. WBB-trees, as well as the MCSTL, offer an interface for bulk insertions and deletions, which take a tree and a sorted array and either insert the elements from the array into the tree, or delete them. Bulk effectively gives a UNION, which we refer to this as an array-tree UNION as opposed to our symmetric tree-tree UNION. If the array is the smaller input, array-tree unions have an inherent advantage over tree-tree unions since accessing an array is much more cache efficient than accessing an tree. Also, the WBB-tree itself has a more cache-aware layout (8 keys per cache line as opposed to 1), leading to a better cache utilization compared to both the MCSTL and our implementation. In this section, we test the

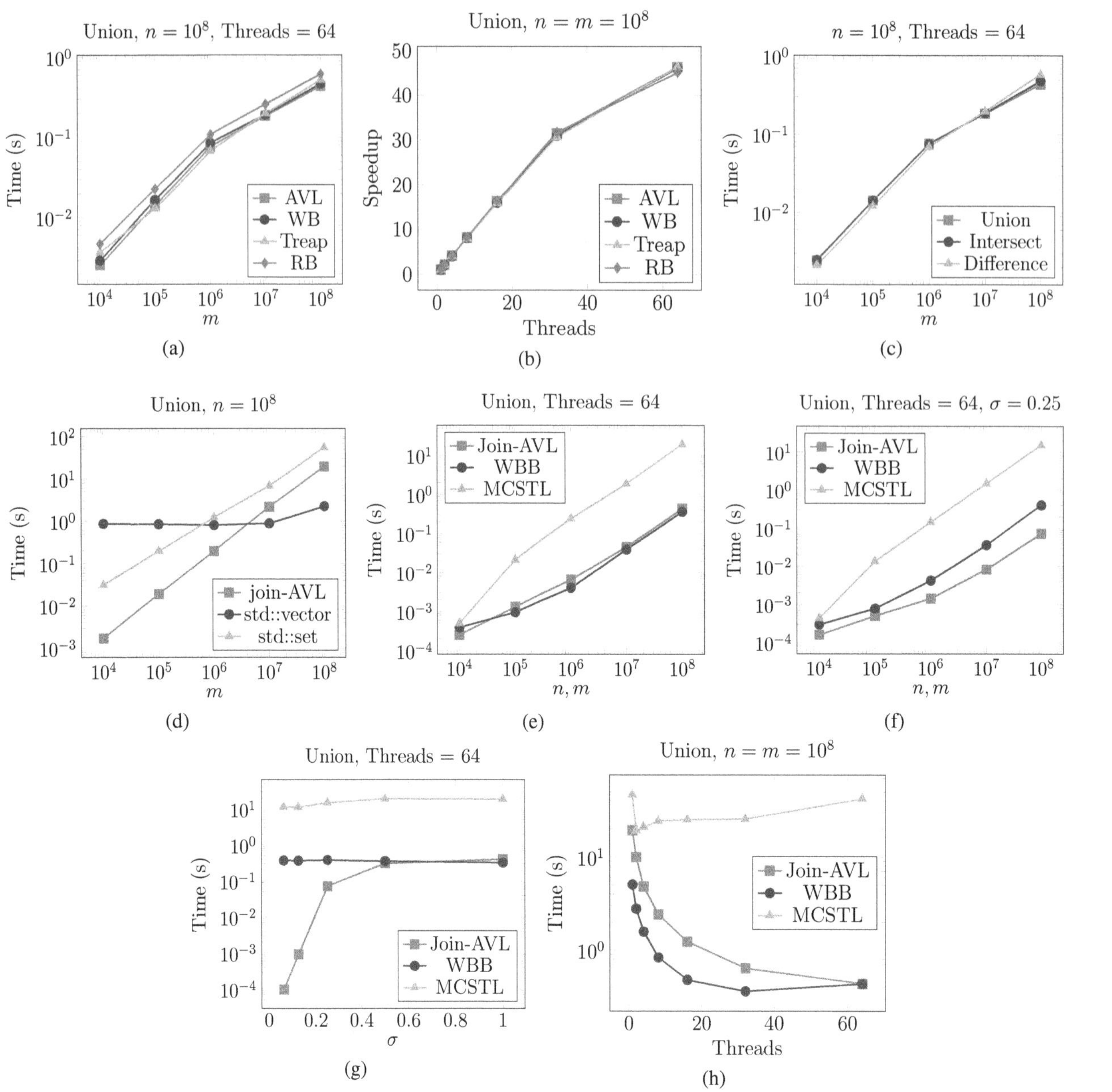

Figure 11: (a) Times for UNION as a function of size ($n = 10^8$) for different BBSTs; (b) speed up of UNION for different BBSTs; (c) times for various operations on AVL trees as a function of size ($n = 10^8$); (d) comparing STLs `set_union` with our UNION; (e, f, g, h) comparing our UNION to other parallel search trees; (e, h) input keys are uniformly distributed doubles in the range of [0, 1]; (f, g) inputs keys follow a normal distribution of doubles - the mean of the main tree is always $\mu_1 = 0$, while the mean of the bulk is $\mu_2 = 1$. Figure (f) uses a standard deviation of $\sigma = 0.25$, while Figure (g) shows the performance across different standard deviations.

performance of our implementation of JOIN-based UNION, WBB-trees and the MCSTL library on different input distributions.

In Figure 11 (e) we show the result of UNION on uniformly distributed doubles in the range of [0,1] across 64 cores. We set the input size to $n = m = 10^i$, i from 4 to 8. The three implementations have similar performance when $n = m = 10^4$. As the input size increases, MCSTL shows much worse performance than the other two because of the lack of parallelism (Figure 11 (h) is a good indication), and the WBB-tree implementation is slightly better than ours. This is likely due to better cache performance as discussed above.

Figure 11 (f) shows the result of a Gaussian distribution with doubles, also on all 64 cores with set sizes of $n = m = 10^i$ for $i = 4$ through 8. The distributions of the two sets have means at 0 and 1 respectively, and both having a standard deviation of 0.25, meaning that the data in the two sets have less overlap comparing to a uniform distribution (as in (e)). In this case our code achieves better performance than the other two implementations. For our algorithms less overlap in the data means more parts of the trees will be untouched, and therefore less nodes will be operated on. This in turn leads to less processing time.

We also do a study on how the overlap of the data sets affects the performance of each algorithm. We generate two sets of size $n = m = 10^8$, each from a Gaussian distribution. The distributions of the two sets have means at 0 and 1 respectively, and both have an equal standard deviation varying in $\{1, 1/2, 1/4, 1/8, 1/16\}$. The different standard deviations are to control the overlap of the two sets, and ideally less overlap should simplify the problem. Figure 11 (g) shows the result of the three parallel implementations on a Gaussian distribution with different standard deviations. From the figure we can see that MCSTL and WBB-tree are not affected by different standard deviations, while our join-based union takes advantage of less overlapping and achieves a much better performance when σ is small. This is not surprising since when the two sets are less overlapped, e.g., totally disjoint, our UNION will degenerate to a simple JOIN, which costs only $O(\log n)$ work. This behavior is consistent with the "adaptive" property (not always the worst-case) in [13]. This indicates that our algorithm is the only one among the three parallel implementations that can detect and take advantage of less overlapping in data, hence have a much better performance when the two operated sets are less overlapped.

We also compare the parallelism of these implementations. In Figure 11 (h) we show their performance across 64 cores. The inputs are both of size 10^8, and generated from an uniform distribution of doubles. It is easy to see that MCSTL does not achieve good parallelism beyond 16 cores, which explains why the MCSTL always performs the worst on 64 cores in all settings. As we mentioned earlier, the WBB-tree are slightly faster than our code, but when it comes to all 64 cores, both algorithms have similar performance. This indicates that our algorithm achieves better parallelism.

To conclude, in terms of parallel performance, our code and WBB-trees are always much better than the MCSTL because of MCSTL's lack of parallelism. WBB-trees achieve a slightly better performance than ours on uniformly distributed data, but it does not improve when the two sets are less overlapped. Thus our code is much better than the other two implementations on less overlapped data.

Comparing to a concurrent data structure.

We also compare our algorithm to an implementation of concurrent AVL trees [11]. UNION can be implemented by concurrent insertions of the smaller set into a larger set, and hence requires $\Omega(m \log n)$ work. We could not get their open-source implementation to run efficiently, so we compare to their previously reported times. As reported in Figure 15, top left of [11], they process 7 million keys per second (insertions and deletions) on 16 threads (for 1 million keys). Ours does 80 million keys per second when unioning two sequences each of length 1-10 million, again on 16 threads. This is 11x faster than theirs.[7] We note, however, that this comparison is not really fair since they support concurrent operations (searches, insertions, deletions, etc.), which we do not.

7. CONCLUSIONS

In this paper, we study ordered sets implemented with balanced binary search trees. We show for the first time that a very simple "classroom-ready" set of algorithms due to Adams' are indeed work optimal when used with four different balancing schemes–AVL, RB, WB trees and treaps—and also highly parallel. The only tree-specific algorithm that is necessary is the JOIN, and even the JOINS are quite simple, as simple as INSERT or DELETE. It seems it is not sufficient to give a time bound to JOIN and base analysis on it. Indeed if this were the case it would have been done years ago. Instead our approach defines the notion of a rank (differently for different trees) and shows invariants on the rank. It is important that the cost of JOIN is proportional to the difference in ranks. It is also important that when joining two trees the resulting rank is only a constant bigger than the larger rank of the inputs. This insures that when joins are used in a recursive tree, as in UNION, the ranks of the results in a pair of recursive calls does not differ much on the two sides. This then ensures that the set functions are efficient.

We also test the performance of our algorithm. Our experiments show that our sequential algorithm is about 3x faster for union on two maps of size 10^8 compared to the STL red-black tree implementation. In parallel settings our code is much better than the two baseline algorithms (MCSTL and WBB-tree) on less overlapped data, while still achieves similar performances with WBB-tree when the two sets are more intermixed. Our code also achieves 45x speedup on 64 cores.

[7]Although on different processors, their processors are faster (2.66Ghz vs. 2.4Ghz).

Acknowledgments

This research was supported in part by NSF grants CCF-1314590 and CCF-1533858, and the Intel Science and Technology Center for Cloud Computing.

8. REFERENCES

[1] S. Adams. Implementing sets effciently in a functional language. Technical Report CSTR 92-10, University of Southampton, 1992.

[2] S. Adams. Efficient sets—a balancing act. *Journal of functional programming*, 3(04):553–561, 1993.

[3] G. Adelson-Velsky and E. M. Landis. An algorithm for the organization of information. *Proc. of the USSR Academy of Sciences*, 145:263–266, 1962. In Russian, English translation by Myron J. Ricci in Soviet Doklady, 3:1259-1263, 1962.

[4] Y. Akhremtsev and P. Sanders. Fast parallel operations on search trees. *arXiv preprint arXiv:1510.05433*, 2015.

[5] R. Bayer. Symmetric binary b-trees: Data structure and maintenance algorithms. *Acta Informatica*, 1:290–306, 1972.

[6] G. Blelloch, D. Ferizovic, and Y. Sun. Just join for parallel ordered sets. *arXiv preprint arXiv:1602.02120*, 2016.

[7] G. E. Blelloch and M. Reid-Miller. Fast set operations using treaps. In *Proc. ACM Symposium on Parallel Algorithms and Architectures (SPAA)*, pages 16 26, 1998.

[8] N. Blum and K. Mehlhorn. On the average number of rebalancing operations in weight-balanced trees. *Theoretical Computer Science*, 11(3):303–320, 1980.

[9] R. D. Blumofe and C. E. Leiserson. Space-efficient scheduling of multithreaded computations. *SIAM J. on Computing*, 27(1):202–229, 1998.

[10] R. P. Brent. The parallel evaluation of general arithmetic expressions. *Journal of the ACM*, 21(2):201–206, Apr. 1974.

[11] N. G. Bronson, J. Casper, H. Chafi, and K. Olukotun. A practical concurrent binary search tree. In *Proc. ACM SIGPLAN Symp. on Principles and Practice of Parallel Programming (PPoPP)*, pages 257–268, 2010.

[12] M. R. Brown and R. E. Tarjan. A fast merging algorithm. *Journal of the ACM (JACM)*, 26(2):211–226, 1979.

[13] E. D. Demaine, A. López-Ortiz, and J. I. Munro. Adaptive set intersections, unions, and differences. In *In Proceedings of the 11th Annual ACM-SIAM Symposium on Discrete Algorithms (SODA)*, 2000.

[14] S. Erb, M. Kobitzsch, and P. Sanders. Parallel bi-objective shortest paths using weight-balanced b-trees with bulk updates. In *Experimental Algorithms*, pages 111–122. Springer, 2014.

[15] L. Frias and J. Singler. Parallelization of bulk operations for STL dictionaries. In *Euro-Par 2007 Workshops: Parallel Processing, HPPC 2007, UNICORE Summit 2007, and VHPC 2007*, pages 49–58, 2007.

[16] Y. Hirai and K. Yamamoto. Balancing weight-balanced trees. *Journal of Functional Programming*, 21(03):287–307, 2011.

[17] F. K. Hwang and S. Lin. A simple algorithm for merging two disjoint linearly ordered sets. *SIAM J. on Computing*, 1(1):31–39, 1972.

[18] J. Katajainen. Efficient parallel algorithms for manipulating sorted sets. In *Proceedings of the 17th Annual Computer Science Conference*. University of Canterbury, 1994.

[19] H. T. Kung and P. L. Lehman. Concurrent manipulation of binary search trees. *ACM Trans. Database Syst.*, 5(3):354–382, 1980.

[20] K. S. Larsen. AVL trees with relaxed balance. *J. Comput. Syst. Sci.*, 61(3):508–522, 2000.

[21] S. Marlow et al. Haskell 2010 language report. *Available online http://www. haskell. org/(May 2011)*, 2010.

[22] D. R. Musser, G. J. Derge, and A. Saini. *STL tutorial and reference guide: C++ programming with the standard template library*. Addison-Wesley Professional, 2009.

[23] A. Natarajan and N. Mittal. Fast concurrent lock-free binary search trees. In *Proc. ACM SIGPLAN Symp. on Principles and Practice of Parallel Programming (PPoPP)*, pages 317–328, 2014.

[24] J. Nievergelt and E. M. Reingold. Binary search trees of bounded balance. *SIAM J. Comput.*, 2(1):33–43, 1973.

[25] H. Park and K. Park. Parallel algorithms for red–black trees. *Theoretical Computer Science*, 262(1):415–435, 2001.

[26] W. J. Paul, U. Vishkin, and H. Wagener. Parallel dictionaries in 2-3 trees. In *Proc. Intl. Colloq. on Automata, Languages and Programming (ICALP)*, pages 597–609, 1983.

[27] R. Seidel and C. R. Aragon. Randomized search trees. *Algorithmica*, 16:464–497, 1996.

[28] D. D. Sleator and R. E. Tarjan. Self-adjusting binary search trees. *Journal of the ACM (JACM)*, 32(3):652–686, 1985.

[29] M. Straka. Adams' trees revisited. In *Trends in Functional Programming*, pages 130–145. Springer, 2012.

[30] R. E. Tarjan. *Data Structures and Network Algorithms*. Society for Industrial and Applied Mathematics, Philadelphia, PA, USA, 1983.

APPENDIX

A. PROOFS FOR SOME LEMMAS

A.1 Proof for Lemma 8

PROOF. One observation in WB trees and treaps is that all nodes attached to a single layer root form a chain. This is true because if two children of one node v are both in layer i, the weight of v is more than 2^{i+1}, meaning that v should be layer $i+1$.

For a layer root v in a WB tree on layer k, $w(v)$ is at most 2^{k+1}. Considering the balance invariant that its child has weight at most $(1-\alpha)w(v)$, the weight of the t-th generation of its descendants is no more than $2^{k+1}(1-\alpha)^t$. This means that after $t^* = \log_{\frac{1}{1-\alpha}} 2$ generations, the weight should decrease to less than 2^k. Thus $d(v) \leq \log_{\frac{1}{1-\alpha}} 2$, which is a constant.

For treaps consider a layer root v on layer k that has weight $N \in [2^k, 2^{k+1})$. The probability that $d(v) \geq 2$ is equal to the probability that one of its grandchildren has weight at least 2^k. This probability P is:

$$P = \frac{1}{2^k} \sum_{i=2^k+1}^{N} \frac{i-2^k}{i} \tag{7}$$

$$\leq \frac{1}{2^k} \sum_{i=2^k+1}^{2^{k+1}} \frac{i-2^k}{i} \tag{8}$$

$$\approx 1 - \ln 2 \tag{9}$$

We denote $1-\ln 2$ as p_c. Similarly, the probability that $d(v) \geq 4$ should be less than p_c^2, and the probability shrink geometrically as $d(v)$ increase. Thus the expected value of $d(v)$ is a constant.

Since treaps come from a random permutation, all $s(v)$ are i.i.d. □

A.2 Proof for Lemma 5

PROOF. We are trying to show that for T_r =UNION(T_p, T_d) on AVL, RB or WB trees, if $r(T_p) > r(T_d)$ then $r(T_r) \leq r(T_p) + r(T_d)$.

For AVL and RB trees we use induction on $r(T_p)+r(T_d)$. When $r(T_d)+r(T_p) = 1$ the conclusion is trivial. If $r = r(T_p) > r(T_d)$, T_p will be split into two subtrees, with rank at most $r(T_p) - 1$ since we remove the root. T_d will be split into two trees with height at most $r(T_d)$ (Theorem 2). Using the inductive hypothesis, the two recursive calls will return two trees of height at most $r(T_p) - 1 + r(T_d)$. The result of the final JOIN is therefore at most $r(T_p) + r(T_d)$.

For WB trees, $|T| \leq |T_p| + |T_d| \leq 2|T_p|$. Thus $r(T) \leq r(T_p) + 1 \leq r(T_p) + r(T_d)$. □

Parallel Equivalence Class Sorting: Algorithms, Lower Bounds, and Distribution-Based Analysis

William E. Devanny
Dept. of Computer Science
Univ. of California, Irvine
Irvine, CA 92697 USA
wdevanny@uci.edu

Michael T. Goodrich
Dept. of Computer Science
Univ. of California, Irvine
Irvine, CA 92697 USA
goodrich@uci.edu

Kristopher Jetviroj
Dept. of Computer Science
Univ. of California, Irvine
Irvine, CA 92697 USA
kjetviro@uci.edu

ABSTRACT

We study parallel comparison-based algorithms for finding all equivalence classes of a set of n elements, where sorting according to some total order is not possible. Such scenarios arise, for example, in applications, such as in distributed computer security, where each of n agents are working to identify the private group to which they belong, with the only operation available to them being a zero-knowledge pairwise-comparison (which is sometimes called a "secret handshake") that reveals only whether two agents are in the same group or in different groups. We provide new parallel algorithms for this problem, as well as new lower bounds and distribution-based analysis.

1. INTRODUCTION

In the *Equivalence Class Sorting* problem, we are given a set, S, of n elements and an equivalence relation, and we are asked to group the elements of the set into their equivalence classes by only making pairwise equivalence tests (e.g., see [15]). For example, imagine a convention of n political interns where each person at the convention belongs to one of k political parties, such as Republican, Democrat, Green, Labor, Libertarian, etc., but no intern wants to openly express his or her party affiliation unless they know they are talking with someone of their same party. Suppose further that each party has a secret handshake that two people can perform that allows them to determine whether they are in the same political party (or they belong to different unidentified parties). We are interested in this paper in the computational complexity of the equivalence class sorting problem in distributed and parallel settings, where we would like to minimize the total number of parallel comparison rounds and/or the total number of comparisons needed in order to classify every element in S.

An important property of the equivalence class sorting problem is that it is not possible to order the elements in S according to some total ordering that is consistent with the equivalence classes. Such a restriction could come from a general lack of such an ordering or from security or privacy concerns. For example, consider the following applications:

- *Generalized fault diagnosis.* Suppose that each of n different computers are in one of k distinct malware states, depending on whether they have been infected with various computer worms. Each worm does not wish to reveal its presence, but it nevertheless has an ability to detect when another computer is already infected with it (or risk autodetection by an exponential cascade, as occurred with the Morris worm [18]). But a worm on one computer is unlikely to be able to detect a different kind of worm on another computer. Thus, two computers can only compare each other to determine if they have exactly the same kinds of infections or not. The generalized fault diagnosis problem, therefore, is to have the n computers classify themselves into k malware groups depending on their infections, where the only testing method available is for two computers to perform a pairwise comparison that tells them that they are either in the same malware state or they are in different states. This is a generalization of the classic fault diagnosis problem, where there are only two states, "faulty" or "good," which is studied in a number of interesting papers, including one from the very first SPAA conference (e.g., see [4–6, 11, 20, 21]).
- *Group classification via secret handshakes.* This is a cryptographic analogue to the motivating example given above of interns at a political convention. In this case, n agents are each assigned to one of k groups, such that any two agents can perform a cryptographic "secret handshake" protocol that results in them learning only whether they belong to the same group or not (e.g., see [7, 14, 23, 25]). The problem is to perform an efficient number of pairwise secret-handshake tests in a few parallel rounds so that each agent identifies itself with the others of its group.
- *Graph mining.* Graph mining is the study of structure in collections of graphs [9]. One of the algorithmic problems in this area is to classify which of a collection of n graphs are isomorphic to one another (e.g., see [19]). That is, testing if two graphs are in the same group involves performing a graph isomorphism comparison of the two graphs, which is a computation that tends to be nontrivial but is nevertheless computationally feasible in some contexts (e.g., see [3]).

SPAA '16, July 11 - 13, 2016, Pacific Grove, CA, USA

ISBN 978-1-4503-4210-0/16/07...$15.00

DOI: http://dx.doi.org/10.1145/2935764.2935778

Note that each of these applications contains two important features that form the essence of the equivalence class sorting problem:

1. In each application, it is not possible to sort elements according to a known total order, either because no such total order exists or because it would break a security/privacy condition to provide such a total order.
2. The equivalence or nonequivalence between two elements can be determined only through pairwise comparisons.

There are nevertheless some interesting differences between these applications, as well, which motivate our study of two different versions of the equivalence class sorting problem. Namely, in the first two applications, the comparisons done in any given round in an algorithm must be disjoint, since the elements themselves are performing the comparisons. In the latter two applications, however, the elements are the objects of the comparisons, and we could, in principle, allow for comparisons involving multiple copies of the same element in each round. For this reason, we allow for two versions of the equivalence class sorting problem:

- *Exclusive-Read (ER)* version. In this version, each element in S can be involved in at most a single comparison of itself and another element in S in any given comparison round.
- *Concurrent-Read (CR)* version. In this version, each element in S can be involved in multiple comparisons of itself and other elements in S in any comparison round.

In either version, we are interested in minimizing the number of parallel comparison rounds and/or the total number of comparisons needed to classify every element of S into its group.

Because we expect the number parallel comparison rounds and the total number of comparisons to be the main performance bottlenecks, we are interested here in studying the equivalence class sorting problem in Valiant's parallel comparison model [24], which only counts steps in which comparisons are made. This is a synchronous computation model that does not count any steps done between comparison steps, for example, to aggregate groups of equivalent elements based on comparisons done in previous steps.

1.1 Related Prior Work

In addition to the references cited above that motivate the equivalence class sorting problem or study the special case when the number of groups, k, is two, Jayapaul *et al.* [15] study the general equivalence class sorting problem, albeit strictly from a sequential perspective. For example, they show that one can solve the equivalence class sorting problem using $O(n^2/\ell)$ comparisons, where ℓ is the size of the smallest equivalence class. They also show that this problem has a lower bound of $\Omega(n^2/\ell^2)$ even if the value of ℓ is known in advance.

The equivalence class sorting problem is, of course, related to comparison-based algorithms for computing the majority or mode of a set of elements, for which there is an extensive set of prior research (e.g., see [1, 2, 10, 22]). None of these algorithms for majority or mode result in efficient parallel algorithms for the equivalence class sorting problem, however.

1.2 Our Results

In this paper, we study the equivalence class sorting (ECS) problem from a parallel perspective, providing a number of new results, including the following:

1. The CR version of the ECS problem can be solved in $O(k + \log\log n)$ parallel rounds using n processors, were k is the number of equivalence classes.
2. The ER version of the ECS problem can be solved in $O(k \log n)$ parallel rounds using n processors, were k is the number of equivalence classes.
3. The ER version of the ECS problem can be solved in $O(1)$ parallel rounds using n processors, for the case when ℓ is at least λn, for a fixed constant $0 < \lambda \leq 0.4$, where ℓ is the size of the smallest equivalence class.
4. If every equivalence class is of size f, then solving the ECS problem requires $\Omega(n^2/f)$ total comparisons. This improves a lower bound of $\Omega(n^2/f^2)$ by Jayapaul *et al.* [15].
5. Solving the ECS problem requires $\Omega(n^2/\ell)$ total comparisons, where ℓ is the size of the smallest equivalence class. This improves a lower bound of $\Omega(n^2/\ell^2)$ by Jayapaul *et al.* [15].
6. In Section 4, we study how to efficiently solve the ECS problem when the input is drawn from a known distribution on equivalence classes. In this setting, we assume n elements have been sampled and fed as input to the algorithm. We establish a relationship between the mean of the distribution and the algorithm's total number of comparisons, obtaining upper bounds with high probability for a variety of interesting distributions.
7. We provide the results of several experiments to validate the results from Section 4 and study how total comparison counts change as parameters of the distributions change.

Our methods are based on several novel techniques, including a two-phased compounding-comparison technique for the parallel upper bounds and the use of a new coloring argument for the lower bounds.

2. PARALLEL ALGORITHMS

In this section, we provide efficient parallel algorithms for solving the equivalence class sorting (ECS) problem in Valiant's parallel model of computation [24]. We focus on both the exclusive-read (ER) and concurrent-read (CR) versions of the problem, and we assume we have n processors, each of which can be assigned to one equivalence comparison test to perform in a given parallel round. Note, therefore, that any lower bound, $T(n)$, on the total number of comparisons needed to solve the ECS problem (e.g., as given by Jayapaul *et al.* [15] and as we discuss in Section 3), immediately implies a lower bound of $\Omega(T(n)/n)$ for the number of parallel rounds of computation using n processors per round. For instance, these lower bounds imply that the number of parallel rounds for solving the ECS problem with n processors must be $\Omega(n/\ell)$ and $\Omega(k)$, respectively, where k is the number of equivalence classes and ℓ is the size of the smallest equivalence class.

With respect to upper bounds, recall that Jayapaul *et al.* [15] studied the ECS problem from a sequential perspective. Unfortunately, their algorithm cannot be easily parallelized, because the comparisons performed in a "round" of their algorithm depend on the results from other comparisons in that same round. Thus, new parallel ECS algorithms are needed.

2.1 Algorithms Based on the Number of Groups

In this subsection, we describe CR and ER algorithms based on knowledge of the number of groups, k.

If two sets of elements are sorted into their equivalence classes, merging the two answers into the answer for the union requires at most k^2 equivalence tests by simply performing a comparison between every pair of equivalence class one from the first answer and one from the second. This idea leads to the following algorithm, which uses a two-phased compounding-comparison technique to solve the ECS problem:

1. Initialize a list of n answers containing the individual input elements.
2. While the number of processors per answer is less than $4k^2$, merge pairs of answers by performing k^2 tests.
3. While there is more than one answer, let ck^2 be the number of processors available per answer and merge c answers together by performing at most $\binom{c}{2}k^2$ tests between each of the answers.

We analyze this algorithm in the following two lemmas and we illustrate it in Figure 1.

LEMMA 1. *The first while loop takes $O(k)$ rounds to complete.*

PROOF. In each round the number of equivalence classes in an answer at most doubles until it reaches the upper bound of k. In loop iteration $i \leq \lceil \log k \rceil$, the answers are size at most 2^i and there are 2^i processors per answer. Therefore it takes at most 2^i rounds to merge two answers. The number of rounds to reach the $\lceil \log k \rceil$ loop iteration is $O(k)$. For loop iterations $\lceil \log k \rceil < i < \lceil \log k \rceil^2$, the answers are size at most k, but there are still at most 2^i processors per answer. The number of rounds needed for these iterations is also $O(k)$, as it forms a geometric sum that adds up to be $O(k)$. This part of the algorithm is illustrated in the bottom half of Figure 1. □

LEMMA 2. *The second while loop takes $O(\log \log n)$ rounds to complete.*

PROOF. When entering the second while, there are more processors per answer than needed to merge just two answers at a time. If an answer has access to ck^2 processors, then a group of $\binom{c}{2}$ answers can merge into one answer in a single round. This means that if there are $n/(ck^2)$ answers at the start of a round, then we merge groups of $c^2/2$ answers into one answer and there are $n/(c^3k/2)$ answers remaining. Because $c \geq 4$ by the condition of the first while loop, in the iteration i of the second while loop, there are at most $n/(2^{2^i}k)$ answers. And so the second while loop will terminate after $O(\log \log n)$ rounds with the single answer for the entire input. This is illustrated in the top half of Figure 1. □

Combining these two lemmas, we get the following.

THEOREM 1. *The CR version of the equivalence class sorting problem on n elements and k equivalence classes can be solved in $O(k+\log \log n)$ parallel rounds of equivalence tests, using n processors in Valiant's parallel comparison model.*

PROOF. Lemmas 1 and 2. □

We also have the following.

THEOREM 2. *The ER version of the equivalence class sorting problem on n elements and k equivalence classes can be solved in $O(k \log n)$ parallel rounds of equivalence tests, using n processors in Valiant's parallel comparison model.*

PROOF. Merging two answers for the ER version of the ECS problem model will always take at most k rounds. Repeatedly merging answers will arrive at one answer in $\log n$ iterations. So equivalence class sorting can be done in $O(k \log n)$ parallel rounds of equivalence tests. □

2.2 Algorithms Based on the Smallest Group Size

In this subsection, we describe ER algorithms based on knowledge of ℓ, the size of the smallest equivalence class. We assume in this section that $\ell \geq \lambda n$, for some constant $\lambda > 0$, and we show how to solve the ECS problem in this scenario using $O(1)$ parallel comparison rounds. Our methods are generalizations of previous methods for the parallel fault diagnosis problem when there are only two classes, "good" and "faulty" [4-6,11]. Let us assume, therefore, that there are at least 3 equivalence classes.

We begin with a theorem from Goodrich [11].

THEOREM 3 (GOODRICH [11]). *Let V be a set of n vertices, and let $0 < \gamma, \lambda < 1$. Let $H_d = (V, E)$ be a directed graph defined by the union of d independent randomly-chosen[1] Hamiltonian cycles on V (with all such cycles equally likely). Then, for all subsets W of V of λn vertices, H_d induces at least one strongly connected component on W of size greater than $\gamma \lambda n$, with probability at least*

$$1 - e^{n[(1+\lambda)\ln 2 + d(\alpha \ln \alpha + \beta \ln \beta - (1-\lambda)\ln(1-\lambda))] + O(1)},$$

where $\alpha = 1 - \frac{1-\gamma}{2}\lambda$ and $\beta = 1 - \frac{1+\gamma}{2}\lambda$.

In the context of the present paper, let us take $\gamma = 1/4$, so $\alpha = 1 - (3/8)\lambda$ and $\beta = 1 - (5/8)\lambda$. Let us also assume that $\lambda \leq 0.4$, since we are considering the case when the number of equivalence classes is at least 3; hence, the smallest equivalence class is of size at most $n/3$.

Unfortunately, using standard approximations for the natural logarithm is not sufficient for us to employ the above probability bound for small values of λ. So instead we use the following inequalities, which hold for x in the range $[0, 0.4]$ (e.g., see [16]), and are based on the Taylor series for the natural logarithm:

$$-x - \frac{x^2}{2} - \frac{x^3}{2} \leq \ln(1-x) \leq -x - \frac{x^2}{2} - \frac{x^3}{4}.$$

[1]That is, H_d is defined by the union of cycles determined by d random permutations of the n vertices in V, so H_d is, by definition, a simple directed graph.

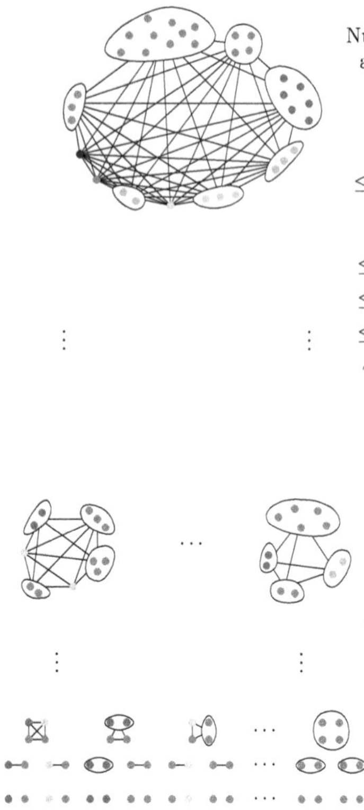

Number of answers	Processors per answer	Answer size	Rounds needed	Answer reduction factor
1	n	k		
$\vdots$	$\vdots$	$\vdots$	$\vdots$	$\vdots$
$\leq n/2^{2^i}k^2$	$\geq 2^{2^i}k^2$	$\leq k$	1	$\sim 2^{2^i}$
$\vdots$	$\vdots$	$\vdots$	$\vdots$	$\vdots$
$\leq n/2^8k^2$	$\geq 2^8k^2$	$\leq k$	1	$\sim 2^8$
$\leq n/2^4k^2$	$\geq 2^4k^2$	$\leq k$	1	2^4
$\leq n/2^2k^2$	$\geq 2^2k^2$	$\leq k$	1	2^2
$\sim n/2k^2$	$\sim 2k^2$	$\leq k$	1	2
$\sim n/k^2$	$\sim k^2$	$\leq k$	1	2
$\vdots$	$\vdots$	$\vdots$	$\vdots$	$\vdots$
$\sim n/2k$	$\sim 2k$	$\leq k$	$k/2$	2
$\sim n/k$	$\sim k$	$\leq k$	k	2
$\sim 2n/k$	$\sim k/2$	$\leq k/2$	$k/2$	2
$\vdots$	$\vdots$	$\vdots$	$\vdots$	$\vdots$
n/4	4	≤ 4	4	2
$n/2$	2	≤ 2	2	2
n	1	1	1	2

Second while loop phase (rows from 1 through $\leq n/2^2k^2$)

First while loop phase (rows from $\sim n/2k^2$ through n)

Figure 1: A visualization of the parallel algorithm with a table on the right keeping track of relevant numbers for each loop iteration.

These bounds allow us to bound the main term, t, in the above probability of Theorem 3 (for $\gamma = 1/4$) as follows:

$$\begin{aligned} t &= \alpha \ln \alpha + \beta \ln \beta - (1-\lambda)\ln(1-\lambda) \\ &= (1-\frac{3}{8}\lambda)\ln(1-\frac{3}{8}\lambda) + (1-\frac{5}{8}\lambda)\ln(1-\frac{5}{8}\lambda) \\ &\quad - (1-\lambda)\ln(1-\lambda) \\ &\leq (1-\frac{3}{8}\lambda)\left(-\frac{3}{8}\lambda - \frac{1}{2}\left(\frac{3}{8}\lambda\right)^2 - \frac{1}{4}\left(\frac{3}{8}\lambda\right)^3\right) \\ &\quad + (1-\frac{5}{8}\lambda)\left(-\frac{5}{8}\lambda - \frac{1}{2}\left(\frac{5}{8}\lambda\right)^2 - \frac{1}{4}\left(\frac{5}{8}\lambda\right)^3\right) \\ &\quad - (1-\lambda)\left(-\lambda - \frac{\lambda^2}{2} - \frac{\lambda^3}{2}\right) \\ &\leq -\frac{3743}{8192}\lambda^4 + \frac{19}{256}\lambda^3 - \frac{15}{64}\lambda^2, \end{aligned}$$

which, in turn, is at most

$$-\frac{\lambda^2}{8},$$

for $0 < \lambda \leq 0.4$. Thus, since this bound is negative for any constant $0 < \lambda \leq 0.4$, we can set d to be a constant (depending on λ) so that Theorem 3 holds with high probability.

Our ECS algorithm, then, is as follows:

1. Construct a graph, H_d, as in Theorem 3, as described above, with d set to a constant so that the theorem holds for the fixed λ in the range $(0, 0.4]$ that is given. Note that this step does not require any comparisons; hence, we do not count the time for this step in our analysis (and the theorem holds with high probability in any case).
2. Note that H_d is a union of d Hamiltonian cycles. Thus, let us perform all the comparisons in H_d in $2d$ rounds. Furthermore, we can do this set of comparisons even for the ER version of the problem. Moreover, since d is $O(1)$, this step involves a constant number of parallel rounds (of $O(n)$ comparisons per round).
3. For each strongly connected component, C, in H_d consisting of elements of the same equivalence class, compare the elements in C with the other elements in S, taking $|C|$ at a time. By Theorem 3, $|C| \geq \lambda n/8$. Thus, this step can be performed in $O(1/\lambda) = O(1)$ rounds for each connected component; hence it requires $O(1)$ parallel rounds in total. Moreover, after this step completes, we will necessarily have identified all the members of each equivalence class.

We summarize as follows.

THEOREM 4. *Suppose S is a set of n elements, such that the smallest equivalence class in S is of size at least λn, for a fixed constant, λ, in the range $(0, 0.4]$. Then the ER version of the equivalence class sorting problem on S can be solved in $O(1)$ parallel rounds using n processors in Valiant's parallel comparison model.*

This theorem is true regardless of whether or not λ is known. If the value of λ is not known, it is possible to repeatedly run the ECS algorithm starting with an arbitrary constant of 0.4 for λ and halving the constant whenever the algorithm fails. Once the value is less than the unknown λ, the algorithm will succeed and the number of rounds will be independent of n and a function of only the constant λ.

As we show in the next section, this performance is optimal when $\ell \geq \lambda n$, for a fixed constant $\lambda \in (0, 0.4]$.

3. LOWER BOUNDS

The following lower bound questions were left open by Jayapaul *et al.* [15]:

- If every equivalence class has size f, the total number of comparisons needed to solve the equivalence class sorting problem $\Theta(n^2/f)$ or $\Theta(n^2/f^2)$?
- Is the total number of comparisons for finding an element in the smallest equivalence class $\Theta(n^2/\ell)$ or $\Theta(n^2/\ell^2)$?

Speaking loosely these lower bounds can be thought of as a question of how difficult it is for an element to locate its equivalence class. The $\Theta(n^2/f)$ and $\Theta(n^2/\ell)$ bounds can be interpreted as saying the average element needs to compare to at least one element in most of the other equivalence classes before it finds an equivalent element. Because there must be $\binom{x}{2}$ comparisons between x equivalence classes, the $\Theta(n^2/f^2)$ and $\Theta(n^2/\ell^2)$ bounds say we do not need too many more comparisons then the very minimal number needed just to differentiate the equivalence classes. It seems unlikely that so few comparisons are required and we prove that this intuition is correct by proving lower bounds of $\Omega(n^2/f)$ and $\Omega(n^2/\ell)$ comparisons.

Note that these lower bounds are on the total number of comparisons needed to accomplish a task, that is they bound the work a parallel algorithm would need to perform. By dividing by n, they also give simple bounds on the number of rounds needed in either the ER or CR models.

With respect to such lower bound questions as these, let us maintain the state of an algorithm's knowledge about element relationships in a simple graph. At each step, the vertex set of this graph is a partition of the elements where each set is a partially discovered equivalence class for S. Thus, each element in S is associated with exactly one vertex in this graph at each step of the algorithm, and a vertex can have multiple elements from S associated with it. If a pair of elements was compared and found to not be equal, then there should be an edge in between the two vertices containing those elements. So initially the graph has a vertex for each element and no edges. When an algorithm tests equivalence for a pair of elements, then, if the elements are not equivalent, the appropriate edge is added (if it is absent) and, if the elements are equivalent, the two corresponding vertices are contracted into a new vertex whose set is the union of the two. A depiction of this is shown in Figure 2. An algorithm has finished sorting once this graph is a clique and the vertex sets are the corresponding equivalence classes.

An *equitable k-coloring* of a graph is a proper coloring of a graph such that the size of each color class is either $\lfloor n/k \rfloor$ or $\lceil n/k \rceil$. A *weighted equitable k-coloring* of a vertex weighted graph is a proper coloring of a graph such that the sum of the weight in each color class is either $\lfloor n/k \rfloor$ or $\lceil n/k \rceil$. Examples of these can be seen in Figure 3.

An adversary for the problem of equivalence class sorting when every equivalence class has the same size f (so f divides n) must maintain that the graph has a weighted equitable n/f-coloring where the weights are the size of the vertex sets. The adversary we describe here will maintain such a coloring and additionally mark the elements and the color classes in a special way. It proceeds as follows.

First, initialize an arbitrary equitable coloring on the starting graph that consists of n vertices and no edges. For each comparison of two elements done by the adversary algorithm, let us characterize how we react based on the following case analysis:

- If either of the elements is unmarked and this comparison would increase its degree to higher than $n/4f$, then mark it as having "high" element degree.
- If either element is still unmarked, they currently have the same color, and there is another unmarked vertex such that it is not adjacent to a vertex with the color involved in the comparison and no vertex with its color is adjacent to the unmarked vertex in the comparison (i.e. we can have it swap colors with one of the vertices in the comparison), then swap the color of that element and the unmarked element in the comparison.
- If either element is still unmarked, they currently have the same color, and there is no other unmarked vertex with a different unmarked color not adjacent to the color of the two elements being compared, then mark all elements with the color involved in the comparison as having "high" color degree and mark the color as having "high" degree.
- At this point, either both elements are marked and we answer based on their color, or one of the elements is unmarked and they have different colors, so we answer "not equal" to the adversary algorithm.

At all times, the vertices that contain unmarked elements all have weight one, because the adversary only answers equivalent for comparisons once both vertices are marked. When a color class is marked, all elements in that color class are marked as having "high" color degree. A few of the cases the adversary goes through are depicted in Figure 4.

LEMMA 3. *If $n/8$ elements are marked during the execution of an algorithm, then $\Omega(n^2/f)$ comparisons were performed.*

PROOF. There are three types of marked vertices: those with "high" element degree marks, those with "high" color degree marks, and those with both marks.

The color classes must have been marked as having "high" degree when a comparison was being performed between two elements of that color class and there were no unmarked color candidates to swap colors with. Because one of the elements in the comparison had degree less than $n/4f$, only a quarter of the elements have a color class it cannot be swapped with. So if there were at least $n - n/4$ unmarked elements in total, then the elements in the newly marked color class must have been in a comparison $n/2$ times.

The "high" element degree elements were involved in at least $n/4f$ comparisons each. So if i color classes were marked and j elements were only marked with "high" element degree, then the marked elements must have been a part of a test at least $ni/2 + nj/4f \geq (i + j/f)n/4$ times. Once $if + j \geq n/8$, then at least $n^2/64f$ equivalence tests were performed. □

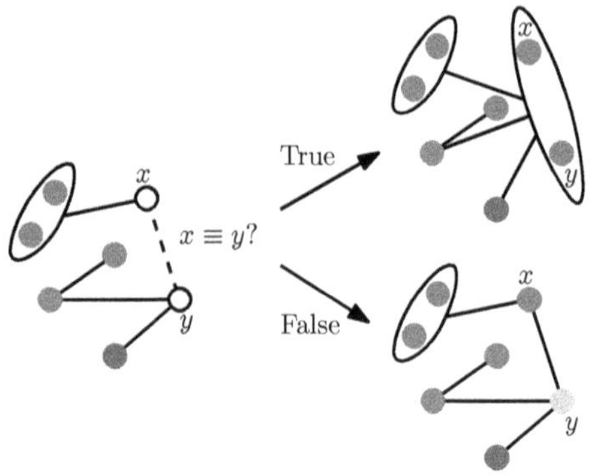

Figure 2: We test if x and y are in the same equivalence class. If they are, their vertices are contracted together. If they are not, an edge is added.

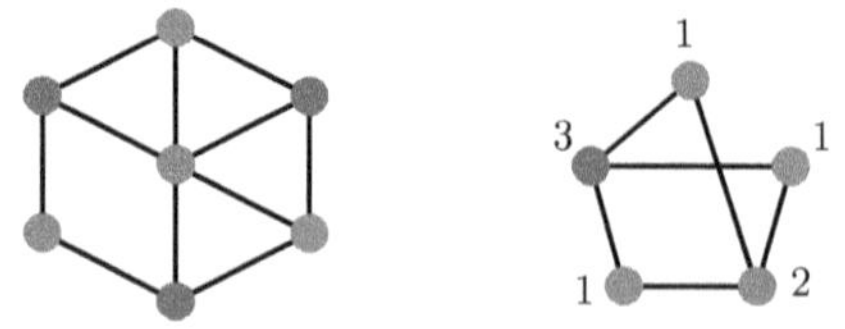

Figure 3: On the left we have a graph with an equitable 3-coloring and on the right we have a graph with a weighted equitable 3-coloring.

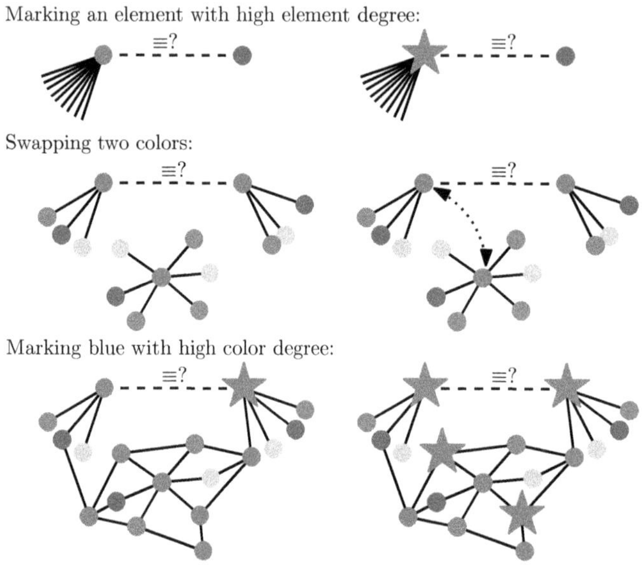

Figure 4: Three cases of how the adversary works to mark vertices and swap colors. The dashed line indicates the two elements being compared. Marked vertices are denoted with stars.

THEOREM 5. *If every equivalence class has the same size f, then sorting requires at least $\Omega(n^2/f)$ equivalence comparisons.*

PROOF. When an algorithm finishes sorting, each vertex will have weight f and so the elements must all be marked. Thus, by Lemma 3, at least $\Omega(n^2/f)$ comparisons must have been performed. □

We also have the following lower bound as well.

THEOREM 6. *Finding an element in the smallest equivalence class, whose size is ℓ, requires at least $\Omega(n^2/\ell)$ equivalence comparisons.*

PROOF. We use an adversary argument similar to the previous one, but we start with ℓ vertices colored a special *smallest class color (scc)* and seperate the remaining $n-\ell$ vertices into $\lfloor (n-\ell)/(\ell+1) \rfloor$ color classes of size $\frac{n}{\lfloor (n-\ell)/(\ell+1) \rfloor}$ or $\frac{n}{\lfloor (n-\ell)/(\ell+1) \rfloor} + 1$.

There are two changes to the previous adversary responses. First, the degree requirement for having "high" degree is now $n/4\ell$. Second, if an scc element is about to be marked as having "high" degree, we attempt to swap its color with any valid unmarked vertex. Otherwise, we proceed exactly as before.

If an algorithm attempts to identify an element as belonging to the smallest equivalence class, no scc elements are marked, and there have been fewer than $n/8$ elements marked, then the identified element must be able to be swapped with a different color and the algorithm made a mistake. Therefore, to derive a lower bound for the total number of comparisons, it suffices to derive a lower bound for the number of equivalence tests until an scc element is marked.

The scc color class cannot be marked as having "high" color degree until at least one scc element has high element degree. However, as long as fewer than $n/8$ elements are marked, we will never mark an scc element with "high" degree. So at least $n/8$ elements need to be marked as having "high" element degree or "high" color degree and, by the same type of counting as in Lemma 3, $\Omega(n^2/\ell)$ equivalence tests are needed. □

4. SORTING DISTRIBUTIONS

In this subsection, we study a version of the equivalence class sorting problem where we are given a distribution, D, on a countable set, S, and we wish to enumerate the set in order of most likely to least likely, $s_0, s_1, s_2, \ldots$. For example, consider the following distributions:

- Uniform: In this case, D is a distribution on k equivalence classes, with each equivalence class being equally likely for every element of S.
- Geometric: Here, D is a distribution such that the ith most probable equivalence class has probability $p^i(1-p)$. Each element "flips" a biased coin where "heads" occurs with probability p until it comes up "tails." Then that element is in equivalence class i if it flipped i heads.
- Poisson: In this case, D is model of the number of times an event occurs in an interval of time, with an expected number of events determined by a parameter λ. Equivalence class i is defined to be all the samples that have the same number of events occurring, where the probability of i events occurring is
$$\frac{\lambda^i e^{-\lambda}}{i!}.$$
- Zeta: This distribution, D, is related to Zipf's law, and models when the sizes of the equivalence classes follows a power law, based on a parameter, $s > 1$, which is common in many real-world scenarios, such as the frequency of words in natural language documents. With respect to equivalence classes, the ith equivalence class has probability
$$\frac{i^{-s}}{\zeta(s)},$$
where $\zeta(s)$ is Riemann zeta function (which normalizes the probabilities to sum to 1).

So as to number equivalence classes from most likely to least likely, as $i = 0, 1, \ldots$, define $D_{\mathbb{N}}$ to be a distribution on the natural numbers such that
$$\Pr_{x\sim D_{\mathbb{N}}}[x=i] = \Pr_{y\sim D}[y = s_i].$$
Furthermore, so as to "cut off" this distribution at n, define $D_{\mathbb{N}}(n)$ to be a distribution on the natural numbers less than or equal to n such that, for $0 \le i < n$,
$$\Pr_{x\sim D_{\mathbb{N}}(n)}[x=i] = \Pr_{y\sim D_{\mathbb{N}}}[y=i]$$
and
$$\Pr_{x\sim D_{\mathbb{N}}(n)}[x=n] = \Pr_{y\sim D_{\mathbb{N}}}[y\ge n].$$
That is, we are "piling up" the tail of the $D_{\mathbb{N}}$ distribution on n.

The following theorem shows that we can use $D_{\mathbb{N}}(n)$ to bound the number of comparisons in an ECS algorithm when the equivalence classes are drawn from D. In particular, we focus here on an algorithm by Jayapaul *et al.* [15] for equivalence class sorting, which involves a round-robin testing regiment, such that each element, x, initiates a comparison with the next element, y, with an unknown relationship to x, until all equivalence classes are known.

THEOREM 7. *Given a distribution, D, on a set of equivalence classes, then n elements who have corresponding equivalence class independently drawn from D can be equivalence class sorted using a total number of comparisons stochastically dominated by twice the sum of n draws from the distribution $D_{\mathbb{N}}(n)$.*

PROOF. Let V_i denote the random variable that is equal to the natural number corresponding to the equivalence class of element i in $D_{\mathbb{N}}(n)$. We denote the number of elements in equivalence class i as Y_i. Let us denote the number of equivalence tests performed by the algorithm by Jayapaul *et al.* [15] using the random variable, R.

By a lemma from [15], for any pair of equivalence classes, i and j, the round-robin ECS algorithm performs at most $2\min(Y_i, Y_j)$ equivalence tests in total. Thus, the total number of equivalence tests in our distribution-based analysis is upper bounded by

$$\begin{aligned}
R &\le \sum_{i=0}^{\infty}\sum_{j=0}^{i-1} 2\min(Y_i, Y_j) \\
&= 2\sum_{i=0}^{n}\sum_{j=0}^{i-1}\min(Y_i,Y_j) + 2\sum_{i=n+1}^{\infty}\sum_{j=0}^{i-1}\min(Y_i,Y_j) \\
&\le 2\sum_{i=0}^{n}\sum_{j=0}^{i-1} Y_i + 2\sum_{i=n+1}^{\infty} nY_i \\
&\le 2\left(\sum_{i=0}^{n} iY_i + \sum_{i=n+1}^{\infty} nY_i\right) = 2\sum_{i=1}^{n} V_i
\end{aligned}$$

The second line in the above simplification is a simple separation of the double summation and the third line follows because $\sum_{j=0}^{i-1}\min(Y_i,Y_j)$ is zero if Y_i is zero and at most n, otherwise. So the total number of comparisons in the algorithm is bounded by twice the sum of n draws from $D_{\mathbb{N}}(n)$. □

Given this theorem, we can apply it to a number of distributions to show that the total number of comparisons performed is linear with high probability.

THEOREM 8. *If D is a discrete uniform, a geometric, or a Poisson distribution on a set equivalence classes, then it is possible to equivalence class sort using linear total number of comparisons with exponentially high probability.*

PROOF. The sum of n draws from $D_{\mathbb{N}}(n)$ is stochastically dominated by the sum of n draws from $D_{\mathbb{N}}$. Let us consider each distribution in turn.

- Uniform: The sum of n draws from a discrete uniform distribution is bounded by n times the maximum value.
- Geometric: Let p be the parameter of a geometric distribution and let $X = \sum_{i=0}^{n-1} X_i$ where the X_i are drawn from *Geom*(p), which is, of course, related to the Binomial distribution, *Bin*(n,p), where one flips n coins with probability p and records the number of "heads." Then, by a Chernoff bound for the geometric distribution (e.g., see [17]),
$$\begin{aligned}
\Pr[X-(1/p)n > k] &= \Pr[Bin(k+(1/p)n, p) < n] \\
&\le e^{-2\frac{(pk+n-n)^2}{k+(1/p)n}} \\
\Pr[X > (2/p)n] &\le e^{-np}
\end{aligned}$$

- Poisson: Let λ be the parameter of a Poisson distribution and let $Y = \sum_{i=0}^{n-1} Y_i$ where the Y_i are drawn from $Poisson(\lambda)$. Then, by a Chernoff bound for the Poisson distribution (e.g., see [17]),

$$\begin{aligned} \Pr[Y > (\lambda(e-1)+1)n] &= \Pr[e^Y > e^{(\lambda(e-1)+1)n}] \\ &\le \frac{(E[e^{Y_i}])^n}{e^{(\lambda(e-1)+1)n}} \\ &= \frac{e^{\lambda(e-1)n}}{e^{(\lambda(e-1)+1)n}} = e^{-n} \end{aligned}$$

So, in each case with exponentially high probability, the sum of n draws from the distribution is $O(n)$ and the round-robin algorithm does $O(n)$ total equivalence tests. □

We next address the zeta distribution.

THEOREM 9. *Given a zeta distribution with parameter $s > 2$, n elements who have corresponding equivalence class independently drawn from the zeta distribution can be equivalence class sorted in $O(n)$ work in expectation.*

PROOF. When $s > 2$, the mean of the zeta distribution is

$$\frac{\zeta(s-1)}{\zeta(s)},$$

which is a constant. So the sum of n draws from the distribution is expected to be linear. Therefore, the expected total number of comparisons in the round-robin algorithm is linear. □

Unfortunately, for zeta distributions it is not immediately clear if it is possible to improve the above theorem so that total number of comparisons is shown to be linear when $2 \geq s > 1$ or obtain high probability bounds on these bounds. This uncertainty motivates us to look experimentally at how different values of s cause the runtime to behave. Likewise, our high-probability bounds on the total number of comparisons in the round-robin algorithm for the other distibutions invites experimental analysis as well.

5. EXPERIMENTS

In this section, we report on experimental validatations of the theorems from the previous section and investigations of the behavior of running the round-robin algorithm on the zeta distribution. For the uniform, geometric, and Poisson distributions, we ran ten tests on sizes of $10,000$ to $200,000$ elements incrementing in steps of $10,000$. For the zeta distribution, because setting $s < 2$ seems to lead to a super linear number of comparisons, we reduced the test sizes by a factor of 10 and ran ten tests each on sizes from $1,000$ to $20,000$ in increments of $1,000$. For each distribution we used the following parameter settings for various experiments:

Uniform:	$k = 10, 25, 100$
Geometric:	$p = \frac{1}{2}, \frac{1}{10}, \frac{1}{50}$
Poisson:	$\lambda = 1, 5, 25$
Zeta:	$s = 1.1, 1.5, 2, 2.5$

The results of these tests are plotted in Figure 5. Best fit lines were fitted whenever we have theorems stating that there will be a linear number of comparisons with high probability or in expectation (i.e., everything except for zeta with $s < 2$). We include extra plots of the zeta distribution tests with the $s = 1.1$ data and the $s = 1.1, 1.5$ data removed to better see the other data sets.

We can see from the data that the number of comparisons for the uniform, geometric, and Poisson distributions are so tightly concentrated around the best fit line that only one data point is visible. Contrariwise, the data points for the zeta distributions do not cluster nearly as nicely. Even when we have linear expected comparisons with $s = 2$, the data points vary by as much as 10%.

6. CONCLUSION

In this paper we have studied the equivalence class sorting problem, from a parallel perspective, giving several new algorithms, as well as new lower bounds and distribution-based analysis. We leave as open problems the following interesting questions:

- Is it possible to find all equivalance classes in the ER version of the ECS problem in $O(k)$ parallel rounds, for $k \geq 3$, where k is the number of equivalence classes? Note that the answer is "yes" for $k = 2$, as it follows from previous results for the parallel fault diagnosis problem [4–6].
- Is it possible to bound the number of comparisons away from $O(n^2)$ for the zeta distribution when $s < 2$ even just in expectation?
- Is it possible to prove a high-probability concentration bound for the zeta distribution, similar to the concentration bounds we proved for other distributions?

Acknowledgments

This research was supported in part by the National Science Foundation under grant 1228639 and a gift from the 3M Corporation. William E. Devanny was supported by an NSF Graduate Research Fellowship under grant DGE-1321846. We would like to thank David Eppstein and Ian Munro for several helpful discussions concerning the topics of this paper.

7. REFERENCES

[1] L. Alonso and E. M. Reingold. Analysis of Boyer and Moore's MJRTY algorithm. *Information Processing Letters*, 113(13):495–497, 2013.

[2] L. Alonso, E. M. Reingold, and R. Schott. Determining the majority. *Information Processing Letters*, 47(5):253 – 255, 1993.

[3] L. Babai, P. Erdös, and S. M. Selkow. Random graph isomorphism. *SIAM Journal on Computing*, 9(3):628–635, 1980.

[4] R. Beigel, W. Hurwood, and N. Kahale. Fault diagnosis in a flash. In *36th IEEE Symp. on Foundations of Computer Science (FOCS)*, pages 571–580, 1995.

[5] R. Beigel, S. R. Kosaraju, and G. F. Sullivan. Locating faults in a constant number of parallel testing rounds. In *1st ACM Symp. on Parallel Algorithms and Architectures (SPAA)*, pages 189–198, 1989.

[6] R. Beigel, G. Margulis, and D. A. Spielman. Fault diagnosis in a small constant number of parallel testing rounds. In *5th ACM Symp. on Parallel Algorithms and Architectures (SPAA)*, pages 21–29, 1993.

[7] C. Castelluccia, S. Jarecki, and G. Tsudik. Secret handshakes from CA-oblivious encryption. In P. J. Lee, editor, *Advances in Cryptology - ASIACRYPT*, pages 293–307. Springer, 2004.

[8] J. Clausen, D. D. Keck, W. M. Hiesey, P. Grun, et al. Experimental taxonomy. *Carnegie Institution of Washington. Yearbook No. 48: 1948-1949*, pages 95–103, 1947.

[9] D. J. Cook and L. B. Holder. *Mining Graph Data.* John Wiley & Sons, 2006.

[10] D. Dobkin and J. I. Munro. Determining the mode. *Theoretical Computer Science*, 12(3):255–263, 1980.

[11] M. T. Goodrich. Pipelined algorithms to detect cheating in long-term grid computations. *Theoretical Computer Science*, 408(2–3):199–207, 2008.

[12] J. W. Gregor. Experimental taxonomy. *New Phytologist*, 38(4):293–322, 1939.

[13] J. B. Hagen. Experimentalists and naturalists in twentieth-century botany: Experimental taxonomy, 1920–1950. *Journal of the History of Biology*, 17(2):249–270, 1984.

[14] S. Jarecki and X. Liu. Unlinkable secret handshakes and key-private group key management schemes. In J. Katz and M. Yung, editors, *5th Int. Conf. on Applied Cryptography and Network Security (ACNS)*, pages 270–287. Springer, 2007.

[15] V. Jayapaul, J. I. Munro, V. Raman, and S. R. Satti. Sorting and selection with equality comparisons. In F. Dehne, J.-R. Sack, and U. Stege, editors, *14th Int. Symp. on Algorithms and Data Structures (WADS)*, pages 434–445. Springer, 2015.

[16] L. Kozma. Useful inequalities cheat sheet, 2016. http://www.lkozma.net/inequalities_cheat_sheet/.

[17] M. Mitzenmacher and E. Upfal. *Probability and Computing: Randomized Algorithms and Probabilistic Analysis.* Cambridge University Press, 2005.

[18] H. Orman. The Morris worm: A fifteen-year perspective. *IEEE Security & Privacy*, 1(5):35–43, 2003.

[19] S. Parthasarathy, S. Tatikonda, and D. Ucar. A survey of graph mining techniques for biological datasets. In C. C. Aggarwal and H. Wang, editors, *Managing and Mining Graph Data*, pages 547–580. Springer, 2010.

[20] A. Pelc and E. Upfal. Reliable fault diagnosis with few tests. *Combinatorics, Probability and Computing*, 7:323–333, 1998.

[21] F. P. Preparata, G. Metze, and R. T. Chien. On the connection assignment problem of diagnosable systems. *IEEE Trans. on Electronic Computers*, EC-16(6):848–854, 1967.

[22] M. E. Saks and M. Werman. On computing majority by comparisons. *Combinatorica*, 11(4):383–387, 1991.

[23] A. Sorniotti and R. Molva. A provably secure secret handshake with dynamic controlled matching. *Computers & Security*, 29(5):619–627, 2010.

[24] L. G. Valiant. Parallelism in comparison problems. *SIAM Journal on Computing*, 4(3):348–355, 1975.

[25] S. Xu and M. Yung. K-anonymous secret handshakes with reusable credentials. In *11th ACM Conf. on Computer and Communications Security (CCS)*, pages 158–167, 2004.

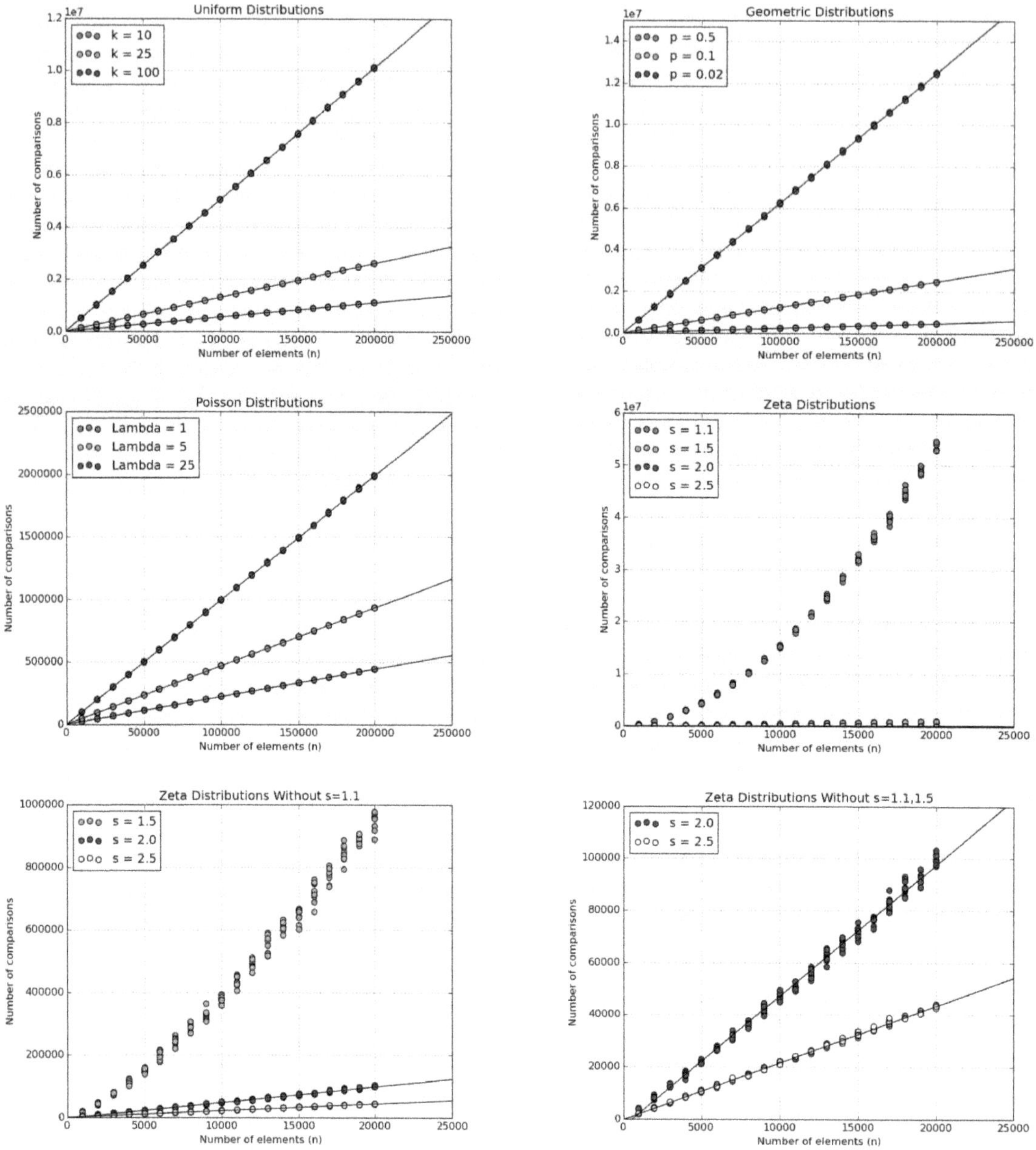

Figure 5: The results of the experiments are plotted and best fit lines are placed when we have a linear number of comparisons with high probability or in expectation.

Parallel Approaches to the String Matching Problem on the GPU

Saman Ashkiani
University of California, Davis
sashkiani@ucdavis.edu

Nina Amenta
University of California, Davis
amenta@cs.ucdavis.edu

John D. Owens
University of California, Davis
jowens@ece.ucdavis.edu

ABSTRACT

We design a family of parallel algorithms and GPU implementations for the exact string matching problem, based on Rabin-Karp (RK) randomized string matching. We describe and analyze three primary parallel approaches to binary string matching: cooperative (CRK), divide-and-conquer (DRK), and a novel hybrid of both (HRK). The CRK is most effective for large patterns (>8K characters), while the DRK approach is superior for shorter patterns. We then generalize the DRK to support any alphabet size without loss of performance. Our DRK method achieves up to a 64 GB/s processing rate on 8-character patterns from an 8-bit alphabet on an NVIDIA Tesla K40c GPU. We next demonstrate a novel parallel two-stage matching method (DRK-2S), which first skims the text for a smaller subset of the pattern and then verifies all potential matches in parallel. Our DRK-2S method is superior for pattern sizes up to 64k compared to the fastest CPU-based string matching implementations. With an 8-bit alphabet and up to 1k-character patterns, we get a geometric mean speedup of 4.81x against the best CPU methods, and can achieve a processing rate of at least 53 GB/s.

1. INTRODUCTION

Classic PRAM algorithms are proving to be a fertile source of ideas for GPU programs solving fundamental computational problems. But in practice, only certain PRAM algorithms actually perform well on GPUs. The PRAM model and the GPU programming model differ in important ways. Particularly important considerations suggest choosing algorithms where parallel threads perform uniform computation without branching or waiting ("uniformity"); where memory accesses across neighboring threads access neighboring memory locations ("coalescing"); and where the algorithm and memory accesses can take advantage of the computational and memory hierarchy of the modern GPU ("hierarchy"). Although these choices are usually the foremost considerations in GPU *implementations*, as in Schatz and Trapnell [1] and Lin et al. [2], they rarely play an important role in the process of *algorithm design*. In other words, they are considered optimization opportunities for programmers rather than desirable features of the algorithm itself.

In this paper we address this issue through a case study. We consider the exact string matching problem, which is interesting in that it admits several different styles of parallelization. We focus on a classical PRAM algorithm of Karp and Rabin [3]. Forty years of research into serial string matching has resulted in a plethora of elegant serial algorithms that perform very well in practice, but parallel algorithms are less well explored, particularly in the context of newer hierarchical parallel architectures like GPUs. We implement several variants of the Rabin-Karp algorithm (RK) on NVIDIA GPUs using the CUDA programming environment. Our experience leads us to believe that our general results apply to a broader set of hierarchical parallel processors, with either a compute hierarchy (multiple parallel processors, each with multiple parallel cores or functional units), a memory hierarchy (globally shared memory shared by all processors and faster locally shared memory of limited size shared by all cores within a processor), or both. Examples include other GPUs, accelerators such as the Intel Xeon Phi, and parallel multicore CPUs with vector instructions.

We begin with two main approaches to exploiting parallelism: *cooperative* and *divide-and-conquer*. In the former, all threads cooperate in computing a global solution, and in the latter, the main task is divided into smaller pieces, each piece is processed separately, and the results are combined. Rabin-Karp makes a good test case because it can be parallelized in both ways. In RK, the pattern of length m and all text substrings of length m are hashed (e.g., into a positive integer), and then the hashes are compared instead of the strings. Sting matching is inherently amenable to divide-and-conquer; the text can be divided into as many parallel sub-texts as needed, and the only drawback is due to overlap. RK is also amenable to cooperative parallelization, as described in the original 1987 paper, because with a wise choice of hash functions, the text can be hashed using a cooperative algorithm based on scan (aka parallel-prefix) operations. Fast implementation of scan operations has been one of the great successes in GPU software development for general computation. In both cases, the RK algorithm fits well with the GPU model in terms of uniformity, coalescing, and memory hierarchy. The downside of RK is that it always reads the entire text, while the best sequential algorithms are designed to skip as much as possible, so that they work

SPAA '16, July 11–13, 2016, Pacific Grove, CA, USA

ISBN 978-1-4503-4210-0/16/07…$15.00

DOI: http://dx.doi.org/10.1145/2935764.2935800

especially well on "real data", such as natural language text, genomics data, and internet traffic.

We experimented extensively with two different parallel versions of RK, one with the cooperative strategy (CRK), and the other on using a simple divide-and-conquer strategy (DRK). We find that for short patterns (up to about 800 characters), DRK is much faster than leading sequential codes running on an 8-core CPU. This is mostly because of its uniform load balance, relatively cheap operations, and high memory bandwidth due to coalesced memory accesses. The performance gap is especially large for very short patterns (e.g., 8 characters).

We then leverage the high performance of DRK's short-pattern matching to design a two-stage matching algorithm for longer patterns. It does a first round of searching on a small subset of the original pattern, and then groups of threads cooperate to verify all the potential matches. This new GPU-friendly algorithm outperforms the best multi-core sequential codes for patterns of size up to almost 64k characters. This approach opens up some very interesting opportunities for skipping parts of the text and for doing approximate matching.

Our work provides both good news and bad news for parallel algorithm design. The good news is that parallel algorithms that pay attention to memory access patterns and load balancing can lead directly to high-performance GPU implementations. The bad news is that although scan operations can now be implemented very efficiently in the GPU environment, complex scans are still not necessarily competitive with more straightforward parallelization approaches.

We divide this paper into the following parts:

- We propose three major RK-based binary matching algorithms: cooperative, divide-and-conquer, and a combination of both (hybrid). Using both theoretical demonstration and experimental validation, we address the following question: *for a given pattern and text size, what is the best method to use and why?* At a high level, we show that the divide-and-conquer approach is better for smaller patterns, while cooperative is superior for very large patterns (Sections 3–4).

- We provide several optimizations: both in terms of the general algorithm and computations, as well as some hardware specific ones (Section 6).

- We extend our RK-based algorithms to support characters from any general alphabets (Section 7.1).

- Using the divide-and-conquer approach, which is the fastest we have found for processing short patterns, we propose a novel two-stage matching method to process patterns of any size efficiently. In this method, we first *skim* the text for a random small subset of the main pattern, and then *verify* all potential matches efficiently in parallel (Section 7.2).

2. PRIOR WORK

A naive approach to solve the single-pattern scenario is to compare all the possible strings of length m in our text with our pattern ($O(mn)$ time steps). There are several methods proposed so far to improve such quadratic running time. For instance, the KMP algorithm [4] saves work by jumping to the next possible index in case of a mismatch. The Boyer-Moore (BM) algorithm [5] is similar to KMP but starts its comparison from right to left. Some algorithms combine the existing tricks in other algorithms to enhance their performance. For example, the HASHq algorithm [6] hashes (similar to RK) all suffixes of shorter length (e.g., at most of length 8) and performs the matching on them. In case of a mismatch, like KMP, it shifts to the next potential match and like BM, starts comparing from the rightmost characters of each word. Faro and Lecroq's survey provides a comprehensive introduction and comparison between these and other methods [7].

Some of the earliest parallel work was from Galil [8] and Vishkin [9], who proposed a series of parallel string matching methods over a concurrent-read-concurrent-write PRAM memory model. The GPU literature features numerous papers that target related problems, but none of them address the fundamental problem of matching a single non-preprocessed pattern, implemented entirely on the GPU. Both Lin et al. [2] and Zha and Sahni [10] target multiple patterns (which is easier to parallelize) with an approach that leverages offline pattern compilation; the latter paper concludes that CPU implementations are still faster. Schatz and Trapnell used a CPU-compiled suffix tree for their matching [1]. Seamans and Alexander's virus scanner targeted multiple patterns with a two-step approach, but performed the second step on the CPU [11]. Kouzinopoulos and Margaritis [12] implement a brute-force non-preprocessed search and compare it to preprocessed-pattern methods.

3. PRELIMINARIES

In this section we explain some of the basic algorithms and primitive parallel operations. Readers familiar with the graphics processing unit (GPU) terminology (Section 3.1), the serial RK algorithm (Section 3.2), and its parallel formulation (Section 3.3), can skip to Section 4.

In the basic scenario, $X = x_0 \dots x_{m-1}$ is a binary pattern of length m to be found in a binary text $Y = y_0 \dots y_{n-1}$ of length $n \geq m$. If $Y[r] = y_r y_{r+1} \dots y_{r+m-1}$, then our objective is to find all indices r such that $Y[r] = X$ for $0 \leq r < n - m + 1$. We will later generalize our results to arbitrary alphabets.

3.1 Graphics Processing Units (GPUs)

The GPU is a highly parallel processor that features both a computational hierarchy and a memory hierarchy. In this work we use NVIDIA's CUDA programming model and its related terminology [13]; parenthetical values indicate specific values for the NVIDIA Tesla K40c that we use in evaluating this work. NVIDIA GPUs have one or more parallel *cores* (15 in the K40c, called "streaming multiprocessors" or SMs). Within each core, the hardware runs a *warp* of 32 threads together as a single SIMD unit. These GPUs thus exhibit parallelism across cores and within each core. Programmers express GPU programs as parallel threads that are grouped into blocks (virtualized cores), and typical GPU programs are run on many blocks at the same time. The GPU hardware efficiently assigns blocks to cores as cores become available. The memory hierarchy has three levels, ordered from fastest/smallest to slowest/largest: *registers*, local to each thread (up to 1 KB); *locally shared* memory, shared by threads within a block (up to 48 KB); and *globally shared* memory, available to all threads (12 GB). Bandwidth to globally shared memory is maximized with *coalesced* memory accesses, where nearby threads access nearby memory addresses.

3.2 Serial Rabin-Karp

The main idea of the RK algorithm is to hash the pattern X and all the possible strings of length m in the text Y. The hashes are known as *fingerprints*, and any two strings with the same fingerprint match with high probability. Karp and Rabin proposed two families of hash functions [3]. The first produces integers as its fingerprints: for any $X \in \{0,1\}^m$: $F(X) = 2^{m-1}x_0 + \cdots + 2x_{m-2} + x_{m-1}$. In order to avoid overflow, the result is computed modulo a random prime number $p \in (1, nm^2)$, so that $F_p(X) \stackrel{p}{\equiv} F(x)$. The second family of fingerprints is defined as follows. Define two matrices,

$$\mathbf{K}(0) = \begin{bmatrix} 1 & 0 \\ 1 & 1 \end{bmatrix} \qquad \mathbf{K}(1) = \begin{bmatrix} 1 & 1 \\ 0 & 1 \end{bmatrix}. \tag{1}$$

Then for any binary string $X = x_0 \dots x_{m-1} \in \{0,1\}^m$, we define its fingerprint to be the product $\mathbf{K}(X) = \mathbf{K}(x_0)\dots\mathbf{K}(x_{m-1})$. Again to avoid overflows, the result is computed modulo a random prime number $p \in (1, mn^2)$ (i.e., $\mathbf{K}_p(X) \stackrel{p}{\equiv} \mathbf{K}(X)$). Regardless of which fingerprints we use, the RK algorithm can then be summarized as (1) choose a random prime number $p \in (1, mn^2)$; (2) compute all fingerprints (e.g., $\mathbf{F}_p(X)$, and $\mathbf{F}_p(Y[r])$ for $r \in [0, n-m+1)$); and (3) compare: e.g., if $\mathbf{F}_p(Y[r])$ and $\mathbf{F}_p(X)$ are equal, then X and $Y[r]$ are equal with high probability, otherwise there is no match.

Step 2 can be done quite efficiently in a sequential manner [3]. In case we use the first class of fingerprints, $\mathbf{F}_p(Y[r+1])$ can be computed by using $\mathbf{F}_p(Y[r])$:

$$\mathbf{F}_p(Y[r+1]) \stackrel{p}{\equiv} 2\left(\mathbf{F}_p(Y[r]) - 2^{m-1}y_r\right) + y_{r+m+1}. \tag{2}$$

In case of the second class of fingerprints, we compute $\mathbf{K}_p(Y[r+1])$ based on $\mathbf{K}_p(Y[r])$ by a few operations:

$$\mathbf{K}_p(Y[r+1]) \stackrel{p}{\equiv} \mathbf{A}_p(y_r)\mathbf{K}_p(Y[r])\mathbf{K}_p(y_{r+m+1}), \tag{3}$$

where for any binary value $x \in \{0,1\}$, $\mathbf{A}_p(x)$ is defined as the left inverse of $\mathbf{K}_p(x)$ modulo p (i.e., $\mathbf{A}_p(x)\mathbf{K}_p(x) \stackrel{p}{\equiv} \mathbf{I}$ where $\mathbf{I}$ is an identity matrix). For each read text character, equation (2) requires two multiplications (each can be done by bitwise shift operation), two summations, and a modulo operation. Equation (3), on the other hand, requires 16 integer multiplications, 8 summations and 4 modulo operations per text character. As a result, the first class of fingerprints are significantly simpler to compute. We refer to sequential RK with first class of fingerprints as SRK algorithm. On the other hand, the second class of fingerprints can be updated using an associative operator, which can be leveraged in the following parallel formulation.

3.3 Cooperative Rabin-Karp

Karp and Rabin showed that the second class of fingerprints can be computed in parallel [3] using scan operations. It is well known that the *scan operation* takes a vector of input elements $\mathbf{u}$ and an associative binary operator $\oplus$, and returns an output vector $\mathbf{v}$ of the same size as $\mathbf{u}$. In exclusive (resp., inclusive) scan, $v_i = u_0 \oplus \cdots \oplus u_{i-1}$ (resp., 0 to i). A parallel scan on a vector of length n can be done with $O(\log n)$ depth and in $O(n)$ computations. With p processors, it is easy to show that a scan can be computed in $O(n/p + \log p)$ time steps. On the GPU, there are now highly optimized generic scan implementations that take an arbitrary associative operator as an input.

Let $\mathcal{K} = [\mathbf{K}_p(y_i)]_{i=0}^{n-1}$ and $\mathcal{A} = [\mathbf{A}_p(y_j)]_{j=0}^{n-m}$ represent vectors of all the required fingerprints and their inverses. We then define $\mathcal{S}$ and $\mathcal{T}$ vectors as follows:

$$\mathcal{S} = [\mathbf{K}_p(y_0), \mathbf{K}_p(y_0)\mathbf{K}_p(y_1), \dots, \mathbf{K}_p(y_0)\dots\mathbf{K}_p(y_{n-1})],$$
$$\mathcal{T} = [\mathbf{I}, \mathbf{A}_p(y_0), \mathbf{A}_p(y_1)\mathbf{A}_p(y_0), \dots, \mathbf{A}_p(y_{n-m})\dots\mathbf{A}_p(y_0)].$$

So $\mathcal{S}$ is an inclusive scan over vector $\mathcal{K}$ with right matrix multiplication modulo prime p as its associative operator. Similarly, $\mathcal{T}$ is an exclusive scan over vector $\mathcal{A}$ with left matrix multiplication modulo prime p as its associative operator. Then, it is clear that for $0 \le r < n - m + 1$:

$$\mathbf{K}_p(Y[r]) = \mathcal{T}[r]\mathcal{S}[r+m-1] \tag{4}$$
$$= [\mathbf{A}_p(y_{r-1})\dots\mathbf{A}_p(y_0)] \times$$
$$[\mathbf{K}_p(y_0)\dots\mathbf{K}_p(y_{r-1})\mathbf{K}_p(y_r)\dots\mathbf{K}_p(y_{r+m-1})] \tag{5}$$
$$= \mathbf{K}_p(y_r)\dots\mathbf{K}_p(y_{r+m-1}), \tag{6}$$

Thus, after computing two scans (i.e., computing $\mathcal{S}$ and $\mathcal{T}$), we can compute any required fingerprint by computing a single matrix multiplication (as in (4)). Based on Eq. (5), it is important to use different matrix multiplications (i.e., left/right) for each operator in order that each pair of matrices and their inverses correctly cancel each other out. Throughout this paper, we refer to this method as Cooperative Rabin-Karp (CRK), because scan operations can be computed cooperatively by a set of independent threads or processors.

Our cooperative implementation uses this second fingerprint, but we should point out that it might be possible to improve the performance of the cooperative algorithm using a variant of the first fingerprint. Blelloch [14] points out, among many other things, that any sequential scan operation whose output can be represented by a recurrence of the form $x_i = a_i x_{i-1} + b_i$, where a_i and b_i are fixed input arrays and can be computed by a scan operation. In our case, $a_i = 2$, we have $b_i = y_i - 2^m y_{i-m}$, which can be computed in $O(1)$ from the input y, and all operations are done modulo p. Specialized to this situation, Blelloch's method is to define an associative operator $\cdot$ on pairs $c_i = (a_i, b_i)$, where $c_i \cdot c_j = (a_i a_j, b_i a_j + b_j)$. He proves that this is an associative operator on the set of pairs, and so it can be implemented using a scan operation. In addition to requiring many fewer operations than the second fingerprint, implementing this would only require one scan operation, not two. In practice, we have observed that this function produced more false positives due to hash collisions than the matrix-fingerprint, unless we used more expensive 64-bit operations. Thus our initial attempt to implement this did not lead to much of an improvement over our current CRK implementation. In any case, we expect neither approach would compete with our best methods, as we shall see in Section 8.

4. DIVIDE-AND-CONQUER STRATEGY

Cooperative RK (Section 3.3) elegant exploits parallelism by having all of the processors cooperate through the two large scan operations. These parallel scans require intermediate communication between different processors and cores (threads from different blocks). However, CRK benefits little from the computational or memory hierarchy in its implementation (all operations are device-wide and global), so we also explored a straightforward *divide-and-conquer* approach. Dealing with smaller subproblems gives us a lot of flexibility in our design choices (e.g., work distribution among processors/cores, and exploiting the memory hierarchy), which allows us to tailor the computation to the GPU's strengths.

Divide and conquer is a natural approach to string matching; the easiest way to divide the work is to assign different parts of the text to different processors and process each part seperately. The final result is simply a union of matching results for each subproblem. In order to maintain independence between different subproblems, and to avoid extra communication between processors, this division should be done in an intelligent way. We must consider an overlap of length $m-1$ characters between consecutive subtexts to avoid losing any potential matches at the boundaries. Let L denote the number of subtexts, or equivalently, the granularity of the divide-and-conquer approach. Then, if we show each subtext as Y^ℓ, for $0 \le \ell < L$, the division process can be shown as:

$$Y^\ell = \underbrace{y_{\ell g} y_{\ell g+1} \cdots y_{\ell g+g-1}}_{\text{exclusive characters}} \underbrace{y_{(\ell+1)g} \cdots y_{(\ell+1)g+m-1}}_{\text{overlapped characters}}, \quad (7)$$

where each subtext has $g = (n-m+1)/L$ *exclusive* characters, plus $m-1$ *overlapped* characters. For simplicity we assume that $(n-m+1)$ is a multiple of L, otherwise we can easily extend our text (increasing n with enough dummy characters) to be such a number. Now, each of these subtexts have $\bar{n} = g+m-1$ characters and are independent from each other [1].

In general, the possible cases for the number of subtexts is from $1 \le L \le n-m+1$. We define *Divide-and-conquer RK* (DRK) as a method in which each processor performs the SRK on its own subtext individually. $L = 1$ corresponds to SRK applied to the whole text. We can also combine ideas of both the CRK and the DRK methods and form a *hybrid* method. We define *Hybrid RK* (HRK) as a method in which the main text is divided into subtexts (Eq. (7)) and then each subtext is assigned to a group of processors, which will perform CRK on it. If $L = 1$, HRK will be identical to CRK. Figure 1 shows our four possible formulations—serial, cooperative, divide-and-conquer, and hybrid—schematically.

Intuitively, a larger number of subtexts L (i.e., a finer granularity) yields more parallelism. At the same time, it means more potential overlaps and hence more redundant work because the total number of overlapped characters is $L(m-1)$. One important question in this work is to determine the optimal choice of L depending on the method and other machine and problem characteristics.

4.1 Theoretical analysis with finite processors

In the following, we want to investigate each method's depth-work analysis under equal and finite number of p processors. We also assume that all processors have access to a globally shared memory.

[1]This approach has commonality with stencil methods that operate over a large domain on hierarchical parallel machines: the domain is divided across cores and parallelism is exploited within a core. Typically, each core is assigned not only its own subdomain but also an overlapping region with its neighbors (the "halo"). Larger halos result in less communication at the cost of more redundant computation. In string matching, the overlap size is fixed, but the total overlap (i.e., total redundant work) is changed by the granularity of our division. Our objective will then be reaching a trade-off between minimizing redundant work (overlap) and maximizing achieved parallelism (maximizing the granularity).

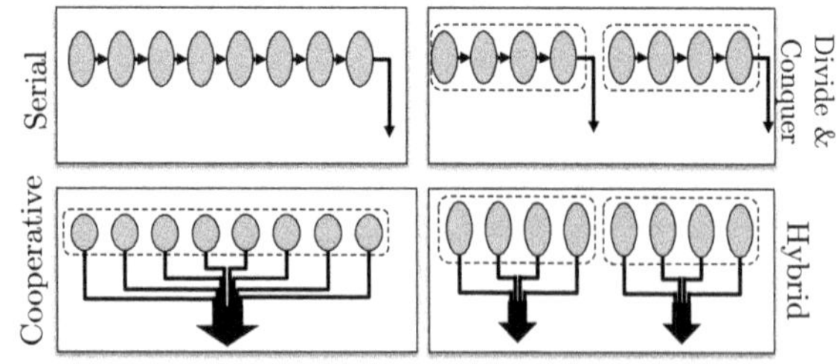

Figure 1: Schematic view of the four approaches considered in this paper. The picture is simplified and shows the work distribution in each method. Dashed lines indicate subproblems.

Method	Step complexity	Work complexity
CRK	$O(n/p + \log p)$	$O(n)$
DRK	$O((n+mL)/p)$	$O(n+mL)$
HRK	$O((n+mL)/p + (L/p_1)\log p_2)$	$O(n+mL)$

Table 1: Step-work complexity for our methods with p processors (p_1 groups with p_2 processors in each).

We know that scan operations can be done with $O(n/p + \log p)$ depth complexity and $O(n)$ work. The CRK method requires two scan operations, followed by a constant round of final multiplications and comparisons, and $O(n)$ added work. Overall, the CRK requires $O(n)$ work and its running time will be

$$T_{\text{CRK}}(n,p) = O(n/p + \log p). \quad (8)$$

In the DRK method, each subtext is assigned to a processor. If we have $L > p$ subtexts of length $g+m-1$, each subtext can be processed sequentially using SRK in $O(g+m-1)$ time steps. Total work will be $O(n+Lm)$. Since at most p processors can be used at a time, $T_{\text{DRK}}(n,p)$ will be

$$T_{\text{DRK}}(n,p) = \frac{L}{p} O(g+m-1) = O(\frac{n+Lm}{p}). \quad (9)$$

For the HRK, we assign each subtext to a group of processors, and each group runs CRK with its processors. Here we have a new degree of freedom: fewer groups of processors with more processors per group or vice versa. We assume p_1 groups and p_2 processors per group, for a total of $p = p_1 p_2$ processors. Subtexts are assigned to groups (p_1 at a time), while each subtext can be processed in parallel as in CRK with $O((g+m-1)/p_2 + \log p_2)$. Overall, the running time $T_{\text{HRK}}(n,p)$ will be

$$\begin{aligned} T_{\text{HRK}}(n,p) &= \frac{L}{p_1} O(\frac{g+m-1}{p_2} + \log p_2) \\ &= O(\frac{n+Lm}{p} + \frac{L}{p_1}\log p_2). \end{aligned} \quad (10)$$

For a fixed n, m, L and p, the runtime component $(L/p_1)\log p_2$ is minimized if $p_2 = 1$ and $p_1 = p$. It is interesting to note that in such case, HRK will be identical to the DRK method. For HRK, then, it is better to have more groups with fewer processors in each than fewer groups with more processors. Also, total work will be $O(n+Lm)$.

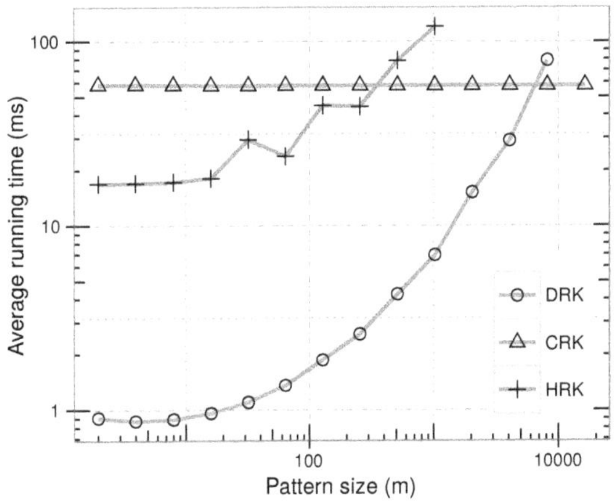

Figure 2: Average running time (ms) versus pattern size m, for a fixed binary text of size $n = 2^{25}$.

4.2 Theoretical Conclusions

Table 1 summarizes the step and work complexity for our three parallel methods with an equal number of processors. Although we have considered some simplifying assumptions in the above analysis, we can make some interesting general conclusions. First of all, since the sequential RK method is linear in time, as text size increases we expect to see an approximate linear increase in the running time of all our parallel alternatives (because of the $O(n/p)$ term in Eq. (8), (9), and (10)).

As the pattern size m increases, more overlapped characters are included in DRK and HRK. These overlaps are redundant work and thus, there always exists a pattern size for which CRK is superior to the other algorithms, and for all larger patterns. This can also be seen in step complexities and the fact that CRK does not have any factor of pattern size in it. Also, with fixed number of processors (fixed p) and for large sizes of text and pattern our asymptotic analysis gets more accurate and hence we expect the DRK method to be asymptotically superior to the HRK method. However, for smaller text or pattern sizes, the order may differ.

5. SUMMARY OF RESULTS

At this point in the paper, we have introduced and analyzed three parallel algorithm formulations based on the RK algorithm: cooperative (CRK), divide-and-conquer (DRK), and hybrid (HRK). In Section 4.1 we analyzed the theoretical behavior of these algorithms and in Section 4.2, predicted their implementation behavior. Figure 2 shows the performance of these three algorithms, all implemented on an NVIDIA K40c GPU, with a fixed text size and varying pattern sizes. We observe that DRK is superior to the other methods for small patterns, but degrades as pattern size increases. Because CRK's performance is independent of pattern size, we note a crossover point where for all larger patterns the CRK method is superior. While HRK is better than CRK for small patterns, it is always inferior to the DRK method.

In the next three sections, we will build from the algorithms we detailed above, both analyzing and improving their performance as well as extending them to address practical concerns such as non-binary alphabets. We address the following issues:

1. In Section 6, we provide implementation details for each of our parallel algorithms and describe a series of optimizations that improve their performance.
2. Karp and Rabin [3] only discussed binary alphabets and at this point in the paper, so have we. In Section 7.1 we modify our algorithms to support any alphabet size.
3. Figure 2 demonstrates a large performance gap between DRK and CRK: DRK is up to 65x faster than CRK for small patterns. However, as pattern size increases, this performance gap narrows. We wish to preserve DRK's high performance for any pattern size and in Section 7.2, we propose a novel two-stage method (DRK-2S) based on the original DRK method that achieves this goal.
4. In Section 8 we thoroughly analyze the performance of all of our algorithms. Section 8.1 identifies the best parallel algorithm for any text and pattern size for binary alphabets. Then in Section 8.2, we compare our binary algorithms with the existing fastest CPU methods, and in Sections 8.3 and 8.4, extend this comparison for general alphabets. All our experiments up to this point are on randomly generated texts. In Section 8.5, we expand our performance analysis to real-world text.

6. IMPLEMENTATION DETAILS

In the previous sections, we concentrated on our theoretical approach to parallel RK-based pattern matching. In this section, we dive into our implementation strategy. Since all our implementations are based on C, we assume that any character has a size of one byte; binary strings are handled as sequences of bytes. Throughout this section and beyond, some of our decisions we make are influenced by the CUDA programming model and GPU hardware.

6.1 Cooperative RK

For the CRK method we described in Section 3.3, we used the second class of fingerprints. We begin by mapping the input text to form the intermediate vectors $\mathcal{K}$ and $\mathcal{A}$. Then we perform two device-wide scan operations on these intermediate vectors to compute $\mathcal{S}$ and $\mathcal{T}$. In order to perform these scans, we use the scan operations provided by the Thrust library [15], with input and output stored in global memory and left/right matrix multiplications modulo a given prime number as their associative operators, respectively. All intermediate results are in the form of arrays of 2-by-2 integer matrices (as shown in Section 3.3): $\mathcal{K}$, $\mathcal{A}$, $\mathcal{S}$ and $\mathcal{T}$ each requires 16B per input character. As a result, our CRK implementation not only uses the more computationally heavy fingerprints (second class), but also requires more global memory accesses per text character read.

6.2 Divide-and-Conquer RK

Our DRK implementations use the first class of fingerprints. Modulo operators do not have hardware implementations on current GPUs and hence are very slow compared to other operations. The only reason that we need this operator in equation (2) is to avoid overflows and hash the results; however, we can avoid these operations by making sure that an overflow never happens. For binary patterns of size less than or equal to 32 characters, we can use 32-bit registers (or 64-bit registers for $m \leq 64$) and guarantee no overflows. This change can significantly improve the performance for small patterns compared to the original updates. First, let us consider the most general case. Consider equation (2) and suppose we have previously computed 2^{m-1} modulo prime p and stored it in a register (called `base`). Then, if we denote y_r by `y_old` and y_{n+r-1} by `y_new`, the updated fingerprint `F` will be `F` $\leftarrow$ `((F + p - R)` $\ll$ `1) + y_new) % p`, where `R` $\leftarrow$ `(base * y_old) % p`.

For 32-bit registers, if $p < 2^{30}$, then `R` and `F` never overflow (`base` is itself modulo `p`). Originally we should have `F-R` instead of `F+p-R`. But since `F` and `R` are both positive and less than `p`, we add a `p` value (neutral to modulo operator) to assure the result is positive before shifting ($0 \leq F+p-R < 2p$). The choice of the maximum of 30 bits is required because the result of both lines must not overflow before the modulo operator. Now, for patterns smaller than 32 characters we can have `F` $\leftarrow$ `((F & mask)` $\ll$ `1) + y_new`, where `mask` $\leftarrow$ `~(1` $\ll$ `m)`. Since we use the binary representation of characters as their fingerprints (exact hashing with theoretical zero collision), we can mask out the effect of y_r by an AND operation and avoid using an extra subtraction here. `mask` can be computed once, so on average we have one bitwise AND, one shift and one summation per character in this case. We refer to this version as DRK without modulo (DRK-WOM-32bit). With minimal (but non-zero) performance degradation, we can instead use 64-bit registers and support binary patterns up to 64 characters (DRK-WOM-64bit).

In DRK (or DRK-WOM), each thread is supposed to process $g+m-1$ consecutive characters from the text and verify whether or not there is a match for its g exclusive strings (Section 4). This is not an ideal memory access pattern for high-performance GPU implementation. We would instead prefer coalesced accesses, where consecutive threads within a warp access consecutive elements. To alleviate this problem, with N_T threads per block, we initially load N_T consecutive subtexts into each block's shared memory in a coalesced manner (total of $gN_T + m - 1$ characters per block), and then each thread reads its own subtext locally from much faster shared memory (where coalescing is less important). In GPUs, memory accesses are in 4B alignments. Therefore we read elements as `char4` vectors (4 consecutive characters) to better exploit the available memory bandwidth[2].

6.3 Hybrid RK

As discussed in Section 4, HRK assigns each subtext to a group of processors, where a CRK method is performed on each subtext. On the GPU, we assign each subtext to a block, and threads within each block perform CRK on their own subtext. We use a block-wide scan operation from the CUB library [17]. In order to use CRK on each subtext, we need to store intermediate vectors in shared memory ($\mathcal{S}$ and $\mathcal{T}$ when using the second fingerprint). Current GPUs have very limited shared memory of at most 48 KB per block, so the extra storage forces us to either have fewer threads per block (small N_T) or very small subtext sizes (small g) and equivalently too many blocks (large L). In neither scenario are we utilizing our hardware's full potential, and consequently our HRK implementation compares poorly to our DRK- and CRK-based implementations.

[2] `char4` is a built-in CUDA vector type with 4B alignment [16, Ch. B.3.].

7. EXPANDING BEYOND THE SIMPLE RK

7.1 General alphabets

In their original paper, Karp and Rabin only considered binary alphabets [3]; we now extend this to general alphabets. Suppose we have an alphabet set Σ such that each character $a \in \Sigma$ requires at most $\sigma = \lceil \log \Sigma \rceil$ bits of information. Then, for any arbitrary pattern $X = x_0 \ldots x_{m-1} \in \Sigma^m$, we can extend our first class of fingerprints to be $F_p(X) \overset{p}{\equiv} \sum_{i=0}^{m-1} x_i 2^{\sigma(m-i-1)}$. So, for this first class of fingerprints, the new update equation will be

$$F_p(Y[r+1]) \overset{p}{\equiv} 2^{\sigma}\left(F_p(Y[r]) - 2^{\sigma(m-1)} y_r\right) + y_{r+m+1}. \quad (11)$$

This update equation has a similar computational cost as equation (2). Its implementation will also be similar to what we outlined in Section 6.2. The `base` register we used in Section 6.2 is now precomputed to be $2^{\sigma(m-1)}$ modulo p. In order to avoid overflows, with the same reasoning as we had before, we should make sure that $p \leq 2^{31-\sigma}$. We also update our DRK-WOM implementation to incorporate σ: `F` $\leftarrow$ `((F & mask)` $\ll$ σ`) + y_new`, where `mask` $\leftarrow$ `~(((1`$\ll$ σ`) - 1)` $\ll$ `m)`. Here `mask` is intended to wipe out any possible remainder from the oldest added character. By using 64-bit registers, we can support pattern lengths of $m \leq 64/\sigma$, i.e., up to eight 8-bit ASCII characters.

For the second class of fingerprints, we first identify our fundamental fingerprints $\mathbf{K}_0 \ldots \mathbf{K}_{2^\sigma - 1}$. Suppose we have an arbitrary character $z = c_{\sigma-1} \ldots c_0$ where $c_i \in \{0, 1\}$. Then, $\mathbf{K}_z = \mathbf{K}_{c_{\sigma-1}} \times \cdots \times \mathbf{K}_{c_0}$. Inverse fingerprints are similarly defined as $\mathbf{A}_p(z) = \mathbf{A}_p(c_0) \times \cdots \times \mathbf{A}_p(c_{\sigma-1})$. These fundamental fingerprints and their inverses can either be precomputed and looked up from a table at runtime or else can be computed on the fly. In either case, the amount of computation can become up to σ times more expensive and not any better than the binary CRK method, and hence for general alphabets, we prefer the first class of fingerprints and the DRK method.

7.2 Two-stage matching

For small patterns, our DRK implementations outperform our other methods on GPUs as well as the fastest CPU-based codes (Section 8 has more details). DRK-WOM, for instance, achieves up to a 66 GB/s processing rate. However, it works only for fairly small patterns (up to $64/\sigma$ characters if we use our 64-bit version). As the pattern size increases, DRK is the superior method up to almost 512 characters (for $1 \leq \sigma \leq 8$). However, DRK's performance degrades gradually as the pattern size increases for two reasons. 1) As m increases, the total number of characters that each thread must read until it can process g strings increases linearly ($g + m - 1$). 2) As m increases, the total number of characters stored in shared memory also increases ($gN_T + m - 1$) and hence our device occupancy (and overall performance) gradually decrease.

As we have discussed earlier in this paper, the RK algorithm does not depend on the content of either the text or the pattern. This is a desirable property: the performance of RK implementations only depends on text and pattern sizes (n and m). We make no runtime decisions (e.g., branches) based on pattern or text content, which is beneficial for the uniformity goal we outlined in the introduction. In practice, most of our resources can be assigned statically at compile time (like the amount of required shared memory per block).

But an RK-based implementation processes every possible substring of length m in the text. Many well-known sequential matching algorithms (such as those introduced in Section 2) use different techniques to avoid this unnecessary work. In this subsection, we propose an algorithm that balances between the uniform workload of RK and avoids the unnecessary work of checking every possible substring.

Our *two-stage* DRK matching method (DRK-2S) first *skims* the text for a random small substring of the pattern and then *verifies* the potential matches that we identify. Suppose we search for a smaller substring of the pattern ("subpattern") of length $\bar{m} < m$. This subpattern can be chosen arbitrarily: it can be a prefix, a suffix, or any other arbitrary alignment from the main pattern. We then search our text using one of our DRK methods (preferably the DRK-WOM). Each thread stores its potential matches, if any, into a local register-level stack. We note that any sequential method could be used for the skimming stage, but we focus on using one of our DRK methods because their implementations on GPUs balance load efficiently across the GPU.

For final verification, we expect that by choosing a large enough subpattern size, the expected number of potential matches will be much less than the text size n. As a result, we group threads together to verify potential matches altogether in parallel rather than individually and sequentially. In our implementation, we use a warp (32 threads) as the primary unit of verification. By doing so, we can have an efficient implementation by using warp-synchronous programming features and warp-wide voting schemes.

Initially we divide our pattern into several consecutive chunks of 32 characters. For each chunk, we compute the substring's fingerprint as $F_p(x_0 \ldots x_{31}) \stackrel{p}{\equiv} \sum_{i=0}^{31} x_i 2^{\sigma(31-i)}$ by using a random prime number p as before. For example, for a pattern of length $m = 128$, we would compute 4 different fingerprints: $F_p(x_0 \ldots x_{31}), \ldots, F_p(x_{96} \ldots x_{127})$. Now, we should verify whether for each potential match beginning at index r, $F_p(y_r \ldots y_{r+31}), \ldots, F_p(y_{r+96} \ldots y_{r+127})$ are all equal to their pattern's counterparts.

After the skimming stage, each thread has a local stack of its own potential matches. Threads can find out about the existence of any non-empty stack within their warp (using a ballot). We start the verification based on threads' lane IDs (priority from 0 to 31). At this point all threads ask about the beginning index (say r) of that specific potential match (by using a shuffle) and then continue by coalesced reading of a chunk of 32 consecutive characters (from y_r until y_{r+31}). Then, by using at most five rounds of shuffles (performing a warp-wide reduction), we can compute the fingerprint corresponding to that chunk and compare it to that of the pattern's. In case it does not match, that specific potential match is not a final match and it is popped out of its thread's local stack. Otherwise, we continue to the next chunk of characters until all chunks are verified. The whole process is continued until all local stacks are empty. Algorithm 1 shows the high-level procedure of the DRK-2S.

We expect the DRK-2S method will significantly outperform the DRK method in dealing with large patterns, because we incur the cost of verifying a potential match (including reading m characters from the text) *only* when we first identify a subpattern. Consequently, we significantly reduce the memory bandwidth requirements compared to DRK, and as we will see in the next section, achieve large speedups in practice.

Algorithm 1 Two-stage matching method (DRK-2S)

for each warp w **parallel do**
  for each thread t within w **parallel do**
    Search for subpattern of length $\bar{m} < m$ using DRK
    $S_t \leftarrow$ potential matches
    $R_t \leftarrow$ beginning indices of S_t
  end for
  for each index $r \in \bigcup_{t \in w}\{R_t\}$ **do**
    for $0 \leq k < \lceil m/32 \rceil$ **do**
      Compute $F \leftarrow F_p(y_{(r+32k)} \cdots y_{(r+31+32k)})$
      if F is not equal to $F_p(x_{32k} \ldots x_{(32k+31)})$ **then**
        r is not a match
      end if
    end for
    if all above k fingerprints matched **then**
      r is a match
    end if
  end for
end for

8. PERFORMANCE EVALUATION

In this section, we experimentally assess the performance of all our proposed algorithms. Unless otherwise stated (Section 8.5), we use randomly generated texts and patterns with arbitrary alphabet sizes[3]. All our parallel methods are run on an NVIDIA Tesla K40c GPU, and compiled with NVIDIA's nvcc compiler (version 7.5.17). All our sequential codes are run on an Intel Xeon E5-2637 v2 3.50 GHz CPU, with 16 GB of DDR3 DRAM memory. We used OpenMP v3.0 to run our CPU codes in parallel over 8 cores (2 threads per core). All parallel GPU implementations are by the authors, while all CPU codes are from SMART library [18] and run in a divide-and-conquer fashion over our multi-core platform.

In this section, all our experiments are averaged over at least 200 independent random trials. All results in this section—average running times (ms) and processing rates (GB/s)—are measured without considering the transfer time (from disk or from CPU to GPU). In other words, for all GPU methods we assume that text is already stored on the off-chip DRAM memory of the device. As we will see shortly, our processing rates are indeed currently much faster than PCIe 3.0 transfer time. However, the recently announced CPU-GPU NVLink would allow us to eliminate this bottleneck by feeding the GPU at the rate of our fastest string matching implementations.

All our GPU codes are run with $N_T = 256$ threads per block. Based on the utilized number of registers per thread and also the size of shared memory per block, this amount of N_T has given us a very high occupancy ratio on our GPU device. Another important parameter in our divide-and-conquer methods is the total number of subtexts L, i.e., the total number of launched threads. Instead of optimizing for L, we instead optimize for $g = (n-m+1)/L$, since it directly expresses the amount of work assigned to each thread, i.e., g is the total number of exclusive characters in each subtext. An advantage of RK-based methods is that by running a

[3]Because the RK algorithm is independent of the content of the text or pattern, the runtime for any text or pattern for a fixed (m, n) will be identical.

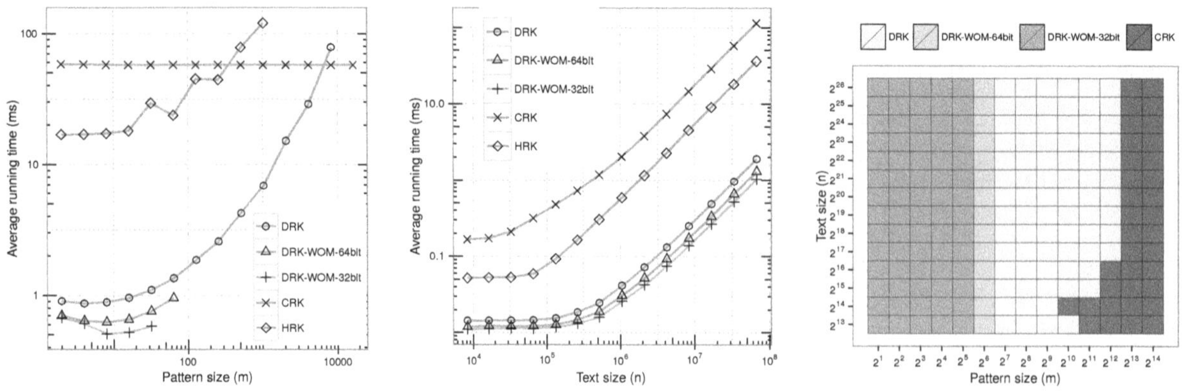

(a) Avg. running time vs. m; $n = 2^{25}$ (b) Avg. running time vs. n; $m = 16$ (c) Superior Algorithms

Figure 3: Average running time vs. (a) pattern length (m) and (b) text length (n). (c) Superior algorithms in the input parametric space (m, n), where m is the pattern length and n is the text length. All GPU methods are implemented by the authors.

few tests on randomly generated texts and patterns, we can tune the optimum amount of g to fully exploit available GPU resources. Our simulations showed that the range of $12 \leq g \leq 44$ for $2 \leq m \leq 2^{16}$ achieves the best results.

8.1 Algorithm behavior in problem domains

In this part, we revisit the question of "which method is best suited for text size n and pattern size m?" We begin with a fixed text size n and varying pattern sizes m for a binary alphabet. Based on our earlier discussions, we expect all of our DRK family algorithms to perform better than CRK and HRK because of 1) significantly cheaper computations with the first class of fingerprints and 2) fewer and coalesced global memory accesses. All DRK methods only read text characters once and report results back to global memory only if necessary; however, CRK (and to some extent HRK) first process the text into 2-by-2 integer matrices and perform several device-wide computations over these intermediate vectors (requiring additional global memory operations). However, we also predicted that as pattern size becomes large, DRK methods fall behind CRK because of 1) excessive work due to overlap and 2) the limited capacity of available per-block shared memory in current GPUs.

Figure 3a shows the average running time over 200 independent random trials on texts with 32 M characters and various pattern sizes ($2 \leq m \leq 2^{16}$). In this simulation, the DRK methods are superior to CRK for $m < 2^{13}$. In addition, HRK performs better than CRK for $m \leq 256$ (because most intermediate operations are performed locally in each block), but it is never competitive to the DRK methods. All DRK methods have similar memory access behavior; the only difference is between their update costs. Consequently, on pattern sizes where they are applicable, DRK-WOM-32bit is better than DRK-WOM-64bit, and both are better than the regular DRK method, because they avoid expensive modulo operators.

We expected that all parallel algorithms would show linear performance with respect to text size (summarized in Table 1). Figure 3b depicts average running time versus varying text sizes and a fixed pattern size $m = 16$ for binary characters. This expected linear behavior is evident after we reach a certain text size, which is large enough to fully exploit GPU resources under each scenario's algorithmic and implementation limitations.

Let's turn from the above snapshots from the (m, n) problem domain to the overall behavior of our algorithms across the whole problem domain. Figure 3c shows the superior algorithms across the (m, n) space. As we expect, the DRK family is superior for small patterns, and the CRK method for larger patterns, but the crossover point differs based on the text size. Within the DRK family, the DRK-WOM-32bit has the cheapest computational cost and is hence dominant. However, it can only be used for patterns with $m \leq 32$ characters. The next best choice is the DRK-WOM-64bit, which supports up to $m \leq 64$ characters. For larger patterns we should choose the regular DRK method, per Section 6.2.

8.2 Binary sequential algorithms

Now that we have studied the competitive behavior of our parallel algorithms with each other, we compare their performance with the best sequential binary matching algorithms. Faro and Lecroq's comprehensive survey [7] covers the fastest sequential methods. We begin with available source codes from the SMART library [18][4] and parallelize them in a divide-and-conquer fashion (as described in Section 4) but distributed over 8 CPU cores (total of 16 CPU threads). We compile and run the results in parallel using OpenMP v3.0 with -O3 optimizations. Figure 4a shows the average running time of the best CPU implementations against our parallel algorithms implemented on the GPU.

We note that the CPU algorithms perform better as the pattern size increases. Most of these algorithms use different techniques to avoid unnecessary processing of text based on the content of read characters and the pattern (as we also leverage in our DRK-2S from Section 7.2). As the pattern size increases, this strategy avoids more work on average (the methods can take larger jumps through the text). On the other hand, as we noted previously, our DRK method

[4] We compare against all top-performing algorithms from Faro and Lecroq's survey [7] and SMART library [18] except for SSEF, which in our experiments did not deliver competitive performance.

		Pattern size (m)				
	Algorithm	4	16	64	256	1024
CPU	SRK	0.95	1.11	1.15	1.16	1.16
	SA	**1.57**	3.41	4.1	4.09	4.01
	AOSO2	0.80	4.25	4.53	4.54	4.54
	HASH5	—	**4.69**	5.25	5.68	5.63
	HASH8	—	4.62	**5.93**	**6.33**	**5.98**
GPU	CRK	0.58	0.58	0.58	0.58	0.58
	DRK	38.5	34.91	24.75	**12.98**	**4.86**
	DRK-WOM-32bit	**54.84**	**64.50**	—	—	—
	DRK-WOM-64bit	52.40	51.07	**35.06**	—	—
Speedup (GPU/CPU)		34.9x	13.8x	5.9x	2.1x	0.8x

Table 2: Processing rate (throughput) in GB/s. Texts and patterns are randomly chosen using a binary alphabet.

		Pattern size (m)				
	Algorithm	4	16	64	256	1024
CPU	SA	3.96	4.20	4.92	4.91	5.26
	HASH3	2.24	9.69	11.16	12.89	12.08
	HASH5	-	7.22	10.29	11.63	12.21
	HASH8	-	7.33	11.56	10.69	12.18
	FJS	4.27	5.80	7.13	6.95	7.77
	SBNDM-BMH	4.82	5.22	6.90	7.03	7.80
	GRASPm	3.89	5.69	7.32	7.01	8.25
	FS	4.01	6.19	7.22	6.70	8.05
	SSECP	**7.66**	9.43	9.32	9.71	9.87
	EPSM	7.58	5.34	10.35	12.08	3.27
	FSBNDM	7.71	**11.00**	**12.55**	**12.92**	**14.59**
	EBOM	5.49	8.04	9.48	4.18	2.59
GPU	DRK	40.31	34.94	24.75	12.98	4.86
	DRK-2S	**62.68**	**53.77**	**53.73**	**53.51**	**53.04**
Speedup (GPU/CPU)		8.18x	4.89x	4.28x	4.14x	3.63x

Table 3: Processing rate (throughput) in GB/s. Text and patterns are randomly chosen with alphabet $\sigma = 8$ (8-bit ASCII characters).

degrades as the pattern size increases. As a result, our DRK family of implementations is superior to all binary CPU methods for patterns up to almost 1024 characters. Table 2 reports processing rate (throughput) for some specific pattern sizes measured over random texts with 2^{25} binary characters.

8.3 General sequential algorithms

Except for very minor low-level differences, our DRK implementations with any non-binary alphabet should perform as well as our binary DRK implementation. Figure 4b shows some of the fastest matching algorithms for $\sigma = 8$ (based on the survey from Faro and Lecroq [7]). As with our binary sequential comparison, we parallelize codes from the SMART library [18] across 8 CPU cores/16 threads. For the DRK-2S method, we used the DRK-WOM-64bit as our matching method for the skimming stage. Here, since we have $\sigma = 8$, we can use up to $\bar{m} = 8$ characters for our subpatterns.

Table 3 summarizes our achieved processing rates on random texts with 2^{25} 8-bit characters. Our DRK-2S method achieves a geometric mean speedup of 4.81x over the fastest CPU methods. Although we consider patterns up to 1024 characters in this table, the DRK-2S continues to be superior to all the CPU methods up to patterns of almost 64k characters. For example, with 32k characters DRK-2S achieves 9.19 GB/s while the best CPU method, the FS-BNDM, achieves 5.89 GB/s. The main reason behind our performance degradation for very large patterns is an increased number of memory accesses for each potential match

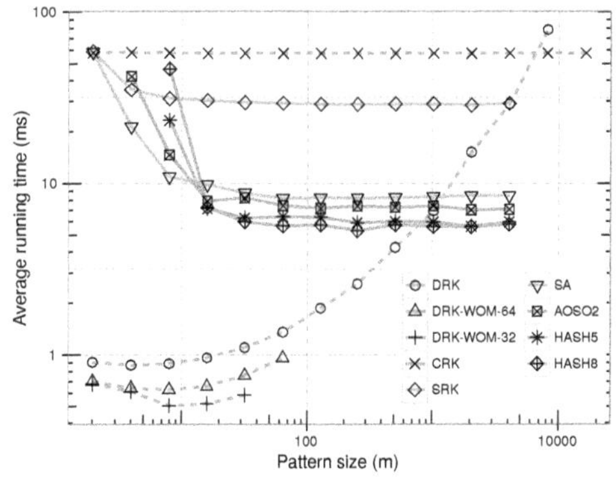

(a) Binary alphabet ($\sigma = 1$)

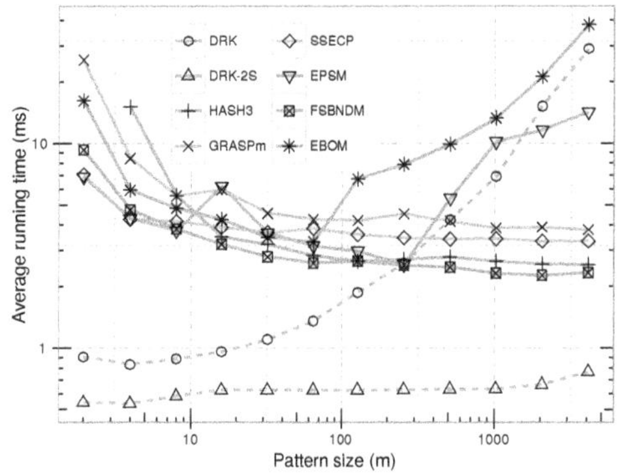

(b) 8-bit alphabet ($\sigma = 8$)

Figure 4: Average running time (ms) versus pattern size m with fixed text size $n = 2^{25}$ for (a) $\sigma = 1$ and (b) $\sigma = 8$. Solid and dashed lines correspond to CPU and GPU implementations respectively.

($O(m/32)$ accesses). We could potentially address this issue by modifying DRK-2S to consider chunks of 128 characters (instead of 32) and use `char4` memory accesses in its verification stage as well; this would reduce the number of accesses by a factor of 4. However, for realistic pattern sizes this modification would not significantly improve our performance.

8.4 Dependency on alphabet size

In the last two parts, we have evaluated our parallel GPU methods against the best CPU methods for two cases of binary characters (Section 8.2) and general 8-bit characters (Section 8.3). In this section, we focus on the DRK-2S method and continue our discussion over randomly generated texts over various alphabet sizes ($\Sigma = 2^{\sigma}$). Table 4 shows the processing rate of the DRK-2S for $1 \leq \sigma \leq 8$ and $4 \leq m \leq 1024$. For the skimming stage, we use a subpattern length of $\bar{m} = 16$ for $1 \leq \sigma \leq 4$ and $\bar{m} = 8$ otherwise.

It is interesting to note that with a fixed pattern size, our performance increases as the alphabet size increases. This is mainly due to the fact that for randomly generated texts and with a fixed pattern size, as alphabet size increases, we get less likely to visit a match in our skimming stage (probability of $\sigma^{-\bar{m}}$), and hence fewer verifications are required in the second stage. It is also interesting to note the sudden performance degradation for $m > \bar{m}$ with each alphabet size, which is

	Pattern size (m)						
σ	4	8	16	32	64	256	1024
1	52.40	56.55	55.04	49.96	49.86	49.74	49.23
2	59.98	58.91	55.75	51.04	51.03	51.01	50.15
3	60.57	58.94	55.86	51.13	51.11	50.91	50.45
4	60.58	58.85	55.78	51.09	51.01	50.71	49.82
5	60.59	58.88	53.47	53.52	53.44	53.38	52.76
6	60.63	58.94	52.36	53.46	53.42	53.30	52.29
7	60.59	58.87	53.50	53.45	53.42	53.18	52.11
8	62.68	63.66	53.77	53.69	53.73	53.51	53.04

Table 4: Processing rate (throughput) in GB/s of our DRK-2S method for various alphabet sizes ($\Sigma = 2^\sigma$) and different pattern lengths (m).

	Pattern size (m)						
Algorithm	4	8	16	32	64	256	1024
SA	16.68	17.23	17.51	17.19	15.08	16.20	15.67
HASH3	20.95	10.97	6.29	5.75	**4.67**	4.98	**3.77**
HASH5	–	14.56	7.40	5.99	5.32	4.96	5.77
HASH8	–	49.15	10.00	5.97	5.46	5.57	5.31
FJS	12.98	9.80	7.95	6.50	6.31	7.58	4.82
SBNDM-BMH	10.19	9.88	7.73	6.53	6.22	6.16	6.78
GRASPm	13.17	9.31	7.04	6.41	6.20	6.78	6.60
FS	13.06	9.58	7.43	5.73	6.06	6.38	6.52
FSBNDM	8.51	6.31	5.21	**4.92**	4.97	4.61	5.16
EBOM	7.55	6.17	**5.05**	5.42	5.25	5.49	6.47
SSECP	5.35	6.97	6.27	6.23	6.99	7.05	5.81
EPSM	**5.05**	**5.15**	5.69	5.43	4.75	**3.78**	6.64
DRK	2.46	2.62	2.84	3.25	3.99	7.59	20.34
DRK-2S	**1.58**	**1.63**	**1.88**	**1.84**	**1.84**	**1.84**	**1.83**
Speedup	3.2x	3.16x	2.69x	2.67x	2.54x	2.05x	2.06x

Table 5: Average running time (ms) for finding patterns of different sizes (m) on a sample text from Wikipedia with 100 M characters. The last row reports the achieved speedup of our DRK-2S method over the best CPU method.

directly related to whether or not we have to perform the verification stage. For $m > \bar{m}$ as the pattern size increases, we witness a very mild rate decrease mainly due to the number of times that a consecutive number characters are verified (line 8 in Alg. 1). Overall, as we discussed earlier, we do not expect our performance to be affected much by change in alphabet size (evident in update equation (11)), which is also clear from this table as well.

8.5 Real-world scenarios

So far, we have only used randomly generated texts and patterns for our experiments, because all of our RK-based methods have performance independence of the content of the text and the pattern. For DRK-2S, however, the total number of verifications directly depends on the number of potential matches found in the skimming stage. As a result, the algorithm is no longer data-independent. In this part, we consider some real-world scenarios for evaluation:

Natural language text: Table 5 shows the average running time (ms) of the DRK-2S method as well as all the high-performing CPU algorithms from Section 8.3 in finding several patterns of different sizes in a 100 MB sample text from Wikipedia[5]. Here DRK-2S achieves a geometric mean speedup of 2.59x against the best CPU codes.

[5]The enwik8 dataset includes the first 100 MB text from Wikipedia as of March 2006: http://prize.hutter1.net/.

	Pattern size (m)						
Algorithm	4	8	16	32	64	256	1024
SA	1.10	1.01	1.03	1.01	0.98	0.98	1.00
HASH3	1.35	0.80	0.60	**0.52**	0.49	**0.46**	0.52
HASH5	–	1.05	0.60	0.54	**0.44**	0.49	0.45
HASH8	–	2.74	0.73	0.54	0.45	0.52	**0.44**
FJS	1.83	1.51	1.55	1.47	1.64	1.59	1.50
SBNDM-BMH	1.32	1.01	0.79	0.56	0.58	0.57	0.65
GRASPm	1.36	1.09	1.07	0.83	0.74	0.71	0.67
FS	1.37	1.16	1.07	1.02	0.90	0.82	0.72
FSBNDM	1.24	0.88	0.64	0.56	0.54	0.58	0.61
EBOM	0.96	0.92	0.74	0.65	0.61	0.82	1.21
SSECP	**0.52**	**0.50**	0.74	0.65	0.66	0.65	0.65
EPSM	0.54	0.76	**0.50**	0.61	0.50	0.48	0.67
DRK	0.162	0.121	0.137	0.175	0.264	0.855	0.954
DRK-2S	**0.075**	**0.077**	**0.093**	**0.093**	**0.093**	**0.093**	**0.098**
Speedup	6.93x	6.49x	5.38x	5.59x	4.73x	4.94x	4.49x

Table 6: Average running time (ms) for finding patterns of different sizes (m) on E. coli genome with 4.6M characters. The last row reports the achieved speedup of our DRK-2S method over the best CPU method.

	Pattern size (m)						
Algorithm	4	8	16	32	64	256	1024
SA	0.84	0.84	0.84	0.88	0.78	0.78	0.78
HASH3	1.18	0.67	0.49	**0.43**	0.44	0.44	0.43
HASH5	–	0.86	0.60	0.49	0.46	0.47	0.50
HASH8	–	1.96	0.57	0.44	0.46	**0.43**	0.44
FJS	0.72	0.63	0.61	0.54	0.49	0.51	0.56
SBNDM-BMH	0.76	0.68	0.56	0.44	0.50	0.49	0.48
GRASPm	0.88	0.68	0.55	0.55	0.56	0.48	0.45
FS	0.79	0.60	0.54	0.51	0.46	0.46	0.49
FSBNDM	0.62	0.47	**0.45**	0.50	**0.41**	0.46	**0.43**
EBOM	0.51	0.48	0.53	0.55	0.53	0.63	1.46
SSECP	**0.45**	**0.41**	0.49	0.49	0.51	0.48	0.49
EPSM	0.56	0.53	0.55	0.50	0.46	0.53	0.66
DRK	0.080	0.086	0.098	0.125	0.188	0.609	0.684
DRK-2S	**0.053**	**0.055**	**0.065**	**0.065**	**0.065**	**0.065**	**0.071**
Speedup	8.49x	7.45x	6.92x	6.61x	6.31x	6.62x	6.01x

Table 7: Average running time (ms) for finding patterns of different sizes (m) on the Homo sapiens protein sequence with 3.3M characters. The last row reports the achieved speedup of our DRK-2S method over the best CPU method.

DNA sequences: Table 6 shows the average running time (ms) of regular DRK and DRK-2S methods as well as some of the best sequential algorithms over the E. coli genome sequence[6]. This is a text with almost 4.6 million characters drawn from four different possible characters ($\Sigma = 4$). The DRK-2S method achieves a geometric mean speedup of 5.45x against the best CPU codes.

Protein sequences: Table 7 shows the average running time (ms) of our DRK-based methods compared to the best CPU methods over processing of the Homo sapiens protein sequence, with 3.3 million characters and alphabet of 19 characters[6]. The DRK-2S method achieves a geometric mean speedup of 6.88x against the best CPU codes.

8.6 False positives

The RK algorithm, and hence all the proposed methods in this article so far, are randomized algorithms whose randomness comes from our choice of prime number and hashing process. While RK algorithms will always be successful in finding matches, it is possible to have false positives, i.e., multiple strings that hash to the same value. In the original RK algorithm, it is shown that if the chosen prime number

[6]Data available in SMART library: http://www.dmi.unict.it/~faro/smart/corpus.php

is less than $n(n-m+1)^2$, then the probability of error is upper-bounded by $2.511/(n-m+1)$ [3]. Even by using 64-bit variables and operations, that leaves us with a non-zero probability of false positives. On the other hand, all our DRK-WOM methods assign a unique fingerprint to their strings, and hence false positives are not possible. Our DRK-2S has a great advantage here. First of all, by using a DRK-WOM method in the skimming stage, we significantly reduce the total number of potential matches. Secondly, DRK-2S divides the pattern into multiple smaller-sized chunks of size 32 and hashes them with a random prime number. So for a pattern to result in a false positive, all of its chunks should independently hash to the same values as the original pattern's. So the probability is exponentially decreased. We did not encounter any false positives in our experiments with the DRK-2S. Still, we could arbitrarily decrease the false positive probability even more by hashing each chunk with a different prime number (or even using multiple prime numbers and multiple hashing per chunk). This would increase our computational load in the verification stage, but since the total number of potential matches after the skimming stage is significantly fewer than n, the impact on the overall performance would be negligible.

9. CONCLUSION

Our final outcome from this work is a novel two-stage algorithm that addresses the string matching problem. The DRK-2S algorithm fully exploits GPU computational and memory resources in its skimming stage, where we efficiently process the whole text to identify potential matches. We then test these potential matches using cooperative groups of threads. The result is a highly efficient string matching algorithm for patterns of any size, which we believe to be the fastest string-matching implementation on any commodity processor for pattern sizes up to nearly 64k characters. Though very efficient, our string matching method can only be used for *exact* matching of a *single* pattern (or at least very few). We hope that this algorithm and the presented ideas embodied in it can be used as a cornerstone for other high-throughput string processing applications such as in regular expressions and approximate matching algorithms, as well as for multiple-pattern matching scenarios where a text is matched against a dictionary of patterns (e.g., in intrusion detection systems).

Acknowledgments

Thanks to Martin Farach-Colton for helpful comments on the paper. Also, thanks to NVIDIA for providing the GPUs that made this research possible. We appreciate the funding support from UC Lab Fees Research Program Award 12-LR-238449, Sandia LDRD award #13-0144, and NSF award CCF-1017399.

10. REFERENCES

[1] M. C. Schatz and C. Trapnell, "Fast exact string matching on the GPU," University of Maryland, Tech. Rep., 2007.

[2] C.-H. Lin, C.-H. Liu, and S.-C. Chang, "Accelerating regular expression matching using hierarchical parallel machines on GPU," in *IEEE Global Telecommunications Conference*, ser. GLOBECOMM 2011. IEEE, Dec. 2011, pp. 1–5.

[3] R. M. Karp and M. O. Rabin, "Efficient randomized pattern-matching algorithms," *IBM Journal of Research and Development*, vol. 31, no. 2, pp. 249–260, Mar. 1987.

[4] D. E. Knuth, J. H. Morris, Jr, and V. R. Pratt, "Fast pattern matching in strings," *SIAM Journal on Computing*, vol. 6, no. 2, pp. 323–350, 1977.

[5] R. S. Boyer and J. S. Moore, "A fast string searching algorithm," *Communications of the ACM*, vol. 20, no. 10, pp. 762–772, Oct. 1977.

[6] T. Lecroq, "Fast exact string matching algorithms," *Information Processing Letters*, vol. 102, no. 6, pp. 229–235, Jun. 2007.

[7] S. Faro and T. Lecroq, "The exact online string matching problem: A review of the most recent results," *ACM Computing Surveys (CSUR)*, vol. 45, no. 2, p. 13, Feb. 2013.

[8] Z. Galil, "Optimal parallel algorithms for string matching," *Information and Control*, vol. 67, no. 1–3, pp. 144–157, Oct.–Dec. 1985.

[9] U. Vishkin, "Optimal parallel pattern matching in strings," *Information and Control*, vol. 67, no. 1–3, pp. 91–113, Oct.–Dec. 1985.

[10] X. Zha and S. Sahni, "GPU-to-GPU and host-to-host multipattern string matching on a GPU," *IEEE Transactions on Computers*, vol. 62, no. 6, pp. 1156–1169, Jun. 2013.

[11] E. Seamans and T. Alexander, "Fast virus signature matching on the GPU," in *GPU Gems 3*, H. Nguyen, Ed. Addison-Wesley, Aug. 2007, ch. 35, pp. 771–783.

[12] C. S. Kouzinopoulos and K. G. Margaritis, "String matching on a multicore GPU using CUDA," in *13th Panhellenic Conference on Informatics*, ser. PCI '09. IEEE, Sep. 2009, pp. 14–18.

[13] J. Nickolls, I. Buck, M. Garland, and K. Skadron, "Scalable parallel programming with CUDA," *ACM Queue*, pp. 40–53, Mar./Apr. 2008.

[14] G. E. Blelloch, "Prefix sums and their applications," School of Computer Science, Carnegie Mellon University, Tech. Rep. CMU-CS-90-190, Nov. 1990.

[15] N. Bell and J. Hoberock, "Thrust: A productivity-oriented library for CUDA," in *GPU Computing Gems*, W. W. Hwu, Ed. Morgan Kaufmann, Oct. 2011, vol. 2, ch. 26, pp. 359–371.

[16] NVIDIA Corporation, "NVIDIA CUDA C programming guide," Sep. 2015, pG-02829-001_v7.5.

[17] D. Merrill, "CUB," 2011. [Online]. Available: nvlabs.github.io/cub/

[18] S. Faro and T. Lecroq, "Smart: a string matching algorithm research tool," 2011. [Online]. Available: http://www.dmi.unict.it/~faro/smart/

Brief Announcement: MIC++: Accelerating Maximal Information Coefficient Calculation with GPUs and FPGAs

Chao Wang, Xi Li, Aili Wang, and Xuehai Zhou
School of Computer Science, University of Science and Technology of China, Hefei, China
School of Software Engineering, University of Science and Technology of China, Suzhou, China
{cswang,llxx,wangal,xhzhou}@ustc.edu.cn

ABSTRACT

To discover relationships and associations between pairs of variables in large data sets have become one of the most significant challenges for bioinformatics scientists. To tackle this problem, maximal information coefficient (MIC) is widely applied as a measure of the linear or non-linear association between two variables. To improve the performance of MIC calculation, in this work we present MIC++, a parallel approach based on the heterogeneous accelerators including Graphic Processing Unit (GPU) and Field Programmable Gate Array (FPGA) engines, focusing on both coarse-grained and fine-grained parallelism. As the evaluation of MIC++, we have demonstrated the performance on the state-of-the-art GPU accelerators and the FPGA-based accelerators. Preliminary estimated results show that the proposed parallel implementation can significantly achieve more than 6X-14X speedup using GPU, and 4X-13X using FPGA-based accelerators.

Keywords

MIC; Accelerator; GPU; FPGA

1. INTRODUCTION AND CONTRIBUTION

Large scale data analysis is posing significant challenges to state-of-the-art bioinformatics computing machines and technologies. The problem of identifying whether two or more variables are independent or have some kinds of associations (functional or non-functional) is called the *Detecting Association Problem* [1]. This problem is becoming g increasingly important in different fields growing with the explosive data scale. To tackle this issue, David N.Reshef [2] has established the generality of maximal information coefficient (MIC) calculation method, showing its equitability on functional relationships through simulations, and observe the intuitively equitable behavior on more general associations. However, this MIC computation algorithm is entirely computational and data intensive so that it is not feasible to employ traditional machine on large data sets. Billions of samples and thousands of variables make the computing impossible and time-consuming. To our best knowledge, although there has been some preliminary research on the acceleration of MIC calculation using cloud-based distributed system [4] or GPU-based accelerators [3], so far no hardware accelerating techniques like using FPGA-based platforms have been implemented.

To solve this problem, in this paper, we propose MIC++, an accelerator framework based on heterogeneous GPU and FPGA hardware accelerators. We extended the current sequential algorithm which is based on dynamic programming, and can achieve higher performance without any correctness penalty and insignificant overheads. We claim following contributions of this work:

- In this work, we analyze the behavior of the MIC calculation with four steps and propose a parallelized implementation of the MIC calculation with hierarchical coarse-grained and fine-grained parallelisms, named MIC++. We can use parallelized MIC++ algorithm to different accelerators like GPU and FPGA based architectures.
- We implement the parallel MIC++ approach on NVIDIA GTX 750 GPU, and Xilinx Virtex-7 NetFPGA SUME real hardware platforms. Experimental results demonstrate the MIC++ accelerator can achieve 6X-14X speedup with ignorable hardware cost. Finally, we believe the MIC accelerator can be utilized in a wider range such as data processing in machine learning areas.

2. MIC PARALLELIZATION

Fig.1 illustrates the parallel MIC++ architecture. In particular, Fig.1 (a) demonstrates the coarse-grained parallelism on accelerator based cluster architectures, while Fig.1 (b) and Fig.1 (c) illustrate the fine-grained parallelism on accelerating threads.

2.1 Coarse-grained parallelism

Regarding the MIC calculation process, Each element of MICM (MIC matrix) is defined as $I(x, y)$, which stands for the maximum entropy when partitioning all the two-variable pairs in x rows and y columns. The computing process of MICM starts by sorting all pairs in ascendant order by the Y value. Thus, each column of MICM uses the same initial partition. Then, we use accelerator based architecture to compute MICM in parallel. In the coarse-grained parallelism step, we only focus on the sorting of the input data set D, while the fine-grained parallelism step handles actual accelerating for computing MICM. When processing large data sets, sorting steps (step 1 and 3) take intolerable long time when using serial sorting algorithms such as QuickSort or MergeSort. By contrast, Bitonic sorting networks have been introduced to run sorting steps in parallel. Bitonic sorting networks have been proved as efficient measures for GPU computing not only for its time complexity but also for its data-dependency, meaning that the time consumption of sorting depends on the size of the data set but not the

SPAA '16 July 11-13, 2016, Pacific Grove, CA, USA

ACM ISBN 978-1-4503-4210-0/16/07.
DOI: http://dx.doi.org/10.1145/2935764.2935804

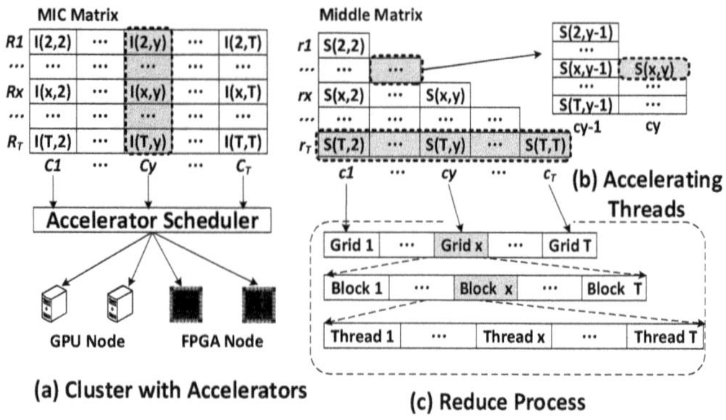

Figure 1: Architecture of the parallel algorithm, the MIC matrix is first processed by GPU cluster scheduler (in a), and then organized into a Middle Matrix, which will be operated in CUDA threads (b and c).

original sequence of it. The time complexity of Bitonic sorting is $O(log_2(N))$, and it is a comparator based sorting network. Thus, no additional memory is required as in Quicksort. The other two steps of initial partition are not suitable for coarse-grained parallelization due to the inter-task dependencies between them. Finally, it can be concluded that the steps 1 and 3 run on accelerators while steps 2 and 4 run on CPU. Though data transmission takes place between CPU and accelerators in Bitonic sorting networks, the overall performance is still significantly improved than the serial algorithms. Besides, when the CPU is executing step 2, execution of step 3 on GPU can be fully overlapped, reducing the overall time consumption of the implementation of the algorithm. When the coarse-grained parallelism finishes, a series of two-dimensional vectors (TDVs) are stored. The TDVs contain the partitions of each (x, y) pair, which will be used to compute the MIC in the fine-grained parallelism.

2.2 Fine-grained parallelism

In the coarse-grained parallelism, the TDV that holds the necessary data for computing a certain column of MICM is generated. In this section, we design a parallel algorithm to accelerate the computing process at each node. Fig.1 (b) presents the computing process of each column of MICM. The left part of Fig.1 (b) is a middle matrix (MM) that temporarily stores the intermediate results. Each element of MM is $S(x, y)$, which refers to the maximum entropy when partitioning the first x columns of TDV into y columns. MM is a lower triangular matrix, where the last row finally stores the results of the column of MICM, e.g. the data of rT in Fig.1(b) is cy in Fig.1(a) after transposition, both rT and cy are surrounded with dashed line. The right part of Fig.1(b) demonstrates the data dependencies when computing an element in MM. Each S(x,y) only relies on the elements whose x-axis index is no more than x of the $(y-1)$ column, as shown in the right part of Fig.1(b), the dark elements will affect the value of $S(x, y)$. When computing $S(x, y)$, each element produces a new entropy and then $S(x, y)$ selects the maximum one of the final value. Based on the above analysis, accelerator threads are organized at three levels, Grid level, Block level, and Thread level, respectively, as illustrated in Fig.1 (c).

Grid level: Each column of MM is calculated simultaneously. As adjacent columns have data dependencies, thus each column is organized as a grid in the middleware (like CUDA), a synchronization function is inserted between adjacent grids. The kth column is corresponding to the kth grid.

Block level: Different elements of a column have different data dependencies as described above. To efficiently use the shared memory of each block, each separate component is organized as a block.

Thread level: As shown in the right part of Fig.1 (b), the computation of $S(x, y)$ has $(x-1)$ separate intermediate calculations, and finally, the peak value is selected. So the uth block has $(u-1)$ threads, a parallel reduce process is applied to find the maximum value and its position.

If thread index exceeds the maximum number allowed by accelerators, the associating block is then automatically divided into smaller subblocks. Accordingly, the reduce process is also divided into subsequences, and a merge process will be handled after all the sub-tasks are finished.

2.3 Preliminary results and analysis

To evaluate the effectiveness of the MIC++ accelerators using GPU and FPGA-based accelerators, we compare it against a CPU with 256-bit SIMD (Intel Core i5 4460 3.3Hz, 8GB memory) over different data scales. We take a modern GPU card (NVIDIA GTX 750, 1.04 TFlops peak, 2GB GDDR5, 80.2 GB/s memory bandwidth, 28nm technology, CUDA SDK5.5) as the baseline. We use the MovieLen1M Benchmark to evaluate the speedup and hardware cost. 1000 movies are selected, and each movie is represented by a 6040*32bit vector.

We have evaluated four case studies for users and items in the benchmark, with specific parts of the application offloaded to accelerator. Preliminary estimated results show that the GPU accelerator achieves an average kernel speedup of 6X-14X on the SIMD CPU implementation. By contrast, the FPGA based hardware accelerator achieves 4X-13X in estimation, which is slightly lower than the GPU-based accelerators. By the further data analysis, it can be concluded that the GPU can access the data with up to 80.2 GB/s memory bandwidth while the FPGA accelerators only have a peak bandwidth at 14.9GB/s. The reason that GPU and FPGA are achieving similar speedup is that although FPGA is faster than GPU accelerators, the bandwidth of the FPGA development board limits the peak speedup. Regarding the hardware cost, simulation shows that the area utilization for each FPGA-based accelerator is less than 5%, which means a modern FPGA platform can accommodate about 20 accelerators. In that case, the speedup of a single FPGA chip can achieve 260X kernel speedup against state-of-the-art processors. Meanwhile, the power consumption for a single accelerator is only 210mW, which is much more energy-efficient than CPU and GPU-based parallel approaches. Therefore, GPU and FPGA-based accelerators have great potential to accelerate MIC application.

Acknowledgment. This work was supported by the NSFC No. 61379040, 61272131, Jiangsu Provincial NSF SBK201240198, Anhui Provincial NSF 1608085QF128, State Key Lab of Computer Architecture, and CCF-Tencent Open Research Fund. Xi Li and Aili Wang are the corresponding authors of this paper.

3. REFERENCES

[1] Karpinets T.V., et al., Analyzing large biological datasets with association networks. Nucleic Acids Res, 2012. 40(17):e131.

[2] Reshef, D.N., et al., Detecting Novel Associations in Large Data Sets. Science, 2011. 334: p. 1518-1524.

[3] Tang, D., et al., RapidMic: Rapid Computation of the Maximal Information Coefficient. Evolutionary Bioinformatics, 2014.

[4] Wang, C., et al., Accelerating Computation of Large Biological Datasets using MapReduce Framework, IEEE/ACM Trans. on Computational Biology and Bioinformatics, 2016.

Universal Shape Formation for Programmable Matter

Zahra Derakhshandeh
Arizona State University
zderakhs@asu.edu

Robert Gmyr
Paderborn University
gmyr@mail.upb.de

Andréa W. Richa
Arizona State University
aricha@asu.edu

Christian Scheideler
Paderborn University
scheideler@upb.de

Thim Strothmann
Paderborn University
thim@mail.upb.de

ABSTRACT

We envision programmable matter consisting of systems of computationally limited devices (which we call *particles*) that are able to self-organize in order to achieve a desired collective goal without the need for central control or external intervention. Central problems for these particle systems are shape formation and coating problems. In this paper, we present a *universal* shape formation algorithm which takes an arbitrary shape composed of a constant number of equilateral triangles of unit size and lets the particles build that shape at a scale depending on the number of particles in the system. Our algorithm runs in $O(\sqrt{n})$ asynchronous execution rounds, where n is the number of particles in the system, provided we start from a well-initialized configuration of the particles. This is optimal in a sense that for any shape deviating from the initial configuration, any movement strategy would require $\Omega(\sqrt{n})$ rounds in the worst case (over all asynchronous activations of the particles). Our algorithm relies only on local information (e.g., particles do not have ids, nor do they know n, or have any sort of global coordinate system), and requires only a constant-size memory per particle.

Keywords

Self-Organizing Systems; Programmable Matter; Distributed Algorithms

1. INTRODUCTION

The vision behind *programmable matter* is to have a piece of matter that can change its physical properties like shape, density, conductivity, or color in a programmable fashion based on either user input or autonomous sensing. Many realizations of programmable matter have been proposed — ranging from DNA tiles, shape-changing molecules, and synthetic cells, to reconfigurable modular robotics — each pursuing solutions for specific application scenarios with their own, special capabilities and constraints. We envision programmable matter to consist of a system of computationally limited devices (which we refer to as particles) which can move and bond and exchange information in order to solve the given goal in a collective manner and without any outside intervention. One can envision a number of applications for these particle systems, most prominently shape formation and coating problems. Various algorithms for the formation of specific shapes have already been proposed within our model, but they are all inherently sequential: starting with a seed particle, the particles bond to each other in a chain-like fashion till the desired shape has been constructed. So for n particles $\Omega(n)$ rounds are needed to finish the shape formation. In this work we do not only show how to design a universal shape formation algorithm but we also show that for any shape composed of a constant number of equilateral triangles of unit size, our approach just needs $O(\sqrt{n})$ rounds to arrive at the desired shape, when starting in a well-initialized shape. We also show that this bound is best possible. Our shape formation approach is based on the geometric amoebot model [11], which we briefly describe in the next section.

SPAA '16, July 11-13, 2016, Pacific Grove, CA, USA
© 2016 ACM. ISBN 978-1-4503-4210-0/16/07...$15.00
DOI: http://dx.doi.org/10.1145/2935764.2935784

1.1 Amoebot model

We assume that any structure the particle system can form can be represented as a subgraph of an infinite graph $G = (V, E)$ where V represents all possible positions the particles can occupy relative to their structure, and E represents all possible atomic transitions a particle can perform as well as all places where neighboring particles can bond to each other. In the *geometric amoebot model*, we assume that $G = G_{\text{eqt}}$, where G_{eqt} is the infinite regular triangular grid graph. Figure 1(a) illustrates the standard planar embedding of G_{eqt}.

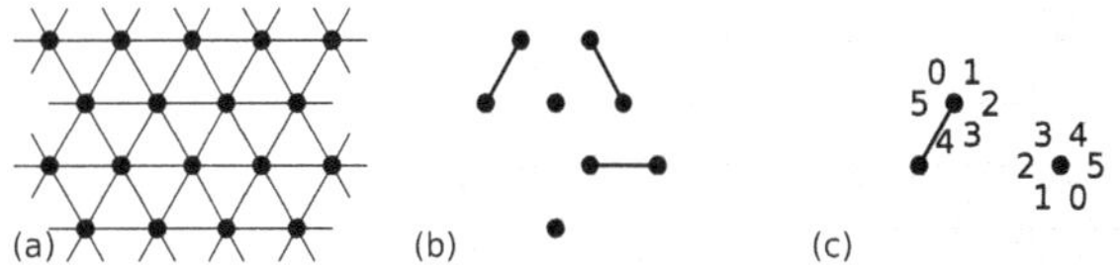

Figure 1: (a) shows a section of G_{eqt}. Nodes of G_{eqt} are shown as black circles. (b) shows five particles on G_{eqt}. The underlying graph G_{eqt} is depicted as a gray mesh. A particle occupying a single node is depicted as a black circle, and a particle occupying two nodes is depicted as two black circles connected by an edge. (c) depicts two particles occupying two non-adjacent positions on G_{eqt}. The particles have different offsets for their head port labelings.

We recall the main properties of the geometric amoebot model from [11]. Each particle occupies either a single node or a pair of adjacent nodes in G_{eqt}, and every node can be occupied by at most one particle. Two particles occupying adjacent nodes are *connected* by a *bond*, and we refer to such particles as *neighbors*. The bonds do not just ensure that the particles form a connected structure but they are also used for exchanging information as explained below.

Particles move through *expansions* and *contractions*: If a particle occupies one node (i.e., it is *contracted*), it can expand to an unoccupied adjacent node to occupy two nodes. If a particle occupies two nodes (i.e., it is *expanded*), it can contract to one of these nodes to occupy only a single node. Figure 1(b) illustrates a set of particles (some contracted, some expanded) on the underlying graph G_{eqt}. For an expanded particle, we denote the node the particle last expanded into as the *head* of the particle and call the other occupied node its *tail*. For a contracted particle, the single node occupied by the particle is both its head and its tail. A *handover* allows particles to stay connected as they move. Two scenarios are possible here: (1) a contracted particle p can "push" a neighboring expanded particle q and expand into the neighboring node previously occupied by q, forcing q to contract, or (2) an expanded particle p can "pull" a neighboring contracted particle q to node v it occupies thereby causing q to expand into v, which allows p to contract.

Particles are *anonymous*. Each particle has a collection of *ports*, one for each edge incident to the nodes occupied by it, that have unique labels from the local perspective of that particle. Adjacent particles establish bonds through the ports facing each other. We assume that the particles have a common *chirality*, i.e., they all have the same notion of *clockwise direction*, which allows a particle to order the port labels of its head and tail in clockwise order. However, particles do not have a common sense of orientation since they can have different offsets of the labelings, see Figure 1(c). Without loss of generality, we assume that each particle labels its head and tail ports from 0 to 5 in clockwise order. Whenever a particle p is connected through some port to a particle q, we assume that p knows the label of q's port that lies opposite of the respective port of p. Futhermore, we assume that p knows whether q's port belongs to the head or tail of q.

Each particle has a constant-size shared local memory that can be read and written to by any neighboring particle. This allows a particle to exchange information with a neighboring particle by simply writing it into the other particle's memory. A particle always knows whether it is contracted or expanded, and in the latter case it also knows along which head port label it is expanded. We assume that this information is also available to the neighboring particles (by publishing that label in its local shared memory). Particles do not know the total number of particles, nor do they have any estimate on this number.

We assume the standard asynchronous model from distributed computing, where the particle system progresses through a sequence of *particle activations*, i.e., only one particle is active at a time. Whenever a particle is activated, it can perform an arbitrary bounded amount of computation (involving its local memory as well as the shared memories of its neighbors) and at most one movement. We define a *round* to be over once each particle has been activated at least once.

The *configuration* C of the system at the beginning of time t consists of the nodes in G_{eqt} occupied by the set of particles; in addition, for every particle p, C contains the current state of p, including whether the particle is expanded or contracted, its port labeling, and the contents of its local memory. For more details on the model, please refer to [11].

1.2 Related work

Many approaches have already been proposed that can potentially be used for shape formation. One can distinguish between active and passive systems. In passive systems the particles either do not have any intelligence at all (but just move and bond based on their structural properties or due to chemical interactions with the environment), or they have limited computational capabilities but cannot control their movements. Examples of research on shape formation in *passive systems* appear in DNA self-assembly systems (see, e.g., [9, 17, 20]), and also the surveys in [16, 23]). In particular, [17] presents an approach to fold long single-stranded DNA molecules into arbitrary 2D shapes. In [15, 14], the authors study network topology and shape construction problems under a variation of the population protocols model [1], focusing on specific simple structures, such as a spanning line, a spanning star, or a spanning square.

In *active systems*, computational particles can control the way they act and possibly move in order to solve a specific task. Robotic swarms, modular robotic systems, and cellular automata are some examples of active programmable matter systems. In *swarm robotics*, one usually has a collection of autonomous robots that have limited sensing, often including vision, and communication ranges, and that can freely move in a given area. They follow a variety of goals, including shape formation (e.g., [18, 2, 12]). For example, in [18], the authors demonstrate that programmable self-assembly of complex two-dimensional shapes with hundreds or thousands of simple robots called *kilobots* is possible; however their approach differs considerably from ours, since the algorithms rely on a global pre-processing phase for shape formation that directly depends on the number of robots in the system. In [2], the authors explore a method to build and repair arbitrary two-dimensional shapes on a 2D coordinate system with a swarm of self-assembly robots. In [12], the authors study the algorithmic limitations of building a predefined exact shape by a set of autonomous mobile robots. Samples of other representative work can be found in e.g., [19, 7, 8]. While the analytic techniques developed in the area of swarm robotics and natural swarms are of some relevance for this work, the individual units in those systems have more powerful communication and processing capabilities than the systems we consider.

Beyond conventional actuation, sensing, and control typically found in fixed-morphology robots, *self-reconfigurable robots* are also able to adapt to form desired shapes (see e.g., [25, 26, 27]). *Metamorphic robots* form a subclass of self-reconfigurable robots that share some characteristics of our geometric model [6]. The hardware development in the field of self-reconfigurable robotics has been complemented by a number of algorithmic advances (e.g., [3, 22, 18]), but so far mechanisms that scale from a few to hundreds or thousands of individual units are still under investigation. While pattern formation has been extensively studied in the *cellular automata* model (e.g., in [21, 4, 13]), these studies differ from our model since particles can replicate (or die) at will.

The *nubot* model [24, 5] aims at providing the theoretical framework that would allow for a more rigorous algorithmic study of biomolecular-inspired systems, more specifically of self-assembly systems with active molecular components. One of the main results of [24] is to efficiently construct two-dimensional geometric shapes in polylogarithmic time in the size of the shape. While bio-molecular inspired systems share many similarities with self-organizing particle systems, there are differences — e.g., the system allows for an additional (non-local) notion of rigid-body movement.

Finally, in [10], we presented a preliminary algorithmic framework in the geometric amoebot model that allows particles to to build simple shapes, such as a hexagon or a triangle. The number of rounds required by the algorithms presented in this work is at least linear on the number of particles in the worst-case.

1.3 Our Contributions

In this paper, we present a universal shape formation algorithm for self-organizing particle systems which takes as input an arbitrary shape composed of a constant number of equilateral triangles and lets the particles build that shape at a scale depending on the number of particles in the system. We limit the number of triangles to a constant because in this case every particle can store the entire shape description, which can be seen as the base case for the study of universal shape formation algorithms. More complex scenarios (i.e., a shape description is spread across multiple particles, or the shape is only implicitly defined via some algorithm) are left for future research. Our algorithm runs in $O(\sqrt{n})$ asynchronous execution rounds, where n is the number of particles in the system, provided we start from a well-initialized configuration in which the particles form a (not necessarily complete) triangle. Starting in a shape with $O(\sqrt{n})$ diameter, like a triangle, is important because if the initial shape had $\omega(\sqrt{n})$ diameter, a runtime bound of $O(\sqrt{n})$ can no longer be guaranteed, no matter which algorithm is used for the shape formation. We chose the triangle as the initial structure since it turned out to be most convenient for the design of a universal shape formation algorithm. Our algorithm relies only on local information (e.g., particles do not have ids, nor do they know n, the total number of particles, or have any sort of global coordinate system), and requires only a constant-size memory per particle.

Note that the $O(\sqrt{n})$ runtime bound is much better than the runtime bounds of $O(n)$ that were previously shown for specific shapes [10]. The reason for this is that the approach in [10] is inherently sequential while we make full use of the available parallelism in this paper. In fact, *any* shape formation algorithm would need $\Omega(\sqrt{n})$ rounds to form *any* shape that is not just a single triangle, so our runtime bound is best possible.

2. PROBLEM STATEMENT

In the *shape formation problem*, a particle system has to reconfigure into a given shape. Formally, let S be a set of faces in the standard planar embedding of G_{eqt}. Hence, S is a set of nodes in the dual graph of G_{eqt}. We say two faces of G_{eqt} are *connected* if their corresponding nodes in the dual graph of G_{eqt} are connected. We say S is connected if the induced subgraph of the dual graph of G_{eqt} is connected. We define a *shape* to be a connected set of faces that has constant size. Consider any transformation of S into a geometric shape S' defined by a translation, a rotation by a multiple of 60°, and an isotropic scaling with the restriction that the vertices of the triangles forming S' all coincide with vertices in G_{eqt}. Consider the set of nodes $V(S') \subseteq V(G_{\text{eqt}})$ that lie on a vertex of S', on an edge of S', or inside of S'. We call $V(S')$ a *representation* of the shape S. Figure 2 illustrates this definition by an example.

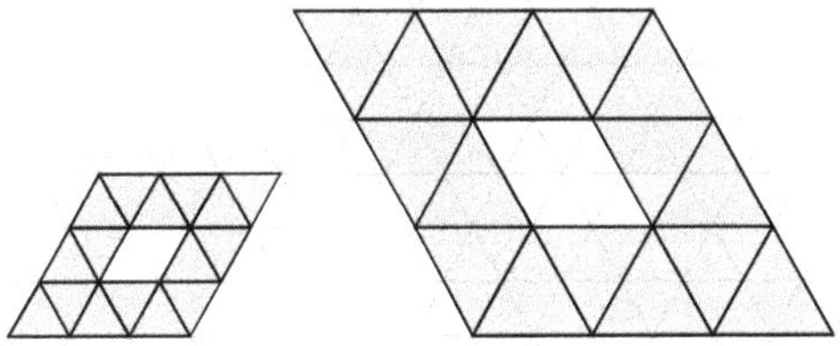

Figure 2: Two representations of a shape S consisting of 16 faces. For ease of presentation, we will often represent sets of particles via geometric shapes. In this example, each position inside a triangle, on a side of a triangle, and on a vertex of a triangle is occupied by a particle. The left part shows a representation in which the triangles coincide with the faces of G_{eqt}. Note that in this very small representation of S the hole suggested by the triangles is actually closed and therefore the representation is a solid quadrilateral. The right part shows a representation that is rotated counter-clockwise by 120° compared to the left representation and in which each triangle consists of four faces in G_{eqt}.

For the shape formation problem, we assume that initially all particles are contracted and they are arranged in a triangle. All particles are in the same *idle* state except for a unique *leader particle* that occupies one of the vertices of the *initial triangle* and that stores the desired shape S in its local memory (note that a leader particle could also be established by letting the particles occupying the vertices of the initial triangle engange in a competition using random coin flips that are transmitted along the sides of the triangle in a pipelined fashion). If the number of particles in the system n is not a triangular number, the last row of the initial triangle is not completely filled. For ease of presentation, we assume for now that n is a triangular number and hence the particles initially form a perfect triangle. We show how to avoid this assumption at the end of Section 5. To solve the shape formation problem, the system has to reconfigure so that the set of positions occupied by the particles is some representation of S. We allow particles in the final configuration to be expanded.

3. MOVEMENT PRIMITIVES

The shape formation algorithm reconfigures the system by using primitives for moving connected sets of particles. The simplest of these primitives moves a *chain* of particles along a path: Consider a simple directed path P of length ℓ in G_{eqt}. Let the first m nodes of P be occupied by contracted particles for some $m \leq \ell$. The goal is to let the particles *traverse* P, that is, the particles should move only through the nodes in P, they have to stay connected at all times, and in the end the particles should all be contracted and should occupy the last m nodes of P. This is achieved by letting the particles move as a connected chain using handovers. Lemma 1 bounds the number of rounds required for the particles to traverse P. Section 3.1 provides more detail about particle chain movement.

LEMMA 1. *A chain of particles of size $m \leq \ell$ can traverse a path P of length ℓ in G_{eqt} in $O(\ell)$ rounds.*

For the remaining primitives, consider a set of contracted particles that forms a triangle in G_{eqt}. Let one of the vertices of the triangle be occupied by a distinguished particle that we call the *coordinator* of the triangle. Furthermore, let the particles on the boundary of the triangle span a path oriented counter-clockwise around the triangle.

We define four primitive operations on triangles, namely *expansion*, *contraction*, *rotation*, and *shift*. Expansion, contraction, and rotation are shown in Figure 3. A shift of a triangle simply moves all particles of the triangle in a common direction by one position. A movement is initiated and controlled by the coordinator of a triangle. We give a detailed description of a local-control protocol for the expansion of a triangle in Section 3.2. Based on the general ideas presented in that section, it is easy to design protocols for the remaining operations. We have the following lemma.

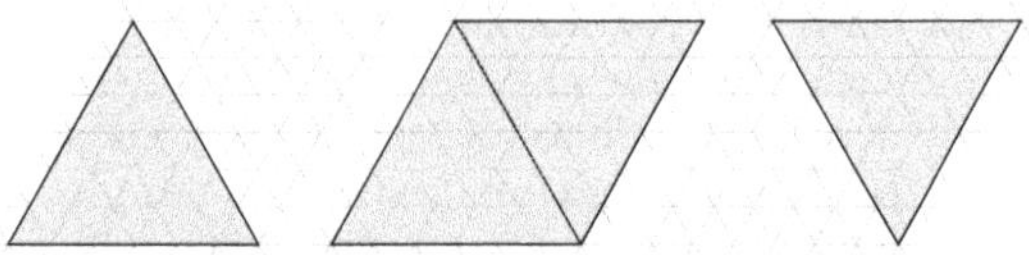

Figure 3: A triangle (left) can expand to form an expanded triangle (middle). An expanded triangle can contract back to a simple triangle (right). Concatening an expansion and a contraction effectively rotates a triangle.

LEMMA 2. *A triangle of side length ℓ can be expanded, contracted, rotated, and shifted in $O(\ell)$ rounds.*

Note that a triangle consisting of m particles has a side length of $O(\sqrt{m})$. Therefore, the primitives move such a triangle in $O(\sqrt{m})$ rounds.

3.1 Particle Chain Movement

A *movement schedule* is a sequence of particle system configurations $C_0, C_1, \ldots, C_k$. A movement schedule is called a *valid parallel schedule* (or simply *valid*) if every C_i represents a connected particle system and for every $i \geq 0$, C_{i+1} is reached from C_i in a way that for every particle p one of the following properties holds:

1. p occupies the same positions in C_i and C_{i+1}, or
2. p expands into a node that was empty in C_i, or
3. p contracts, leaving the node occupied by its tail empty in C_{i+1}, or
4. p is part of a handover with another particle p'.

Note that this means that several particles are allowed to move from C_i to C_{i+1}.

A *particle chain* is a sequence of particles $(p_1, p_2, \ldots, p_m)$ forming an arbitrary connected path of contracted or expanded particles in G_{eqt}. A *line schedule* is a valid movement schedule in which the particles initially form a particle chain and all particles move forward along the same, simple path of nodes in G_{eqt} (i.e., no node is traversed more than once by a particle) in their given order, so at the end the particles still form a particle chain of the same order as initially. Let $P = (v_1, \ldots, v_\ell)$ be the path used in a given line schedule, where v_1 is the node occupied by the tail of p_1 (the trailing particle in the particle chain) at the beginning of the schedule and v_ℓ is the node occupied by the head of p_m (the leading particle) at the end of the schedule. For any configuration C of the particle chain and any particle p_i in that chain we define its head position $h(C, i)$ to be the index of the node in P occupied by the head of p_i in C and its tail position $t(C, i)$ to be the index of the node occupied by the tail of p_i in C. Certainly, $t(C, i) \in \{h(C, i), h(C, i) - 1\}$, depending on whether p_i is contracted or expanded. For any two chain configurations C_1 and C_2 and any particle p_i we say that C_1 *dominates* C_2 w.r.t. p_i (or short, $C_1(p_i) \geq C_2(p_i)$) if and only if $h(C_1, i) \geq h(C_2, i)$ and $t(C_1, i) \geq t(C_2, i)$. Altogether, we say that C_1 *dominates* C_2 (or short, $C_1 \geq C_2$) if and only if C_1 dominates C_2 w.r.t. every particle.

We say that a given particle chain *emulates* a line schedule S if it starts in the initial configuration of S and every particle greedily aims at reaching its final position in S. That is, whenever p_i has not yet reached its final position in S, it tries to expand, contract, or use a handover whenever activated in order to advance towards its final position. However, it will only do so if this does not disconnect the particle chain.

LEMMA 3. *For any line schedule $C_0, \ldots, C_k$ that a particle chain wants to emulate and any activation sequence of the particles it holds for the configuration C'_i of the particles after round i that $C'_i \geq C_i$.*

PROOF. We will prove the lemma by induction. Initially, $C'_0 = C_0$ by assumption. Hence, suppose that for some $i \geq 0$ it holds that $C'_i \geq C_i$. Let us consider some fixed particle p_j. If $h(C'_i, j) > h(C_i, j)$ or $t(C'_i, j) > t(C_i, j)$, then certainly $C'_{i+1}(p_j) \geq C_{i+1}(p_j)$. Thus, it remains to consider the case that $h(C'_i, j) = h(C_i, j)$ and $t(C'_i, j) = t(C_i, j)$. Here, we consider the following subcases:

- If $C_{i+1}(p_j) = C_i(p_j)$, it certainly holds that $C'_{i+1}(p_j) \geq C_{i+1}(p_j)$. So for the remaining cases we assume that $C_{i+1}(p_j) > C_i(p_j)$.

- If p_j is contracted in C_i, it must be expanded in C_{i+1}, which means that p_{j+1} is expanded in C_i (or the position in front of it is empty, i.e., $j = m$). Since p_j is also contracted in C'_i, the particles must form a connected chain, and $C'_i \geq C_i$, this means that p_{j+1} must also be expanded in C'_i. No matter which of p_j and p_{j+1} is activated first, a handover will happen between them, which implies that $C'_{i+1}(p_j) \geq C_{i+1}(p_j)$. p_j cannot be involved in a handover with p_{j+1} before that because for that it would have to be expanded.

- If p_j is expanded in C_i, it must be contracted in C_{i+1}, which means that p_{j-1} is contracted in C_i (or the position behind it was empty, i.e., $j = 1$). Since p_j is also expanded in C'_i, the particles must form a connected chain, and $C'_i \geq C_i$, this means that p_{j-1} must also be contracted in C'_i. No matter which of p_j and p_{j-1} is activated first, a handover will happen between them, which implies that $C'_{i+1}(p_j) \geq C_{i+1}(p_j)$. p_j cannot be involved in a handover with p_{j-1} before that because for that it would have to be contracted.

Hence, in any case, $C'_{i+1}(p_j) \geq C_{i+1}(p_j)$ for all p_j, which proves the lemma. □

Consider a chain of contracted particles that should move along a path P of length ℓ. It is easy to see that there is a line schedule of length $O(\ell)$ that lets the particle chain traverse P. Therefore, Lemma 3 implies that by greedily moving forward the particle chain traverses P in $O(\ell)$ rounds independently of the activation order of the particles. Hence, Lemma 1 holds.

3.2 Triangle Expansion

A triangle coordinator p can *expand* its triangle to form an *expanded triangle*, i.e., two triangles of the same size of the original triangle that share a common side as illustrated in Figure 4. Let T be the set of nodes occupied by the

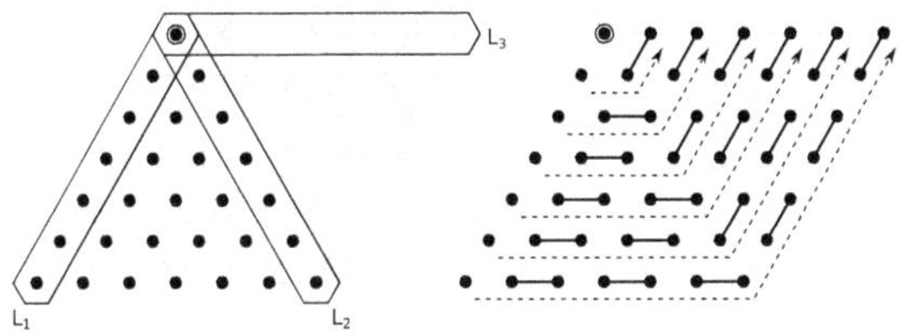

Figure 4: An example of a counter-clockwise triangle expansion. The coordinator p is highlighted by a black circle. Every row of particles expands independently as a chain (i.e., without disconnecting) around p. The resulting trajectories are shown as dashed arrows in the right part of the figure. Once every particle that did not occupy a position in L_1 is expanded, the triangle expansion is complete.

particles before the expansion and let ET be the set of positions occupied after the expansion. Let L_1 be the set of positions on the side of the initial triangle that occurs first when traversing the path on the boundary of the triangle starting from the coordinator in counter-clockwise direction. Let L_2 be the set of positions on the side of the initial triangle that corresponds to rotating L_1 counter-clockwise by 60° around p, and let L_3 be the set of positions on the side of the expanded triangle that corresponds to rotating L_1 counter-clockwise by 120°. Let a *row* of a triangle be a subset of T that forms a straight line in G_{eqt} that is parallel to the side of the initial triangle opposite of p.

An expansion is coordinated using the following token passing scheme. To initiate the expansion, p sends an *activation token* along L_1. Once a particle receives the activation token, it forwards the token along L_1 and sends a *row token* along its row. A particle that receives a row token forwards it along the row. Furthermore, it considers the particle it forwards the token to as its parent and it will follow that particle using handovers. In each row there is a unique particle that occupies L_2. Once this particle receives the expansion token it starts moving as depicted in Figure 4. In this way, all particles not on L_1 eventually expand, hence forming the expanded triangle. To determine when the expansion of the triangle is complete, the coordinator p proceeds as follows. After p sent out the activation token it sends a *validation token* along L_3. This token can only be forwarded to a specific row when the expansion of the particles in that row is complete. After the validation token completely traversed L_3, it is sent back to p along L_3. Once p receives the validation token, it knows that the expansion is completed.

Since the tokens in this scheme only traverse distances of $O(\ell)$, the corresponding parts of the algorithm can be easily realised using $O(\ell)$ rounds. Each row of the triangle acts as a chain of particles and expands independently over a distance of at most $O(\ell)$. By arguments analogous to those in the proof of Lemma 3, this movement takes $O(\ell)$ rounds. Therefore, Lemma 2 holds.

4. INTERMEDIATE STRUCTURE

The goal of this section is to reorganize the particles from the initially given triangle into an intermediate structure that simplifies the actual shape formation process. The intermediate structure we aim for is shown in Figure 5. It con-

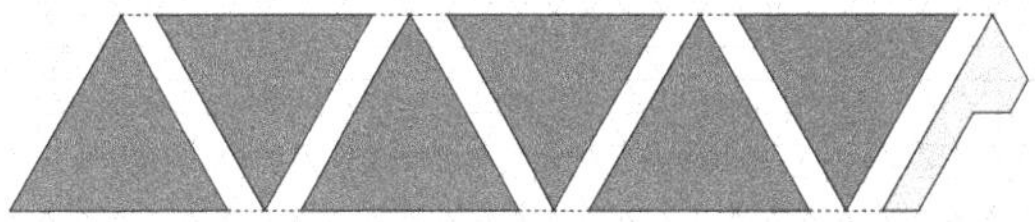

Figure 5: The intermediate structure.

sists of Δ many equilateral triangles of side length ℓ (shown in dark gray) that are arranged in a straight line and a remainder of particles (light gray) that is too small to form an additional triangle. All particles in this structure are contracted. Note that the algorithm we present in this section might actually create a structure that is slightly worse in the sense that it might leave a larger remainder of particles. We will come back to this at the end of the section; for now we assume that we can build the ideal structure.

Given a certain number of particles, the value of Δ is completely determined by the value of ℓ. Let $s = |S|$. For the intermediate structure to be useful, we want to choose ℓ such that $\frac{3}{4}s + 1 \leq \Delta \leq s - 3$. We will elaborate on these bounds in the following section; for now our focus remains on building the intermediate structure. Let L be the side length of the initial triangle. We choose $\ell = \lceil L / \lfloor c \cdot \sqrt{s} \rfloor \rceil$ with $c = 80/81$. Lemma 4 shows that this choice is appropriate for sufficiently large s and L; we omit the proof.

LEMMA 4. *If $s \geq 123$ and $L \geq 34\lfloor\sqrt{s}\rfloor$, we have that $\frac{3}{4}s + 1 \leq \Delta \leq s - 3$.*

Note that the bounds on s and L given in Lemma 4 could be lowered by a better choice of c and a tighter analysis.

We now turn to the construction of the intermediate structure. First, the particles have to determine ℓ. Note that in general no single particle can store ℓ as $\ell = \Theta(\sqrt{n})$ and the particles only have constant memory. Hence, we have to store ℓ in a distributed fashion over multiple particles. To determine ℓ we use the following token passing scheme: The leader particle, which occupies a vertex of the initial triangle, sends a *counter token* along an adjacent edge of the initial triangle. This token stores a counter that counts the number of steps it takes along the edge modulo $\lfloor c \cdot \sqrt{s} \rfloor$. Since c and s are constants, the leader can use a hard-coded table to determine $\lfloor c \cdot \sqrt{s} \rfloor$ and the token only requires constant memory. Initially, the value stored in the counter token is 0. When a particle holds the counter token while its value is 0, that particle will create a *marker token* (note that also the leader creates a marker token). Once the counter token completely traversed the edge of the initial triangle, it is simply consumed by the particle occupying the corresponding vertex of the initial triangle. The consuming particle will then create a *terminal token.* Both the marker tokens and the terminal token travel in the opposite direction of the counter token (i.e., towards the leader). Each particle is only allowed to store either one marker token or the terminal token. The only exception to this rule is the particle that creates the terminal token. This particle might also have created a marker token. In this case, the particle can temporarily store both tokens and has to first pass the marker token and then the terminal token. Since the tokens all move towards the leader, they will eventually occupy a segment of consecutive particles starting with the leader particle and ending with the particle that holds the terminal token. To detect when this state is reached, each marker token stores a boolean value that is initially false and becomes true if either the marker token occupies the leader particle or the marker token has another marker token in front of it with its value set to true. Once the terminal token has a marker token with its value set to true in front of it, it knows that all tokens are done moving and sends a final token towards the leader to inform him that the token passing scheme has terminated. It is easy to check that the length of the segment occupied by the tokens is exactly ℓ. Furthermore, it is easy to show that the token passing scheme requires $O(\sqrt{n})$ rounds and only uses constant memory.

Once ℓ has been established, the intermediate structure can be built using a globally synchronized process. This simple process is coordinated by the leader and only uses triangle shifts and triangle rotations, as illustrated in Figure 6. For simplicity, we assume a global perspective to

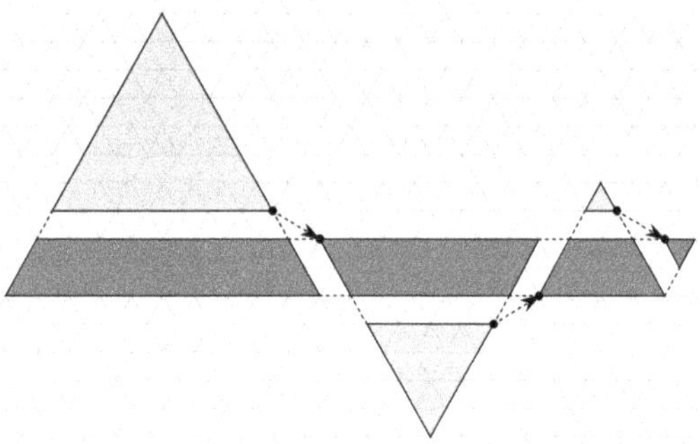

Figure 6: Construction of the intermediate structure. The parts forming the intermediate structure is shown in dark gray. The triangles that are shifted and rotated are shown in light gray. For each dotted arrow, the circles at the origin and the tip of the arrow marks the same particle before and after the respective triangle is moved. As an example, the left-most triangle is rotated clockwise by 60° around the vertex at the origin of the corresponding arrow, then it is shifted once to the right and once to the bottom-right, and finally it is rotated clockwise by 120° around the vertex at the tip of the arrow.

describe this process; a local-control protocol implementing this process is easy to design. The process is executed recursively starting with the initial triangle. It splits the triangle into a wedge of height ℓ and a smaller triangle. The wedge becomes the first part of the intermediate structure. The triangle is rotated, shifted twice, and rotated again as described in the caption of Figure 6. Then the process recurs. Note that the orientation of the rotations and the direction of the shifts changes with every recurrence. The process ends after moving the first triangle that has a side length less or equal to ℓ.

The final part of our algorithm divides the structure into triangles, each having its own coordinator, by assigning structural information to the particles. From a global perspective, the intermediate structure is simply divided into triangles that are arranged as in Figure 5. This process ends once no more triangle can be formed in this way. The process can be easily implemented locally as a traversal of the intermediate structure using token passing that is globally coordinated by the leader. Note that in this traversal the token(s) only have to move along the edges of the prospective triangles. We assume that during the process the leader counts the number of triangles Δ' that have been built, and that in the end the leader token moves back to its initial position. Concerning the number of rounds required to build the intermediate structure we have the following lemma.

LEMMA 5. *The algorithm terminates after $O(\sqrt{n})$ rounds.*

PROOF SKETCH. The recursive part of the algorithm terminates after $\lceil L/\ell \rceil = O(1)$ recursions. Each recursion requires a constant number of triangle rotations and shifts, each of which takes $O(\sqrt{n})$ rounds. The remainder of the recursive part of the algorithm as well as the final part of the algorithm that divides the intermediate structure into triangles can be implemented via token passing schemes requiring $O(\sqrt{n})$ rounds. □

As mentioned earlier, the given algorithm builds a structure that is slightly different from the ideal intermediate structure shown in Figure 5. Roughly speaking, the end of the structure is not necessarily perfectly suited for the purpose of dividing the structure into triangles of side length ℓ. Consequently, the number of triangles Δ' in the intermediate structure might be one less than the number of triangles Δ in an ideal intermediate structure, as we show in Lemma 6.

LEMMA 6. *The algorithm builds an intermediate structure containing Δ' triangles where $\Delta - 1 \leq \Delta' \leq \Delta$. The particles that are not included in any triangle are arranged as shown in Figure 7.*

PROOF. We first need the following simple observation: The end of the structure built by the algorithm can take on one of the three different forms illustrated in the first three parts of Figure 7. If the last triangle moved by the algorithm

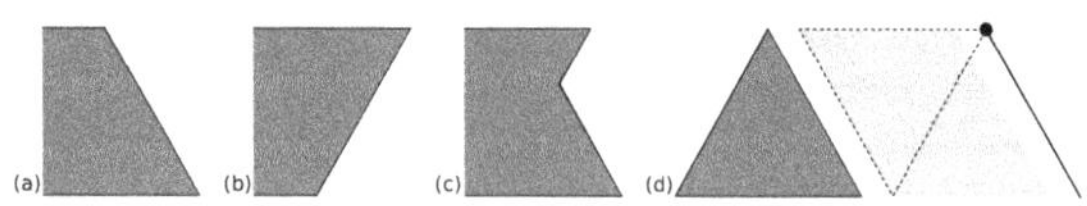

Figure 7: The end of the intermediate structure.

has side length greater or equal than $\ell - 1$, one of the forms in (a) and (b) is created. Otherwise, the end of the structure will look similar to part (c) of Figure 7.

For the rest of the proof consider part (d) of Figure 7. Without loss of generality, let the last triangle formed by the algorithm lie as shown in dark gray. The potential next triangle, shown as a dashed outline, cannot be formed. Consequently, the vertex of that triangle marked by a circle cannot be occupied. This holds because if it were occupied all positions of the dashed triangle would be occupied, no matter which of the forms the end of the structure assumes. By the same argument, all positions on the bold line have to be unoccupied and also every position to the right of that line has to be unoccupied. Hence, all particles of the intermediate structure that are not part of a triangle have to lie in the light gray area. This area contains $\ell(\ell-1)$ positions. Since a triangle of side length ℓ contains $\ell(\ell+1)/2$ positions, the particles that are not part of any triangle could form at most one additional triangle. Therefore, the lemma holds. □

The following theorem follows immediately from the lemmas presented throughout this section.

THEOREM 1. *For $s \geq 123$ and $L \geq 34\lfloor\sqrt{s}\rfloor$, the algorithm builds an intermediate structure consisting of Δ' triangles where $\frac{3}{4}s \leq \Delta' \leq s-3$. The particles that are not included in any triangle are arranged as shown in Figure 7.*

5. SHAPE FORMATION ALGORITHM

We now turn to the actual shape formation algorithm. From this point onwards we will use the term *face* exclusively to refer to a triangular face of G_{eqt} and the term *triangle* exclusively to refer to a set of particles occupying nodes in G_{eqt} that form a triangle. The algorithm we present can be interpreted as a sequential global algorithm that is coordinated by the leader and that operates almost exclusively on triangles. Recall that for a given shape S we want to build a representation $R(S)$. We will use the shape in the left part of Figure 8 as a running example to illustrate the intermediate steps of the shape formation algorithm. Observe

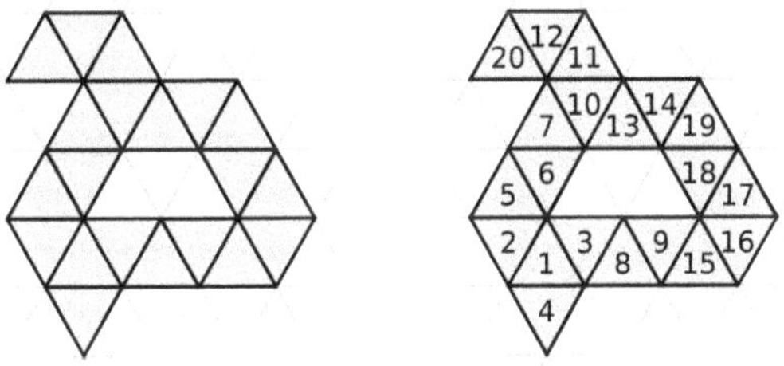

Figure 8: The running example of Section 5. The left part shows the example shape. The right part shows a corresponding construction schedule CS. The number inside a face indicates its rank in CS.

that building $R(S)$ generally requires triangles of different side lengths, namely ℓ, $\ell-1$, and $\ell-2$ (see Figure 9), since nodes in G_{eqt} can only be occupied by one particle.

Before building $R(S)$, the leader computes a *construction schedule* CS, i.e., a permutation of the faces that dictates the chronological order in which the corresponding triangles are placed. The schedule is computed backwards, i.e., the leader starts with determining which triangles to place last.

Let G_S be the subgraph of the dual graph of G_{eqt} induced by S. For the computation of CS, let D (resp. ND) be the subset of S that contains the faces that already have an assigned chronological ranking in CS (resp. have not been assigned yet). Initially, $D=\emptyset$ and $ND=S$. As long

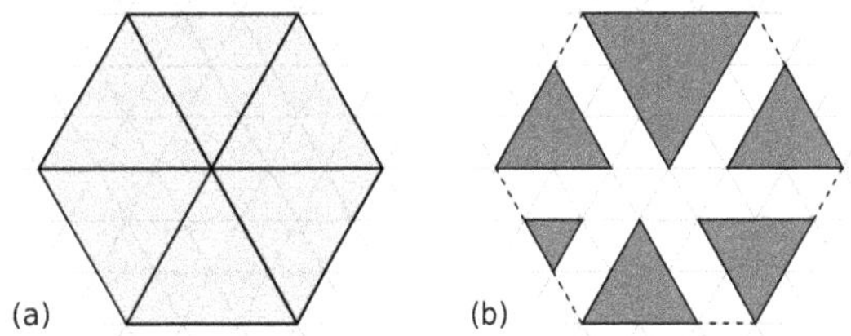

Figure 9: Part (a) shows a representation of a shape with six faces. Part (b) shows the triangles forming that representation which requires triangles of three different sizes.

as $ND \neq \emptyset$ the leader determines the next face in CS (in backwards order), removes the corresponding face from ND, and adds it to D, according to the following two rules.

1. Let G_{ND} be the subgraph of G_S induced by the nodes of ND. Mark all nodes as prospects that can be removed from G_{ND} without disconnecting the graph.
2. Instead of specifying the second rule as a graph property, it is easier and more useful to specify the condition geometrically. Interpret the nodes of G_{ND} as triangles in the Euclidean plane according to the standard embedding (see Figure 1(a)). Since G_{ND} is connected, we can combine the triangles to a single geometric shape (e.g., see Figure 10). Pick a prospect that has an edge on the outer boundary of said shape.

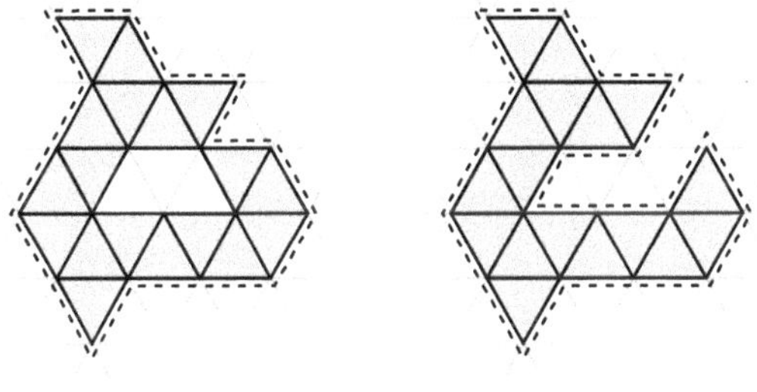

Figure 10: Two steps of the computation of CS. The left part shows the current shape after the faces of rank 20 and 19 have been chosen by the rules. The dotted line indicates the outer boundary of the current shape. Note that even though the two faces in the upper right corner are not connected, the hole of the polygon is not part of the outer boundary because the faces share a vertex. The right part shows the shape after the subsequent application of the rules (i.e. face 18 is chosen). Now the former hole is part of the boundary of the shape.

We call the chronological position of a face $a \in S$ in CS the *rank* of a in CS (i.e., the face chosen first by the rules has rank s and the one chosen last rank 1). See the right part of Figure 8 for a complete construction schedule for the running example. Informally speaking, the first rule guarantees that the schedule respects the connectivity requirements of a shape. The second rule ensures that we build $R(S)$ from the inside outwards, since outside faces are chosen early (i.e., they appear late in CS). The following lemma shows that our algorithm always computes a correct schedule.

LEMMA 7. *The algorithm assigns a rank to each face.*

PROOF. It is sufficient to show that in each step there exists at least one face of ND that fulfills both rules. We will consider the two rules in reversed order. Let ND_2 be the set of faces in ND that have an edge that lies on the outer boundary of the polygon as specified in the second rule. If there is a node in ND_2 with degree 1 in G_{ND_2} (i.e., the subgraph of G_S induced by the nodes of ND_2), that node trivially fulfills both rules. Therefore, assume that all nodes of ND_2 have a degree ≥ 2 in G_{ND_2}. Consequently, there has to exist at least one simple cycle among a subset of nodes of ND_2. In each simple cycle there has to exist at least one node with degree exactly two, since otherwise the cycle would not be on the outer boundary of the polygon. Naturally, we can remove this node from a cycle without disconnecting G_{ND}. Thus, in each step the two rules find a node that can be removed from ND. □

Moreover, we show that the C fulfills two properties that we need in order to build $R(S)$. The *prefix of length* i of a construction schedule CS is a subschedule of CS containing only the first i elements of CS.

LEMMA 8. *Consider CS as computed by our set of rules. For any prefix of length $i \in \{1, \dots, n\}$ it holds that: (i) the subgraph of G_S induced by the prefix is connected and (ii) the face of rank i in CS has an edge that lies on the outer boundary of the shape corresponding to the prefix.*

PROOF. The first statement of the lemma follows immediately from the first rule for computing CS, and the second statement follows immediately from the second rule. □

Once CS is computed, the building of $R(S)$ does not start immediately. Section 4 pointed out that the intermediate structure is not perfect (see Figure 7), but has a remainder, i.e., particles that are not included in any triangle of the intermediate structure. Instead of ignoring the remainder, we want to incorporate it into $R(S)$ without moving it. Ultimately, we aim at building one of the two subshapes shown in Figure 11 (a) and (b) first (possibly rotated by a multiple of 60°). These subshapes have the advantage that there are two adjacent (inner) faces (shown in dark grey in Figure 11) such that both face are also adjacent to another face (light grey). The remainder will (partially) occupy the triangles

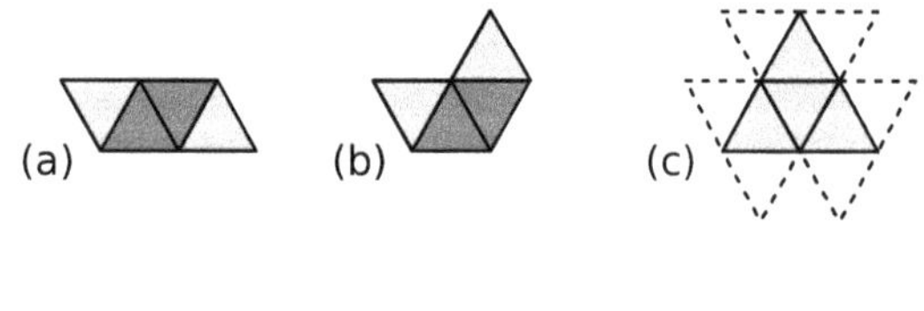

Figure 11: Three subshapes of S. We aim at building a rotated version of subshape (a) or (b) first. The subshape shown in (c) is the one we want to avoid building first. The faces with a dashed boundary are all possible locations to attach a fifth face.

corresponding to the two inner faces. We then use two triangles from the intermediate structure to represent the outer faces (see left part of Figure 12). Finally, the two triangles will use the expansion primitive to occupy all nodes in the inner triangles that are not occupied by the remainder (see

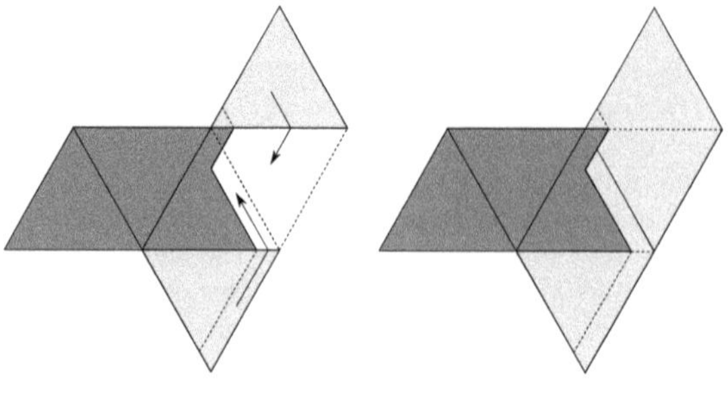

Figure 12: A conceptual sketch of how to incorporate the remainder of the intermediate structure into $R(S)$. As shown in Lemma 6 the remainder can at most occupy the nodes of two adjacent triangles of side length $\ell - 1$ (here, we abstract from concrete side lengths). The left part illustrates how the first two triangles (light grey), one of side length ℓ the other of side length $\ell - 1$, are placed adjacent to the remainder. The rows of those triangles that can expand into the white area do so (as depicted by the arrows). In the right part the rows have expanded as far as possible. The remainder and the two partially expanded triangles together form four faces of S.

right part of Figure 12). For this initial construction step two expanded triangles are necessary.

However, it is possible that the first four faces in CS do not form one of the subshapes shown in Figure 11 (a) and (b), but the one shown in Figure 11 (c) (apart from 60° rotation of those shapes there are no other possibilities, since faces have to be connected). Note that this subshape does not have two adjacent faces such that each has another adjacent face. For case (c) consider all possibilities for the fifth face in CS (i.e., faces with dashed boundary in Figure 11 (c)). No matter where it is placed, the resulting shape contains one of the two desired shapes as a subshape. Consequently, by switching the order of the first five faces in CS, we get an adjusted schedule CS' that starts with a desired subshape. In the running example, the first four faces of CS form the subshape of figure Figure 11 (c) (see right part of Figure 8); CS' is chosen accordingly (see left part of Figure 13).

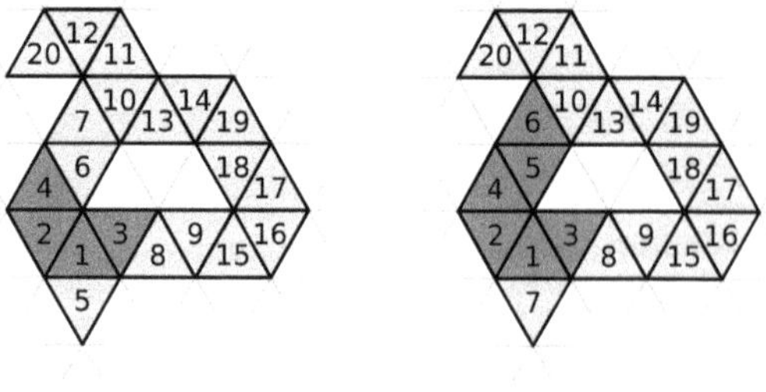

Figure 13: The two adjusted construction schedules of CS. The left part shows the adjusted construction schedule CS'. The first four faces (dark gray) now form a desired subshape. The right part illustrates CS''. The root is the subshape shown in dark gray.

Once the remainder of the intermediate structure has been incorporated as described, the algorithm performs one intermediate step before constructing the rest of $R(S)$. As already mentioned, triangles of three possible sizes are needed. Therefore, each triangle is pruned to its desired size while it is still in the intermediate structure. We will elaborate later how the leader decides which triangles to prune to a certain size; for now we focus on the pruning itself and *waste particles* arising from that pruning (i.e., particles that are removed from triangles). The pruning of a triangle is done by removing (i.e., moving away) the lower one or two rows. The number of waste particles introduced through this pruning procedure is $O(\sqrt{n})$, since the number of triangles is constant and each triangle is pruned by at most two rows. In order to incorporate the waste in $R(S)$, we want to construct an expanded triangle next (corresponding to faces ranked 5 and 6 in CS'). Note that the faces of rank 5 and 6 of CS' are not necessarily adjacent. Similar to the first four faces we can adjust CS' to get a schedule that has the desired property. To be more precise, consider the subshapes in Figure 11 (a) and (b) (i.e., the two possible subshapes we fixed for the first four triangles). If we add seven more faces to the subshape, the resulting shape will have at least another pair of adjacent faces. Therefore, it is sufficient to swap the order among the faces of rank 5 to 11 in CS' to get an adjusted schedule CS'' that has two adjacent faces at rank 5 and 6 which are connected to the faces with ranks 1 through 4, while still having the properties of Lemma 8. The schedule CS'' for the running example is shown in the right part of Figure 13. We call the substructure consisting of the first six faces in CS'' the *root* of the shape. During the construction of the root, we use particle chain movement to move the waste particles to some position that does not interfere with the construction of the root. Once the the root is constructed, we again use particle chain movement to move the waste particles to the expanded triangle forming the faces with rank 5 and 6. This completely expanded triangle then contracts as many particles as necessary to incorporate all of the waste particles. Note that the fact that we need at least three expanded triangles for the construction of the root matches the upper bound $\Delta' \leq s-3$ from to Section 4.

Note that CS'' is oblivious to the fact that $\frac{3}{4}s \leq \Delta' \leq s-3$. Consequently, it might be that more than the three already mentioned expanded triangles are needed to build $R(S)$. Due to our lower bound on Δ', we certainly have enough triangles. Nevertheless, the leader has to determine which pairs of faces to construct using expanded triangles. Let $\eta = s - \Delta'$, i.e., at most η many expanded triangles are needed to built $R(S)$.

LEMMA 9. *For any shape S the leader can identify at least η many disjoint pairs of adjacent faces.*

PROOF. For a shape S consider the adjusted schedule CS''. Let $r(a)$ denote the rank of a face $a \in S$ in CS''. Additionally, let the predecessor $pred(a)$ of a be the face $b \in S$ such that a and b are connected, $r(a) > r(b)$, and $r(b)$ is minimal. Note that every face has a predecessor except for the face with rank 1. Let T be the spanning tree of G_S induced by CS'', i.e., $T = (V, E^*)$ with $E^* = \{\{a,b\} \mid pred(a) = b\}$ (see left part of Figure 14).

In order to show that the leader can identify enough pairs of faces, we give the following two rules to deconstruct T

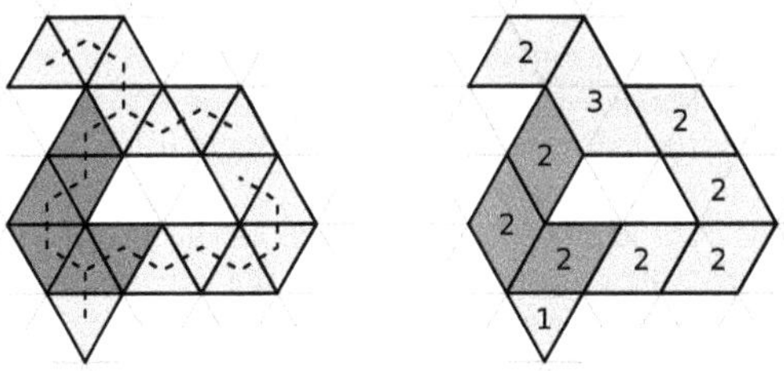

Figure 14: A graphical representation of the two intermediate steps of the proof of Lemma 9. The left part illustrates the spanning tree T (indicated by the dotted lines). The right part shors the deconstruction of T. The numbers indicate the different possibilities of the rules: (1) a single face connected to the root, (2) a pair of faces that was found by the first rule, and (3) three faces that the second rule was applied to.

and count ρ, the number of pairs found. Since we already know how to build the root, we do not apply the rules to these six nodes, i.e., the process stops once T solely consist of the six root nodes and constantly many leaves that the rules cannot be applied to.

1. Remove a leaf and its predecessor from T if that removal does not disconnect the remaining tree. By definition such a pair can be represented by an expanded triangle.
2. If the first rule is not applicable, each predecessor of a leaf is a predecessor for two leafs. Remove all three nodes from T, i.e., a pair and a singleton node. We can represent these three faces by one expanded and one contracted triangle.

The right part of Figure 14 shows the deconstruction of T for our running example. The lemma holds if $\eta \leq \rho$. Note that ρ is minimized if we always have to apply the second rule. Futhermore, note that at most 8 faces of S are adjacent to the root. So overall, since the root consists of 6 faces, we get that $\rho \geq \frac{1}{3}(s-6-8)+3$. Additionally, it holds that $\eta \leq \frac{1}{4}s$ due to our lower bound on Δ'. Thus, $\eta \leq \rho$ if $s \geq 20$, which holds according to the lower bound on s (see Theorem 1). □

As a consequence, the leader exactly knows how many expanded triangles it needs and has a simple rule to determine where to use an expanded triangle. The leader still has to specify which triangles have to be pruned. However, with CS'' and the information gained from the deconstruction of T, it can easily do so: It iterates over CS'' and determines for each face whether the face is represented by a triangle of size $\ell-2$, $\ell-1$, or ℓ. In case two adjacent faces are represented by an expanded triangle, it is important that either both faces are assigned the same size or that the lower ranked face gets the bigger size. Otherwise, the expansion would fail, since a triangle of size $\ell-1$ has not enough particles to occupy all nodes of a triangle of size ℓ and and a triangle of size $\ell-1$. Afterwards, the leader can prune the triangles in the intermediate structure accordingly. Thus, the building process of $R(S)$ according to CS'' is in general straightforward. Once the root is built as described, the leader sequentially builds $R(S)$ according to CS'' by either moving a triangle with triangle rotations and triangle shifts from the intermediate structure or by expanding an already placed triangle.

Finally note that CS'' is oblivious to the position of the intermediate structure. If we keep the structure fixed in its initial position, it might get in the way of the construction of the shape or it might get walled-in, i.e., it might get completely surrounded by already placed triangles. We can avoid both of these problems as follows: Before moving a triangle in CS'', the leader can easily check whether the intermediate structure is in the way or would get walled in. If this is the case, it simply moves the entire intermediate structure, triangle by triangle, to a different position that is still adjacent to the already placed triangles but where it does not interfere with the construction. We now show that CS'' is a correct schedule, i.e., we can actually build $R(S)$ if we follow the order of the construction schedule.

LEMMA 10. *For any shape S our algorithm computes a construction schedule CS'' that allows the construction of $R(S)$.*

PROOF. First note that the intermediate structure does not interfere with the construction process since it is moved out of the way when necessary. We have already shown how to build the root. It remains to show for $i > 6$ that if the first $i-1$ faces have been built, we can always build the the face of rank i in CS''. There are two cases: Either an already built triangle has to expand or a new triangle has to be moved from the intermediate structure to the desired position. First consider the former case. There already exists a triangle a that corresponds to a face of rank strictly less than i that is adjacent to the face of rank i. Since the triangle corresponding to a has the same size or a larger size than the triangle corrsponding to the face with rank i, the i-th triangle can in fact be built using triangle expansion. Now consider the second case, i.e., a triangle has to be moved. According to property 1 of Lemma 8, the i-th face is connected to at least one of the first $i-1$ faces. According to property 2 of Lemma 8, there exists a path along which the new triangle can be moved from the intermediate structure to the desired position. Thus, we can always build $R(S)$ according to CS''. □

We conclude our section with the following theorem.

THEOREM 2. *The shape formation algorithm solves the shape formation problem in $O(\sqrt{n})$ rounds.*

PROOF. By Lemma 10 we can build $R(S)$ according to CS''. Moreover, consider the following observation.

OBSERVATION 1. *Consider two triangles of the same size that are arranged such that two vertices of one triangle are adjacent to a position of the other triangle (e.g., two triangles in the intermediate structure shown in Figure 5). We can rotate one triangle completely around the other using only a constant number of triangle rotations and shifts.*

The computation of CS with its adjustments is done locally by the leader. Building the root takes $O(\sqrt{n})$ rounds. Pruning the triangles and moving the waste particles takes $O(\sqrt{n})$ rounds according to Lemma 1. For each face in the schedule we either need to expand an already placed triangle or move a triangle to its desired position. The former case takes $O(\sqrt{n})$ rounds according to Lemma 2. For the latter case, we have to move the triangle along all other triangles in the worst case. Doing so takes at most $O(\sqrt{n})$ rounds, due to Lemma 2 and Observation 1). Additionally, it might be possible that we have to move the whole intermediate structure every time a new triangle is moved. We move the structure triangle by triangle to its new position which takes $O(\sqrt{n})$ rounds. □

The following theorem shows that our algorithm is actually *optimal* in terms of worst-case number of rounds.

THEOREM 3. *Let S be any shape except for a triangle. Our algorithm is $O(1)$-competitive against* any *algorithm that solves the shape formation problem with regards to number of rounds.*

PROOF. First note that an algorithm that solves the shape formation problem cannot control the activation order of particles, thus, every particle moves only a distance of at most 1 per round in the worst case. If S is not a triangle there exists at least one particle that has to move at distance of $\Omega(\sqrt{n})$ in order to form the desired shape. Therefore, any algorithm needs at least $\Omega(\sqrt{n})$ rounds to solve the shape formation problem in the worst case. □

Finally, we explain how to get rid of the assumption that the number of particles is a triangular number (see Section 2). As a consequence, the initial triangle of particles is not necessarily perfect anymore, i.e., the last row of the initial triangle is not completely filled with particles. Note that there are at most $O(\sqrt{n})$ particles in the last row and the leader can determine by a token passing scheme whether the last row is complete. While the intermediate structure is constructed, the incomplete row is moved to a safe location (by using the particle chain movement from Section 3) such that it does not interfere with the process described in Section 4. During the construction of the representation of S we move the incomplete row together with the intermediate structure if necessary. We incorporate the row into $R(S)$ early on by moving it into the third expanded triangle we construct, which is similar to the way the waste particles are handled. There is enough space for the waste particles and the incomplete row since both amounts are in $O(\sqrt{n})$ and the expanded triangle can incorporate $\Omega(n)$ many particles. During the entire algorithm, the incomplete row only has to move a distance of $O(\sqrt{n})$, which is in line with the given runtime bound.

6. CONCLUSION

We presented a universal shape formation algorithm for self-organizing particle systems which takes as input an arbitrary shape composed of a constant number of equilateral triangles and lets the particles build that shape at a scale depending on the number of particles in the system. For future work, it would be interesting to investigate more complex descriptions of the shape that has to be built: a shape description of non-constant size could be spread across multiple particles, or the shape could be defined only implicitly via some algorithm. Furthermore, initial configurations of diameter $O(\sqrt{n})$ other than the triangle could be considered.

7. ACKNOWLEDGMENTS

This work was partially supported by the NSF under the Awards CCF-1353089 and CCF-1422603. Furthermore, it was partially supported by DFG grant SCHE 1592/3-1.

8. REFERENCES

[1] D. Angluin, J. Aspnes, Z. Diamadi, M. J. Fischer, and R. Peralta. Computation in networks of passively mobile finite-state sensors. *Distributed Computing*, 18(4):235–253, 2006.

[2] D. Arbuckle and A. Requicha. Self-assembly and self-repair of arbitrary shapes by a swarm of reactive robots: algorithms and simulations. *Autonomous Robots*, 28(2):197–211, 2010.

[3] Z. J. Butler, K. Kotay, D. Rus, and K. Tomita. Generic decentralized control for lattice-based self-reconfigurable robots. *International Journal of Robotics Research*, 23(9):919–937, 2004.

[4] A. Chavoya and Y. Duthen. Using a genetic algorithm to evolve cellular automata for 2d/3d computational development. In *8th annual conference on genetic and evolutionary computation*, pages 231–232, 2006.

[5] M. Chen, D. Xin, and D. Woods. Parallel computation using active self-assembly. In *DNA Computing and Molecular Programming*, pages 16–30. Springer, 2013.

[6] G. Chirikjian. Kinematics of a metamorphic robotic system. In *Proceedings of ICRA '94*, volume 1, pages 449–455, 1994.

[7] S. Das, P. Flocchini, N. Santoro, and M. Yamashita. On the computational power of oblivious robots: forming a series of geometric patterns. In *Proceedings of PODC 2010*, pages 267–276, 2010.

[8] X. Defago and S. Souissi. Non-uniform circle formation algorithm for oblivious mobile robots with convergence toward uniformity. *Theoretical Computer Science*, 396(1-3):97–112, 2008.

[9] E. D. Demaine, M. J. Patitz, R. T. Schweller, and S. M. Summers. Self-assembly of arbitrary shapes using RNAse enzymes: Meeting the kolmogorov bound with small scale factor (extended abstract). In *Proceedings of STACS '11*, pages 201–212, 2011.

[10] Z. Derakhshandeh, R. Gmyr, A. W. Richa, C. Scheideler, and T. Strothmann. An algorithmic framework for shape formation problems in self-organizing particle systems. In *Proceedings of NANOCOM 2015*, 2015.

[11] Z. Derakhshandeh, R. Gmyr, T. Strothmann, R. A. Bazzi, A. W. Richa, and C. Scheideler. Leader election and shape formation with self-organizing programmable matter. In *DNA Computing and Molecular Programming (DNA 21)*, pages 117–132, 2015.

[12] P. Flocchini, G. Prencipe, N. Santoro, and P. Widmayer. Arbitrary pattern formation by asynchronous, anonymous, oblivious robots. *Theoretical Computer Science*, 407(1):412–447, 2008.

[13] K. Imai, Y. Kasai, Y. Sonoyama, C. Iwamoto, and K. Morita. Self-reproduction and shape formation in two and three dimensional cellular automata with conservative constraints. In *Proceedings of the Eighth International Symposium on Artificial Life and Robotics*, pages 377–380, 2003.

[14] O. Michail. Terminating distributed construction of shapes and patterns in a fair solution of automata. In *Proceedings of PODC 2015*, pages 37–46, 2015.

[15] O. Michail and P. G. Spirakis. Simple and efficient local codes for distributed stable network construction. In *Proceedings of PODC 2014*, pages 76–85, 2014.

[16] M. J. Patitz. An introduction to tile-based self-assembly and a survey of recent results. *Natural Computing*, 13(2):195–224, 2014.

[17] P. W. Rothemund. Folding DNA to create nanoscale shapes and patterns. *Nature*, 440(7082):297–302, 2006.

[18] M. Rubenstein, A. Cornejo, and R. Nagpal. Programmable self-assembly in a thousand-robot swarm. *Science*, 345(6198):795–799, 2014.

[19] M. Rubenstein and W.-M. Shen. Automatic scalable size selection for the shape of a distributed robotic collective. In *Proceedings of IROS 2010*, pages 508–513. IEEE, 2010.

[20] N. Schiefer and E. Winfree. Universal computation and optimal construction in the chemical reaction network-controlled tile assembly model. In *DNA Computing and Molecular Programming (DNA 21)*, pages 34–54, 2015.

[21] J. L. Schiff. *Cellular automata: a discrete view of the world*, volume 45. John Wiley & Sons, 2011.

[22] J. E. Walter, J. L. Welch, and N. M. Amato. Distributed reconfiguration of metamorphic robot chains. *Distributed Computing*, 17(2):171–189, 2004.

[23] D. Woods. Intrinsic universality and the computational power of self-assembly. In *Proceedings of MCU 2013*, pages 16–22, 2013.

[24] D. Woods, H.-L. Chen, S. Goodfriend, N. Dabby, E. Winfree, and P. Yin. Active self-assembly of algorithmic shapes and patterns in polylogarithmic time. In *ITCS*, pages 353–354, 2013.

[25] K. Yeom. Bio-inspired automatic shape formation for swarms of self-reconfigurable modular robots. In *Proceedings of BIC-TA 2010*, pages 469–476, 2010.

[26] K. Yeom and B.-J. You. Agent based morphological approach for collaborative shape formation of self-organizable unmanned aerial vehicles. In *Proceedings of HPCC_EUC 2013*, pages 85–92, 2013.

[27] M. Yim, W.-M. Shen, B. Salemi, D. Rus, M. Moll, H. Lipson, E. Klavins, and G. S. Chirikjian. Modular self-reconfigurable robot systems. *IEEE Robotics Automation Magazine*, 14(1):43–52, 2007.

Asymptotically Optimal Gathering on a Grid

Andreas Cord-Landwehr
Heinz Nixdorf Institute &
Computer Science Dept.
Paderborn University
cola@upb.de

Matthias Fischer
Heinz Nixdorf Institute &
Computer Science Dept.
Paderborn University
mafi@upb.de

Daniel Jung
Heinz Nixdorf Institute &
Computer Science Dept.
Paderborn University
Daniel.Jung@upb.de

Friedhelm Meyer auf der Heide
Heinz Nixdorf Institute &
Computer Science Dept.
Paderborn University
fmadh@upb.de

ABSTRACT

In this paper, we solve the local gathering problem of a swarm of n indistinguishable, point-shaped robots on a two-dimensional grid in asymptotically optimal time $\mathcal{O}(n)$ in the fully synchronous $\mathcal{FSYNC}$ time model. Given an arbitrarily distributed (yet connected) swarm of robots, the gathering problem on the grid is to locate all robots within a 2×2-sized area that is not known beforehand. Two robots are connected if they are vertical or horizontal neighbors on the grid. The locality constraint means that no global control, no compass, no global communication and only local vision is available; hence, a robot can see its grid neighbors only up to a constant L_1-distance, which also limits its movements. A robot can move to one of its eight neighboring grid cells and if two or more robots move to the same location they are *merged* to be only one robot. The locality constraint is the significant challenging issue here, since robot movements must not harm the (only globally checkable) swarm connectivity. For solving the gathering problem, we provide a synchronous algorithm – executed by every robot – which ensures that robots merge without breaking the swarm connectivity. In our model, robots can obtain a special state, which marks such a robot to be performing specific connectivity preserving movements in order to allow later merge operations of the swarm. Compared to the grid, for gathering in the Euclidean plane for the same robot and time model the best known upper bound is $\mathcal{O}(n^2)$ [6].

Keywords

autonomous robots; distributed algorithms; gathering problem; runtime bound; robot formation problems

SPAA '16, July 11-13, 2016, Pacific Grove, CA, USA

DOI: http://dx.doi.org/10.1145/2935764.2935789

1. INTRODUCTION

In the field of robot formation problems, there is a strong interest in what is feasible when robots only have very limited capabilities. Runtime bounds are intrinsically hard for such problems and tight results are rarely provided. One common formation problem is the gathering, where robots have to gather in one, beforehand unspecified point.

There are essentially three significant approaches that try to tackle this problem: The first approach [6] is a gathering algorithm for n autonomous, indistinguishable and point-shaped connected robots in the Euclidean plane. A local robot model is used, where the robots especially have only a local vision and no compass. The gathering algorithm works in the $\mathcal{FSYNC}$ time model and runs in time $\mathcal{O}(n^2)$. It is still unknown whether the model-specific time bound is tight for the general case, too. The second approach [10] deals with gathering on a grid in the $\mathcal{ASYNC}$ time model. The robots have global vision and can move unbounded (finite) steps. The gathering strategy is optimal concerning the total number of movements. The third approach [2] (accepted for IPDPS 2016, preliminary version [1]) is an asymptotically optimal gathering strategy for robots, connected as a closed chain on a grid, which is linear in the number of robots in the $\mathcal{FSYNC}$ time model. Like the first approach [6], the robot model is local, especially only local vision and no compass.

In this work, we use an idea from our gathering algorithm for a closed chain [2], yet drop the chain connectivity for sake of solving the general gathering on a grid under the same robot and time model. Our solution for the general gathering problem on the grid is a distributed synchronous algorithm that solves the problem asymptotically optimally in the total number of rounds. Note that the $\mathcal{FSYNC}$ time model is (like in [2]) one of the main parameters that makes the construction and the analysis of an algorithm very challenging. The combination of preventing symmetry issues due the distributed robot behavior and constant length rounds require the presented complex solution. Contrary, if one would assume a fair scheduler in the $\mathcal{ASYNC}$ time model, which allows only one robot to be active at a time and finishes a round after every robot has been active at least once, a simple strategy could achieve the same $\mathcal{O}(n)$ rounds. Specifically when compared to gathering on the Euclidean plane in the $\mathcal{FSYNC}$ time model, our runtime of $\mathcal{O}(n)$ is a noteworthy result and beats the best known algorithm, which requires time $\mathcal{O}(n^2)$ for gathering a swarm of n robots.

Our Local Grid Model.

Our mobile robots need only simple capabilities: A robot moves on a two-dimensional grid and can change its position to one of its eight horizontal, vertical or diagonal neighboring grid points. A robot can see other robots only within a constant *viewing radius* (measured in L_1-distance). We call the range of visible robots *viewing range*. The robots controlled by our algorithm need L_1-distance 20, which can still be optimized. The robots have no compass, no global control, no IDs and no global communication. A robot has a fixed small amount of memory to store a constant number of states. A robot can see the states of all robots inside the viewing range.

Our algorithm uses the fully synchronous time model $\mathcal{FSYNC}$. Time is subdivided into equally sized rounds of constant lengths. In every round all robots simultaneously execute their operations in the common *look-compute-move model* [5], which divides one operation into three steps. In the *look step*, the robot gets a snapshot of the current scenario from its own perspective, restricted to its constant-sized viewing range. During the *compute step*, the robot computes its action, and eventually performs it in the *move step*.

Outline of the Algorithm.

The starting point for our problem is our strategy for the gathering of an arbitrary closed chain of robots on a grid [2]. All operations to shorten the chain are based on the strong definition of the robot's connectivity. Each robot of a chain has exactly two well defined neighbors given by the input of the problem.

The main difference to the general gathering problem is that the connectivity of the chain is missing and so the algorithm of [2] could not be applied. This makes general gathering more challenging than in the closed chain case. The idea of this paper is to find a substitute for the chain and the chain's connectivity in order to transmit the ideas of the algorithm.

The substitute of the chain's connectivity is the following: We call two robots *connected* if they are horizontal or vertical neighbors on the grid. This means that a robot is connected to at least one and at most four robots. Initially, under the restriction that the swarm is connected, the robots are arbitrarily distributed on the grid. A swarm is connected, if the robots cannot be separated into two subsets such that no robot of the one subset is connected to any robot of the other subset and vice versa.

In order to find a substitute for the chain we define the so-called boundaries: The boundaries consist of all robots who have at least one unconnected side. The black robots of Figure 1 are part of the *outer boundary* and the hatched robots are part of *inner boundaries*. By that definition the swarm consists of one single outer boundary and typically multiple inner boundaries. A robot can detect if it is located on some boundary of the swarm, but because of its limited viewing range it does not know if it is located on the outer boundary or on some inner boundary.

The outer boundary has the role of a closed chain and the goal of our algorithm is to shorten the outer boundary. However, the outer boundary does not have the same structure as the chain because the outer boundary can have multiple fringes. Thus our algorithm has to tackle two problems: First, we have to ensure that the algorithm will shorten the outer boundary. Second, we have to ensure that the shortening of the inner boundaries does not disturb the shortening of the outer boundary. Because the robots can not distinguish between the inner and outer boundary our algorithm will also shorten the inner boundary.

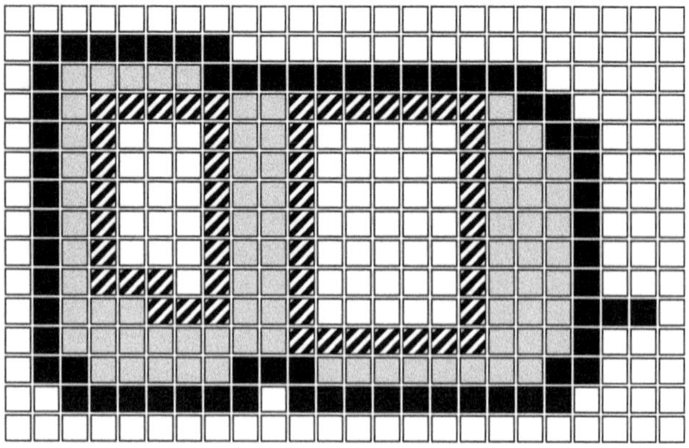

Figure 1: The hatched robots are part of *inner boundaries* and the black robots are part of the *outer boundary*.

The main idea for our algorithm is the following: Our algorithm achieves progress in the gathering by performing *merge operations*. A merge operation is a *hop* of a robot located on the boundary onto the same grid cell as one of its neighbors and we remove one of them. A merge operation is allowed only if it does not disconnect the swarm. Sometimes no merge is possible without disconnecting the swarm.

In that case we want the robots of the boundary to reshape the swarm. Reshapement means that the robots reach positions such that new merges are possible, which does not break the connectivity. Reshapement operations consist of two types: Starting a reshapement and continuing a reshapement.

Starting a reshapement is allowed only for a robot that is located on a boundary and can see a certain configuration of robot positions in its viewing range. The robots that are allowed to start a reshapement generate a so-called *run state*, hop to another position, and give the run state to neighbors on the boundary. Robots receiving the run state are called *runners* and are allowed to continue the reshapement by hopping in following rounds and giving the state to neighbors of the boundary. In that way the run state will be moved along the boundary by the runners. If two runners converge and see each other inside their viewing ranges, a merge can be performed. Gathering is finished when all robots are located within a 2×2 square, since in our model that situation cannot be simplified anymore. In order to simplify the description of our algorithm, we sometimes allow a robot to reconfigure the positions of the robots in its viewing range.

For counting the progress of our algorithm, it is sufficient to consider the merges of the outer boundary only, i.e., we look at the shortening of the outer boundary. After a constant number of rounds either a merge is possible or a new run state will be generated. A new generated run state will provide at least two runners that converge and enable a merge after $\mathcal{O}(n)$ rounds. The runners move in parallel and our strategy ensures that the runners do not disturb each other. Different started run states result in different merges. Therefore the algorithm gathers a swarm of n robots in time $\mathcal{O}(n)$. Our result is asymptotically optimal for worst case swarms.

2. RELATED WORK

There is vast literature on robot problems, researching how specific coordination problems can be solved by a swarm of robots given a certain limited set of abilities. The robots are usually point-shaped (hence collisions are neglected) and positioned in the Euclidean plane. They can be equipped with a memory or are *oblivious*, i.e., the robots do not remember anything from the past and perform their actions only on their current views. If robots are anonymous, they do not carry any IDs and cannot be distinguished by their neighbors. Another type of constraint is the compass model: If all robots have the same coordinate system, some tasks are easier to solve than if all robots' coordinate systems are distorted. In [15, 14] a classification of these two and also of dynamically changing compass models, as well as their effects regarding the gathering problem in the Euclidean plane, is considered. The operation of a robot is considered in the *look-compute-move model* [5]. How the steps of several robots are aligned is given by the *time model*, which can range from an asynchronous $\mathcal{ASYNC}$ model (for example, see [5]), where even the single steps of the robots' steps may be interleaved, to a fully synchronous $\mathcal{FSYNC}$ model (for example, see [3]), where all steps are performed simultaneously. A collection of recent algorithmic results concerning distributed solving of basic problems like gathering and pattern formation, using robots with very limited capabilities, can be found in [13].

One basic robot formation problem is the shortening and maintenance of a communication chain between two fixed endpoints. The robots then only have a local vision, no compass, and a static connectivity is defined by neighborhoods along the chain. For this several results have been published in the $\mathcal{FSYNC}$ time model. The first shown runtime bound was $\mathcal{O}(n^2 \log(n))$ [11]. Later, this has been improved [17]: In the Euclidean plane, the *Hopper* strategy delivers a $\sqrt{2}$-approximation of the shortest communication chain in time $\mathcal{O}(n)$. Restricted to a grid, the *Manhattan Hopper* strategy delivers an optimal solution in time $\mathcal{O}(n)$.

One of the most natural problems is to gather a swarm of robots in a single point. Usually, the swarm consists of point-shaped, oblivious, and anonymous robots. The problem is widely studied in the Euclidean plane. Having point-shaped robots, collisions are understood as merges/fusions of robots and interpreted as gathering progress [7]. In [4] the first gathering algorithm for the $\mathcal{ASYNC}$ time model with multiplicity detection (i.e., a robot can detect if other robots are also located at its own position) and global views is provided. Gathering in the local setting was studied in [3]. In [19] situations when no gathering is possible are studied. The question of gathering on graphs instead of gathering in the plane was considered in [18, 8, 16]. In [9] the authors assume global vision, the $\mathcal{ASYNC}$ time model and furthermore allow unbounded (finite) movements. They show optimal bounds concerning the number of robot movements for special graph topologies like trees and rings.

Concerning the gathering on grids, in [12] it is shown that multiplicity detection is not needed and the authors further provide a characterization of solvable gathering configurations on finite grids. In [10], these results are extended to infinite grids, assuming global vision. The authors characterize *gatherable* grid configurations concerning exact gathering in a single point. Under their robot model and the $\mathcal{ASYNC}$ time model, the authors present an algorithm which gathers *gatherable* configurations optimally concerning the total number of movements.

Assuming only local capabilities of the robots, esp. only local vision and no compass, makes gathering challenging. For example, with a given global vision or alternatively just the knowledge of a global compass, the robots could compute the center of the globally smallest enclosing square or circle and just move to this point (global vision) or all robots with local neighbors in front of them could simply move to the south-eastern direction, for example, and would finally meet (global compass).

In the $\mathcal{FSYNC}$ time model, the total running time is a quality measurement of an algorithm. In this time model and additionally under the restriction, that the robots do not have a compass and have only local vision, i.e., they can only see other robots up to a constant distance instead of a global vision of the whole scenery, there exist several results that prove runtime bounds. One of these are the strategies for shortening communication chains, which we introduced above.: i.e., [11] which needs time $\mathcal{O}(n^2 \log(n))$ and [17] which needs time $\mathcal{O}(n)$ in the Euclidean plane as well as on a grid.

Our recent result gathers a closed chain on a grid asymptotically optimal in time $\mathcal{O}(n)$ [2],[1]. There, connectivity is statically given by a chain structure. For the more general gathering, i.e., using connectivity dynamically given by local vision in the Euclidean plane, an $\mathcal{O}(n^2)$ runtime bound has been shown [6]. There, every robot synchronously computes the smallest enclosing circle only of the robots within its restricted viewing range and then moves towards its center. Repeatingly executing this synchronous behaviour finally solves the gathering. The authors also prove that for their algorithm the $\mathcal{O}(n^2)$ bound is tight. For the problem itself, under this local model, a tight bound for the running time is still unknown.

In the present paper, we tighten this bound to the asymptotically optimal value of $\mathcal{O}(n)$ using the same time- and robot model, but for robots on a grid.

3. THE ALGORITHM

In our model, merges/removal of robots mean progress of the gathering. Then, at the latest after $n-1$ removals the gathering is done. In our model, a robot can be removed, if two robots are located at the same grid cell. Then, one of them is removed.

Because a robot's viewing range is restricted to just a constant size, these removals cannot be performed easily in general. Our algorithm performs two basic operations. More precisely, we have to deal with two cases:

1. Some neighboring robots perform a single hop such that afterwards at least two robots are located at the same position, while preserving the swarm connectiv-

ity. Then, we remove one of them. This is a so-called *merge* and is further discussed in Subsection 3.1.

2. If on some parts of the swarm merges are impossible, we perform so-called reshapements to reshape the swarm in order to prepare merges in succeeding steps. They are explained in Subsection 3.2.

In Subsection 3.1, we now start with case 1. For the sake of simpler descriptions, we use terms such as *horizontal, vertical, downwards, left, ...* Since our robots do not have a common sense for this, the descriptions/figures are also to be understood in a mirrored or rotated manner.

3.1 Merges

A *merge operation*, or simpler a *merge*, is the simultaneous local operation of a sequence of neighboring robots that merges at least one robot, while not harming the overall connectivity of the swarm. There are different merge operations, all parametrized by a parameter k, as depicted in Figure 2. In the figure, the case $k = 1$ denotes the simplest variant, where only a single robot hops onto a grid cell occupied by another robot. Because the robot's viewing radius is > 1, namely 20, also bigger merges are possible within the local vision. Then, to not break the swarm's connectivity, multiple robots (the black ones in the figure) have to hop simultaneously: Using the local information about the occupied and empty cells in a viewing range, every robot can decide individually, based on its local knowledge, if it participates in the simultaneous merge operation or not. Specifically, the marked white grid cells must not contain any robot, any further marked cell must contain a robot, and the maximal size k of a merge configuration is limited by the viewing radius. Moreover, all not explicitly depicted cells are ignored for the decision.

The k robots that constitute a merge form a subboundary of the swarm. When operating, these subboundary robots simultaneously hop one grid cell in the same direction (in the illustration, this means downwards). The swarm's connectivity is ensured, since a merge is performed only when the depicted white cells are empty. By requiring at least one grey cell, i.e., a robot that does not move, after the hops of the subboundary robots at least one robot from a grey cell will be located at the same cell as a robot from a formerly black cell and hence one robot is merged.

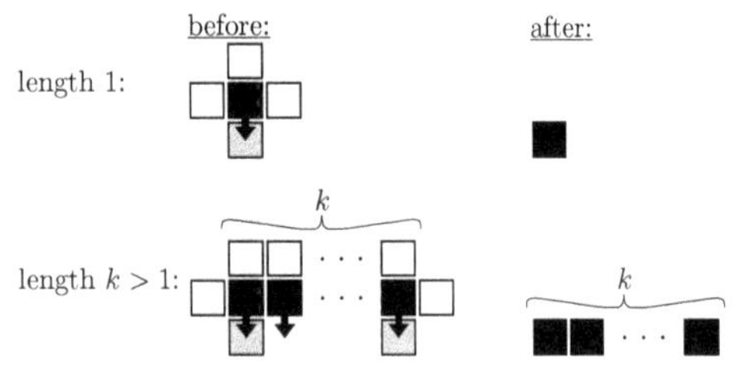

Figure 2: Robot subboundaries that allow progress hops (*merge operations*). The value of the *length* k indicates the number of robots (the black ones) of the subboundary. k is upper bounded by a robot's constant viewing radius. The operations are performed only, if the cells, marked by white squares, are empty. Else, the swarm's connectivity might break.

Possibly, several simultaneous merges can occur at different parts of the swarm. The problematic cases we have to discuss are those, where two of the robot subsets participating in the merge operations, i.e., the subboundaries, consisting of the black and grey robots of Figure 2, overlap (cf. Figure 3). Precisely, two cases need a closer look (We refer to the black and grey robots of Figure 2.):

1. The beginnings and endings of the subboundaries overlap by two robots.

2. The beginnings and endings of the subboundaries overlap by three robots.

An example for 1) can be seen in Figure 3.*a*): The robots of the subboundaries 1,2,3 all perform the hop as the black ones during the merge operation (Figure 2). The difference is that afterwards, for example, the robot a is not located at the same position as b and vice versa. So, no robot can be removed. But the outermost grey robots of Figure 3.*a*) do not move and there a merge occurs.

An example for 2) is shown in Figure 3.*b*). Here, the robot r belongs to both subboundaries 1 and 2: i.e, concerning subboundary 1, r would hop downwards, but concerning subboundary 2 it would hop to the left. In this case, r performs a diagonal hop to the lower left, while the other robots perform their usual hops. Afterwards, r, a, b occupy the same grid cell and a, b are removed without breaking the connectivity.

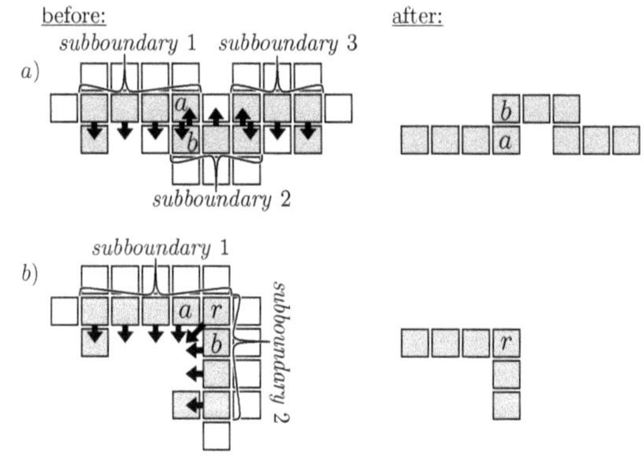

Figure 3: Overlapping merges. (significant examples)

3.2 Reshapement of the Swarm by Runners

From the global perspective, if globally the algorithm's local merge operation is not possible anywhere in the swarm, then we call it a *Mergeless Swarm*. In this case, our goal is to perform certain *reshapements* of the swarm's outer boundary in order to make merge operations possible. Still considering the swarm from a global perspective, if there is a subboundary as depicted in Figure 4 by the black robots, then we continuously let an outermost robot of this subboundary perform the depicted diagonal hops. Eventually, this will shorten the subboundary enough to allow a (local) merge operation (cf. Figure 2). We say, these hops *reshape* the subboundary.

For an individual robot with its limited viewing range this raises some challenges.

1. When a robot decides to start the reshapement, within its restricted viewing range it does not know if its task of performing diagonal hops will lead to merges (in Figure 4, this is the left outermost black one in round i).
2. In the following rounds, due to the local viewing ranges and skewed coordinate systems, the local view of an outermost black robot may be the same as that of its grey neighbor. So, we have to ensure that the reshapement is continued by the outermost black robots instead of by their grey neighbors.
3. When robots decide to start the reshapement, symmetries of the subboundary's local shape may lead to breaking of the swarm's connectivity. In Figure 5 this is the case if both r and r' start the reshapement.

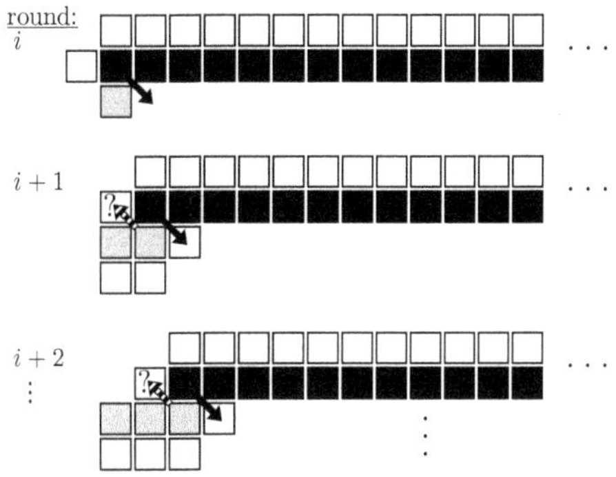

Figure 4: If the length of the black subboundary (i.e., the value of k in Figure 2) is larger than the robots' viewing radius, we shrink it by letting one or both of the outermost black robots perform diagonal hops. We indicate such hops by diagonal arrows.

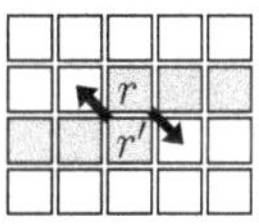

Figure 5: If r and r' both start reshaping the subboundary, the connectivity might break.

In the following, we tackle these challenges by introducing certain (local) states of a robot, which we call the *run* state. We call a robot with an active run state a *runner*. Robots can achieve this state in two different ways:

start runstate: If the local subboundary within a robot's viewing range has a certain configuration, i.e., the relative positions of other robots and empty cells, then the robot decides on its own to generate the run state. We say, such a robot starts a run. Based on the configuration of the local subboundary, the run state gets a fixed moving direction along the boundary. A robot can start and store up to two run states at the same time. Figure 7 shows how the local configurations must look like.

move runstate: A runner $R(S)$ can move the run state S to its boundary neighbor r' in the moving direction of S. We say the run state has moved from $R(S)$ to r', while its in "start runstate" initially set moving direction always remains unchanged. Afterwards, r' is identified by $R(S)$.

Once a run state has been started in "start runstate", "move runstate" is executed in every of the following rounds. This means that the run moves along the boundary at constant speed and in the initially settled moving direction.

When starting runs, the shapes of Start-A and Start-B in Figure 7 ensure that the run starts cannot break the swarm's connectivity. For this, in a situation like in Figure 5 we do not start any runs. We name subboundaries, consisting of shapes like in the figure, *quasi lines*. Figure 6 gives an example of a quasi line.

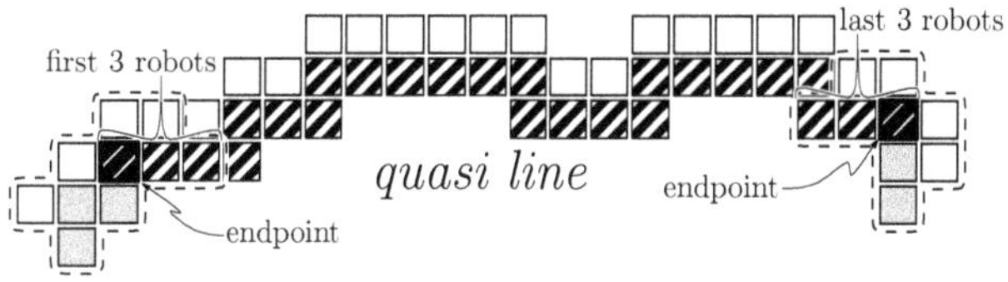

Figure 6: Example of a quasi line. The fat robots are its endpoints.

Definition 1 (Quasi line). *We call a subboundary a horizontal* quasi line*, if the following points hold:*

1. *At least its first and last three robots are horizontally aligned.*
2. *All its subboundaries of horizontally aligned robots contain at least three robots.*
3. *All its subboundaries of vertically aligned robots contain at most two robots.*

In a Mergeless Swarm, at both ends of a quasi line a run starting subboundary Start-A or Start-B of Figure 7 in a matching rotation or reflection occurs. (If the swarm is not mergeless, then the subboundaries outside the quasi line's endpoints may also have other shapes than these.)

The definition of a vertical quasi line *follows analogously.*

We let runs start at endpoints of quasi lines. We let them move along such quasi lines and, while doing this, perform reshapements of the boundary. For this, depending on the local shape of the subboundary, we require the run operations, shown in Figure 8.

a) OP-A: The runner and at least the next 3 robots are located on a straight line. Here, the runner first performs a diagonal hop, then moves the run to the next robot.

b) OP-B: The runner and only the next 2 robots are located on a straight line. Then, for 3 times the runners just move the run to the next robot without any diagonal hops. Afterwards, it is located at the target corner c.

c) OP-C: This one is needed at most once for a new run, if started at the run starting subboundary Start-B (Figure 7.(ii)).

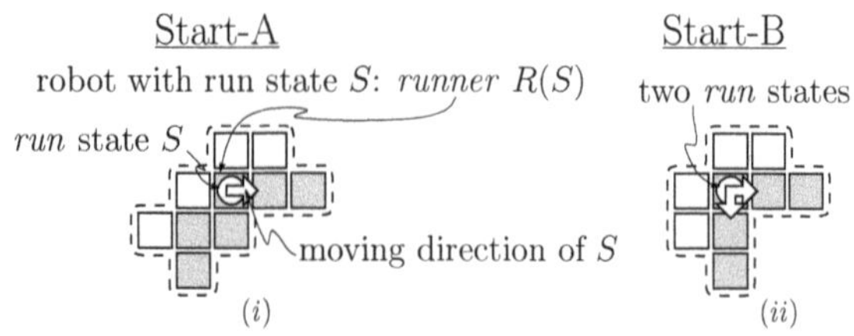

Figure 7: Run starting subboundaries: The robots marked by white circles decide to start the run states, based only on the relative positions of the marked robots and empty cells. Here, grey squares denote robots, while white squares denote cells that must be empty. The white arrows indicate the moving direction of the runs. This is the notation, we will use for marking a runner. $R(S)$ identifies the runner/robot which currently has the run state S. In (*ii*), Start-B, the robot marked by the circle is the endpoint of a horizontally and a vertically aligned subboundary at the same time. Here, we must start two runs, moving in both directions along the boundary.

These operations shall finally enable merges.

Two properties let multiple runs be active in parallel.

1. Usually, at different positions, the whole swarm contains multiple run starting subboundaries (cf. Figure 7) at the same point in time.
2. No matter, if previously started runs are still active, every constant number of $L = 25$ rounds all robots simultaneously check if they can start new runs (cf. Figure 7) and if so, they do so.

So, we have to deal with two runs, meeting on a quasi line. Then, we distinguish two cases (Cf. Figure 9.). *a*) This run pair has enabled the desired merge. *b*) This pair is oriented in a way that does not enable a merge. We let the runs of such pairs pass along each other. Figure 9.*b*) shows how this is performed for the case that both runs are located on the same quasi line: At the time when their distance along the boundary (i.e., the number of robots on the subboundary connecting both +1) is 3 or less, they only keep moving along the boundary, but the runners do not perform reshapement hops. We call 3 the *run passing distance*. This is repeated until S_1 is located at its target robot c_2 (then also S_2 is located at its target c_1). We call this the *run passing* operation. Afterwards, the normal reshapement operations are continued. In the appendix in Section A, we provide a full explanation of all possible situations of needed run passing operations. While in the easy case a viewing radius of 11 is the minimum value that suffices, we then need the unoptimized value of 20.

3.3 Stopping Runs

We use the example of Figure 10 for introducing some terms when speaking about runs: Because S_1, S_2 are moving in the same direction, we call them *sequent* runs, while relative to their moving direction S_1 is located *in front of* S_2. The *distance* between them is defined as the number of robots on the subboundary connecting both +1. We say S_1 is *visible* to S_2 if the *distance* between them is ≤ 20.

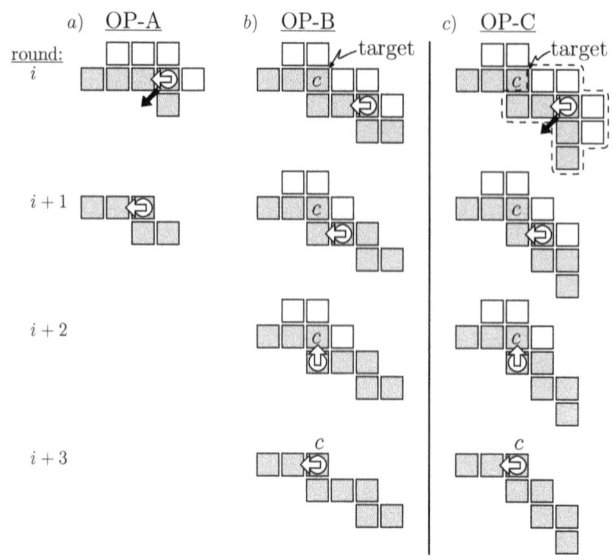

Figure 8: *a*) OP-A: Reshapement by a runner. The operation takes only one round. *b*) OP-B: No diagonal hops are performed until the target corner *c* is reached. *c*) OP-C: Special case when new runs start: First, perform one diagonal hop, then no diagonal hops until the target corner *c* is reached.

In order to ensure that runs, being active at the same time, can work correctly, some of them have to stop in certain situations. More precisely, we let a runner $R(S)$ stop/terminate its run S if one of the conditions of Table 1 is true.

We give some more detailed explanations concerning some of the conditions of Table 1:

1) For example, because of merges two sequent runs may come too close to each other, which then might hinder the pipelining. The affected runners can detect this on their own. The criterion for this is that the next sequent run in front of them becomes visible. Then, the termination condition 1) matches and the run behind stops.

4) We assume that in Figure 9.*b*) to the right of robot c_2 another run S_3, moving in the same direction as S_2, is located. During the rounds in which S_1 and S_2 are performing their run passing operation, S_3 keeps moving towards c_2. Now, for example, it may happen that because of the reshapements of S_3, c_2 becomes part of a merge operation. Then, c_2 would hop downwards such that the corner shape does not exist anymore. Because this corner has been the target of S_1, S_1 could not continue its reshapements after the run passing, so it terminates.

Summarizing, all robots synchronously execute the algorithm, shown in Figure 11.

4. WHY THE STRATEGY PRODUCES PROGRESS IN GATHERING

For measuring progress, we only consider runs that started pairwise at both ends of certain quasi lines. The kind of run pairs which in any case lead to a merge, are called *good pairs*.

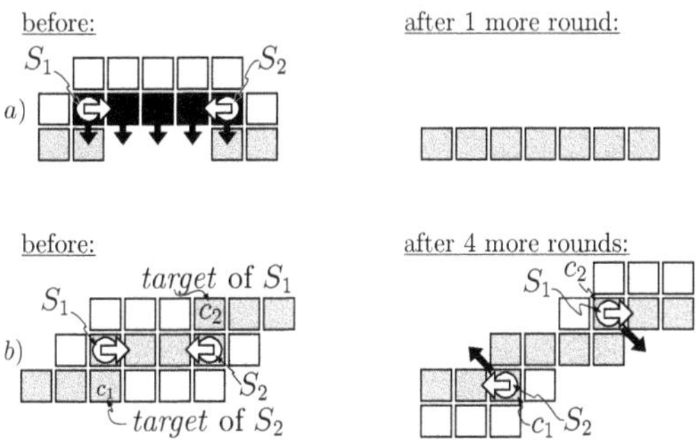

Figure 9: *a) Merge* operation: The reshapements of the runs S_1, S_2 have enabled a merge. This merge is performed and both are stopped. The operation takes only one round. *b) Run passing* operation: The runs S_1, S_2 cannot enable a merge. If their distance along the boundary is less or equal 3, then they pass each other by only keeping moving but without making the runners perform diagonal hops. Afterwards, i.e., when S_1, S_2 have reached their target robots/-corners c_2, c_1, they return to normal operation.

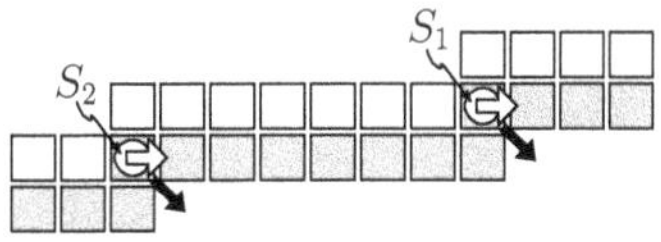

Figure 10: The *distance* between S_1, S_2 is 8.

4.1 Good Pairs

Assume a newly started run pair, connected by a quasi line. We call this pair a *good pair* if the following is true (cf. Figure 12): The exterior neighbors (the fat bordered robots in the figure) of the run pair are both located downwards and the whole (global) area above the connecting quasi line does not contain any robot (The same definition analogously holds for any rotation.). Looking at our run operations OP-A, OP-B and OP-C as well as the run passing operation and merges, we notice that none of them could let a robot which is not part of the considered quasi line hop into this empty area.

Such good pairs always enable a merge if they have been moving close enough together and then terminate. Figure 13 shows an example of a good pair where the shape of the quasi line connecting both, is a straight line. The example of the figure shows that using runs, we solve the problem we have had in Figure 4, where it was impossible to locally decide by the robots which of them has to perform the reshapement hop. Figure 14 shows an example for a more general case of a quasi line: Again, the black subboundary will be reshaped for performing a merge. But now, several run operations (cf. Figure 8) are needed until a runner arrives at an endpoint of the black subboundary: Until round $i + 4$, the runners execute only the operation OP-A (cf. Figure 8). Afterwards, the runner $R(S_r)$ starts operation OP-B, while $R(S_\ell)$ still executes OP-A. After operation OP-B has been processed completely, S_r finally is located at the right end of the black subboundary (round $i+8$). Now, its runners start shortening this subboundary by executing OP-A until the merge can be performed. Afterwards, S_ℓ is still active and keeps moving and will stop at the latest when an endpoint of the quasi line becomes visible.

A runner stops/terminates its run, if at least one of the following conditions is true:

1. It can see the next sequent run in front of it. (This happens if sequent runs have come too close to each other, e.g., because of merge operations.)
2. It can see the quasi line's endpoint in front of it.
3. It was part of a merge operation.
4. While it performs the run passing operation (Figure 9.*b*)), some change of the subboundary's shape prevents the operation from being completed successfully. (This can happen because of a merge.)
5. While it performs the operation OP-B or OP-C (Figure 8), some change of the subboundary's shape prevents the operation from being completed successfully. (This can happen because of a merge.)
6. While it performs the operation OP-A or OP-C, it has hopped onto an occupied cell. (Then, one of both robots is removed.)

Table 1: Conditions which let a run terminate.

Many of the started runs do not belong to good pairs. In Section 5, we will prove the actual existence of good pairs.

4.2 Pipelining

We will show that even if multiple good pairs are nested into each other, different good pairs will enable different merges. This is what we call *pipelining*. Figure 15 shows an example for the case that the quasi line has the shape of a straight line. The more general case works analog to this.

As runs are moving with constant speed, the runs of the inner good pair will meet and as the result enable a merge and stop, first. Then, obviously the outer good pair will also enable a (different) merge, some rounds later.

5. CORRECTNESS AND RUNNING TIME

Our basic argumentation for the total running time is the following: If every round a merge can be performed, then the time needed for the gathering is obviously upper bounded by n, with n being the number of robots. If no merge can be performed, then every $L = 25$ rounds a *good pair* can be started which reshapes the swarm such that a merge can be performed after at most n further rounds. As L is a constant, this then leads to a linear total running time $\mathcal{O}(n)$.

In this section, we give the formal proofs. Our goal is the proof of the correctness and the linear running time (Theorem 1). In our main approach, we want to enable merges by good pairs if else no merge could be performed. The following two lemmas prove that this actually works. They are the base for the proof of the theorem. The proofs of the lemmas can be found in Subsection 5.1 and B.1 (appendix).

Progress pairs.

Because of the local vision, new runs and maybe also good pairs are started every $L = 25$ rounds, regardless of whether

Every robot r in every round checks the following 3 steps:

1. Merge: If r detects a possible merge within its viewing range then
   - if r is one of the black robots in Figure 2, it hops downwards.
   - if afterwards r is located at the same position as one of the grey robots, the grey one is removed without breaking the connectivity.
2. Run Operations: If r is a *runner*, then
   (a) Its run terminates/stops if any of the conditions of Table 1 is true.
   (b) Runner's Movement and Reshapement
   - Run passing:
     - If r is currently in progress of executing the run passing operation (Figure 9.b)), then this operation is continued.
     - Else, if r can see a run in front of it, such that both are moving towards each other and the distance between them is less or equal than the *run passing distance*, then r starts the run passing op.
   - If r is not in progress of passing, then
     - If r is in progress of executing a run operation OP-B or OP-C (cf. Figure 8), which take more than one round, then this one is continued.
     - Else: r executes the matching new run operation OP-A, OP-B or OP-C.
3. Start new runs: Every ($L = 25$)th round, r checks if it can start a new run:
   If r is one of the robots marked by circles, of the run starting subboundaries Start-A or Start-B (cf. Figure 7), then it starts one resp. two runs.

Figure 11: The algorithm.

or not merges can be performed at somewhere in the swarm. In the following analysis, we will only argue with new good pairs which are started if no merge has been performed during the last $L-1$ and the current round in the whole swarm. We distinguish such good pairs from others by calling them *progress pairs*.

LEMMA 1. *Every $L = 25$ rounds either a merge has been performed or else a new* progress pair *is started.*

LEMMA 2. *For all* progress pairs *the following properties hold.*

a) Every progress pair enables a merge (after at most n rounds).

b) Different progress pairs enable different merges.

Using these two lemmas, we can now prove the total linear running time.

THEOREM 1. *Given a swarm of n robots, then, after $\mathcal{O}(n)$ rounds gathering is done. This is asymptotically optimal.*

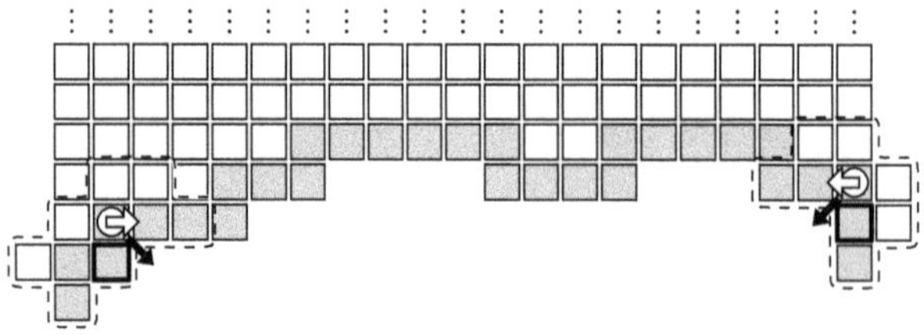

Figure 12: Pair of runs, connected by a quasi line. The runs are a *good pair* if the outer subboundary neighbors (the fat robots) are both located downwards and globally the whole area above does not contain any robots.

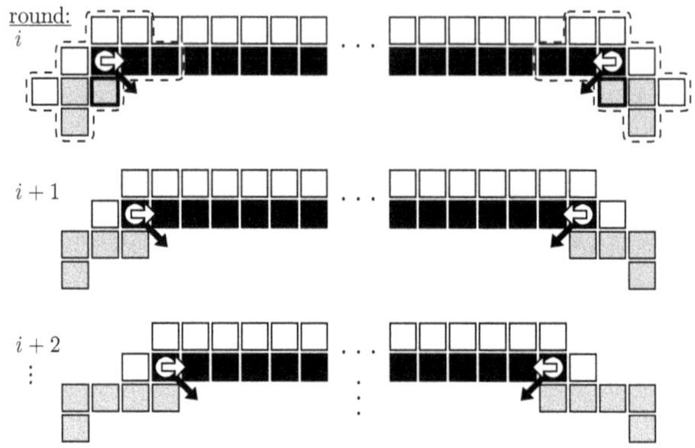

Figure 13: A *good pair* of runs. In round i, the new runs start (cf. Figure 7). Afterwards, the action OP-A of Figure 8 is repeatingly executed. The runs are moving closer and closer together. If the runs have moved close enough, a merge can be performed.

PROOF. We subdivide time into intervals of lengths L, where L denotes a number of rounds. Merges can be performed during at most n such intervals, because every merge removes at least one robot. In all other intervals a new progress pair starts (Lemma 1). Each of these progress pairs leads to a merge (Lemma 2.a)). Because no two of them lead to the same merge (Lemma 2.b)), the number of intervals without merges is also upper bounded by n.

By Lemma 2, a progress pair needs at most n rounds until it has led to a merge. We assume the worst case, which is that in the last of the $2 \cdot n$ intervals the last progress pair was started. Then the total running time is upper bounded by $2n \cdot L + n$, which proves the upper bound of the theorem, because L is a constant.

In our model, the diameter of the initial configuration provides the worst case lower bound $\Omega(n)$ for any gathering strategy. □

5.1 Proof of Lemma 1

PROOF. The lemma requires that the swarm is a *Mergeless Swarm*. As the basis of our proof, we start by showing that then the outer boundary of the swarm only consists of quasi lines and stairways (cf. Figure 16). First, we assume that every robot is connected to only two other robots. Then, especially no robots are located at the inside of the swarm, and the swarm consists only of its *outer boundary*. We start with the assumption that merges are possible only

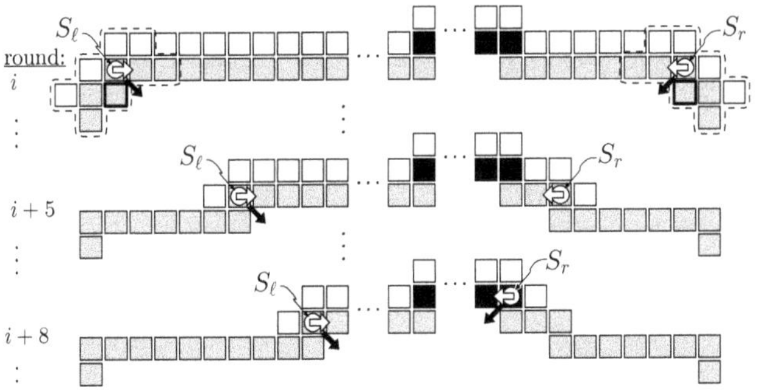

Figure 14: A good pair, started on a quasi line in order to shorten the black subboundary. Several and different run operations are needed.

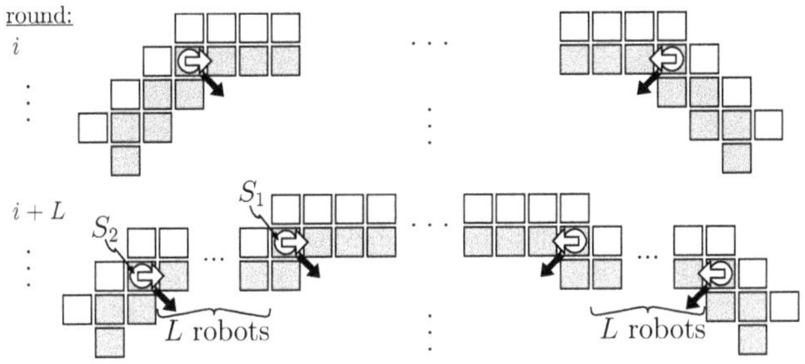

Figure 15: Pipelining of runs. New runs are started every $L = 25$ rounds.

up to the length 2 (cf. Figure 2). Then, as by definition all horizontal subchains of a horizontal quasi line consist of at least 3 robots, no merge can be performed on them. In order to connect two horizontal or two vertical quasi lines without enabling a merge, they must be connected by so-called *stairways.* Stairways can have arbitrary length and are subchains of alternating left and right turns. Figure 16 shows an example. The bicolored robots are the connection points between the quasi lines and the stairway. All differently shaped con-

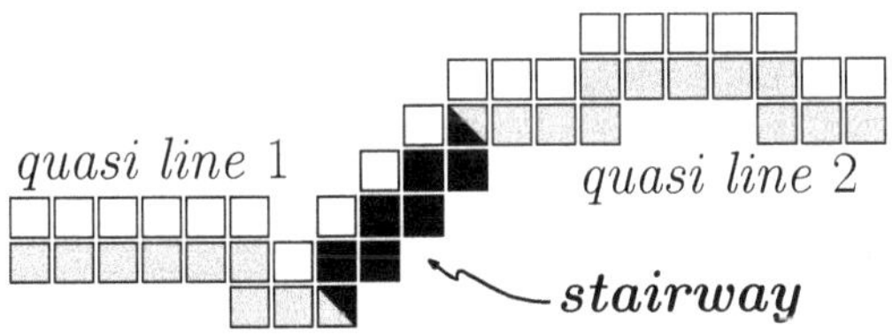

Figure 16: Two quasi lines, connected by a *stairway.*

necting subchains would allow merges. So, assuming that every robot is connected to only two other robots, the whole outer boundary consists only of quasi lines and stairways. This clearly is also the case if longer merges are allowed, because for horizontal quasi lines this increases the number of horizontally aligned robots but decreases the number of vertically aligned ones (cf. Definition 1 and Figure 2).

Now, we also allow connectivities bigger than 2. Then robots may also be located at the swarm's inside or some parts of the outer boundary may be neighboring (i.e., if at that position the diameter = 2). Such robots can hinder merges. Figure 17 shows examples for configurations with

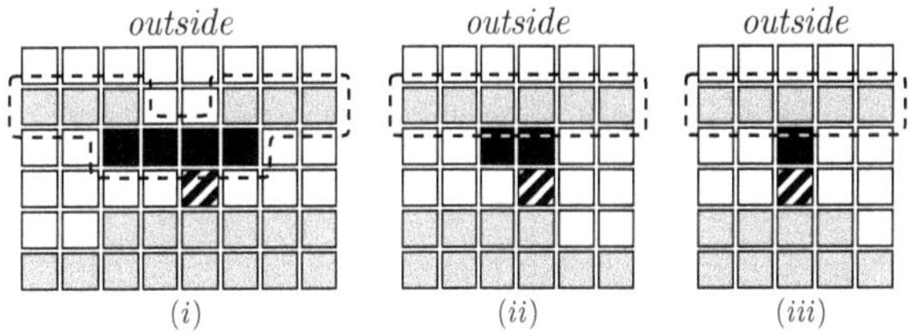

Figure 17: The hatched robot prevents the merge.

existing inside robots. In the figure, the dashed bordered robots are part of the outer boundary. The hatched robots prevent the black ones from performing a merge for which the black ones needed to hop upwards. So, although the swarm is mergeless, the outer boundary may still contain mergable shapes. For merges of length > 2 ((*i*) in the Figure), the outer boundary then still is a quasi line. For merges of length 1 and 2 ((*i*, *ii*) in the Figure), the black robots are not part of the outer boundary. So, in every *Mergeless Swarm*, the outer boundary consists only of quasi lines and stairways.

Now we can show that in a *Mergeless Swarm* always a progress pair exists. For this, we assume a global north and west and construct a vector chain along the swarm's outer boundary as follows. We consider the upper envelope of the swarm and take its left- and rightmost robots s respectively t. Because s, t must be located on the boundary of the swarm's smallest enclosing rectangle and the swarm is mergeless, below each of them must exist two additional robots (cf. Figure 18). We start from the left at the vector $\vec{v_0}$ constructing a vector chain in clockwise orientation along the outer boundary of the swarm, ending at the vector $\vec{v_m}$. The figure shows a significant example of this construction. Here, the grey colored robots denote the corresponding part of the swarm's outer boundary. Starting from its left end,

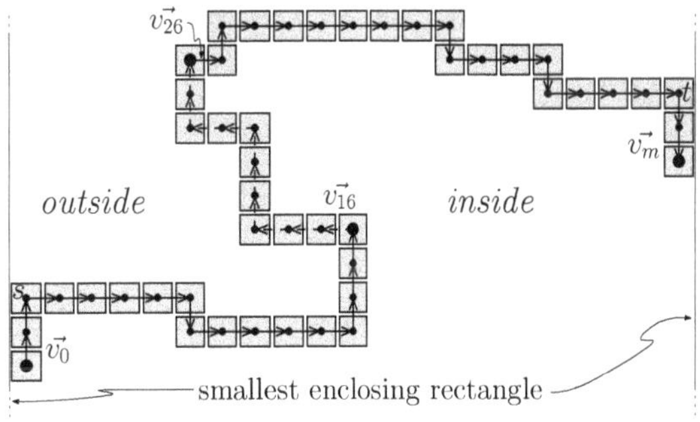

Figure 18: Constructing a vector chain along the swarm's outer boundary.

we divide this vector chain into longest x-monotone subchains. The vector, originated at s, by construction points to the east. The second subchain starts when the first vector points to the west. The third subchain starts when the first vector points to the east again, and so forth. In the figure, these are the vectors $\vec{v_{16}}$ respectively $\vec{v_{26}}$. The constructed vector chain may overlap itself at places where the diameter of the swarm's boundary amounts only 1, but cannot contain any crossings. Because all constructed subchains are x-monotone, at least one of them is fully part of the upper envelope. Let $\mathcal{C}$ denote this subchain. If we consider $\mathcal{C}$, then, as the swarm is mergeless, both predecessors of its first vector must point to the north, i.e., the corresponding robots are located downwards. By the same arguments, both successors of its last vector must point to the south, i.e., the corresponding robots are also located downwards. This also holds if s or t is an endpoint of this vector chain. Then, on both sides are three neighboring robots on a vertical straight line. By Definition 1 of a quasi line, these robots must be part of vertical quasi lines.

In contrast, if looking at the subchain $\mathcal{C}$, then because the swarm is mergeless, $\mathcal{C}$ must contain at least two succeeding vectors, both pointing to the east. The three connected robots then must be part of a horizontal quasi line. At the transition between horizontal and vertical quasi lines, possibly connected by stairways, the shape matches the starting subboundaries Start-A or Start-B of Figure 7. As both vertical quasi lines are located downwards w.r.t. the horizontal quasi line of $\mathcal{C}$, a good pair can be started (cf. Subsection 4.1). Because we have assumed that the swarm has been a Mergeless Swarm also during the previous $L-1$ rounds, this good pair is a progress pair. □

6. ACKNOWLEDGMENTS

This work was partially supported by the German Research Foundation (DFG) within the Collaborative Research Centre "On-The-Fly Computing" (SFB 901).

7. REFERENCES

[1] S. Abshoff, A. Cord-Landwehr, M. Fischer, D. Jung, and F. Meyer auf der Heide. Gathering a closed chain of robots on a grid. *CoRR*, abs/1510.05454, 2015.

[2] S. Abshoff, A. Cord-Landwehr, M. Fischer, D. Jung, and F. Meyer auf der Heide. Gathering a closed chain of robots on a grid. In *IPDPS '16*. IEEE, to appear, May 2016.

[3] H. Ando, Y. Suzuki, and M. Yamashita. Formation and agreement problems for synchronous mobile robots with limited visibility. In *ISIC '95*, pages 453–460, Aug. 1995.

[4] M. Cieliebak, P. Flocchini, G. Prencipe, and N. Santoro. Solving the Robots Gathering Problem. In *ICALP '03*, pages 1181–1196, 2003.

[5] R. Cohen and D. Peleg. Robot Convergence via Center-of-Gravity Algorithms. In *SIROCCO '04*, volume 3104 of *LNCS*, pages 79–88, 2004.

[6] B. Degener, B. Kempkes, T. Langner, F. Meyer auf der Heide, P. Pietrzyk, and R. Wattenhofer. A tight runtime bound for synchronous gathering of autonomous robots with limited visibility. In *SPAA '11*, pages 139–148, 2011.

[7] B. Degener, B. Kempkes, and F. Meyer auf der Heide. A local $O(n^2)$ gathering algorithm. In *SPAA '10*, pages 217–223, 2010.

[8] A. Dessmark, P. Fraigniaud, D. R. Kowalski, and A. Pelc. Deterministic Rendezvous in Graphs. *Algorithmica*, 46(1):69–96, 2006.

[9] G. Di Stefano and A. Navarra. Optimal Gathering of Oblivious Robots in Anonymous Graphs. *LNCS*, 8179:213–224, 2013.

[10] G. Di Stefano and A. Navarra. Optimal Gathering on Infinite Grids. In *SSS '14*, pages 211–225. 2014.

[11] M. Dynia, J. Kutylowski, P. Lorek, and F. Meyer auf der Heide. Maintaining communication between an explorer and a base station. In *IFIP TC10*, pages 137–146, 1 Jan. 2006.

[12] G. D'Angelo, G. Di Stefano, R. Klasing, and A. Navarra. Gathering of robots on anonymous grids without multiplicity detection. In *SIROCCO '12*, volume 7355 of *LNCS*, pages 327–338. 2012.

[13] P. Flocchini, G. Prencipe, and N. Santoro. *Distributed Computing by Oblivious Mobile Robots*. Synthesis Lectures on Distributed Computing Theory. Morgan & Claypool, 2012.

[14] T. Izumi, S. Souissi, Y. Katayama, N. Inuzuka, X. Défago, K. Wada, and M. Yamashita. The Gathering Problem for Two Oblivious Robots with Unreliable Compasses. *SICOMP*, 41(1):26–46, 2012.

[15] Y. Katayama, Y. Tomida, H. Imazu, N. Inuzuka, and K. Wada. Dynamic Compass Models and Gathering Algorithms for Autonomous Mobile Robots. In *SIROCCO '07*, volume 4474 of *LNCS*, pages 274–288, 2007.

[16] R. Klasing, E. Markou, and A. Pelc. Gathering asynchronous oblivious mobile robots in a ring. *TCS*, 390(1):27–39, 2008.

[17] J. Kutylowski and F. Meyer auf der Heide. Optimal strategies for maintaining a chain of relays between an explorer and a base camp. *TCS*, 410(36):3391–3405, 2009.

[18] S. Martînez. Practical multiagent rendezvous through modified circumcenter algorithms. *Automatica*, 45(9):2010–2017, 2009.

[19] G. Prencipe. Impossibility of gathering by a set of autonomous mobile robots. *TCS*, 384(2-3):222–231, 2007.

APPENDIX

A. RUN PASSING OPERATION IN DETAIL

If two runs S, S' that are moving towards each other but do not enable a merge have come too close to each other, then we let them pass along each other with a constant movement speed but without performing diagonal hops, in order to prevent the connectivity from breaking or destroying the quasi line property. We call this the *run passing* operation. If they have come this close that the operation is needed, then also S can see S' within its constant viewing range and vice versa. For the run passing operation, it is important to assign a target corner to every such run so that it can continue its reshapements afterwards. Cf. Figure 19. The subfigures show two runs S, S' that need to pass along each other. The curve q, originating at S, symbolizes the quasi line that belongs to S. Analogously, the quasi line q' belongs to S'. We can assume that locally no robots are located in the area above q and below q', because else the corresponding run S respectively S' could not be part of a good pair so that it is allowed to stop itself. Then, the run passing is not needed anymore. If a run passing operation is necessary, then, between the locations of S, S', the quasi lines q, q' must in some way overlap. We now explain that in all possible cases of overlappings suitable target corners can always be assigned to both of the runs so that they can continue their reshapements after the passing. We refer to Figure 19.

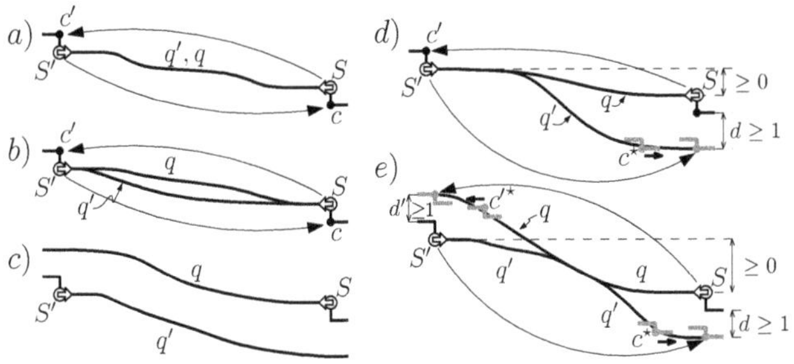

Figure 19: Classification of all possible cases that can occur if two runs need to pass along each other.

a) q, q' are identical. Then the run passing operation executes in the way explained in Section 3.2.

b) q, q' overlap at the location of S and at the location of S'. Then by the same arguments as in a), the target corners c, c' must exist.

c) q, q' are disjoint. Then the runners calculate whether their reshapements would make q and q' overlap. If so, then this overlapping would lead to the removal/merge of robots, so that we can credit this merge to the good pair and both runs are allowed to stop. Else, the runs continue their normal reshapement operations.

d) q, q' overlap only at the location of S'. Then, the vertical distance between S and S' must be ≥ 0 because else a merge would make a run passing superfluous. As on the right, q' is located below q ($d \geq 1$), there must exist some corner $c^\star$ with the same rotation as the corner at which S' is located. The robots then reconfigure the robots of q' in such a way that $c^\star$ is located at the right endpoint of the sub quasi line. Afterwards, S' can move to this corner and then continue its reshapements. In contrast, S can simply move to c'.

e) q, q' overlap but are disjoint at both endpoints. Then, by the same arguments as in d), both target corners exist.

B. PROOFS

B.1 Proof of Lemma 2

For the proof, we need the run invariants of Lemma 3.

LEMMA 3. *The value $L = 25$ and the value 20 for the viewing radius ensure that for every run S until it terminates, the following invariants holds.*

1. *Every round, S moves one robot further in the moving direction.*
2. *After the first three rounds after its start, the reshapements of the runner $R(S)$ do not violate the quasi line Definition 1 of its own quasi line.*
3. *The reshapements of $R(S)$ do not violate the quasi line shape of other quasi lines if they belong to good pairs.*
4. *S cannot see other sequent runs in front of it.*
5. *S is either in progress of passing along another run or the runner $R(S)$ executes one of the operations OP-A, OP-B or OP-C (Figure 8).*
6. *Good pairs stay being good pairs.*

Now, we can prove Lemma 2:

PROOF. *a)* : At the time a progress pair S, S' is started, the subboundary connecting both is a quasi line. Because of Lemma 3.2) and 3), this also does not change if other runs are located on this quasi line or next to it. And also merges preserve the quasi line properties. So, if not stopped, S and S' keep moving towards each other (Lemma 3.1)). Because of Lemma 3.6) a merge can be performed at the latest when they meet, which takes at most n rounds.

It remains to show that S, S' are not stopped by the algorithm's termination conditions (Table 1) before the merge could be performed. In the following, we check all these conditions. In this proof, we denote the quasi line, on which S, S' are located by the variable q. Let $S^\star$ be the next sequent run in front of S. 1): By definition of a progress pair, no merge has been performed since the last time new runs have been started. This means that if no run from outside the quasi line q has interfered with q, the distance between S and $S^\star$ is at least $L - 1$ (cf. the proof of Lemma 3.5)) which is bigger than the viewing radius. (The same analogously holds for S'.) So then, the runs of a progress pair cannot be stopped by this termination condition. So, we assume that other runs have interfered with q. If $S^\star$ originates from a different quasi line, S and $S^\star$ can be oriented only in the way shown in Figure 20, because the run operations require the cells "above" be empty. If these quasi lines shall meet, then at least one of them cannot be y-monotone. But then a merge would have removed at least one of them before both runs have come too close. So $S^\star$ cannot originate from a different quasi line.

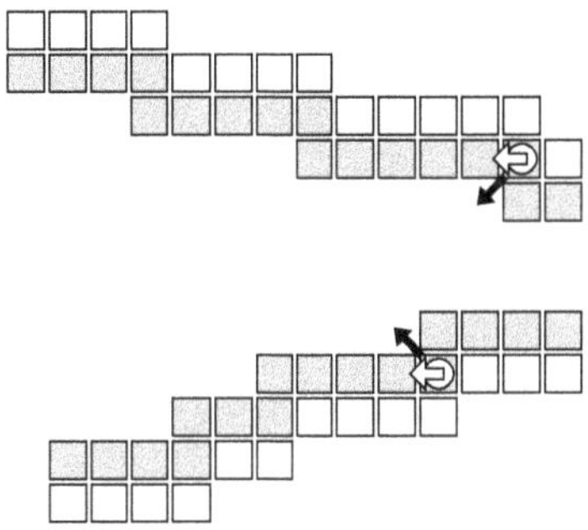

Figure 20: Too close sequent runs cannot originate from different quasi lines.

So, a run on a different quasi line (lying alongside q) must have shortened the part of q that connects S and $S^\star$. This can only have happened because of a merge operation, but this is not possible, because S, S' is a progress pair.

2): If a run of a progress pair can see an endpoint of the quasi line in front of it, then the other run of the progress pair must have previously been stopped (Using the properties of Lemma 3.2) and 3).). Then, because a run of a progress pair cannot be stopped by condition 1), it instead must have been stopped because of a merge. So, a termination because of condition 2) is allowed.

4, 5): The change of the quasi lines shape could either have happened because of the reshapement of a sequent run or because of a merge operation. Because we have ensured the minimum distance of two sequent runs to be large enough, the first case cannot happened. So, a merge must have been the reason. Then, this merge must have been enabled by another run $S^\star$, moving towards S. If $S^\star$ is the partner run of S, then stopping is allowed. Else, because progress pairs are nested into each other, $S^\star$ either was not a run of a progress pair or its partner run has previously been stopped. In the latter case, because runs of progress pairs cannot be stopped because of condition 1), the run must have been stopped by an earlier merge. In both cases, the current merge can be credited to the progress pair of S.

3): By the same arguments, this merge does not need to be also credited to a different progress pair. This then also proves b) of the lemma. □

The missing proof of Lemma 3 can be found in Subsection B.2.

B.2 Proof of Lemma 3

PROOF. Let q be the quasi line S is located on and we w.l.o.g. assume that q is a horizontal quasi line. 1): This directly follows by the run definition in Subsection 3.2.

2): Cf. Figure 8. OP-A ensures that on horizontal quasi lines only horizontal subchains of lengths > 2 are shortened and vertical subchains remain unextended. OP-B does not reshape. OP-C can be executed only during the first three rounds after S has been started. Our design of the run passing operation also ensures that the quasi line properties are maintained.

3): Because of the run stopping condition of Table 1.2), $R(S)$ can reshape a quasi line $q^\star$ only if $q^\star$ is also a horizontal one. As the run operation OP-C cannot be applied inside $q^\star$, we only need to consider OP-A. If the cell onto which $R(S)$ hops is empty, then OP-A (because of the cells that are required to be empty) can be executed only if S is also located on $q^\star$. But then, by the same arguments as in 2), the reshapements of $R(S)$ cannot violate the quasi line definition. If in contrast the cell onto the $R(S)$ hops is occupied by some of the robots of $q^\star$, then this operation does not modify the shape of $q^\star$.

4): This is ensured by the run termination condition of Table 1.1).

5): Cf. Figure 8. All run operations OP-A, OP-B and OP-C ensure that if S was located at some corner c_1 when the operation started, it afterwards either is located at some other corner c_2 such that both corners are rotated equally or terminates if the target corner has been removed during the operation (cf. Table 1.5, 4)). Then, because still located on a quasi line (cf. 2)), again a) or b) can be applied or run passing is started.

The run passing needs a closer look, because it interrupts other operations. In order to ensure a regulated behavior, we chose the distance between sequent runs big enough such that a run does not have to execute a new run passing operation before it has finished its previous one. As the value of the constant L controls the length of the waiting intervals between the start of two sequent runs and our stopping conditions maintain this minimum distance by stopping a run if the next sequent run in front of it becomes visible, we need to settle the values for these constants appropriately. At this place, we only analyze the case that was explained in Section 3.2, i.e., all participating runs are located on the same quasi line. The other cases (Section A in the appendix) can be proven similarly. We look at two sequent runs S_1 and S_1^{succ} such that S_1^{succ} has been started after S_1. Their distance D is at least $L-3$. This value is achieved if at the start of S_1 the operation OP-C and then OP-B (Figure 8) was executed.

Now we chose the value for the constant D big enough for ensuring that while some run S_2 is passing along S_1, S_1^{succ} becomes visible to S_2 the earliest when the passing operation with S_1 has been completed. Figure 21 shows an example for the longest possible duration of a run passing operation. Here, it takes 6 rounds until S_2 has arrived at its target

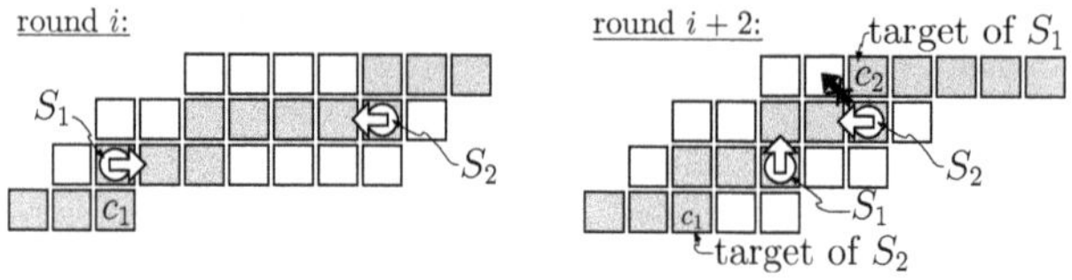

Figure 21: Runs passing along each other while the runner $R(S_1)$ is executing the operation OP-B (cf. Figure 8).

corner. Because the run passing operation starts when the distance between S_1 and S_2 is ≤ 3, after the passing operation, the distance between S_2 and S_1^{succ} equals $D-9$. We then want this to still be ≥ 3. So we choose $D \geq 12$ and together with the above argumentation concerning the minimum distance between sequent runs follows $L \geq 15$. In order to detect that the distance has become smaller than 12 (and solve this problem), the viewing radius must be 11 (cf. Table 1.1)).

Using the same construction, but including all other possible cases of run passings (Section A in the appendix), we can show that for (unoptimized) values of $L = 25$ a viewing radius of 20 suffice.

6): When defining good pairs in Subsection 3.2, good pairs have been characterized by the relative position of the outer direct neighbors of the good pair according to the quasi line. The first part of the proof of 5) finishes the proof. □

Better Bounds for Coalescing-Branching Random Walks

Michael Mitzenmacher *
Harvard University
michaelm@eecs.harvard.edu

Rajmohan Rajaraman †
Northeastern University
rraj@ccs.neu.edu

Scott Roche ‡
Northeastern University and
Akamai Technologies
str7@cornell.edu

ABSTRACT

Coalescing-branching random walks, or *cobra walks* for short, are a natural variant of random walks on graphs that can model the spread of disease through contacts or the spread of information in networks. In a k-cobra walk, at each time step a subset of the vertices are active; each active vertex chooses k random neighbors (sampled independently and uniformly with replacement) that become active at the next step, and these are the only active vertices at the next step. A natural quantity to study for cobra walks is the cover time, which corresponds to the expected time when all nodes have become infected or received the disseminated information.

In this work, we extend previous results for cobra walks in multiple ways. We show that the cover time for the 2-cobra walk on an n-vertex d-dimensional grid is $O(n^{1/d})$ (where the order notation hides constant factors that depend on d); previous work had shown the cover time was $O(n^{1/d} \cdot \text{polylog}(n))$. We show that the cover time for a 2-cobra walk on an n-vertex d-regular graph with conductance ϕ_G is $O(d^4 \phi_G^{-2} \log^2 n)$, significantly generalizing a previous result that held only for expander graphs with sufficiently high expansion. And finally we show that the cover time for a 2-cobra walk on a graph with n vertices is always $O(n^{11/4} \log n)$; this is the first result showing that the bound of $\Theta(n^3)$ for the worst-case cover time for random walks can be beaten using 2-cobra walks.

Categories and Subject Descriptors

G.3 [**Probability and Statistics**]: Stochastic processes; Probabilistic Algorithms; G.2.2 [**Discrete Mathematics: Graph Theory**]: Graph algorithms

*This work was supported in part by NSF grants CNS-1228598, CCF-1320231, and CCF-1535795.

†Supported in part by NSF CCF-1422715, NSF CCF-1535929, and an ONR grant

‡Supported in part by NSF CCF-1216038 and NSF CCF-1422715.

SPAA '16, July 11 - 13, 2016, Pacific Grove, CA, USA

ISBN 978-1-4503-4210-0/16/07...$15.00

DOI: http://dx.doi.org/10.1145/2935764.2935791

Keywords

Random Walks; Networks; Information Spreading; Cover Time; Epidemic Processes

1. INTRODUCTION

Random walks provide a fundamental mathematical model for many basic network processes. In disease models, transmission of a virus can be modeled by the virus moving according to a random walk on a graph representing a human contact network; computer viruses can be modeled similarly [18, 26, 13]. Variants of random walks can also be used for information dissemination, using message-passing protocols where a message is passed from neighbor to neighbor via a random walk [9, 17]. Such protocols require little state information and are robust to various types of faults, and are therefore useful in many distributed networks [4]. More generally, random walks provide a fundamental primitive for network algorithms for information propagation, search, routing, and load balancing.

In many of these settings, a central measure of interest is the cover time, the expected time for the random walk to cover all of the vertices of the underlying network. In disease models, this corresponds to the time until all vertices in the network have been exposed to the virus; in message-passing protocols, this corresponds to the time until all vertices have received the message.

Parallel random walks provide a natural generalization of standard random walks, with multiple random walks traversing the network simultaneously, and several papers have analyzed the performance of parallel random walks (as we describe in the related work section). A related variant, less well-studied and understood, are coalescing-branching random walks, or *cobra walks* for short [13]. In a cobra walk, at each time step, a subset of the vertices are active; typically in the initial state a single vertex would be active. At each time step, each active vertex chooses k random neighbors (sampled independently and uniformly with replacement) that become active at the next step. A vertex is active at step t if and only if it was chosen by an active vertex in the previous step. When $k > 1$, each walk branches at that step into multiple walks, but multiple walks then coalesce when they reach the same vertex at the same time. We refer to a cobra walk where at each time step a vertex chooses k active neighbors as a k cobra walk for convenience. (One could further study variations where the branching varied based on the vertex or the time step, or was governed by a random distribution; we do not do that here.)

As examples of cobra walks, in the message passing setting, a k-cobra walk corresponds to a network where a vertex may send k outgoing copies of the message to neighbors during a time step instead of just one. In disease networks, a cobra walk corresponds to an idealized process within the Susceptible Infected Susceptible model (or SIS model): in each time step, an infected agent infects k random neighbors and recovers, but can be infected again (including at the next time step).

In contrast to results in parallel random walks, where the number of walks is a parameter, in cobra walks the number of active vertices varies over time and its behavior depends significantly on the network. One might expect cobra walks to yield significant improvements in the cover time over standard random walks, based on their power to reproduce, even if limited by coalescence. The goal of our work is to formally and theoretically bound the performance of cobra walks, focusing on the cover time. While our results have potential applications to distributed protocols and disease models, as suggested above, we also believe that k-cobra walks are a natural mathematical model worthy of study in their own right.

1.1 Our Results and Techniques

We are motivated by the prior work [13], which obtained bounds on the cover time of cobra walks on trees, grids, and expanders. Our work pushes those results further, in several directions. Our primary results are the following:

- We show that the cover time for the 2-cobra walk on an n-vertex d-dimensional grid is $O(n^{1/d})$, where the constant in the order notation can depend on d. This improves on the previous bound of $O(n^{1/d} \cdot \text{polylog}(n))$ [13]. With respect to n, our result is optimal.
- We show that the cover time for the 2-cobra walk for a d-regular graph with conductance ϕ_G is $O(\phi_G^{-2} \log^2 n)$. This generalizes a similar result in [13] for expander graphs with sufficiently high expansion. Our new result holds for any d-regular graph, and expresses the bound as a function of the conductance.
- We provide a result for general graphs, showing that the cover time for a 2-cobra walk is always $O(n^{11/4} \log n)$. For standard random walks, there are graphs where the cover time is $\Theta(n^3)$. This is the first result showing that cobra walks can beat the corresponding worst-case bound for random walks. We also establish an $O(n^{2-1/d} \log n)$ upper bound on the cover time for arbitrary d-regular graphs, again improving the tight quadratic bound for standard random walks.

Our main techniques involve making use of the parallelism inherent in cobra walks, and by thinking of cobra walks as a *union of biased random walks*. In some settings we can show the cobra walk goes through an initial phase that instantiates a large number of essentially parallel random walks, and then analyze the behavior of these random walks. Here we have to take care of the dependency challenges introduced by coalescing, as random walks can essentially disappear when several collide at a vertex. In other settings, we think of our cobra walk as being a single walk moving toward a specific vertex, and then eventually taking a union bound over all vertices. At each step, we can choose to follow the active vertex that moves toward the target vertex and discard the others. This approach simplifies the analysis by allowing us to focus on a single walk, where now the k choices correspond to a bias in the walk that we can model. The downside of such an analysis, however, is that it does not take full advantage of the power of parallelism inherent to cobra walks.

1.2 Background and Related Work

The cobra walk process has structural similarities with several other fairly diverse stochastic processes: branching processes, gossip protocols, and random walks (including parallel random walks, coalescing random walks, and other variants). Despite these commonalities, cobra walks resist being fully described by any of these other processes; furthermore, analysis techniques used for these other processes often have no clear use or power in analyzing cobra walks.

Branching and coalescing processes. Branching processes appear in many disciplines, from nuclear physics to population genetics, on various discrete and continuous structures [19, 21, 6]. Another related topic is the study of coalescing processes and voter models (see, for example [11]). Naturally, there is also work on processes that contain both branching and coalescing elements [3, 25], although unlike our work these analyses tend to operate in continuous time and on either restricted topologies or infinite spaces. The restriction of cobra walks to discrete time effectively disallows the use of differential-equation based analysis that often yields results in continuous-time processes (see, for example [18, 20, 26]).

Gossip and rumor-spreading mechanisms Gossip-based algorithms have been used successfully to design efficient distributed algorithms for a variety of problems in networks such as information dissemination, aggregate computation, constructing overlay topologies, and database synchronization (e.g., see [9] and the references therein). There are three major variants of gossip-based processes: push-based models, in which the members of the set of informed vertices each select a neighbor and inform that neighbor (if it is not already informed), pull-based models, in which uninformed vertices select neighbors and poll them for information, and push-pull, which is a combination of the first two.

Cobra walks bear the closest resemblance to push-based gossip models. Indeed, [17] show that the push process completes in every undirected graph in $O(n \log n)$ steps with high probability, and this bound has been conjectured to hold for cobra walks [13]. However, the similarity between the two is in many ways superficial. If we view a gossip process as a Markov chain on the state space of the set of all subsets of vertices (representing the sets of possible informed vertices), this Markov chain has a single absorbing state (assuming the graph is connected) in which every vertex is informed. On the other hand, performing a similar projection of a cobra walk onto a Markov chain of the 2^n possible subsets of vertices that could be active at any time, we see that there is no absorbing state and with the addition of self-loops, the chain can be made ergodic.

Random walks and parallel random walks. Cobra walks also resemble standard random walks and parallel variants. For simple random walks, the now classic work of Feige [15, 16] showed that the cover time on any graph lies between $\Theta(\log n)$ and $O(n^3)$. A formal model of biased random walks was introduced in [5] with the motivation of studying imperfect sources of randomness. Specifically, these biased walks allow a controller to fix, at each step of the walk, the next step with a small probability, with the aim of increasing the stationary probability at a target set of vertices. A variant of the biased walk of [5] plays a significant role in our analysis of cobra walks for general graphs.

Additional work has considered speeding up the cover time by modifying the underlying process. Adler et al [1] studied a process on the hypercube in which in each round a vertex is chosen uniformly at random and covered; if the chosen vertex was already covered, then an uncovered neighbor of the vertex is chosen uniformly at random and covered. For any d-regular graph, Dimitrov and Plaxton showed that a similar process achieves a cover time of $O(n + (n \log n)/d)$ [12]. For expander graphs, Berenbrink et al showed a simple variant of the standard random walk that achieves a linear (i.e., $O(n)$) cover time [7].

Parallel random walks, first studied in [8] for the special case where the starting vertices are drawn from the stationary distribution and in [2] for arbitrary starting vertices, also appear related to cobra walks. Nearly-tight results on the speedup of cover time as a function of the number of parallel walks have been obtained by [14] for several graph classes including the cycle, d-dimensional meshes, hypercube, and expanders. However, again the similarity is somewhat superficial. A parallel random walk with k independent walks can be mapped to anundirected random walk on a graph known as the tensor product. As such, much of the machinery of the analysis of simple random walks can be applied to the parallel case. Applying a similar approach to a cobra walk is not feasible, although for cobra walks one can convert the tensor product into a directed graph, changing the topology significantly. As such, generally the techniques that can be used for parallel random walks cannot be used directly for the cobra walk. Indeed, one can view the dependencies on the locations of the other active nodes in a cobra walk as a manifestation of this difference. Cobra walks suffer from the "time's arrow" effect: locally, most individual steps are reversible, but as a cobra walk expands, the likelihood that it will coalesce back to a single vertex grows exponentially unlikely. Despite these difficulties, the tensor product graph can be useful when studying the movement of a small number of pebbles in a cobra walk, and we make use of this technique in obtaining a general bound based on conductance.

2. PRELIMINARIES

Let G be a connected graph with vertex set V and edge set E, and let $|V| = n$, except for the case when we are analyzing the grid, in which case we let $V = [0, n]^d$. A k-coalescing-branching (k-cobra) walk is defined as follows: It starts at time $t = 0$ at an arbitrary vertex v, at which a pebble is placed. In the next and every subsequent time step, every pebble in G clones itself $k - 1$ times (so that there are now k indistinguishable pebbles at each vertex that originally had a pebble). Each pebble then independently selects a neighbor of its current vertex uniformly at random and moves to it. Once all pebbles have made their moves, the coalescing phase begins: if two or more pebbles are at the same vertex they coalesce into a single pebble, and the next round begins.

For time step t, S_t is the **active set**, which is the set of all vertices of G that have a pebble. Define the **cover time** of a cobra walk to be the maximum over all vertices v of expectation of the minimum time T at which all vertices have belonged to some S_t for $t \leq T$ when the cobra walk is started at v. We note that while our results are stated as bounds on the cover time, all of the results in this paper actually give bounds on the time to cover all the vertices in the graph with high probability, as is clear from the proofs. Hence we may also refer to the time at which all vertices have been covered, where the meaning is clear. The **hitting time** $H(u, v)$ is the expectation of the minimum time it takes for any pebble originating from a cobra walk that starts at u to reach v. The **maximum hitting time** $h_{\max}$ is $max_{u,v \in V} H(u, v)$.

We make use of an extension of Matthews' Theorem, which relates the cover time of a random walk to the maximum hitting time. The following theorem was proven in [13]:

THEOREM 1. *Let G be a connected graph on n vertices. Let W be a cobra walk on G starting at an arbitrary vertex. Then the cover time of W on G is bounded above by $O(h_{\max} \log n)$; in fact W covers all of G in $O(h_{\max} \log n)$ steps with high probability.*

Finally, we make use of a combinatorial property of the graph, the conductance. Define the conductance of a set $S \subseteq V$ as $\phi(S) = |\partial(S)|/vol(S)$, where $\partial(S) = \sum_{(u,v):u \in S, v \notin S} 1$ and $vol(S) = \sum_{u \in S} d(u)$. Then the conductance Φ_G of the graph is $\min_{S:vol(S) \leq vol(V)/2} \phi(S)$. For the purposes of this paper, we say that a d-regular graph is an ϵ-expander if the conductance of the graph is greater than or equal to ϵ.

3. TIGHT RESULTS FOR GRIDS

We show that the cover time for the d-dimensional grid using a 2-cobra walk $[0, N]^d$ is $O(N)$, where the order notation hides constant factors and other terms that depend on d; indeed, we show all vertices are covered in $O(N)$ steps with high probability. Previous work has shown that the cover time is $O(N\text{polylog}(N))$ [13]. We note that the results of [13] use a slightly different notation, working with n total nodes, or $[0, n^{1/d} - 1]^d$. We have opted to work over $[0, N]^d$ for convenience, with conversion factor $N = n^{1/d} - 1$. Our result is clearly tight in its dependence on N. Moreover, it shows that in some circumstances one can avoid using tools such as Matthews' Theorem, which had been used previously in this setting [13], and necessarily adds in an additional logarithmic factor in the number of vertices over the hitting time.

The case of $d = 2$ is simple and instructive; we sketch a proof, but do not go into full detail as we have a more detailed proof for the general case.

LEMMA 2. *The 2-cobra walk on $[0, N]^2$ has cover time $O(N)$.*

PROOF. Let v_0 be the starting vertex of the walk. We show that with high probability all vertices are reached within $O(N)$ steps, and the result follows, because if every vertex is hit within T steps with probability p, the expected time to cover all vertices is bounded above by T/p.

Let $v_1 = (x_1, y_1)$ be some other vertex on the grid. Let X_t be the Manhattan distance between the closest pebble of the cobra walk and v_1 after t steps, which we will refer to as time t. (All distances in this section will refer to Manhattan distances.) Let $u_t = (a_t, b_t)$ be some arbitrary vertex with a pebble of distance X_t from v_1 at time t. We show by cases that there is drift so that the expectation of X_t decreases linearly over time, even when at each step we pessimistically consider only the single vertex u_t and not other additional pebbles; it follows from standard results in random walks v_1 is reached after $O(N)$ steps with probability $1 - O(1/N^3)$. Hence all vertices are covered after $O(N)$ steps with probability $1 - O(1/N)$, and the result follows.

If $x_1 \neq a_t$ and $y_1 \neq b_t$, the probability that at least one of the two pebbles at u_t moves closer to v_1 is at least $1 - (1/2)^2 = 3/4$, since each pebble moves closer to v_1 with probability at least 1/2. (It can be more if a pebble v_1 is on the boundary of a grid.) If either $x_1 = a_t$ or $y_1 = b_t$ but not both, the probability that at least one of the two pebbles at u_t moves closer to v_1 could be as small as $1 - (3/4)^2 = 7/16 < 1/2$, since each pebble could move closer to v_1 with probability only 1/4. (This probability would be $1 - (2/3)^2 = 5/9$ if for example $x_1 = a_t = n$, but off the grid boundary this is not the case.) Over one step, then, the expected distance may be increasing. So we instead consider two steps. It is important to note that if the distance increases on the first of the two steps but (at least) one pebble moves so that $x_1 \neq a_t$ and $y_1 \neq b_t$ after the first step, it improves our probability that the distance decreases in the second step. We find taking cases, assuming that u_t is at least distance 2 from the boundary and from v_1, that X_t increases by 2 by with probability $\frac{1}{16}\frac{9}{16} + \frac{1}{2}\frac{1}{4} = \frac{41}{256}$. X_t decreases by 2 by with probability $\frac{7}{16}\frac{7}{16} = \frac{49}{256}$. (Similar (better) results can be shown when u_t is near a boundary.)

We therefore see that X_t has negative drift (except at $X_t = 1$, where the drift is slightly positive), and therefore the time to reach 0 can be shown to be $O(N)$ with probability $1 - O(1/N)$ as claimed. □

The analysis above suggests technical difficulties to overcome with a direct approach for general d; the behavior is slightly different at the boundaries of the grid (though one could always work on the toroidal grid), and when coordinates match in one or more dimensions, it makes analyzing the drift more difficult. The analysis makes clear that for any fixed d, there should be a large enough constant value of k so that the cover time for the k-cobra walk is $O(N)$ on the d-dimensional grid $[0, N]^d$. One just needs a large enough value of k so that the pebble nearest a target vertex drifts toward that vertex.

We actually show the stronger result that the 2-cobra walk has cover time $O(N)$ on the d-dimensional grid $[0, N]^d$, where the order notation hides constants that depend on d. We prove this below; we have not aimed to optimize the constant factors. The intuition for the proof is the following. If we look at the distance between the closest point on the cobra walk and our target vertex in any single dimension, it behaves like a biased random walk, with a bias toward 0. Hence, after $O(N)$ steps, each individual dimension has matched coordinates, with high probability. Indeed, if each chain was an independent biased random walk with constant bias (independent of d), after $O(dN)$ steps we would expect each independent walk to be near its stationary distribution, in which case each chain would be at 0 with some constant probability γ, and hence it would take roughly γ^d steps for all chains to be at 0 simultaneously. Sadly, as usual, the fact that the chains are not themselves independent causes significant technical challenges.

THEOREM 3. *The 2-cobra walk has cover time $O(N)$ on the d-dimensional grid $[0, N]^d$ for any constant d.*

PROOF. We break the proof into steps. As in Lemma 2, we consider the distance to a target vertex over all dimensions for some pebble generated by the 2-cobra walk. We pessimistically keep track of only a single pebble. Specifically, our state at time t can be defined as follows. Let $(z_{1,0}, z_{2,0}, \ldots, z_{d,0})$ be such that the distance from the initial pebble to the target vertex is $z_{i,0}$ for the ith grid dimension. More generally, assume there is some pebble at the tth step so that $(z_{1,t}, z_{2,t}, \ldots, z_{d,t})$ gives the distance from that pebble to the target vertex in each dimension. We update the $z_{i,t}$ values over time steps as follows. If our two choices of pebbles generated from that pebble move in the same dimension, we choose the pebble that moves closer to the target, if such a pebble exists. If our two choices of pebbles generated from that pebble move in different dimensions i and j, there are several cases. If $z_{i,t} = 0$ but $z_{j,t} \neq 0$, we choose the pebble that moves in dimension j. If $z_{i,t} = 0$ and $z_{j,t} = 0$, we choose the pebble randomly. If $z_{i,t} \neq 0$ and $z_{j,t} \neq 0$, if both choices of pebbles move closer or both move farther away from the target, we choose the pebble randomly; otherwise we choose the pebble that moves closer.

LEMMA 4. *In each dimension, we have that if $z_{i,t} \neq 0$, then $z_{i,t}$ changes in the next step with probability at least $1/(2d-1)$, and conditioned on the ith dimension being the value that changes, it decreases with probability at least $1/2 + 1/(8d-4)$. If $z_{i,t} = 0$, it increases in the next step with probability at most $2/(d+1)$.*

PROOF. This follows directly from the description above. We note that worst case with regard to the bias is when one dimension has $z_{i,t} \neq 0$ and $z_{j,t} \neq 0$ for $j \neq i$. In this case, the only bias that favors the ith dimension decreasing rather than increasing stems for both choices being in the ith dimension. With probability $2(d-1)/d^2$ the pebble is chosen to move in the ith dimension and some other dimension, in which case the pebble is equally likely to move closer or further to the target. With probability $1/d^2$ dimension i is chosen for both moves, in which case it moves closer with probability 3/4. Hence, conditioned on $z_{i,t}$ changing, it increases with probability

$$\frac{(d-1)/d^2 + (3/4)/d^2}{2(d-1)/d^2 + 1/d^2} = \frac{d - 1/4}{2d-1} = \frac{1}{2} + \frac{1}{8d-4}$$

as claimed.

With regard to which dimension moves, we notice that when $z_{i,t} \neq 0$, the probability of moving is least when we are on the boundary in the ith dimension (and hence there is just one move in that dimension), and other dimensions are not. When $z_{i,t} = 0$, that dimension is most likely to move if all others are on the boundary. The above bounds reflect these cases. □

Our multi-dimensional biased random walk has a natural interpretation as a discrete time queueing system, where customers arrive and wait at a randomly chosen queue, where the arrival rate is slightly smaller than the departure rate (except when a queue is empty). In this setting, our question concerns the time until the system empties from a given starting state. Surprisingly, despite this connection, we could not find a statement corresponding to our desired result in the literature.

The following follows easily from the bias shown above.

LEMMA 5. *In each individual dimension, the walk starting at $z_{i,0}$ with probability $1 - O(1/N^{d+1})$, $z_{i,t}$ hits 0 in $O(d^2N)$ steps.*

PROOF. Let X be the number of steps taken in the ith dimension over the first $64d^2N$ steps. Then by Lemma 4, $\mathbb{E}[X] > 32dN$, and using a Chernoff bound (e.g., [24, Exercise 4.7])

$$\Pr(X \le 16dN) \le (e/2)^{-8dN}.$$

The expected difference between the number of steps that decrease $z_{i,t}$ and the number of steps that increase $z_{i,t}$ grows with X, so we pessimistically condition on $X \ge 16dN$. Suppose that in this case that 0 is never reached, so the bias remains in effect over all $16dN$ steps. Let Y be number of decreases in the first $16dN$ steps. Then $\mathbb{E}[Y] \ge 8dN + 2N$, and again using a Chernoff bound (e.g., [24, Exercise 4.7])

$$\Pr(Y \le 8dN + N \mid X \ge 16dN) \le \left(\frac{e^{-\delta}}{(1-\delta)^{(1-\delta)}}\right)^{-8dN+2N},$$

where $\delta = 1/(8d+2)$. Notice that if $Y \ge 8dN + N$ then in fact 0 was reached. Hence the total probability that 0 is not reached is bounded above by

$$\Pr(Y \le 8dN+N \mid X \ge 16dN)+\Pr(X \le 16dN) \le (e/2)^{-8dN}$$

which is clearly $O(1/N^{d+1})$. □

Similarly, the following result is standard for biased random walks.

LEMMA 6. *Once $z_{i,t}$ hits 0, with probability $1-O(1/N^{d+2})$, it will remain below $c_d \ln N$ for some constant c_d (depending on d) over the next $100d^2N^2$ steps.*

PROOF. We may pessimistically assume that all N^2 steps are performed in the ith dimension. By the natural coupling we have that the probability that $z_{i,t}$ reaches $c_d \ln N$ in exactly k steps after it hits 0 is less than the probability in equilibrium that a biased random walk with probability $\frac{1}{2} + \frac{1}{8d-4}$ is at $c_d \ln N$. (Technically, the biased random walk doesn't have an equilibrium distribution, because of parity; it will be an even number of steps from its starting point after an even number of steps. We can add an arbitrarily small self-loop probability and increase the number of steps accordingly; we use N^2 steps and assume the appropriate equilibrium distribution for convenience.) The equilibrium distribution for this biased random walk, where π_j is the probability of being at j in equilibrium, is easily found by detailed balance equations, which yield

$$\pi_j = \frac{2}{4d-1}\left(\frac{4d-3}{4d-1}\right)^k.$$

As π_j is geometrically decreasing, for $j = c_d \ln n$ for some constant c_d we have π_k will be less than $1/(100d^2N^{d+4})$, and hence over the $100d^2N^2$ time steps we see $z_{i,t}$ never reaches $c_d \ln N$ with probability $1 - O(1/N^{d+2})$. □

We now use the following lemma, which in a slightly different form appears in Theorem 7 of [13]. We sketch the proof for completeness.

LEMMA 7. *Starting from $(z_{1,t}, z_{2,t}, \ldots, z_{d,t})$, where each $z_{i,t}$ is at most $c_d \ln N$, with probability $\Omega(1/(\ln\ln N)^c)$ for some constant c, there is a $u = \alpha \ln n$ such that for some $k \le u$, $z_{i,t+k} = 0$ for all $i = 1, \ldots, d$.*

PROOF. The analysis is broken into phases. The first phase is of length $O(\ln N)$, the second phase is of length $O((\ln N)^{1/2})$, and the jth phase is of length $O((\ln N)^{1/2^{j-1}})$. All phases have the same basic structure, except for the last. Within each phase, there are d subphases. In the ith subphase, we assume that the ith coordinate $z_{i,t}$ moves according to a biased random walk as previously described; in all other phases, we pessimistically assume that it moves according to an unbiased random walk. Our goal is to show that in each phase, each dimension moves closer to zero; in particular, after the jth phase, all the $z_{i,t}$ are at $O((\ln N)^{1/2^j})$ with constant probability. This is shown using Chernoff bounds (see Theorem 7 of [13] for the corresponding calculation). It follows that after $O(\ln\ln\ln N)$ phases each $z_{i,t}$ will be bounded by a constant with probability $\Omega(1)^{O(\ln\ln\ln N)} = \Omega(1/(\ln\ln N)^c)$. At that point, there is a constant probability that the target vertex will be reached in a constant number of steps. □

Putting this all together now yields the theorem that the cover time for the 2-cobra random walk on $[0, N]^d$ is $O(N)$ where the order notation hides constant factors that can depend on d. Lemma 5 shows that for each dimension i, $z_{i,t}$ hits 0 within the first $64d^2N^2$ steps with high probability. Hence, by Lemma 6, after $64d^2N^2$ steps all $z_{i,t}$ are at most $c_d \ln N$ with high probability. We are therefore in a state where we reach the target vertex within an additional $O(\ln N)$ steps with probability $\Omega(1/(\ln\ln N)^c)$. If we have not reached the target vertex, however, we are still within $c_d \ln N$ distance in each dimension with high probability. That is, let $\mathcal{E}_1$ be the event that we did not reach the target vertex within the $\alpha \ln N$ steps of Lemma 7, and let $\mathcal{E}_2$ be the event that some $z_{i,t}$ is more than $c_d \ln n$ after those $\alpha \ln N$ steps. We have by Lemma 6 that this is a low probability event (at least up through an additional $36d^2N^2$ steps), so we can consider a polylogarithmic number of repeated trials of $\alpha \ln N$ steps. As each trial succeeds with probability $\Omega(1/(\ln\ln N)^c)$, we can conclude that we hit the target vertex with probability at least $1-O(1/N^{d+1})$ within $O(N)$ steps. It follows via a union bound that with probability $1 - O(1/N)$ all vertices are hit within $O(N)$ steps, from which it readily follows that the cover time is $O(N)$.

We remark that this proof, while achieving $O(N)$ bounds, appears quite loose in the constant factors. As our proof does not directly take advantage of the large number of pebbles within the system, we believe the bounds could be tightened with respect to the dependence on d. Even with this bound, we expect there remains further work to fully understand the behavior of cobra walks on grids.

We also remark that the multi-step case analysis used in Lemma 2 can similarly be used to show that 2-cobra walks on k-ary trees have cover times that are proportional to the graph's diameter when $k = 2$ or $k = 3$. We conjecture that in fact the cover time for 2-cobra walks on k-ary trees is proportional to the diameter for every constant k, where the constant of proportionality may depend on k, similar to Theorem 3 for grids.

4. COVER TIME FOR A GRAPH WITH ARBITRARY CONDUCTANCE

In this section, we significantly improve and extend the results first developed in [13], which provided an $O(\log^2 n)$ bound for the cover time of a k-cobra walk on a d-regular expander with an expansion only achieved by graphs such as random $d-$regular expanders and Ramanujan expanders. Here, we provide the first known bound for the cover time of cobra walks on a d-regular graph of *arbitrary* conductance Φ. While the upper bound is not useful for graphs with very low conductance, there are a wide class of graphs beyond expanders for which this guarantees rapid coverage,, e.g. the hypercube, power-law graphs, and random geometric graphs. For this section and the rest of the paper, we work exclusively with 2-cobra walks, and use cobra walks to mean 2-cobra walks where the meaning is clear.

THEOREM 8. *Let G be a d-regular graph with conductance Φ_G. Then a cobra-walk starting at any vertex will cover G in $O(d^4\Phi_G^{-2}\log^2(n))$ rounds, with high probability.*

From this general bound, we have the following corollary, which improves the previous result of [13].

COROLLARY 9. *Let G be a bounded-degree d-regular ϵ-expander graph. Then a cobra walk starting at any vertex v will cover G in $O(\log^2(n))$ rounds with high probability when d is specifically bounded by a constant.*

Due to the extreme difficulty of analyzing the progress of a cobra walk explicitly, we follow [13] and analyze a process that, while conceptually similar to a cobra walk, has more structured rules which allow us to analyze walks taken by individual pebbles with only limited dependence on one another. Furthermore, this process stochastically dominates the cobra walk when starting from the same vertex with respect to the time to cover all of the vertices. Any upper bound on the cover time for this process therefore automatically applies to the cover time of a cobra walk as well.

This process, which we refer to as W_{alt}, can be defined as follows: We start with δn pebbles for some constant $\delta \leq 1/2$, distributed arbitrarily among the vertex set V, including the possibility for more than one pebble to to start at the same vertex. Furthermore, we assume that the pebbles have a total ordering, and that each pebble knows its position in the ordering. In this process, unlike in the cobra walk, no pebbles split or coalesce - the total number of pebbles is an invariant. Pebbles interact with one another according to two simple rules. For each time step:

1. If one or two pebbles are co-located in time and space: at vertex v at time t, each pebble chooses a random neighbor from $N(v)$ independently u.a.r and moves to that vertex.

2. If three or more pebbles are at v at time t, the two pebbles with the lowest order each pick a vertex independently from $N(v)$ u.a.r. and move to their chosen vertex. Label these vertices u, w (keeping in mind that $u = w$ is allowed). The remaining pebble(s) at v then each independently pick u with probability $1/2$ or w with probability $1/2$ and move to the vertex they have chosen.

If we are observing, for a single time step, a vertex v at which two or more pebbles (or zero, trivially) have landed, we would be unable to distinguish between a cobra walk and a W_{alt} process. On the other hand, if we observe a vertex v at which a single pebble has landed, we *would* be able to distinguish. In W_{alt}, in the next step, the pebble at v will act like a simple random walk and move to a single neighbor. On the other hand, in the cobra walk, there is some probability p two neighbors will receive a pebble from v, and probability $1 - p$ only one neighbor will. Thus, the active set of W_{alt} can be viewed as a (possibly proper) subset of the active set of a cobra walk when both are started from the same initial state. Therefore, at any future time t, the size of the active set of a cobra walk (viewed as a random variable) stochastically dominates the size of the active set of W_{alt}. We can then "invert" this argument to show that the cover time of W_{alt} stochastically dominates the cover time of the cobra walk. For a formal proof, we refer to the full paper [23].

Finally, for technical reasons, we make the W_{alt} process a *lazy* process. That is, at each step, with probability 1/2 all pebbles remain in their same position. With probability 1/2 a step proceeds with the probabilities described above. (Thus, to obtain the unconditioned probabilities of any particular action, we need to multiply the above probabilities through by 1/2.)

We are now ready to prove Theorem 8. This proof builds on the machinery developed in [13, Theorem 16 and Lemma 17]. Here we will outline the proof technique, making note of the new ideas needed to provide a general bound on the cover time in terms of the conductance of the graph. We have refactored the full proof for completeness, and it is available in the full paper [23].

One significant difference with previous work is the following. The previous analysis consisted of two stages, with the first stage providing an exponential growth in the number of pebbles, but requiring the graph to have extremely high expansion. In contrast, we begin our analysis of W_{alt} with a large number of pebbles, *all of which are located at a single initial, arbitrary vertex v*, and compare this to a cobra walk that starts at v. In the first stage of Since the stochastic dominance of the cover time of W_{alt} over a cobra walk holds for all starting distributions of the pebbles on the vertices of G, it also therefore holds for the starting distribution in which all δn pebbles begin at the same vertex. This allows us to work exclusively with W_{alt} for the entire analysis, bypassing the analysis of the cobra walk as it grows from one active node to a linear number of active nodes and therefore dropping the requirement that G have extremely high expansion.

The second contribution of our new analysis is the derivation of bounds on the probability of coverage of vertices in terms of the conductance of the graph. As a consequence, we are able to derive bounds that hold for regular graphs with arbitrary values of d and arbitrary Φ_G.

Proof of Theorem 8: To prove the theorem, we break up W_{alt} into epochs of length s, where $s \in O(\Phi_G^m \log n)$, for m a constant to be defined later. We show that each vertex v has a constant probability of being hit by at least one pebble at the exact time step the epoch ends. We then go through $O(\log n)$ epochs to boost the probability v is covered to a sufficiently high probability and then take a union bound over every vertex to obtain the result.

We first prove that in a particular epoch vertex v will be hit by at least one pebble with constant probability. Define E_i to be the event that pebble i for $i \in 1, \ldots, \delta n$ covers an arbitrary vertex v at time s. Then the event that v is hit by at least one pebble is $\bigcup E_i$. Note that for any two pebbles i, j it is not safe to assume that E_i and E_j are independent, since i and j may cross paths during their walks and have their transition probabilities affected by the rules of W_{alt}. However, we can use a second-order inclusion-exclusion inequality to lower-bound the probability:

$$\Pr\left[\bigcup_i E_i\right] \geq \sum_i \Pr[E_i] - \sum_{i,j:i \neq j} \Pr[E_i \cup E_j]$$

Thus, we need to show that, for the r.h.s., the first quantity is a constant and the second quantity is smaller.

The first part is fairly straightforward and makes use of well-known results regarding simple random walks on graphs of a given conductance. We point the reader to the full version of the proof.

Next we establish an upper bound for $\Pr[E_i \cap E_j]$ using the joint (dependent) walks of pebbles i and j. Without loss of generality, assume that i has a lower order than j, and that if i and j are co-located in time and space, then not only is i the lower order, but j must behave like a third-or-greater priority pebble and choose the same vertex that i next hops to with probability $1/2$. (Note that under this assumption, the total probability that j moves to the same vertex as i is $1/2 + 1/2d$, a fact which will be important shortly).

We can view the random walks of i and j as a random walk over a graph with the topology of the tensor product graph $G \times G$. The tensor product graph has the Cartesian product $V(G) \times V(G)$ as its vertex set, and an edge set defined as follows: vertex $(u, u') \in V(G \times G)$ has an edge to $(v, v') \in V(G \times G)$ if and only if $(u, v), (u', v') \in E(G)$. The random walk we construct on $G \times G$ is slightly different than a simple random walk on the same graph: we make the edges directed, and we attach weights to them such that the walk on the directed graph $D(G \times G)$ is isomorphic to the movement of pebbles i,j in a W_{alt} on G.

We will show in the next Lemma that the walk on $D(G \times G)$ has a stationary distribution, that this stationary distribution is close to $1/n^2$, and that the walk converges rapidly to it. Thus, after s steps, the probability that i and j are at the same vertex in G is bounded from above by $2/(n^2 + n) + 1/n^4$.

Once we have established bounds for $\Pr[E_i], \Pr[E_i \cap E_j]$, we can apply them to the full expression and get:

$$\begin{aligned}
\Pr\left[\bigcup E_i\right] &\geq \sum_i \Pr[E_i] - \frac{1}{2}\sum_{i \neq j} \Pr[E_j \cap E_i] \\
&\geq \delta n \frac{1}{2n} - \frac{1}{2}\binom{\delta n}{2}\left(\frac{2}{n^2+n} + \frac{1}{n^4}\right) \\
&\geq \frac{\delta}{2} - \frac{\delta}{4}(\delta n^2 - n)\left(\frac{2}{n^2+n} + \frac{1}{n^4}\right) \\
&\geq \frac{\delta}{2} - \frac{2\delta^2}{4}
\end{aligned}$$

Finally, to complete the proof, we have the following lemma:

LEMMA 10. *Let G and s be defined as in Theorem 8. Let i, j be two pebbles walking on G according to the rules of W_{alt} If $E_i \cap E_j$ are defined as the event in which i and j are both located at (arbitrarily chosen) vertex v at time s, then* $\Pr[E_i \cap E_j] \leq \dfrac{2}{n^2+2} + \dfrac{1}{n^4}$.

Here we provide a brief sketch of the proof, full details of which are provided in the long version. We first create a directed graph $\mathcal{D}(G \times G) = \mathcal{D}$ through some minor modifications of the edge set of $G \times G$. These changes are such that the transition probability matrix of $\mathcal{D}$ is isomorphic to W_{alt} on G. We make use of the fact that $\mathcal{D}$ is an Eulerian digraph to calculate the stationary distribution π of the walk on $\mathcal{D}$. We then show that $\Phi_G = \Phi_{G \times G}$ and, making use of the work of [10], demonstrate through the use of the directed Cheeger inequalities that the second smallest eigenvalue of the normalized Laplacian of $\mathcal{D}$ is bounded from below by $O(\Phi_G^{-2})$. We then apply Theorem 7.3 of [10] to show that this walk converges in $O(\Phi^{-2} \log n)$ time to the stationary distribution of $\Theta(1/n^2)$ for each vertex in $\mathcal{D}$.

This concludes the proof of Theorem 8. It follows immediately that when d is a constant and G is any expander with conductance Φ_G bounded away from zero by a constant, a cobra walk will cover G in at most $O(\log^2 n)$ time. □

5. COVER TIME FOR GENERAL GRAPHS

In this section, we show that the cover time of 2-cobra walks for general graphs is $O(n^{11/4} \log n)$. For d-regular graphs, we obtain an improved bound of $O(n^{2-1/d} \log n)$. We establish the bounds on the cover time by proving that for any start vertex u and any target vertex v, the hitting time from u to v, denoted by $H(u, v)$, is $O(n^{11/4})$ for general graphs and $O(n^{2-1/d})$ for d-regular graphs. We then apply Matthews' Theorem (Theorem 1), which actually give a high probability result.

To analyze the cobra walk, we consider biased versions of the standard random walk; in each step, with some probability, instead of moving to a neighbor chosen uniformly at random, the walk moves to a vertex as determined by a memoryless controller whose aim is to reach a certain target vertex. The biased walk we analyze is a variant of *ϵ-biased walks* defined in [5]. In Section 5.1, we review the ϵ-biased walks of [5] and introduce and analyze our variant, which we call *inverse-degree biased* walks. In Section 5.2, we use $1/d$-biased walks to derive an $O(n^{2-1/d})$ bound on the hitting time of the cobra walk on d-regular graphs, improving on the quadratic bound for standard random walks. In Section 5.3, we use inverse-degree-biased walks to derive an $O(n^{11/4})$ bound on the hitting time of the cobra walk on nonregular graphs, improving on the cubic bound for standard random walks.

5.1 Biased random walks

An *ϵ-biased walk* on G is defined as follows: in each step, with probability $1 - \epsilon$ one of the neighbors is selected uniformly at random, and the walk moves there; with probability ϵ, a controller gets to select which neighbor to move to. The controller can be probabilistic, but it is time independent. The primary motivation for biased random walks is to study how much can a controller increase the occupancy probabilities at a targeted subset S of the vertices in the stationary distribution. A central result of [5] is the following lower bound achieved by an optimal controller in an ϵ-biased walk.

THEOREM 11 (THEOREM 2 OF [5]). *Let $G = (V, E)$ be a connected graph, $S \subset V$, $v \in S$ and $x \in V$. Let $\Delta(x, v)$ be the length of the shortest path between vertices x and v in G and $\Delta(x, S) = \min_{v \in S} \Delta(x, v)$. Let $\beta = 1 - \epsilon$. There is an ϵ-bias strategy for which the stationary probability at S (i.e. the sum of the stationary probabilities of $v \in S$) is at least*

$$\frac{\sum_{v \in S} \delta(v)}{\sum_{v \in S} \delta(v) + \sum_{x \notin S} \beta^{\Delta(x,S)-1} \delta(x)}. \quad (1)$$

The bias in an ϵ-biased walk is constant (ϵ) at each vertex. To analyze the cobra walk, we define a biased walk in which the bias available to the controller at each vertex of the graph varies with the vertex. Specifically, we define the *inverse-degree-biased walk* with target x: if the walk is at x, then the next vertex visited is a neighbor of x chosen uniformly at random; if the walk is at vertex $v \neq x$, then with probability $1 - 1/\delta(v)$ one of the neighbors is selected uniformly at random and the walk moves there, and with probability $1/\delta(v)$ a controller gets to select which neighbor to move to. The goal of the controller is to minimize the hitting time to x.

Our main motivation for introducing inverse-degree-biased walks is the following dominance argument. For any pair of vertices u and v, let $H^*(u, v)$ denote the smallest hitting time to v achievable by an inverse-degree-biased walk with target v, starting at u. Recall that $H(u, v)$ denotes the hitting time at v for a cobra walk starting at u.

LEMMA 12. *For any pair of vertices u and v, $H(u, v) \leq H^*(u, v)$.*

PROOF. Our proof is by a coupling argument. Consider the cobra walk starting at u at time 0. For any vertex x and any time t, let $E_t^*(x)$ denote the event that x is active in the cobra walk at the start of round t. For any vertex x, any neighbor y of x, and any time t, let $P_t^*(x, y)$ be the probability that y is active at the start of round $t+1$ conditioned on the event that x is active at the start of round t. That is,

$$P_t^*(x, y) = \Pr[E_{t+1}^*(y) \mid E_t^*(x)].$$

We next consider any inverse-degree-biased walk starting from u. Let $E_t(x)$ denote the event that the walk is at vertex x at the start of round t. Let $P_t'(x, y)$ be the probability that the inverse-degree-biased walk is at y at the start of round $t+1$, conditioned on the event that the walk is at x at the start of round t. By the definition of the cobra walk and the inverse-degree-biased walk, we have the straightforward derivation.

$$\begin{aligned} P_t^*(x, y) &= 1 - \left(1 - \frac{1}{\delta(u)}\right)^2 \\ &\geq \frac{2}{\delta(u)} - \frac{1}{\delta(u)^2} \\ &= \frac{1}{\delta(u)} + \left(1 - \frac{1}{\delta(u)}\right)\frac{1}{\delta(u)} \\ &\geq P_t'(x, y). \end{aligned}$$

We now invoke a standard coupling argument to obtain that for any round t and any vertex x, the probability that x is active in the cobra walk at the start of round t is at least the probability that the inverse-degree-biased walk is at x at the start of round t. This also implies that the expected time for u to become active in the cobra walk is at most the expected time to hit x in the inverse-degree-biased walk. Setting $x = v$ and choosing the inverse-degree-biased walk to be one that minimizes the hitting time to v yields $H(u, v) \leq H^*(u, v)$. □

5.2 $O(n^{2-1/d})$ hitting time for d-regular graphs

THEOREM 13. *Let G be a finite, d-regular graph. Then the hitting time of a cobra walk on G is in $O(n^{2-\frac{1}{d}})$, for any constant d.*

PROOF. For the case of d-regular graphs, the inverse-degree-biased walk with target v is exactly a $1/d$-biased walk with target v. We invoke Theorem 11 for d-regular graphs with $\beta = 1 - 1/d$, and letting S equal $\{v\}$. We calculate a lower bound on stationary probability at v of the $1/d$-biased walk with target v, we need to determine the maximum value that $\sum_{x \neq v} \beta^{\Delta(x,v)-1}$ can take. We calculate this maximum value, over all graphs with maximum degree d, hence yielding an upper bound for d-regular graphs as well. Let n_i denote the number of vertices within i hops of v. Then, we have

$$\sum_{x \neq v} \beta^{\Delta(v,x)-1} = \sum_{i \geq 1} n_i \beta^{i-1}.$$

Since the degree is at most d, we have the following constraints on the n_is, given by the number of vertices within a certain number of hops from v.

$$\sum_{1 \leq i \leq j} n_i \leq \min \left\{ n - 1, d \left(1 + \sum_{1 \leq i < j} (d-1)^i \right) \right\}.$$

Since $\beta < 1$, and the total number of vertices is bounded by n, the sum $\sum_{i \geq 1} n_i \beta^{i-1}$ is maximized when

$$\begin{aligned} n_1 &= d \\ n_j &= d(d-1)^j \; 1 < j < L, \end{aligned}$$

where L is the smallest j such that $d\left(1 + \sum_{1 \leq i < j}(d-1)^i\right)$ is at least $n - 1$. Then, we have $n_L = n - 1 - \sum_{j < L} n_j$. With elementary algebra, we calculate the value of L as

$$L = \log_{(d-1)} \left[\frac{(n-1)}{d}(d-2) + 1 \right].$$

We now bound $\sum_{x \neq v} \beta^{\Delta(x,v)-1}$ as follows.

$$\begin{aligned} \sum_{x \neq v} \beta^{\Delta(v,x)-1} &= d\beta^0 + (d-1)d\beta^2 + d(d-1)^2\beta^2 \\ &\quad + \ldots + d(d-1)^{L-1}\beta^{L-1} \\ &= d\left(\sum_{i=0}^{L-1}((d-1)\beta)^i\right) \\ &= d\left[\frac{((d-1)\beta)^L - 1}{(d-1)\beta - 1}\right] \\ &\leq C\left[((d-1)\beta)^L\right] \end{aligned}$$

where $C = d/((d-1)\beta - 1)$.

With some minimal algebra, we can see that:

$$(d-1)^{\log_{d-1}(n-1)(d-2)/d+1} = (n-1)(d-2)/d + 1 < n$$

and that

$$\begin{aligned}
\beta^L &= (1-1/d)^{\log_{d-1}(n-1)(d-2)/(d-1)+1} \\
&\leq (d-1)^{(-1/d)\log_{d-1}((n-1)(d-1)/(d-2)+1)} \\
&= \left[\frac{(n-1)(d-2)+d}{d}\right]^{-1/d} < n^{-1/d}.
\end{aligned}$$

Therefore, the stationary probability at v is at least $1/(1+n^{1-1/d})$, giving a return time to v of at most $1+n^{1-1/d}$. Using the tree-traversal argument and noting that it will take, in expectation, d returns to current vertex v to make one "progress" step in the traversal in expectation for a total cost of $dn^{1-1/d}$ per progress step. Thus, the total cost of coverage will be $2dCn^{2-1/d} = O(n^{2-1/d})$ for constant d. □

5.3 $O(n^{11/4})$ hitting time for general graphs

To bound $H(u,v)$ in a general graphs, let P be a shortest-hop path from u to v, given by the sequence of vertices $u = u_0, u_1, u_2, \ldots, u_{|P|} = v$. Then

$$H(u,v) \leq \sum_{i=0}^{|P|-1} H(u_i, u_{i+1}). \tag{2}$$

Let $R(x)$ denote the minimum return time to x among all inverse-degree-biased walks with target x. We have

$$R(x) = 1 + \sum_{y\in N(x)} \frac{H^*(y,x)}{\delta(x)}. \tag{3}$$

Furthermore, we have

$$\begin{aligned}
H(u_i,u_{i+1}) &\leq 1 + \sum_{y\in N(u_i), y\neq u_{i+1}} H(y,u_{i+1})/\delta(u_i) \\
&\leq 1 + \sum_{y\in N(u_i), y\neq u_{i+1}} \frac{H(y,u_i)+H(u_i,u_{i+1})}{\delta(u_i)} \\
&\leq 1 + \sum_{y\in N(u_i), y\neq u_{i+1}} \frac{H^*(y,u_i)+H(u_i,u_{i+1})}{\delta(u_i)} \\
&\leq R(u_i) + \sum_{y\in N(u_i), y\neq u_{i+1}} H(u_i,u_{i+1})/\delta(u_i) \\
&= R(u_i) + \left(1-\frac{1}{\delta(u_i)}\right) H(u_i,u_{i+1}).
\end{aligned}$$

(The second step follows from the fact that the hitting time from y to u_{i+1} is at most the sum of the hitting times from y to u_i and from u_i to u_{i+1}. The third step follows from Lemma 12. The fourth step follows from Equation 3. The final equality holds since u_i has $\delta(u_i)$ neighbors.)

The above equation easily yields $H(u_i,u_{i+1}) \leq \delta(u_i)R(u_i)$, which combined with Equation 2 yields

$$H(u,v) \leq \sum_{i=0}^{|P|-1} H(u_i,u_{i+1}) \leq \sum_{i=0}^{|P|-1} \delta(u_i)R(u_i). \tag{4}$$

We prove the following extension of Theorem 11, applied to inverse-degree-biased walks. For the sake of completeness, we include the proof, which essentially mimics the proof of Theorem 2 in [5].

Lemma 14. *Let $G = (V,E)$ be a connected graph and S be an arbitrary subset of V. For a given path P, let $\sigma(P)$ denote the product $\prod_{y\in P}(1-1/\delta(y))$. For $v \in S$ and $x \in V-S$, let $\widehat{\sigma}(x,v)$ denote the maximum, over all paths P from x to v, of $\sigma(P)$. Let $\widehat{\sigma}(x,S)$ denote the maximum, over all $v\in S$, of $\widehat{\sigma}(x,v)$. There is an inverse-degree-biased walk for which the stationary probability at S (i.e. the sum of the stationary probabilities of $v \in S$) is at least*

$$\frac{\sum_{v\in S}\delta(v)}{\sum_{v\in S}\delta(v) + \sum_{x\notin S}(\widehat{\sigma}(x,S)\delta(x))}.$$

Proof. Define a probability distribution π^M: $\pi^M(v) = \gamma\delta(v)$ for $v\in S$ and $\pi^M(x) = \gamma\widehat{\sigma}(x,S)\delta(x)$ for $x\notin S$, where

$$\gamma = \frac{1}{\sum_{v\in S}\delta(v) + \sum_{x\notin S}(\widehat{\sigma}(x,S)\delta(x))}.$$

Let M be the transition probability matrix for which the stationary distribution given by Metropolis Theorem [5, Theorem 1] [22] is π^M. Define the following transition probability matrix: $P_{x,x} = 0$ for all $x \in V$, and for $y \neq x$, $P_{x,y} = M_{x,y}/(1-M_{x,x})$. We now argue that $M_{x,y} \geq (1-1/\delta(x))/\delta(x)$ for any neighbor y of x. By the Metropolis Theorem, $M_{x,y}$ is either $1/\delta(x)$ or $\pi^M(y)/(\delta(y)\pi^M(x))$. In the former case, the desired lower bound on $M_{x,y}$ is trivial. In the latter case, we have

$$M_{x,y} = \frac{\widehat{\sigma}(y,S)}{\delta(x)\widehat{\sigma}(x,S)} \geq \frac{1-1/\delta(x)}{\delta(x)},$$

where the last inequality follows from the fact that $\widehat{\sigma}(y,S) \geq (1-1/\delta(x))\widehat{\sigma}(x,S)$. We thus obtain $P_{x,y} \geq M_{x,y} \geq (1-1/\delta(x))/\delta(x)$ for any neighbor y of x. So P is a transition probability matrix of an inverse-degree-biased walk.

We next show that for each vertex in S, its stationary probability under P is at least its stationary probability under M. Let $H^M(x,v)$ and $H^P(x,v)$ denote the hitting time to v under the walks defined by P and M, respectively, with start vertex x. For each vertex $x \neq v$, we have

$$H^M(x,v) = 1 + M_{x,x}H^M(x,v) + \sum_{y\in N(x)} M_{x,y}H^M(y,v),$$

which yields

$$\begin{aligned}
H^M(x,v) &= \frac{1}{1-M_{x,x}} + \sum_{y\in N(x)} \frac{M_{x,y}}{1-M_{x,x}} H^M(y,v) \\
&\geq 1 + \sum_{y\in N(x)} P_{x,y}H^M(y,v).
\end{aligned}$$

By [5, Lemma 1], for every $x\in V$ and $v \in S$, $H^M(x,v) \geq H^P(x,v)$. If we denote the return time to vertex v in the walks under P and M by $R^P(v)$ and $R^M(v)$, respectively, we obtain that

$$\begin{aligned}
R^M(v) &= 1 + \sum_{y\in N(v)} M_{v,y}H^M(y,v) \\
&= 1 + \sum_{y\in N(v)} P_{v,y}H^M(y,v) \\
&\geq 1 + \sum_{y\in N(v)} P_{v,y}H^P(y,v) \\
&= R^P(v).
\end{aligned}$$

(The second step follows from the fact that for any v in S, and neighbor y of v, $M_{v,y} = P_{v,y} = 1/d(v)$.) We thus have

$$\pi^P(S) \geq \pi^M(S) = \frac{\sum_{v\in S}\delta(v)}{\sum_{v\in S}\delta(v) + \sum_{x\notin S}\delta(x)\widehat{\sigma}(x,S)}.$$

□

COROLLARY 15. *Let v be an arbitrary vertex of G. There exists a bias strategy for the inverse-degree-biased walk such that the return time to v in the walk is at most*

$$\frac{\delta(v) + \sum_{x \neq v} \widehat{\sigma}(x, v)\delta(x)}{\delta(v)}.$$

PROOF. The result follows from Lemma 14, setting $S = \{v\}$ and noting that the return time to v equals the inverse of the stationary probability at v. □

For our analysis, it is more convenient to work with an upper bound on $\widehat{\sigma}(x, v)$ (for each x and v) as given the following lemma. Let $p(y, x)$ denote the weight of the shortest path from y to x in G, where we assign a weight of $1/\delta(z)$ for each vertex z.

LEMMA 16. *For all vertices x and v, $\widehat{\sigma}(x, v)$ is at most $e^{-p(x,v)}$.*

PROOF. Let P' denote a path between x and v such that $\widehat{\sigma}(x, v) = \sigma(P)$. Then, we have

$$\widehat{\sigma}(x, v) = \prod_{y \in P'} (1 - 1/\delta(y)) \leq \prod_{y \in P'} e^{-1/\delta(y)} = e^{-p(x,v)}.$$

□

LEMMA 17. *For start vertex u and target v, let P be a shortest-hop path from u to v, given by the sequence of vertices $u = u_0, u_1, u_2, \ldots, u_{|P|} = v$. Then, we have*

$$\sum_{i=0}^{|P|-1} \delta(u_i) R(u_i) = O(n^{11/4}).$$

PROOF. By Lemma 12 and Corollary 15, we have

$$\begin{aligned}
\sum_{i=0}^{|P|-1} \delta(u_i)R(u_i) &\leq \sum_{i=0}^{|P|-1} \delta(u_i)R(u_i) \\
&\leq \sum_{i=0}^{|P|-1} \delta(u_i) \left(\frac{\delta(u_i) + \sum_{x \neq u} \widehat{\sigma}(x, u)\delta(x)}{\delta(u_i)} \right) \\
&\leq \sum_{i=0}^{|P|-1} \left(\delta(u_i) + \sum_{x \neq u_i} \delta(x) e^{-p(x,u_i)} \right) \\
&\leq 3n + \sum_{i=1}^{|P|-1} \sum_{x \neq u_i} \delta(x) e^{-p(x,u_i)} \\
&\leq 3n + \sum_{x \in V} \left(\delta(x) \sum_{i=1}^{|P|-1} e^{-p(x,u_i)} \right).
\end{aligned}$$

(The second step follows from Corollary 15. The third step follows from Lemma 16. The fourth step follows from the elementary claim that the sum of the degrees of vertices along any shortest path in an n-vertex graph is at most $3n$; e.g., see [17, Proof of Theorem 2.1]. The final step is obtained by rearranging the summations.)

We next place an upper bound on $\sum_{x \in V} \left(\delta(x) \sum_{i=1}^{|P|-1} e^{-p(x,u_i)} \right)$. We claim that the number of vertices u_i in P to which any vertex x has paths of length at most L is at most $2L$. This is because two vertices a and b that are more than $2L$ hops away in P would have a path of $2L$ hops via x, a contradiction.

Consider a vertex u_i, for some i. Consider any path from x to u_i that minimizes $p(x, u_i)$. No vertex in the graph has edges to more than $\sqrt{n}$ vertices along this path. If it did, then we could short-cut and decrease the sum of the reciprocals of the degrees $1/\sqrt{n} < \sqrt{n}/(n-1)$. Therefore, any path that minimizes $p(x, u_i)$ has a total degree of at most $n^{3/2}$. If the length L of the path is less than $\sqrt{n}$, then $p(x, u_i) \geq 0$; otherwise, $p(x, u_i) \geq L^2/n^{3/2}$.

We now show that for any vertex x, $\sum_{i=1}^{|P|-1} e^{-p(x,u_i)}$ is $O(n^{3/4})$. We partition the u_i according to their hop-distance from x. Fix j and consider all vertices in P that are distance between 2^{j-1} and 2^j from x. By our claim above, there are at most 2^j such vertices. If $2^j \leq \sqrt{n}$, then we use the trivial bound of 1; otherwise, we use the bound $2^{2j}/n^{3/2}$. So we have

$$\begin{aligned}
\sum_{u_i \in P} e^{-p(x,u_i)} &= \sum_{j: 2^j \leq \sqrt{n}} O(2^j) + \sum_{j: 2^j > \sqrt{n}} \left(2^j * e^{-2^{2j}/n^{3/2}} \right) \\
&= O(n^{1/2}) + O(n^{3/4}) = O(n^{3/4}).
\end{aligned}$$

Since $\delta(x)$ for each x is at most $n-1$ and the length of P is at most n, we get the desired bound of $O(n^{11/4})$. □

THEOREM 18. *The hitting and cover times for a 2-cobra walk on a graph with n vertices are $O(n^{11/4})$ and $O(n^{11/4} \log n)$, respectively.*

PROOF. For any start vertex u and target vertex v, let P be a shortest-hop path from u to v, given by the sequence of vertices $u = u_0, u_1, u_2, \ldots, u_{|P|} = v$. By Lemma 12 and Equation 4 we have

$$H(u, v) \leq H^*(u, v) \leq \sum_{i=0}^{|P|-1} \delta(u_i) R(u_i),$$

which, by Lemma 17, is $O(n^{11/4})$. The bound on the cover time follows from Matthews' Theorem, Theorem 1. □

6. CONCLUSION

We have derived several improved results for cobra walks. However, there remain many open problems, and corresponding gaps in our understanding. We have shown that for d-dimensional grids on $[0, n]^d$ the cover time is proportional to n, even for 2-cobra walks. The dependence on d, however, has not been determined, and more generally we would like to find a larger collection of graph types for which the cover time for 2-cobra walks is proportional to the diameter. Better results for general graphs are still open; we optimistically conjecture that for 2-cobra walks the worst case cover time on a graph with n vertices is only $O(n \log n)$. (The star graph shows that it can be $\Omega(n \log n)$.) Perhaps most importantly, we believe there should be better methods available for analyzing cobra walks. Our results utilize techniques based on parallelism and bias, but we do not believe they are as yet taking full advantage of the power of cobra walks.

7. REFERENCES

[1] Micah Adler, Eran Halperin, Richard M. Karp, and Vijay V. Vazirani. A stochastic process on the hypercube with applications to peer-to-peer networks. In *Proceedings of the Thirty-fifth Annual ACM Symposium on Theory of Computing*, STOC '03, pages 575–584, New York, NY, USA, 2003. ACM.

[2] Noga Alon, Chen Avin, Michal Koucky, Gady Kozma, Zvi Lotker, and Mark R. Tuttle. Many random walks are faster than one. In *Proceedings of the Twentieth Annual Symposium on Parallelism in Algorithms and Architectures*, SPAA '08, pages 119–128, New York, NY, USA, 2008. ACM.

[3] Siva R. Arthreya and Jan M Swart. Branching-coalescing particle systems. *Probability Theory and Related Fields*, 131(3):376–414, 2005.

[4] J. Augustine, G. Pandurangan, P. Robinson, S. Roche, and E. Upfal. Enabling robust and efficient distributed computation in dynamic peer-to-peer networks. In *Foundations of Computer Science (FOCS), 2015 IEEE 56th Annual Symposium on*, pages 350–369, Oct 2015.

[5] Yossi Azar, Andrei Z Broder, Anna R Karlin, Nathan Linial, and Steven Phillips. Biased random walks. In *Proceedings of the twenty-fourth annual ACM symposium on Theory of computing*, pages 1–9. ACM, 1992.

[6] Itai Benjamini and Sebastian Müller. On the trace of branching random walks. *arXiv preprint arXiv:1002.2781*, 2010.

[7] Petra Berenbrink, Colin Cooper, Robert Elsässer, Tomasz Radzik, and Thomas Sauerwald. Speeding up random walks with neighborhood exploration. In *Proceedings of the Twenty-first Annual ACM-SIAM Symposium on Discrete Algorithms*, SODA '10, pages 1422–1435, Philadelphia, PA, USA, 2010. Society for Industrial and Applied Mathematics.

[8] Andrei Broder. Generating random spanning trees. In *Foundations of Computer Science, 1989., 30th Annual Symposium on*, pages 442–447, Oct 1989.

[9] Jen-Yeu Chen and Gopal Pandurangan. Almost-optimal gossip-based aggregate computation. *SIAM J. Comput.*, 41(3):455–483, 2012.

[10] F. Chung. Laplacians and the cheeger inequality for directed graphs. *Annals of Combinatorics*, 9:1–19, 2005.

[11] Colin Cooper, Robert Elsässer, Hirotaka Ono, and Tomasz Radzik. Coalescing random walks and voting on graphs. In *Proceedings of the 2012 ACM Symposium on Principles of Distributed Computing*, PODC '12, pages 47–56, New York, NY, USA, 2012. ACM.

[12] Nedialko B. Dimitrov and C. Greg Plaxton. Optimal cover time for a graph-based coupon collector process. In *Proceedings of the 32Nd International Conference on Automata, Languages and Programming*, ICALP'05, pages 702–716, Berlin, Heidelberg, 2005. Springer-Verlag.

[13] Chinmoy Dutta, Gopal Pandurangan, Rajmohan Rajaraman, and Scott Roche. Coalescing-branching random walks on graphs. *ACM Trans. Parallel Comput.*, 2(3):20:1–20:29, November 2015.

[14] Robert Elsasser and Thomas Sauerwald. Tight bounds for the cover time of multiple random walks. volume 412, pages 2623 – 2641, 2011. Selected Papers from 36th International Colloquium on Automata, Languages and Programming (ICALP 2009).

[15] U. Feige. A tight upper bound on the cover time for random walks on graphs. 1993.

[16] Uriel Feige. A tight lower bound on the cover time for random walks on graphs. *Random Struct. Algorithms*, 6(4):433–438, July 1995.

[17] Uriel Feige, David Peleg, Prabhakar Raghavan, and Eli Upfal. Randomized broadcast in networks. *Random Structures & Algorithms*, pages 447–460, 1990.

[18] Ayalvadi J. Ganesh, Laurent Massouli, and Donald F. Towsley. The effect of network topology on the spread of epidemics. In *INFOCOM*, pages 1455–1466. IEEE, 2005.

[19] Theodore E. Harris. *The theory of branching processes.* Die Grundlehren der Mathematischen Wissenschaften, Bd. 119. Springer-Verlag, Berlin, 1963.

[20] David A. Kessler. Epidemic size in the sis model of endemic infections. *Journal of Applied Probability*, 45(3):757–778, 09 2008.

[21] Neal Madras and Rinaldo Schinazi. Branching random walks on trees. *Stochastic Processes and their Applications*, 42(2):255 – 267, 1992.

[22] M. Metropolis, A. Rosenbluth, M. Rosenbluth, A. Teller, and M. Teller. Equation of state calculations by fast computing machines. *Journal of Chemical Physics*, 21:1087–1092, 1953.

[23] Michael Mitzenmacher, Rajmohan Rajaraman, and Scott Roche. Better bounds for coalescing-branching random walks, 2016. arXiv:1603.06109.

[24] Michael Mitzenmacher and Eli Upfal. *Probability and computing: Randomized algorithms and probabilistic analysis.* Cambridge University Press, 2005.

[25] Rongfeng Sun and Jan M Swart. The brownian net. *The Annals of Probability*, 36(3):1153–1208, 2008.

[26] Piet Van Mieghem. The n-intertwined sis epidemic network model. *Computing*, 93(2-4):147–169, December 2011.

Lock-free Transactions without Rollbacks for Linked Data Structures

Deli Zhang
de-li.zhang@knights.ucf.edu

Damian Dechev
dechev@cs.ucf.edu

Department of Computer Science
University of Central Florida
Orlando, FL 32817, USA

ABSTRACT

Non-blocking data structures allow scalable and thread-safe accesses to shared data. They provide individual operations that appear to execute atomically. However, it is often desirable to execute multiple operations atomically in a transactional manner. Previous solutions, such as software transactional memory (STM) and transactional boosting, manage transaction synchronization in an external layer separated from the data structure's own thread-level concurrency control. Although this reduces programming effort, it leads to overhead associated with additional synchronization and the need to rollback aborted transactions.

In this work, we present a new methodology for transforming high-performance lock-free linked data structures into high-performance lock-free transactional linked data structures without revamping the data structures' original synchronization design. Our approach leverages the semantic knowledge of the data structure to eliminate the overhead of false conflicts and rollbacks. We encapsulate all operations, operands, and transaction status in a transaction descriptor, which is shared among the nodes accessed by the same transaction. We coordinate threads to help finish the remaining operations of delayed transactions based on their transaction descriptors. When transaction fails, we recover the correct abstract state by reversely interpreting the logical status of a node.

In our experimental evaluation using transactions with randomly generated operations, our lock-free transactional lists and skiplist outperform the transactional boosted ones by 40% on average and as much as 125% for large transactions. They also outperform the alternative STM-based approaches by a factor of 3 to 10 across all scenarios. More importantly, we achieve 4 to 6 orders of magnitude less spurious aborts than the alternatives.

CCS Concepts

•**Computing methodologies** → **Concurrent algorithms;**

SPAA '16, July 11-13, 2016, Pacific Grove, CA, USA

DOI: http://dx.doi.org/10.1145/2935764.2935780

Keywords

Transactional Data Structure, Lock-free, Transactional Memory, Transactional Boosting

1. INTRODUCTION

With the growing prevalence of multi-core systems numerous highly concurrent non-blocking data structures have emerged [8,27,31,39]. Researchers and advanced users have been using libraries like LibCDS [1], Tervel [2] and Intel TBB [3], which are packed with efficient concurrent implementations of fundamental data structures. High level programming languages such as C#, JAVA and Scala also introduce concurrent libraries, which allow users who are unaware of the pitfalls of concurrent programming to safely take advantage of the performance benefits of increased concurrency. These libraries provide operations that appear to execute atomically when invoked individually. However, they fall short when users need to execute a sequence of operations atomically (i.e., compose operations in the manner of a transaction). For example, given a concurrent map data structure, the following code snippet implementing a simple COMPUTEIFABSENT pattern [11] is error prone.

```
if(!map.containsKey(key)) {
    value = ... // some computation
    map.put(key, value); }
```

The intention of this code is to compute a value and store it in the map, if and only if the map does not already contain the given key. The code snippet fails to achieve this since another thread may have stored a value associated with the same key right after the execution of CONTAINSKEY and before the invocation of PUT. As a result, the thread will overwrite the value inserted by the other thread upon the completion of PUT. Programmers may experience unexpected behavior due to the violation of the intended semantics of COMPUTEIFABSENT. Many Java programs encounter bugs that are caused by such non-atomic composition of operations [36]. Because of such hazards, users are often forced to fall back to locking and even coarse-grained locking, which has a negative impact on performance and annihilates the non-blocking progress guarantees provided by some concurrent containers.

The problem of implementing high-performance transac-

[1]http://libcds.sourceforge.net/
[2]http://ucf-cs.github.io/Tervel/
[3]https://www.threadingbuildingblocks.org/

tional data structures [4] is important and has recently gained much attention [2,11,12,13,19,21,26]. We refer to a transaction as sequence of linearizable operations on a concurrent data structure. This can be seen as a special case of memory transactions where the granularity of synchronization is on the data structure operation level instead of memory word level. We consider a concurrent data structure "transactional" if it supports executing transactions 1) atomically (i.e., if one operation fails, the entire transaction should abort), and 2) in isolation (i.e., concurrent executions of transactions appear to take effect in some sequential order).

Software transactional memory (STM) [22,37] can be used to conveniently construct transactional data structures from their sequential counterparts: operations executed within an STM transaction are guaranteed to be transactional. Despite the appeal of straightforward implementation, this approach has yet to gain practical acceptance due to its significant runtime overhead [3]. An STM instruments threads' memory accesses by recording the locations a thread reads in a *read set*, and the locations it writes in a *write set*. Conflicts are detected among the *read/write sets* of different threads. In the presence of conflicts, only one transaction is allowed to commit while the others are aborted and restarted. Apart from the overhead of metadata management, excessive transaction aborts in the presence of data structure "hot-spots" (memory locations that are constantly accessed by threads, e.g., the head node of a linked list) limit the overall concurrency [21]. The inherent disadvantage of STM concurrency control is that *low-level memory access conflicts do not necessarily correspond to high-level semantic conflicts.*

In this paper, we present *lock-free transactional transformation*: a methodology for transforming high-performance lock-free *base data structures* into high-performance lock-free transactional data structures. Our approach is applicable to a large class of linked data structures—ones that comprise a set of data nodes organized by references. We focus our discussion here on the data structures that implement the set *abstract data type* with three canonical operations INSERT, DELETE, and FIND. Linked data structures are desirable for concurrent applications because their distributed memory layout alleviates contention [38]. The specification for the base data structures thus defines an *abstract state*, which is the set of integer keys, and a *concrete state*, which consists of all accessible nodes. Lock-free transactional transformation treats the base data structure as a *white box*, and introduces a new code path for transaction-level synchronization using only the single-word COMPARE-ANDSWAP (CAS) synchronization primitive. The two key challenges for high-performance data structure transaction executions are: 1) to efficiently buffer write operations so that their modifications are invisible to operations outside the transaction scope; and 2) to minimize the penalty of rollbacks when aborting partially executed transactions.

To overcome the first challenge, we employ a cooperative transaction execution scheme in which threads help each other finish delayed transactions so that the delay does not propagate across the system. We embed a reference to a *transaction descriptor* in each node, which stores the instructions and arguments for operations along with a flag indicating the status of the transaction (i.e., active, committed, or aborted). A transaction descriptor is shared among a group of nodes accessed by the same transaction. When an operation tries to access a node, it first reads the node's descriptor and proceeds with its modification only if the descriptor indicates the previous transaction has committed or aborted. Otherwise, the operation helps execute the active transaction according to the instructions in the descriptor.

To overcome the second challenge, we introduce *logical rollback*—a process integrated into the transformed data structure to interpret the *logical status* of the nodes. This process interprets the logical status of the nodes left behind by an aborted transaction in such a way that concurrent operations observe a consistent abstract state as if the aborted transaction has been revoked. The logical status defines how the concrete state of a data structure (i.e., set of nodes) should be mapped to its abstract state (i.e., set of keys). Usually the mapping is simple—every node in the concrete state corresponds to a key in the abstract state. Previous works on lock-free data structures have been using *logical deletion* [18], in which a key is considered removed from the abstract state if the corresponding node is bit-marked. Logical deletion encodes a binary logical status so that a node maps to a key only if its reference has not been bit-marked. We generalize this technique by interpreting a node's logical status based on the combination of transaction status and operation type. The intuition behind our approach is that operations can recover the correct abstract state by *inversely interpreting* the logical status of the nodes with a descriptor indicating an aborted transaction. For example, if a transaction with two operations INSERT(3) and DELETE(4) fails because key 4 does not exist, the logical status of the newly inserted node with key 3 will be interpreted as *not inserted*.

We applied lock-free transaction transformation on an existing lock-free linked list and a lock-free skiplist to obtain their lock-free transactional counterparts. In our experimental evaluation, we compare them against the transactional data structures constructed from transactional boosting, a word-based STM, and an object-based STM. We execute a micro-benchmark on a 64-core NUMA system to measure the throughput and number of aborts under three types of workloads. The results show that our transactional data structures achieve an average of 40% speedup over transactional boosting based approaches, an average of 10 times speedup over the word-based STM, and an average of 3 times over the object-based STM. Moreover, the number of aborts generated by our approach are 4 orders of magnitude less than transactional boosting and 6 orders of magnitude less than STMs.

This paper makes the following contributions:

- To the best of our knowledge, lock-free transactional transformation is the first methodology that provides both lock-free progress and semantic conflict detection for data structure transactions.
- We introduce a node-based conflict detection scheme that does not rely on STM nor require the use of an additional data structure. This enables us to augment linked data structures with native transaction support.
- We propose an efficient recovery strategy based on interpreting the logical status of the nodes instead of explicitly revoking executed operations in an aborted transaction.

[4] Also referred as *atomic composite operations* [11]

- Data structures transformed by our approach gain substantial speedup over alternatives based on transactional boosting and the best-of-breed STMs; Due to cooperative execution in our approach, the number of aborts caused by node access conflict is brought down to a minimum.
- Because our transaction-level synchronization is compatible with the base data structure's thread-level synchronization, we are able to exploit the considerable amount of effort devoted to the development of lock-free data structures.

The rest of the paper is organized as follows. In Section 2, we explain our methodology in details. We present the template for building transactional linked lists and skiplists in Section 3. We reason about the correctness and progress properties of our algorithms in Section 4. The performance evaluation is presented in Section 5. In Section 6, we review existing approaches on constructing transactional data structures. We conclude the paper in Section 7.

2. LOCK-FREE TRANSACTIONAL TRANSFORMATION

Any transactional data structure must cope with two tasks: conflict detection and recovery. In previous works [12, 21], locks were commonly used to prevent access conflict, and undo logs were often used to discard speculative changes when a transaction aborts. In this work we introduce *lock-free transactional transformation*: a methodology that streamlines the execution of a transaction by abolishing locks and undo logs. Our lock-free transactional transformation combines three key ideas: 1) node-based semantic conflict detection; 2) interpretation-based logical rollback; and 3) cooperative transaction execution. In this section, we explain these ideas and introduce the core procedures that will be used by transformed data structures: a) the procedure to interpret the logical status of a node; b) the procedure to update an existing node with a new transaction descriptor; and c) the transaction execution procedure that orchestrates concurrent executions.

For clarity, we list the constants and data type definitions in Algorithm 1. In addition to the fields used by the base lock-free data structure, we introduce a new field *info* in NODE. NODEINFO stores *desc*, a reference to the shared transaction descriptor, and an index *opid*, which provides a history record on the last access (i.e., given a node n, $n.info.desc.ops[n.desc.opid]$ is the most recent operation that accessed it). A node is considered *active* when the last transaction that accessed the node had an active status (i.e., $n.info.desc.status$ = Active). A descriptor [24] is a shared object commonly used in lock-free programming to announce steps that cannot be done by a single atomic primitive. The functionalities of our transaction descriptor is twofold: 1) it stores all the necessary context for helping finish a delayed transaction; and 2) it shares the transaction status among all nodes participating in the same transaction. For set operations, we pack the high-level instructions including the operation type and the operand using only 8 bytes per operation. We also employ the pointer marking technique described by Harris [18] to designate logically deleted nodes. The macros for pointer marking are defined in Algorithm 2. The *Mark* flag is co-located with the *info* pointers.

Algorithm 1 Type Definitions

```
enum TxStatus
    Active
    Committed
    Aborted
enum OpType
    Insert
    Delete
    Find
struct Operation
    OpType type
    int key
struct Desc
    int size
    TxStauts status
    Operation ops[ ]
struct NodeInfo
    Desc* desc
    int opid
struct Node
    NodeInfo* info
    int key
    ...
```

Algorithm 2 Pointer Marking

```
int Mark ← 0x1
define SetMark(p) (p | Mark)
define ClearMark(p) (p & ∼ Mark)
define IsMarked(p) (p & Mark)
```

2.1 Node-based Conflict Detection

In our approach, conflicts are detected at the granularity of a node. If two transactions access different nodes (i.e. the method calls in them commute [21]), they are allowed to proceed concurrently. In this case, shared-memory accesses are coordinated by the concurrency control protocol in the base data structure. Otherwise, threads proceed in a cooperative manner as detailed in Section 2.4. For set data types, each node is associated with a unique key, thus our conflict detection operates at the same granularity as the abstract locking used by transactional boosting.

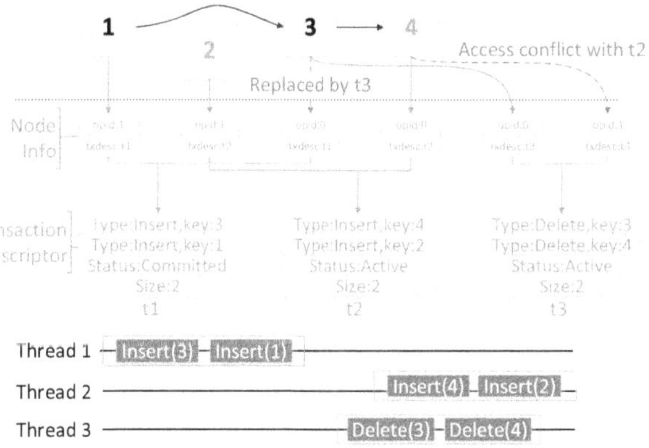

Figure 1: Transaction Execution and Conflict

We illustrate an example of node access conflict in Figure 1. At the beginning, Thread 1 committed a transaction *t1* inserting keys 1 and 3. Thread 2 attempted to insert keys 4 and 2 in transaction *t2*, while Thread 3 was concurrently executing transaction *t3* to delete keys 3 and 4. Thread 3 was able to perform its first operation by updating the *info* pointer on node 3 with a new NODEINFO. However, it encounters a conflict when attempting to update node 4 because Thread 2 has yet to finish its second operation. To enforce serialization, operations must not modify an active node. In order to guarantee lock-free progress, the later

Algorithm 3 Logical Status

```
function IsNodePresent(Node* n, int key)
    return n.key = key
function IsKeyPresent(NodeInfo* info, Desc* desc)
    OpType op ← info.desc.ops[info.opid]
    TxStatus status ← info.desc.status
    switch (status)
      case: Active
        if info.desc = desc then
          return op = Find or op = Insert
        else
          return op = Find or op = Delete
      case: Committed
        return op = Find or op = Insert
      case: Aborted
        return op = Find or op = Delete
```

Algorithm 4 Update NodeInfo

```
1:  function UpdateInfo(Node* n, NodeInfo* info,
    bool, wantkey)
2:    NodeInfo* oldinfo ← n.info
3:    if IsMarked(oldinfo) then
4:      Do_Delete(n)
5:      return retry
6:    if oldinfo.desc ≠ info.desc then
7:      ExecuteOps(oldinfo.desc, oldinfo.opid + 1)
8:    else if oldinfo.opid ≥ info.opid then
9:      return success
10:   bool haskey ← IsKeyPresent(oldinfo)
11:   if (!haskey and wantkey) or (haskey and !wantkey)
    then
12:     return fail
13:   if info.desc.status ≠ Active then
14:     return fail
15:   if CAS(&n.info, oldinfo, info) then
16:     return success
17:   else
18:     return retry
```

transaction must help carry out the remaining operations in the other active transaction.

Our synchronization protocol is *pessimistic* in that it assigns a node to a transaction as soon as an operation requires it, for the duration of the transaction. Moreover, node-based conflict detection effectively compartmentalizes the execution of transactions. Completed operations will not be affected should a later operation in the transaction experience contention and need to retry (most lock-free data structures use CAS-based retry loops). Each node acts as a checkpoint; once an operation successfully updates a node, the transaction advances one step towards completion. Data-based conflict detection, due to the lack of such algorithm-specific knowledge, has to restart the whole transaction upon conflict.

2.2 Logical Status Interpretation

To achieve isolation in transaction executions, a write operation needs to buffer or "hide" its update until the transaction commits; and to achieve atomicity it needs to revoke its modifications upon transaction abort. In the context of data structure transactions, existing strategies undo the operations by invoking their inverse operations [21]. This would incur a significant penalty because the compute cycles spent on the inverse operations do not contribute to the overall throughput and introduce additional contention. We approach the recovery task from another angle: an aborted transaction does not need to physically invoke the inverse methods; executed operations in an aborted transaction just need to *appear to have be undone.* We achieve this by having operations *inversely interpret* the logical status of nodes accessed by operations in an aborted transaction. Both physical undo and our logical undo reach the same goal of restoring the abstract state of the data structure.

In Algorithm 3, we list the function to interpret the logical status of a node according to the value of the transaction descriptor. Function IsNodePresent, verifies that a node associated with a specific key is present. This is a common test found in existing linked data structures. Given a node's presence, function IsKeyPresent verifies if the key should be logically included in the abstract state, and returns a boolean value based on the combination of operation type and transaction status. For a node most recently accessed by an Insert operation, its key is considered present if the transaction has successfully *committed.* On the contrary, according to the semantics of Delete, a successful operation must remove the key from the set. Thus for a node most recently accessed by a Delete operation, its key is considered present if the transaction has *aborted.* These two opposite interpretations also match previous observations that Insert and Delete are a pair of inverse operations [21]. Since the Find operation is read-only, no rollback is needed. The node's key is always present regardless the status of the transaction. A special case is the operations in an active transaction, which we treat as committed but are visible only to subsequent operations within the same transaction scope.

2.3 Logical Status Update

As mentioned above, the logical status of a node depends on the interpretation of its transaction descriptor. In a transformed data structure, an operation needs to change a node's logical status before performing any necessary low-level node manipulations. This is done by updating the node's NodeInfo pointer as shown in Algorithm 4. Given a node n, the function UpdateInfo reads its current $info$ field (line 4.2 [5]), verifies its sanity, and attempts to update $n.info$ through the use of CAS (line 4.15). It returns a tri-state value indicating whether the operation succeeded, failed, or should be retried. We make sure that any other active transaction accessing n is completed by helping execute its remaining operations (line 4.7). However, we have to avoid helping the same transaction because of the hazard of infinite recursions. This is prevented by the condition check on line 4.6. We also skip the update and report success if the operation has already been performed by other threads (line 4.8). Due to the use of the helping mechanism, the same operation may be executed multiple times by different threads. The condition check on line 4.8 allows us to identify the node accessed by threads that execute the same transaction, and ensures consistent results. We validate the presence of the key on line 4.10 and test if the key's presence

[5]We denote line b from algroithm a by $a.b$

Algorithm 5 Transaction Execution

```
1: thread_local Stack helpstack
2: function ExecuteTransaction(Desc* desc)
3:     helpstack.Init()
4:     ExecuteOps(desc, 0)
5:     return desc.status = Committed

6: function ExecuteOps(Desc* desc, int opid)
7:     bool ret ← true
8:     set delnodes
9:     if helpstack.Contains(desc) then
10:        CAS(&desc.flag, Active, Aborted)
11:        return
12:    helpstack.Push(desc)
13:    while desc.status = Active and ret and opid <
       desc.size do
14:        Operation* op ← desc.ops[opid]
15:        if op.type = Find then
16:            ret ← Find(op.key, desc, opid)
17:        else if op.type = Insert then
18:            ret ← Insert(op.key, desc, opid)
19:        else if op.type = Delete then
20:            Node* del
21:            ret ← Delete(op.key, desc, opid, del)
22:            delnodes.Insert(del)
23:        opid ← opid + 1
24:    helpstack.Pop()
25:    if ret = true then
26:        if CAS(&desc.flag, Active, Committed) then
27:            MarkDelete(delnodes, desc)
28:    else
29:        CAS(&desc.flag, Active, Aborted)
```

(as required by deletions and finds), or lack of presence (as required by insertions), is desired on line 4.11. The boolean flag *wantkey* is passed on by the caller function to indicate if the presence of key is desired. The operation reports failure when *wantkey* contradicts *haskey*. Finally, we validate that the transaction is still active (line 4.13) to prevent a terminated transaction from erroneously overwriting *n.info*.

2.4 Transaction Execution

We consider the transaction execution model in which a transaction explicitly aborts upon the first operation failure. The ExecuteTransaction in Algorithm 5 is the entry point of transaction execution, which is invoked by the thread that initiates a transaction. The ExecuteOps function executes operations in sequence starting from *opid*. For threads that help to execute a delayed transaction, the *opid* could be in the range of [1, *desc.size*]. In each step of the while loop (line 5.13), the return value of the previous operation is verified. We require the operations to return a boolean value indicating if the executions are successful. A false value indicates the precondition required by the operation is unsatisfied and the transaction will abort. Once all operations complete successfully we atomically update the transaction status with a *Committed* flag (line 5.26). It is not necessary to retry this CAS operation as a failed CAS indicates that some other thread must have successfully updated the transaction status. The thread that successfully executed the CAS will be responsible for performing physical node deletion (line 5.27), which will be explained in Section 3.

By adopting cooperative transaction execution, our approach is able to eliminate the majority of aborts caused by access conflicts. Although rare, potential livelock is possible if two threads were to access two of the same nodes in opposite order. In such cases, both threads will be trapped in infinite recursions helping execute each other's transaction. We detect and recover from this hazard by using a per-thread *help stack*, which is a simple stack containing *Desc* pointers. This is similar to a function call stack, except it records the invocation of ExecuteOps. A thread initializes its help stack before initiating a transaction. Each time a thread begins to help another transaction, it pushes the transaction descriptor onto its help stack. A thread pops its help stack once the help completes. Cyclic dependencies among transactions can be detected by checking for duplicate entries in the help stack (line 5.9). We recover by aborting one of the transactions as shown on line 5.10.

3. APPLICATION EXAMPLES

In this section we demonstrate the application of our lock-free transaction transformation on linked lists and skiplists based sets. The process involves two steps: 1) identify and encapsulate the base data structure's methods for locating, inserting, and deleting nodes; and 2) integrate the UpdateInfo function (Algorithm 4) in each operation using the templates provided in this section.

The first step is necessary because we still rely on the base algorithm and its concurrency control to add, update, and remove linkage among nodes. This is a refactoring process, as we do not alter the functionality of the base implementations. Although implementation details such as argument types and return values may vary, we need to extract the following three functions: Do_LocatePred, Do_Insert, and Do_Delete. We add a prefix Do_ to indicate these are the methods provided by the base data structures. For brevity, we omit detailed code listings, but express the general functionality specifications. Given a key, Do_LocatePred returns the target node (and any necessary variables for linking and unlinking a node, e.g., its predecessor). Do_Insert creates the necessary linkage to correctly place the new node in the data structure. Do_Delete removes any references to the node. Note that some lock-free data structures [10, 18] employ a two-phased deletion algorithm, where the actual node removal is delayed or even separated from the first phase of logical deletion. In this case, we only expect Do_Delete to perform the logical deletion as nodes will be physically removed during the next traversal.

Algorithm 6 lists the template for the transformed Insert function. The function resembles the base node insertion algorithm with a CAS-based while loop (line 6.4). The only addition is the code path for invoking UpdateInfo on line 6.7. The logic is simple: on line 6.6 we check if the data structure already contains a node with the target key. If so, we try to update the node's logical status, otherwise we fall back to the base code path to insert a new node. Should any of the two code paths indicate a retry due to contention, we start the traversal over again.

The Delete operation listed in Algorithm 8 is identical to Insert except it terminates with failure when the target node does not exist (line 8.13). We also adopt a two-phase process for unlinking nodes from the data structure: deleted

Algorithm 6 Template for Transformed Insert Function

```
function Insert(int key, Desc* desc, int opid)
    NodeInfo* info ← new NodeInfo
    info.desc ← desc, info.opid ← opid
    while true do
        Node* curr ← Do_LocatePred(key)
        if IsNodePresent(curr, key) then
            ret ← UpdateInfo(curr, info, false)
        else
            Node* n ← new Node
            n.key ← key, n.info ← info
            ret ← Do_Insert(n)
        if ret = success then
            return true
        else if ret = fail then
            return false
```

Algorithm 7 Template for Transformed Find Function

```
function Find(int key, Desc* desc, int opid)
    NodeInfo* info ← new NodeInfo
    info.desc ← desc, info.opid ← opid
    while true do
        Node* curr ← Do_LocatePred(key)
        if IsNodePresent(curr, key) then
            ret ← UpdateInfo(curr, info, true)
        else
            ret ← fail
        if ret = success then
            return true
        else if ret = fail then
            return false
```

Algorithm 8 Template for Transformed Delete Function

```
1: function Delete(int key, Desc* desc, int opid,
   ref Node* del)
2:     NodeInfo* info ← new NodeInfo
3:     info.desc ← desc, info.opid ← opid
4:     while true do
5:         Node* curr ← Do_LocatePred(key)
6:         if IsNodePresent(curr, key) then
7:             ret ← UpdateInfo(curr, info, true)
8:         else
9:             ret ← fail
10:        if ret = success then
11:            del ← curr
12:            return true
13:        else if ret = fail then
14:            del ← NIL
15:            return false

16: function MarkDelete(set delnodes, Desc* desc)
17:    for del ∈ delnodes do
18:        if del = NIL then
19:            continue
20:        NodeInfo* info ← del.info
21:        if info.desc ≠ desc then
22:            continue
23:        if CAS(del.info, info, SetMark(info)) then
24:            Do_Delete(del)
```

nodes will firstly be buffered in a local set in ExecuteOps, and when the transaction commits, the *info* field of buffered nodes will be marked (line 8.23) and consequently unlinked from the data structure by invoking the base data structures' Do_Delete. One advantage of our logical status interpretation is that unlinking nodes from the data structure is optional, whereas in transactional boosting nodes must be physically unlinked to restore the abstract state. This opens up opportunities to optimize performance based on application scenarios. Timely unlinking deleted nodes is important for linked lists because the number of "zombie" nodes has linear impact on sequential search time. Leaving delete nodes in the data structure may be beneficial for skiplists because the overhead and contention introduced by unlinking nodes may outweigh the slight increase in sequential search time ($\mathcal{O}(logn)$).

The Find operation listed in Algorithm 7 also needs to update the node's *info* pointer. Without this, concurrent deletions may remove the node after Find has returned and before the transaction commits. Since we have extracted the core functionality of interpreting and updating logical status into a common subroutine, the transformation process is generic and straightforward. To use a transformed data structure, the application should first initialize and fill a Desc structure, then invoke ExecuteTransaction (Algorithm 5) with it as an argument. The allocation of the transaction descriptor contributes to most of the transaction execution overhead. We discuss this in more details in Section 5.

4. CORRECTNESS

We base our correctness discussion on the notion of commutativity isolation [21], which states that the history of committed transactions is *strictly serializable* for any transactional data structure that provides linearizable operations and obeys commutativity isolation [6]. STM systems may prefer more strict correctness criteria, such as opacity [16], because they need to account for the consistency of intermediate memory access. In the case of data structure transactions, the intermediate computation is managed by linearizable methods, and only the end result of a transaction is accessible to users. Strict serializability [33], which is the analogue of linearizability [25] for transactions, provides enough semantics for such cases.

4.1 Definitions

We provide a brief recapitulation of the definitions and correctness rules from Herlihy and Koskinen's work [21]. A *history* of computation is a sequence of instantaneous events. Events associated with a method call include invocation I and response R. A single transaction running in isolation defines a *sequential history.* A *sequential specification* for a data structure defines a set of *legal histories* for that data structure.

Definition 1. *A history h is strictly serializable if the subsequence of h consisting of all events of committed transac-*

[6]We omit the discussion of rules on compensating actions and disposable methods because they are not applicable to our approach

tions is equivalent to a legal history in which these transactions execute sequentially in the order they commit.

Definition 2. *Two method calls I, R and I', R' commute if: for all histories h, if $h \cdot I \cdot R$ and $h \cdot I' \cdot R'$ are both legal, then $h \cdot I \cdot R \cdot I' \cdot R'$ and $h \cdot I' \cdot R' \cdot I \cdot R$ are both legal and define the same abstract state.*

Commutativity identifies operations that have no dependencies on each other. Executing commutative operations in any order yields the same abstract state. The commutativity specification for set operations is as follows:

$$\begin{aligned} \text{INSERT}(x) &\leftrightarrow \text{INSERT}(y),\ x \neq y \\ \text{DELETE}(x) &\leftrightarrow \text{DELETE}(y),\ x \neq y \\ \text{INSERT}(x) &\leftrightarrow \text{DELETE}(y),\ x \neq y \\ \text{FIND}(x) \leftrightarrow \text{INSERT}(x)/false &\leftrightarrow \text{DELETE}(x)/false \end{aligned} \tag{1}$$

Rule 1. ***Linearizability:*** *For any history h, two concurrent invocations I and I' must be equivalent to either the history $h \cdot I \cdot R \cdot I' \cdot R'$ or the history $h \cdot I' \cdot R' \cdot I \cdot R$*

Rule 2. ***Commutativity Isolation:*** *For any non-commutative method calls $I_1, R_1 \in T_1$ and $I_2, R_2 \in T_2$, either T_1 commits or aborts before any additional method calls in T_2 are invoked, or vice-versa.*

4.2 Serializability and Recoverability

We now show that lock-free transactional transformation meets the two above correctness requirements. We denote the concrete state of a set as an node set N. At any time, the abstract state observed by transaction T_i is $S_i = \{n.key \mid n \in N \land \text{ISKEYPRESENT}(n.info,\ desc_i)\}$, where $desc_i$ is the descriptor of T_i.

Linearizability requires that concurrent operations appear as if they took place instantaneously at some points between their invocations and responses. We show the transformed operations are linearizable by identifying their *linearization points*. Additionally, we use the notion of decision points and state-read points to facilitate our reasoning. The decision point of an operation is defined as the atomic statement that finitely decides the result of an operation, i.e. independent of the result of any subsequent instruction after that point. A state-read point is defined as the atomic statement where the state of the dictionary, which determines the outcome of the decision point, is read.

Lemma 1. *The set operations* INSERT, DELETE, *and* FIND *are linearizable.*

Proof. For the transformed INSERT operation, the execution is divided into two code paths by the condition check on line 6.6. The code path on line 6.7 updates the existing node's logical status. Note that if the operation reports failure on line 4.12 and 4.14, no write operation will be performed to change the logical status of the node. The state-read point for the former case is when the previous transaction status is read from *oldinfo.desc.status* on line 3.5. The state-read point for the later case is when the current transaction status is read from *info.desc.status* on line 4.13. The abstract states S' observed by all transactions immediately after the reads are unchanged, i.e., $\forall i, S'_i = S_i$. For a successful logical status update, the decision point for it to take effect is when the CAS operation on line 4.15 succeeds. The abstract states S' observed by the transactions T_d executing this operation immediately after the CAS is $i = d \implies S'_i = S_i \cup n.key$. For all other transactions $i \neq d \implies S'_i = S_i$. In all cases, the update of abstract states conforms to the sequential specification of the insert operation. The code path for physically adding linkage to the new node (line 6.11) is linearizable because the corresponding DO_INSERT operation in the base data structure is linearizable.

The same reasoning process applies to the transformed DELETE and FIND operations because they share the same logical status update procedure with INSERT. □

The commutativity isolation rule prevents operations that are not commutative from being executed concurrently.

Lemma 2. *Conflict detection in lock-free transactional transformation satisfies the commutativity isolation rule.*

Proof. As identified in Equation 1, two set operations commute if they access the different keys. Because of the one-to-one mapping from node to keys, we have $\forall n_x, n_y \in N, x \neq y \implies n_x \neq n_y \implies n_x.key \neq n_y.key$. This means that two set operations commute if they access two different nodes. Let T_1 denotes a transaction that currently accesses node n_1, i.e., $n_1.info.desc = desc_1 \land desc_1.status = Active$. If another transaction T_2 were to access n_1, it must perform EXECUTEOPS for T_1 on line 4.7 because EXECUTEOPS always update the transaction status when it returns on line 5.26 or 5.29 (note that failed CAS also means the transaction status has been set, but another thread). We thus ensure that $desc_1.status = Committed \lor desc_1.status = Aborted$ before T_2 proceeds. □

Theorem 1. *For a data structure generated by lock-free transactional transform, the history of committed transactions is strictly serializable.*

Proof. Follow Lemma 1, and 2, and the conclusion in Herlihy and Koskinen's work [21], the theorem holds. □

Theorem 2. *For a data structure generated by lock-free transactional transformation, any history defines the same abstract state as a history with aborted transactions removed.*

Proof. Let T_1 be an aborted transaction with descriptor $desc_1$. We denote S as the abstract state immediately after T_1 aborts. Let history $h = F_1 \cdot F'_1 \cdots F_2 \cdot F'_2 \cdot F_x \cdots F'_y$ be the sequence of linearizable method calls after T_1 starts and until T_1 aborts, where $F_i, 1 \leq i \leq x$ denotes the method calls successfully executed by T_1, and $F'_i, 1 \leq i \leq y$ denotes the method calls executed by other transactions. The interleaving of these method calls is arbitrary. Follow commutativity isolation in Lemma 2 we assure that the method calls after F_x must commute with F_x, thus we can swap them without changing the abstract state. By progressively doing this for $F_i, 1 \leq i \leq x$, we obtain an equivalent history $h = h' = F'_1 \cdots F'_2 \cdots F'_y \cdots F_1 \cdot F_2 \cdots F_x$. Let n_x be the node accessed by F_x we denote S' as the abstract state before the invocation of F_x. Because of the inverse interpretation of logical status we can assert $n_x.key \in S' \implies n_x.key \in S \land n_x.key \notin S' \implies n_x.key \notin S$. Thus, we have $S' = S$ and we can remove F_x from h' without altering the abstract state. Doing this for $F_i, 1 \leq i \leq x$, we obtain $h = h' = h'' = F'_1 \cdots F'_2 \cdots F'_y \cdots$, hence T_1 is removed from the history. □

4.3 Progress Guarantees

Lock-free transaction transform provides lock-free progress because it guarantees that for every possible execution scenario, at least one thread makes progress in finite steps by either committing or aborting a transaction. We reason about this property by examining unbounded loops in all possible executions paths, which can delay the termination of the operations. For a system with i threads, the upper bound of the number of active transactions is i. Consider the while loop that executes the operations on line 5.13. This loop is bounded by the maximum number of operations in a transaction, denoted as j, but threads may set out to help each other during the execution of each of the operations. The number of recursive helping invocations is bound by the number of active transactions. In the worst case where only 1 thread remains live and $i-1$ threads have failed, the system guarantees a transaction will commit in at most $i * j$ steps. In the presence of cyclic dependencies among transactions, the system guarantees that a duplicate transaction descriptor will be detected within $i * j$ steps.

Our cooperative contention management strategy requires that the users specify all operations in a transaction beforehand. It is possible to allow dynamic transaction executions by adopting aggressive contention management (i.e., the later transaction always forcibly aborts the competitor). In this case, the progress guarantee provided by the system degrades to obstruction-free. We focus on the lock-free implementations because the obstruction-free versions can be trivially obtained by disabling the helping mechanism in the lock-free version.

5. PERFORMANCE EVALUATION

We compare the overhead and scalability of our lock-free transactional list and skiplist against the implementations based on transaction boosting, NOrec STM from Rochester Software Transactional Memory package [29] and Fraser's lock-free object-based STM [10]. RSTM is the best available comprehensive suite of prevailing STM implementations. In our test, TML [5] and its extension NOrec [5] are among the fastest on our platform. They have extreme low overhead and good scalability due to elimination of ownership records. We choose NOrec as the representative implementation because its value-based validation allows for more concurrency for readers with no actual conflict.

For transaction boosting, we implement the lookup of abstract lock using Intel TBB's concurrent hash map. Although the transaction boosting is designed to be used in tandem with STMs for replaying undo logs, it is not necessary in our test case as the data structures are tested in isolation. To reduce the runtime overhead, we scrap the STM environment and implement a lightweight per-thread undo log for the boosted data structures. We employ a micro-benchmark to evaluate performance in three types of workloads: write dominated, read dominated, and mixed. This canonical evaluation method [5, 18] consists of a tight loop that randomly chooses to perform a fixed size transaction with a mixture of INSERT, DELETE and FIND operations according to the workload type. We also vary the transaction size (i.e., the number of operations in a transaction) from 1 to 16 to measure the performance impact of rollbacks. The tests are conducted on a 64-core NUMA system (4 AMD opteron 6272 CPUs with 16 cores per chip @2.1 GHz). Both the micro-benchmark and the data structure implementations are compiled with GCC 4.7 with C++11 features and O3 optimizations. [7]

5.1 Transactional List

We show the throughput and the number of spurious aborts in Figure 2 for all three types of lists. The throughput is measured in terms of number of completed operations per second, which is the product of the number of committed transactions and transaction size. The number of spurious aborts takes into account the number of aborted transactions except self-aborted ones (i.e., those that abort due to failed operations). This is an indicator for the effectiveness of the contention management strategy. Each thread performs 10^5 transactions and the key range is set up to 10^4. Our lock-free transactional list is denoted by LFT, the boosted list by BST, and the NOrec STM list by NTM. The underlying list implementations for both LFT and BST were based on Harris' lock-free design [18]. The linked list for NTM is taken directly from the benchmark implementation in RSTM suite. Since the lock-free list and the RSTM list use different memory management scheme, we disable node reclamation for fair comparison of the synchronization protocols. For each list legend annotation, we append a numeric postfix to denote the transaction size (e.g., BST-4 means the boosted list tested with 4 operations in one transaction).

In Figure 2a, threads perform solely write operations. The upper half of the graph shows the throughput with both y- and x-axes in logarithm scale. Starting with transaction of size 1, the throughput curve of BST-1 and LFT-1 essentially expose the overhead difference between the two transaction synchronization protocols. Because each transaction contains only one operation, the code paths for transaction rollback in BST and transaction helping in LFT will not be taken. For each node operation, BST-1 needs to acquire and release a mutex lock, while LFT-1 needs to allocate a transaction descriptor. For executions within one CPU chip (no more than 16 threads), LFT-1 maintains a moderate performance advantage to BST-1, averaging more than 15% speedup. As the execution spawns across multiple chips, LFT-1's performance is setback by the use of descriptor, which incurs more remote memory accesses. This trend can be observed for all scenarios with different transaction sizes. Another noticeable trend is that LFT lists gain better performance as the transaction size grows. For example, on 64 threads the throughput of LFT-2 slightly falls short behind that of BST-2, then the performance of LFT-4 is on par with BST-4, and finally LFT-8 and LFT-16 outperforms their BST counterpart by as much as 50%. Two factors contribute to the great scalability of LFT lists in handling large transactions: 1) its helping mechanism manages conflict and greatly reduces spurious aborts whereas in BST such aborts cause a significant amount of rollbacks; 2) the number of allocated transaction descriptors decreases as the transaction size grows whereas in BST the number of required lock acquisitions stays the same.

Generally, we observe that for small transaction sizes (no more than 4 operations), BST and LFT lists explore fine-grained parallelism and exhibit similar scalability trends. The throughput increases linearly until 16 threads, and continues to increase at a slower pace until 64 threads. Because

[7] All source code can be downloaded from http://cse.eecs.ucf.edu/gitlab/deli/transactional-linked-data-structure

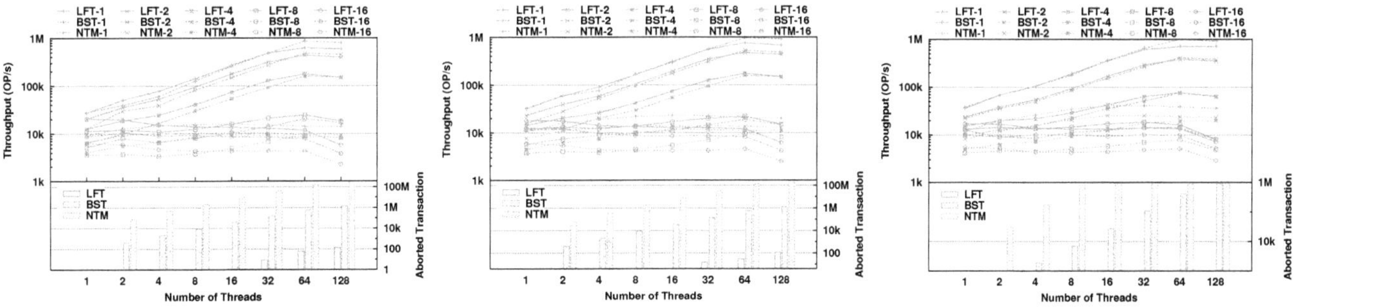

(a) 50% INSERT, 50% DELETE, 0% FIND (b) 33% INSERT, 33% DELETE, 34% FIND (c) 15% INSERT, 5% DELETE, 80% FIND

Figure 2: Throughput and Spurious Abort Counts for Transaction Lists (10K Key Range)

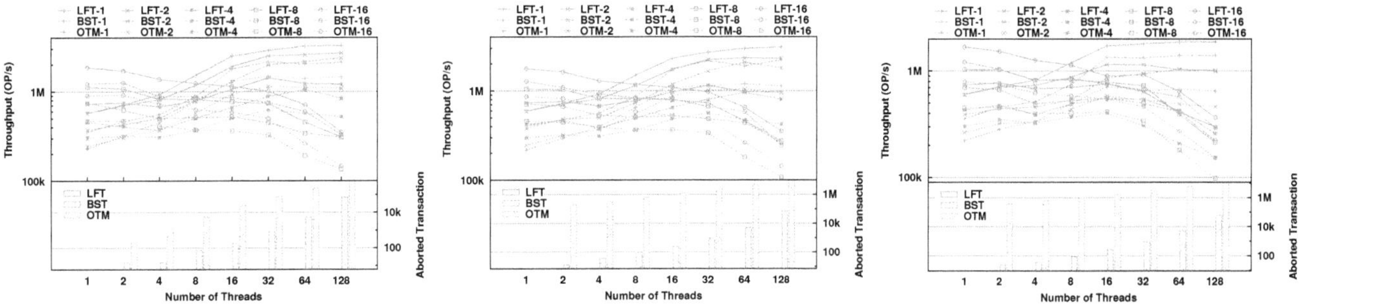

(a) 50% INSERT, 50% DELETE, 0% FIND (b) 33% INSERT, 33% DELETE, 34% FIND (c) 15% INSERT, 5% DELETE, 80% FIND

Figure 3: Throughput and Spurious Abort Counts for Transaction Skiplists (1M Key Range)

executions beyond 16 threads span across multiple chips, the performance growth is slightly reduced due to the cost of remote memory accesses. The executions are no longer fully concurrent beyond 64 threads, thus the overall throughput is capped and may even reduce due to context switching overhead. LFT lists obtain an average of 25% speedup over BST lists. For large transactions, the throughputs of both LFT and BST list do not scale well. This could be attributed to the semantic and the randomness of the benchmark. As the transaction size grows, the probability of a randomly generated sequence of operations will all succeed is inherently smaller. Most of the transactions were self-aborted due to some failed attempts to locate the target element. LFT lists outperforms BST lists by an average of 40% in these scenarios. On the other hand, the throughput of all NTM lists stagnates as the number of threads increases. Since NTM uses a single writer lock, concurrency is precluded for this write-dominated test case. On 64 threads, both BST and LFT lists are able to achieve as much as 10 times better performance than NTM lists.

On the bottom half of Figure 2a, we illustrate the histogram of spurious aborts across all transaction sizes and cluster them by thread counts. The y-axis is in logarithmic scale. For BST lists and NTM lists the number of spurious aborts grows linearly with the increase of threads. BST lists have about 100 times less aborts than NTM lists, which matches our intuition that semantic conflict detection can remarkably reduce the number of false conflicts. Also as expected no approach incurs spurious aborts in single thread scenario. Remarkably, LFT lists do not introduce spurious aborts until 32 threads, and the number of aborts is 4 orders of magnitude smaller than that of BST lists. The helping mechanism of LFT is able to resolve majority of the conflicts in a cooperative manner, and aborts only when cyclic dependencies exist among transactions.

We show the results from mixed and read-dominated workloads in Figure 2b and 2c. The throughputs follow the same pattern as in Figure 2a with LFT lists' performance advantage slightly diminishes in read-dominated workload. This is because the FIND operations in LFT lists also update descriptors in nodes, which requires extra cycles compared with read-only BST FIND operations. Nevertheless, LFT lists still maintain an average of 20% speedup over BST lists in these scenarios and achieves as much as 40% throughput gain for large transactions. Because of allowing reader concurrency, NTM lists also exhibit some degree of scalability in read-dominated scenarios.

5.2 Transactional Skiplist

In Figure 3, we show the throughput and the number of spurious aborts for three types of transactional skiplists. All of them are based on Fraser's open source lock-free skiplist [10], and the epoch-based garbage collection is enabled in all three. The naming convention for BST and LFT skiplists remain the same as in Figure 2. We denote the STM based skiplist as OTM because it uses Fraser's object-based STM. Compared with word-based STMs, an object-based STM groups memory into blocks thus reducing metadata overhead. Since skiplists have logarithmic search time, we are able to stress the algorithms with heavier workloads: each threads now performs 1 million transactions and the key range is also boosted to 1 million.

Overall, with a peak throughput of more than 3 million (OP/s), transaction execution on skiplists is considerably more efficient than on linked lists. Also both OTM and BST skiplists generates 2 orders or magnitude less spurious aborts than their list counterparts. Because skiplist algorithms traverse exponentially less nodes than list algorithms, a single operation can finish much sooner, which greatly reduces the probability of memory access conflicts in STM and lock acquisition time out in transaction boosting. Another noteworthy difference is that the divergent scalability trends of large and small transactions. As we can see in Figure 3a, large transaction such as LFT-8 and LFT-16 achieves maximum throughputs on a single thread, then their throughputs steadily fall as the number of threads increases. On the contrary, the throughputs of small transactions such as LFT-2 and LFT-4 start low, but gain momentum as more threads are added. Large transactions have lower synchronization overhead but are vulnerable to conflict. As the number of threads increases, a failed large transaction could easily forfeit a considerable amount of operations. On the flip side, small transactions incur greater synchronization overhead, but are less likely to encounter conflicts when more threads contend with each other.

Despite the differences, we still observe performance results generally similar to that of transaction lists. LFT and BST skiplists outperform OTM skiplists by as much as 3 times across all scenarios, while LFT skiplists maintain an average of 60% speedup over BST for large transactions. For example, in Figure 3a on 32 threads LFT-8 outperforms BST-8 by 125%. Even for small transactions, LFT skiplists begin to set the throughput apart from BST skiplists further than what is in Figure 2. For example, in Figure 3b on 32 threads LFT-2 achieves an 30% speedup over BST-2.

6. RELATED WORK

Non-blocking linked data structures have been extensively studied because their distributed memory layout provides data access parallelism and scalability under high levels of contention [18, 27, 31, 39]. To the best of our knowledge, there is no existing linked data structure that provides native support for transactions. A transactional execution of data structure operations can be seen as a restricted form of *software transactions* [17], in which the memory layout and the semantics of the operations are well defined according to the specification of the data structure. Straightforward generic constructions can be implemented by executing all shared memory accesses in coarse-grained *atomic sections*, which can employ either optimistic (e.g., STM) or pessimistic (e.g., lock inference) concurrency control. More sophisticated approaches [2, 12, 21] exploit semantic conflict detection for transaction-level synchronization to reduce benign conflicts. We draw inspirations from previous semantic based conflict detection approaches. However, with the specific knowledge on linked data structure, we further optimize the transaction execution by performing in-place conflict detection and contention management on existing nodes.

6.1 Transactional Memory

Initially proposed as a set of hardware extensions by Herlihy and Moss [23], transactional memory was intended to facilitate the development of lock-free data structures. However, due to current HTM's cache-coherency based conflict detection scheme, transactions are subject to spurious failures during page faults and context switches [6]. This makes HTM less desirable for data structure implementations. Considerable amount of work and ingenuity has instead gone into designing lock-free data structures using low-level synchronization primitives such as COMPAREANDSWAP, which empowers researchers to devise algorithm-specific fine-grained concurrency control protocol.

The first software transactional memory was proposed by Shavit and Touitou [37], which is lock-free but only supports a static set of data items. Herlihy, et al., later presented DSTM [22] that supports dynamic data sets on the condition that the progress guarantee is relaxed to obstruction-freedom. Over the years, a large number of STM implementations have been proposed [5, 7, 10, 29, 35]. We omit complete reviews because it is out of the scope of this paper. As more design choices were explored [28], we have seen emerging discussions on the issues of STM regarding usability [34], performance [3], and expressiveness [15]. There is also an increasing realization that the read/write conflicts inherently provide insufficient support for concurrency when shared objects are subject to contention [26]. It has been suggested that "STM may not deliver the promised efficiency and simplicity for *all* scenario, and multitude of approaches should be explored catering to different needs" [1].

6.2 Lock Inference

STM implementations are typically *optimistic*, which means they execute under the assumption that interferences are unlikely to occur. They maintain computationally expensive redo or undo logs to allow replay or rollback in case a transaction experiences interference. In light of this shortcoming, pessimistic alternatives based on lock inference have been proposed [30]. These algorithms synthesize enough locks through static analysis to prevent data races in atomic sections. The choice of locking granularity has an impact on the trade-off between concurrency and overhead. Some approaches require programmers' annotation [11] to specify the granularity, others automatically infer locks at a fixed granularity [9] or even multiple granularities [4]. Nevertheless, most approaches associate locks with memory locations, which may lead to reduced parallelism due to false conflicts as seen in STM. Applying these approaches to real-world programs also faces scalability changes in the presence of large libraries [14] because of the high complexity involved in the static analysis process. Moreover, the use of locks degrades any non-blocking progress guarantee one might expect from using a non-blocking library.

6.3 Semantic Conflict Detection

Considering the imprecise nature of data-based conflict detection, semantic-based approaches have been proposed to identify conflicts at a high-level (e.g., two commutative operations would not raise conflict even though they may access and modify the same memory data) which enables greater parallelism. Because semantically independent transactions may have low-level memory access conflicts, some other concurrency control protocol must be used to protect accesses to the underlying data structure. This results in a two-layer concurrency control. Transactional boosting proposed by Herlihy [21] is the first dedicated treatment on building highly concurrent transactional data structures using a semantic layer of abstract locks. The idea behind boosting is intuitive: if two operations commute they are allowed to proceed without interference (i.e., thread-level synchronization happens within the operations); otherwise they need to be synchronized at the transaction level. It treats the base data structure as a black box and uses *abstract locking* to ensure that non-commutative method calls do not occur concurrently. For each operation in a transaction, the boosted data structure calls the corresponding method of the underlying linearizable data structure after acquiring the abstract lock associated with that call. A transaction aborts when it fails to acquire an abstract lock, and it recovers from failure by invoking the inverses of already executed calls. Its semantic-based conflict detection approach eliminates excessive false conflicts associated with STM-based transactional data structures, but it still suffers from performance penalties due to the rollbacks of partially executed transactions. Moreover, when applied to non-blocking data structures, the progress guarantee of the boosted data structure is degraded because of the locks used for transactional-level synchronization. Transactional boosting is pessimistic in that it acquires locks eagerly before the method calls, but it still requires operation rollback because not all locks are acquired at once. Koskinen et al. [26] later generalized this work and introduce a formal framework called coarse-grained transactions. Bronson et al. proposed transaction prediction, which maps the abstract state of a set into memory blocks called predicate and relies on STM to synchronize transactional accesses [2]. Hassan et al. [20] proposed an optimistic version of boosting, which employs a white box design and provides throughput and usability benefits over the original boosting approach. Other STM variants, such open nested transactions [32] support a more relaxed transaction model that leverages some semantic knowledge based on programmers' input. The relaxation of STM systems and its implication on composability have been studied by Gramoli et al. [13]. The work by Golan-Gueta et al. [12] applies commutativity specification obtained from programmers' input to inferring locks for abstract data types.

7. CONCLUSION

We introduced a methodology for transforming lock-free linked data structures into high-performance lock-free transactional data structures. Our approach embeds the transaction metadata in each node, which enables resolving transaction conflicts cooperatively through thread-level synchronization. No undo logs nor rollbacks are needed because operations can correctly interpret the logical status of nodes left over by aborted transactions. Data structures that guarantees lock-free or weaker progress will be able to maintain their progress properties during the transformation. We demonstrated the application of our lock-free transactional transformation on two fundamental data structures: a linked list and a skiplist. The performance evaluation results show that our transaction synchronization protocol has low overhead and high scalability–providing an average of 40% speedup over our good-faith transaction boosting implementations across all scenarios and as much as 125% more throughput for large transactions. The performance gain over STMs are even more substantial: more than 10 times over the alternative word-based STM and 3 times over the object-based STM. Besides the performance advantages, our approach decreases spurious aborts to a minimum, which is desirable because transaction success rate is a decisive factor for a majority of the applications.

We defer describing the methodology to encompass dictionary API to future work. The key change is to add two value fields (old, and current) in the NODEINFO structure so that the old version can be recovered if update fails. We also plan to further evaluate our approach on SMP systems to verify potential performance gains under low memory latency.

8. ACKNOWLEDGMENTS

This work is supported by the National Science Foundation under ACI Award No. 1440530.

9. REFERENCES

[1] H. Attiya. The inherent complexity of transactional memory and what to do about it. In *Proceedings of the 29th ACM SIGACT-SIGOPS symposium on Principles of distributed computing*, pages 1–5. ACM, 2010.

[2] N. G. Bronson, J. Casper, H. Chafi, and K. Olukotun. Transactional predication: high-performance concurrent sets and maps for stm. In *Proceedings of the 29th ACM SIGACT-SIGOPS symposium on Principles of distributed computing*, pages 6–15. ACM, 2010.

[3] C. Cascaval, C. Blundell, M. Michael, H. W. Cain, P. Wu, S. Chiras, and S. Chatterjee. Software transactional memory: Why is it only a research toy? *Queue*, 6(5):40, 2008.

[4] S. Cherem, T. Chilimbi, and S. Gulwani. Inferring locks for atomic sections. In *ACM SIGPLAN Notices*, volume 43, pages 304–315. ACM, 2008.

[5] L. Dalessandro, M. F. Spear, and M. L. Scott. Norec: streamlining stm by abolishing ownership records. In *ACM Sigplan Notices*, volume 45, pages 67–78. ACM, 2010.

[6] D. Dice, Y. Lev, M. Moir, D. Nussbaum, and M. Olszewski. Early experience with a commercial hardware transactional memory implementation. 2009.

[7] D. Dice, O. Shalev, and N. Shavit. Transactional locking ii. In *Distributed Computing*, pages 194–208. Springer, 2006.

[8] F. Ellen, P. Fatourou, E. Ruppert, and F. van Breugel. Non-blocking binary search trees. In *Proceedings of the 29th ACM SIGACT-SIGOPS symposium on Principles of distributed computing*, pages 131–140. ACM, 2010.

[9] M. Emmi, J. S. Fischer, R. Jhala, and R. Majumdar. Lock allocation. In *ACM SIGPLAN Notices*, volume 42, pages 291–296. ACM, 2007.

[10] K. Fraser. *Practical lock-freedom*. PhD thesis, PhD thesis, Cambridge University Computer Laboratory, 2003. Also available as Technical Report UCAM-CL-TR-579, 2004.

[11] G. Golan-Gueta, G. Ramalingam, M. Sagiv, and E. Yahav. Concurrent libraries with foresight. In *ACM SIGPLAN Notices*, volume 48, pages 263–274. ACM, 2013.

[12] G. Golan-Gueta, G. Ramalingam, M. Sagiv, and E. Yahav. Automatic scalable atomicity via semantic locking. In *Proceedings of the 20th ACM SIGPLAN Symposium on Principles and Practice of Parallel Programming*, pages 31–41. ACM, 2015.

[13] V. Gramoli, R. Guerraoui, and M. Letia. Composing relaxed transactions. In *Parallel & Distributed*

Processing (IPDPS), 2013 IEEE 27th International Symposium on, pages 1171–1182. IEEE, 2013.

[14] K. Gudka, T. Harris, and S. Eisenbach. Lock inference in the presence of large libraries. In *ECOOP 2012–Object-Oriented Programming*, pages 308–332. Springer, 2012.

[15] R. Guerraoui and M. Kapalka. On obstruction-free transactions. In *Proceedings of the twentieth annual symposium on Parallelism in algorithms and architectures*, pages 304–313. ACM, 2008.

[16] R. Guerraoui and M. Kapalka. On the correctness of transactional memory. In *Proceedings of the 13th ACM SIGPLAN Symposium on Principles and practice of parallel programming*, pages 175–184. ACM, 2008.

[17] T. Harris, J. Larus, and R. Rajwar. Transactional memory. *Synthesis Lectures on Computer Architecture*, 5(1):1–263, 2010.

[18] T. L. Harris. A pragmatic implementation of non-blocking linked-lists. In *Distributed Computing*, pages 300–314. Springer, 2001.

[19] A. Hassan, R. Palmieri, and B. Ravindran. Integrating transactionally boosted data structures with stm frameworks: A case study on set. In *9th ACM SIGPLAN Workshop on Transactional Computing (TRANSACT)*, 2014.

[20] A. Hassan, R. Palmieri, and B. Ravindran. On developing optimistic transactional lazy set. In *Principles of Distributed Systems*, pages 437–452. Springer, 2014.

[21] M. Herlihy and E. Koskinen. Transactional boosting: a methodology for highly-concurrent transactional objects. In *Proceedings of the 13th ACM SIGPLAN Symposium on Principles and practice of parallel programming*, pages 207–216. ACM, 2008.

[22] M. Herlihy, V. Luchangco, M. Moir, and W. N. Scherer III. Software transactional memory for dynamic-sized data structures. In *Proceedings of the twenty-second annual symposium on Principles of distributed computing*, pages 92–101. ACM, 2003.

[23] M. Herlihy and J. E. B. Moss. Transactional memory: Architectural support for lock-free data structures. In *Proceedings of the 20th Annual International Symposium on Computer Architecture*, ISCA '93, pages 289–300, New York, NY, USA, 1993. ACM.

[24] M. Herlihy and N. Shavit. *The Art of Multiprocessor Programming, Revised Reprint*. Elsevier, 2012.

[25] M. P. Herlihy and J. M. Wing. Linearizability: A correctness condition for concurrent objects. *ACM Transactions on Programming Languages and Systems (TOPLAS)*, 12(3):463–492, 1990.

[26] E. Koskinen, M. Parkinson, and M. Herlihy. Coarse-grained transactions. *ACM Sigplan Notices*, 45(1):19–30, 2010.

[27] J. Lindén and B. Jonsson. A skiplist-based concurrent priority queue with minimal memory contention. In *Principles of Distributed Systems*, pages 206–220. Springer, 2013.

[28] V. J. Marathe, W. N. Scherer, and M. L. Scott. Design tradeoffs in modern software transactional memory systems. In *Proceedings of the 7th workshop on Workshop on languages, compilers, and run-time support for scalable systems*, pages 1–7. ACM, 2004.

[29] V. J. Marathe, M. F. Spear, C. Heriot, A. Acharya, D. Eisenstat, W. N. Scherer III, and M. L. Scott. Lowering the overhead of nonblocking software transactional memory. In *Workshop on Languages, Compilers, and Hardware Support for Transactional Computing (TRANSACT)*, 2006.

[30] B. McCloskey, F. Zhou, D. Gay, and E. Brewer. Autolocker: synchronization inference for atomic sections. *ACM SIGPLAN Notices*, 41(1):346–358, 2006.

[31] M. M. Michael. High performance dynamic lock-free hash tables and list-based sets. In *Proceedings of the fourteenth annual ACM symposium on Parallel algorithms and architectures*, pages 73–82. ACM, 2002.

[32] Y. Ni, V. S. Menon, A.-R. Adl-Tabatabai, A. L. Hosking, R. L. Hudson, J. E. B. Moss, B. Saha, and T. Shpeisman. Open nesting in software transactional memory. In *Proceedings of the 12th ACM SIGPLAN symposium on Principles and practice of parallel programming*, pages 68–78. ACM, 2007.

[33] C. H. Papadimitriou. The serializability of concurrent database updates. *Journal of the ACM (JACM)*, 26(4):631–653, 1979.

[34] C. J. Rossbach, O. S. Hofmann, and E. Witchel. Is transactional programming actually easier? In *Proceedings of the 15th ACM SIGPLAN Symposium on Principles and Practice of Parallel Programming*, PPoPP '10, pages 47–56, New York, NY, USA, 2010. ACM.

[35] B. Saha, A.-R. Adl-Tabatabai, R. L. Hudson, C. C. Minh, and B. Hertzberg. Mcrt-stm: a high performance software transactional memory system for a multi-core runtime. In *Proceedings of the eleventh ACM SIGPLAN symposium on Principles and practice of parallel programming*, pages 187–197. ACM, 2006.

[36] O. Shacham, N. Bronson, A. Aiken, M. Sagiv, M. Vechev, and E. Yahav. Testing atomicity of composed concurrent operations. *ACM SIGPLAN Notices*, 46(10):51–64, 2011.

[37] N. Shavit and D. Touitou. Software transactional memory. *Distributed Computing*, 10(2):99–116, 1997.

[38] N. Shavit and A. Zemach. Scalable concurrent priority queue algorithms. In *Proceedings of the eighteenth annual ACM symposium on Principles of distributed computing*, pages 113–122. ACM, 1999.

[39] D. Zhang and D. Dechev. A lock-free priority queue design based on multi-dimensional linked lists. *IEEE Transactions on Parallel and Distributed Systems*, PP(99):1–1, 2015.

Concurrent Search Data Structures Can Be Blocking and Practically Wait-Free

Tudor David
EPFL
tudor.david@epfl.ch

Rachid Guerraoui
EPFL
rachid.guerraoui@epfl.ch

ABSTRACT

We argue that there is virtually no practical situation in which one should seek a "theoretically wait-free" algorithm at the expense of a state-of-the-art blocking algorithm in the case of search data structures: blocking algorithms are simple, fast, and can be made "practically wait-free".

We draw this conclusion based on the most exhaustive study of blocking search data structures to date. We consider (a) different search data structures of different sizes, (b) numerous uniform and non-uniform workloads, representative of a wide range of practical scenarios, with different percentages of update operations, (c) with and without delayed threads, (d) on different hardware technologies, including processors providing HTM instructions.

We explain our claim that blocking search data structures are practically wait-free through an analogy with the birthday paradox, revealing that, in state-of-the-art algorithms implementing such data structures, the probability of conflicts is extremely small. When conflicts occur as a result of context switches and interrupts, we show that HTM-based locks enable blocking algorithms to cope with them.

1. INTRODUCTION

With multi-core architectures being ubiquitous, concurrent data structures have become performance-critical components in many widely-used applications and software systems. In particular, *search data structures* are heavily used by numerous popular systems, such as Memcached [42], RocksDB [15], LevelDB [20], MySQL [50], MongoDB [49], MonetDB [48] and the Linux kernel [40]. Basically, search data structures are implementations of the *set* abstraction: they provide operations to search for a particular element, to insert, and to remove an element. The most common examples include *linked lists*, *skip lists*, *hash tables*, and *binary-search trees (BSTs)*.

However, despite the fact that a large body of work has been dedicated to concurrent search data structure (CSDS) algorithms [6, 9, 11, 13, 14, 18, 23, 24, 28, 32, 37, 39, 43, 51, 53, 57, 58], their design and implementation remains an onerous task. The difficulty lies in providing implementations that are both correct, i.e., linearizable [31], as well as efficient. Essentially, an ideal concurrent data structure (i) is easy to design, implement and reason about, (ii) provides high aggregate throughput and scalability, and (iii) ensures limited latency delays due to concurrency for all requests.

SPAA'16, July 11–13, 2016, Pacific Grove, California, USA.
 ISBN 978-1-4503-4210-0/16/07...$15.00
DOI: http://dx.doi.org/10.1145/2935764.2935774

In theory, *wait-free* algorithms [27, 30] are the only ones that satisfy requirement (iii). These algorithms prevent known issues of locking (i.e., convoying, deadlocks, priority inversions), without the risk of starvation. In essence, a wait-free algorithm guarantees that every thread completes its operation in a finite number of its own steps, thus promising limited latency, even under high contention.

Nevertheless, despite the significant amount of research dedicated to the design of wait-free CSDSs [2, 16, 27, 37, 38, 57, 58], these algorithms exhibit low throughput, roughly half of that of a state-of-the-art *blocking* or *lock-free* search data structure (as we show experimentally in the paper). Essentially, the reason for the difference in throughput between wait-free algorithms on the one hand, and lock-free and blocking algorithms one the other hand, is related to the amount of concurrency-related information that needs to be associated with the data. While in the case of lock-free and blocking algorithms, data and concurrency-related information can be efficiently manipulated in an atomic manner, this is not the case for wait-free algorithms. This results in more pointer chasing and thus slower traversals of the structures.

Lock-free algorithms have been shown to provide high aggregate throughput in the case of CSDSs [9] (and have been proven to ensure wait-freedom with high probability for a large class of schedulers [3]). However, they are difficult to design and implement correctly [21], with memory management making the task even more complex [7, 44].

Blocking algorithms are considered to be significantly easier to implement and use, mainly because data can only be modified in critical sections protected through mutual exclusion mechanisms. It is thus natural to ask whether it is possible to have blocking CSDS algorithms that provide high aggregate throughput, but also ensure that on realistic workloads, no individual request is significantly delayed due to contention, i.e., these algorithms are *practically wait-free*.

We believe this question can only be answered empirically. To this end, we conduct the most exhaustive study of blocking CSDSs to date. We deploy a wide variety of state-of-the-art CSDS algorithms, on the latest hardware technology. In particular, we enable locks to use Hardware Transactional Memory (HTM) in order to prevent threads from holding locks while not scheduled, which is a rather novel use-case for HTM. Our evaluation is extensive both in the metrics we collect, as well as in the scenarios we study: we consider numerous uniform and non-uniform workloads, representative of a wide range of practical scenarios. We also test different data structures with varying sizes and percentages of update operations, with and without delayed threads.

Our results indicate that state-of-the-art blocking implementations of search data structures behave practically wait-free in all realistic scenarios. Even in scenarios of extreme contention, requests experience acceptable delays with blocking CSDSs. The usage of HTM reveals effective in the face of frequent context switches and other interrupts.

The main conclusion we draw from our study is that there is virtually no practical situation in which one needs to seek an algorithm providing a strong theoretical progress guarantee at the expense of a state-of-the-art blocking algorithm in the case of search data structures: blocking algorithms provide good throughput and latency, even under high contention, and are much simpler than their non-blocking counterparts.

Our explanation for this fact is that state-of-the-art blocking CSDSs are specifically devised to minimize the probability of high contention for any memory address. This reason is different from the perspective taken by recent work [3], namely that if thread accesses are scheduled stochastically, lock-free algorithms behave in a wait-free manner even if there is high contention for a particular memory address. Our conclusion suggests instead that the main reason for non-wait-free CSDS algorithms, in the theoretical sense, to behave wait-free in the practical sense is the small probability of actual contention for a surprisingly wide spectrum of workloads. This follows from the fact that, in the case of state-of-the-art CSDSs, only short portions of the update operations may cause conflicts when occurring concurrently. State-of-the-art blocking algorithms simply go through the nodes and follow the next pointers, and only lock the area which needs to be modified. Indeed, the time needed to traverse the structure in order to reach the point where the operation needs to actually be performed generally dominates the total execution time. In addition, problematic scenarios, such as large delays that may occur due to context switches or interrupts can often be handled efficiently using HTM technologies available in commodity processors.

The probability of conflicts can be modeled using variations of the *birthday paradox*. We show that in common workloads, this probability is below 1%, with the probability of repeated conflicts for the same request being much smaller. Even in contended situations with a high number of conflicts, it is extremely rare that a wait-free algorithm outperforms state-of-the-art blocking algorithms.

Three remarks are, however, in order. (1) We do not claim that blocking search data structure algorithms behave in a wait-free manner under *every* conceivable scenario. We could create a scenario where (i) the data structure has a small number of nodes, (ii) these are accessed repeatedly, (iii) by a very large number of concurrent threads, and (iv) with a high update rate, and in which latency would indeed suffer.[1] (2) Our conclusion only applies to search data structures. Indeed, we show in the paper that in the case of data structures which have the potential of inducing much more contention on a small number of memory addresses, such as queues and stacks, a blocking algorithm is not ideal. (3) We do not claim that non-blocking algorithms cannot offer the same performance as blocking ones. In fact, several lock-free algorithms are known to provide performance comparable to blocking algorithms. Rather, we show that state-of-the-art blocking algorithms, which are often much simpler to design and implement than their non-blocking counterparts, provide no disadvantage.

The rest of the paper is structured as follows. We discuss CSDSs in Section 2. We present our experimental methodology and settings in Section 3. In Section 4, we show that blocking CSDSs provide high throughput and scalability, while in Section 5 we perform an extensive evaluation of the degree to which blocking CSDS algorithms are practically wait-free. Section 6 discusses the analogy with the birthday paradox. We examine the extent to which our conclusions apply to structures other than CSDSs in Section 7. Section 8 presents related work. We conclude the paper in Section 9.

2. CONCURRENT SEARCH DATA STRUCTURES: FROM THEORY TO PRACTICE

In this section, we look at the metric types indicative of the performance of a concurrent algorithm: coarse-grained and fine-grained. Moreover, we clarify why theoretically wait-free algorithms fail to perform well in the former, and explain what we mean by practical wait-freedom in the context of blocking algorithms.

2.1 Performance and progress

The performance of concurrent algorithms is usually evaluated according to two main types of metrics:

- *coarse-grained performance metrics*: these capture the overall performance of the system, and usually include metrics such as throughput (the number of requests completed system-wide per unit of time), average latency (average duration of an operation), scalability (variation in throughput and latency as more threads are added to the system), and fairness (the difference in observed throughput and average latency between threads);
- *fine-grained performance metrics*: these metrics capture the behavior of individual requests; these include for example metrics such as latency distribution, variability, outliers, as well as other algorithm-specific metrics. Such metrics might be useful, for instance, to identify the quantity of particularly slow requests in a system.

An ideal algorithm would provide good results for both these metric types. However, optimizing for one of them can have a negative impact on the other. For example, attempting to maximize system throughput might result in an algorithm with a large variability in the operation latencies. Ensuring bounded latencies for all requests is likewise likely to limit throughput.

One of the main knobs used to adjust the relative importance of these metrics is the progress guarantee provided by the algorithm. The vast majority of published algorithms are either (i) *blocking*, (ii) *lock-free*, or (iii) *wait-free* [30].

- *Blocking* algorithms ensure mutually exclusive access to (parts of) the data structure using, for example, mechanisms such as locks. More broadly, threads have to explicitly release resources before others can use them, thus potentially preventing the progress of other threads indefinitely.
- *Lock-free* algorithms ensure that at least one thread in the system is able to make progress at any point in time.
- *Wait-free* algorithms ensure that every thread in the system will eventually complete its operation.

[1] We do however claim this does simply not occur in the vast majority of practical situations. Practitioners, which often have some knowledge about their workloads and system requirements, can use our work to decide when blocking implementations are sufficient.

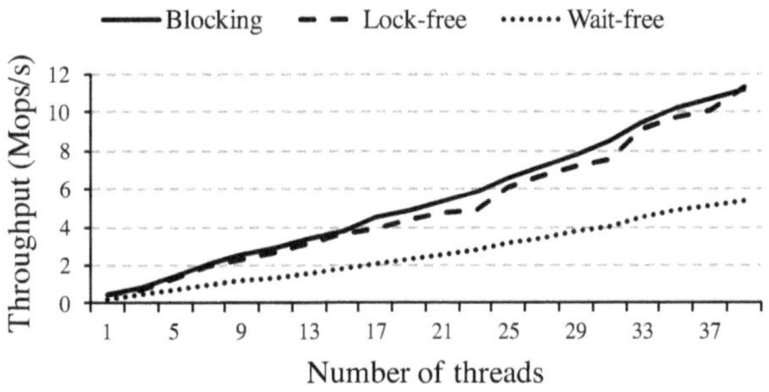

Figure 1: The throughput of blocking, lock-free and wait-free linked lists of size 1024, with 10% of the operations being updates.

As we pointed out, blocking algorithms are generally simple. The downsides are the potential of several threads being indefinitely delayed by a slow thread holding a lock, deadlocks, livelocks, convoying or priority inversions. Lock-free algorithms present the risk of some threads starving. In theory, wait-freedom is the most desirable property for a concurrent algorithm. It ensures that no request is indefinitely delayed due to contention.

A significant amount of effort has been dedicated in recent years [16, 37, 38, 57, 58] to dispel the belief that wait-free algorithms provide low throughput in practice [17, 30]. In the context of search data structures however, such algorithms still lag significantly behind alternatives providing weaker progress guarantees in terms of system-wide throughput, as we will discuss below.

2.2 A closer look at wait-free CSDS algorithms

A search data structure contains a set of elements, and allows access to each of them, regardless of their position in the data structure. These structures store elements of arbitrary sizes, indexed using keys, and are usually implemented as linked data structures. They have a simple base interface, consisting of three operations:

- *get(k)* returns the value associated with key k in case such an entry exists, or returns false in case the entry is not present;
- *put(k,v)* inserts a key-value pair in case an entry for key k is not present, or returns false otherwise;
- *remove(k)* removes the entry corresponding to key k in case it exists in the data structure, or returns false otherwise.

Given the practical importance of these structures, a lot of effort has been dedicated to their efficient concurrent implementations.

In the following, we illustrate the current difference in throughput between a state-of-the-art wait-free algorithm [58], a state-of-the-art blocking algorithm [24] and a lock-free algorithm [23] for a linked list (for space limitations, we only give results for the linked list; we also experimented with a skip-list, a BST and a hash table). We use a recent 20-core (40 hardware threads) Intel server. We depict the throughput of a linked list with 1024 elements and 10% updates (5% inserts, 5% removes) as we increase the number of threads from 1 to 40.

As conveyed in Figure 1, the throughput of the wait-free algorithm is around 50% of its blocking and lock-free counterparts. This trend pertains to other CSDSs as well (skip lists, BSTs and hash-tables[2]).

[2]In the case of a hash table with average occupancy per bucket equal to 1, and hence on average no linked components, the wait-free algorithm is only around 33% slower. For the others, it is also 50%.

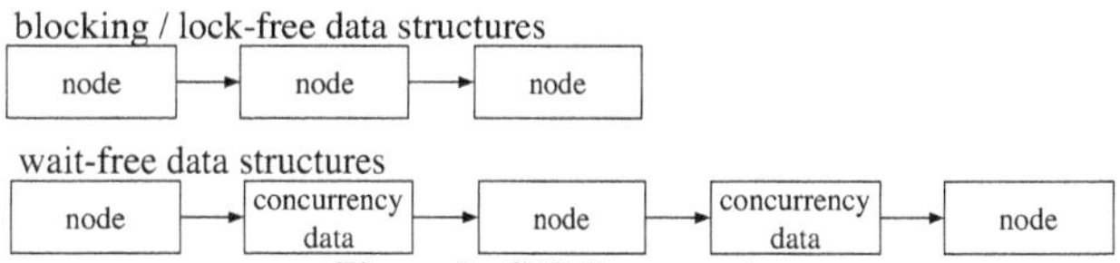

Figure 2: CSDS traversals.

The main reason for the difference in throughput between wait-free and blocking CSDSs is that in a CSDS, the time needed to traverse the structure in order to reach the point where the operation needs to actually be performed generally dominates the total execution time. In essence, the smaller the number of memory locations an operation needs to read or write, the faster the operation. Due to their simpler nature, blocking algorithms have to chase a smaller number of pointers during an operation: the most efficient such algorithms simply have to go through the nodes and follow the next pointers, and only lock the area which needs to be modified.

In the case of wait-free algorithms, the underlying reason for their inefficiency is a fundamental mismatch between current architectures and the complexity of wait-free algorithms. In non-blocking CSDS algorithms, the common approach is to associate some concurrency information with each *next* pointer of a node, and update this information and the pointer atomically. While the unused three least significant bits of a pointer (in a 64-bit architecture) are generally sufficient for this concurrency information in the case of lock-free algorithms, this is not the case for the most efficient wait-free algorithms (which might need, for example, version numbers associated with next pointers). In terms of practical implementations, this usually translates in additional objects being interposed between data structure nodes, resulting in slower traversals of the structure. This is illustrated in Figure 2. Thus, wait-free algorithms fail to provide at least one of the characteristics of an ideal concurrent algorithm we have previously identified: high aggregate throughput.

Of course, our experiment tells only half of the story: the main goal of wait-freedom is not high system-wide throughput, but rather the promise that every request will eventually return (fine-grain latency). In the rest of the paper, we focus on showing that in addition to providing good coarse-grained performance metrics (Section 4), blocking CSDS algorithms also exhibit "wait-free behavior" for a very wide variety of workloads (Section 5).

2.3 Practical wait-freedom

We now look at how the theoretical guarantees of wait-free algorithms manifest in practice in the context of concurrent search data structures.

In theory, threads may crash. Wait-free algorithms ensure that despite the crash of a thread, the requests of other threads still get served. In practice, threads usually do not crash, and when they do, they do not crash independently: even when software bugs occur in a multi-threaded program, it is preferable to stop or restart the entire application rather than work with state that might have been corrupted.

Threads can however be temporarily delayed due to I/O, context switches, scheduling decisions or other interrupts. In practice, we expect wait-freedom to translate to a bound in the delay a request can suffer due to contention, i.e., all requests finishing before a certain deadline as long as the thread itself is scheduled (i.e., taking steps).

We thus argue that a data structure implementation which has a negligible percentage of requests that exhibit significant delays due to other concurrent threads in the system for a wide array of

Linked lists	Skip lists	Hash tables	BSTs
Lock-coupling list [30]	Pugh skip list [53]	Lock-coupling hash table [30]	Practical binary tree [6]
Lazy linked list [24]	Herlihy skip list [28]	Lazy hash table [24]	Logical ordering tree [13]
Pugh linked list [53]		Pugh hash table [53]	BST-TK tree [9]
Copy-on-write linked list [52]		Copy-on-write hash table [52]	
		ConcurrentHashMap [39]	
		Intel TBB [34]	
		URCU hash table [11]	

Table 1: Blocking search data structure algorithms considered in our evaluation.

workloads is *practically wait-free*. In practice, most systems indeed provide a Service Level Agreement (SLA) tolerating small percentages (e.g. 0.1% or 1%) of slow requests. Hence, what we call practical wait-freedom is bounded delays due to contention, for all but a potentially infinitesimal percentage of requests, under all realistic workloads.

This characteristic of an implementation does not imply a particular theoretical guarantee provided by the algorithm. It simply identifies implementations whose execution (in terms of request delays due to contention and fairness) cannot be distinguished from that of an algorithm that actually provides the theoretical guarantee of wait-freedom.

In the context of blocking CSDSs, there are two possible causes for which a thread's operation can be delayed by other concurrent threads: *locks* and *restarts*. To quantify the extent to which a thread is delayed as a result of them, we can measure the time an operation waits in order to acquire locks, as well as the number of times an operation has to restart. These two fine-grained metrics are indicative of different sources of delays to which wait-free algorithms may serve as better alternatives:

- Large average waiting times to acquire locks can be for the most part linked with i) other threads suffering delays while holding locks or ii) a large number of threads attempting to acquire the same lock. In the following sections, we show that in the context of state-of-the-art blocking CSDS algorithms, the latter case occurs only extremely rarely.
- In contrast, restarts capture a pattern present in a large fraction of the state-of-the-art blocking CSDS algorithms: if at some point during an operation, a state which does not allow it to progress correctly is encountered, the operation is restarted. These possible inconsistencies triggering restarts are a result of the fine-grained locking and optimistic approaches used in state-of-the-art algorithms. In general, a large percentage of requests having to be restarted repeatedly can be linked to high contention for a particular area of the data structure. The theoretical possibility of triggering restarts indefinitely might result in threads suffering from starvation.

We note that a more generic metric such as latency distribution is not appropriate in the case of all linked search data structures, given the fact that request latencies are often dominated by the time needed to reach the point of the data structure which needs to be accessed. Therefore, accesses to different parts of the data structure naturally have very different latencies. In addition, if context switches or other interrupts occur, threads may not even be taking steps, resulting in potentially unbounded latencies even for a theoretically wait-free algorithm.

In the following, we look at the extent to which blocking CSDSs provide the desired coarse-grained performance metrics, as well as the fine-grained performance metrics indicative of practical wait-freedom discussed above.

3. EXPERIMENTAL SETTING

For our study, we evaluated a wide range of blocking CSDS algorithms, summarized in Table 1, and part of ASCYLIB [5], an open source library implemented in C containing blocking and lock-free CSDSs. We report on their behavior under a wide range of conditions, representative of a wide variety of workloads. We enhance the library with benchmarks allowing us to report on the metrics presented in this paper. Roughly, we argue that the state-of-the-art algorithms have good throughput, scalability and behave practically wait-free regardless of the search data structure, thus representing ideal implementations for the vast majority of workloads.

For clarity, in the following experiments, we only highlight the behavior of the blocking algorithm exhibiting the best performance in our tests for each data structure, as our intention is to show that at least one practically wait-free algorithms exists for each structure type. Nevertheless, the conclusions we draw are in fact valid for multiple state-of-the-art algorithms for each data structure.

The best performing algorithms per data structure (which are shown in the following figures) are the lazy linked list, Herlihy's skip-list, the lazy linked list-based hash table (one lazy linked list per bucket, with per-bucket locks, with average load factor per bucket set to 1), and the BST-TK external binary search tree.

3.1 State-of-the art algorithms

Before we go into any details, it is important to understand the principles according to which the best performing blocking CSDS algorithms operate today [9]:

- Read operations do not perform any stores, and do not trigger any restarts;
- Update operations can be divided into a parse phase and a write phase: in the parse phase, the area of the data structure where the update needs to be applied is reached in a synchronization-free manner, while during the write phase, the actual updates are applied by writing to a small neighborhood of nodes in the data structure.
- Conflicts arise between two threads if they are executing their write phase concurrently, and the nodes accessed during these phases by the two threads intersect.
- Parses and reads are not obstructed by concurrent updates.

In short, in all these algorithms, the only blocking portions are short sequences of code in the update operations in which the actual modifications to the data structures are performed.

3.2 Implementation details

Our structures use either test-and-set locks or ticket locks in our experiments. We observe no benefits from using more complex locks, such as MCS locks, due the low degree of contention for any particular lock in these data structures. In addition, it has been

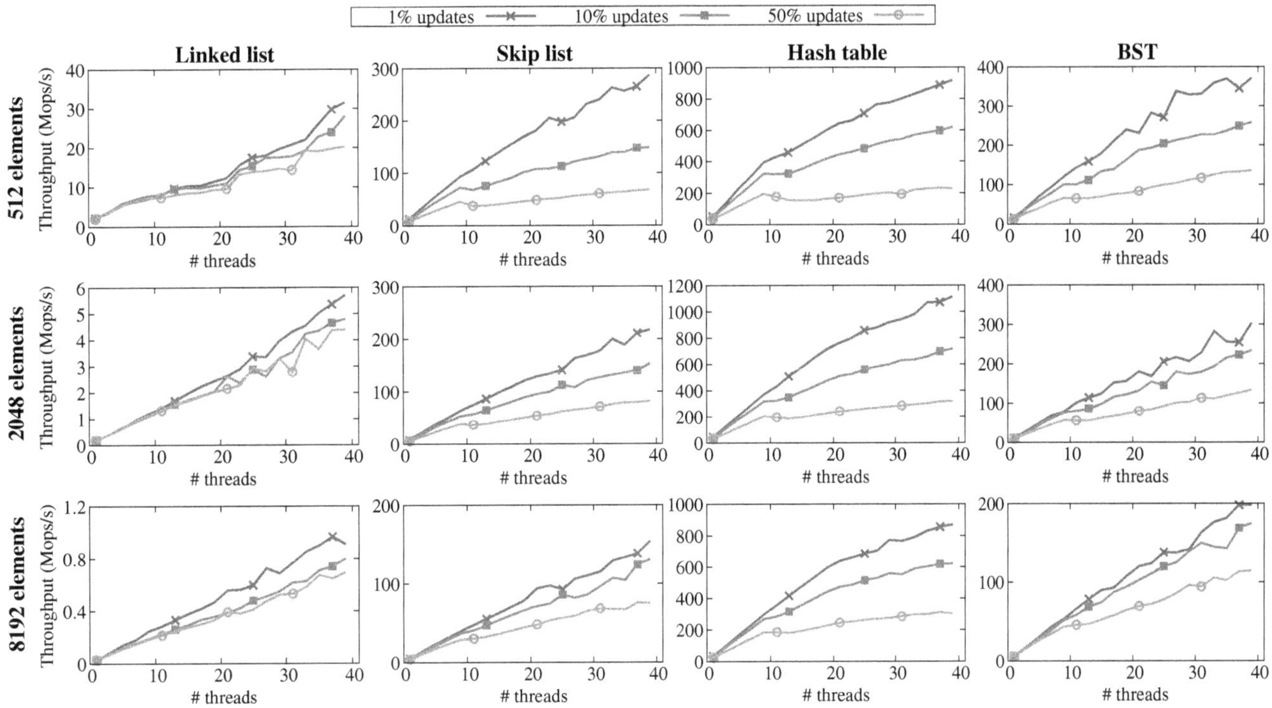

Figure 3: Throughput scalability of blocking implementations.

shown that these simple locks often perform well in practice [10], even for moderately high degrees of contention. Our implementations use an epoch-based memory management scheme, similar in principle to RCU [41].

In order to test our implementations, we use an Intel machine having two Xeon E5-2680 v2 Ivy Bridge processors with 10 cores each (20 cores in total). In addition, each core supports two hardware threads. The cores run at 2.8 GHz and have caches of sizes 32KB (L1), 256 KB (L2) and 25 MB (LLC per processor). The machine runs Ubuntu Linux 14.04 (kernel version 3.13.0). We bind threads to cores such that threads first use all physical cores before using both hardware contexts of the same core.

3.3 Methodology

We present results for different structure sizes and update ratios, which we believe to be representative of those used in practical systems. We consider structures consisting of 512, 2048 and 8192 key-value pairs, and percentages of update requests of 1%, 10%, and 50%. Half of the updates are inserts, and the other are removes. These parameters, are, in fact, similar to the ones we observe in real systems (e.g., in LevelDB [20], RocksDB [15], Memcached [42], MySQL [50], MongoDB [49], MonetDB [48]). We also address smaller structures and higher degrees of contention in a separate experiment.

We evaluate the extent to which blocking CSDSs provide the two main features of an ideal concurrent algorithm: (i) high system-wide performance, and (ii) practical wait-freedom. We start by showing that blocking CSDSs provide the desired coarse-grained performance metrics, after which we look at the fine-grained metrics indicative of wait-freedom, and study how they evolve as we modify the parameters of our workload and environment.

Unless otherwise specified, the distribution of accesses over the key space is uniform. Keys and values have 64 bits in size. Using larger values is straightforward: instead of the 64-bit value we would simply manipulate pointers to these larger values. Each of the worker threads in our benchmarks continuously issues requests.

In each of the workloads, we consider a key space twice as large as the structure size. Given that our workloads have an equal number of inserts and removes, this ensures that on average the data structure size remains close to the initial size throughout the experiment. We use runs of 5 seconds and report the average results of 11 runs.

In order to capture the system-wide performance and the degree to which the individual requests of these algorithms are delayed, we consider the following metrics: (a) the throughput as we increase the number of threads from 1 to 40 (the maximum number of hardware threads on our machine), (b) the average throughput per thread and the standard deviation of this quantity, (c) the average percentage of time spent waiting for locks by each thread and the standard deviation, and the (d) percentage of operations that have to restart at least once. We also look at the distribution of the values for the last two metrics among requests to identify any outliers. Where not specified, measurements are taken using 20 concurrent threads.

4. COARSE-GRAINED METRICS

In this section, we evaluate the first performance characteristic of an ideal CSDS: we verify the extent to which blocking CSDSs provide good aggregate throughput and scalability for various structure sizes and update ratios.

Figure 3 presents the evolution of the throughput as a function of the number of threads. We note that the structures exhibit no decrease in scalability as the number of concurrent threads increases. Of course, as we increase the percentage of updates more cache invalidations are generated, resulting in slightly larger latencies and overall lower throughput increases. However, the scalability trends remain the same. This is particularly noticeable in the case of the hash table, due to the much higher incurred throughput and the lower latencies of the requests. Once we have to use both sockets of the multi-core (for more than 10 threads), the scalability slope

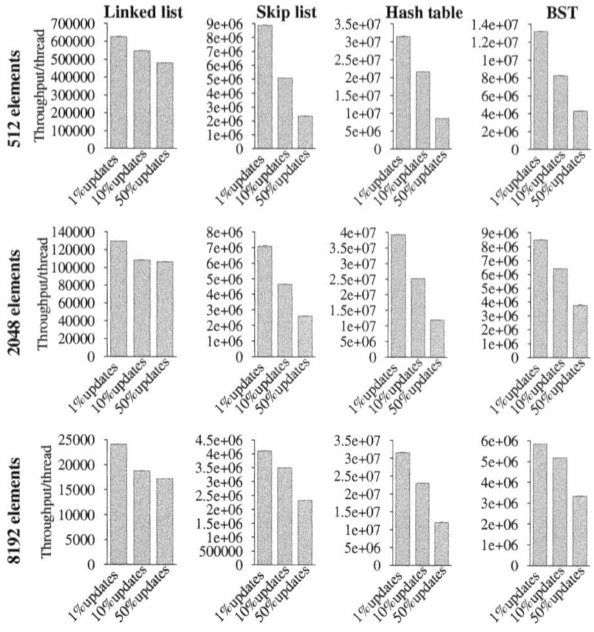

Figure 4: Per-thread throughput (and standard deviation).

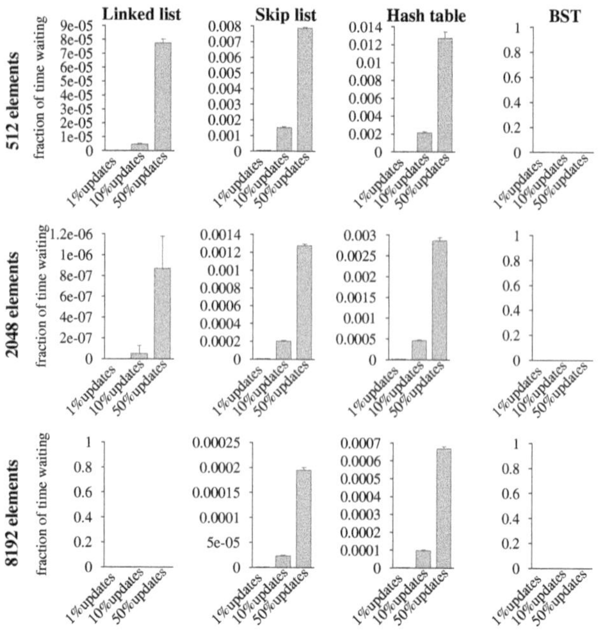

Figure 5: Fraction of time threads spend waiting for locks (and standard deviation).

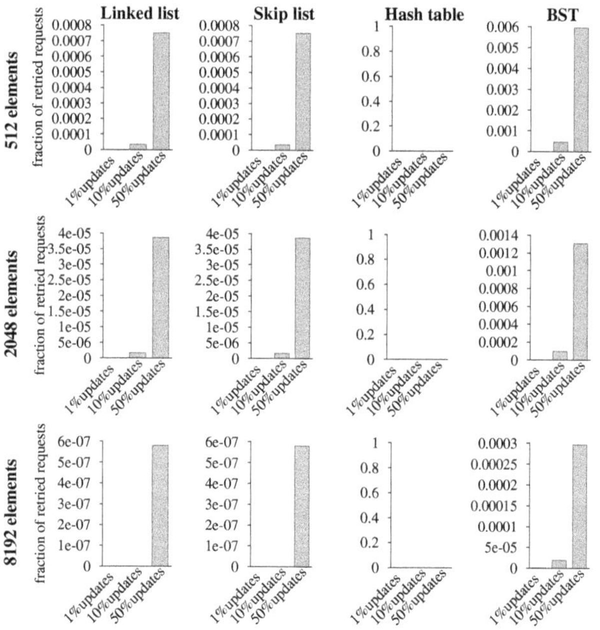

Figure 6: Fraction of requests that are restarted.

slightly reduces due to increased latencies to access data. This effect of the higher cache coherence latencies on the total throughput is inherent to each data structure, and cannot be bypassed regardless of the algorithm and its progress guarantees [9, 10].

In addition, in Figure 4, we also present the average throughput per thread and the standard deviation of this metric. We depict the standard deviation using error bars. On average, the standard deviation is 0.2% of the average per-thread throughput. This quantity is so small compared to the per-thread throughput, that it is not visible on the graphs. This is valid for all the data structures and for all the workloads. Given that threads continuously issue requests, we can also conclude that the average latency is identical among threads. The observation we extract from this experiment is thus that blocking CSDSs ensure a high degree of fairness.

The conclusion we can draw from these experiments is that the blocking nature of these algorithms is not an obstacle to high throughput or scalability, even as we modify the size of the structure or the percentage of update operations. In addition, all threads exhibit high performance: there is no skew between the throughputs of the threads.

5. PRACTICAL WAIT-FREEDOM

While as we have shown in the previous experiments, blocking algorithms have good throughput scalability and are fair, in this section we look closer at the fine-grained performance metrics indicative of practical wait freedom. As presented in Section 2, these metrics are the amount of blocking and retries as we vary the data structure size and update ratio.

We study how these metrics evolve as we very the percentage of updates, decrease the size of the data structure, use non-uniform workloads, cause threads to become unresponsive, and induce frequent context switches.

5.1 Structure size and update ratio

In this experiment we collect the performance metrics as we vary the structure size and the update ratio. Figure 5 presents the percentage of time threads spend waiting for locks. The percentage is relative to the total execution time when threads are continuously issuing requests. We measure this amount of time by using ticket locks: once a thread has acquired its ticket, if it is not immediately its turn to be served, we measure the time until this event occurs. We note that this percentage is under 2% in all situations, with most values being significantly below this percentage. In the case of the 8192-element linked list, for example, no thread has to wait in order to acquire locks. For the 2048-element linked list, the standard deviation is large due to the fact that the waiting times are between 0 and a few hundred cycles: even one brief delay waiting for a lock makes a thread an outlier. In the case of the BST, the tested algorithm uses trylocks, and restarts the operation in case the locking attempt fails. Therefore, the time spent waiting for locks is zero, but this is compensated by the slightly higher percentage of operations that are restarted.

Similarly, as shown in Figure 6, the percentage of operations delayed due to restarts is significantly smaller than 1% in all situations. This value is 0 in the case of the hash table: each bucket is protected by a lock, so once the operations have acquired the lock they never restart.

We also run an experiment in which we look at the distribution of the two sources of delays (the number of restarts and the time spent blocked) on a per-request basis. We want to identify any outliers: requests significantly delayed due to concurrency, which would violate practical wait-freedom. We consider a workload using a linked list of 512 elements, 40 threads and 10% updates. Only 0.01% of the requests had to wait for locks, with no requests waiting for more than 6μs. In addition, out of the 26 million operations, 2900 had to restart once, 9 had to restart 2 times, and none had to restart more than that.

The conclusion we can draw from these experiments is that blocking CSDS algorithms cause negligible request delays due to concurrency, thus allowing threads to complete their requests in a finite number of their own steps. When these small delays do occur, there are no requests that are affected significantly more than others.

These metrics also allow us to confirm the fact that our conclusion applies to the state-of-the-art search data structure algorithms, and not to more naive implementations, which have more frequent or longer critical sections. For example, we consider a lock-coupling linked list [30]. This algorithm, while using fine-grained locks, acquires locks as the structure is traversed. We measure the percentage of time threads spend waiting for locks for this algorithm. With 20 concurrent threads and just 1% updates, threads spend around 10% of their time waiting for locks, regardless of the structure size. Therefore, we do not claim such algorithms are practically wait-free.

5.2 Non-uniform workloads

We now look at non-uniform workloads, in which some keys are more popular than others. We use a Zipfian distribution of requests over the key space with $s = 0.8$. Zipfian distributions are known to model a large percentage of real workloads [8]. We show results for each of the data structures, using a workload with 20 threads, 2048 data structure size and 10% updates. We provide numbers for the time threads have to wait for locks, and the average number of retries that have to be performed. The results of this experiment are depicted in Figure 7. While the values observed in this experiment are slightly higher than for uniform workloads, the delays remain very low: threads spent at most 1% of their time waiting for locks, and only restart at most 0.30% of their operations regardless of the data structure.

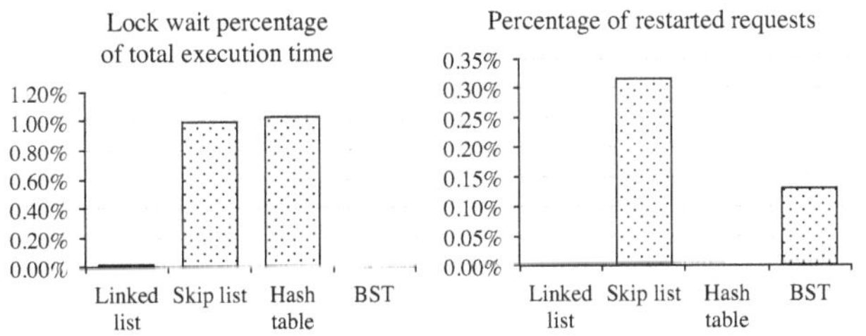

Figure 7: Percentage of time spent waiting for locks and percentage of requests restarted for blocking search data structures on a workload with a Zipfian request distribution.

Thus, we can conclude that blocking CSDS algorithms behave practically wait-free on such non-uniform workloads as well.

5.3 High contention

We present the following experiment: we consider a scenario in which 40 threads concurrently access a data structure, with 25% of the operations being updates. We start with a structure having 512 elements and in subsequent runs reduce its size down to an extreme-contention configuration with a structure consisting of 16 elements on average out of 32 possible keys. We report the percentage of time threads spend waiting for locks, as well as the percentage of update operations that restart at least once, and more than three times (reads do not restart). The percentage of updates restarted at least three times provides a measure of the number of such requests that are significantly delayed. As before, the hash table does not restart (as we use per-bucket locks), while the BST does not wait for locks.

Figure 8 presents the results of this experiment. In the case of the linked list, in the most extreme contention configuration, with only 16 elements in the structure, threads spend about 30% of their time waiting for locks, with 20% of the operations restarting at least once, and 1.8% of the operations restarting more than three times. Arguably, these numbers stretch the limits of what could be considered as practical wait-freedom, and in this particular configuration non-blocking algorithms may represent a better alternative. However, a data structure of size 32 already spends only around 1% of the time waiting for locks, restarts only 0.6% of its operations and repeatedly restarts only 0.02% of them, thus warranting the claim of practical wait-freedom. The values of these metrics continue to decrease steeply with the increasing data-structure size. With a linked list of 512 elements, practically no requests are significantly delayed or restarted more than three times.

Other data structures behave similarly: while for the very smallest structures our metrics can be non-negligible, they decrease exponentially as we increase data structure size. In the case of the hash table, since there are no restarts and we use per-bucket locks, the time spent waiting for very small hash tables is somewhat larger than for the other structures. This can be addressed by using finer-grained locks: i.e, use per-node locks instead of per-bucket locks. Nevertheless, since the hash tables used in practice are usually large in size, we use per-bucket locks throughout the paper.

The conclusion we can draw from this experiment is that there are indeed some extreme cases in which blocking data structures exhibit a non-negligible percentage of delays. However, these cases require extremely small data structures, a very high degree of concurrency and relatively high update ratios. We argue that such particular situations are rare in practice in the context of CSDSs. In fact, we have not observed such highly contested structures in popular practical systems which use CSDSs. In the majority of cases, even under high contention, blocking CSDSs still behave practically wait-free.

5.4 Unresponsive threads

We now look at a scenario in which threads become slow. In the first instance, we cause a thread to be delayed for a random interval between 1000 and 100000 ns every 10 updates, while holding locks. This range of delays captures many of the events that might occur in practice, such as accessing data from memory, SSD, or sending packets over the network. In essence, given that threads usually hold locks for short intervals only, this experiment looks at a worst-case scenario, where delays only happen while the locks are held. We present results for a workload having 20 concurrent threads, using data structures consisting of 2048 key-value pairs

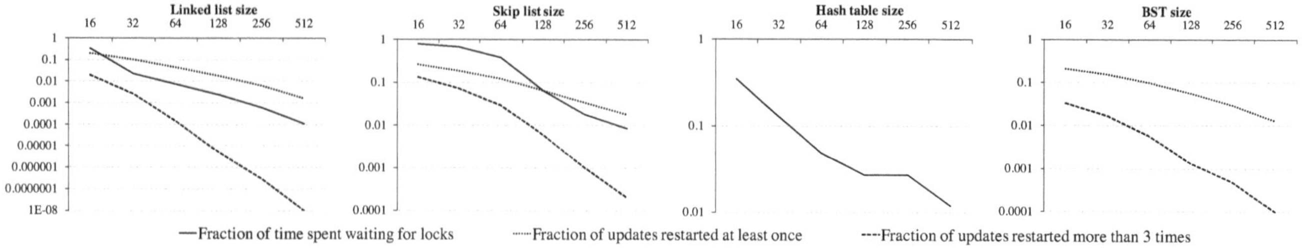

Figure 8: Delayed requests and time spent waiting for locks as a function of structure size.

and 10% update operations. In Figure 9, we provide results for the time spent waiting for locks and the number of restarted requests. Given that BST-TK uses trylocks [22], the waiting time for locks is normally 0. However, to better capture the effects of a slow thread on this algorithm, we depict the average time spent by threads on retries due to trylock failures. We note that threads spend at most 1% of their execution time waiting for locks. In fact, aside from the hash table, the percentages for the other data structures are significantly lower. We can lower this percentage for the hash table as well by replacing the per-bucket locks with finer grained locks for the linked lists representing each bucket. The percentage of restarted requests is also small: at most 0.015% for the skip-list. Thus, even under such workloads with temporary delays, the practically wait-free behavior of blocking CSDSs is not affected.

There is of course a limit up to which threads can be delayed before the system behavior is affected and practical wait-freedom jeopardized. In essence, an unresponsive thread might be problematic if (i) the delay happens while a thread is holding a lock and (ii) the thread is unresponsive for a large period of time. We find that such a scenario is possible, for example, in workloads where the number of threads significantly outnumbers the available cores (multi-programming). In an example using 4 threads per hardware context (160 threads in total), we find that around 3300 context switches occur every second. Roughly, that means that every thread executes for 12 ms, after which it is swapped out for 37 ms. Although critical sections in our algorithms are very short, a few of these context switches are bound to happen while locks are held. In such scenarios, while algorithms' performance is affected regardless of their progress guarantee, we find this to be more obvious in the case of blocking algorithms, particularly under workloads with higher update ratios.

To address this issue, we propose using hardware features recently introduced on modern architectures, such as Intel's Transactional Synchronization Extensions (TSX) [33], which allow us to elide locks. One characteristic of Intel's TSX implementations is the fact that hardware transactions are aborted when interrupts occur. While this is often regarded as a limitation [47, 61], we use

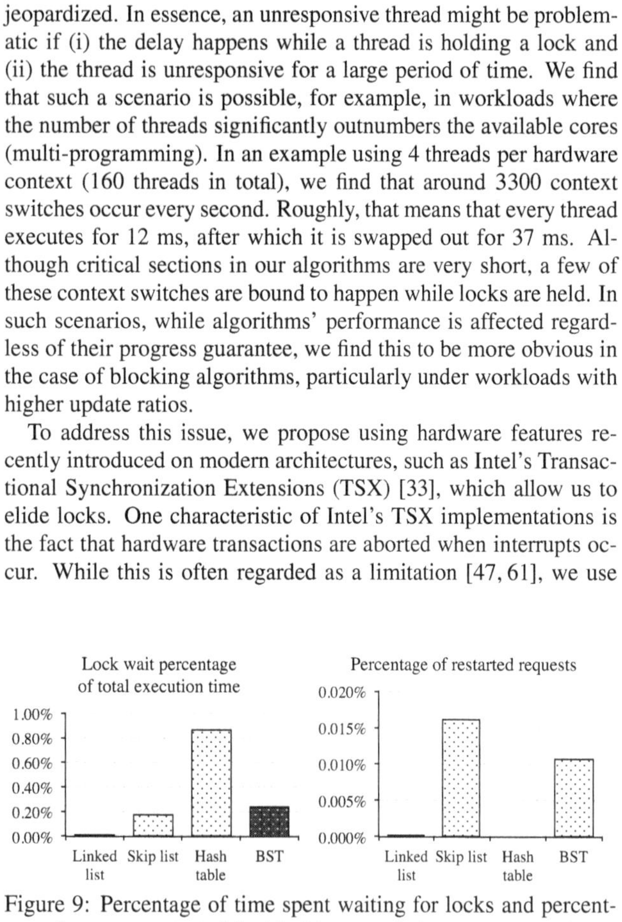

Figure 9: Percentage of time spent waiting for locks and percentage of requests restarted for blocking search data structures when a thread repeatedly suffers delays.

the abort-on-interrupt characteristic of TSX to our advantage, as it enables us to maintain the practically wait-free behavior of CSDS algorithms even in the case of frequent context switches, I/O, or other interrupts: even if a thread is within a critical section when the interrupt occurs, the hardware transaction is aborted and locks are not held when threads are not scheduled. This technique does not change the blocking nature of the algorithms: since Intel TSX is best-effort only, we need to provide a fall-back path which uses the actual locks for the situation when a speculative execution of a critical section is repeatedly aborted. The effectiveness of this approach is thus contingent on hardware transactions not aborting extremely frequently.

As we have observed in our evaluation, and as we will further show in Section 6, the probability of contention between two threads is small. Therefore, only a very limited percentage of updates will be repeatedly aborted due to data conflicts, even when contention is high. In addition, the short critical sections in the write phase do not trigger interrupts in the common case. While it is possible for page faults to occur within a critical section, we argue that this is a fairly rare event, and, given that by using TSX we can re-try the optimistic transactional approach multiple times before reverting back to the pessimistic path, this does not jeopardize wait-freedom. Additionally, TSX also provides us with a degree of tolerance to failed threads. Although in general one would stop a concurrent system rather than work with corrupted state, using TSX-enabled locks could also prevent failed threads from leaving the system in an inconsistent state, or holding locks after crashing.

We validate our hypothesis using a 3 GHz 4-core (8 hardware threads) Intel Haswell Core i7-4770 machine. The processor has 32 KB L1, 256 KB L2, and 8 MB L3 caches. Our algorithms remain unchanged: we only add TSX instructions to the acquire and release methods of the locks. Except for BST-TK, which uses ticket trylocks, all the other algorithms use test-and-set locks. We show results for a workload using 32 concurrent threads (8/physical core), with data structures consisting of 1024 key-value pairs and workloads with varying update ratios. Given the frequent context switches, measuring the amount of time threads spend waiting to acquire locks is not an appropriate metric here. Instead, we measure the number of operations that fail to elide the locks and fall back to normal lock acquisition: it is only these operations that have the potential of delaying other threads for longer amounts of time. We report this as a fraction of the total number of lock acquisition calls. The results are shown in Table 2. We note that in most cases the percentage of operations that acquire the locks is well below 1%. This number is slightly larger in the case of the skip-list, which needs to take multiple locks per update. The conclusion we can draw from this experiment is that the probability of a thread being de-scheduled while holding a lock is extremely small: an interrupt would have to occur while a thread is (i) in the write phase of an update operation and (ii) after the thread failed repeatedly to

Update ratio	Linked list	Skip list	Hash table	BST
20	0.001	0.011	0.001	0.000
50	0.001	0.012	0.001	0.000
100	0.001	0.014	0.002	0.001

Table 2: Fraction of critical sections falling back to acquiring locks using 8 threads/physical core (32 threads in total) with data structures of size 1024.

Update ratio	Linked list	Skip list	Hash table	BST
20	1.11	10.6	2.46	2.21
50	1.23	20.21	3.06	2.65
100	2.26	53.28	2.75	2.56

Table 3: Throughput improvements of TSX-enabled versions vs. default implementations using 8 threads/physical core (32 threads in total) with data structures of size 1024.

elide the locks. We theoretically estimate this probability in Section 6.

We also measure the increase in throughput we obtain in these scenarios when using TSX. Table 3 shows the ratio between the throughput of the TSX-enhanced versions of the algorithms and the default implementations. We note important improvements in all data structures. The benefits of using TSX are particularly impressive in the case of the skip list. This is due to the lager number of locks per update operation, which increases the potential of a thread being de-scheduled while holding a lock.[3]

The behavior revealed in the previous experiments allows us to conclude that TSX indeed enables us to maintain practically wait-free behavior even in the face of frequent context switches, which is a scenario particularly well-known for causing issues in the context of concurrent systems.

Depending on the level of privilege of the code, an alternative to our solution could be to make the critical sections non-preemptable. However, even this might be problematic in the context of virtualization: scheduling multiple virtual machines in the presence of locks is a well-known challenge [19, 36, 55, 59]. Essentially, the guest OS does not have control over the scheduling decisions of the hypervisor. Our proposed approach would maintain the practical wait-freedom of CSDS algorithms even in such a situation, and may prove beneficial for other applications in virtualized environments as well.

In this section, we have shown that blocking algorithms behave practically wait-free on structures of different sizes, with different percentages of updates, under non-uniform workloads, under extreme contention and with frequently unresponsive threads. While it is extremely difficult for an evaluation to address every possible scenario, we argue that these experiments cover most situations that arise in practical systems using CSDSs. Thus, given the behavior of blocking CSDSs observed in this section, we conclude that in practice, for the vast majority of workloads, blocking CSDSs behave practically wait-free.

6. THE BIRTHDAY PARADOX

In essence, the explanation for the wait-free behavior of blocking CSDSs is that the probability of threads being delayed due to contention is very small. We say that a *conflict* occurs when a thread is blocked or restarted by another thread. In state-of-the-art CSDS algorithms, a thread can generally encounter a conflict only during the write phase of an update operation. We provide an estimation of this conflict probability using an analogy with the *birthday paradox*.

Assuming threads that continuously issue requests, we first estimate the fraction of time a thread spends doing update operations (in a concurrent execution, including the acquisition and release of locks):

$$f_u = \frac{u \times dur_u}{u \times dur_u + (1-u) \times dur_r} \tag{1}$$

Here u is the update ratio (the fraction of operations that are updates), dur_u is the average duration of an update, and dur_r is the average duration of a read.

We then estimate the fraction of time a thread spends in its write phase, where d_w is the average duration of the write phase, and d_p is the average duration of the parse phase (recall that in state-of-the-art algorithms updates have a parse phase and an update phase):

$$f_w = f_u \times \frac{d_w}{d_w + d_p} \tag{2}$$

It is then a matter of computing the probability of conflict between threads concurrently executing their write phase. This is highly specific to the data structure, the implementation, and the request distribution. In general however, it can be reduced to variations of the birthday paradox: the probability of randomly chosen variables being similar enough to each other to cause conflicts. We denote by $B_s(k,n)$ the probability that if k threads are concurrently executing their write phases on a structure s of size n, at least one conflict will arise.

The probability of conflict in a system with t threads is thus:

$$p_{conflict} = \sum_{k=1}^{t} \binom{t}{k} {f_w}^k (1-f_w)^{t-k} B_s(k,n) \tag{3}$$

We now provide numeric examples for some of the structures and workloads employed in this paper.

6.1 Hash table

Our hash table implementation has the particularity of using one lock per bucket. Hence, in the above equations, d_p is 0: the lock is acquired immediately after the update starts. In the case of the hash table, since conflicts only appear if two threads want to write to the same bucket concurrently, the problem reduces to the classical version of the birthday paradox. We therefore have:

$$B_{ht}(k,n) = 1 - \frac{\prod_{i=1}^{k-1}(n-i)}{n^{k-1}} \tag{4}$$

We first assume a uniform workload for simplicity (see below for a non-uniform case). In this scenario, an update operation takes approximatively twice as long as a read operation. We assume a scenario with 1024 buckets and 20 threads, with 10% of the operations being updates. f_u is then 0.18, f_w has the same value (given that d_p is 0), and thus, using the formulas above, we obtain $p_{conflict} = 0.0058$. Therefore, the probability of any thread being delayed due to concurrency at any point in time is about 0.58%, a small enough percent to lead to wait-free behavior.

6.2 Linked list

In the case of other data structures, this computation is slightly more complex. For example, in our linked list, in which a remove operation has to lock two consecutive nodes, we can use the solution to the "almost birthday paradox" [1] to provide an upper bound

[3] We notice no important difference between the default and TSX-enabled implementations in other experiments used in this paper.

to the probability of conflict. In this case, we have:

$$B_{ll}(k,n) = 1 - \frac{(n-k-1)!}{(n-2k)!n^{k-1}} \quad (5)$$

We provide a numerical example, considering a slightly higher contention example, with a list of 512 elements, 40 concurrent threads and 20% updates. An important distinction with the hash table is that the parse phase dominates the latency of an update operation. In fact, on average, the write phase takes only around 10% of the parse phase duration. That also means that updates are only one tenth more expensive than reads. Applying the presented formulas, we obtain $f_w \approx 0.0215$. We apply the formula for computing the probability of conflict in the case of the almost birthday paradox and obtain $p_{conflict} = 0.0021$. In the case of the linked list, the probability of conflict is thus 0.21%, again a percentage permitting wait-free executions.

6.3 Uniform vs. non-uniform workloads

In the above, we have considered uniform workloads. Of course, one could also repeat the computations considering non-uniform accesses. In that case, a variation of the birthday paradox using non-uniform probability distributions would have to be employed. For instance, using a Poisson approximation to model the probability of conflicts in such scenarios, we have:

$$B_{non-uniform}(k,n) = 1 - e^{-\binom{k}{2}\sum_{i=1}^{n} p_i^2} \quad (6)$$

Here, p_i denotes the probability of element i in the structure to be accessed. Using our linked list example from above and a Zipfian workload with $s = 0.8$, the probability of conflict is 0.47%. This value is slightly larger than in the uniform case, but still well below 1%, allowing practically wait-free executions.

These examples do not take into account slow threads, assuming similar speeds for all participants. One could model a slow thread, by assuming that while a thread t_{slow} writes to a set of memory locations, the other threads do multiple operations, writing to multiple such sets of locations. We give below an intuition for the probability of conflict when using TSX to avoid threads holding locks being interrupted.

6.4 TSX-based algorithms

In the algorithm versions in which the critical sections are wrapped with TSX instructions, speculative execution can be attempted several times. We assume each transactional region is tried five times before falling back to actually taking the locks. In these versions of the algorithms, conflicts occur if data that is being written during the critical section is read or written by another thread, or if data read during the critical section is written by another thread. Hence, while as before, only threads which are in the write phase may be the victims of a conflict, in this case all other threads may be causing the conflict, even those in the process of reading data. We can continue to use Equation 2 in order to estimate the probability of a conflict. However, given that threads during their read or parse phases also need to be taken into account, the computation of the term $B_s(k,n)$ will be different, as we will illustrate in the following. With five re-tries before reverting to locking, we can estimate the probability of a thread reverting to locking as $p_{lock} = p_{conflict}^5$.

We use the same hash table and linked list examples as above. In the case of the hash table, by taking reads into account when computing the probability of conflict with k current writers on a hash table of size n, we have:

$$B_{ht-tsx}(k,n) = 1 - \frac{(n-k)^{t-k}\prod_{i=1}^{k-1}(n-i)}{n^{t-1}} \quad (7)$$

With the same numeric values as before, $p_{lock} = 0.0005\%$.

In the case of the TSX-enhanced linked list, we have:

$$B_{ll-tsx}(k,n) = 1 - \frac{(n-k-1)!}{(n-2k)!n^{k-1}}\left(\frac{(n-2k)(n-2k-1)}{n(n-k-1)}\right)^{t-k} \quad (8)$$

For our linked list example, this results in $p_{lock} = 0.001\%$ (in the case of this fairly contended linked list, the probability of at least a re-try of the transactional region is however non-negligible: 16%).

It is important to note the significance of the low probabilities of conflict computed throughout this section: it simply means that there is a 1% chance that *some* thread in the system is delayed at any point in time. This delay, as shown by our practical evaluation, is likely to be insignificant for any particular thread. In addition, after such small delays the thread quickly returns to its steady state, with no changes to the parameters considered in this section.

7. BEYOND SEARCH DATA STRUCTURES

In the previous sections, we focused our attention on search data structures. One of the main reasons we are able to obtain a practically wait-free behavior for a large spectrum of workloads in the case of state-of-the-art CSDSs is the low probability of conflicts between concurrent operations: accesses are distributed over all the nodes contained in the structure. In this section, we briefly present the limits of our conclusion when applied to concurrent objects other than search data structures.

7.1 Intuition

Intuitively, in the case of data structures such as queues, stacks, priority queues, and counters, the accesses are not distributed among multiple memory addresses, but rather concentrated on a small number of "hotspots". In this case, blocking algorithms essentially serialize operations by only allowing one (or a small number) to execute at a time. Thus, each thread spends a significant amount of time waiting for its turn. HTM-based techniques, which mitigate delays due to interrupts for search data structures, are also not applicable for such data structures: virtually all hardware transactions would repeatedly abort due to data conflicts. In a search data structure, it is only possible to encounter similar scenarios if (i) only a handful of nodes in the CSDS are accessed (ii) continuously by a large number of threads (iii) with a large fraction of the accesses being updates.

7.2 Experimentation

We quantify the extent to which these characteristics hinder practical wait-freedom using standard lock-based algorithms for a queue and a stack. Figure 10 shows the fraction of time threads spend waiting for locks in the case of these data structures. We use 20 concurrent threads, with 50% of the operations being inserts (enqueue/push), and 50% removes (dequeue/pop). The structures contain 1024 nodes. We note that the fraction of time threads spend waiting quickly approaches 1 as we increase the number of threads. This behavior is clearly not compliant with practical wait-freedom.

In the case of such data structures therefore, one can expect to obtain better performance by using lock-free or wait-free algorithms, to the design of which much work has been dedicated [16, 26, 35, 38, 46, 56, 60]. Another technique which has proved effective for such data structures is flat combining [25]. A further avenue which has been pursued in recent years in order to reduce the contention for any particular node in such structures is to relax the semantics of the data structure operations [4, 12, 62].

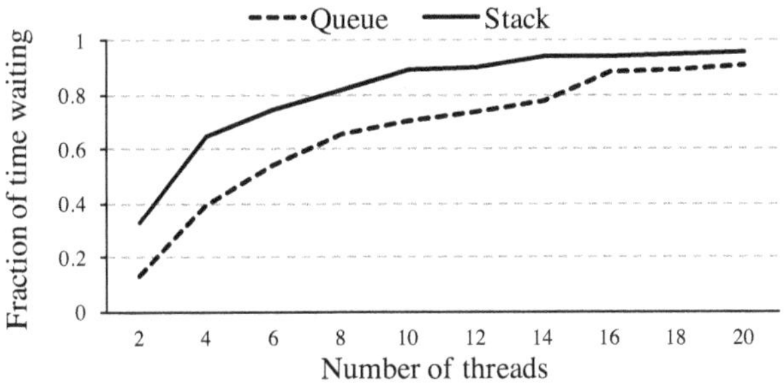

Figure 10: Percentage of time threads spend waiting in blocking queue and stack implementations.

8. RELATED WORK

Asynchronized concurrency [9] is a set of patterns for the design of CSDS algorithms resulting in implementations with nearly-optimal throughput. The choice between blocking or lock-free CSDS algorithms is shown to not be of fundamental importance from the point of view of performance (i.e., throughput, average latency) as long as these patterns are applied. However, the authors only focus on the aggregate, system-wide performance metrics, and do not study metrics indicative of the behavior of individual requests. Similarly, Gramoli [21] studies different classes of concurrent data structures, and observes no inherent difference in aggregate throughput between lock-free and lock-based search data structures. In this paper, we look at CSDSs through the perspective of a different criterion: practical wait-freedom.

We are not the first to ask whether algorithms with weaker progress guarantees do not actually provide wait-freedom, given some assumptions about the execution environment. We are however the first to look at blocking algorithms. In doing so, we also provide the first practical quantification of the effects of progress guarantees on CSDSs. Ellen et al. [17] show that under an unknown-bound synchronous model, obstruction-free algorithms can behave practically wait-free. Herlihy and Shavit [29] suggest that on realistic schedulers, lock-free algorithms behave in a wait-free manner. Alistarh et al. [3] prove that assuming a stochastic scheduler which determines the ordering of accesses to a memory location, lock-free algorithms behave practically wait-free. Our work suggests that in the case of CSDSs, given the fact that the probability of contention for any memory location is low, the characteristics of the scheduler governing the order of memory accesses might not be a determining factor.

Michael [45] also studies the practical trade-offs between different progress guarantees. However, his analysis only discusses non-blocking algorithms, and does not focus on CSDSs, but mostly on objects where a single point of contention is likely, such as counters and queues. As we have shown in this paper, the properties of state-of-the-art concurrent algorithms for search data structures are significantly different from other concurrent structures.

Rajwar and Goodman [54] propose a hardware mechanism for transactions and identify it as conductive to non-blocking behavior in lock-based programs. However, the transactional support they propose provides starvation freedom, which is not the case in practical implementations such as Intel TSX. In the context of blocking CSDSs, we show that HTM support is needed for wait-free behavior in a particular set of circumstances only. This observation is, we believe, interesting in its own right. We also show that wait-free behavior is possible even with best-effort transactional memory which may revert to locking, and explain why this conclusion does not extend to other concurrent structures beyond CSDSs.

9. CONCLUDING REMARKS

The main conclusion we can draw from this paper is that, practically, one can achieve the behavior of wait-free CSDS algorithms in terms of individual thread progress with blocking implementations. The nature of search data structures is such that there is no single contention point in the structure, rendering locks less problematic than they might be for structures such as concurrent queues, stacks, and counters. Our conclusions only concern CSDSs: we do not claim blocking implementations of objects such as queues and stacks are practically wait-free. It is also important to note that we do not claim that *every* blocking CSDS algorithm is practically wait-free. Rather, we considered state-of-the-art blocking algorithms, which generally have synchronization-free reads and writes with minimal and extremely fine-grained synchronization. We find such practically wait-free algorithms for each data structure we study. In addition to showing that these algorithms are practically wait-free, this work also represents the first detailed quantification of the effects of a progress guarantee on the behavior of practical CSDSs. Moreover, we have shown how new technologies such as Intel TSX can be leveraged to provide the desired performance characteristics of CSDSs. We also note that while the experiments presented in this paper were run on an Intel Xeon server, we have verified our conclusions on other architectures as well, including servers from AMD and Oracle.

Acknowledgements. This work has been supported in part by a VMware Fellowship.

10. REFERENCES

[1] Morton Abramson and WOJ Moser. More birthday surprises. *American Mathematical Monthly*, pages 856–858, 1970.

[2] Yehuda Afek, Dalia Dauber, and Dan Touitou. Wait-free Made Fast. STOC 1995.

[3] Dan Alistarh, Keren Censor-Hillel, and Nir Shavit. Are Lock-free Concurrent Algorithms Practically Wait-free? STOC 2014.

[4] Dan Alistarh, Justin Kopinsky, Jerry Li, and Nir Shavit. The SprayList: A Scalable Relaxed Priority Queue. PPoPP 2015.

[5] ASCYLIB. http://github.com/LPD-EPFL/ASCYLIB.

[6] Nathan G. Bronson, Jared Casper, Hassan Chafi, and Kunle Olukotun. A Practical Concurrent Binary Search Tree. PPoPP 2010.

[7] Nachshon Cohen and Erez Petrank. Efficient Memory Management for Lock-Free Data Structures with Optimistic Access. SPAA 2015.

[8] Brian F. Cooper, Adam Silberstein, Erwin Tam, Raghu Ramakrishnan, and Russell Sears. Benchmarking Cloud Serving Systems with YCSB. SoCC 2010.

[9] Tudor David, Rachid Guerraoui, and Vasileios Trigonakis. Asynchronized Concurrency: The Secret to Scaling Concurrent Search Data Structures. ASPLOS 2015.

[10] Tudor David, Rachid Guerraoui, and Vasileios Trigonakis. Everything You Always Wanted to Know About Synchronization but Were Afraid to Ask. SOSP 2013.

[11] Mathieu Desnoyers, Paul E McKenney, Alan S Stern, Michel R Dagenais, and Jonathan Walpole. User-level implementations of read-copy update. *Parallel and Distributed Systems, IEEE Transactions on*, 23(2):375–382, 2012.

[12] Dave Dice, Yossi Lev, and Mark Moir. Scalable Statistics Counters. SPAA 2013.

[13] Dana Drachsler, Martin Vechev, and Eran Yahav. Practical

Concurrent Binary Search Trees via Logical Ordering. PPoPP 2014.

[14] Faith Ellen, Panagiota Fatourou, Eric Ruppert, and Franck van Breugel. Non-blocking Binary Search Trees. PODC 2010.

[15] Facebook. RocksDB. http://rocksdb.org.

[16] Panagiota Fatourou and Nikolaos D. Kallimanis. A Highly-efficient Wait-free Universal Construction. SPAA 2011.

[17] Faith Ellen Fich, Victor Luchangco, Mark Moir, Nir Shavit, and Sun Microsystems Laboratories. Obstruction-Free algorithms can be practically wait-free. DISC 2005.

[18] Keir Fraser. *Practical Lock-Freedom*. PhD thesis, University of Cambridge, 2004.

[19] Thomas Friebel and Sebastian Biemueller. How to Deal with Lock Holder Preemption. Xen Summit North America 2008.

[20] Google. LevelDB. http://leveldb.org.

[21] Vincent Gramoli. More Than You Ever Wanted to Know About Synchronization: Synchrobench, Measuring the Impact of the Synchronization on Concurrent Algorithms. PPoPP 2015.

[22] Rachid Guerraoui and Vasileios Trigonakis. Optimistic Concurrency with OPTIK. PPoPP 2016.

[23] Timothy L Harris. A Pragmatic Implementation of Non-blocking Linked Lists. DISC 2001.

[24] Steve Heller, Maurice Herlihy, Victor Luchangco, Mark Moir, III Scherer, William N., and Nir Shavit. A Lazy Concurrent List-Based Set Algorithm. In *Principles of Distributed Systems*, volume 3974. 2006.

[25] Danny Hendler, Itai Incze, Nir Shavit, and Moran Tzafrir. Flat combining and the synchronization-parallelism tradeoff. SPAA 2010.

[26] Danny Hendler, Nir Shavit, and Lena Yerushalmi. A Scalable Lock-free Stack Algorithm. SPAA 2004.

[27] Maurice Herlihy. Wait-free Synchronization. *ACM Trans. Program. Lang. Syst.*, 13(1):124–149, 1991.

[28] Maurice Herlihy, Yossi Lev, Victor Luchangco, and Nir Shavit. A simple optimistic skiplist algorithm. SIROCCO 2007.

[29] Maurice Herlihy and Nir Shavit. On the Nature of Progress. OPODIS 2011.

[30] Maurice Herlihy and Nir Shavit. *The Art of Multiprocessor Programming, Revised First Edition*. 2012.

[31] Maurice P Herlihy and Jeannette M Wing. Linearizability: A correctness condition for concurrent objects. *ACM Transactions on Programming Languages and Systems*, 12(3):463–492, 1990.

[32] Shane V Howley and Jeremy Jones. A non-blocking internal binary search tree. SPAA 2012.

[33] Intel. Intel Transactional Synchronization Extensions Overview. 2013.

[34] Intel Thread Building Blocks. https://www.threadingbuildingblocks.org.

[35] Amos Israeli and Lihu Rappoport. Efficient wait-free implementation of a concurrent priority queue.

[36] Avi Kivity, Dor Laor, Glauber Costa, Pekka Enberg, Nadav Har'El, Don Marti, and Vlad Zolotarov. OSv—Optimizing the Operating System for Virtual Machines. Usenix ATC 2014.

[37] Alex Kogan and Erez Petrank. A Methodology for Creating Fast Wait-free Data Structures. PPoPP 2012.

[38] Alex Kogan and Erez Petrank. Wait-free Queues with Multiple Enqueuers and Dequeuers. PPoPP 2011.

[39] Doug Lea. Overview of package util.concurrent Release 1.3.4. http://gee.cs.oswego.edu/dl/classes/EDU/oswego/cs/dl/util/concurrent/intro.html, 2003.

[40] Paul E. McKenney, Dipankar Sarma, and Maneesh Soni. Scaling Dcache with RCU. *Linux Journal*, 2004(117), January 2004.

[41] Paul E McKenney and John D Slingwine. Read-copy update: Using execution history to solve concurrency problems. In *Parallel and Distributed Computing and Systems*, pages 509–518, 1998.

[42] Memcached. http://www.memcached.org.

[43] Maged M Michael. High performance dynamic lock-free hash tables and list-based sets. SPAA 2002.

[44] Maged M Michael. Hazard pointers: Safe memory reclamation for lock-free objects. *Parallel and Distributed Systems, IEEE Transactions on*, 15(6):491–504, 2004.

[45] Maged M. Michael. The Balancing Act of Choosing Nonblocking Features. *ACM Queue*, 11(7):50–61, 2013.

[46] Maged M. Michael and Michael L. Scott. Simple, Fast, and Practical Non-blocking and Blocking Concurrent Queue Algorithms. PODC 1996.

[47] Mohamed Mohamedin, Roberto Palmieri, Ahmed Hassan, and Binoy Ravindran. Brief announcement: Managing resource limitation of best-effort HTM. SPAA 2015.

[48] Monetdb. http://www.monetdb.org.

[49] Mongodb. http://www.mongodb.org.

[50] Mysql. http://www.mysql.com.

[51] Aravind Natarajan and Neeraj Mittal. Fast Concurrent Lock-free Binary Search Trees. PPoPP 2014.

[52] Oracle. CopyOnWriteArrayList in Java docs. http://docs.oracle.com/javase/7/docs/api/java/util/concurrent/CopyOnWriteArrayList.html.

[53] William Pugh. Concurrent Maintenance of Skip Lists. Technical report, 1990.

[54] Ravi Rajwar and James R. Goodman. Transactional Lock-free Execution of Lock-based Programs. ASPLOS 2002.

[55] Xiang Song, Jicheng Shi, Haibo Chen, and Binyu Zang. Schedule Processes, Not VCPUs. APSys 2013.

[56] Håkan Sundell and Philippas Tsigas. Fast and lock-free concurrent priority queues for multi-thread systems. IPDPS 2003.

[57] Shahar Timnat, Anastasia Braginsky, Alex Kogan, and Erez Petrank. Wait-free linked-lists. OPODIS 2012.

[58] Shahar Timnat and Erez Petrank. A Practical Wait-free Simulation for Lock-free Data Structures. PPoPP 2014.

[59] Volkmar Uhlig, Joshua LeVasseur, Espen Skoglund, and Uwe Dannowski. Towards Scalable Multiprocessor Virtual Machines. VM 2004.

[60] Valois, John D. Implementing lock-free queues. ICPDCS 1994.

[61] Zhaoguo Wang, Hao Qian, Haibo Chen, and Jinyang Li. Opportunities and Pitfalls of Multi-core Scaling Using Hardware Transaction Memory. APSys 2013.

[62] Martin Wimmer, Jakob Gruber, Jesper Larsson Träff, and Philippas Tsigas. The lock-free k-LSM relaxed priority queue. PPoPP 2015.

Fast and Robust Memory Reclamation for Concurrent Data Structures

Oana Balmau
EPFL

Rachid Guerraoui
EPFL

Maurice Herlihy
Brown University

Igor Zablotchi
EPFL

ABSTRACT

In concurrent systems without automatic garbage collection, it is challenging to determine when it is safe to reclaim memory, especially for lock-free data structures. Existing concurrent memory reclamation schemes are either fast but do not tolerate process delays, robust to delays but with high overhead, or both robust and fast but narrowly applicable.

This paper proposes QSense, a novel concurrent memory reclamation technique. QSense is a hybrid technique with a fast path and a fallback path. In the common case (without process delays), a high-performing memory reclamation scheme is used (fast path). If process delays block memory reclamation through the fast path, a robust fallback path is used to guarantee progress. The fallback path uses hazard pointers, but avoids their notorious need for frequent and expensive memory fences.

QSense is widely applicable, as we illustrate through several lock-free data structure algorithms. Our experimental evaluation shows that QSense has an overhead comparable to the fastest memory reclamation techniques, while still tolerating prolonged process delays.

1. INTRODUCTION

1.1 The Problem

Any realistic application requires its data structures to grow and shrink dynamically and hence to reclaim memory that is no longer being used. For the foreseeable future, many high-performing applications, such as operating systems and databases, will be written in languages where programmers manage memory explicitly (such as C or C++). There is thus a clear need for concurrent data structures that scale *and* efficiently allocate/free memory. Designing such data structures is however challenging, as it is not clear when it is safe to free memory, especially when locks are prohibited (lock-free constructions [12, 19]).

To illustrate the difficulty, consider, as illustrated in Figure 1, two processes p_1 and p_2 concurrently accessing a

SPAA '16, July 11-13, 2016, Pacific Grove, CA, USA

DOI: http://dx.doi.org/10.1145/2935764.2935790

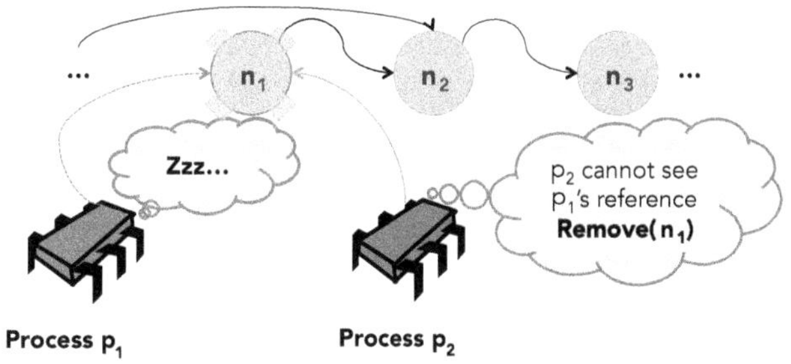

Figure 1: The concurrent memory reclamation problem.

linked list of several nodes. Process p_1 is reading node n_1, while p_2 is concurrently removing node n_1. Assume p_2 unlinks n_1 from the list. Then, p_2 needs to decide whether n_1's memory can be freed. If p_2 were allowed to block p_1 and inspect p_1's references, then it could easily determine whether freeing n_1 is safe. But in a lock-free context, p_2 has a priori no way of knowing if p_1 is still accessing n_1 or not. So, if p_2 goes ahead and frees node n_1, it triggers an illegal access next time p_1 tries to use n_1.

1.2 The Trade-off

Various approaches have been proposed to address the issue of concurrent, programmer-controlled memory reclamation for lock-free data structures. *Hazard pointers* (HP) [26] (which we recall in more details in § 3) is perhaps the most widely-used method. Basically, the programmer publishes the addresses (hazard pointers) of nodes for as long as they cannot be safely reclaimed. A reclaiming process must ensure that a node it is about to free is not marked by any other process. The hazard pointer methodology holds two important advantages: (1) it is wait-free and (2) it is applicable to a wide range of data structures. However, hazard pointers also have a notable drawback: as we explain in § 3.2, they require a memory fence instruction for every node traversed in the data structure. This can decrease performance by up to 75% (as we will see in § 7).

Most memory reclamation techniques that seek to overcome the performance penalty of hazard pointers have been analyzed in terms of amortized overhead [1, 6, 7, 15]: the overhead of reclamation operations is spread across several node accesses or across several operations, thus considerably reducing their impact on performance. *Quiescent State Based Reclamation* (QSBR) (which we recall in § 3), is among the most popular schemes applying the amortized overhead principle [7, 15]. QSBR is fast and can be applied to virtually any data structure. However, QSBR is *blocking*: if a process is delayed for a long time (a process failure is

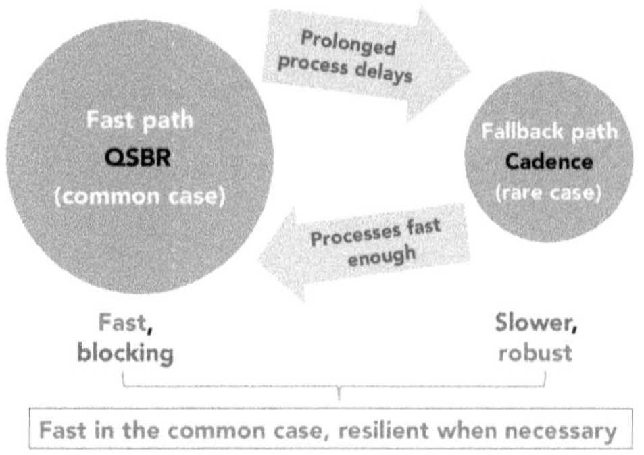

Figure 2: A high-level view of QSense.

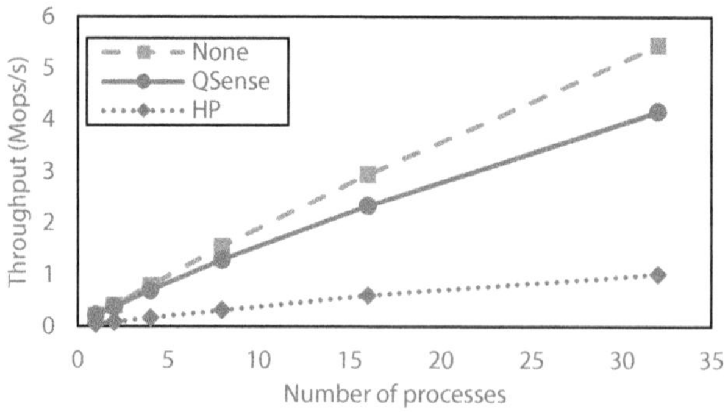

Figure 3: QSense, HP and no reclamation on a linked list of 2000 elements, with a 10% updates workload.

a particular type of delay), an unbounded amount of memory might remain unreclaimed. As such, using QSBR with lock-free data structures would negate one of the main advantages of lock-freedom: *robustness* to process delays.

There have indeed been several proposals for achieving both lock-freedom and low amortized overhead [6, 7]. Yet, these are ad-hoc methods that apply only to certain well-chosen data structures. They require significant effort to be adapted to other data structures (as we discuss in § 8).

Overall, the current prevalent solutions for concurrent memory reclamation are either *wait-free* but *with high overhead*, *fast* but *blocking*, or *ad-hoc*, lacking a clear and systematic methodology on how to apply them.

1.3 The Contributions

We design, implement and evaluate *QSense*, a novel technique for concurrent memory reclamation that is, at the same time, easily applicable to a wide range of concurrent data structures (including lock-free ones), robust, and fast.

QSense uses a hybrid approach to provide fast and robust memory reclamation. Figure 2 depicts a high-level view of QSense. In the common case (i.e. when processes do not undergo prolonged delays), the fast QSBR scheme is employed. A delay could be caused, for instance, by cache misses, application-related delays, or being descheduled by the operating system. By *prolonged delay*, we refer to a delay of a process p_1 that is long enough such that a large number of nodes (larger than a given configurable threshold) are removed but cannot be safely reclaimed by another concurrent process p_2. If prolonged process delays are detected, QSense automatically switches to a fall-back memory reclamation scheme that is robust. When all processes are active again (no more prolonged delays), the system automatically switches back to the fast path. By *robustness* we mean that any process performing operations on the data structure (called *worker process*) will finish any action related to memory reclamation within a bounded number of steps, regardless of the progress of other worker processes. To guarantee this progress, we require certain timing assumptions about a set of auxiliary background processes, that do not participate in the actual data structure operations (all assumptions are discussed in § 5).

The fall-back path consists of a subprotocol we call *Cadence*, a novel amortized variant of the widely-used hazard pointer mechanism. Cadence overcomes the necessity for per-node memory barriers during data structure traversal, significantly increasing performance. We achieve this through two new concepts. The first is *rooster processes*: background processes that periodically wake up and generate context switches, which act as memory barriers. The periodic context switches ensure that any hazard pointer becomes visible to other processes within a bounded time T. The second concept is *deferred reclamation*: a process p only reclaims a removed node n after n has been awaiting reclamation for longer than T. This ensures any hazard pointer potentially protecting n must be visible. Therefore, n's memory can be safely freed provided no hazard pointers are protecting n. Cadence can be used either as part of QSense or as a stand-alone memory reclamation scheme.

QSense requires minimal additions to the data structure code, consisting only of a number of calls to functions provided by the QSense interface. We present a simple set of rules that determine where to place these calls. QSense communicates with data structures through three functions: `manage_qsense_state`, `assign_HP` and `free_node_later`. The rules concerning where to call these three functions are:

1. Call `manage_qsense_state` in states where no references to shared objects are held by the processes (usually in between data structure operations).
2. Call `assign_HP` before using a reference to a node so as to inform other processes that the node's memory should not be reclaimed yet.
3. Call `free_node_later` whenever a node is removed from the data structure (where `free` would be called in a sequential setting).

We show empirically that QSense achieves good performance in a wide range of scenarios, while providing the same progress guarantees as a hazard pointer based scheme. Our experiments in § 7 show that QSense achieves a 29% overhead on average over leaky implementations of a lock-free concurrent linked list, a skip list and a binary search tree. Moreover, QSense outperforms the popular hazard pointers technique by two to three times. To illustrate this point, Figure 3 shows sample results from our experiments, comparing QSense to hazard pointers and no memory reclamation (leaky implementation) on a concurrent linked list.

Roadmap. The rest of this paper is organized as follows. In § 2, we pose the problem. In § 3, we recall prior work that inspired QSense. In § 4, we give an overview of QSense. Then, in § 5, we dive into the details of Cadence and detail the assumptions needed for its correctness. In § 6, we prove safety and liveness properties of QSense. In § 7, we compare QSense's performance against that of popular memory reclamation schemes. Finally, in § 8, we describe related work and we conclude in § 9.

2. MODEL AND PROBLEM DEFINITION

We consider a set of n processes that communicate through a set of shared memory locations using primitive memory access operations. A *node* is a set of memory locations that can be viewed as a logical entity. A *data structure* consists of one or more fixed nodes that can always be accessed directly by the processes, called *roots*, and the set of nodes that are reachable by following pointers from the roots.

2.1 Node States

At any given time, a node can be in one of five states [26]: (1) *Allocated* — the node has been allocated by a process, but not yet inserted into the data structure. (2) *Reachable* — the node is reachable by following pointers from the roots of the data structure. (3) *Removed* — the node is no longer *reachable*, but may still be in use by some processes. (4) *Retired* — the node is removed and cannot be used by any process, but is not yet *free*. (5) *Free* — the node's memory is available for allocation.

2.2 The Memory Reclamation Problem

We can now state the *memory reclamation problem* as follows: given some *removed* nodes, make them available for re-allocation (i.e. change their state to *free*) after it is no longer possible for any process (except the reclaiming process) to access them (i.e. after they have become *retired*).

The problem is distinct from garbage collection. Here, we are only concerned with the reclamation of memory used by data structure nodes, and not the reclamation of arbitrary memory regions. Moreover, the nodes whose memory needs to be reclaimed are expressly marked by the programmer after they have been explicitly unlinked from the data structure and are no longer reachable.

2.3 Terminology

Safe: A node n is *safe* [26] for a process p if: (1) n is *allocated* and p is the process that allocated it, or (2) n is *reachable*, or (3) n is *removed* or *retired* and p is the process that removed n from the data structure.

Possibly unsafe: A node n is *possibly unsafe* [26] for a processes p if it is impossible, using only knowledge of p's private variables and the semantics of the data structure algorithm used, to positively establish that n is *safe* for p. Informally, a node is *possibly unsafe* if it is impossible to determine using only local process data and knowledge of the data structure algorithm whether accessing n will trigger an access violation (e.g. if n has been reclaimed in the meanwhile).

Access hazard: An *access hazard* [26] is a step in the algorithm that might result in accessing a *possibly unsafe* node for the process that is executing the algorithm.

Hazardous reference: A process p holds a *hazardous reference* [26] to a node n if one of p's private variables holds n's address and p will reach an *access hazard* that uses n's address. Informally, a *hazardous reference* is an address that will be used later in a hazardous manner (i.e. to access *possibly unsafe* memory) without further verification of safety.

3. BACKGROUND

In this section we recall quiescent state based reclamation and hazard pointers, the techniques QSense builds upon.

3.1 Quiescent State Based Reclamation

Quiescent State Based Reclamation (QSBR) is a technique which emerged in the context of memory management in operating system kernels [4]. Quiescence-based schemes are fast, outrunning popular pointer-based schemes under a variety of workloads [15]. Therefore, in QSense, we chose a quiescence technique for the fast path. Though not a contribution of this paper, QSBR is detailed below, for completeness. QSBR makes use of *quiescent states* (at process level) and *grace periods* (at system level).

A process is in a *quiescent state* if it does not hold references to any shared objects in the data structure. Quiescent states need to be specified at the application level. Typically, a process is in a quiescent state whenever it is in between operations (read/insert/delete). In practice, quiescent states are declared after processes have finished a larger number of operations — called the *quiescence threshold* — as batching operations in this way boosts performance.

A *grace period* is a time interval in the execution during which each worker process in the system goes through at least one quiescent state. If the time interval $[a, b]$ is a grace period, after time b no process holds hazardous references to nodes that were removed before time a. The occurrence of grace periods is managed through an epoch-based technique [7, 15]. At every step of the execution, every process is in one of three logical epochs. Each process has three lists in which removed nodes are stored, called *limbo lists* (one per epoch). If a node n has been removed when a process p was in epoch i, n will be added to p's i^{th} limbo list. Each process keeps track of its local epoch and all processes have access to a shared global epoch. When a process p declares a quiescent state, it does the following. If p's local epoch e_p is different than the global epoch e_G, then p updates e_p to e_G. Else, if all processes have their local epoch equal to e_G (including p), p increments e_G by 1.

The Problem of Robustness in QSBR. The main advantage of QSBR is the low overhead. Nevertheless, its lack of robustness to significant process delays makes its out of the box use unsuitable for some practical applications. As we show in § 7, if achieving a grace period is no longer possible or takes a significant amount of time, the system might run out of memory and eventually block. In § 5, we show how we address the problem of resilience to prolonged process delays in QSense.

3.2 Hazard Pointers (HP)

The main idea behind the hazard pointers scheme [26] is to associate with each process a number of single-writer multi-reader pointers. These pointers — called *hazard pointers* — are used by processes to indicate which nodes they might be about to access without further validation. The nodes marked by hazard pointers are unsafe to reclaim.

The hazard pointer scheme mainly consists of *node marking* and *node reclamation*. *Node marking* is the assignment of hazard pointers to nodes. This ensures that the reclaiming process can discern which of the nodes that were removed from the data structure are *retired* (and thus safe to reclaim). *Node reclamation* is a procedure that makes nodes available for re-allocation. Every time a process removes a node from a data structure, the process adds a reference to the node in a local list of removed nodes. After a given number of node removals, each process will go through its list of removed nodes and will free those nodes that are not protected by any hazard pointers. The programmer needs to ensure the following condition:

CONDITION 1. *At the time of any hazardous access by a process p to the memory location of a node n (access hazard), n has been continuously protected by one of p's hazard pointers since a time when n was definitely safe for p.*

Michael [26] provides a *methodology* for programmers to enforce this condition: (1) Identify all hazardous references and access hazards in the data structure code. (2) For each hazardous reference, determine the step when the reference is created and the last access hazard where the reference is used. This is the period when the reference needs to be protected by a hazard pointer. (3) Examine the overlap of the periods from step 2. The maximum number of hazard pointers is the maximum number of distinct hazardous references that exist simultaneously for the same process. (4) For each hazardous reference, assign a hazard pointer to it and immediately afterwards, verify if the reference (the node) is still safe. If the verification fails, follow the path of the original algorithm that corresponds to failure due to contention (e.g. try again, backoff etc.).

The Problem of Instruction Reordering in HP. An important practical consideration when applying the above methodology is instruction reordering [19, 22]. In most modern processors, instructions may be executed out of order for performance considerations. In particular, in the widespread x86/AMD 64/SPARC TSO memory models, stores may be executed after loads, even if the stores occur before loads in the program code [22, 29]. Instruction reordering is relevant in the case of hazard pointers due to step 4 in the methodology above. We assign a hazard pointer and then verify that the node is still safe, thus ensuring that the hazard pointer starts protecting that node from a time when the node is definitely safe. However, if assigning the hazard pointer (a store) is reordered after the validation (a load), then we can no longer be certain that the node is still safe when the hazard pointer becomes visible to other processes. Therefore, it is necessary for the programmer to insert a *memory barrier* between the hazard pointer assignment and the validation. Algorithm 1 shows the high-level instructions that need to be added to the data structure code when accessing a node, if hazard pointers are used (lines 2–4).

```
1 Read reference to node n
2 Assign a hazard pointer to n
3 Perform a memory barrier
4 Check if node n is still valid
5 Access n's memory
6 Release reference to n (e.g. move to successor node)
```

Algorithm 1: High-level steps taken when accessing a node in a data structure using *hazard pointers.*

A *memory barrier* [19] (or fence) is an instruction that ensures no memory operation is reordered around it. In particular, all stores that occur before a memory barrier in program order will be visible to other processes before any loads appearing after the barrier is executed. Therefore, when validating that a node is still safe (as per step 4 in the methodology), we can be certain that the hazard pointer is already visible.

Memory barriers are expensive instructions. They can take hundreds of processor cycles. This cost results in a significant performance overhead for hazard pointer implementations, especially in read-only data structure operations (update operations typically use other expensive synchronization primitives such as compare-and-swap, so the marginal cost of memory barriers due to hazard pointers is much lower than for read-only operations). Moreover, these memory barriers must be performed on a per-element basis, which causes the performance of hazard pointers to scale poorly with data structure size.

4. AN OVERVIEW OF QSENSE

Combining QSBR's high-performance with hazard pointers' robustness in a hybrid memory reclamation scheme is appealing. In this section, we first argue why merging QSBR with the original hazard pointers technique is also however a challenge. Then, we give a high-level view of QSense.

4.1 Rationale

One could imagine a hybrid scheme where QSBR and hazard pointers are two separate entities, with the switch between the two schemes triggered by a *signal* or *flag*. QSBR would run in the common case (when no process delays are observed) and hazard pointers would be employed when a long process delay makes quiescence impossible. However, after a switch to hazard pointers based reclamation, hazardous references from when the system was running in QSBR mode would need to be protected as well. So, hazard pointers should be protecting nodes during the entire execution of the system, regardless of the mode of operation the system is currently in. As discussed above, the original hazard pointers algorithm requires a memory barrier call after every hazard pointer update, to ensure correctness. However, ideally, when the system operates in QSBR mode, the per-node memory barriers required by hazard pointers should be eliminated. Per-node memory barriers should be placed as specified in the HP algorithm only when the system goes into fallback mode. Nonetheless, such an approach is not correct. The scenario in Algorithm 2 illustrates why.

```
R1. Read a pointer to a node n (Load)
R2. Assign a hazard pointer to n (Store)
R3. If fallback mode is active (Load) execute a memory
      barrier (here, suppose fallback mode is
      inactive and the memory barrier is not
      executed)
R4. Recheck n (Load)
R5. Use n (Loads and Stores)

D1. Remove n
D2. Check fallback−flag (here, suppose fallback
      mode was activated)
D3. Scan hazard pointers
D4. Free n (assuming no hazard pointer protects it)
```

Algorithm 2: Example of illegal operation interleaving

Consider two processes, P_R and P_D, at a time t when the system makes the switch from the fast path to the fallback path. P_R is a reader process performing steps R_1 to R_5 and P_D is a deleting process performing steps D_1 to D_4, during which it detects that it must switch to the fallback scheme.

Assume that P_D's steps are not reordered (we can use memory barriers to ensure this, since we are mainly concerned with removing memory barriers from read-only operations, but not necessarily from deletion operations). However, P_R's steps can be reordered; more precisely, in the TSO model, the R_2 store can be delayed past all subsequent reads [22, 29] if P_R does not detect that the fallback-flag is turned on and does not perform a memory barrier.

Next, consider the following interleaving of P_R's and P_D's steps. Initially the fallback-flag is off (the system is running in the fast path). The reader will read a reference to n (R_1) and assign a hazard pointer to n (R_2). At R_3 the fallback-flag is off, so the memory barrier is not executed. Thus, the store of the hazard pointer (R_2) can be delayed past all subsequent reads. Then, P_R rechecks n (R_4) and finds that it is still a valid node. Now, suppose that another process P activates the fallback path. This is where P_D steps in and executes D_1 through D_4. Since P_R's store of the hazard pointer was delayed, P_D is free to reclaim the node in question. Finally, in step R_5, P_R will try to use the reference to n that it had acquired without publishing the hazard pointer via a memory barrier and thus attempt to access a reclaimed node, which is incorrect.

If a memory barrier was called after the update of each hazard pointer in both the fast and fallback paths, the QSBR/HP hybrid would function correctly. However, adding per-node memory barriers when running the fast path means re-introducing the main performance bottleneck of the fallback scheme into the fast path. Consequently, the performance of the hybrid in QSBR mode would be similar to its performance in HP mode, what we initially set out to avoid.

The challenge is to eliminate the traversal memory barriers when the system operates in the fast path (QSBR), while optimistically updating the hazard pointer values. We address this challenge by designing Cadence, a hazard pointer inspired memory reclamation scheme which does not require per-node memory barriers upon traversal. Cadence is presented in § 5. Then, in § 6 we show that Cadence is a good candidate for the fallback scheme in QSense, preserving the safety properties of the algorithm, while not hindering the performance of QSBR in the fast path.

4.2 QSense in a Nutshell

QSense is a hybrid scheme, unifying the high-performing approach provided by QSBR and the robustness provided by hazard pointers. QSense is an adaptive scheme, using two paths (a fast path and a fallback path) and automatically deciding when it should switch paths. QSBR constitutes the fast path and is used in the common case, when all processes are active in the system. As QSBR was presented in prior work [7, 15], we omit the implementation details.

When one or more processes experience prolonged delays (e.g. blocked in I/O), there is a risk of exhausting the available memory, because quiescence is not possible. In this case, Cadence serves as a safety net. Cadence guarantees that QSense continues to function within a bounded amount of memory. Cadence eliminates the expensive per-node memory fences needed for data structure traversal, the main drawback of the original hazard pointer scheme. Instead of using memory barriers, Cadence forces periodic context switches in order to make outstanding hazard pointer writes visible. Since the cost of expensive operations (in our case context switches) is spread across a large number of operations, Cadence achieves scalability that is up to three times as good as the original hazard pointer scheme, while maintaining the same safety guarantees. Moreover, using Cadence as the fallback path allows the elimination of memory barriers when running in the fast path. QSense automatically detects the need to switch to the fallback scheme and triggers the switch through a shared flag. Similarly, when all the processes become active again in the system (e.g. return from a routine incurring a long delay), QSense re-establishes the quiescence-based reclamation mechanism automatically.

Applicability. QSense can be used with any data structure for which both the fast path and the slow path are applicable. Since Cadence does not introduce any additional usability constraints compared to hazard pointers, and QSBR can be applied to virtually any data structure, this means that QSense can be used with any data structure for which hazard pointers are applicable. Applying QSense to a data structure is done in three steps: (1) Call `manage_qsense_state` to declare a quiescent state (e.g. between every two data structure operations). The function automatically handles amortizing overhead by executing the memory reclamation code only once every Q calls to `manage_qsense_state` (where Q is the quiescence threshold introduced in § 3.1). (2) Following the methodology from § 3.2, protect hazardous references by calling `assign_HP`. (3) To reclaim memory, call `free_node_later` when `free` would be called in a sequential setting. An example of how to apply QSense to a concurrent linked list can be found in [5].

5. CADENCE

In this section, we present Cadence, our fallback path for QSense. We first describe Cadence as a stand-alone memory reclamation technique and then show how we integrate Cadence with QSBR in our QSense scheme.

5.1 The Fallback Path

Cadence builds upon hazard pointers, eliminating the need to use per-node memory barriers when traversing the data structure. Note that while Cadence is the fallback path in QSense, it could also be used as a stand alone memory reclamation scheme. Algorithm 3 presents the pseudocode of the main functions of Cadence. This scheme is based on two new concepts: *rooster processes* and *deferred reclamation*.

1. **Rooster processes** are a mechanism used to ensure that all new hazard pointer writes become globally visible after at most a period of time T (the sleep interval, a configurable parameter). For every core or hardware context on which a worker process is running, we create a rooster process and pin it to run on that core. Every rooster process has the task of sleeping for a predetermined amount of time T, waking up, and going back to sleep again, in an infinite loop. In this way, every worker process is guaranteed to be switched out periodically, and thus the worker processes' outstanding writes, *including hazard pointers*, will become visible to the other processes (as detailed in *Note on assumptions* below). Therefore, for every time t, all hazard pointers that were published before time $t-T$ are visible to all processes.

2. **Deferred reclamation.** Figure 4 illustrates the main idea of how rooster processes and deferred reclamation

work together. By verifying that a node n is *old enough* (pseudocode shown in Algorithm 3, lines 35–39), the reclaiming process makes sure that at least one rooster process wake-up has occurred since n was removed from the data structure and thus that any hazard pointers protecting n have become visible. If n is removed by a process at time t_0, then at time $t > t_0 + T$, any potential hazard pointers protecting n are visible. This is because these hazard pointers were written before t_0 (by the methodology in § 3.2) and at least one rooster process wake-up has occurred between t_0 and t. Therefore, at t, the reclaiming process can safely free the node's memory provided that no hazard pointers are protecting it.

```
1  // *** Cadence ***
2  timestamped_node {
3   node* actual_node;
4   timestamp time_created;
5   timestamped_node* next;};
6  HP_array HP; // Shared HP array
7
8  void assign_HP(node* target, int HP_index) {
9    // Assign hazard pointer to target node.
10   HP[HP_index] = target;
11   // No need for a memory barrier here.
12 }
13
14 void scan(timestamped_node* removed_nodes_list)
15 {
16   // Insert non-null values in HP_in_use.
17   HP_array HP_in_use = get_protected_nodes(HP);
18   // Free non-hazardous nodes
19   timestamped_node* tmplist;
20   tmplist = removed_nodes_list;
21   removed_nodes_list = NULL;
22   timestamped_node* cur_node;
23   while (tmplist != NULL) {
24    cur_node = tmplist;
25    tmplist = tmplist->next;
26    // Deferred reclamation
27    if (!is_old_enough(cur_node) ||
28    HP_in_use.find(cur_node->actual_node)) {
29     cur_node->next = removed_nodes_list;
30     removed_nodes_list = cur_node;
31    } else {
32     free(cur_node->actual_node);
33     free(cur_node);
34 } } }
35
36 boolean is_old_enough(timestamped_node*
       wrapper_node) {
37   current_time = get_current_time();
38   age = current_time - wrapper_node->
       time_created;
39   return (age >= (ROOSTER_SLEEP_INTERVAL +
       EPSILON));
40 }
```

Algorithm 3: Main functions of Cadence

When a node n is removed from the data structure (when the `free` function would be called in a sequential setting), n is *timestamped* and placed inside the removing process' local list of nodes awaiting reclamation. Once every R such node removals, a `scan` of the list is performed (see Algorithm 3, lines 14–33). A `scan` inspects the process' removed nodes list and frees those nodes that are safe to reclaim (retired). Nodes that are *old enough and are not protected by any hazard pointers* are freed; hazard pointers of all the worker processes are checked, not only the reclaiming process'. The rest of the nodes — which are either not old enough, or are protected — are left in the removed nodes list, to be reclaimed at a later time (Algorithm 3, lines 26–30).

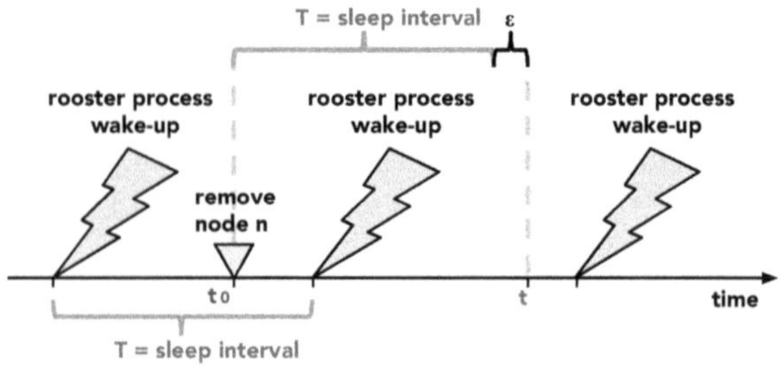

Figure 4: Rooster processes and deferred reclamation

From the programmer's perspective, using Cadence is essentially identical to using hazard pointers. The difference is that no memory barriers are needed after publishing a new hazard pointer, thus making Cadence up to three times as fast than the original hazard pointers (as we will see in § 7). Algorithm 4 shows the steps taken when accessing a node, when Cadence is used.

1. Read reference to node n
2. Assign a hazard pointer to n
3. ~~Perform a memory barrier~~
4. Check if n is still valid
5. Access n's memory
6. Release reference to n (e.g. move to successor node)

Algorithm 4: High-level steps taken when accessing a node in a data structure using *Cadence*.

Note on assumptions. For correctness, Cadence relies on the following assumptions. First, we assume that the only instruction reorderings possible are the ones between loads and subsequent reads, as in the TSO model. We assume this in § 3.2 to determine the memory barrier placement and in § 5.1 to justify that the memory barrier is no longer needed.

Second, we require that a context switch implies a memory barrier for the process being switched out. This is necessary to guarantee that hazard pointers published by a process p become visible at the latest right after p is switched out by a rooster process. The low-level locking required to perform a context switch automatically provides a memory barrier for the process being switched out. Although this property is architecture dependent and might not be generally true if architectures change in the future, it does hold for most modern architectures [20, 22].

Third, we assume that rooster processes never fail. This is a reasonable assumption, considering that rooster processes do not take any steps that could produce exceptions: their only actions are going to sleep and waking up. However, small timing inconsistencies might appear, in the form of (1) rooster processes possibly taking slightly longer than T between wake-ups, i.e. "oversleeping" (it is reasonable to assume that this difference is small, since modern operating systems use fair schedulers [21]) and (2) different cores seeing slightly different times when creating and comparing timestamps. We make the assumption that these inconsistencies are bounded and introduce a tolerance ϵ to account for them. We use ϵ explicitly, as shown in Figure 4: to verify if a removed node n is old enough, we compute the difference between the current value of the system clock and n's timestamp. If the time difference is larger than $T + \epsilon$, then n is old enough.

Note that we are making no assumptions about the *worker processes* (i.e. the processes performing read or write operations on the data structure). In particular, they may be delayed for an arbitrary amount of time. Therefore, the model under which our construction is correct and wait-free is partly asynchronous (the worker processes) and partly synchronous (the rooster processes).

5.2 Merging the Fast and Fallback Paths

In QSense, from a high-level design point of view, the fast path (QSBR) and the fallback path (Cadence) can be viewed as two separate entities, functioning independently. The switch between the two modes is triggered via a shared flag, called the *fallback-flag*. However, even if the two modes of operation are logically distinct, there are elements of the two schemes that have been merged or that are continuously active. Even if QSense is running in the fast path, hazard pointers still have to be set. As explained in § 4.1, this is necessary because in the case of a switch to the fallback path, hazardous references need to be protected. Furthermore, for similar reasons, timestamps need to be recorded when a node is removed, regardless of the mode of operation of QSense. Moreover, when running in fallback mode and performing a `scan`, QSBR's `limbo_list` (with all three epochs) becomes the `removed_nodes_list` scanned by Cadence. Pseudocode for the main functions used by QSense is shown in Algorithm 5 (unless stated otherwise, all pseudocode references in this section refer to Algorithm 5).

Any of the worker processes can trigger the switch between the fast and fallback paths. The switch can be split into the following sub-problems:

1. **Detecting the need to switch to the fallback path.** QSense triggers the switch from QSBR to Cadence when a process detects that its removed (but not freed) nodes list reached a size C, where C is a parameter of the system (lines 53–60). Reaching a large removed nodes list size for one process indicates that quiescence was not possible for an extended period.
2. **Switching from the fast path to the fallback path.** QSense signals the switch from QSBR to Cadence through the *fallback-flag*. The process that has detected the need for the switch sets the shared *fallback-flag*. The *fallback-flag* is checked by all processes when performing node reclamation (i.e. calling the `free_node_later` function, shown in lines 35–60), so the path switch will eventually be detected by all active processes (line 41). If the flag is set to *fallback mode*, a hazard pointer style `scan` as described in § 5.1 is immediately performed to reclaim nodes (lines 42–47; `scan` shown in Algorithm 3).
3. **Detecting when it is safe to switch back to the fast path.** To determine when to switch from the fallback path to the fast path we need to verify if all processes have once again become active in the system. While the system operates in fallback mode, there is at least one process which cannot participate, because using the fallback path implies that one of the processes was delayed and quiescence was not possible. To assess whether all the processes have become active in the meantime, we

```
1  //*** QSENSE interface ***
2  void manage_qsense_state();
3  void assign_HP(node* target, int HP_index);
4  void free_node_later(node* n);
5
6  // One limbo list per epoch
7  timestamped_node* limbo_list[3];
8  int call_count = 0;
9  int free_node_later_call_count = 0;
10
11 // *** QSENSE main functions***
12 void manage_qsense_state(){
13  // Batch operations
14  call_count += 1;
15  if (call_count % QUIESCENCE_THRESHOLD != 0) {
16   return;
17  }
18  // Signal that the process is active
19  is_active(process_id);
20  seen_fallback_flag = fallback_flag;
21  if (seen_fallback_flag == FAST_PATH) {
22   // Common case: run the fast path
23   quiescent_state();
24   prev_seen_fallback_flag = FAST_PATH;
25  } else if (seen_fallback_flag == FALLBACK_PATH
       ) {
26   // Try to switch to fast path
27   if ( all_processes_active() ) {
28    // Trigger switch to the fast path
29    fallback_flag = FAST_PATH;
30    prev_seen_fallback_flag = FAST_PATH;
31    quiescent_state();
32   }
33   prev_seen_fallback_flag = FALLBACK_PATH;
34 } }
35
36 void free_node_later (node* n) {
37  // Create timestamped wrapper node
38  timestamped_node* wrapper_node = alloc(size(
      timestamped_node));
39  wrapper_node->actual_node = n;
40  wrapper_node->time_created = get_current_time
      ();
41  limbo_list[my_current_epoch].add(wrapper_node)
      ;
42  seen_fallback_flag = fallback_flag;
43  if (seen_fallback_flag == FALLBACK_PATH &&
44  ++free_node_later_call_count % R == 0) {
45   // Running in fallback mode. All three epochs
        in limbo list are scanned.
46   scan(limbo_list[0]); scan(limbo_list[1]);
47   scan(limbo_list[2]);
48   prev_seen_fallback_flag = FALLBACK_PATH;
49  } else if ( prev_seen_fallback_flag ==
       FALLBACK_PATH &&
50    seen_fallback_flag == FAST_PATH) {
51   // QSBR mode switch triggered by another
        process.
52   quiescent_state();
53   prev_seen_fallback_flag = FAST_PATH;
54  } else if (size(limbo_list) >= C &&
55    prev_seen_fallback_flag == FAST_PATH) {
56   // Trigger switch to fallback mode:
57   fallback_flag = FALLBACK_PATH;
58   prev_seen_fallback_flag = FALLBACK_PATH;
59   scan(limbo_list[0]); scan(limbo_list[1]);
60   scan(limbo_list[2]);
61 } }
```

Algorithm 5: Main QSense functions

keep an array of *presence-flags* (one flag per worker process), which is reset periodically. After each operation (or batch of operations) on the data structure, processes set their corresponding *presence-flags* to true, to signal that they are active (line 18). Then, processes scan the *presence-flag* array (line 26). If one of the processes sees all of the presence flags set to true, it infers that all processes might be active again in the system and a switch from fallback path to fast path is attempted.

4. **Switching from the fallback path to the fast path.** If QSense runs in fallback mode, but all processes have become present in the meantime, the possibility to switch from Cadence back to QSBR is detected, as described above. Similarly to switching from the fast path to the fallback path, the switch in the opposite direction is signaled through setting the value of the shared *fallback-flag* and immediately declaring a quiescent state (lines 27–30). If the switch to the fast path was already triggered by another process, the new value of the *fallback-flag* will be seen upon retiring a node (in the `free_node_later` function, lines 48–52).

The current version of QSense does not support dynamic membership: processes cannot join or leave the system as an algorithm is running. Also, if a process crashes and never recovers, QSense will switch to fallback mode and stay there forever. Both of these issues can be addressed by adding mechanisms for processes to announce entering or leaving the system and for evicting participating processes that have not quiesced in a long time. We leave these extensions for future work.

6. CORRECTNESS & COMPLEXITY

In this section we argue for the safety and liveness of Cadence and QSense. For completeness, safety and liveness proofs for QSBR can be found in [5].

6.1 Cadence

PROPERTY 1. (SAFETY) *If at time t, a node n is identified in the* `scan` *function as eligible to be reused by process p, then no process $q \neq p$ holds a hazardous reference to n at time t.*

PROOF. Assume by contradiction that (1) n is identified as eligible for reuse by p at time t and (2) there exists another process q that holds a hazardous reference to n at t. Then by (1) and the `scan` algorithm, at time t, p inspects n's timestamp and finds that n is old enough, meaning that n has been removed from the data structure at a time $t' \leq t-T$ (where T is the rooster process sleep interval, including the tolerance ϵ). Therefore, by Condition 1 in § 3.2, q has had a hazard pointer *hp* dedicated to n since a time $t'' \leq t'$. Since $t - t'' \geq T$, the write by q to *hp* at t'' is visible to p at time t. Therefore, by the `scan` algorithm, p will not identify n as eligible for reuse (since it is protected by a hazard pointer). □

LEMMA 1. *For any process p, at the end of a call to* `scan` *by p, p can have at most $NK+T$ retired nodes in its removed nodes list, where N is the number of processes, K is the number of hazard pointers per process and T is the rooster process sleep interval.*

PROOF. At the time of the `scan`, there can be at most NK nodes protected by hazard pointers (since NK is the total number of hazard pointers), and there can be at most T nodes that are not yet old enough (for clarity, we assume that p can remove at most one node per time unit). □

PROPERTY 2. (LIVENESS) *At any time, there are at most $N(K+T+R)$ retired nodes in the system, where R is the number of nodes a process can remove before it invokes* `scan`.

PROOF. Fix a process p and examine how many nodes can be removed by p but not yet reclaimed. Using Lemma 1, it follows that between two `scan` calls, the number of nodes in p's removed nodes list can grow up to $NK+T+R$, before the next `scan` call is triggered, lowering the size of the removed nodes list to $NK+T$ again. So the maximum size of a process' removed nodes list is $NK+T+R$, where the NK term comes from the nodes that are protected by hazard pointers. When considering the entire system, we can have at most NK HP-protected nodes, and at most $N(T+R)$ non-HP-protected nodes, so the maximum number of retired nodes is $N(K+T+R)$. □

6.2 QSense

PROPERTY 3. (SAFETY) *If a node n is identified at time t by process p as eligible for reuse, then no process $q \neq p$ holds a hazardous reference to n.*

PROOF. Since all processes keep track of both hazard pointers (exactly as in Cadence) and of epochs (exactly as in QSBR), regardless of whether the system is in the fast path or in the fallback path, the safety guarantees of both methods are maintained. □

For the next property, we define a *legal* value of C, the threshold introduced in step 1 of § 5.2. C refers to the size of the removed nodes list and is used for determining when to switch to the fallback path. We say that C is legal if $C > \max(mQ, NK+T, (K+T+R)/2)$, where Q is the quiescence threshold introduced in § 3, m is the maximum number of nodes that can be removed by a single operation, and N, K and T are as in § 6.1. Picking a legal value for C is always possible since C is a configurable parameter.

PROPERTY 4. (LIVENESS) *If C has a legal value then, at any time, there can be no more than $2NC$ retired nodes in the system.*

PROOF. Assume by contradiction that there is a time t when there are $U > 2NC$ retired nodes in the system. Then there exists a process p such that at time t, p has more than $2C$ retired nodes.

Let $t_1 < t$ be the time of the last quiescent state called by p before t. Since t_1, p has completed at most Q operations (otherwise p would have gone through another quiescent state before t) and has therefore removed at most mQ nodes. Therefore, at t_1, p has at least $2C - mQ > C$ (using the fact that $C > mQ$) retired nodes and therefore triggers a switch to the fallback path. This means that p will call a hazard pointers `scan` before starting any other operation, by construction of the QSense algorithm (step 2 in § 5.2). Let t_2 be the time of this first `scan` after t_1. After this scan is complete, p can have at most $NK+T$ retired nodes, by Lemma 1. If $t > t_2$, then at t, p can have at most $NK+T+mQ < 2C$ retired nodes ($NK+T$ at most at the end of the scan plus mQ because p has completed at most Q operations since t_2), a contradiction. Therefore it must be the case that $t_1 < t < t_2$. Since the scan at t_2 is called immediately after the quiescent state at t_1, without other operations being started by p (by step 2 in § 5.2), the number of retired nodes does not increase between t_1 and t. So at t_1, p has more than $2C$ retired nodes. We now show this to be impossible.

Let t_3 be the time of the last quiescent state called by p before t_1. Since p performed Q operations between t_3 and t_1, it follows that at t_3, p had at least $2C - mQ > C$ retired nodes, thus triggering a switch to the fallback state and a scan at time t_4, $t_3 < t_4 < t_1$. After this scan, p had at most $NK + T$ retired nodes and therefore, at t_1, p had at most $NK + T + mQ < 2C$ retired nodes, a contradiction because we had shown that p had more than $2C$ retired nodes at t_1. This completes the proof. □

7. EXPERIMENTAL EVALUATION

We first describe the experimental setup of our evaluation. We proceed with presenting the methodology of our experiments and we finally discuss our evaluation results.

7.1 Experimental Setting

We apply QSense to a lock-free linked list [25], a lock-free skip list [12] and a binary search tree [28]. The base implementations of these data structures are taken from ASCYLIB [9]. The code to reproduce our experiments is available at https://github.com/zablotchi/qsense. We compare the performance of QSense to that of QSBR, HP and a leaky implementation. Our evaluation was performed on a 48 core AMD Opteron with four 12-core 2.1 GHz Processors and 128 GB of RAM, running Ubuntu 14.04. Our code was compiled with GCC 4.8.4 and the -O3 optimization level.

Each experiment consists of a number of processes concurrently performing data structure operations (searching, inserting or deleting keys) for a predefined amount of time. Each operation is chosen at random, according to a given probability distribution, with a randomly chosen key. An initialization is performed before each experiment, where one process fills the data structure up to half the key-range.

7.2 Methodology

The purpose of our evaluation is two-fold. First, we aim to determine whether QSense performs similarly to QSBR in the base case. It is important to highlight the base case behavior of QSense (i.e. when no processes undergo prolonged delays), since this is the expected execution path in most scenarios. To this end, we run a set of tests emphasizing the scalability with respect to the number of cores. For this first category of tests, the system throughput is recorded as a function of the number of cores (each process is pinned to a different core). The number of cores is varied from 1 to 32, the operation distribution is fixed at 50% reads and 50% updates (i.e. 25% inserts, 25% deletes) and the key range sizes are fixed at 2000 for the linked list, 20000 for the skip list and 2000000 for the binary search tree.

The second goal of the evaluation is to examine the behavior of QSense in case of prolonged process delays. To this end, we run a set of tests that include periodic process disruptions and measure the system throughput as a function of *time*. We observe the switch from QSBR to Cadence when the system senses that one of the processes was delayed and the switch back to QSBR when all the processes became active in the system again. We seek to trigger a switch between the paths (QSBR to Cadence or oppositely) every 10 seconds. To induce the system switch, every 20 seconds one of the processes is delayed for a period of 10 seconds. The operation distribution and key range sizes are fixed as above and the number of processes is fixed at 8. As before, the data structure is filled up to half of its capacity, processes start simultaneously, then run for 100 seconds. The throughput is recorded as a function of time and is measured every second.

7.3 Results

The top row of Figure 5 shows the behavior of QSBR, QSense, HP and None (the leaky implementation) on the linked list, on the skip list and on the binary search tree in the common case, when no process delays occur. The throughput of the algorithms is plotted as a function of number of cores (higher is better). Due to its amortized overhead, QSBR maintains a 2.3% overhead on average compared to None. As expected, HP achieves the lowest overall throughput, with an average overhead of 80% over the leaky implementation. This is due to the expensive per-node memory barriers used upon data structure traversal. QSense achieves two to three times better throughput than HP and has an average overhead of 29% over None. While close to QSBR in all scenarios, QSense does not match its performance. Even if QSense follows a quiescence-based reclamation scheme in the base case, it still has to maintain the hazard pointer and timestamp values updated. This induces increased overhead, compared to QSBR. Despite the fact that no memory barriers are used upon updating the hazard pointers, the process-local variable updates alone add sequential complexity. This explains why the performance gap between QSBR and QSense is larger for the skip list than for the linked list, or the tree: whereas the linked list only uses two hazard pointers per process and the tree uses six, the skip list can use up to 35 hazard pointers per process.

QSense does not completely match the performance of QSBR but, unlike QSBR, it can recover from long process delays. The bottom row of Figure 5 illustrates this. The throughput of QSense is shown alongside QSBR and HP. In this experiment, one of the processes is delayed in the 10-20, 30-40, 50-60, 70-80 and 90-100 time intervals. A similar pattern can be observed for all three data structures. Note that the first time a process is delayed (after 10 seconds), QSBR (shown in orange) can no longer quiesce. Consequently, the system runs out of memory and eventually fails. In contrast, QSense (shown in green) continues to run. When quiescence is no longer possible, QSense switches to Cadence and then switches back to QSBR as soon as the delayed process becomes active. The sequence of fallbacks and recoveries is continued throughout the entire experiment run. As intended, the throughput achieved by QSense is similar to QSBR during the fast path. When QSense is running in the fallback path, it can be seen that Cadence outperforms the original hazard pointer scheme by a factor of 3x on average, because it avoids per-node memory barriers upon data structure traversal.

8. RELATED WORK

Reference counting (RC) [10, 13, 16, 31] assigns shared counters to each node in the data structure, representing the number of references to the nodes held at every given time. When a node's counter reaches zero, the node is safe to

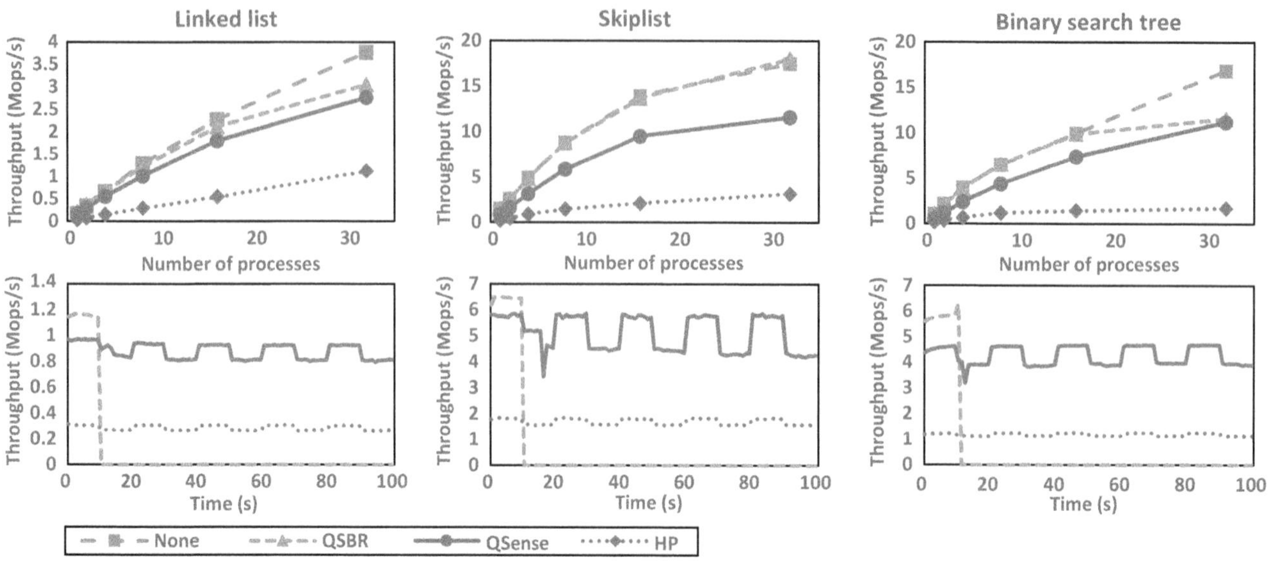

Figure 5: Scalability of memory reclamation on a linked list (2000 elements), a skip list (20000 elements) and a BST (2000000 elements) with 50% updates (top row); Path switching with process delays (8 processes, 50% updates) (bottom row).

reclaim. Though easy to implement, RC requires expensive atomic operations on every access to maintain consistent counters.

Pointer-based techniques. Hazard pointers (HP) [26], or Pass-the-Buck [17] rely on the programmer marking nodes that are unsafe to reclaim before performing memory accesses to their locations. A reclaiming process must ensure that a node it is about to deallocate is not marked. An advantage of these schemes is that they maintain the lock-free property of data structures. Yet, their implementation requires a memory fence instruction to be issued for every node traversed, which significantly hinders the performance of read-only operations [15].

Improvements on HP. Morrison et al. [27] introduce a new, strengthened version of the Total Store Ordering (TSO) memory model [29] in which there is a known bound on the time it takes for writes in the store buffer to become visible in main memory. A variant of HP which does not need memory barriers is proposed. While this solution is similar to Cadence, it relies on hardware guarantees that do not exist yet in practice. McKenney et al. [23] describe a method to force quiescent states by creating a high-priority daemon process that executes on each CPU in turn, but this method has never been applied to HP. Finally, Aghazadeh et al. [1] provide an improvement on HP by reducing the number of hazard-pointer-to-node comparisons per scan call to one, at the cost of increasing the amount of time between node removal and node reclamation.

Epoch-based techniques. These techniques [14, 15, 24] rely on the assumption that live processes will eventually drop references they hold on a node (i.e. if a reclaiming process waits long enough, all other processes will eventually stop holding references to the deleted nodes, which will thus become safe to reclaim). Though epoch-based techniques have good performance [15], their main drawback is that they are blocking.

Ad-hoc techniques. Drop the Anchor (DTA) [6] combines timestamping with a HP-inspired technique. Processes use timestamps to track their progress and they place anchor pointers in the data structure upon traversal. When a process delay occurs, the other processes work together to reconstruct the data structure using the anchors. Similarly to QSense, DTA spreads the cost of expensive operations across a large number of operations. However, the applicability of DTA to other data structures, besides the linked list implementation provided by the authors, is unclear. In contrast, QSense is as easy to apply as HP, for which a well established methodology exists.

DEBRA+ [7] uses a variant of QSBR when processes are making progress in the common case and has a slower mechanism for treating delays. When a delayed process is preventing other processes from quiescing for too long, the slow process is *neutralized*, using an OS signal. Upon resuming execution, a neutralized process runs special *recovery code* to clean up any inconsistencies it might have left in the data structure before it was neutralized. Like QSense, DEBRA+ has a fast path and a recovery path. Unlike QSense, DEBRA+ relies on OS-specific instructions. Moreover, DEBRA+ is only easy to apply to lock-free data structures that have (1) an explicit help function and an explicit descriptor record containing all the information required by the help function and (2) operation code that follows a certain pattern (quiescent preamble – non-quiescent body – quiescent postamble). It is unclear how to extend DEBRA+ to state-of-the-art algorithms not satisfying the above properties.

Automatic memory reclamation. ThreadScan [3] is an automatic technique for concurrent memory reclamation. Processes add references to removed nodes to a shared *delete buffer*. Periodically, a scan is initiated by sending a signal to all processes. Each process examines its stack and registers and marks the corresponding entry in the delete buffer if there is a match, to indicate that the node is in use. After all processes complete the scan, unmarked nodes can be freed. ThreadScan amortizes the overhead of memory reclamation, similarly to QSense. Unlike QSense, ThreadScan has the advantage of being completely automatic. However,

ThreadScan makes critical assumptions about the synchrony of its *worker processes* and about the layout of process stacks in memory. Cohen and Petrank [8] present an automatic memory reclamation scheme for lock-free data structures, inspired by mark-and-sweep garbage collection. This technique relies on the data structure operations being in normalized form [30]. While such implementations of lock-free data structures exist, there is no clear methodology on how to normalize lock-free data structure implementations.

HTM techniques. Another direction for concurrent memory reclamation is the use of Hardware Transactional Memory (HTM) [18]. Dragojevic et al. [11] use HTM to produce faster and simpler solutions to a common subproblem in prior memory reclamation techniques. StackTrack [2] uses the bookkeeping facilities of HTM directly to track node references. The downside of this class of solutions is that they rely on the presence of HTM on the target machine, which is rare in practice.

9. CONCLUSION

QSense offers a fast, robust and highly applicable solution to the concurrent memory reclamation problem. Whenever possible, the fast QSBR technique is used. In case of prolonged process delays, QSense switches to Cadence, a novel hazard pointer inspired scheme, that is robust to process delays. QSense can be integrated in data structures making use of the popular hazard pointer based schemes almost effortlessly, a significant advantage from the applicability standpoint. We show experimentally that QSense achieves performance similar to the highest-performing techniques in the common case (i.e. when all worker processes are active in the system), while tolerating process delays.

10. REFERENCES

[1] Z. Aghazadeh, W. Golab, and P. Woelfel. Making objects writable. PODC 2014.

[2] D. Alistarh, P. Eugster, M. Herlihy, A. Matveev, and N. Shavit. StackTrack: An automated transactional approach to concurrent memory reclamation. EuroSys 2014.

[3] D. Alistarh, W. M. Leiserson, A. Matveev, and N. Shavit. Threadscan: Automatic and scalable memory reclamation. SPAA 2015.

[4] A. Arcangeli, M. Cao, P. E. McKenney, and D. Sarma. Using read-copy-update techniques for System V IPC in the Linux 2.5 kernel. USENIX Annual Technical Conference 2003.

[5] O. Balmau, R. Guerraoui, M. Herlihy, and I. Zablotchi. Fast and Robust Memory Reclamation for Concurrent Data Structures. Technical report, EPFL, 2016.

[6] A. Braginsky, A. Kogan, and E. Petrank. Drop the anchor: Lightweight memory management for non-blocking data structures. SPAA 2013.

[7] T. A. Brown. Reclaiming memory for lock-free data structures: There has to be a better way. PODC 2015.

[8] N. Cohen and E. Petrank. Automatic memory reclamation for lock-free data structures. OOPSLA 2015.

[9] T. David, R. Guerraoui, and V. Trigonakis. Asynchronized concurrency: The secret to scaling concurrent search data structures. ASPLOS 2015.

[10] D. L. Detlefs, P. A. Martin, M. Moir, and G. L. Steele, Jr. Lock-free reference counting. PODC 2001.

[11] A. Dragojević, M. Herlihy, Y. Lev, and M. Moir. On the power of hardware transactional memory to simplify memory management. PODC 2011.

[12] K. Fraser. *Practical lock-freedom.* PhD thesis, University of Cambridge Computer Laboratory, 2004.

[13] A. Gidenstam, M. Papatriantafilou, H. Sundell, and P. Tsigas. Efficient and reliable lock-free memory reclamation based on reference counting. *IEEE Trans. Parallel Distrib. Syst.*, 20(8), 2008.

[14] T. L. Harris. A pragmatic implementation of non-blocking linked-lists. DISC 2001.

[15] T. E. Hart, P. E. McKenney, A. D. Brown, and J. Walpole. Performance of memory reclamation for lockless synchronization. *Journal of Parallel and Distributed Computing*, 67(12), 2007.

[16] M. Herlihy, V. Luchangco, P. Martin, and M. Moir. Nonblocking memory management support for dynamic-sized data structures. *ACM Trans. Comput. Syst.*, 23(2), 2005.

[17] M. Herlihy, V. Luchangco, and M. Moir. The repeat offender problem: A mechanism for supporting dynamic-sized, lock-free data structures. DISC 2002.

[18] M. Herlihy and J. E. B. Moss. Transactional memory: Architectural support for lock-free data structures. ISCA 1993.

[19] M. Herlihy and N. Shavit. *The Art of Multiprocessor Programming, Revised Reprint.* 1st edition, 2012.

[20] E. Ladan-Mozes, I.-T. A. Lee, and D. Vyukov. Location-based memory fences. SPAA 2011.

[21] R. Love. *Linux System Programming: Talking Directly to the Kernel and C Library, 2nd Edition.* O'Reilly Media, Inc.

[22] P. E. McKenney. Memory barriers: a hardware view for software hackers. 2010.

[23] P. E. McKenney, D. Sarma, A. Arcangeli, A. Kleen, O. Krieger, and R. Russell. Read copy update. Ottawa Linux Symposium 2001.

[24] P. E. McKenney and J. D. Slingwine. Read-copy update: Using execution history to solve concurrency problems. PDCS 1998.

[25] M. M. Michael. High performance dynamic lock-free hash tables and list-based sets. SPAA 2002.

[26] M. M. Michael. Hazard pointers: Safe memory reclamation for lock-free objects. *IEEE Trans. Parallel Distrib. Syst.*, 15(6), 2004.

[27] A. Morrison and Y. Afek. Temporally bounding TSO for fence-free asymmetric synchronization. ASPLOS 2015.

[28] A. Natarajan and N. Mittal. Fast concurrent lock-free binary search trees. PPoPP 2014.

[29] S. Owens, S. Sarkar, and P. Sewell. A better x86 memory model: X86-TSO. TPHOLs 2009.

[30] S. Timnat and E. Petrank. A practical wait-free simulation for lock-free data structures. PPoPP 2014.

[31] J. D. Valois. Lock-free linked lists using compare-and-swap. PODC 1995.

Brief Announcement: Benchmarking Concurrent Priority Queues

Performance of k-LSM and Related Data Structures

Jakob Gruber
TU Wien, Austria
gruber@par.tuwien.ac.at

Jesper Larsson Träff
TU Wien, Austria
traff@par.tuwien.ac.at

Martin Wimmer
Google
wimmerm@google.com

Keywords

Priority Queues, Concurrency, Relaxation, Benchmarking

ABSTRACT

A number of concurrent, relaxed priority queues have recently been proposed and implemented. Results are commonly reported for a *throughput benchmark* that uses a uniform distribution of keys from a large integer range, a balanced mixture of operations, and mostly for single systems. We have conducted more extensive benchmarking of three recent, relaxed priority queues on four different types of systems with different key ranges and distributions. While we can show superior throughput and scalability for our own k-LSM priority queue for the uniform key distribution, the picture changes drastically for other distributions, both with respect to achieved throughput and relative merit of the priority queues. The throughput benchmark alone is thus not sufficient to characterize the performance of concurrent priority queues. Our priority queue, benchmark code and full set of results are publicly available to foster comparison.

1. CONCURRENT PRIORITY QUEUES

Due to the increasing number of processors in modern computer systems, there is strong interest in concurrent data structures with scalable performance that goes beyond a few dozen processor-cores. However, data structures (e.g., priority queues) with strict sequential semantics present (inherent) scalability bottlenecks (e.g., the `delete_min` operation), which motivates weaker correctness conditions or data structures with relaxed semantics (e.g., one of the smallest k items for some k may be deleted). Applications can often accommodate such relaxations, and in many such cases (discrete event simulation, shortest path algorithms, branch-and-bound), the priority queue is a key data structure.

Many lock-free queues have been based on Skiplists [6, 8, 9]. In contrast, the recently proposed, relaxed k-LSM priority queue [10] is based on a deterministic Log-Structured Merge-Tree (LSM), and combines a thread-local variant for scalability with a shared, relaxed variant for semantic guarantees. The k-LSM priority queue is lock-free, linearizable and provides configurable guarantees of `delete_min` returning one of the kP smallest items, with k a configuration parameter and P the number of cores (threads). The SprayList [1] uses a lock-free Skiplist, and allows `delete_min` to remove a random element from the $O(P \log^3 P)$ items at the head of the list. MultiQueues [7] randomly spread insertions and deletions over cP local priority queues, each protected by a lock, with tuning parameter c, and gives no obvious guarantees on the order of deleted elements.

SPAA '16 July 11-13, 2016, Pacific Grove, CA, USA

ACM ISBN 978-1-4503-4210-0/16/07.

DOI: http://dx.doi.org/10.1145/2935764.2935803

2. A CONFIGURABLE BENCHMARK

Priority queue performance is often measured by counting the number of `insert` and `delete_min` operations that can be performed in a given amount of time, i.e., the *throughput*, which would ideally increase linearly with the number of threads. Like recent studies [1, 6, 8, 9, 10], we also measure throughput, but additionally we experiment with different *workloads*: (a) *uniform*, where each thread performs 50% insertions and 50% deletions, randomly chosen, (b) *split*, where half the threads perform only insertions, and the other half only deletions; and (integer) *key distributions*: (a) *uniform*, where keys are drawn uniformly at random from the range of 32-bit, 16-bit, or 8-bit integers, and (b) *ascending (descending)*, where keys are drawn from a 10-bit integer range which is shifted upwards (downwards) at each operation (plus/minus one).

Queues are prefilled with 10^6 elements with keys taken from the chosen distribution. This benchmark provides more scope for investigating locality (split workload), distribution and range sensitivity. The benchmark could be parameterized further [2, 3] to provide for wider synthetic workloads, e.g., sorting as in [5]. To some extent, our ascending/descending distributions correspond to the *hold model* advocated in [4].

For relaxed priority queues, it is as important to characterize the deviation from strict priority queue behavior, also for verifying whether claimed relaxation bounds hold. We have implemented a rank error benchmark as in [7], where the rank of an item is its position within the priority queue as it is deleted.

3. EXPERIMENTAL RESULTS

We have benchmarked variants of the k-LSM priority queue [10] with different relaxation settings (`klsm128`, `klsm256`, `klsm4096`) against a Skiplist based queue [6] (`linden`), the MultiQueue [7] (`multiq`) and the SprayList [1] (`spray`). As a baseline we have used a sequential heap protected by a lock (`globallock`). The benchmarks ran on four different machines, but we give only results from an 80-core Intel Xeon

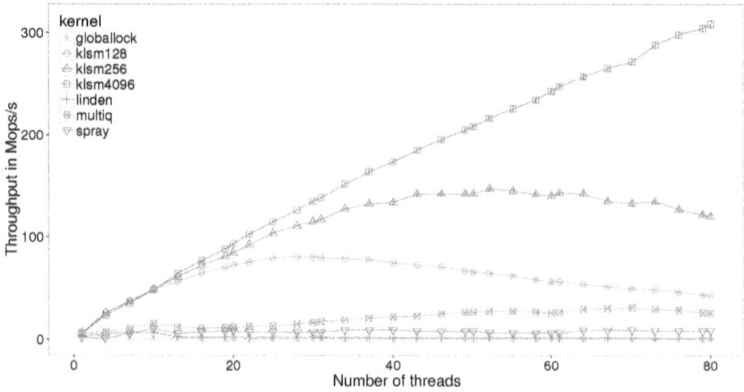

Figure 1: `mars`: Uniform workload, uniform keys.

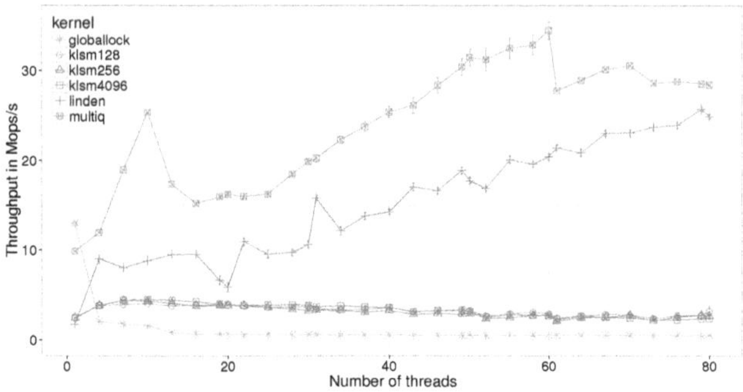

Figure 2: `mars`: Split workload, ascending keys.

E7-8850 2 GHz system (`mars`) here (without hyperthreading); see the report [3] for full details and results. Each benchmark is executed 30 times, and we report on the mean values and confidence intervals. Our benchmark code can be found at https://github.com/klsmpq/klsm.

Figure 1 compares the seven priority queue variants under *uniform workload, uniform keys*. The k-LSM variant with $k = 4096$ exhibits superior scalability and throughput of more than 300 million operations per second (MOps/s), and vastly outperforms the other priority queues. Changing to a *split workload* and *ascending keys*, the picture changes dramatically: As shown in Figure 2 the throughput drops by a factor of 10. Here `multiq` performs and scales best, surprisingly closely followed by `linden`. Restricting the key range likewise dramatically reduces the throughput, but the k-LSM performs better in this case (Figure 3). In the latter two benchmark configurations, the SprayList code was not stable and it was not possible to gather results. Similar behavior and sensitivity can be observed for the other three machines. Hyperthreading only in rare cases leads to a throughput increase. Overall, `multiq` delivers the most consistent performance.

The rank error results in Table 1 for the uniform workload, uniform key situation show that `delete_min` for all queues return keys that are not far from the minimum, much better than the the worst-case analyses predict.

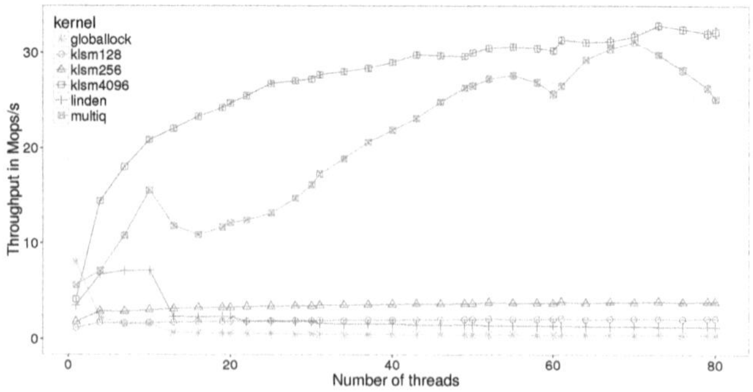

Figure 3: `mars`: Uniform workload, 8-bit restricted keys.

Table 1: `mars`: Rank error, uniform workload and keys.

	20 threads		40 threads		80 threads	
	Mean	St.D.	Mean	St.D.	Mean	St.D.
klsm128	32	29	57	48	298	288
klsm256	42	42	68	57	635	464
klsm4096	422	729	1124	1287	13469	13980
multiq	1163	3607	2296	7881	3753	12856

References

[1] D. Alistarh et al. "The SprayList: A Scalable Relaxed Priority Queue". In: *20th ACM Symposium on Principles and Practice of Parallel Programming.* 2015, pp. 11–20.

[2] V. Gramoli. "More than you ever wanted to know about synchronization: synchrobench, measuring the impact of the synchronization on concurrent algorithms". In: *20th ACM Symposium on Principles and Practice of Parallel Programming.* 2015, pp. 1–10.

[3] J. Gruber, J. L. Träff, and M. Wimmer. *Benchmarking Concurrent Priority Queues: Performance of k-LSM and Related Data Structures.* arXiv:1603.05047. 2016.

[4] D. W. Jones. "An Empirical Comparison of Priority-Queue and Event-Set Implementations". In: *Comm. ACM* 29.4 (1986), pp. 300–311.

[5] D. H. Larkin, S. Sen, and R. E. Tarjan. "A Back-to-Basics Empirical Study of Priority Queues". In: *16th Workshop on Algorithm Engineering and Experiments.* 2014, pp. 61–72.

[6] J. Lindén and B. Jonsson. "A Skiplist-Based Concurrent Priority Queue with Minimal Memory Contention". In: *Principles of Distributed Systems.* Vol. 8304. Lecture Notes in Computer Science. 2013, pp. 206–220.

[7] H. Rihani, P. Sanders, and R. Dementiev. "Brief Announcement: MultiQueues: Simple Relaxed Concurrent Priority Queues". In: *27th ACM Symposium on Parallelism in Algorithms and Architectures.* 2015, pp. 80–82.

[8] N. Shavit and I. Lotan. "Skiplist-Based Concurrent Priority Queues". In: *14th International Parallel and Distributed Processing Symposium.* 2000, pp. 263–268.

[9] H. Sundell and P. Tsigas. "Fast and lock-free concurrent priority queues for multi-thread systems". In: *Journal of Parallel and Distributed Computing* 65.5 (2005), pp. 609–627.

[10] M. Wimmer et al. "The Lock-free k-LSM Relaxed Priority Queue". In: *20th ACM Symposium on Principles and Practice of Parallel Programming.* 2015.

Brief Announcement: Fast Concurrent Cuckoo Kick-Out Eviction Schemes for High-Density Tables

William Kuszmaul
Stanford University
william.kuszmaul@gmail.com

ABSTRACT

Cuckoo hashing guarantees constant-time lookups regardless of table density, making it a viable candidate for high-density tables. Cuckoo hashing insertions perform poorly at high table densities, however. In this paper, we mitigate this problem through the introduction of novel kick-out eviction algorithms. Experimentally, our algorithms reduce the number of bins viewed per insertion for high-density tables by as much as a factor of ten.

We also implement an optimistic concurrency scheme for serializable multi-writer cuckoo hash tables (not using hardware transactional memory). For delete-light loads, one of our kick-out schemes avoids all competition between insertions with high probability, and significantly reduces transaction-abort frequency. This result is extended to arbitrary workloads using a new mechanism called a claim flag.

1 Introduction

Unlike traditional hashing, Cuckoo hashing maps each key to two distinct bins using two hash functions. To insert a key, we simply look at the bins identified by the two hash functions and insert into the first containing a free slot. If neither bin contains an empty slot, then we pick one of the two bins and *kick out* one of the keys it contains. The displaced key, the *victim*, is then recursively reinserted into the table. The sequence of kick-outs that results from the initial insert is called a *kick-out chain*.

Unfortunately, whereas cuckoo hashing reads are guaranteed constant time, inserts become very slow for high-density tables. The kick-out chain resulting from an insertion in a high-density table results in the viewing of dozens (or hundreds) of bins, making cache-friendly or multi-threaded cuckoo hashing difficult [2]. Commonly kick-out victims are selected in one of two manners: *random kicking* selects the victim randomly; and *breadth-first search (BFS)* performs a search to find the shortest possible kick-out chain. Experimentally, at high table densities both kick-out schemes are equally bad in terms of bins viewed per insertion (Figure 1).

SPAA '16 July 11-13, 2016, Pacific Grove, CA, USA

ACM ISBN 978-1-4503-4210-0/16/07.
DOI: http://dx.doi.org/10.1145/2935764.2935814

Our research suggests that simple algorithmic changes to both BFS and random kicking can yield significant improvements. In Section 2, we describe and evaluate experimentally three such techniques, ghost insertions, queue kicking, and sorted search. When combined, ghost insertions and sorted search yield as much as a factor-of-ten reduction in bins viewed per insertion for high-density tables.

Surprisingly, queue kicking can be further harnessed as a concurrency mechanism for planning concurrent kick-out chains. In Section 3, we describe this mechanism along with an extension of it called claim flagging, both of which avoid competition between inserts with high probability. We then implement a serializable multi-writer cuckoo hash table and are able to apply queue kicking and claim flags in order to significantly reduce transaction-abort frequency.

For an extended version of this paper, see [1].

2 Reducing Bins Viewed

In this section, we describe three mechanisms for reducing bins viewed per insertion.

Ghost insertions: When both of a record's bins have free space, ghost insertions allow a record to reside in both bins at once, marked as a duplicate in each. Duplicates make good kick-out victims because they are guaranteed not to cause additional kick-outs. By prioritizing duplicates as kick-out victims, we can therefore obtain a reduction in bins viewed per insertion.

Sorted Search: Whereas BFS can be implemented by maintaining a queue of records whose children bins have not yet been examined, sorted search instead maintains a list sorted by a statistic called *spawn count*; records with small spawn counts are more likely to lead to small kick-out chains. (Note that unlike for BFS, however, for sorted search one must be careful to detect/avoid cycles in the search.)

The *spawn count* of a record in bin b is the number of times since the conception of the hash table that any search has previously visited the children bins of a record that was, at the time, contained in b. Surprisingly, even statistics using information specific to the record (and not just the bin) appear unable to perform better than spawn count.

Queue Kicking: To select kick-out victims, queue kicking picks the record present in the bin for the longest. Consequently, queue kicking prioritizes against victims that have already been kicked around recently. We may not be the first to observe the benefits of queue kicking; in fact, it is the kick-out scheme used by Kennith Ross in his high-performance cuckoo hash table implementation [3].

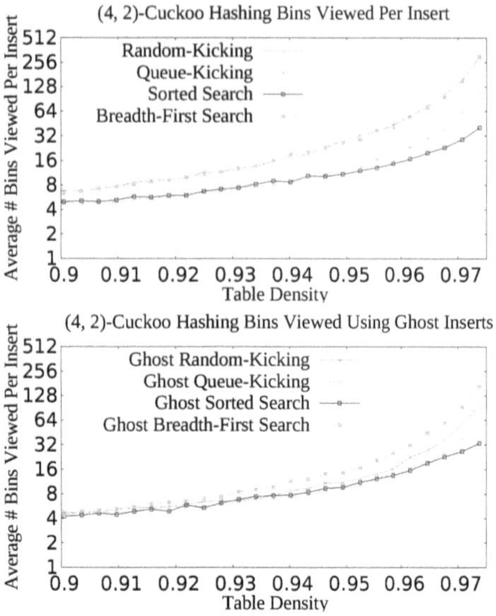

Figure 1: The average number of bins viewed per insertion according to table density.

Figure 1 evaluates these mechanisms according to bins viewed per insertion, which according to the Disk Access Machine model will be proportional to cache misses. We evaluate each mechanism, along with random-kicking and BFS, both with and without ghost insertions. For each algorithm, we fill 1,000 hash tables, each containing 2^{13} 4-slot bins, to 97.5% full and graph the average number of bins viewed for insertions at each density.

In each experiment, hashes are generated uniformly randomly. Moreover, insertions are not responsible for verifying that the key being inserted is not already present. Each experiment appears to scale. That is, for tables with arbitrarily many bins, the data-points remain essentially unchanged.

3 Avoiding Overlapping Chains

One problem with long kick-out chains is that, in multi-threaded systems, two concurrent insertions may plan overlapping chains, forcing one of the insertions to start over [2]. As we will see in Section 3.3, this can lead to a problematic number of transaction aborts in the context of serializable cuckoo hashing. In particular, in serializable cuckoo hashing, hundreds or thousands of inserts may be planned before any of them are committed to the table. Any overlaps in their planned kick-out chains will force one of the insertions' entire transaction to abort. Worse still, if two kick-out chains terminate in the same bin which contains only a single free slot, they are guaranteed to compete for the slot.

In this section, we describe two concurrency mechanisms which avoid overlapping kick-out chains with high probability. The first uses *hit counters*, which are a simple extension of queue kicking from Section 2. The second uses *claim flags*, which restrict write-access to a slot but not read-access.

We then evaluate our concurrency mechanisms on a serializable cuckoo hash table. Starting with a concurrency scheme similar to that of SILO, a high-performance in-memory database [4], we use hit counters and claim flags to obtain significant reductions in transaction-abort frequencies. For example, In our experiments for delete-heavy loads, claim flags bring the percent of transaction attempts that abort down from more than 5% to approximately .02% at low table densities, and from more than 10% to approximately .5% at high table densities. These percentages will vary depending on the size of the table, the number of threads, and the number of operations per transaction. For example, a larger table with the same number of threads and number of operations per transaction will yield smaller percentages.

3.1 Hit counters and Claim Flags

In Section 2, we used queue kicking to reduce bins viewed per insertion. By preemptively updating the queue, we can extend queue kicking to prevent concurrently planned kick-out chains from overlapping. In particular, for delete-light loads, the queue can be approximated by a *hit counter*, whose value modulo the bin size B is incremented atomically[1]on each insertion in the bin, and whose value designates a (possibly non-empty) slot for the next insertion to use.

Only if more than B insertions touch a given bin at a time is there risk of contention. Proposition 3.1 tells us with high probability, however, that this will never happen.

Proposition 3.1. *Suppose t threads concurrently each perform $O(n)$ operations, with each operation randomly touching at most j slots, on a table with n B-slot bins. With probability $O((tj)^{B+1}n^{1-B})$ no bin will ever simultaneously receive more than B touches.*

Hit counters will result in longer-than-necessary kick-out chains for delete-heavy loads, however, because they can result in a kick-out in a bin which has free slots. To achieve similar results for arbitrary loads, we introduce to every slot a mechanism called a *claim flag*, indicating whether the slot is claimed. Claim flags restrict other threads from planning to write to that slot, without restricting read-access.

Insertions and kick-outs select only out of the slots which are not already claimed in a bin, and then claim that slot atomically. Additionally, overwrites and deletes can claim slots in order to prevent insertions from using them.

Just as for queue kicking, as long as fewer than $B+1$ insertions use a given bin at a time, they avoid the risk of overlapping chains. Thus Proposition 3.1 tells us once again that with high probability no two insertions will ever compete during a table's $O(n)$-operation lifespan.

In order to avoid deadlock, no insertion can ever wait on a claim flag. Additionally, in the context of serializable cuckoo hashing, since many operations can be in a single transaction, any operation waiting on a claim flag risks deadlock. Consequently, when overwrites, insertions, or deletes see a claimed slot, they must abort the transaction. In the same situation without claim flags, however, one of the conflicting transactions would have been forced to abort regardless.

3.2 A Serializable Implementation

In serializable cuckoo hashing, each user transaction may consist of many interdependent insertions, overwrites, deletes, and reads. *Serializability* is the guarantee that the execution of a series of transactions is equivalent to some serial execution of those transactions.

[1]In practice, the increment can even be non-atomic, since the critical region is a single instruction.

In order to test hit counters and claim flags, we implemented a serializable cuckoo hash table using a concurrency scheme similar to that of SILO [4]. The basic scheme follows.

Planning Out a Transaction: Each slot in each bin is assigned a version ID which is updated each time it is overwritten. When planning out a transaction, a worker stores the version ID of each slot which it reads and of each slot which it plans to overwrite (in a *read-set* and *write-set* respectively). In addition, to guarantee the consistency of a given read, the worker must verify that the version ID of a slot is the same before and after the read.

Commiting a Transaction: To commit the transaction, the worker locks each slot in its write-set (in some global order to avoid deadlock), and then verifies the version IDs of the keys in both the read and write sets have not changed since the worker recorded them. Should verification succeed, then the worker can apply the transaction without violating serializability; otherwise, the worker must abort. After applying the transaction, and before releasing the locks on the overwritten slots, the worker must update the IDs of the overwritten slots. The worker assigns them an ID one more than the largest ID in either the read-set or write set. This ID is called the transaction's *transaction ID.*

Intuitively, we could simply increment each slot's ID rather than resetting it to the transaction ID. Setting it to the transaction ID has a subtle advantage, however. In particular, one can prove that the actual execution of transactions is equivalent to any serial execution in which the transactions are ordered weakly by their transaction IDs.

In addition to this basic scheme, we implemented a technique which we call *local retrying*, which allows for operations to verify that a given record is not present, without risking an abort later just because one of the slots which could contain the record has been updated. This is accomplished by assigning each bin a version ID which is updated only when a record is inserted into that bin. If a transaction wishes to verify that a bin b does not contain a key k, it places bin b's version ID, along with the key k, into its read-set. If, in the commit phase, a bin version ID from the read set has changed, the worker simply releases its locks, re-verifies that the bin doesn't contain the relevant record, and retries the commit phase using the bin's new version ID.

3.3 Experimental Evaluation

Races between concurrent transactions can force one of the transactions to completely abort. Aborts mean wasted work. Consequently abort-frequency is a good metric for measuring the efficacy of hit counters and claim flags.

We gather data on three variants of serialized cuckoo hashing, the base implementation from Section 3.2 which uses neither claim flags nor hit counters, an implementation which uses hit counters, and and implementation which uses claim-flags. For a delete-light workload, hit counters both decimate transaction aborts and shorten kick-out chains. In turn, claim flags appear to significantly reduce abort frequency in both delete-light and delete-heavy workloads.

We run tests on a table with 2^{14} bins, each containing 8 slots. We consider two workloads, one of which is light on deletes and one of which is delete heavy; the relative frequencies of inserts, deletes, overwrites, and reads is 1:0:1:1 and 2:1:2:2 in the two tests. Our experiments use 15 threads, each of which runs transactions batching together 100 operations. Each insert uses a randomly generated pair of hashes

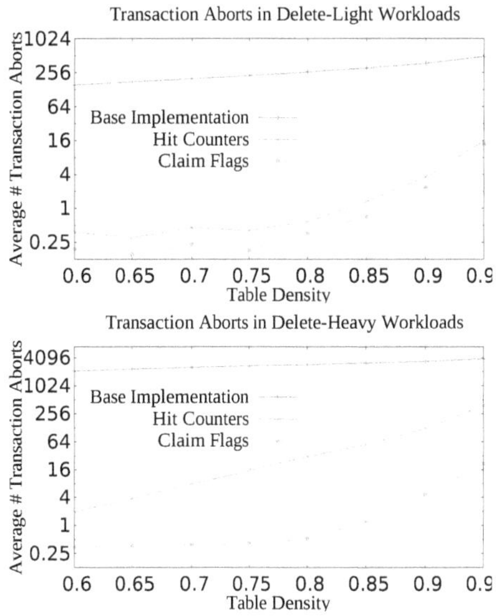

Figure 2: The average number of transaction aborts over the lifetime of tables filled to varying densities.

and a randomly generated integer payload. To randomly select a record for an overwrite, delete, or read, a thread picks out of all records ever inserted into the table by the thread.

Figure 2 graphs the average over 100 trials of the total number of aborts for a table filled to each density.

In general, one expects the total number of aborts to grow proportionally to the number of threads and number of operations per transaction, but to not depend on table size. Experiments on tables with varying parameters indicate this to be roughly the case; it would be interesting to further study the scaling properties of the tables.

4 Acknowledgments

This research was performed at HP Labs. The author thanks Harumi Kuno, Hideaki Kimura, and Bradley Kuszmaul for offering advice on exposition and directions of research.

5 References

[1] W. Kuszmaul. Fast concurrent cuckoo kick-out eviction schemes for high-density tables. *arXiv preprint arXiv:1605.05236*, 2016.

[2] X. Li, D. G. Andersen, M. Kaminsky, and M. J. Freedman. Algorithmic improvements for fast concurrent cuckoo hashing. In *Proc. 9th EuroSys*, page 27. ACM, 2014.

[3] K. A. Ross. Efficient hash probes on modern processors. In *Proc. 23rd ICDE*, pages 1297–1301. IEEE, 2007.

[4] S. Tu, W. Zheng, E. Kohler, B. Liskov, and S. Madden. Speedy transactions in multicore in-memory databases. In *Proc. 24th SOSP*, pages 18–32. ACM, 2013.

The Family Holiday Gathering Problem or Fair and Periodic Scheduling of Independent Sets

Amihood Amir
Bar Ilan University, Israel
Johns Hopkins University, USA
amir@cs.biu.ac.il

Oren Kapah
Bar Ilan University, Israel
orenkapah.ac@gmail.com

Tsvi Kopelowitz
University of Michigan, USA
kopelot@gmail.com

Moni Naor*
Weizmann Institute of Science, Israel
moni.naor@weizmann.ac.il

Ely Porat
Bar Ilan University, Israel
porat@cs.biu.ac.il

ABSTRACT

We introduce the *Holiday Gathering Problem* which models the difficulty in scheduling non-interfering transmissions in (wireless) networks. Our goal is to schedule transmission rounds so that the antennas that transmit in a given round will not interfere with each other, i.e. all of the other antennas that can interfere will not transmit in that round, while minimizing the number of consecutive rounds in which antennas do not transmit.

Following a long tradition in Computer Science, we introduce the problem by an intuitive story. Assume we live in a perfect world where families enjoy being together. Consequently, parents, whose children are in a monogamous relation, would like to have *all* their children at home for the holiday meal (i.e. there is a special pleasure gained by hosting all the children simultaneously and they wish to have this event occur as frequently as possible). However, the conflict is that the in-laws would also be happiest if all their children come to them. Our goal can be described as scheduling an infinite sequence of "guest lists" in a distributed setting so that each child knows where it will spend the holiday. The holiday gathering problem is closely related to several classical problems in computer science, such as the *dining philosophers problem* on a general graph and periodic scheduling.

The process of the scheduling should be done with no further communication after initialization, by using a small amount of local data. The result should minimize the number of consecutive holidays where the family is not together. In a good sequence this number depends on local properties of the parents (e.g., their number of children). Furthermore, solutions that are periodic, i.e. a gathering occurs every fixed number of rounds, are useful for maintaining a small amount of information at each node and reducing the amount of ongoing communication and computation.

Our algorithmic techniques show interesting connections between periodic scheduling, coloring, and universal prefix free encodings. We develop a coloring-based construction where the period of each node colored with the c is at most $2^{1+\log^* c} \cdot \prod_{i=0}^{\log^* c} \log^{(i)} c$ (where $\log^{(i)}$ means iterating the log function i times). This is achieved via a connection with *prefix-free encodings*. We prove that this is the best possible for coloring-based solutions. We also show a construction with period at most $2d$ for a node of degree d.

*Incumbent of the Judith Kleeman Professorial Chair.

SPAA '16, July 11 - 13, 2016, Pacific Grove, CA, USA

ISBN 978-1-4503-4210-0/16/07...$15.00
DOI: http://dx.doi.org/10.1145/2935764.2935788

1. INTRODUCTION

We examine the problem of scheduling an infinite sequence of independent sets in a given graph G in a *distributed* manner, with the following three objectives:

- *Periodicity.* For every node v, if v appears in the ith independent set then the next independent set containing v is the $(i+\pi_v)$th independent set, where π_v is a fixed positive integer. We say that π_v is the *period* of v. Periodicity is useful since it allows each node v to maintain a small amount of information in order to determine the subsequence of independent sets in which it participates. In particular, a periodic schedule guarantees that once the period is set the amount of communication and computation is minimized, saving both bandwidth and energy.

- *Locality.* π_v depends only on local properties of v (such as its degree), and not global properties of the graph (such as the maximum degree or the diameter). Locality provides a sense of fairness since for every node the length of its period only depends on properties of that node.

- *Minimize Starvation.* The periods should collectively be as small as possible.

This problem has direct applications in the realm of common resource scheduling. Suppose that in a world with many agents, each agent requires some shared resources in order to perform some job. For example, it would be beneficial if wireless radios could guarantee that when they broadcast on a particular frequency, none of the other radios interfere. In this application the shared resource is the air which is within transmission radius of more than one radio. We can model this as radios being vertices and two radios which share some air are modelled as an edge.

In the Computer Science tradition of defining systems problems as "social" problems, e.g. the dining philosophers problem, we view the wireless radios model as a "holiday gathering" problem. One of the anxiety-causing problems before the holidays is where to go for the holiday dinner? Parents, whose children are in a monogamous relationship, would obviously (?!) like to have *all* their children at home for the holiday meal (i.e. there is a special pleasure gained by the festive experience of hosting all the children simultaneously and intuitively the goal is to have this event occur as frequently as possible). We say that such parents wish to be *happy* during the holiday. However, the conflict is that the in-laws would also be happy if all their children come to them.

This problem is closely related to the classic *dining philosophers problem*, which we discuss later. Furthermore, scheduling problems are part of our mainstay, and these problems are indeed scheduling problems. To this end, we focus on algorithms whose goal is to schedule which parents are happy during any given holiday in a *distributed* manner with the objective of minimizing the number of consecutive holidays in which a parent is not happy[1].

Connection to coloring.

As in many problems in computer science, for some special inputs the holiday gathering problem is simple. For example, if G is bipartite with two sets of nodes A and B, then there is a very good sequence: during odd rounds the independent set will be all of A and during the even rounds the independent set will be all of B. The reason this example works out so well is because it is based on covering all of the nodes using as few independent sets as possible - a coloring problem. In the bipartite case, two colors suffice. In the setting of wireless networks the topology of the network may also lead to a low chromatic number.

In a general graph where Δ is the largest degree, it is immediate that one can color the graph in $\Delta + 1$ colors. Such a coloring can be obtained in a distributed manner by applying, for example, the recent randomized algorithm of Barenboim, Elkin, Pettie, and Schneider [5] (denoted by the BEPS algorithm for short) running in $O(\log \Delta + 2^{O(\sqrt{\log \log n})})$ rounds. The coloring leads to a scheduling of independent sets where the period of each node is exactly $\Delta + 1$. This scheduling is obtained by partitioning the sequence into phases of $\Delta + 1$ independent sets, and in each phase the ith round corresponds to all of the nodes colored i. However, such a sequence is not local as the length of any period depends on a global graph parameter (the maximum degree), and so this approach requires some refinement.

[1]One may consider the problem of maximizing happiness for a given year, but this problem is $\mathbb{NP}$-hard. One may also consider an objective function relating to the satisfaction of parents. Details for both can be seen in the Appendix.

What is the fair share of parents? Defining fairness is the subject of much debate in philosophy, game theory and theology. Much of cooperative game theory deals with fair allocation of resources. In our case the problem seems hard: given the tight relationship with coloring and maximum independent set, we cannot even determine efficiently the 'value' of the full coalition (see Appendix B.2). On the other hand, consider the following simple 'chaotic' process called "first come first grab": parents wake up at a random time and grab their available (those who have not been grabbed) children. The probability that a node p manages to grab *all* its children is $1/(deg(p) + 1)$, where $deg(p)$ is the degree of p. So the expected time until hosting all the children is $deg(p)$ and this is the landmark we will try to obtain, i.e. we would like every parent to host a holiday with all their children every $O(deg(p))$ years. It is also clear that in general we cannot hope to get a better than $deg(p) + 1$ result, if the conflict graph is a clique. Nevertheless, when the input graph has a small chromatic number, as discussed above, we can do better.

1.1 Our Results and Techniques

The main contributions of this paper are, thus:

1. A **Color-bound** solution for the holiday gathering problem which is based on any given coloring of the graph. The length of a period for a node v with color c is at most $\pi_v \leq 2^{1+\log^* c} \cdot \prod_{i=0}^{\log^* c} \log^{(i)} c$ where $\log^{(i)} c$ is the iterative log function of c taken i times. This is achieved by introducing an interesting new technique that utilizes a connection with *prefix-free encoding*. We also show that, for color-based techniques, our algorithm is close to optimal. This is done by proving a lower bound on the length of a period of $\pi_v \geq \prod_{i=0}^{\log^* c} \log^{(i)} c$ for any scheduling algorithm based on graph coloring. This lower bound makes use of the Cauchy condensation test.

2. A **Degree-bound** solution for the holiday gathering problem where π_v for a node v with degree d children is exactly $2^{\lceil \log d \rceil} \leq 2d$.

We emphasize that it is always possible to color the graph where the color of a node of degree d is at most $d + 1$ (for example using the BEPS algorithm, see [6] for a more recent version). If, in a given coloring, all of the colors are much smaller than the respective degrees (like a 2-coloring of a bipartite graph) then clearly the first algorithm is preferable. However, in terms of worst-case dependence on the degree of a node, the second algorithm is preferable.

We are mainly interested in periodic scheduling, but we also discuss some non-periodic solutions in Appendix A that serve as a sanity check and help us understand what is the best one could hope for without any constraints.

1.2 Related Work

As mentioned, the holiday gathering problem is related to several lines of investigation in computer science (not to mention other scholastic activities). Issues related to calendrical calculations have attracted the best minds since antiquity (see Dershowitz and Reingold [11]). No lesser than al-Khwarizmi (after whom the term 'algorithm' is named) wrote a treatise on the Hebrew Calendar ("Risala fi istikhraj ta'arikh al-yahud"), see Knuth [21]. Some calendars are fixed in the sense the that it is known in advance when each holiday will occur, as is the case with the Western (Gregorian) calendar and the Hebrew calendar, while others, like the Muslim Calendar or the Old Hebrew Calendar are determined on-the-fly, e.g. based on lunar observations. This is reminiscent of some of the issues that arise in our algorithms (the one in Appendix A vs. those of Sections 3 and 4).

The dining philosophers problem is the famous resource allocation problem introduced by Dijkstra [12], see Lynch [25]. In this problem, there is a given conflict graph where each node represents a processor and each edge represents a resource (a "fork" in the story where the processors are philosophers who would like to eat) which is shared by the two endpoint processors. At any time, a fork can be "owned" by at most one of the processors that share it. Each processor can be in one of three states: resting, hungry, or eating. A resting processor can become hungry at any time. In order to eat, a processor must obtain all the forks on its adjacent edges. A processor eats for at most a bounded time, after which it returns to the resting state. The problem, and its many variations, have played a major role in concurrent programming and distributed computation. For this problem there are solutions that minimize the wait chain, based on coloring of the edge or the nodes (see [24, 33, 10, 29, 26]). The main difference between the focus of this work and most work on the dining philosophers problem is that we assume that the philosophers want to eat *all* the time (i.e. they become hungry right after they finish eating)[2] and that the meal takes a fixed amount of time and the main issue is how can we provide an efficient and high throughput solution while guaranteeing some reasonably fair allocation.

Problems related to ours have appeared frequently in the scheduling literature, starting perhaps from the Chairman Assignment Problem of Tijdeman [34]. The assumption is that there is one resource and all users are interested in using it. Each user or task has a weight and the goal is to schedule the users so that they obtain the resource proportionally to their weight. Sometime there are multiple identical resources, but each task can be assigned to one resource concurrently [7, 23]. This is similar to our setting when the graph is a clique (or composed of components that are cliques) and all the weights are the same. In a 'perfectly periodic scheduling' the goal is to schedule the users in a *periodic way* (every user i gets the resource every τ_i rounds) where each user gets its weight (see [3]). The algorithms of Sections 3 and 4 are perfectly periodic. In the chromatic sum problem (see [2]) one tries to find a coloring that minimizes the the total sum of the colors (where the assumption is that the colors are in $\mathbb{N}$). The motivation is, again, from scheduling with the goal of minimizing *average* waiting time, rather than the maximum waiting time as a function of the degree, as is our goal.

Fairness in online scheduling has received some attention as well, for instance the carpool problem [14, 1, 28], that can also be viewed as a generalization of the Chairman Assignment Problem of Tijdeman [34].

The $\mathcal{LOCAL}$ model of computation in distributed computing was first considered by Linial [22] and much developed since then, see Peleg [31]. The problems of interest are especially those of coloring and maximal independent set. For both of these problem good randomized algorithms are known, see the monograph by Barenboim and Elkin for a survey of recent results [4]. Coming up with deterministic polylog in n algorithms for these problems is a major open problem in the area.

[2]So one may call the problem "The Fressing Philosophers Problem", as suggested by Cynthia Dwork.

Minimizing interference in wireless networks.

There has been a lot of research focusing on scheduling devices in wireless networks so as to minimize interference. This work has focused on determining which nodes may transmit on which time-frequency slot, while optimizing fairness and throughput [17]. This line of work leverages the specific topology of wireless networks. For example, some research has looked at conflict graphs that represent geometric intersection graphs such as the unit disk graph [15]. However, many believe that such graphs do not do a good job of representing the reality of wireless graphs (see [27]). Thus, a lot of recent work has focused on the SINR model where signals decays as it travels. In this model the success of a transition depends on its strength at the receiver relative to the strength of other interfering transmissions [18, 16].

In light of the above, we emphasize that our color-based schemes allow to implicitly account for special topologies that have a conflict graph with a low chromatic number, as one may expect from a wireless network. Moreover, the previous line of work has focused on scheduling transmissions in several channels in order to minimize interference, while our focus is on one channel that does not allow any interference.

2. PRELIMINARIES

Our universe is a graph $G = (V, E)$ where $|V| = n$. Let $deg(v)$ be the degree of a node $v \in V$. Most of this work assumes that the G is fixed, but we also consider the dynamic case and briefly discuss it in Section 5.

DEFINITION 2.1. *For a given independent set h we say that node $v \in V$ is* happy *in h if v participates in h.*

DEFINITION 2.2. *Let $H = h_i$, $i = 1, \ldots, \infty$ be a sequence of independent sets and denote the subsequence $h_i, ..., h_j$ by $h[i:j]$. If $v \in V$ is not happy at any $h \in h[i:j]$ then we call the interval $h[i:j]$ an* unhappiness interval *for v and call the longest such interval a* maximum unhappiness interval *of v and denote its length by $mui_H(v)$ (or $mui(v)$ when H is clear from the context). If all (locally) maximal unhappiness intervals of v are of the same length π_v (except for possibly the first interval which may be shorter) then we say that H is periodic for v and π_v is the length of the period of v. We say that H is* periodic-for-all *if it is periodic for all of the nodes in V.*

The combinatorial definition of the Holiday Gathering Problem is: given a graph G, find an infinite sequence H of independent-sets of G. The objective function is to minimize, for every node v, the maximal gap between two appearances of v. Intuitively, our goal is to devise a sequence H of independent sets that is periodic-for-all, while minimizing π_v for each $v \in V$.

Algorithm Scheme

1. Color G.
2. At holiday i, if $decode(i) = col(p)$ then make p happy.

end Algorithm

Figure 1: Generic coloring based scheme for the Holiday Gathering problem.

Elias omega code Algorithm

1. Color G.
2. At holiday i, if $LSB(B(i)) = \omega(p)^R$ then make p happy.

end Algorithm

Figure 2: Scheduling for the Holiday Gathering problem based on the Elias omega code.

3. A PERIODIC COLOR-BOUND ALGORITHM

We are now interested in providing a mechanism whereby the decision of when a node is happy is dependent on *local* properties of that node. We present a general scheme for such a mechanism that depends on the color nodes receive during an initial coloring algorithm. To obtain such a coloring we begin by distributively coloring the graph (for example using the BEPS algorithm). However, we do not make any assumptions on the coloring algorithm, and so this algorithm works for any graph coloring, including the (possibly difficult to obtain) optimal one.

We consider a mapping of the independent set numbers to colors. The mapping needs to satisfy two conditions: (1) Every independent set number is mapped to at most one color, and (2) The resulting sequence guarantees that nodes do not have very large periods.

The basic idea is captured by the following algorithm (see Figure 1). We first color the G with some coloring algorithm, and then we use a decoding scheme so that at round i if the decoding of i is the color of v then v is part of the ith independent set.

Examples:

Trivial: Consider the trivial example where the nodes are colored sequentially from 1 to n. At independent set i, make $v = i \bmod n$ happy. No two adjacent nodes are encoded to the same number, but $\forall v \in V$ we have $\pi_v = n$, which means that it depends on global properties of G.

Prefix Free Color Code: Apply on G the BEPS distributed graph coloring algorithm that colors each graph node v by a color not exceeding $deg(v)+1$. Now encode the colors using some prefix-free binary code. On independent set i, consider the binary representation of i from right to left (with an infinite sequence of 0's padded to it). Any node v is made happy if the prefix-free encoding of $col(v)$ is a prefix of i. The solution is appropriate, since no two adjacent nodes will be made happy concurrently at any given independent set i: they will be assigned different colors and the two different colors are encoded in a prefix-free code and hence the binary representation of i cannot encode both of them. For every $v \in V$, we have that π_v of this procedure is dependent on the length of the prefix-free encoding of v's color.

We will indeed use prefix-free binary codes in our algorithm. Notice that if a node is given a color c which uses x_c bits in its prefix-free code, then the schedule of when that node is happy is periodic with period 2^{x_c}. In other words, every 2^{x_c} independent sets the node will be happy

3.1 Upper Bound - Elias Code

We recursively define the function $\phi : \mathbb{N} \to \mathbb{R}$. For $i \leq 1$ we have $\phi(i) = 1$. Otherwise, $\phi(i) = i \cdot \phi(\log i)$. Explicitly, $\phi(i) = i \cdot \log i \cdot \log\log i \cdot \log\log\log i \cdots 1$, or $\phi(i) = \prod_{i=0}^{\log^* c} \log^{(i)} c$, where $\log^{(i)}$ means iterating the log function i times.

In this section we present an algorithm that will guarantee that no two nodes with different colors are made happy during the same independent set, and that $\pi_v = \phi(c)2^{\log^* c+1}$, where c is the color of v. This algorithm is based on the *Elias omega code*. The Elias omega code is a universal code for the natural numbers developed by Peter Elias [13]. It is one of the prefix-free codes that represents the integers by a number of bits relative to their size. While the omega code is not the most practical code, it is theoretically the most efficient Elias code. Our algorithm in Figure 2 is correct for all Elias codes, but we chose the omega code for its almost optimal complexity.

Details of the Elias omega code are given in Appendix C. The important properties that we need from the code are that it is a prefix free code, and that the length of the coding of i is given by:

$$\begin{aligned}\rho(i) =& 1 + \lceil\log(i)\rceil + \lceil\log(\lceil\log(i)\rceil - 1)\rceil \\ &+ \lceil\log(\lceil\log(\lceil\log(i)\rceil - 1)\rceil - 1)\rceil + \cdots .\end{aligned}$$

Our algorithm will use the Elias omega code of the colors in reverse. Denote by S^R the string S reversed. For example, $(abcdef)^R = fedcba$. Denote by $LSB(S,k)$ the suffix of S of length k, or the k least significant bits of S. Denote by $B(x)$ the binary representation of x, i.e. $B(x)$ is a string over alphabet $\{0,1\}$ which is the representation of n in base 2 with no leading zeros.

THEOREM 3.1. *The Elias omega code algorithm guarantees happiness for node $v \in V$ in every cycle of length bounded above by $\phi(c)2^{\log^* c+1}$, where c is the color of v.*

PROOF. The time between happy independent sets for v is $2^{\rho(c)}$. Notice that $\rho(c) \leq 1+\sum_{i=1}^{\log^* c}\lceil\log^{(i)} c\rceil \leq 1+\log^* c+\sum_{i=1}^{\log^* c}\log^{(i)} c$. The $\log^* c$ term is a result of the rounding up of the log at every recursion of $\rho(n)$, since the number of bits cannot be a fraction. For some colors this term may be less than $\log^* c$, or even a constant, but it will never exceed $\log^* c$. Now, the time between happy independent sets is $2^{\rho(c)} \leq 2^{1+\log^* c} \cdot \prod_{i=0}^{\log^* c-1}\log^{(i)} c = 2^{1+\log^* c}\phi(c)$. $\square$

3.2 Lower Bounds

The coloring-based algorithm scheme of Theorem 3.1 starts by assigning colors to the nodes in G. We would like every node to use its color in order to compute a period π such that every π years that node is happy. In this section we compute lower bounds on that period as a function of the color. This defines the best period one can hope to achieve by the coloring-based scheme. Our lower bound almost matches the algorithm of Theorem 3.1.

THEOREM 3.2. *Let G be legally colored and every node $v \in V$ has a color c_v. Let sequence $H = h_i,\ i = 1, ..., \infty$ of independent sets be such that there is no independent set h_{i_0} in which the nodes of two different colors, $c_1 \neq c_2$ are happy. If there exists a function $f : \mathbb{N} \to \mathbb{N}$ such that for every $v \in V$ we have $\pi_v = f(c_v)$, then $f(c) \in \Omega(\phi(c))$.*

PROOF. Consider a subsequence $h[i_0 : j_0]$ of length m. We require that at any independent set in the sequence, there is at most one color c which is happy. The conclusion is that there are at least $\lceil \frac{m}{f(c)} \rceil$ occurrences in the sequence where nodes of color c are happy. This is true for all colors c that get mapped to the subsequence. Let $C = \{c | c \text{ is a color mapped to } h[i_0 : j_0]\}$. Then we have $\sum_{c \in C} \lceil \frac{m}{f(c)} \rceil \leq m \Rightarrow \sum_{c \in C} \frac{1}{f(c)} \leq 1$. Taking into account all possible sets C as the size of G goes to infinity, we have $\sum_{c=1}^{\infty} \frac{1}{f(c)} \leq 1$. Clearly this will not hold if we have $f(c) = c$. It holds when $f(c) = 2^c$ and even when $f(c) = c^{1+\epsilon}$ for any constant $\epsilon > 0$. According to Cauchy's condensation test [9] the smallest function for which this inequality holds is $f(c) = \phi(c)$, i.e. $f(c) = \prod_{i=0}^{\log^* c} \log^{(i)} c$. □

4. A PERIODIC DEGREE-BOUND ALGORITHM

While many graphs have a low chromatic number that may be obtainable[3], other graphs do not. Furthermore, while some classes of graphs may have a low chromatic number, it is not clear how to obtain algorithms that achieve $o(\Delta)$ colors for some of these classes. In such cases a color-bound algorithm may not suffice considering the inherent lower-bound. We could use the bound of $c \leq d+1$ for a node v with color c and degree d, to obtain a guaranteed degree-bound of $\pi_v \leq \phi(d+1)2^{\log^*(d+1)+1}$ using Theorem 3.1, but we can do better.

To this end, we present a second local algorithm which is degree-bound, i.e. π_v is bounded by a function of $d = deg(v)$. In particular, our algorithm guarantees that this bound is at most $2d$, which is very close to the bound $d+1$ obtained by the non-periodic algorithm of Appendix A. We first describe a sequential version of our algorithm, and later show how to convert it to the distributed setting.

A Sequential Algorithm.

The periodic scheduling is obtained using a greedy algorithm, where nodes are arranged in a *non-increasing* order of their degrees and each node v in its turn chooses a non-negative integer. Thus, when v with degree d has to chose an integer, none of its smaller than degree d neighbors has chosen an integer. Let $j = \lceil \log(d+1) \rceil$. When it is v's turn to pick an integer, there must be at least one integer x in the range $[0, 2^j - 1]$ such that no neighbor of v has chosen a number x' where $x = x' \bmod 2^j$. So v picks x to be its integer.

The independent set i now is determined by checking whether $i \equiv x \mod 2^j$. If 'yes' then v is happy in independent set i, otherwise it is not. We can immediately see that v is happy once every $2^j - 2^{\lceil \log(d+1) \rceil} \leq 2d$ independent sets. We will now show that there are no conflicts.

[3]For instance, for triangle-free graphs Pettie and Su [32] very recently gave an $O(\Delta/\log\Delta)$ distributed coloring.

Algorithm – Distributed degree-bound algorithm

1. For $i = \lceil \log(\Delta+1) \rceil$ to 0
   (a) Let $P_i = \{p \in P$ such that $\lceil \log(\deg(p)+1) \rceil = i\}$
   (b) For each $p \in P_i$ restrict the palette of p to integers that are not equal modulo 2^i with any integer already picked by a neighbor of p.
   (c) Run the BEPS algorithm on P_i with the restricted palettes.

end Algorithm

Figure 3: A degree based scheme for the Holiday Gathering problem.

LEMMA 4.1. *Let v_1 and v_2 be two adjacent nodes in G sharing an edge with degrees d_1 and d_2 respectively. Let $j_1 = \lceil \log(d_1+1) \rceil$ and $j_2 = \lceil \log(d_2+1) \rceil$, and let x_1 and x_2 be the integers picked by v_1 and v_2 respectively using the above algorithm. Then v_1 and v_2 will never be in the same independent set.*

PROOF. Without loss of generality let $d_1 \leq d_2$. Assume, for the sake of contradiction, that at independent set i both v_1 and v_2 try to host. This implies that $i = x_1 + a_1 2^{j_1} = x_2 + a_2 2^{j_2}$. But this also means that $x_1 \equiv x_2 \mod 2^{j_1}$, and so when it was the turn of v_1 to pick its integer the algorithm could not pick x_1 for v_1, giving a contradiction. □

The Distributed Algorithm.

For the distributed setting we run $\lceil \log(\Delta+1) \rceil$ phases of the BEPS algorithm with the following modification. Starting with $i = \lceil \log(\Delta+1) \rceil$ and going to $i = 0$, during phase i all of the nodes with degree d such that $\lceil \log(d+1) \rceil = i$ will participate in the coloring algorithm for that phase. However, we must restrict the palette of colors for each node v to be comprised only of integers that do not collide (under modulo 2^i) with integers of neighbors of v that already participated in early phases. We emphasize that Barenboim et.al. [6] show that the analysis of the BEPS algorithm does not change with this restriction. The algorithm appears in detail in Figure 3.

Each phase takes $O(\log\Delta + 2^{O(\sqrt{\log\log n})})$ rounds, and we have $O(\log\Delta)$ phases, for a total of $O(\log^2\Delta + \log\Delta \cdot 2^{O(\sqrt{\log\log n})})$ rounds. In a manner similar to Lemma 4.1 we can show that a conflict can never arise.

THEOREM 4.2. *The distributed degree-bound algorithm guarantees happiness for node $v \in V$ in every cycle of length bounded above by $2d$, where d is the degree of v.*

5. THE DYNAMIC SETTING AND OPEN PROBLEMS

So far we have assumed that the conflict graph is fixed and does not change throughout the lifetime of the system. However, as we know, relationships are not fixed and new connections may be created or old connections may dissolve. How do our algorithms fare under such conditions? Clearly two nodes that become adjacent and were scheduled to host the same upcoming independent set need to recolor themselves.

In the algorithm of Section 3 all we needed is a valid coloring. So if two nodes v and u that have the same color become connected, one of them, say v, needs to find a new color. But this is relatively simple since v's palette should grow by one more color, since d=$deg(v)$ was increased by 1. So given the new color, the new periodic schedule for v is derived from the prefix-free encoding of the new color. This means that after at most $\phi(d)2^{\log^* d+1}$ rounds after quiescence v will get to host. Note that in this algorithm, if there are w events of adding new neighbors, then the time a node hosts a independent set may be postponed up to $w \cdot \phi(d)2^{\log^* d+1}$ rounds. In the event of deletion of edges, presumably there is nothing to be done. However, if this happens too frequently, then the rate of hosting becomes disproportional to the current degree and we will need to recolor the node (again simple even give the smaller palette).

Our Algorithm of Section 4 does not fare so well in a dynamic graphs. It is very important in that algorithm to let the higher degree nodes color themselves before the lower degree ones (since the latter's frequency is much higher and they will occupy available slots if colored before the higher degree).

So a main open problem this work presents is whether it is possible to have a degree bound algorithm that works in a dynamic graph. Another issue is whether it is possible to get to the bound of Appendix A of frequency $d+1$ in a periodic or at least succinctly defined manner.

A lower bound conjecture for periodic scheduling.
In Section 4 we showed an algorithm that achieves a $2d$ upper bound on the period of a node with degree d. This is in contrast to the non periodic scheduling obtained in Appendix A where we can obtain a $d+1$ guarantee. We conjecture that there is a separation between what is obtainable when one requires periodicity versus the general case, and we leave as an open problem to prove that if one requires a periodic schedule then the best guarantee obtainable is $d+\omega(1)$.

6. ACKNOWLEDGMENTS

This work is partially supported by ISF grants 571/14 and 4/11, BSF grants 2014028 and 2012348, NSF grants CCF-1217338, CNS-1318294, and CCF-1514383, and the I-CORE Program of the Planning and Budgeting Committee.

We thank Amotz Bar-Noy for helpful comments.

7. REFERENCES

[1] Miklós Ajtai, James Aspnes, Moni Naor, Yuval Rabani, Leonard J. Schulman, and Orli Waarts. Fairness in scheduling. *J. Algorithms*, 29(2):306–357, 1998.

[2] Amotz Bar-Noy, Mihir Bellare, Magnús M. Halldórsson, Hadas Shachnai, and Tami Tamir. On chromatic sums and distributed resource allocation. *Inf. Comput.*, 140(2):183–202, 1998.

[3] Amotz Bar-Noy, Aviv Nisgav, and Boaz Patt-Shamir. Nearly optimal perfectly periodic schedules. *Distributed Computing*, 15(4):207–220, 2002.

[4] Leonid Barenboim and Michael Elkin. *Distributed Graph Coloring*. `http://www.cs.bgu.ac.il/~elkinm/BarenboimElkin-monograph.pdf`, 2013.

[5] Leonid Barenboim, Michael Elkin, Seth Pettie, and Johannes Schneider. The locality of distributed symmetry breaking. In *53rd Annual IEEE Symposium on Foundations of Computer Science, (FOCS)*, pages 321–330, 2012.

[6] Leonid Barenboim, Michael Elkin, Seth Pettie, and Johannes Schneider. The locality of distributed symmetry breaking. *CoRR*, abs/1202.1983, 2015.

[7] S. K. Baruah, N. K. Cohen, C. G. Plaxton, and D. A. Varvel. Proportionate progress: a notion of fairness in resource allocation. In *Proceedings of the twenty-fifth annual ACM symposium on Theory of computing*, STOC '93, pages 345–354, New York, NY, USA, 1993. ACM.

[8] P. Berman and T. Fujito. On approximation properties of the independent set problem for degree 3 graphs. In *Workshop on Algorithms and Data Structures (WADS)*, volume 955 of *LNCS*, pages 449–460. Springer, 1995.

[9] D. D. Bonar, Jr. M. J. Khoury, and M. Khoury. *Real Infinite Series*. The Mathematical Association of America, 2006.

[10] Manhoi Choy and Ambuj K. Singh. Efficient fault-tolerant algorithms for distributed resource allocation. *ACM Trans. Program. Lang. Syst.*, 17(3):535–559, 1995.

[11] Nachum Dershowitz and Edward M. Reingold. *Calendrical Calculations*. Cambridge University Press, New York, NY, USA, 3rd edition, 2007.

[12] Edsger W. Dijkstra. Hierarchical ordering of sequential processes. *Acta Inf.*, 1:115–138, 1971.

[13] P. Elias. Universal codeword sets and representations of the integers. *Information Theory, IEEE Transactions on*, 21(2):194–203, Mar 1975.

[14] Ronald Fagin and John H. Williams. A fair carpool scheduling algorithm. *IBM Journal of Research and Development*, 27(2):133–139, 1983.

[15] Piyush Gupta and P. R. Kumar. The capacity of wireless networks. *IEEE Transactions on Information Theory*, 46(2):388–404, 2000.

[16] Magnús M. Halldórsson, Stephan Holzer, Pradipta Mitra, and Roger Wattenhofer. The power of non-uniform wireless power. In *Proceedings of the Twenty-Fourth Annual ACM-SIAM Symposium on Discrete Algorithms, SODA*, pages 1595–1606, 2013.

[17] Magnús M. Halldórsson and Pradipta Mitra. Nearly optimal bounds for distributed wireless scheduling in the SINR model. In *Automata, Languages and Programming - 38th International Colloquium, ICALP, Part II*, pages 625–636, 2011.

[18] Magnús M. Halldórsson and Tigran Tonoyan. How well can graphs represent wireless interference? In *Proceedings of the Forty-Seventh Annual ACM on Symposium on Theory of Computing, STOC*, pages 635–644, 2015.

[19] Johan Håstad. Clique is hard to approximate within $n^{1-\epsilon}$. *Acta Mathematica*, 182(1):105–142, 1999.

[20] J. Hopcroft and R. Karp. An $n^{5/2}$ algorithm for maximum matchings in bipartite graphs. *SIAM J. Computing*, 2(4):225–231, 1973.

[21] Donald E. Knuth. Algorithms in modern mathematics and computer science. In Andrei P. Ershov and Donald E. Knuth, editors, *Algorithms in Modern Mathematics and Computer Science*, volume 122 of *Lecture Notes in Computer Science*, pages 82–99. Springer, 1979.

[22] Nathan Linial. Locality in distributed graph algorithms. *SIAM J. Comput.*, 21(1):193–201, 1992.

[23] Ami Litman and Shiri Moran-Schein. On centralized smooth scheduling. *Algorithmica*, 60(2):464–480, 2011.

[24] Nancy A. Lynch. Upper bounds for static resource allocation in a distributed system. *J. Comput. Syst. Sci.*, 23(2):254–278, 1981.

[25] Nancy A. Lynch. *Distributed Algorithms*. Morgan Kaufmann Publishers,, San Mateo, CA, USA, 1996.

[26] Alain J. Mayer, Moni Naor, and Larry J. Stockmeyer. Local computations on static and dynamic graphs. In *ISTCS*, pages 268–278, 1995.

[27] Thomas Moscibroda, Roger Wattenhofer, and Aaron Zollinger. Topology control meets SINR: the scheduling complexity of arbitrary topologies. In *Proceedings of the 7th ACM Interational Symposium on Mobile Ad Hoc Networking and Computing, (MobiHoc)*.

[28] Moni Naor. On fairness in the carpool problem. *Journal of Algorithms*, 55(1):93 – 98, 2005.

[29] Moni Naor and Larry J. Stockmeyer. What can be computed locally? *SIAM J. Comput.*, 24(6):1259–1277, 1995.

[30] Martin J. Osborne and Ariel Rubinstein. *A Course in Game Theory*. MIT Press, Cambridge, MA, USA, 1994.

[31] David Peleg. *Distributed computing: a locality-sensitive approach*. Society for Industrial and Applied Mathematics, Philadelphia, PA, USA, 2000.

[32] Seth Pettie and Hsin-Hao Su. Fast distributed coloring algorithms for triangle-free graphs. In Fedor V. Fomin, Rusins Freivalds, Marta Z. Kwiatkowska, and David Peleg, editors, *ICALP (2)*, volume 7966 of *Lecture Notes in Computer Science*, pages 681–693. Springer, 2013.

[33] Eugene Styer and Gary L. Peterson. Improved algorithms for distributed resource allocation. In Danny Dolev, editor, *PODC*, pages 105–116. ACM, 1988.

[34] R. Tijdeman. The chairman assignment problem. *Discrete Mathematics*, 32(3):323 – 330, 1980.

APPENDIX

Appendix

A. THE NON-PERIODIC DEGREE-BOUND ALGORITHM

Our goal here is to guarantee *happiness* to every node within a reasonable number of independent sets, but not necessarily in a periodic sequence. We present[4] an algorithm guaranteeing that a node of degree d has to wait at most $d+1$ steps till it is happy. However, the node does not know in advance all the times in which it will host the independent set, just the next time it will do so.

[4]We remark here that while this algorithm is less interesting from a technical perspective, it is useful for set up, and gives us a benchmark for comparison when attempting to understand the strengths of the lightweight algorithms.

Algorithm – Phased Greedy Coloring

1. **Initialization:** Assign every node p a color.
2. For $i = 1$ to ∞
   (a) For every node $p \in P$: if $col(p) = i$ then make p happy and recolor p:
      i. Let $p_1, ..., p_\ell$ be the nodes adjacent to p in P.
         A. Let $s = min\{t | i < t \leq i + \ell + 1, t \notin \{col(p_1), ..., c(p_\ell)\}\}$.
         B. $col(p) \leftarrow s$.

end Algorithm

Figure 4: The phased greedy coloring algorithm.

The algorithm we consider starts with a *distributed graph coloring algorithm*. As mentioned in Section 1, there is a simple mechanism using a $\Delta+1$ coloring to obtain a sequence H such that for every node $v \in V$ we have $mui_H(p) = \Delta+1$. Such a coloring can be obtained in a distributed manner by applying, for example, the recent randomized algorithm of Barenboim, Elkin, Pettie, and Schneider [5] (denoted by the BEPS algorithm for short) running in $O(\log \Delta + 2^{O(\sqrt{\log \log n})})$ rounds. The BEPS algorithm also has the property that the color c picked for a node with degree d will always be bound by $c \leq d+1$ (see [6] for details). So at first the smaller degree nodes will be happy pretty quickly. However, for their next turn they will have to wait time proportional to Δ. As mentioned, we seek an efficient mechanism for constructing a sequence H where $mui_H(p)$ depends on local properties of v.

To solve this problem we will use a phased algorithm where colors are reassigned every phase (independent set), providing a sequence of independent sets. The initial coloring is the one obtained by the BEPS algorithm.

At independent set i, greedily, recolor the nodes whose current color is i: color each such node v with the smallest number $j > i$ such that none of v's neighbors has color j. At independent set i the nodes colored i are happy.

The algorithm appears in detail in Figure 4. We denote by $col(p) \in \mathbb{N}$ the current color of node v.

For every phase i we perform $O(1)$ rounds of communication, This is true since every node needs to only communicate with its neighbors and choose the smallest number that is both greater than i and different from the color of all its neighbors.

THEOREM A.1. *There is a independent set scheduling algorithm, whose initialization takes $O(\log \Delta + 2^{O(\sqrt{\log \log n})})$ rounds, and executing each independent set takes another $O(1)$ rounds, which guarantees that for all $v \in V$ we have $mui_S(v) \leq deg(v) + 1$. In words, for every node v, within every sequence of $deg(v) + 1$ independent sets v is happy at least once.*

PROOF. Apply the Phased Greedy Coloring algorithm. The number of rounds is $O(\log \Delta + 2^{O(\sqrt{\log \log n})})$ for the initialization and another $O(1)$ for every phase. For every node $v \in V$, if it is made happy at phase i then in phase $i+1$ it is re-colored. The number it chooses is the smallest number that exceeds i and is not equal to the number of any of its neighbors. However, since it has $deg(v)$ neighbors then the color it gets can not exceed $i + deg(v) + 1$. □

Recall that if we think of the "first come first grab" where nodes wake up at random at grab all there available neighbors the probability of happiness of a node is $1/(d+1)$, so the expected time till happiness is $d+1$. This algorithm can be seen as providing a guarantee for the waiting time.

Notice that this algorithm generally does *not* give a periodic schedule. Also, it requires communication to take place at every phase, which implies the need to invest a lot of energy if we are considering an application such as cellular communication. An alternative solution would be to have each node know and remember *all* of the conflict graph locally (and then simulate the algorithm locally to obtain determine when it should host). But such an approach requires a lot of local memory, may be unfeasible, and may cause privacy issues.

B. THE COMPLEXITY OF HAPPINESS AND SATISFACTION

In this section we consider the problems of maximizing happiness (all children are hosted) or satisfaction (at least one child is hosted) at a given round with no thought of the other rounds.

B.1 Achieving Maximum Happiness in Hard

Maximizing happiness at a given year means finding the largest set of nodes that can each host all their children. It is hard to maximize happiness and this follows from the tight relationship with the maximum independent set.

OBSERVATION B.1. *Maximizing Happiness is $\mathcal{MAXSNP}$-hard.*

PROOF. Consider the conflict graph G as defined in Section 2, It is easy to see that maximizing happiness means finding the maximum independent set which is $\mathcal{MAXSNP}$-hard even for degree 3 graphs [8]. □

B.2 On the Hardness of Being Fair

The observation on the hardness of maximizing happiness also implies that any sort of fairness based on maximum happiness will be hard to compute (and hence hard to achieve). For instance, consider the coalitional game defined by the conflict graph $G = (V, E)$ where for each subset $S \subseteq V$ of nodes the value $v(S)$ is the size of the maximum independent set (MIS) of the subgraph induced by S (which represents the maximum happiness the parents in S can collectively obtain even if all the other nodes give up). Then clearly it is hard to compute $v(S)$. Moreover, we claim that solution concepts such as the *Shapley Value*[5] of this game are hard to compute: take an arbitrary order of the nodes and consider the total (i.e. sum of) marginal contributions of the nodes according to this order. It is always equal to the size of the MIS of the graph, since the number of times $MIS(S)$ can grow as S goes from the empty set to the full set is exactly the size of the MIS on the full set of nodes. Therefore any system that approximates the shares according to this definition can also be used to approximate the size of the MIS on the full graph: take the total happiness over a long enough period of time and it should approximate the MIS size. The inapproximability of the MIS problem to a factor of $n^{1-\varepsilon}$ (see [19]) implies a large difference between the average rate of hosting for a random node (which should be close to the fair share) and the size of the MIS divided by n. Thus, we left without a more sophisticated choice than competing with the 'chaotic' "first-come-first-grab" scheme described in the Introduction.

[5]The Shapley Value of a player is based on the expected *marginal contribution* of a player to the value of the game when the players are ordered at random; see more details in Osborne and Rubinstein [30] and [28] for its application in the carpool problem.

B.3 Maximum Satisfaction is Linear-Time computable

We say that parents are satisfied if at least one of their children comes home for the holiday.

In contrast to maximizing happiness, the problem of maximizing satisfaction is computationally easy.

THEOREM B.2. *Maximum satisfaction can be achieved in linear time.*

PROOF. Maximizing satisfaction means finding the maximum bipartite matching of the bipartite graph $G' = (V + C, E')$ where the set of nodes corresponds to the vertices V and edges $C = E$ from G and there is an edge between nodes corresponding to a node from V and the nodes corresponding to its edges in E. This can be done in time $O(\sqrt{n}|E'|)$ by the Hopcroft-Karp algorithm [20].

However, a general algorithm for maximum matching in bipartite graphs is an overkill for this problem given that every node in C has exactly two edges: it is possible to find a maximum matching by starting from the nodes in V parents that have just neighbor in G'; each such node is matched with its child (if two such nodes are share the same edge in G, then the satisfied one is decided arbitrarily). Nodes who became nodes with degree one since their other neighbors in G' have been matched are treated similarly. This continues until there are no degree one nodes in V. Then all the remaining nodes can be satisfied: pick an arbitrary neighbor and match it to a the node. At any point there can be at most one node with degree one. Match it to its only neighbor. □

Note that this solution cannot be found in a distributed manner quickly, given that maximum matching requires $\Omega(n)$ distance communication in some graphs, such as the cycle of length n.

While achieving maximum satisfaction is fast, the solution is not socially acceptable, since the same nodes will be happy every round while others will never be happy. Note that if we want a scheme whereby all nodes are guaranteed to be happy within some cycle of time, then we can guarantee that a node will not be unsatisfied for more than one round: each edge simply alternates between its vertices.

C. DETAILS FOR THE ELIAS OMEGA CODE

DEFINITION C.1. *Let $i \in \mathbb{N}$. Denote by $B(i)$ the binary representation of i, i.e. $B(i)$ is a string over $\{0, 1\}$ which is the representation of i in base 2 with no leading zeros. Denote the number of bits in $B(i)$ (the highest power of 2, b such that $2^b \leq i$) by $|B(i)|$. Let S be a binary number.*

Denote by $LSB(S,k)$ the suffix of S of length k, or the k least significant bits of S.

Let i be a positive integer. Denote the empty string by λ. Given two strings u and v, denote by $u \circ v$ the concatenation of u and v. Recursively define a binary string $re(i)$ as follows:

$$re(i) = \begin{cases} \lambda & \text{if } i{=}1, \\ re(|B(i)| - 1) \circ B(i) & \text{if } i > 1. \end{cases}$$

The Elias omega encoding *of i, is $re(i) \circ 0$ and is denoted by $\omega(i)$.*

Example: Consider the Elias omega code of the following numbers:

1. $i = 1$: $re(1) = \lambda$. *Elias omega code*: 0.
2. $i = 9$: $B(9) = 1001$. $|B(9)| - 1 = 3$. $B(3) = 11$. $|B(3)| - 1 = 1$. Therefore $re(9) = re(1)B(3)B(9) = \lambda\ 11\ 1001$
   Elias omega code: 11 1001 0.
3. The Elias omega codes of the numbers 1 to 15 are: 0, 10 0, 11 0, 10 100 0, 10 101 0, 10 110 0, 10 111 0, 11 1000 0, 11 1001 0, 11 1010 0, 11 1011 0, 11 1100 0, 11 1101 0, 11 1110 0, 11 1111 0.

PROPERTIES 1.

1. *The Elias omega code is a prefix-free code.*
2. *The Elias omega code uses $\rho(i) = 1 + rb(i)$ bits to represent the number i, where $rb(i)$ is recursively defined as follows:*

$$rb(i) = \begin{cases} 0 & \text{if } i{=}1, \\ \lceil \log(i) \rceil + rb(\lceil \log(i) \rceil - 1) & \text{if } i > 1. \end{cases}$$

   Explicitly, $\rho(i) = 1 + \lceil \log(i) \rceil + \lceil \log(\lceil \log(i) \rceil - 1) \rceil + \lceil \log(\lceil \log(\lceil \log(i) \rceil - 1) \rceil - 1) \rceil + \cdots$.

Election vs. Selection: How Much Advice is Needed to Find the Largest Node in a Graph?

Avery Miller
University of Manitoba
avery@averymiller.ca

Andrzej Pelc*
Université du Québec en Outaouais
andrzej.pelc@uqo.ca

ABSTRACT

Finding the node with the largest label in a labeled network, modeled as an undirected connected graph, is one of the fundamental problems in distributed computing. This is the way in which *leader election* is usually solved. We consider two distinct tasks in which the largest-labeled node is found deterministically. In *selection*, this node has to output 1 and all other nodes have to output 0. In *election*, the other nodes must additionally learn the largest label (everybody has to know who is the elected leader). Our aim is to compare the difficulty of these two seemingly similar tasks executed under stringent running time constraints. The measure of difficulty is the amount of information that nodes of the network must initially possess, in order to solve the given task in an imposed amount of time. Following the standard framework of *algorithms with advice*, this information (a single binary string) is provided to all nodes at the start by an oracle knowing the entire graph. The length of this string is called the *size of advice*. The paradigm of algorithms with advice has a far-reaching importance in the realm of network algorithms. Lower bounds on the size of advice give us impossibility results based strictly on the *amount* of initial knowledge outlined in a model's description. This more general approach should be contrasted with traditional results that focus on specific *kinds* of information available to nodes, such as the size, diameter, or maximum node degree.

Consider the class of n-node graphs with any diameter $diam \leq D$, for some integer D. If time is larger than $diam$, then both tasks can be solved without advice. For the task of *election*, we show that if time is smaller than $diam$, then the optimal size of advice is $\Theta(\log n)$, and if time is exactly $diam$, then the optimal size of advice is $\Theta(\log D)$. For the task of *selection*, the situation changes dramatically, even within the class of rings. Indeed, for the class of rings, we show that, if time is $O(diam^{\epsilon})$, for any $\epsilon < 1$, then the optimal size of advice is $\Theta(\log D)$, and, if time is $\Theta(diam)$ (and at most $diam$) then this optimal size is $\Theta(\log \log D)$. Thus there is an *exponential* increase of difficulty (measured by the size of advice) between selection in time $O(diam^{\epsilon})$, for any $\epsilon < 1$, and selection in time $\Theta(diam)$. As for the comparison between election and selection, our results show that, perhaps surprisingly, while for small time, the difficulty of these two tasks on rings is similar, for time $\Theta(diam)$ the difficulty of election (measured by the size of advice) is exponentially larger than that of selection.

Keywords

election, selection, maximum finding, advice, deterministic distributed algorithm, time.

1. INTRODUCTION

Background. Finding the node with the largest label in a labeled network is one of the fundamental problems in distributed computing. This is the way in which *leader election* is usually solved. (In leader election, one node of a network has to become a *leader* and all other nodes have to become *non-leaders*). In fact, to the best of our knowledge, all existing leader election algorithms performed in labeled networks choose, as leader, the node with the largest label or the node with the smallest label [35]. The classic problem of leader election first appeared in the study of local area token ring networks [34], where, at all times, exactly one node (the owner of a circulating token) has the right to initiate communication. When the token is accidentally lost, a leader is elected as the initial owner of the token.

Model and Problem Description. The network is modeled as an undirected connected graph with n labeled nodes and with diameter $diam$ at most D. We denote by $diam(G)$ the diameter of graph G. Labels are drawn from the set of integers $\{1, \dots, L\}$, where L is polynomial in n. Each node has a distinct label. Initially each node knows its label and its degree. The node with the largest label in a graph will be called its *largest node*.

We use the extensively studied $\mathcal{LOCAL}$ communication model [38]. In this model, communication proceeds in synchronous rounds and all nodes start simultaneously. In each round, each node can exchange arbitrary messages with all of its neighbours and perform arbitrary local computations. For any $r \geq 0$ and any node v, we use $K(r, v)$ to denote the knowledge acquired by v within r rounds. Thus, $K(r, v)$ consists of the subgraph induced by all nodes at distance at

*Partially supported by NSERC discovery grant and by the Research Chair in Distributed Computing at the Université du Québec en Outaouais.

SPAA '16, July 11–13, 2016, Pacific Grove, CA, USA

DOI: http://dx.doi.org/10.1145/2935764.2935772

most r from v, except for the edges joining nodes at distance exactly r from v, and of degrees (in the entire graph) of all nodes at distance exactly r from v. Hence, if no additional knowledge is provided *a priori* to the nodes, the decisions of v in round r in any deterministic algorithm are a function of $K(r, v)$. We denote by $\lambda(r, v)$ the set of labels of nodes in the subgraph induced by all nodes at distance at most r from v. The *time* of a task is the minimum number of rounds sufficient to complete it by all nodes.

It is well known that the synchronous $\mathcal{LOCAL}$ model can be simulated in an asynchronous network. This can be achieved by defining for each node separately its asynchronous round i; in this round, a node performs local computations, then sends messages stamped i to all neighbours, and waits until it gets messages stamped i from all neighbours. To make this work, every node is required to send at least one (possibly empty) message with each stamp, until termination. All of our results can be translated for asynchronous networks by replacing "time of completing a task" by "the maximum number of asynchronous rounds to complete it, taken over all nodes".

We consider two distinct tasks in which the largest node is found deterministically. In *selection*, this node has to output 1 and all other nodes have to output 0. In *election*, all nodes must output the largest label. Note that in election all nodes perform selection and additionally learn the identity of the largest node. Both variations are useful in different applications. In the aforementioned application of recovering a lost token, selection is enough, as the chosen node will be the only one to get a single token and then the token will be passed from node to node. In this case, other nodes do not need to know the identity of the chosen leader. The situation is different if all nodes must agree on a label of one of the nodes, e.g., to use it later as a common parameter for further computations. Then the full strength of election is needed. Likewise, learning the largest label by all nodes is important when labels carry some additional information apart from the identities of nodes, e.g., some values obtained by sensors located in nodes. Our results also remain valid in such situations, as long as the "informative label" can be represented as an integer polynomial in n.

Our aim is to compare the difficulty of the two seemingly similar tasks of selection and election executed under stringent running time constraints. The measure of difficulty is the amount of information that nodes of the network must initially possess in order to solve the given task in an imposed amount of time. Following the standard framework of *algorithms with advice*, see, e.g., [11, 14, 16, 19, 23, 29, 37], an *advice oracle* is a function from the class of labeled graphs to the set of finite binary sequences. For a given labeled network G, the output of the oracle when applied to G is a single *advice string* that is provided to all nodes in G at the start of the algorithm's execution. Note that this string is the same for all nodes. The length of this string is called the *size of advice*.

The paradigm of algorithms with advice has a far-reaching importance in the realm of network algorithms. Establishing a tight bound on the minimum size of advice sufficient to accomplish a given task permits to rule out entire classes of algorithms and thus focus only on possible candidates. For example, if we prove that $\Theta(\log n)$ bits of advice are needed to perform a certain task in n-node graphs, this rules out all potential algorithms that can work using only some linear upper bound on the size of the network, as such an upper bound could be given to the nodes using $\Theta(\log \log n)$ bits by providing them with $\lceil \log n \rceil$. Lower bounds on the size of advice give us impossibility results based strictly on the *amount* of initial knowledge outlined in a model's description. This more general approach should be contrasted with traditional results that focus on specific *kinds* of information available to nodes, such as the size, diameter, or maximum node degree.

Our results. Consider the class of n-node graphs with any diameter $diam \leq D$, for some integer D. First observe that if time is larger than $diam$, then both tasks can be solved without advice, as nodes learn the entire network and *learn that they have learned it.* Thus they can just choose the maximum of all labels seen.

For the task of *election*, we show that if time is smaller than $diam$, then the optimal size of advice is $\Theta(\log n)$, and if time is exactly $diam$, then the optimal size of advice is $\Theta(\log D)$. Here our contribution consists in proving two lower bounds on the size of advice. We prove one lower bound by exhibiting, for any positive integers $D < n$, networks of size $\Theta(n)$ and diameter $\Theta(D)$, for which $\Omega(\log n)$ bits of advice are needed for election in time below $diam$. To prove the other lower bound, we present, for any positive integer D, networks of diameter $diam \leq D$ for which $\Omega(\log D)$ bits of advice are needed for election in time exactly $diam$. These lower bounds are clearly tight, as even for time 0, $O(\log n)$ bits of advice are enough to provide the largest label in the network, and, for time $diam$ – when nodes know the entire network, but they *do not know that they know it* – $O(\log D)$ bits of advice are enough to give the diameter $diam$ to all nodes and thus reassure them that they have seen everything. In this case, they can safely choose the maximum of all labels seen.

Hence, a high-level statement of our results for election is the following. If time is too small for all nodes to see everything, then no more efficient help in election is possible than just giving the largest label. If time is sufficient for all nodes to see everything, but too small for them to realize that they do, i.e., the time is exactly $diam$, then no more efficient help in election is possible than providing $diam$, which supplies nodes with the missing certainty that they have seen everything.

It should be noted that n could be exponential in D, as in hypercubes, or D can even be constant with respect to arbitrarily large n. Thus, our results for election show that, for some networks, there is an exponential (or even larger) gap of difficulty of election (measured by the size of advice) between time smaller than $diam$ and time exactly $diam$. Another such huge gap is between time $diam$, when advice of size $\Theta(\log D)$ is optimal, and time larger than $diam$, when 0 advice is enough. These gaps could be called *intra-task* jumps in difficulty for election with respect to time.

For the task of *selection*, the situation changes dramatically, even within the class of rings. Indeed, for the class of rings, we show that, if time is $O(diam^{\epsilon})$, for any $\epsilon < 1$, then the optimal size of advice is $\Theta(\log D)$, and, if time is $\Theta(diam)$ (and at most $diam$) then this optimal size is $\Theta(\log \log D)$. Here our contribution is three-fold. For selection in time $O(diam^{\epsilon})$, for any $\epsilon < 1$, we exhibit, for any positive integer D, a class of rings with diameter at most D which requires advice of size $\Omega(\log D)$. As before, this lower bound is tight, even for time 0. Further, for selection in time at most $\alpha \cdot diam$, for $\alpha \leq 1$, we construct a class of rings with diameter $diam \leq D$ which requires advice of size $\Omega(\log\log D)$. At first glance, it might seem that this lower bound is too weak. Indeed, providing either the diameter or the largest label, which are both natural choices of advice, would not give a tight upper bound, as this may require $\Theta(\log D)$ bits. However, we use a more sophisticated idea that permits us to construct a very compact advice (of matching size $O(\log\log D)$) and we design a selection algorithm, working for all rings of diameter $diam \leq D$ in time at most $\alpha \cdot diam$, for which this advice is enough.

Hence, a high-level statement of our results for selection is the following. If time is large enough, i.e., $\alpha \cdot diam$ for $\alpha \leq 1$, then there are many nodes that see larger labels in their view, and these nodes immediately drop out from the competition. For the few remaining nodes, only a small amount of advice is needed to select the largest. In contrast, for smaller time, i.e., $O(diam^{\epsilon})$ for any $\epsilon < 1$, so many nodes are the largest in their limited view that no more efficient help is possible than indicating the largest label.

Thus, there is an *exponential* increase of difficulty (as measured by the size of advice) between selection in time $O(diam^{\epsilon})$, for any $\epsilon < 1$, and selection in time $\Theta(diam)$. As in the case of election, another huge increase of difficulty occurs between time *diam* and time larger than *diam*. These gaps could be called *intra-task* jumps of difficulty for selection with respect to time.

As for the comparison between election and selection, our results show that, perhaps surprisingly, while for small time, the difficulty of these two tasks on rings is similar, for time $\Theta(diam)$ the difficulty of election (measured by the size of advice) is exponentially larger than that of selection, even for the class of rings. While both in selection and in election the unique leader having the maximum label is chosen, these tasks differ in how widely this label is known. It follows from our results that, if linear time (not larger than the diameter) is available, then the increase of difficulty (in terms of advice) of making this knowledge widely known is exponential. This could be called the *inter-task* jump of difficulty between election and selection. Figure 1 provides a summary of our results.

Election for diam $\leq D$	
Time	Advice
> diam	0
diam	$\Theta(\log D)$
< diam	$\Theta(\log n)$

Selection for diam $\leq D$	
Time	Advice
> diam	0
$\alpha\cdot$ diam $0 < \alpha \leq 1$	$\Theta(\log\log D)$
diam$^{\epsilon}$ $\epsilon < 1$	$\Theta(\log D)$

(solid arrow) : denotes an intra-task jump

(dashed arrow) : denotes an inter-task jump

Figure 1: Tight bounds on the size of advice for election and selection in arbitrary graphs and rings (respectively) with diameter diam $\leq D$

Related work. The leader election problem was introduced in [34]. This problem has been extensively studied in the scenario adopted in the present paper, i.e., where all nodes have distinct labels. As far as we know, this task was always solved by finding either the node with the largest or that with the smallest label. Leader election was first studied for rings. A synchronous algorithm based on label comparisons and using $O(n \log n)$ messages was given in [28]. It was proved in [20] that this complexity is optimal for comparison-based algorithms. On the other hand, the authors showed an algorithm using a linear number of messages but requiring very large running time. An asynchronous algorithm using $O(n \log n)$ messages was given, e.g., in [39], and the optimality of this message complexity was shown in [7]. Deterministic leader election in radio networks has been studied, e.g., in [30, 33, 36], as well as randomized leader election, e.g., in [41]. In [27], the leader election problem was approached in a model based on mobile agents for networks with labeled nodes.

Many authors [2, 3, 4, 6, 42, 43] studied leader election in anonymous networks. In particular, [5, 43] characterize message-passing networks in which leader election can be achieved when nodes are anonymous. In [42], the authors study the problem of leader election in general networks under the assumption that node labels are not unique. They characterize networks in which this can be done and give an algorithm which performs election when it is feasible. In [15], the authors study feasibility and message complexity of leader election in rings with possibly nonunique labels, while, in [13], the authors provide algorithms for a generalized leader election problem in rings with arbitrary labels, unknown (and arbitrary) size of the ring, and for both synchronous and asynchronous communication. Characterizations of feasible instances for leader election were provided in [9, 10]. Memory needed for leader election in unlabeled networks was studied in [23]. In [22], the authors investigated the time of leader election in anonymous networks by characterizing this time in terms of the network size, the diameter of the network, and an additional parameter called level of symmetry, which measures how deeply nodes have to inspect the network in order to notice differences in their views of it. In [12], the authors studied the feasibility of leader election among anonymous agents that navigate in a network in an asynchronous way.

Providing nodes or agents with arbitrary kinds of information that can be used to perform network tasks more efficiently has previously been proposed in [1, 8, 11, 14, 16, 17, 18, 19, 23, 24, 25, 29, 31, 32, 37, 40]. This approach was referred to as *algorithms with advice*. The advice is given either to nodes of the network or to mobile agents performing some network task. In the first case, instead of advice, the term *informative labeling schemes* is sometimes used, if (unlike in our scenario) different nodes can get different information.

Several authors studied the minimum size of advice required to solve network problems in an efficient way. In [32], given a distributed representation of a solution for a problem, the authors investigated the number of bits of communication needed to verify the legality of the represented solution. In [17], the authors compared the minimum size of advice required to solve two information dissemination problems using a linear number of messages. In [19], it was shown that advice of constant size given to the nodes enables the distributed construction of a minimum spanning tree in logarithmic time. In [14], the advice paradigm was used for online problems. In [16], the authors established lower bounds on the size of advice needed to beat time $\Theta(\log^* n)$

for 3-coloring cycles and to achieve time $\Theta(\log^* n)$ for 3-coloring unoriented trees. In the case of [37], the issue was not efficiency but feasibility: it was shown that $\Theta(n \log n)$ is the minimum size of advice required to perform monotone connected graph clearing. In [29], the authors studied radio networks for which it is possible to perform centralized broadcasting in constant time. They proved that constant time is achievable with $O(n)$ bits of advice in such networks, while $o(n)$ bits are not enough. In [24], the authors studied the problem of topology recognition with advice given to nodes. In [11], the task of drawing an isomorphic map by an agent in a graph was considered, and the problem was to determine the minimum advice that has to be given to the agent for the task to be feasible. In [26], the authors studied the size of advice needed for fast leader election in anonymous trees. The main difference between [26] and the present paper is that we study networks with labeled nodes. Our results imply that breaking symmetry can be done with much less advice in this setting.

2. ELECTION

Notice that in order to perform election in a graph G in time larger than its diameter, no advice is needed. Indeed, after time $diam(G)+1$, all nodes know the labels of all other nodes, and they are aware that they have this knowledge. This is because, in round $diam(G)+1$, no messages containing new labels are received by any node. So, it suffices for all nodes to output the largest of the labels that they have seen up until round $diam(G)+1$.

Our first result shows that, if election time is no more than the diameter of the graph, then the size of advice must be at least logarithmic in the diameter. This demonstrates a dramatic difference between the difficulty of election in time $diam(G)$ and election in time $diam(G)+1$, measured by the minimum size of advice.

THEOREM 2.1. *Consider any algorithm $\mathcal{A}$ such that, for every graph G, algorithm $\mathcal{A}$ solves election within* diam(G) *rounds. For every integer $D \geq 2$, there exists a ring of diameter at most D for which algorithm $\mathcal{A}$ requires advice of size $\Omega(\log D)$.*

Note that the lower bound established in Theorem 2.1 is asymptotically tight. Indeed, to achieve election in time $diam(G)$ for any graph G, it is enough to provide the value of $diam(G)$ to the nodes of the graph and have each node elect the node with the largest label it has seen up until round $diam(G)$. Hence we have the following corollary for the class of graphs of diameter at most D.

COROLLARY 2.2. *The optimal size of advice to complete election in any graph in time at most equal to its diameter is $\Theta(\log D)$.*

We next consider accomplishing election in time less than the diameter of the graph. One way to do it is to provide the maximum label to all nodes as advice. This yields election in time 0 and uses advice of size $O(\log n)$, where n is the size of the graph, since the space of labels is of size L polynomial in n. The following result shows that this size of advice cannot be improved for election in *any* time below the diameter. This result, when compared to Corollary 2.2, again shows the dramatic difference in the difficulty of election (measured by the minimum size of advice) but now between times $diam(G)-1$ and $diam(G)$.

THEOREM 2.3. *Consider any positive integers $D < \tilde{n}$. There exists $n \in \Theta(\tilde{n})$ such that, for any election algorithm $\mathcal{A}$ in which every execution halts within $D-1$ rounds, there exists an n-node graph of diameter D for which the size of advice needed by $\mathcal{A}$ is $\Omega(\log n)$.*

PROOF. The high-level idea of the proof is the following. We first construct a family of "ring-like" graphs. For a given number of advice strings, we obtain a lower bound on the number of such graphs for which the same advice is given. On the other hand, an upper bound on this number is obtained by exploiting the fact that no node can see the entire graph within $D-1$ rounds. Comparing these bounds gives the desired bound on the size of advice.

Let n be the smallest integer greater than $\tilde{n}$ that is divisible by 2D (and note that $n \in \Theta(\tilde{n})$).

Consider a family $\mathcal{C}$ of n^3 pairwise disjoint sets, each of size $\frac{n}{2D}$. In particular, let $\mathcal{C} = \{C_0, \ldots, C_{n^3-1}\}$, where $C_i = \{\frac{ni}{2D}+1, \ldots, \frac{n(i+1)}{2D}\}$.

We construct a family $\mathcal{G}$ of n-node graphs. Each graph in $\mathcal{G}$ is obtained by first choosing an arbitrary sequence of $2D$ sets from $\mathcal{C}$, say $(H_0, \ldots, H_{2D-1})$. The nodes of the graph are the elements of these sets (which are integers), and this induces a natural labeling of the nodes. Next, for each $j \in \{0, \ldots, 2D-1\}$, add all edges between pairs of elements of the set H_j, as well as all edges between every element in H_j and every element in H_{j+1} (where the indices are taken modulo $2D$). In other words, each graph in $\mathcal{G}$ is a "fat ring" composed of cliques. Due to the cyclic symmetry of each graph in $\mathcal{G}$, we uniquely associate each graph in $\mathcal{G}$ with the sequence of sets $(H_0, \ldots, H_{2D-1})$, where H_0 contains the smallest label, and the smallest label in H_1 is smaller than all labels in H_{2D-1}. The size of $\mathcal{G}$ is calculated in the following claim.

CLAIM 2.4. $|\mathcal{G}| = \binom{n^3}{2D}(2D-1)!/2$.

To prove the claim, first note that the number of sequences $(H_0, \ldots, H_{2D-1})$ consisting of $2D$ distinct sets from $\mathcal{C}$ is $\binom{n^3}{2D}(2D)!$. To count the number of such sequences belonging to $\mathcal{G}$, we first divide this integer by $2D$ to eliminate those sequences in which H_0 does not contain the smallest label. Then, we divide the result by 2 to eliminate those sequences in which the labels in H_{2D-1} are smaller than those in H_1. This completes the proof of the claim.

Next, let b be the maximum number of advice bits provided to $\mathcal{A}$, taken over all graphs in $\mathcal{G}$. By the Pigeonhole Principle, there exists a family S of at least $\frac{|\mathcal{G}|}{2^{b+1}}$ graphs in $\mathcal{G}$ such that the algorithm receives the same advice string when executed on each graph in S. The following claim will be used to find an upper bound on the size of S.

CLAIM 2.5. *Consider two graphs from S, namely $S_1 = (A_0, \ldots, A_{2D-1})$ and $S_2 = (B_0, \ldots, B_{2D-1})$. Suppose that, for some $i \in \{0, \ldots, 2D-1\}$, algorithm $\mathcal{A}$ elects a node from set A_i when executed on S_1 and elects a node from set B_i when executed on S_2. If $A_j = B_j$ for each $j \neq i$, then $A_i = B_i$.*

To prove the claim, let $k = i + D \pmod{2D}$. Since $A_j = B_j$ for all $j \neq i$, it follows that each node $v \in A_k$ is also an element of B_k, and, moreover, for each such v, knowledge $K(D-1, v)$ in S_1 is equal to knowledge $K(D-1, v)$ in S_2. The nodes of A_k output some label ℓ at the end of the execution of $\mathcal{A}$ on S_1. Since we assumed that every execution of $\mathcal{A}$ halts within $D-1$ rounds, and the same advice is given for S_1 and S_2, the nodes of B_k also output label ℓ at the end of execution of $\mathcal{A}$ on S_2. Since $\mathcal{A}$ elects a node from A_i when executed on S_1 and elects a node from B_i when executed on S_2, it follows that ℓ is a label that appears in both A_i and B_i. As the sets in $\mathcal{C}$ are pairwise disjoint, it follows that $A_i = B_i$. This concludes the proof of the claim.

Using Claim 2.5, we now obtain an upper bound on the size of S. In particular, for each $i \in \{0, \ldots, 2D-1\}$, consider the subfamily of graphs $(H_0, \ldots, H_{2D-1})$ in S such that algorithm $\mathcal{A}$ elects a node from H_i. By the claim, for each choice of the $2D-1$ sets $H_0, \ldots, H_{i-1}, H_{i+1}, \ldots, H_{2D-1}$, there is exactly one set H_i such that $(H_0, \ldots, H_{2D-1})$ belongs to S. The number of such choices is bounded above by $(n^3)(n^3-1)\cdots(n^3-2D+2) = \binom{n^3}{2D-1}(2D-1)!$. Since this is true for all $2D$ possible values for i, we get that $|S| \leq 2D\binom{n^3}{2D-1}(2D-1)!$. Comparing this upper bound to our lower bound on $|S|$, it follows from Claim 2.4 that $2D\binom{n^3}{2D-1}(2D-1)! \geq \frac{\binom{n^3}{2D}(2D-1)!/2}{2^{b+1}}$. Re-arranging this inequality, we get that $2^{b+1} \geq \frac{\binom{n^3}{2D}}{4D\binom{n^3}{2D-1}} = \frac{n^3-2D+1}{8D^2} \in \Omega(n)$, and hence $b \in \Omega(\log n)$. □

Hence we have the following corollary.

COROLLARY 2.6. *The optimal size of advice to solve election in any graph in time less than its diameter is* $\Theta(\log n)$.

3. SELECTION

In this section, we study the selection problem for the class of rings. It turns out that significant differences between election and selection can be exhibited already for this class. As in the case of election, and for the same reasons, selection in time larger than the diameter can be accomplished without any advice. Hence, in the rest of the section, we consider selection in time at most equal to the diameter. For any ring R and any selection algorithm $\mathcal{A}$, denote by $\text{adv}_{\mathcal{A}}(R)$ the advice string provided to all nodes in R when they execute algorithm $\mathcal{A}$. Denote by $\max_{\mathcal{A}}(R)$ the node that outputs 1 in the execution of algorithm $\mathcal{A}$ on ring R. We first look at selection algorithms working in time at most $\alpha \cdot diam(R)$, for any ring R and any constant $0 < \alpha \leq 1$.

3.1 Selection in time linear in the diameter

We start with the lower bound on the size of advice needed by any selection algorithm working in time equal to the diameter of the ring. This lower bound shows that, for any positive integer D, there exists a ring with diameter at most D for which such an algorithm requires $\Omega(\log\log D)$ bits of advice. Of course, this implies the same lower bound on the size of advice for selection in any smaller time.

The following theorem provides our first lower bound on the size of advice for selection.

THEOREM 3.1. *Consider any selection algorithm $\mathcal{A}$ such that, for any ring R, algorithm $\mathcal{A}$ halts within $diam(R)$ rounds. For every positive integer D, there exists a ring R of diameter at most D for which algorithm $\mathcal{A}$ requires advice of size $\Omega(\log\log D)$.*

PROOF. At a high level, we consider a "rings-into-bins" problem, in which each bin represents a distinct advice string. We recursively construct sets of rings, such that the rings constructed at a given recursion level cannot be put into the same bin as previously-constructed rings. We continue the construction long enough to run out of bins. With few bins, the number of levels of recursion is sufficiently small to keep the diameters of the constructed rings bounded by D.

The following claim will be used to show that a particular ring that we construct will cause algorithm $\mathcal{A}$ to fail. We will use the following *chopping* operation in our constructions. For any selection algorithm $\mathcal{A}$ and any ring R of odd size, we define the *chop* of R, denoted by $\text{chop}(R)$, to be the path obtained from R by removing the edge between the two nodes at distance $diam(R)$ from $\max_{\mathcal{A}}(R)$ (see Figure 2(a)).

CLAIM 3.2. *Consider any selection algorithm $\mathcal{A}$ such that, for any ring R, algorithm $\mathcal{A}$ halts within $diam(R)$ rounds. Consider two disjoint rings R_1, R_2 of odd size such that $\text{adv}_{\mathcal{A}}(R_1) = \text{adv}_{\mathcal{A}}(R_2)$. For any ring R_3 that contains $\text{chop}(R_1)$ and $\text{chop}(R_2)$ as subgraphs such that $\text{adv}_{\mathcal{A}}(R_3) = \text{adv}_{\mathcal{A}}(R_1) = \text{adv}_{\mathcal{A}}(R_2)$, two distinct nodes in R_3 output 1 when executing $\mathcal{A}$.*

In order to prove the claim, consider the execution of $\mathcal{A}$ by the nodes of R_3. Using the definition of $\text{chop}(R_1)$, it can be shown that knowledge $K(diam(R_1), \max_{\mathcal{A}}(R_1))$ in R_3 is equal to knowledge $K(diam(R_1), \max_{\mathcal{A}}(R_1))$ in R_1. Therefore, the execution of $\mathcal{A}$ at node $\max_{\mathcal{A}}(R_1)$ in R_3 halts in round $diam(R_1)$, and $\max_{\mathcal{A}}(R_1)$ outputs 1. Similarly, the execution of $\mathcal{A}$ at node $\max_{\mathcal{A}}(R_2)$ in R_3 halts in round $diam(R_2)$, and $\max_{\mathcal{A}}(R_2)$ outputs 1. Since R_1 and R_2 are disjoint, we have that $\max_{\mathcal{A}}(R_1) \neq \max_{\mathcal{A}}(R_2)$. Hence, two distinct nodes in R_3 output 1 when executing $\mathcal{A}$. This proves the claim.

It is enough to prove the theorem for sufficiently large D. Fix any integer $D \geq 2^{17}$ and set the label space to be $\{1, \ldots, 2D\}$. To obtain a contradiction, assume that $A < \sqrt{\log D}$ different advice strings suffice.

Form a family $\mathcal{T}$ of $2^A A!$ disjoint sequences of integers, each of size 3. More specifically, let $\mathcal{T} = \{(3i, 3i+1, 3i+2) \mid i \in \{0, \ldots, 2^A A! - 1\}\}$. Let $\mathcal{E} = \{3(2^A A!) + 1, 3(2^A A!) + 2, \ldots, 4(2^A A!)\}$. Note that $\mathcal{E}$ is a set of integer labels, each of which is larger than all of the labels that belong to sequences in $\mathcal{T}$. To verify that we have enough labels to define these sets, note that the largest label $\ell = 4(2^A A!) < 4(2^{\sqrt{\log D}}[\sqrt{\log D}]!)$. Using the inequality $\log n! \leq n \log n$, we get that $\log \ell < 2 + \sqrt{\log D} + \sqrt{\log D}\log(\sqrt{\log D})$. When $D \geq 2^{17}$, one can verify that $\log(\sqrt{\log D}) \leq \sqrt[3]{\log D}$, and $2 + \sqrt{\log D} + \sqrt[6]{(\log D)^5} < \log D$, so $\log \ell < \log D$. It follows that $\ell < D < L$.

Next, we construct a special family $\mathcal{R}$ of rings of diameter at most D. We will add rings to $\mathcal{R}$ by following a procedure that we will describe shortly. Each new ring that we add to $\mathcal{R}$ will be the result of at most one 'gluing' operation, denoted by $\text{glue}(R_1, R_2)$, that takes two disjoint odd-sized rings R_1, R_2 and forms a new odd-sized ring R_3. More specifically, the ith gluing operation takes two disjoint odd-sized rings R_1 and R_2 and forms the new ring defined as follows: construct paths $\text{chop}(R_1)$ and $\text{chop}(R_2)$, add a new edge between the leaf of $\text{chop}(R_1)$ with smaller label and the leaf of $\text{chop}(R_2)$ with smaller label, add a new node with label $3(2^A A!) + i$, and add edges from this new node to the two remaining leaves. The gluing operation is illustrated in Figure 2(b). The additional node is introduced so that the resulting ring has an odd number of nodes. Note that this additional node's label comes from $\mathcal{E}$, which ensures that the new ring formed by a gluing operation does not contain duplicate labels. Further, note that, due to the dependence of the additional node's label on i, no two gluing operations introduce additional nodes with the same label.

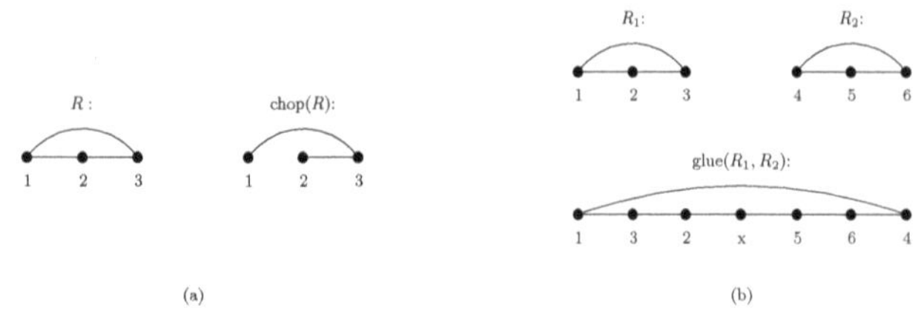

Figure 2: (a) The chop operation on a ring of size 3: the edge between the two nodes at distance $diam(R) = 1$ from node $\max_{\mathcal{A}}(R) = 3$ is removed. (b) The glue operation on two rings of size 3: concatenate paths $\text{chop}(R_1)$, $\text{chop}(R_2)$ and add an additional node x with a label from $\mathcal{E}$.

We now describe the procedure for adding rings to $\mathcal{R}$. In stage 1, we consider the set G_1 of 3-cliques obtained from each sequence in $\mathcal{T}$ by identifying each integer with a node and adding all edges between them. We take a subset $H_1 \subseteq G_1$ of size at least $2^A(A-1)!$ such that the same advice string is provided to the algorithm for each ring in H_1. The rings in H_1 are added to $\mathcal{R}$, which concludes stage 1. In each stage $j \in \{2,\dots,A\}$, we consider the set H_{j-1} of rings that were added to $\mathcal{R}$ in stage $j-1$. The elements of H_{j-1} are partitioned into $|H_{j-1}|/2$ pairs of rings in an arbitrary way. For each such pair R_1, R_2, we perform $\text{glue}(R_1, R_2)$. Define G_j to be the set of all of the resulting rings. We take a subset $H_j \subseteq G_j$ of size at least $|G_j|/(A-j+1)$ such that the same advice string is provided to the algorithm for each ring in H_j. The rings in H_j are added to $\mathcal{R}$, which concludes stage j. This concludes the construction of $\mathcal{R}$.

It is not immediately clear that this construction can always be carried out. In particular, in order to define H_j in each stage $j \in \{1,\dots,A\}$, there must exist $|G_j|/(A-j+1)$ rings in G_j such that the same advice string is provided to the algorithm for each of them. To prove this fact, and to obtain the desired contradiction to prove the theorem, we will use the following two claims.

Claim 3.3. *Consider any $k \in \{1,\dots,A\}$ and any ring $R \in H_k$. For every $j < k$, there exists a ring $Q_j \in H_j$ such that $\text{chop}(R)$ contains $\text{chop}(Q_j)$ as a subgraph.*

To prove the claim, we proceed by induction on k. The case where $k = 1$ is trivial. Next, assume that, for some $k \in \{1,\dots,A\}$ and any ring $R \in H_k$, for every $j < k$, there exists a ring $Q_j \in H_j$ such that $\text{chop}(R)$ contains $\text{chop}(Q_j)$ as a subgraph. We now prove that, for any $R \in H_{k+1}$, there exists a ring $Q_k \in H_k$ such that $\text{chop}(R)$ contains $\text{chop}(Q_k)$ as a subgraph. By construction, $R = \text{glue}(R_1, R_2)$ for some disjoint rings $R_1, R_2 \in H_k$. By the definition of the gluing operation, R contains both $\text{chop}(R_1)$ and $\text{chop}(R_2)$ as disjoint subgraphs. Since $\text{chop}(R)$ has one fewer edge than R, at least one of $\text{chop}(R_1)$ and $\text{chop}(R_2)$ is a subgraph of $\text{chop}(R)$. By induction, this proves Claim 3.3.

Claim 3.4. *Consider any $j,k \in \{1,\dots,A\}$ with $j < k$. For any ring $W \in H_k$, there exist disjoint $P_j, Q_j \in H_j$ such that W contains $\text{chop}(P_j)$ and $\text{chop}(Q_j)$ as subgraphs.*

To prove the claim, note that, by our construction, $W = \text{glue}(R_1, R_2)$ for some disjoint $R_1, R_2 \in H_{k-1}$. It follows that $\text{chop}(R_1)$ and $\text{chop}(R_2)$ are disjoint subgraphs of W. If $j = k-1$, setting $P_j = R_1$ and $Q_j = R_2$ satisfies the statement of the claim. If $j < k-1$, then, by Claim 3.3, there exists a ring $P_j \in H_j$ such that $\text{chop}(R_1)$ contains $\text{chop}(P_j)$ as a subgraph. Similarly, there exists a ring $Q_j \in H_j$ such that $\text{chop}(R_2)$ contains $\text{chop}(Q_j)$ as a subgraph. Note that, since R_1 and R_2 are disjoint, it follows that $\text{chop}(P_j)$ and $\text{chop}(Q_j)$ are disjoint, so P_j and Q_j are disjoint. Thus, P_j and Q_j satisfy the statement of the claim, which concludes its proof.

We now show that, in any fixed stage of the above construction of $\mathcal{R}$, the advice string that is provided for the rings added to $\mathcal{R}$ in this stage is different than the advice strings provided for the rings added to $\mathcal{R}$ in all previous stages.

Claim 3.5. *Consider any $j,k \in \{1,\dots,A\}$ with $j < k$. For any ring $W_1 \in H_j$ and any ring $W_2 \in H_k$, we have $\text{adv}_{\mathcal{A}}(W_1) \neq \text{adv}_{\mathcal{A}}(W_2)$.*

In order to prove the claim, notice that, by Claim 3.4, there exist disjoint $P_j, Q_j \in H_j$ such that W_2 contains $\text{chop}(P_j)$ and $\text{chop}(Q_j)$ as subgraphs. Recall that the algorithm is provided the same advice string for all graphs in H_j, so $\text{adv}_{\mathcal{A}}(P_j) = \text{adv}_{\mathcal{A}}(Q_j) = \text{adv}_{\mathcal{A}}(W_1)$. By Claim 3.2 and the correctness of $\mathcal{A}$, it follows that $\text{adv}_{\mathcal{A}}(W_2) \neq \text{adv}_{\mathcal{A}}(P_j)$. Hence, $\text{adv}_{\mathcal{A}}(W_2) \neq \text{adv}_{\mathcal{A}}(W_1)$, which completes the proof of Claim 3.5.

We show that the construction of $\mathcal{R}$ can always be carried out.

Claim 3.6. *For all $k \in \{1,\dots,A\}$, in stage k of the construction, there exist at least $|G_k|/(A-k+1)$ rings in G_k such that the same advice string is provided to the algorithm for each of them.*

To prove the claim, first note that, for $k = 1$, there are A different strings that could be used as advice for rings in G_1. So, by the Pigeonhole Principle, there are at least $|G_1|/A$ rings in G_1 such that the same advice string is provided to the algorithm for each of them. Next, for any $k \in \{2,\dots,A\}$, Claim 3.5 implies that there are $k-1$ strings that are not provided to the algorithm as advice for rings in G_k. Namely, there are at most $A-k+1$ different strings used as advice for rings in G_k. By the Pigeonhole Principle, there are at least $|G_k|/(A-k+1)$ rings in G_k such that the same advice string is provided to the algorithm for each of them, which proves the claim.

The following claim implies that $|H_j| \geq 2$, for all $j \leq A$. Later, we will use two rings from some H_j to obtain the desired contradiction needed to complete the proof of the theorem.

Claim 3.7. *For all $j \in \{1,\dots,A\}$, at the end of stage j, $|H_j| \geq 2^{A-j+1}(A-j)!$.*

We prove the claim by induction on j. When $j = 1$, we have $|G_1| = |\mathcal{T}| = 2^A A!$. By Claim 3.6, there exist at least $|G_1|/A = 2^A(A-1)!$ rings in G_1 such that the same advice string is provided to the algorithm for each of them.

This implies that $|H_1| \geq 2^A(A-1)!$, as required. As induction hypothesis, assume that, at the end of some stage $j \in \{1, \ldots, A-1\}$, $|H_j| \geq 2^{A-j+1}(A-j)!$. In stage $j+1$, the set H_j is partitioned into pairs and G_{j+1} consists of one (glued) ring for each such pair. Thus, $|G_{j+1}| = 2^{A-j}(A-j)!$. By Claim 3.6, there exist at least $|G_{j+1}|/(A-j) = 2^{A-j}(A-j-1)!$ rings in G_{j+1} such that the same advice string is provided to the algorithm for each of them. This implies that $|H_{j+1}| \geq 2^{A-j}(A-j-1)!$, as required. This concludes the proof of Claim 3.7.

Finally, we construct a ring X on which algorithm $\mathcal{A}$ fails. Note that the rings in $\mathcal{R}$ all have node labels from the sets $\mathcal{T}$ and $\mathcal{E}$, and we proved that the largest integer in these sets is less than D. Thus, the rings in $\mathcal{R}$ all have node labels from the range $\{1, \ldots, D\}$. To construct X, we take any two (disjoint) rings $R_1, R_2 \in H_A$ (which exist by Claim 3.7) and form a ring X consisting of the concatenation of paths chop(R_1), chop(R_2), and the path of D nodes with labels $D+1, \ldots, 2D$. Recall that, in the construction, all rings in H_j, for any fixed $j \leq A$, get the same advice string. By Claim 3.5, each of the A distinct advice strings is used for rings in some H_j. Therefore, there exists a stage j such that the advice provided for all graphs in H_j is the string $\text{adv}_{\mathcal{A}}(X)$. By Claim 3.3, there exists a ring $P_j \in H_j$ such that chop(R_1) contains chop(P_j) as a subgraph, and, there exists a ring $Q_j \in H_j$ such that chop(R_2) contains chop(Q_j). It follows that X contains chop(P_j) and chop(Q_j) as subgraphs, and $\text{adv}_{\mathcal{A}}(X) = \text{adv}_{\mathcal{A}}(P_j) = \text{adv}_{\mathcal{A}}(Q_j)$. By Claim 3.2, when algorithm $\mathcal{A}$ is executed by the nodes of ring X, two distinct nodes output 1, which contradicts the correctness of $\mathcal{A}$. Note that the size of X is at least D and at most $2D$, which implies that the size of the label space is linear in the size of X. The obtained contradiction was due to the assumption that $A < \sqrt{\log D}$. Hence the number A of different advice strings is at least $\sqrt{\log D}$, which implies that the size of advice is $\Omega(\log \log D)$ for some ring of diameter at most D. □

Since imposing less time cannot make the selection task easier, we have the following corollary.

COROLLARY 3.8. *For any constant $\alpha \leq 1$, consider any selection algorithm $\mathcal{A}$ such that, for any ring R, algorithm $\mathcal{A}$ halts within $\alpha \cdot diam(R)$ rounds. For every positive integer D, there exists a ring R of diameter at most D for which algorithm $\mathcal{A}$ requires advice of size $\Omega(\log \log D)$.*

We now establish an upper bound on the size of advice that matches the lower bound from Theorem 3.1. Let D be any positive integer and let L be a power of 2. We consider algorithms that solve selection on the class of rings with diameter at most D and labels from $\{1, \ldots, L\}$. Recall that we assume that L is polynomial in the size of the ring, and hence also in D.

In order to prove the upper bound, we propose a family of selection algorithms such that, for each fixed $\alpha \in (0, 1]$, there is an algorithm in the family that takes $O(\log \log D)$ bits of advice, and, for each ring R, halts within $\alpha \cdot diam(R)$ rounds.

We start with an informal description of the algorithm and the advice for any fixed $\alpha \in (0, 1]$. The algorithm consists of two stages, and the advice consists of two substrings A_1 and A_2.

For any ring R, the substring A_1 of the advice is the binary representation of the integer $a_1 = \lfloor \log(diam(R)) \rfloor$. The size of this advice is $O(\log \log D)$. Note that $2^{a_1} \leq diam(R) < 2^{a_1+1}$.

In stage 1 of the algorithm the nodes perform $r = \lfloor \alpha 2^{a_1} \rfloor$ communication rounds, after which each node v has acquired knowledge $K(r, v)$. Next, each node v checks if its own label is the largest of the labels it has seen within r communication rounds, i.e., the largest in the set $\lambda(r, v)$. If not, then v outputs 0 and halts immediately. Let C_R be the set of *candidate nodes*, i.e., nodes v whose label is the largest in $\lambda(r, v)$. Clearly, the largest node in R is in C_R, and every node knows if it belongs to C_R. Nodes in C_R proceed to the next stage of the algorithm.

In stage 2 of the algorithm, each node in C_R determines whether or not it is the largest node in R, without using any further communication rounds. This is achieved using A_2, the second substring of the advice. The string A_2 describes a set of indices such that the largest node is the only candidate whose label, as a binary string, has a 1 at each of the indices. Each of the candidates with a 0 in at least one of the indices outputs 0, and the candidate that has 1 at all of the given indices outputs 1. This concludes the high-level description of the algorithm.

We now give a formal description of the advice and of the algorithm.

Advice Construction, for fixed $\alpha \in (0, 1]$

Input: Ring R with diameter at most D

1: $a_1 := \lfloor \log(diam(R)) \rfloor$
2: $A_1 :=$ binary representation of a_1
3: $C_R := \{v \mid \text{node } v \text{ has the largest label in } \lambda(\lfloor \alpha 2^{a_1} \rfloor, v)\}$
4: $(\gamma_0, \ldots, \gamma_{|C_R|-1}) :=$ binary reps. of labels of nodes in C_R, sorted in descending order
5: $S = \{x_j \mid j \in \{1, \ldots, |C_R|-1\}, \gamma_0[x_j] = 1 \neq \gamma_j[x_j]\}$
6: $A_2 :=$ binary encoding of S
7: Advice := (A_1, A_2)

Algorithm `Select` at node v with label ℓ, for fixed $\alpha \in (0, 1]$

Input: Advice (A_1, A_2)

1: $a_1 :=$ integer value represented by A_1
2: Acquire knowledge $K(\lfloor \alpha 2^{a_1} \rfloor, v)$ using $\lfloor \alpha 2^{a_1} \rfloor$ communication rounds
3: **if** ℓ is not the largest label in $\lambda(\lfloor \alpha 2^{a_1} \rfloor, v)$ **then**
4: Output 0 and halt.
5: $a_2 :=$ set of integers encoded in A_2
6: **if** there exists $i \in a_2$ such that $\ell[i] = 0$ **then**
7: Output 0 and halt.
8: **else**
9: Output 1 and halt.

THEOREM 3.9. *Consider any fixed $\alpha \in (0, 1]$ and any positive integer D. For any ring R with diameter at most D, Algorithm* `Select` *solves selection in the ring R in time $\alpha \cdot diam(R)$ and with advice of size $O(\log \log D)$.*

PROOF. Notice that Algorithm `Select` halts within $\alpha \cdot diam(R)$ communication rounds. Indeed, by line 2 of the algorithm, every node uses exactly $\lfloor \alpha 2^{a_1} \rfloor$ communication rounds, and $2^{a_1} \leq diam(R)$. Next, note that since A_1 is the binary representation of $\lfloor \log(diam(R)) \rfloor \leq \log D$, the length of A_1 is $O(\log \log D)$. To determine an upper bound on the length of A_2, we note that, at line 5 of the Advice Construction, $|S| \leq |C_R| - 1$, and each element of S is an integer whose value is bounded above by the length of the binary representation of a node's label, i.e., $\log L$. Therefore, from line 6, we see that A_2 is a binary encoding of fewer than $|C_R|$ different integers, each of which can be encoded using $O(\log\log L) = O(\log\log D)$ bits. It follows that the length of A_2 can be bounded above by $O(|C_R| * \log\log D)$. The following claim shows that, for rings, the number of candidate nodes is bounded by a constant that depends only on α. (This is the only place in the analysis that uses the fact that the network is a ring). We conclude that the length of A_2 is $O(\log\log D)$, and hence the total size of advice is $O(\log\log D)$.

CLAIM 3.10. $1 \le |C_R| < 8/\alpha$.

To prove the claim, first note that $|C_R| \ge 1$ since the largest node v in R also has the largest label in $\lambda(r, v)$. If $diam(R) < 2/\alpha$, then $|C_R|$ is at most the number of nodes in R, i.e., at most $2 \cdot diam(R) + 1$, which is at most $5/\alpha$. Hence we may assume that $diam(R) \ge 2/\alpha$. Next, note that there cannot be two candidate nodes v_1, v_2 such that the distance between them is at most r. Indeed, if $v_1 \in \lambda(r, v_2)$ and $v_2 \in \lambda(r, v_1)$, then the node in $\{v_1, v_2\}$ with smaller label will not be a candidate. Since the number of nodes in R is $2 \cdot diam(R) < 2^{a_1+2}$, it follows that the number of candidate nodes is less than $(2^{a_1+2})/r = (2^{a_1+2})/(\lfloor \alpha 2^{a_1} \rfloor)$. Since $diam(R) \ge 2/\alpha$ and $a_1 = \lfloor \log(diam(R)) \rfloor$, it can be shown that $(2^{a_1+2})/(\lfloor \alpha 2^{a_1} \rfloor)$ is at most $(2^{a_1+2})/(\alpha 2^{a_1-1}) = 8/\alpha$. This completes the proof of the claim.

Finally, we prove the correctness of the algorithm for an arbitrary ring R. First, note that the construction of the advice string can indeed be carried out. We must show that, at line 5 in the Advice Construction, for each node label γ_j that is not the largest (i.e., $j > 0$), there exists an index x_j such that $\gamma_j[x_j] = 0$ and $\gamma_0[x_j] = 1$. Indeed, the largest index where the binary representation of γ_j and γ_0 differ satisfies this condition.

We can now conclude that Algorithm `Select` solves selection in the entire ring. Indeed, in lines 1 – 4, each node that learns about the existence of a node with a larger label than itself outputs 0 and halts. The remaining nodes, namely those in C_R (which necessarily includes the largest node), proceed to lines 5 – 9. From line 5 of the Advice Construction, the node with largest label will be the only node that has a 1 at all indices in a_2 at line 6 of Algorithm `Select`, which implies that the node with largest label outputs 1 at line 9, while all other candidates output 0 at line 7. □

Corollary 3.8 and Theorem 3.9 imply the following tight bound on the size of advice.

COROLLARY 3.11. *The optimal size of advice to complete selection in any ring in time linear in its diameter (and not exceeding it) is* $\Theta(\log\log D)$.

3.2 Selection in time D^ϵ where $0 \le \epsilon < 1$

We now turn attention to very fast selection for rings of diameter D. Since every such ring has size n linear in D, and since L is polynomial in n, selection (and even election) can be accomplished using $O(\log D)$ bits of advice without any communication by providing the largest label as advice. It turns out that, even when the available time is D^ϵ, for any constant $0 \le \epsilon < 1$, this size of advice is necessary. Compared to Theorem 3.9, this shows that selection in time D^ϵ where $0 \le \epsilon < 1$, requires exponentially more advice than selection in time $\Theta(D)$.

THEOREM 3.12. *For any constant $0 \le \epsilon < 1$, any selection algorithm $\mathcal{A}$ for rings of diameter D that works in time at most D^ϵ requires $\Omega(\log D)$ bits of advice.*

PROOF. It is enough to consider sufficiently large values of D. Let $U = \{1, \dots, 2D-1\}$, and let $W = \{2D, \dots, L\}$. We start by defining a special class of rings, and then proceed to show that algorithm $\mathcal{A}$ requires $\Omega(\log D)$ bits of advice for this class. For the sake of clarity, we will use the notation $x = \lceil D^\epsilon \rceil$ and $y = \frac{1}{2}\lceil D^{1-\epsilon} \rceil$. We consider sufficiently large D such that $y \ge 2$.

First, we define a set of paths $\mathcal{P} = \{P_1, \dots, P_y\}$ as follows. Each path consists of $1 + 2x$ nodes with labels from W, with the middle node of the path having the largest label. More specifically, path P_i is obtained by considering the path of nodes with labels $2Di, \dots, 2Di + 2x$, respectively, and reversing the order of the last $x+1$ labels. Formally, for each $i \in \{1, \dots, y\}$, let P_i be the path of nodes whose labels form the sequence $(2Di, \dots, 2Di + x - 1, 2Di + 2x, 2Di + 2x - 1, \dots, 2Di + x)$.

Next, we define a set $\mathcal{R}$ of rings $\{R_1, \dots, R_y\}$. Each ring R_i will consist of the paths $P_1, \dots, P_i \in \mathcal{P}$ along with enough nodes with labels from U to ensure that R_i has size $2D$. In order to define the ring R_i, we first construct a path J_i by taking the paths $P_1, \dots, P_i$, and, for each $j \in \{2, \dots, i\}$, connecting the last node of path P_{j-1} with the first node of path P_j. More specifically, J_i is obtained by taking the union of the paths $P_1, \dots, P_i$, and, for each $j \in \{2, \dots, i\}$, adding an edge between the nodes with labels $2Dj - 2D + x$ and $2Dj$. Next, we construct a path K_i whose labels form the sequence $(1, \dots, 2D - |J_i|)$. Since the number of nodes in J_i is at most $y(1 + 2x)$, which, for sufficiently large D, is strictly less than $2D$, it follows that path K_i has at least one node. Finally, the ring R_i is obtained by joining the paths J_i and K_i. More specifically, R_i is obtained by taking the union of the paths J_i and K_i and adding the edges $\{1, 2Di + x\}$ and $\{2D - |J_i|, 2D\}$. The paths and rings constructed above are illustrated in Figure 3.

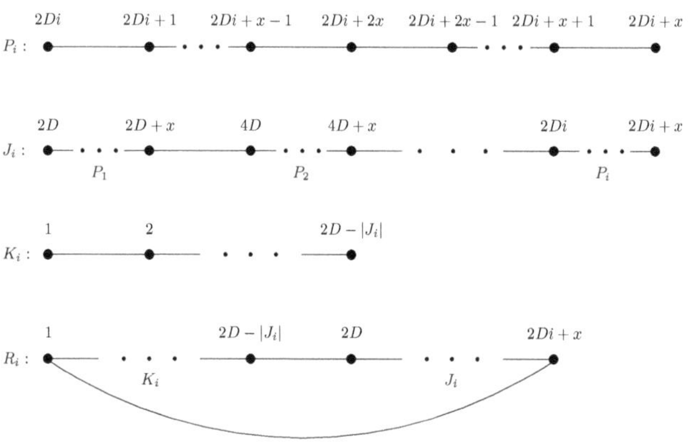

Figure 3: Graphs used in the construction of R_i

The following claim asserts that, in any two rings in $\mathcal{R}$ that contain path P_i as a subgraph, the middle node of this path in both rings acquires the same knowledge when executing algorithm $\mathcal{A}$.

CLAIM 3.13. *Consider any $i \in \{1, \dots, y\}$ and any $j \in \{i, \dots, y\}$. Let v_i be the node in R_i with label $2Di + 2x$ and* *let v_j be the node in R_j with label $2Di+2x$. Then, knowledge $K(x, v_i)$ in R_i is equal to knowledge $K(x, v_j)$ in R_j.*

To prove the claim, note that, in both R_i and R_j, the node with label $2Di + 2x$ is the middle node of path P_i. Since the path P_i has length $1 + 2x$, it follows that, within x communication rounds, node v_i does not learn about any nodes in R_i outside of P_i. Similarly, node v_j does not learn about any nodes in R_j outside of P_i. This implies that knowledge $K(x, v_i)$ in R_i is equal to knowledge $K(x, v_j)$ in R_j, which completes the proof of the claim.

We proceed to prove the theorem by way of contradiction. Assume that the number of bits of advice needed by algorithm $\mathcal{A}$ for the rings in $\mathcal{R}$ is less than $\left(\frac{1-\epsilon}{2}\right) \log D$. It follows that the number of distinct advice strings that are provided to algorithm $\mathcal{A}$ for the rings in $\mathcal{R}$ is strictly less than $2D^{(1-\epsilon)/2}$, which, for sufficiently large D, is strictly less than y. However, since the class $\mathcal{R}$ consists of $y \geq 2$ rings, this means that there exist two rings in $\mathcal{R}$, say R_a, R_b with $a < b$, such that $\text{adv}_{\mathcal{A}}(R_a) = \text{adv}_{\mathcal{A}}(R_b)$.

First, consider the execution of $\mathcal{A}$ by the nodes of ring R_a. Let v_a be the node in R_a with label $2Da+2x$, and note that v_a is the largest node in R_a. It follows that, in this execution, node v_a outputs 1. Next, consider the execution of $\mathcal{A}$ by the nodes of ring R_b. Let v_b be the node in R_b with the label $2Da + 2x$. By Claim 3.13, $K(x, v_a)$ in R_a is equal to $K(x, v_b)$ in R_b. Moreover, algorithm $\mathcal{A}$ halts within x rounds and $\text{adv}_{\mathcal{A}}(R_a) = \text{adv}_{\mathcal{A}}(R_b)$. It follows that the execution of $\mathcal{A}$ by v_a in R_a is identical to the execution of $\mathcal{A}$ by v_b in R_b. Hence, v_b outputs 1 in the execution of $\mathcal{A}$ in R_b. However, node v_b is not the largest in R_b. Indeed, v_b's label is $2Da + 2x$, whereas path P_b (and, hence, ring R_b) contains a node labeled $2Db + 2x > 2Da + 2x$. This contradicts the correctness of $\mathcal{A}$. □

COROLLARY 3.14. *For any constant $0 \leq \epsilon < 1$, the optimal size of advice to complete selection in any ring of diameter at most D in time D^ϵ is $\Theta(\log D)$.*

4. CONCLUSION

We established tradeoffs between the time of choosing the largest node in a network and the amount of *a priori* information (advice) needed to accomplish two variations of this task: election and selection. For the election problem, the tradeoff is complete and tight up to multiplicative constants in the advice size. Moreover, it holds for the class of arbitrary connected graphs. For selection, our results are for the class of rings and a small gap remains in the picture. We proved that in rings with diameter *diam* at most D, the optimal size of advice is $\Theta(\log D)$ if time is $O(diam^\epsilon)$ for any $\epsilon < 1$, and that it is $\Theta(\log \log D)$ if time is at most *diam*. Hence, the first open problem is to establish the optimal size of advice to perform selection for rings when the time is in the small remaining gap, for example, in time $\Theta(diam/\log diam)$. We can also consider a model with larger label spaces, i.e., where L is super-polynomial in n. All of the results in this paper would apply in that scenario as well, except for the following cases: for election in time $<$ diam, the upper and lower bounds on advice size would be $\Theta(\log L)$ instead of $\Theta(\log n)$, and the upper bounds on advice size for selection would be in $O(\log \log L)$ and $O(\log L)$ instead of $O(\log \log D)$ and $O(\log D)$, respectively. It would be interesting to close these resulting gaps. Another problem is to extend the tradeoff obtained for selection in rings to the class of arbitrary connected graphs. In particular, it would be interesting to investigate whether the optimal advice needed to perform fast selection in graphs of size much larger than the diameter depends on their size (like in the case of election) or on their diameter.

As noted in the introduction, all known leader election algorithms in labeled networks choose as leader either the node with the largest label or that with the smallest label. It is worth noting that the situation is not always symmetric here. For example, the Time Slice algorithm for leader election [35] (which elects the leader using exactly n messages in n-node rings, at the expense of possibly huge time) finds the node with the smallest label, and it does not seem to be possible to convert it directly to finding the node with the largest label. (Of course it is possible to first find the node with the smallest label and then to use this leader to find the node with the largest label, but this takes additional time and communication.) In our case, however, the situation is completely symmetric with respect to the order of labels: our results hold without change, if finding the largest node is replaced by finding the smallest. It is an open question whether they also remain valid if electing the largest node is replaced by general leader election (i.e., the task in which a single *arbitrary* node becomes the leader, and all other nodes become non-leaders and also learn the identity of the leader) and if selecting the largest node is replaced by general leader selection (i.e., the task in which a single *arbitrary* node becomes the leader, and all other nodes become non-leaders). Our lower bound for election in time at most the diameter and our algorithms for selection use the ordering in an essential way, and it is not clear if smaller advice would be enough to elect or select some arbitrary node in a given time.

Acknowledgments: We are grateful to the anonymous reviewer for pointing out the simplification of the algorithm showing the upper bound in Theorem 3.9.

5. REFERENCES

[1] S. Abiteboul, H. Kaplan, T. Milo, Compact labeling schemes for ancestor queries, Proc. 12th Annual ACM-SIAM Symposium on Discrete Algorithms (SODA 2001), 547–556.

[2] D. Angluin, Local and global properties in networks of processors. Proc. 12th Annual ACM Symposium on Theory of Computing (STOC 1980), 82–93.

[3] H. Attiya and M. Snir, Better Computing on the Anonymous Ring, *Journal of Algorithms* 12, (1991), 204-238.

[4] H. Attiya, M. Snir, and M. Warmuth, Computing on an Anonymous Ring, *Journal of the ACM* 35, (1988), 845-875.

[5] P. Boldi, S. Shammah, S. Vigna, B. Codenotti, P. Gemmell, and J. Simon, Symmetry Breaking in Anonymous Networks: Characterizations. *Proc. 4th Israel Symposium on Theory of Computing and Systems, (ISTCS 1996)*, 16-26.

[6] P. Boldi and S. Vigna, Computing Anonymously with Arbitrary Knowledge, *Proc. 18th ACM Symp. on Principles of Distributed Computing (PODC 1999)*, 181-188.

[7] J.E. Burns, A Formal Model for Message Passing Systems, *Tech. Report TR-91*, Computer Science

Department, Indiana University, Bloomington, September 1980.

[8] S. Caminiti, I. Finocchi, R. Petreschi, Engineering tree labeling schemes: a case study on least common ancestor, Proc. 16th Annual European Symposium on Algorithms (ESA 2008), 234–245.

[9] J. Chalopin, Local Computations on Closed Unlabelled Edges: The Election Problem and the Naming Problem *Proc. 31st Conference on Current Trends in Theory and Practice of Computer Science (SOFSEM 2005)*, 82-91.

[10] J. Chalopin and Y. Métivier, Election and Local Computations on Edges. *Proc. Foundations of Software Science and Computation Structures (FoSSaCS 2004)*, 90-104.

[11] D. Dereniowski, A. Pelc, Drawing maps with advice, Journal of Parallel and Distributed Computing 72 (2012), 132–143.

[12] D. Dereniowski, A. Pelc, Leader election for anonymous asynchronous agents in arbitrary networks, *Distributed Computing* 27 (2014), 21-38.

[13] S. Dobrev and A. Pelc, Leader Election in Rings with Nonunique Labels, *Fundamenta Informaticae* 59 (2004), 333-347.

[14] Y. Emek, P. Fraigniaud, A. Korman, A. Rosen, Online computation with advice, Theoretical Computer Science 412 (2011), 2642–2656.

[15] P. Flocchini, E. Kranakis, D. Krizanc, F.L. Luccio and N. Santoro, Sorting and Election in Anonymous Asynchronous Rings, *Journal of Parallel and Distributed Computing* 64 (2004), 254-265.

[16] P. Fraigniaud, C. Gavoille, D. Ilcinkas, A. Pelc, Distributed computing with advice: Information sensitivity of graph coloring, Distributed Computing 21 (2009), 395–403.

[17] P. Fraigniaud, D. Ilcinkas, A. Pelc, Communication algorithms with advice, Journal of Computer and System Sciences 76 (2010), 222–232.

[18] P. Fraigniaud, D. Ilcinkas, A. Pelc, Tree exploration with advice, Information and Computation 206 (2008), 1276–1287.

[19] P. Fraigniaud, A. Korman, E. Lebhar, Local MST computation with short advice, Theory of Computing Systems 47 (2010), 920–933.

[20] G.N. Fredrickson and N.A. Lynch, Electing a Leader in a Synchronous Ring, *Journal of the ACM* 34 (1987), 98-115.

[21] E. Fusco, A. Pelc, How Much Memory is Needed for Leader Election, *Distributed Computing* 24 (2011), 65-78.

[22] E. Fusco, A. Pelc, Knowledge, level of symmetry, and time of leader election, Proc. 20th Annual European Symposium on Algorithms (ESA 2012), LNCS 7501, 479-490.

[23] E. Fusco, A. Pelc, Trade-offs between the size of advice and broadcasting time in trees, Algorithmica 60 (2011), 719–734.

[24] E. Fusco, A. Pelc, R. Petreschi, Use knowledge to learn faster: Topology recognition with advice, Proc. 27th International Symposium on Distributed Computing (DISC 2013), 31-45.

[25] C. Gavoille, D. Peleg, S. Pérennes, R. Raz. Distance labeling in graphs, Journal of Algorithms 53 (2004), 85-112.

[26] C. Glacet, A. Miller, A. Pelc, Time vs. Information Tradeoffs for Leader Election in Anonymous Trees, arXiv:1505.04308.

[27] M.A. Haddar, A.H. Kacem, Y. Métivier, M. Mosbah, and M. Jmaiel, Electing a Leader in the Local Computation Model using Mobile Agents. *Proc. 6th ACS/IEEE International Conference on Computer Systems and Applications (AICCSA 2008)*, 473-480.

[28] D.S. Hirschberg, and J.B. Sinclair, Decentralized Extrema-Finding in Circular Configurations of Processes, *Communications of the ACM* 23 (1980), 627-628.

[29] D. Ilcinkas, D. Kowalski, A. Pelc, Fast radio broadcasting with advice, Theoretical Computer Science, 411 (2012), 1544–1557.

[30] T. Jurdzinski, M. Kutylowski, and J. Zatopianski, Efficient Algorithms for Leader Election in Radio Networks. *Proc., 21st ACM Symp. on Principles of Distributed Computing (PODC 2002)*, 51-57.

[31] M. Katz, N. Katz, A. Korman, D. Peleg, Labeling schemes for flow and connectivity, SIAM Journal of Computing 34 (2004), 23–40.

[32] A. Korman, S. Kutten, D. Peleg, Proof labeling schemes, Distributed Computing 22 (2010), 215–233.

[33] D. Kowalski, and A. Pelc, Leader Election in Ad Hoc Radio Networks: A Keen Ear Helps, *Proc. 36th International Colloquium on Automata, Languages and Programming (ICALP 2009), LNCS* 5556, 521-533.

[34] G. Le Lann, Distributed Systems - Towards a Formal Approach, *Proc. IFIP Congress*, 1977, 155–160, North Holland.

[35] N.L. Lynch, Distributed algorithms, Morgan Kaufmann Publ. Inc., San Francisco, USA, 1996.

[36] K. Nakano and S. Olariu, Uniform Leader Election Protocols for Radio Networks, *IEEE Transactions on Parallel and Distributed Systems* 13 (2002), 516-526.

[37] N. Nisse, D. Soguet, Graph searching with advice, Theoretical Computer Science 410 (2009), 1307–1318.

[38] D. Peleg, Distributed Computing, A Locality-Sensitive Approach, SIAM Monographs on Discrete Mathematics and Applications, Philadelphia 2000.

[39] G.L. Peterson, An $O(n \log n)$ Unidirectional Distributed Algorithm for the Circular Extrema Problem, *ACM Transactions on Programming Languages and Systems* 4 (1982), 758-762.

[40] M. Thorup, U. Zwick, Approximate distance oracles, Journal of the ACM, 52 (2005), 1–24.

[41] D.E. Willard, Log-logarithmic Selection Resolution Protocols in a Multiple Access Channel, *SIAM J. on Computing* 15 (1986), 468-477.

[42] M. Yamashita and T. Kameda, Electing a Leader when Procesor Identity Numbers are not Distinct, *Proc. 3rd Workshop on Distributed Algorithms (WDAG 1989), LNCS* 392, 303-314.

[43] M. Yamashita and T. Kameda, Computing on Anonymous Networks: Part I - Characterizing the Solvable Cases, *IEEE Trans. Parallel and Distributed Systems* 7 (1996), 69-89.

Near-Optimal Distributed Algorithms for Fault-Tolerant Tree Structures

Mohsen Ghaffari
MIT
ghaffari@mit.edu

Merav Parter
MIT
parter@mit.edu

ABSTRACT

Tree structures such as *breadth-first search* (BFS) trees and *minimum spanning trees* (MST) are among the most fundamental graph structures in distributed network algorithms. However, by definition, these structures are not robust against failures and even a single edge's removal can disrupt their functionality. A well-studied concept which attempts to circumvent this issue is *Fault-Tolerant Tree Structures*, where the tree gets augmented with additional edges from the network so that the functionality of the structure is maintained even when an edge fails. These structures, or other equivalent formulations, have been studied extensively from a centralized viewpoint [PP13, NSW97, CP10, GW12]. However, despite the fact that the main motivations come from distributed networks, their distributed construction has not been addressed before.

In this paper, we present distributed algorithms for constructing fault tolerant BFS and MST structures. The time complexity of our algorithms are nearly optimal in the following strong sense: they almost match even the lower bounds of constructing (basic) BFS and MST trees.

1. INTRODUCTION

Fault-Tolerant Tree Structures are well-studied concepts that attempt to add failure resilience to standard spanning tree structures. Spanning trees are among the most basic infrastructures used for communication in distributed networks. Two key examples are BFS and MST: Breadth First Search (BFS) trees are the main backbone in many communication tasks such as broadcast and routing as they provide the shallowest possible tree and shortest source-wise paths; Minimum Spanning Trees (MST) gets used because they provide the cheapest structure that keeps the graph connected. A downside of spanning trees is their sensitivity to faults, because even the failure of a single link disconnects the tree, which may lead to a complete loss of functionality. As the vertices and edges of the network may occasionally fail or malfunction, it is desirable to make these tree structures robust to failures.

A *Fault-Tolerant (FT) Tree Structure* augments the tree with additional edges from the base graph G in a way that provides it some redundancy and flexibility. As this augmentation carries certain costs, it is desirable to minimize the number of added edges. The motivation for this arises in settings where the graph edges represent the channels of a communication network, and the system designer would like to purchase or lease a minimal collection of channels (i.e., a subgraph $G' \subseteq G$) that maintain its functionality under faults. Another motivation for pre-computing fault tolerant tree structures arises in scenarios of *transient edge failures*: here, re-computing the structure after each failure is inefficient, as the failures are temporary, and instead one has to be prepared for each single edge's removal.

Indeed, time-efficient constructions of sparse FT tree structures have been studied extensively in the *centralized* setting for various notions of trees, see e.g., [NSW97, GW12, PP13, BK13, PP14, BGLP14]. Yet, albeit the fact that the key motivations come from distributed networks and these structures can be considered as *reliable* skeletons for distributed communication, their distributed construction has not been studied thoroughly before. In this paper, our objective is to provide *fast* distributed constructions of *sparse* FT tree structures. We next formalize this:

Model: We work with the standard distributed message passing model called CONGEST [Pel00]: communications occur in synchronous rounds; per round $O(\log n)$ bits can be sent along each link.

Problem Definitions: We focus on two fundamental tree structures, BFS and MST. The fault tolerant analogues of these structures are defined as follows: A *fault-tolerant BFS* (FT-BFS) structure is a sparse subgraph H of the given network G and a source node s that contains a BFS rooted at s in $G \setminus \{e\}$ for every failing of the edge $e \in G$. Thus, subsequent to the failure of a single edge $e \in G$, the surviving part $H \setminus \{e\}$ of H still contains a BFS tree of $G \setminus \{e\}$. Moreover, H preserves the source-wise distances as in the original graph G following the failing of a single edge. Similarly, a *fault-tolerant MST* (FT-MST) structure is a sparse subgraph H of the given network G that contains an MST in $G \setminus \{e\}$ for every failing of the edge $e \in G$. Given these definitions, our problems boil down to the following:

The research in this work was partially funded by the following grants: AFOSR FA9550-13-1-0042, NSF CCF-1461559, CCF-1217506, CCF-0939370.

SPAA '16, July 11-13, 2016, Pacific Grove, CA, USA
© 2016 ACM. ISBN 978-1-4503-4210-0/16/07...$15.00
DOI: http://dx.doi.org/10.1145/2935764.2935795

> ***Core Problem:*** *Distributedly construct BFS trees (or MST trees) of graphs $G \setminus \{e\}$ for all $e \in G$.*

Although this specification suggests we need to compute m trees, where m is the number of edges of G, in reality we just need to compute n (potentially) distinct trees: one is the BFS or MST tree T_0 of the base graph G, and $n-1$ additional BFS or MST trees, one for $G \setminus \{e\}$ for each $e \in T$.

We use the standard distributed representation for trees. In particular, for BFS trees, each vertex knows its parent. Our algorithms also provide the additional information of each vertex knowing its children in the tree, and its distance from the source. For MST trees, in the output, every vertex knows which of its incident edges are in the MST.

Our Contribution: We show somewhat surprisingly that these sparse fault tolerant tree structures can be computed within almost the same number of rounds as the corresponding *non-resilient* counterparts, i.e., the time to compute just one of the trees. We present distributed algorithms for constructing FT-BFS in $O(D \log n)$ rounds and FT-MST $O(D + \sqrt{n} \log n)$. These round complexities are nearly optimal in the sense they almost match even the lower bounds of constructing BFS and MST trees, respectively. Our constructions lead to sparse structures by simple connections with previous works. Hence, our main focus would be on the running time.

THEOREM 1.1 (**Distributed FT-BFS**). *Given an unweighted undirected n-vertex graph $G = (V, E)$ of diameter D, the collection of m BFS structures $\mathtt{BFS}(G \setminus \{e\}, s)$ for every $e \in G$, containing at most $O(n^{3/2})$ edges, can be constructed in $O(D \log n)$ rounds, with high probability*[1].

THEOREM 1.2 (**Distributed FT-MST**). *Given a weighted undirected n-vertex graph $G = (V, E, W)$ of diameter D, the collection of m MST trees $\mathtt{MST}(G \setminus \{e\})$ for each $e \in G$, containing at most $2(n-1)$ edges, can be constructed in $O(D + \sqrt{n} \log n)$ rounds, with high probability.*

The above two round complexity bounds are nearly optimal, because of the following: computing even one BFS requires at least $\Omega(D)$ rounds (a trivial and folklore lower bound), and computing even one MST requires at least $\Omega(D + \sqrt{\frac{n}{\log n}})$ rounds, by lower bounds of Das Sarma et al. [DSHK+11] and its predecessors [PR99, Elk04].

We also note that our $O(D \log n)$ round FT-BFS construction leads to $O(D \log n)$ round distributed algorithms for single-source replacement paths and also BFS sensitivity analysis, and our $O(D + \sqrt{n} \log n)$ round FT-MST construction leads to an $(D + \sqrt{n} \log n)$ round distributed algorithm for MST sensitivity analysis. The definition of these problems are discussed in the next section.

2. RELATED WORK

2.1 Works Related to FT-BFS Structures

The notion of sparse FT-BFS structure was introduced in [PP13]. The authors showed that one can obtain an FT-BFS structure with $O(n^{3/2})$ edges, simply by doing the following; take the union of m BFS structures, one for subgraph $G \setminus \{e\}$, for each $e \in E$, while breaking ties in a consistent manner. They also provide a matching lower bound, by presenting a family of graphs for which $\Omega(n^{3/2})$ edges are necessary.

The FT-BFS structure is closely related to the problem of constructing *replacement paths*. For a pair of vertices s and t and a an edge e, the replacement path $P_{s,t,e}$ is the $s-t$ shortest path that avoids e. In the *replacement-path* problem, one is given a graph $G = (V, E)$ and a pair of vertices $s-t$, it is then required to compute the collection of all replacement paths $P_{s,t,e}$ for every edge e. s

For undirected graphs on m edges, Malik et al. [MMG89] gave an algorithm for solving the replacement path problem with time complexity of $\widetilde{O}(m)$. Gotthilf and Lewenstein [GL09] showed an $O(mn \cdot n^2 \log \log n)$ time algorithm for directed graphs with arbitrary edge weights. For unweighted directed graphs, Roditty and Zwick [RZ12] gave a randomized algorithm which runs in time $\widetilde{O}(m\sqrt{n})$. Weimann and Yuster [WY13] were the first to apply fast matrix multiplication techniques to the problem and obtained an $O(Mn^{2.584})$-time randomized algorithm for directed graphs with integer weights in $[-M, M]$. In [Wil11], Vassilevska Williams showed that the replacement paths problem in directed graphs is equivalent to the all pairs shortest paths problem (APSP), under subcubic reductions. She also provided a deterministic algorithm for this problem with improved rum time of $\widetilde{O}(Mn^{\omega})$ where ω is the exponent of matrix multiplication.

FT-BFS structures are in particular related to the *single source* variant of the replacement-path problem, namely, the *single-source replacement paths* problem, studied in [GW12]. That problem requires to compute the collection $\mathcal{P}_s$ of all $s-t$ replacement paths $P_{s,t,e}$ for every $t \in V$ and every failed edge e that appears on the $s-t$ shortest-path in G. Grandoni and Vassilevska Williams [GW12] showed that the single source replacement path problem can be solved within nearly the same centralized time complexity as that of computing all-pairs shortest paths in a graph. Since the collection of paths $\mathcal{P}_s$ is precisely an FT-BFS structure with respect to s, the best algorithm for computing an FT-BFS structure in the centralized setting is almost as that of computing the all pairs distances.

The replacement-path problem and its single source variant have been studied so far only in the centralized setting. These problems have applications for computing the k shortest simple $s-t$ paths [RZ12] and for computing the *Vickrey pricing* of edges in a network [NR99, HS01]. We note that our distributed construction of a sparse FT-BFS structure can also be viewed as a distributed computation of the single-source replacement paths.

2.2 Works related to FT-MST Structures

FT-MST structures were introduced by Nardelli et al. [NSW97] for the geometric setting. They showed that the problem of computing the minimum (with respect to total edge weights) FT-MST structure is NP-hard already for the single failure case. This problem has been later studied by Chechik and Peleg [CP10] in the *general* graph setting where they showed an $O(\log n)$-approximation algorithm for an arbitrary constant number f of edge faults.

The first distributed construction of FT-MST structures resilient against single *vertex* or edge faults was given by Flocchini at el. [FEP+12]. They provide an $O(n)$-round al-

[1]As standard, we use the phrase *with high probability* (w.h.p.) to indicate that the probability of an event is at least $1 - 1/n^c$, for a desired fixed constant $c \geq 2$.

gorithm with message complexity of $O(n^2)$. Linear time algorithm for constructing FT-MST (via the edge swapping approach) was also given by Datta et al. [DLPP13]. Moreover, Gfeller et al. [GSW11] provide $O(n)$-round algorithm for finding the fault tolerant MST of minimum diameter.

Finally, the concept of FT-BFS and FT-MST structures is closely related to the *sensitivity analysis problem* [Tar82]. In this problem, one is given an optimal tree (with respect to some function), and it is required to measure by how much one can perturb each edge individually (e.g., by changing the weight of the edge or deleting it entirely) without changing the optimality of the tree (compared to other tree solutions in the graph). The best centralized bounds for computing an FT-MST structure are given by solving the MST sensitivity problem: given a graph G and minimum spanning tree $T = MST(G)$, decide how much each individual edge weight can be perturbed without invalidating the identity of T_0 (i.e., that T_0 is still an MST for the perturbed graph). Tarjan showed that the MST sensitivity analysis can be perform in $O(m\alpha(m,n))$ time, where m in the number of edges, n is the number of vertices, and α is the inverse-Ackermann function. This was later improved by Pettie to an $O(m\log(\alpha(m,n)))$ time algorithm [Pet05]. Our distributed constructions for FT-BFS and FT-BFS can also be viewed as solving the sensitivity analysis problems for BFS and MST trees.

3. FAULT-TOLERANT BFS

In this section, we explain a distributed algorithm that given a source node s, in $O(D\log n)$ rounds computes an FT-BFS structure rooted in s that is tolerant against the failure of each one edge. Recall that to compute an FT-BFS structure, we need to compute BFS trees in graph $G \setminus \{e\}$ for each edge $e \in G$, which as we discuss next, boils down to computing only n BFSs. By [PP13], it is sufficient to break shortest-paths ties consistently. To do that, in our distributed BFS construction, each node would break the ties among its potential parents in the BFS tree by selecting the one of minimum ID.

A basic BFS tree $T_0 = BFS(G, s)$ rooted in node s can be computed in $O(D)$ rounds, using the standard approach of synchronously growing the BFS-tree one hop per round, starting from the source s. Besides this base BFS tree, what remains to be computed is $n-1$ additional BFS trees rooted in s, one in each graph $G \setminus \{e\}$ for each edge $e \in T_0$.

As a side remark, we note that this problem is reminiscent of the problem of computing all-to-all shortest paths in G, i.e., computing n BFS trees, one rooted in each node $v \in G$. Holzer and Wattenhofer [HW12] showed how to compute these n BFS trees simultaneously in $O(n)$ rounds, using a simple and elegant scheduling idea. We will show that in our case, the $n-1$ BFSs can be computed much faster in $O(D\log n)$ rounds, thanks to their structure.

3.1 Naive Approaches

We first discuss two simpler and natural approaches that do not leverage the special structure of these BFSs and lead to results much weaker than our end goal of $O(D\log n)$.

Straw Man Approach 1: The most naive method for solving this problem would be to run the BFSs one by one, sequentially. That would lead to a round complexity of $O(Dn)$, a far cry from our goal of $O(D\log n)$ rounds.

Straw Man Approach 2: The second method would be to use the classic idea of *random delays* due to Leighton, Maggs, and Rao [LMR94,Gha15] to schedule the $n-1$ BFSs. Particularly, we would divide time into phases of $O(\log n)$ rounds, and delay the start of each BFS T_e by a random delay of t_e phases where t_e is a random variable with a uniform distribution in $\{1, 2, \ldots, \frac{n}{\log n}\}$. Once a BFS algorithm starts, the related BFS grows at a synchronous speed of one hop per phase. One can see that in this way, w.h.p., per phase and per edge $e' = (v, u)$, there are at most $O(\log n)$ BFS tokens scheduled to go through edge e' from v to u, in this phase. The reason is as follows: for each BFS, the phase number in which the BFS arrives at v and goes to u is exactly equal to the distance of v from s in the corresponding graph plus the random delay of that BFS. Now due to the fact that the random delay is picked uniformly from a range of size $\frac{n}{\log n}$, the probability of this summation being equal to each exact given value is at most $\log n/n$. Hence, over all the n BFSs, we expect to have at most $\log n$ BFS token that try to go from v to u per phase. By Chernoff bound, we know the number of such BFS tokens is at most $O(\log n)$, with high probability. Since each phase has $O(\log n)$ rounds, this means the phase has enough capacity to admit all the messages of all the BFSs through e. Thus, once started, the BFSs will be able to continually grow with the speed of one hop per phase. Therefore, the finishing time of this routine is $O((D + \frac{n}{\log n}))$ phases, which is $O(D\log n + n)$ rounds.

This bound is again far from our goal of $O(D\log n)$ rounds, due to the additive $O(n)$ term. This undesirable additive $O(n)$ term comes from the range of the random delay, which was $\frac{n}{\log n}$ phases. This range size was chosen to ensure that per phase no more than $O(\log n)$ of the n BFSs try to go through each edge. In fact, this is unavoidable unless we change the BFS algorithms, because if for an edge e', each of the $n-1$ BFSs should send one messages through e', any scheduling of these BFSs clearly requires $n-1$ rounds.

As a side note, we remark that albeit its shortcoming in our case, the above simple and general approach is quite useful. Particularly, it can be used to compute all-to-all shortest paths in $O(D\log n + n)$ rounds, which is only slightly worse than the $O(n)$ result of [HW12].

3.2 The Intuition of Our Approach

To get to the bound of $O(D\log n)$, we will have to zoom in on the BFSs that we are trying to build and leverage their structure. Particularly, as noted above, it is vital to make sure that per edge e, not all the $n-1$ BFSs need to transmit independent messages through edge e—as that would require at least $n-1$ rounds. For that, consider one edge $e' = (v, u)$, and let us zoom in on what messages need to be sent from v to u for various BFSs.

In a synchronous growth of a BFS tree $T_e = BFS(G\setminus e, s)$, the key thing that matters for each node v is when is the first time that the BFS token arrives at v (as well as who is the related parent). Note that this time indicates the distance of v from the source, in the corresponding graph. For edge $e' = (v, u)$, we need to send the BFS token from v to u if in $G \setminus \{e\}$, node v is closer to s compared to u. Moreover, in that case, what u needs to learn is the time that this token will be sent from v to u. This time is equal to $dist_{G\setminus\{e\}}(s, u) + t_e$, where the latter term is the starting time of the BFS T_e. A key observation is that, for many of the $n-1$ BFSs T_e that we are trying to run, we can make u know this time $dist_{G\setminus\{e\}}(s, u) + t_e$ without actually running that BFS through edge e. Note that in each tree T_e, node u receives messages from all its potential parents at the same time, namely, at time $dist_{G\setminus\{e\}}(s,u)+t_e$. It would then select as its parent the node of minimum ID, which would guarantee that the shortest path ties are broken an a consistent manner, leading to a sparse structure with $O(n^{3/2})$ edges.

Let P_v be the shortest path connecting s to v in G. If $e \notin P_v$, then $dist_{G\setminus\{e\}}(s,v) = dist_G(s,v)$. So, for each $e \notin P_v$, the $BFS(G\setminus\{e\},s)$ arrives at v at time $dist_G(s,v)+t_e$. Thus, we can avoid running all these BFSs through edge e if we could make node u know three things: (1) the distance $dist_G(s,v)$ in the base graph G, (2) the edges e on shortest path P_v in the base graph G, (3) the starting time for $BFS(G\setminus\{e\},s)$ for each of these $e \notin P_v$.

We will explain that we will be able to make each node u have this information about each of its neighbors v, using just $O(D+\log n)$ rounds of communication. Hence, the only BFSs that need to actually send a token through edge $e'=(v,u)$ from v to u are those T_e for $e\in P_v$. This is a total of D many BFSs, so using the random delays technique, we will be able to schedule these remaining BFSs in a short span of time. However, having these random delays creates a complication, as we need to make nodes know the starting time of (essentially) all BFSs, as needed in item (3) above. We will explain how using classic pseudo-random generators, and via spreading only $O(\log^2 n)$ bits of independent randomness in the network, we can simulate a large string of sufficiently-independent bits of randomness to be able to schedule these BFSs while nodes know their starting times.

3.3 Our Algorithm

We first describe the algorithm assuming that all nodes know a string SR of shared randomness, where $SR[i]$ for $i\in[n-1]$ describes a random value in range $\{1,\ldots,\Theta(D)\}$. Later, we explain how to generate SR in $O(D+\log n)$ rounds.

The Distributed FT-BFS Algorithm:

1. Construct a BFS tree $T_0 = BFS(G,s)$ rooted in node s, in $O(D)$ rounds.
2. Number the edges of T_0 by numbers 1 to $n-1$ in an arbitrary way, in $O(D)$ rounds.
3. Make each node v know the numbers of the edges on its shortest path P_v to s in T_0, in $O(D)$ rounds.
4. Let each node v send to each of its neighbors u the numbers of the edges on the shortest path P_v, in $O(D)$ rounds.
5. Divide time into phases of $\Theta(\log n)$ rounds each.
6. Generate the string SR of shared randomness, in $O(D+\log n)$ rounds.
7. Start $BFS(G\setminus\{e\},s)$ for each $e\in T_0$ with a delay of t_e phases, picked uniformly at random from $\{1,2,\ldots,D\}$, by setting it equal to $SR[i]$ where i is the edge-number of e. Since SR is publicly known, all nodes know t_e.
8. Run each $BFS(G\setminus\{e\},s)$ at a speed of one hop per phase, following these rules:
   - For each $e'=(v,u)$, each $BFS(G\setminus\{e\},s)$ is permitted to send its token from v to u only if $e\in P_v$. As v knows the edges on P_v, it can identify the permitted BFSs.
   - For each $e\notin P_v$, if v is u's parent in T_0, then u sets its parent in $BFS(G\setminus\{e\},s)$ to be also v. In that case, u proceeds $BFS(G\setminus\{e\},s)$ as if the related BFS token arrived from v to u in phase number $dist_G(s,v)+t_e+1$. Note that node u can do this for all edges $e\notin P_v$ as u knows the numbers of edges $e\in P_v$.

The correctness of the computed BFSs is immediate as for each $BFS(G\setminus\{e\},s)$, each node v will receive the related BFS token in the phase number $dist_{G\setminus\{e\}}(s,v)+t_e$, which since v knows t_e, means v also learns its distance in that BFS, as well as its parent in the BFS. As for the time complexity, each of the first four steps can be performed in $O(D)$ rounds using the standard approach. Steps 4 and 6 are just for explanation and they do not need any communication rounds. We will discuss step 5 later in Lemma 3.2. The execution of the last step finishes within $O(D)$ phases, which is $O(D\log n)$ rounds. This is because each BFS will start at the latest by phase D and after that, it can continue for at most $2D$ additional phases[2].

The only two things that remain to be discussed are as follows: (1) we should show that w.h.p., per phase, at most $O(\log n)$ BFS tokens will need to pass through each edge, (2) we need to explain how to generate the string of shared randomness SR.

LEMMA 3.1. *W.h.p., at most $O(\log n)$ BFS tokens need to go through each edge, per phase.*

PROOF. We show that w.h.p., in each phase number t and for each edge $e'=(v,u)$, at most $O(\log n)$ BFS tokens will need to go through e' from v to u in phase t.

Note that the only BFSs that are now permitted to send a token from v to u are those trees $BFS(G\setminus\{e\},s)$ for $e\in P_v$, which by definition of P_v, is a total of at most D BFSs. For each such $BFS(G\setminus\{e\},s)$, the token will have to go through e' from v to u in phase t if and only if $dist_{G\setminus\{e\}}(v,s)+t_e=t$. Since t_e is chosen randomly from a range of size D, the probability of this event is at most $1/D$. Hence, over the set of D BFSs for $e\in P_v$, we expect to see at most 1 scheduled to go from v to u in phase t. If the random delay values t_e where completely independent, by an application of Chernoff bound, we would have that this number is at most $O(\log n)$, w.h.p. This will not be exactly true in our case, as we produce SR using a pseudo-random generators, but we will have k-wise independence on the generated string, for $k=\Theta(\log n)$ as we discuss later, and from a result of Schmidt et al. [SSS95], it is known that for this application of Chernoff bound, it suffices to have k-wise independence between the random values, for $k=\Theta(\log n)$. □

LEMMA 3.2. *The string of shared randomness SR can be generated and delivered to all nodes in $O(D+\log n)$ rounds.*

[2]It is easy to see that the diameter of each BFS in $G\setminus\{e\}$ is at most $2D$. For general number of faults $f\geq 1$, see [CG84].

PROOF. What SR needs to contain is $n-1$ values of randomness, each from a range of size $\Theta(D)$, where these values have $O(\log n)$-wise independent. Suppose that we share $O(\log^2 n)$ random bits that are completely random and independent between all nodes. Note that this can be done in $O(D+\log n)$ rounds, by having the source node s sample these bits using its private randomness, putting them in $O(\log n)$ messages, and then downcasting these messages on the BFS using the standard method. Then, we can feed these bits of true randomness to a pseudo-random number generator. Particularly, each node v feeds these $\Theta(\log^2 n)$ bits into one of the classical k-wise independent, for $k=\Theta(\log n)$, pseudo-randomness constructions (e.g., [AS04, Theorem 15.2.1][3]). This pseudo-random number generator produces n random values, each in range $[\Theta(D)]$, with $\Theta(\log n)$-wise independence between the values. □

4. FAULT-TOLERANT MST

In this section, we explain a distributed algorithm that in $O(D+\sqrt{n}\log n)$ rounds computes an FT-MST structure that is tolerant against failure of each one edge. Recall that to compute an FT-MST structure, we need to compute MST trees in graph $G\setminus\{e\}$ for each edge $e\in G$, which as we discuss next, boils down to computing only n MSTs.

A basic MST tree $T_0 = MST(G)$ can be computed in $O(D+\sqrt{n}\log^* n)$ rounds, using the classic algorithm of Kutten and Peleg [KP95]. Besides this base MST tree, what remains to be computed is $n-1$ additional MST trees, one in each graph $G\setminus\{e\}$ for each edge $e\in T_0$. To compute these MSTs, we essentially need to compute $n-1$ swap edges, as we formalize next.

For a given MST $T_0\subseteq G$ and an edge $e\in T_0$, we call edge $e'=(u,v)$ a *swap edge* for e if adding e' to $T_0\setminus\{e\}$ restores the connectivity of T_0 when e fails. It is easy to see that an edge $e'=(u,v)$ is a swap edge for e iff the edge e is on the unique T_0-path connecting u and v. In other words, edge $e'=(u,v)\in G$ is a swap edge for e if and only if the following conditions are satisfied: (1) edge e appears on the T_0-path connecting the root r to v or to u, and (2) the Least Common Ancestor (LCA) of v and u is above e. See Figure 1.

Given this definition, it is easy to see that when a T_0-edge e fails, to restore the MST, what we need to do is to compute the lightest swap edge for e. Particularly, we have the following fact:

DEFINITION 4.1. *For each edge $e\in T_0$, let $\mathsf{SE}(e)$ be the set of all swap edges for e, by defining $\mathsf{SE}(e)=\{e' \mid (T_0\setminus\{e\})\cup\{e'\}$ is connected$\}$. Moreover, define the best swap edge $\mathsf{SE}^*(e)$ of e to be the lightest edge e' in $\mathsf{SE}(e)$. Note that the tree $T_0\setminus\{e\}\cup\{\mathsf{SE}^*(e)\}$ is an MST of $G\setminus\{e\}$.*

Hence, an FT-MST structure H consists of the edges of the MST tree T_0 along with at most $(n-1)$ best swap edges, one $\mathsf{SE}^*(e)$ for each $e\in T_0$. Thus, to compute FT-MST structures, we need to distributedly compute all $(n-1)$ best swap edges, one $\mathsf{SE}^*(e)$ for each $e\in T_0$.

[3]We note that [AS04, Theorem 15.2.1] only describes the construction for GF(2) which yields k-wise independent bit. However, as also described in [Cou, Section 3], the construction readily extends to $GF(p)$, for any prime number $p\in \text{poly}(n)$. Furthermore, when desiring random delays in range $[\Theta(D)]$, we can pick them from a range $\{1,\ldots,p\}$ for a prime $p\in[D,10D]$, which exists by Bertrand's postulate.

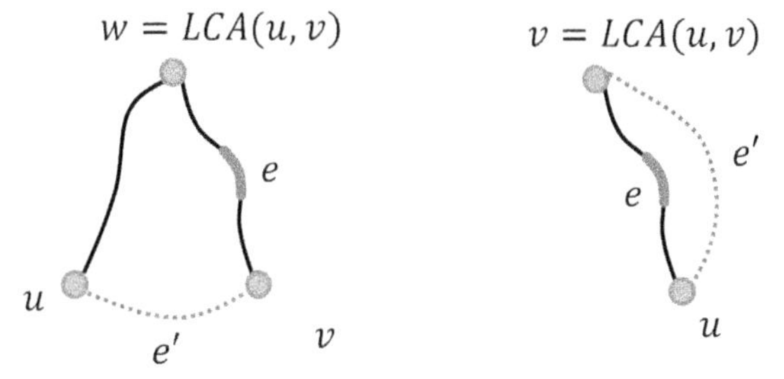

Figure 1: An illustration of a swap edge e' for edge e, in two possible shapes. The solid edges are those of the MST tree T_0, the T_0 edge e is indicated with a red color, and the dashed line indicates e'.

As a warm up, we begin in Section 4.1 by describing an algorithm that computes all these swap edges in $O(D_{MST})$ rounds, where D_{MST} is the diameter of the tree $T_0 = MST(G)$. Notice that D_{MST} can possibly be much larger than the diameter D of graph G. In Section 4.2, we explain how to extend this idea and get an algorithm with round complexity $O(D+\sqrt{n}\log n)$. For that, in a nutshell, we will decompose the tree into $O(\sqrt{n}\log n)$ *segments*, each of diameter $O(\sqrt{n}\log n)$, and we will also use a *virtual skeleton tree* that captures the structure between these segments.

Throughout, we consider the node r with the minimum ID to be the root of T_0 and we consider the edges of T_0 to be directed away from the root r. A vertex v is said to be *above* an edge e in the tree T_0 if it is closer (in hops) to the root r in T_0.

4.1 Warm Up: FT-MST in $O(D_{MST})$ rounds

To compute the swap edges, we make each vertex v know the T_0 path $\pi(r,v)$ connecting root r to v and moreover, we make each two neighboring vertices exchange these path descriptions. Note that this can be easily done in $O(D_{MST})$ rounds, using standard methods: computing the path $\pi(r,v)$ can be done by downcasting the parent IDs from the root to the leaves. Then, each two neighbors need to exchange at most $O(D_{MST})$ path edges, which clearly can be done in $O(D_{MST})$ rounds. At the end, each two neighboring vertices u and v connected via edge e' can know all T_0-edges e for which e' is a swap edge for e. Particularly, v and u compute their LCA w in T_0 and then edge e' is a swap edge for each T_0-edge $e\in\pi(r,v)\cup\pi(r,u)$ that is below w. That is, if e' is on the unique T_0-path connecting v and u.

The algorithm proceeds as follows: each vertex v evaluates which of its incident edges e' are swap edges for each T_0-edge $e\in\pi(r,v)$. Specifically, vertex v defines its swap proposal $\mathsf{SE}^*(e,v)$ for each edge $e\in\pi(r,v)$ to be the lightest edge e' incident on v that is a swap edge for e.

Next, the edges $\mathsf{SE}^*(e,v)$ along with their weights are upcasted towards the head endpoint y of the edge $e=(x,y)$ in the following pipeline manner: Letting $\pi(r,v)=[e_1,\ldots,e_k]$, each vertex v maintains a list of edges $\mathsf{SE}^*(e_1,v),\ldots,\mathsf{SE}^*(e_k,v)$, where each such edge $\mathsf{SE}^*(e_i,v)$ is the current best swap edge for e_i that v knows. Initially, the $\mathsf{SE}^*(e_i,v)$ edges are those incident to v. During the upcast, upon receiving values from its descendants, these values may correspond to edges with endpoint in the subtree of v. The vertex v keeps on forward-

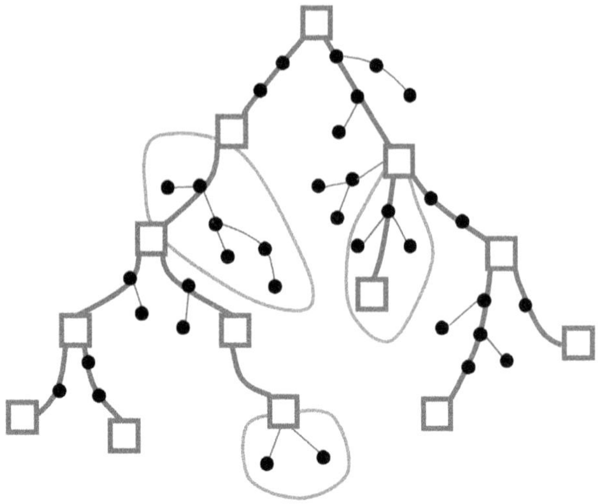

Figure 2: A schematic depiction of the decomposition of the MST and its skeleton tree. The marked nodes are depicted as blue boxes, while small black circles indicate non-marked nodes. One can obtain the *skeleton tree* by erasing the non-marked nodes, i.e., keeping only the thicker blue lines between the boxes. The three green curves show three sample segments; for simplicity, we do not highlight all the segments in the picture.

ing to its parent in T_0 arbitrary stored items that have not been upcast so far; upon receiving an edge $\mathtt{SE}^*(e_i, u)$ from a descendant u, the vertex v updates its $\mathtt{SE}^*(e, v)$ values only if the swap edge suggested by u is better, i.e., of smaller weight. Since overall every vertex v computes the minimum of $O(D_{MST})$ functions in its subtree T_v, this piplelined upcast finishes in $O(D_{MST})$ rounds (cf., [Pel00]).

By the end of this process, we get that every vertex v holds the best swap edge $\mathtt{SE}^*(e_v)$ where e_v is the incoming edge to v in T_0. By rewinding the tape of the communication, the endpoints of the selected swap edges $\mathtt{SE}^*(e_v)$ for every v are notified, learning that their edge is the best swap edge for e_v. They can then add these edges to the FT-MST structure H. This completes the description for our warm up $O(D_{MST})$ round algorithm.

4.2 FT-MST in $O(D + \sqrt{n}\log n)$ rounds

We start the description of the algorithm by defining a decomposition of the MST tree into a number of *segments* and a skeleton tree capturing this decomposition. For simplicity, we then first explain how to use these structures to compute the best swap edges, and only later come back to the description of distributed construction of these structures.

Pre-processing—Segments and Skeleton Tree: To define the tree decomposition into segments, we mark a number of nodes on the MST tree T_0 such that these marked nodes satisfy the following three properties: (P1) the root r is a marked node and for each node $v \neq r$, there is a marked node ancestor u of v such that $\mathtt{dist}_{T_0}(u, v) \leq O(\sqrt{n}\log n)$, (P2) for each two marked nodes u and v, their least common ancestor is also a marked node, and (P3) the number of the marked nodes is at most $O(\sqrt{n}\log n)$. See Figure 2.

Given these marked nodes, we decompose the MST tree T_0 into segments as follows: for each node v, define its lowest ancestor marked node $LAM(v)$ and its highest descendant marked node $HDM(v)$, if such exists, and $\emptyset$ otherwise. Each segment is defined to include the set of all nodes with the same pair LAM and HDM. Note that these segments are not vertex-disjoint, as they overlap in marked nodes, but they are edge-disjoint, and therefore, we can perform independent communications in different segments in parallel.

Due to properties (P1) and (P3), we have $O(\sqrt{n}\log n)$ segments, each with a diameter of $O(\sqrt{n}\log n)$ hops. Having these segments, we further define a virtual *skeleton tree* T_S whose vertices are the marked nodes and a marked node v is the T_S-parent of marked node u iff $v = LAM(u)$. Putting it in intuitive (and imprecise) words, the skeleton tree can be obtained simply by erasing all non marked nodes, while paths going through them are maintained and turn into virtual edges. See Figure 2.

In the following, we assume that vertices have the following knowledge about these structures:

(K1) each vertex v knows the identifier of its segment, namely $LAM(v)$ and $HDM(v)$,

(K2) each vertex v knows the identifiers of the T_0-edges on the unique path from v to each of these two vertices $LAM(v)$ and $HDM(v)$, and

(K3) all vertices know the full topology (vertices and edges) of the skeleton tree T_S.

We will explain later in Section 4.3 that all this knowledge can be attained in $O(D + \sqrt{n}\log n)$ rounds. For now, we assume this knowledge as given, and proceed to explain how to compute the best swap edges, using these structures.

Classifying swap edges to short, mid, and long ranges: Given a T_0-edge e and a swap edge of it $e' = (u', v') \in \mathtt{SE}(e)$, we call e' a *short-range*, *mid-range*, or *long-range* swap for e if and only if, respectively, two, one or zero of the endpoints u' and v' of e' are in the same segment as e. See Figure 3 for some examples.

The *best short-range* swap for e is the *lightest* short-range edge $e' \in \mathtt{SE}(e)$; the *best mid-range* and *best long-range* swaps for e are defined analogously. We compute the *best short-range*, the *best mid-range*, and the *best long-range* swaps separately. At the end, we set the best swap edge of each T_0-edge e to be simply the lightest of its best swaps in these three categories.

Computing short-range swap edges: The computations of short-range swaps in different segments happen independently and in parallel, each via communicating only on the edges of that segment. Before starting that computation of these swap edges, we make every two neighbors exchange their segment identifiers.

We focus on one segment S_i and the T_0-subtree T_i induced by vertices of S_i. Our goal is to compute the best short-range swap edge $\mathtt{SE}^*_{short}(e)$ for each tree edge $e = (x, y) \in T_i$. To do that, we employ the algorithm described in the previous subsection, restricted to tree T_i, as follows: Assume that all edges of T_i are directed away from the root r_i. We let every two neighboring vertices v and u in the same segment, connected via edge $e' = (u, v)$, exchange items (K2) of their knowledge, i.e., their T_0-paths to $LAM(v) = LAM(u)$. Notice that this can be performed in $O(\sqrt{n}\log n)$ rounds, as

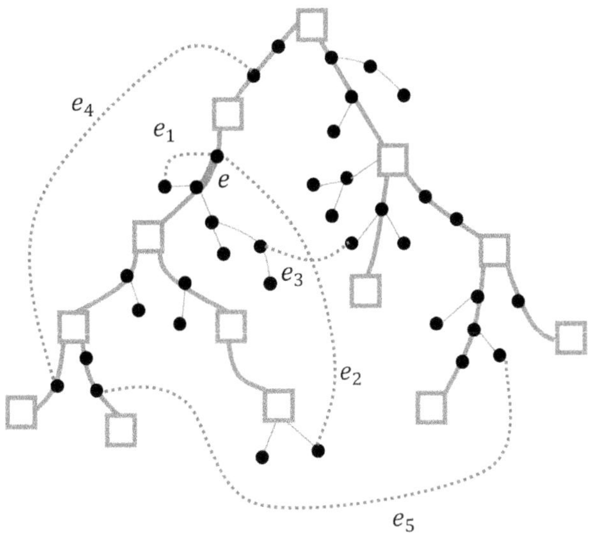

Figure 3: For the T_0-edge e indicated with a red color, the edge e_1 is a short-range swap, the edges e_2 and e_3 are mid-range swaps, and the edges e_4 and e_5 are long-range swaps.

each of these paths has length $O(\sqrt{n}\log n)$. Using this information, nodes v and u can compute the unique T_0-path connecting v and u. Then, v and u include edge e' in their computations of swap proposals for all T_0-edges on this path. The rest of the computation for finding the best short-range swap edge is a simple upcast, exactly as described in the previous subsection.

Computing mid-range swap edges: Similar to the short-range swaps, the mid-range swaps of different segments happen independently and in parallel, after nodes know the segment identifiers of their neighbors. Let us focus on one segment S_i. Consider a node $v \in S_i$ and a neighbor of it u in a different segment S_j, connected to v via edge $e' = (v, u)$. We say that segments S_i and S_j are *dependent* if either all nodes of S_i are in the T_0-subtree below (the lowest marked node of) S_j, or all nodes of S_j are in the T_0-subtree below S_i. Otherwise, we say these two segments are *independent*. We next examine these two cases separately:

- **Independent Segments S_i and S_j:** In this case, the LCA of v and u is above $LAM(v)$ and e' is a mid-range swap edge for all edges on the T_0-path connecting v to its lowest ancestor marked ndoe $LAM(v)$.
- **Dependent Segments S_i and S_j:** This case breaks into two possibilities: either S_j is a descendant of S_i or S_i is a descendant of S_j. In the former possibility, the LCA of v and u is in S_i and e' is a mid-range swap edge for all edges on the T_0-path connecting v to $HDM(v)$. In the latter possibility, the LCA of v and u is in S_j and e' is a mid-range swap edge for all edges on the T_0-path connecting v to $LAM(v)$.

Since v knows the segment identifier of u as well as the full skeleton tree structure T_S, node v can identify in which of the above cases we are. Furthermore, since v knows its paths to its own $LAM(v)$ and $HDM(v)$, node v knows which T_0-edges of segment S_i can use e' as a mid-range swap edge. To have the best mid-range computed, we have each such node v put its proposals for each of the relevant T_0-edges e. We then perform one upcast in $T_0[S_i]$ towards $LAM(v) = LAM(S_i)$, thus obtaining the best mid-range swaps for which the segment endpoint of the swap edge is below the swapped edge. Afterward, we also perform a downcast towards $HDM(S_i)$, thus obtaining the best mid-range swaps for which the segment endpoint of the swap edge is above the swapped edge. Each of these upcast and downcast is essentially identical to, or reverse of, the upcast in the algorithm of the previous subsection. Hence, after at most $O(\sqrt{n}\log n)$ rounds, all edges know their best mid-range swaps.

Computing long-range swap edges: For this part, we use the skeleton tree. We consider $O(\sqrt{n}\log n)$ minimization problems, one for each skeleton edge. For each edge $e' = (u, v) \in G$, the two endpoints u and v can easily find the skeleton edges e for which e' is a swap edge, that is, the skeleton edges e which reside on the skeleton path connecting the closest marked nodes of the segments of u and v. Then, v and u include e' in their proposal for swap edges of e. We perform a pipelined upcast for these $O(\sqrt{n}\log n)$ minimization problems on the BFS tree of the graph G. For each problem, each node always maintains the lightest solution for that problem seen so far, and passes it to its parent in the BFS tree. A final downcast then delivers these solutions to all nodes. At the end, since for each physical edge $e'' \in T_0$, the endpoints know to which virtual skeleton edge e does edge e'' belong, they can take the solution of the minimization of e as the best long range swap for e''. Note that in this manner, we are treating all the physical edges that are on the same virtual skeleton edge essentially the same, for the purpose of their long-range swaps. We next formally argue that this indeed is correct, which means we compute the best long-range swaps for all T_0-edges.

PROPOSITION 4.2. *Let e_1, e_2 be two T_0-edges in the same segment and suppose that e_1' and e_2' are the best long-range swap edges for e_1 and e_2, respectively. Then, the two best long-range swap edges are the same and we have $e_1' = e_2'$.*

PROOF. Notice that since e_1 and e_2 have long range swaps, they both must be on the main path of their segment which connects their lowest ancestor marked node w_1 to their highest descendant marked node w_2. Now, since e_1' is long range swap edges for e_1, it must be the case the T_0-path connecting w_1 and w_2 is a subpath of the T_0-path connecting the two endpoints of e_1'. A similar thing is also true for e_2'. Hence, e_1' and e_2' are both long range swaps for both of e_1 and e_2. Since e_1' and e_2' are the best long-range swap edges for e_1 and e_2, by the uniqueness of the edge weights, we then get that $e_1' = e_2'$. □

Putting things together: At the end, for each T_0-edge e, the best swap edge e' is the lightest of its best short-range, mid-range, and long-range swaps. Since the endpoints of e know the best of each category, they can easily find the best swap edge. Finally, we can reverse the direction and time order of all these communications, i.e., essentially rewinding the tape of communications backwards, and thus let the endpoints of each best swap edge e' know that it is the best swap edge for some T_0-edge e. The endpoints of e' can then add e' to the FT-MST structure H. This completes the

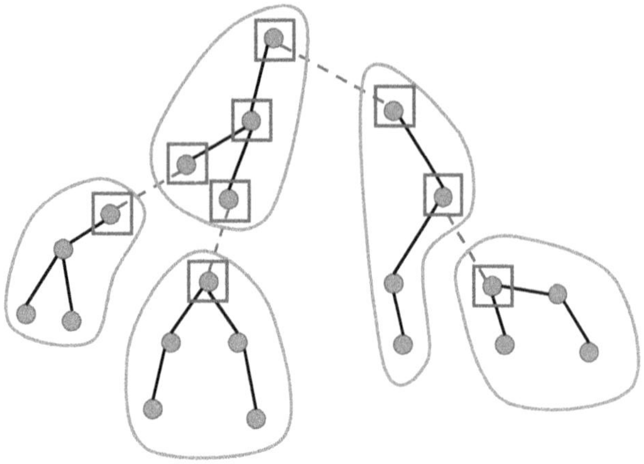

Figure 4: The components in the decomposition are marked with green curves, the sampled edges are depicted as dashed red edges, and red boxes indicate marked nodes, i.e., the nodes of virtual skeleton tree.

description of how we compute the swap edges, using the skeleton structure and the segments. We next go back to explain how we compute these structures in $O(D+\sqrt{n}\log n)$ rounds, as claimed.

4.3 Constructing the Segments and the Skeleton Tree

Here, we explain how to identify the marked nodes such that they satisfy the properties (P1) to (P3), stated in Section 4.2. We then explain how to use these marks to identify the segments and the skeleton tree and let each node v have the knowledge items (K1) to (K3), stated in Section 4.2.

First, define a random subset of MST edges $R \subseteq T_0$ by including each T_0-edge in E independently with probability $1/\sqrt{n}$. First, we show that w.h.p. $T_0 \setminus R$ has $O(\sqrt{n}\log n)$ connected components, each with a diameter of at most $O(\sqrt{n}\log n)$. See Figure 4.

LEMMA 4.3. *W.h.p., $T_0 \setminus R$ has $O(\sqrt{n}\log n)$ connected components, each with a diameter of at most $O(\sqrt{n}\log n)$.*

PROOF. Since every edge in T_0 is added to R with probability $p = 1/\sqrt{n}$, by Chernoff bound, we get that $|R| = O(\sqrt{n} \cdot \log n)$, with high probability. Hence, the number of connected components of $T_0 \setminus R$ is $O(\sqrt{n} \cdot \log n)$.

We next bound the diameter of the tree induced by the vertices of each component C_i in $T_0 \setminus R$. Consider all pairs $\mathcal{P}$ of vertices u and v whose distance in the tree T_0 is exactly $c \cdot \log n \cdot \sqrt{n}$. That is letting $\pi(u,v)$ be the $u-v$ path in T_0, then $\mathcal{P} = \{\langle u,v\rangle \mid |\pi(u,v)| = c \cdot \log n \cdot \sqrt{n}\}$. We claim that w.h.p. $R \cap E(\pi(u,v)) \neq \emptyset$ for every $\langle u,v\rangle \in \mathcal{P}$. To see this, consider one pair u and v in $\mathcal{P}$. The probability that none of the edges on $\pi(u,v)$ has been sampled into R is $(1-1/\sqrt{n})^{c\cdot\log n\cdot\sqrt{n}} = 1/n^c$. Hence, by union bound over at most $O(n^2)$ pairs, we get that w.h.p the tree paths of all pairs in $\mathcal{P}$ intersect R. Therefore, w.h.p., the diameter of every component of $T \setminus R$ is $O(\sqrt{n}\log n)$. □

We now proceed to use these components for defining the marked nodes, the segments, and the skeleton. First, we start with orienting the tree of each component downward, with respect to the global root. We then use these oriented component trees to define the marked nodes. At the end, we use these marked nodes to construct the segments and the skeleton tree.

Pre-processing Step 1—Defining a rooted subtree $T_i' \subseteq T$ for each component C_i: First, remove the edges of R and perform a minimum ID flooding on edges of $T_0 \setminus R$. Thus, within $O(\sqrt{n}\log n)$ rounds, all nodes of each component C_i of $T_0 \setminus R$ have the smallest ID of that component.

We next wish to define a root r_i' for each component C_i. In particular, assuming that all edges of T_0 are directed away from the global root r, the root r_i' of the component C_i is the vertex with incoming degree zero in the subtree T_i' induced on the vertices of C_i. To let every vertex know the root of its component, we define an intermediate virtual tree T' obtained by contracting every component C_i of $T_0 \setminus R$ into a single vertex. By exchanging the component IDs with the neighbors, the edges of T' can become global knowledge within $O(D+\sqrt{n}\log n)$ rounds, w.h.p. This is because there are $O(\sqrt{n}\log n)$ components (w.h.p.) and the T_0-edges connecting vertices of different components, which are those in R, can be communicated to the entire graph using an upcast on the BFS tree, in $O(D+\sqrt{n}\log n)$ rounds. Hence, by rooting the intermediate virtual tree T' at the component of the root vertex r, each vertex can know the root of its own component, all in $O(D+\sqrt{n}\log n)$ rounds. Then, by performing a downcast from the root of each component on the edges of $T_0 \setminus R$, in $O(D+\sqrt{n}\log n)$ rounds, we get that each component of $T_0 \setminus R$ is directed outwards from its root and each node knows its parent—that is, its unique incoming neighbor—in this orientation.

Pre-processing Step 2—Marking nodes, inside components C_i: First, mark each vertex that is incident on a sampled edge in R, as well as the root r of T_0. Then, we start an upcast in each component C_i, on the tree of $T_0[C_i]$ from the leaves towards the root. During this process, we identify and mark nodes of $T_0[C_i]$ that are LCA of two of these sampled edges (i.e., their marked nodes). Particularly, any leaf v that is a marked node sends the identifier of its sampled edge to its parent, indicating that v is marked. Then, when the upcast reaches a node u, (1) if u itself is incident on a sampled edge, then u is marked and it passes the ID of one such sampled edge to its parent, (2) if u is not marked and it receives only one sampled edge from its children, it simply passes this sampled edge to its parent, and (3) if node u is not marked but it receives two or more sampled edges from its children, then u becomes marked and it passes only one of these sampled edges to its parent.

LEMMA 4.4. *The set of marked nodes satisfy the following properties: (P1) the root r is marked and for each node $v \neq r$, there is a marked node ancestor u of v such that $\texttt{dist}_{T_0}(u,v) \leq O(\sqrt{n}\log n)$, (P2) for each two marked nodes u and v, their least common ancestor is also a marked node, and (P3) the number of the marked nodes is $O(\sqrt{n}\log n)$.*

PROOF. Property (P1) follows immediately because each component has depth at most $O(\sqrt{n}\log n)$ and the root of each component is marked, as either it is the root of T_0, or it is incident on a sampled edge in R.

For property (P2), consider two marked nodes u and v. If v is a descendant or ancestor of u, then their LCA is u

or v, respectively, which is marked. So suppose that v is not a descendant or ancestor of u. Suppose that u and v are in the same connected component. Then, all edges on the T_0-path connecting these two nodes will carry marks, while we perform the upcast explained above. This means that their LCA receives at least two sampled edges from its children and thus it becomes marked, too. Now suppose that v and u are in two different component. Then, consider the component that includes the LCA w of these two nodes, and the parts of the paths from w to v and from w to u that are in this component. Clearly, these paths end at two different sampled edges. Thus, these endpoints are marked. This means node w is in fact the LCA of two marked nodes in the same component. As we argued above, in this case, we know that node w is marked.

Finally, for (P3), note that the initial set of marked nodes is those vertices that are incident on sampled edges, and since $|R| = O(\sqrt{n} \log n)$, the set of initial marked nodes has size $O(\sqrt{n} \log n)$. Now, as we perform the upcast of marking, each new node w that we mark receives at least two sampled edges from its children, but it passes only one sampled edge to its parent. Hence, we can charge the marking of w to one of the sampled edges that it received but did not pass up to its parent. This shows that the number of additional marks that we introduce during the marking upcast is one per sampled edge, which is at most $O(\sqrt{n} \log n)$. □

Pre-processing Step 3—Defining the Segments and the Skeleton tree T_S: To define the edges of the skeleton tree T_S, we perform an upcast inside each component, where each marked node v that is not the root of a component sends its ID up to its parent. We continue this upcast and the ID gets passed on to the parent until it reaches the lowest ancestor marked node w. Then, w knows that it is the parent of v in the skeleton tree T_S, and there is a virtual edge between w and v in T_S. Since there are $O(\sqrt{n} \log n)$ marked nodes, there are also $O(\sqrt{n} \log n)$ such virtual edges in the skeleton tree. We broadcast all these virtual edges to all nodes, in $O(D + \sqrt{n} \log n)$ rounds. This ensures that all nodes know the skeleton tree, i.e., it satisfies knowledge item (K3) in Section 4.2. Then, by performing a downcast from each marked node, and after that also an upcast from each marked node, and stopping these downcast and upcast once they reach the first next marked node, we can make each nodes v know the identifiers of its lowest ancestor marked node $LAM(v)$ and its highest descendant marked node $HDM(v)$. This is the segment identifier of v and thus it satisfies knowledge item (K1). Finally, by repeating these upcasts and downcast while also carrying the names of all visited edges, we can make each node v know the IDs of the edges on its paths to $LAM(v)$ and its highest descendant marked node $HDM(v)$, thus satisfying (K2). This finishes our description of the knowledge items (K1) to (K3), and hence also the construction of the segments and the skeleton tree.

5. REFERENCES

[AS04] Noga Alon and Joel H Spencer. *The probabilistic method.* John Wiley & Sons, 2004.

[BGLP14] Davide Bilò, Luciano Gualà, Stefano Leucci, and Guido Proietti. Fault-tolerant approximate shortest-path trees. In *Algorithms-ESA 2014*, pages 137–148. Springer, 2014.

[BK13] Surender Baswana and Neelesh Khanna. Approximate shortest paths avoiding a failed vertex: Near optimal data structures for undirected unweighted graphs. *Algorithmica*, 66(1):18–50, 2013.

[CG84] FRK Chung and MR Garey. Diameter bounds for altered graphs. *Journal of Graph Theory*, 8(4):511–534, 1984.

[Cou] Lecture notes on k-wise uniform (randomness) generators. http://pages.cs.wisc.edu/~dieter/Courses/2013s-CS880/Scribes/PDF/lecture04.pdf. Accessed: 2015-02.

[CP10] Shiri Chechik and David Peleg. Rigid and competitive fault tolerance for logical information structures in networks. In *Electrical and Electronics Engineers in Israel (IEEEI), 2010 IEEE 26th Convention of*, pages 000024–000025. IEEE, 2010.

[DLPP13] Ajoy K Datta, Lawrence L Larmore, Linda Pagli, and Giuseppe Prencipe. Linear time distributed swap edge algorithms. In *Algorithms and Complexity*, pages 122–133. Springer, 2013.

[DSHK+11] Atish Das Sarma, Stephan Holzer, Liah Kor, Amos Korman, Danupon Nanongkai, Gopal Pandurangan, David Peleg, and Roger Wattenhofer. Distributed verification and hardness of distributed approximation. In *Proc. of the Symp. on Theory of Comp. (STOC)*, pages 363–372, 2011.

[Elk04] Michael Elkin. Unconditional lower bounds on the time-approximation tradeoffs for the distributed minimum spanning tree problem. In *Proc. of the Symp. on Theory of Comp. (STOC)*, pages 331–340, 2004.

[FEP+12] Paola Flocchini, T Enriquez, Linda Pagli, Giuseppe Prencipe, and Nicola Santoro. Distributed minimum spanning tree maintenance for transient node failures. *Computers, IEEE Transactions on*, 61(3):408–414, 2012.

[Gha15] Mohsen Ghaffari. Near-optimal scheduling of distributed algorithms. In *the Proc. of the Int'l Symp. on Princ. of Dist. Comp. (PODC)*, pages 3–12, 2015.

[GL09] Zvi Gotthilf and Moshe Lewenstein. Improved algorithms for the k simple shortest paths and the replacement paths problems. *Information Processing Letters*, 109(7):352–355, 2009.

[GSW11] Beat Gfeller, Nicola Santoro, and Peter Widmayer. A distributed algorithm for finding all best swap edges of a minimum-diameter spanning tree. *Dependable and Secure Computing, IEEE Transactions on*, 8(1):1–12, 2011.

[GW12] Fabrizio Grandoni and Virginia Vassilevska Williams. Improved distance sensitivity oracles via fast single-source replacement paths. In *Foundations of Computer Science*

(FOCS), 2012 IEEE 53rd Annual Symposium on, pages 748–757. IEEE, 2012.

[HS01] John Hershberger and Subhash Suri. Vickrey prices and shortest paths: What is an edge worth? In *Foundations of Computer Science, 2001. Proceedings. 42nd IEEE Symposium on*, pages 252–259. IEEE, 2001.

[HW12] Stephan Holzer and Roger Wattenhofer. Optimal distributed all pairs shortest paths and applications. In *the Proc. of the Int'l Symp. on Princ. of Dist. Comp. (PODC)*, pages 355–364, 2012.

[KP95] Shay Kutten and David Peleg. Fast distributed construction of k-dominating sets and applications. In *the Proc. of the Int'l Symp. on Princ. of Dist. Comp. (PODC)*, pages 238–251, 1995.

[LMR94] Frank Thomson Leighton, Bruce M Maggs, and Satish B Rao. Packet routing and job-shop scheduling in O(congestion+ dilation) steps. *Combinatorica*, 14(2):167–186, 1994.

[MMG89] Kavindra Malik, AK Mittal, and Santosh K Gupta. The k most vital arcs in the shortest path problem. *Operations Research Letters*, 8(4):223–227, 1989.

[NR99] Noam Nisan and Amir Ronen. Algorithmic mechanism design. In *Proceedings of the thirty-first annual ACM symposium on Theory of computing*, pages 129–140. ACM, 1999.

[NSW97] Enrico Nardelli, Ulrike Stege, and Peter Widmayer. *Low-cost Fault-tolerant Spanning Graphs for Point Aets in the Euclidean Plane.* 1997.

[Pel00] David Peleg. *Distributed Computing: A Locality-sensitive Approach.* Society for Industrial and Applied Mathematics, Philadelphia, PA, USA, 2000.

[Pet05] Seth Pettie. Sensitivity analysis of minimum spanning trees in sub-inverse-ackermann time. *Algorithms and Computation*, pages 964–973, 2005.

[PP13] Merav Parter and David Peleg. Sparse fault-tolerant BFS trees. In *the Proceedings of the Annual European Symposium on Algorithms*, pages 779–790, 2013.

[PP14] Merav Parter and David Peleg. Fault tolerant approximate bfs structures. In *Proceedings of the Twenty-Fifth Annual ACM-SIAM Symposium on Discrete Algorithms*, pages 1073–1092. SIAM, 2014.

[PR99] David Peleg and Vitaly Rubinovich. A near-tight lower bound on the time complexity of distributed MST construction. In *Proc. of the Symp. on Found. of Comp. Sci. (FOCS)*, pages 253–, 1999.

[RZ12] Liam Roditty and Uri Zwick. Replacement paths and k simple shortest paths in unweighted directed graphs. *ACM Transactions on Algorithms (TALG)*, 8(4):33, 2012.

[SSS95] Jeanette P Schmidt, Alan Siegel, and Aravind Srinivasan. Chernoff-hoeffding bounds for applications with limited independence. *SIAM Journal on Discrete Mathematics*, 8(2):223–250, 1995.

[Tar82] Robert Endre Tarjan. Sensitivity Analysis of Minimum Spanning Trees and Shortest Path Trees. *Inf. Process. Lett.*, 14(1):30–33, 1982.

[Wil11] Virginia Vassilevska Williams. Faster replacement paths. In *Proceedings of the twenty-second annual ACM-SIAM symposium on Discrete Algorithms*, pages 1337–1346. SIAM, 2011.

[WY13] Oren Weimann and Raphael Yuster. Replacement paths and distance sensitivity oracles via fast matrix multiplication. *ACM Transactions on Algorithms (TALG)*, 9(2):14, 2013.

Brief Announement: Applications of Uniform Sampling: Densest Subgraph and Beyond*

Hossein Esfandiari
University of Maryland
Hossein@cs.umd.edu

MohammadTaghi Hajiaghayi†
University of Maryland
hajiagha@cs.umd.edu

David P. Woodruff
IBM Almaden
dpwoodru@us.ibm.com

ABSTRACT

In this paper we provide a framework to analyze the effect of uniform sampling on graph optimization problems. Interestingly, we apply this framework to a general class of graph optimization problems that we call *heavy subgraph problems*, and show that uniform sampling preserves a $1-\epsilon$ approximate solution to these problems. This class contains many interesting problems such as densest subgraph, directed densest subgraph, densest bipartite subgraph, d-max cut, and d-sum-max clustering. As an immediate impact of this result, one can use uniform sampling to solve these problems in streaming, turnstile or Map-Reduce settings. Indeed, our results by characterizing heavy subgraph problems address Open Problem 13 at the IITK Workshop on Algorithms for Data Streams in 2006 regarding the effects of subsampling, in the context of graph streams.

Recently Bhattacharya et al. in STOC 2015 provide the first one pass algorithm for the densest subgraph problem in the streaming model with additions and deletions to its edges, i.e., for dynamic graph streams. They present a $(0.5-\epsilon)$-approximation algorithm using $\tilde{O}(n)$ space, where factors of ϵ and $\log(n)$ are suppressed in the $\tilde{O}$ notation. In this paper we improve the $(0.5-\epsilon)$-approximation algorithm of Bhattacharya et al. by providing a $(1-\epsilon)$-approximation algorithm using $\tilde{O}(n)$ space.

1. INTRODUCTION

In this paper we consider a general class of graph optimization problems that we call *heavy subgraph problems* in the streaming setting with additions and deletions, i.e., in dynamic graph streams. We show that many interesting problems such as densest subgraph, directed densest subgraph, densest bipartite subgraph, d-max cut, and d-sum-max clustering fit in this general class of problems. To the best of our knowledge, we are the first to consider densest bipartite subgraph and d-sum-max clustering in the streaming setting.

Finding the densest subgraph of a graph is one of the fundamental problems in computer science. This problem has many applications across different areas that deal with massive datasets such as Community detection [5, 19, 9, 7], Link spam detection [11], distance query indexing [8, 13], analyzing communication in social networks [9], and, Computational biology [20] among others. We refer to [16] for a survey of applications of the densest subgraph problem.

In an instance of the *densest subgraph problem* we are given a graph G and want to find a subgraph $sol \subseteq G$, that maximizes $\frac{|E_{sol}|}{|V_{sol}|}$, where V_{sol} and E_{sol} are the vertex set and the edge set of sol, respectively. Similarly, in an instance of the *directed densest subgraph problem* we are given a directed graph $G=(V_G,E_G)$ and want to find a pair $A,B\subseteq V_G$, that maximizes $\frac{|E(A,B)|}{\sqrt{|A|\cdot|B|}}$, where $E(A,B)$ is the number of edges from A to B in E_G.

There are polynomial time algorithms for the densest subgraph problem in the classical setting [6, 10, 12, 15]. Specifically, Charikar [6] studies the densest subgraph problem in the classical setting and provides an exact algorithm with $\tilde{O}(nm)$ running time, where n and m are the number of vertices and edges, respectively. He also provides a 0.5-approximation algorithm with running time $O(n+m)$. To the best of our knowledge, this is the fastest known constant factor approximation algorithm for the densest subgraph problem. Moreover, he provides a 0.5-approximation algorithm for the directed densest subgraph problem as well.

Later, Bahmani, Kumar and Vassilvitskii [3], consider the densest subgraph problem and the directed densest subgraph problem in the streaming setting with only insertions of edges. For both problems, they present streaming algorithms with a $\frac{1}{2(1+\epsilon)}$-approximation factor using $\log_{1+\epsilon}(n)$ passes over the input. To the best of our knowledge, their results for directed graphs are the only non-trivial results for the directed densest subgraph problem in the streaming setting, prior to our work. Recently, Bahmani, Goel and Munagala [2] improve this result and provide a $(1-\epsilon)$-approximation algorithm using $O(\log(\frac{n}{\epsilon^2}))$ passes over the input.

Very recently, Bhattacharya et al. [4] present the first single pass streaming algorithm for dynamic graph streams.

*A full version of this paper is available at: http://arxiv.org/abs/1506.04505

†Supported in part by NSF CAREER award CCF-1053605, NSF BIGDATA grant IIS-1546108, NSF AF:Medium grant CCF-1161365, DARPA GRAPHS/AFOSR grant FA9550-12-1-0423, and another DARPA SIMPLEX grant.

SPAA '16 July 11-13, 2016, Pacific Grove, CA, USA

ACM ISBN 978-1-4503-4210-0/16/07.

DOI: http://dx.doi.org/10.1145/2935764.2935813

Their first algorithm provides a $(0.5-\epsilon)$-approximation using $\tilde{O}(n)$ bits of space. The update time of this algorithm is $\tilde{O}(1)$, though the query time is inefficient. They provide a second algorithm with a $(0.25-\epsilon)$-approximation factor for which the update time and query time are only $\tilde{O}(1)$, again using $\tilde{O}(n)$ bits of space.

In the *d-max cut* problem, we are given a graph G, and we want to decompose the vertices of G into d partitions such that the number of edges between different partitions is maximized. To the best of our knowledge, we are the first to consider this problem for general d in the streaming setting. A restricted version of this problem where $d=2$, is the classic max cut problem. One can store a sparsifier [1] of the input graph in $\tilde{O}(n)$ space, and preserve a $(1-\epsilon)$-approximation of the max cut. However, it is not clear if sparsifiers preserve d-max cut or not. Recently, Kapralov, Khanna and Sudan [14] show that any $(1-\epsilon)$-approximation to the max cut problem in the streaming setting requires $n^{1-O(\epsilon)}$ space.

1.1 Our Results

In this paper, we first consider the densest subgraph problem in the streaming setting where we have both insertions and deletions to the edges as they arrive in the stream, i.e., in a dynamic graph stream. We improve the $(0.5-\epsilon)$-approximation algorithm of Bhattacharya et al. (STOC'15) [4] by providing a $(1-\epsilon)$-approximation algorithm for this problem using $\tilde{O}(n)$ space. Indeed, our algorithm simply samples $\tilde{O}(n)$ edges uniformly at random, and finds the densest subgraph on the sampled graph. We also achieve update time $\tilde{O}(1)$. To achieve this, we use min-wise independent hashing together with fast multi-point polynomial evaluation.

THEOREM 1.1. *There exists a semi-streaming algorithm in dynamic graph streams for the densest subgraph problem with space $\tilde{O}(n)$ which gives a $(1-\epsilon)$-approximate solution, with probability $1-1/n$. The update time is $\tilde{O}(1)$.*

We note that Bhattacharya et al. [4] provide a $(0.25-\epsilon)$ approximation streaming algorithm with update time and query time $\tilde{O}(1)$ as well. Our update time matches their $\tilde{O}(1)$ update time, which is important since it multiplies the time to process each stream update. We note, though, that they provide a better query time, which is useful if one repeatedly queries the data structure, as may often be the case in the study of dynamic graph algorithms. However, especially in the data stream setting, which is the setting considered in this paper, getting a $(1-\epsilon)$-approximation instead of a $(0.25-\epsilon)$-approximation is often more important. This is true if one is only interested in querying the data structure at the end of the stream, or at a few intermediate positions, for which one can amortize the cost of the query, which is at most $\tilde{O}(n)$, over the next n stream updates. We also note that the query time of [4] et al. can be as large as $\tilde{\Omega}(n)$, that is, it is proportional to the current number of nodes of the densest subgraph, so to take advantage of it one should apply it to graphs with small densest subgraphs.

Next, we extend our results to a general family of graph optimization problems that we call *heavy subgraph problems*. Interestingly, we show that by uniformly sampling edges we obtain enough information about the solution of any heavy subgraph problem. Since the solution of a heavy subgraph problem itself may be as large as the whole graph, here we just claim that we can estimate the size of the optimum solution. However, in some cases, like for the densest subgraph problem, it might be possible to also obtain the optimum solution itself, and not just the size, from the sampled graph.

A graph optimization problem is defined by, an input graph G, a set of feasible solutions Sol_G, which are subgraphs of G, and an objective function $f : Sol \to \mathbb{R}$. In a graph optimization problem we aim to find a solution $sol \in Sol_G$ that maximizes f. In fact, the number of feasible solutions for a graph G may be exponential in the size of G. We say a graph optimization problem on graph G is a (γ, l)-*heavy subgraph problem* if there exist l [not necessarily disjoint] sets $Sol_G^1, Sol_G^2, \ldots, Sol_G^l$, such that $Sol_G = \cup_{k=1}^{l} Sol_G^k$ and for any k:

- **Local Linearity:** There exists a number $f_k \geq 1$ such that for any solution $sol \in Sol_G^k$, we have $f(sol) = f_k \cdot |E_{sol}|$, where E_{sol} is the edge set of sol. Without loss of generality we assume $f_1 \geq f_2 \geq \cdots \geq f_l = 1$.
- **Hereditary Property:** For any spanning subgraph $H \subseteq G$, we have $sol_H \in Sol_H^k$ if and only if there exists a solution $sol_G \in Sol_G^k$ such that $sol_H = sol_G \cap H$.
- **γ Bound:** γ is chosen such that the optimum solution is lower bounded by $\gamma \log(|Sol_G^k|) f_k \frac{m}{n}$.

Let $\mathcal{P}(\gamma, l)$ be a heavy subgraph problem, and let *Alg* be an α-approximation algorithm for $\mathcal{P}$. Algorithm 1 samples $O(\frac{n\delta \log(l)}{\gamma\epsilon^2})$ edges of the input graph and runs *Alg* on the sampled graph. Interestingly, the following Theorem shows Algorithm 1 is an $(\alpha-\epsilon)$-approximation algorithm for $\mathcal{P}$ on G.

THEOREM 1.2. *Let $\mathcal{P}(\gamma, l)$ be a heavy subgraph problem. Let G be an arbitrary graph, and let Alg be an α-approximation algorithm for $\mathcal{P}$. With probability $1-e^{-\delta}$, Algorithm 1 is an $(\alpha-\epsilon)$-approximation algorithm for $\mathcal{P}$ on G, using $O(\frac{n\delta \log(l)}{\gamma\epsilon^2})$ space.*

Finally, we show several applications of Theorem 1.2. Indeed, we show that directed densest subgraph, densest bipartite subgraph, d-max cut and d-sum-max clustering all fits in the general family of heavy subgraph problems, and thus, Theorem 1.2 holds for them.

THEOREM 1.3. *The following statements hold.*

- *Densest bipartite subgraph is a $(\gamma = \frac{1}{2(\log(n)+1)}, l = n)$ heavy subgraph problem.*
- *Directed densest subgraph is a $(\gamma = \frac{1}{2\sqrt{n}\log(n)}, l = n^2)$ heavy subgraph problem.*
- *d-max cut is a $(\gamma = \frac{1}{2\log(d)}, l = 1)$ heavy subgraph problem.*
- *d-sum-max clustering is a $(\gamma = \frac{n-2d}{n\log(d)}, l = 1)$ heavy subgraph problem.*

In fact, understanding the structure of the problems that can be solved using sampling, and specifically uniform sampling, is a well-motivated challenge, which was highlighted as a direction in the IITK Workshop on Algorithms for Data

Algorithm 1 A General Algorithm

Input: A graph G, a heavy subgraph problem $\mathcal{P}(\gamma, l)$ and an α approximation algorithm Alg for $\mathcal{P}$.
Output: An $\alpha - \epsilon$ estimator of $\mathcal{P}$ on graph G, w.pr. $1 - e^{-\delta}$.

1: Set $C = \frac{12n(4+\delta)\log(l)}{\gamma\epsilon^2}$
2: **if** $|E| \leq C$ **then**
3: Return $Alg(G)$.
4: **else**
5: Sample C edges uniformly at random, without replacement from G.
6: Let H be the sampled graph.
7: Return $\frac{|E|}{C} Alg(H)$.

Streams in 2006. Our structural results, as well as our characterization for heavy subgraph problems, give partial answers to this open question in the context of graphs.

In simultaneous and independent work McGregor et al. [17] present a single pass $(1 - \epsilon)$-approximation algorithm for the densest sugraph problem in the dynamic graph streaming model with update time $\tilde{O}(1)$, that uses $\tilde{O}(n)$ space. Also, simultaneously and independently of our work, Mitzenmacher et al. [18] show if one samples each edge with a small probability, then with high probability the sampled graph preserves the densest subgraph of the input graph. Mitzenmacher et al. do not provide a way to implement the sampling efficiently in dynamic graph streams.

2. REFERENCES

[1] K. J. Ahn, S. Guha, and A. McGregor. Graph sketches: sparsification, spanners, and subgraphs. In *Proceedings of the 31st symposium on Principles of Database Systems*, pages 5–14. ACM, 2012.

[2] B. Bahmani, A. Goel, and K. Munagala. Efficient primal-dual graph algorithms for mapreduce. In *Algorithms and Models for the Web Graph - 11th International Workshop, WAW 2014, Beijing, China, December 17-18, 2014, Proceedings*, pages 59–78. Springer, 2014.

[3] B. Bahmani, R. Kumar, and S. Vassilvitskii. Densest subgraph in streaming and mapreduce. *Proceedings of the VLDB Endowment*, 5(5):454–465, 2012.

[4] S. Bhattacharya, M. Henzinger, D. Nanongkai, and C. E. Tsourakakis. Space-and time-efficient algorithm for maintaining dense subgraphs on one-pass dynamic streams. In *STOC*, 2015.

[5] G. Buehrer and K. Chellapilla. A scalable pattern mining approach to web graph compression with communities. In *Proceedings of the 2008 International Conference on Web Search and Data Mining*, pages 95–106. ACM, 2008.

[6] M. Charikar. Greedy approximation algorithms for finding dense components in a graph. In *Approximation Algorithms for Combinatorial Optimization*, pages 84–95. Springer, 2000.

[7] J. Chen and Y. Saad. Dense subgraph extraction with application to community detection. *Knowledge and Data Engineering, IEEE Transactions on*, 24(7):1216–1230, 2012.

[8] E. Cohen, E. Halperin, H. Kaplan, and U. Zwick. Reachability and distance queries via 2-hop labels. *SIAM Journal on Computing*, 32(5):1338–1355, 2003.

[9] Y. Dourisboure, F. Geraci, and M. Pellegrini. Extraction and classification of dense communities in the web. In *Proceedings of the 16th international conference on World Wide Web*, pages 461–470. ACM, 2007.

[10] G. Gallo, M. D. Grigoriadis, and R. E. Tarjan. A fast parametric maximum flow algorithm and applications. *SIAM Journal on Computing*, 18(1):30–55, 1989.

[11] D. Gibson, R. Kumar, and A. Tomkins. Discovering large dense subgraphs in massive graphs. In *Proceedings of the 31st international conference on Very large data bases*, pages 721–732. VLDB Endowment, 2005.

[12] A. V. Goldberg. *Finding a maximum density subgraph.* University of California Berkeley, CA, 1984.

[13] R. Jin, Y. Xiang, N. Ruan, and D. Fuhry. 3-hop: a high-compression indexing scheme for reachability query. In *Proceedings of the 2009 ACM SIGMOD International Conference on Management of data*, pages 813–826. ACM, 2009.

[14] M. Kapralov, S. Khanna, and M. Sudan. Streaming lower bounds for approximating max-cut. In *Proceedings of the Twenty-Sixth Annual ACM-SIAM Symposium on Discrete Algorithms*, pages 1263–1282. SIAM, 2015.

[15] S. Khuller and B. Saha. On finding dense subgraphs. In *Automata, Languages and Programming*, pages 597–608. Springer, 2009.

[16] V. E. Lee, N. Ruan, R. Jin, and C. Aggarwal. A survey of algorithms for dense subgraph discovery. In *Managing and Mining Graph Data*, pages 303–336. Springer, 2010.

[17] A. McGregor, D. Tench, S. Vorotnikova, and H. T. Vu. Densest subgraph in dynamic graph streams. In *Mathematical Foundations of Computer Science 2015*, pages 472–482. Springer, 2015.

[18] M. Mitzenmacher, J. Pachocki, R. Peng, C. Tsourakakis, and S. C. Xu. Scalable large near-clique detection in large-scale networks via sampling. In *Proceedings of the 21th ACM SIGKDD International Conference on Knowledge Discovery and Data Mining*, pages 815–824. ACM, 2015.

[19] M. E. Newman. Modularity and community structure in networks. *Proceedings of the National Academy of Sciences*, 103(23):8577–8582, 2006.

[20] B. Saha, A. Hoch, S. Khuller, L. Raschid, and X.-N. Zhang. Dense subgraphs with restrictions and applications to gene annotation graphs. In *Research in Computational Molecular Biology*, pages 456–472. Springer, 2010.

Brief Announcement: Relaxed Byzantine Vector Consensus*

Zhuolun Xiang
Institute for Interdisciplinary Information Sciences
Tsinghua University
xiangzhuolun@gmail.com

Nitin H. Vaidya
Department of Electrical and Computer Engineering
University of Illinois at Urbana-Champaign
nhv@illinois.edu

ABSTRACT

Byzantine vector consensus requires that non-faulty processes reach agreement on a decision (or output) that is in the convex hull of the inputs at the non-faulty processes. Recent work has shown that, for n processes with up to f Byzantine failures, when the inputs are d-dimensional vectors of reals, $n \geq \max(3f+1, (d+1)f+1)$ is the tight bound for synchronous systems, and $n \geq (d+2)f+1$ is tight for approximate consensus in asynchronous systems.

Due to the dependence of the lower bound on vector dimension d, the number of processes necessary becomes large when the vector dimension is large. With the hope of reducing the lower bound on n, we propose relaxed versions of Byzantine vector consensus: k-relaxed Byzantine vector consensus and (δ, p)-relaxed Byzantine vector consensus. k-relaxed consensus only requires consensus for projections of inputs on every subset of k dimensions. (δ, p)-relaxed consensus requires that the output be within distance δ of the convex hull of the non-faulty inputs, where distance is defined using the L_p-norm. An input-dependent δ allows the distance from the non-faulty convex hull to be dependent on the maximum distance between the non-faulty inputs.

We show that for k-relaxed consensus and (δ, p)-relaxed consensus with constant $\delta \geq 0$, the bound on n is identical to the bound stated above for the original vector consensus problem. On the other hand, when δ depends on the inputs, we show that the bound on n is smaller when $d \geq 3$. Input-dependent δ may be of interest in practice – in essence, input-dependent δ scales with the spread of the inputs.

Keywords

Byzantine consensus; vector inputs; relaxed validity conditions

*This research is supported in part by National Science Foundation award 1421918. Any opinions, findings, and conclusions or recommendations expressed here are those of the authors and do not necessarily reflect the views of the funding agency or the U.S. government.

SPAA '16 July 11-13, 2016, Pacific Grove, CA, USA

ACM ISBN 978-1-4503-4210-0/16/07.
DOI: http://dx.doi.org/10.1145/2935764.2935808

1. INTRODUCTION

This paper considers Byzantine consensus in a complete network consisting of n processes of which up to f processes may be Byzantine faulty [2]. Recent work has shown that when the inputs are d-dimensional vectors of reals, $n \geq \max(3f+1, (d+1)f+1)$ is the tight bound on the number of processes n to be able to achieve exact Byzantine consensus in a synchronous system, and $n \geq (d+2)f+1$ is tight for approximate Byzantine consensus in an asynchronous system [4, 5].

Due to the dependence of the lower bound on vector dimension d, the number of processes necessary becomes large when the vector dimension is large. With the hope of reducing the lower bound on n, we consider *relaxed* versions of Byzantine vector consensus: k-relaxed Byzantine vector consensus and (δ, p)-relaxed Byzantine vector consensus. For brevity, we will often refer to these as k-relaxed consensus and (δ, p)-relaxed consensus, respectively. For (δ, p)-relaxed consensus, we consider two formulations: constant δ and input-dependent δ, respectively. These problems are defined formally in Sections 2 and 3.

The vector consensus problem defined in [4, 5] is obtained as a special case of the above relaxed versions. In particular, as should be clearer soon, the previous vector consensus problem is identical to d-relaxed consensus and $(0, 2)$-relaxed consensus. Also note that when $d = 1$, the inputs are scalar, and all the L_p norms are identical. For the case of $d = 1$, (δ, p)-relaxed consensus with constant $\delta > 0$ is equivalent to a problem that was addressed in prior work [1]. So (δ, p)-relaxed consensus extends the prior work [1] to higher dimensions. Before we conclude this section, we define exact Byzantine vector consensus [5].

The input of each process is a d-dimensional vector of reals (i.e., the input is in $\mathbb{R}^d$). For convenience, we also view a d-dimensional vector in $\mathbb{R}^d$ as a point in the d-dimensional Euclidean space.

Exact Byzantine vector consensus must satisfy the following three conditions [5]:

1. *Agreement:* The decision (or output) vector at all the non-faulty processes must be identical.

2. *Validity:* The decision vector at each non-faulty process must be in the convex hull of the input vectors at the non-faulty processes.

3. *Termination:* Each non-faulty process must terminate after a finite amount of time.

The *approximate* Byzantine vector consensus problem is defined by replacing the (exact) agreement condition above by an approximate agreement condition [4, 5].

The relaxed consensus problems defined below weaken the above *validity* condition for Byzantine vector consensus. In Sections 2 and 3, we define these relaxations, and present our key results. At the end of the paper, we also present an open problem.

2. K-RELAXED CONSENSUS

As seen above, Byzantine vector consensus requires that the output be in the convex hull of the d-dimensional non-faulty inputs. The goal of k-relaxed consensus is to choose an output vector that is in the convex hull of projections of non-faulty inputs along any k dimensions. In particular, 1-relaxed consensus is equivalent to performing Byzantine consensus (with scalar inputs) on each coordinate of the input vector separately. To formally define k-relaxed consensus, we first present other definitions. Recall that the input of each process is a d-dimensional vector in $\mathbb{R}^d$, where $d \geq 1$. Also, $1 \leq k \leq d$. For a vector v, let $v[i]$ denote the i-th coordinate of v.

DEFINITION 1 (PROJECTION g_D). *Let $D = \{d_1, d_2, \cdots, d_k\}$ where $k \leq d$, and $1 \leq d_i < d_j \leq d$ for $1 \leq i < j \leq k$. For $u \in \mathbb{R}^d$, define projection $g_D(u) = v$ where $v \in \mathbb{R}^k$ and $v[i] = u[d_i]$.*

For example, suppose that $d = 4$, $D = \{1, 3\}$, and $u = (7, -4, -2, 0)$. Then $g_D(u) = (7, -2)$.

DEFINITION 2. *Define $\mathcal{D}_k$ to be the set of all size k subsets of $[1, d]$. That is,*

$$\mathcal{D}_k = \{D \mid D \subseteq [1, d], \; |D| = k\}.$$

For a given $D \in \mathcal{D}_k$, $g_D(S)$ defined next is the set of projections of all the vectors in S.

DEFINITION 3. *For $D \in \mathcal{D}_k$ and $S \subset \mathbb{R}^d$, define*

$$g_D(S) = \{g_D(u) \mid u \in S\}.$$

Let $\mathcal{H}(S)$ denote the convex hull of the vectors in S.

DEFINITION 4. *k-relaxed convex hull of $S \subset \mathbb{R}^d$ is defined as*

$$\{\, u \mid g_D(u) \in \mathcal{H}(g_D(S)), \;\; \forall D \in \mathcal{D}_k\}$$

Now we can define k-relaxed consensus. In particular, k-relaxed consensus must satisfy the *Agreement* and *Termination* conditions in Section 1, and the following *relaxed* validity condition.

k-relaxed validity: The decision vector at each non-faulty process must be in the *k-relaxed convex hull* of the set of input vectors at the non-faulty processes.

When $k = 1$, it should be easy to see that 1-relaxed consensus can be achieved simply by performing d instances of Byzantine consensus (with scalar inputs), with the i-th instance using as input of each process the i-th coordinate of its input vector. Thus, 1-relaxed consensus for any $d \geq 1$ is achievable with just $3f + 1$ processes. That is, for $k = 1$, the relaxation allows us to solve the problem with fewer processes than the vector consensus bound in Section 1.

Main result for k-relaxed consensus: Observe that the k-relaxed convex hull contains the convex hull of the non-faulty inputs. Thus, k-relaxed consensus allows the output to come from a larger set than the original vector consensus problem. However, for $k > 1$, this relaxation does not help in reducing the number of processes necessary to achieve k-relaxed consensus.

THEOREM 1. *$n \geq \max(3f + 1, (d + 1)f + 1)$ is necessary and sufficient for k-relaxed consensus in a synchronous system when $k > 1$.*

Since $d \geq k$, the above result applies to $d \geq 2$. The above bound is identical to the bound in Section 1 for the original vector consensus problem (for $d \geq 2$) in synchronous systems [5]. Similarly, if we relax the agreement condition to *approximate* agreement, then we can show the bound below for asynchronous systems, which is identical to the bound for approximate Byzantine vector consensus in [4, 5]. Thus, no benefit is achieved by the above relaxation when $k > 1$.

THEOREM 2. *$n \geq (d+2)f + 1$ is necessary and sufficient for* approximate *k-relaxed consensus in an asynchronous system when $k > 1$.*

3. (δ, P)-RELAXED CONSENSUS

The second relaxation allows the output to be *outside* the convex hull of inputs of the non-faulty processes, up to some distance δ of that convex hull. In particular, (δ, p)-relaxed consensus uses the following relaxed notion of a convex hull.

DEFINITION 5. *For $\delta \geq 0$ and $p \geq 1$, (δ, p)-relaxed convex hull of $S \subseteq \mathbb{R}^d$ is defined as*

$$\{u \mid \|u - v\|_p \leq \delta, \;\; v \in \mathcal{H}(S)\}$$

where $\|u - v\|_p$ is the L_p-norm distance between u and v.

Recall that $\mathcal{H}(S)$ is convex hull of S. Observe that when $\delta = 0$, the $(0, p)$-relaxed convex hull of S equals $\mathcal{H}(S)$.

Now we can define (δ, p)-relaxed consensus. In particular, (δ, p)-relaxed consensus must satisfy the *Agreement* and *Termination* conditions stated in Section 1, and the following *relaxed* validity condition.

(δ, p)-relaxed validity: The decision vector at each non-faulty process must be in the *(δ, p)-relaxed convex hull* of the set of input vectors at the non-faulty processes.

We consider two ways to specify δ: (i) δ may be specified as a constant, or (ii) δ may be input-dependent, in particular, specified as a function of the distance between the inputs at the non-faulty processes.

3.1 Constant δ

For constant δ, the relaxation of the validity condition in (δ, p)-relaxed consensus does not reduce the number of processes necessary to solve the problem, as stated below.

THEOREM 3. *$n \geq \max(3f+1, (d+1)f+1)$ is necessary and sufficient for (δ, p)-relaxed consensus in a synchronous system.*

THEOREM 4. *$n \geq (d+2)f+1$ is necessary and sufficient for* approximate *(δ, p)-relaxed consensus in an asynchronous system.*

3.2 Input-dependent δ

Unlike the above results, for input-dependent δ, we can achieve a reduction in the number of processes necessary to solve the relaxed consensus problem. Intuitively, if the inputs at the non-faulty processes are far apart, then we allow the output to be farther away from the convex hull of the non-faulty inputs. In particular, we impose the restriction that δ value must be upper bounded as follows:

$$\delta \leq \kappa(n, f, d, p)\ d_{max}$$

where (i) d_{max} is the largest distance between the inputs of non-faulty processes, where the distance is computed using the L_p-norm, and (ii) $\kappa(n, f, d, p)$ is a finite constant that may depend on n, f, d and the L_p-norm used for the distance metric, but *not* on the inputs.

For brevity, we limit the discussion below to synchronous systems. Analogous results are also obtained for asynchronous systems [6]. Similarly, for brevity, we focus on the case when $p = 2$. Results for $p > 2$ are derived from the results presented here [6].

Main results for input-dependent δ:

Similar to the well-known bound for scalar Byzantine consensus [3], it can be shown that (δ, p)-relaxed consensus is impossible when $n \leq 3f$ [6]. Therefore, we only consider $n \geq 3f+1$ below. Secondly, when $n \geq \max(3f+1, (d+1)f+1)$, the original Byzantine vector consensus problem is solvable, or equivalently, $(0, p)$-relaxed consensus is achievable. Thus, for relaxed consensus, only smaller n values are of interest. Similarly, for $d = 2$, $n \geq 3f+1$ also suffices to achieve $(0, p)$-relaxed consensus. Therefore, in the following discussion, we assume that $d \geq 3$ and $3f+1 \leq n \leq (d+1)f$ **without stating this explicitly again**.

In a given execution, let G denote the set of inputs at the non-faulty processes. Let $d_{max}(G)$ and $d_{min}(G)$ denote the maximum and minimum distance, respectively, between the points in G (distance measured using L_2-norm, i.e., $p = 2$).

We have constructively shown [6] that there exists an algorithm that achieves $(\delta(G), 2)$-relaxed consensus where $\delta(G)$ can be bounded as shown below in two special cases: (i) $f = 1$, and (ii) $f > 1$, and $n = (d+1)f$. Recall that the vectors in G can be viewed as points in a d-dimensional Euclidean space.

- $\boldsymbol{f = 1}$: If the points in G are *not* affinely independent, then $(0, 2)$-relaxed consensus can be achieved. If the points in G are affinely independent, then $(\delta(G), 2)$-relaxed consensus can be achieved, where

$$\delta(G) < \min\left(\frac{d_{min}(G)}{2}, \frac{d_{max}(G)}{n-2}\right)$$

- $\boldsymbol{f > 1}$ **and** $\boldsymbol{n = (d+1)f}$: $(\delta(G), 2)$-relaxed consensus can be achieved, where

$$\delta(G) < \frac{d_{max}(G)}{d-1}$$

The above results show that input-dependent δ can indeed be achieved using number of processes smaller than the bound for the original Byzantine vector consensus problem.

Open Problem: The above results for $f > 1$ are incomplete in that we do not have a bound on $\delta(G)$ for $n < (d+1)f$. Proving the conjecture below remains an open problem.

CONJECTURE 1. *For $d \geq 3$, $f > 1$ and $3f+1 \leq n < (d+1)f$, $(\delta(G), 2)$-relaxed consensus is achievable, where*

$$\delta(G) < \frac{d_{max}(G)}{\lfloor n/f \rfloor - 2}$$

4. REFERENCES

[1] M. J. Fischer, N. A. Lynch, and M. Merritt. *Easy impossibility proofs for distributed consensus problems.* Springer, 1990.

[2] L. Lamport, R. Shostak, and M. Pease. The byzantine generals problem. *ACM Transactions on Programming Languages and Systems (TOPLAS)*, 4(3):382–401, 1982.

[3] N. Lynch. A hundred impossibility proofs for distributed computing. In *Proceedings of the eighth annual ACM Symposium on Principles of distributed computing*, pages 1–28. ACM, 1989.

[4] H. Mendes and M. Herlihy. Multidimensional approximate agreement in byzantine asynchronous systems. In *Proceedings of the forty-fifth annual ACM symposium on Theory of computing*, pages 391–400. ACM, 2013.

[5] N. H. Vaidya and V. K. Garg. Byzantine vector consensus in complete graphs. In *Proceedings of the 2013 ACM symposium on Principles of distributed computing*, pages 65–73. ACM, 2013.

[6] Z. Xiang and N. H. Vaidya. Relaxed byzantine vector consensus. *arXiv preprint arXiv:1601.08067*, 2016.

The Cost of Unknown Diameter in Dynamic Networks*

[Extended Abstract] †

Haifeng Yu
Dept. of Computer Science
National Univ. of Singapore
haifeng@comp.nus.edu.sg

Yuda Zhao
Dept. of Computer Science
National Univ. of Singapore
yuda@comp.nus.edu.sg

Irvan Jahja
Dept. of Computer Science
National Univ. of Singapore
irvan@comp.nus.edu.sg

ABSTRACT

For dynamic networks with *unknown diameter*, we prove novel lower bounds on the time complexity of a range of basic distributed computing problems. Together with trivial upper bounds under dynamic networks with *known diameter* for these problems, our lower bounds show that the complexities of all these problems are *sensitive* to whether the diameter is known to the protocol beforehand: Not knowing the diameter increases the time complexities by a large poly(N) factor as compared to when the diameter is known, resulting in an exponential gap. Here N is the number of nodes in the network. Our lower bounds are obtained via communication complexity arguments and by reducing from the two-party DISJOINTNESSCP problem. We further prove that sometimes this large poly(N) cost can be completely avoided if the protocol is given a good estimate of N. In other words, having such an estimate makes some problems no longer sensitive to unknown diameter.

Keywords

unknown network diameter, dynamic networks, communication complexity, lower bounds

1. INTRODUCTION

Background and motivation. It is well-known that smaller network diameter often implies smaller time complexity for distributed computing problems. If the diameter D is known beforehand to the protocol (e.g., specified as an input parameter to the protocol), then the protocol needs to guarantee correctness *only* for the given D, and does not need to provide any guarantee for other D values. This allows the protocol to incur as small a complexity as possible for the given D. If D is not known beforehand, in typical static networks, D can still be efficiently estimated by building a spanning tree in just $O(D)$ rounds. This estimate can then be plugged into protocols requiring the knowledge of D. Hence, the complexities of problems in static networks are usually not *sensitive* to unknown diameter, or more rigorously, not *sensitive* to whether the diameter is known beforehand.

In recent years, there has been a growing interest in *dynamic networks* [17], where the network topology may change over time. Similar to static networks, a dynamic network's *diameter* [17] is the smallest D such that any node can causally affect any other node in the network within D rounds (see Section 2 for the formal definition). A dynamic network's diameter depends on the future behavior of the network, and hence is usually unknown to the protocol. Within such a context, we focus on the following question:

In dynamic networks, do any problems (or which problems) have complexities sensitive to unknown diameter?

The answer to this question can have broad implications: If many basic problems are sensitive, it means that different from static networks, unknown diameter in dynamic networks incurs a fundamental cost. If most problems are not sensitive, then there could be great opportunities in improving many existing protocols for dynamic networks (e.g., [5, 7, 11, 12, 14]): Some of these protocols need the diameter D to be specified as an input parameter. When D is not known beforehand, one is forced to pessimistically set $D = N$ to ensure correctness (N being the total number of nodes). Other protocols do not need such an input, but internally implicitly use N as the diameter. In summary, these protocols have not yet explored potentially reducing the complexity when D is unknown, but turns out to be much smaller than N.

To our knowledge, so far the only problem that has been proved to be sensitive to unknown diameter in dynamic networks is the *simultaneous consensus* problem. Specifically, Kuhn et al. [15] investigate a dynamic network model that ignores congestion. Using a knowledge-based proof, they show that the time complexity of simultaneous consensus can increase by a large poly(N) factor if the diameter is not known beforehand, as compared to when the diameter is known. (See later for more discussion on related work.)

Overview of our results. This paper is the first to approach the previous question without ignoring congestion. Doing so perhaps is more realistic since real systems do

*The first two authors of this paper are alphabetically ordered.
†A full version of this paper is available at `http://www.comp.nus.edu.sg/%7Eyuhf/TRA4-16.pdf`

SPAA '16, July 11 - 13, 2016, Pacific Grove, CA, USA

ISBN 978-1-4503-4210-0/16/07...$15.00
DOI: http://dx.doi.org/10.1145/2935764.2935781

not have unlimited bandwidth. We adopt the standard $\mathcal{CONGEST}$ model [19], with $O(\log N)$ message sizes. Via communication complexity arguments, we prove several novel lower bounds for *confirmed flooding*, *consensus*, and *leader election* (all defined later) in dynamic networks with unknown diameter. Our results also carry over to the HEAR-FROM-N-NODES problem [16] (see the full version [21] of this paper), which in turn, reduces to computing globally-sensitive functions [16] such as MAX.

Our lower bounds show that all these basic problems are sensitive to unknown diameter: Not knowing the diameter increases the time complexity by a poly(N) factor, as compared to when the diameter is known. Such extra complexity is due to the protocol's need to be correct under all possible diameters, even though any given execution only experiences a certain (and potentially small) diameter. Without knowing the actual diameter beforehand, the protocol is forced to be conservative. On the other hand, interestingly, we further prove that sometimes this large cost can be completely avoided if the protocol is given a good estimate of N. In other words, having such an estimate makes some problems no longer sensitive to unknown diameter.

Our results differ from Kuhn et al. [13]'s at a fundamental level: We show that when congestion is taken into account, many more basic problems (besides simultaneous consensus[1]) are sensitive to unknown diameter. Furthermore, considering congestion is *necessary* to reveal the sensitivity of these problems — in their model ignoring congestion, Kuhn et al. actually have implicitly shown that *none* of these problems is sensitive.

Our setting and our problems. In our model, nodes proceed in synchronous rounds. In each round, each node may choose to either send $O(\log N)$ bits or receive, as determined by the randomized protocol executed by the node. A message sent is received by all the sender's neighbors who are receiving in that round. The topology in each round is determined by an adversary and can be an arbitrary connected graph. (See full details of our model in Section 2.) Such a dynamic network model is similar to the evolving-graph model [2] and the T-interval model [14]. All our results and proofs also extend to the dual graph model [9, 13] without any modification.

In *confirmed flooding* (CFLOOD), a certain node V needs to propagate a token of size $O(\log N)$ bits to all nodes. V further, intuitively, wants to confirm that all nodes have received the token.[2] More rigorously, a CFLOOD protocol *terminates* when V outputs a special symbol, and the output is correct if by the time that V outputs, the token has been received by all nodes. In *consensus* (CONSENSUS), each node has an initial binary value, and they aim to achieve a consensus. The standard requirements of termination, agreement, and validity apply. The protocol *terminates* when every node decides. *Leader election* (LEADERELECT) aims to elect a leader and the protocol *terminates* when every node outputs the leader's id. The *time complexity* of a protocol captures the number of rounds needed for the protocol to terminate. To discuss the time complexity under different topologies with different diameters in a consistent way, we will often describe the time complexity under a given dynamic network in terms of *flooding rounds*, with each flooding round having D rounds. We say that a protocol has a time complexity of $s(N)$ flooding rounds if it terminates within $s(N)$ flooding rounds on all dynamic networks of size no more than N. When the context is clear, we also write $s(N)$ as s.

With known diameter, the above three problems can all be solved in $O(\log N)$ flooding rounds. With known diameter, $O(\log N)$ protocols also exist for HEAR-FROM-N-NODES, MAX, and estimating N. See the full version [21] of this paper for all these trivial upper bounds. Under unknown diameter, it was not clear whether $O(\log N)$ flooding rounds is still sufficient, and there have been no prior non-trivial lower bounds.

Our main results. Under unknown diameter, we prove the first non-trivial lower bounds of $\Omega(\sqrt[4]{N/\log N})$ flooding rounds for CFLOOD, CONSENSUS, and LEADERELECT. Such lower bounds are at least *exponentially* larger than the upper bounds when the diameter is known, resulting in an exponential gap. It is worth noting that for obtaining these lower bounds, the topologies we construct for each round all have the same diameter (asymptotically), and the dynamic network's diameter also remains fixed (asymptotically) throughout.[3] In other words, these lower bounds are *not* due to changing diameters (or increasing diameters) in each round. Rather, they are due to the difficulty of confirming whether certain information has reached a sufficient number of nodes.

Our lower bound for CFLOOD holds even if N is known, while the lower bounds for CONSENSUS and LEADERELECT hold even if the protocol knows an estimate N' of N that guarantees $|\frac{N'-N}{N}| \leq \frac{1}{3}$. On the other hand, when there exists a positive constant c such that N' guarantees $|\frac{N'-N}{N}| \leq \frac{1}{3} - c$, we further propose novel CONSENSUS and LEADERELECT protocols that do not require prior knowledge of D and yet need only $O(\log N)$ flooding rounds.

Our upper bound protocols suggest that interestingly, the cost of unknown diameter sometimes can be avoided if a good estimate of N is known. The upper bounds also imply that obtaining an N' such that $|\frac{N'-N}{N}| \leq \frac{1}{3} - c$ needs $\Omega(\sqrt[4]{N/\log N})$ flooding rounds, under unknown diameter. When the diameter is known, the full version [21] of this paper explains how to obtain such an N' in only $O(\log N)$ flooding rounds. Hence, obtaining such an N' itself is also a problem that is sensitive to unknown diameter.

Our main techniques. Our lower bounds are from communication complexity arguments, and more specifically, via reductions from the recently introduced two-party DISJOINTNESSCP [4] problem. Our reductions not only are novel themselves, but also rely on some interesting techniques that have not been exploited in related reductions in other contexts [4, 6, 16, 20, 22]:

- We design three novel types of *subnetworks* as building blocks. We then prove a general *composition* lemma that enables flexible composition of these subnetworks.
- In our reduction, we allow the two parties in the DIS-

[1]Kuhn et al.'s results on simultaneous consensus trivially carry over to the $\mathcal{CONGEST}$ model as well.

[2]V may potentially confirm without explicit acknowledgements, such as by counting the number of rounds.

[3]If needed, one can trivially modify our construction so that the diameter is always fixed, and not just fixed asymptotically.

$\mathcal{G}$	a dynamic network	Γ, Λ, Υ	3 types of subnetworks
N	number of nodes in the dynamic network	A_Γ, B_Γ	special nodes in the type-Γ subnetwork
N'	estimate of N	A_Λ, B_Λ	special nodes in the type-Λ subnetwork
D	diameter of the dynamic network	A_Υ, B_Υ	special nodes in the type-Υ subnetwork
		U, V, W	generic nodes in the network
n	size of the DISJOINTNESSCP problem	$\mathbf{x}$, $\mathbf{y}$	input strings to DISJOINTNESSCP
q	parameter in the DISJOINTNESSCP problem	x_i, y_i	ith character of $\mathbf{x}$, $\mathbf{y}$

Table 1: Key notations.

JOINTNESSCP problem to *disagree* on the dynamic network that they simulate, which is quite different from reductions in other efforts [4, 6, 16, 20, 22].

Additional related work. For static networks, Kuhn et al. [16] show that the time complexity of the HEAR-FROM-N-NODES problem is sensitive to unknown diameter in *directed static* networks. Specifically, they prove that HEAR-FROM-N-NODES needs $\tilde{\Omega}(\sqrt{N})$ flooding rounds under unknown diameter, even though it takes only a single flooding round under known diameter. Their proof uses a reduction from the classic DISJOINTNESS problem, and critically relies on the directed edges to avoid "leaking" one party's input to the other party. In comparison, our setting is undirected dynamic networks. Neither setting can be reduced to the other. Our reductions face different challenges and are perhaps more complex than the one in [16]: Our reductions need to i) reduce from a more complex and recently proposed DISJOINTNESSCP problem, ii) allow the two parties to disagree on the dynamic network that they simulate, iii) continuously change the topology (e.g., cascading edge removals), and iv) give up simulating certain nodes as the simulation progresses.

Some researchers have obtained various lower bounds under unknown diameter, for other settings such as *asynchronous* networks with edge failures [1, 10] and *anonymous* static networks without congestion [8]. These proofs all critically rely on the specifics of their settings, and have little relevance to this work. Ghaffari et al. [9] have proved that broadcasting needs $\Omega(N/\log N)$ rounds under some constant-diameter dual graph. This lower bound is, however, not due to the lack of knowledge of the diameter. Finally, this paper builds upon our own previous work [4] on the communication complexity of computing aggregate functions, and we adopt the DISJOINTNESSCP problem from there. But the actual reductions in this paper are quite different from and are more complex than those in [4]. In particular, this paper relies on multiple unique techniques as mentioned earlier.

Roadmap. The next section formalizes our model and definitions. Section 3 gives an overview of our lower bounds under unknown diameter, with details in Section 4 through 6. Section 7 presents upper bounds showing that having a good estimate of N makes some problems no longer sensitive to unknown diameter.

2. MODEL AND DEFINITIONS

Dynamic network. The dynamic network has N nodes (see Table 1 for the notation summary), each with a unique id of $\Theta(\log N)$ bits. The timing model is synchronous, and all nodes start executing the protocol from round 1 simultaneously. For convenience, we also discuss round 0, where the protocol does nothing. The set of N nodes is always fixed, but the (undirected) edges among the N nodes may change arbitrarily from round to round, subject to the constraint that the topology at any specific point of time must be connected.

For convenience, we say that the topology is determined by an *adversary.* In each round, the nodes first flip their coins (for the randomized protocol). The adversary then determines the topology for the current round, based on the randomized protocol, all the coin flip outcomes so far, and the states of the nodes. (The adversary cannot predict future coin flip outcomes.) Next each node does some local processing, and then either sends or receives, as decided by the randomized protocol.[4]

In a round, a node that chooses to send can send a single message of $O(\log N)$ bits. All neighboring nodes that choose to receive in that round will receive that message. A node may receive multiple messages from multiple neighbors in a round. The topology in each round is unknown to each node, and a node does not know its neighbors unless it receives messages from them.

Following [15], given any round $r \geq 0$ and any two nodes U and V, we say that $(U, r) \rightarrow (V, r+1)$ if either (U, V) is an edge in the dynamic network in round $r+1$ or $U = V$. We define "$\rightsquigarrow$" as the transitive closure of "$\rightarrow$": Intuitively, $(U, r) \rightsquigarrow (V, r+z)$ means that U's behavior/state in round r may potentially influence V's behavior/state in round $r+z$. The *(dynamic) diameter* of the dynamic network is defined as the minimum D such that for any round $r \geq 0$ and any two nodes U and V, $(U, r) \rightsquigarrow (V, r+D)$.

Time complexity. Since this paper mainly focuses on lower bounds, we consider Monte Carlo protocols with δ error probability (or simply called *δ-error protocols*) for solving various distributed computing problems, and we define time complexity over average coin flips and worst-case input. For lower bounds, the coins will be public, while for upper bounds the coins will be private. This enables all

[4]Such an adversary model and send/receive model have been used in prior work on dynamic networks as well (e.g., [3, 9, 13]). There have also been alternative prior models (e.g. [7, 14]) that allow a node to both send and receive in a round (e.g., if the rounds are sufficiently long to accommodate both a send and a receive). All our results continue to hold under such an alternative model, as long as the dynamic network's topology may potentially change in the middle of a round. In fact, when a round contains multiple operations, it is perhaps more realistic not to rule out potential topology changes in the middle of a round. As an analogy, for classic fault-tolerant distributed consensus in synchronous systems, researchers have always considered the possibility of a node failing in the middle of a round, where the node has completed some but not all of the operations it intended to do in that round.

our lower bounds to trivially extend to worst-case coin flips, Las Vegas protocols, and private coin protocols. To discuss the time complexities of these protocols under different topologies with different diameters in a consistent way, we will often describe the time complexity under a given dynamic network in terms of *flooding rounds*, with each flooding rounds being exactly D rounds. Given a dynamic network $\mathcal{G}$, a protocol's *time complexity over* $\mathcal{G}$ is defined as the number of flooding rounds needed for the protocol to terminate, over average coin flips and worst-case input over $\mathcal{G}$. The protocol's *time complexity* is defined as the largest time complexity over all possible $\mathcal{G}$'s with no more than N nodes.

Communication complexity. For positive integer n and positive odd integer $q \geq 3$, DisjointnessCP$_{n,q}$ [4] is a two-party communication complexity problem where Alice and Bob have input strings $\mathbf{x}$ and $\mathbf{y}$, respectively. Here $\mathbf{x}$ and $\mathbf{y}$ each have n characters, with each character being an integer in $[0, q-1]$. Let x_i (y_i) denote the ith character in $\mathbf{x}$ ($\mathbf{y}$), for $1 \leq i \leq n$. Alice and Bob aim to compute DisjointnessCP$(\mathbf{x}, \mathbf{y})$, which is defined to be 0 if there exists any i such that $x_i = y_i = 0$, and 1 otherwise. The inputs $\mathbf{x}$ and $\mathbf{y}$ must satisfy the *cycle promise* [4] in the sense that for any $i \in [1, n]$, we must have either i) $y_i = x_i - 1$, or ii) $y_i = x_i + 1$, or iii) $(x_i, y_i) = (0, 0)$, or iv) $(x_i, y_i) = (q-1, q-1)$. Chen et al. [4] have shown that the cycle promise is not an ad hoc promise — for a wide class of reductions, the cycle promise can in some sense be "derived" from the reduction. Larger q in DisjointnessCP$_{n,q}$ means that some character will have a small number of occurrences in $\mathbf{x}$ and $\mathbf{y}$, and this can be exploited by the upper bound protocol [4] to solve DisjointnessCP$_{n,q}$ more efficiently. The following lower bound is from [4]:

Theorem 1. (From [4].) *A $\frac{1}{5}$-error public coin Monte Carlo protocol for* DisjointnessCP$_{n,q}$ *must incur at least $\Omega(\frac{n}{q^2}) - O(\log n)$ bits of communication between Alice and Bob, over worst-case $\mathbf{x}$, $\mathbf{y}$, and worst-case coin flips.*

For this paper, we will need the following corollary (see the full version [21] of this paper for the simple proof):

Corollary 2. *For any $\frac{1}{6}$-error public coin Monte Carlo protocol for* DisjointnessCP$_{n,q}$, *there exist $\mathbf{x}_0$ and $\mathbf{y}_0$ such that* DisjointnessCP$_{n,q}(\mathbf{x}_0, \mathbf{y}_0) = 1$ *and the protocol incurs at least $\Omega(\frac{n}{q^2}) - O(\log n)$ bits over $\mathbf{x}_0$, $\mathbf{y}_0$, and average coin flips.*

3. OVERVIEW OF OUR LOWER BOUNDS

This section provides an overview of our lower bound proofs for CFlood and Consensus. Consensus can be easily reduced to LeaderElect (see the full version [21] of this paper), so we do not need to separately prove a lower bound for LeaderElect.

3.1 High-level Structure of Our Proof

Our lower bound proofs for CFlood and Consensus have similar high-level structures, and we use CFlood as an example. Our lower bound for CFlood is based on a reduction from DisjointnessCP. Putting it another way, given a (black-box) oracle protocol for solving CFlood, Alice and Bob will solve DisjointnessCP$(\mathbf{x}, \mathbf{y})$ by simulating the execution of that oracle protocol under a certain dynamic network.

The specifics of this dynamic network depend on the values of both $\mathbf{x}$ and $\mathbf{y}$: The dynamic network is constructed in such a way that it has $O(1)$ diameter if DisjointnessCP$(\mathbf{x}, \mathbf{y}) = 1$, and $\Omega(q)$ diameter if DisjointnessCP$(\mathbf{x}, \mathbf{y}) = 0$. Assume that the CFlood oracle protocol promises to terminate within s flooding rounds. We can then show that i) if DisjointnessCP$(\mathbf{x}, \mathbf{y}) = 1$, then the CFlood protocol under the corresponding network should terminate within $O(s)$ rounds, and ii) if DisjointnessCP$(\mathbf{x}, \mathbf{y}) = 0$, then the CFlood protocol under the corresponding network takes $\Omega(q)$ rounds to terminate. (Note that it is not $\Omega(qs)$ rounds since the protocol may terminate in less than s flooding rounds.)

We will choose a proper value of q to ensure a gap between $O(s)$ and $\Omega(q)$. Alice and Bob will simulate the execution of the CFlood oracle protocol for $O(s)$ rounds. If the CFlood protocol terminates within these $O(s)$ rounds, then Alice and Bob claim DisjointnessCP$(\mathbf{x}, \mathbf{y}) = 1$. Otherwise they claim DisjointnessCP$(\mathbf{x}, \mathbf{y}) = 0$. In such a way, Alice and Bob successfully solve DisjointnessCP after simulating the CFlood oracle protocol for $O(s)$ rounds.

Alice and Bob will need to incur communication during this simulation, as following. There are two special nodes A_Γ and A_Λ in the dynamic network. During each round of the simulation, to enable the simulation to later continue onto the next round, Alice needs to forward to Bob all messages sent by A_Γ and A_Λ in the CFlood oracle protocol in that round. Under the $\mathcal{CONGEST}$ model, A_Γ and A_Λ will altogether send at most $O(\log N)$ bits in one round. Hence Alice will send at most $O(\log N)$ bits to Bob in one round of the simulation, and $O(s \log N)$ bits throughout the simulation. Similarly, there are two additional special nodes B_Γ and B_Λ in the dynamic network, and Bob will forward to Alice all messages sent by B_Γ and B_Λ. Altogether, the number of bits exchanged between Alice and Bob during the simulation is $O(s \log N)$ bits. (This is where the time complexity upper bound of s gets connected to the communication complexity upper bound of $O(s \log N)$.)

Finally, by the communication complexity lower bound on DisjointnessCP, Alice and Bob need to exchange at least $\Omega(\frac{n}{q^2}) - O(\log n)$ bits to solve DisjointnessCP. This gives us the equation $O(s \log N) = \Omega(\frac{n}{q^2}) - O(\log n)$. Solving this equation gives us a lower bound on s.

3.2 Adversaries and Subnetworks

The 3 adversaries. As explained above, the specifics of the dynamic network used in the reduction depends on the value of both $\mathbf{x}$ and $\mathbf{y}$. More precisely, we say that the dynamic network's topology in each round is determined by a *reference adversary*, whose behavior is a function of $\mathbf{x}$ and $\mathbf{y}$. Since Alice does not see $\mathbf{y}$, Alice does not know the reference adversary. Hence the crux in the reduction is to enable Alice to still properly simulate without seeing $\mathbf{y}$. Putting it another way, we want the dynamic network to be "indistinguishable" from Alice's perspective, as long as $\mathbf{x}$ remains fixed and regardless of $\mathbf{y}$. Such discussions symmetrically apply to Bob as well.

To this end, we will exploit the properties of the cycle promise in the DisjointnessCP problem. Furthermore, our reduction will let Alice simulate her own adversary based on **x**, and Bob simulate his own adversary based on **y**. We will allow the 3 adversaries (i.e., the reference adversary, Alice's simulated adversary, and Bob's simulated adversary) to be pairwise slightly different. We will nevertheless ensure that the entire simulation is still "meaningful".

The subnetworks. The dynamic networks we use to prove our lower bounds are obtained by composing various novel types of subnetworks (type-Γ, type-Λ, and type-Υ). Each type of subnetwork is itself a dynamic network uniquely determined by the given **x** and **y**. We will also describe the 3 adversaries for each subnetwork. Unless otherwise stated, each subnetwork has $\Theta(nq)$ nodes, and by itself does not need to be connected in each round. Section 4 and Section 5 will the present the details of these subnetworks. The following provides an overview:

- Type-Γ subnetwork: If DISJOINTNESSCP$(\mathbf{x},\mathbf{y}) = 0$, then there exist $\Omega(q)$ nodes in the type-Γ subnetwork that are disconnected from the rest of the type-Γ subnetwork, starting from the beginning of round 1. These $\Omega(q)$ nodes are arranged into a line, and will connect to some other subnetwork. If DISJOINTNESSCP$(\mathbf{x},\mathbf{y}) = 1$, then the type-$\Gamma$ subnetwork is always connected with $O(1)$ diameter.
- Type-Λ subnetwork: If DISJOINTNESSCP$(\mathbf{x},\mathbf{y}) = 0$, then the type-$\Lambda$ subnetwork will contain at least one node as a *mounting point*. It takes $\Omega(q)$ rounds for a mounting point to causally affect all other nodes in the subnetwork. If DISJOINTNESSCP $(\mathbf{x},\mathbf{y}) = 1$, then there is no mounting point and the diameter of the type-Λ subnetwork is $O(1)$.
- Type-Υ subnetwork: If DISJOINTNESSCP$(\mathbf{x},\mathbf{y}) = 0$, the type-$\Upsilon$ subnetwork is the same as the type-Λ subnetwork. If DISJOINTNESSCP $(\mathbf{x},\mathbf{y}) = 1$, the type-$\Upsilon$ subnetwork is empty and has no nodes.

3.3 Composing Subnetworks to Obtain Lower Bounds for CFLOOD and CONSENSUS

To prove the lower bound on CFLOOD (details in Section 6), we will compose the type-Γ subnetwork with the type-Λ subnetwork together:

- When DISJOINTNESSCP$(\mathbf{x},\mathbf{y}) = 1$, our composition will connect the type-Γ subnetwork with the type-Λ subnetwork together using one edge. Since each of these subnetworks is itself connected and has a diameter of $O(1)$, doing so will result in a dynamic network with $O(1)$ diameter.
- When DISJOINTNESSCP$(\mathbf{x},\mathbf{y}) = 0$, there will be $\Omega(q)$ nodes disconnected from the rest of the type-Γ subnetwork. Our composition will arrange them into a line and then connect them to a mounting point in the type-Λ subnetwork. (We still connect the rest of the type-Γ subnetwork with the type-Λ subnetwork together using one edge as earlier.) This leads to a dynamic network over which the CFLOOD protocol needs to take $\Omega(q)$ rounds to terminate.

To prove the lower bound on CONSENSUS, one way is to reduce from CFLOOD. Specifically, Kuhn et al. describe a reduction from HEAR-FROM-N-NODES to CONSENSUS [15], while CFLOOD reduces to HEAR-FROM-N-NODES (see the full version [21] of this paper). But Kuhn et al.'s reduction does not directly capture our model — for example, we consider Monte Carlo protocols. While we could adapt that reduction, since we already have the composition lemma, we will conveniently prove a lower bound on CONSENSUS by composing the type-Λ subnetwork with the type-Υ subnetwork (details in Section 6):

- When DISJOINTNESSCP$(\mathbf{x},\mathbf{y}) = 1$, the type-$\Upsilon$ subnetwork is empty. The dynamic network resulted from our composition will simply be the type-Λ subnetwork with $O(1)$ diameter.
- When DISJOINTNESSCP$(\mathbf{x},\mathbf{y}) = 0$, both the type-$\Lambda$ subnetwork and the type-Υ subnetwork have a mounting point. Our composition connects some arbitrary mounting point in the type-Λ subnetwork with some arbitrary mounting point in the type-Υ subnetwork. Recall that in the CONSENSUS problem, each node has a binary initial value. We set the initial values so that all nodes in the type-Λ subnetwork have the same initial values, while all nodes in the type-Υ subnetwork have the opposite initial values. We will prove that over such a dynamic network, the CONSENSUS protocol takes $\Omega(q)$ rounds to terminate on all nodes.

Finally, note that the number of nodes in the type-Υ subnetwork is not fixed, and depends on **x** and **y**. Hence Alice and Bob, without knowing the other party's input, cannot determine the number of nodes in the type-Υ subnetwork. Thus the CONSENSUS lower bound here does not hold when N is known. But Alice and Bob can nevertheless produce an N' with limited accuracy (i.e., $|\frac{N'-N}{N}| \le \frac{1}{3}$) to feed into the oracle protocol if needed.

4. TYPE-Γ SUBNETWORK

The reference adversary. Given **x** and **y**, Figure 1 illustrates the type-Γ subnetwork. In round 0, it has n groups of vertical chains, where each group has $\frac{q-1}{2}$ vertical chains. Each chain has three nodes and two edges. We call the edge adjacent to the top node (bottom node) as the *top edge* (*bottom edge*). We connect the top node on every chain to a special node A_Γ, and the bottom node on every chain to a special node B_Γ. For $1 \le i \le n$, all the $\frac{q-1}{2}$ top nodes (bottom nodes) in the ith group are labeled x_i (y_i). We use $|_y^x$ to denote a chain whose top node is labeled x and whose bottom node is labeled y.

Let t be any non-negative integer. The reference adversary for the type-Γ subnetwork manipulates certain chains according to the following rules:

1. For every chain in the form of $|_{2t-1}^{2t}$, the adversary removes the top edge at the beginning of round $t+1$.
2. For every chain in the form of $|_{2t}^{2t-1}$, the adversary removes the bottom edge at the beginning of round $t+1$.
3. For every chain in the form of $|_{2t+1}^{2t}$, the adversary removes the top edge at the beginning of either round $t+2$ (if the middle node on the chain is receiving in round $t+1$) or round $t+1$ (otherwise).

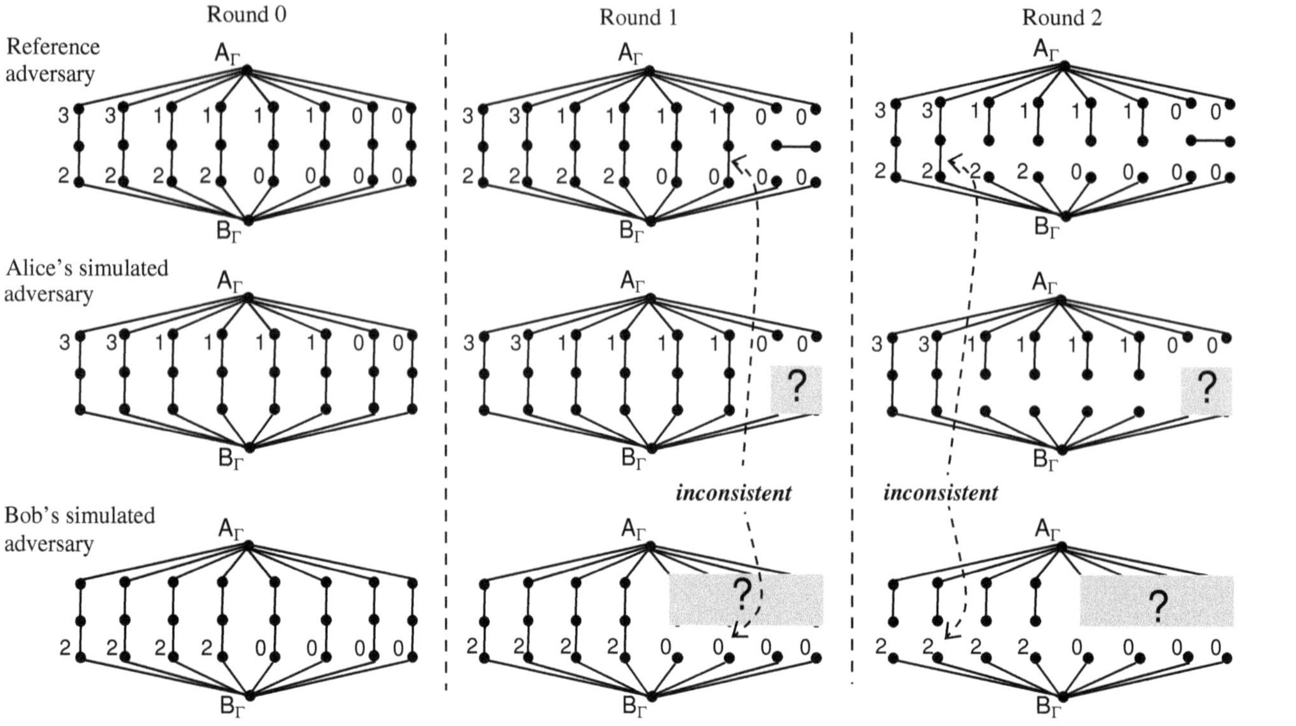

Figure 1: The three adversaries of the type-Γ subnetwork, for $n = 4$, $q = 5$, $\mathbf{x} = 3110$, and $\mathbf{y} = 2200$. The numbers beside the nodes are labels. This example assumes that the middle nodes on all the chains are receiving.

4. For every chain in the form of $|^{2t+1}_{2t}$, the adversary removes the bottom edge at the beginning of either round $t+2$ (if the middle node on the chain is receiving in round $t+1$) or round $t+1$ (otherwise).

5. For all chains in the form of $|^{0}_{0}$, the adversary removes both the top edges and the bottoms edges at the beginning of round 1, hence disconnecting all the middle nodes on these chains. The adversary connects all such middle nodes into a line. Obviously, we will have at least $\frac{q-1}{2}$ chains in the form of $|^{0}_{0}$ if DISJOINTNESSCP$(\mathbf{x}, \mathbf{y}) = 0$. In such a case, we will have a line of $\Omega(q)$ nodes which can be connected to some other subnetwork to boost the diameter.

Finally, the adversary does not manipulate $|^{q-1}_{q-1}$ chains, which are the only remaining kind of chains.

Adversaries simulated by Alice and Bob. Alice will not be able to simulate this reference adversary, because Alice does not know $\mathbf{y}$ and hence does not know the labels of the bottom nodes. Overcoming this issue is a key challenge in the reduction. Let "*" be a wildcard label and let t be any non-negative integer. Based on only $\mathbf{x}$, Alice simulates the following adversary (called *Alice's simulated adversary*) instead:

- For every chain in the form of $|^{2t}_{*}$, the adversary removes the top edge at the beginning of round $t+1$.
- For every chain in the form of $|^{2t+1}_{*}$, the adversary removes the bottom edge at the beginning of round $t+2$.

Our simulation will only last for $\frac{q-1}{2}$ rounds, and hence Alice's adversary will not have removed any edges from $|^{q-1}_{*}$ chains and $|^{q-2}_{*}$ chains by the end of the simulation.

Similarly, Bob simulates the following adversary (called *Bob's simulated adversary*):

- For every chain in the form of $|^{*}_{2t}$, the adversary removes the bottom edge at the beginning of round $t+1$.
- For every chain in the form of $|^{*}_{2t+1}$, the adversary removes the top edge at the beginning of round $t+2$.

Note that Alice's simulated adversary and Bob's simulated adversary diverge. For example, for a $|^{2t}_{2t+1}$ chain, Alice's simulated adversary removes the top edge in round $t+1$, while Bob's simulated adversary does so in round $t+2$.

Communication between Alice and Bob. To allow the simulation to continue properly, during every round of the simulation, Alice will always forward to Bob the message sent by the node A_Γ (if any). We will later show that Alice can always generate those messages. Similarly, Bob will forward to Alice all messages sent by B_Γ.

A concrete example. Part of our proof will need to show that even though the three adversaries (i.e., the reference adversary, Alice's simulated adversary, and Bob's simulated adversary) can be pairwise different and inconsistent, the behavior of the oracle protocol under the three different adversaries will nevertheless be "consistent enough" to enable simulation.

To get some intuition, Figure 1 illustrates the three adversaries. In round 0, the topology is the same under all three adversaries. Next in round 1, under the reference adversary, all the edges in the two $|^0_0$ chains are removed. Under Alice's simulated adversary, the top edges of the two $|^0_*$ chains are removed. Alice cannot infer (as indicated by "?" in the figure) whether the bottom edges are removed under the reference adversary. But since the top edges on these two chains have already been removed, the behavior of the nodes in the "?" region cannot causally affect other nodes, without passing through B_Γ first. Since Bob will forward to Alice all the messages sent by B_Γ, Alice can afford to simply give up simulating those nodes in the "?" region. Similar arguments apply to Bob.

Next consider the $|^1_0$ chains in round 1 and $|^3_2$ chains in round 2. In Figure 1, Bob's simulated adversary removes the bottom edge of every $|^1_0$ chain at the beginning of round 1, while the reference adversary will not remove those edges until round 2. Here this edge removal will causally affect B_Γ, preventing Bob from properly simulating B_Γ. We will leverage the following observation to address this issue. Let the three nodes on a $|^1_0$ chain be U, V, and W, from the top to the bottom. If V is receiving in round 1 (as in Figure 1), then W cannot tell whether the bottom edge is removed in round 1 or round 2. Hence even though Bob simulates edge removal in round 1, so far as the protocol is concerned, it is equivalent to removing the bottom edge in round 2. The case for V sending in round 1 is similar.

Correctness arguments. We next formalize the correctness arguments. In any round, a node is defined to be either *spoiled* or *non-spoiled* with respect to Alice. Intuitively, the behavior of a non-spoiled node for Alice depends only on Alice's input $\mathbf{x}$ and messages sent by B_Γ. We will eventually aim to prove that Alice can properly simulate the execution of the oracle protocol on a node in a round r ($r \le \frac{q-1}{2}$), if it is non-spoiled for Alice in that round. Let t be any non-negative integer. Consider any given chain and let the three nodes on the chain be U, V, and W, from the top to the bottom:

- If the chain is in the form of $|^{2t}_*$, then V and W become spoiled since the beginning of round $t+1$.
- If the chain is in the form of $|^{2t+1}_*$, then W becomes spoiled since the beginning of round $t+1$.

We define B_Γ to be spoiled for Alice from the beginning of round 1. A node is *non-spoiled* for Alice unless it is spoiled for Alice. In particular, A_Γ is always non-spoiled for Alice.

We similarly define these concepts for Bob:

- If the chain is in the form of $|^*_{2t}$, then V and U become spoiled since the beginning of round $t+1$.
- If the chain is in the form of $|^*_{2t+1}$, then U becomes spoiled since the beginning of round $t+1$.

We define A_Γ to be spoiled for Bob from the beginning of round 1. A node is *non-spoiled* to Bob unless it is spoiled for Bob. B_Γ is always non-spoiled for Bob.

The following lemma claims that for any node Z that is non-spoiled for Alice in a round and is receiving in that round, Alice is able to determine which nodes can potentially send messages to Z in that round under the reference adversary, by simply simulating her own adversary based on $\mathbf{x}$. The lemma further claims that any node that is sending messages to Z must be either non-spoiled for Alice or the node B_Γ. All these will allow us to later prove in Section 6, via an induction, that Alice can simulate all her non-spoiled nodes.

LEMMA 3. *Consider any round r where $1 \le r \le \frac{q-1}{2}$ in the type-Γ subnetwork. For any non-spoiled node Z for Alice (Bob) in round r that is receiving in round r, let $\mathcal{S}$ be the set of Z's neighbors under the reference adversary in round r, and $\mathcal{S}'$ be the set of Z's neighbors under the adversary simulated by Alice (Bob) in round r. Then i) all nodes in $(\mathcal{S} \setminus \mathcal{S}') \cup (\mathcal{S}' \setminus \mathcal{S})$ are receiving in round r, and ii) a node in $\mathcal{S}'$ is either the node B_Γ (A_Γ) or a non-spoiled node for Alice (Bob) in round $r-1$.*

PROOF. It suffices to prove the lemma for Alice. In the following, the notions of spoiled and non-spoiled nodes are always with respect to Alice. First, B_Γ is always spoiled in all rounds, and A_Γ is always non-spoiled. For A_Γ, we have $\mathcal{S} = \mathcal{S}'$ and they contain all the top nodes on all the chains. None of these top nodes are ever spoiled for Alice. Next we consider the non-spoiled nodes on all the chains. Consider any given chain, and let U, V, and W be the nodes on the chain from the top to the bottom. We will enumerate all 6 kinds of chains. Let t be any non-negative integer.

For a $|^{2t}_{2t+1}$ chain, U is always non-spoiled, and V and W are non-spoiled iff $r \le t$:

- For node U, we exhaustively enumerate all scenarios: i) If $r \le t$, then $\mathcal{S} = \mathcal{S}' = \{A_\Gamma, V\}$. By definition, both A_Γ and V are non-spoiled in round $r-1$. ii) If $r \ge t+2$, then $\mathcal{S} = \mathcal{S}' = \{A_\Gamma\}$. By definition, A_Γ is non-spoiled in round $r-1$. iii) If $r = t+1$ and V is sending in round $t+1$, then $\mathcal{S} = \mathcal{S}' = \{A_\Gamma\}$ and A_Γ is non-spoiled in round $r-1$. iv) If $r = t+1$ and V is receiving in round $t+1$, then $\mathcal{S} = \{A_\Gamma, V\}$ and $\mathcal{S}' = \{A_\Gamma\}$. Again, A_Γ is non-spoiled in round $r-1$.
- For node V and $r \le t$, we have $\mathcal{S} = \mathcal{S}' = \{U, W\}$, and both nodes are non-spoiled in round $r-1$.
- For node W and $r \le t$, we have $\mathcal{S} = \mathcal{S}' = \{V, B_\Gamma\}$, where V is non-spoiled in round $r-1$.

For a $|^{2t}_{2t-1}$ chain, U is always non-spoiled, and V and W are non-spoiled iff $r \le t$:

- For node U, we exhaustively enumerate all scenarios: i) If $r \le t$, then $\mathcal{S} = \mathcal{S}' = \{A_\Gamma, V\}$. By definition, both A_Γ and V are non-spoiled in round $r-1$. ii) If $r \ge t+1$, then $\mathcal{S} = \mathcal{S}' = \{A_\Gamma\}$. By definition, A_Γ is non-spoiled in round $r-1$.
- For node V and $r \le t$, we have $\mathcal{S} = \mathcal{S}' = \{U, W\}$, and both nodes are non-spoiled in round $r-1$.
- For node W and $r \le t$, we have $\mathcal{S} = \mathcal{S}' = \{V, B_\Gamma\}$, where V is non-spoiled in round $r-1$.

For a $|^{2t+1}_{2t}$ chain, U and V are always non-spoiled, and W is non-spoiled iff $r \le t$:

- For node U, $\mathcal{S} = \mathcal{S}' = \{A_\Gamma, V\}$. By definition, both A_Γ and V are non-spoiled in round $r-1$.
- For node V, we exhaustively enumerate all scenarios: i) If $r \le t$, we have $\mathcal{S} = \mathcal{S}' = \{U, W\}$, and both nodes are non-spoiled in round $r-1$. ii) If $r \ge t+2$,

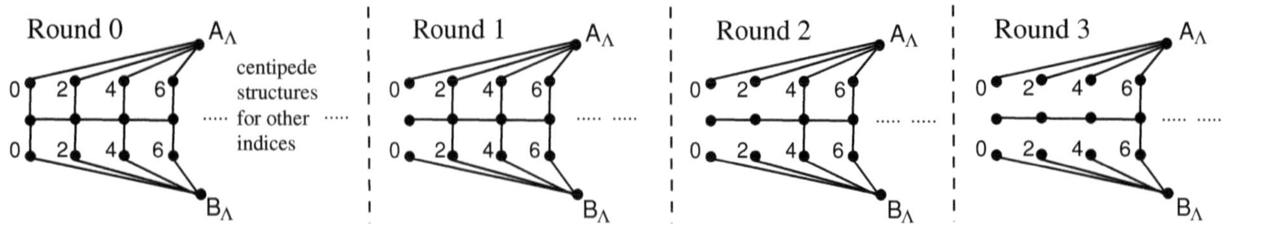

Figure 2: The ith centipede structure in the type-Λ subnetwork under the reference adversary, for $x_i = y_i = 0$ and $q = 7$.

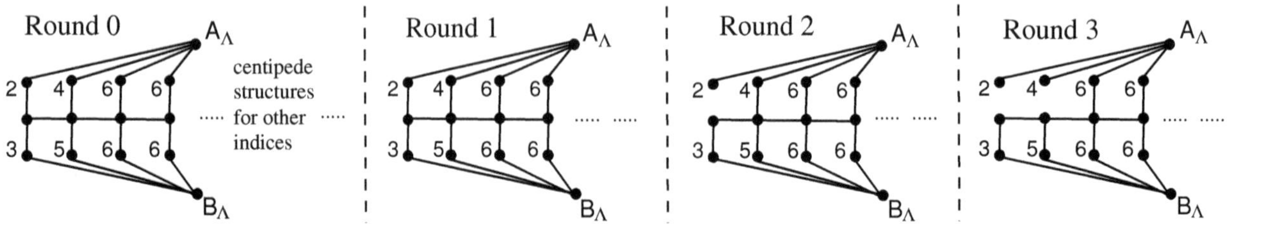

Figure 3: The ith centipede structure in the type-Λ subnetwork under the reference adversary, for $x_i = 2$, $y_i = 3$, and $q = 7$, assuming all middle nodes on all chains are sending.

then $\mathcal{S} = \mathcal{S}' = \{U\}$. By definition, U is non-spoiled in round $r-1$. iii) If $r = t+1$, recall that we only need to consider the case where V is receiving in round $t+1$. We have $\mathcal{S} = \mathcal{S}' = \{U, W\}$, and both U and W are non-spoiled in round $r-1$.

- For node W and $r \leq t$, we have $\mathcal{S} = \mathcal{S}' = \{V, B_\Gamma\}$, where V is non-spoiled in round $r-1$.

For a $|_{2t}^{2t-1}$ chain, U and V are always non-spoiled, and W is non-spoiled iff $r \leq t-1$:

- For node U, $\mathcal{S} = \mathcal{S}' = \{A_\Gamma, V\}$. By definition, both A_Γ and V are non-spoiled in round $r-1$.

- For node V, we enumerate all scenarios: i) If $r \leq t$, we have $\mathcal{S} = \mathcal{S}' = \{U, W\}$, and both nodes are non-spoiled in round $r-1$. ii) If $r \geq t+1$, then $\mathcal{S} = \mathcal{S}' = \{U\}$. By definition, U is non-spoiled in round $r-1$.

- For node W and $r \leq t-1$, we have $\mathcal{S} = \mathcal{S}' = \{V, B_\Gamma\}$, where V is non-spoiled in round $r-1$.

For a $|_{q-1}^{q-1}$ chain, U, V, and W are always non-spoiled for all $r \leq \frac{q-1}{2}$:

- For node U , we have $\mathcal{S} = \mathcal{S}' = \{A_\Gamma, V\}$. By definition, both A_Γ and V are non-spoiled in round $r-1$.

- For node V, we have $\mathcal{S} = \mathcal{S}' = \{U, W\}$. By definition, both U and W are non-spoiled in round $r-1$.

- For node W, we have $\mathcal{S} = \mathcal{S}' = \{B_\Gamma, W\}$. By definition, W is non-spoiled in round $r-1$.

Finally, for a $|_0^0$ chain, only U can be non-spoiled for $r \geq 1$. We have $\mathcal{S} = \mathcal{S}' = \{A_\Gamma\}$, where A_Γ is always non-spoiled. $\square$

5. TYPE-Λ AND TYPE-Υ SUBNETWORKS

We describe type-Λ subnetwork first and type-Υ subnetwork next.

Mounting points. Recall from Section 3 that the type-Λ subnetwork should contain at least one node as a *mounting point* when DisjointnessCP$(\mathbf{x}, \mathbf{y}) = 0$. This allows us to later attach nodes to a mounting point when needed. Whether a mounting point exists depends on both $\mathbf{x}$ and $\mathbf{y}$. Hence if a mounting point exists, without seeing both $\mathbf{x}$ and $\mathbf{y}$, neither Alice nor Bob can properly simulate it. Intuitively, a mounting point is always spoiled for both Alice and Bob. We need to prevent a mounting point from quickly affecting all other nodes, since any nodes causally affected by a mounting point intuitively become spoiled as well. We will carefully remove edges to achieve this. On the other hand, the type-Λ subnetwork needs to have $O(1)$ diameter when DisjointnessCP$(\mathbf{x}, \mathbf{y}) = 1$. Thus the crux here is that such edge removals should not increase the diameter of the type-Λ subnetwork when DisjointnessCP$(\mathbf{x}, \mathbf{y}) = 1$. While we will still use the trick of having three different adversaries, that trick by itself no longer suffices here. We will need an additional technique of *cascading edge removals* over novel *centipede structures*.

The 3 adversaries and the spoiled nodes. Given $\mathbf{x}$ and $\mathbf{y}$, Figure 2 and 3 illustrate the type-Λ subnetwork. In round 0, the topology has n *centipede structures*, one for each index $i \in [1, n]$. Each centipede structure has $\frac{q+1}{2}$ vertical chains, and each chain has three nodes. The middle nodes on all chains in a centipede structure are connected and form a horizontal line. The top (bottom) nodes on all chains of all centipede structures connect to a special node A_Λ (B_Λ). Consider the jth chain in the ith centipede structure for $1 \leq j \leq \frac{q+1}{2}$ and $1 \leq i \leq n$, and let the three nodes on the chain be U, V, and W, from the top to the bottom. We label U and W as $\min(x_i + 2j - 2, q-1)$ and $\min(y_i + 2j - 2, q-1)$, respectively. The middle nodes of all $|_0^0$ chains are defined as mounting points. The reference adversary for the type-Λ

subnetwork follows the same rules as the reference adversary for the type-Γ subnetwork in Section 4, except that the 5th rule is replaced by:

5. Let t be any integer in $[0, \frac{q-3}{2}]$. For all chains in the form of $|_{2t}^{2t}$, the adversary removes both the top edges and the bottom edges at the beginning of round $t+1$.

Note that cascading edge removals are implicit here — edge removals following all the rules will be cascading.

Finally, the adversary simulated by Alice (Bob) in the type-Λ subnetwork follows the exact same rules (but now based on the labels in the type-Λ subnetwork) as earlier in the type-Γ subnetwork in Section 4. Spoiled/non-spoiled nodes are also defined according to exactly the same rules as in Section 4 (after replacing A_Γ with A_Λ, and replacing B_Γ with B_Λ). In the simulation, Alice will always forward to Bob all messages sent by A_Λ. (We will later show that Alice can always generate those messages.) Similarly, Bob will forward all messages sent by B_Λ.

A concrete example. We aim to highlight here the role of cascading edge removals, while focusing on the reference adversary. Figure 2 illustrates the ith centipede structure when $x_i = y_i = 0$. This structure has a mounting point, which is the middle node of the $|_0^0$ chain. A mounting point is spoiled from the beginning of round 1 for both Alice and Bob. To prevent it from causally affecting A_Λ and B_Λ, we remove the two edges on the $|_0^0$ chain at the beginning of round 1, remove the edges on the $|_2^2$ chain at the beginning of round 2, and so on.

One may wonder why we cannot simply remove the edges on all these chains at the same time. To understand, imagine that the two edges on the $|_4^4$ chain in Figure 2 are removed in round 1 instead of in round 3. Once we do this in the reference adversary, Alice (Bob) will no longer be able to simulate the middle node V on this chain, since based on $\mathbf{x}$ ($\mathbf{y}$), Alice (Bob) cannot tell whether both edges on the chain have been removed. Intuitively, V becomes spoiled. V may now causally affect A_Λ and B_Λ, via the $|_6^6$ chain. This can happen rather quickly since V is just next to the $|_6^6$ chain.

Finally, we will also need to remove edges in the ith centipede structure when $x_i + y_i > 0$, as illustrated in Figure 3 where $x_i = 2$ and $y_i = 3$. While not immediately obvious, cascading edge removals play a critical role here as well: The middle node V on the $|_3^2$ chain becomes spoiled for Alice at the beginning of round 2, and cascading edge removals prevent V from causally affecting A_Λ via the $|_5^4$ chain.

Correctness arguments. The following lemma (whose proof is in the full version [21] of this paper) is the same as Lemma 3 except that it is now for the type-Λ subnetwork:

LEMMA 4. *Consider any round r where $1 \le r \le \frac{q-1}{2}$ in the type-Λ subnetwork. For any non-spoiled node Z for Alice (Bob) in round r that is receiving in round r, let $\mathcal{S}$ be the set of Z's neighbors under the reference adversary in round r, and $\mathcal{S}'$ be the set of Z's neighbors under the adversary simulated by Alice (Bob) in round r. Then i) all nodes in $(\mathcal{S} \setminus \mathcal{S}') \cup (\mathcal{S}' \setminus \mathcal{S})$ are receiving in round r, and ii) a node in $\mathcal{S}'$ is either B_Λ (A_Λ) or a non-spoiled node for Alice (Bob) in round $r-1$.*

Type-Υ subnetwork. So far we have only described the type-Λ subnetwork, and we now move on to the type-Υ subnetwork.. Under the reference adversary, the type-Υ subnetwork is the same as the type-Λ subnetwork when DISJOINTNESSCP$(\mathbf{x}, \mathbf{y}) = 0$. To avoid confusion, we rename A_Λ (B_Λ) to be A_Υ (B_Υ) in the type-Υ subnetwork. When DISJOINTNESSCP$(\mathbf{x}, \mathbf{y}) = 1$, the type-$\Upsilon$ subnetwork is an empty network with no nodes. Under Alice's and Bob's simulated adversary, the type-Υ subnetwork is always empty (even when DISJOINTNESSCP$(\mathbf{x}, \mathbf{y}) = 0$). We define all nodes (if any) in the type-Υ subnetwork as always spoiled for both Alice and Bob. In the simulation, Alice (Bob) does not need to forward messages sent by A_Υ (B_Υ) to the other party.

6. LOWER BOUNDS FOR CFLOOD AND CONSENSUS

The composition lemma. We first present a lemma to enable the composition of multiple subnetworks. While this lemma can be extremely general, to simplify discussion, we only present a restricted form. Given a dynamic network $\mathcal{G}$ and a round, we use $\mathcal{G}^N$ and $\mathcal{G}^E$ to denote the set of vertices and edges in that round, respectively. A dynamic network $\mathcal{G}$ is the *composition network* of two dynamic networks $\mathcal{G}_1$ and $\mathcal{G}_2$ via *bridging edge set* $\mathcal{E}$ if for every round, $\mathcal{G}^N = \mathcal{G}_1^N \cup \mathcal{G}_2^N$ and $\mathcal{G}^E = \mathcal{G}_1^E \cup \mathcal{G}_2^E \cup \mathcal{E}$. All edges (called *bridging edges*) in the bridging edge set $\mathcal{E}$ are required to span $\mathcal{G}_1$ and $\mathcal{G}_2$. Note that $\mathcal{E}$ does not change from round to round. A mapping from DISJOINTNESSCP instances to dynamic networks is called a *composition mapping* of type-φ_1 and type-φ_2 subnetworks ($\varphi_1, \varphi_2 \in \{\Gamma, \Lambda, \Upsilon\}$), if the mapped dynamic network $\mathcal{G}$ is always a composition network of the corresponding type-φ_1 subnetwork and type-φ_2 subnetwork for the given DISJOINTNESSCP instance. Note that the bridging edge set is allowed to differ under different DISJOINTNESSCP instances. A bridging edge in a dynamic network appeared in a composition mapping is *sensitive for Alice (Bob)* if at least one of its end points is a non-spoiled node for Alice (Bob) in that dynamic network in the first round. A composition mapping is called a *simple composition mapping* if i) both end points of every sensitive bridging edge for Alice (Bob) are always non-spoiled for Alice (Bob) up to round $\frac{q-1}{2}$, and ii) every sensitive bridging edge for Alice (Bob) appears in every dynamic network in the composition mapping.

LEMMA 5. *Consider any given simple composition mapping of type-φ_1 and type-φ_2 subnetworks ($\varphi_1, \varphi_2 \in \{\Gamma, \Lambda, \Upsilon\}$), and any given inputs $\mathbf{x}$ and $\mathbf{y}$ to the* DISJOINTNESSCP *problem. Let $\mathcal{G}$ be the dynamic network corresponding to $\mathbf{x}$ and $\mathbf{y}$, under this simple composition mapping. Consider the execution of any given oracle protocol over $\mathcal{G}$, under certain inputs to the nodes and certain public coin flip outcomes. Then for all round r where $0 \le r \le \frac{q-1}{2}$, Alice (Bob) can determine both the incoming and the outgoing messages of a node V in round r of that execution, based on only $\mathbf{x}$ ($\mathbf{y}$), if:*

- *V is non-spoiled for Alice (Bob) in round r.*
- *Alice (Bob) knows the oracle protocol and the public coin flip outcomes.*
- *Alice (Bob) knows the inputs to all her (his) corresponding non-spoiled nodes in the first round.*

- *Bob (Alice) always forwards to the other party all messages sent by B_Γ and B_Λ (A_Γ and A_Λ) in all rounds, as long as those nodes exist and if he (she) can determine those messages.*

PROOF. We prove via an induction on r. The lemma trivially holds for round 0. Assume that the lemma holds for all rounds before round r, and we prove the lemma for round r. It suffices to prove for Alice. Consider any non-spoiled node V for Alice in round r. Since knowing a node's initial input and its incoming messages up to a certain round immediately allows Alice to generate all its outgoing messages by simulating the oracle protocol, it suffices to prove that Alice can determine the incoming messages for V in round r if V is receiving in that round. By definition of a composition mapping, we know that V's incoming messages are either from V's neighbors in V's subnetwork or from nodes in the other subnetwork via bridging edges.

We first consider V's incoming messages from V's own subnetwork. Note that V must not be in a type-Υ subnetwork since V is non-spoiled. Lemma 3 and 4 tell us that if V is receiving in a round, then Alice can determine a set $\mathcal{S}'$ (by simulating her adversary) such that all the messages sent in that round by nodes in $\mathcal{S}'$ will exactly be those incoming messages to V in its subnetwork in that round. Also by Lemma 3 and 4, a node W in $\mathcal{S}'$ is either node B_Γ or B_Λ, or a non-spoiled node for Alice in the previous round. If W is B_Γ or B_Λ, note that B_Γ and B_Λ are non-spoiled for Bob. By inductive hypothesis, Bob can determine all the incoming messages to B_Γ and B_Λ up to and including round $r-1$. Hence Bob can generate the outgoing message from B_Γ and B_Λ in round r, if B_Γ and B_Λ are sending in round r. By condition in the lemma, Bob will have already forwarded these messages to Alice, so Alice knows these messages (as incoming messages to V). Second, if W is a non-spoiled node for Alice in the previous round, by inductive hypothesis, Alice can determine all incoming messages to W up to and including round $r-1$. Alice hence can also generate the message sent by W in round r if W is sending.

We next consider V's incoming messages via the bridging edges. Since V is non-spoiled in round r, it must be non-spoiled in the first round. Thus any bridging edge incidental to V must be sensitive for Alice. Let the other end of the bridging edge be W. By definition of a simple composition mapping, we know that W must be V's neighbor regardless of the DISJOINTNESSCP instance, and W must always be non-spoiled for Alice. By inductive hypothesis, Alice can determine all the incoming messages to W up to and including round $r-1$. Based on these messages and W's input, Alice can determine whether W is sending in round r, by simulating the oracle protocol on W. If W is sending, Alice can further determine W's outgoing message. Thus Alice can determine the incoming messages (if any) to V via the bridging edges. □

Lower bounds for CFLOOD **and** CONSENSUS. Using Lemma 5 and following the intuition described in Section 3, we can eventually obtain the following two main theorems.

THEOREM 6. *If the diameter D is unknown to the protocol beforehand, then a $\frac{1}{6}$-error Monte Carlo protocol for* CFLOOD *must have a time complexity of $\Omega(\sqrt[4]{N/\log N})$ flooding rounds. Furthermore, this holds even if the protocol knows N and the nodes' ids are from 1 to N.*

PROOF. Consider any $\frac{1}{6}$-error CFLOOD protocol that promises to terminate within s flooding rounds over average coin flips and over every dynamic network with no more than N nodes. Let $q = 120s+1$ and $n = \frac{N-4}{3q}$. Alice and Bob in the two-party DISJOINTNESSCP$_{n,q}(\mathbf{x},\mathbf{y})$ problem will use this oracle CFLOOD protocol to solve DISJOINTNESSCP with error probability of at most $\frac{1}{6}$, which will eventually lead to the lower bound. The proof is obtained via the following steps:

- *Constructing a simple composition mapping.* We first construct a mapping from DISJOINTNESSCP instances to dynamic networks, and then show that this mapping is a simple composition mapping. Given $\mathbf{x}$ and $\mathbf{y}$, we start from the corresponding type-Γ subnetwork and type-Λ subnetwork. It is easy to verify that the type-Γ subnetwork and the type-Λ subnetwork have $\frac{3}{2}n(q-1)+2$ and $\frac{3}{2}n(q+1)+2$ nodes, respectively. Hence the total number of nodes is N. If DISJOINTNESSCP$_{n,q}(\mathbf{x},\mathbf{y}) = 1$, we let the bridging edge set be $\{(A_\Gamma, A_\Lambda), (B_\Gamma, B_\Lambda)\}$. Here A_Γ and B_Γ (A_Λ and B_Λ) are the two special nodes in the type-Γ subnetwork (type-Λ subnetwork), as described in Section 4 (Section 5). If DISJOINTNESSCP$_{n,q}(\mathbf{x},\mathbf{y}) = 0$, then the type-$\Gamma$ subnetwork must have $\Omega(q)$ disconnected nodes that are arranged into a line. Let one end of this line be node L_Γ. The type-Λ subnetwork must have at least one $|^0_0$ chain. Let L_Λ be the middle node of an arbitrary $|^0_0$ chain in the type-Λ subnetwork. We connect the two subnetworks using the bridging edge set $\{(A_\Gamma, A_\Lambda), (B_\Gamma, B_\Lambda), (L_\Gamma, L_\Lambda)\}$.

  It is obvious that this mapping is a composition mapping. We next show that it is a simple composition mapping. For Alice, the bridging edge (A_Γ, A_Λ) is sensitive, and both end points of this edge are always non-spoiled for Alice up to round $\frac{q-1}{2}$. Furthermore, this edge is present in every dynamic network that appeared in the mapping. The other two bridging edges, (B_Γ, B_Λ) and (L_Γ, L_Λ), are not sensitive to Alice. Similar arguments apply to Bob.

- *Simulating the* CFLOOD *oracle protocol.* Given $\mathbf{x}$ and $\mathbf{y}$, Alice and Bob will simulate the execution of the given CFLOOD protocol over the dynamic network obtained from the above simple composition mapping, while feeding public coin flips into this oracle protocol. The nodes in the dynamic network will have ids from 1 to N, and A_Γ will be the special node that needs to flood the token in the CFLOOD problem. Since the ids do not depend on $\mathbf{x}$ and $\mathbf{y}$, Alice and Bob know all such information. Alice (Bob) will always forward to the other party all messages sent by A_Γ and A_Λ (B_Γ and B_Λ) in all rounds, as long as she (he) can determine those messages.

Based on these conditions, Lemma 5 tells us that Alice will be able to determine the incoming and outgoing messages of all her non-spoiled nodes in all round r where $0 \le r \le \frac{q-1}{2}$. Since A_Γ is always non-spoiled for Alice, Alice can determine all the incoming messages to A_Γ. Using all these incoming messages and by simulating the CFLOOD protocol on A_Γ, Alice monitors whether A_Γ outputs by round $\frac{q-1}{2}$ (which would indicate that the CFLOOD protocol has terminated). If yes,

Alice claims that $\text{DISJOINTNESSCP}_{n,q}(\mathbf{x}, \mathbf{y}) = 1$. Otherwise Alice claims that $\text{DISJOINTNESSCP}_{n,q}(\mathbf{x}, \mathbf{y}) = 0$.

- *Correctness of Alice's output.* We next prove that Alice's claim is correct with probability at least $\frac{5}{6}$, making the above a valid reduction. If $\text{DISJOINTNESSCP}(\mathbf{x}, \mathbf{y}) = 1$, then there are no $|^0_0$ chains in the two subnetworks, and one can easily verify that the diameter of the entire dynamic network is at most 10. Since the oracle CFLOOD protocol promises to terminate (over average coin flips) within s flooding rounds, it should terminate (over average coin flips) within $10s$ rounds on this dynamic network. By Markov's inequality, with probability at least $\frac{5}{6}$, it terminates by round $60s = \frac{q-1}{2}$, making Alice claim that $\text{DISJOINTNESSCP}(\mathbf{x}, \mathbf{y}) = 1$.

  If $\text{DISJOINTNESSCP}(\mathbf{x}, \mathbf{y}) = 0$, then the type-$\Gamma$ subnetwork has at least $\frac{q-1}{2}$ chains in the form of $|^0_0$. The middle nodes of all these chains are arranged into a line, and the line is connected to the type-Λ subnetwork via the (L_Γ, L_Λ) edge. It is impossible for the farthest node on the line to receive A_Γ's token in the CFLOOD protocol within $\frac{q-1}{2} = 60s$ rounds. Since the CFLOOD protocol has an error probability at most $\frac{1}{6}$, with probability at least $\frac{5}{6}$, the CFLOOD oracle protocol cannot terminate within $60s$ rounds. Hence Alice's claim is correct with probability at least $\frac{5}{6}$.

- *From communication complexity to time complexity.* We have shown above that by simulating the CFLOOD oracle protocol, Alice and Bob can solve any $\text{DISJOINTNESSCP}_{n,q}$ instance. During such simulation, Alice (Bob) only needs to forward to the other party all messages sent by A_Γ and A_Λ (B_Γ and B_Λ). By Corollary 2, there exist $\mathbf{x}_0$ and $\mathbf{y}_0$ such that i) $\text{DISJOINTNESSCP}_{n,q}(\mathbf{x}_0, \mathbf{y}_0) = 1$, and ii) Alice and Bob incur $\Omega(\frac{n}{q^2}) - O(\log n)$ bits over $\mathbf{x}_0$, $\mathbf{y}_0$, and average coin flips. Hence under such $\mathbf{x}_0$ and $\mathbf{y}_0$, at least one node out of A_Γ, A_Λ, B_Γ, and B_Λ must have sent $\Omega(\frac{n}{q^2}) - O(\log n)$ bit. The dynamic network corresponding to $\mathbf{x}_0$ and $\mathbf{y}_0$ has $O(1)$ diameter. This means that under this dynamic network and under the $\mathcal{CONGEST}$ model, the oracle protocol must take $\Omega(\frac{n}{q^2 \log N})$ rounds and also $\Omega(\frac{n}{q^2 \log N})$ flooding rounds to terminate over average coin flips. Since the oracle protocol promised to terminate within s flooding rounds, we have $s = \Omega(\frac{n}{q^2 \log N}) = \Omega(\frac{N}{s^3 \log N})$, implying $s = \Omega(\sqrt[4]{N/\log N})$.

□

THEOREM 7. *If the diameter D is unknown to the protocol beforehand, then a $\frac{1}{18}$-error Monte Carlo protocol for* CONSENSUS *must have a time complexity of $\Omega(\sqrt[4]{N/\log N})$ flooding rounds. Furthermore, this holds even if the protocol knows an estimate N' for N that guarantees $|\frac{N'-N}{N}| \le \frac{1}{3}$.*

PROOF. See the full version [21] of this paper. □

7. UPPER BOUND FOR CONSENSUS AND LEADERELECT — EFFECT OF A GOOD ESTIMATE OF N

Our lower bounds on CONSENSUS and LEADERELECT no longer hold when N' promises to satisfy $|\frac{N'-N}{N}| \le \frac{1}{3} - c$, for any positive constant c. For such N', this section presents a novel LEADERELECT protocol that does not require any prior knowledge of D and yet has a time complexity of only $O(\log N)$ flooding rounds.[5] Since CONSENSUS can be trivially reduced to LEADERELECT (see the full version [21] of this paper), such an upper bound applies to CONSENSUS as well. The following provides the intuition for the protocol, with the pseudo-code and the proofs deferred to the full version [21] of this paper. At the high level, the protocol proceeds in phases and keeps a guess D' for D, with D' doubling in each phase.

Majority counting. Our LEADERELECT protocol needs the following *majority counting* subroutine. Imagine that each node holds some input value. The subroutine uses well-known techniques [18] to count the total number of nodes holding a given node's input, and determines whether it is a majority of all the nodes in the system, within $O(D' \log N)$ rounds. There may be many distinct input values in the system, in which case the subroutine counts all these input values in parallel, while still having $O(\log N)$ message sizes. When $D' < D$ or when there are multiple distinct input values, the subroutine may under-count. With high probability, the subroutine does not over-count. If $D' \ge D$ and if there is a unique input value in the system, the subroutine will claim a majority with high probability. In other words, the subroutine is rather conservative in claiming a majority, and has one-sided error (with high probability). When determining the majority, we will need to use the condition of $|\frac{N'-N}{N}| \le \frac{1}{3} - c$.

Locking a majority. Given a D', our LEADERELECT protocol tries to elect the node with the largest id as the leader. Conceptually, it does so by simply flooding the ids of all the nodes for D' rounds, with only the largest id seen so far surviving in the flooding. If a node V finds that its id is the largest id it has seen after D' rounds, it tries to become a leader. (There can be multiple such V's when $D' < D$.) To do so, V will try to lock at least a majority of all the nodes, by flooding V's lock message for D' rounds. Whoever receives this message will get locked, unless it has already been locked by someone else. Next, V uses majority counting to see whether it has locked a majority. If so, V declares itself as the leader, and floods its id in future phases to notify all other nodes of the leader's id. Otherwise V floods an unlock message in future phases to roll back.

Avoid excessive lock roll back. If there are many such V's that fail to lock a majority, there will be many unlock messages to be propagated, which would result in excessive communication overhead and hence time complexity. Our key technique to overcome this is to have a separate stage before V actually acquires locks. Specifically, if V finds that

[5]Kuhn et al. [15] also notice that their reduction from HEAR-FROM-N-NODES to CONSENSUS no longer works when $|\frac{N'-N}{N}| \le \frac{1}{3} - c$, but their claim does not rule out the possibility of obtaining a good lower bound on CONSENSUS via other means.

its id is the largest id it has seen after the D' rounds of initial flooding, before V acquires locks, V uses majority counting to check whether a majority of nodes have seen V's id. V will only acquire the locks if it finds a majority. This separate stage ensures (with high probability) that in a given phase, there is only at most one node that tries to acquire locks and hence may potentially need to unlock later.

It is worth noting that our protocol invokes majority counting twice — once for counting the nodes seeing V's id, and once for counting the nodes locked by V. These two invocations cannot be replaced by one: The largest id seen by a node may change from phase to phase. But once a node is locked, it will remain locked in all future phases unless it is explicitly unlocked.

Correctness. Intuitively, the correctness of the protocol comes from two facts. First, once a node declares itself as the leader, it must have locked a majority of the nodes (with high probability). This prevents other nodes from becoming leaders later. Second, once D' reaches D, all unsuccessful lockings done in previous phases will be fully rolled back, and also all nodes will now see the largest id in the system. The node with the largest id will then get the majority (with high probability) in both steps, and become the leader. For space limitations, we leave the pseudo-code and the proof of the following theorem to the full version [21] of this paper:

THEOREM 8. *Let $c \in (0, \frac{1}{3}]$ be any given constant and N' be any value such that $|\frac{N'-N}{N}| \leq \frac{1}{3} - c$. Consider the* LEADERELECT *problem where c and N' are known to the protocol. Then even if the diameter D is unknown to the protocol beforehand, there exists a $\frac{1}{N}$-error Monte Carlo* LEADERELECT *protocol with a time complexity of $O(\log N)$ flooding rounds.*

8. ACKNOWLEDGMENTS

We thank Kartik Sankaran and the SPAA anonymous reviewers for their helpful feedbacks. This work is partly supported by the research grant MOE2014-T2-2-030 from Singapore Ministry of Education Academic Research Fund Tier-2.

9. REFERENCES

[1] Y. Afek and D. Hendler. On the complexity of global computation in the presence of link failures: the general case. *Distributed Computing*, 8(3):115–120, 1995.

[2] C. Avin, M. Koucký, and Z. Lotker. How to explore a fast-changing world (cover time of a simple random walk on evolving graphs). In *ICALP*, July 2008.

[3] K. Censor-Hillel, S. Gilbert, F. Kuhn, N. Lynch, and C. Newport. Structuring unreliable radio networks. In *PODC*, June 2011.

[4] B. Chen, H. Yu, Y. Zhao, and P. B. Gibbons. The cost of fault tolerance in multi-party communication complexity. *Journal of the ACM*, 61(3), May 2014.

[5] A. Cornejo, S. Gilbert, and C. Newport. Aggregation in dynamic networks. In *PODC*, July 2012.

[6] A. Drucker, F. Kuhn, and R. Oshman. The communication complexity of distributed task allocation. In *PODC*, July 2012.

[7] C. Dutta, G. Pandurangan, R. Rajaraman, Z. Sun, and E. Viola. On the complexity of information spreading in dynamic networks. In *SODA*, Jan. 2013.

[8] E. Fusco and A. Pelc. Knowledge, level of symmetry, and time of leader election. In *ESA*, Sept. 2012.

[9] M. Ghaffari, N. Lynch, and C. Newport. The cost of radio network broadcast for different models of unreliable links. In *PODC*, July 2013.

[10] O. Goldreich and L. Shrira. On the complexity of computation in the presence of link failures: the case of a ring. *Distributed Computing*, 5(3), 1991.

[11] B. Haeupler and D. Karger. Faster information dissemination in dynamic networks via network coding. In *PODC*, June 2011.

[12] B. Haeupler and F. Kuhn. Lower bounds on information dissemination in dynamic networks. In *DISC*, Oct. 2012.

[13] F. Kuhn, N. Lynch, C. Newport, R. Oshman, and A. Richa. Broadcasting in unreliable radio networks. In *PODC*, July 2010.

[14] F. Kuhn, N. Lynch, and R. Oshman. Distributed computation in dynamic networks. In *STOC*, June 2010.

[15] F. Kuhn, Y. Moses, and R. Oshman. Coordinated consensus in dynamic networks. In *PODC*, June 2011.

[16] F. Kuhn and R. Oshman. The complexity of data aggregation in directed networks. In *DISC*, Sept. 2011.

[17] F. Kuhn and R. Oshman. Dynamic networks: models and algorithms. *SIGACT News*, 42(1):82–96, Mar. 2011.

[18] D. Mosk-Aoyama and D. Shah. Fast distributed algorithms for computing separable functions. *IEEE Transactions on Information Theory*, 54(7):2997–3007, 2008.

[19] D. Peleg. *Distributed computing: a locality-sensitive approach.* Society for Industrial and Applied Mathematics, 1987.

[20] A. Sarma, S. Holzer, L. Kor, A. Korman, D. Nanongkai, G. Pandurangan, D. Peleg, and R. Wattenhofer. Distributed verification and hardness of distributed approximation. In *STOC*, 2011.

[21] H. Yu, Y. Zhao, and I. Jahja. The Cost of Unknown Diameter in Dynamic Networks. Technical Report TRA4/16, School of Computing, National University of Singapore, April 2016. Also available at `http://www.comp.nus.edu.sg/%7Eyuhf/TRA4-16.pdf`.

[22] Y. Zhao, H. Yu, and B. Chen. Near-optimal communication-time tradeoff in fault-tolerant computation of aggregate functions. *Distributed Computing*, 29(1):17–38, Feb 2016.

Churn- and DoS-resistant Overlay Networks Based on Network Reconfiguration

Maximilian Drees
Paderborn University
maxdrees@mail.upb.de

Robert Gmyr
Paderborn University
gmyr@mail.upb.de

Christian Scheideler
Paderborn University
scheideler@upb.de

ABSTRACT

We present three robust overlay networks: First, we present a network that organizes the nodes into an expander and is resistant to even massive adversarial churn. Second, we develop a network based on the hypercube that maintains connectivity under adversarial DoS-attacks. For the DoS-attacks we use the notion of a $\Omega(\log\log n)$-late adversary which only has access to topological information that is at least $\Omega(\log\log n)$ rounds old. Finally, we develop a network that combines both churn- and DoS-resistance. The networks gain their robustness through constant network reconfiguration, i.e., the topology of the networks changes constantly. Our reconfiguration algorithms are based on node sampling primitives for expanders and hypercubes that allow each node to sample a logarithmic number of nodes uniformly at random in $O(\log\log n)$ communication rounds. These primitives are specific to overlay networks and their optimal runtime represents an exponential improvement over known techniques. Our results have a wide range of applications, for example in the area of scalable and robust peer-to-peer systems.

Keywords

Churn; DoS-Attack; Expander; Hypercube; Overlay Network; Random Walks

1. INTRODUCTION

Large-scale and highly decentralized overlay networks have become increasingly popular since the rise of peer-to-peer systems and social networks. Issues like churn (the membership rapidly changes over time) and adversarial attacks pose significant challenges for these networks, so a significant amount of work has been invested in recent years to find effective ways of protecting overlay networks against churn and attacks. A standard approach for this is to continuously refresh the topology of the overlay network so that defects in the network caused by churn or attacks are repaired. Early attempts in practice go back to solutions like JXTA, where at the core the peers continuously exchange random neighbors with their neighbors in an attempt to keep the network well-connected. In theory, it is already known that there are simple rules for randomly switching edges in a local fashion so that eventually a random graph emerges (e.g., [12, 24]). However, the runtime bounds shown so far for these rules are fairly large, and a rigorous analysis showing that such a rule would be sufficient to get to a random graph in polylogarithmically many parallel rounds seems to be out of reach so far, even if there is no churn. An alternative approach is to keep the nodes in some hypercubic topology and to perform load balancing under churn in order to make sure that all places of the hypercubic topology are kept well-occupied by the nodes (e.g., [21]). However, here the best result known so far is a solution that can just tolerate a logarithmic churn per round. Currently, the most promising approach to rigorously handle a high churn is to perform random walks, which is also the approach used in our paper. However, instead of just using random walks in a standard fashion, which would take $\Omega(\log n/\log\log n)$ communication rounds in graphs of polylogarithmic degree in order to sample nodes uniformly at random, we combine random walks with pointer doubling, which *exponentially* improves the runtime needed for random walks to sample nodes uniformly at random. Pointer doubling (i.e., a node introduces its neighbors to its neighbors) is a well-known technique in the area of parallel computing [19], but to our great surprise, it seems that it has never been combined with random walks so far. With our rapid node sampling approach we can significantly improve the state of the art concerning the maximum churn rate that we can allow and the number of nodes that can be blocked by an adversary in each round while preserving connectivity among the remaining nodes.

SPAA '16, July 11 - 13, 2016, Pacific Grove, CA, USA

ISBN 978-1-4503-4210-0/16/07... $15.00

DOI: http://dx.doi.org/10.1145/2935764.2935783

1.1 Model and Problem Statement

We assume that we have a set of nodes V that can potentially change over time, where n denotes the current size of V. Every node v is assumed to have a unique identifier id(v) of size $O(\log n)$ (which, in reality, is its IP address or MAC address) that has to be known by a node w to send messages to it. The nodes aim at maintaining a topology for their overlay network that can be represented as a bidirected graph $G = (V, E)$, i.e., if $(v, w) \in E$ then also $(w, v) \in E$, where $(v, w) \in E$ requires v to know id(w). Apart from the ids needed for G, each node v may hold additional ids that it does not currently use for communication, so they do not appear in E. Since G is bidirected, we will henceforth simply consider G to be undirected. An undirected graph $G = (V, E)$ is *connected* if for every pair of nodes $v, w \in V$

there is a path along edges in E from v to w. We consider the synchronous message passing model for our protocols, which means that all nodes operate in synchronized *rounds*. Each round consists of three steps. In the first step, a node v receives all messages sent to it in the previous round, in the second step, it may perform any kind of local computation, and in the third step, it may send out a distinct message to each of its neighbors, where the *neighborhood* of a node v is defined as $N(v) = \{w \in V \mid (v, w) \in E\}$.

We consider the problem of *maintaining connectivity* in overlay networks under *large-scale adversarial churn* or *adversarial DoS-attacks* (or both) using only polylogarithmic communication work for each node in each round, where the *communication work* of a node is defined as the total number of bits that it receives and sends in a round. In the following, we define the exact nature of the attacks we consider.

Adversarial churn. Here, we assume that there is an adversary that for each round i prescribes a set of nodes W_i. However, the network has some flexibility in adapting its node set to the W_i's, as described below. The adversary has a *churn rate* of r if for all i, $|W_i|/r \leq |W_{i+1}| \leq r \cdot |W_i|$. For each node $v \in W_{i+1} \setminus W_i$ (i.e., a *new* node added to the system), we require that it is introduced to exactly one node in $W_i \cap W_{i+1}$ (i.e., a node *staying* in the system), and altogether at most $\lceil r \rceil$ new nodes are introduced to any node in a round. Formally, whenever a node w is introduced to a node v, it means that v learns about id(w). A node v is *leaving* if $v \in W_i \setminus W_{i+1}$. For simplicity, we assume that every node v is prescribed to enter and leave the system only once (or more precisely, every id can be used at most once). The decisions of the adversary can be based on any information about the past or current state of the system, so we allow it to be omniscient.

We allow the network to adapt its node set to the prescribed node sets within a certain delay T, i.e., the goal is to exclude the leaving nodes from G and to integrate the new nodes into G within T rounds while maintaining connectivity, where T is as small as possible. Let V_i be the set of nodes that are part of the network in round i. Formally, we require for each i that $\bigcap_{j=i-T}^{i} W_j \subseteq V_i \subseteq \bigcup_{j=i-T}^{i} W_j$. The protocols presented in this work all satisfy $T = O(\log\log n)$. Furthermore, we require the network to be monotonic in the sense that there is a unique round i where $v \in V_{i+1} \setminus V_i$ (i.e., v is entering V) and a unique round $j > i$ where $v \in V_j \setminus V_{j+1}$ (i.e., v is excluded from V). Our approach to satisfy these conditions is to keep V fixed over certain periods of time. In addition to that, any new node v introduced to a node w not yet in V will be delegated to the node in V that w was delegated (or introduced) to itself, so that w.l.o.g. we will assume in our protocols that a new node is always introduced to a node in V.

Adversarial DoS-attacks. In this case, we allow an r*-bounded* adversary to block any r-fraction of the current nodes in a round. A blocked node cannot send or receive messages in that round. We assume that a message sent out from node v to node w at round i can only be successfully received and processed by node w if v is non-blocked in round i and w is non-blocked in round i and $i+1$. In this case, we also call w *available* in round $i+1$. Note that for a protocol to make progress, it is crucial that nodes available in round i can send messages to nodes available in round $i+1$ for any i. The *only* information about the state of the system that the adversary is allowed to use for its DoS-attacks is the topology of the overlay network, i.e., we do not allow it to inspect messages or the state of nodes or even count the number of messages sent along an edge (which can easily be made uniform in our protocols, so it would not be of any use). An adversary is called t*-late* if it only has access to topological information that is at least t rounds old. We say that an overlay network is connected under a DoS-attack if the network restricted to its non-blocked nodes is still connected. Certainly, an overlay network of degree d cannot maintain connectivity under a r-bounded 0-late DoS-attack as long as $r > d/n$ because it would be very easy for such an adversary to isolate individual nodes.

1.2 Related Work

A central idea used throughout this work is network reconfiguration, i.e., switching the topology of an overlay network to a new topology that is independent of the old topology. Various ways of achieving this have already been studied in the literature. One way is to use random local edge switching rules in order to eventually obtain a random graph (e.g., [7, 12, 24]). However, the runtime bounds shown so far for these rules are fairly large, and a rigorous analysis showing that such a rule would be sufficient to get to a random graph in polylogarithmically many parallel rounds seems to be out of reach so far, even without churn.

A much simpler approach is to use routing or sorting, with the goal of randomly reordering the nodes in an overlay network. To illustrate that, consider the skip graph, which is known to be an expander with high probability [2]. Suppose that the skip graph is formed by nodes with labels that are chosen uniformly at random from $[0, 1]$. Then the formation of a new, independent skip graph can essentially be reduced to a routing problem in the old skip graph where each node v sends a message to the node w closest to a randomly chosen $x \in [0, 1]$, which is supposed to be v's new label. Once the routing has completed, it is easy to use the old skip graph to establish a skip graph on the new labels in altogether just $O(\log n)$ communication rounds. However, with overlay networks of polylogarithmic degree, routing or sorting cannot be done faster than in $o(\log n / \log\log n)$ time while just allowing a polylogarithmic communication work at each node in each round.

There are various other approaches of maintaining connectivity under churn. A standard approach in practice is to use a multi-tier architecture where the older, more stable peers form the actual overlay network while the young peers just connect to one or more of the stable peers (see, e.g., [33] and the references therein). Another way is to keep the nodes in some hypercubic topology and to perform local load-balancing in order to make sure that all places of the hypercubic topology are kept well-occupied by nodes under churn (e.g., [1, 21]). However, just eventual recovery from adversarial churn, or adversarial churn allowing only a logarithmic number of arrivals and departures per round has been considered there. Various other solutions have been proposed in theory that can handle either stochastic churn or adversarial churn that does not cause disconnectivity in a round, either by using a high enough degree or by constraining the adversary (e.g., [5, 16, 18, 26, 29]). Also, self-healing networks (e.g., [27]) have been proposed, but in these networks each insertion or deletion of a constant number of nodes is followed by some process of repairing the network. Finally, self-stabilizing overlay networks can be used to handle churn (e.g., [6, 14, 17]), but no concrete bounds on the churn rate are known for these.

Some of the solutions above cannot just handle churn but also limited-DoS attacks (e.g., [5, 21, 29, 33]). Within our model, DoS-attacks are more severe than churn in a sense that if an adversary decides to block a node, it will be instantly blocked without warning. If the adversary is not aware of the network topology, a standard approach to prevent disconnectivity is to randomly spread nodes in an overlay network and to use redundant connections, which is satisfied by numerous peer-to-peer networks. However, once the adversary knows the topology, nothing can be done to prevent disconnectivity unless the degree (defined as the maximum number of edges into or out of a node) is higher than the maximum number of nodes that the adversary can block at the same time: if an adversary wants to isolate node v, it simply blocks all nodes w that can either send a message to v or receive a message from v. Apart from blocking nodes, also other attacks on the connectivity of an overlay network have been studied like Sybil-attacks [9] and Eclipse-attacks [32]. There have also been several works on protecting distributed hash tables (DHTs) against DoS-attacks from outsiders [20], past insiders [4], or even insiders [10], but for past insiders and insiders the nodes are assumed to form a clique to avoid disconnectivity problems.

In [3] the authors show that under a model similar to ours it is impossible to maintain connectivity when a topology-oblivious adversary can subject $\Omega(\sqrt{n})$ nodes to churn in each round. The key difference between the model in [3] and our model is that in [3] nodes that are prescribed by the adversary to leave the network have to do so *immediately* while we allow the nodes to leave within the next $T = O(\log \log n)$ rounds. This shows that allowing a very small delay is sufficient to handle churn rates that would otherwise be impossible to handle.

Our network reconfiguration algorithms are based on node sampling primitives that combine random walks with pointer doubling. Pointer doubling is a well-known technique in the area of parallel computing [19]. It has originally been applied to rapidly contract trees by each node continuously introducing its current parent as the new parent to its children. In this way, a tree of depth D can be contracted in $O(\log D)$ parallel rounds to a tree of depth 1. Another application of pointer doubling is to rapidly form a clique: if in a graph of diameter D every node continuously introduces its neighbors to each other, then it just takes $O(\log D)$ communication rounds until a clique is formed. However, the communication work per round when using message passing is huge towards the end for both cases. To the best of our knowledge, pointer doubling has not been applied in the context of random walks yet.

The presented node sampling primitives allow each node in a network to sample a logarithmic number of nodes uniformly at random from the set of nodes in the network using only $O(\log \log n)$ communication rounds. The primitives are specific to overlay networks, i.e., they exploit the fact that a node can send a message to any other node whose identifier is known to it. Also, our primitives are restricted to $\mathbb{H}$-graphs (or, more generally, regular multigraphs with appropriate expansion properties) and hypercubes. For the case of arbitrary networks in which only nodes sharing an edge can communicate, Das Sarma et al. [30, 31] provide distributed algorithms for different variations of the problem of creating random walks. For the problem of letting each node in the network sample a logarithmic number of nodes uniformly at random using random walks, we achieve an exponential improvement in running time compared to Das Sarma et al., breaking through the lower bound of Nanongkai et al. [25], and an exponential improvement in message complexity (though it should be mentioned that their work did not aim at minimizing the message complexity).

1.3 Our Contribution

We develop three overlay networks: First, we present a network that organizes the nodes into an expander and maintains connectivity under adversarial churn by an omniscient adversary with constant churn rate. Second, we develop a network based on the hypercube that maintains connectivity under DoS-attacks by a $(1/2-\varepsilon)$-bounded $\Omega(\log \log n)$-late adversary for any $0 < \varepsilon \leq 1/2$. We finally extend this approach to get a network that maintains connectivity under DoS-attacks and adversarial churn by a $(1/2-\varepsilon)$-bounded $\Omega(\log \log n)$-late adversary with churn rate $\gamma^{1/\Theta(\log \log n)}$ for any $0 < \varepsilon \leq 1/2$ and any constant γ. All of our overlay networks have polylogarithmic degree and require polylogarithmic communication work for each node in each round. Our algorithms are based on novel node sampling primitives for expanders and hypercubes that allow each node to sample a logarithmic number of nodes uniformly at random in $O(\log \log n)$ communication rounds. These primitives are specific to overlay networks and their optimal runtime represents an exponential improvement over known techniques. Our results have a wide range of applications in the area of scalable and robust P2P-networks and beyond; we outline some applications in a dedicated section. Due to space constraints, most of the proofs have been omitted.

2. PRELIMINARIES

Before we get to the main part of this work, we introduce some basic tools, network topologies, and node sampling techniques for overlay networks.

2.1 Chernoff Bounds

We extensively use the following bounds which are known as *Chernoff bounds*.

LEMMA 1. *Suppose that $X_1, \ldots, X_n$ are independent binary random variables, let $X = \sum_{i=1}^{n} X_i$ and $\mu = \mathrm{E}[X]$. Then it holds for all $\delta > 0$ that*

$$\Pr[X \geq (1+\delta)\mu] \leq e^{-\min\{\delta^2,\delta\}\cdot\mu/3}.$$

Furthermore, it holds for all $0 < \delta < 1$ that

$$\Pr[X \leq (1-\delta)\mu] \leq e^{-\delta^2\mu/2}.$$

2.2 Network Topologies

We use two different network topologies throughout this work, namely the well-known *hypercube* and a graph class we refer to as $\mathbb{H}$-*graphs*, following the notation used in [22]. A d-dimensional hypercube is an undirected, simple graph $G = (V, E)$ where $V = \{0,1\}^d$ is the set of all binary d-tuples and E is such that two vertices are connected if and only if they differ in exactly one coordinate. Our definition of $\mathbb{H}$-graphs slightly differs from the definition given in [22]. Let $d \geq 8$ be an even constant. An $\mathbb{H}$-graph is an undirected multi-graph $G = (V, E)$ where $E = \bigcup_{i=1}^{d/2} C_i$ such that each C_i is a set of edges that forms a Hamilton cycle over the nodes in V.[1] Each C_i has an orientation, that is, a node u stores a reference to its predecessor and its successor in C_i. Note that a $\mathbb{H}$-graph is a connected d-regular multi-graph that can have parallel edges but no loops. We refer to the set of all possible $\mathbb{H}$-graphs over n nodes as $\mathbb{H}_n$. We can sample a graph from $\mathbb{H}_n$ by choosing the Hamilton cycles $C_1, C_2, \ldots, C_{d/2}$ independently and uniformly at random from the set of all possible Hamilton cycles over V.

2.3 Node Sampling

Our algorithms heavily rely on the ability of nodes to efficiently sample nodes uniformly at random from a network. In the d-dimensional hypercube we can achieve uniform node sampling using the following well-known random walk technique: A node u in the hypercube creates a token containing $\mathrm{id}(u)$ that traverses the graph for d rounds. Let $v = (b_1, \ldots, b_d)$ be the node that holds this token in round i. The node v flips a fair coin. If the coin comes up tails, v keeps the token; otherwise v forwards the token to the neighboring node $n_i(v) := (b_1, \ldots, b_{i-1}, 1 - b_i, b_{i+1}, \ldots, b_d)$. The node w that holds the token at the end of the random walk sends $\mathrm{id}(w)$ to u. It is easy to see that w is chosen uniformly at random from V. Therefore, a node in a d-dimensional hypercube can perform uniform node sampling in $O(\log n)$ rounds.

For $\mathbb{H}$-graphs we can also use a random walk to perform node sampling with a probability distribution that deviates only slightly from the uniform distribution over V. For a given n and $d \geq 8$ let G be a graph chosen uniformly at random from $\mathbb{H}_n$. Consider the simple random walk over G, that is, at a node u the random walk chooses an edge incident to u uniformly at random and then moves along that edge to another node. Since G is a d-regular graph, the stationary distribution of this random walk is the uniform distribution over V. Furthermore, for a graph G chosen uniformly at random from $\mathbb{H}_n$ we have the following theorem shown by Friedman [15].

THEOREM 1 (FRIEDMAN [15]). *For any fixed real $\epsilon > 0$ there is a constant c such that*

$$\Pr\left[\ |\lambda_i| \leq 2\sqrt{d-1} + \epsilon \ \ \forall i > 1\ \right] \geq 1 - \frac{c}{n^\tau}$$

where λ_i are the eigenvalues of the adjacency matrix of G in descending order and $\tau = \lceil\sqrt{d-1}\rceil - 1$.

Theorem 1 implies the following corollary.

COROLLARY 1. *For d and n sufficiently large we have $|\lambda_i| \leq 2\sqrt{d}$ for all $i > 1$, w.h.p.*[2]

By Corollary 1, G is an expander with diameter $O(\log n)$, w.h.p. As a result, the simple random walk on G is rapidly mixing, that is, it quickly approaches the stationary distribution. Formally, we have the following lemma, which is a consequence of Theorem 5.1 in [23].

LEMMA 2. *Let G be a d-regular multi-graph with $|\lambda_i| \leq 2\sqrt{d}$ for all $i > 1$ and let $t = \lceil 2\alpha \log_{d/4} n\rceil$ for any constant $\alpha \geq 1$. Consider the simple random walk of length t starting at a node u. Then for any node $v \in V$, we have*

$$\left|\Pr[\textit{random walk ends at } v] - \frac{1}{n}\right| \leq n^{-\alpha}.$$

We refer to the probability distribution given in Lemma 2 as *almost uniform*. If n and d are sufficiently large, a node in a random $\mathbb{H}$-graph can perform almost uniform node sampling in $O(\log n)$ communication rounds, w.h.p. Lemma 2 immediately implies the following lemma, which allows us to ignore the imperfectness of the random walks in our applications to overlay networks.

LEMMA 3. *For any set of k independent random walks of length $t = \lceil 2\alpha \log_{d/4} n\rceil$ with $\alpha > 2$ and any $v_1, \ldots, v_k \in V$ we have*

$$\left|\Pr[\textit{for all } i, \textit{ random walk } i \textit{ ends in } v_i] - \frac{1}{n^k}\right| \leq 2n^{2-\alpha} \cdot \frac{1}{n^k}.$$

3. RAPID NODE SAMPLING

In this section, we show how pointer doubling can be used to achieve an exponential speed-up in the random walk techniques for node sampling presented in Section 2.3. Our goal is to let each node in a network sample at least $\beta \log n$ nodes uniformly and independently at random from the set of all nodes in the network for any given constant β. The presented *rapid node sampling* primitives solve this problem in $O(\log\log n)$ communication rounds for both $\mathbb{H}$-graphs and hypercubes. The following lemma implies that this is optimal.

LEMMA 4. *Let $G = (V, E)$ be a graph with diameter d. Any algorithm that allows a node u to sample a node from V uniformly at random requires $\Omega(\log d)$ rounds.*

PROOF. Let $u, v \in V$ be such that the shortest path between the nodes is d. Consider the following algorithm: In each round every node mutually introduces all its neighbors by sending all references it holds to all nodes it knows. This algorithm requires $\Omega(\log d)$ rounds to introduce v to u. Clearly, no algorithm can introduce v to u faster than this algorithm. Hence, for any algorithm that samples a node from V and stores it at u in $o(\log d)$ rounds we have $\Pr[u \text{ chooses } v] = 0$. Therefore, no algorithm that uses $o(\log d)$ rounds can perform uniform node sampling over V. □

Throughout this section we assume that all nodes know n. However, when we use the primitives in the following sections, we explain how to circumvent this assumption.

3.1 H-Graphs

In our rapid node sampling primitives, the nodes collaborate to construct random walks of length $\Theta(\log n)$ in $O(\log\log n)$ rounds. Each node locally executes the algorithm shown in Algorithm 1. The algorithm is divided into four phases. While Phase 1 is executed only once, the remaining phases are executed in a loop. The execution of a phase corresponds to one communication round. The variable T in line 5 determines the length of the generated random walks. To generate random walks of length at least $\lceil 2\alpha \log_{d/4} n\rceil$, we choose $T = \lceil\log(2\alpha \log_{d/4} n)\rceil \leq \log\log n + O(1)$. Each node uses a multiset M holding ids of

[1]The union in the definition of the edge set E is a multi-set union.

[2]We write *w.h.p.* (i.e., *with high probability*) to refer to an event that occurs with probability at least $1 - n^{-c}$ for any constant $c > 1$.

nodes. During the execution of the algorithm, M is repeatedly emptied and then filled to a certain size. Specifically, the size of M before the first iteration of the loop in line 5 is defined as m_0 and the size of M after the i-th iteration of the loop is defined to be m_i. After the execution of the algorithm, M contains ids that were chosen uniformly at random from V.

Algorithm 1 Rapid Node Sampling in $\mathbb{H}$-Graphs

Phase 1:
1: $M \leftarrow \emptyset$
2: **for** $j \leftarrow 1$ to m_0 **do**
3: choose neighbor v uniformly at random
4: $M \leftarrow M \cup \{v\}$
5: **for** $i \leftarrow 1$ to T **do**
Phase 2:
6: **for** $j \leftarrow 1$ to m_i **do**
7: choose and remove $v \in M$ uniformly at random
8: send request to v
Phase 3:
9: receive k requests from nodes $u_1, u_2, \ldots, u_k$
10: **for** $j \leftarrow 1$ to k **do**
11: choose and remove $v \in M$ uniformly at random
12: send response v to u_j
Phase 4:
13: receive responses $v_1, v_2, \ldots, v_{m_i}$
14: $M \leftarrow \{v_1, v_2, \ldots, v_{m_i}\}$

The correctness of the algorithm depends on the choice of the sizes m_i: an inappropriate choice might lead to M being empty when an element should be extracted from it in line 7 or 11. We say the algorithm *succeeds for node v in iteration i* if in the i-th iteration of the loop in line 5 during the execution of the algorithm by v, M is never empty when an element is extracted. We say the algorithm *succeeds* if it succeeds for all nodes and for all iterations. Before we turn to the choice of the m_i, we show that the algorithm is correct under the assumption that it succeeds. Specifically, we show that after the execution of the algorithm, M contains nodes that were chosen by following independent random walks of length at least $\lceil 2\alpha \log_{d/4} n \rceil$.

LEMMA 5. *The algorithm satisfies the following invariant: After the i-th iteration of the loop in line 5, M contains ids of nodes that were chosen by following independent random walks of length 2^i.*

In Lemma 7 we establish a choice for the m_i such that the algorithm succeeds, w.h.p., and it holds $m_T \geq \beta \log n$ for any given β. The proof of Lemma 7 requires the following auxiliary lemma.

LEMMA 6. *Consider a regular undirected multi-graph $G = (V, E)$. Assume that each node in V creates $k \in \mathbb{N}$ tokens. The tokens traverse G in synchronous rounds according to a simple random walk. For $v \in V$ and $t \in \mathbb{N}$ let X be the number of tokens at node v after t rounds. Then X is a sum of independent binary random variables and $\mathrm{E}[X] = k$.*

LEMMA 7. *For any $0 < \varepsilon \leq 1$ we can choose a constant $c \geq \beta$ such that with $m_i = (2+\varepsilon)^{T-i} c \log n$, the algorithm succeeds, w.h.p.*

PROOF. Consider the i-th iteration of the algorithm in the execution by a node v. Let X_i denote the number of requests received by v in Phase 3 (denoted by k in the pseudo-code). It is easy to see that the algorithm succeeds for v in iteration i if $m_{i-1} \geq m_i + X_i$. By the definition of m_i we have

$$\begin{aligned}\Pr[m_i + X_i \geq m_{i-1}] &= \Pr[m_i + X_i \geq (2+\varepsilon)\, m_i] \\ &= \Pr[X_i \geq (1+\varepsilon)\, m_i].\end{aligned}$$

By Lemma 6, X_i is a sum of independent binary random variables and we have $\mathrm{E}[X_i] = m_i$. Therefore, we can apply Chernoff bounds to get

$$\Pr[X_i \geq (1+\varepsilon)\, m_i] \leq e^{-\varepsilon^2 m_i/3} \leq e^{-\varepsilon^2 c \log n/3},$$

where the second inequality holds because $m_i \geq c \log n$. The lemma follows by applying the union bound. □

The following theorem summarizes our analysis of Algorithm 1.

THEOREM 2. *For any $0 < \varepsilon \leq 1$ and any β, the algorithm samples at least $\beta \log n$ nodes almost uniformly at random from V in $O(\log \log n)$ rounds, and the communication work for every node in every round is $O(\log^{2+\log(2+\varepsilon)} n)$, w.h.p.*

PROOF. The correctness of the algorithm follows by Lemmas 5 and 7. The upper bound on the number of rounds immediately follows from our choice of T. Since $m_{i+1} \leq m_i$, the number of identifiers sent or received by a node in every round is at most $m_0 = (2+\varepsilon)^T c \log n = O(\log^{1+\log(2+\varepsilon)} n)$ which immediately implies the given bound on the communication work. □

Note that the presented primitive does not use any properties of $\mathbb{H}$-graphs aside from their regularity and their expansion. Accordingly, the presented primitive works for arbitrary regular graphs with appropriate expansion properties.

3.2 Hypercube

The rapid node sampling algorithm for the hypercube and its analysis are analogous to the above, though technically slightly more involved. We only provide the algorithm and the main results. For ease of presentation we assume that $d = 2^k$ for some $k \in \mathbb{N}$. Each node of the hypercube executes the algorithm given in Algorithm 2. In the pseudo-code we refer to the node executing the algorithm as u.

LEMMA 8. *Consider the execution by a node u. The following invariant holds: After the i-th iteration of the loop in line 8 for any $1 \leq j \leq \log n$ such that $j \equiv 1 \mod 2^i$ we have that for any node $v \in M_j$ the coordinates $j, \ldots, j + 2^i - 1$ of v were chosen independently and uniformly at random while the remaining coordinates of v are identical to the corresponding coordinates of u.*

LEMMA 9. *For $0 < \varepsilon \leq 1$ we can choose a constant $c \geq \beta$ such that with $m_i = (1+\varepsilon)^{\log \log n - i} c \log n$, the algorithm succeeds, w.h.p.*

THEOREM 3. *For any $0 < \varepsilon \leq 1$ and any β, the algorithm samples at least $\beta \log n$ nodes uniformly at random from V in $O(\log \log n)$ rounds, and the communication work for every node in every round is $O(\log^{2+\log(1+\varepsilon)} n)$, w.h.p.*

Algorithm 2 Rapid Node Sampling in the Hypercube

Phase 1:
for $j \leftarrow 1$ to $\log n$ **do**
  $M_j \leftarrow \emptyset$
  for $k \leftarrow 1$ to m_0 **do**
    if coin flip comes up heads **then**
      $M_j \leftarrow M_j \cup \{n_j(u)\}$ ▷ see Section 2
    else
      $M_j \leftarrow M_j \cup \{u\}$
for $i \leftarrow 1$ to $\log \log n$ **do**
  Phase 2:
  for $j \leftarrow 1$ to $\log n$ with step-size 2^i **do**
    for $k \leftarrow 1$ to m_i **do**
      choose and remove $v \in M_k$ unif. at random
      send request (u, j) to v
  Phase 3:
  receive requests $(u_1, j_1), \ldots, (u_\ell, j_\ell)$
  for $k \leftarrow 1$ to ℓ **do**
    choose and remove $v \in M_{j_k+2^{i-1}}$ unif. at random
    send response (v, j_k) to u_k
  Phase 4:
  for $j \leftarrow 1$ to $\log n$ **do**
    $M_j \leftarrow \emptyset$
  receive responses $(u_1, j_1), \ldots, (u_\ell, j_\ell)$
  for $k \leftarrow 1$ to ℓ **do**
    $M_{j_k} \leftarrow M_{j_k} \cup \{u_k\}$

4. MAINTAINING CONNECTIVITY UNDER ADVERSARIAL CHURN

The rapid node sampling primitives will be our primary tools for the rest of the paper. In this section, we use rapid node sampling for the fast reconfiguration of an overlay network based on the $\mathbb{H}$-graph topology. The new network structure is chosen uniformly at random. Our reconfiguration process only takes $O(\log \log n)$ communication rounds, enabling the nodes to handle continuous adversarial churn with any constant churn rate.

We present the network reconfiguration algorithm shown in Algorithm 3. Executed locally by each node, it transforms an existing Hamilton cycle into a new one, which is chosen uniformly at random. To reconfigure the whole overlay network, every node executes $d/2$ independent instances of the algorithm simultaneously, one instance for each Hamilton cycle. As soon as the reconfiguration is finished, a new iteration begins. As a result, the network structure changes periodically. For the rest of this section, unless otherwise noted, we always consider the execution of the algorithm with respect to a fixed Hamilton cycle. Similar to the rapid node sampling primitive, we split the algorithm into phases for ease of presentation. This time, however, a phase may take multiple communication rounds. Our approach requires the nodes to have some knowledge of the size of the network. Specifically, we need estimates on $\log \log n$ and $\log n$ (for example, both are required for the rapid node sampling primitive for $\mathbb{H}$-graphs, see Section 3.1, which is used in our approach). Since polynomial changes in n just cause additive changes in $\log \log n$ and for all realistic values of n, $\log \log n$ is very small, we assume for simplicity that the nodes have an upper bound k on $\log \log n$ that is precise up to some additive deviation of at most some constant c (i.e., $k - c \leq \log \log n \leq k$). Accordingly, we can use 2^k as an estimate for $\log n$ that is precise up to a constant multiplicative factor.

Algorithm 3 Network Reconfiguration

Phase 1:
choose node $u \in V$ via rapid node sampling primitive
send own id to u
Phase 2:
$U \leftarrow$ set of all received ids
$m \leftarrow |U|$
if $U \neq \emptyset$ **then**
  $(u_1, u_2, \ldots, u_m) \leftarrow$ unif. random permutation of U
Phase 3:
if $U \neq \emptyset$ **then**
  send u_1 to closest active predecessor
  send u_m to closest active successor
  receive u_0 from closest active predecessor
  receive u_{m+1} from closest active successor
Phase 4:
for $i = 1$ to m **do**
  send (u_{i-1}, u_{i+1}) to u_i
receive (u_p, u_s), predecessor $\leftarrow u_p$, successor $\leftarrow u_s$

Algorithm 3 reconfigures the network without considering churn. Phase 1 of the algorithm relies on rapid node sampling to randomly choose a node from the network. If a node u is chosen in Phase 1 by at least one node, we call u *active* in the respective Hamilton cycle. At the end of the reconfiguration algorithm, each node receives its new neighbors in a randomly chosen Hamilton cycle. We extend the reconfiguration algorithm to handle churn in the following way: When a new node v joins the network, it is introduced to a node w. In Phase 1 of the next reconfiguration, w sends id(v) to a randomly chosen node in the network for each node v that was introduced to w (along with its own id to another random node as usual). As a result, at the end of the reconfiguration each new node receives the ids of its neighbors in the newly build Hamilton cycle. We are going to show that our algorithm takes $O(\log \log n)$ communication rounds to reconfigure the network. Therefore, the number of new nodes being introduced to w is at most $r^{c \cdot \log \log n} = (\log n)^{c \cdot \log r}$ for some constant c. To provide a sufficiently large number of random nodes in Phase 1, polylogarithmically many instances of the rapid node sampling primitive have to be executed in parallel. If a node w wants to leave the network, it simply skips sending its own id to a random node in Phase 1 of the next reconfiguration. Therefore, w will not be incorporated in the newly build cycle. However, w still has to take part in the reconfiguration which includes sending the ids of nodes that were introduced to w before the adversary determined that w should leave the network. Once the reconfiguration is complete, w can leave the network.

To prove the utility of our algorithm, we first show that the new topology is chosen uniformly at random from the set $\mathbb{H}_n$, provided n is the number of nodes after reconfiguration.

LEMMA 10. *Consider Hamilton cycles C, C_1, and C_2 with $|V_{C_1}| = |V_{C_2}|$ and denote the probability that Algorithm 3 reconfigures C into C_j with $\Pr_C[C_j]$. We have $\Pr_C[C_1] = \Pr_C[C_2]$.*

Next, we prove that the total congestion caused by all instances of Algorithm 3 is small. Since the number of Hamilton cycles is constant, it suffices to bound the congestion for a single cycle.

LEMMA 11. *For a fixed Hamilton cycle and n sufficiently large, the number of times a node is chosen in Phase 1 is at most polylogarithmic, w.h.p.*

To realize Phase 3 efficiently, we use pointer doubling to quickly bridge the distance between active nodes. We have to show that these distances are logarithmic in n, so that Phase 3 can be executed in $O(\log\log n)$ communication rounds. For this, we introduce the concept of *empty segments*. For an Hamilton cycle C and $v \in V_C$, denote the successor of v with respect to the orientation of C as $\text{succ}(v)$. For $u, v \in V_C$, let $[u, v] := \{u, \text{succ}(u), \text{succ}(\text{succ}(u)), \ldots, v\}$. We call $[u, v]$ an empty segment if $\text{succ}(v)$ is active but no node in $[u, v]$ is active.

LEMMA 12. *For a fixed Hamilton cycle, the size of the largest empty segment is at most polylogarithmic, w.h.p.*

Finally, we show that the complete reconfiguration process is asymptotically as fast the rapid node sampling method it relies upon.

LEMMA 13. *Algorithm 3 terminates after $O(\log\log n)$ communication rounds.*

We now state the main results of this section.

THEOREM 4. *Let $G \in \mathbb{H}_n$ and $G' \in \mathbb{H}_m$, assuming m is the number of nodes which want to join or remain in the network. Algorithm 3 reconfigures G into G' with probability $1/|\mathbb{H}_m|$ in $O(\log\log n)$ communication rounds. The communication work is polylogarithmic, w.h.p.*

By Theorem 4, the continuous reconfiguration based on Algorithm 3 correctly transforms the network into a new $\mathbb{H}$-graph every $O(\log\log n)$ rounds, even under churn. This implies the following Theorem.

THEOREM 5. *The given procedure maintains the connectivity of the network under adversarial churn by an omniscient adversary with any constant churn rate, w.h.p.*

5. MAINTAINING CONNECTIVITY UNDER ADVERSARIAL DOS-ATTACKS

Next we present an overlay network that maintains connectivity under constantly changing DoS-attacks. In this section we assume that the number of nodes n is fixed; we lift this restriction in Section 6. We consider a $(1/2 - \varepsilon)$-bounded $\Omega(\log\log n)$-late adversary and our goal is to maintain connectivity among the non-blocked nodes.

In our approach, we organize the nodes into a topology that is derived from the d-dimensional hypercube where d is the largest integer such that $2^d \leq n/(c \log n)$ for some constant c that is chosen throughout the analysis. We denote the number of nodes in the hypercube as $N = 2^d$. To distinguish the nodes of the hypercube from the physical nodes in the network, we refer to them as *supernodes*. For each supernode x there is a set of nodes $R(x)$ that we call the *group of representatives* (or just *group*) of x and that has logarithmic size in n. Each node is part of exactly one group. We say that two groups are neighbors if their corresponding supernodes are neighbors. The exact topology of our network generally depends on which nodes are blocked. However, if no node is blocked, it has the following simple structure: The nodes in a group are connected to a clique, and nodes of neighboring groups form a complete bipartite graph. Our goal is to make it difficult for the adversary to block a large fraction of any group. To achieve this, we randomly rebuild the groups every $\Theta(\log\log n)$ rounds so that the $\Omega(\log\log n)$-late adversary never knows which nodes currently form a group. We assume that initially the network is such that each node chose its group independently and uniformly at random and that the nodes are connected as described above. We then rebuild the groups as follows.

First, the groups simulate the rapid node sampling primitive for their respective supernodes in the hypercube. We denote the state of the rapid node sampling primitive for a supernode x as $S(x)$. $S(x)$ contains all variables used by the primitive and a counter that represents the current iteration and phase. $S(x)$ further contains references to all nodes in $R(x)$ as well as reference to all nodes in $R(y)$ for every supernode y stored in x. The simulation proceeds in *steps*. Each step consists of two rounds and corresponds to one round of the rapid node sampling primitive for the supernodes. In addition to the simulation described below, each available node sends $S(x)$ to all nodes in $R(x)$ in every round. This ensures that newly available nodes can join the simulation and guarantees that as long as there is at least one available node per group in each round the network stays connected. Initially, all nodes in $R(x)$ know the initial state of x. Afterwards, each step is executed as follows for each supernode x.

- **Simulation round**: First, all available nodes in $R(x)$ receive the messages that x is supposed to receive in that round. Afterwards, each available node v simulates the local computation of x and sends a message m_v to all nodes in $R(x)$ containing the new state of x from the viewpoint of v including all messages that x is supposed to send out in that round. Note that m_v might differ because of different random decisions.
- **Synchronization round**: Every available node u in $R(x)$ first receives all messages sent out in the simulation round and chooses among these the message m_v of the node v of lowest $\text{id}(v)$. It then adopts the new state of x as given in m_v and for each message m that x is supposed to send out to some node in y, u sends m to all nodes in $R(y)$.

The following lemma is easy to show by induction on the number of rounds.

LEMMA 14. *If every $R(x)$ contains at least one available node in every round, the nodes can correctly simulate the rapid node sampling primitive for their respective supernodes.*

Hence, it follows from Theorem 3 that at the end of the simulation $S(x)$ contains $\beta \log n$ many supernodes (represented by their groups) that were sampled uniformly at random. Let $R(x) = \{v_1, v_2, \ldots, v_k\}$, where the nodes are ordered according to their ids, i.e., $\text{id}(v_1) < \text{id}(v_2) < \ldots < \text{id}(v_k)$, and let $x_1, x_2, \ldots, x_k$ be the first k supernodes that were sampled. In a final phase, these supernodes are used in the following way to reorganize the groups, given that $|R(x)| \leq \beta \log n$ for each x.

- First, every available node in $R(x)$ assigns v_i to $R(x_i)$ for every i by sending out messages to all nodes in $R(x_i)$ informing them about v_i.
- Afterwards, every available node in $R(x)$ collects all nodes sent to it from the previous round and sets them to $R'(x)$, the new group representing supernode x. It then sends $R'(x)$ to all nodes in $R(x)$ as well as all nodes in $R(y)$ where y is a neighbor of x.
- After collecting $R'(x)$ and $R'(y)$ for all neighbors y of x, each available node in $R(x)$ sends $R'(x)$ and $R'(y)$ for all neighbors y of x to all nodes in $R'(x)$.
- Each available node v collects $R'(x')$ of the new supernode x' that was assigned to v and also $R'(y)$ for all neighbors y of x'.

Note that at the end of the last round, all available nodes know their new supernode x in form of references to the nodes in $R(x)$ as well as the new groups of the neighbors of x, given that every old group always had at least one available node. We therefore have the following lemma.

LEMMA 15. *If $|R(x)| \leq \beta \log n$ and $R(x)$ contains at least one available node in every round for every supernode x, then the nodes can correctly reconfigure the network by assigning nodes to groups uniformly at random.*

We now turn to the analysis of the given reconfiguration procedure. First we establish bounds for the sizes of the groups.

LEMMA 16. *For any $0 < \delta < 1$ we can choose a constant c such that, w.h.p., for every supernode x it holds $(1-\delta)c \log n \leq (1-\delta)n/N < |R(x)| < (1+\delta)n/N < 2(1+\delta)c \log n$.*

Based on Lemma 16 and Theorem 3 it is easy to verify that the reconfiguration procedure outlined above requires $\Theta(\log \log n)$ rounds and polylogarithmic communication work per node in each round. Now let t be the exact number of rounds required by the procedure. A $2t$-late adversary has no knowledge about the current organization of nodes into groups. In fact, in the exact round in which the adversary would gain first information about the execution of the reconfiguration procedure that led to the current composition of the groups, a new reconfiguration of the groups finishes. Therefore, the current assignment of nodes to groups is random from the perspective of the adversary. This gives us the following lemma.

LEMMA 17. *For any $0 < \varepsilon \leq 1/2$ we can choose a constant c so that if the adversary blocks any set of $(1/2-\varepsilon)n$ nodes we have that for every supernode x the adversary blocks strictly less than $|R(x)|/2$ nodes in $R(x)$, w.h.p.*

With the above lemmas we have everything in place to show the following theorem.

THEOREM 6. *The given procedure maintains the connectivity of the network under DoS-attacks by a $(1/2-\varepsilon)$-bounded $\Omega(\log \log n)$-late adversary for any $0 < \varepsilon \leq 1/2$, w.h.p. The communication work per node in each round is polylogarithmic.*

PROOF. The following statements hold by induction over the executions of the reconfiguration procedure: Since the reconfiguration procedure requires $t = \Theta(\log \log n)$ rounds, a $2t$-late adversary has no knowledge about the current composition of the groups. Therefore, by Lemma 17 at least one node is available in each group in every round. By Lemma 16 it is sufficient to choose $\beta = 2(1+\delta)c$ to satisfy the requirements of Lemma 15. Hence, Lemmas 14 and 15 imply that the reconfiguration succeeds. The bound on the communication work follows immediately from Lemma 16 and Theorem 3 as stated above. □

6. MAINTAINING CONNECTIVITY UNDER DOS-ATTACKS AND CHURN

In this section, we extend the network presented in the previous section to get a network that is resistant to both DoS-attacks and churn. We consider a $(1/2-\varepsilon)$-bounded $\Omega(\log \log n)$-late adversary with a churn rate of $\gamma^{1/\Theta(\log \log n)}$ for any constant γ. A node in the network that receives a reference to a new node u adds u to its group by broadcasting its id within the group. A new node will always be included in the newly built groups. A leaving node informs its group so that it will not be included in the formation of the new groups. In this way, nodes enter or leave the network once a reconfiguration is completed, so both the join- and leave-operation require $O(\log \log n)$ rounds.

To successfully extend the approach to handle churn, we have to keep the group sizes within a suitable range: If the groups become too small, the adversary has a high chance to block an entire group. If the groups become large, the communication work increases. The main idea of our extension is to split and merge supernodes and their groups in order to adapt the group sizes. A supernode $x = (b_1, b_2, \ldots b_\ell)$ splits by changing its label to $x = (b_1, b_2, \ldots b_\ell, 0)$ and creating a new supernode $x' = (b_1, b_2, \ldots b_\ell, 1)$. The nodes in $R(x)$ are divided between the supernodes x and x' uniformly at random. A supernode $x = (b_1, b_2, \ldots b_\ell)$ that decides to merge informs its sibling $x' = (b_1, b_2, \ldots, 1-b_\ell)$ about its decision. It then changes its label to $x = (b_1, b_2, \ldots b_{\ell-1})$ and takes over the group of its sibling so that $R(x) \leftarrow R(x) \cup R(x')$. If a sibling y of a supernode x does not exist, because y was at some point split, x forces the subtree below y (or more specifically the leaves of that subtree) to merge until y is created; x then merges with y. We refer to the length of the label of a supernode x as the *dimension* $d(x)$ of the supernode. We enforce for every supernode x that

$$c \cdot d(x) - c \leq |R(x)| \leq 2c \cdot d(x) \tag{1}$$

for some positive constant c. Hence, x splits into two nodes if $|R(x)| > 2c \cdot d(x)$, and x merges with its sibling if $|R(x)| < c \cdot d(x) - c$. We assume that initially all supernodes satisfy this restriction and that for all supernodes x, y it holds $|d(x) - d(y)| \leq 2$. We define two supernodes x and y with $d(x) \leq d(y)$ to be connected if the first $d(x)$ bits of their labels differ in exactly one coordinate, and we modify the rapid node sampling primitive for hypercubes such that each supernode x is chosen with probability $2^{-d(x)}$.

The following lemma establishes the main properties of our approach.

LEMMA 18. *For all supernodes x, y it holds $|d(x)-d(y)| \leq 2$, and for each supernode x it holds $0.5 \log n < d(x) < \log n + 2$, w.h.p.*

PROOF. We show this by induction over the reconfigurations. Initially, the lemma holds by our assumptions. For the inductive step, consider a network that has to reconfigure from n nodes to n' nodes. Let d be the unique integer such that $2^d \cdot 2cd < n' \leq 2^{d+1} \cdot 2c(d+1)$. Note that the first inequality gives us $d < d+1 < \log n'$ for $d > 0$. Combining the respective second inequality in the two equations above gives us $d > 0.5 \log n'$ for n' sufficiently large. Hence, we have $0.5 \log n' < d < \log n'$. Consider a supernode x for which $d(x) < d$ before the reconfiguration. Let X be the number of nodes that are assigned to x in the random assignment of nodes to supernodes. It holds $\mathrm{E}[X] = n' \cdot 2^{-d(x)}$ and therefore by our choice of d it holds $\mathrm{E}[X] > 4c \cdot d(x)$. We have

$$\begin{aligned}\Pr[X \text{ does not split}] &= \Pr[X \leq 2c \cdot d(x)] \\ &= \Pr[X \leq (1-\delta)\mathrm{E}[X]]\end{aligned}$$

for some $0.5 < \delta < 1$. Hence, we can apply Chernoff bounds to get

$$\Pr[X \leq (1-\delta)\mathrm{E}[X]] \leq e^{-\delta \mathrm{E}[X]/2} \leq e^{-c \cdot d(x)}.$$

Since $d(x) > 0.5 \log n$ by our induction hypothesis, x splits w.h.p. Upon splitting, x distributes the nodes in $R(x)$ uniformly at random between the two new supernodes. As a consequence, one can show using Chernoff bounds and the union bound that once all supernodes are done splitting, it holds $d(x) \geq d$ for all x. By analogous arguments, one can show that once all supernodes are done merging, it holds $d(x) \leq d+2$ for all x. Hence, if the reconfiguration terminates, we have for all x that $d \leq d(x) \leq d+2$. So to prove the first part of the lemma, it remains to show termination. Note that by the arguments above, any supernode x merges or splits a finite number of times until $d \leq d(x) \leq d+2$. It is easy to show that a supernode x with $d(x) = d$ never merges and a supernode with $d(x) = d+2$ never splits. Therefore, a supernode never leaves the specified interval of values for $d(x)$. Furthermore, note that by the restriction on $|R(x)|$ given in Equation 1 there is no group size that is at the same time too large to be accommodated by a single supernode x and too small to be accommodated by the two supernodes resulting from splitting x. Therefore, within the specified interval in the worst case the supernodes merge to build supernodes of dimension d and then split to form supernodes of dimension $d+2$ to evenly distribute the nodes in the respective groups. Hence, once the specified interval is reached, only a constant number of rounds is needed to execute the merges and splits in an organized fashion. The second part of the lemma follows by combining the bounds on the dimension of the supernodes with the bound on d. □

According to Lemma 18, as long as n stays unchanged (i.e., the number of leaving nodes is equal to the number of joining nodes), also the interval of possible values of $d(x)$ remains unchanged, and therefore the merging and splitting of groups can be realized in an organized fashion using only a constant number of rounds. The specified churn rate of $\gamma^{1/\Theta(\log \log n)}$ means that if the network has n nodes at the beginning of a reconfiguration and n' nodes at the end of that reconfiguration we have $n/\gamma \leq n' \leq \gamma n$. By the arguments given in the proof of Lemma 18, the interval for the values of $d(x)$ can shift up or down by at most $\log \gamma$ during one reconfiguration. Hence, even under churn a constant number of rounds is sufficient to execute all merges and splits.

The lower and upper bounds on $d(x)$ given in Lemma 18 provide an estimate on $\log n$ which is required by the rapid node sampling primitive. Since $|d(x) - d(y)| \leq 2$ for all supernodes x, y, a supernode is connected to at most constantly many other supernodes. Applying the bounds on $d(x)$ to Equation 1 shows that the group sizes are in $O(\log n)$ so the communication work stays polylogarithmic. At the same time, by choosing an appropriate c the group sizes can be made large enough so that, according to Lemma 17 from the previous section, each group contains at least one available node at all times. Therefore, we have the following theorem.

THEOREM 7. *The given procedure maintains the connectivity of the network under DoS-attacks and simultaneous adversarial churn by a $(1/2-\varepsilon)$-bounded $\Omega(\log\log n)$-late adversary with churn rate $\gamma^{1/\Theta(\log \log n)}$ for any $0 < \varepsilon \leq 1/2$ and any constant γ, w.h.p. The communication work per node in each round is polylogarithmic.*

One may wonder whether the churn rate in the theorem can be extended to include crash failures. However, for that it must be possible to distinguish a crash failure from a node that is under DoS-attack. If this is possible, then the departure of a crashed node can simply be emulated by the other nodes in its groups. Otherwise, the nodes do not know how long they have to keep up emulating a non-responding node v in the system. If they do not emulate it long enough, v will be excluded, which will make it hard for it to be reintegrated since after $O(\log \log n)$ steps the adversary will know about all nodes that know v and that are known to v, so a dedicated DoS-attack can easily isolate v.

7. APPLICATIONS

Finally, we demonstrate that our results have many applications including scalable anonymizers, DHTs and publish-subscribe systems that are robust against massive DoS-attacks by $\Omega(\log \log n)$-late adversaries.

7.1 Robust Anonymous Routing

A standard approach to preserve anonymity in a distributed system is to exchange information through relays. A prominent example is the Tor network [8], which consists of several thousand servers spread all over the world so that there is no single authority having access to a significant fraction of its servers. In simple terms, we have a (possibly variable) set U of users and a fixed set V of servers that are used as relays to anonymize the source of a request. The goal of the servers is to ensure that whenever a user v wants to send a request to user w, w can receive the request and send a reply back to v via the servers without knowing v. More precisely, we would like to have a server system satisfying the following minimal set of requirements:

1. For every request, the request and its reply can be delivered reliably under the given attacker (robustness),
2. every message will exit the server system at a server chosen uniformly at random with respect to the current knowledge of the attacker (anonymity), and
3. at any time the servers form a network of polylogarithmic degree and the communication work per server

is polylogarithmic in each round given that in each round every server only receives a constant number of requests (scalability).

We added "with respect to the current knowledge of the attacker" in item 2 because all that matters is that based on its current knowledge, the attacker cannot make a better guess on which servers to monitor than a uniform distribution. If it learns about the final server in hindsight, this is uncritical as long as it does not have any monitoring data for that server since in that case it does not learn about the destination w. Using our reconfiguration techniques, we can set up a server system satisfying all of these requirements w.h.p. against a $\Omega(\log\log n)$-late adversary. It works as follows:

We organize the servers in a hypercube as described in Section 5. Recall that in each reconfiguration round, $\Theta(\log n)$ random supernodes are selected for each server so that after the reconfiguration, $|R(x)| = \Theta(\log n)$ for every supernode x, w.h.p. In addition to that, for each server v, a specific supernode x that v belongs to is picked, and $D(v) = R(x)\setminus\{v\}$ is defined as its *destination group*. Note that since every server in $D(v)$ has selected supernode x uniformly at random, it holds that if v picks a server out of $D(v)$ (using a rule that does not take any server properties into account), then this corresponds to a server chosen uniformly at random from V.

Suppose now that a user v wants to send a message to user w. We assume that v can contact some currently non-blocked server $s(v)$. $s(v)$ will then forward the message to all servers in $D(v)$, which will forward it to w (if they are non-blocked) and remember v. Once w has sent its reply back to (all non-blocked servers it received the message from in) $D(v)$, $D(v)$ will send the reply back to v.

Using our insights from Section 5, we immediately get:

COROLLARY 2. *Our server system exchanges messages between users via the servers in a reliable, anonymous, and robust fashion using only $O(1)$ communication rounds for each request and just polylogarithmic communication work even if the servers are under DoS-attack by a $(1/2-\epsilon)$-bounded $\Omega(\log\log n)$-late adversary for any constant $0 < \epsilon \le 1/2$.*

Of course, there are still various ways of attacking our system, and various more advanced defenses have already been proposed (e.g., [13]), but here we just wanted to give a basic idea of how our techniques can be used to provide a robust anonymizing system.

7.2 Robust DHTs

Another important application area of our techniques are distributed hash tables. At first glance, one may think that a continuous reconfiguration of the network also requires the data in a DHT to be continuously moved. But this is not needed when using the DHT named RoBuSt proposed in [11]. In this paper, a DHT on top of a fixed set of n reliable servers is presented that can correctly serve any set of read and write requests with at most one request per non-blocked server with just polylogarithmic work per server even if it is attacked by a 0-late adversary that can block up to $\gamma n^{1/\log\log n}$ many servers for a sufficiently small constant $\gamma > 0$. The work bound includes any movements of data needed to keep the system in a state that protects itself against the ongoing DoS-attacks. However, for RoBuSt to work, the servers have to be completely interconnected, i.e., every server knows all other servers in the system. Also, the adversary can only make a blocking decision every $O(\log^3 n)$ rounds (but whenever it can make a blocking decision, it can take the entire current state of the system into account).

First, we describe how to get rid of the completely interconnected network. It turns out that this is needed so that no matter which servers are blocked by the adversary, the remaining servers still form a connected network. In fact, they are still completely interconnected, which allows them to quickly organize themselves so that they can emulate a d-dimensional k-ary butterfly, which is needed for the routing of messages. In order to emulate a d-dimensional k-ary butterfly, the servers will establish connections forming a k-ary hypercube, which is defined as follows.

DEFINITION 1. *A d-dimensional k-ary hypercube is a graph $G = (V, E)$ with $V = \{0, \dots, k-1\}^d$, in which two nodes $(v_1, \dots, v_d)$, $(w_1, \dots, w_d) \in V$ are connected by an edge if and only if they differ in only one coordinate.*

It is easy to verify that a d-dimensional k-ary hypercube consists of k^d nodes and has a degree of $(k-1)\cdot d$ and a diameter of d. For the particular case that $d = k/\log k$ (which is the case in [11]), this results in a degree of $O(\log^2 n/\log\log n)$ and a diameter of $\log n/\log\log n$, where $n = 2^k$ is the number of nodes in the hypercube.

It is straightforward to extend the reconfiguration procedure for the binary hypercube in Section 5 to the k-ary hypercube. Then we have a network that is robust against a $(1/2-\epsilon)$-bounded $\Omega(\log\log n)$-late adversary. Whenever a request in the original RoBuSt system needs to fetch some data from a node v, we simply exchange messages between the group $R(v)$ representing v in the k-ary hypercube and v. In that way, all results in [11] carry over so that we get the following result.

THEOREM 8. *With only logarithmic redundancy, the extended RoBuSt system correctly serves any set of read and write requests (at most $O(1)$ per non-blocked server) in at most $O(\log^3 n)$ communication rounds with a congestion of at most $O(\log^3 n)$ at every server for any $\Omega(\log\log n)$-late adversary that can block at most $\gamma n^{1/\log\log n}$ servers at a time.*

7.3 Robust Publish-Subscribe Systems

Finally, we also note how to construct a robust publish-subscribe system with our reconfiguration procedures. A publish-subscribe system can easily be emulated by a server-based DHT as described above: each subscriber group is identified some unique key k, and we store k together with the number of publications $m(k)$ already done for k together with k in a DHT. For any set of publications with at most one per server, first the keys of the publications are aggregated to determine the number of publications for each used key. This can be done in time $O(\log n/\log\log n)$ in the k-ary hypercube that is reconfigured as described above using, for example, Ranade's routing scheme [28]. Once this number, $m'(k)$, is known for some k, $m(k)$ can be updated to $m(k) + m'(k)$ and unique numbers from $m(k) + 1$ to $m(k) + m'(k)$ can be given to the publications so that publication i for key k can be stored under the key $(k, m(k)+i)$ in the DHT. Whenever a subscriber for group k wants to access the latest publications, it simply needs to access $m(k)$ and can then request all publications with keys till $(k, m(k))$.

Overall, we can then obtain the same result for publish-subscribe systems as for DHTs above if at most $O(1)$ publish or retrieve requests are issued per non-blocked server.

8. CONCLUSION AND FUTURE WORK

We demonstrated how efficient network reconfiguration can be used to construct overlay networks that maintain connectivity under large-scale adversarial churn and adversarial DoS-attacks. Possible future work includes the extension of the churn- and DoS-resistant network presented in Section 6 to handle constant churn rates. In less immediate future work, it would be interesting to investigate the efficient reconfiguration of other topologies and further applications of our rapid node sampling primitives.

9. ACKNOWLEDGMENTS

This work was partially supported by the German Research Foundation (DFG) within the Collaborative Research Center "On-The-Fly Computing" (SFB 901) and by the EU within FET project MULTIPLEX under contract no. 317532.

10. REFERENCES

[1] I. Abraham, B. Awerbuch, Y. Azar, Y. Bartal, D. Malkhi, and E. Pavlov. A generic scheme for building overlay networks in adversarial scenarios. In *Proc. of IPDPS*, page 40, 2003.

[2] J. Aspnes and U. Wieder. The expansion and mixing time of skip graphs with applications. *Distributed Computing*, 21(6):385–393, 2009.

[3] J. Augustine, G. Pandurangan, P. Robinson, S. Roche, and E. Upfal. Enabling robust and efficient distributed computation in dynamic peer-to-peer networks. In *Proc. of FOCS*, pages 350–369, 2015.

[4] B. Awerbuch and C. Scheideler. A denial-of-service resistant DHT. In *Proc. of DISC*, pages 33–47, 2007.

[5] B. Awerbuch and C. Scheideler. Towards scalable and robust overlay networks. In *Proc. of IPTPS*, 2007.

[6] A. Berns, S. Ghosh, and S. V. Pemmaraju. Building self-stabilizing overlay networks with the transitive closure framework. *TCS*, 512, 2013.

[7] C. Cooper, M. Dyer, and A. J. Handley. The flip markov chain and a randomising p2p protocol. In *Proc. of PODC*, pages 141–150, 2009.

[8] R. Dingledine, N. Mathewson, and P. Syverson. Tor: the second-generation onion router. In *Proc. SSYM*, 2004.

[9] J. R. Douceur. The sybil attack. In *Proc. of IPTPS*, pages 251–260, 2002.

[10] M. Eikel and C. Scheideler. IRIS: a robust information system against insider dos-attacks. In *Proc. of SPAA*, pages 119–129, 2013.

[11] M. Eikel, C. Scheideler, and A. Setzer. RoBuSt: A crash-failure-resistant distributed storage system. In *Proc. of OPODIS*, pages 107–122, 2014.

[12] T. Feder, A. Guetz, M. Mihail, and A. Saberi. A local switch markov chain on given degree graphs with application in connectivity of peer-to-peer networks. In *Proc. of FOCS*, pages 69–76, 2006.

[13] J. Feigenbaum, A. Johnson, and P. Syverson. Preventing active timing attacks in low-latency anonymous communication. In *Prof. of PETS*, pages 166–183, 2010.

[14] D. Foreback, A. Koutsopoulos, M. Nesterenko, C. Scheideler, and T. Strothmann. On stabilizing departures in overlay networks. In *Proc. of SSS*, 2014.

[15] J. Friedman. *A Proof of Alon's Second Eigenvalue Conjecture and Related Problems*, volume 195 of *Memoirs of the AMS*. 2008.

[16] T. P. Hayes, J. Saia, and A. Trehan. The forgiving graph: a distributed data structure for low stretch under adversarial attack. In *Proc. of PODC*, 2009.

[17] R. Jacob, A. W. Richa, C. Scheideler, S. Schmid, and H. Täubig. A distributed polylogarithmic time algorithm for self-stabilizing skip graphs. In *Proc. of PODC*, pages 131–140, 2009.

[18] T. Jacobs and G. Pandurangan. Stochastic analysis of a churn-tolerant structured peer-to-peer scheme. *Peer-to-Peer Networking and Applications*, 6(1), 2013.

[19] J. JaJa. *An Introduction to Parallel Algorithms*. Addison Wesley, 1992.

[20] A. Keromytis, V. Misra, and D. Rubenstein. SOS: Secure Overlay Services. In *Proc. of the ACM SIGCOMM*, pages 61–72, 2002.

[21] F. Kuhn, S. Schmid, and R. Wattenhofer. A self-repairing peer-to-peer system resilient to dynamic adversarial churn. In *Proc. of IPTPS*, 2005.

[22] C. Law and K.-Y. Siu. Distributed construction of random expander networks. In *Proc. of INFOCOM*, volume 3, pages 2133–2143 vol.3, March 2003.

[23] L. Lovasz. Random walks on graphs: A survey, 1993.

[24] P. Mahlmann and C. Schindelhauer. Distributed random digraph transformations for peer-to-peer networks. In *Proc. of SPAA*, pages 308–317, 2006.

[25] D. Nanongkai, A. D. Sarma, and G. Pandurangan. A tight unconditional lower bound on distributed randomwalk computation. In *Proc. of PODC*, 2011.

[26] M. Naor and U. Wieder. Novel architectures for P2P applications: the continuous-discrete approach. In *Proc. of SPAA*, pages 50–59, 2003.

[27] G. Pandurangan, P. Robinson, and A. Trehan. Dex: Self-healing expanders. In *Proc. of IPDPS*, 2014.

[28] A. Ranade. How to emulate shared memory. *Journal of Computer and System Sciences*, 42(3):307–326, 1991.

[29] J. Saia and A. Trehan. Picking up the pieces: Self-healing in reconfigurable networks. In *Proc. of IPDPS*, pages 1–12, 2008.

[30] A. D. Sarma, D. Nanongkai, and G. Pandurangan. Fast distributed random walks. In *Proc. of PODC*, 2009.

[31] A. D. Sarma, D. Nanongkai, G. Pandurangan, and P. Tetali. Distributed random walks. *Journal of the ACM*, 60:2:1–2:31, 2013.

[32] A. Singh, T. Ngan, P. Druschel, and D. S. Wallach. Eclipse attacks on overlay networks: Threats and defenses. In *Proc. of the INFOCOM*, 2006.

[33] K. Suto, H. Nishiyama, N. Kato, T. Nakachi, T. Fujii, and A. Takahara. THUP: A P2P network robust to churn and DoS attack based on bimodal degree distribution. *IEEE Journal on Selected Areas of Communication*, 31(9):247–256, 2013.

Fast Distributed Algorithms for Connectivity and MST in Large Graphs

Gopal Pandurangan*
Dept. of Computer Science
University of Houston
gopalpandurangan@gmail.com

Peter Robinson
Royal Holloway
University of London
peter.robinson@rhul.ac.uk

Michele Scquizzato
Dept. of Computer Science
University of Houston
michele@cs.uh.edu

ABSTRACT

Motivated by the increasing need to understand the algorithmic foundations of distributed large-scale graph computations, we study a number of fundamental graph problems in a message-passing model for distributed computing where $k \geq 2$ machines jointly perform computations on graphs with n nodes (typically, $n \gg k$). The input graph is assumed to be initially randomly partitioned among the k machines, a common implementation in many real-world systems. Communication is point-to-point, and the goal is to minimize the number of communication rounds of the computation.

Our main result is an (almost) optimal distributed randomized algorithm for graph connectivity. Our algorithm runs in $\tilde{O}(n/k^2)$ rounds ($\tilde{O}$ notation hides a polylog(n) factor and an additive polylog(n) term). This improves over the best previously known bound of $\tilde{O}(n/k)$ [Klauck et al., SODA 2015], and is optimal (up to a polylogarithmic factor) in view of an existing lower bound of $\tilde{\Omega}(n/k^2)$. Our improved algorithm uses a bunch of techniques, including linear graph sketching, that prove useful in the design of efficient distributed graph algorithms. We then present fast randomized algorithms for computing minimum spanning trees, (approximate) min-cuts, and for many graph verification problems. All these algorithms take $\tilde{O}(n/k^2)$ rounds, and are optimal up to polylogarithmic factors. We also show an almost matching lower bound of $\tilde{\Omega}(n/k^2)$ for many graph verification problems using lower bounds in random-partition communication complexity.

Keywords

Distributed graph algorithms; massive graphs; graph sketching; graph connectivity; minimum spanning trees

*Supported, in part, by US-Israel Binational Science Foundation grant 2008348, NSF grant CCF-1527867, and NSF grant CCF-1540512.

SPAA '16, July 11 - 13, 2016, Pacific Grove, CA, USA

ISBN 978-1-4503-4210-0/16/07...$15.00

DOI: http://dx.doi.org/10.1145/2935764.2935785

1. INTRODUCTION

The focus of this paper is on distributed computation on large-scale graphs, which is increasingly becoming important with the rise of massive graphs such as the Web graph, social networks, biological networks, and other graph-structured data and the consequent need for fast algorithms to process such graphs. Several large-scale graph processing systems such as Pregel [27] and Giraph [1] have been recently designed based on the message-passing distributed computing model [26, 34]. We study a number of fundamental graph problems in a model which abstracts the essence of these graph-processing systems, and present almost tight bounds on the time complexity needed to solve these problems. In this model, introduced in [19] and explained in detail in Section 1.1, the input graph is distributed across a group of $k \geq 2$ machines that are pairwise interconnected via a communication network. The k machines jointly perform computations on an arbitrary n-vertex input graph, where typically $n \gg k$. The input graph is assumed to be initially randomly partitioned among the k machines (a common implementation in many real world graph processing systems [27, 36]). Communication is point-to-point via message passing. The computation advances in synchronous rounds, and there is a constraint on the amount of data that can cross each link of the network in each round. The goal is to minimize the time complexity, i.e., the number of rounds required by the computation. This model is aimed at investigating the amount of "speed-up" possible vis-a-vis the number of available machines, in the following sense: when k machines are used, how does the time complexity scale in k? Which problems admit linear scaling? Is it possible to achieve super-linear scaling?

[19] presents lower and upper bounds for several fundamental graph problems in the k-machine model. In particular, for the graph connectivity problem it shows a lower bound of $\tilde{\Omega}(n/k^2)$ rounds.[1] It also presents an $\tilde{O}(n/k)$-round algorithm for graph connectivity and spanning tree (ST) verification. This algorithm thus exhibits a scaling linear in the number of machines k. The question of existence of a faster algorithm, and in particular of an algorithm matching the $\tilde{\Omega}(n/k^2)$ lower bound, was left open in [19]. In this paper we answer this question affirmatively by presenting an $\tilde{O}(n/k^2)$-round algorithm for graph connectivity, thus achieving a speedup quadratic in k. This is optimal up to polylogarithmic (in n) factors.

[1]Throughout this paper $\tilde{O}(f(n))$ denotes $O(f(n) \operatorname{polylog} n + \operatorname{polylog} n)$, and $\tilde{\Omega}(f(n))$ denotes $\Omega(f(n)/\operatorname{polylog} n)$.

This result is important for two reasons. First, it shows that there are non-trivial graph problems for which we can obtain *superlinear* (in k) speed-up. To elaborate further on this point, we shall take a closer look at the proof of the lower bound for connectivity shown in [19]. Using communication complexity techniques, that proof shows that any (possibly randomized) algorithm for the graph connectivity problem has to exchange $\tilde{\Omega}(n)$ bits of information across the k machines, for any $k \geq 2$. Since there are $k(k-1)/2$ links in a complete network with k machines, when each link can carry $O(\text{polylog}(n))$ bits per round, in each single round the network can deliver at most $\tilde{\Theta}(k^2)$ bits of information, and thus a lower bound of $\tilde{\Omega}(n/k^2)$ rounds follows. The connectivity algorithm of this paper thus shows that the optimal speed-up factor of $\Theta(k^2)$ is attainable. Second, this implies that many other important graph problems can be solved in $\tilde{O}(n/k^2)$ rounds as well. These include computing a spanning tree, minimum spanning tree (MST), approximate min-cut, and many verification problems such as spanning connected subgraph, cycle containment, and bipartiteness.

It is important to note that under a different output requirement (explained next) there exists a $\tilde{\Omega}(n/k)$-round lower bound for computing a spanning tree of a graph [19], which also implies the same lower bound for other fundamental problems such as computing an MST, breadth-first tree, and shortest paths tree. However, this lower bound holds under the requirement that each vertex (i.e., the machine which hosts the vertex) must know at the end of the computation the "status" of all of its incident edges, that is, whether they belong to a ST or not, and output their respective status. (This is the output criterion that is usually required in distributed algorithms [26, 34].) The proof of the lower bound exploits this criterion to show that any algorithm will require some machine receiving $\Omega(n)$ bits of information, and since any machine has $k-1$ incident links, this results in a $\tilde{\Omega}(n/k)$ lower bound. On the other hand, if we relax the output criterion to require the final status of each edge to be known by *some* machine (different machines might know the status of different edges), then we show that this can be accomplished in $\tilde{O}(n/k^2)$ rounds using the fast connectivity algorithm of this paper.

1.1 The Model

We now describe the adopted model of distributed computation, the *k-machine model* (a.k.a. the *Big Data model*), introduced in [19] and further investigated in [9, 35, 33]. The model consists of a set of $k \geq 2$ machines $N = \{M_1, M_2, \ldots, M_k\}$ that are pairwise interconnected by bidirectional point-to-point communication links. Each machine executes an instance of a distributed algorithm. The computation advances in synchronous rounds where, in each round, machines can exchange messages over their communication links and perform some local computation. Each link is assumed to have a bandwidth of $O(\text{polylog}(n))$ bits per round, i.e., $O(\text{polylog}(n))$ bits can be transmitted over each link in each round. (As discussed in [19] (cf. Theorem 4.1), it is easy to rewrite bounds to scale in terms of the actual inter-machine bandwidth.) Machines do not share any memory and have no other means of communication. There is an alternate (but equivalent) way to view this communication restriction: instead of putting a bandwidth restriction on the links, we can put a restriction on the amount of information that each *machine* can communicate (i.e., send/receive) in each round. The results that we obtain in the bandwidth-restricted model will also apply to the latter model [19]. Local computation within a machine is considered to happen instantaneously at zero cost, while the exchange of messages between machines is the costly operation. (However, we note that in all the algorithms of this paper, every machine in every round performs a computation bounded by a polynomial in n.) We assume that each machine has access to a private source of true random bits.

Although the k-machine model is a fairly general model of computation, we are mostly interested in studying graph problems in it. Specifically, we are given an input graph G with n vertices, each associated with a unique integer ID from $[n]$, and m edges. To avoid trivialities, we will assume that $n \geq k$ (typically, $n \gg k$). Initially, the entire graph G is not known by any single machine, but rather partitioned among the k machines in a "balanced" fashion, i.e., the nodes and/or edges of G are partitioned approximately evenly among the machines. We assume a *vertex-partition* model, whereby vertices, along with information of their incident edges, are partitioned across machines. Specifically, the type of partition that we will assume throughout is the *random vertex partition (RVP)*, that is, each vertex of the input graph is assigned randomly to one machine. (This is the typical way used by many real systems, such as Pregel [27], to partition the input graph among the machines; it is easy to accomplish, e.g., via hashing.[2]) However, we notice that our upper bounds also hold under the much weaker assumption whereby it is only required that nodes and edges of the input graph are partitioned approximately evenly among the machines; on the other hand, lower bounds under RVP clearly apply to worst-case partitions as well.

More formally, in the random vertex partition variant, each vertex of G is assigned independently and uniformly at random to one of the k machines. If a vertex v is assigned to machine M_i we say that M_i is the *home machine* of v and, with a slight abuse of notation, write $v \in M_i$. When a vertex is assigned to a machine, *all its incident edges* are assigned to that machine as well; i.e., the home machine will know the IDs of the neighbors of that vertex as well as the identity of the home machines of the neighboring vertices (and the weights of the corresponding edges in case G is weighted). Note that an immediate property of the RVP model is that the number of vertices at each machine is *balanced*, i.e., each machine is the home machine of $\tilde{\Theta}(n/k)$ vertices with high probability. A convenient way to implement the RVP model is through hashing: each vertex (ID) is hashed to one of the k machines. Hence, if a machine knows a vertex ID, it also knows where it is hashed to.

Eventually, each machine M_i, for each $1 \leq i \leq k$, must set a designated local output variable o_i (which need not depend on the set of vertices assigned to M_i), and the *output configuration* $o = \langle o_1, \ldots, o_k \rangle$ must satisfy certain feasibility conditions for the problem at hand. For example, for the minimum spanning tree problem each o_i corresponds to a set of edges, and the edges in the union of such sets must form an MST of the input graph. The *time complexity* of an algorithm is the maximum number of rounds until termination.

[2]In Section 1.3 we will discuss an alternate partitioning model, the *random edge partition (REP)* model, where each edge of G is assigned independently and randomly to one of the k machines, and show how the results in the random vertex partition model can be related to the random edge partition model.

1.2 Our Contributions and Techniques

The main result of this paper, presented in Section 2, is a randomized Monte Carlo algorithm in the k-machine model that determines the connected components of an undirected graph G correctly with high probability and that terminates in $\tilde{O}(n/k^2)$ rounds.[3] This improves upon the previous best bound of $\tilde{O}(n/k)$ [19], since it is strictly superior in the wide range of parameter $k = \Theta(n^\epsilon)$, for all constants $\epsilon \in (0, 1)$. Improving over this bound is non-trivial since various attempts to get a faster connectivity algorithm fail due to the fact that they end up congesting a particular machine too much, i.e., up to n bits may need to be sent/received by a machine, leading to a $\tilde{O}(n/k)$ bound (as a machine has only $k-1$ links). For example, a simple algorithm for connectivity is simply flooding: each vertex floods the lowest labeled vertex that it has seen so far; at the end each vertex will have the label of the lowest labeled vertex in its component.[4] It can be shown that the above algorithm takes $\Theta(n/k + D)$ rounds (where D is the graph diameter) in the k-machine model by using the Conversion Theorem of [19]. Hence new techniques are needed to break the n/k-round barrier.

Our connectivity algorithm is the result of the application of the following three techniques.

1. Randomized Proxy Computation. This technique, similar to known techniques used in randomized routing algorithms [39], is used to load-balance congestion at any given machine by redistributing it evenly across the k machines. This is achieved, roughly speaking, by re-assigning the executions of individual nodes uniformly at random among the machines. It is crucial to distribute the computation *and* communication across machines to avoid congestion at any particular machine. In fact, this allows one to move away from the communication pattern imposed by the topology of the input graph (which can cause congestion at a particular machine) to a more balanced communication.

2. Distributed Random Ranking (DRR). DRR [8] is a simple technique that will be used to build trees of low height in the connectivity algorithm. Our connectivity algorithm is divided into phases, in each of which we do the following: each current component (in the first phase, each vertex is a component by itself) chooses one *outgoing edge* and then components are combined by merging them along outgoing edges. If done naively, this may result in a long chain of merges, resulting in a component tree of high diameter; communication along this tree will then take a long time. To avoid this we resort to DRR, which suitably reduces the number of merges. With DRR, each component chooses a random *rank*, which is simply a random number, say in the interval $[1, n^3]$; a component (say C_1) will merge with the component on the other side of its selected outgoing edge (say C_2) if and only if the rank of C_2 is larger than the rank of C_1. If the rank of C_1 is higher, then C_1 does not merge with C_2 and thus it becomes the root of a DRR tree, which is a tree induced by the components and the set of the outgoing edges that have been used in the above merging procedure. We will show that the height of a DRR tree is bounded by $O(\log n)$ with high probability.

3. Linear Graph Sketching. Linear graph sketching [2, 3, 28] is crucially helpful in efficiently finding an outgoing edge of a component. A *sketch* for a vertex (or a component) is a short ($O(\text{polylog}\, n)$) bit vector that efficiently encodes the adjacency list of the vertex. Sampling from this sketch gives a random (outgoing) edge of this vertex (component). A very useful property is the linearity of the sketches: adding the sketches of a set of vertices gives the sketch of the component obtained by combining the vertices; the edges between the vertices (i.e., the intra-component edges) are automatically "cancelled", leaving only a sketch of the outgoing edges. Linear graph sketches were originally used to process dynamic graphs in the (semi-) streaming model [2, 3, 28]. Here, in a distributed setting, we use them to reduce the amount of communication needed to find an outgoing edge; in particular, graph sketches will avoid us from checking whether an edge is an inter-component or an intra-component edge, and this will crucially reduce communication across machines. We note that earlier distributed algorithms such as the classical GHS algorithm [14] for the MST problem would incur too much communication since they involve checking the status of each edge of the graph.

We observe that it does not seem straightforward to effectively exploit these techniques in the k-machine model: for example, linear sketches can be easily applied in the distributed streaming model by sending to a coordinator machine the sketches of the partial stream, which then will be added to obtain the sketch of the entire stream. Mimicking this trivial strategy in the k-machine model model would cause too much congestion at one node, leading to a $\tilde{O}(n/k)$ time bound.

Using the above techniques and the fast connectivity algorithm, in Section 3 we give algorithms for many other important graph problems. In particular, we present a $\tilde{O}(n/k^2)$-round algorithm for computing an MST (and hence an ST). We also present $\tilde{O}(n/k^2)$-round algorithms for approximate min-cut, and for many graph verification problems including spanning connected subgraph, cycle containment, and bipartiteness. All these algorithms are optimal up to a polylogarithmic factor. In Section 4 we show a lower bound of $\tilde{\Omega}(n/k^2)$ rounds for many verification problems by simulating the k-machine model in a 2-party model of communication complexity where the inputs are randomly assigned to the players. This simulation has to be done in a careful manner since the k-machine model is synchronous, whereas the communication complexity model is asynchronous.

1.3 Related Work and Comparison

The theoretical study of large-scale graph computations in distributed systems is relatively new. Several works have been devoted to developing MapReduce graph algorithms (see, e.g., [18, 21, 24] and references therein). We note that the flavor of the theory developed for MapReduce is quite different compared to the one for the k-machine model. Minimizing communication is also the key goal in MapReduce algorithms; however this is usually achieved by making sure that the data is made small enough quickly (that is, in a small number of MapReduce rounds) to fit into the memory of a single machine (see, e.g., the MapReduce algorithm for MST in [21]).

For a comparison of the k-machine model (a.k.a Big Data

[3]Since the focus is on the scaling of the time complexity with respect to k, we omit explicitly stating the polylogarithmic factors in our run time bounds. However, the hidden polylogarithmic factor is not large—at most $O(\log^3 n)$.

[4]This algorithm has been implemented in a variant of Giraph [38].

model) with other parallel and distributed models proposed for large-scale data processing, including Bulk-Synchronous Parallel (BSP) model [40], MapReduce [18], and the congested clique, we refer to [41]. In particular, according to [41], "Among all models with restricted communication the "big data" [k-machine] model is the one most similar to the MapReduce model".

The k-machine model is closely related to the BSP model; it can be considered to be a simplified version of BSP, where local computation is ignored and synchronization happens at the end of every round (the synchronization cost is ignored). Unlike the BSP and refinements thereof, which have several different parameters that make analysis of algorithms complicated [41], the k-machine model is characterized by just one parameter, the number of machines, and this might ease the job of designing and analyzing algorithms.

The k-machine model is related to the classical $\mathcal{CONGEST}$ model [34], and in particular to the *congested clique* model, which recently has received considerable attention (see, e.g., [25, 23, 22, 12, 30, 7, 15]). The main difference is that the k-machine model is aimed at the study of large-scale computations, where the size n of the input is significantly bigger than the number of available machines k, and thus many vertices of the input graph are mapped to the same machine, whereas the two aforementioned models are aimed at the study of distributed network algorithms, where $n = k$ and thus each vertex corresponds to a dedicated machine. More "local knowledge" is available per vertex (since it can access for free information about other vertices in the same machine) in the k-machine model compared to the other two models. On the other hand, all vertices assigned to a machine have to communicate through the links incident on this machine, which can limit the bandwidth (unlike the other two models where each vertex has a dedicated processor). These differences manifest in the time complexity. In particular, the fastest known distributed algorithm in the congested clique model for a given problem may not give rise to the fastest algorithm in the k-machine model. For example, the fastest algorithms for MST in the congested clique model ([25, 15]) require $\Theta(n^2)$ messages; implementing these algorithms in the k-machine model requires $\Theta(n^2/k^2)$ rounds. Conversely, the slower GHS algorithm [14] gives an $\tilde{O}(n/k)$ bound in the k-machine model. The recently developed techniques (see, e.g., [11, 31, 13, 15, 12]) used to prove time lower bounds in the standard $\mathcal{CONGEST}$ model and in the congested clique model are not directly applicable here.

The work closest in spirit to ours is the recent work of Woodruff and Zhang [42]. This paper considers a number of basic statistical and graph problems in a distributed message-passing model similar to the k-machine model. However, there are some important differences. First, their model is asynchronous, and the cost function is the communication complexity, which refers to the total number of bits exchanged by the machines during the computation. Second, a *worst-case* distribution of the input is assumed, while we assume a random distribution. Third, which is an important difference, they assume an edge partition model for the problems on graphs, that is, the edges of the graph (as opposed to its vertices) are partitioned across the k machines. In particular, for the connectivity problem, they show a message complexity lower bound of $\tilde{\Omega}(nk)$ which essentially translates to a $\tilde{\Omega}(n/k)$ round lower bound in the k-machine model; it can be shown by using their proof technique that this lower bound also applies to the *random edge partition (REP)* model, where edges are partitioned randomly among machines, as well. On the other hand, it is easy to show an $\tilde{O}(n/k)$ upper bound for the connectivity in the REP model for connectivity and MST.[5] Hence, in the REP model, $\tilde{\Theta}(n/k)$ is a tight bound for connectivity and other related problems such as MST. However, in contrast, in the RVP model (arguably, a more natural partition model), we show that $\tilde{\Theta}(n/k^2)$ is the tight bound. Our results are a step towards a better understanding of the complexity of distributed graph computation vis-a-vis the partition model.

2. THE CONNECTIVITY ALGORITHM

In this section we present our main result, a Monte Carlo randomized algorithm for the k-machine model that determines the connected components of an undirected graph G correctly with high probability and that terminates in $\tilde{O}(n/k^2)$ rounds with high probability (Theorem 1). This algorithm is optimal (up to polylog(n)-factors) by virtue of a matching lower bound of $\tilde{\Omega}(n/k^2)$ rounds, which was shown in [19] by a reduction from the 2-party communication complexity of set disjointness under random input partitions.

Before delving into the details of our algorithm, as a warm-up we briefly discuss simpler, but less efficient, approaches. The easiest way to solve *any* problem in our model is to first collect all available graph data at a single machine and then solve the problem locally. For example, one could first elect a referee among the machines, which requires $O(1)$ rounds [20], and then instruct every machine to send its local data to the referee machine. Since the referee machine needs to receive $O(m)$ information in total but has only $k-1$ links of bounded bandwidth, this requires $\Omega(m/k)$ rounds.

A more refined approach to obtain a distributed algorithm for the k-machine model is to use the Conversion Theorem of [19], which provides a simulation of a congested clique algorithm $\mathcal{A}$ in $\tilde{O}(M/k^2 + \Delta' T/k)$ rounds in the k-machine model, where M is the message complexity of $\mathcal{A}$, T is its round complexity, and Δ' is an upper bound to the total number of messages sent (or received) by a single node in a single round. (All these parameters refer to the performance of $\mathcal{A}$ in the congested clique model.) Unfortunately, existing algorithms (e.g., [14, 37]) typically require Δ' to scale to the maximum node degree, and thus the converted time complexity bound in the k-machine model becomes $\tilde{\Omega}(n/k)$ at best. Therefore, in order to break the $\tilde{\Omega}(n/k)$ barrier, we must develop new techniques that directly exploit the additional locality available in the k-machine model.

In the next subsection we give a high level overview of our algorithm, and then formally present all the technical details in the subsequent subsections.

2.1 Overview of the Algorithm

Our algorithm follows a Boruvka-style strategy [6], that is, it repeatedly merges adjacent *components* of the input graph,

[5]The high-level idea of the MST algorithm in the REP model is: (1) First "filter" the edges assigned to one machine using the cut and cycle properties of a MST [17]; this leaves each machine with $O(n)$ edges; (2) Convert this edge distribution to a RVP which can be accomplished in $\tilde{O}(n/k)$ rounds via hashing the vertices randomly to machines and then routing the edges appropriately; then apply the RVP bound.

which are connected subgraphs, to form larger (connected) components. The output of each of these phases is a *labeling* of the nodes of G such that nodes that belong to the same current component have the same label. At the beginning of the first phase, each node is labeled with its own unique ID, forms a distinct component, and is also the *component proxy* of its own component. Note that, at any phase, a component contains up to n nodes, which might be spread across different machines; we use the term *component part* to refer to all those nodes of the component that are held by the same machine. Hence, at any phase every component is partitioned in at most k component parts. At the end of the algorithm, every node $v \in G$ will have a component label $\ell(v)$ such that two nodes have the same label if and only if they belong to the same connected component of G.

Our algorithm relies on *linear graph sketches* as a tool to enable communication-efficient merging of multiple components. Intuitively speaking, a (random) linear sketch $\mathbf{s}_u$ of a node u's graph neighborhood returns a sample chosen uniformly at random from u's incident edges. Interestingly, such a linear sketch can be represented as matrices using only $O(\text{polylog}(n))$ bits [16, 28]. A crucial property of these sketches is that they are linear: that is, given sketches $\mathbf{s}_u$ and $\mathbf{s}_v$, the *combined sketch* $\mathbf{s}_u + \mathbf{s}_v$ ("+" refers to matrix addition) has the property that, w.h.p., it yields a random sample of the edges incident to (u, v) in a graph where we have contracted the edge (u, v) to a single node. We describe the technical details in Section 2.3.

We now describe how to communicate these graph sketches in an efficient manner: Consider a component C that is split into j parts $P_1, P_2, \ldots, P_j$, the nodes of which are hosted at machines $M_1, M_2, \ldots, M_j$. To find an outgoing edge for C, we first instruct each machine M_i to construct a linear sketch of the graph neighborhood of each of the nodes in part P_i. Then, we sum up these $|P_i|$ sketches, yielding a sketch $\mathbf{s}_{P_i}$ for the neighborhood of part P_i. To combine the sketches of the j distinct parts, we now select a *random component proxy* machine $M_{C,r}$ for the current component C at round r (see Section 2.2). Next, machine M_i sends $\mathbf{s}_{P_i}$ to machine $M_{C,r}$; note that this causes at most k messages to be sent to the component proxy. Finally, machine $M_{C,r}$ computes $\mathbf{s}_C = \sum_{i=1}^{j} \mathbf{s}_{P_i}$, and then uses $\mathbf{s}_C$ to sample an edge incident to some node in C, which, by construction, is guaranteed to have its endpoint in a distinct component C'. (See Section 2.4.)

At this point, each component proxy has sampled an inter-component edge inducing the edges of a *component graph* $\mathcal{C}$ where each vertex corresponds to a component. To enable the efficient merging of components, we employ the *distributed random ranking* (DRR) technique of [8] to break up any long paths of $\mathcal{C}$ into more manageable directed trees of depth $O(\log n)$. To this end, every component chooses a rank independently and uniformly at random from $[0, 1]$,[6] and each component (virtually) connects to its neighboring component (according to $\mathcal{C}$) via a (conceptual) directed edge if and only if the latter has a higher rank. Thus, this process results in a collection of disjoint rooted trees, rooted at the node of highest (local) rank. We show in Section 2.5 that each of such trees has depth $O(\log n)$.

The merging of the components of each tree $\mathcal{T}$ proceeds from the leafs upward (in parallel for each tree). In the first merging phase, each leaf C_j of $\mathcal{T}$ merges with its parent C' by relabeling the component labels of all of their nodes with the label of C'. Note that the proxy M_{C_j} knows the labeling of C', as it has computed the outgoing edge from a vertex in C_j to a vertex in C'. Therefore, machine M_{C_j} sends the label of C_j to all the machines that hold a part of C_j. In Section 2.5 we show that this can be done in parallel (for all leafs of all trees) in $\tilde{O}(n/k^2)$ rounds. Repeating this merging procedure $O(\log n)$ times, guarantees that each tree has been merged to a single component.

Finally, in Section 2.6 we prove that $O(\log n)$ repetitions of the above process suffice to ensure that the components at the end of the last phase correspond to the connected components of the input graph G.

[6]It is easy to see that an accuracy of $\Theta(\log n)$ bits suffices to break ties w.h.p.

2.2 Communication via Random Proxy Machines

Recall that our algorithm iteratively groups vertices into "components" (which are connected subgraphs of the actual components of G) and subsequently merges such components according to the topology of G. Each of these components may be split into multiple component parts spanning multiple machines. Hence, to ensure efficient load balancing of the messages that machines need to send on behalf of the component parts that they hold, the algorithm performs all communication via *proxy machines*.

Our algorithm proceeds in phases and each phase consists of iterations. Consider the ρ-iteration of the j-th phase of the algorithm, with $\rho, j \geq 1$. We construct a "sufficiently" random hash function $h_{j,\rho}$, such that, for each component C, the machine with ID $h_{j,\rho}(C) \in [k]$ is selected as the proxy machine for component C. First, machine M_1 generates $\ell = \tilde{\Theta}(n/k)$ random bits from its private source of randomness. M_1 will distribute these random bits to all other machines via the following simple routing mechanism that proceeds in sequences of two rounds. M_1 selects k bits $b_1, b_2, \ldots, b_{k-1}$ from the set of its ℓ private random bits that remain to be distributed, and sends bit b_i across its i-th link to machine M_{i+1}. Upon receiving b_i, machine M_{i+1} broadcasts b_i to all machines in the next round. This ensures that bits $b_1, b_2, \ldots, b_{k-1}$ become common knowledge within two rounds. Repeating this process to distribute all the $\ell = \Theta(n/k)$ bits takes $\tilde{O}(n/k^2)$ rounds, after those all the machines have the ℓ random bits generated by M_1. We leverage a result of [4] (cf. in its formulation as Theorem 2.1 in [5]), which tells us that we can generate a random hash function such that it is d-wise independent by using only $O(d \log n)$ true random bits. We instruct machine M_1 to disseminate $d = \ell \log n = n\, \text{polylog}(n)/k$ of its random bits according to the above routing process and then each machine locally constructs the same hash function $h_{j,\rho}$, which is then used to determine the component proxies throughout iteration ρ of phase j.

We now show that communication via such proxy machines is fast in the k-machine model.

Lemma 1. *Suppose that each machine M generates a message of size $O(\text{polylog}(n))$ bits for each component part residing on M; let m_i denote the message of part P_i and let C be the component of which P_i is a part. If each m_i is addressed to the proxy machine M_C of component C, then all messages are delivered within $\tilde{O}(n/k^2)$ rounds with high probability.*

Proof. Observe that, except for the very first phase of

the algorithm, the claim does not immediately follow from a standard balls-into-bins argument because not all the destinations of the messages are chosen independently and uniformly at random, as any two messages m_i and $m_{i'}$ of the same component have the same destination.

Let us stipulate that any component part held by machine M_i is the i-th component part of its component, and denote this part with $P_{i,j}$, $i \in [k]$, $j \in [n]$, where $P_{i,j} = \emptyset$ means that in machine i there is no component part for component j. Suppose that the algorithm is in phase j' and iteration ρ. By construction, the hash function $h_{j',\rho}$ is $\tilde{\Theta}(n/k)$-wise independent, and all the component parts held by a single machine are parts of different components. Since M_i has at most $\tilde{\Theta}(n/k)$ distinct component parts w.h.p., it follows that all the proxy machines selected by the component parts held by machine M_i are distributed independently and uniformly at random. Let y be the number of distinct component parts held by a machine M_i that is, $y = |\{P_{i,j} : P_{i,j} \neq \emptyset\}| = \tilde{O}(n/k)$ (w.h.p.).

Consider a link of M_i connecting it to another machine M_1. Let X_t be the indicator variable that takes value 1 if M_1 is the component proxy of part t (of M_i), and let $X_t = 0$ otherwise. Let $X = \sum_{i=1}^{y} X_i$ be the number of component parts that chose their proxy machine at the endpoint of link (M_i, M_1). Since $\Pr(X_i = 1) = 1/(k-1)$, we have that the expected number of messages that have to be sent by this machine over any specific link is $\mathrm{E}[X] = y/(k-1)$.

First, consider the case $y \geq 11k \log n$. As the X_i's are $\tilde{\Theta}(n/k)$-wise independent, all proxies by the component parts of M_i are chosen independently and thus we can apply a standard Chernoff bound (see, e.g., [29]), which gives

$$\Pr\left(X \geq \frac{7y}{4(k-1)}\right) \leq e^{-3y/16(k-1)} < e^{\frac{-2k\log n}{k}} < \frac{1}{n^2}.$$

By applying the union bound over the $k \leq n$ machines we conclude that w.h.p. every machine sends $\tilde{O}(n/k^2)$ messages to each proxy machine, and this requires $\tilde{O}(n/k^2)$ rounds.

Consider now the case $y < 11k \log n$. It holds that $6\mathrm{E}[X] = 6y/(k-1) < 6 \cdot 11k \log n/(k-1) \leq 132 \log n$, and thus, by a standard Chernoff bound,

$$\Pr(X \geq 132 \log n) \leq 2^{-132 \log n} = \frac{1}{n^{132}}.$$

Analogously to the first case, applying the union bound over the $k \leq n$ machines yields the result. □

2.3 Linear Graph Sketches

As we will see in Section 2.5, our algorithm proceeds by merging components across randomly chosen inter-component edges. In this subsection we show how to provide these sampling capabilities in a communication-efficient way in the k-machine model by implementing random linear graph sketches. Our description follows the notation of [28].

Recall that each vertex u of G is associated with a unique integer ID from $[n]$ (known to its home machine) which, for simplicity, we also denote by u.[7] For each vertex u we define the *incidence vector* $\mathbf{a}_u \in \{-1,0,1\}^{\binom{n}{2}}$ *of* u, which describes the incident edges of u, as follows: $\mathbf{a}_u[(x,y)] = 0$ if $(x,y) \notin E(G)$ or, if $(x,y) \in E(G)$, then $\mathbf{a}_u[(x,y)] = 1$ if $u = x < y$, or $a_u[(x,y)] = -1$ if $x < u = y$. Note that the vector $\mathbf{a}_u + \mathbf{a}_v$ corresponds to the incidence vector of the contracted edge (u,v). Intuitively speaking, summing up incidence vectors "zeroes out" edges between the corresponding vertices, hence the vector $\sum_{u \in C} \mathbf{a}_u$ represents the outgoing edges of a component C.

Since each incidence vector $\mathbf{a}_u$ requires polynomial space, it would be inefficient to directly communicate vectors to component proxies. Instead, we construct a random linear sketch $\mathbf{s}_u$ of polylog(n)-size that has the property of allowing us to sample uniformly at random a nonzero entry of $\mathbf{a}_u$ (i.e., an edge incident to u). (This is referred to as ℓ_0-sampling in the streaming literature, see e.g. [28].) It is shown in [16] that ℓ_0-sampling can be performed by linear projections. Therefore, at the beginning of each phase j of our algorithm, we instruct each machine to to create a new (common) polylog$(n) \times \binom{n}{2}$ sketch matrix L_j, which we call *phase j sketch matrix*.[8] Then, each machine M creates a sketch $\mathbf{s}_u = L_j \cdot \mathbf{a}_u$ for each vertex u that resides on M. Hence, each $\mathbf{s}_u$ can be represented by a polylogarithmic number of bits.

Observe that, by linearity, we have $L_j \cdot \mathbf{a}_u + L_j \cdot \mathbf{a}_v = L_j \cdot (\mathbf{a}_u + \mathbf{a}_v)$. In other words, a crucial property of sketches is that the sum $\mathbf{s}_u + \mathbf{s}_v$ is itself a sketch that allows us to sample an edge incident to the contracted edge (u,v). We summarize these properties in the following statement.

LEMMA 2. *Consider a phase j, and let P a subgraph of G induced by vertices $\{u_1, \ldots, u_\ell\}$. Let $\mathbf{s}_{u_1}, \ldots, \mathbf{s}_{u_\ell}$ be the associated sketches of vertices in P constructed by applying the* phase j sketch matrix *to the respective incidence vectors. Then, the combined sketch $\mathbf{s}_P = \sum_{i=1}^{\ell} \mathbf{s}_{u_i}$ can be represented using $O(\text{polylog}(n))$ bits and, by querying $\mathbf{s}_P$, it is possible (w.h.p.) to sample a random edge incident to P (in G) that has its other endpoint in $G \setminus P$.*

Constructing Linear Sketches Without Shared Randomness. Our construction of the linear sketches described so far requires $\tilde{O}(n)$ fully independent random bits that would need to be shared by all machines. It is shown in Theorem 1 (cf. also Corollary 1) of [10] that it is possible to construct such an ℓ_0-sampler (having the same linearity properties) by using $\Theta(n)$ random bits that are only $\Theta(\log n)$-wise independent. Analogously as in Section 2.2, we can generate the required $\Theta(\log^2 n)$ true random bits at machine M_1, distribute them among all other machines in $O(1)$ rounds, and then invoke Theorem 2.1 of [5] at each machine in parallel to generate the required (shared) $\Theta(\log n)$-wise independent random bits for constructing the sketches.

2.4 Outgoing Edge Selection

Now that we know how to construct a sketch of the graph neighborhood of any set of vertices, we will describe how to combine these sketches in a communication-efficient way in the k-machine model. The goal of this step is, for each (current) component C, to find an outgoing edge that connects C to some other component C'.

Recall that C itself might be split into parts $P_1, P_2, \ldots, P_j$ across multiple machines. Therefore, as a first step, each machine M_i locally constructs the combined sketch for each part that resides in M_i. By Lemma 2, the resulting sketches

[7]Note that the asymptotics of our results do not change if the size of the ID space is $O(\text{poly}(n))$.

[8]Here we describe the construction as if nodes have access to a source of shared randomness (to create the sketch matrix). We later show how to remove this assumption.

have polylogarithmic size each and present a sketch of the incidences of their respective component parts. Next, we combine the sketches of the individual parts of each component C to a sketch of C, by instructing the machines to send the sketch of each part P_i (of component C) to the proxy machine of C. By virtue of Lemma 1, all of these messages are delivered to the component proxies within $\tilde{O}(n/k^2)$ rounds. Finally, the component proxy machine of C combines the received sketches to yield a sketch of C, and randomly samples an outgoing edge of C (see Lemma 2). Thus, at the end of this procedure, every component (randomly) selected exactly one neighboring component. We now show that the complexity of this procedure is $\tilde{O}(n/k^2)$ w.h.p.

LEMMA 3. *Every component can select exactly one outgoing edge in $\tilde{O}(n/k^2)$ rounds with high probability.*

PROOF. Clearly, since at every moment each node has a unique component's label, each machine holds $\tilde{O}(n/k)$ component's parts w.h.p. Each of these parts selected at most one edge, and thus each machine "selected" $\tilde{O}(n/k)$ edges w.h.p. All these edges have to be sent to the corresponding proxy. By Lemma 1, this requires $\tilde{O}(n/k^2)$ rounds.

The procedure is completed when the proxies communicate the decision to each of the at most k components' parts. This entails as many messages as in the first part to be routed using exactly the same machines' links used in the first part, with the only difference being that messages now travel in the opposite direction. The lemma follows. □

2.5 Merging of Components

After the proxy machine of each component C has selected one edge connecting C to a different component, all the neighboring components are merged so as to become a new, bigger component. This is accomplished by relabeling the nodes of the graph such that all the nodes in the same (new) component have the same label. Notice that the merging is thus only virtual, that is, component parts that compose a new component are not moved to a common machine; rather, nodes (and their incident edges) remain in their home machine, and just get (possibly) assigned a new label.

We can think of the components along with the sampled outgoing edges as a *component graph* $\mathcal{C}$. We use the *distributed random ranking* (DRR) technique [8] to avoid having long chains of components (i.e., long paths in $\mathcal{C}$). That is, we will (conceptually) construct a forest of directed trees that is a subgraph (modulo edge directions) of the component graph $\mathcal{C}$ and where each tree has depth $O(\log n)$.[9] The component proxy of each component C chooses a rank independently and uniformly at random from $[0, 1]$. (It is easy to show that $\Theta(\log n)$ bits provide sufficient accuracy to break ties w.h.p.) Now, the proxy machine of C (virtually) connects C to its neighboring component C' if and only if the rank chosen by the latter's proxy is higher. In this case, we say that C' becomes the *parent* of C and C is a *child* of C'.

LEMMA 4. *After $\tilde{O}(n/k^2)$ rounds, the structure of the DRR-tree is completed with high probability.*

[9]Instead of using DRR trees, an alternate and simpler idea is the following. Let every component select a number in [0, 1]. A merging can be done only if the outgoing edge (obtained from the sketch) connects a component with ID 0 to a component with ID 1. One can show that this merging procedure also gives the same time bound.

PROOF. We need to show that every proxy machine of a non-root component knows its smaller-ranking parent component and every root proxy machine knows that it is root. Note that during this step the proxy machines of the child components communicate with the respective parent proxy machines. Moreover, the number of messages sent for determining the ordering of the DRR-trees is guaranteed to be $O(n)$ with high probability, since $\mathcal{C}$ has only $O(n)$ edges. By instantiating Lemma 1, it follows that the delivery of these messages can be completed in $\tilde{O}(n/k^2)$ rounds w.h.p.

Since links are bidirectional, the parent proxies are able to send their replies within the same number of rounds, by re-running the message schedule of the child-to-parent communication in reverse order. □

If a component has the highest rank among all its neighbors (in $\mathcal{C}$), we call it a *root component*. Since every component except root components connects to a component with higher rank, the resulting structure is a set of disjoint rooted trees.

In the next step, we will merge all components of each tree into a single new component such that all vertices that are part of some component in this tree receive the label of the root. Consider a tree $\mathcal{T}$. We proceed level-wise (in parallel for all trees) and start the merging of components at the leafs that are connected to a (lower-ranking) parent component C.

LEMMA 5. *There is a distributed algorithm that merges all trees of the DRR forest in $\tilde{O}(dn/k^2)$ rounds with high probability, where d is the largest depth of any tree.*

PROOF. We proceed in d iterations by merging the (current) leaf components with their parents in the tree. Thus it is sufficient to analyze the time complexity of a single iteration. To this end, we describe a procedure that changes the component labels of all vertices that are in leaf components in the DRR forest to the label of the respective parent in $\tilde{O}(n/k^2)$ rounds.

At the beginning of each iteration, we select a new proxy for each component C by querying the shared hash function $h_{j,\rho}(C)$, where ρ is the current iteration number. This ensures that there are no dependencies between the proxies used in each iteration. We know from Lemma 4 that there is a message schedule such that leaf proxies can communicate with their respective parent proxy in $\tilde{O}(n/k^2)$ rounds (w.h.p.) and vice versa, and thus every leaf proxy knows the component label of its parent. We have already shown in Lemma 3 that we can deliver a message from each component part to its respective proxy (when combining the sketches) in $\tilde{O}(n/k^2)$ rounds. Hence, by re-running this message schedule, we can broadcast the parent label from the leaf proxy to each component part in the same time. Each machine that receives the parent label locally changes the component label of the vertices that are in the corresponding part. □

The following result is proved in [8, Theorem 11].

LEMMA 6. *The depth of each DRR tree is $O(\log n)$ with high probability.*

2.6 Analysis of the Time Complexity

We now show that the number of phases required by the algorithm to determine the connected components of the input graph is $O(\log n)$. At the beginning of each phase

i, distributed across the k machines there are c_i distinct components. At the beginning of the algorithm each node is identified as a component, and thus $c_0 = n$. The algorithm ends at the completion of phase φ, where φ is the smallest integer such that $c_\varphi = cc(G)$, where $cc(G)$ denotes the number of connected components of the input graph G. If pairs of components were merged in each phase, it would be straightforward to show that the process would terminate in at most $O(\log n)$ phases. However, in our algorithm each component connects to its neighboring component if and only if the latter has a higher rank. Nevertheless, it is not difficult to show that this slightly different process also terminates in $O(\log n)$ phases w.h.p. (that is, components gets merged "often enough"). The intuition for this result is that, since components' ranks are taken randomly, for each component the probability that its neighboring component has a higher rank is exactly one half. Hence, on average half of the components will not be merged with their own neighbor: each of these components thus becomes a root of one component, which means that, on average, the number of new components will be half as well.

LEMMA 7. *After* $12 \log n$ *phases, the component labels of the vertices correspond to the connected components of* G *with high probability.*

PROOF. Replace the c_i's with corresponding random variables C_i's, and consider the stochastic process defined by the sequence $C_0, C_1, \ldots, C_\varphi$. Let $\bar{C}_i$ be the random variable that counts the number of components that actually participate at the merging process of phase i, because they do have an outgoing edge to another component. Call these components *participating components*. Clearly, by definition, $\bar{C}_i \leq C_i$.

We now show that, for every phase $i \in [\varphi - 1]$, $\mathrm{E}[\mathrm{E}[\bar{C}_{i+1} \mid \bar{C}_i]] \leq \mathrm{E}[\bar{C}_i]/2$. To this end, fix a generic phase i and a random ordering of its $\bar{C}_i$ participating components. Define random variables $X_{i,1}, X_{i,2}, \ldots, X_{i,\bar{C}_i}$ where $X_{i,j}$ takes value 1 if the j-th participating component will be a root of a participating tree/component for phase $i+1$, and 0 otherwise. Then, $\bar{C}_{i+1} \mid \bar{C}_i = \sum_{j=1}^{\bar{C}_i} X_{i,j}$ is the number of participating components for phase $i+1$. As we noticed before, for any $i \in [\varphi - 1]$ and $j \in [\bar{C}_i]$, the probability that a participating component will not be merged to its neighboring component, and thus become a root of a tree/component for phase $i+1$ is exactly one half. Therefore, $\Pr(X_{i,j} = 1) \leq 1/2$. Hence, by the linearity of expectation, we have that

$$\mathrm{E}[\bar{C}_{i+1} \mid \bar{C}_i] = \sum_{j=1}^{\bar{C}_i} \mathrm{E}[X_{i,j}] = \sum_{j=1}^{\bar{C}_i} \Pr(X_{i,j} = 1) \leq \frac{\bar{C}_i}{2}.$$

Then, using again the linearity of expectation,

$$\mathrm{E}[\mathrm{E}[\bar{C}_{i+1} \mid \bar{C}_i]] \leq \mathrm{E}\left[\frac{\bar{C}_i}{2}\right] = \frac{\mathrm{E}[\bar{C}_i]}{2}.$$

We now leverage this result to prove the claimed statement. Let us call a phase *successful* if it reduces the number of participating components by a factor of at most 3/4. By Markov's inequality, the probability that phase i is not successful is

$$\Pr\left(\mathrm{E}[\bar{C}_{i+1} \mid \bar{C}_i] > \frac{3}{4}\mathrm{E}[\bar{C}_i]\right) < \frac{\mathrm{E}[\mathrm{E}[\bar{C}_{i+1} \mid \bar{C}_i]]}{(3/4)\mathrm{E}[\bar{C}_i]} \leq \frac{\mathrm{E}[\bar{C}_i]}{2} \cdot \frac{4}{3\mathrm{E}[\bar{C}_i]} = \frac{2}{3},$$

and thus the probability that a phase of the algorithm is successful is at least 1/3. Now consider a sequence of $12 \log n$ phases of the algorithm. We shall prove that within that many phases the algorithm w.h.p. has reduced the number of participating components a sufficient number of times so that the algorithm has terminated, that is, $\varphi \leq 12 \log n$ w.h.p. Let X_i be an indicator variable that takes value 1 if phase i is successful, and 0 otherwise (this also includes the case that the i-th phase does not take place because the algorithm already terminated). Let $X = \sum_{i=1}^{12 \log n} X_i$ be the number of successful phases out of the at most $12 \log n$ phases of the algorithm. Since $\Pr(X_i = 1) \geq 1/3$, by the linearity of expectation we have that

$$\mathrm{E}[X] = \sum_{i=1}^{12 \log n} \mathrm{E}[X_i] = \sum_{i=1}^{12 \log n} \Pr(X_i = 1) \geq \frac{12 \log n}{3} = 4 \log n.$$

As the X_i's are independent we can apply a standard Chernoff bound, which gives

$$\Pr(X \leq \log n) \leq e^{-4 \log n (3/4)^2/2} = e^{-\frac{9}{8} \log n} < \frac{1}{n}.$$

Hence, with high probability $12 \log n$ phases are enough to determine all the components of the input graph. □

THEOREM 1. *There is a distributed algorithm in the* k*-machine model that determines the connected components of a graph* G *in* $\tilde{O}(n/k^2)$ *rounds with high probability.*

PROOF. By Lemma 7, the algorithm finishes in $O(\log n)$ phases with high probability. To analyze the time complexity of an individual phase, recall that it takes $\tilde{O}(n/k^2)$ rounds to sample an outgoing edge (see Lemma 3). Then, building the DRR forest requires $\tilde{O}(n/k^2)$ additional rounds, according to Lemma 4. Merging each DRR tree $\mathcal{T}$ in a level-wise fashion (in parallel) takes $\tilde{O}(dn/k^2)$ rounds (see Lemma 5), where d is the depth of $\mathcal{T}$ which, by virtue of Lemma 6, is bounded by $O(\log n)$. Since each of these time bounds hold with high probability, and the algorithm consists of $O(\log n)$ phases with high probability, by the union bound we conclude that the total time complexity of the algorithm is $\tilde{O}(n/k^2)$ with high probability. □

We conclude the section by noticing that it is easy to output the actual number of connected components after the termination of our algorithm: every machine just needs to send "YES" directly to the proxies of each of the components' labels it holds, and subsequently such proxies will send the labels of the components for which they received "YES" to one predetermined machine. Since the communication is performed via the components' proxies, it follows from Lemma 1 that the first step takes $\tilde{O}(n/k^2)$ rounds w.h.p., and the second step takes only $O(\log n)$ rounds w.h.p.

3. APPLICATIONS

In this section we describe how to use our fast connectivity algorithm as a building block to solve several other fundamental problems in the k-machine model in time $\tilde{O}(n/k^2)$. Here we consider the problem of constructing a minimum spanning tree (MST), and defer the treatment of other problems (namely, approximate min-cut and several graph verification problems) to the full version of the paper [32].

The minimum spanning tree (MST) problem requires the machines to jointly output a set of edges that form a tree, connect all nodes, and have the minimum possible total weight. Interestingly, [19] shows that $\tilde{\Omega}(n/k)$ rounds are necessary for constructing *any* spanning tree (ST), assuming that, for every spanning tree edge (u,v), the home machine of u and the home machine of v must *both* eventually output (u,v) as being part of the ST. We now show that we can break the $\tilde{\Omega}(n/k)$ barrier, under the slightly less stringent requirement that at least *one* machine outputs each spanning tree edge e, but not necessarily any of the home machines of e. Note that for the MST problem we assume that each edge $e=(u,v)$ of the input graph G has an associated *edge weight* $w(e)$ that is known to the home machines of u and v.

Our algorithm mimics the multi-pass MST construction procedure of [2], originally devised for the (centralized) streaming model. To this end we modify our connectivity procedure of Section 2, by ensuring that when a component proxy C chooses an outgoing edge e, this is the *minimum weight outgoing edge* (MWOE) of C with high probability.

We now describe the i-the phase of this MST construction in more detail: Analogously to our algorithm in Section 2, the proxy of each component C determines an outgoing edge e_0 which, by the guarantees of our sketch construction (Lemma 2), is chosen uniformly at random from all possible outgoing edges of C.

We then repeat the following edge-elimination process $t=\Theta(\log n)$ times: The proxy broadcasts $w(e_0)$ to every component part of C. Recall from Lemma 3 that this communication is possible in $\tilde{O}(n/k^2)$ rounds. Upon receiving this message, the machine M of a part P of C now constructs a new sketch $\mathbf{s}_u$ for each $u \in P$, but first zeroes out all entries in $\mathbf{a}_u$ that refer to edges of weight $> w(e_0)$. (See Section 2.3 for a more detailed description of $\mathbf{a}_u$ and $\mathbf{s}_u$.) Again, we combine the sketches of all vertices of all parts of C at the proxy of C, which in turn samples a new outgoing edge e_1 for C. Since each time we sample a randomly chosen edge and eliminate all higher weight edges, it is easy to see that the edge e_t is the MWOE of C w.h.p. Thus, the proxy machine of C includes the edge e_t as part of the MST output. Note that this additional elimination procedure incurs only a logarithmic time complexity overhead.

At the end of each phase, we proceed by (virtually) merging the components along their MWOEs in a similar manner as for the connectivity algorithm (see Section 2.5), thus requiring $\tilde{O}(n/k^2)$ rounds in total.

Let E be the set of added outgoing edges. Since the components of the connectivity algorithm eventually match the actual components of the input graph, the graph H on the vertices $V(G)$ induced by E connects all vertices of G. Moreover, since components are merged according to the trees of the DRR-process (see Section 2.5), it follows that H is cycle-free.

We can now fully classify the complexity of the MST problem in the k-machine model:

THEOREM 2. *There exists an algorithm for the k-machine model that outputs an MST in*

- *$\tilde{O}(n/k^2)$ rounds, if each MST-edge is output by at least one machine, or in*
- *$\tilde{O}(n/k)$ rounds, if each MST-edge e is output by both machines that hold an endpoint of e.*

Both bounds are tight up to polylogarithmic factors.

4. LOWER BOUNDS FOR VERIFICATION PROBLEMS

In this section we show that $\tilde{\Omega}(n/k^2)$ rounds is a fundamental lower bound for many graph verification problems in the k-machine model. Even though many verification problems are known to satisfy a lower bound of $\tilde{\Omega}(D+\sqrt{n})$ in the classic distributed $\mathcal{CONGEST}$ model [11], the reduction of [11] encodes a $\Theta(\sqrt{n})$-instance of set disjointness, requiring at least one node to receive $\tilde{\Theta}(\sqrt{n})$ information across a single short "highway" path or via $\Theta(\sqrt{n})$ longer paths of length $\Theta(\sqrt{n})$. Moreover, we assume the random vertex partition model, whereas the results of [11] assume a worst case distribution. Lastly, any pair of machines can communicate directly in the k-machine model, thus breaking the $\Omega(D)$ bound for the $\mathcal{CONGEST}$ model. Our complexity bounds follows from the communication complexity of 2-player set disjointness in the *random input partition model* (see [19]). The main result of the section is the following theorem. The proof is deferred to the full version of the paper [32].

THEOREM 3. *There exists a constant $\gamma > 0$ such that any γ-error algorithm $\mathcal{A}$ has round complexity of $\tilde{\Omega}(n/k^2)$ on an n-node vertex graph of diameter 2 in the k-machine model, if $\mathcal{A}$ solves any of the following problems: connectivity [19], spanning connected subgraph, cycle containment, e-cycle containment, s-t-connectivity, cut, edge on all paths, and s-t-cut.*

5. CONCLUSIONS

There are several natural directions for future work. Our connectivity algorithm is randomized: it would be interesting to study the deterministic complexity of graph connectivity in the k-machine model. Specifically, does graph connectivity admit a $\tilde{O}(n/k^2)$ deterministic algorithm? Investigating higher-order connectivity, such as 2-edge/vertex connectivity, is also an interesting research direction. A general question motivated by the algorithms presented in this paper is whether one can design algorithms that have superlinear scaling in k for other fundamental graph problems. Some recent results in this directions are in [33].

Acknowledgments. The authors would like to thank Mohsen Ghaffari, Seth Gilbert, Andrew McGregor, Danupon Nanongkai, and Sriram V. Pemmaraju for helpful discussions, and the anonymous reviewers for their helpful comments.

6. REFERENCES

[1] Giraph, http://giraph.apache.org/.

[2] K. J. Ahn, S. Guha, and A. McGregor. Analyzing graph structure via linear measurements. In *ACM-SIAM SODA*, pages 459–467, 2012.

[3] K. J. Ahn, S. Guha, and A. McGregor. Graph sketches: sparsification, spanners, and subgraphs. In *ACM PODS*, pages 5–14, 2012.

[4] N. Alon, L. Babai, and A. Itai. A fast and simple randomized parallel algorithm for the maximal independent set problem. *J. Algorithms*, 7(4):567–583, 1986.

[5] N. Alon, R. Rubinfeld, S. Vardi, and N. Xie. Space-efficient local computation algorithms. In *ACM-SIAM SODA*, pages 1132–1139, 2012.

[6] O. Boruvka. O Jistém Problému Minimálním (About a Certain Minimal Problem). *Práce Mor. Přírodověd. Spol. v Brne III*, 3, 1926.

[7] K. Censor-Hillel, P. Kaski, J. H. Korhonen, C. Lenzen, A. Paz, and J. Suomela. Algebraic methods in the congested clique. In *PODC*, pages 143–152, 2015.

[8] J. Chen and G. Pandurangan. Almost-optimal gossip-based aggregate computation. *SIAM J. Comput.*, 41(3):455–483, 2012.

[9] F. Chung and O. Simpson. Distributed algorithms for finding local clusters using heat kernel pagerank. In *WAW*, pages 77–189, 2015.

[10] G. Cormode and D. Firmani. A unifying framework for ℓ_0-sampling algorithms. *Distributed and Parallel Databases*, 32(3):315–335, 2014.

[11] A. Das Sarma, S. Holzer, L. Kor, A. Korman, D. Nanongkai, G. Pandurangan, D. Peleg, and R. Wattenhofer. Distributed verification and hardness of distributed approximation. *SIAM J. Comput.*, 41(5):1235–1265, 2012.

[12] A. Drucker, F. Kuhn, and R. Oshman. On the power of the congested clique model. In *PODC*, pages 367–376, 2014.

[13] M. Elkin, H. Klauck, D. Nanongkai, and G. Pandurangan. Can quantum communication speed up distributed computation? In *ACM PODC*, pages 166–175, 2014.

[14] R. G. Gallager, P. A. Humblet, and P. M. Spira. A distributed algorithm for minimum-weight spanning trees. *ACM Trans. Program. Lang. Syst.*, 5(1):66–77, 1983.

[15] J. W. Hegeman, G. Pandurangan, S. V. Pemmaraju, V. B. Sardeshmukh, and M. Scquizzato. Toward optimal bounds in the congested clique: Graph connectivity and MST. In *PODC*, pages 91–100, 2015.

[16] H. Jowhari, M. Saglam, and G. Tardos. Tight bounds for L_p samplers, finding duplicates in streams, and related problems. In *ACM PODS*, pages 49–58, 2011.

[17] D. R. Karger, P. N. Klein, and R. E. Tarjan. A randomized linear-time algorithm to find minimum spanning trees. *J. ACM*, 42(2):321–328, 1995.

[18] H. J. Karloff, S. Suri, and S. Vassilvitskii. A model of computation for MapReduce. In *ACM-SIAM SODA*, pages 938–948, 2010.

[19] H. Klauck, D. Nanongkai, G. Pandurangan, and P. Robinson. Distributed computation of large-scale graph problems. In *ACM-SIAM SODA*, pages 391–410, 2015.

[20] S. Kutten, G. Pandurangan, D. Peleg, P. Robinson, and A. Trehan. Sublinear bounds for randomized leader election. *Theoret. Comput. Sci.*, 561:134–143, 2015.

[21] S. Lattanzi, B. Moseley, S. Suri, and S. Vassilvitskii. Filtering: a method for solving graph problems in MapReduce. In *ACM SPAA*, pages 85–94, 2011.

[22] C. Lenzen. Optimal deterministic routing and sorting on the congested clique. In *PODC*, pages 42–50, 2013.

[23] C. Lenzen and R. Wattenhofer. Tight bounds for parallel randomized load balancing. *Distrib. Comput.*, 29(2):127–142, 2016.

[24] J. Leskovec, A. Rajaraman, and J. D. Ullman. *Mining of Massive Datasets.* Cambridge University Press, 2014.

[25] Z. Lotker, B. Patt-Shamir, E. Pavlov, and D. Peleg. Minimum-weight spanning tree construction in $O(\log \log n)$ communication rounds. *SIAM J. Comput.*, 35(1):120–131, 2005.

[26] N. A. Lynch. *Distributed Algorithms.* Morgan Kaufmann Publishers Inc., 1996.

[27] G. Malewicz, M. H. Austern, A. J. C. Bik, J. C. Dehnert, I. Horn, N. Leiser, and G. Czajkowski. Pregel: a system for large-scale graph processing. In *ACM SIGMOD*, pages 135–146, 2010.

[28] A. McGregor. Graph stream algorithms: a survey. *SIGMOD Record*, 43(1):9–20, 2014.

[29] M. Mitzenmacher and E. Upfal. *Probability and Computing: Randomized Algorithms and Probabilistic Analysis.* Cambridge University Press, 2005.

[30] D. Nanongkai. Distributed approximation algorithms for weighted shortest paths. In *STOC*, pages 565–573, 2014.

[31] D. Nanongkai, A. D. Sarma, and G. Pandurangan. A tight unconditional lower bound on distributed randomwalk computation. In *ACM PODC*, pages 257–266, 2011.

[32] G. Pandurangan, P. Robinson, and M. Scquizzato. Fast distributed algorithms for connectivity and MST in large graphs. *CoRR*, abs/1503.02353, 2016.

[33] G. Pandurangan, P. Robinson, and M. Scquizzato. Tight bounds for distributed graph computations. *CoRR*, abs/1602.08481, 2016.

[34] D. Peleg. *Distributed Computing: A Locality-Sensitive Approach.* Society for Industrial and Applied Mathematics, 2000.

[35] J. Qiu, S. Jha, A. Luckow, and G. C. Fox. Towards HPC-ABDS: An initial high-performance big data stack. 2014. Available: http://grids.ucs.indiana.edu/ptliupages/publications/nist-hpc-abds.pdf.

[36] I. Stanton. Streaming balanced graph partitioning algorithms for random graphs. In *ACM-SIAM SODA*, pages 1287–1301, 2014.

[37] R. Thurimella. Sub-linear distributed algorithms for sparse certificates and biconnected components. *J. Algorithms*, 23(1):160–179, 1997.

[38] Y. Tian, A. Balmin, S. A. Corsten, S. Tatikonda, and J. McPherson. From "think like a vertex" to "think like a graph". *PVLDB*, 7(3):193–204, 2013.

[39] L. G. Valiant. A scheme for fast parallel communication. *SIAM J. Comput.*, 11(2):350–361, 1982.

[40] L. G. Valiant. A bridging model for parallel computation. *Commun. ACM*, 33(8):103–111, 1990.

[41] S. Vassilvitskii. Models for parallel computation (a hitchhikers' guide to massively parallel universes), http://grigory.us/blog/massively-parallel-universes/, 2015.

[42] D. P. Woodruff and Q. Zhang. When distributed computation is communication expensive. *Distrib. Comput.*, to appear.

Brief Announcement: A Tight Distributed Algorithm for All Pairs Shortest Paths and Applications*

Qiang-Sheng Hua
Services Computing Technology and System Lab, School of Computer Science and Technology, Huazhong University of Science and Technology, China

Haoqiang Fan
The Institute for Interdisciplinary Information Sciences, Tsinghua University, China

Lixiang Qian, Ming Ai, Yangyang Li, Xuanhua Shi, Hai Jin
Services Computing Technology and System Lab, School of Computer Science and Technology, Huazhong University of Science and Technology, China

ABSTRACT

Given an unweighted and undirected graph, this paper aims to give a tight distributed algorithm for computing the all pairs shortest paths (APSP) under synchronous communications and the $\mathcal{CONGEST}(\mathcal{B})$ model, where each node can only transfer B bits of information along each incident edge in a round. The best previous results for distributively computing APSP need $O(N + D)$ time where N is the number of nodes and D is the diameter [1, 2]. However, there is still a B factor gap from the lower bound $\Omega(N/B + D)$ [1]. In order to close this gap, we propose a multiplexing technique to push the parallelization of distributed BFS tree constructions to the limit such that we can solve APSP in $O(N/B+D)$ time which meets the lower bound. This result also implies a $\Theta(N/B + D)$ time distributed algorithm for diameter. In addition, we extend our distributed algorithm to compute girth which is the length of the shortest cycle and clustering coefficient (CC) which is related to counting the number of triangles incident to each node. The time complexities for computing these two graph properties are also $O(N/B + D)$.

1. INTRODUCTION

Computing all pairs shortest paths (APSP) is a fundamental problem in computer science. For unweighted graphs, APSP can be solved by fast matrix multiplication [3] and the time complexity is $O(N^{\omega} \log N)$ where N is the number of nodes and ω is the exponent of the fast matrix multiplication algorithm[1]. For weighted graphs, the up-to-date fastest algorithm [5] can solve APSP in time $O(N^3/2^{\Omega(\sqrt{\log N})})$. Whether we can design faster APSP algorithms than the above time complexities is an open problem.

However, there is another story when it comes to distributed algorithms. In the distributed algorithms, we consider synchronous communications and each node can only send a bounded size message to each neighbor in a round. Typically, if we restrict each node can only send B bits of information, it's called the $\mathcal{CONGEST}(\mathcal{B})$ model. If we set $B = O(\log N)$, this is the extensively used $\mathcal{CONGEST}$ model used in the distributed computing community [6].

For an undirected and unweighted graph $G = (V, E)$, where $|V| = N$ and $|E| = M$, computing APSP boils down to computing N Breadth-First-Search (BFS) trees. Distributively computing one BFS tree takes $O(D)$ time where D is the graph diameter. So a naive way to distributively computing APSP takes $O(ND)$ time by sequentially computing a distributed BFS tree rooted for each node. Surprisingly, recent elegant results [1, 2] show that APSP can be done in $O(N + D)$ time by scheduling N parallel distributed BFS tree constructions under the $\mathcal{CONGEST}$ model. This result is nearly optimal since the lower bound is $\Omega(N/B + D)$ [1]. However, there's still a B factor gap from the lower bound. A natural question is: Can we design a distributed algorithm for APSP that matches the lower bound under the $\mathcal{CONGEST}(\mathcal{B})$ model? In this paper, we give an affirmative answer to this question.

The basic idea of our distributed algorithm is that we utilize the multiplexing technique to take full advantage of the bandwidth B. Our algorithm divides the bandwidth into multiple channels and divides the nodes into several groups. The algorithm then performs parallel distributed Breadth-First-Search (BFS) processes for the nodes in the corresponding groups on each channel. In order to avoid message transmission collisions on the same channel (i.e., to satisfy the $\mathcal{CONGEST}(\mathcal{B})$ model), we will schedule the starting time of BFS processes in each channel. Since the distributed BFS processes don't interfere on different channels, there will be another dimension of freedom to increase the parallelism of the distributed BFS processes. Therefore,

*This paper is partly supported by the NSFC under grant No. 61572216 and 61433019, International Science & Technology Cooperation Program of China under grant No. 2015DFE12860, National 863 Hi-Tech Research and Development Program under grant 2014AA01A301.

SPAA '16 July 11-13, 2016, Pacific Grove, CA, USA

ACM ISBN 978-1-4503-4210-0/16/07.
DOI: http://dx.doi.org/10.1145/2935764.2935812

[1]The state-of-the-art fast matrix multiplication shows this exponent is around 2.372864 [4].

we give a tight distributed algorithm for APSP that meets the lower bound. This algorithm also implies a tight distributed algorithm for diameter since the lower bound for distributively computing diameter is also $\Omega(N/B + D)$ [7]. In addition, our algorithm can be extended to distributively compute the girth and the clustering coefficient (CC) whose time complexities are also $O(N/B + D)$.

2. OUR RESULTS

The main results of this paper are summarized in Table 1. In this paper we mainly focus on distributed algorithms for exactly computing APSP. Furthermore, we can extend our distributed APSP algorithm to compute diameter, girth and clustering coefficient. Our contributions are as follows:

1. We present a distributed algorithm for computing APSP in time $O(N/B + D)$. This improves previous upper bound of $O(N+D)$ in [1, 2]. Our distributed algorithm matches the lower bound $\Omega(N/B + D)$ of computing APSP in [1].
2. We introduce three applications of our distributed APSP algorithm: diameter, girth and clustering coefficient. All of them can be computed in time $O(D + N/B)$.

Table 1: Previous works and our results

Task	Precision	Previous Works	This Work
APSP	exact	$O(N)$[1][2] *	$\Theta(D+N/B)$
Girth	exact	$O(N)$[1][2] *	$O(D+N/B)$
CC	exact	$O(N)^{*\dagger}$	$O(D+N/B)$
Diameter	exact	$O(N)$[1][2] *	$\Theta(D+N/B)$

* All these works are based on $\mathcal{CONGEST}$ model. Our work is under the $\mathcal{CONGEST}(\mathcal{B})$ model. Note that if $B = O(\log N)$, $\mathcal{CONGEST}(\mathcal{B})$ model is the same as the $\mathcal{CONGEST}$ model.
† We are unaware of any previous work for computing this graph property under the $\mathcal{CONGEST}$ model. But we can derive this result based on the $O(N)$ time distributed APSP algorithm [1].

3. NAME-INDEPENDENT SHORTEST PATHS

In distributed APSP, $O(NM)$ messages have to be exchanged to construct N BFS trees. Following the distributed BFS approach, we cannot avoid a message complexity of $O(NM)$. But in one time step, at most $O(BM)$ bits can flow over the edges. So if the message size is B bits, the total $O(NBM)$ bits need to be exchanged. Thus, the time complexity will be $O(D + N)$. In order to reduce the time complexity to $O(D+N/B)$ and to meet the $\Omega(D+N/B)$ lower bound in [1], the message size can only be $O(1)$ bits such that we only need to exchange $O(NM)$ bits in the graph. In this case, the time complexity will be $O(D + N/B)$. However, if the message size is $O(1)$, we cannot include the node ID into the message (each node ID will be $O(\log N)$ bits) to distinguish messages from different sources in the BFS process. Thus, our major concern is to avoid sending nodes' IDs.

In this section, we present the method to compute name-independent APSP in $O(D+N/B)$ time. In order to match this bound, we first relabel the nodes to avoid sending nodes' IDs in subsection 3.1. That is, the new ID of each node does not need to be sent any more. For making the best use of the B bandwidth, we divide the bandwidth into multiple channels and perform BFS processes in each channel in subsection 3.2. Considering there may be collisions in each channel (violating the $\mathcal{CONGEST}(\mathcal{B})$ model), we present an algorithm scheduling the starting time of BFS processes to avoid it.

3.1 Relabel the Nodes

Given a spanning tree, we imagine a pebble [1] traversing the tree by DFS (Depth-First-Search), and at each step it records the node it visits. Denote a_k the time a pebble k-th time visits a node. So a_0 is the time a pebble enters node v for the first time and a_k is the time a pebble leaves node v for the last time if v only has k successors. We aim to get an array that records $a_0, \cdots, a_k$ for each node. Denote this array as τ where $\tau(i) = j$ means node j is visited by the pebble at time i.

To get array τ efficiently, we first compute the sizes of subtrees rooted at each node. This allows us to simulate DFS process by the sizes of subtrees. For a node v, if the size of its k-th subtree is s_k, we have $a_k = a_{k-1} + 2s_k$. It is easy for the root of the tree to compute a_k since a_0 is 0, then the root broadcasts a_{k-1} to its k-th successor and this successor takes $a_{k-1} + 1$ as its own a_0. We formulate this algorithm below.

- **Step 1:** Select a node to construct a BFS tree.
- **Step 2:** Each node in the tree computes its subtrees' sizes by convergecasting.
- **Step 3:** The root of the tree computes $a_0, a_1, \cdots, a_k$ where $a_0 = 0$ and $a_k = a_{k-1} + 2s_k$ if the root has k successors, then broadcasting a_{i-1} to its i-th successor where $0 < i \le k$.
- **Step 4:** The i-th node which receives a_{i-1} sets $a_0 = a_{i-1} + 1$ and does the same operation as Step 3.
- **Step 5:** After all the leaves of the BFS tree finished Step 4, each node gets its local array τ.

We use array τ as the new labels of nodes. Since the new label implies the order of nodes visited in the DFS process, we get the following LEMMA 1 showing the relationship between distance and new labels.

LEMMA 1. *Denote the distance from u to v as $d(u, v)$. For each node, it maintains a local τ where $\tau(x) = y$ means node y is visited by the pebble at time x so that*

$$d(\tau(i), \tau(j)) \le |i - j|.$$

Observe that nodes do not need to send the distance value in the BFS process. They only need to send a bit as a pebble. The problem is s_v and a_k can be as large as $O(N)$. We use pipelining to address this problem. That is, each node divides s_v into several messages of size B, then it sends the number of B bits at a time, from the least significant bits to the most significant bits. The pipelining takes $O(D + (\log N)/B)$ time. We conclude the time complexity of relabeling the nodes in LEMMA 2.

LEMMA 2. *Nodes can be relabeled in $O(D + (\log N)/B)$ time.*

3.2 Multiplexing

Recall that the basic idea of our algorithm is dividing the bandwidth into multiple channels and running the distributed BFS algorithm in each channel. If we divide the nodes into several groups and put them into different channels, there is no collision among the groups. So we only concern the schedule on one channel.

For the sake of generality, let b denote the size of messages used in the BFS process. Since only b bits are needed in one round when building each BFS tree, we divide the bandwidth into $R = \Theta(\min\{B/b, N\})$ channels. We partition the nodes relabeled in the subsection 3.1 into R groups:

$$U_i = \{\tau(j) | \lfloor \frac{i}{R}(2N-1) \rfloor \leq j < \lfloor \frac{i+1}{R}(2N-1) \rfloor\},$$

where U_i denotes the i-th group $(0 \leq i < R)$, and $0 \leq j < 2N-1$ denotes the index of nodes in τ. Since a node appears many times in τ, it can be contained in multiple groups. In order to avoid repeatedly computing the distance between two nodes, we only allow each node to perform one BFS process. Note that we only deliver a pebble as the BFS message instead of sending nodes' IDs, so b is $O(1)$. The message's traveling time between two nodes implies the distance between them. If each node knows where the messages originate from, we can figure out the distance by the messages' arriving time. Due to the limit of space, we just give a sketch of the multiplexing technique below.

- **Step 1:** Divide the nodes into R groups U_i where $0 \leq i < R$. Each group corresponds to a channel.
- **Step 2:** In one group, the nodes perform BFS one by one according to their ranks in the group. We set the time interval between two BFS processes as three rounds.
- **Step 3:** The node which receives a BFS message deduces where the message originates from. Since this node could receive duplicated messages from the same source during three continuous rounds, we ignore messages in the latter two rounds.
- **Step 4:** This node computes the distance from the message's originating node to itself.
- **Step 5:** The algorithm is finished if all nodes in the groups finished their BFS process.

We only concern one channel in Steps 2-4. In Step 3, a node may receive several messages from its neighbors in three continuous rounds and these messages originate from one source. Since we only need the messages which travel along the shortest paths, the messages which travel along longer paths must arrive at the latter two rounds and should be ignored. We set time interval as three rounds to avoid ignoring messages originating from different sources so that the messages arriving at different time intervals must originate from different nodes. That is, the first batch of messages a node received must originate from the first node in the group. The second batch of messages which are not ignored must originate from the second node in the group. This allows us to compute the distance between two nodes by messages' arriving time. By using LEMMA 1, we show that there is no collision in one group in LEMMA 3.

LEMMA 3. *Denote BFS_v as a BFS performed by node v. When node j and node k are both in the same group, at no time a node is simultaneously visited by both BFS_j and BFS_k.*

By using LEMMA 2 and LEMMA 3, we conclude the time complexity of name-independent APSP in THEOREM 1.

THEOREM 1. *The name-independent APSP can be solved in $O(D + N/B)$ time by using Relabeling and Multiplexing techniques.*

4. APPLICATIONS

In this section, we introduce three applications using Relabeling and Multiplexing techniques. Due to the limit of space, we directly give the time complexities of these applications.

THEOREM 2. *The diameter can be computed in $O(N/B + D)$ rounds. This matches the lower bound of computing diameter $\Omega(N/B + D)$ in [1].*

THEOREM 3. *Girth can be computed in time $O(D+N/B)$.*

THEOREM 4. *Clustering coefficient of vertices can be computed in time $O(D + N/B)$.*

5. CONCLUSION

In this paper, we studied the distributed computation of APSP on an undirected and unweighted graph under synchronous communications and the $\mathcal{CONGEST}(\mathcal{B})$ model. By dividing the limited B bandwidth into multiple channels and by utilizing the multiplexing technique, we can push the parallelization of the distributed BFS processes to the limit such that the time complexity for distributively computing APSP can be reduced from $O(N+D)$ to $O(N/B+D)$ which meets the lower bound $\Omega(N/B + D)$. This technique might be of independent interest to tackle some other problems under the $\mathcal{CONGEST}(\mathcal{B})$ model.

Our distributed algorithm also implies a tight distributed algorithm for computing diameter whose time complexity is $\Theta(N/B + D)$. In addition, we also extend our distributed algorithm to compute the girth and the clustering coefficient in $O(N/D + B)$ time.

6. REFERENCES

[1] Stephan Holzer and Roger Wattenhofer. Optimal distributed all pairs shortest paths and applications. In *Proc. PODC*, 2012.

[2] David Peleg, Liam Roditty, and Elad Tal. Distributed algorithms for network diameter and girth. In *Proc. ICALP*, 2012.

[3] Raimund Seidel. On the all-pairs-shortest-path problem in unweighted undirected graphs. *J. Comput. Syst. Sci.*, 51(3):400–403, 1995.

[4] François Le Gall. Powers of tensors and fast matrix multiplication. In *Proc. ISSAC*, 2014.

[5] Ryan Williams. Faster all-pairs shortest paths via circuit complexity. In *Proc. STOC*, 2014.

[6] David Peleg. Distributed computing: a locality sensitive approach. *SIAM Monographs on discrete mathematics and applications*, 5, 2000.

[7] Silvio Frischknecht, Stephan Holzer, and Roger Wattenhofer. Networks cannot compute their diameter in sublinear time. In *Proc. SODA*, 2012.

Parallel Shortest Paths Using Radius Stepping

Guy E. Blelloch
Carnegie Mellon University
guyb@cs.cmu.edu

Yan Gu
Carnegie Mellon University
yan.gu@cs.cmu.edu

Yihan Sun
Carnegie Mellon University
yihans@cs.cmu.edu

Kanat Tangwongsan*
Mahidol University
International College
kanat.tan@mahidol.edu

ABSTRACT

The single-source shortest path problem (SSSP) with nonnegative edge weights is notoriously difficult to solve efficiently in parallel—it is one of the graph problems said to suffer from the transitive-closure bottleneck. Yet, in practice, the Δ-stepping algorithm of Meyer and Sanders (*J. Algorithms, 2003*) often works efficiently but has no known theoretical bounds on general graphs. The algorithm takes a sequence of steps, each increasing the radius by a user-specified value Δ. Each step settles the vertices in its annulus but can take $\Theta(n)$ substeps, each requiring $\Theta(m)$ work (n vertices and m edges).

Building on the success of Δ-stepping, this paper describes RADIUS-STEPPING, an algorithm with one of the best-known tradeoffs between work and depth bounds for SSSP with nearly-linear ($\widetilde{O}(m)$) work. The algorithm is a Δ-stepping-like algorithm but uses a variable instead of a fixed-size increase in radii, allowing us to prove a bound on the number of steps. In particular, by using what we define as a vertex k-radius, each step takes at most $k + 2$ substeps. Furthermore, we define a (k, ρ)-graph property and show that if an undirected graph has this property, then the number of steps can be bounded by $O(n/\rho \cdot \log \rho L)$, for a total of $O(kn/\rho \cdot \log \rho L)$ substeps, each parallel. We describe how to preprocess a graph to have this property. Altogether, for an arbitrary input graph with n vertices and m edges, RADIUS-STEPPING, after preprocessing, takes $O((m+n\rho)\log n)$ work and $O(n/\rho \cdot \log n \log(\rho L))$ depth per source. The preprocessing step takes $O(m \log n + n\rho^2)$ work and $O(\rho \log \rho)$ depth, adding no more than $O(n\rho)$ edges.

1. INTRODUCTION

The single-source shortest path problem (SSSP) is a fundamental graph problem that is extremely well-studied and has numerous practical and theoretical applications. For a weighted graph $G = (V, E, w)$ with $n = |V|$ vertices and $m = |E|$ edges, and a source vertex $s \in V$, the SSSP problem with nonnegative edge weights is to find the shortest (i.e., minimum weight) path from s to every $v \in V$, according to the weight function $w: E \to \mathbb{R}_+$, which assigns to every edge a real-valued nonnegative weight ("distance"). We assume without loss of generality that the lightest nonzero edge has weight 1, i.e, $\min_{e:w(e)>0} w(e) = 1$. Throughout, we let $L = \max_e w(e)$ denote the heaviest edge in the graph.

In the sequential setting, Dijkstra's algorithm [8] implemented with the Fibonacci heap [10] solves this problem in $O(m + n \log n)$ time. This is the best theoretical running time for general nonnegative edge weights although faster algorithms exist for certain special cases. Thorup [27], for example, gives an $O(m + n)$-time algorithm for undirected graphs when the edge weights are positive integers.

In the parallel setting, the holy grail of parallel SSSP is an algorithm with Dijkstra's work bound (i.e., work efficient) that runs in small depth. Although tens of algorithms for the problem have been proposed over the last several decades, none of the existing algorithms that take the same amount of work as Dijkstra's have polylogarithmic or even $o(n)$ depth. This has led Karp and Ramachandran to coin the term *transitive closure bottleneck* [15].

Apart from the theoretical quest for a polylogarithmic-depth, work-efficient algorithm, one could aim for an algorithm with a high degree of parallelism ($\mathbb{P} = W/D$) that is work efficient or nearly work-efficient. From a performance standpoint, both factors are important because work efficiency is a prerequisite for the algorithm to quickly gain speedups over the sequential algorithm, and the parallelism factor $\mathbb{P}$ indicates how well it will scale with processors.

This observation has fueled the design of SSSP algorithms with substantial parallelism that are nearly work-efficient. Spencer [26] shows that SSSP can be solved in $O(n/\rho \cdot \log n \log(\rho L))$ depth and $O((n\rho^2 \log \rho + m)\log(n\rho L))$ work, using limited path-doubling to determine the shortest-path distances to about ρ vertices in each round. Later, by precomputing about ρ closest neighbors of every vertex, Shi and Spencer [25] solve SSSP in $O(n/\rho \cdot \log n)$ depth, and $O(n\rho^2 \log n \log \rho + m \log n)$ or $O((\rho^3 + m\rho)\log n)$ work; the preprocessing takes $O(n\rho^2 \log n \log \rho + m)$ work and $O(\log n \log \rho)$ depth. We further discuss these results, as well as other related algorithms, in Section 6.

On the empirical side, the Δ-stepping algorithm of Meyer and Sanders [19] works well on many kinds of graphs. The algorithm has been analyzed for random graphs, but no theoretical guarantees are known for the general case. Δ-stepping is a hybrid of Dijkstra's algorithm and the Bellman-Ford algorithm. It determines the correct distances from s in increments of Δ, settling in step i all the vertices whose shortest-path distances are between $i\Delta$ and $(i + 1)\Delta$. Within each step, the algorithm resorts to running Bellman-Ford as substeps to determine the distances to such vertices. Altogether, the algorithm performs up to a total of LK/Δ rounds of substeps, where K is the shortest-path distance to the farthest vertex from s.

*Corresponding author.

SPAA '16, July 11-13, 2016, Pacific Grove, CA, USA

DOI: http://dx.doi.org/10.1145/2935764.2935765

Our Contributions

In this paper, we investigate the single-source shortest-path problem for weighted, undirected graphs. We begin by introducing the notion of a (k, ρ)-graph to capture structural properties that enable computing SSSP in a few parallel steps. Informally, a (k, ρ)-graph is a graph in which every vertex can reach its ρ closest vertices within k hops. Based on this notion, our main results are as follows:

THEOREM 1.1 (SHORTEST PATH). *There is an algorithm, RADIUS-STEPPING, that on input a (k, ρ)-graph with m edges and n vertices and a source vertex, computes the shortest path to every vertex in $O(km \log n)$ work and $O(kn/\rho \cdot \log n \log(\rho L))$ depth.*

However, not all graphs are (k, ρ)-graphs as given. We prove that by adding a small number of extra edges ("shortcuts"), every graph can be turned into a $(1, \rho)$-graph at a modest cost:

THEOREM 1.2 (PREPROCESSING). *There is an algorithm that on input an undirected, weighted graph G with n vertices and m edges, computes a $(1, \rho)$-graph out of G in $O(m \log n + n\rho^2)$ work and $O(\rho \log \rho)$ depth by adding at most $n\rho$ extra edges.*

Together, this means that given as input an *arbitrary* undirected, weighted graph with n vertices and m edges, we can make it a $(1, \rho)$-graph in $O(m \log n + n\rho^2)$ work and $O(\rho \log \rho)$ depth. The graph then has $m' = m + n\rho$ edges, whose weight is at most ρL each. Hence, after preprocessing, the shortest path from any given source can be computed in $O((m + n\rho) \log n)$ work and $O(n/\rho \cdot \log n \log(\rho L))$ depth[1].

Compared to a standard Dijkstra's implementation, the algorithm, excluding preprocessing, is work-efficient up to only a $\log n$ factor. Using $\rho = \text{polylog}(n)$, the algorithm offers at least polylogarithmic parallelism. Using $\rho = \Omega(n^{\epsilon})$, the algorithm has sublinear depth. As far as we know, this is one of the best tradeoffs between work and depth for the problem and has the potential to perform better on real graphs than what the theoretical bounds suggest.

In broad strokes, our algorithm RADIUS-STEPPING (Section 3) can be seen as a hybrid variant of Δ-stepping and Spencer's algorithm, though simpler. It also bears some similarity to Shi and Spencer's algorithm but is again simpler. Like Δ-stepping, it performs Dijkstra's-like steps in the outer loop, finding and settling multiple vertices at a time using (restricted) Bellman-Ford as substeps. Unlike Δ-stepping, however, the algorithm judiciously picks a new step size (Δ) every time. The step size is chosen so that, like in Spencer's algorithm, about ρ new vertices are settled in every step, or otherwise it doubles the distance explored. Yet, unlike Spencer's algorithm, RADIUS-STEPPING does not perform path doubling in every iteration, leading to a conceptually simpler algorithm with fewer moving parts. Ultimately, the steps of RADIUS-STEPPING mirror Dijkstra's execution steps, and the only invariant necessary is a natural generalization of Dijkstra's invariant.

Provided that the input is a (k, ρ)-graph, RADIUS-STEPPING runs in $O(\frac{n}{\rho} \log(\rho L))$ steps, each running up to $O(k)$ substeps, leading to the bounds in Theorem 1.1. For unweighted graphs, it only takes $O(k(m + n))$ work and $O(k\frac{n}{\rho} \log \rho \log^* \rho)$ depth.

As not all graphs are (k, ρ)-graphs as given, Section 4 describes preprocessing strategies to make a graph a (k, ρ)-graph. They involve running restricted Dijkstra's to discover the ρ-closest vertices for all vertices in parallel. To derive a $(1, \rho)$-graph, the preprocessing step effectively adds up to $n\rho$ shortcut edges to the input graph. The number of shortcut edges can be reduced if we use a larger k. Although this saves some memory, RADIUS-STEPPING will have to do slightly more work when computing the shortest paths. For $k > 1$, it is less trivial to generate a (k, ρ)-graph that adds only a small number of edges. We present some heuristics in Section 4 and empirically study their quality in Section 5.

Our experiments study the number of edges added by preprocessing and the number of steps taken by RADIUS-STEPPING. This is a good proxy for measuring the depth of the algorithm experimentally. The results confirm our theory: the number of steps taken (that is, roughly the depth) is inversely proportional to ρ for both the weighted and unweighted cases. They further show that with an appropriate heuristic (such as the dynamic programming heuristic from Section 4.2) and choice of parameters, preprocessing will add a reasonably small number of edges (at most $O(m)$), thereby increasing the total work by at most a constant.

[1]The heaviest edge is technically heavier by a ρ-factor, affecting the $\log(\rho L)$ term only by a constant.

2. PRELIMINARIES

Let $G = (V, E, w)$ be an undirected, simple, weighted graph. We assume without loss of generality that G is a connected, simple graph (i.e., no self-loops nor parallel edges). For $S \subseteq V$, define $N(S) = \cup_{u \in S}\{v \mid (u, v) \in E\}$ to be the ***neighbor set*** of S. During the execution of standard breadth-first search (BFS) or Dijkstra's algorithm, the ***frontier*** is the neighbor set of all visited vertices. Let $d(u, v)$ denote the shortest-path distance in G between two vertices u and v. The ***enclosed ball*** of a vertex u is $B(u, r) = \{v \in V \mid d(u, v) \leqslant r\}$.

A ***shortest-path tree*** rooted at vertex u is a spanning tree T of G (a subtree if disconnected) such that the path distance from the root u to any other vertex $v \in T$ is the shortest-path distance from v to u in G. A graph is ***unweighted*** if $w(e) = 1$ for all $e \in E$ (so $L = 1$).

We assume the standard PRAM model that allows for concurrent reads and writes, and analyze the performance of our parallel algorithms in terms of work and depth [14], where ***work*** W is equal to the total number of operations performed and ***depth (span)*** D is equal to the longest sequence of dependent operations. Nonetheless, all of our algorithms can also be implemented on machines with exclusive writes. An algorithm is ***work efficient*** if it does the same amount of work as the best sequential counterpart, up to constants.

Consider two ordered sets A and B stored in balanced BSTs with $|A| \leqslant |B|$. Recent research work shows that set union and set difference can be computed either in $O(|A| \log |B|)$ work and $O(\log |B|)$ depth [24, 22, 23], or in $O(|A| \log |B|/|A|)$ work and $O(\log |A| \log |B|)$ depth [3, 2]. For this paper, it suffices that both set operations take $O(|A| \log |B|)$ work and $O(\log |B|)$ depth. Also, to split a tree A by a certain key costs $O(\log |A|)$ work and depth [2].

Finally, we need a few definitions for our algorithms:

DEFINITION 1 (HOP DISTANCE). *Let $\hat{d}(u, v)$ be the number of edges on the shortest (weighted) path between u and v that uses the fewest edges.*

DEFINITION 2 (k-RADIUS). *For $u \in V$, the k-radius of u, denoted by $\bar{r}_k(u)$, is $\min_{v \in V, \hat{d}(u,v) > k} d(u, v)$—that is, the closest distance to u which is more than k hops away.*

The k-radii of vertices are widely used in our algorithm analysis. However, computing them can be costly, so instead, we provide the concepts of ρ-nearest distance and (k, ρ)-graph, and our algorithm is based on both the k-radius and ρ-nearest distance of each vertex.

DEFINITION 3 (ρ-NEAREST DISTANCE). *For $v \in V$, the ρ-nearest distance of v, denoted by $r_\rho(v)$, is the distance from v to the ρ-th closest vertex to v.*

Algorithm 1: The Radius-Stepping Algorithm.

Input: A graph $G = (V, E, w)$, vertex radii $r(\cdot)$, and a source vertex s.
Output: The graph distances $\delta(\cdot)$ from s.

1 $\delta(\cdot) \leftarrow +\infty, \delta(s) \leftarrow 0$
2 **foreach** $v \in N(s)$ **do** $\delta(v) \leftarrow w(s, v)$
3 $S_0 \leftarrow \{s\}, i \leftarrow 1$
4 **while** $|S_{i-1}| < |V|$ **do**
5 $\quad d_i \leftarrow \min_{v \in V \setminus S_{i-1}} \{\delta(v) + r(v)\}$
6 $\quad$ **repeat**
7 $\quad\quad$ **foreach** $u \in V \setminus S_{i-1}$ *s.t.* $\delta(u) \leqslant d_i$ **do**
8 $\quad\quad\quad$ **foreach** $v \in N(u) \setminus S_{i-1}$ **do**
9 $\quad\quad\quad\quad \delta(v) \leftarrow \min\{\delta(v), \delta(u) + w(u, v)\}$
10 $\quad$ **until** *no* $\delta(v) \leqslant d_i$ *was updated*
11 $\quad S_i = \{v \mid \delta(v) \leqslant d_i\}$
12 $\quad i = i + 1$
13 **return** $\delta(\cdot)$

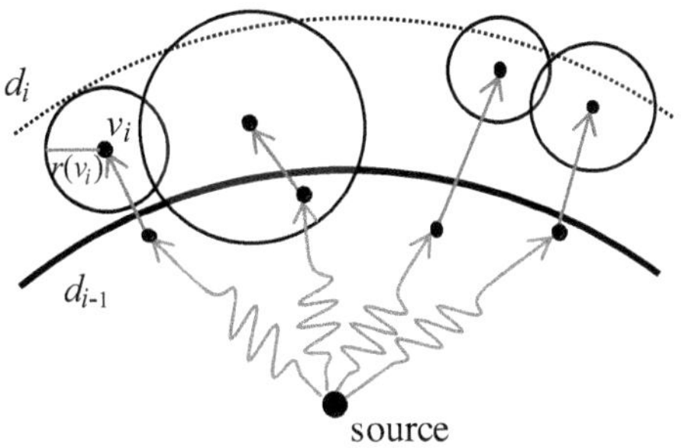

Figure 1: Illustration of a step of Radius-Stepping: For all vertices whose neighbors are within d_i, we pick v_i, the lead node in the i-th step, that minimizes the tentative distance plus the vertex radius of this vertex. The step distance d_i is set to $\delta(v_i) + r(v_i)$.

Definition 4 (((k, ρ)-ball and (k, ρ)-graph). *We say that a vertex $v \in V$ has a (k, ρ)-ball if $r_\rho(v) \leqslant \bar{r}_k(v)$. A graph is a (k, ρ)-graph if each vertex in the graph forms a (k, ρ)-ball.*

The following lemma then follows directly from these definitions:

Lemma 2.1. *For a graph G, if we let $r(v) = r_\rho(v)$ for all $v \in V$ and G is a (k, ρ)-graph, then $r(v) \leqslant \bar{r}_k(v)$ and $|B(v, r(v))| \geqslant \rho$.*

3. THE RADIUS-STEPPING ALGORITHM

This section describes our algorithm for parallel SSSP called Radius-Stepping and discusses its performance analysis. We begin with a high-level description, which we analyze for the number of steps. Following that, we give a detailed implementation, which we analyze for work and depth.

The Radius-Stepping algorithm is presented in Algorithm 1. At a high level, it works as follows: The input to the algorithm is a weighted, undirected graph, a source vertex, and a target radius value for every vertex, given as a function $r : V \to \mathbb{R}_+$. In the algorithm we use $\delta(\cdot)$ to denote the tentative distance. The algorithm has the same basic structure as the Δ-stepping algorithm; both are effectively a hybrid of Dijkstra's algorithm and the Bellman-Ford algorithm. Like Dijkstra's algorithm, they visit vertices in increasing distance from the source s, settling each vertex v—i.e., determining its correct distance $d(s, v)$. However, instead of visiting one vertex at a time, the algorithms visit vertices in ***steps*** (the while loop in Line 5–12). In each step i, Radius-Stepping increments the radius centered at s from d_{i-1} to d_i, and settles all vertices v in the annulus $d_{i-1} < d(s, v) \leqslant d_i$. This is illustrated in Figure 1.

Settling these vertices involves multiple ***substeps*** (the do loop in Lines 6–10) of what is effectively Bellman-Ford's algorithm. Each substep is easily parallelized. In Δ-stepping, the step distance $d_i = d_{i-1} + \Delta$ increases the radius by a fixed amount on each step. This can require $\Theta(n)$ substeps in the worst case, which is not efficient since each substep will process the same set of vertices and their edges. In the worst case, it could take $O(nm)$ work.

In the Radius-Stepping algorithm, a new step distance d_i is decided on each step with the goal of bounding the number of substeps. The algorithm takes a radius $r(v)$ for each vertex and selects a d_i on step i by taking the minimum of $\delta(v) + r(v)$ over all v in the frontier (Line 5). Lines 6–10 then run the Bellman-Ford substeps until all vertices with radius less than d_i are settled. Vertices within d_i are then added to the visited set S_i.

The algorithm is correct for any radii $r(\cdot)$, but by setting it appropriately, it can be used to control the number of substeps per step and the number of steps. If $r(v) = 0$, then the algorithm is effectively Dijkstra's, and the inner step is run only once. It may, however, visit multiple vertices with the same distance. If $r(v) = \infty$, then the algorithm is effectively the Bellman-Ford algorithm, and the substeps will run until all vertices are settled, and hence there will be a single step. If $r(v) = \Delta$, then the algorithm is almost Δ-stepping, but not quite since Δ is added to the distance of the nearest frontier vertex instead of to d_{i-1}.

In this paper, we aim to set $r(v)$ to be close, but no more, than the k-radius $\bar{r}_k(v)$. By making $r(v)$ no more than the k-radius, it guarantees that the algorithm will run at most $(k + 2)$ Bellman-Ford substeps. For our theoretical bounds, we set $k = 1$ so the algorithm only does constant substeps.

In addition to bounding the number of substeps, we want to bound the number of steps. To do this, we can make use of properties of the input graph. In particular, if every vertex v has ρ vertices that are within a distance $r(v)$, i.e. $r_\rho(v) \leqslant r(v)$ (indicating $|B(v, r(v))| \geqslant \rho$), then we can bound the number of steps by $O(\frac{n}{\rho} \log(\rho L))$, where L is the longest edge in the graph.

Theorem 3.1 (Correctness). *After the i-th step of Radius-Stepping, each vertex v with $d_{i-1} < d(s, v) \leqslant d_i$ will have $\delta(v) = d(s, v)$ and will be included in S_i.*

Correctness of the algorithm is straightforward since it is essentially the Δ-stepping algorithm with a variable step size: At the end of the inner loop, all vertices within the step distance are settled, and all of their direct neighbors are relaxed.

To analyze the parallelism of this algorithm, we observe that the inner-most loops for each Bellman-Ford step (Lines 7 and 8) are readily parallelizable, so the longest chain of dependencies (i.e., the depth) is bounded by the number of steps (Line 5) and substeps (Line 6), as given below:

Theorem 3.2 (The number of substeps). *The repeat-until loop (Lines 6–10) runs at most $k + 2$ times provided that $r(v) \leqslant \bar{r}_k(v)$ for all $v \in V$.*

Theorem 3.3 (The number of steps). *The while loop (Lines 5–12) requires no more than*

$$\left\lceil \frac{n}{\rho} \right\rceil (1 + \lceil \log_2 \rho L \rceil) = O\left(\frac{n}{\rho} \log(\rho L)\right)$$

steps provided that $r_\rho(v) \leqslant r(v)$ for all $v \in V$.

We prove these theorems in Sections 3.1 and 3.2 that follow, and give implementation details of the algorithm in Section 3.3.

In the following analysis, we define the ***lead node*** in step i as the vertex v that attains d_i in Line 5 and denote it by v_i.

3.1 Number of Substeps

Let k be such that $r(v) \leqslant \bar{r}_k(v)$ for all $v \in V$. To bound the number of substeps, we use the fact that vertices with distances no more than the step distance in the previous step (d_{i-1}) are all correctly computed, as given by Theorem 3.1. Observe that their neighbors are also relaxed, since the distances to none of these vertices are updated in the last substep of the previous step (the termination condition in Line 10).

Lemma 3.4. *For a vertex $v \in V$, if $d_{i-1} < d(s,v) \leqslant d_i$, then its distance is correctly computed after $k+1$ substeps of the i-th step, i.e. $\delta(v) = d(s,v)$.*

Proof. Consider the shortest path from s to v that uses the fewest hops. Let u be the first vertex on this path with distance larger than d_{i-1}. By Theorem 3.1, we have that $\delta(u)$ is relaxed to $d(s,u)$ at the end of the $(i-1)$-th step.

Now we prove that v must be within $(k+1)$ hops from u. Assume to the contrary that the hop distance $\hat{d}(u,v) > k+1$. Let v' be the vertex on the shortest path from s to v which appears right before v, then $d(u,v') < d(u,v) \leqslant d_i - \delta(u) \leqslant r(u) \leqslant \bar{r}_k(u)$, which contradicts the condition that $\hat{d}(u,v') = \hat{d}(u,v) - 1 > k$ (the definition of k-radius $\bar{r}_k(u)$ prevents this from happening). Hence, we have $\hat{d}(u,v) \leqslant k+1$, and the distance of v can be computed within $k+1$ substeps along the shortest path from u to v. □

By Lemma 3.4, all vertices with distances no more than d_i can be computed within $k+1$ substeps. We need an extra substep to relax all of their direct neighbors, and to ensure no $\delta(v) \leqslant d_i$ was updated. This proves Theorem 3.2.

3.2 Number of Steps

Let $\rho > 0$ be such that the condition $r(v) \geqslant r_\rho(v)$ (or $B(v, r(v)) \geqslant \rho$) holds for all $v \in V$. We prove Theorem 3.3 by showing the following lemma:

Lemma 3.5. *In any $t = 1 + \lceil \log_2 \rho L \rceil$ consecutive steps, except possibly in the last step of the algorithm, we have $|S_{i+t} - S_i| \geqslant \rho$.*

The lemma says that Radius-Stepping will visit at least ρ vertices in any $t = 1 + \lceil \log \rho L \rceil$ consecutive steps, except perhaps in the last one. Hence, all vertices will be visited in no more than $\lceil n/t \rceil = \lceil n/\rho \rceil (1 + \lceil \log_2 \rho L \rceil)$ steps.

To prove this lemma, we show that in a step j, $i < j \leqslant i+t$, either ρ vertices have already been visited in the j-step (i.e. $|S_{j+1} - S_i| \geqslant \rho$), or the difference in the step distance doubles (i.e. $d_j - d_i \geqslant 2(d_{j-1} - d_i)$). In the latter case, if that happens for t consecutive steps, then $d_t - d_i \geqslant 2^{t-1} > \rho L$, which has at least ρ nodes in this range.We begin the proof by showing some basic facts about the algorithm: The lemma below shows a property of the enclosed ball of the lead node v_j.

Lemma 3.6. *Let $i < j$. For a lead node v_j, if $r(v_j) < d(s, v_j) - d_i$, then $B(v_j, r(v_j)) \subseteq (S_j - S_i)$.*

Proof. Consider a vertex $v \in B(v_j, r(v_j))$. First, v cannot be visited after the j-th step, since $d(s,v) \leqslant d(s,v_j) + d(v_j,v) \leqslant \delta(v_j) + r(v_j) = d_j$. Similarly, v cannot be visited in the first i steps since $d(s,v) \geqslant d(s,v_j) - d(v_j,v) > d_i + r(v_j) - d(v_j,v) \geqslant d_i$. □

The next property states that starting from the i-th step, either we reach ρ vertices, or the distance we explore in each step doubles.

Lemma 3.7. *Let i be given. If $|B(v_j, r(v_j))| \geqslant \rho$, then $\forall j > i$, either $|S_j - S_i| \geqslant \rho$, or $d_j - d_i \geqslant 2(d_{j-1} - d_i) \geqslant 2^{j-i-1}$.*

Proof. Lemma 3.6 already shows that if $r(v_j) < d(s,v_j) - d_i$ then we have $|S_j - S_i| \geqslant |B(v_j, r(v_j))| \geqslant \rho$. Otherwise, since $\delta(v_j) \geqslant d(s, v_j)$,

$$\begin{aligned} d_j - d_i &= \delta(v_j) + r(v_j) - d_i \\ &\geqslant d(s,v_j) + \big(d(s,v_j) - d_i\big) - d_i \\ &= 2(d(s,v_j) - d_i) \geqslant 2(d_{j-1} - d_i), \end{aligned}$$

where the last step used the fact that $d(s,v_j) \geqslant d_{j-1}$ (Line 5). Since the minimum edge weight is 1, we have that $d_{i+1} - d_i \geqslant 1$ and further that $d_j - d_i \geqslant 2^{j-i-1}$. □

With Lemma 3.7, we now prove Lemma 3.5, which is equivalent to proving Theorem 3.3.

Proof of Lemma 3.5. If $|B(v_j, r(v_j))| \geqslant \rho$ and $|S_{i+t} - S_i| < \rho$, then based on Lemma 3.7, $d_{i+t} - d_i \geqslant 2^{t-1} \geqslant \rho L$. Consider the node $u^* = \arg\min_{u \in V \setminus S_{i+t}} d(s,u)$. Let $\{u_1 = s, u_2, \cdots, u_k = u^*\}$ be the ancestors to reach u^* on the shortest-path tree. From the definition of u^* we have $\{u_1 = s, u_2, \cdots, u_{k-1}\} \subseteq S_{i+t}$. Meanwhile, since the longest edge in G has edge weight L, for any j that $k - \rho \leqslant j \leqslant k-1$, the shortest-path distance to u_j satisfies that $d(s,u_j) \geqslant d(s,u^*) - (k-j)L \geqslant d(s,u^*) - \rho L > d_{i+t} - \rho L \geqslant d_i$, which means $u_j \notin S_i$. Therefore, $\{u_{k-\rho}, u_{k-\rho+1}, \cdots, u_{k-1}\} \in S_{i+t} - S_i$, and $|S_{i+t} - S_i| \geqslant \rho$. □

3.3 Work and Depth

We now analyze the work and depth of Radius-Stepping. Algorithm 1 is a high-level description, and an efficient implementation with priority queues is shown in Algorithm 2. Throughout the complexity analysis, we assume $r_\rho(v) \leqslant r(v) \leqslant \bar{r}_k(v)$ for all $v \in V$ (we show how to prepare the graph to guarantee this property in the next section).

There are mainly two steps in Algorithm 1 that are costly and require efficient solutions: the calculation of the step distance d_i (Line 5) and the discovery of all unvisited vertices with tentative distances less than d_i (Line 7).

To efficiently support these two types of queries, we use two ordered sets Q and R, implemented as balanced binary search trees (BSTs) to store the tentative distance ($\delta(u)$) for each unvisited vertex and the tentative distance plus the vertex radius ($\delta(u) + r(u)$). With these BSTs, the selection of step distance corresponds to finding the minimum in the tree R, and picking vertices within a certain distance is a split operation on the BST Q. Both operations require $O(\log n)$ work.

Let A_i be the ***active set*** that contains the elements visited in the i-th step (all vertices u in line 7 in Algorithm 1). This can be computed by splitting the BST Q (Line 7 in Algorithm 2). To maintain the priority queues sequentially, we relax all neighbors of vertices in A_i for $k+2$ substeps. Other than updating the tentative distance, we update each neighbor vertex (referred to as v) as follows:

(1) if the previous distance of v is already no more than d_i, v is already removed from Q and R earlier in this step, so we do nothing;

(2) if the previous distance is larger than d_i while the updated value is no more than d_i, we remove v from Q and R, and add v to the active set A_i; and

(3) if the updated distance is still larger than d_i, we decrease the keys corresponding to v in Q and R.

It can be checked that the efficient implementation with BSTs Q and R (Algorithm 2) visits the same vertices in each step as Algorithm 1 and hence computes the shortest-path distances correctly.

The key step to parallelize Algorithm 2 is to handle the inner loop (Line 10), which can be separated into two parts: (1) update the tentative distances and (2) update the BSTs. We process these two steps in turn. To update the tentative distances, we just use priority-write (WRITEMIN) to relax the other endpoints for all edges that have endpoints in A_i. After all tentative distances are updated, each edge checks whether the relaxation (priority-write) is successful. If successful, the edge will *own* this vertex (called u), and create a BST node that contains a pair of keys (lexicographical ordering): the current tentative distance of u as the first key, and the vertex label of u as the second key. Then, we create a BST that contains all these nodes using standard parallel packing and sorting process. With this BST, we first apply set DIFFERENCE to remove out-of-date keys in Q, then we SPLIT this BST into two parts by d_i, and UNION each part separately with A_i and Q. It is easy to see that in this parallel version, we apply asymptotically the same number of operations to Q compared to the sequential version. We can maintain R in a similar way.

Let us now analyze the work and depth of the parallel version. Each vertex is in the active set in only one step, so each of its neighbors is relaxed $k+2$ times, once in each substep. In the worst case (all the relaxation succeeded), there are $O(m)$ updates for Q and R; each can be done for no more than $O(k)$ times when $r(v) \leqslant \bar{r}_k(v)$.

Suppose there are t steps and the number of updates in step i is a_i. Then, we have $\sum_{i=1}^{t} a_i = m$, and $t = O(\frac{n}{\rho}\log \rho L)$ as $r_\rho(v) \leqslant r(v)$. The work and depth for set DIFFERENCE and UNION are $O(p\log q)$ and $O(\log q)$ for two sets with size p and q, $q \geqslant p$. The overall work W for all set operations is no more than $\sum_{i=1}^{t} a_i \cdot k\log n = O(km\log n)$. The depth D is no larger than

$$O\left(\sum_{i=1}^{t} k\log n\right) = O\left(k\frac{n}{\rho}\log \rho L\log n\right)$$

All other steps in Algorithm 2 are dominated by the cost to maintain the BSTs. The total work and depth can be summarized in the following lemma.

LEMMA 3.8. *Assuming $r_\rho(v) \leqslant r(v) \leqslant \bar{r}_k(v)$ for all $v \in V$, the RADIUS-STEPPING algorithm computes single source shortest paths in $O(km\log n)$ work and $O\left(k\frac{n}{\rho}\log n\log \rho L\right)$ depth.*

3.4 Unweighted Cases

The implementation we just discussed also works on unweighted graphs. But the performance can be further improved in this case. A special property of the unweighted case is that all vertices in the frontier have the same tentative distances. This means that we do not need search trees or priority queues to maintain the ordering. Hence, a similar approach to parallel BFS can be directly used here, and each step takes $O(n')$ work and $O(\log^* n')$ depth on the CRCW PRAM model [2] where n' is the number of vertices and their associated edges in each step. The additional step to compute the step distance uses one priority-write. Because of concavity, the worst case appears when n' is the same in every step.

LEMMA 3.9. *The RADIUS-STEPPING algorithm computes single-source shortest paths on unweighted graph in $O(m+n)$ work and $O(n/\rho \cdot \log \rho \log^* \rho)$ depth.*

[2]The bound changes with different models, and a more practical solution is to use semisort [12].

Algorithm 2: The Shortest-path Algorithm.

Input: A graph $G = (V, E, w)$, vertex radii $r(\cdot)$ and a source node s.

Output: The graph distances $\delta(\cdot)$ from s.

1 $\delta(\cdot) \leftarrow +\infty$, $\delta(s) \leftarrow 0$
2 $i \leftarrow 1$
3 $Q = \{w(s,u) \mid u \in N(s)\}$
4 $R = \{w(s,u) + r(u) \mid u \in N(s)\}$
5 **while** $|Q| > 0$ **do**
6     $d_i \leftarrow R$.EXTRACT-MIN()
7     $\{A_i, Q\} = Q$.SPLIT(d_i)
8   **foreach** $u \in A_i$ **do** R.REMOVE(u)
9   **repeat**
10   **foreach** $u \in A_i, v \in N(u)$ **do**
11   **if** $\delta(v) > \delta(u) + w(u,v)$ **then**
12   **if** $\delta(v) > d_i$ and $\delta(u) + w(u,v) \leqslant d_i$ **then**
13   R.REMOVE(v)
14   Q.REMOVE(v)
15   A_i.INSERT(v)
16                 $\delta(v) = \delta(u) + w(u,v)$
17   **if** $\delta(v) > d_i$ **then**
18   Q.DECREASE-KEY($v, \delta(v)$)
19   R.DECREASE-KEY($v, \delta(v) + r(v)$)
20   **until** *no $\delta(v)$ that $v \in A_i$ is updated*
21     $i = i + 1$
22 **return** $\delta(\cdot)$

4. SHORTCUTS AND PREPROCESSING

This section describes how to prepare an arbitrary undirected graph so that RADIUS-STEPPING can run efficiently afterward. As shown earlier, the cost of RADIUS-STEPPING is a function of k and ρ provided that the input to the algorithm is a (k,ρ)-graph. But not every graph as given meets this condition with k and ρ that one desires. Our aim here is to prepare the input graph by adding a small number of edges (shortcuts) to satisfy the condition for k and ρ that the user chooses. The process will also generate an appropriate vertex radius $r(v)$ for every $v \in V$.

Any graph can be turned into a (k,ρ)-graph by adding up to $n\rho$ edges (put shortcut edges from every vertex to its ρ-nearest vertices). For $k = 1$, this strategy adds the minimum number of edges possible. For $k > 1$, however, one can usually do better. Below, we discuss efficient preprocessing strategies and their cost.

4.1 Heuristics for $(1,\rho)$-graph

The simplest case of a (k,ρ)-graph is $k = 1$. In this case, we have to ensure that every vertex is a $(1,\rho)$-ball, so all the ρ-closest vertices from a vertex u are added to u's neighbor list with edge weight $d(u,\cdot)$. To do so for all the vertices, we can, in parallel, start n Dijkstra's execution (or BFS for unweighted graphs) and compute the ρ-closest vertices in each run.

LEMMA 4.1. *Given a graph G, generating $(1,\rho)$-balls for all vertices takes $O(m\log n + n\rho^2)$ work and $O(\rho\log\rho)$ depth.*

PROOF. Initially, we sort all edges from each vertex by their weights, requiring $O(m\log n)$ work and $O(\log n)$ depth. This can be skipped if the edges are presorted or the graph is unweighted. Then, run parallel Dijkstra's [4] from each vertex for ρ rounds. For each vertex, we only consider the lightest ρ edges as only these edges may be needed to reach the ρ-closest vertices. So, the search from each vertex explores no more than ρ^2 edges (ρ^2 DECREASE-KEYS

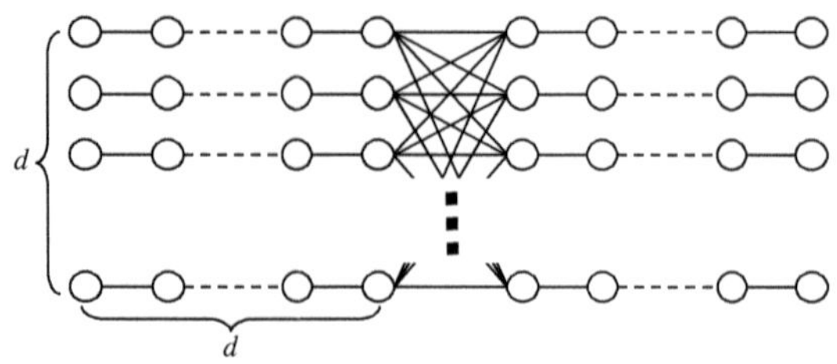

Figure 2: Example of a sparse graph that requires BFS to look at $O(d^2)$ edges from any vertex to reach $3d$ vertices.

in the Fibonacci Heap) and visits ρ vertices (ρ DELETE-MINS in the Fibonacci Heap), leading to $O(\rho^2)$ work for each source node—or in total, $O(\rho \log \rho)$ depth and $O(n\rho^2)$ work.

We can then add ρ shortcut edges from the source to all these vertices. When the algorithm stops in the ρ-th round, we also have the value of $r_\rho(v)$, the distance from the source to ρ-th nearest neighbor. Clearly, we have $r_\rho(v) \leqslant \bar{r}_1(v)$ at this time. □

For the unweighted case, a parallel BFS from the source vertex to reach ρ-nearest neighbors takes $O(\rho^2)$ work and $O(\rho \log^* \rho)$ depth.

Combining Lemmas 4.1, 2.1, and 3.9 proves the main theorems. Notie that after preprocessing, the graph now has $O(m + n\rho)$ edges.

It is worth mentioning that even when the given graph is unweighted and sparse, we may still need to look at $O(\rho^2)$ edges to reach ρ vertices. We give an example of a carefully-constructed graph with that behavior in Figure 2. If $d = \lfloor \rho/3 \rfloor - 1$, then the BFS search from any vertex has to visit $O(d^2)$ edges to reach $\rho > 3d$ vertices. However, Section 5.3 shows empirically that this scenario is not common in real-world graphs. Furthermore, if the input graph has constant-bounded degrees, the work for this step is $O(n\rho)$.

4.2 Heuristics for (k, ρ)-graphs

The construction of a $(1, \rho)$-graph can add up to $n\rho$ extra edges, potentially too many to be useful for many graphs in practice. Using a small $k > 1$ creates an opportunity to add fewer shortcut edges, by taking better advantange of the original edges.

To construct a (k, ρ)-graph, we will still run the algorithm in Lemma 4.1. But for each vertex s, instead of adding a shortcut edge for each of the ρ closest vertices, we derive a shortest-path tree T_s (at no additional cost) from s that reaches out to its ρ nearest vertices. We then work with these trees with the goal of adding as few edges as possible while ensuring that every $v \in V(T_s)$ can be reached within k hops using the combination of the original edges and the added edges E'.

We propose two heuristics below, both relying on the following claim, which shows that from the perspective of a single source vertex, the most beneficial shortcut edge goes directly from the source itself. The proof is straightforward and is omitted.

CLAIM 4.2. *Let s be a source vertex. A shortcut edge (u, v), $u \neq s$, can be exchanged for (s, v) with an appropriate weight without increasing the overall hop count.*

Shortcut using Greedy: The greedy heuristic eliminates vertices that are more than k hops away in T_s by adding edges from s to all $(ki + 1)$-th hop vertices for $i \in \mathbb{Z}_+$. It is simple and easy to implement, but may end up adding far too many edges. For example, consider a shortest-path tree that first forms a chain of length k from the source, then the remaining $\rho - k - 2$ vertices all lie in the $(k + 1)$-st level. The greedy heuristic will shortcut to all these $\rho - k - 2$ vertices, while we can only add one edge from the source to the node in the k-th layer to include all vertices in k hops.

Shortcut using Dynamic Programming (DP): The DP heuristic solves a dynamic program that adds the optimal number of edges from the perspective of one vertex. Consider, among all shortest-path trees from s, one where for every $v \in T_s$, the path $s \rightarrow v$ on T has the smallest hop count possible. The optimal number of edges needed for a certain node can be computed using the following dynamic program. Let $F(u, t)$ be the number of edges into the subtree of T_s rooted at u so that every node in the subtree is at most k hops away from s provided that parent(u) is at t hops away from s. Then, for all $u \neq s$, $F(u, t)$ is given by

$$\begin{cases} 1 + \sum\limits_{w \in N^+(u)} F(w, 1) & \text{if } t = k \\ \min\left(1 + \sum\limits_{w \in N^+(u)} F(w, 1),\ \sum\limits_{w \in N^+(u)} F(w, t+1)\right) & \text{if } t < k \end{cases}$$

The number of edges needed in the end is $\sum_{u \in N^+(s)} F(u, 0)$. The actual edges to add can be traced from the recurrence. We note that this dynamic program can be solved in $O(k\rho)$ (as $|T_s| = \rho$) work and $O(\rho \log n)$ depth by resolving the recurrence bottom up. We apply this to all n vertices in parallel, requiring $O(nk\rho)$ work and $O(\rho \log n)$ depth overall.

Note that although the dynamic programming solution gives an optimal solution for each shortest-path tree individually, the overall solution is not necessary the global optimal. Adding globally smallest number of edges to construct (k, ρ)-ball appears to be much more involved. Yet, we show empirically in Section 5 that the dynamic programming (DP) heuristic performs very well on a wide variety of graphs—and even the greedy heuristic does well on well-structured graphs.

5. EXPERIMENTAL ANALYSIS

This section empirically investigates how the settings of k and ρ, and the choice of shortcutting heuristics affect the number of shortcut edges added, as well as the number of steps RADIUS-STEPPING requires. These quantities provide insights into how a well-engineered implementation would perform in practice and how much parallelism RADIUS-STEPPING is able to derive.

5.1 Experiment Setup

We use graphs of various types from the SNAP datasets [18], including the road networks in Pennsylvania and Texas (real-world planer graphs) and the web graphs of the University of Notre Dame and Stanford University (real-world networks). In the case of web graphs, each edge represents a hyperlink between two web pages. We also use synthetic graphs of 2D and 3D grids (structured and unstructured grids). For each of the graphs used, the number of vertices and the number of edges are given in the table below.

Graph	# Vertices	# Edges
Road map: Pennsylvania	1.09M	3.08M
Road map: Texas	1.39M	3.84M
Web graph: Notre Dame	325K	2.20M
Web graph: Stanford	281K	3.98M
Grid: 2D	1M	2.00M
Grid: 3D	1M	5.94M

In practical applications, such graphs are used both in the weighted and unweighted settings. In the weighted setting, for instance, the distances in road networks and grids can represent real distances, while the edge weights in network graphs (e.g., social networks) also have real-world meanings, such as the time required to pass a message between two users, or (the logarithm of) the probability to pass a message. In our experiments, if a graph does not come equipped with weights, we assign to every edge a random integer between 1 and 10,000.

We construct (k, ρ)-balls using the heuristics described in Section 4.2, except that the implementation has the following modifications: instead of breaking ties arbitrarily and taking exactly ρ neighbors, we continue until all vertices with distance $r_\rho(\cdot)$ are visited. This has the same implementation complexity as the theoretical description but is more deterministic. Using this, our results are a pessimistic estimate of the original heuristics as more than ρ edges may be found for some sources. However, in all our experiments, we found the difference to be negligible in most instances.

To improve our confidence in the results, two of the authors have independently implemented and conducted the experiments, and arrived at the same results, even without introducing a tie-breaker.

5.2 The Number of Shortcut Edges

Of the heuristics in Section 4.2 for making a (k, ρ)-graph, *how many extra edges are generated by each heuristic?* To answer this question, we use 3 representative graphs in our analysis: (1) road networks in Pennsylvania, (2) a webgraph of Stanford University, and (3) a synthetic 1000-by-1000 2D grid. All these graphs have about 1 million vertices, and between 2 and 3 million edges. We show experimental results for unweighted graphs since the performance of the heuristics is independent of edge weights.

Figure 3 shows the number of added edges in terms of the fraction of the original edges for $k = 3$ as the value of ρ is varied between 10 and 1,000. More detailed results are given in Tables 8 and 9. Evidently, both heuristics achieve similar results on the road map and 2D grid. This is because road maps and grids are relatively regular, in fact almost planar. Thus, even naïvely shortcutting to the $(ki + 1)$-hop performs well: for small k, both heuristics add only a small number of edges. As k becomes larger, the gap between the greedy and the DP heuristic increases. When ρ reaches 1000, both DP and greedy add a large number of edges (more than 100x edges). This is because in road maps and grids, the degree of a vertex is usually a small constant, making the shortest-path tree deep.

On web graphs, which is less regular, DP only adds 4x the number of original edges even when ρ is as large as 1000 while greedy still adds 100x the original edges. This is because web graphs not only are far more irregular but also have a very skewed degree distribution. As a known scale-free network [1], it has some "super stars" (or more precisely, the "hubs") in the network. In this case, the bad example in Section 4.2 occurs frequently when these hubs are not at the exact $(ki + 1)$-th layer in the shortest-path tree, while the DP heuristic can discover the hubs accurately. This also explains the phenomena that only a few edges are added on web graphs by the DP heuristic even when ρ is large, since the hubs already significantly reduce the depth of the shortest path tree, and it only takes a few edges to shortcut to the hubs. This property holds for many kinds of real-world graphs such as social networks, airline networks, protein networks, and so on. In such graphs, a relatively optimal heuristic is necessary to construct the enclosed balls; a naïve method often has bad performance. As can be seen, the DP solution achieves satisfactory performance on web graphs, adding only about 10% more edges with $k = 3$ and $\rho = 100$.

5.3 The Number of Visited Edges

Theoretically, the preprocessing step has to examine $O(\rho^2)$ edges per source vertex (Section 4.1). This bound is indeed tight even on sparse unweighted graphs (Figure 2). In practice, the number of visited edges tends to be much smaller: *on all real-world graphs studied, we find that the number of visited edges appears proportional to ρ for $\rho \leqslant 1000$.*

ρ	Road Maps		Web Graphs		Grids	
	Penn	*Texas*	*Notre Dame*	*Stanford*	*2D*	*3D*
10	1.47	1.47	1.06	1.18	1.24	1.20
20	1.72	1.71	1.10	1.27	1.84	1.66
50	1.99	1.96	1.20	1.52	2.61	2.32
100	2.16	2.12	1.29	1.70	2.94	2.90
200	2.29	2.24	1.35	1.72	3.26	3.45
500	2.43	2.38	1.34	1.97	3.52	4.00
1000	2.51	2.46	1.73	1.98	3.66	4.40

Table 1: The average number of edges visited from each source node divided by $n\rho$ for different unweighted graphs.

ρ	Road Maps		Web Graphs		Grids	
	Penn	*Texas*	*Notre Dame*	*Stanford*	*2D*	*3D*
10	1.69	1.68	1.49	1.74	1.76	1.84
20	2.01	1.99	1.80	2.00	2.19	2.20
50	2.31	2.28	2.29	2.73	2.72	2.63
100	2.47	2.44	2.67	2.85	3.04	2.95
200	2.59	2.55	2.99	3.20	3.28	3.27
500	2.69	2.66	3.41	3.89	3.51	3.68
1000	2.75	2.72	4.02	4.73	3.64	3.97

Table 2: The average number of edges visited from each source node divided by $n\rho$ for different weighted graphs.

For the unweighted case, our implementation of preprocessing is just a standard BFS, and it terminates as soon as ρ vertices are added to the visited set. For the weighted case, it is slightly more complex, and we use a BST to maintain the priority queue with size no more than ρ. Then, a standard Dijkstra's is run from every source node. Since the edges from each vertex are sorted by weights, if the current relaxed distance is larger than the ρ-th nearest node from the source (can be checked in $O(1)$ cost), then we can skip all the remaining edges. Therefore, it is possible that even fewer edges are visited in the preprocessing for the weighted case, compared to the unweighted case on the same graph.

Tables 1 and 2 show the average number of edges visited from each source node divided by ρ on both unweighted and weighted cases. We can see that on all input instances, the average number of visited edges is never more than 5x compared to ρ, so it is much closer to $O(\rho)$ than $O(\rho^2)$. The ratio slightly increases with larger ρ, but the growth is much slower.

5.4 The Number of Steps

How many steps does Radius-Stepping *take for each setting of ρ?* We ran our Radius-Stepping on both weighted and unweighted graphs and counted the number of steps as we change ρ. Notice that the number of steps is independent of k and is only affected by ρ. (The value of k only affects the number of substeps within a step.) We discuss the performance of our algorithm on all six graphs after preprocessing the graphs with the corresponding ρ. Since the cost of SSSP potentially varies with the source and we cannot afford to try all possible sources, we take 1000 random sample sources for each graph. We use the same 1000 sources for all our experiments for both the weighted and unweighted cases. We report the arithmetic mean over the sampled sources.

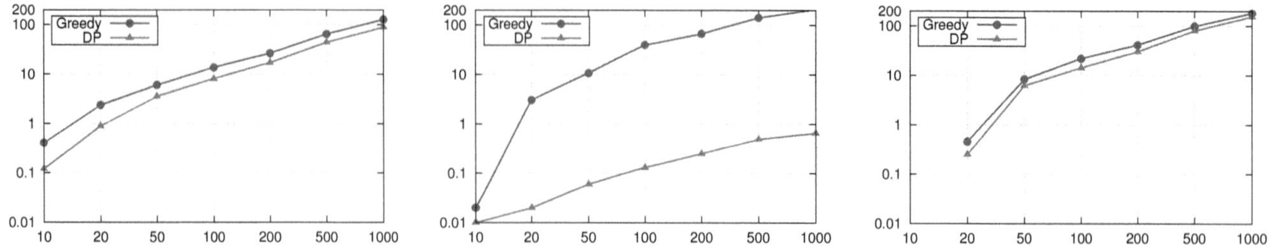

(a) Road map of Pennsylvania **(b) Web graph of Stanford** **(c) 2D-grid**

Figure 3: The ratio of extra edges to the original edges (y-axis) to generate ($k = 3, \rho$)-graph using greedy and dynamic programming (DP) for different types of graphs as ρ (x-axis) is varied.

ρ	Road Maps		Web Graphs		Grids	
	Penn	*Texas*	*Notre Dame*	*Stanford*	*2D*	*3D*
1	619.12	761.06	28.09	108.92	1504.00	223.50
2	309.32	380.31	13.77	54.23	751.76	111.50
5	308.47	379.34	13.44	43.27	751.74	111.50
10	206.30	253.71	13.32	31.29	501.14	74.50
20	165.73	196.30	13.17	21.67	375.62	74.48
50	123.01	151.13	12.38	14.13	250.32	55.48
100	101.41	124.07	9.78	10.63	187.46	44.08
200	78.61	96.92	8.47	8.56	136.24	36.48
500	58.44	70.75	6.63	7.30	87.86	27.36
1000	45.95	55.39	5.69	7.18	64.88	21.74
2000	35.66	42.58	5.27	6.72	44.82	17.94
5000	24.95	29.17	4.14	5.84	28.82	12.50
10000	18.54	21.33	3.83	5.76	20.18	10.00

Table 3: The average number of steps with different settings of ρ for different unweighted graphs.

ρ	Road Maps		Web Graphs		Grids	
	Penn	*Texas*	*Notre Dame*	*Stanford*	*2D*	*3D*
2	2.00	2.00	2.04	2.01	2.00	2.00
5	2.01	2.01	2.09	2.52	2.00	2.00
10	3.00	3.00	2.11	3.48	3.00	3.00
20	3.74	3.88	2.13	5.03	4.00	3.00
50	5.03	5.04	2.27	7.71	6.01	4.03
100	6.11	6.13	2.87	10.25	8.02	5.07
200	7.88	7.85	3.32	12.72	11.04	6.13
500	10.59	10.76	4.24	14.92	17.12	8.17
1000	13.47	13.74	4.94	15.17	23.18	10.28
2000	17.36	17.87	5.33	16.21	33.56	12.46
5000	24.81	26.09	6.79	18.65	52.19	17.88
10000	33.39	35.68	7.33	18.91	74.53	22.35

Table 4: The number steps required by Radius-Stepping unweighted graphs divided by the number of BFS steps.

Unweighted Graphs (BFS): Figure 4 shows, for the unweighted case, the average number of steps taken by Radius-Stepping as ρ is varied. More results appear in Tables 3 and 4, which compare the number of steps taken by Radius-Stepping with that of a conventional BFS implementation.

Several things are clear: on a log-log scale[3], the trends are downward linear as ρ increases except for the Notre Dame web graph (not completely regular but shows a similar trend). This suggests that the average number of steps is inversely proportional to ρ, which is consistent with our theoretical analysis.

The web graph has a relatively smoother slope. The reason is that once the "super stars" are included in the enclosed balls, which usually only need a few hops, then most of the vertices will be visited in a few steps (20–100 steps vs. 200–1,500 steps on the other graphs when $\rho = 1$). However, we will later see that in the weighted case, the performances on these graphs are even better than the other graphs. For the road maps and grids, the number of steps reduces steadily. Furthermore, the number of steps shown in the experiments is much less than the theoretical upper bound ($\frac{n}{\rho}\log\rho$) because most real-world graphs tend to have a hop radius that is much smaller than n.

On all the graphs studied, ρ can be as small as 10 and already reduces the number of steps by 3x. When $\rho = 100$, the reduction is about 10x. As the results show, we can obtain more than 20x reduction when thousands of vertices are in the balls. This experimentally supports our theoretical analysis.

What should an unweighted graph look like so that Radius-Stepping can significantly reduce the steps after adding no more than m edges? At first thought, the answer might be a grid or a road map with a large diameter, so that there is more space to be reduced. However, our experiments give the opposite answer: Radius-Stepping, in fact, performs better on web graphs with smaller diameters. On web graphs, Radius-Stepping can reduce the number of steps by 15x by adding no more than m edges (choosing $\rho = 1000$ and $k = 3$), while on road maps and grids, a 5x reduction in steps requires $4m$ to $6m$ edges. Even though the number of steps reduces more steadily and quickly on road maps and grids with larger ρ, the number of added edges in turn increases more rapidly (100x times more edges added to achieve 20x reduction on the number of steps). On scale-free networks, however, Radius-Stepping improves standard BFS by more than 10x without adding many extra edges, and an efficient implementation of Radius-Stepping on these networks might be worthwhile in the future.

Weighted Graphs: Figure 5 shows, for the weighted case, the average number of steps taken by Radius-Stepping as ρ is varied. More results appear in Tables 5 and 6, which compare the number of steps taken by Radius-Stepping to when $\rho = 1$. Notice that when $\rho = 1$, Radius-Stepping becomes essentially Dijkstra's except vertices with the same distance are extracted together.

Similar to the unweighted case, the trends in Figure 5 are also nearly-linear, indicating an inverse-proportion relationship between

[3]The vertical axis is drawn on a log scale and the horizontal axis closely approximates a log scale.

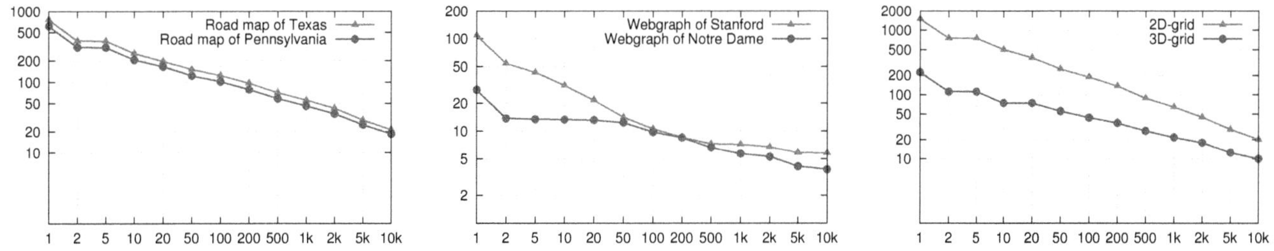

(a) Road maps (b) Web graphs (c) Grids

Figure 4: Unweighted graphs—the average number of RADIUS-STEPPING steps (y-axis) as ρ (x-axis) is varied.

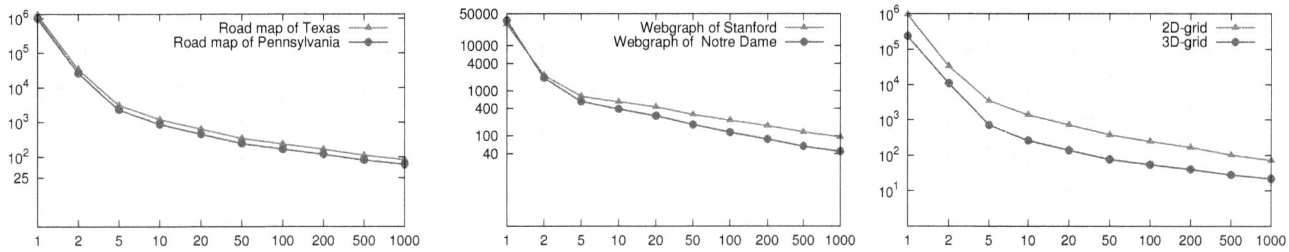

(a) Road maps (b) Web graphs (c) Grids

Figure 5: Weighted graphs—the average number of RADIUS-STEPPING steps (y-axis) as ρ (x-axis) is varied.

ρ	**Road Maps**		**Web Graphs**		**Grids**	
	Penn	*Texas*	*Notre Dame*	*Stanford*	*2D*	*3D*
1	986K	1252K	35.6K	30.0K	965K	239K
2	26479.9	34673.4	1953.7	2203.3	33592.2	11046.1
5	2294.5	3123.5	571.3	759.2	3495.8	722.4
10	872.6	1206.5	387.2	562.3	1385.0	261.9
20	455.0	634.1	274.9	432.2	722.9	137.8
50	245.0	343.0	174.6	293.7	375.1	76.1
100	167.2	233.7	118.8	219.3	246.9	54.1
200	119.8	166.9	83.7	166.0	166.9	40.2
500	81.1	111.3	58.4	120.0	102.1	28.1
1000	61.1	83.2	45.0	93.6	71.1	21.7

Table 5: The average number of steps with different settings of ρ for weighted graphs.

ρ	**Road Maps**		**Web Graphs**		**Grids**	
	Penn	*Texas*	*Notre Dame*	*Stanford*	*2D*	*3D*
2	37.2	36.1	18.2	13.6	28.7	21.6
5	429.7	400.8	62.3	39.6	276.1	330.6
10	1130.0	1037.7	92.0	53.4	696.8	912.0
20	2167.0	1974.5	129.5	69.5	1334.9	1733.3
50	4024.5	3650.1	203.9	102.3	2572.7	3138.5
100	5897.1	5357.3	299.7	137.0	3908.6	4414.9
200	8230.4	7501.5	425.4	180.9	5782.0	5941.4
500	12157.8	11248.9	609.7	250.3	9451.7	8499.8
1000	16137.5	15048.1	791.2	320.9	13572.8	11006.6

Table 6: The number of steps taken by RADIUS-STEPPING on weighted graphs divided by the number of steps taken by RADIUS-STEPPING itself when using $\rho = 1$.

the number of steps and ρ, which is consistent with our theory. In the weighted case, however, we can visit much fewer vertices in each step than those in the unweighted case because most vertices have different distances to the source. Thus, Dijkstra's algorithm (or when $\rho = 1$) requires almost n steps to finish. As a result, considering the inverse-proportion relationship, even a small ρ can greatly reduce the number of steps. Indeed, the number of steps taken by RADIUS-STEPPING is far fewer than the predicted theoretical upper bound ($O(\frac{n}{\rho}\log \rho L)$ with $L = 10^4$ here). We also notice that the number of steps decreases much faster when ρ is small compared to larger values of ρ.

The reduction in the number of steps is significant. Even $\rho = 10$ leads to about 1000x fewer steps on road maps and grids, and about 50–100x on the web graphs. When $\rho = 100$, we only need a few hundreds of steps on all graphs, which can already provide considerable parallelism. The number of steps further decreases to 20–80 when $\rho = 1000$. This provides some evidence that the algorithm has the potential to deliver substantial speedups when many more cores on a shared-memory machine are made available.

Another trend is that the reduction factors on the web graphs are always less than the other two types of graphs. The reason is that the web graphs are scale-free, and even when we do not use enclosed balls to traverse the graph, not many steps are required. The "hubs" substantially bring down the diameter of the graph. For more uniformly distributed graphs, such as the road maps and grids, increasing ρ to a big value reduces the number of steps required to perform SSSP more rapidly.

5.5 How to choose the parameters?

What is the best combination of k and ρ? The choice of k and ρ offers a tradeoff between the number of added edges (hence additional space and work) and the parallelism of the algorithm. In general, we do not want to increase the number of edges substantially, the total number of edges should be around $O(m)$. On every graph tested, $k = 3$ or 4 works reasonably well whereas ρ in the range 50–100 for weighted graph yields the best bang for the buck. A larger ρ can reduce the number of steps in RADIUS-STEPPING but in turn, increases the preprocessing time and the number of edges required to be added. A larger k will reduce the number of added edges but at the same time, increases the number of visited edges, as well as the overall depth[4].

On unweighted graphs, RADIUS-STEPPING performs better on web graphs, but less efficient on grids and road maps. Finally, since preprocessing is only run once, if SSSP will be run from multiple sources, we suggest increasing ρ and decreasing k: the cost for preprocessing is amortized over more sources.

6. PRIOR AND RELATED WORK

This secton discusses prior results on parallel single-source shortest paths that are most relevant to ours (for a more comprehensive survey, see [19] and the references therein). Throughout, we assume the input is an *arbitrary* undirected graph with n vertices and m nonnegative edges.

Some early algorithms achieve a high degree of parallelism (polylogarithm depth) but with substantially more work than Dijkstra's algorithm. Using matrix multiplications over semirings, Han et al. [13] gives an algorithm with $O(\log^2 n)$ depth and $O(n^3(\log\log n/\log n)^{1/3})$ work that, in fact, solves the *all-pairs* shortest-path problem. With randomization, this algorithm can be implemented in $O(\log n)$ depth and $O(n^3 \log n)$ work [11].

In another line of work, Driscoll et al. [9], refining the approach of Paige and Kruskal [21], present an $O(n \log n)$-depth algorithm with Dijkstra's work bound. Later, Brodal et al. [4] improve the depth to $O(n)$; however, the algorithm needs $O(m \log n)$ work. We summarize in Table 7 the cost bounds for exact SSSP algorithms that have subcubic work.

By allowing a slight increase in work in exchange for a better depth bound, many algorithms have been proposed. Ullman and Yannakakis [29] describe a randomized parallel breadth-first search (BFS) that solves unweighted SSSP in $\tilde{O}(m + n\rho)$ work and $\tilde{O}(n/\rho)$. The algorithm works by performing limited searches from a number of locations and adding shortcut edges with appropriate distances to speed up later traversal. Extending this idea to weighted graphs, Klein and Subramanian [17] derive an algorithm that runs in $O(\sqrt{n}\log L \log^2 n)$ depth and $O(m\sqrt{n}\log L \log^2 n)$ work. For undirected graphs, Cohen [6] presents an algorithm with $O(n/\rho \cdot \text{polylog}(n))$ depth and $O(n^2 \log L + n\rho^2)$ work. Shi and Spencer [25] show an algorithm with $\Theta(n/\rho \cdot \log n)$ depth, and $O(n\rho^2 \log n \log \rho + m \log n)$ or $O((\rho^3 + m\rho)\log n)$ work. This not only has a smaller depth bound than our algorithm but also is the only algorithm in Table 7 with strongly-polynomial depth. However, since the search is based on vertices instead of distances, the work and depth bounds here are tight, promising $O(\rho^2)$ parallelism on any input instances but leaving no room for more parallelism on "nice" input graphs. By contrast, the experiments in this paper show that our algorithm can attain a much higher degree of parallelism on many real-world graphs.

More recently, Meyers and Sanders [19] describe an algorithm called Δ-stepping and analyze it for various random graph settings. Although the algorithm works well on general graphs in practice, no theoretical guarantees are known.

In addition to these results, better algorithms have been developed for special classes of graphs such as planar graphs (e.g., [28, 16]) and separator-decomposable graphs [5].

There have also been approximation algorithms for SSSP. Cohen [7] describes a $(1+\varepsilon)$-algorithm for undirected graphs that runs in $O(\text{polylog}(n))$ depth and $O((m+n)n^{\alpha})$ work for $\alpha > 0$. Using an alternative hopset construction of Miller et al. [20], Cohen's algorithm can be made to run in $O(m \cdot \text{polylog}(n))$ work and $O(n^{1-\alpha})$ depth for $\alpha > 0$.

[4] As mentioned at the beginning of Section 5.4, a larger k will not increase the number of steps, but the number of the overall substeps, which is the inner loop of RADIUS-STEPPING, hence an increase in the overall depth.

7. CONCLUSION

We presented a parallel algorithm for single-source shortest paths that runs in two phases. The preprocessing requires $O(n\rho^2)$ work and $O(\rho \log \rho)$ depth, adding $O(n\rho)$ edges (shortcuts) where ρ is a user-defined parameter. Then, the single-source shortest paths can be computed with $O((m+n\rho)\log n)$ work and $O(\frac{n}{\rho}\log n \log \rho L)$ depth for any arbitrary graph with nonnegative weights. The algorithm is simple and has the potential to be practical. Our experiments further show that the theoretical bounds are pessimistic for real-world graphs; the actual costs are often much less.

Acknowledgments

This research was supported in part by NSF grants CCF-1314590 and CCF-1533858, and the Intel Science and Technology Center for Cloud Computing.

8. REFERENCES

[1] A.-L. Barabási and R. Albert. Emergence of scaling in random networks. *Science*, 286(5439):509–512, 1999.

[2] G. E. Blelloch, D. Ferizovic, and Y. Sun. Parallel ordered sets using join. In *ACM Symposium on Parallel Algorithms and Architectures (SPAA)*. ACM, 2016.

[3] G. E. Blelloch and M. Reid-Miller. Fast set operations using treaps. In *ACM Symposium on Parallel Algorithms and Architectures (SPAA)*, pages 16–26. ACM, 1998.

[4] G. S. Brodal, J. L. Träff, and C. D. Zaroliagis. A parallel priority queue with constant time operations. *Journal of Parallel and Distributed Computing*, 49(1):4–21, 1998.

[5] E. Cohen. Efficient parallel shortest-paths in digraphs with a separator decomposition. *Journal of Algorithms*, 21(2):331–357, 1996.

[6] E. Cohen. Using selective path-doubling for parallel shortest-path computations. *Journal of Algorithms*, 22(1):30–56, 1997.

[7] E. Cohen. Polylog-time and near-linear work approximation scheme for undirected shortest paths. *Journal of the ACM (JACM)*, 47(1):132–166, 2000.

[8] E. W. Dijkstra. A note on two problems in connexion with graphs. *Numerische mathematik*, 1(1):269–271, 1959.

[9] J. R. Driscoll, H. N. Gabow, R. Shrairman, and R. E. Tarjan. Relaxed heaps: An alternative to fibonacci heaps with applications to parallel computation. *Communications of the ACM*, 31(11):1343–1354, 1988.

[10] M. L. Fredman and R. E. Tarjan. Fibonacci heaps and their uses in improved network optimization algorithms. *Journal of the ACM (JACM)*, 34(3):596–615, 1987.

[11] A. M. Frieze and L. Rudolph. *A parallel algorithm for all pairs shortest paths in a random graph.* Management Sciences Research Group, Graduate School of Industrial Administration, Carnegie-Mellon University, 1984.

[12] Y. Gu, J. Shun, Y. Sun, and G. E. Blelloch. A top-down parallel semisort. In *ACM Symposium on Parallelism in Algorithms and Architectures (SPAA)*, pages 24–34. ACM, 2015.

[13] Y. Han, V. Pan, and J. Reif. Efficient parallel algorithms for computing all pair shortest paths in directed graphs. In *ACM*

	Algorithm	Preprocessing		Shortest Path	
		Work	Depth	Work	Depth
Unweighted	Standard BFS	–	–	$O(m+n)$	$O(n)$
	Ullman and Yannakakis [29]	$O(m\rho+\rho^3)$	$O(\frac{n}{\rho}\log n\log^* n)$	$O(m+n\rho)$	$O(\frac{n}{\rho}\log n\log^* n)$
	Spencer [26]	–	–	$O(m\log\rho+n\rho^2\log^2\rho)$	$O(\frac{n}{\rho}\log^2\rho)$
	*This work**	$O(n\rho^2)$	$O(\rho\log^* n)$	$O(m+n\rho)$	$O(\frac{n}{\rho}\log\rho\log^* n)$
Weighted	Parallel Dijkstra's [21]	–	–	$O(m+n\log n)$	$O(n\log n)$
	Parallel Dijkstra's [4]	–	–	$O(m\log n+n)$	$O(n)$
	Klein and Subramanian [17]	–	–	$O(m\sqrt{n}\log^2 n\log L)$	$O(\sqrt{n}\log^2 n\log L)$
	Spencer [26]	–	–	$O((n\rho^2\log\rho+m)\log n\rho L)$	$O(\frac{n}{\rho}\log n\log\rho L)$
	Shi and Spencer [25]*	$O(n\rho^2\log n\log\rho+m)$	$O(\log n\log\rho)$	$O((m+n\rho)\log n)$	$O(\frac{n}{\rho}\log n)$
	Cohen [6]*	$O(m+n\rho^2\log^2 n)$	$O(\log^2 n)$	$O(n^2\log^3 n\log L)$	$O(\frac{n}{\rho}\log^3 n\log L)$
	*This work**	$O(m\log n+n\rho^2)$	$O(\rho\log\rho)$	$O((m+n\rho)\log n)$	$O(\frac{n}{\rho}\log n\log\rho L)$

* the presented bounds only apply to undirected graphs.

Table 7: Cost bounds for exact SSSP algorithms that have subcubic work, broken down into (i) the cost of preprocessing and (ii) the cost of only the shortest-path computation, where m is the number of edges in the initial input graph and n is the number of vertices in the initial input graph. The bounds already account for alterations made, if any, by preprocessing.

Symposium on Parallel Algorithms and Architectures (SPAA), pages 353–362. ACM, 1992.

[14] J. Jaja. *Introduction to Parallel Algorithms*. Addison-Wesley Professional, 1992.

[15] R. M. Karp and V. Ramachandran. *Parallel algorithms for shared-memory machines*. Handbook of theoretical computer science (vol. a): algorithms and complexity, 1991.

[16] P. N. Klein and S. Subramanian. A linear-processor polylog-time algorithm for shortest paths in planar graphs. *Symposium on Foundations of Computer Science (FOCS)*. IEEE, 1993.

[17] P. N. Klein and S. Subramanian. A randomized parallel algorithm for single-source shortest paths. *Journal of Algorithms*, 25(2):205–220, 1997.

[18] J. Leskovec and A. Krevl. SNAP Datasets: Stanford large network dataset collection. 2014.

[19] U. Meyer and P. Sanders. Δ-stepping: a parallelizable shortest path algorithm. *Journal of Algorithms*, 49(1), 2003.

[20] G. L. Miller, R. Peng, A. Vladu, and S. C. Xu. Improved parallel algorithms for spanners and hopsets. In *ACM Symposium on Parallelism in Algorithms and Architectures, SPAA*, pages 192–201, 2015.

[21] R. C. Paige and C. P. Kruskal. Parallel algorithms for shortest path problems. In *International Conference on Parallel Processing (ICPP)*, pages 14–20, 1985.

[22] H. Park and K. Park. Parallel algorithms for red–black trees. *Theoretical Computer Science*, 262(1):415–435, 2001.

[23] W. Paul, U. Vishkin, and H. Wagener. Parallel computation on 2-3-trees. *RAIRO, Informatique théorique*, 17(4):397–404, 1983.

[24] W. J. Paul, U. Vishkin, and H. Wagener. Parallel dictionaries in 2-3 trees. In *Intl. Colloq. on Automata, Languages and Programming (ICALP)*, pages 597–609, 1983.

[25] H. Shi and T. H. Spencer. Time-work tradeoffs of the single-source shortest paths problem. *Journal of Algorithms*, 30(1):19–32, 1999.

[26] T. H. Spencer. Time-work tradeoffs for parallel algorithms. *Journal of the ACM (JACM)*, 44(5):742–778, 1997.

[27] M. Thorup. Undirected single-source shortest paths with positive integer weights in linear time. *Journal of the ACM (JACM)*, 46(3):362–394, 1999.

[28] J. L. Träff and C. D. Zaroliagis. A simple parallel algorithm for the single-source shortest path problem on planar digraphs. *Journal of Parallel and Distributed Computing* 60.9 (2000): 1103-1124.

[29] J. D. Ullman and M. Yannakakis. High-probability parallel transitive-closure algorithms. *SIAM Journal on Computing*, 20(1):100–125, 1991.

ρ	Road map of Pennsylvania k 2	3	4	5	reduced steps	Web graph of Stanford k 2	3	4	5	reduced steps	2D-grid k 2	3	4	5	reduced steps
10	1.67	0.41	0.05	0.01	3.00	3.11	0.02	0.01	0.00	3.48	0.36	0.00	0.00	0.00	3.00
20	3.79	2.38	0.84	0.23	3.88	9.91	3.06	0.09	0.01	5.03	5.75	0.46	0.00	0.00	4.00
50	10.34	6.05	5.65	3.71	5.04	47.57	10.74	3.40	0.13	7.71	16.05	8.40	9.54	0.67	6.01
100	20.33	13.64	8.85	8.16	6.13	109.98	39.99	20.96	8.73	10.25	29.59	22.02	10.52	11.43	8.02
200	39.92	26.35	20.15	14.51	7.85	188.92	67.25	45.54	17.96	12.72	48.40	41.34	28.03	12.73	11.04
500	97.58	64.72	48.49	37.64	10.76	337.34	141.58	119.03	63.69	14.92	126.09	99.22	55.62	64.75	17.12
1000	192.00	127.45	95.55	75.84	13.74	529.14	208.66	219.21	149.20	15.17	243.12	181.50	129.26	108.37	23.18

Table 8: The ratio of created shortcut edges to the original edges when using the **greedy** heuristic as ρ and k are varied. The "reduced steps" columns are from Table 4 as a reference.

ρ	Road map of Pennsylvania k 2	3	4	5	reduced steps	Web graph of Stanford k 2	3	4	5	reduced steps	2D-grid k 2	3	4	5	reduced steps
10	0.95	0.12	0.01	0.00	3.00	0.02	0.01	0.01	0.00	3.48	0.25	0.00	0.00	0.00	3.00
20	2.70	0.90	0.18	0.04	3.88	0.05	0.02	0.01	0.01	5.03	3.95	0.25	0.00	0.00	4.00
50	7.78	3.59	1.89	0.72	5.04	0.20	0.06	0.04	0.03	7.71	12.16	6.21	4.06	0.36	6.01
100	16.09	8.09	4.40	2.58	6.13	0.51	0.13	0.08	0.06	10.25	24.22	14.27	8.32	6.06	8.02
200	32.60	17.04	9.89	6.03	7.85	0.99	0.25	0.15	0.11	12.72	48.35	30.23	20.28	12.45	11.04
500	81.75	44.14	26.65	17.11	10.76	2.18	0.50	0.30	0.22	14.92	125.96	80.09	54.44	42.26	17.12
1000	162.91	89.30	54.82	35.95	13.74	3.92	0.66	0.34	0.24	15.17	241.30	154.97	110.87	84.87	23.18

Table 9: The ratio of created shortcut edges to the original edges when using the **DP** heuristic as ρ and k are varied. The "reduced steps" columns are from Table 4 as a reference.

Parallel Metric Tree Embedding based on an Algebraic View on Moore-Bellman-Ford

[Extended Abstract]*

Stephan Friedrichs
Max Planck Institute for Informatics
Saarbrücken, Germany
Saarbrücken Graduate School
of Computer Science
sfriedri@mpi-inf.mpg.de

Christoph Lenzen
Max Planck Institute for Informatics
Saarbrücken, Germany
clenzen@mpi-inf.mpg.de

ABSTRACT

A *metric tree embedding* of expected *stretch* α maps a weighted n-node graph $G = (V, E, \omega)$ to a weighted tree $T = (V_T, E_T, \omega_T)$ with $V \subseteq V_T$, and $\operatorname{dist}(v, w, G) \leq \operatorname{dist}(v, w, T)$ and $\mathbb{E}[\operatorname{dist}(v, w, T)] \leq \alpha \operatorname{dist}(v, w, G)$ for all $v, w \in V$. Such embeddings are highly useful for designing fast approximation algorithms, as many hard problems are easy to solve on tree instances. However, to date the best parallel polylog n depth algorithm that achieves an asymptotically optimal expected stretch of $\alpha \in \mathrm{O}(\log n)$ uses $\Omega(n^2)$ work and requires a metric as input.

In this paper, we show how to achieve the same guarantees using $\tilde{\mathrm{O}}(m^{1+\varepsilon})$ work, where m is the number of edges of G and $\varepsilon > 0$ is an arbitrarily small constant. Moreover, one may reduce the work further to $\tilde{\mathrm{O}}(m + n^{1+\varepsilon})$, at the expense of increasing the expected stretch α to $\mathrm{O}(\varepsilon^{-1} \log n)$ using the spanner construction of Baswana and Sen as preprocessing step.

Our main tool in deriving these parallel algorithms is an algebraic characterization of a generalization of the classic Moore-Bellman-Ford algorithm. We consider this framework, which subsumes a large variety of previous "Moore-Bellman-Ford-flavored" algorithms, to be of independent interest.

Keywords

Parallel Algorithm; Distributed Algorithm; Randomized Algorithm; Tree Embedding; Congruence Relation on Semimodules

*Full version available at http://arxiv.org/abs/1509.09047

SPAA'16, July 11–13, 2016, Pacific Grove, California, USA.

ISBN 978-1-4503-4210-0/16/07...$15.00

DOI: http://dx.doi.org/10.1145/2935764.2935777

1. INTRODUCTION

In a variety of fundamental graph problems the objective is closely related to distances in the graph. Prominent examples are shortest path problems, minimum weight spanning trees, a plethora of Steiner-type problems [20], the traveling salesman, finding a longest simple path, and many more. The hardness of such problems ranges from P over NP-complete to APX-hard.

If approximation is viable or mandatory, a successful strategy is to make use of *metric embeddings,* mapping a graph $G = (V, E, \omega)$ to $G' = (V', E', \omega')$ such that $V \subseteq V'$ and $\operatorname{dist}(v, w, G) \leq \operatorname{dist}(v, w, G') \leq \alpha \operatorname{dist}(v, w, G)$ for some $\alpha \geq 1$ referred to as *stretch.*[1] A convenient class of metric embeddings are *metric tree embeddings,* because very few problems are hard to solve on trees. They allow, despite their extremely simple topology, to randomly construct an embedding of any graph G into a tree T so that the *expected stretch* $\alpha = \max\{\mathbb{E}_T[\operatorname{dist}(v, w, T)] / \operatorname{dist}(v, w, G) \mid v, w \in V\}$ satisfies $\alpha \in \mathrm{O}(\log n)$; Fakcharoenphol, Rao, and Talwar (FRT) introduced such a random distribution of tree embeddings [17].

Unfortunately, the known parallel algorithms of polylog n depth constructing such embeddings require $\Omega(n^2)$ work, and even this only under the assumption that the input is given by direct query access to the distance metric [9]. Reducing the work to sample from the FRT tree embeddings in graphs with $m \ll n^2$ without sacrificing the depth bound of polylog n is the primary motivation of this paper.

Our Contribution. We obtain the following results.

- For any constant $\varepsilon > 0$, there is a randomized parallel algorithm of depth polylog n and work $\tilde{\mathrm{O}}(m^{1+\varepsilon})$ that computes a metric tree embedding of expected stretch $\mathrm{O}(\log n)$ w.h.p.
- The work can be reduced to $\tilde{\mathrm{O}}(m + n^{1+\mathrm{O}(\varepsilon)})$ when stretch $\mathrm{O}(\varepsilon^{-1} \log n)$ is acceptable, by applying the spanner construction of Baswana and Sen [7] as a preprocessing step.
- Our key tool in achieving this goal is an algebraic interpretation of "Moore-Bellman-Ford-like" (MBF-like) algorithms. Since our framework subsumes a large class of previous algorithms and explains them from a dif-

[1] By $\operatorname{dist}(v, w, G)$ we refer to the distance between v and w in G; $\operatorname{dist}(\cdot, \cdot, G)$ gives rise to a metric space.

ferent perspective, we consider it to be of independent interest.

- We illustrate the utility of our main results by providing efficient approximation algorithms for k-median and buy-at-bulk network design.
- Furthermore, our techniques allow to improve over previous distributed algorithms computing tree embeddings in the Congest model [29].

Our Approach. Khan et al. show how to compute an FRT embedding by a distributed algorithm [22] in the Congest model. Their algorithm gives rise to an $\tilde{O}(\mathrm{SPD}(G))$ depth parallel algorithm, where the *shortest-path diameter (SPD)* is the maximum over all pairs of nodes $v, w \in V$ of the minimum hop-length of a path p from v to w with $\omega(p) = \mathrm{dist}(v, w, G)$. Intuitively, $\mathrm{SPD}(G)$ captures the number of iterations of MBF-like algorithms: Each iteration updates distances (see below), so the $(\mathrm{SPD}(G)+1)$-th iteration does not yield new information. Unfortunately, $\mathrm{SPD}(G) = n - 1$ is possible, so applying this algorithm naively results in poor performance.

A natural idea is to reduce the number of iterations the algorithm by Khan et al. requires by adding a hop set to the graph [12]: A *(d, ε)-hop set* is a set of additional edges E' such that $\mathrm{dist}(v, w, G) \leq \mathrm{dist}(v, w, G') \leq (1+\varepsilon)\,\mathrm{dist}(v, w, G)$ for all $v, w \in V$, where G' is G augmented with E'. Adding a suitable hop set ensures that, in the augmented graph, examining paths of few hops already yields $(1+o(1))$-approximate distances. One may now jump to the conclusion that the efficient parallel hop set construction by Cohen [12] together with the algorithm by Khan et al. [22] readily yields an efficient embedding algorithm, but this is incorrect: The FRT construction crucially relies on the fact that the distances form a metric, i.e., satisfy the triangle inequality, which is not true for approximate distances.

Choosing a different hop set does not solve the problem: Hop sets guarantee that d-hop distances *approximate* distances, but any hop set fulfilling the triangle inequality on d-hop distances has to reduce the shortest path diameter of the graph to at most d, i.e., yield *exact* distances.

OBSERVATION 1.1. *Let G be a graph augmented with a (d, ε)-hop set. If $\mathrm{dist}^d(\cdot, \cdot, G)$ is a metric, then $\mathrm{dist}^d(\cdot, \cdot, G) = \mathrm{dist}(\cdot, \cdot, G)$, i.e., $\mathrm{SPD}(G) \leq d$.*

We overcome this obstacle by embedding G' (G augmented with a hop set) into a complete graph H on the same node set that $(1 + o(1))$-approximates distances in G, but fulfills $\mathrm{SPD}(H) \in \mathrm{polylog}\, n$. In other words, where Cohen preserves distances *exactly* and ensures existence of *approximately* shortest paths with few hops, we preserve *distances* approximately, but guarantee that we obtain *exact* shortest paths with few hops. This, however, introduces a new challenge: As H is complete, we cannot explicitly compute H without incurring $\Omega(n^2)$ work.

MBF-like Algorithms. This is where our novel perspective on MBF-like algorithms comes into play. It is well-known [1, 30] that distance computations can be performed by multiplication with the (weighted) adjacency matrix A over the min-plus semiring[2] $\mathcal{S}_{\min,+} = (\mathbb{R}_{\geq 0} \cup \{\infty\}, \min, +)$. For instance, if $B = A^h$ with $h \geq \mathrm{SPD}(G)$, then $b_{vw} = \mathrm{dist}(v, w, G)$.

In an iteration of an MBF-like algorithm

(1) the information stored at each node is *propagated* to its neighbors,
(2) each node *aggregates* the received information, and
(3) optionally *filters* out uninteresting parts.

In terms of the semiring, propagation is the "multiplication" with an edge weight, and aggregation is "summation." The $(i+1)$-th iteration results in $x^{(i+1)} = r^V A x^{(i)}$, where r^V is vertex-wise filtering, A as above, and $x \in M^V$ the node values. Both M and M^V form semimodules[3] over $\mathcal{S}_{\min,+}$.

In other words, in an h-iteration MBF-like algorithm each node determines its part of the output based on its h-hop distances to all other nodes. However, for efficiency reasons, various algorithms [2, 5, 6, 21, 23, 24, 25] compute only a subset of these distances. The role of the filter is to remove the remaining values to allow for better efficiency. The core feature of an MBF-like algorithm is that filtering is *compatible* with propagation and aggregation: If a node discards information and then propagates it, the discarded parts must be "uninteresting" at the receiving node as well. We model this as *equivalence classes* of node states; filters simply pick suitable (efficiently encodable) representatives of such classes, and the equivalence relation has to be a *congruence relation* on the semimodule of possible node states.

This helps us to determine an FRT embedding as follows. First, we observe that acquiring the information required to represent an FRT embedding can be done by an MBF-like algorithm. Second, we can *simulate arbitrary MBF-like algorithms* on the complete graph H, without explicitly storing H, using polylogarithmic overhead and MBF-like iterations on G' (G augmented with a hop set): Due to the way H is constructed, we can — loosely speaking — represent one multiplication with its adjacency matrix A_H by $\mathrm{polylog}\, n$ multiplications with the adjacency matrix of G'. As filtering preserves equivalence classes, we may apply it in between each of these MBF relaxation steps, resulting in a work-efficient decomposition of A_H of polylogarithmic depth. We obtain a metric tree embedding with asymptotically optimal stretch, depth $\mathrm{polylog}\, n$, and work $\tilde{O}(m^{1+\varepsilon})$.

Overview. The remaining paper is structured as follows. After discussing related work, defining the model, and fixing basic notation, the main body of the paper deals with presenting our framework and applying it to the FRT construction. The framework, i.e., the proposed algebraic characterization of MBF-like algorithms, is presented in Section 2. As outlined above, applying it to the FRT embedding entails the following main steps.

(1) Add a hop set to G, resulting in graph G'.
(2) Embed G' into H with stretch $1 + o(1)$, such that $\mathrm{SPD}(H) \in \mathrm{polylog}\, n$.
(3) Execute an MBF-like algorithm on H, resulting in an (implicit) representation of (a sample from) the FRT embedding of H.

For Step (1), we may use any suitable hop set construction. To date, to the best of our knowledge the only work-efficient $\mathrm{polylog}\, n$ depth construction is Cohen's [12]. In Section 3,

[2] A semiring is a ring without inverse elements w.r.t. the semiring's addition (here min).

[3] A semimodule supports scalar multiplication (propagation) and provides a semigroup (representing aggregation).

regarding step (2), we describe the construction of H and prove the desired properties.

Concerning step (3), we first discuss how an iteration of an MBF-like algorithm on H can be decomposed into polylog n MBF-like iterations on G' in Section 4. This is key to circumventing the $\Omega(n^2)$ work that would result from any explicit use of H. In Section 5, we prove that the desired implicit representation of the embedding, LE lists (see Definition 5.2 and prior work [9, 11, 13, 19, 22]), can indeed be computed by an MBF-like algorithm. Together with the results from the previous sections and standard parallelization techniques, we then arrive at our main result, Theorem 5.8.

Finally, Sections 6.1 and 6.2 summarize the improved parallel algorithms for k-median and buy-at-bulk network design that follow from our results, and Section 6.3 applies our framework to FRT construction in the Congest model; Section 7 wraps up the paper. We remark that due to space constraints, most proofs are partially or fully omitted from this extended abstract; we refer to the full version of the paper for details.

1.1 Related Work

Classical Distance Computations. The earliest and possibly also most basic algorithms for single-source shortest paths (SSSP) computation are Dijkstra's algorithm [16] and the Moore-Bellman-Ford (henceforth MBF) algorithm [8, 18, 28]. From the perspective of parallel algorithms, Dijkstra's algorithm performs excellent in terms of work, requiring $\tilde{O}(m)$ computational steps, but suffers from being inherently sequential, processing one vertex at a time. While the MBF algorithm also has depth $\Omega(n)$ in the worst case and may require $\Omega(nm)$ work, it can perform substantially better.

Algebraic Distance Computations. Concretely, the MBF algorithm can be interpreted as a fixpoint iteration $Ax^{(i+1)} = Ax^{(i)}$, where A is the adjacency matrix of the graph G and "multiplication" and "addition" are replaced by $+$ and min, respectively. This structure is known as the the min-plus semiring — a.k.a. tropical semiring — $\mathcal{S}_{\min,+} = (\mathbb{R}_{\geq 0} \cup \{\infty\}, \min, +)$ which is a well-established tool for distance computations [1, 30]. From this point of view, the *shortest path diameter (SPD)* of G, $\operatorname{SPD}(G)$, is the number of iterations until a fixpoint is reached. More precisely, MBF thus has depth $\tilde{O}(\operatorname{SPD}(G))$ and work $\tilde{O}(m \operatorname{SPD}(G))$, and it is possible that $\operatorname{SPD}(G) \in O(1)$.

One may overcome the issue of large depth by performing the fixpoint iteration on the matrix instead: setting $A^{(0)} := A$ and iterating $A^{(i+1)} := A^{(i)}A^{(i)}$, after $\lceil \log \operatorname{SPD}(G) \rceil \leq \lceil \log n \rceil$ iterations a fixpoint is reached [14]. The final matrix then, in fact, has as entries exactly the pairwise node distances, and the computation has polylogarithmic depth. This comes at the cost of $\Omega(n^3)$ work (even if $m \ll n^2$), but in dense graphs it is as efficient in terms of work as (n instances of) Dijkstra's algorithm for solving APSP, without having depth $\Omega(n)$.

Mohri [27] solved various shortest-distance problems using the $\mathcal{S}_{\min,+}$ semiring and variants thereof. Each problem is formulated as an appropriate semiring, and solved by a general algorithm. Our approach is more generic and easier to use: Where Mohri lifts problem-specific information into a new semiring for each problem, we always use $\mathcal{S}_{\min,+}$ and combine it with an appropriate semimodule carrying problem-specific information. While the semimodule can be exchanged, it is reusable for most considered problems. Typically, all that needs to be specified is a problem-specific congruence relation on the same standard semimodule. This covers many, if not most, distance problems, and it avoids introducing an (in this context artificial) semiring multiplication on the elements of the semimodule.

Approximate Distances. In a seminal paper, Cohen [12] proved that SSSP can be approximately solved with depth polylog n and near-optimal $\tilde{O}(m^{1+\varepsilon})$ work, for any constant choice of $\varepsilon > 0$. Her approach is based on an efficient randomized parallel hop set construction, adding $\tilde{O}(m^{1+\varepsilon})$ edges so that, for some $d \in$ polylog n, it holds that d-hop distances are at most by factor $1 + 1/\operatorname{polylog} n$ larger (and never smaller) than the original distances. Henziger et al. [21] show that a hop set yielding $(1 + 1/\operatorname{polylog} n)$-approximate distances for $d \in 2^{O(\sqrt{\log n})} \subset n^{o(1)}$ can be deterministically computed with depth $2^{O(\sqrt{\log n})} \subset n^{o(1)}$ and work $m2^{O(\sqrt{\log n})} \subset m^{1+o(1)}$.[4]

Metric Tree Embeddings. When metrically embedding into a tree, it is impossible to guarantee a small stretch. For instance, when the graph is a cycle with unit edge weights, it is impossible to embed it into a tree without having at least one edge with stretch $\Omega(n)$. However, *on average,* the edges in this example are stretched by a constant factor only, justifying the hope that one may have a small *expected* stretch. A number of elegant algorithms [2, 5, 6, 17] compute metric tree embeddings, culminating in the one by Fakcharoenphol, Rao, and Talwar (FRT) [17] that achieves stretch $O(\log n)$ in expectation. This stretch bound is optimal in the worst case, as illustrated by expander graphs [6]. Mendel and Schwob show how to sample from the FRT distribution in $\tilde{O}(m)$ steps [26], matching the trivial $\Omega(m)$ lower bound up to polylogarithmic factors. However, their approach relies on a pruned version of Dijkstra's algorithm for distance computations and hence does not parallelize well.

Several parallel and distributed algorithms compute FRT embeddings [9, 19, 22]. These algorithms and ours have in common that they (essentially) represent the embedding by *least element (LE) lists,* which were introduced in [11, 13]. In the parallel case, the state-of-the-art solution due to Blelloch et al. [9] achieves $O(\log^2 n)$ depth and $O(n^2 \log n)$ work. However, Blelloch et al. assume the input to be given as an n-point *metric,* where the distance between two points can be queried at constant cost. We note that our approach is more general, as we can interpret the metric as a complete weighted graph (using the query access to determine edge weights) of shortest path diameter 1 and then solve in a single MBF iteration; this reproduces the result by Blelloch et al. For graph inputs, we are not aware of any algorithms achieving polylog n depth at a non-trivial work bound, i.e., not incurring the $\Omega(n^3)$ work caused by relying on matrix-matrix multiplication.

1.2 Notation and Preliminaries

We consider weighted, undirected graphs $G = (V, E, \omega)$ without loops or parallel edges. We set $n := |V|$, $m := |E|$,

[4]The authors focus on Congest algorithms, which can be interpreted in our framework to infer the stated bounds.

and $V = \{v_1, \dots v_n\}$. For an edge $e = \{v, w\} \in E$, we write $\omega(v, w) := \omega(e)$, and fix $\omega(v, v) := 0$ for $v \in V$ and $\omega(v, w) := \infty$ for $\{v, w\} \notin E$. We assume that the ratio between maximum and minimum edge weight is polynomially bounded in n and that each edge weight and constant can be stored with sufficient precision in a single register.[5] We assume that G is given in the form of an adjacency list. W.l.o.g., we assume that there are no isolated nodes; in particular, $n \in \mathrm{O}(m)$. Furthermore, $0 \in \mathbb{N}$, and $[k] := \{0, \dots, k\}$.

Let $p \subseteq E$ be a path. p has $|p|$ *hops*, and *weight* $\omega(p) := \sum_{e \in p} \omega(e)$. For the nodes $v, w \in V$ let $\mathrm{P}(v, w, G)$ denote the set of paths from v to w, and $\mathrm{P}^h(v, w, G)$ the set of such paths using at most h hops. We denote by $\mathrm{dist}^h(v, w, G) := \min\{\omega(p) \mid p \in \mathrm{P}^h(v, w, G)\}$ the minimum weight of an h-hop path from v to w, where (by slight abuse of notation) $\min \emptyset := \infty$; the *distance* between v and w is $\mathrm{dist}(v, w, G) := \mathrm{dist}^n(v, w, G)$. The *shortest path hop distance* between v and w is $\mathrm{hop}(v, w, G) := \min\{|p| \mid p \in \mathrm{P}(v, w, G) \wedge \omega(p) = \mathrm{dist}(v, w, G)\}$; $\mathrm{MHSP}(v, w, G) := \{p \in \mathrm{P}^{\mathrm{hop}(v,w,G)}(v, w, G) \mid \omega(p) = \mathrm{dist}(v, w, G)\}$ denotes all *min-hop shortest paths* from v to w. Finally, the *shortest path diameter (SPD)* of G is $\mathrm{SPD}(G) := \max\{\mathrm{hop}(v, w, G) \mid v, w \in V\}$.

For a set N and $k \in \mathbb{N}$ we define $\binom{N}{k} := \{M \subseteq N \mid |M| = k\}$ and denote by $\mathrm{id}\colon N \to N$ the identity function. We use weak asymptotic notation hiding polylogarithmic factors in n: $\mathrm{O}(f(n) \operatorname{polylog}(n)) = \tilde{\mathrm{O}}(f(n))$, etc.

Probability. A claim holds *with high probability (w.h.p.)*, if it occurs with a probability of at least $1 - n^{-c}$ for any fixed choice of $c \in \mathbb{R}_{\geq 1}$, where c is a constant in terms of O-notation.

OBSERVATION 1.2. *Let $\mathcal{E}_1, \dots, \mathcal{E}_k$, $k \in \operatorname{poly} n$, be events occurring w.h.p., then $\mathcal{E}_1 \cap \dots \cap \mathcal{E}_k$ occurs w.h.p.*

Model of Computation. We use an abstract model of parallel computation similar to those used in circuit complexity. The computation is represented by a directed acyclic graph (DAG) with constantly bounded maximum indegree, where nodes represent words of memory that are given as input (indegree 0), or computed out of previously determined memory contents (non-zero indegree). When a word is computed, this happens with a constant number of basic instructions, e.g., addition, multiplication, comparison, etc.; here, we also allow for the use of (independent) randomness.

An algorithm defines, given the input, the DAG and how the nodes' content is computed, as well as which nodes represent the output. Given an instance of the problem, the *work* is the number of nodes of the corresponding DAG and the *depth* is its longest path. Assuming that there are no read or write conflicts, the work is thus (proportional to) the time required by a single processor (of uniform speed) to complete the computation, whereas the depth is the time required by an infinite number of processors.

Hop Sets. Graph $G = (V, E, \omega)$, *contains a (d, ε)-hop set* if

$$\forall v, w \in V\colon \quad \mathrm{dist}^d(v, w, G) \leq (1 + \varepsilon) \, \mathrm{dist}(v, w, G), \quad (1.1)$$

i.e., if its d-hop distances are a $(1 + \varepsilon)$-approximation of its distances. This definition is based on Cohen [12], who describes how to efficiently add edges to G to establish this property.

Distance Metrics. The min-plus algebra $\mathcal{S}_{\min,+} = (\mathbb{R}_{\geq 0} \cup \{\infty\}, \min, +)$ forms a semiring, i.e., a ring without additive inverses. For the sake of presentation, we associate $\oplus$ and $\odot$ with the addition and multiplication of the underlying ring throughout the paper; in this case we use $a \oplus b := \min\{a, b\}$ and $a \odot b := a + b$. Observe that ∞ and 0 are the neutral elements w.r.t. $\oplus$ and $\odot$, respectively. We follow the standard convention to occasionally leave out $\odot$ and give it priority over $\oplus$, e.g., interpret $ab \oplus c$ as $(a \odot b) \oplus c$ for all $a, b, c \in \mathbb{R}_{\geq 0} \cup \{\infty\}$.

The min-plus algebra is a well-established tool to determine pairwise distances in a graph via the distance product [1, 30]. Let $G = (V, E, \omega)$ be a weighted graph and let $A \in (\mathbb{R}_{\geq 0} \cup \{\infty\})^{V \times V}$ be its *adjacency matrix* A, given by $a_{vw} = \omega(v, w)$. Throughout this paper, the operations involved in matrix multiplication are induced by the ring operations of $\mathcal{S}_{\min,+}$, i.e., for square matrices A, B with row and column index set V, we have

$$(A \oplus B)_{vw} = \min\{a_{vw}, b_{vw}\}, \text{ and} \quad (1.2)$$

$$(AB)_{vw} = \min_{u \in V}\{a_{vu} + b_{uw}\}. \quad (1.3)$$

The *distance product* A^h corresponds to h-hop distances, i.e., $(A^h)_{vw} = \mathrm{dist}^h(v, w, G)$ [1]. In particular, this corresponds to the exact distances between all pairs of nodes for $h \geq \mathrm{SPD}(G)$.

2. MBF-LIKE ALGORITHMS

The Moore-Bellman-Ford (MBF) algorithm [8, 18, 28] is both fundamental and elegant. Over the years, numerous algorithms emerged that use similar iterative schemes for distributing information [2, 5, 6, 17, 21, 23, 24, 25]. In this section, we propose a characterization for this class of algorithms. The common denominator of these algorithms is the following:

- The initial state vector $x^{(0)}$ contains information initially known to the nodes.
- In each *iteration,* information is first *propagated* along all edges.
- All nodes then *aggregate* the received information. This and the previous step are precisely the same as updating the state vector $x^{(i)}$ by the matrix-vector product $x^{(i+1)} = Ax^{(i)}$ over the min-plus semiring.
- Finally, redundancies are *filtered* out before moving on to the next iteration.

As a concrete example, consider the task of determining for each node the list of its k closest nodes. To this end, one needs to consider all nodes as sources, i.e., run the multi-source variant of the classic MBF algorithm with all nodes as sources. Nodes store values in $(\mathbb{R}_{\geq 0} \cup \{\infty\})^V$, so that in iteration i each node $v \in V$ learns $\mathrm{dist}^i(v, w, G) \in \mathbb{R}_{\geq 0} \cup \{\infty\}$ for all $w \in V$. Initially, $x^{(0)}_{vw} = 0$ at $v = w$ and ∞ everywhere else (the 0-hop distances). *Propagating* these distances over an edge of weight $\omega(e)$ means uniformly increasing all these distances by $\omega(e)$. During *aggregation,* the vertex-wise minimal distance is picked. This is costly due to possibly maintaining at each node non-∞ distance values for *all* other nodes. To increase efficiency, we *filter* out, in each iteration and at each node, all source/distance pairs but the k pairs

[5] As we are interested in approximation algorithms, $\mathrm{O}(\log n)$ bits suffice to encode values with sufficient precision.

with smallest distance. This reduces the amount of work by a factor of $\Theta(n/k)$ compared to the naive approach.

The filtering step thus generalizes from a classic APSP-MBF to an "MBF-like" algorithm, with the goal of reducing work. The crucial characteristics exploited by this idea are the following.

- Propagation and aggregation are interchangeable. It makes no difference whether two pieces of information are propagated separately to their destination, or as a single aggregated piece of information.
- Filtering or not filtering after aggregation has no impact on the output, only on efficiency.

2.1 Propagation and Aggregation

Let M be the set of possible values that an MBF-like algorithm can store at a vertex. We represent propagation of $x \in M$ over an edge of weight $s \in \mathbb{R}_{\geq 0} \cup \{\infty\}$ by $s \odot x$ and aggregation of $x, y \in M$ at some node by $x \oplus y$. We require that $\mathcal{M} = (M, \oplus, \odot)$ is a zero-preserving semimodule over $\mathcal{S}_{\min,+}$ with zero $\bot \in M$, i.e., that for all $s, t \in \mathbb{R}_{\geq 0} \cup \{\infty\}$ and $x, y \in M$:

$$0 \odot x = x, \tag{2.1}$$
$$\infty \odot x = \bot, \tag{2.2}$$
$$s \odot (x \oplus y) = (s \odot x) \oplus (s \odot y), \tag{2.3}$$
$$(s \oplus t) \odot x = (s \odot x) \oplus (t \odot x), \text{ and} \tag{2.4}$$
$$(s \odot t) \odot x = s \odot (t \odot x). \tag{2.5}$$

We write $x \in \mathcal{M}$ to indicate that $x \in M$ and $\oplus$ and $\odot$ operations involving x are those of $\mathcal{M}$. The straightforward choice of $\mathcal{M}$, the direct product of $|V|$ copies of $\mathbb{R}_{\geq 0} \cup \{\infty\}$, is suitable for most applications we consider.

Definition 2.1 (Distance Map). *The* distance map semimodule $\mathcal{D} := ((\mathbb{R}_{\geq 0} \cup \{\infty\})^V, \oplus, \odot)$ *is given by, for all* $s \in \mathbb{R}_{\geq 0} \cup \{\infty\}$ *and* $x, y \in (\mathbb{R}_{\geq 0} \cup \{\infty\})^V$, $(x \oplus y)_v = \min\{x_v, y_v\}$ *and* $(s \odot x)_v = s + x_v$, *where* $\bot := (\infty, \ldots, \infty) \in (\mathbb{R}_{\geq 0} \cup \{\infty\})^V$ *is the neutral element w.r.t.* $\oplus$.

Observation 2.2. *$\mathcal{D}$ is a zero-preserving semimodule with zero* $\bot = (\infty, \ldots, \infty)$.

Distance maps can be represented by only storing those distances (and their indices from V) that are not ∞. In the following, we denote by $|x|$ the number of non-∞ entries of $x \in \mathcal{D}$.

Lemma 2.3. *Suppose $x_1, \ldots, x_n \in \mathcal{D}$ are stored in lists of index/distance pairs as above. Then $\bigoplus_{i=1}^{n} x_i$ can be computed with $O(\log n)$ depth and $O(\sum_{i=1}^{n} |x_i| \log n)$ work.*

2.2 Filtering

MBF-like algorithms maintain efficiency by propagating only a filtered (small) representative of the information they obtained. We capture this with a congruence relation on the node states, and a representative projection that picks a suitable representative of an equivalence class.

Definition 2.4 (Congruence Relation). *Let* $\mathcal{M} = (M, \oplus, \odot)$ *be a semimodule and* $\sim$ *an equivalence relation on* M. *We call* $\sim$ *a* congruence relation *on* $\mathcal{M}$ *iff*

$$\forall s \in \mathbb{R}_{\geq 0} \cup \{\infty\}, \forall x, x' \in M : x \sim x' \Rightarrow sx \sim sx' \tag{2.6}$$
$$\forall x, x', y, y' \in M : x \sim x' \wedge y \sim y' \Rightarrow x \oplus y \sim x' \oplus y'. \tag{2.7}$$

A congruence relation induces a quotient semimodule.

Observation 2.5. *Denote by $[x]$ the equivalence class of $x \in M$ under the congruence relation $\sim$ of semimodule $\mathcal{M} = (M, \oplus, \odot)$. Set $M/_\sim := \{[x] \mid x \in M\}$. Then $\mathcal{M}/_\sim = (M/_\sim, \oplus, \odot)$ is a semimodule with the operations $[x] \oplus [y] := [x \oplus y]$ and $s \odot [x] = [sx]$.*

An MBF-like algorithm implicitly operates on this quotient semimodule, meaning that it operates on suitable representatives of the equivalence classes that allow efficient computations. Obtaining such representatives is the task of the filtering step.

Definition 2.6 (Representative Projection). *Let* $\mathcal{M} = (M, \oplus, \odot)$ *be a semimodule and* $\sim$ *a congruence relation on* $\mathcal{M}$. *The function* $r \colon M \to M$ *is a* representative projection *w.r.t.* $\sim$ *iff*

$$\forall x \in M : \quad x \sim r(x) \tag{2.8}$$
$$\forall x, y \in M : \quad x \sim y \Rightarrow r(x) = r(y). \tag{2.9}$$

An MBF-like algorithm has to behave in a compatible way for all vertices in that each vertex follows the same propagation, aggregation, and filtering rules. This induces a semimodule structure on the (possible) state vectors of the algorithm in a natural way.

Definition 2.7 (Power Semimodule). *Given a node set V and a zero-preserving semimodule $\mathcal{M} = (M, \oplus, \odot)$, we define $\mathcal{M}^V = (M^V, \oplus, \odot)$ by applying the operations of $\mathcal{M}$ coordinatewise. Furthermore, by r^V we denote the componentwise application of a representative projection r of $\mathcal{M}$ and define the equivalence relation $\sim$ via $x \sim y$ iff $x_v \sim y_v$ for all $v \in V$.*

Observation 2.8. *$\mathcal{M}^V$ is a zero-preserving semimodule with neutral element $\bot^V := (\bot, \ldots, \bot) \in M^V$, where $\bot$ is the neutral element of $\mathcal{M}$. The equivalence relation $\sim$ induced by r^V is a congruence relation on $\mathcal{M}^V$ with representative projection r^V.*

2.3 Definition

Definition 2.9 (MBF-like Algorithm). *An* MBF-like algorithm $\mathcal{A}$ *is determined by*

1. *a zero-preserving semimodule $\mathcal{M} = (M, \oplus, \odot)$ over $\mathcal{S}_{\min,+} = (\mathbb{R}_{\geq 0} \cup \{\infty\}, \min, +)$,*
2. *a congruence relation on $\mathcal{M}$ with representative projection r, and*
3. *initial values $x^{(0)} \in \mathcal{M}^V$ for the nodes,*

where $x^{(0)}$ depends on the input graph. On a weighted graph G, h iterations of $\mathcal{A}$ determine

$$\mathcal{A}^h(G) := x^{(h)} := r^V A^h x^{(0)}, \tag{2.10}$$

where A is the adjacency matrix of G.

The i-th iteration of $\mathcal{A}$ determines $x^{(i)} := r^V A x^{(i-1)}$ (propagate, aggregate, filter). Thus, h iterations yield $(r^V A)^h x^{(0)}$, which we show to be identical to $r^V A^h x^{(0)}$ below.

2.4 State Manipulations

The operations of interest to us are linear functions on the semimodule $\mathcal{M}^V$, like multiplication with an adjacency matrix. However, these operations are not arbitrary linear functions on $\mathcal{M}^V$, but only those that act in a "simple" way on each of the n copies of $\mathcal{M}$ making up $\mathcal{M}^V$. We give the proofs of this section in the full paper.

Definition 2.10 (Simple Linear Function). *Consider $\mathcal{M} = (M, \oplus, \odot)$, a semimodule over $\mathcal{S}_{\min,+}$. A matrix $A \in (\mathbb{R}_{\geq 0} \cup \{\infty\})^{V \times V}$ defines a* simple linear function *$A \colon M^V \to M^V$ (and vice versa) by*

$$(A(x))_v := (Ax)_v = \bigoplus_{w \in V} a_{vw} x_w. \tag{2.11}$$

Thus, each iteration of an MBF-like algorithm is an application of the simple linear function given by the adjacency matrix, followed by application of r^V.

Example 2.11 (Non-simple Linear Function). *We remark that not all linear functions on $\mathcal{M}^V$ are simple. For a counter-example, suppose $V = \{1,2\}$, $\mathcal{M} = \mathcal{S}_{\min,+}^V$, and consider $f \colon \mathcal{M}^V \to \mathcal{M}^V$ given by $((f(x))_1)_1 = (x_1)_1 \oplus (x_1)_2$ and $((f(x))_v)_w = \infty$ for $v \neq 1$ or $w \neq 1$. Clearly f is linear, but since it acts on x_1 in a non-trivial way, it is not simple.*

An intermediate lemma states that equivalence is preserved by linear combinations.

Lemma 2.12. *Let $\mathcal{M} = (M, \oplus, \odot)$ be a semimodule and $\sim$ a congruence relation on $\mathcal{M}$. Furthermore, for $k \in \mathbb{N}$, let $x_1, \dots, x_k, x'_1, \dots, x'_k \in \mathcal{M}$ such that $x_i \sim x'_i$ for all $1 \leq i \leq k$. Then for all $s_1, \dots, s_k \in \mathbb{R}_{\geq 0} \cup \{\infty\}$, it holds that*

$$\bigoplus_{i=1}^{k} s_i x_i \sim \bigoplus_{i=1}^{k} s_i x'_i. \tag{2.12}$$

We establish some key properties of simple linear functions: They map equivalent inputs to equivalent results (crucial for dealing with filtered and unfiltered states), and matrix multiplication and addition behave as expected.

Lemma 2.13. *Let A and B be simple linear functions and $x \sim x' \in M^V$. Then*

$$Ax \sim Ax', \tag{2.13}$$

$$(A \oplus B)(x) = (A \oplus B)x, \text{ and} \tag{2.14}$$

$$(A \circ B)(x) = ABx. \tag{2.15}$$

Due to the above lemma, we identify simple linear functions and their matrices. We proceed to formalize in what manner an MBF-like algorithm operates on $\mathcal{M}/_\sim$.

Lemma 2.14 (Simple Linear Function Semirings). *Denote by F the set of simple linear functions on semimodule $\mathcal{M}$ and let $\sim$ be a congruence relation on $\mathcal{M}$ with representative projection r.*

1. *$\mathcal{F} = (F, \oplus, \circ)$ is a semiring.*
2. *For $A \in F$, $[A][x] := [Ax]$ defines a simple linear function on $\mathcal{M}/_\sim$.*
3. *For $A, B \in F$, $[A] \oplus [B] = [A \oplus B]$ and $[A] \circ [B] = [AB]$.*
4. *Setting $F/_\sim := \{[A] \mid A \in F\}$, $\mathcal{F}/_\sim := (F/_\sim, \oplus, \circ)$ is a semiring.*
5. *$[r^V]x := [r^V x]$ defines a simple linear function on $F/_\sim$, which in fact is the multiplicative identity of the semiring.*

The following corollary is the key result required throughout the paper. It allows applying filters whenever convenient.

Corollary 2.15 ($r^V \sim \mathrm{id}$). *For a simple linear function A and representative projection r on $\mathcal{M}$, it holds that*

$$r^V A \sim A r^V \sim A, \tag{2.16}$$

where $\sim$ extends to functions by $A \sim B$ iff $A(x) \sim B(x)$ for all $x \in \mathcal{M}^V$. In particular, for any MBF-like algorithm $\mathcal{A}$, we have that

$$\mathcal{A}^h(G) = (r^V A)^h x^{(0)} = r^V A^h x^{(0)}. \tag{2.17}$$

We stress that both the restriction to simple linear functions and the componentwise application of r to determine r^V are crucial:

Example 2.16 (Non-simple Linear Function). *Let V, $\mathcal{M}$, and f be defined as in Example 2.11. If $r(x) = (x_1, \infty)$ for all $x \in \mathcal{M}$, we have that*

$$r^V f\begin{pmatrix}(2,1)\\ \bot\end{pmatrix} = \begin{pmatrix}(1,\infty)\\ \bot\end{pmatrix} \not\sim \begin{pmatrix}(2,\infty)\\ \bot\end{pmatrix} = f r^V \begin{pmatrix}(2,1)\\ \bot\end{pmatrix},$$

implying that $r^V f \not\sim f r^V$.

Example 2.17 (Non-component-wise Filter). *Let a simple linear function be given by $fx = \binom{x_1 \oplus x_2}{\bot}$, and filter with $r^V(x) = \binom{x_1}{\bot}$, i.e., r^V is not componentwise application of some representative projection r on $\mathcal{M}$, but still a representative projection on $\mathcal{M}^V$. Then we have that*

$$r^V f\begin{pmatrix}(2,\infty)\\ (1,\infty)\end{pmatrix} = \begin{pmatrix}(1,\infty)\\ \bot\end{pmatrix} \not\sim \begin{pmatrix}(2,\infty)\\ \bot\end{pmatrix} = f r^V \begin{pmatrix}(2,\infty)\\ (1,\infty)\end{pmatrix},$$

again implying that $r^V f \not\sim f r^V$.

2.5 Algorithms

For the purpose of illustration, we give some basic MBF-like algorithms; correctness is shown in the full version.

Example 2.18 (SSSP). *Single-source shortest paths is to determine the h-hop distance to $s \in V$ for all $v \in V$. It is solved by an MBF-like algorithm with $\mathcal{M} = \mathcal{S}_{\min,+}$, $r = \mathrm{id}$, and $x_s^{(0)} = 0$, $x_v^{(0)} = \infty$ for all $v \neq s$.*

Example 2.19 (k-SP). *k-shortest paths means to determine, for each node, the k closest nodes in terms of the h-hop distance $\mathrm{dist}^h(\cdot,\cdot,G)$. It is solved by an MBF-like algorithm, as can be seen by choosing $\mathcal{M} = \mathcal{D}$,*

$$r(x)_v \mapsto \begin{cases} x_v & \text{if } x_v \text{ is among the } k \text{ smallest entries of } x \\ \infty & \text{otherwise,} \end{cases}$$

ties broken by index, and $x_v^{(0)} = (\infty, \dots, \infty, 0, \infty, \dots, \infty)$.

Example 2.20 (APSP). *All-pairs shortest paths is n-SP (resulting in $r = \mathrm{id}$).*

Example 2.21 (Forest Fires). *The goal is to detect, for each node, if there is a forest fire within distance d, where every node initially knows if it is on fire. For an MBF-like algorithm solving it, pick, e.g., $\mathcal{M} = \mathcal{S}_{\min,+}$,*

$$r(x) = \begin{cases} x & \text{if } x \leq d \\ \infty & \text{otherwise,} \end{cases}$$

and $x_v^{(0)} = 0$ if v is on fire and $x_v^{(0)} = \infty$ otherwise.

3. THE SIMULATED GRAPH

In order to determine the tree into which G is embedded, we need to determine LE lists (compare Section 5). These are the result of an MBF-like algorithm, where r ensures that $|r(x^{(i)})_v| \in \mathrm{O}(\log n)$ w.h.p. for all $0 \leq i \leq h$ and $v \in V$, allowing to perform an iteration with $\tilde{\mathrm{O}}(m)$ work. However, doing so on G requires $h \geq \mathrm{SPD}(G)$, which in general can be as large as $n-1$. In this section, we embed G into a complete graph H with $\mathrm{SPD}(H) \in \tilde{\mathrm{O}}(1)$ and small stretch.

Our construction requires to first add a hop set to G. For the sake of presentation, we assume G to already contain a (d, ε)-hop set throughout this section.

We begin our construction of H by geometrically sampling levels for the vertices V: Every vertex starts at level 0. In step $\lambda \geq 1$, each vertex in level $\lambda - 1$ is raised to level λ with probability 1/2. We continue until the first step $\Lambda + 1$ where no node is sampled. $\lambda(v)$ refers to the level of $v \in V$, and $\lambda(v, w) := \lambda(\{v, w\}) := \min\{\lambda(v), \lambda(w)\}$ for $\{v, w\} \in E$.

LEMMA 3.1. *W.h.p., $\Lambda \in \mathrm{O}(\log n)$.*

The idea is to use the levels in the following way. We devise a complete graph H on V. An edge of H with level λ is weighted with the d-hop distance between its endpoints in G (which is a $(1+\varepsilon)$-approximation of their exact distance due to the hop set), but multiplied with a penalty of $(1+\varepsilon)^{\Lambda-\lambda}$. This way, high-level edges are "more attractive" for shortest paths, because they receive smaller penalties.

DEFINITION 3.2. *Let $G = (V, E, \omega)$ be a graph that contains a (d, ε)-hop set with levels sampled as above. We define the complete graph H as*

$$H := \left(V, \binom{V}{2}, \omega_\Lambda\right) \tag{3.1}$$

$$\omega_\Lambda(\{v, w\}) \mapsto (1+\varepsilon)^{\Lambda - \lambda(v,w)} \operatorname{dist}^d(v, w, G). \tag{3.2}$$

LEMMA 3.3. *Consider $v, w \in V$, and $p \in \mathrm{MHSP}(v, w, H)$. Then all $e \in p$ have $\lambda(e) \geq \lambda(w, v)$.*

PROOF SKETCH. Due to the factor $(1+\varepsilon)$-penalty in edge weights per level and G containing a (d, ε)-hop set, a v-w-path of level smaller than $\lambda(v, w)$ is at least as heavy as $\omega_\Lambda(v, w)$. □

Thus, edge levels in a min-hop shortest path p never locally decrease. Instead, the edge levels in p first monotonically increase to some maximum and then monotonically decrease. It remains to bound the number of hops spent on each level.

LEMMA 3.4. *Consider vertices v and w of H with $\lambda(v) = \lambda(w) \geq \lambda$. Then w.h.p. one of the following statements holds:*

$$\operatorname{hop}(v, w, H) \in \mathrm{O}(\log n), \text{ or} \tag{3.3}$$

$$\forall p \in \mathrm{MHSP}(v, w, H)\ \exists e \in p\colon\ \lambda(e) \geq \lambda + 1. \tag{3.4}$$

PROOF. Condition on the event $\mathcal{E}_{V_\lambda}$ that $V_\lambda \subseteq V$ is the set of nodes with level λ or higher (with level $\lambda+1$ not yet sampled). Let $H_\lambda := (V_\lambda, \binom{V_\lambda}{2}, \omega_\lambda)$ with $\omega_\lambda(\{v, w\}) \mapsto (1+\varepsilon)^{\Lambda-\lambda} \operatorname{dist}^d(v, w, G)$ denote the subgraph of H spanned by V_λ and capped at level λ.

Consider $p \in \mathrm{MHSP}(v, w, H_\lambda)$. Observe that $\mathbb{P}[\lambda(u) \geq \lambda + 1 \mid \mathcal{E}_{V_\lambda}] = \frac{1}{2}$ independently for all $u \in V_\lambda$, and hence $\mathbb{P}[\lambda(e) \geq \lambda + 1 \mid \mathcal{E}_{V_\lambda}] = \frac{1}{4}$ for all $e \in p$. The latter events are independent for any subset of non-adjacent edges of p. Selecting every other edge, we obtain such a subset of size at least $\frac{|p|}{2}$. If $|p| \geq 2c\log_{4/3} n$ for some choice of $c \in \mathbb{R}_{\geq 1}$, the probability that p contains no edge of level $\lambda+1$ or higher is bounded from above by $(\frac{3}{4})^{|p|/2} \leq (\frac{3}{4})^{c\log_{4/3} n} = n^{-c}$, so p contains such an edge w.h.p.

We show that for all $q \in \mathrm{MHSP}(v, w, H)$, w.h.p. (3.3) or (3.4) holds. Observe that $\omega_\Lambda(q) \leq \omega_\Lambda(p)$. Furthermore, q uses only edges of level λ or higher by Lemma 3.3. If q contains an edge of level $\lambda+1$ or higher, (3.4) holds for q. Otherwise, we have $\omega_\lambda(q) = \omega_\Lambda(q)$, and distinguish two cases:

Case $|p| \geq 2c\log_{4/3} n$: Recall that w.h.p. p has an edge of level $\lambda+1$ or higher. This yields $\omega_\Lambda(p) < \omega_\lambda(p)$, implying

$$\omega_\Lambda(p) \overset{\text{w.h.p.}}{<} \omega_\lambda(p) \leq \omega_\lambda(q) = \omega_\Lambda(q), \tag{3.5}$$

which contradicts $q \in \mathrm{MHSP}(v, w, H)$.

Case $|p| < 2c\log_{4/3} n$: Not unlike above, we have

$$\omega_\Lambda(p) \leq \omega_\lambda(p) \leq \omega_\lambda(q) = \omega_\Lambda(q), \tag{3.6}$$

so $\omega_\Lambda(q) = \omega_\Lambda(p)$ and $|q| \leq |p| \in \mathrm{O}(\log n)$ follows.

Let $\mathcal{E}_{vw}$ denote the event that (3.3) or (3.4) holds for $v, w \in V$. We conclude that

$$\begin{aligned}
&\mathbb{P}[\mathcal{E}_{vw} \mid \lambda(v, w) \geq \lambda] && (3.7)\\
&= \sum_{V_\lambda \subseteq V} \mathbb{P}[\mathcal{E}_{V_\lambda} \mid \lambda(v, w) \geq \lambda]\, \mathbb{P}[\mathcal{E}_{vw} \mid \mathcal{E}_{V_\lambda}] && (3.8)\\
&= \sum_{\{v,w\} \subseteq V_\lambda \subseteq V} \mathbb{P}[\mathcal{E}_{V_\lambda} \mid \lambda(v, w) \geq \lambda]\, \mathbb{P}[\mathcal{E}_{vw} \mid \mathcal{E}_{V_\lambda}] && (3.9)\\
&\geq \sum_{\{v,w\} \subseteq V_\lambda \subseteq V} \mathbb{P}[\mathcal{E}_{V_\lambda} \mid \lambda(v, w) \geq \lambda](1 - n^{-c}) && (3.10)\\
&= (1 - n^{-c}) \sum_{V_\lambda \subseteq V} \mathbb{P}[\mathcal{E}_{V_\lambda} \mid \lambda(v, w) \geq \lambda] = 1 - n^{-c}, && (3.11)
\end{aligned}$$

which is precisely the statement of the lemma. □

Min-hop shortest paths traverse at most $\Lambda \in \mathrm{O}(\log n)$ levels spending $\mathrm{O}(\log n)$ hops in each, bounding $\mathrm{SPD}(H)$. Weights increase by a factor of at most $(1+\varepsilon)$ per level.

THEOREM 3.5. *W.h.p., $\mathrm{SPD}(H) \in \mathrm{O}(\log^2 n)$. Furthermore, w.h.p. for all $v, w \in V$,*

$$\begin{aligned}
&\operatorname{dist}(v, w, H) \geq \operatorname{dist}(v, w, G), \text{ and}\\
&\operatorname{dist}(v, w, H) \leq (1+\varepsilon)^{\mathrm{O}(\log n)} \operatorname{dist}(v, w, G).
\end{aligned} \tag{3.12}$$

4. THE ORACLE

As H is a complete graph, we cannot hope to achieve $\mathrm{o}(n^2)$ work when operating on it explicitly. Instead, we exploit the properties of MBF-like algorithms discussed in Section 2 to simulate iterations of $\mathcal{A}$ on H using a polylogarithmic number of matrix-vector multiplications with A_G, the adjacency matrix of G. Here, we again assume for the sake of presentation that G already contains a (d, ε)-hop set.

The idea is to simulate one iteration of an MBF-like algorithm $\mathcal{A}$ on H using d iterations on G, which in turn suffices to evaluate $\omega_\Lambda(v, w) = (1+\varepsilon)^{\Lambda - \lambda(v,w)} \operatorname{dist}^d(v, w, G)$. This is done separately for each level $\lambda \in [\Lambda]$ in parallel. For level λ, we run $\mathcal{A}$ for d iterations on G with edge weights scaled up by $(1+\varepsilon)^{\Lambda-\lambda}$, where the initial vector is obtained by discarding all information at nodes $v \notin V_\lambda := \{v \in V \mid \lambda(v) \geq \lambda\}$. Afterwards, we again discard everything stored at vertices not in V_λ. To formalize this, we define the operator discarding all information from levels smaller than λ. For $\lambda \in [\Lambda]$, denote by P_λ the $\mathcal{M}^V$-projection to coordinates V_λ:

$$(P_\lambda x)_v = \begin{cases} x_v & \text{if } \lambda(v) \geq \lambda \\ \bot & \text{otherwise.} \end{cases} \tag{4.1}$$

Observe that P_λ is a simple linear function on $\mathcal{M}^V$, where $(P_\lambda)_{vw} = 0$ if $v = w \in V_\lambda$ and $(P_\lambda)_{vw} = \infty$ otherwise. This gives us the tools to decompose A_H as discussed above.

LEMMA 4.1. *With $(A_\lambda)_{vw} := (1+\varepsilon)^{\Lambda-\lambda}(A_G)_{vw}$, we have*

$$A_H = \bigoplus_{\lambda=0}^{\Lambda} P_\lambda A_\lambda^d P_\lambda. \tag{4.2}$$

Leveraging that $A_\lambda \sim r^V A_\lambda$ by Corollary 2.15, the above shows that we can apply $r^V A_H$ efficiently provided we can do so for $r^V A_\lambda$.

THEOREM 4.2. *Suppose that $\mathcal{M} = \mathcal{D}$ and, for each intermediate state vector $y = (r^V A_\lambda)^f x^{(i)}$ for some $f \in [d]$, $i \in [h]$, and $\lambda \in [\Lambda]$, we can compute $r^V A_\lambda y$ with depth D and work W. Then, w.h.p., $\mathcal{A}^{\mathrm{SPD}(H)}(H)$ can be executed with $\tilde{\mathrm{O}}(dD)$ depth and $\tilde{\mathrm{O}}(dW)$ work.*

PROOF SKETCH. By Lemma 3.1 and Theorem 3.5, w.h.p. $\Lambda \in \mathrm{O}(\log n)$ and $\mathrm{SPD}(H) \leq h \in \mathrm{O}(\log^2 n)$. By construction — h iterations on H, each simulated by d iterations on G, run in parallel for each level — we have to compute

$$\mathcal{A}(H) = r^V \left(\bigoplus_{\lambda=0}^{\Lambda} P_\lambda (r^V A_\lambda)^d P_\lambda \right)^h r^V x^{(0)}. \tag{4.3}$$

The claim follows by showing that applying P_λ and aggregating over λ does not affect depth and work too much. □

5. FRT CONSTRUCTION

As discussed in the full paper and related work [9, 11, 13, 19, 22], sampling from the FRT distribution, which we do for the graph H from Section 3, boils down to computing LE lists (see below) for H.

The first step of the construction is to choose a uniformly random total order of the nodes (i.e., a uniformly random permutation). In the following, $v < w$ means that v is smaller than w w.r.t. to this order. The *least element (LE) list* of $v \in V$ is obtained by deleting from $\{(\mathrm{dist}(v,w,H), w) \mid w \in V\}$ all pairs $(\mathrm{dist}(v,w,H), w)$ for which there is some $u \in V$ with $\mathrm{dist}(v,u,H) \leq \mathrm{dist}(v,w,H)$ and $u < w$. Essentially, v learns, for every distance d, the smallest node within distance d or less, i.e., $\min\{w \in V \mid \mathrm{dist}(v,w,G) \leq d\}$.

LEMMA 5.1. *Given LE lists of length $\mathrm{O}(\log n)$ for all vertices $v \in V$, the corresponding FRT embedding can be determined using $\mathrm{O}(n \log^2 n \log\log n)$ work and $\mathrm{O}(\log n \log\log n)$ depth.*

5.1 Determining LE Lists is MBF-like

In the following, we use the distance map module $\mathcal{D}$ from Definition 2.1. We show that LE lists are the image of a representative projection r, which by Definition 2.9 means that they are the output of the respective MBF-like algorithm.

DEFINITION 5.2. *For $x, y \in \mathcal{D}$, define $x \sim y \Leftrightarrow r(x) = r(y)$, where*

$$r(x)_v := \begin{cases} \infty & \exists w < v \colon x_w \leq x_v \\ x_v & \textit{otherwise.} \end{cases} \tag{5.1}$$

In other words, $r(x)$ is the LE list of $v \in V$ if $x_w = \mathrm{dist}(v,w,H)$, and we consider two lists equivalent iff they result in the same (intermediate) LE list.

The following lemma prepares the proof that retrieving LE lists is an MBF-like algorithm. It first states that filtering keeps the interesting information: If a node/distance pair is dominated by an entry in a distance map (smaller vertex ID and at least as close), then the filtered distance map also contains a (possibly different) dominating entry; in this sense, filtering keeps the relevant information. Similar statements hold when filtering is applied before aggregation.

LEMMA 5.3. *Consider arbitrary $x, y \in \mathcal{D}$, $v \in V$, and $s \in \mathbb{R}_{\geq 0} \cup \{\infty\}$. Then*

$$\exists w < v \colon x_w \leq s \Leftrightarrow \exists w < v \colon r(x)_w \leq s, \tag{5.2}$$

$$\begin{aligned} &\exists w < v \colon (x \oplus y)_w \leq (x \oplus y)_v \\ &\Leftrightarrow \exists w < v \colon (r(x) \oplus r(y))_w \leq (r(x) \oplus r(y))_v, \textit{ and} \end{aligned} \tag{5.3}$$

$$\begin{aligned} &\nexists w < v \colon (x \oplus y)_w \leq (x \oplus y)_v \\ &\Rightarrow (x \oplus y)_v = (r(x) \oplus r(y))_v. \end{aligned} \tag{5.4}$$

PROOF SKETCH. Observe that the necessity "$\Leftarrow$" in (5.2) is trivial. As for sufficiency, suppose that for given s and v there is $w < v$ such that $x_w \leq s$. If $r(x)_w = x_w$, we are done. Otherwise, there must be some $u < w < v$ satisfying $x_u \leq x_w \leq x_v$. Since $|V|$ is finite, an inductive repetition of the argument yields that there is some $w' < v$ with $r(x)_{w'} = x_{w'} \leq s$. The other two statements follow from (5.2) by basic (but non-trivial) reasoning. □

Equipped with this lemma, we now can prove that $\sim$ is a congruence relation on $\mathcal{D}$ with representative projection r.

LEMMA 5.4. *The equivalence relation $\sim$, compare Definition 5.2, is a congruence relation on the zero-preserving semimodule $\mathcal{D}$. The function r from Definition 5.2 is a representative projection w.r.t. $\sim$.*

PROOF SKETCH. The challenge is to prove that $r(x \oplus y) = r(r(x) \oplus r(y))$ for all $x, y \in \mathcal{D}$, which implies (2.7). This is done componentwise, by distinguishing the cases $x_v \oplus y_v = r(x)_v \oplus r(y)_v = \infty$, $(x \oplus y)_v \neq r(x \oplus y)_v = \infty$ and $(x \oplus y)_v = r(x \oplus y)_v < \infty$, repeatedly applying Lemma 5.3. □

5.2 Efficient LE list computation

To show that the computation is efficient, we make use of Theorem 4.2. To this end, it remains to prove that we can perform the matrix-vector multiplication with A_λ (a scaled version of A_G, the adjacency matrix of G) and apply r^V efficiently. To this end, we first show that LE lists are always short, a slight generalization from known results [19, 22].

LEMMA 5.5. *Suppose that $x \in \mathcal{D}$ is arbitrary, but independent of the random order on the nodes. Then $|r(x)| \in \mathrm{O}(\log n)$ w.h.p.*

Having shown that intermediate LE lists are short w.h.p., next we establish that such lists can be computed efficiently.

LEMMA 5.6. *For $x \in \mathcal{D}$, $r(x)$ can be computed using depth $\mathrm{O}(|r(x)| \log n)$ and work $\mathrm{O}(|x|(|r(x)| + \log n))$.*

PROOF SKETCH. Use a tournament tree to determine the smallest entry, eliminate the selected entry and all entries it dominates, and iterate $|r(x)|$ times. □

We next show that intermediate results can be computed efficiently. Any such intermediate result is of the form

$$y = (r^V A_\mu)^f P_\mu \underbrace{\left(r^V \left(\bigoplus_{\lambda=0}^{\Lambda} P_\lambda (r^V A_\lambda)^d P_\lambda\right)\right)^h r^V x^{(0)}}_{=:x^{(h)}}, \quad (5.5)$$

where $x^{(h)} = (r^V A_H^h)x^{(0)} = \mathcal{A}^h(H)$ is the intermediate result of h iterations on H, and $(r^V A_\mu)^f P_\mu$ represents another f iterations on G used by the oracle to simulate the $(h+1)$-th iteration on H regarding level μ.

LEMMA 5.7. *Suppose $x^{(0)} \in \mathcal{D}^V$ is given by $(x_v)_w = 0$ for $v = w$ and $(x_v)_w = \infty$ everywhere else ($x_v^{(0)}$ is the v-th unit vector w.r.t. $\mathcal{D}$). For arbitrary $d, h \in \mathbb{N}$, $f \in [d]$, and $\mu \in [\Lambda]$, suppose that*

$$y = (r^V A_\mu)^f P_\mu \left(r^V \left(\bigoplus_{\lambda=0}^{\Lambda} P_\lambda (r^V A_\lambda)^d P_\lambda\right)\right)^h r^V x^{(0)}. \quad (5.6)$$

Then $A_\mu y$ and $r^V A_\mu y$ can be computed using $O(m \log^2 n)$ work and depth $O(\log^2 n)$.

PROOF. By (2.16) and (4.3), we have

$$y = (r^V A_\mu)^f P_\mu \left(r^V \left(\bigoplus_{\lambda=0}^{\Lambda} P_\lambda (r^V A_\lambda)^d P_\lambda\right)\right)^h r^V x^{(0)} \quad (5.7)$$

$$= r^V A_\mu^f P_\mu \left(\bigoplus_{\lambda=0}^{\Lambda} P_\lambda A_\lambda^d P_\lambda\right)^h x^{(0)} =: r^V y'. \quad (5.8)$$

Since y' does not depend on the random order of V, we know from Lemma 5.5 that, for all $v \in V$, $|y_v| \in O(\log n)$ w.h.p. We compute $(A_\mu y)_v$ in parallel for each $v \in V$. By Lemma 2.3, this can be done with depth $O(\log n)$ and work

$$O\left(\sum_{v \in V} \sum_{\substack{w \in V \\ \{v,w\} \in E}} |y_w| \log n\right) = O\left(\sum_{\{v,w\} \in E} |y_w| \log n\right) \quad (5.9)$$

$$\subseteq O(m \log^2 n) \quad (5.10)$$

w.h.p., where we note that the cost of propagation (i.e., addition of the edge weights) is asymptotically dominated by the aggregation (i.e., the min operations) with respect to both depth and work. To bound the cost of computing $r^V A_\mu y$, we again invoke (4.3), showing that

$$r^V A_\mu y = r^V A_\mu r^V y' = r^V A_\mu y', \quad (5.11)$$

and Lemma 5.5, showing that $|(r^V A_\mu y)_v| \in O(\log n)$ w.h.p. for all $v \in V$. By Lemma 5.6, we deduce that w.h.p. $r^V A_\mu y$ can be computed from $A_\mu y$ with depth $O(\log^2 n)$ and work

$$O\left(\sum_{v \in V} |(A_\mu y)_v| \log n\right) \subseteq O\left(\sum_{v \in V} \sum_{\substack{w \in V \\ \{v,w\} \in E}} |y_w| \log n\right)$$

$$= O\left(\sum_{\{v,w\} \in E} |y_w| \log n\right) \subseteq O(m \log^2 n). \quad \square \quad (5.12)$$

5.3 Main Result

We have shown that determining LE lists on H yields a probabilistic tree embedding for G with expected stretch $O(\log n)$, is the result of an MBF-like algorithm, and this algorithm is efficient by Lemma 5.7 and Theorem 4.2, which relies on the graph containing a suitable hop set.

THEOREM 5.8. *Given a graph $G = (V, E, \omega)$ containing a (d, ε)-hop set, we can compute, w.h.p., a tree embedding of G of expected stretch $O((1+\varepsilon)^{O(\log n)} \log n)$ with depth $\tilde{O}(d)$ and work $\tilde{O}(md)$.*

The requirement of a hop set is removed by invoking Cohen's construction [12] first.

COROLLARY 5.9. *For any constant $\varepsilon > 0$, w.h.p. we can compute a tree embedding of G of expected stretch $O(\log n)$ with depth* polylog n *and work $\tilde{O}(m^{1+\varepsilon})$.*

We can trade in approximation quality for less work by computing a spanner of G first.

COROLLARY 5.10. *For any constant $\varepsilon > 0$, w.h.p. we can compute a tree embedding of expected stretch $O(\varepsilon^{-1} \log n)$ with depth* polylog n *and work $\tilde{O}(m + n^{1+\varepsilon})$.*

6. FURTHER RESULTS

In Sections 6.1 and 6.2 we consider two applications of the embedding that were given by Blelloch et al. [9] and show how their results are improved by applying our techniques. The main difference is that Blelloch et al. assume the metric to be given by query access, whereas we work on a graph. This is more general, as the metric can be interpreted as a complete graph of shortest path diameter 1. The use of hop sets, however, restricts us to polynomially bounded edge ratios. The details for these results are given in the full version of this paper.

In Section 6.3, we show how existing distributed FRT constructions can be concisely interpreted in our framework. We then apply our approach to obtain an improved distributed FRT construction.

6.1 k-Median

In the k-median problem, the task is to determine $F \subseteq V$, $|F| \leq k$, such that $\sum_{v \in V} \operatorname{dist}(v, F, G)$ is minimized, where $\operatorname{dist}(v, F, G) := \min_{f \in F}\{\operatorname{dist}(v, f, G)\}$ is the distance of v to the set F. In [9], an $O(\log k)$-approximation with depth $O(\log^2 n)$ and work $\tilde{O}(nk + k^3)$ is given for $k \geq \log n$; the special case $k < \log n$ admits an $\tilde{O}(n)$-work solution with the same depth [10].

COROLLARY 6.1. *For any fixed constant $\varepsilon > 0$, an expected $O(\log k)$-approximation to k-median can be computed with depth* polylog n *and work $\tilde{O}(m^{1+\varepsilon} + k^3)$.*

Recall that, in general, one may need to examine $\Omega(m)$ edge weights to determine a reasonable approximation of the distance between two nodes, i.e., the dependence of the work on m is near-optimal. Blelloch et al. achieve a smaller complexity for $k \ll m/n$ due to their assumption that the distance metric is already precomputed.

6.2 Buy-at-Bulk Network Design

In this problem, one is given a weighted graph G, demands $(s_i, t_i, d_i) \in V \times V \times \mathbb{R}_{>0}$, $i \in [k]$, and a set of cable types, where the cable of type j has capacity u_j and costs $c_j\, \omega(e)$ when purchased for edge e. The goal is to find an assignment of cable types to edges minimizing the total cost such that the resulting edge capacities allow to simultaneously route d_i units of (distinct) flow from s_i to t_i (for all $i \in [k]$). Andrews shows that this problem is hard to approximate better than factor $\log^{1/2-o(1)} n$ [3].

Blelloch et al. [9] give an expected $O(\log n)$-approximation with polylog n depth and $O(n^3 \log n)$ work for this problem, which is a straightforward parallelization of the algorithm by Awerbuch and Azar [4].

Corollary 6.2. *For any constant $\varepsilon > 0$, an $O(\log n)$-approximation to buy-at-bulk network design can be computed with depth* polylog n *and work* $\tilde{O}(\min\{m^{1+\varepsilon}, n^2\} + \min\{k, n\}\,\mathrm{SPD}(G)) \subseteq \tilde{O}(n^2)$.

6.3 Distributed FRT Construction

In this section we fix $\sim$ to be the congruence relation given in Definition 5.2. Furthermore, let $G = (V, E, \omega)$ be a weighted graph with adjacency matrix $A_G \in (\mathbb{R}_{\geq 0} \cup \{\infty\})^{V \times V}$. Distributed algorithms for constructing FRT-type tree embeddings in the Congest model [29] are covered by our framework as well. For the sake of brevity, we do not formally introduce this model of computation here. The key aspects are the following:

- Computation proceeds by nodes exchanging $O(\log n)$-sized messages over the edges of the graph in synchronous rounds. Recall that edge weights, and by extension all path weights relevant to our computations, can be encoded using $O(\log n)$ bits, i.e., one message can basically carry one index/distance pair.
- Nodes initially know their neighbors and the weight of their incident edges. They need to compute only "their" part of the output. As pointed out in Section 5, sampling a tree from the distribution boils down to computing LE lists, so each node needs to compute its LE list.
- Local computations are free. The goal is to minimize the number of communication rounds.

We first briefly summarize the distributed FRT algorithms by Kahn et al. [22], and Ghaffari and Lenzen [19]. Then we demonstrate how to reduce an n^{ε} overhead of [19] to one of $n^{o(1)}$, using our machinery and a distributed hop set construction due to Henziger et al. [21].

The Algorithm by Khan et al. In our terminology, the algorithm due to Khan et al. [22] computes $r^V A_G^h x^{(0)} = (r^V A_G)^h x^{(0)}$, where $h = \mathrm{SPD}(G)$ and $x^{(0)} \in \mathcal{D}^V$ (see Definitions 2.1 and 2.7) given by $x_v^{(0)} = e_v$, i.e., $x_{vw}^{(0)} = 0$ iff $v = w$ and ∞ otherwise. It does so in the straightforward way: One initializes $x^{(0)}$ as above and iteratively computes $x^{(i+1)} := r^V A_G x^{(i)}$ until a fixpoint is reached, i.e., $x^{(i+1)} = r^V A_G x^{(i)}$. As $(r^V A_G)^i x^{(0)} = r^V A_G^i x^{(0)}$ by (2.16), Lemma 5.5 shows that, w.h.p., $|x_v^{(i)}| \in O(\log n)$ for all $i \in [h]$ and all $v \in V$. Therefore, $v \in V$ can transmit $x_v^{(i)}$ to all of its neighbors using $O(\log n)$ messages, and upon reception of its neighbors' lists compute $x_v^{(i+1)}$ locally. Thus, each iteration takes $O(\log n)$ rounds w.h.p., readily implying the round complexity of $O(\mathrm{SPD}(G) \log n)$ w.h.p. shown in [22].

The Algorithm by Ghaffari and Lenzen. The strongest lower bound for constructing a (low-stretch) metric tree embedding of G in the Congest model is $\tilde{\Omega}(\sqrt{n} + D)$ [15, 19], where D is the hop diameter of the graph. If $\mathrm{SPD}(G) \gg D + \sqrt{n}$, one may thus hope for a solution that runs in $\tilde{o}(\mathrm{SPD}(G))$ rounds. For $\varepsilon > 0$, in [19] a running time of $\tilde{O}(n^{1/2+\varepsilon} + D)$ is achieved by the following strategy.

1. Abbreviate $\ell := \lceil \sqrt{n} \rceil$. For a sufficiently large constant c, sample $\lceil c\ell \log n \rceil$ nodes uniform at random; call this set S. The *skeleton graph* $G_S = (S, E_S, \omega_S)$ is defined such that for $s, t \in S$, we set $\omega_S(s, t) = \mathrm{dist}^{\ell}(s, t, G)$, i.e., $\{s, t\} \in E_S$ iff $\mathrm{dist}^{\ell}(s, t, G) \neq \infty$. Then, w.h.p., $\mathrm{dist}(s, t, G_S) = \mathrm{dist}(s, t, G)$ for all $s, t \in S$ (Lemma 4.6 of [23]).
2. For $k \in \Theta(1/\varepsilon)$, construct a $(2k-1)$-spanner G'_S of the skeleton that has $\tilde{O}(\ell^{1+1/k}) \subseteq \tilde{O}(n^{1/2+\varepsilon})$ edges (Lemma 4.9 of [23]). Make the spanner globally known by broadcasting it via a BFS tree of G ($\tilde{O}(n^{1/2+\varepsilon} + D)$ rounds).
3. Define $H = (V, E_H, \omega_H)$ by E_H being the union of the skeleton spanner edges with E. Edge $e \in E_H$ has weight $\omega_H(e) := \omega_S(e)$ if e is in the skeleton spanner and $\omega_H(e) := (2k-1)\,\omega(e)$ otherwise. Thus, by construction G embeds into H with stretch $2k-1$, i.e., $\mathrm{dist}(v, w, G) \leq \mathrm{dist}(v, w, H) \leq (2k-1)\,\mathrm{dist}(v, w, G)$.
4. Choose uniform permutations of S and $V \setminus S$. We extend these permutations to a permutation of all nodes by ruling that for all $s \in S$ and $v \in V \setminus S$, we have $s < w$. The LE lists of H corresponding to this permutation induce an embedding of H into a tree T with expected stretch $O(\log n)$, see Lemma 4.9 of [19]. Accordingly, G embeds into T with expected stretch $O(k \log n) = O(\varepsilon^{-1} \log n)$.

It is then shown that LE lists of H can be computed fast in the Congest model. To this end, one exploits that (min-hop) shortest paths in H contain only a single (maximal) subpath consisting of spanner edges, where the maximal subpaths of non-spanner edges have at most $\ell \in \Theta(\sqrt{n})$ hops w.h.p.[6] Given that $s < v$ for all $s \in S$ and $v \in V \setminus S$, it follows that for each $v \in V$ and each entry $(w, \mathrm{dist}(v, w, H))$ of its LE list, w.h.p. there is a min-hop shortest path from v to w that consists of a prefix of at most ℓ non-spanner edges followed by a shortest path in G'_S. This entails that

$$r^V A_H^{\mathrm{SPD}(H)} x^{(0)} = r^V A_{G,2k-1}^{\ell} A_{G'_S}^{|S|} x^{(0)} \tag{6.1}$$

$$= r^V A_{G,2k-1}^{\ell} \left(r^V A_{G'_S}^{|S|} x^{(0)} \right), \tag{6.2}$$

where $x^{(0)}$ is as above, A_G is the adjacency matrix of a graph G, and $A_{G,s}$ is A_G with entries multiplied by factor $s \in \mathbb{R}_{\geq 0} \cup \{\infty\}$. Here, $A_{G'_S}$ is interpreted as an adjacency matrix for node set V by setting $(A_{G'_S})_{vw} = \infty$ if $\{v, w\} \not\subseteq S$. Clearly, $A_H x \leq A_{G,2k-1} x$ and $A_H x \leq A_{G'_S} x$ for all x (where $\leq$ is to be read componentwise), while $A_{G'_S}^{|S|} x^{(0)}$ yields distances in G'_S and $A_{G,2k-1}^{\ell}$ propagates information via non-spanner edges for ℓ hops.

[6]This follows analogously to Lemma 3.4, with 2 levels and a sampling probability of $\tilde{\Theta}(1/\sqrt{n})$ instead of 1/2.

Because G'_S is known to all nodes, each $v \in V$ can compute $\bar{x}_v^{(0)} := (A_{G'_S}^{|S|} x^{(0)})_v$ locally. Subsequently, nodes determine their component of $r^V A_{G,2k-1}^{\ell} \bar{x}^{(0)} = (r^V A_{G,2k-1})^{\ell} \bar{x}^{(0)}$ via ℓ iterations $\bar{x}^{(i+1)} := r^V A(G, 2k-1)\bar{x}^{(i)}$. Here, one exploits that, for all i, $|\bar{x}_v^{(i)}| \in O(\log n)$ w.h.p. by Lemma 5.5,[7] and thus each iteration can be performed by sending $O(\log n)$ messages over each edge. The time complexity of $\tilde{O}(n^{1/2+\varepsilon} + D)$ for an embedding of expected stretch $O(\varepsilon^{-1} \log n)$ shown in [19] follows.

Achieving Stretch $O(\log n)$ *in Near-Optimal Time.* The factor n^{ε} overhead is due to constructing and broadcasting the skeleton spanner. We can improve on this by relying on hop sets, just as we do in our parallel construction. In recent work, Henziger et al. [21] show how to compute an $(n^{o(1)}, o(1))$-hop set of the skeleton (in the sense that nodes learn their incident edges and their weights) in $n^{1/2+o(1)} + D^{1+o(1)}$ rounds.

The prerequisite of the algorithm is that the skeleton nodes learn their skeleton edges and their weights. Unfortunately, doing so precisely would require $\tilde{\Omega}(n)$ rounds in the Congest model [25]. Instead, we $(1 + o(1/\log n))$-approximate $\mathrm{dist}^{\ell}(s, t, G)$ for all $s, t \in S$, which can be done in $\tilde{O}(\sqrt{n})$ rounds [25]. Here, $s \in S$ learns the approximate ℓ-hop distance to each $t \in S$. This can be seen as metrically embedding the skeleton graph with stretch $1 + o(1/\log n)$, and the representation of the resulting graph allows to apply the algorithm from [21]. Overall, we obtain a graph G'_S satisfying for all $s, t \in G$ that $\mathrm{dist}(s, t, G) \leq \mathrm{dist}^{n^{o(1)}}(s, t, G'_S) \in (1 + o(1/\log n)) \mathrm{dist}(v, w, G)$ w.h.p., where nodes in S know their incident edges in this graph.

Now we can apply the machinery established for the parallel setting. First, we embed G'_S into H_S as in Section 3, where $d \in n^{o(1)}$. To this end, nodes determine their level locally and broadcast it over a BFS tree, which takes $O(|S| + D) \subset \tilde{O}(\sqrt{n} + D)$ rounds; thus, $s \in S$ knows the level of $\{s, t\} \in E_{H_S}$ for each $t \in S$.

We define H as above, but with H_S taking the role of the skeleton spanner. Since, by Theorem 3.5 for $\varepsilon \in o(1/\log n)$, for all $s, t \in V$ we have $\mathrm{dist}(s, t, H_S) \in (1 + o(1)) \mathrm{dist}(s, t, G)$ w.h.p., it suffices to increase the weight of edges from G by factor $1 + o(1)$, i.e., G embeds into H with stretch $1 + o(1)$.

To determine the LE lists for H, we must compute

$$r^V A_H^{\mathrm{SPD}(H)} x^{(0)} = (r^V A_{G,1+o(1)})^{\ell} (r^V A_{H_S})^{\mathrm{SPD}(H_S)} x^{(0)}, \tag{6.3}$$

where $A_{G,1+o(1)}$ is given by multiplying each entry of A_G by a sufficiently large factor $f \in 1 + o(1)$ and A_{H_S} is extended to an adjacency matrix on the node set V as above. Applying $r^V A_{G,1+o(1)}$ is the same as before, taking in total $\tilde{O}(\ell) = \tilde{O}(\sqrt{n})$ rounds. Concerning A_{H_S}, we follow the same strategy as in Theorem 4.2, i.e., it suffices to show that we can efficiently perform a matrix-vector multiplication $A_{G'_S} x$ for any x that may occur during the computation (applying r^V is a local operation and thus free), assuming that each node $v \in V$ knows x_v and its row of the matrix. As multiplications with $A_{G'_S}$ affects only lists at nodes $s \in S$, this can be done by local computations once all nodes know x_s for each $s \in S$. As before, $|x_s| \in O(\log n)$ w.h.p., so $\sum_{s \in S} |x_s| \in O(|S| \log n) \subset \tilde{O}(\sqrt{n})$ w.h.p. We broadcast these lists over a BFS tree (of G) to all nodes, taking $\tilde{O}(\sqrt{n} + D)$ rounds per matrix-vector multiplication. Overall, this results in round complexity $n^{1/2+o(1)} + D^{1+o(1)}$.

THEOREM 6.3. *There is a randomized distributed algorithm computing a metric tree embedding of expected stretch* $O(\log n)$ *in* $(\sqrt{n} + D) 2^{O(\sqrt{\log n})}$ *rounds of the Congest model.*

PROOF SKETCH. Follows from the above discussion, noting that the $n^{o(1)}$ and $D^{o(1)}$ factors from [21] are, more precisely, $2^{O(\sqrt{\log n})}$ factors, $\mathrm{SPD}(H_S) \in O(\log^2 n)$ w.h.p. by Theorem 3.5, and multiplication with A_{H_S} requires $\tilde{O}(d) \subset 2^{O(\sqrt{\log n})}$ multiplications with $A_{G'_S}$. □

Note that by combining this result with the algorithm by Khan et al., we obtain a round complexity of $\min\{n^{1/2+o(1)} + D^{1+o(1)}, \tilde{O}(\mathrm{SPD})\}$.

7. CONCLUSION

In this work, we show how to sample from an FRT-style distribution of metric tree embeddings at low depth and near-optimal work, provided that the maximum ratio between edge weights is polynomially bounded. While we consider the polylogarithmic factors too large for our algorithm to be of practical interest, this result motivates the search for solutions that achieve low depth despite having work comparable to the currently best known sequential bound of $O(m \log^3 n)$ [26]. Concretely, better hop set constructions could readily be plugged into our machinery to yield improved bounds, and one may seek to reduce the number of logarithmic factors incurred by the remaining construction.

Our second main contribution is an algebraic interpretation of MBF-like algorithms, reducing the task of devising and analyzing such algorithms to the following recipe:

1. Determine a node-wise filter r and initial values $x^{(0)}$ so that $r^V A_G^h x^{(0)}$ is the desired output.
2. Verify that r induces a congruence relation on a suitable $\mathcal{S}_{\min,+}$-semimodule $\mathcal{M} \ni x^{(0)}$.
3. Leverage (repeated use of) r^V to ensure that iterations can be implemented efficiently.

As can be seen by example of our metric tree embedding algorithm, further steps may be required to control the number of iterations h. Nevertheless, we believe that our framework unifies and simplifies the interpretation and analysis of MBF-like algorithms, as illustrated by the examples listed in Section 2.5 and the discussion of distributed tree embeddings in Section 6.3. Therefore, we hope that our framework will be of use in the design of efficient MBF-like algorithms in the future.

[7] More precisely, one applies the lemma twice, as it requires the considered module elements to be independent of the randomness of the permutation. First, one considers the computation starting from $(y_v)_w = 0$ if $v = w \in S$ and $(y_v)_w = \infty$ else. Since $s < v$ for all $s \in S$ and $v \in V \setminus S$, this shows that the (sub)lists concerning nodes from S have $O(\log n)$ non-∞ entries w.h.p. Then one applies the lemma to $(r^V A(G, k))^i z = r^V A(G, k)^i z$, $i \in \{1, \ldots, \ell\}$, with $(z_v)_w = 0$ if $v = w \in V \setminus S$ and $(z_v)_w = \infty$ else, and argues that the sublists concerning nodes from $V \setminus S$ have length $O(\log n)$ w.h.p., too, because they are sublists of $(r^V A(G, k))^i z = r^V A(G, k)^i z$ for some i.

8. REFERENCES

[1] N. Alon, Z. Galil, and O. Margalit. On the exponent of the all pairs shortest path problem. *Journal of Computer and System Science*, 54(2):255–262, 1997.

[2] N. Alon, R. M. Karp, D. Peleg, and D. B. West. A graph-theoretic game and its application to the k-server problem. *SIAM Journal on Computing*, 24(1):78–100, 1995.

[3] M. Andrews. Hardness of buy-at-bulk network design. In *Proceedings of the 45th Symposium on Foundations of Computer Science (FOCS)*, pages 115–124, 2004.

[4] B. Awerbuch and Y. Azar. Buy-at-bulk network design. In *Proceedings of the 38th Annual Symposium on Foundations of Computer Science (FOCS)*, pages 542–547, 1997.

[5] Y. Bartal. Probabilistic approximations of metric spaces and its algorithmic applications. In *Proceedings of the 37th Annual Symposium on Foundations of Computer Science (FOCS)*, pages 184–193, 1996.

[6] Y. Bartal. On approximating arbitrary metrices by tree metrics. In *Proceedings of the 30th Annual ACM Symposium on the Theory of Computing*, pages 161–168, 1998.

[7] S. Baswana and S. Sen. A simple and linear time randomized algorithm for computing sparse spanners in weighted graphs. *Random Structures & Algorithms*, 30(4):532–563, 2007.

[8] R. E. Bellman. On a routing problem. *Quarterly Applied Mathematics*, 16:87–90, 1958.

[9] G. E. Blelloch, A. Gupta, and K. Tangwongsan. Parallel probabilistic tree embeddings, k-median, and buy-at-bulk network design. In *Proceedings of the 24th ACM Symposium on Parallelism in Algorithms and Architectures (SPAA)*, pages 205–213, 2012.

[10] G. E. Blelloch and K. Tangwongsan. Parallel approximation algorithms for facility-location problems. In *Proceedings of the 22nd ACM Symposium on Parallelism in Algorithms and Architectures (SPAA)*, pages 315–324, 2010.

[11] E. Cohen. Size-estimation framework with applications to transitive closure and reachability. *Journal of Computer and System Sciences*, 55(3):441–453, 1997.

[12] E. Cohen. Polylog-time and near-linear work approximation scheme for undirected shortest paths. *Journal of the ACM*, 47(1):132–166, 2000.

[13] E. Cohen and H. Kaplan. Spatially-decaying aggregation over a network. *Journal of Computer and System Sciences*, 73(3):265–288, 2007.

[14] T. H. Cormen, C. E. Leiserson, R. L. Rivest, and C. Stein. *Introduction to Algorithms (3rd edition)*. MIT Press, 2009.

[15] A. Das Sarma, S. Holzer, L. Kor, A. Korman, D. Nanongkai, G. Pandurangan, D. Peleg, and R. Wattenhofer. Distributed verification and hardness of distributed approximation. *SIAM Journal on Computing*, 41(5):1235–1265, 2012.

[16] E. W. Dijkstra. A note on two problems in connexion with graphs. *Numerische Mathematik*, 1(1):269–271, 1959.

[17] J. Fakcharoenphol, S. Rao, and K. Talwar. A tight bound on approximating arbitrary metrics by tree metrics. *Journal of Computer and System Sciences*, 69(3):485–497, 2004.

[18] L. R. Ford. Network flow theory. 1956.

[19] M. Ghaffari and C. Lenzen. Near-optimal distributed tree embedding. In *Proceedings of the 28th International Symposium on Distributed Computing (DISC)*, pages 197–211, 2014.

[20] M. Hauptmann and M. Karpinski. A compendium on Steiner tree problems. http://theory.cs.uni-bonn.de/info5/steinerkompendium/netcompendium.html. Visited 2016-05-12.

[21] M. Henzinger, S. Krinninger, and D. Nanongkai. An almost-tight distributed algorithm for computing single-source shortest paths. *CoRR*, abs/1504.07056, 2015.

[22] M. Khan, F. Kuhn, D. Malkhi, G. Pandurangan, and K. Talwar. Efficient distributed approximation algorithms via probabilistic tree embeddings. *Distributed Computing*, 25(3):189–205, 2012.

[23] C. Lenzen and B. Patt-Shamir. Fast routing table construction using small messages: extended abstract. In *Symposium on Theory of Computing Conference (STOC)*, pages 381–390, 2013.

[24] C. Lenzen and B. Patt-Shamir. Improved distributed Steiner forest construction. In *Proceedings of the ACM Symposium on Principles of Distributed Computing (PODC)*, pages 262–271, 2014.

[25] C. Lenzen and B. Patt-Shamir. Fast partial distance estimation and applications. In *Proceedings of the ACM Symposium on Principles of Distributed Computing (PODC)*, pages 153–162, 2015.

[26] M. Mendel and C. Schwob. Fast C-K-R partitions of sparse graphs. *Chicago Journal of Theoretical Computer Science*, 2009, 2009.

[27] M. Mohri. Semiring frameworks and algorithms for shortest-distance problems. *Journal of Automata, Languages and Combinatorics*, 7(3):321–350, 2002.

[28] E. F. Moore. The shortest path through a maze. In *Symposium on the Theory of Switching*, pages 87–90, 1959.

[29] D. Peleg. *Distributed Computing: A Locality-Sensitive Approach*. SIAM, Philadelphia, 2000.

[30] U. Zwick. All pairs shortest paths using bridging sets and rectangular matrix multiplication. *Journal of the ACM*, 49(3):289–317, 2002.

Parallelism in Randomized Incremental Algorithms

Guy E. Blelloch
Carnegie Mellon University
guyb@cs.cmu.edu

Yan Gu
Carnegie Mellon University
yan.gu@cs.cmu.edu

Julian Shun
UC Berkeley
jshun@eecs.berkeley.edu

Yihan Sun
Carnegie Mellon University
yihans@cs.cmu.edu

ABSTRACT

In this paper we show that many sequential randomized incremental algorithms are in fact parallel. We consider several random incremental algorithms including algorithms for comparison sorting and Delaunay triangulation; linear programming, closest pair, and smallest enclosing disk in constant dimensions; as well as least-element lists and strongly connected components on graphs.

We analyze the dependence between iterations in an algorithm, and show that the dependence structure is shallow for all of the algorithms, implying high parallelism. We identify three types of dependences found in the algorithms studied and present a framework for analyzing each type of algorithm. Using the framework gives work-efficient polylogarithmic-depth parallel algorithms for most of the problems that we study. Some of these algorithms are straightforward (e.g., sorting and linear programming), while others are more novel and require more effort to obtain the desired bounds (e.g., Delaunay triangulation and strongly connected components). The most surprising of these results is for planar Delaunay triangulation for which the incremental approach is by far the most commonly used in practice, but for which it was not previously known whether it is theoretically efficient in parallel.

1. INTRODUCTION

The randomized incremental approach has been an extremely useful paradigm for generating simple and efficient algorithms for a variety of problems. There have been dozens of papers on the topic (e.g., see the surveys [57, 48]). Much of the early work was in the context of computational geometry, but the approach has more recently been applied to graph algorithms [20, 23]. The main idea is to insert elements one-by-one in random order while maintaining a desired structure. The random order ensures that the insertions are somehow spread out, and worst-case behaviors are unlikely.

The incremental process would appear sequential since it is iterative, but in practice incremental algorithms are widely used in parallel implementations by allowing some iterations to start in parallel and using some form of locking to avoid conflicts. Many parallel implementations for Delaunay triangulation and convex hull, for example, are based on the randomized incremental approach [17, 26, 18, 46, 5, 33, 15, 50, 59]. In theory, however, after 25 years, there are still no known bounds for parallel Delaunay triangulation using the incremental approach, nor for many other problems.

In this paper we show that the incremental approach for Delaunay and many other problem is actually parallel, at least with the right incremental algorithms, and leads to work-efficient polylogarithmic-depth (time) algorithms for the problems. The results are based on analyzing the dependence graph. This technique has recently been used to analyze the parallelism available in a variety of sequential algorithms, including the simple greedy algorithm for maximal independent set [7], the Knuth shuffle for random permutation [60], greedy graph coloring [40], and correlation clustering [49]. The advantage of this method is that one can use standard sequential algorithms with modest change to make them parallel, often leading to very simple parallel solutions. It has also been shown experimentally that this approach leads to quite practical parallel algorithms [6], and to deterministic parallelism [12, 6].

The contributions of the paper can be summarized as follows.

1. We describe a framework for analyzing parallelism in randomized incremental algorithms, and give general bounds on the depth of algorithms with certain dependence probabilities (Section 2).
2. We show that randomly ordered insertion into a binary search tree is inherently parallel, leading to an almost trivial comparison sorting algorithm taking $O(\log n)$ depth and $O(n \log n)$ work (i.e., n processors), both with high probability on the priority-write CRCW PRAM (Section 3). Surprisingly, we know of no previous description and analysis of this parallel algorithm.
3. We propose a new randomized incremental algorithm for planar Delaunay triangulation, and then describe a simple way to parallelize it (Section 4). The algorithm takes $O(\log^2 n)$ depth with high probability, and $O(n \log n)$ work (i.e., $n/\log n$ processors) in expectation, on the CRCW PRAM. It would seem to be by far the simplest work-efficient parallel Delaunay triangulation algorithm.
4. We show that classic sequential randomized incremental algorithms for constant-dimensional linear programming, closest pair, and smallest enclosing disk can be parallelized (Section 5). This leads to very simple linear-work and polylogarithmic-depth randomized parallel algorithms for all three problems.
5. For two incremental graph algorithms, instead of forcing the parallel version to abide by all dependences, we allow some dependences to be violated, but show that this does not asymptotically increase work, or change the result. We use this approach for a sequential algorithm for computing least-element lists, leading to an efficient parallel implementation (Section 6.1). Least-element lists have applications for probabilistic tree embeddings on graph metrics [30, 10], and estimating neighborhood sizes in

SPAA'16, July 11–13, 2016, Pacific Grove, California, USA.

DOI: http://dx.doi.org/10.1145/2935764.2935766

Problem	Work (expected)	Depth (with high probability)
Comparison sorting (Section 3)	$O(n \log n)$	$O(\log n)$
Planar Delaunay triangulation (Section 4)	$O(n \log n)$	$O(\log^2 n)$
2D linear programming (Section 5.1)	$O(n)$	$O(\log n)$
2D closest pair (Section 5.2)	$O(n)$	$O(\log n \log^* n)$
Smallest enclosing disk (Section 5.3)	$O(n)$	$O(\log^2 n)$
Least-element lists (Section 6.1)	$O(W_{SP}(n,m) \log n)$	$O(D_{SP}(n,m) \log n)$
Strongly connected components (Section 6.2)	$O(W_R(n,m) \log n)$	$O(D_R(n,m) \log n)$

Table 1: Work and depth bounds for our parallel randomized incremental algorithms. $W_{SP}(n,m)$ and $D_{SP}(n,m)$ denote the work and depth, respectively, of a single-source shortest paths algorithm. $W_R(n,m)$ and $D_R(n,m)$ denote the work and depth, respectively, of performing a reachability query.

graphs [21]. We also use the approach to parallelize an elegant algorithm for strongly connected components [23] (Section 6.2).

Other than the graph algorithms, which call subroutines that are known to be hard to parallelize, all of our solutions are work-efficient and run in polylogarithmic depth (time). The bounds for all of our parallel randomized incremental algorithms can be found in Table 1.

Preliminaries

We analyze parallel algorithms in the work-depth paradigm [42]. An algorithm proceeds in a sequence of D (depth) rounds, with round i doing w_i work in parallel. The total work is therefore $W = \sum_{i=1}^{D} w_i$. We account for the cost of allocating processors and compaction in our depth. Therefore the bounds on a PRAM with P processors is $O(W/P + D)$ time [14]. We use the concurrent-read and concurrent-writes (CRCW) PRAM model. By default, we assume the arbitrary-write CRCW model, but when stated use the priority-write model. We say $O(f(n))$ ***with high probability (w.h.p.)*** to indicate $O(kf(n))$ with probability at least $1 - 1/n^k$.

2. ITERATION DEPENDENCES

An ***iterative algorithm*** is an algorithm that runs in a sequence of ***steps*** (iterations) in order. When applied to a particular input, we refer to the computation as an ***iterative computation***. Each step i of an iterative computation does some work $W(i)$, and has some depth $D(i)$ (the steps themselves can be parallel). Step j is said to ***depend*** on step $i < j$ if the computation of step j is affected by the computation of step i. The particular dependences, or even the number of steps, can be a function of the input, and can be modeled as a directed acyclic graph (DAG)—the steps ($I = 1, \ldots, n$) are vertices and dependences between them are arcs (directed edges).

DEFINITION 1 (ITERATION DEPENDENCE GRAPH [60]). *An* ***iteration dependence graph*** *for an iterative computation is a (directed acyclic) graph $G(I, E)$ such that if every step $i \in I$ runs after all predecessor steps in G have completed, then every step will do the same computation as in the sequential order.*

We are interested in the depth (longest directed path) of iteration dependence graphs since shallow dependence graphs imply high parallelism—at least if the dependences can be determined online, and depth of each step $D(i)$ can be appropriately bounded. We refer to the depth of the DAG as the ***iteration depth***, and denote it as $D(G)$. In this paper, we are interested in probabilistic bounds on the iteration depth over random input orders.

An ***incremental algorithm*** is an iterative algorithm that maintains some property over elements while ***inserting*** a new element on each step. We will use $E = \{e_1, \ldots, e_n\}$ to indicate the insertion order of n elements. A ***randomized incremental algorithm*** is an incremental algorithm in which the elements are added in a uniformly random order. In randomized incremental algorithms, the presence of a dependence arc between steps i and j will have a probability p_{ij} based on all possible orders (each of the $n!$ orders is a primitive event in the sample space). We are interested in upper bounds on these probabilities, which we will refer to as $\hat{p}_{ij}$. A subtle point is that the exact probabilities p_{ij} are sometimes not independent (e.g., along a path), but the upper bounds $\hat{p}_{ij}$ are, allowing them to be multiplied. We will use backwards analysis [57]—we consider "removing" randomly selected elements one at a time from the end, noting that the analysis of elements $1, \ldots, i$ does not depend on the elements $j > i$.

In this paper, we consider three types of incremental algorithms, which we refer to as Type 1, 2, and 3, for lack of better names.

Type 1 Algorithms. In these algorithms we analyze the dependence depth by considering all possible paths in the iteration dependence graph and taking a union bound over the probability of each. We describe two algorithms of this type—sorting by insertion into a binary search tree, and incremental planar Delaunay triangulation. In the algorithms (and indeed in just about all incremental algorithms) inserting an element j between two elements $i < j$ and $k > j$ will never add a dependence between i and k (although it might remove one). The property means that we only need to consider the dependence between positions i and $i+1$ when calculating an upper bound on the probability $\hat{p}_{ij}$ ($j > i$). In particular, for all $j \geq i+1$ we use $\hat{p}_{i(i+1)} \geq \hat{p}_{ij} \geq p_{ij}$. We use the following lemma.

LEMMA 2.1. *Consider an iteration dependence graph G of n iterations with $\hat{p}_{ij} = f(i) \geq 1/n$, independent along any path, then*

$$\Pr(D(G) \geq l) < n\left(\frac{e\sum_{i=1}^{n} f(i)}{l}\right)^l$$

PROOF. Consider a path of length $l-1$, and let $K \subseteq \{1, \ldots, n\}$ be the vertices on the path ($|K| = l$). We have that the probability of the path existing is upper bounded by:

$$P(K) = n \prod_{k \in K} f(k) .$$

The multiplicative factor of n is needed to account for the fact that the last element of Kdoes not contribute to the probability of the path and can be as small as $1/n$. We can now take the union bound over all possible paths of length $l-1$, giving:

$$\Pr(D(G) > l-1) \leq X(G) = \sum_{K \subseteq \{1,\ldots,n\}, |K|=l} P(K)$$

If $f(i)$ is a constant with value $\hat{p}$ we have:

$$X(G) = \binom{n}{l} n\hat{p}^l < n\left(\frac{en\hat{p}}{l}\right)^l = n\left(\frac{e\sum_{i=1}^{n} f(i)}{l}\right)^l$$

where we use the inequality $\binom{n}{m} < \left(\frac{en}{m}\right)^m$.

We now show that unequal (non-constant) probabilities that maintain the same sum $\sum_{i=1}^{n} f(i)$ will only reduce $X(G)$ and hence the upper bound on $\Pr(D(G) \geq l)$. Therefore the probability is maximized by the equation above. Consider two locations i and j such that $f(i) \neq f(j)$. We show that changing these probabilities both to $\hat{p}_m = (f(i) + f(j))/2$ will increase $X(G)$. A path will either go through i but not j, j but not i, neither or both. Clearly the ones through neither will not affect the total sum. For every path through just i there is a path through just j going through the same set of other vertices. If P_r is the product of probabilities of the other vertices in one of these pairs of paths then the contribution to the union bound of both is $f(i)P_r + f(j)P_r = 2\hat{p}_m P_r$. The contribution from these paths is therefore not changed by changing $f(i)$ and $f(j)$ to $\hat{p}_m$. However, the contribution from paths going through both will increase since the old product is $f(i)f(j)P_r$ while the new one is $\hat{p}_m^2 P_r$, which has to be at least as large. □

COROLLARY 2.2. *Consider an iteration dependence graph G of n iterations with $\hat{p}_{ij} \leq c/i$, independent along any path. Then for any $k \geq 2ce^2$ we have*

$$\Pr(D(G) > k \ln n) \in O(1/n^{k-1}) .$$

PROOF. Plugging into Lemma 2.1 gives:

$$\begin{aligned} \Pr(D(G) \geq k \ln n) &< n\left(\frac{ec\sum_{i=1}^{n} 1/i}{k \ln n}\right)^{k \ln n} \\ &< n\left(\frac{ec(1+\ln n)}{k \ln n}\right)^{k \ln n} \\ &\leq n(1/e)^{k \ln n} = 1/n^{k-1} \end{aligned}$$ □

To apply the previous lemma or corollary requires showing independence of the upper $\hat{p}_{ij}$ along every path. For sorting this is easy. For Delaunay triangulation the probabilities are not independent among the iterations corresponding to points, but we divide the iterations into sub-iterations, corresponding to the creation of triangles, for which they are independent.

The Type 1 algorithms that we describe can be parallelized by running a sequence of rounds. Each round checks all remaining steps to see if their dependences have been satisfied and runs the steps if so. The algorithms require at most $O(n)$ work per round to check violations. By Theorem 2.2, the number of rounds will be $O(\log n)$ w.h.p. The total expected work is therefore $O(n \log n)$ for the checks, plus the work for the steps, which is the same as for the sequential variants—$O(n \log n)$ in expectation. The total work is therefore $O(n \log n)$ in expectation.

Type 1 incremental algorithms can be implemented in two ways: one completely online, only seeing a new element at the start of each step, and the other offline, keeping track of all elements from the beginning. In the first case, a structure based on the history of all updates can be built during the algorithm that allows us to efficiently locate the "position" of a new element (e.g., [38]), and in the second case the position of each uninserted element is kept up-to-date on every step (e.g., [19]). The bounds on work are typically the same in either case. Our incremental sort uses an online style algorithm, and the Delaunay triangulation uses an offline one.

Type 2 Algorithms. Here we describe a class of incremental algorithms, called Type 2 algorithms, that have a special structure. The iteration dependence graph for these algorithms is formed as follows: each step j independently has probability at most c/j of being a ***special step*** for some constant c; each special step j has dependence arcs to all steps $i < j$; and all non-special steps have one dependence arc to the closest earlier special step. For Type 2 algorithms, when a special step i is processed, it will check all previous steps, requiring $O(i)$ work and $d(i)$ depth, and when a non-special step is processed it does $O(1)$ work. It can be shown that in expectation each step takes $O(1)$ work, so this means that sequential implementations of Type 2 algorithms take $O(n)$ work in expectation.

THEOREM 2.3. *A Type 2 incremental algorithm has an iteration dependence depth of $O(\log n)$ w.h.p., and can be implemented to run in $O(n)$ expected work and $O(d(n) \log n)$ depth w.h.p., where $d(n)$ is the depth of processing a special step.*

PROOF. Since the probabilities are independent and the expectation is $\sum_{j=1}^{n} c/j = O(\log n)$, using a Chernoff bound, it is easy to show that the number of special steps is $O(\log n)$ w.h.p. With this bound, we can show that the iteration dependence depth, or the length of the longest path in the dependence graph, is $O(\log n)$ w.h.p. by noticing that there cannot be two consecutive non-special steps in a path (i.e., in the worst case every other vertex in the path is a special step, and there are only $O(\log n)$ of them w.h.p.).

We now show how parallel linear-work implementations can be obtained. A parallel implementation needs to execute the special steps one-by-one, and for each special step it can do its computation in parallel. For the non-special steps whose closest earlier special step has been executed, their computation can all be done in parallel. To maintain work-efficiency, we cannot afford to keep all unfinished steps active on each round. Instead, we start with a constant number of the earliest steps on the first round and on each round geometrically increase the number of steps processed, similar to the prefix methods described in earlier work on parallelizing iterative algorithms [7].

Without loss of generality, assume $n = 2^k$ for some integer k. We can process batched steps in $k + 1$ rounds—the first round runs the first task and the i-th round ($i > 1$) runs the second half of the first 2^{i-1} tasks (we refer to each batch as a ***prefix***). Each time a prefix is processed it checks all steps, finds the earliest unfinished special step, applies the computation associated with that step, and marks that special step and all earlier steps as finished. Since each step takes $O(1)$ work in expectation, each time a prefix is processed, it applies some computation with work $O(2^{i-2})$ and depth $d(n)$. The maximum/minimum of n elements can be computed in $O(n)$ work and $O(1)$ depth w.h.p. on an arbitrary CRCW PRAM [66], so finding the earliest special step can be done in $O(2^{i-2})$ work and $O(1)$ depth w.h.p. Marking steps as finished can be done in the same bounds. The number of times a prefix needs to be executed is equal to the number of special steps in the prefix, which for any prefix k is bounded by $\sum_{i=2^{k-2}}^{2^{k-1}} c/i = O(1)$ in expectation. Therefore, the work per prefix is $O(2^{i-2})$ in expectation, and summed over all rounds is $O(1)+\sum_{i=2}^{\log n} O(2^{i-2}) = O(n)$ in expectation. Summed across all prefixes, the total number of times they are processed is equal to the iteration dependence depth, which is $O(\log n)$ w.h.p., and so we have an overall depth of $O(d(n) \log n)$ w.h.p. □

Type 3 Algorithms. In the third type of incremental algorithms, instead of fully abiding by the dependence arcs and bounding the iteration depth, we allow for violations of the dependence arcs, and hence allow computations to differ from the sequential ordering possibly doing some extra work. However, we bound the extra work and show how to resolve the conflicts so the results are the same as in the sequential algorithm.

Consider a set of elements S. We assume that each element $x \in S$ defines a total ordering $<_x$ on all S. This ordering can be the same for each $x \in S$, or different. For example, in sorting the total ordering would be the order of the keys and the same for all $x \in S$. We say the computation has ***separating dependences*** if the following condition is satisfied.

DEFINITION 2 (SEPARATING DEPENDENCES). *For any three elements $a, b, c \in S$, if $a <_c b <_c c$ or $c <_c b <_c a$, then c can only depend on a if a is inserted first among the three.*

In other words, if b separates a from c in the total ordering for c, and runs first, it will separate the dependence between a and c (also if c runs before a, of course, there is no dependence from a to c). Again using sorting as an example, if we insert b into a BST first (or use it as a pivot in quicksort), it will separate a from c and they will never be compared (each comparison corresponds to a dependence).

LEMMA 2.4. *In a randomized incremental algorithm that has separating dependences, $\hat{p}_{ij} = 2/i$ is an upper bound on p_{ij}.*

PROOF. Consider the total ordering $<_j$. The elements are inserted in random order, and so the probability that i is the nearest element before j among the first i is at most $1/i$. If it is not the nearest, it has already been separated from j by an earlier insertion. Similarly for the nearest element after j, giving a total probability of $2/i$. □

COROLLARY 2.5. *The number of dependences in a randomized incremental algorithm with separating dependences is $O(n \log n)$ in expectation.*[1]

This comes simply from the sum $\sum_{j=2}^{n} \sum_{i=1}^{j-1} p_{ij}$ which is bounded by $2n \ln n$. This leads to yet another proof that quicksort, or randomized insertion into a binary search tree, does $O(n \log n)$ comparisons in expectation. This is not the standard proof based on $p_{ij} = 2/(j - i + 1)$ being the probability that the i'th and j'th smallest elements are compared. Here the p_{ij} represent the probability that the i'th and j'th elements in the random order are compared.

In this paper we introduce graph algorithms that have separating dependences with respect to insertion of the vertices, and there is a dependence from vertex i to vertex j if a search from i (e.g., shortest path or reachability) visits j.

To allow for parallelism we permit iterations to run concurrently in rounds. This means that we might not separate elements that were separated in the sequential order (for example, if i separated j from k in the sequential order, but we run i and j concurrently, then they might both have a dependence to k). Also, for each algorithm we describe a way to combine results from steps that run in parallel so they give an identical result as the sequential order. If all elements are randomly permuted and the rounds are of geometrically increasing size starting with constant size, as with Type 2 algorithms, the approach wastes at most a constant factor in extra dependences (extra visited vertices in our graph algorithms).

THEOREM 2.6. *A randomized incremental algorithm with separating dependences can run in $O(\log n)$ parallel rounds over the iterations and every element will have $O(\log n)$ incoming dependence arcs in expectation (for a total of $O(n \log n)$).*

PROOF. As in the proof of Theorem 2.3, assume without loss of generality $n = 2^k - 1$ for some integer k, and we process batched steps in k rounds where the batch size increases by powers of 2 $(1, 2, 4, 8, \ldots)$. Clearly the number of rounds is $O(\log n)$. Consider the number of incoming arcs to the last element x to be inserted since it is the worst case in expectation. We can consider all elements at each round happening at the very beginning of the round, since in a parallel execution no other elements in the round will separate any elements in the round from x (although all previous rounds can). For round i, the beginning of the round is at position 2^{i-1}. Therefore by Lemma 2.4, the probability from any element in round i is $2/2^{i-1}$, and there are 2^{i-1} such elements giving 2 as the expected number of incoming arcs to x from elements in round i. When summed across the $\log n$ rounds we get $2 \log n$, which gives us the $O(\log n)$ bound on incoming arcs as claimed. □

[1] Also true w.h.p.

Algorithm 1: INCREMENTALSORT

```
Input: A sequence K = {k_1, ..., k_n} of keys.
Output: A binary search tree over the keys in K.
// *P reads indirectly through the pointer P.
// The check on Line 8 is only needed for the parallel version.
1  Root ← a pointer to a new empty location
2  for i ← 1 to n do
3      N ← newNode(k_i)
4      P ← Root
5      while true do
6          if *P = null then
7              write N into the location pointed to by P
8              if *P = N then
9                  break
10         if N.key < *P.key then
11             P ← pointer to *P.left
12         else
13             P ← pointer to *P.right
14 return Root
```

As a side remark we note that by batching we have increased the number of incoming arcs over the sequential algorithm by a factor of about $(2 \log_2 n)/(2 \ln n) = \log_2 e \approx 1.44$.

3. COMPARISON SORTING

The first algorithm that we consider is sorting by incrementally inserting into a binary search tree (BST) with no rebalancing (w.l.o.g. we assume that no two keys are equal). It is well-known that for a random insertion order, this takes $O(n \log n)$ expected time. We apply our approach to show that the sequential incremental algorithm is also efficient in parallel. Algorithm 1 gives pseudocode that works either sequentially or in parallel. A step is one iteration of the **for** loop on Line 2. For the parallel version, the **for** loop should be interpreted as a **parallel for**, and the assignment on Line 7 should be considered a priority-write—i.e., all writes happen synchronously across the n iterations, and when there are writes to the same location, the smallest value gets written. The sequential version does not need the check on Line 8 since it is always true.

The dependence between iterations in the algorithm is in the check if $^*P$ is empty in Line 6. This means that iteration j depends on $i < j$ if and only if the node for i is on the path to j. This leads to the following lemma.

LEMMA 3.1. *For keys in random order,* INCREMENTALSORT *iteration j depends on iteration $i < j$ with probability at most $2/i$, and this upper bound is independent of all choices for $k > i$.*

PROOF. The proof follows the standard analysis (e.g. [57]). We consider the probability for steps i and $i + 1$ (and hence an upper bound for all $j > i$). Since it was inserted last, node i is a leaf in the BST when $i + 1$ is inserted. Node i will therefore only be on the path to $i + 1$ if they are neighbors in **sorted**$(1, \ldots, i + 1)$.

Node $i + 1$ has at most two neighbors, each which is added on step i with probability $1/i$ (independent of all choices of $k > i$), giving $\hat{p}_i = 2/i$. □

Along with Corollary 2.2 this implies the following.

COROLLARY 3.2. *Insertion of n keys into a binary search tree in random order has iteration dependence depth $O(\log n)$ w.h.p.*

We note that since iterations only depend on the path to the key, the transitive reduction of the iteration dependence graph is simply the BST itself. In general, e.g. Delaunay triangulation in the next section, the dependence structure is not a tree.

THEOREM 3.3. *The parallel version of* INCREMENTALSORT *generates the same tree as the sequential version, and for a random order of n keys runs in $O(n \log n)$ work and $O(\log n)$ depth w.h.p. on a priority-write CRCW PRAM.*

PROOF. They generate the same tree since whenever there is a dependence, the earliest step wins. The number of rounds of the while loop is bounded by the iteration depth ($O(\log n)$ w.h.p.) since for each iteration, each round checks a new dependence (i.e. each round traverses one level of the iteration dependence graph). Since each round takes constant depth on the priority-write CRCW PRAM with n processors, this gives the required bounds. □

Note that this gives a much simpler work-optimal logarithmic-depth algorithm for comparison sorting than Cole's mergesort algorithm [22], although it is on a stronger model (priority-write CRCW instead of EREW) and is randomized.

4. PLANAR DELAUNAY TRIANGULATION

A Delaunay triangulation (DT) in the plane is a triangulation of a set of points P such that no point in P is inside the circumcircle of any triangle (the circle defined by the triangle's three corner points). We say a point ***encroaches*** on a triangle if it is in the triangle's circumcircle, and will assume for simplicity that the points are in general position (no three points on a line or four points on a circle). Delaunay triangulation can be solved sequentially in optimal $O(n \log n)$ work. There are also several work-efficient parallel algorithms that run in polylogarithmic depth [54, 3, 11], but they are all quite complicated.

The widely-used incremental Delaunay algorithms, due to their simplicity, date back to the 1970s [36]. They are based on the rip-and-tent idea: for each point p in order, rip out the triangles p encroaches on and tent over the resulting cavity with a ring of triangles centered at p. The algorithms differ in how the encroached triangles are found, and how they are ripped and tented. Clarkson and Shor [19] first showed that randomized incremental 3D convex hull is efficient, running in $O(n \log n)$ time in expectation, which by reduction implies the same results for DT. Guibas et al. (GKS) showed a simpler direct incremental algorithm for DT [38] with the same bounds, and this has become the standard version described in textbooks [48, 24, 29] and often used in practice. The GKS algorithm uses a history of triangle updates to locate the triangle t that p is in. It then searches out for all other encroached triangles. The algorithm, however, is inherently sequential since for certain inputs and certain points in the input, the search from t will likely have depth $\Theta(n)$, and hence a single step can take linear depth.

Our goal is to use an incremental DT algorithm for which the steps themselves can be parallelized. For this purpose we use an offline variant of an algorithm by Boissonnat and Teillaud [13]. We show that the iteration depth is $O(\log n)$ w.h.p. although this requires analyzing substeps. We further show that each step can be parallelized leading to a simple parallel algorithm with $O(n \log n)$ work in expectation and $O(\log^2 n)$ depth w.h.p.

Algorithm 2: INCREMENTALDT

Input: A sequence $V = \{v_1, \ldots, v_n\}$ of points in the plane.
Output: DT(V).
Maintains: A set of triangles M, and for each $t \in M$, the points that encroach on it, $E(t)$.

$t_b \leftarrow$ a sufficiently large bounding triangle
$E(t_b) \leftarrow V$
$M \leftarrow \{t_b\}$
for $i \leftarrow 1$ *to* n **do**
  foreach *triangle* $t \in M$ *with* $v_i \in E(t)$ **do**
    REPLACETRIANGLE(M,t,v_i)
return M

function REPLACETRIANGLE(M,t,v)
  foreach *edge* $(u, w) \in t$ *(three of them)* **do**
    if (u, w) *is a boundary of v's encroached region* **then**
      $t_o \leftarrow$ the other triangle sharing (u, w)
      $t' \leftarrow (u, w, v)$
      $E(t') \leftarrow \{v' \in E(t) \cup E(t_o) \mid \text{INCIRCLE}(v', t')\}$
      $M \leftarrow M \cup \{t'\}$
  $M \leftarrow M \setminus \{t\}$

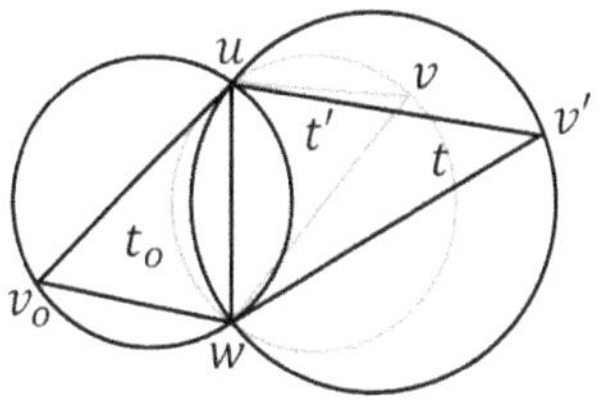

Figure 1: An illustration of the procedure of REPLACETRIANGLE. For each edge (u, w) that is a boundary of v's encroached triangle t, we find the triangle t_o on the other side of (u, w), generate the new triangle t', and recompute the encroaching set $E(t')$. Notice that the new (colored) circumcircle for t' (the encroaching region for t') can only contain points that are in the circumcircles of t and t_o.

Our variant is described in Algorithm 2. For each triangle $t \in M$ it maintains the set of uninserted points that encroach on t, denoted as $E(t)$. On each step i the algorithm selects the triangles that point i encroach on (all already known), removes these triangles and replaces them with new ones (see Figure 1). All work on uninserted points is done in determining $E(t')$ for each new triangle t', and for each new triangle only requires going through two existing sets, $E(t)$ and $E(t')$. This justified by Fact 4.1 [13]. Determining which triangles encroach on a point can be implemented by keeping a mapping of points to encroached triangles.

FACT 4.1. *When adding a triangle $t' = (u, w, v)$ for a new point v, and for the two old triangles t and t_o that shared the edge (u, w), we have $E(t) \cap E(t_o) \subseteq E(t') \subseteq E(t) \cup E(t_o)$.*

PROOF. Let $t = (u, w, v')$ be the triangle being removed and $t_o = (w, u, v_o)$ be the other triangle sharing the edge (u, w). The new point v must be in the circumcircle of t since it is removing it, but cannot be in the circumcircle of t_o since then it would be removing t_o as well and (u, w) would not be a boundary. The circumcircle of t' therefore must be contained in the union of the circumcircles of t and t_o, and must contain the intersection (see Figure 1). □

A time bound for INCREMENTALDT of $O(n \log n)$ follows from the analysis of Boissonnat and Teillaud [13], and more indirectly from Clarkson and Shor [19]. However for completeness and to show precise (within constant factor) bounds we include a bound on the number of INCIRCLE tests here. We note that due to Fact 4.1, the INCIRCLE test is not required for points that appear in both $E(t_o)$ and $E(t)$.

THEOREM 4.2. INCREMENTALDT *on n points in random order does at most* $24n \ln n + O(n)$ INCIRCLE *tests in expectation.*

PROOF. On step i, for each point at $j > i$ we consider the boundary of the region j encroaches on. We define each of the boundary edges by its two endpoints (u, w) along with the (up to) two points sharing a triangle with (u, w). Note that in REPLACETRIANGLE a point is only tested for encroachment on the triangle (u, w, v) if its boundary (u, w, v_o, v') is being deleted and replaced with (u, w, v_o, v). We can therefore charge every comparison to the creation of a boundary of a point, and spend it when deleted.

Consider steps i and $i+1$ (recall we can use $i+1$ as a surrogate for any $j > i$). By Euler's formula, the average degree of a node in a planar graph is at most 6. Therefore, since $i+1$ is selected uniformly at random (among $1, \ldots, i+1$), its expected boundary size will be at most 6. Each boundary involves up to 4 points from $1, \ldots, i$, so the probability that the random point removed on step i is one of them is at most $4/i$. Therefore, the total expected number of boundaries of $i+1$ (and hence any $j > i$) added on step i is at most $6 \times 4/i = 24/i$. If C is the number of in-circle tests, this gives:

$$\mathbb{E}[C] \leq 3n + \sum_{j=2}^{n} \sum_{i=1}^{j} 24/i \leq 24n \ln n + O(n)$$

where the $3n$ term comes from having to charge for the creation of the initial bounding triangle. □

Parallel Version and Analysis

We now consider the dependence depth of our algorithm. One approach to parallelizing the algorithm is to on each parallel round have every uninserted point check if its dependences are satisfied, and insert itself if so. It turns out that two points i and $i+1$ are dependent if and only if immediately before either is added, their encroached regions overlap by at least an edge. Unfortunately this means that the probabilities of the dependence arcs (i, j) and (j, k) are not independent. In particular if j has a large encroached region, this increases both p_{ij} and p_{jk}. For example, consider a wagon wheel—$(n-1)$ points nearly on a circle, and a single point at the hub. When the hub point is inserted at j, it will have dependence arcs from all previous points, and to all future points.

We therefore consider a more fine-grained dependence structure that relaxes the dependences. The observation is that not all triangles added by a point need to be added on the same round. In particular, REPLACETRIANGLE only depends on the triangle it is replacing and the three neighbors. We therefore can run REPLACETRIANGLE(M, t, v) as long as among the points encroaching on t and the three neighbors of t, there is no earlier point than v. An equal point is fine, since that would be the same point.

Algorithm 3 describes such a parallel variant. Since the triangles for a given point can be added on different rounds, the mesh is not necessarily self consistent after each round. We therefore assume that if a neighboring triangle (i.e., t_1, t_2 or t_3) is already deleted it can be ignored, and if not yet added, then REPLACETRIANGLE cannot proceed until added. A hash table mapping pairs of vertices representing edges to their up to two adjacent triangles can be used to find neighboring triangles. We assume that there is a synchronization point before Line 8.

Algorithm 3: PARINCREMENTALDT

Input: A sequence $V = \{v_1, \ldots, v_n\}$ of points in the plane.
Output: DT(V).
Maintains: $E(t)$, the points that encroach on each triangle t.

```
1 t_b ← a sufficiently large bounding triangle
2 E(t_b) ← V
3 M ← {t_b}
4 while E(t) ≠ ∅ for any t ∈ M do
5     parallel foreach triangle t ∈ M do
6         Let t_1, t_2, t_3 be the three neighboring triangles
7         if min(E(t)) ≤ min(E(t_1) ∪ E(t_2) ∪ E(t_3)) then
8             REPLACETRIANGLE(M, t, min(E(t)))
9 return M
```

Note that there is a one-to-one correspondence between the calls to REPLACETRIANGLE in the sequential and parallel algorithm—i.e., they are the "same" algorithm but just with a different ordering. We believe that this parallel version is even simpler than the sequential version since it does not require a mapping from points to encroached triangles.

For a sequence of points V, let $G_T(V) = (T, E)$ be the dependence graph defined by PARINCREMENTALDT(V) in the following way. The vertices T corresponds to triangles created by the algorithm, and for each call to REPLACETRIANGLE(M, t, v_i) we place an arc from triangle t and its three neighbors (t_1, t_2 and t_3) to each of the one, two, or three triangles created by REPLACETRIANGLE. Note that we can associate each triangle with the point v_i that created it. This is an iteration dependence graph over all iterations, including subiterations that create triangles.

THEOREM 4.3. *For points V in random order,* $D(G_T(V)) = O(\log n)$ *w.h.p.*

PROOF. For a sequence of points V let $T(V, i)$ be the set of triangles created by point v_i, and let $E_{t,t'}(V)$ be the indicator variable for a dependence arc from triangle t to t' given V. Let $\hat{p}_{ij}$ be an upper bound for the total probability that triangles created by v_i have an arc to any single triangle created by v_j (uniformly random over all permutations of the input). More precisely:

$$\hat{p}_{ij} \geq \frac{1}{|V|!} \left(\sum_{V' \in \text{perms}(V)} \left(\max_{t \in T(V', j)} \left(\sum_{t' \in T(V', i)} E_{t,t'}(V') \right) \right) \right).$$

Consider a path going through a triangle created by each point $K \subseteq \{1, \ldots, n\}$. If the $\hat{p}_{ij}$ are independent along any path, then the probability of such a path is bounded by the product of the $\hat{p}_{ij}$ along the path and the expectation on the number of triangles on the last point (which is 6 and independent of the $\hat{p}_{ij}$). For $\hat{p}_{ij} = f(i) \geq 1/n$ this gives a total bounded by $6n \prod_{k \in K} f(k)$. We can now apply the proof of Lemma 2.1, where the $\hat{p}_{ij}$ are interpreted in this new way, and the probability along a path $K \subseteq \{1, \ldots, n\}$ is interpreted as the probability that any path exists involving triangles created by those points. As in the proof of Lemma 2.1, the union bound over all possible subsets K of length l gives an overall upper bound on the probability of any path of length $l-1$:

$$\Pr(D(G_T(V)) > l - 1) \leq \sum_{K \subseteq \{1, \ldots, n\}, |K| = l} 6n \prod_{k \in K} f(k)$$

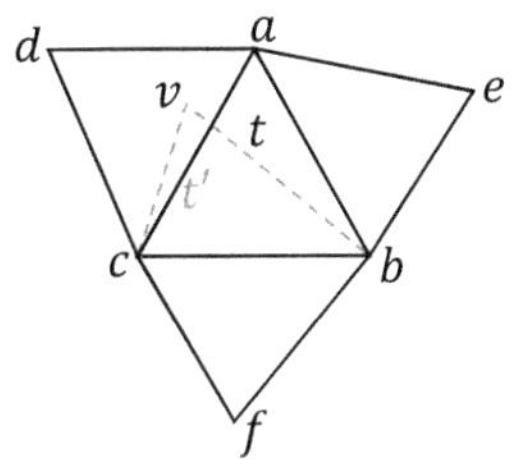

Figure 2: The dependence of t' on four previously created triangles.

and assuming that $\hat{p}_{ij} = f(i) = O(1/i)$ gives $O(\log n)$ depth w.h.p. (the argument about equal probabilities being the worst case still holds).

We are therefore left with showing that the $\hat{p}_{ij} = O(1/i)$ is a valid upper bound, and that this bound is independent along any path (allowing us to multiply them). As usual we consider steps (points) i and $j = i+1$, and hence an upper bound for any $j > i$. We consider one triangle t' created at $i+1$. Every triangle t' depends on 4 triangles—the t that was sacrificed for it in REPLACETRIANGLE, and its three neighbors (see Figure 2). These 4 triangles have six corners in total, any one of which could be the point i. Three of those points (a, b and c in the figure) would create three triangles that t' depends on. The other three (d, e and f in the figure) only create one triangle t' depends on. Therefore given that the point i is selected uniformly at random from i points the total probability that triangles at i have an arc to t' (a triangle at $i + 1$) is bounded by $\hat{p}_{ij} = (3 \cdot 3 + 3 \cdot 1)/i = 12/i$.

The probabilities are independent since $\hat{p}_{ij} = 12/i$ does not depend on the point j, or indeed any of the points selected in positions $(i + 1), \ldots, n$. For example, conditioned on the center of the wagon wheel being at j, $\hat{p}_{ij} = 12/i$ is still an upper bound. With $\hat{p}_{ij} = O(1/i)$, and independence of the $\hat{p}_{ij}$ along paths, we can apply our variant of Lemma 2.1 (described above), and Corollary 2.2 for the result. □

THEOREM 4.4. PARINCREMENTALDT *(Algorithm 3) runs in $O(n \log n)$ work in expectation and $O(\log^2 n)$ depth w.h.p. on the CRCW PRAM.*

PROOF. The number of rounds of PARINCREMENTALDT is $D(G_T(V))$ since the iteration dependence graph is defined by the algorithm. Each round has depth $O(\log n)$ for merging the encroached sets and load balancing, for an overall depth of $O(\log^2 n)$ (w.h.p.). Assuming each triangle maintains its minimum index, checking if a triangle is safe to process takes constant work. Since there are be at most $O(n)$ triangles on any round (true even though the mesh is not necessarily consistent), each round does at most $O(n)$ work to check all the triangles, for a total of $O(n \log n)$ work across rounds (w.h.p.). The rest of the work is no more than the sequential version, which is $O(n \log n)$ in expectation. □

5. LINEAR-WORK ALGORITHMS

In this section, we study several problems from low-dimensional computational geometry that have linear-work randomized incremental algorithms. These algorithms fall into the Type 2 category of algorithms defined in Section 2, and their iteration depth is polylogarithmic w.h.p. To obtain linear-work parallel algorithms, we process the steps in prefixes, as described in Section 2. For simplicity, we describe the algorithms for these problems in two dimensions, and and briefly note how they can be extended to any fixed number of dimensions.

5.1 Linear Programming

Constant-dimensional linear programming (LP) has received significant attention in the computational geometry literature, and several parallel algorithms for the problem have been developed [16, 25, 35, 28, 1, 34, 58, 2]. We consider linear programming in two dimensions. We assume that the constraints are given in general position and the solution is either infeasible or bounded. We note that these assumptions can be removed without affecting the asymptotic cost of the algorithm [56]. The standard randomized incremental algorithm [56] adds the constraints one-by-one in a random order, while maintaining the optimum point at any time. If a newly added constraint causes the optimum to no longer be feasible (a tight constraint), we find a new feasible optimum point on the line corresponding to the newly added constraint by solving a one-dimension linear program, i.e., taking the minimum or maximum of the set of intersection points of other earlier constraints with the line. If no feasible point is found, then the algorithm reports the problem as infeasible.

The iteration dependence graph is defined with the constraints as steps, and fits in the framework of Type 2 algorithms from Section 2. The steps corresponding to inserting a tight constraint are the special steps. Special steps depend on all earlier steps because when a tight constraint executes, it needs to look at all earlier constraints. Non-special steps depend on the closest earlier special step i because it must wait for step i to execute before executing itself to retain the sequential execution (we can ignore all of the earlier constraints since i will depend on them). Using backwards analysis, a step j has a probability of at most $2/j$ of being a special step because the optimum is defined by at most two constraints and the constraints are in a randomized order. Furthermore, the probabilities are independent among different steps. This gives us a dependence depth of $O(\log n)$ w.h.p. as discussed in Section 2.

As described in the proof of Theorem 2.3, our parallel algorithm executes the steps in prefixes. Each time a prefix is processed, it checks all of the constraints and finds the earliest one that causes the current optimum to be infeasible using line-side tests. The check per step takes $O(1)$ work and processing a violating constraint at step i takes $O(i)$ work and $O(1)$ depth w.h.p. to solve the one-dimensional linear program which involves minimum/maximum operations. Applying Theorem 2.3 with $d(n) = O(1)$ gives the following theorem.

THEOREM 5.1. *The randomized incremental algorithm for 2D linear programming can be parallelized to run in $O(n)$ work in expectation and $O(\log n)$ depth w.h.p. on an arbitrary-CRCW PRAM.*

We note that the algorithm can be extended to the case where the dimension d is greater than two by having a randomized incremental d-dimensional LP algorithm recursively call a randomized incremental algorithm for solving $(d-1)$-dimensional LPs. This increases the iteration dependence depth (and hence the depth of the algorithm) to $O(d! \log^{d-1} n)$ w.h.p. and increases the expected work to $O(d!n)$. We note that we can generate the random permutation only once and reuse it for the sub-problems. Although we lose independence, the expectation is not affected, and since there are only a constant (a function of d) number of sub-problems with high probability, the high probability bound for the depth is not affected.

5.2 Closest Pair

The ***closest pair*** problem takes as input a set of points in the plane and returns the pair of points with the smallest distance between each other. We assume that no pair of points have the same distance. A well-known expected linear-work algorithm [51, 44, 32, 39] works by maintaining a grid and inserting the points into the grid in a random order. The grid partitions the plane into regions of size $r \times r$ where each non-empty region stores the points inside the region and r is the distance of the closest pair so far (initialized to the distance between the first two points). It is maintained using a hash table. Whenever a new point is inserted, one can check the region the point belongs in and the eight adjacency regions to see whether the new value of r has decreased, and if so, the grid is rebuilt with the new value of r. The check takes $O(1)$ work as each region can contain at most nine points, otherwise the grid would have been rebuilt earlier. Therefore insertion takes $O(1)$ work, and rebuilding the grid takes $O(i)$ work where i is the number of points inserted so far. Using backwards analysis, one can show that point i has probability at most $2/i$ of causing the value of r to decrease, so the expected work is $\sum_{i=1}^{n} O(i) \cdot (2/i) = O(n)$.

This is a Type 2 algorithm, and the iteration dependence graph is similar to that of linear programming. The special steps are the ones that cause the grid to be rebuilt, and the dependence depth is $O(\log n)$ w.h.p. Rebuilding the grid involves hashing, and can be done in parallel in $O(i)$ work and $O(\log^* i)$ depth w.h.p. for a set of i points [31]. We also assume that the points in each region are stored in a hash table, to enable efficient parallel insertion and lookup in linear work and $O(\log^* i)$ depth. To obtain a linear-work parallel algorithm, we again execute the algorithm in prefixes. Applying Theorem 2.3 with $d(n) = O(\log^* n)$ gives the following theorem.

THEOREM 5.2. *The randomized incremental algorithm for closest pair can be parallelized to run in $O(n)$ work in expectation and $O(\log n \log^* n)$ depth w.h.p. on an arbitrary-CRCW PRAM.*

We note that the algorithm can be extended to d dimensions where the depth is $O(\log d \log n \log^* n)$ w.h.p. and expected work is $O(c_d n)$ where c_d is some constant that depends on d.

5.3 Smallest Enclosing Disk

The ***smallest enclosing disk*** problem takes as input a set of points in two dimensions and returns the smallest disk that contains all of the points. We assume that no four points lie on a circle. Linear-work algorithms for this problem have been described [47, 67], and in this section we will study Welzl's randomized incremental algorithm [67]. The algorithm inserts the points one-by-one in a random order, and maintains the smallest enclosing disk so far (initialized to the smallest disk defined by the first two points). Let v_i be the point inserted on the i'th iteration. If an inserted point v_i lies outside the current disk, then a new smallest enclosing disk is computed. We know that v_i must be on the smallest enclosing disk. We first define the smallest disk containing v_1 and v_i, and scan through v_2 to v_{i-1}, checking if any are outside the disk (call this procedure **Update1**). Whenever v_j ($j < i$) is outside the disk, we update the disk by defining the disk containing v_i and v_j and scanning through v_1 to v_{j-1} to find the third point on the boundary of the disk (call this procedure **Update2**). **Update2** takes $O(j)$ work, and **Update1** takes $O(i)$ work plus the work for calling **Update2**. With the points given in a random order, the probability that the j'th iteration of **Update1** calls **Update2** is at most $2/j$ by a backwards analysis argument, so the expected work of **Update1** is $O(i) + \sum_{j=1}^{i}(2/j) \cdot O(j) = O(i)$. The probability that **Update1** is called when the i'th point is inserted is at most $3/i$ using a backwards analysis argument, so the expected work of this algorithm is $\sum_{i=1}^{n}(3/i) \cdot O(i) = O(n)$.

This is another Type 2 algorithm whose iteration dependence graph is similar to that of linear programming and closest pair. The points are the steps, and the special steps are the ones that cause **Update1** to be called, which for step i has at most $3/i$ probability of happening. The dependence depth is again $O(\log n)$ w.h.p. as discussed in Section 2.

Our work-efficient parallel algorithm again uses prefixes, both when inserting the points, and on every call to **Update1**. We repeatedly find the earliest point that is outside the current disk by checking all points in the prefix with an in-circle test and taking the minimum among the ones that are outside. **Update1** is work-efficient and makes $O(\log n)$ calls to **Update2** w.h.p., where each call takes $O(1)$ depth w.h.p. as it does in-circle tests and takes a maximum. As in the sequential algorithm, each step takes $O(1)$ work in expectation. Applying Theorem 2.3 with $d(n) = O(\log n)$ w.h.p. (the depth of a executing a step and calling **Update1**) gives the following theorem.

THEOREM 5.3. *The randomized incremental algorithm for smallest enclosing disk can be parallelized to run in $O(n)$ work in expectation and $O(\log^2 n)$ depth w.h.p. on an arbitrary-CRCW PRAM.*

The algorithm can be extended to d dimension, with $O(d! \log^d n)$ depth w.h.p., and $O(c_d n)$ expected work for some constant c_d that depends on d. Again, we can use the same randomized order for all sub-problems.

6. ITERATIVE GRAPH ALGORITHMS

In this section we study two sequential graph algorithms that can be viewed as offline versions of randomized incremental algorithms. We show that the algorithms are Type 3 algorithms, as described in Section 2, and also that steps executing in parallel can be combined efficiently. This gives us simple parallel algorithms for the problems. The algorithms use single-source shortest paths and reachability as (black-box) subroutines, which is the dominating cost. Our algorithms are within a logarithmic factor in work and depth of a single call to these subroutines on the input graph.

6.1 Least-Element Lists

The concept of Least-Element lists (LE-lists) for a graph (either unweighted or with non-negative weights) was first proposed by Cohen [20] for estimating the neighborhood sizes of vertices. The idea has subsequently been used in many applications related to estimating the influence of vertices in a network (e.g., [21, 27] among many others), and generating probabilistic tree embeddings of a graph [43, 8], which itself is a useful component in a number of network optimization problems and in constructing distance oracles [8]. For $d(u, v)$ being the shortest path from u to v in G, we have:

DEFINITION 3 (LE-LIST). *Given a graph $G = (V, E)$ with $V = \{v_1, \ldots, v_n\}$, the* ***LE-lists*** *are*

$$L(v_i) = \left\{ v_j \in V \mid d(v_i, v_j) < \min_{k=1}^{j-1} d(v_i, v_k) \right\}$$

sorted by $d(v_i, v_j)$.

In other words, a vertex u is in vertex v's LE-list if and only if there are no earlier vertices (than u) that are closer to v. Often one stores with each vertex v_j in $L(v_i)$ the distance of $d(v_i, v_j)$.

Algorithm 4 provides a sequential iterative (incremental) construction of the LE-lists, where the i'th step is the i'th iteration of the for-loop. The set S captures all vertices that are closer to the i'th vertex than earlier vertices (the previous closest distance is stored in $\delta(\cdot)$). Line 3 involves computing S with a single-source shortest paths (SSSP) algorithm (e.g., Dijkstra's algorithm for weighted graphs and BFS for unweighted graphs, or other algorithms [62, 65, 45, 9] with more work but less depth). Note that the only minor

Algorithm 4: The iterative LE-lists construction [20]

Input: A graph $G = (V, E)$ with $V = \{v_1, \ldots, v_n\}$
Output: The LE-lists $L(\cdot)$ of G

```
Set δ(v) ← +∞ and L(v) ← ∅ for all v ∈ V.
for i ← 1 to n do
    Let S = {u ∈ V | d(v_i, u) < δ(u)}
    for u ∈ S do
        δ(u) ← d(v_i, u)
        concatenate ⟨v_i, d(v_i, u)⟩ to the end of L(u)
return L(·)
```

change to these algorithms is to remove the initialization of the tentative distances before we run SSSP, and instead use the $\delta(\cdot)$ values from previous steps in Algorithm 4. Thus the search will only explore S and its outgoing edges. Cohen [20] showed that if the vertices are in random order, then each LE-list has size $O(\log n)$ w.h.p., and that using Dijkstra, with distances initialized with $\delta(\cdot)$, the algorithm runs in $O(\log n(m + n \log n))$ time. Here we show that the algorithm is in fact parallel, and in particular a Type 3 incremental algorithm.

In this paper, we treat the shortest paths algorithm as a black box that computes the set S in depth $D_{SP}(n', m')$ and work $W_{SP}(n', m')$, where $n' = |S|$ and m' is the sum of the degrees of S. We also assume the cost functions are convex, i.e. $W_{SP}(n_1, m_1) + W_{SP}(n_2, m_2) \leq W_{SP}(n, m)$ for $n_1 + n_2 \leq n$ and $m_1 + m_2 \leq m$, which holds for all existing shortest paths algorithms.

For the separating dependences: v_j depends on v_i if and only if $v_i \in L(v_j)$, (i.e., was searched by v_i), and we use the total orderings $i <_k j$ if $d(v_k, v_i) < d(v_k, v_j)$. This gives:

LEMMA 6.1. *Algorithm 4 has a separating dependence for the dependences and orderings $<_v$ defined above.*

PROOF. By Definition 2, we need to show that for any three vertices $v_a, v_b, v_c \in V$, if $v_a <_c v_b <_c v_c$ or $v_c <_c v_b <_c v_a$, then v_c can only be visited on v_a's step if v_a's step is the first among the three.

Clearly the statement holds if v_c's step is the earliest among the three. We now consider the case when v_b's step is the first among the three. Since $d(v_c, v_c) = 0$, $v_a <_c v_b <_c v_c$ cannot happen, so we only need to consider the case $v_c <_c v_b <_c v_a$. Since $d(v_c, v_b) < d(v_c, v_a)$ and $b < a$, based on the definition of the LE-lists, $v_a \notin L(v_c)$. As a result, v_c can only be visited in v_a's step if v_a's step is first among the three. □

To parallelize the algorithm, we execute prefixes of vertices in batches that are geometrically increasing in size. Multiple searches will be executing in parallel in a round, so some dependences will be violated. We discuss how to fix these violations in a post-processing phase, which effectively combines the steps so we can apply Theorem 2.6 and Lemma 6.1 to obtain the following theorem.

THEOREM 6.2. *The LE-lists of a graph with the vertices in random order can be constructed in $O(W_{SP}(n, m) \log n)$ expected work and $O(D_{SP}(n, m) \log n)$ depth w.h.p. on the CRCW PRAM.*

PROOF. First we bound the cost of the algorithm excluding the post-processing step. Note that here visiting each vertex is no longer the same cost but based on the number of outgoing edges. However, since each vertex is visited no more than $O(\log n)$ times, the cost can be averaged. Assuming random input order, we can apply Theorem 2.6 and Lemma 6.1 with the convexity of the work complexity, and this is within the claimed bounds.

Since we execute multiple searches in parallel, there may be entries in the LE-lists that would not have been generated in the sequential algorithm. These extra entries violate the property that entries have to be strictly increasing in distance. We fix this with a post-processing phase, which effectively combines the steps executing in parallel. If the elements in the list are sorted by order of the vertices, we can sequentially filter out the extra entries in the list by finding the ones that are out of order by their distance (distances should be in reverse order). The size of the LE-lists can be shown to be $O(\log n)$ w.h.p. [20, 57], so the overall cost of the scan is $O(n \log n)$ work and $O(\log n)$ depth w.h.p.

We now show that we can efficiently sort the list. Without loss of generality, assume $n = 2^k$ for some integer k. Since the order of vertices in lists can only be violated inside a round, we only need to sort the entries within rounds. Consider the last vertex v_n (which is the worst case) and let X_i be the indicator variable for the event that v_i is in the LE-list of v_n. Thus $\mathbb{E}[X_i] = 1/i$ when $i < n$ and $\mathbb{E}[X_i] = 1$ when $i = n$. Note that two random variables X_i and X_j are independent. We analyze the cost of sorting the LE-list of v_n in a round, which executes a prefix of the steps. Assume that we use a loose upper bound of quadratic work for sorting and let $s = 2^{k-2}$ and $t = 2^{k-1}$. The expected work in round 1 is clearly $O(1)$ and in round $k > 1$ is:

$$\mathbb{E}\left[(\sum_{j=s+1}^{t} X_j)^2\right] = \mathbb{E}\left[\sum_{j=s+1}^{t} X_j^2\right] + 2 \cdot \mathbb{E}\left[\sum_{j=s+1}^{t} \sum_{j'=j+1}^{t} X_j X_{j'}\right]$$
$$< s \cdot \frac{1}{s} + 2 \cdot \frac{1}{s^2} \cdot s(s-1) = O(1)$$

Since there are $O(\log n)$ rounds, the expected work to sort this LE-list is $O(\log n) \cdot O(1) = O(\log n)$. The only exception is X_n, which is 1 with probability 1 instead of $1/n$. In the worst case, this adds at most $O(\log n)$ to the work to compare it to all elements in the list. Thus the expected work to sort one LE-list in the worst case is $O(\log n)$, and is $O(n \log n)$ when summed over all lists. The depth for sorting is $O(\log n)$ [22], which is within the claimed bounds. □

6.2 Strongly Connected Components

Given a directed unweighted graph $G = (V, E)$, a ***strongly connected component*** (SCC) is a maximal set of vertices $C \subseteq V$ such that for every pair of vertices u and v in C, there are directed paths both from u to v and from v to u. Tarjan's algorithm [63] finds all strongly connected components of a graph using a single pass of depth-first search (DFS) in $O(|V| + |E|)$ work. However, DFS is generally considered to be hard to parallelize [53], so a divide-and-conquer SCC algorithm [23] is usually used in parallel settings [41, 4, 61, 64].

The basic idea of the divide-and-conquer algorithm is similar to quicksort. It applies forward and backward reachability queries for a specific "pivot" vertex v, which partitions the remaining vertices into four subsets of the graph, based on whether it is forward reachable from v, backward reachable, both, or neither. The subset of vertices reachable from both directions form a strongly connected component, and the algorithm is applied recursively to the three remaining subsets. Coppersmith et al. [23] show that if the vertex v is selected uniformly at random, then the algorithm sequentially runs in $O(m \log n)$ work in expectation.

Although divide-and-conquer is generally good for parallelism, a problem with this algorithm is that the divide-and-conquer tree can be very unbalanced. The issue is that if the input graph is very sparse such that most of the reachability searches only visit a few vertices, then most of the vertices will fall into the subset of un-

Algorithm 5: The sequential iterative SCC algorithm

Input: A directed graph $G = (V, E)$ with $V = \{v_1, \ldots, v_n\}$.
Output: The set of strongly connected components of G.

```
1  𝒱 ← {{v_1, v_2, ..., v_n}}     (Initial Partition)
2  S_scc ← {}
3  for i ← 1 to n do
4  |  Let S ∈ 𝒱 be the subgraph that contains v_i
5  |  if S = ∅ then go to the next iteration;
6  |  R⁺ ← FORWARD-REACHABILITY(S, v_i)
7  |  R⁻ ← BACKWARD-REACHABILITY(S, v_i)
8  |  V_scc ← R⁺ ∩ R⁻
9  |  𝒱 ← 𝒱\{S} ∪ {R⁺\V_scc, R⁻\V_scc, S\(R⁺ ∪ R⁻)}
10 |  S_scc ← S_scc ∪ {V_scc}
11 return S_scc
```

reachable vertices from v, creating unbalanced partitions with $\Theta(n)$ recursion depth. Schudy describes a technique to better balance the partitions [55], however the approach requires a factor of $O(\log n)$ extra work compared to the original algorithm and the depth is equal to the depth of $O(\log^2 n)$ reachability queries. Tomkins et al. describe another parallel approach [64], although the analysis is quite complicated.[2]

The divide-and-conquer algorithm [23] can also be viewed as an incremental algorithm as described in Algorithm 5. A random ordering is equivalent to picking the pivots at random. This is the algorithm we will analyze as a Type 3 algorithm. Our analysis is significantly simpler than those of [55, 64], and furthermore the work of our algorithm matches that of the sequential algorithm.

As in previous work on parallel SCC algorithms, we treat the algorithm for performing reachability queries as a black box with $W_R(n, m)$ work and $D_R(n, m)$ depth, where n are the number of reachable vertices and m is the sum of their degrees. It can be implemented using a variety of algorithms with strong theoretical bounds [62, 65] or simply with a breadth-first search for low-diameter graphs. We also assume convexity on the work $W_R(n, m)$, which holds for existing reachability algorithms.

We first show that the algorithm has separating dependences. Here a dependence from i to j corresponds to a forward or backward reachability search from i visiting j (Lines 6 and 7 in Algorithm 5). Let $T = (t_1, t_2, \ldots, t_n)$ be an arbitrary topological order of components in the given graph G, with vertices of the same component arbitrarily ordered within the component. T is not constructed explicitly, but only used in analysis. To define the total order for vertex v_i, i.e., $<_{v_i}$, we take all vertices of T that are forward or backward reachable from v_i (including v_i itself) and put them at the beginning of the ordering (maintaining their relative order), and put the unreachable vertices after them. Given this ordering we have the following lemma.

LEMMA 6.3. *Algorithm 5 has a separating dependence for the dependences and orderings $<_v$ defined above.*

PROOF. By Definition 2, we need to show that for any three vertices $v_a, v_b, v_c \in V$, if $v_a <_c v_b <_c v_c$ or $v_c <_c v_b <_c v_a$, v_c can only be reached (forward or backward) in v_a's step if v_a's step is the first among the three.

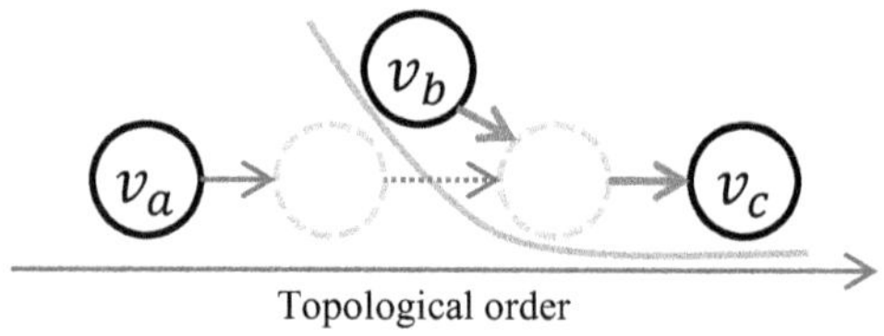

Figure 3: An illustration for the proof of Lemma 6.3.

Clearly the statement is true if v_c is earliest. We now consider the case when v_b's step is first among the three vertices. We give the argument for the forward direction, and the backward direction is true by symmetry. If v_b is in the same SCC as either v_a or v_c, then in v_b's step either v_a or v_c is marked in one SCC and removed from the subgraph set $\mathcal{V}$. Otherwise, since v_b and v_a are not in the same SCC, when $v_c <_c v_b <_c v_a$, v_c cannot be forward reachable in v_a's step, and when $v_a <_c v_b <_c v_c$, v_a cannot be forward reachable from v_b's step. In the second case, after v_b's step, the forward reachability search from v_b reaches v_c but not v_a, so v_a and v_c fall into different components in $\mathcal{V}$ (shown in Figure 3). As a result, v_c is also not reachable in v_a's step.

In conclusion, v_c can only be reached (forward or backward) in v_a's step if v_a's step is first among the three. □

Note that this separating dependence implies that the sequential algorithm on a random ordering does $O(m \log n)$ work since each vertex v_j is visited $\sum_{i=1}^{j} 2/i = O(\log n)$ times in expectation using Lemma 2.4, and the expectation is independent of the degrees. Since $W_R(n, m) = O(m)$ sequentially, e.g., using BFS, this gives $O(m \log n)$ work.

We now consider a parallel version based on rounds. To implement the parallel version, we need a way to efficiently combine the steps that run in the same round. First, there might be multiple vertices (sources) that obtain the same SCC in the same round and we want to avoid having duplicates in the final output. Second, since multiple reachability queries are performed in parallel, we want them to partition the subgraph set $\mathcal{V}$ consistently. The solution for combining steps is have all steps do a priority-write into a data field associated with the vertices that they visit during the reachability queries, and synchronize after the reachability queries.

To partition the graph, all edges with endpoints that hold different data values or differ in whether they are forward or backward reachable are removed (marked) from the graph, and this disconnects the graph into appropriate subgraphs. Also, all nodes that are reachable from the sources in both directions, which can be checked by their data fields, form SCCs and are removed (marked) from graph. All of these extra steps take linear work and constant depth. Finally, after all $O(\log n)$ rounds are complete, we group the vertices to form SCCs based on the vertex labels in data fields, which requires linear work and $O(\log n)$ depth [52, 37]. Note that this implementation yields exactly the same intermediate state as the sequential algorithm after each round, making it deterministic.

THEOREM 6.4. *For a random order of the input vertices, the incremental SCC algorithm does $O(W_R(n, m) \log n)$ expected work and has $O(D_R(n, m) \log n)$ depth on a priority-write CRCW PRAM.*

PROOF. The overall extra work is $O(m \log n)$ and no more than the work for executing the reachability queries. The depth for the additional operations is constant in each round and $O(\log n)$ at the end of the algorithm. Therefore if the input vertices are randomly

[2] Tomkins et al. [64] claim that their algorithm takes the same amount of work as the sequential algorithm, however it seems that there are errors in their analysis. For example, the goal of the analysis is to show that in each round their algorithm visits $O(n)$ vertices in expectation, which they claimed to imply visiting $O(m)$ edges in expectation. This is not generally true since the vertices do not necessarily have the same probabilities of being visited. Other than this, their work contains many interesting ideas that motivated us to look at this problem.

permuted, we can apply Theorem 2.6 with Lemma 6.3 and the convexity of the work cost to bound the expected work and depth of the algorithm. □

7. CONCLUSION

In this paper, we have analyzed the dependence structure in a collection of known randomized incremental algorithms (or slight variants) and shown that there is inherently high parallelism in all of the algorithms. The approach leads to particularly simple parallel algorithms for the problems—only marginally more complicated (if at all) than some of the very simplest efficient sequential algorithms that are known for the problems. Furthermore the approach allows us to borrow much of the analysis already done for the sequential versions (e.g., with regard to total work and correctness). We presented three general classes of algorithms, and tools and general theorems that are useful for multiple algorithms within each class. We expect that there are many other algorithms that can be analyzed with these tools and theorems.

Acknowledgments

This research was supported in part by NSF grants CCF-1314590 and CCF-1533858, the Intel Science and Technology Center for Cloud Computing, and the Miller Institute for Basic Research in Science at UC Berkeley.

8. REFERENCES

[1] M. Ajtai and N. Megiddo. A deterministic poly($\log\log n$)-time n-processor algorithm for linear programming in fixed dimension. In *ACM Symposium on Theory of Computing (STOC)*, pages 327–338, 1992.

[2] N. Alon and N. Megiddo. Parallel linear programming in fixed dimension almost surely in constant time. *J. ACM (JACM)*, 41(2):422–434, Mar. 1994.

[3] M. Atallah and M. Goodrich. Deterministic parallel computational geometry. In *Synthesis of Parallel Algorithms*, pages 497–536. Morgan Kaufmann, 1993.

[4] J. Barnat, P. Bauch, L. Brim, and M. Ceska. Computing strongly connected components in parallel on CUDA. In *International Parallel & Distributed Processing Symposium (IPDPS)*, pages 544–555, 2011.

[5] D. K. Blandford, G. E. Blelloch, and C. Kadow. Engineering a compact parallel Delaunay algorithm in 3D. In *ACM Symposium on Computational Geometry (SoCG)*, pages 292–300, 2006.

[6] G. E. Blelloch, J. T. Fineman, P. B. Gibbons, and J. Shun. Internally deterministic algorithms can be fast. In *Principles and Practice of Parallel Programming (PPoPP)*, pages 181–192, 2012.

[7] G. E. Blelloch, J. T. Fineman, and J. Shun. Greedy sequential maximal independent set and matching are parallel on average. In *ACM Symposium on Parallelism in Algorithms and Architectures (SPAA)*, pages 308–317, 2012.

[8] G. E. Blelloch, Y. Gu, and Y. Sun. Efficient construction of probabilistic tree embeddings. *arXiv preprint: 1605.04651*, 2016.

[9] G. E. Blelloch, Y. Gu, Y. Sun, and K. Tangwongsan. Parallel shortest-paths using radius stepping. In *ACM Symposium on Parallelism in Algorithms and Architectures (SPAA)*, 2016.

[10] G. E. Blelloch, A. Gupta, and K. Tangwongsan. Parallel probabilistic tree embeddings, k-median, and buy-at-bulk network design. In *ACM Symposium on Parallelism in Algorithms and Architectures (SPAA)*, pages 205–213, 2012.

[11] G. E. Blelloch, J. C. Hardwick, G. L. Miller, and D. Talmor. Design and implementation of a practical parallel Delaunay algorithm. *Algorithmica*, 24(3-4):243–269, 1999.

[12] R. L. Bocchino, V. S. Adve, S. V. Adve, and M. Snir. Parallel programming must be deterministic by default. In *Usenix HotPar*, 2009.

[13] J.-D. Boissonnat and M. Teillaud. On the randomized construction of the delaunay tree. *Theoretical Computer Science*, 112(2):339–354, 1993.

[14] R. P. Brent. The parallel evaluation of general arithmetic expressions. *J. ACM (JACM)*, 21(2):201–206, 1974.

[15] C. Cao Minh, J. Chung, C. Kozyrakis, and K. Olukotun. STAMP: Stanford transactional applications for multi-processing. In *IEEE International Symposium on Workload Characterization (IISWC)*, 2008.

[16] D. Z. Chen and J. Xu. Two-variable linear programming in parallel. *Computational Geometry*, 21(3):155 – 165, 2002.

[17] P. Cignoni, C. Montani, R. Perego, and R. Scopigno. Parallel 3D delaunay triangulation. *Computer Graphics Forum*, 12(3):129–142, 1993.

[18] M. Cintra, D. R. Llanos, and B. Palop. International conference on computational science and its applications. In *Speculative Parallelization of a Randomized Incremental Convex Hull Algorithm*, pages 188–197, 2004.

[19] K. L. Clarkson and P. W. Shor. Applications of random sampling in computational geometry, II. *Discrete & Computational Geometry*, 4(5):387–421, 1989.

[20] E. Cohen. Size-estimation framework with applications to transitive closure and reachability. *Journal of Computer and System Sciences*, 55(3):441–453, 1997.

[21] E. Cohen and H. Kaplan. Efficient estimation algorithms for neighborhood variance and other moments. In *ACM-SIAM Symposium on Discrete Algorithms (SODA)*, pages 157–166, 2004.

[22] R. Cole. Parallel merge sort. *SIAM J. Comput.*, 17(4):770–785, 1988.

[23] D. Coppersmith, L. Fleischer, B. Hendrickson, and A. Pinar. A divide-and-conquer algorithm for identifying strongly connected components. Technical Report RC23744, IBM, 2003.

[24] M. de Berg, O. Cheong, M. van Kreveld, and M. Overmars. *Computational Geometry: Algorithms and Applications*. Springer-Verlag, 2008.

[25] X. Deng. An optimal parallel algorithm for linear programming in the plane. *Information Processing Letters*, 35(4):213 – 217, 1990.

[26] P. Diaz, D. R. Llanos, and B. Palop. Parallelizing 2D-convex hulls on clusters: Sorting matters. *Jornadas De Paralelismo*, 2004.

[27] N. Du, L. Song, M. Gomez-Rodriguez, and H. Zha. Scalable influence estimation in continuous-time diffusion networks. In *Advances in Neural Information Processing Systems (NIPS)*, pages 3147–3155, 2013.

[28] M. Dyer. A parallel algorithm for linear programming in fixed dimension. In *Symposium on Computational Geometry (SoCG)*, pages 345–349, 1995.

[29] H. Edelsbrunner. *Geometry and Topology for Mesh Generation*. Cambridge University Press, 2006.

[30] J. Fakcharoenphol, S. Rao, and K. Talwar. A tight bound on approximating arbitrary metrics by tree metrics. *Journal of Computer and System Sciences (JCSS)*, 69(3):485–497, 2004.

[31] J. Gil, Y. Matias, and U. Vishkin. Towards a theory of nearly constant time parallel algorithms. In *Foundations of Computer Science (FOCS)*, pages 698–710, 1991.

[32] M. Golin, R. Raman, C. Schwarz, and M. Smid. Simple randomized algorithms for closest pair problems. *Nordic J. of Computing*, 2(1):3–27, Mar. 1995.

[33] A. Gonzalez-Escribano, D. R. Llanos, D. Orden, and B. Palop. Parallelization alternatives and their performance for the convex hull problem. *Applied Mathematical Modelling*, 30(7):563 – 577, 2006.

[34] M. T. Goodrich. Fixed-dimensional parallel linear programming via relative ϵ-approximations. In *ACM-SIAM Symposium on Discrete Algorithms (SODA)*, pages 132–141, 1996.

[35] M. T. Goodrich and E. A. Ramos. Bounded-independence derandomization of geometric partitioning with applications to parallel fixed-dimensional linear programming. *Discrete & Computational Geometry*, 18(4):397–420, 1997.

[36] P. J. Green and R. Sibson. Computing Dirichlet tessellations in the plane. *The Computer Journal*, 21(2):168–173, 1978.

[37] Y. Gu, J. Shun, Y. Sun, and G. E. Blelloch. A top-down parallel semisort. In *ACM Symposium on Parallelism in Algorithms and Architectures (SPAA)*, pages 24–34, 2015.

[38] L. J. Guibas, D. E. Knuth, and M. Sharir. Randomized incremental construction of Delaunay and Voronoi diagrams. *Algorithmica*, 7(4):381–413, 1992.

[39] S. Har-peled. *Geometric Approximation Algorithms*. American Mathematical Society, 2011.

[40] W. Hasenplaugh, T. Kaler, T. B. Schardl, and C. E. Leiserson. Ordering heuristics for parallel graph coloring. In *ACM Symposium on Parallelism in Algorithms and Architectures (SPAA)*, pages 166–177, 2014.

[41] S. Hong, N. C. Rodia, and K. Olukotun. On fast parallel detection of strongly connected components (SCC) in small-world graphs. In *International Conference for High Performance Computing, Networking, Storage and Analysis (SC)*, pages 1–11, 2013.

[42] J. Jaja. *Introduction to Parallel Algorithms*. Addison-Wesley Professional, 1992.

[43] M. Khan, F. Kuhn, D. Malkhi, G. Pandurangan, and K. Talwar. Efficient distributed approximation algorithms via probabilistic tree embeddings. *Distributed Computing*, 25(3):189–205, 2012.

[44] S. Khuller and Y. Matias. A simple randomized sieve algorithm for the closest-pair problem. *Information and Computation*, 118(1):34–37, 1995.

[45] P. N. Klein and S. Subramanian. A randomized parallel algorithm for single-source shortest paths. *Journal of Algorithms*, 25(2):205–220, 1997.

[46] D. R. Llanos, D. Orden, and B. Palop. Meseta: A new scheduling strategy for speculative parallelization of randomized incremental algorithms. *International Conference on Parallel Processing Workshops*, pages 121–128, 2005.

[47] N. Megiddo. Linear-time algorithms for linear programming in R^3 and related problems. *SIAM Journal on Computing*, 1983.

[48] K. Mulmuley. *Computational geometry - an introduction through randomized algorithms*. Prentice Hall, 1994.

[49] X. Pan, D. Papailiopoulos, S. Oymak, B. Recht, K. Ramchandran, and M. I. Jordan. Parallel correlation clustering on big graphs. In *Advances in Neural Information Processing Systems (NIPS)*, 2015.

[50] K. Pingali, D. Nguyen, M. Kulkarni, M. Burtscher, M. A. Hassaan, R. Kaleem, T.-H. Lee, A. Lenharth, R. Manevich, M. Méndez-Lojo, D. Prountzos, and X. Sui. The tao of parallelism in algorithms. In *ACM SIGPLAN conference on Programming Language Design and Implementation (PLDI)*, 2011.

[51] M. O. Rabin. Probabilistic algorithms. *Algorithms and Complexity: New Directions and Recent Results*, pages 21–39, 1976.

[52] S. Rajasekaran and J. H. Reif. Optimal and sublogarithmic time randomized parallel sorting algorithms. *SIAM J. Comput.*, 18(3):594–607, 1989.

[53] J. H. Reif. Depth-first search is inherently sequential. *Information Processing Letters*, 20(5):229–234, 1985.

[54] J. H. Reif and S. Sen. Optimal randomized parallel algorithms for computational geometry. *Algorithmica*, 7(1-6):91–117, 1992.

[55] W. Schudy. Finding strongly connected components in parallel using $O(\log^2 n)$ reachability queries. In *ACM Symposium on Parallelism in Algorithms and Architectures (SPAA)*, pages 146–151, 2008.

[56] R. Seidel. Small-dimensional linear programming and convex hulls made easy. *Discrete & Computational Geometry*, 6(3):423–434, 1991.

[57] R. Seidel. Backwards analysis of randomized geometric algorithms. In *New Trends in Discrete and Computational Geometry*, pages 37–67. 1993.

[58] S. Sen. A deterministic $poly(\log\log n)$ time optimal CRCW PRAM algorithm for linear programming in fixed dimensions. Technical report, Department of Computer Science, University of Newcastle, 1995.

[59] J. Shun, G. E. Blelloch, J. T. Fineman, P. B. Gibbons, A. Kyrola, H. V. Simhadri, and K. Tangwongsan. Brief announcement: the Problem Based Benchmark Suite. In *ACM Symposium on Parallelism in Algorithms and Architectures (SPAA)*, pages 68–70, 2012.

[60] J. Shun, Y. Gu, G. Blelloch, J. Fineman, and P. Gibbons. Sequential random permutation, list contraction and tree contraction are highly parallel. In *ACM-SIAM Symposium on Discrete Algorithms (SODA)*, pages 431–448, 2015.

[61] G. M. Slota, S. Rajamanickam, and K. Madduri. BFS and Coloring-based parallel algorithms for strongly connected components and related problems. In *International Parallel and Distributed Processing Symposium (IPDPS)*, 2014.

[62] T. H. Spencer. Time-work tradeoffs for parallel algorithms. *Journal of the ACM (JACM)*, 44(5):742–778, 1997.

[63] R. Tarjan. Depth-first search and linear graph algorithms. *SIAM Journal on Computing*, 1(2):146–160, 1972.

[64] D. Tomkins, T. Smith, N. M. Amato, and L. Rauchwerger. Efficient, reachability-based, parallel algorithms for finding strongly connected components. Technical report, Texas A&M University, 2015.

[65] J. D. Ullman and M. Yannakakis. High-probability parallel transitive-closure algorithms. *SIAM Journal on Computing*, 20(1):100–125, 1991.

[66] U. Vishkin. Thinking in Parallel: Some Basic Data-Parallel Algorithms and Techniques. 2010.

[67] E. Welzl. Smallest enclosing disks (balls and ellipsoids). In *New Results and New Trends in Computer Science*, 1991.

Author Index

www.ingramcontent.com/pod-product-compliance
Ingram Content Group UK Ltd.
Pitfield, Milton Keynes, MK11 3LW, UK
UKHW051414290926
15471UKWH00009B/1598

9 781450 346092